Garage Sale & Flea Market

ANNUAL

EIGHTH EDITION
CASHING IN ON
TODAY'S LUCRATIVE
COLLECTIBLES MARKET

cb
COLLECTOR BOOKS
A Division of Schroeder Publishing Co., Inc.

CURRENT VALUES ON: **TODAY'S COLLECTIBLES**
TOMORROW'S ANTIQUES

Searching For A Publisher?

We are always looking for knowledgeable people considered to be experts within their fields. If you feel that there is a real need for a book on your collectible subject and have a large comprehensive collection, contact Collector Books.

Front cover: No. 610 Pyramid Creamer and Sugar, pink, $30.00 each; Hull Bow-Knot Whisk Broom Wall Pocket, B-27, 8", $265.00 – 300.00; Nesbitt's California Orange Thermometer, 1950s, 26", $125.00; *Nightmare Before Christmas* Tie, $30.00 (courtesy Pamela Apkarian-Russell); Tammy's Mom Doll, MIB, $65.00 (courtesy Cindy Sabulis); *Fun with Dick and Jane,* juvenile series hardcover, Scott Foresman, 1946 – 1947, NM, $350.00 (courtesy June Moon); Indianapolis Motor Speedway Pennant, May 30, 1938, 28½", $200.00 (courtesy Eric Jungnickel).

Title page: Colonial Boy and Girl Advertising Dolls, 1976, 10", M, $65.00 – 80.00 each (courtesy Dan and Micki Young); Abingdon What-Not Vases, C-6, $70.00, A-3, $60.00, B-3, $70.00; Dakin Smokey Figure, 1970s, 8", M, $45.00 (courtesy June Moon).

Cover design by Beth Summers
Book design by Terri Hunter and Beth Ray

COLLECTOR BOOKS
P.O. Box 3009
Paducah, Kentucky 42002-3009
www.collectorbooks.com

A Word From the Editor

I'm sure you've heard the old adage 'Nothing's certain but death and taxes,' and we that have lived a few more years than we care to think about will nod in melancholy agreement. But there's one more thing we can add to that, I've learned: 'nothing will stay the same' — things *will* change. Just when you're settling into a routine you're really comfortable and happy with, someone or something will 'throw a kink in the works,' as my dear old dad used to say. The annual fishing trips you've taken for at least twenty years are cancelled because your old-but-heretofore-reliable boat broke and can't be fixed. The cat dies. The little girl that used to be your shadow has grown up and generally prefers the company of boys to yours, and you miss her. The factory where you've worked so long closed and moved to Mexico, and somebody, somewhere invented the Internet.

Sure, Internet sales were around before, but their impact on the antiques and collectibles field during 1999 hit like a meteorite. Shock waves were felt allover, all the way down from the finest antique shows to the smallest out-of-the way flea markets. Suddenly, anyone with a PC and a modem became a 'dealer.' Veterans, tired from packing and unpacking their merchandise, decided to stay at home and sell from the comfort of their swivel chairs. Buyers found it ever-so-much fun to select their goodies from online auctions that had more hard-to-find merchandise than they'd ever seen in one place before. Mall dealers held out their best stuff to put on the Internet. Those things were the 'crater' — here are the shock waves: Show promoters reported decreased attendance and empty booths. Malls suffered from lack of quality merchandise, and tradepapers that once overflowed with 'for sale' ads shrank into near oblivion. When the dust began to settle, we found the online market in a state of complete confusion due to the 'more supply, less demand' principle that caused the prices of the more accessible items to plummet. Rare items, on the other hand, were pounced on by the core of the more affluent collectors of a worldwide audience, and winning bids were often astronomical.

As I observed these results, I began to be concerned about the influence they would or should have on books such as this one, so I polled my advisors with this question: What effect do you see the Internet phenomenon having on established market values? Like observers of a traffic accident, they all see it a little differently, but by and large, the consensus was that because of the excessive polarity occurring between the selling prices of common versus rare items, they should not be factored in. As one advisor put it: 'Internet final-auction bid prices indicate what one person is willing to pay to add a new or different piece to a personal collection and may not necessarily reflect any established value.' This quote is from another advisor: '...certain collectors are willing to pay outrageous sums to win the objects of their desire...resulting in the winner paying a price which far exceeds the collectible's true market value.' One of our advisors says she expects the 'extreme highs of now will soon die

down to a more reasonable pace,' noting that a certain piece went for $177.00 but when an identical item turned up for sale a few weeks later, it brought only $77.00. She believes 'many of the purchases are made by Internet-savy people who have discovered a whole new pastime.' Still another observes: '(this) has created a multitude of brand new collectors that know little about values. They then overbid and along with having auction fever drive up prices to unreal levels on many items (noting that he has seen a $20.00 item sell for $500.00 and a brand new $50.00 item go for more than $200.00). And this final quote: 'As a result, market volatility prevails with little regard to the proper description of the items offered and in many cases results in bids with no relation to true value. Inconsistency is the rule.' He summarizes: 'The Internet market must be taken with a grain of salt, and in many cases, not as an indicator of true market value.'

So for this edition, we will will stick to the tried and true, fully aware that Internet auctions may indeed be the reality of the future, and that the collectibles market as we know it may at some point be completely altered and restructured by a fierce online power that will have to be reckoned with, but not today.

Call me technologically impaired if you will, but I must admit I liked things just the way they were — just the way we had them for years, since way back in the '60s. I yearn for those old flea markets — remember Washington Court House (Ohio)? The epitome of the flea market! Great buys on wonderful Depression glass. Fiesta was just beginning to surface, so were McCoy cookie jars. That show could keep you buying and buying for days. But the flea market venue has seen drastic change. As we all know, where there were once many, today there are few. But it's still very possible, though perhaps not as often as in the past, to find wonderful items at outdoor flea markets. And there are those of us who still prefer the 'hands-on' method of shopping, so I truly can't foresee a time when the flea market will no longer be.

Thank the gods for garage sales — at least we still have them… primal, uncomplicated, and totally unaffected by the Internet, at least for now. (Here's a disconcerting thought: you think they'll ever go online?) I love yard sales, garage sales, tag sales, estate sales — whatever. Here in the Midwest, there's a cult — garage salers (and we are legion) who zealously watch for the first break in the winter weather that signals their onset. We, who hope our daughters will plan a December wedding rather than have to miss one Saturday of sales, who would turn down an invitation to a White House luncheon for fear of having to cut short our shopping, who even with a throbbing toothache would postpone seeing the dentist until all area sales were covered, are Garage Salers of the First Order! We're charter members of GSA (Garage Salers Anonymous). But not only is it tremendous fun, I can assure you it can be profitable as well.

Since I personally enjoy passing on to you some of the wonderful buys we make each season, I've kept a list, and

I'd like to share some of our better finds with you. The first weekend out was very good for us. In addition to the area we routinely cover, a small village in Illinois was having its annual town-wide rummage, so we had a heyday. In Pfaltzgraff, we bought three boxes of Village for $60.00, including some very nice serving pieces, and a three-piece condiment set in Gourmet Royal for $5.00; we found a Vernon Kiln Organdie pitcher for $1.50, a Noritake lemon tray for 50¢; a wonderful pair of redbirds by Goebel for $1.00; and some Metlox Nostalgia pieces — a large surrey (no horse) and two of the four riders that came with it for $5.00. Of course, not every weekend was this good, but throughout the season we were able to pick up nice items on a basis regular enough to more than keep us happy — the McCoy Wedding Jar (cookie jar) for $1.00; the Cardinal Chinaman laundry sprinkler for 50¢, and a Lionstone Fireman decanter, still full, for $2.00 (it booked at $110.00 several years ago). In glassware, we found the Moon and Star (amber) water pitcher and two tumblers at a sale here in town, and several other more common items in that pattern; I paid $5.00 for a ruffled Fenton Hobnail cake stand in milk glass (that's going to be a hard item to part with), and bought $400.00 worth of Cape Cod by Imperial for $15.00. We found a large cut crystal bell with a West Germany sticker for just $2.00 and several interesting pieces of Depression glass here and there.

Other fun buys included a Hall Aladdin teapot in sapphire blue for $5.00, two TV lamps (both a pair of Siamese cats, each under $5.00), Van Tellingen huggy bear shakers for 50¢, a pair of Lefton rabbits (50¢), various vintage record albums and jewelry, and a collection of California Raisins (we paid $10.00, it booked out at $250.00). This purchase went way beyond fun, it was absolutely fantastic — a set of six dinner plates and cups and saucers in the Rodeo pattern by Wallace for $50.00! A cup and saucer set books at $75.00, while the dinner plates go for around $85.00 each.

Our summer might be described as a Pfaltzgraff summer. In addition to the items we found on our first weekend, we found forty pieces of Yorktowne for $17.00 and some wonderful Village at giveaway prices that we purchased from a consignment shop. Pfaltzgraff sells very well for us, as long as we keep prices reasonable. There's still an abundance of Village around (it was made for years in an unbelievable assortment), but now that it's been discontinued, those who've been using it all along are rebuilding and enlarging their services, and as is always the case, now that it's no longer available from the company, it has become most attractive to collectors (that's just the way we are). This is by no mean all of our purchases for the season, there were 'men' things that I had no interest in recording, as well as many more trivial but saleable items. As those of you who buy our book on a regular basis are aware, we 'do' a flea market only once a year, marketing all our garage sale finds except those we have trouble parting with and end up keeping for ourselves. It's very profitable, even though this flea market is in rural central Indiana, and we price things to move (usually about 60% to 70% of book). Considering the prices we pay are always low, and since we have very little overhead, we can do that. As a rule, we will realize about $3,500.00 after expenses. We've had a summer full of fun and made money as well — what other hobby can you say that about!

But whether you regard it as a hobby or a more serious money-making opportunity, to make it work for you, become familiar with the market. This book will serve as a tool to educate you toward becoming a wise shopper. The key is knowledge. We'll suggest references for in-depth study, all written by by today's leading experts. We're going to zero in on items from the 1940s on, since that's where the market's activity is strongest today. We'll list clubs and newsletters related to many specific areas; we recommend all of them very highly. There is much knowledge to be gleaned by networking through clubs with collectors whose interests are similar to yours. Trade papers are listed as well; they contain a wealth of timely information. If you're not already subscribing, see about getting sample copies.

As usual, this year's edition contains several new categories, most of which you'll never find in any other guide. These will tip you off to new collectibles well before the general public becomes aware of them, and you'll be able to make some fantastic buys before competition becomes so intense.

An exclusive feature of this book is the section called Special Interests. It contains the addresses of authors, collectors, and dealers sorted by specific collectible categories. Not only are these people potential buyers, but under most circumstances, they'll be willing to help you with questions that remain after you've made an honest attempt at your own research. Please, read the text. Then go to your library; you should be able to find most of the books we reference. Check them out for study — they're all wonderful. Just remember if you do write one of our people, you will have to include an SASE if you want a response. And if you call, please consider the differences in time zones.

If you'd like to collect some nice pieces to decorate your home or if you're interested in becoming a dealer but find there's no room in the budget for extra spending, we'll show you how to realize a profit from holding your own garage sale. And we'll give you some timely pointers on how to set up at your first flea market.

Remember that our prices in no way reflect what you will be paying at garage sales — our values are well established and generally accepted by seasoned collectors and authorities and have been checked over before publication by people well versed in their particular fields.

How to Hold Your Own Garage Sale

Just as we promised we would, here are our suggestions for holding your own garage sale. If you're toying with the idea of getting involved in the business of buying and selling antiques and collectibles but find yourself short of any extra cash to back your venture, this is the way we always recommend you get started. Everyone has items they no longer use; get rid of them! Use them to your advantage. Here's how.

Get Organized. Gather up your merchandise. Though there's not a lot of money in selling clothing, this is the perfect time to unload things you're not using. Kids' clothing does best, since it's usually outgrown before it's worn out, and there's a lot of budget-minded parents who realize this and think it makes good sense to invest as little as possible in their own children's wardrobes. Everything should of course be clean and relatively unwrinkled to sell at all, and try to get the better items on hangers. Leave no stone unturned. Clean out the attic, the basement, the garage — then your parent's attic, basement, and garage. If you're really into it, bake cookies, make some crafts. Divide your house plants; pot the starts in attractive little containers — ladies love 'em. Discarded and outgrown toys sell well. Framed prints and silk flower arrangements you no longer use, recipe books and paperbacks, tapes, records, and that kitchen appliance that's more trouble to store than it's worth can be turned into cash to get you off and running!

After you've gathered up your merchandise, you'll need to price it. Realistically, clothing will bring at the most about 15% to 25% of what you had to pay for it, if it's still in excellent, ready-to-wear shape and basically still in style. There's tons of used clothing out there, and no one is going to buy much of anything with buttons missing or otherwise showing signs of wear. If you have good brand-name clothing that has been worn very little, you would probably do better by taking it to a resale or consignment shop. They normally price things at about one-third of retail, with their cut being 30% of that. Not much difference money-wise, but the garage-sale shopper that passes up that $150.00 suit you're asking $25.00 for will probably give $50.00 for it at the consignment shop, simply because like department stores, many have dressing rooms with mirrors so you can try things on and check them for fit before you buy. Even at $25.00, the suit is no bargain if you can't use it when you get it home.

Remember that garage-sale buyers expect to find low prices. Depending on how long you plan on staying open, you'll have one day, possibly two to move everything. If you start out too high, you'll probably be stuck with a lot of leftover merchandise, most of which you've already decided is worthless to you. The majority of your better buyers will hit early on; make prices attractive to them and you'll do all right. If you come up with some 'low-end' collectibles — fast-food toys, character glasses, played-with action figures, etc. — don't expect to get much out of them at a garage sale. Your competition down the block may underprice you. But if you have a few things you think have good resale potential, offer them at about half of 'book' price. If they don't sell at your garage sale, take them to a flea market or a consignment shop. You'll probably find they sell better on that level, since people expect to find prices higher there than at garage sales.

You can use pressure-sensitive labels or masking tape for price tags on many items. But *please* do not use either of these on things where damage is likely to occur when they are removed. For instance, (as one reader pointed out) on boxes containing toys, board games, puzzles, etc.; on record labels or album covers; or on ceramics or glass with gold trim or unfired, painted decoration. Unless a friend or a neighbor is going in on the sale with you, price tags won't have to be removed; the profit will all be yours. Of course, you'll have to keep tabs if others are involved. You can use a sheet of paper divided into columns, one for each of you, and write the amount of each sale down under the appropriate person's name, or remove the tags and restick them on a piece of poster board, one for each seller. I've even seen people use straight pins to attach small squares of paper which they remove and separate into plastic butter tubs. When several go together to have a sale, the extra help is nice, but don't let things get out of hand. Your sale can get *too* big. Things become too congested, and it's hard to display so much to good advantage.

Advertise. Place your ad in your local paper or on your town's cable TV information channel. It's important to make your ad interesting and upbeat. Though most sales usually start early on Friday or Saturday mornings, some people are now holding their sales in the early evening, and they seem to be having good crowds. This gives people with day jobs an opportunity to attend. You *might* want to hold your sale for two days, but you'll do 90% of your selling during the first two or three hours, and a two-day sale can really drag on. Make signs — smaller ones for street corners near your home to help direct passers-by, and a large one for your yard. You might even want to make another saying 'Clothing ½-Price after 12:00.' (It'll cut way down on leftovers that you'll otherwise have to dispose of yourself.) Be sure that you use a wide-tipped felt marker and print in letters big enough that the signs can be read from the street. Put the smaller signs up a few days in advance unless you're expecting rain. (If you are, you might want to include a rain date in your advertising unless your sale will be held under roof.) Make sure you have a lot of boxes and bags and plenty of change. If you price your items in increments of 25¢, you won't need anything but a few rolls of quarters, maybe ten or fifteen ones, and a few five-dollar bills. Then on the day of the sale, put the large sign up in a prominent place out front with some balloons to attract the crowd. Take a deep breath, brace yourself, and raise the garage door!

What to Do With What's Left. After the sale, pack up any good collectibles that didn't sell. Think about that consignment shop or setting up at a flea market. (We'll talk about that later on.) Sort out the better items of clothing for Goodwill or a similar charity, unless your city has someone who will take your leftovers and sell them on consignment. This is a fairly new concept, but some of the larger cities have such 'bargain centers.'

Learning to Become a Successful Bargain Hunter

Let me assure you, anyone who takes the time to become an informed, experienced bargain hunter will be successful. There is enough good merchandise out there to make it well worthwhile, at all levels. Once you learn what to look for, what has good resale potential, and what price these items will probably bring for you, you'll be equipped and ready for any hunting trip. You'll be the one to find treasures. They are out there!

Garage sales are absolutely wonderful for finding bargains. But you'll have to get up early! Even non-collectors can spot quality merchandise, and at those low garage sale prices (low unless of course held by an owner who's done his homework) those items will be the first to move.

In order for you to be a successful garage sale shopper, you have to learn how to get yourself organized. It's important to conserve your time. The sales you hit during the first early-morning hour will prove to be the best nine times out of ten, so you must have a plan before you ever leave home. Plot your course. Your local paper will have a section on garage sale ads, and local cable TV channels may also carry garage sale advertising. Most people hold their sales on the weekend, but some may start earlier in the week, so be sure to turn to the 'Garage Sales' ads daily. Write them down and try to organize them by areas — northwest, northeast, etc. At first, you'll probably need your city map, but you'll be surprised at how quickly the streets will become familiar to you. Upper middle-class neighborhoods generally have the best sales and the best merchandise, so concentrate on those areas, though sales in older areas may offer older items. (Here's where you have to interpret those sale ads.) When you've decided where you want to start, go early! If the ad says 8:00, be there at 7:00. This may seem rude and pushy, but if you can bring yourself to do it, it will pay off. And chances are when you get there an hour early, you'll not be their first customer. If they're obviously not ready for business, just politely inquire if you may look. If you're charming and their nerves aren't completely frayed from trying to get things ready, chances are they won't mind.

Competition can be fierce during those important early-morning hours. Learn to scan the tables quickly, then move to the area that looks the most promising. Don't be afraid to ask for a better price if you feel it's too high, but most people have already priced garage sale merchandise so that it will sell. Keep a notebook to jot down items you didn't buy the first time around but think you might be interested in if the price were reduced later on. After going through dozens of sales (I've done as many as thirty or so in one morning), you won't remember where you saw what! Often by noon, at least by mid-afternoon, veteran garage sale buyers are finished with their rounds and attendance becomes very thin. Owners are usually much more receptive to the idea of lowering their prices, so it may pay you to make a second pass. In fact some people find it advantageous to go to the better sales on the last day as well as the first. They'll make an offer for everything that's left, and since most of the time the owner is about ready to *pay* someone to take it at that point, they can usually name their price. Although most of the collectibles will normally be gone at this point, there are nearly always some useable household items and several pieces of good, serviceable clothing left. The household items will sell at flea markets or consignment shops, and if there are worthwhile clothing items, take them to a resale boutique. They'll either charge the 30% commission fee or buy the items outright for about half of the amount they feel they can ask, a new practice some resale shops are beginning to follow. Because they want only clothing that is in style, in season, and like new, their prices may be a little higher than others shops, so half of that asking price is a good deal.

Tag sales are common in the larger cities. They are normally held in lieu of an auction, when estates are being dispersed, or when families are moving. Sometimes only a few buyers are admitted at one time, and as one leaves another is allowed to take his place. So just as is true with garage sales, the early bird gets the goodies. Really serious shoppers begin to arrive as much as an hour or two before the scheduled opening time. I know of one who will spend the night in his van and camp on the 'doorstep' if he thinks the sale is especially promising. And he can tell you fantastic success stories! But since it's customary to have tag sale items appraised before values are set, be prepared to pay higher prices. That's not to say, though, that you won't find bargains here. If you think an item is overpriced, leave a bid. Just don't forget to follow through on it, since if it doesn't sell at their asking price, they may end up holding it for you. It's a good idea to check back on the last day of the sale. Often the prices on unsold items may have been drastically reduced.

Auctions can go either way. Depending on the crowd and what items are for sale, you can sometimes spend all day and never be able to buy anything anywhere near 'book' price. On the other hand, there are often 'sleepers' that can be bought cheaply enough to resell at a good profit. Toys, dolls, Hummels, Royal Doultons, banks, cut glass, and other 'high-profile' collectibles usually go high, but white ironstone, dinnerware sets from the '20s through the '50s, silver plated hollow ware, books, records, and linens, for instance, often pass relatively unnoticed by the majority of the buyers.

If there is a consignment auction house in your area, check it out. These are usually operated by local auctioneers and the sales they hold in-house often involve low-income estates. You won't find something every time, so try to investigate the merchandise ahead of schedule to see if it's going to be worth your time to attend. Competition is probably less at one of these than in any of the other types of sales we've mentioned, and wonderful buys have been made from time to time.

Flea markets are often wonderful places to find bargains. I don't like the small ones — not that I don't find anything there, but I've learned to move through them so fast (to get ahead of the crowd), I don't get my 'fix'; I just leave wanting more. If you've never been to a large flea market, you don't know what you're missing. Even if you're not a born-again collector, I guarantee you will love it. And they're excellent places to study the market. You'll be able to see where the buying activity is; you can check and compare prices, talk with dealers and collectors, and do hands-on inspections. I've found that if I first study a particular subject by reading a book or a magazine article, this type of exposure to that collectible really 'locks in' what I have learned.

Because there are many types of flea market dealers, there are plenty of bargains. The casual, once-in-a-while dealer may not always keep up with changing market values. Some of them simply price their items by what they themselves had to pay for it. Just as being early at garage sales is important, here it's a must. If you've ever been in line waiting for a flea market to open, you know that cars are often backed up for several blocks, and people will be standing in line waiting to be admitted hours before the gate opens. Browsers? Window shoppers? Not likely. Competition! So if you're going to have a chance at all, you'd better be in line yourself. Take a partner and split up on the first pass so that you can cover the grounds more quickly. It's a common sight to see the serious buyers conversing with their partners via walkie-talkies, and if you like to discuss possible purchases with each other before you actually buy, this is a good way to do it.

Learn to bargain with dealers. Their prices are usually negotiable, and most will come down by 10% to 20%. Be polite and fair, and you can expect the same treatment in return. Unpriced items are harder to deal for. I have no problem offering to give $8.00 if an item is marked $10.00, but it's difficult for me to have to ask the price and then make a counter offer. So I'll just say 'This isn't marked. Will you take...?' I'm not an aggressive barterer, so this works for me.

There are so many reproductions on the flea market level (and at malls and co-ops), that you need to be suspicious of anything that looks too new! Some fields of collecting have been especially hard hit. Whenever a collectible becomes so much in demand that prices are high, reproductions are bound to make an appearance. For instance, Black Americana, Nippon, Roseville, banks, toys of all types, teddy bears, lamps, glassware, doorstops, cookie jars, prints, advertising items, and many other fields have been especially vulnerable. Learn to check for telltale signs — paint that is too bright, joints that don't fit, variations in sizes or colors, creases in paper that you can see but not feel, and so on. Remember that zip codes have been used only since 1963, and this can sometimes help you date an item in question. Check glassware for areas of wavy irregularities often seen in new glass. A publication we would highly recommend to you is called *Antique and Collector Reproduction News*, a monthly report of 'Fakes, Frauds, and Facts.' To subscribe, call 1-800-227-5531. You can find them on the web at www.repronews.com. Rates are very reasonable compared to the money you may save by learning to recognize reproductions.

Antique malls and co-ops should be visited on a regular basis. Many mall dealers restock day after day, and traffic and buying competition is usually fierce. As a rule, you won't often find great bargains here; what you do save on is time. And if time is what you're short of, you'll be able to see a lot of good merchandise under one roof, on display by people who've already done the leg work and invested *their* time, hence the higher prices. But there are always underpriced items as well, and if you've taken the time to do your homework, you'll be able to spot them right away.

Unless the dealer who rents the booth happens to be there, though, mall and co-op prices are usually firm. But often times they'll run sales — '20% off everything in booth #101.' If you have a dealer's license, and you really should get one, most will give you a courtesy 10% discount on items over $10.00, unless you want to pay with a credit card.

Antique shows are exciting to visit, but obviously if a dealer is paying several hundred dollars to set up for a three-day show, he's going to be asking top price to offset expenses. So even though bargains will be few, the merchandise is usually superior, and you may be able to find that special item you've been looking for.

Mail order buying is not only very easy, but most of the time economical as well. Many people will place an ad in 'For Sale' sections of tradepapers. Some will describe and price their merchandise in their ad, while others offer lists of items they have in exchange for a SASE (stamped, self-addressed envelope). You're out no gas or food expenses, their overhead is minimal so their prices are usually very reasonable, so it works out great for both buyer and seller. I've made a lot of good buys this way, and I've always been fairly and honestly dealt with. You may want to send a money order or cashier's check to save time, otherwise (especially on transactions involving larger sums of money) the seller might want to wait until your personal check clears.

Goodwill stores and re-sale shops are usually listed in the telephone book. When you travel, it will pay you to check them out. If there's one in your area, visit it often. You never know what may turn up there.

Internet shopping is really catching on. There are set-price antique malls and online auctions. The great thing is the fact that there will be a higher concentration of your specific collectible interest available to you at the click of a mouse than you will ever find under one roof anywhere else. It's collectibles heaven. I've been able to buy items I didn't even know existed right from my own swivel chair. I haven't found things to be any more expensive than they would be from the other sources we've mentioned; in fact, I feel that some of my purchases have been real bargains. In every collecting category, there will always be those extremely rare and desirable pieces where the sky is the limit, and when such an item comes up for bid, I've seen some astronomical prices realized, but this has always been true, well before online shopping. For more information, we recommend the *Collector's Guide to Buying, Selling, and Trading on the Internet, Second Edition,* by Nancy Hix, and *Antiquing and Collecting on the Internet* by Karima Perry. Both are available from Collector Books.

What's Hot on Today's Market

Though the market remains strong, in many areas we saw some leveling off during the past year. This plateau continued well into late fall, when in some instances we finally saw the beginning of an upswing. Several factors influenced the market — no doubt the strongest of them was the Internet. Items regarded as rare suddenly turned up in triplicate. And reproductions took their toll — the cookie jar market has been very hard hit, so has Roseville, and to an extent, Fiesta as well. But in general, we predict that Y2K will be exciting for collectors. We polled some of our key advisors in various fields to get their opinions concerning what collectibles would bear watching for the coming year. Here's what we learned from them:

Toys. Young people well out of college and employed long enough to have accumulated a little extra money, dictate the focus of the toy market. Right now it's toys from the '70s they're after. They buy things they remember having as a child. TV show/character memorabilia is hot. GI Joe remains strong; so do vintage Barbies. (Some of the newer Barbies have cooled down because collectors are finding themselves overwhelmed with an over abundance of dolls who vary only in the color of their hair.) Fisher-Price toys are good, so are action figures. Interest is especially high on the early wrestling figures. Slot cars continue to be a good investment. Among diecasts, Hot Wheels are #1, while early Matchboxes are slow right now. Transformers and Micronauts are popular. Pokemon is hot, Tickle Me Elmo is not. The Beanie Baby market is in limbo, waiting to see what exactly Ty is planning next. Caution: if you must buy limited editions and collector series toys, do it strictly for the enjoyment of owning them, not as an investment.

Pottery and Porcelain. American pottery is always a good investment. Most of the most beautiful art pottery ever made was produced in the USA; and, rightly so, Americans are proud of it and eager to own it. Roseville continues strong as does Rookwood, Weller, Hull, and McCoy, but the products of the smaller pottery companies and studio potters are wonderful in their own right. California studio potters have been on top for several years and continue to be today, among them Kay Finch, Florence Ceramics, Brayton Laguna, and many others whose output may not have been quite as extensive: Brad Keeler, Will-George, Dorothy Kindell, Cleminson, Max Weil, Hedi Schoop, Sascha Brastoff, Howard Pierce, and Matthew Adams, for instance. Each possess diverse characteristics of their own that endear them to collectors. New books often fuel interest in their particular area of focus, and there are some wonderful new references on Muncie, Cowan, Camark, Royal Copley, Van Briggle, Shawnee, and Red Wing. Royal Haeger has stole the show for two years running at APEC in Illinois. Ceramic Arts Studio, Josef, Rosemeade, and Lefton produced some fantastic figurines, and all are very popular; we find they sell very well. Holt Howard pixies are still on top. Kreiss novelties, especially the Psycho Ceramic line are unbelievably expensive, and Weeping Gold items are inspiring active bidding on the Internet auctions. Head vases, salt and pepper shakers, wall pockets, string holders, reamers, and clothes sprinkler bottles continue to be popular.

In dinnerware, restaurant china is attracting a lot of attention, and there are two volumes of in-depth information available on the subject. Most of it is of the heavy ironstone variety, but some of it was produced by makers of fine china as well. Just look for the logos of the various restaurants, airlines, institutions, government facilities, corporations, etc., that commissioned the ware. Fiesta is still strong, and besides the vintage colors, watch for items in lilac — they're often as desirable as the old line. Hall dinnerware seems to be perpetually in the spotlight as does Russel Wright, Franciscan, Metlox, Blue Ridge, Homer Laughlin, Stangl, Watt, Purington, and Red Wing. Pick up Pfaltzgraff when you can get nice serving and accessory pieces, especially in America, Gourmet, and Village. Several lines of Johnson Brothers dinnerware have become very collectible. Chintz patterns are very desirable, and Lipper's Blue Danube is starting to draw a lot of attention. Lefton's Holly lines are always good, and Rooster and Roses, another Japanese-made dinnerware line, continues to be worth watching as well.

Glassware. Gene Florence keeps the focus on Depression glass, and collectors seem never to tire of it. Largely because of his efforts, the market for Fire-King glassware, especially their Jade-ite, has been very active. Kitchen glassware, the colored items in particular — reamers, salt and pepper shakers, batter bowls, knives, etc. — continues to grow in value. Crackle glass is well worth looking for, and you'll sometimes be able to pick up some nice Fenton items well underpriced — never pass them by. Westmoreland's mid-century carnival glass, milk glass, and giftware items are appreciating at a very nice pace. There's absolutely no interest in generic stemware, no matter how lovely, so don't be tempted to buy it up, unless you plan to use it yourself. Imperial, Heisey, Fostoria, Tiffin, New Martinsville, Paden City, and the like have for years been safe investments, and no doubt always will be. You'll probably find some Murano clowns, roosters, or animal figures; these are very collectible right now.

Jewelry. Costume jewelry by well-known designers sometimes sells for as much or even more than fine jewelry items. Look for quality workmanship and check the metal mounts for names such as Miriam Haskell, Eisenberg, Trifari, Hollycraft, and Hobè. (There are many others, see our jewelry section for references that will clue you in on all the designers.) Sarah Coventry pieces turn up on occasion, as do those by Coro. Though not quite as pricey, they're still worth your attention. Bakelite or Lucite bracelets, brooches, and earrings have sold at auction this past year bringing prices in a range you might find hard to believe. Remember the plastic fruit jewelry? A simple choker can fetch as much as $100.00, if not more. Aurora Borealis and rhinestone pieces so popular in the '50s and '60s are very collectible. Don't pass up quality items that are unsigned; we predict them to be the stars of the next wave of jewelry collecting.

Furniture. Arts and Crafts style furniture is considered very trendy now; watch for pieces still in their original finish. Signed examples can be very pricey. Fifties Modern pieces such as the boomerang tables and the cube chairs are very good; chairs made of molded fiberglass or with a leather sling seat or an aluminum or wire-work frame typify this genre. Heywood-Wakefield furniture has a devoted following. And don't overlook the clocks and lighting fixtures from that era; good examples by noted designers often sell for several hundred dollars each.

Other Collectibles. Good hand-wrought aluminum is still of interest to collectors, especially signed pieces. Barware items, in particular cocktail shakers with a decidedly Art Deco design, are hot. Old fishing lures are very collectible, some of the more desirable carry price tags of more than several hundred dollars. Old fountain pens, souvenir spoons, and inkwells certainly deserve a close look. TV lamps are very popular right now, so are motion lamps. Good Christmas items are always collectible, even examples from the '50s and '60s. Of course, Coca-Cola memorabilia is holding its own. In fact, soda-related advertising of any type is good; so is breweriana. Advertising characters are still very desirable — watch for Reddy Kilowatt, Campbell Kids, the Energizer Bunny, Charlie the Tuna, Tony the Tiger, Mr. Peanut, Colonel Sanders, and all the others. Black Americana is strong, and Rock 'n Roll collectibles, especially Elvis, Beatles, and KISS memorabilia, have a devoted following.

How to Evaluate Your Holdings

When viewed in its entirety, granted, the antiques and collectibles market can be overwhelming. But in each line of glassware, any type of pottery or toys, or any other field I could mention, there are examples that are more desirable than others, and these are the ones you need to be able to recognize. If you're a novice, it will probably be best at first to choose a few areas that you find most interesting and learn just what particular examples or types of items are most in demand within that field. Concentrate on the top 25%. This is where you'll do 75% of your business. Do your homework. Quality sells. Obviously no one can be an expert in everything, but gradually you can begin to broaden your knowledge. As an added feature of our guide, information on clubs and newsletters, always a wonderful source of up-to-date information on any subject, is contained in each category when available. (Advisor's names are listed as well. We highly recommend that you exhaust all other resources before you contact them with your inquiries. Their role is simply to check over our data before we go to press to make sure it is as accurate as we and they can possibly make it for you; they do not agree to answer readers' questions, though some may. If you do write, you must send them an SASE. If you call, please take the time zones into consideration. Some of our advisors are professionals and may charge an appraisal fee, so be sure to ask. Please, do *not* be offended if they do not respond to your contacts, they are under no obligation to do so.)

There are many fields other than those we've already mentioned that are strong and have been for a long time — Elegant and Carnival glass; photographica; ephemera such as valentines and sheet music; dolls; and railroadiana. It's impossible to list them all. But we've left very little out of this book; at least we've tried to represent each category to some extent and where at all possible to refer you to a source of further information. It's up to you to read, observe the market, and become acquainted with it to the point that you feel confident enough to become a part of today's antiques and collectibles industry.

The thousands of current values found in this book will increase your awareness of today's wonderful world of buying, selling, and collecting antiques and collectibles. Use it to educate yourself to the point that you'll be the one with the foresight to know what and how to buy as well as where and how to turn those sleepers into cold, hard cash.

In addition to this one, there are several other very fine price guides on the market. One of the best is *Schroeder's Antiques Price Guide*; another is *The Flea Market Trader*. Both are published by Collector Books. *The Antique Trader Antiques and Collectibles Price Guide, Warman's Antiques and Their Prices,* and *Kovel's Antiques and Collectibles Price List* are others. You may want to invest in a copy of each. Where you decide to sell will have a direct bearing on how you price your merchandise, and nothing will affect an item's worth more than condition.

If you're not familiar with using a price guide, here's a few tips that may help you. When convenient and reasonable, antiques will be sorted by manufacturer. This is especially true of pottery and most glassware. If you don't find the item you're looking for under manufacturer, look under a broader heading, for instance, cat collectibles, napkin dolls, cookie jars, etc. And don't forget to use the index. Most guides of this type have very comprehensive indexes — a real boon to the novice collector. If you don't find the exact item you're trying to price, look for something similar. For instance, if it's a McCoy rabbit planter you're researching, go through the McCoy section and see what price range other animal planters are in. Or if you have a frame-tray puzzle with Snow White and the Seven Dwarfs, see what other Disney frame-trays are priced at. Just be careful not to compare apples to oranges. You can judge the value of a 7" Roseville Magnolia vase that's not listed; just look at the price given for one a little larger or smaller and adjust it up or down. Pricing collectibles is certainly not a science; the bottom line is simply where the buyer and the seller finally agree to do business. Circumstances dictate sale price, and we can only make suggestions, which we base on current sales, market observations, and the expert opinions of our advisors.

Once you've found 'book' price, decide how much less you can take for it. 'Book' price represents a high average retail. A collectible will often change hands many times, and obviously it will not always be sold at book price. How quickly do you want to realize a profit? Will you be patient enough to hold out for top dollar, or would you rather price your merchandise lower so it will turn over more quickly? Just as there are both types of dealers, there are two types of collectors. Many are bargain hunters. They shop around — do the legwork themselves. On the other hand, there are those who are willing to pay whatever the asking price is to avoid spending precious time searching out pieces they especially want, but they represent the minority. You'll often see tradepaper ads listing good merchandise (from that top 25% we mentioned before) at prices well above book value. This is a good example of a dealer who knows that his merchandise is good enough to entice the buyer who is able to pay a little more and doesn't mind waiting for him (or her) to come along, and that's his prerogative.

Don't neglect to assess the condition of the item you want to sell. Most people, especially inexperienced buyers and sellers, have a tendency to overlook some flaws and to overrate merchandise. Mint condition means that an item is complete and undamaged — in effect, just as it looked the day it was made. Glassware, china, and pottery may often be found in mint condition, though signs of wear will downgrade anything. Unless a toy is still in its original box and has never been played with, you seldom see a toy in mint condition. Paper collectibles are almost never found without deterioration or damage. Most price guides will list values that apply to glass and ceramics that are mint (unless another condition is specifically indicated within some descriptions). Other items are usually evaluated on the assumption that they are in the best as-found condition common to that area of collecting, for instance magazines are simply never found in mint condition. Grade your merchandise as though you were the buyer, not the seller. You'll be building a reputation that will go a long way toward contributing to your success. If it's glassware or pottery you're assessing, an item in less than excellent condition will be mighty hard to sell at any price. Just as a guideline (a basis to begin your evaluation, though other things will factor in), use a scale of one to five with Good being a one, Excellent being a three, and Mint being a five. As an example, a beer tray worth $250.00 in mint condition would then be worth $150.00 if excellent and $50.00 if only good. Remember, the first rule of buying (for resale or investment) is 'Don't put your money in damaged goods.' And the second rule should be be, 'If you do sell damaged items, indicate 'as is' on the price tag, and don't price the item as though it were mint.' The Golden Rule applies just as well to us as antique dealers as it does in any other interaction. Some shops and co-ops have poor lighting — your honesty will be greatly appreciated. If you include identification on your tags as well, be sure it's accurate. If you're not positive, say so. Better yet, let the buyer decide.

Deciding Where to Best Sell Your Merchandise

Personal transactions are just one of many options. Overhead and expenses will vary with each and must be factored into your final pricing. If you have some especially nice items and can contact a collector willing to pay top dollar, that's obviously the best of the lot. Or you may decide to sell to a dealer who may be willing to pay you only half of book. Either way, your expenses won't amount to much more than a little gas or a phone call.

Classified ads are another way to get a good price for your more valuable merchandise without investing much money or time. Place a 'For Sale' ad or run a mail bid in one of the collector magazines or newsletters, several of which are listed in the back of this book. Many people have had excellent results this way. One of the best to reach collectors in general is *The Antique Trader Weekly* (P.O. Box 1050, Dubuque, Iowa 52004). It covers virtually every type of antique and collectible and has a very large circulation. If you have glassware, china, or pottery from the Depression era, you should have good results through *The Depression Glass Daze* (Box 57, Otisville, Michigan 48463). If you have several items and the cost of listing them all is prohibitive, simply place an ad saying (for instance) 'Several pieces of Royal Copley (or whatever) for sale, send SASE for list.' Be sure to give your correct address and phone number.

When you're making out your list or talking with a prospective buyer by phone, try to draw a picture with words. Describe any damage in full; it's much better than having a disgruntled customer to deal with later, and you'll be on your way to establishing yourself as a reputable dealer. Sometimes it's wise to send out photographs. Seeing the item exactly as it is will often help the prospective buyer make up his or her mind. Send an SASE along and ask that your photos be returned to you, so that you can send them out again, if need be. A less expensive alternative is to have your item photocopied. This works great for many smaller items, not just flat shapes but things with some dimension as well. It's wonderful for hard-to-describe dinnerware patterns or for showing their trademarks.

If you've made that 'buy of a lifetime' or an item you've hung onto for a few years has turned out to be a scarce, highly sought collectible, a mail bid is often the best way to get top dollar for your prize. This is how you'll want your ad to read. 'Mail Bid. Popeye cookie jar by American Bisque, slight wear (or 'mint' — briefly indicate condition), closing 6/31/95, right to refuse' (standard self-protection clause meaning you will refuse ridiculously low bids), and give your phone number. Don't commit the sale to any bidder until after the closing date, since some may wait until the last minute to try to place the winning bid.

Be sure to let your buyer know what form of payment you prefer. Some dealers will not ship merchandise until personal checks have cleared. This delay may make the buyer a bit unhappy. So you may want to request a money order or a cashier's check.

Be very careful about how you pack your merchandise for shipment. Breakables need to be well protected. There are several things you can use. Plastic bubble wrap is excellent, or scraps of foam rubber such as carpet padding (check with a carpet-laying service or confiscate some from family and friends who are getting new carpet installed). I've received items wrapped in pieces of egg-crate type mattress pads (watch for these at garage sales!). If there is a computer business near you, check their dumpsters for discarded foam wrapping and other protective packaging. It's best not to let newspaper come in direct contact with your merchandise, since the newsprint may stain certain surfaces. After you've wrapped them well, you'll need boxes. Find smaller boxes (one or several, whatever best fits your needs) that you can fit into a larger one with several inches of space between them. First pack your well-wrapped items snugly into the smaller box, using crushed newspaper to keep them from shifting. Place it into the larger box, using more crushed paper underneath and along the sides, so that it will not move during transit. Remember, if it arrives broken, it's still your merchandise, even though you have received payment. You may want to insure the shipment; check with your carrier. Some have automatic insurance up to a specified amount.

After you've mailed your box, it's good to follow it up with a phone call after a few days. Make sure it arrived in good condition and that your customer is pleased with the merchandise. Most people who sell by mail allow a 10-day return privilege, providing their original price tag is still intact. For this purpose, you can simply initial a gummed label or use one of those pre-printed return address labels that most of us have around the house.

For very large or heavy items such as furniture or slot machines, ask your buyer for his preferred method of shipment. If the distance involved is not too great, he may even want to pick it up himself.

Flea market selling can either be a lot of fun, or it can turn out to be one of the worst experiences of your life.

Obviously you will have to deal with whatever weather conditions prevail, so be sure to listen to weather reports so that you can dress accordingly. You'll see some inventive shelters you might want to copy. Even a simple patio umbrella will offer respite from the blazing sun or a sudden downpour. I've recently been seeing stands catering just to the needs of the flea market dealer — how's that for being enterprising! Not only do they carry specific items the dealers might want, but they've even had framework and tarpaulins, and they'll erect shelters right on the spot!

Be sure to have plastic table covering in case of rain and some large clips to hold it down if there's much wind. The type of clip you'll need depends on how your table is made, so be sure to try them out before you actually get caught in a storm. Glass can blow over, paper items can be ruined, and very quickly your career as a flea market dealer may be cut short for lack of merchandise!

Price your things, allowing yourself a little bargaining room. Unless you want to collect tax separately on each sale (for this you'd need a lot of small change), mentally calculate the amount and add this on as well. Sell the item 'tax included.' Everybody does.

Take snacks, drinks, paper bags, plenty of change, and somebody who can relieve you occasionally. Collectors are some of the nicest people around. I guarantee that you'll enjoy this chance to meet and talk them, and often you can make valuable contacts that may help you locate items you're especially looking for yourself.

Auction houses are listed in the back of this book. If you have an item you feel might be worth selling at auction, be sure to contact one of them. Many have appraisal services; some are free while others charge a fee, dependent on number of items and time spent. We suggest you first make a telephone inquiry before you send in a formal request.

Internet selling works. In fact, I know some dealers who have quit doing shows and simply work out of their home. No more unpacking, travel expense, disappointing attendance, or inconvenience of any kind to endure. You may sell through a set-price online mall or an auction. If you choose the auction (eBay is the most widely used right now), you can put a 'reserve' on everything you sell, a safeguard that protects the seller and prevents an item from going at an unreasonably low figure should there be few bidders.

In Summation

As a long-time collector myself, I can say with certainty that becoming involved in the antiques and collectibles field can be a very enjoyable and profitable pursuit. Those people that are the most successful are those who will devote hours of their time doing research, attending shows, and networking with other collectors. Knowledge is the key to success, and the time you invest in pursuing understanding of the field in every way you can devise will pay off handsomely as you enjoy the hunt for today's collectibles, tomorrow's antiques.

Abbreviations

dia — diameter
ea — each
EX — excellent
G — good condition
gal — gallon
L — long, length
lg — large
M — mint condition

med — medium
MIB — mint in (original) box
MIP — mint in package
MOC — mint on card
NM — near mint
oz — ounce
pc — piece
pr — pair

pt — pint
qt — quart
sm — small
VG — very good
w — wide
w/ — with

Abingdon

You may find smaller pieces of Abingdon around, but it's not common to find many larger items. This company operated in Abingdon, Illinois, from 1934 until 1950, making not only nice vases and figural pieces but some kitchen items as well. Their cookie jars are very well done and popular with collectors. They sometimes used floral decals and gold to decorate their wares, and a highly decorated item is worth a minimum of 25% more than the same shape with no decoration. Some of their glazes also add extra value. If you find a piece in black, bronze, or red, you can add 25% to those as well. Note that if you talk by phone about Abingdon to a collector, be sure to mention the mold number on the base.

For more information we recommend *Abingdon Pottery Artware, 1934 – 50, Stepchild of the Great Depression,* by Joe Paradis (Schiffer).

See also Cookie Jars.

Club: Abingdon Pottery Collectors Club
Elaine Westover, Membership and Treasurer
210 Knox Hwy. 5, Abingdon, IL 61410; 309-462-3267

Ashtray, #334, 5½" $22.50
Ashtray, Daisy, #386, 4½" $20.00
Ashtray, leaf, #660, 5½" $22.00

Bookend/planter, dolphin, decorated, #444, 6", $35.00.

Bowl, #311, 6½" $40.00
Bowl, #684, 5" W $17.50
Bowl, leaf, #408, 6½" $50.00
Bowl, oval, #541, 15x9" $45.00
Bowl, Scallop, scalloped rim, #564, 11" L $18.00
Bowl, Shell, #501, 10½" $22.50
Bowl, Tulip, #642, 6½" $50.00
Box, rosebud finial, #585D, 4½" $80.00
Cache pot, #558, 4¾" $24.00
Candle holder, double, #575, 5", pr $22.50
Chessman, King, #03905K, 5½" $100.00
Figurine, gull, #562, 5" $50.00
Figurine, swan, #661, 3¾" $50.00
Flowerpot, La Fleur, #150, 4" $18.00

Flowerpot w/saucer, La Fleur, 6" $25.00
Jar, grease; Daisy, #679, 4½" $35.00
Jar, Ming, #301, 7¼" $85.00
Lamp base, Swirl, #252, 20½" $100.00
Pitcher, cream; Daisy, #682, 2½" $20.00
Planter, dog, #670, 4" $45.00
Planter, donkey, #673, 4½" $42.00
Plate, Apple Blossom, #415, 11" $45.00
Plate, coupe salad; #342, 7½" $45.00
Rose bowl, #407, 6" $35.00
Sculpture, Scarf Dancer, #3902, 13" $275.00
Urn, Regency, #539, 7" $30.00
Vase, bud; #483, 8" $35.00
Vase, Capri, #351, 5¾" $120.00
Vase, cornucopia; double, #581, 8¼" $45.00
Vase, Dutch girl, #470, 8" $75.00
Vase, embossed anchor, #632, 7½" $35.00
Vase, embossed bird, #468, 7½" $38.00
Vase, w/handles, #630, 9" $45.00
Vase, Ionic, #511, 8" $35.00
Vase, Morning Glory, #391, 7¾" $40.00
Vase, Oak Leaf, #706, 9¼" $55.00
Vase, Rhythm, #380, 7¾" $42.00
Vase, Rosette, #598D, 7¼" $45.00
Vase, Sea Horse, #596D, 8" $60.00
Vase, trumpet form w/handles, #597, 9" $45.00

Vases, What-Nots: C-6, $70.00; A-3, $60.00; B-3, $70.00.

Vase, wreath w/star, #467, 8" $50.00
Wall pocket, butterfly, #601D, 8½" $80.00
Water jug, #113, 7½" $110.00
Window box, sunburst, #448, 9" L $35.00

Advertising Character Collectibles

The advertising field holds a special fascination for many of today's collectors. It's vast and varied, so its appeal is universal; but the characters of the ad world are its stars right now. Nearly every fast-food restaurant and manufacturer of a consumer product has a character logo. Keep your eyes open on your garage sale outings; it's not at all uncommon to find the cloth and plush dolls, plastic banks and mugs, bendies, etc., such as we've listed here. There are several books on the market that are geared specifically toward these types of collectibles. Among them are *Advertising Character Collectibles* by Warren Dotz; *Zany Characters of the Ad World* by Mary Jane Lamphier; and *Cereal Box Bonanza, The 1950s* by Scott Bruce. All are published by Collector Books. Others you'll enjoy reading are *Collectible Aunt Jemima* by Jean Williams Turner (Schiffer); *Cereal Boxes and Prizes, The 1960s* by Scott Bruce (Flake World Publishing); and *Hake's Guide to Advertising Collectibles* by Ted Hake (Wallace-Homestead). *Huxford's Collectible Advertising* offers a more general overview of the market but nevertheless includes many listings and values for character-related items as well. *Schroeder's Collectible Toys, Antique to Modern,* is another source. (The latter two are also published by Collector Books.)

See also Advertising Watches; Breweriana; Bubble Bath Containers; Cereal Boxes and Premiums; Character Clocks and Watches; Character and Promotional Drinking Glasses; Coca-Cola Collectibles; Fast-Food Collectibles; Novelty Radios; Novelty Telephones; Pez Candy Containers; Pin-Back Buttons; Salt and Pepper Shakers; Soda Pop Memorabilia.

Newsletter: *FLAKE, The Breakfast Nostalgia Magazine*
P.O. Box 481
Cambridge, MA 02140; 617-492-5004

Aunt Jemima

One of the most widely recognized ad characters of them all, Aunt Jemima has decorated bags and boxes of pancake flour for more than ninety years. In fact, the original milling company carried her name, but by 1926 it had become part of the Quaker Oats Company. She and Uncle Mose were produced in plastic by the F&F Mold and Die Works in the 1950s, and the salt and pepper shakers, syrup pitchers, cookie jars, etc., they made are perhaps the most sought-after of the hundreds of items available today. (Watch for reproductions.) Age is a big worth-assessing factor for memorabilia such as we've listed below, of course, but so is condition. Watch for very chipped or worn paint on the F&F products, and avoid buying soiled cloth dolls.

Advisor: Judy Posner (See Directory, Advertising)

Banner, Here Today! Aunt Jemima in Person Serving Her Famous Pancakes, cloth, w/graphics, red, yellow, white, 34x58", EX $500.00
Box, 24 Packages Aunt Jemima Pancake Flour, red & black image of Aunt Jemima & lettering on brown cardboard, 14x13x9", VG $150.00
Brochure, Aunt Jemima's Kitchen/As You Travel..., lists locations of 28 restaurants & planned locations, 1950s, EX $45.00
Canister, features various Aunt Jemima products on colorful nostalgic background, dated, 1983, 6x5¼" dia, EX ..$42.00

Clock, Lucite w/wooden base, battery-operated, Seal in the Freshness... Aunt Jemima Waffles Stay-Fresh Bag, 6" square, MIB $225.00
Cookie jar, Aunt Jemima plastic figural, F&F Mold & Die Co, NM $500.00
Creamer, Uncle Mose, F&F Mold & Die Co, EX $80.00
Doll, Breakfast Bear, blue plush, in chef's hat, apron & bandanna, 13", M $175.00
Junior Chef Pancake Set, Argo Industries, 1949, EX .$150.00
Magazine ad, Lenten Meal w/Real Appeal...the Lightest Pancakes Ever! Celebrate Pancake Day Feb 26, 1952, 13x11", EX $22.00
Magazine ad, Perfect Corn Bread, New Easy Mix From Aunt Jemima, w/color graphics, 1958, 13x10", EX $18.00
Pancake mold, aluminum w/center handle & 4 animal shapes, Aunt Jemima embossed on surface, 8½" dia, EX, from $165 to $195.00
Pancake shaker, yellow plastic, Perfect Pancakes In 10 Shakes...Aunt Jemima embossed on lid, 1940s-50s, 9", EX $90.00
Place mat, The Story of Aunt Jemima.../Aunt Jemima at Disneyland, drawings based on NC Wyeth art, 1955, 10x14", EX $35.00
Plate, white w/Aunt Jemima's Kitchen Restaurant logo, scalloped edge, Wellsville China, 1950s, 10" dia, EX ..$225.00
Promotional poster book, Mr Grocer Here's Your Year-Round Promotional Parade!, shows ad layouts, etc, spiral, 1940s, EX $550.00
Recipe booklet, Pancakes Unlimited, full color, 31 pages, 1959, 6x4½", EX $55.00
Recipe cards, I Know You Will Enjoy These...As Much as I Enjoy Sending Them..., complete set of 16, M, from $265 to .$250.00
Restaurant table card, diecut relief, ...Time for Aunt Jemima Pancakes, trademark image w/breakfast, 1953, 3x4¾", M $45.00
Salt & pepper shakers, Aunt Jemima & Uncle Mose, F&F Mold & Die Co, 3½", NM, pr $55.00
Salt & pepper shakers, Aunt Jemima & Uncle Mose, F&F Mold & Die Co, 5", pr $75.00
Sign, cardboard stand-up, Aunt Jemima Pancake Flour/Self Rising & Ready Mixed..., diecut image in center, 20x13", VG+ $375.00
Sign, cardboard stand-up, Aunt Jemima Says: Here's the Place to Get Eatin'est Hot Cakes in Town!, 15x21", EX .$100.00

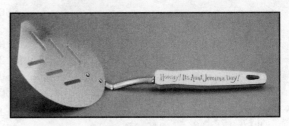

Spatula, plastic handle, $45.00.

Spice shaker, figural, F&F Mold & Die Co, from set of 6, ea $50.00

Sugar bowl, Aunt Jemima figural, w/lid, F&F Mold & Die, 5½", EX..**$90.00**
Syrup pitcher, Aunt Jemima figural, F&F Mold & Die Co, 5½"..**$70.00**

Table sign, $40.00. (Photo courtesy Judy Posner)

Big Boy and Friends

Bob's Big Boy, home of the nationally famous Big Boy, the original double-deck hamburger, was founded by Robert C. 'Bob' Wian in Glendale, California, in 1938. He'd just graduated from high school, and he had a dream. With the $300.00 realized from the sale of the car he so treasured, he bought a run-down building and enough basic equipment to open his business. Through much hard work and ingenuity, Bob turned his little restaurant into a multimillion-dollar empire. Not only does he have the double-deck two-patty burger to his credit, but carhops and drive-in restaurants were his creation as well.

With business beginning to flourish, Bob felt he needed a symbol — something that people would recognize. One day in walked a chubby lad of six, his sagging trousers held up by reluctant suspenders. Bob took one look at him and named him Big Boy, and that was it! It was a natural name for his double-deck hamburger — descriptive, catchy, and easy to remember. An artist worked out the drawings, and Bob's Pantry was renamed Boy's Big Boy.

The enterprise grew fast, and Bob added location after location. In 1969 when he sold out to the Marriott Corporation, he had 185 restaurants in California, with franchises such as Elias Big Boy, Frisch's Big Boy, and Shoney's Big Boy in other states. The Big Boy burger and logo was recognized by virtually every man, woman, and child in America, and Bob retired knowing he had made a significant contribution to millions of people everywhere.

Since Big Boy has been in business for over sixty years, you'll find many items and numerous variations. Some, such as the large statues, china, and some menus, have been reproduced. If you're in doubt, consult an experienced collector for help. Many items of jewelry, clothing, and kids promotions were put out over the years, too numerous to itemize separately. Values range from $5.00 up to $1,000.00.

Advisor: Steve Soelberg (See Directory, Advertising)

Ashtray, clear w/red logo..............................**$20.00**
Ashtray, gray w/white logo in bottom, round............**$20.00**
Bank, w/ or w/out hamburger, vinyl, M, ea..............**$40.00**

Bob's Diner menu, copyright 1956, M, $150.00. (Photo courtesy Steve Soelberg)

Box, lunch/pencil; red, plastic......................**$25.00**
Button, magnet, lighter, paper bag, current dinner menus, ea...**$10.00**
Button, National Big Boy Club Member.................**$20.00**
Cookie jar, figural.................................**$500.00**
Doll, Dakin, complete w/hamburger & shoes...........**$150.00**
Doll, no burger or shoes, Dakin......................**$50.00**
Figurine, pewter.....................................**$50.00**
Golf ball, pencil, balloons, pen, condiments (ketchup, salt, pepper, sugar, towelette), crayons, yo-yos, ea.......**$5.00**
Hamburger wrapper, white & brown, food design, 1960s.**$50.00**
Hat, painter's; Should He Stay or Go.................**$15.00**
Kite, paper w/Big Boy logo..........................**$500.00**

Lamp base, ceramic, tube in back to contain wiring, 9½", M, $2,500.00. (Photo courtesy Steve Soelberg)

Lithograph, signed & #d, 1976, very colorful.........**$150.00**
Lithograph, 1976 Bicentennial, signed & #d..........**$100.00**
Matchbook collection, 22 early matchbooks in holder.**$500.00**
Mug, Big Boy China, Canoga Park drive-in.............**$25.00**
Night light, plastic, plug-in-socket type, MIB......**$100.00**
Ornament, Christmas; Happy Holidays..................**$20.00**

Pen, Parker, MIB $20.00
Pin, employee service; gold color, man's or woman's, ea .$35.00
Plate, dinner/bread; Elias, w/leaf design $50.00
Playing cards, red, unopened, M.................................$40.00
Radio, transistor; soda can shape, w/logo.................$500.00
Salt & pepper shakers, original, some paint wear, pr..$250.00
Seasoning salt, patch, evolution ruler, sippers, Zippo pen,
    Christmas card, sidewalk chalk, notebook, name badge,
    ea $10.00
Statue, employee award, gold Oscar $450.00
Store display, PVC w/4 figures $100.00
Sweatshirt, dark blue, w/logo, worn, lg $20.00
Trading cards, famous Americans, set of 30 ....$80.00
Watch, gold, quartz, lady's, MIB................................$100.00
Watch, snap; digital, red & white checkered band, man's .$20.00
Watch, Windert, gold, quartz, man's, MIB $150.00

Campbell Kids

The introduction of the world's first canned soup was
announced in 1897. Later improvements in the manufacturing process created an evolutionary condensed soup. The
Campbell's® Soup Company is now the primary beneficiary
of this early entrepreneurial achievement. Easily identified by
their red and white advertising, the company has been built
on a tradition of skillful product marketing through five generations of consumers. Now a household name for all ages,
Campbell's Soups have grown to dominate 80% of the
canned soup market.

The first Campbell's licensed advertising products were
character collectibles offered in 1910 — composition dolls
with heads made from a combination of glue and sawdust.
They were made by the E.I. Horsman Company and sold for
$1.00 each. They were the result of a gifted illustrator, their
creator, Grace Drayton, who in 1904 gave life to the chubby-
faced cherub 'Campbell's Kids.'

In 1994 the Campbell's Soup Kids celebrated their 90th
birthday. They have been revised a number of times to maintain a likeness to modern-day children. Over the years hundreds of licensees have been commissioned to produce collectibles and novelty items with the Campbell's logo in a red
and white theme.

Licensed advertising reached a peak from 1954 through
1956 with thirty-four licensed manufacturers. Unusual items
included baby carriages, toy vacuums, games, and apparel.
Many of the more valuable Campbell's advertising collectibles were made during this period. In 1956 a Campbell's
Kid doll was produced from latex rubber. Called 'Magic Skin,'
it proved to be the most popular mail-in premium ever produced. Campbell's received more than 560,000 requests for
this special girl chef doll.

For more information, we recommend *Campbell's Soup
Collectibles, A Price and Identification Guide,* by David and
Micki Young (Krause Publications). The book may be
ordered through The Soup Collector Club.

Advisors: David and Micki Young (See Directory, Advertising)

Club: The Soup Collector Club
414 Country Lane Ct.
Wauconda, IL 60084
fax/phone: 847-487-4917; e-mail: dyoung@soupcollector.com;
www.soupcollector.com

Bank, Campbell Boy in chef's garb, ceramic, Oriental letter-
    ing w/Campbell's lettered on hat, 1970s, 8", EX ..$45.00
Bank, pail w/lid, metal w/plastic handle, 6 different Campbell
    Kids graphics, Shackman, 1980, 2½", M.................$20.00
Calendar, 1974, linen hanger, M'm! M'm! Good!, Campbell
    Boy as chef, Norcross, 27x16", M $15.00
Christmas ornament, Warm & Hearty Wishes, Kid atop soup
    can, Enesco, 1993, MIB $20.00

Comic book, 'Captain
America & The Campbell
Kids,' promotional, Marvel,
1980, 32 pages, M, $24.00.
(Photo courtesy Dan and
Micki Young)

Cookie jar, ceramic, white w/Campbell Kids graphics,
    Westwood, 1991, MIB..$35.00
Cup, ceramic, Campbell Kids graphics, Westwood, M..$5.00
Cup, ceramic, M'm! M'm! Good!, M...............................$3.00
Cup, ceramic, Salute America, Campbell Kids as Uncle Sam
    & Liberty, 1986, M $17.00
Cup, plastic, M'm! M'm! Good!, Campbell Kids graphics,
    w/lid, microwaveable, 1992, M................................$5.00
Cup, plastic, molded Campbell Kid head, yellow hair, 1976,
    NM $12.00
Decal, Boy chef w/spoon raised in front of barbecue,
    Meyercord, 1954, 5x6x5", M....................................$8.00
Dinnerware, child's set, stoneware, plate, bowl, cup &
    saucer, Campbell Kids graphics, 1992, MIB.........$12.00
Dinnerware, tumbler, bowl & spoon, Campbell Kids graph-
    ics, Zak Designs, 1995, MIP $20.00
Dolls, Campbell Boy & Girl, vinyl, 1970s, 9", set of 2,
    MIB $125.00
Dolls, Campbell Boy & Girl, vinyl w/rooted hair, cloth
    clothes, Globe, 1988, MIB, pr $90.00
Fork & spoon set, Campbell Kids graphics on handles,
    Westwood, 1992, MIB..$8.00
Game, The Campbell Kids Shopping game, Parker Bros,
    1955, scarce, NMIB...$150.00
Hot pad/oven mitt, graphics of Campbell Kid as chef hold-
    ing loaf of bread, 1992, M..$8.00
Jigsaw puzzle, All Aboard, Jaymar, 1986, 28 pieces, MIB ..$25.00
Paperweight, etched glass, 1978, M $45.00

Phone card, Cheering Soup Kids, Collect-A-Card, 1996, unused, M..**$10.00**

Salt & pepper shakers, ceramic, Campbell Kid as dancing chef on sides, Westwood, 1991, MIB, pr.............**$10.00**

Salt & pepper shakers, metal, Campbell Kids graphics on sides, 1996, M, pr...**$10.00**

Salt & pepper shakers, plastic, Campbell Kid figures as chefs, made by F&F, 1950s, 4½", MIB, pr....................**$50.00**

Sign, cardboard diecut, Campbell Kids as baseball player, 1980, 18", EX..**$8.00**

Sign, cardboard diecut, Campbell Kids as pilgrims, 1980, 18", EX...**$8.00**

Sign, tin, ...M'm! M'm! Good!/Ready In A Jiffy, Campbell Kids & list of flavors, red, white & yellow, 1950s, 12x18", NM...**$110.00**

Tea set, child's, porcelain, Chilton, 1992, 9-pc set, MIB (recalled for high lead content)..................**$25.00**

Thimble, china, Campbell Girl at stove, banded top & bottom, Franklin Mint, 1980, ¾", M.....................**$15.00**

Tool caddy w/tools, Chef Kid on sides, Westwood, 1992, M **$8.00**

Wristwatch, dial pictures Campbell Girl holding purse, red vinyl band, Criterion, 1970s, MIB **$45.00**

Dolls, Colonial boy and girl (Paul Revere and Betsy Ross replicas), 1976 premiums, 10", M, from $65.00 to $80.00 each. (Photo courtesy Dan and Micki Young)

Cap'n Crunch

Cap'n Crunch was the creation of Jay Ward, whom you will no doubt remember was also the creator of the Rocky and Bullwinkle show. The Cap'n hails from the '60s and was one of the first heroes of the presweetened cereal crowd. Jean LaFoote was the villain always scheming to steal the Cap'n's cereal.

Advisor: Scott Bruce (See Directory, Advertising)

Bank, Cap'n Crunch figure, painted plastic, 1973, VG..**$65.00**
Bank, Treasure Chest, blue plastic, 1984, NM.............**$10.00**

Baseball, logo: Cap'n Crunch's Home Run Crunch Cereal, sealed in cellophane, M **$10.00**

Beanie, Tiger Shark Meanie, in original printed bag, M, from $16 to..**$20.00**

Big Slick Gyro Car, blue plastic, 1972, MIP **$15.00**

Binoculars, blue plastic, 1972, MIP **$15.00**

Boson whistle, blue & white w/Cap'n & Seadog, ca 1965, EX **$10.00**

Cap'n Crunch Cruiser, plastic, 1987, EX......................**$10.00**

Cap'n Rescue Kit, paper, 1986, MIP **$10.00**

Coloring book, c 1968, Whitman, VG..........................**$20.00**

Comic book, Center of the Earth, 1987, 8-page, EX...**$10.00**

Figure, Cap'n Crunch, blue plastic, 1986, 1½", VG.....**$10.00**

Figure, Cap'n Crunch, vinyl, 1970s, EX, from $40 to..**$50.00**

Figure, Sog Master, silver plastic robot, 1986, 1½", NM..**$15.00**

Figure, Soggie, nearly clear plastic, 1986, 1½", EX.....**$10.00**

Frisbee, blue plastic w/Cap'n in center, MIP, 1970s, EX..**$50.00**

Game, Island Adventure, complete, Warren, 1987, EXIB.**$30.00**

Hand puppet, plastic, 1960s, VG................................**$15.00**

Imprint set, EX...**$45.00**

Iron-ons, 4 characters in original paper pack, M........**$12.50**

Membership kit, Quaker Oats, 1965, mailer: 9½x12½", EX/M, from 200.00 to $300.00. (Photo courtesy Scott Bruce)

Puzzle, Cap'n & crew, Fisher-Price #504, 1971, VG....**$35.00**

Sea Dog spy kit, plastic, w/instructions, M (original mailer)..**$45.00**

Stickers, Cockle, paper, sheet A or B, 1980, M, ea **$15.00**

Storyscope '72, assembled plastic, w/cut-out story disk, NM.**$35.00**

Surfboard rider, fill his head w/baking soda to activate, ca 1975, MIP...**$10.00**

Wallet, thin cardboard, outline of Cap'n's head, 1982, +5 pcs of Cap'n's money, EX...**$10.00**

Charlie Tuna

Poor Charlie, never quite good enough for the Star-Kist folks to can, though he yearns for them to catch him; but since the early 1970s he's done a terrific job working for them as the company logo. A dapper blue-fin tuna in sunglasses and a beret, he's appeared in magazines, done TV commercials, modeled for items as diverse as lamps and banks, but still they deny him his dream. 'Sorry, Charlie.'

Belt buckle, brass oval w/embossed Charlie...............**$35.00**
Camera, Charlie figure, ca 1970, 10", VG **$100.00**
Charm, embossed brass 1½" disk, on brass-link bracelet, 1960s, NM...**$12.00**
Cuff links, bracelet & pendant, copper-tone, ca 1970s, EX.**$30.00**
Doll, plush, 1983, NM.......................................**$40.00**
Figure, vinyl Charlie, arms up (rare version), 1973, 7½", (M, $125) MIB...**$200.00**
Figure, vinyl Charlie, blue, pink hat w/Star-Kist, ca 1973, 7", EX, from $50 to.....................................**$60.00**
Lamp base, Charlie figure reaching upward w/other fin on hip, painted composition w/brown base, Copyright 1970, 13", EX..**$85.00**
Patch, Charlie embroidered on green background w/yellow coral & orange starfish, Sorry Charlie sign, 1975, 3", NM **$12.00**
Radio, bike; Charlie embossed on rectangular case, dated 1973, non-working, VG **$15.00**

Radio, copyright 1970 by Starkist Foods, made in Hong Kong (base not original), 5½x3½", EX, $60.00. (Photo courtesy Marty and Sue Bunis)

Radio, transistor **$55.00**
Ring, metal 1" Charlie figure, adjustable, EX...............**$10.00**
Tape measure, Star-Kist can, ca 1980s, MIB **$15.00**
Telephone, Charlie figure stands on square platform, MIB **$65.00**
Tumbler, Charlie 3X & girl tuna, Tell 'em Charlie Sent You, 3½" **$6.50**

Colonel Sanders

There's nothing fictional about the Colonel — he was a very real guy, who built an empire on the strength of his fried chicken recipe with 'eleven herbs and spices.' In the 1930s, the Colonel operated a small cafe in Corbin, Kentucky. As the years went by, he developed a chain of restaurants which he sold in the mid-'60s. But even after the sale, the new company continued to use the image of the handsome southern gentlemen as their logo. The Colonel died in 1980.

Album, LP, Christmas Day w/Colonel Sanders, RCA 1968, EX...**$25.00**

Bank, 1965, Run Starling Plastics Ltd., 13", NM, from $30.00 to $40.00.

Bank, plastic figure, no base, white w/black necktie, holding bucket of chicken, 1970s, 8", NM, from $20 to....**$30.00**
Bank, plastic figure, w/arm around restaurant building & holding bucket of chicken, white w/red & black trim, 6", EX **$125.00**
Bank, plastic figure, 10" or 13", EX, ea, from $40 to..**$50.00**
Child's tea set, plastic, 1970s, MIB **$110.00**
Coin, Visit the Colonel at Mardi Gras, M....................**$10.00**
Coloring book, Favorite Chicken Stories, 1960s, 11x5½", EX...**$25.00**
KFC Colonel Sanders housebox w/14 3" Colonels in various ethnic attire, limited edition, MIP, from $40 to.....**$50.00**
Lamp shade, glass, painted as fried chicken bucket, unmarked, from $275 to **$325.00**
Magazine ad, featuring the Colonel, 1967, 10x13" **$8.00**
Mask, multicolored plastic, 1960s, M.......................**$38.00**
Nodder, bisque, marked Charlsprod Japan, 1960s, 7½", M, from $100 to...**$125.00**
Nodder, painted skin tone w/white suit, black trim, cane & glasses, holds bucket of chicken, 1960s, 7", EX...**$85.00**
Nodder, papier-mache, Tops Enterprises, c 1967, 7½", MIB...**$150.00**
Pin, Colonel's head, metal, EX.............................**$6.50**
Playset, Let's Play at Kentucky Fried Chicken, Child Guidance, 1970s, EX (EX box) **$140.00**
Poker chip, plastic w/portrait, 1960s, M **$17.50**
Postcard, Colonel's original motel on linen, EX............**$8.00**
Print block, Kentucky Fried Chicken w/smiling face, metal mounted on hardwood, 1960s, 2⅜x1½", EX..........**$9.50**
Salt & pepper shakers, Colonel & Mrs Harland Sanders (busts), marked Marquardt Corp 1972, 3½", pr, from $85 to.**$95.00**
Salt & pepper shakers, plastic Colonel figure, EX, pr.**$45.00**
Salt & pepper shakers, white hard plastic, 1 w/black base, 1 w/white, 4½", pr...**$10.00**
Tie tac, gold-tone molded head w/diamond chip, M.**$65.00**
Toy, figural, wind-up walker, white suit, red bolo tie, glasses & cane, arms move & head nods, 3¼", NM.........**$15.00**

Elsie the Cow and Family

She's the most widely recognized cow in the world; everyone knows Elsie, Borden's mascot. Since the mid-1930s, she's been seen on booklets and posters; modeled for mugs, creamers, dolls, etc.; and appeared on TV, in magazines, and at grocery stores to promote their products. Her husband is Elmer (who once sold Elmer's Glue for the same company), and her twins are best known as Beulah and Beauregard, though they've been renamed in recent years (now they're Bea and Beaumister). Elsie was retired in the 1960s, but due to public demand was soon reinstated to her rightful position and continues today to promote the company's dairy products.

Advisor: Lee Garmon (See Directory, Advertising)

Activity book, Elsie's Funbook/Cut-Out Toys & Games, full color, 1940s, 10x7", EX................$65.00
Bottle topper, Season's Greetings From Borden's And...(space for name) Your Milkman, Elmer in wreath, EX....$35.00
Cookbook, Elsie's Cook Book/By Elsie the Cow/Tested Recipes of Every Variety, 1st edition, 1952, 374 pages, 8x5", EX................$32.00
Cookie cutter, round yellow plastic w/embossed head image of Beulah, 2¼" dia, EX................$48.00

Cookie jar, Pottery Guild (not always marked), 13", from $400.00 to $450.00. (Photo courtesy Lee Garmon)

Creamer, ceramic, Elsie's head w/bow at neck, 1940s, 5", VG+................$80.00
Doll, Elsie sitting, brown plush w/vinyl head, yellow hands & feet, yellow bow w/plastic charm, 16", M......$135.00
Game, board shows barn w/names & head images of Elsie, Elmer & Beulah on daisy background, no box o/w EX................$70.00
Letter opener, red plastic w/round image of Elsie flashing to Borden's Milk 23 Ways Guarded, EX................$70.00
Mug, china, trademark image of Elsie on white Coke-glass shape w/handle, EX................$60.00
Needle book, black & white trademark image of Elsie above phrase on red, 1940s, 5¼", EX................$55.00

Paper hat, 1857/1957 on either side of daisy logo on receding pennant-type graphic, blue & white, 5x11", M......$50.00
Place mat, paper, Elsie Says For Over 125 Years Folks Have Known..., 5 color scenes w/geometric border, 11x17", M................$25.00
Plate, porcelain, daisy logo in center w/embossed design on scalloped rim, gold trim, 6½" dia, M................$125.00
Recipe book, Elsie's Hostess Recipe Book/...Sour Cream/Cottage Cheese/Lite-Line Yogurt, shows Elsie in apron, 1970s, M................$25.00
Recipe leaflet, Try These Nine Such Recipes!, says Elsie, 1949, M................$30.00
Salt & pepper shakers, Beulah w/flowers on head & Beauregard in green shorts, Japan, 3½", EX........$85.00

Salt and pepper shakers, Elsie and her twins, from $75.00 to $85.00. (Photo courtesy Helene Guarnaccia)

Sign, embossed tin button, Borden's Ice Bream, white & blue lettering on red & white w/head image of Elsie, 36" dia, VG................$525.00
Sign, tin, Borden's Ice Cream Very Big On Flavor, daisy logo w/white & red lettering on blue, 1959, 24x45", VG.$150.00
Sweater, V-neck w/embroidered daisy logo, 1960s, M..$40.00
Tablecloth, cotton, printed scene w/Elsie & family at outdoor barbecue, 1940s, 36x56", NM................$145.00
Thermometer, tin, Borden's Ice Cream/Very Big on Flavor, daisy logo above white & red lettering on blue, 1960s, 25", NM................$500.00
Tie clasp, gold-tone metal bar w/encircled image of Elsie hanging from double chain, EX................$55.00
Toy train kit, Elsie's Good Food Line Train, 1940s, unpunched, w/instructions, M (original envelope)................$200.00
Toy truck, Borden's Fresh Milk, metal w/plastic trim, yellow & white w/daisy decal, Buddy L, 1960s, 11", VG+...$125.00
Tumbler, clear glass w/applied graphics of Elmer in tiny car & Beulah w/checkered flag, 1930s, 4¾", M........$55.00

Gerber Baby

Since the late 1920s, the Gerber company has used the smiling face of a baby to promote their line of prepared strained baby food. Several dolls and rubber squeeze toys have been made over the years. Even if you're a novice collector, they'll be easy to spot. Some of the earlier dolls hold a can of product in their hand. Look for the Gerber mark on later dolls. For further information see *A Collector's Guide to the Gerber Baby* by Joan Stryker Grubaugh, Ed.D.

Advisor: Joan Stryker Grubaugh (See Directory, Advertising)

Bib, rubber, animals & baby printed in blue on white, Kleinerts, ca 1936-39.............................**$75.00**
Book, Baby Care Manual, Parent's Magazine, 1943......**$6.00**
Cafeteria tray, 1950s.....................................**$40.00**
Clock, hexagonal wooden frame, time & temperature, 1970s, 1½"...**$40.00**
Cup, silver metal, w/penny-size baby head mounted on side, 1990 ....**$55.00**
Doll, Lucky Ltd, rabbit logo on back, 1982-92, dressed, 6"...**$15.00**
Doll, Musical Dreamy Doll, plush body, wind-up music box plays Rock-a-bye Baby, 1984 Atlanta Novelty......**$75.00**
Doll, Sun Rubber, 1955-59, drinks & wets, head, arms & legs move, 2nd premium, w/accessories....................**$140.00**

Duffel bag, Windjammer, rayon canvas, 1983, $18.00. (Photo courtesy Joan Stryker Grubaugh)

Electronic Discovery Book, 3 levels of learning about animal & object identification, Toy Biz, 1995 ....**$23.00**
Figure, vinyl squeaker, boy or girl, ca 1985, 8", ea **$20.00**
Golf glove, leather, baby screened on front, 1980s **$15.00**
Hat, factory worker's, Quality Is My Job, Gerber screened on front, 1940s...............................**$9.00**
Lapel pin, blue w/Gerber in gold, 1990s.....................**$4.00**
License plate, metal, baby & Gerber, 1981 ....**$14.00**
Mug, ceramic, baby & Safety & Quality Freemont Plant, 1987 in blue on white **$10.00**
Mug, insulated; baby & Gerber in blue on white 1988 ..**$6.00**
Pop can holder, baby on front, Safety Is Just a Thought Away on back..**$10.00**
Ruler, metal, 1960, 13".....................................**$14.00**
T-shirt, toddler's, baby screened on white shirt w/blue sleeves, 1982 ....**$18.00**

Tennis ball, yellow w/blue printed-on baby & Gerber, 1978 ....**$4.00**

Toy phone, Talk-Back, Arrow Products, 1969, $35.00. (Photo courtesy Joan Stryker Grubaugh)

Green Giant

The Jolly Green Giant has been a well-known ad fixture since the 1950s (some research indicates an earlier date); he was originally devised to represent a strain of European peas much larger than the average-size peas Americans had been accustomed to. At any rate, when Minnesota Valley Canning changed its name to Green Giant, he was their obvious choice. Rather a terse individual himself, by 1974 he was joined by Little Green Sprout, with the lively eyes and more talkative personality.

In addition to a variety of toys and other memorabilia already on the market, in 1988 Benjamin Medwin put out a line of Little Green Sprout items. These are listed below.

Advisor: Lil West (See Directory, Advertising)

Bank, Little Sprout, composition, plays Valley of the Jolly Green Giant, 8½"...................................**$50.00**

Brush holder, with four brushes, Benjamin Medwin, MIB, $40.00. (Photo courtesy Lil West)

Clock, Little Sprout holding round dial in front on base, w/talking alarm, 1986, 10½", EX **$25.00**
Cookie jar, Little Sprout, Benjamin Medwin, 1990-1992, MIB..**$65.00**
Dinnerware set, includes plate, cup, knife & fork, 1991, MIB..**$10.00**
Doll, Green Giant, cloth, 1966, 16", M (in original mailer), from $25 to..**$35.00**
Doll, Little Sprout, plush w/cloth outfit, felt leaf hair, 1970s, 12", EX, from $20 to..........................**$30.00**
Doll, talking; Little Sprout, MIP **$55.00**
Fabric, Green Giant & Little Sprout, heavy material, 48x45"...**$20.00**

Farm Factory, with truck workers, Little Sprout finger puppet, and all accessories, MIB, $20.00. (Photo courtesy Lil West)

Figure, Green Giant, vinyl, ca 1975, 9", EX.............**$75.00**
Figure, Little Sprout, soft vinyl, 6" **$15.00**
Flashlight, Little Sprout, MIB.............................**$45.00**
Jump rope, Little Sprout, MIB...........................**$20.00**
Kite, plastic, mail-in premium, late 1960s, 42x48", unused, M **$30.00**
Lamp, Touch-on, Little Sprout holding balloons, 1985-86, 14½", M, from $35 to..................................**$45.00**
Lapel pin, Green Giant.......................................**$7.00**
Planter, Little Sprout, Benjamin Medwin, 1988, MIB...**$35.00**
Record, Green Giant 20th Birthday, 78 rpm, red wax, 7", VG **$10.00**
Salt & pepper shakers, Little Sprout, Benjamin Medwin, 1990-92, MIB, pr **$25.00**
Scouring pad holder w/pad, Little Sprout, Benjamin Medwin, 1988, MIB **$15.00**
Toy, tractor trailer, Green Giant Corn, Nylint, w/all attachments, 21", VG **$55.00**
Toy semi truck, Green Giant, 18-wheeler, Tonka, 1951, M, from $150 to...**$200.00**
Toy stake truck, Green Giant Peas, metal sideboards, Tonka, 1953, EX **$300.00**

Joe Camel

Joe Camel, the ultimate 'cool character,' was only on the scene for a few years as a comic character. The all-around Renaissance beast, he dated beautiful women, drove fast motorcycles and cars, lazed on the beach, played pool, hung around with his pals (the Hard Pack), and dressed formally for dinner and the theatre. He was 'done in' by the anti-cigarette lobby because he smoked. Now reduced to a real camel, his comic strip human persona is avidly collected by both women and men, most of whom don't smoke. Prices have been steadily raising as more and more people come to appreciate him as the great icon he is.

Advisor: C.J. Russell and Pamela E. Apkarian-Russell (See Directory, Halloween)

Ashtray, cobalt glass, 57 Chevy, 1 license plate on front & back, M..**$25.00**

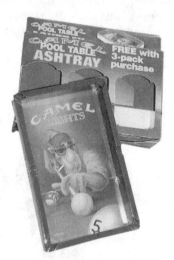

Ashtray, plastic, in original box, $25.00. (Photo courtesy C.J. Russell and Pamela E. Apkarian-Russell)

Auto shade, colorful logo, M......................................**$15.00**
Backpack...**$30.00**
Calendar, 1992, Year in Pictures, MIP **$20.00**
Cap, Camel Club, MIB..**$15.00**
Cap, camouflage, MIB **$15.00**
Cap, Smokin' Joe's Racing embroidered on side, Joe on front, M **$15.00**
Card game, 48 cards, 6 dice, score pad & pencil, M..**$10.00**
Casino Poker set, 6 tubes of clay chips, 2 decks of cards, in original tin, M.......................................**$65.00**
Cigarette pack, Joe at the piano **$8.00**
Clock, Camel Lights, Joe as pool player **$35.00**
Clock, plastic Joe standing by round clock, battery-op, 1992, 20x23", NM.......................................**$90.00**
Coaster set, square, MIB..**$10.00**
Compact mirror, Joe & the gang w/lg Camels sign behind them, city buildings either side, white plastic, 3½x2½"...**$20.00**
Counter mat, Joe in various activities in triangular reserves, EX...**$10.00**
Cup, plastic, 4 different, ea...**$15.00**
Dartboard, arched top, Joe holding dart on front, 2-part front opens, unused, 27x20", M..................................**$65.00**
Drink holder, Camel Joe figure...................................**$20.00**

Duffle bag, 14x9x10½", EX $28.00
Ice bucket, w/4 tumblers, 1992, M $30.00
Jacket, yellow, MIP $12.00
Light, Joe as pool player, 8½x21", EX $30.00
Lighter, black, bronze coin w/embossed Joe, Zippo, in original sleeve w/desert scene, MIB $25.00
Lighter, black w/Joe in tux, Zippo, in original sleeve w/desert scene, M $35.00
Lighter, gold color w/embossed Joe as pool player, Zippo, original case, M $35.00
Lighter, Joe on motorcycle in desert, pyramids in backgound, flip-top refillable, MIB $20.00
Lighter, Joe's 75th anniversary, Zippo, MIB $25.00
Lighters, Camel Club, Floyd, Eddie, Joe, Bustah & Max, 5-pack, unopened, M.....................................$30.00
Mouse pad, various designs, ea..............................$10.00
Paperweight, glass, Hard Pack, 4⅛x2¾x¾", M...........$15.00
Pennant, Smokin' Joe, NASCAR, #23 race car, cloth, on cardboard hanger, rare $50.00
Radio/cassette player, replica of jukebox $75.00

Salt and pepper shakers, Max and Ray, ceramic, $45.00 for the pair. (Photo courtesy C.J. Russell and Pamela E. Apkarian-Russell)

Salt & pepper shakers, plastic figurals, 1993 RJRTC on bottom, 4", EX, pr, from $20 to $40.00
Stein, Octoberfest, ceramic, w/lid $150.00
Store display ashtray, metal, Joe in leather jacket, floor standing, 24", EX..................................$50.00
Thermometer, Joe holding pack, diecut, 18½", EX.....$50.00
Toy funny car dragster, diecast, 1/64 scale, w/case....$50.00
Toy race car, Jimmy Spencer, #23, 1995, 1/64 scale, MIB...$25.00
Vest, Joe's Fish & Game Club logo on right front top pocket, khaki...$20.00
Vest, leather, lined, snap front, man's size................$65.00
Wheel cover, multicolor image of Joe in jeep on blue, 1993.$40.00

M & M Candy Men

Toppers for M&M packaging first appeared about 1988; since then other M&M items have been introduced that portray the clever antics of these colorful characters. Toppers have been issued for seasonal holidays as well as Olympic events.

Advisors: Bill and Pat Poe (See Directory, Fast-Food Collectibles)

Banner, beach scene, plastic, 1995, 26x30" $12.00
Banner, Christmas scene w/train, Holiday Express, plastic, 1996, 26x30" $12.00
Bean bag toys, M&M shape, red, green, blue or yellow, 6", ea $10.00
Bean bag toys, peanut shape, golfer or witch, 6", ea.$20.00
Book, Plain & Peanut & the Missing Christmas Present, 1993...$6.00
Calculator, yellow w/different color M&M keys, MIB.$20.00
Coin holder, set of 6 containers full of mini M&Ms, 1996, per set...$10.00
Cookie cutter, M&M shape, standing w/arms up, red plastic, 3"...$4.00
Dispenser, spaceship shape w/M symbol, press button to dispense candy, battery-op, red, yellow or blue, MOC, ea $8.00
Dispenser, 1991, M&M shape, brown, sm $10.00
Dispenser, 1991, M&M shape, holding bouquet of flowers, yellow, sm $5.00
Dispenser, 1991, M&M shape, red, lg $15.00
Dispenser, 1991, peanut shape, brown, sm................$10.00
Dispenser, 1991, peanut shape, orange, green or yellow, sm, ea...$5.00
Dispenser, 1992, peanut shape, red, lg......................$20.00
Dispenser, 1995, M&M Fun Machine, shaped like a gumball machine $12.00
Dispenser, 1995, peanut shape, football in right hand, helmet in left, yellow, lg....................................$20.00
Dispenser, 1995, peanut shape, yellow, lg $30.00

Dispenser, 1997, peanut shape, basketball player, M, $20.00.

Doll, M&M shape, stuffed plush, red, 12"...................$15.00
Easy Bake Set, cake baking set, w/M&M stencil & spoon, MIB $12.00
Figure, M&M shape, bendable arms & legs, red, 5½" ..$20.00
Figure, peanut shape, bendable arms & legs, blue or yellow, 7", ea $15.00

Magnet, red M&M shape or yellow peanut shape, plush, 2", ea...**$8.00**

Message board, magnetic school bus shape, characters on top & hood of bus, M **$10.00**

Tin, Christmas 1992, dark green w/winter scene........**$12.00**

Tin, Christmas 1993, red w/various scenes.................**$15.00**

Tin, Christmas 1996, Taking a Break at the Diner, rectangular...**$15.00**

Tin, 1988, blue w/stars & M&M's, sm **$10.00**

Tin, 1990, 50th Birthday, lg..**$15.00**

Topper, Christmas, M&M shape, several variations w/Santa hats, square base, ea **$10.00**

Topper, 1989, M&M shape, on ice skates wearing red Santa hat, green, round base **$3.50**

Topper, 1992, M&M shape, going down chimney w/bag of toys in left hand, green, round base **$3.50**

Topper, 1992, peanut shape, arrow in left hand, bow in right hand, brown, heart w/arrow on round base **$7.00**

Topper, 1994, peanut shape, w/paint brush & chick in egg, turquoise, pink, lavender or lime green, round base, ea **$3.50**

Topper, 1995, M&M shape, postman holding pink valentine, red, round base...**$3.50**

Topper, 1995, M&M shape, w/Easter bouquet & watering can, green, turquoise or lavender, round base, ea........**$3.50**

Topper, 1997, peanut shape, bag of toys on shoulder, green, round base...**$3.50**

Utensil holder, 1 in chefs hat holding rolling pin, 3 others holds spoons or a wisk, Mars, 1996, NM................**$5.00**

Wristwatch, M&M skate boarder as second hand, in plastic case w/cardboard sleeve, 1994.............................**$50.00**

Wristwatch, M&M's on face, in padded sleeve, 1993..**$45.00**

Dolls, plush M&M shape, 8", $12.00; 4½", $10.00. (Photo courtesy Bill and Pat Poe)

Michelin Man (Bibendum or Mr. Bib)

Perhaps one of the oldest character logos around today, Mr. Bib actually originated in the late 1800s, inspired by a stack of tires that one of the company founders thought suggested the figure of a man. Over the years his image has changed considerably, but the Michelin Tire Man continues today to represent his company in many countries around the world.

Ashtray, ceramic, Mr Bib seated on rim, 1-rest **$55.00**

Ashtray, hard plastic, 5" Mr Bib sits on edge, brown, 6" dia, EX...**$65.00**

Ashtray, molded cream plastic Mr Bib in black base, 1940s, 6x3¾" dia, from $75 to...**$90.00**

Bank, PVC Mr Bib figural, made for 100-year birthday, 14" **$30.00**

Coffee cup, plastic, Mr Bib on side, EX......................**$5.00**

Costume, nylon and metal with yellow sash, EX, $900.00.

Cuff links, gold-tone w/white Mr Bib on blue ground, ⅞" dia, pr...**$50.00**

Desk ornament/pen holder, ceramic Mr Bib figure, made for 100-year birthday, rare **$50.00**

Figure, ceramic, Mr Bib w/hands at waist, green glaze, 1950s, made in Holland, 12½" **$500.00**

Figure, plastic Mr Bib, 12", NM, from $50 to..............**$75.00**

Figure, plastic Mr Bib on yellow motorcycle, EX **$110.00**

Key chain, 1½" figure of Mr Bib running, EX.............**$15.00**

Playing cards, Mr Bib courts, wide non-standard, VG..**$18.00**

Sign, sm Mr Bib near top, 60s car, NY City, 24x32", EX..**$55.00**

Watch fob, Mr Bib on front, Earth Moving Tires, 1½x1¾", EX..**$20.00**

Yo-yo, Mr Bib in black outline on white, EX.............**$10.00**

Mr. Peanut

The trademark character for the Planters Peanuts Company, Mr. Peanut has been around since 1916. Although his appearance became more stylized in 1961, he is still a common sight on Planters advertising efforts and product containers.

Mr. Peanut has been modeled as banks, salt and pepper shakers, whistles, and many other novelty items. His image has decorated T-shirts, beach towels, playing cards, sports equipment, etc.

Today Mr. Peanut has his own 'fan club,' the collector's organization for those who especially enjoy the Planters Peanuts area of advertising.

Advisors: Judith and Robert Walthall (See Directory, Advertising)

Club: *Peanut Pals*
Judith Walthall, Founder
P.O. Box 4465, Huntsville, AL 35815; 205-881-9198. Dues: $20 per year (+ $3 for each additional member of household). Annual directory and convention news sent to members. For membership, write to PO Box 652, St. Clairsville, OH 43950. Sample newsletter: $2.

Ashtray, gold-plated metal w/Mr Peanut statue in center of round shallow dish, marked 1906-1956, 5¾", MIB w/booklet **$130.00**
Charm bracelet, 6 plastic charms on brass-colored chain, 1941, VG **$35.00**
Container, painted papier-mache composition Mr Peanut figure against lg peanut, 12½x3" dia, VG **$500.00**
Cookie cutter, red plastic figure bowing & tipping hat, EX, from $15 to **$20.00**
Dart board, wood case w/Planters lettered in yellow above Mr Peanut on hinged doors, EX **$25.00**
Doll, jointed wood, Mr Peanut w/yellow body, blue hat, black arms & legs, 1930s, 9", EX **$200.00**
Doll, stuffed cloth, Chase Bag Co, 1967, 21", NM.......**$40.00**
Doll, stuffed cloth, Chase Bag Co, 1970, 18", NM.......**$25.00**
Jar, Barrel, embossed Mr Peanut, original lid w/peanut finial, red & gold label, silver paint, 12¼" **$250.00**
Jar, Clipper, original tin lid, 1938, EX........................**$100.00**
Nodder figure, clayware, 6½", MIB..........................**$150.00**
Oven mitt, Mr Peanut figure on white background, MIP, from $10 to **$15.00**
Parade mask, life-size costume, fiberglass, 1955, EX, from $800 to **$900.00**
Parade mask, life-size costume, molded vacuum-form sheet plastic, 1965 to present, M **$300.00**
Pin, figural, diecut wood w/name Mr Peanut lettered on hat, 2", EX **$75.00**

Radio, distributed by PRI, yellow molded plastic, 10x5", EX, $45.00. (Photo courtesy Marty Bunis and Robert Breed)

Salad fork & spoon set, wood w/ceramic figural Mr Peanut tops, MIB..**$115.00**
Sign, paper, Planters Mr Peanut Sale/Stock Up Now & Save!, Mr Peanut & girl w/sign, blue, 1950s, 15x36", EX **$175.00**

Spoon, nut server; silverplate with Mr. Peanut on handle, 1941 – 61, M, $15.00.

Toy car, molded red plastic peanut shape w/Mr Peanut driver, w/friction motor, 1950s-60s, 5", EX+............**$600.00**
Toy truck, Mr Peanut's Peanut Wagon, yellow & red, Pyro, 1950s, 5", NM...**$350.00**
Toy wind-up figure, green plastic, 1950s, 8½", EX, from $300 to **$350.00**
Tray, The Planters Peanut Co/Fresh Roasted Since 1906, Mr Peanut in center, oval, 1982, 14", M, from $15 to ..**$25.00**
Umbrella, blue & yellow w/single image of Mr Peanut, 1982s, M **$40.00**

Old Crow

Old Crow collectors have learned to date this character by the cut of his vest and the tilt of his head along with other characteristics of his stance and attire. Advertising Kentucky whiskey, he appears as an elegant gent in his tuxedo and top hat.

Advisor: Geneva Addy (See Directory, Dolls)

Almanac/whiskey mixing guide, Taste the Greatness, EX .**$35.00**
Ashtray, black glass, 1¼x3½", EX **$30.00**
Ashtray, ceramic, 3½" **$25.00**
Cuff links & tie clip set, gold-tone crow on black enameling, 1½" ea, M **$75.00**
Decanter, light red vest, yellow cane, Royal Doulton, 12½" **$185.00**
Dice, I Buy, You Buy, image of crow on 1, ½", pr **$45.00**
Drink stirrer, black plastic crow figural, Perfection Plastics, 1950s, 6½" **$10.00**
Figure, brass, black base, brass plaque: We Pour It, 13", EX...**$75.00**
Figure, composition, 1950s, 11½", from $75 to.........**$125.00**
Figure, painted plastic, sand-weighted bottom, 4"......**$40.00**
Figure, plastic, in birdcage, 9" **$125.00**
Figure, plastic, on base w/blue letters, 1960s, 5½", from $15 to **$35.00**
Figure, plastic, on rocking base, 1950s, 10", from $50 to **$95.00**
Figure, plastic, on rocking base, 1970s, 10", from $20 to **$45.00**

Figure, plastic, square black & white base, 1960s, 10", from $25 to **$45.00**

Figure, vinyl, no glasses (post 1956), 14", M, $45.00. (Photo courtesy Joleen Robison and Kay Sellers)

Glass, Bourbon; crow & lettering in black on clear, 4⅞"..**$12.50**
Glass, clear w/crow stem, Libbey................................**$35.00**
Glass, Manhattan; Old Crow & crow figure in black on clear, 4¾"..**$15.00**
Jigger, plastic..**$18.00**
Key chain **$15.00**
Lamp, plastic lantern form w/brass paint, Advertising Novelty Co, 13½"...**$75.00**
Lamp, porcelain, red vest w/gold buttons, ca 1960s, 14", from $145 to...**$195.00**
Lighter, no date, M...**$30.00**
Lipstick tissue booklet, made in USA for Cub Products, 1⅞x3", EX...**$20.00**
Phone dialer, figural hard plastic crow, back embossed Call For..., EX..**$10.00**
Pitcher, glass w/metal ring & handle, 5".....................**$25.00**
Playing cards, Two Crows You See Good Luck to Thee, 1967, 2 decks, EX **$40.00**
Thermometer, Taste the Greatness of Historic Old Crow, red, white & black, 13½", EX.....................................**$200.00**

Poppin' Fresh (Pillsbury Doughboy) and Family

Who could be more lovable than the chubby blue-eyed Doughboy with the infectious giggle introduced by the Pillsbury Company in 1965. Wearing nothing but a neck scarf and a chef's hat, he single-handedly promoted the company's famous biscuits in a tube until about 1969. It was then that the company changed his name to 'Poppin' Fresh' and soon after presented him with a sweet-faced, bonnet-attired mate named Poppie. Before long, they had created a whole family for him. Many premiums such as dolls, salt and pepper shakers, and cookie jars have been produced over the years. In 1988 the Benjamin Medwin Co. made several items for Pillsbury; all of these white ceramic Doughboy items are listed below. Also offered in 1988, the Poppin' Fresh Line featured the plump little fellow holding a plate of cookies; trim

colors were mauve pink and blue. The Funfetti line was produced in 1992, again featuring Poppin' Fresh, this time alongside a cupcake topped with Funfetti icing (at that time a fairly new Pillsbury product), and again the producer was Benjamin Medwin.

Advisor: Lil West (See Directory, Advertising)

Club: The Lovin' Connection
2343 10000 Rd.
Oswego, KS 67356; 316-795-2842

Bulletin & chalkboard, Poppin' Fresh Line, 1988, very hard to find, M, from $50 to **$85.00**
Address book, spiral-bound, Poppin' Fresh on front, EX..**$6.00**
Bank, Doughboy White Ceramic Line, chubby figure, Benjamin Medwin, 1988, MIB..............................**$25.00**
Bank, Poppin' Fresh, ceramic, 1980s mail-in premium, M.**$35.00**
Bean bag toy, Poppin' Fresh, 2 styles, M, ea from $10 to .**$20.00**
Bowl, bread; Doughboy White Ceramic Line, embossed Doughboy, Benjamin Medwin, 1988, 16", rare, MIB, from $150 to...**$200.00**
Bowls, mixing; Doughboy White Ceramic Line, embossed Doughboy, Benjamin Medwin/Portugal, 1988, scarce, set of 3, MIB **$75.00**
Canisters, Doughboy White Ceramic Line, embossed Doughboy, Benjamin Medwin, 1988, very scarce, set of 4, MIB, from $95 to **$135.00**
Canisters, Poppin' Fresh Line, metal, mauve pink & blue on white, Benjamin Medwin, 1988, 4-pc set............**$100.00**
Coffee mug, Poppin' Fresh Line, 1988.........................**$10.00**
Cookie jar, Doughboy White Ceramic Line, Benjamin Medwin, 1988, MIB...**$50.00**

Cookie jar, Funfetti Line, Benjamin Medwin, 1991, $50.00. (Photo courtesy Lil West)

Creamer & sugar bowl w/spoon, Doughboy White Ceramic Line, 1988, MIB...**$35.00**
Doll, Poppin' Fresh, stuffed cloth, 1970s, 14", VG......**$15.00**
Doll, Poppin' Fresh, stuffed cloth, 1972, 11", EX, from $15 to **$20.00**
Doll, Poppin' Fresh, stuffed plush, 1982, M, from $40 to .**$50.00**
Figure, Grandmommer, vinyl, 1974, 5", M, from $75 to....**$95.00**

Figure, Grandpopper, vinyl, 1974, 5¼", M, from $75 to....**$95.00**

Figure, Poppie Fresh, vinyl, 1972, 6", NM **$15.00**

Figure, Poppin' Fresh, vinyl, 1971, 7", NM **$15.00**

Figures, Poppin' & Poppie, vinyl, on stands as a set, M, pr, from $35 to..**$40.00**

Figures, Poppin' Fresh, cold-cast porcelain, set of 4 in various poses, 5", MIB..**$60.00**

Finger puppet, Biscuit (cat), vinyl, 1974......................**$35.00**

Finger puppet, Bun Bun (girl), vinyl, 1974, 3"............**$25.00**

Finger puppet, Flapjack (dog), vinyl, 1974..................**$35.00**

Finger puppet, Popper (boy), vinyl, 1974, 3¼"..........**$25.00**

Finger puppet, Poppie Fresh, vinyl, 1974, 3½"............**$25.00**

Finger puppet, Poppin' Fresh, vinyl, 1974, 4½"..........**$25.00**

Finger puppets, Poppin' Fresh & Pals, set of 3, rare, MIB.**$235.00**

Jell-O mold, Doughboy White Ceramic Line, Benjamin Medwin/Portugal, 1988, IB........................**$35.00**

Jewelry box & jewelry, Poppin' Fresh, pewter, w/pin, necklace & earrings, EX **$15.00**

Key chain, Poppin' Fresh figure, soft vinyl, MOC........**$6.00**

Lotion/soap dispenser, Doughboy White Ceramic Line, embossed Doughboy, Benjamin Medwin, 1988, MIB **$20.00**

Magnets, Doughboy White Ceramic Line, Poppin' & Poppie Fresh, Benjamin Medwin, 1988, 2-pc set, MIB **$20.00**

Magnets, Poppin' Fresh & Poppie, plastic, 1970s premium, 2-pc set, MIP **$35.00**

Memo pad, diecut Poppin' Fresh in upper left corner, 40 sheets, 7x4", EX..**$8.00**

Mug, ceramic, features Poppin' Fresh, 1985, 5", VG...**$15.00**

Mug, plastic Doughboy, 1979, 4½", from $10 to **$15.00**

Napkin holder, Doughboy White Ceramic Line, Benjamin Medwin, 1988, MIB..**$20.00**

Napkin holder, Funfetti Line, Benjamin Medwin, 1992, MIB **$12.00**

Plant holder, Doughboy White Ceramic Line, Benjamin Medwin, 1988, MIB..**$25.00**

Playhouse, vinyl, w/4 finger puppets (Poppin' Fresh, Poppie, Popper & Bun Bun), 1974, rare, complete, from $250 to..**$300.00**

Pop-up can, Poppin' Fresh, blue version, EX **$300.00**

Pop-up can, Poppin' Fresh, orange version, M.........**$200.00**

Potpourri burner, Doughboy White Ceramic Line, Benjamin Medwin, 1988, rare, 3-pc, M **$50.00**

Radio with head phones, MIB, $125.00. (Photo courtesy Lil West)

Salt & pepper shakers, ceramic, Poppin' Fresh, white w/blue details painted over glaze, 1969, 3½", EX, pr.......**$22.00**

Salt & pepper shakers, Funfetti Line, Doughboy & cupcake, 1992, MIB, pr **$20.00**

Salt & pepper shakers, plastic, Poppin' & Poppie Fresh, white w/blue details, dated 1974, 3½ & 4", pr..............**$25.00**

Salt & pepper shakers, range size; Doughboy White Ceramic Line, Benjamin Medwin, 1988, MIB, pr................**$20.00**

School box, Poppin' Fresh, w/pencils, erasers, etc, EX.**$100.00**

Scouring pad holder w/pad, Doughboy White Ceramic Line, Benjamin Medwin, 1988, M **$20.00**

Soap dish, Poppie, Doughboy White Ceramic Line, Benjamin Medwin, 1988, M **$20.00**

Soap dish, Poppin' Fresh, Doughboy White Ceramic Line, Benjamin Medwin, 1988, M **$20.00**

Spoon holder, Funfetti Line, Benjamin Medwin, recent issue but dated 1988, MIB..**$15.00**

Spoon rest, double; Doughboy White Ceramic Line, Poppin' & Poppie, Benjamin Medwin, recent issue but dated 1988, MIB..**$15.00**

Storage jar, glass w/snap-on lid, Poppin' Fresh & checked band, Anchor Hocking, 3 sizes, ea, from $20 to..**$25.00**

Tool holder w/tools, Doughboy White Ceramic Line, Benjamin Medwin, 1988...**$20.00**

Tool holder w/tools, Funfetti Line, Benjamin Medwin 1992, MIB **$20.00**

Towel holder, Poppie, Doughboy White Ceramic Line, Benjamin Medwin, 1988, M **$25.00**

Towel holder, Poppin' Fresh, Doughboy White Ceramic Line, Benjamin Medwin, 1988, M **$25.00**

Towels, Poppin' Fresh Line, Cannon, 1988, 4-pc set, MIP ..**$30.00**

Trivet, Poppin' Fresh Line, 1988, M...........................**$25.00**

Truck, battery-operated; engine, air brake, horn & back-up signal sounds, Nylint, 1989, MIB.....................**$100.00**

Reddy Kilowatt

Reddy was developed during the late 1920s and became very well known during the '50s. His job was to promote electric power companies all over the United States, which he did with aplomb! Reddy memorabilia is highly collectible today, with the small-head plastic figures sometimes selling for $200.00 or more. On Reddy's 65th birthday (1992), a special 'one-time-only' line of commemoratives was issued. This line consisted of approximately thirty different items issued in crystal, gold, pewter, silver, etc. All items were limited editions and quite costly. Because of high collector demand, new merchandise is flooding the market. Watch for items such as a round mirror, a small hand-held game with movable squares, a ring-toss game, etc., marked 'Made in China.'

Advisor: Lee Garmon (See Directory, Advertising)

Apron, She Loves Me above image of Reddy pulling daisy petals, label reads Here Is Your New RK Apron, M..............**$40.00**

Ashtray, hexagonal w/6 rests, shows Reddy by wall plug in center, name below, red, EX **$28.00**

Ashtray, round w/3 rests, Electricity Recycles lettered around Reddy's head in center, red, EX $32.00

Badge, Your Electrical Servant, 2½" $13.00

Charm, brass Reddy, on original card w/poem, c 1954, USA $25.00

Coloring book, ca 1960s, PA Electric Co (PENELEC), 14x10½", G $20.00

Cookie cutter, red plastic Reddy head, 3"...................$10.00

Cuff links, MIB...$65.00

Figure, hard rubber, 1930s, 3"......................................$8.00

Figure, lg head, red & white plastic on black outlet switch-plate base, MCMLXI, 6", minimum value...........$150.00

Figure, sm head, hands & feet, red & white plastic, on base, (harder to find than lg-head version), 6", EX.....$200.00

Light switch, plastic glow-in-the-dark Reddy, MCMLXI, EX $125.00

Lighter, made in Japan for Price Associates, 2x1¼", in original box, EX...$40.00

Measuring glass, shows Reddy holding logo above phrase, red on clear glass, 1930s, 4¾" $42.00

Mirror, reproduction, 3" dia, EX....................................$7.00

Necktie, full-figure Reddy, plugged-in feet, 8 outlets shown, M..$180.00

Necktie, navy blue w/scattered red embroidered Reddy outlines..$45.00

Night light, Panelescent, Sylvania, 3" diameter, from $35.00 to $40.00. (Photo courtesy Lee Garmon)

Note paper holder, 1" Reddy on 3x5" holder, Autopoint, EX...$25.00

Patch, for bowling shirt, full color, ca 1960s, 4x6"......$40.00

Penknife, 2-blade, Zippo, EX...$50.00

Pin-back button, shows Reddy by electrical wall plug & name, Whitehead & Hoag, 1" dia, EX.................$55.00

Pin-back button, 4 power-saving suggestions printed on back, 2" dia, EX $17.50

Pin-back name badge, celluloid, round, ...Your Electrical Servant, red, white & blue, 2¼", dia, NM............$25.00

Plate, 1950s, Syracuse China, 7" $85.00

Playing cards, USPC, in original box, VG....................$20.00

Pot holder, white quilted cloth w/red head image of Reddy, yellow trim, w/magnet inside, 1950s, 6x6", MIP (sealed) $30.00

Sign, diecut hardboard figure, red & white, 10x9", VG .$115.00

Slide-tile puzzle, white w/red & blue graphics, reproduction, 3x3½"...$10.00

Stick pin, figural, gold-tone w/red enamel, 1" $30.00

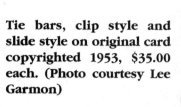

Tie bars, clip style and slide style on original card copyrighted 1953, $35.00 each. (Photo courtesy Lee Garmon)

Smokey Bear

The 50th Anniversary of Smokey Bear, the fire-prevention spokesbear for the State Foresters, Ad Council, and US Forest Service, was in 1994. After ruling out other mascots (including Bambi), by 1944 it had been decided that a bear was best suited for the job, and Smokey was born. When a little cub was rescued from a fire in a New Mexico national forest in 1950, Smokey's role intensified. Over the years his appearance has evolved from one a little more menacing to the lovable bear we know today.

The original act to protect the Smokey Bear image was enacted in 1974. The character name in the 'Smokey Bear Act' is Smokey Bear. Until the early 1960s, when his name appeared on items such as sheet music and Little Golden Books, it was 'Smokey *the* Bear. Generally, from that time on, he became known as simply Smokey Bear.

Advisor: Glen Brady (See Directory, Advertising)

Ashtray, ceramic, embossed Smokey head in center, Smokey Says Prevent Forest Fires, pie-crust rim, pastel colors $225.00

Ashtray, ceramic, figural Smokey sits on rim by trees & fire prevention sign, 4x4½"..$95.00

Ashtray, SnuffIt, magnetized to stay on dashboard.....$25.00

Badge, Junior Forest Ranger, tin w/embossed letters ...$8.00

Bank, ceramic, white w/gold details, EX....................$60.00

Bank, chalkware, Smokey in blue uniform, orange ranger's hat, #975, 1940s, 12", EX..$25.00

Bank, plastic, Smokey stands on stump, holds shovel, Smokey on belt, 8" $25.00

Belt buckle, cast metal, 2½x1¾" $18.00

Belt buckle, 40th anniversary, heavy metal, #414.....$125.00

Big Golden Book, True Story of..., 1973, 13 x 9½", G $18.00

Book & rubber stamp set, Story of..., 10 stamps, pad & poster, M $15.00

Bookmark, paper, Smokey & 8" ruler, dated 1961.......$8.00

Bow biter, Smokey heads to keep tikes from untying shoe-strings, MIP..**$10.00**

Cigarette lighter, chrome, Smokey Says..., Japan, 2¼", M..**$65.00**

Coffee mug, Only You Can..., official, M.....................**$25.00**

Cookie jar, Smokey's head, Prevent Forest Fires on hat, 7½x7", from $275 to..**$325.00**

Doll, 50th anniversary, 12", MIB................................**$30.00**

Figure, Dakin, plastic with cloth trousers, 1970s, 8", M, $45.00. (Photo courtesy June Moon)

Figurine, ceramic Smokey holding remnants of burned tree, marked A-19, M..**$55.00**

Figurine, Smokey planting a tree, kneeling by bear cubs, Lefton, 5½"..**$25.00**

Figurine, Smokey teaching 2 bear cubs from worksheet on stand made from branches, 5½"..................**$30.00**

First day cover, commemorating Prevention of Forest Fires, 1984, M..**$12.00**

Game, Smokey Bear, Milton Bradley, 1968, VG..........**$60.00**

Handkerchief, picnic scenes, 8", EX.........................**$25.00**

Litter bag for car, hard plastic, Keep Highways Clean..., EX..**$40.00**

Magic slate, Watkins-Strathmore, diecut cardboard, 1969, EX..**$85.00**

Mug, milk glass w/brown painted-on Smokey & Help Prevent Forest Fires..**$12.00**

Nodder, dated 1966, 6", EX.....................................**$125.00**

Patch, Ranger, Please Be Careful, Prevent Forest Fires, 4x3"..**$10.00**

Picnic grill, National Can Corp, unused, NM............**$115.00**

Plaque, dimensional Smokey breaking match in half, Norcrest, Japan, 5½", EX...**$90.00**

Poster, Smokey saluting Girl Scouts, dated 1962, 13x10", M..**$65.00**

Poster, 1956, 13x18½", EX.......................................**$20.00**

Printer's block, wood base w/metal top, 2½x2"........**$35.00**

Ruler, Smokey's Friends Don't Play w/Matches............**$8.00**

Safety matches, American Camper, sealed..................**$15.00**

Salt & pepper shakers, 1 w/shovel, 1 w/pail, Japan, pr..**$40.00**

Scarf, cotton, 12x12", EX...**$20.00**

Sign, paper, US Dept Agriculture Forest Service, 60-CFFP-3a, 1959, 13x18½", VG..**$15.00**

Stand-up, diecut Smokey holds chart detailing Forest Fire Danger Today, used at Forest Ranger Stations, 7½"..**$35.00**

Trading cards, Smokey Bear Day, 1987, 12 player cards w/stats, 15 in set, M..**$12.00**

Snap!, Crackle!, and Pop!

Rice Krispies, the talking cereal, was first marketed by Kellogg's in 1928. Capitalizing on the sounds the cereal made in milk, the company chose elves named 'Snap,' 'Crackle,' and 'Pop' as their logos a few years later. The first of the Rice Krispie dolls were introduced in 1948. These were 12" tall, printed on fabric for the consumer to sew and stuff. The same dolls in a 16" size were offered in 1954. Premiums and memorabilia of many types followed over the years, all are very collectible.

Advisor: Scott Bruce (See Directory, Advertising)

Canteen, yellow, white & red plastic, 1973, NM.........**$25.00**

Dolls, jointed vinyl, 1984, set of 3, 6¼", M (individual boxes)..**$175.00**

Drawing template, yellow plastic, 1979, 3x5", NM.....**$15.00**

Figurines, Snap! & Pop!, bisque, Papel, 1984, 4¼", EX, ea..**$35.00**

Key chain, metal, paper & plastic, 1980s, EX............**$10.00**

Magic Color Cards, colors appear when water is applied, set of 4, 1933, 6x4", EX+..**$75.00**

Patch, head images, glow-in-the-dark cloth iron-on, 1974, M (in paper), ea..**$15.00**

Popper, plastic, 1980s, MIP..**$7.00**

Ring, soft rubber face makes different expressions w/spinning dial, brass band, 1950s, EX........................**$175.00**

Salt & pepper shakers, Snap! & Pop! figures, ceramic, Japan, 1950s, 2½", EX, pr..**$85.00**

Squeeze toy, plastic, 1978, EX.....................................**$35.00**

Sticker, glow-in-the-dark paper, 1971, M...................**$10.00**

Tony the Tiger

Kellogg's introduced Tony the Tiger in 1953, and since then he's appeared on every box of their Frosted Flakes. In his deep, rich voice, he's convinced us all that they are indeed 'Gr-r-r-reat'!

Advisor: Scott Bruce (See Directory, Advertising)

Baseball, Tony's face & paw print signature, regulation, M (still in plastic)..**$4.00**

Bowling set, NMIB..**$150.00**

Can, shaped like Kellogg's Racing Car, w/Tony driving, 7⅜x3¼", M..**$5.00**

Decal, sky blue background w/picture of Tony in center, for gas pump, M..**$16.00**

Design maker, Kooky Doodle, 1984, MIP.................**$10.00**

Doll, Bean Bag Bunch, w/tag, Kellogg's, MIP.............**$9.00**

Doll, plush, mail-away item, 1997, 8".............**$8.00**

Doll, squeeze vinyl, Product People, 1970s, 9", NM+..**$100.00**

Doll, stuffed cloth, 1973, 14", EX.............**$40.00**

Duffle bag, cream, picture on front & back, drawstring closure, 17", EX.............**$10.00**

Figure, plastic, diving Tony, 1979, MIP.............**$5.00**

Frisbee, logo on top w/name, copyright & register info on bottom, mini, 4" dia.............**$5.00**

Golf ball, logo on Titleist DT Wound 90, EX.............**$5.50**

Hat, white paper w/graphics, given on plant tour in Battlecreek MI, Kellogg's, 1968, M.............**$25.00**

Hot Wheel car, Terry Labonte's 1997 NASCAR #5 w/special paint scheme, MIB.............**$5.00**

Mug and bowl, cereal premium, Kellogg, 1964, M, $35.00. (Photo courtesy Scott Bruce)

Mug, plastic, 1965-71, G.............**$10.00**

Mug, Tony on ea side, 1993, 3¾".............**$5.00**

Page marker/paper clip, plastic, 1979, NM.............**$3.00**

Patch, glow-in-the-dark cloth, 1974, 2", M (in paper)...**$12.00**

Place mat, vinyl, 1981, EX.............**$10.00**

Recipe book, 1990, 8 pages, 5½x8½", VG.............**$5.00**

Tin, 12th World Hot Air Balloon Championship at Battlecreek MI, 1995, 1¾" deep, 7" dia, VG.............**$6.00**

Watch, digital, 3-D hologram, orange w/black tiger stripes, Canadian, MIP.............**$17.00**

Miscellaneous

Advisor: Jim Rash (See Directory, Dakins)

A&W Root Beer, bear, stuffed plush, 1975, 13", EX, from $25 to.............**$35.00**

Alka-Seltzer, bank, Speedy figure, 1950s, vinyl, 5½", NM, from $250 to.............**$300.00**

Allied Van Lines, doll, stuffed cloth, 1970s, 17", NM, minimum value.............**$25.00**

Blue Bonnet Margarine, doll, Blue Bonnet Sue, 1980s, stuffed cloth w/yellow yarn hair, NM, minimum value.............**$20.00**

Brach's Candy, doll, Scarecrow, stuffed cloth, EX, minimum value.............**$35.00**

Breck, doll, Bonnie Breck, Hasbro, 1972, 9", VG.............**$40.00**

Captain Marine, bank, molded vinyl figure on round base, Marine Bank, 1980s, 8½", NM.............**$35.00**

Ceresota Flour, doll, Ceresota Boy, stuffed cloth, 1972, EX, minimum value.............**$30.00**

Chicken of the Sea Tuna, doll, mermaid, stuffed printed cloth, 1974, 15", NM.............**$20.00**

Chips Ahoy, figure, rubber, Nabisco, 1990s, 5", M.............**$20.00**

Chiquita Bananas, doll, Chiquita Banana girl, stuffed cloth, mail-in premium, 1974, NM, minimum value.............**$20.00**

Chocks Vitamins, doll, Charlie Chocks, stuffed cloth, 1970, 20", NM, minimum value.............**$35.00**

Chrysler, bank, Mr Fleet, plastic figure, all-white version, 10", NM.............**$300.00**

Diaparene, figure, Diaparene Baby, 1980s, vinyl, original diaper, M, from $50 to.............**$75.00**

Dole Pineapple, doll, Bananimal Banabear, stuffed plush, Trudy toys, 1989, original tag, 10", M.............**$15.00**

Dow, figure, Scrubbing Bubble, 1989, vinyl, EX.............**$20.00**

Eskimo Pie, doll, Eskimo Pie boy, stuffed cloth, Chase Bag Co, 1975, 15", NM.............**$25.00**

Fruit Roll Ups, figure, Rollupo the Wizard, bendable, 6", EX.............**$6.00**

Hamburger Helper, doll, Helping Hand, plush, EX.............**$20.00**

Hawaiian Punch, doll, Punchy, stuffed cloth, 20", NM..**$40.00**

Hot Tamales Candies, doll, Tamale Kid, stuffed cloth, 1967-75, 18", NM, minimum value.............**$35.00**

Hushpuppies, bank, dog on round base, vinyl, 1970, 8", NM.............**$45.00**

Jell-O, kite, yellow paper w/red lettering, M.............**$35.00**

Keebler, bank, Ernie the Keebler Elf, marked 1989, 8½", from $40.00 to $45.00. (Photo courtesy Beverly and Jim Mangus)

Kellogg's Pop Tarts, bank, Milton the Toaster, vinyl, 1970s, rare, MIB, minimum value.............**$100.00**

Kleenex, figures, Kleenex bears, mail-in premium, set of 3, NM.............**$50.00**

Kool Cigarettes, figure, Willie the Penguin w/doctor's bag & stethoscope, painted plaster, 1930-40s, 4½", G+..**$65.00**

Kool-Aid, battery-operated Kool-Aid Kid, 8½", $45.00.

Levi's, rag doll, Knickerbocker, MIB, from $50 to.......**$75.00**
Little Debbie, doll, vinyl w/cloth dress & straw hat, 1984, 11", M...**$60.00**
Mr Clean, figure, painted vinyl, Proctor & Gamble, 1961, 8", EX..**$80.00**

Pepto-Bismol, bank, 24-Hour Bug, vinyl, 7", $40.00. (Photo courtesy June Moon)

Raid, bag, cloth, white w/Raid! Bug Out to the Beach in pink lettering on both side, drawstring, 17¼", M **$10.00**
Sara Lee Bagels, bear, stuffed cloth, NM, minimum value **$20.00**
Sunbeam Bread, doll, Little Miss Sunbeam, stuffed cloth, 17", EX **$30.00**
Tastee Freeze, doll, Miss Tastee Freeze, hard plastic, 1950s, 7", NM...**$20.00**
Wrangler, dolls, Cody or Missy, Ertl, 1982, 11½", MIB, ea **$55.00**
5th Avenue Candy Bar, pillow, stuffed cloth, 1970s, EX, minimum value..**$25.00**

Advertising Tins

In her book *Modern Collectible Tins* (Collector Books), Linda McPherson declares these colorful, very attractive tin containers an official new area of collecting. There are so many of these 'new' tins around though (she warns), that you'll probably want to narrow your choices down to either a specific type of product or company to avoid being inundated with them! She says the best of the lot are usually those offered as mail-in premiums and suggests we avoid buying tins with paper labels and plastic lids. Besides the esthetics factor, condition and age also help determine price. The values suggested below represent what you might pay in an antique store for tins in mint condition. But what makes this sort of collecting so much fun is that you'll find them much cheaper at garage sales, Goodwill Stores, and flea markets.

Advisor: Linda McPherson (See Directory, Advertising)

Newsletter: *Tinfax*
Jeannie Tucker
205 Broiley Woods Dr.
Woodstock, GA 30189
Subscription: $25 for 4 issues

Barnum's Animal Crackers, box w/plastic handle, red, yellow & blue w/4 circus animals, 1995, 5x7x4", from $12 to **$16.00**
Big Mac, hamburger shape & graphics, came w/McDonaldland character-shaped gummies, 1996, 4¼", from $8 to...**$10.00**

Bisquick Recipe Box, red banner with white lettering, 3⅝x5⅛x3", from $20.00 to $25.00. (Photo courtesy Linda McPherson)

Butterfinger, short oval, logo on yellow background, 3½x5½x2½", from $8 to.......................................**$10.00**
Campbell's Soups, flat round, Season's Greetings, Campbell Kids building snowman on lid, 1¼x6½", from $4 to..**$7.00**
Campbell's Tomato Soup, soup can bank, 125th Anniversary, 4", from $5 to **$8.00**
Chiclets, short round, lettering on green sides w/lady's framed portrait on lid, Cheinco, 3½", from $18 to..............**$20.00**
Chupa Chups, fruit-crate shape w/graphics of various fruits & end labels, 5x10½x6¼", from $14 to **$16.00**

Chupa Chups, milk can shape w/bail handle, shows cow facing lollipops growing in grass, 3rd edition, 9½", from $18 to..**$20.00**

Cracker Jack, cylinder, 3 panels w/Jack & dog, baseball player & bathing beauty on CJ box, 1992, 8", from $10 to..**$14.00**

Domino Cane Sugar, Confectioners Sugar & Brown Sugar, canisters, yellow, blue & cream, sm, med & lg, set, from $25 to..**$30.00**

Double Bubble, octagonal, brown & cream label on dark blue, 1st edition, 1994, 6", from $8 to..................**$10.00**

Dove Chocolate Eggs, egg shape, various designs, 5x3", from $5 to..**$7.00**

Fig Newton, tall box, resembles a stack of Fig Newton cookies, 1995, 8¼", from $12 to..................................**$16.00**

Fossil Watches, box w/rounded corners, campus football scene w/1954 classic convertible, ½x2½x5½", from $3 to..**$5.00**

Gillette Safety Razor, cylinder, shows baby shaving, Cheinco, 7½", from $20 to..**$25.00**

Hershey's Chocolate, short round, The Great American Chocolate Bar, shows baseball boy, 1¾x6¾" dia, from $4 to..**$6.00**

Hershey's Milk Chocolate, barn shape, shows cows & Amish lady w/little girl, 4¾x3¾x3", from $8 to..............**$10.00**

Hershey's Milk Chocolate Kisses, heart shape, A Kiss for You, red, white & blue w/boy & girl, 1995, 4½", from $3 to..**$5.00**

Jelly Belly Jelly Beans, jelly bean shape, hinged lid, ¾x3¾x2½", from $3 to...**$5.00**

Kellogg's Frosted Flakes, tall box, Tony graphics on dark blue background, 1984, 6½", from $14 to....................**$18.00**

Kellogg's Pep, tall oval, football graphics, brown lid, 1984, 5½", from $14 to...**$18.00**

Land O'Lakes, recipe box w/hinged lid, Indian maiden scouting river bank, 3½x5x3", from $20 to **$25.00**

Log Cabin Syrup, cabin shape w/plastic cap, 100th Anniversary, 1987, 4¾", from $15 to......................**$20.00**

M&M Peanuts, Toy Shop #3 or Diner #4, limited edition Christmas Village series, 1996, 5½" & 8¾", ea, from $5 to..**$8.00**

Milky Way, octagonal, stained-glass poinsettia design, 1995, 2¼x6x9", from $4 to **$6.00**

Nestle Crunch, candy bar w/torn wrapper, 2½x3¾x10", from $12 to..**$14.00**

Oreo Cookies, cylinder, shows stacks of cookies behind red, white & blue graphics, Cheinco, 7½", from $15 to..**$20.00**

Quaker Oats, short round, various labels on dark blue backgound, red lid, limited edition, 1983, 7½" dia, from $6 to..**$10.00**

Quaker Old Fashioned Oats, cyclinder, Quaker man logo on red, white & blue, limited edition, 1982, 7¼", from $10 to..**$15.00**

Quaker Rolled White Oats, tall box, replica of 1886 label on yellow background, 1984, 8", from $12 to...........**$16.00**

Raisinets, box, colorful stage scene w/dancing Raisinets & orchestra, 2¾x6x7¾", from $10 to **$14.00**

Reeses Miniatures, cylinder, brown, 1989, 6¾", from $4 to..**$6.00**

Ritz Crackers, round, 50th Anniversary, 1984, 6x6" dia, from $14 to..**$16.00**

Russel Stover Candies, box w/hinged lid, Barbie series, 1997, 1x3¾x4¼", ea, from $4 to.............................**$6.00**

Russel Stover Candies, egg shape, 4 Barbie designs available, 1996, 2½x4½", ea, from $3 to...............................**$5.00**

Snickers Fun Size, radio, hinged lid, 1990, 4¾x7x3", from $8 to..**$12.00**

Starbucks Coffee Company, box resembling truck loaded w/sacks of coffee beans, 7x10x4", from $18 to....**$23.00**

Tootsie Roll, canister, 100th Anniversary, A Little Piece of History, 1896-1996, 6¼", from $5 to.......................**$8.00**

Trident Sugarless Gum, box w/rounded corners, hinged lid, red, white, blue & black graphics, 1x4x8", from $10 to..**$12.00**

Twizzlers Strawberry Twists, short round, red lips graphics on blue starry sky background, 1994, 2x10" dia, from $10 to..**$12.00**

Uneeda Biscuit, child in yellow rain suit, 5½x4¼x3½", from $4.00 to $7.00. (Photo courtesy Linda McPherson)

Washburn Crosby Co Gold Medal Flour, recipe box w/hinged lid, flour mill on front, 4½x5½x3½", from $18 to.**$22.00**

Werther's Original, oval, The Old World Recipe, embossed village among trees on tan background, 1985, 3x5x7", from $6 to..**$8.00**

Wessex Cake Co, box resembling delivery truck, Silver Crane Co, 7x7½x13½", from $25 to................................**$30.00**

Whitman's Candies, box w/hinged lid, winter cottage, 1992, 2x5½x3¾", from $6 to..**$10.00**

York Peppermint Pattie, lg pattie w/foil wrapper, 2x6", from $5 to..**$8.00**

Zu Zu Ginger Snaps, cylinder, replica of 1916 clown face on brown & gold, 1982, 6", from $25 to....................**$30.00**

Advertising Watches

The concept of the advertising watch is strictly twentieth century. Some were produced through the 1960s, but it wasn't until the early 1970s that watches were increasingly used for advertising. Now, many themes, subjects, and types are available. Collectible ad watches include mechanical/battery-operated pocket watches; mechanical/battery-operated wrist-watches; digital/analog (with hands) watches; dress/sports watches; company logo/character watches; corporate/in-house watches; catalog/store retail watches; and give-away/premium watches.

Condition, originality, cleanliness, scarcity, completeness, cross-collectibility, and buyer demand all affect value. The more recently issued the watch, the better its condition must be. Original mint packaging (including any paperwork) can triple value. Look for original watch offers and order forms on old packaging and magazines; they are desirable for documentation and are collectible in their own right. Look through 'parts boxes'; an old, nonworking ad pocket or wristwatch, even without a strap, may have value. A higher degree of wear is acceptable on an older watch.

A popular character/event will add value. Currently, demand is good for some '70s characters such as Mr. Peanut and Charlie the Tuna, the '80s – '90s M&M watches, and the '90s Pillsbury Doughboy. Demand for a watch that features a forgotten or less popular character may be limited, even if it is an older one, and value could be affected.

Great numbers of watches exist for Coca-Cola, Pepsi, various automobiles, Camel, and other tobacco products. These are usually of most interest to collectors who specialize in those fields. A 'reverse attitude' may exist — the more watches produced for a theme or character, the less desirable it is to the typical ad watch collector.

Copyright dates can lead to confusion about the age of a watch. The date may refer to the publishing date of the character or logo, not the year the watch was made. Date watches by style and features. Generally analog watches are more collectible than digital. A watch need not be working; most are not of high quality. Examine watches displayed in glass cases at outdoor shows for signs of moisture buildup and sun fading. Remove dead batteries only if you can do so without damaging the watch or packaging.

Warning: A new-looking silver-tone digital watch with an expansion bracelet and only a logo on the face may be a 'fantasy' piece. Also sometimes misrepresented: the 'Wal-Mart watches' — twenty Nelsonic watches for Green Giant and Little Sprout, Pillsbury, Wheaties, Cheerios, Trix, and Lucky Charms. They were retailed at $12.82 each in the winter of '98. Wal-Mart later retailed a group of nineteen Pepsi, Dr. Pepper, and Mountain Dew watches. The 1997 – 99 Quisp watch and tin were still available through 12/31/99 for $16.95 with the original order form. These watches are all worth buying at reasonable prices, especially to put away for a few years.

Advisor: Sharon Iranpour (See Directory, Advertising, Watches)

Newsletter: *The Premium Watch Watch©*
Sharon Iranpour, Editor
24 San Rafael Dr.
Rochester, NY 14618-3702; 716-381-9467 or fax: 716-383-9248

e-mail: watcher1@rochester.rr.com
Only newsletter on ad watches; $15 per year, bimonthly. Details on latest watch offers, news, free ads for subscribers. Send LSASE for sample copy.

Pre-1970s

Many mechanical pocket and wristwatches are known; most appeal to 'masculine' interests and professions such as automobiles and related products. As early as the 1920s, Chevrolet gave wristwatches to top-performing salesmen; the watch case was in the shape of a car radiator front. Many commemorative watches were issued for special events like world's fairs.

Buster Brown Pocket Watch, 1928, EX......................**$175.00**
Buster Brown Pocket Watch, 1960s, VG......................**$75.00**
Chevrolet Salesman's Award Wristwatch, 1927, EX...**$400.00**
Ever Ready Safety Razor Pocket Watch, 1959, VG....**$275.00**
Indian Motocycle (note: moto-, not motor-) Pocket Watch, w/fob, 1920s, EX **$325.00**
Mr Peanut Wristwatch, yellow face, 1966, VG.............**$50.00**
Mr Peanut Wristwatch, yellow face w/date window, 1967, VG **$50.00**
NY World's Fair Ingraham Pocket Watch, 1939, VG.**$500.00**
Red Goose Shoes Wristwatch, 1960s, G....................**$130.00**
Reddy Kilowatt Five-Sided Pocket Watch, 1930s, VG.**$250.00**
Rexall Ingersoll Pocket Watch, 1908, EX **$100.00**
Shell Oil Girard-Perregaux Pocket Watch, 1940s, VG.**$350.00**
St Louis World's Fair Ingersoll Pocket Watch, 1904, EX.**$200.00**

The 1970s

The most common were mechanicals with a heavy metal case, often marked Swiss Made. Some had wide straps with snaps or straps with holes. Mechanical digital watches and revolving disks appeared. As a general rule, special packaging had not been created. Wristwatches from the '70s are appearing at Internet auction sites and at shows in greater frequency due to growing interest. They are generally valued from $75.00 to $300.00 in very good to mint condition. Watches listed in this section are all mechanical wristwatches.

Kellogg's Tony the Tiger, 1976 (plain black/orange box exists), MIB, $200.00; Hawaiian Punch, Punchy, digital, $50.00; Goodyear Tires with revolving blimp, $50.00; Starkist's Charlie the Tuna, 1973, $50.00. (Photo courtesy Sharon Iranpour)

Big Boy, watch hands are arms, 1970s, EX **$75.00**
Buster Brown, red costume, VG **$75.00**
Charlie Tuna, faces left, 1971, VG **$50.00**
Count Chocula, Booberry & Frankenberry, Lafayette Watch
    Co, MIB **$300.00**
Ernie Keebler, G **$50.00**
Irish Spring, EX **$10.00**
Mr Peanut, blue face, mechanical, digital, EX **$50.00**
Pals Vitamins, moving eyes, G **$40.00**
Ritz Crackers, 1971, MIB **$200.00**

The 1980s

Digital and analog battery-operated watches became the norm; mechanicals all but disappeared early in the decade. Watches became slim and lightweight with plastic commonly used for both the case and the strap. Electronic hands (visible only when the battery is good), clamshell, and pop-up digital watches appeared; revolving disks were frequently used. Toward the end of the decade, printing on straps began. Specially designed packaging became more commonplace. Hanger cards added design to otherwise plain digital watches. These are most desirable in excellent, unopened condition. Watches from the 1980s are generally valued from $10.00 to $50.00 in mint condition. Watches listed in this section are battery operated unless noted otherwise.

From left: Campbell Kids (one of four), among the last of the mechanicals, MIB, $75.00 each; Hawaiian Punch, Punchy, electronic hands, $10.00; Cracker Jack, clamshell digital, $5.00; Ragu Pasta Meals, $5.00. (Photo courtesy Sharon Iranpour)

Bart Simpson by Butterfingers Candy, M **$20.00**
Captain Midnight by Ovaltine, 1988, M **$40.00**
Charlie the Tuna 25th Anniversary, 1986, MIB **$25.00**
Cherry 7-Up, 1980, M **$15.00**
Dukes of Hazzard (new old stock), several styles, from $5
    to **$10.00**
Kellogg's Atlantis 'Do & Learn Set,' 1983, MIB **$25.00**
Kraft Cheese & Macaroni Club, M **$10.00**
M&Ms, 1987, M **$25.00**

Max Headroom by Coca-Cola, 1987, lady's, M **$10.00**
Max Headroom by Coca-Cola, 1987, man's, M **$25.00**
Ronald McDonald House & Coca-Cola, 1984, MOC, from $3
    to **$5.00**
Stanley Powerlock, M **$45.00**
Swiss Miss, mechanical windup, 1981, EX **$50.00**
Welch's Grape Juice, 1989, M **$20.00**

The 1990s

Case and strap design became innovative. New features were holograms on the watch face, revolving subdials, 'talking' features, water watches (liquid within case/straps), stopwatches and timers, game watches, giga pets, and clip-on clocks. Classic and retro styling became popular. Very well designed packaging including special boxes and printed tins became more common as did printed plastic straps. Clear printed resin straps (Swatch type) and diecut rubber straps emerged. Companies created their own retail catalogs and websites to sell logo merchandise. Licensing agreements produced many tie-ins with movies, TV, and sports events. Most plastic watches currently sell in the $5.00 to $15.00 range; there is little market for the most common. Quality, hard-to-find gold- and silver-tone watches rarely sell beyond $25.00 at the present.

Quaker Chewy Granola Bars Wildlife Hologram, $5.00; Mars Snickers Candy Bar Anniversary, revolving subdial, $35.00; Campbell Kids Vegetable Soup, retail catalog purchase, $50.00; Pillsbury Doughboy Talking Watch, $15.00. (Photo courtesy Sharon Iranpour)

Congo the Movie by Taco Bell, set of 3, 1995, MIB, ea ..**$3.00**
Eggo Waffles Eggosaurus, 1990, M **$15.00**
Fisher-Price Little People Watch, 1997, M **$50.00**
Inspector Gadget by Life Cereal, 1992, M **$3.00**
Kool Aid Hologram, 1991, M **$15.00**
Kraft Superbowl XXX Watch in goal post box, M **$20.00**
Lion King by Kodak, 1995, MIB **$5.00**
Lost World by Burger King, set of 4, 1997, MIB, ea **$3.00**
Mask the Cartoon by Life Cereal, 1996, M **$3.00**
Mr Magoo by Nutrasweet, 1995, M **$30.00**

New Blue M&Ms Watch, & box cover, M $20.00
Nightmare Before Christmas by Burger King, set of 4, 1993, MIB, ea $3.00
Olypmics 1996 by Kodak, man's or lady's, MIB, ea $5.00
Oreo Cookie Watch, M....................$50.00
Snicker's Anniversary, 1990, M $35.00

Airline Memorabilia

Even before the Wright brothers' historic flight prior to the turn of the century, people have been fascinated with flying. What better way to enjoy the evolution and history of this amazing transportation industry than to collect its memorabilia. Today just about any item ever used or made for a commercial (non-military) airline is collectible, especially dishes, glasswares, silver serving pieces and flatware, wings and badges worn by the crew, playing cards, and junior wings given to passengers. Advertising items such as timetables and large travel agency plane models are also widely collected. The earlier, the better! Anything pre-war is good; items from before the 1930s are rare and often very valuable.

Advisor: Dick Wallin (See Directory, Airline)

Baggage sticker, Pan American, blue logo $10.00
Booklet, TAT/Penn RR, 1929, EX................................$250.00
Butter pat, American Airlines, blue & silver $25.00
Carafe, American Airlines Captain's Flagship...............$20.00
Cup & saucer, British Airways Concorde, blue & yellow design $40.00
Cup & saucer, China Airlines, Blue Leaf....................$20.00
Cup & saucer, demitasse; Alitalia, gray & silver logo .$40.00
Cup & saucer, demitasse; Pan American, President (eagles & stars) $35.00
Cup & saucer, TWA, china, marked on side & bottom..$10.00

Cup and saucer, TWA (RA), red stripe, Rosenthal, $15.00; Japanese, 1970s – 80s, $10.00. (Photo courtesy Dick Wallin)

Dishes, Air France, Limoges, ea pc $35.00
Dishes, Northeast, Yellow Bird pattern, ea pc $30.00
Flight bag, Mexicana Airlines, logo on vinyl $10.00
Flight computer, American Airlines, pilot's, in leather pouch, 1933 ....$245.00

Lapel pin, Northrop employee's, gold triangle form, w/hallmark, 1950................................$23.00
Menu, TWA, Collector series $5.00
Patch, Eastern, blue & yellow embroidered block letters, 10x2" $5.00
Plate, Pan American, Collector series, #1....................$80.00
Plate, Pan American, Collector series, #3................$100.00
Plate, Pan American, Collector series, #5....................$50.00
Plate, Pan American, Collector series, #6....................$40.00
Plate, US Air, china, 6¾" $10.00
Playing cards, Ozark Airlines, 1984 World's Fair........$10.00
Playing cards, Western Pacific Airline/Thrifty Car Rental ..$15.00
Print, United DC-6 Mainliner 300, prop plane, 12x15½" matted $35.00
Route map folder, Pan American, winged globe logo, 1950s $10.00
Salt & pepper shakers, Eastern, glass w/metal top, pr .$8.00
Salt & pepper shakers, Singapore Airlines, red & gold on china, pr $45.00
Silverware, American Airlines Flagship, ea pc, from $25 to....................$35.00
Swizzle stick, TWA....................$2.00
Teaspoon, Iberia $25.00
Tumbler, Eastern, commemorative w/Eddie Rickenbacker name on glass $20.00
Wings, Delta, w/logo....................$12.50
Wings, TWA, Junior, metal, VG....................$10.00

Akro Agate

Everybody remembers the 'Aggie' marbles from their childhood; this is the company that made them. They operated in West Virginia from 1914 until 1951, and in addition to their famous marbles they made children's dishes as well as many types of novelties — flowerpots, powder jars with Scottie dogs on top, candlesticks, and ashtrays, for instance — in many colors and patterns. Though some of their glassware was made in solid colors, their most popular products were made of the same swirled colors as their marbles. Nearly everything they produced is marked with their logo: a crow flying through the letter 'A' holding an Aggie in its beak and one in each claw. Some children's dishes may be marked 'JP,' and the novelty items may instead carry one of these trademarks: 'JV Co, Inc,' 'Braun & Corwin,' 'NYC Vogue Merc Co USA,' 'Hamilton Match Co,' and 'Mexicali Pickwick Cosmetic Corp.'

In the children's dinnerware listings below, you'll notice that color is an important worth-assessing factor. As a general rule, an item in green or white opaque is worth only about one-third as much when compared to the same item in any other opaque color. Marbleized pieces are about three times higher than solid opaques, and of the marbleized colors, blue is the most valuable. It's followed closely by red, with green about 25% under red. Lemonade and oxblood is a good color combination, and it's generally three times higher item for item than the transparent colors of green or topaz.

For further study we recommend *The Collector's Encyclopedia of Children's Dishes* by Margaret and Kenn Whitmyer.

Club: Akro Agate Collectors Club
Roger Hardy
10 Bailey St., Clarksburg, WV 26301-2524; 304-624-4523

Chiquita, cup, baked-on colors, 1½"............................**$6.00**
Chiquita, plate, transparent cobalt, 3¾"........................**$7.00**
Chiquita, sugar bowl, baked-on colors, 1½" **$8.00**
Chiquita, 12-pc set, opaque colors other than green, MIB...**$150.00**
Chiquita, 16-pc set, opaque green, MIB **$60.00**
Chiquita, 22-pc set, opaque green, MIB **$80.00**
Concentric Rib, cup, opaque colors other than green or white, 1¼" **$8.00**
Concentric Rib, plate, opaque green or white, 3¼"......**$3.50**
Concentric Rib, saucer, opaque colors other than green or white, 2¾" **$2.50**
Concentric Rib, teapot, opaque colors other than green or white, w/lid, 3⅜" **$18.00**
Concentric Rib, 10-pc set, opaque green or white, MIB..**$55.00**
Concentric Rib, 8-pc set, opaque colors other than green, MIB **$54.00**
Concentric Ring, lg creamer, marbleized blue, 1⅜"....**$50.00**
Concentric Ring, lg cup, pumpkin, 1⅜".......................**$50.00**
Concentric Ring, lg plate, solid opaque colors, 4¼".....**$7.00**
Concentric Ring, lg sugar bowl, solid opaque colors, w/lid, 1⅞"...**$28.00**
Concentric Ring, lg teapot, marbleized blue, w/lid, 3¾"..**$125.00**
Concentric Ring, lg 21-pc set, solid opaque colors, MIB..**$350.00**
Concentric Ring, sm cup, transparent cobalt, 1¼" **$30.00**
Concentric Ring, sm plate, marbleized blue, 3¼" **$22.00**
Concentric Ring, sm teapot, marbleized blue, 3⅜"...**$125.00**
Concentric Ring, sm 16-pc set, solid opaque colors, MIB **$160.00**

Concentric Ring, solid opaque colors: Plate, 3¼", $6.00; Cup, small, $10.00; Saucer, 2¾", $3.50.

Interior Panel, lg cereal bowl, marbleized red & white, 3⅜" **$37.00**

Interior Panel, lg cup, transparent green, 1⅜"..............**$9.00**
Interior Panel, lg plate, marbleized green & white, 4¼" ...**$18.00**
Interior Panel, lg saucer, transparent topaz, 3⅛"..........**$3.50**
Interior Panel, lg teapot, lemonade & oxblood, w/lid, 3¾" **$75.00**
Interior Panel, lg 21-pc set, marbleized red & white, MIB **$600.00**
Interior Panel, lg 21-pc set, pink & green lustre, MIB.**$320.00**
Interior Panel, sm cup, azure blue or yellow, 1¼" **$30.00**
Interior Panel, sm pitcher, transparent green, topaz or green lustre, 2⅞"..**$14.00**
Interior Panel, sm plate, azure blue or yellow, 3¾" ...**$10.00**
Interior Panel, sm sugar bowl, transparent green, topaz, or green lustre, 1¼"..**$20.00**
Interior Panel, sm teapot, opaque cobalt w/white lid, 3⅜"..**$45.00**
Interior Panel, sm tumbler, pink lustre, 2"..................**$55.00**
Interior Panel, sm 8-pc set, marbleized red & white, MIB **$150.00**
Interior Panel, sm 16-pc set, pink lustre, MIB..........**$180.00**
Miss America, creamer, white w/decal, 1¼"................**$65.00**
Miss America, plate, orange & white, 4½"...................**$45.00**
Miss America, saucer, white, 3⅝" **$15.00**
Miss America, teapot, white w/decal, w/lid, 3¼" **$140.00**
Octagonal, lg cereal bowl, dark blue, 3⅜".................**$10.00**
Octagonal, lg creamer, beige or pumpkin, closed handle, 1½" **$15.00**
Octagonal, lg cup, beige, pumpkin, or light blue, open handle, 1½" **$20.00**
Octagonal, lg teapot, pink, yellow, or other opaques, closed handle, 3⅝" **$20.00**
Octagonal, lg 17-pc set, white w/decal, MIB **$150.00**
Octagonal, lg 21-pc set, dark blue, MIB....................**$140.00**
Octagonal, sm cup, lime green, 1¼"...........................**$27.00**
Octagonal, sm pitcher, dark green, blue, or white, 2¾" ..**$18.00**
Octagonal, sm plate, pumpkin, yellow or lime green, 3⅜" **$6.00**
Octagonal, sm sugar bowl, dark green, blue or white, 1¼" **$16.00**
Octagonal, sm teapot, dark green, blue or white, w/lid, 3⅜" **$20.00**
Octagonal, sm tumbler, pumpkin, yellow or lime green, 2"...**$20.00**
Octagonal, sm 21-pc set, dark green, blue or white, MIB **$200.00**

Raised Daisy, solid opaque colors, 13-piece set in original box (with green cups), $245.00.

Raised Daisy, creamer, yellow, 1¾" $50.00
Raised Daisy, cup, green, 1¾" $18.00
Raised Daisy, saucer, yellow, 2½" $10.00
Raised Daisy, sugar bowl, yellow, 1¾" $50.00
Raised Daisy, teapot, yellow, 2⅜" $45.00
Stacked Disc, creamer, opaque green, 1¼" $10.00
Stacked Disc, cup, opaque colors other than green or white,
   1¼" $12.00
Stacked Disc, pitcher, opaque green or white, 3¼"....$15.00
Stacked Disc, saucer, opaque green or white, 2¾".......$3.00
Stacked Disc, sugar bowl, pumpkin, 1¼" $20.00
Stacked Disc, teapot, opaque green or white, w/lid, 3⅜"..$15.00
Stacked Disc, 21-pc set, opaque green or white, MIB..$130.00
Stacked Disc & Interior Panel, lg cereal bowl, solid opaque
   colors, 3⅜" $25.00
Stacked Disc & Interior Panel, lg creamer, solid opaque col-
   ors, 1⅜" $25.00
Stacked Disc & Interior Panel, lg plate, solid opaque colors,
   4¾" $12.00
Stacked Disc & Interior Panel, lg saucer, transparent green,
   3¼" $7.00
Stacked Disc & Interior Panel, lg sugar bowl, solid opaque
   colors, w/lid, 1⅞" $35.00
Stacked Disc & Interior Panel, lg 21-pc set, solid opaque col-
   ors, MIB...$370.00
Stacked Disc & Interior Panel, sm creamer, marbleized blue,
   1¼" $45.00
Stacked Disc & Interior Panel, sm cup, solid opaque colors,
   1¼" $12.00
Stacked Disc & Interior Panel, sm plate, transparent green,
   3¼" $9.00
Stacked Disc & Interior Panel, sm saucer, marbleized blue,
   2¾" $14.00
Stacked Disc & Interior Panel, sm sugar bowl, solid opaque
   colors, 1¼" $18.00
Stacked Disc & Interior Panel, sm tumbler, transparent green,
   2" $14.00
Stacked Disc & Interior Panel, sm 7-pc water set, transparent
   green, MIB...$100.00
Stacked Disc & Interior Panel, sm 16-pc set, transparent
   cobalt, MIB...$300.00
Stippled Band, lg creamer, transparent green, 1½".....$22.00
Stippled band, lg cup, transparent azure, 1½" $25.00
Stippled Band, lg saucer, transparent azure, 3¼"........$12.00
Stippled Band, lg sugar bowl, transparent green, w/lid,
   1⅞" $27.00
Stippled Band, lg teapot, transparent amber, w/lid,
   3¾"..$40.00
Stippled Band, lg 17-pc set, transparent green, MIB...$160.00
Stippled Band, sm cup, transparent amber, 1¼" $8.00
Stippled Band, sm pitcher, transparent amber, 2⅞"....$18.00
Stippled Band, sm plate, transparent green, 3¼" $4.00
Stippled Band, sm saucer, transparent amber, 2¾".......$2.50
Stippled Band, sm tumbler, transparent amber, 1¾"...$12.00
Stippled Band, sm 7-pc set, transparent green, MIB...$70.00
Stippled Band, sm 16-pc set, transparent amber, MIB..$145.00
Stippled Band, sm 28-pc set, transparent green, MIB...$175.00

Aluminum

The aluminum items which have become today's collectibles range from early brite-cut giftware and old kitchen
wares to furniture and club aluminum cooking pans. But the
most collectible, right now, at least, is the giftware of the
1930s through the '50s.

There were probably several hundred makers of aluminum accessories and giftware with each developing their
preferred method of manufacturing. Some pieces were cast;
other products were hammered with patterns created by
either an intaglio method or repousse. Machine embossing
was utilized by some makers; many used faux hammering,
and lightweight items were often decorated with pressed
designs. During one period, spun aluminum and colored
aluminum became very popular.

As early as the 1940s, collectors began to seek out aluminum, sometimes to add to the few pieces received as wedding gifts. By the late 1970s and early '80s, aluminum giftware was found in abundance at almost any flea market, and
prices of $1.00 or less were normal. As more shoppers
became enthralled with the appearance of this lustrous metal
and its patterns, prices began to rise and have not yet peaked
for the products of some companies. A few highly prized
pieces have brought prices of four or five hundred dollars
and occasionally even more.

One of the first to manufacture this type of ware was
Wendell August Forge, when during the late 1920s they
expanded their line of decorative wrought iron and began to
use aluminum, at first making small items as gifts for their
customers. Very soon they were involved in a growing industry estimated at one point to be comprised of several hundred companies, among them Arthur Armour, the
Continental Silver Company, Everlast, Buenilum, Rodney
Kent, and Palmer-Smith. Few of the many original companies
survived the WWII scarcity of aluminum.

Prices differ greatly from one region to another, sometimes without regard to quality or condition, so be sure to
examine each item carefully before you buy. There are two
good books on the subject: *Hammered Aluminum, Hand
Wrought Collectibles* by Dannie Woodard; and *Collectible
Aluminum, An Identification and Value Guide*, by Everett
Grist (Collector Books).

Ashtray, Everlast, bowl shape w/allover bamboo patterns,
   single rest, 5" dia $15.00
Basket, Continental, saddlebag shape w/mum pattern, single
   smooth strap handle, 3x7x11"..............................$25.00
Basket, Federal Silver Co, sailing ship, serrated ruffled rim,
   knotted handle, 9" dia $25.00
Beverage set, unmarked, 8 hammered tumblers nestled in 2-
   tiered tray w/single smooth round handle, 13"....$35.00
Bookends, Bruce Cox, leaping fish figures, 7x3x5",
   pr $185.00
Bowl, Arthur Armour, square w/rounded corners, dogwood
   & butterfly pattern on gold anodize, ribbon & bead rim,
   8" $25.00

Bowl, Kensington, plain-spun w/smooth flared rim, 3½x11" dia **$5.00**

Bowl, Palmer Smith, stylized wheat pattern, smooth rim, 4x14" dia..**$60.00**

Bowl, Rodney Kent, tulip pattern on hammered background, ear handles w/tulip design, serrated rim, 3x10" dia **$20.00**

Breakfast set, unmarked, Lazy Susan w/attached toast rack, 2 glass butter dishes & 2 jam jars w/tulip finials on lids..**$75.00**

Bun server, II Farberware, plain smooth finish w/serrated rim, 3 S-shaped legs w/tulip design, scrolled lid finial, 8x9" **$20.00**

Butter dish, Everlast, bamboo pattern w/bamboo finial, 4x4x7" **$10.00**

Candlesticks, Buenilum, curved handle projects to point on other side of plain cup w/beaded rim, rectangular base, pr..**$25.00**

Candlesticks, Continental, 7¾", $45.00 for the pair. (Photo courtesy Dannie Woodard)

Candlesticks, II Farberware, S-shaped w/tulip decoration, beaded cup rim & base, 8", pr **$45.00**

Candy dish, Neocraft by Everlast, 2 gold anodized butterfly bowls w/center loop handle, 12" **$15.00**

Casserole, Everlast, bamboo pattern w/bamboo handles & lid finial, glass insert, 5x7" dia....................................**$10.00**

Cigarette box, Laird Argental, plain box w/cast duck applied to lid, 1½x3x5"..**$75.00**

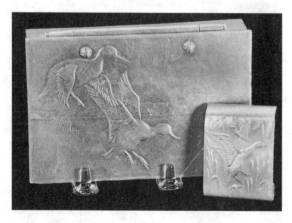

Cigarette case, 5¼x3½", $100.00; Match holder, $25.00.

Coaster set, Rodney Kent, shaped like tulip blossoms, basket holder w/open-work ribbon handle, set of 4.......**$35.00**

Compote, unmarked, allover hammered effect w/tulip & ribbon finial on lid, openwork ribbon pedestal on round base...**$15.00**

Creamer & sugar bowl, World Hand Forged, allover hammered effect w/elbow handles, open flower finial on sugar lid...**$5.00**

Double boiler, Buenilum, highly polished pan w/black wooden handle & lid finial, w/Pyrex liner, 7" dia **$10.00**

Dresser dish, Farberware, single rose pattern on lid w/black wooden finial, glass dish w/beaded rim & 2 handles...........**$10.00**

Fruit bowl w/knives, unmarked, fruit & flowers w/double loop handles, serrated rim, short base, knives in center, 11"..**$15.00**

Gravy boat, Continental, mum pattern w/serrated rim, w/handle & attached underplate, 3x6" dia **$25.00**

Hurricane lamps, Everlast, embossed grape & leaf pattern, ring handles w/thumb supports, glass chimneys, 8½", pr...**$40.00**

Ice bucket, Everlast, allover hammered effect, scalloped rim, barbell-type handles, w/tongs, no lid, 5x10" dia .**$15.00**

Lazy Susan, unmarked, 2-tiered w/tulip spray pattern, serrated pattern, 10"...**$15.00**

Napkin holder, Wendell August Forge, dogwood pattern on curved sides, 3x4x4½" **$30.00**

Nut bowl, Wilson, flower & leaf pattern, serrated ruffled rim, nutcracker & 6 picks in center, low base, 4x7" dia..**$10.00**

Pitcher, Continental, acorn & leaf pattern, wire coil around ear-shaped handle, applied ice lip, 8"...................**$20.00**

Pitcher, Rodney Kent, tulip pattern, ice lip applied to inside spout, serrated rim, ear-shaped handle, 9" **$35.00**

Sandwich tray, unmarked, acorn & leaf pattern, fluted edge, applied barbell-type handles, 11" dia....................**$15.00**

Serving tray, Everlast, bamboo pattern on hammered background, bamboo handles, 12x16"..........................**$15.00**

Serving tray, Rodney Kent, tulip pattern on hammered background, flower & ribbon handles, 14x20".............**$35.00**

Snack tray, Wendell August Forge, sailboat design in center, patterned rim, 5x8"...**$45.00**

Tidbit tray, unmarked, rose pattern, fluted rims, 3-tiered, 11x10" dia..**$5.00**

Trivet, Continental, acorn pattern banded around scalloped & serrated edge, 10" dia...**$10.00**

American Bisque

This was a West Virginia company that operated from 1919 until 1982, producing a wide variety of figural planters and banks, cookie jars, kitchenware, and vases. It has a look all its own; most of the decoration was done by the airbrushing method, and some pieces were gold trimmed. Collectors often identify American Bisque items by the 'wedges' or dry-footed cleats on the bottom of the ware. The most valuable pieces are those modeled after copyrighted characters like Popeye and the Flintstones. If you'd like more information, refer to *American Bisque, Collector's Guide With Prices*, by Mary Jane Giacomini.

See also Cookie Jars.

Advisor: Mary Jane Giacomini (See Directory, American Bisque)

Bank, Bedtime Pig, gold trim, made by APCO, unmarked, 6½"..$40.00
Bank, Bow Pig, marked USA, 5¼"................................$30.00
Bank, Chicken Feed, unmarked, 4½".......................$28.00
Bank, Humpty Dumpty, advertising piece marked Alice in Philcoland, 6"..$125.00
Bank, Little Girl Pig, cold paint, made by APCO, unmarked, 5¾"..$28.00
Bank, Little Girl Rag Doll, unmarked, 5¼"................$30.00
Bank, Popeye Bust, unmarked, 7"..............................$450.00
Bank, Rainy Day Pig, unmarked, 6¼x7½"................$75.00

Condiment jar, no mark, 5¼", $65.00. (Photo courtesy Mary Jane Giacomini)

Figurine, bird, covered entirely in 22-24k gold, made by APCO, 4"..$24.00
Flowerpot, bowl shape, white w/airbrushed color on embossed zigzag design around rim, made by APCO, marked USA, 3"..$5.00
Gravy boat, genie lamp style covered entirely in 22-24k gold, made by APCO, 5"..$60.00
Lamp, clock w/happy face, no shade, unmarked, 7¼"........$55.00
Lamp, Davy Crockett, w/original shade, unmarked, 7½"..$225.00
Night light, Davy Crocket by tree stump w/bear cub, 4½".$45.00
Pitcher, apple shape w/leaves & blossoms, gold handle & trim...$75.00
Pitcher, chick, gold trim, 6¼"......................................$35.00
Pitcher, USA Pig, 8"..$25.00
Planter, bear w/beehive, gold trim, unmarked, 5¾"...$32.00
Planter, circus horse rearing above tub, unmarked, 7"..$32.00
Planter, cockatiel on stump, unmarked, 5".................$14.00
Planter, dog & kitten by stump, marked USA, 4½".....$18.00
Planter, duck face on square basket (no handle), unmarked, 3¼"..$10.00
Planter, Dutch girl w/wooden shoe, unmarked, 6".......$8.00
Planter, elf on mushroom, unmarked, 6".....................$30.00
Planter, elf reclining next to log, unmarked, 2¾".......$10.00

Planter, gazelle w/flower, unmarked, 5"......................$26.00
Planter, kitten w/fishbowl, marked USA or unmarked, 6".$28.00
Planter, kitten wailing, marked USA or unmarked, 5¾".....$22.00
Planter, lovebirds on nest, unmarked, 6½".................$14.00
Planter, mallard duck, gold trim, unmarked, 4¾".......$26.00
Planter, rooster w/corncob, unmarked, 6"...................$10.00
Planter, sailfish jumping from water, unmarked, 8x10"..$50.00
Planter, swan, marked USA 7001, 6"...........................$24.00
Planter, whimsical donkey cart, unmarked, 6½".........$12.00
Planter, winter couple hugging by tree stump, unmarked, 7½"..$30.00
Planter, yarn doll w/block, various colors, unmarked, 5¾"..$20.00
Plate, Christmas tree shape, green airbrushing w/red cold-painted detail & gold garland, unmarked, 14½"..$75.00
Toothpick holder, fluted vessel w/low handles painted gold, gold rim, made by APCO, 2½"...............................$20.00
Vase, cornucopia, plain version, made by APCO, unmarked, 4½"..$14.00
Vase, cornucopia w/flower motif, made by APCO, unmarked, 6"..$16.00
Vase, cornucopia w/rose motif, gold trim, made by APCO, 5"...$24.00
Vase, golf bag, unmarked, 6"..$14.00
Vase, jug w/gold handle & gold-trimmed rose motif, 5"..$20.00
Vase, philodendron leaves, gold trim, unmarked, 7¼"....$30.00

Gift basket, gold trim, metal bail, 6¾", from $65.00 to $75.00. (Photo courtesy Mary Jane Giacomini)

Angels

Angels, Birthday

Not at all hard to find and still reasonably priced, birthday angels are fun to assemble into 12-month sets, and since there are many different series to look for, collecting them can be challenging as well as enjoyable. Generally speaking, angels are priced by the following factors: 1) company — look for Lefton, Napco, Norcrest, and Enesco marks or labels (unmarked or unknown sets are of less value); 2) application of flowers, bows, gold trim, etc. (the more detail, the more valuable); 3) use of rhinestones, which will also increase the price); 4) age; and 5) quality of the workmanship involved, detail, and accuracy of painting.

#1194, angel of the month series, white hair, 5", ea, from $18 to..**$20.00**
#1294, angel of the month, white hair, 5", ea, from $18 to..**$20.00**
#1300, boy angels, wearing suit, white hair, 6", ea, from $22 to..**$25.00**
#1600 Pal Angel, month series of both boy & girl, 4", ea, from $10 to..**$15.00**
Arnart, Kewpies, in choir robes, w/rhinestones, 4½", ea, from $12 to..**$15.00**
Enesco, angels on round base w/flower of the month, gold trim, ea, from $15 to...**$18.00**
High Mountain Quality, colored hair, 7", ea, from $30 to..**$32.00**

Josef/Japan, #1 through #16, 2¾" to 6½", from $16.00 to $20.00 each. (Photo courtesy Jim and Kaye Whitaker)

Kelvin, C-230, holding flower of the month, 4½", ea, from $15 to..**$20.00**
Kelvin, C-250, holding flower of the month, 4½", ea, from $15 to..**$20.00**
Lefton, #1323, angel of the month, bisque, ea, from $18 to..**$22.00**
Lefton, #2600, birthstone on skirt, 3¼", ea, from $25 to..**$30.00**

Lefton, #489, applied flowers, 4", from $25.00 to $35.00. (Photo courtesy Loretta DeLozier)

Lefton, #3332, bisque, w/basket of flowers, 4", ea, from $18 to..**$22.00**
Lefton, #556, boy w/blue wings, 5", ea, from $28 to .**$32.00**
Lefton, #574, day of the week series (like #8281 but not as ornate), ea, from $25 to...**$28.00**
Lefton, #6224, applied flower/birthstone on skirt, 4½", ea, from $18 to..**$20.00**
Lefton, #627, day of the week series, 3½", ea, from $28 to..**$32.00**
Lefton, #6883, square frame, day of the week & months, 3¼x4", ea, from $20 to...**$25.00**
Lefton, #6949, day of the week series in oval frame, 5", ea, from $28 to..**$32.00**
Lefton, #8281, day of the week series, applied roses, ea, from $30 to..**$35.00**
Lefton, #985, flower of the month, 5", ea, from $25 to .**$30.00**
Lefton, AR-1987, w/ponytail, 4", ea, from $18 to........**$22.00**
Lefton, 1987J, w/rhinestones, 4½", ea, from $25 to....**$30.00**
Napco, A1360-1372, angel of the month, ea, from $20 to...**$25.00**
Napco, A1917-1929, boy angel of the month, ea, from $20 to..**$25.00**
Napco, A4307, angel of the month, sm, ea, from $22 to.**$25.00**
Napco, C1361-1373, angel of the month, ea, from $20 to.**$25.00**
Napco, C1921-1933, boy angel of the month, ea, from $20 to..**$25.00**
Napco, S1291, day of the week 'Belle,' ea, from $22 to..**$25.00**
Napco, S1307, bell of the month, ea, from $22 to......**$25.00**
Napco, S1361-1372, angel of the month, ea, from $20 to..**$25.00**
Napco, S1392, oval frame angel of the month, ea, from $25 to..**$30.00**
Napco, S401-413, angel of the month, ea, from $20 to ..**$25.00**
Napco, S429, day of the week angel (also available as planters), ea, from $25 to...**$30.00**
Norcrest, F-120, angel of the month, 4½", ea, from $18 to **$22.00**
Norcrest, F-15, angel of the month, on round base w/raised pattern on dress, 4", ea, from $18 to **$22.00**
Norcrest, F-167, bell of the month, 2¾", ea, from $8 to ..**$12.00**
Norcrest, F-210, day of the week angel, 4½", ea, from $18 to..**$22.00**
Norcrest, F-23, day of the week angel, 4½", ea, from $18 to..**$22.00**
Norcrest, F-340, angel of the month, 5", ea, from $20 to ..**$25.00**
Norcrest, F-535, angel of the month, 4½", ea, from $20 to..**$25.00**
Relco, 4¼", ea, from $15 to **$18.00**
Relco, 6", ea, from $18 to **$22.00**
SR, angel of the month, w/birthstone & 'trait' of the month (i.e. April - innocence), ea, from $20 to **$25.00**
TMJ, angel of the month, w/flower, ea, from $20 to..**$25.00**
Ucagco, white hair, 5¾", from $12 to **$15.00**
Wales, wearing long white gloves, white hair, Made in Japan, 6⅜", ea, from $25 to..**$28.00**

Angels, Zodiac

These china figurines were made and imported by the same companies as the birthday angels. Not as many companies made the Zodiac series, though, which makes them harder to find. Because they're older and were apparently never as popular as the month pieces, they were not made or distributed as long as the birthday angels. Examples tend to be more individualized due to each sign having a specific characteristic associated with it.

Japan, wearing pastel dress w/applied pink rose on head, standing on cloud base w/stars, 4½", ea, from $15 to **$20.00**

Japan, wearing pastel dress w/rhinestones on gold stars, applied pink rose on head, 4", ea, from $20 to ...**$25.00**

Josef, holds tablet w/sign written in gold, 1960-1962, ea, from $30 to..**$40.00**

Josef, no wings, sign written in cursive on dress, 4", ea, from $30 to..**$40.00**

Lefton, K8650, applied flowers & gold stars, 4" when standing (1946-1953), ea, from $32 to **$38.00**

Napco, A2646, wearing gold crown, applied 'coconut' gold trim on dress hem, 5", ea, from $25 to.................**$30.00**

Napco, S1259, 'Your lucky star guardian angel' planter series, 4", ea, from $30 to...**$35.00**

Napco, S980, 'Your lucky star guardian angel,' 4", ea, from $22 to..**$28.00**

Semco, gold wings, applied roses & pleated ruffle on front edge of dress, 5", ea, from $20 to **$25.00**

Animal Dishes with Covers

Made for nearly two centuries, animal dishes with covers are as just about as varied as their manufacturers. Slag, colored, clear, or milk glass types may be found as well as those made of china and pottery. While the hen on the nest (or basketweave base) is the most common theme, birds and animals of nearly every kind have been fashioned into covered dishes. Other figural designs such as ships were produced as well.

Covered Animal Dishes by Everett Grist is an excellent source for more information and covers the products of many manufacturers. Also refer to *American Slag Glass* by Ruth Grizel (Collector Books).

See also Degenhart; Duncan and Miller; Fenton; Imperial; Indiana Glass; L.E. Smith; L.G. Wright; Powder Jars; St. Clair Glass; Viking Glass; Westmoreland.

Advisor: Everett Grist (See Directory, Animal Dishes)

Atterbury duck, milk glass, 11"..................................**$245.00**

Bird on round basketweave base, milk glass, Vallerysthal..**$95.00**

British lion, milk glass, 6¼" **$195.00**

Chick in oblong basket, milk glass w/painted detail, 2¼x4½" **$325.00**

Crawfish on handled scroll base, milk glass, 7¼".....**$185.00**

Deer on fallen tree, clear glass, Flaccus **$185.00**

Duck on split-rib base, milk glass, Kemple reproduction **$65.00**

Elephant powder jar, plain round base, clear glass, 1930s...**$15.00**

Elephant w/rider, clear frosted, Vallerysthal, 7" **$200.00**

Fish lying flat on ribbed base, milk glass, attributed to Fostoria, 8½" **$165.00**

Fish on collared base, clear frosted, Cental Glass Co..**$150.00**

Hen on basket base, light green slag, Kanawah, 7", $135.00. (Photo courtesy Sharon Thoerner)

Hen on basketweave base, milk glass, Vallerysthal, 2"..**$25.00**

Hen on basketweave base, opaque blue w/white head, Wright reproduction..**$85.00**

Hen w/chicks, milk glass w/painted comb & waddle, ribbed base, condiment, McKee, 5½" **$165.00**

Lion on scroll base, milk glass, 5½"............................**$75.00**

Lion on split-rib base, milk glass, McKee, marked ...**$245.00**

Rabbit, clear glass, Vallerysthal....................................**$95.00**

Rabbit emerging from horizontal egg, milk glass w/painted detail, Gillinder & Sons **$65.00**

Rabbit on wheat base, milk glass, Flaccus **$350.00**

Robin on pedestal nest base, milk glass, Vallerysthal.**$75.00**

Setter on detailed footed square base, opaque blue, attributed to Vallerysthal..**$225.00**

Swan, milk glass, Vallerysthal, 5½" **$95.00**

Swan powder jar, ribbed base, clear green, Jeannette, late 1960s...**$15.00**

Turkey standing, clear glass, US Glass, lg **$250.00**

Turtle on tab-handled scoll base, milk glass, 7½" **$185.00**

Ashtrays

Ashtrays, especially for cigarettes, did not become widely used in the United States much before the turn of the century. The first examples were simply receptacles made to hold ashes for pipes, cigars, and cigarettes. Later, rests were incorporated into the design. Ashtrays were made in a variety of materials. Some were purely functional, while others advertised or entertained, and some stopped just short of being works of art. They were made to accommodate smokers in homes, businesses, or wherever they might be. Today their prices range from a few dollars to hundreds. Since they are comparatively new in the collectibles field, values are still fluctuating. For further information see *Collector's Guide to Ashtrays, Second Edition, Identification and Values,* by Nancy Wanvig.

See also specific glass companies and potteries; Japan Ceramics; Disney; Tire Ashtrays; World's Fairs.

Advisor: Nancy Wanvig (See Directory, Ashtrays)

Publication: Ashtray Collectors Directory
Chuck Thompson, Editor/Publisher
10802 Greencreek Dr., Suite 703; Houston, TX 77070
Annual publication listing all known ashtray collectors with addresses and specialties, $9.95 postage paid

Advertising, Old Judge Coffee, old, $95.00. (Photo courtesy Nancy Wanvig)

Advertising, Abbeey Rents, ceramic, bedpan shape, 'Everything for the Sickroom,' 2 rests, 4¼" wide .**$16.00**

Advertising, Agfa Film, figural of photo film box, ceramic, end rests wider than front one, old, 6" wide **$65.00**

Advertising, Ball, clear glass, canning jars, 3 rests, 3½" wide **$18.00**

Advertising, Buick, blue anodized aluminum, chrome logo & name in center, local ad on back, 4⅝" L.............**$15.00**

Advertising, Camel, cobalt glass, name in yellow, palm trees in green, 7¾" L **$35.00**

Advertising, Carlsberg, Danish beer, Pilsner-Lager-Supplied to Royal Courts, brass, very old, 3⅝" square **$23.00**

Advertising, Coors, cream ceramic, common mold, saying in center about forefathers working, 5⅞" dia **$15.00**

Advertising, Courvoisier Cognac, French, The Brandy of Napoleon, milk glass, 3 rests, 5½" dia **$8.00**

Advertising, Culligan, clear glass, 'soft water service,' 4¼" square **$8.00**

Advertising, Cutty Shark, Scotch whiskey, ceramic, ashtray by Seton Pottery, England, 4¼" square **$23.00**

Advertising, Dairy Queen, clear glass, white name on red, 3⅜" L.................**$11.00**

Advertising, Dewar's Scotch Whiskey, White Label, cream ceramic, picture of Dewar Highlander, 7" square ..**$36.00**

Advertising, Dr Pepper, clear glass, red decal w/white letters, 4" wide.................**$9.00**

Advertising, Falstaff, pale amber glass, rings at bottom, 3½" dia **$18.00**

Advertising, GE Sunlamp, painted pink steel, ... Summer Tan Look!, by Smokestone, 5½" dia **$11.00**

Advertising, General Electric, ceramic, gray plastic figural motor on back, 7" L.................**$56.00**

Advertising, Henkels, ceramic, German kitchen knives, picture of stylized man in center, 5¾" dia.................**$18.00**

Advertising, Hershey's, glass w/brown & white paint, 'Chocolate World,' 6" L.....................**$12.00**

Advertising, Holland American Lines, ceramic, cruise ship, name in gold around rim, 4¼" dia.........................**$27.00**

Advertising, Johnnie Walker Red, Scotch, red plastic, bump in center to knock off ashes, 3¾" dia.........................**$6.00**

Advertising, Moet & Chandon Champagne, French, silhouette of Dom Perignon, 4" L **$12.00**

Advertising, Old Judge Coffee, painted tin, 'vacuum packed-Irradiated,' 2⅞" H **$42.00**

Advertising, Olympia, white ceramic, salesman's sample, decal logo, Premium Lager Beer, 4⅛" dia **$15.00**

Advertising, Pizza Hut, clear glass, stylized logo impressed center, 5" dia **$7.00**

Advertising, Playboy Club, white glass, sm black bunny head in center, 1960s, 4" square **$12.00**

Advertising, Ritz Carlton, made by Syracuse China, brown picture of lions logo, 7⅝" dia **$15.00**

Advertising, Urquell, Czech Republic beer, milk glass, older style w/colorful Czech decal, 5¼" dia...................**$15.00**

Advertising, Winston, clear glass w/red decal, 'nothing but taste-NO BULL,' 4½" dia.................**$12.00**

Advertising, Wurlitzer piano, baby grand shape, wood & metal, registered name, w/box, 3⅝" **$83.00**

Art Deco, head w/streaming hair, head is frosted smoky glass, base is chrome, nice face, 6¾" dia **$135.00**

Art Deco, nude smoking, little drapery, solid brass dish shape, background ridge like seashell, 6⅜" L......**$79.00**

Art Deco, reclining bisque nude on back of ceramic ashtray, hand painted, flowers on rise, 6¼" L.................**$78.00**

Art Glass, glass clown sitting, top hat, 2 blue rests (hands), big colorful bowl (lap), Murano, 5¼" L.................**$90.00**

Art Glass, peacock glass bowl w/3 eyes, chrome top w/ornate match holder & cigar cutter, 6¼"........**$375.00**

Art Nouveau, man w/figural cigarette, ceramic, man in relief, cigarette is a rest, 6¼" L......................**$83.00**

Art Nouveau, pipe figural, ceramic, France-1911, painter signed, handle is rest, Limoges-type, 5⅜" L **$35.00**

Arts & Crafts, hammered copper, pig in center, Germany, a card suit marked in ea corner, 4⅝" L....................**$35.00**

Arts & Crafts, Roycroft, hammered copper, octagon, 1 rest, center marks, no patina, 4¾" L **$100.00**

Casino, Landmark, gold letters on rim, Hotel-Las Vegas, green glass, 4⅛" dia **$9.00**

Casino, The Sands, amber glass, Las Vegas, Nevada, red letters & logo in center, hotel now demolished, 4½" dia ...**$8.00**

Fraternal, Rotary International, ceramic figural of cogwheel logo, probably for convention, 5¾" dia.................**$14.00**

Fraternal, Royal American Shrine Club, ceramic, pictures helping children, circus background, 8⅝" dia......**$15.00**

Majolica, smoke set, boy holding plate-basket for cigarettes & matches, tray is green, Austria, 5¼" L.................**$215.00**

Novelty, Black man with drums, four snufferettes, 4", $60.00. (Photo courtesy Nancy Wanvig)

Novelty, cat w/umbrella in center of ashtray, solid brass, 3 rests, 4" **$21.00**

Novelty, nodder, black boy w/cigar in mouth, metal, colorful clothes, Austria, 4⅞" **$185.00**

Novelty, nodder, lady on lounge chair, pink clothes & red shoes, rests on side, legs & fan nods, 6" L...........**$95.00**

Novelty, nodder, man, Yes, Dear, Yes Dear written in center, Japan, 3¼" **$48.00**

Novelty, nodder, Moon Mullins, ceramic, cigar in mouth, Germany, 4⅝" **$150.00**

Novelty, smoker: brown African face, pivoting wire rest, Treasure Craft CA, 1957, 6¼" L.............................**$32.00**

Novelty, smoker: Charlie Chaplin, feet are rests, smoke vents out hole in cigar in mouth, Lego-Japan, 7½" **$70.00**

Novelty, smoker: clown head on book, bee between eyes, rest in mouth, Japan, 4⅛x4⅛" **$57.00**

Novelty, smoker: head w/distorted face, movable button eyes, holes in ears, Sweet Adeline, 5¼" **$80.00**

Novelty, smoker: lion head, teeth & rest in mouth, lots of character, holes in nose, Japan, 3⅝" L..................**$46.50**

Novelty, smoker: skull, teeth are rests, holes in eyes, 'Poor Old Fred—He Smoked in Bed,' Japan, 5⅞" L......**$35.00**

Sports, Indianapolis 500, cranberry-color glass, names of winners from 1911 to 1969 around sides, 8" L.....**$38.00**

Victorian, dragonfly, solid brass tray, lg fly in relief, dark patina, 6 rests, late 1880s, 7" dia **$135.00**

Victorian, monkeys pictured dancing in bottom of tray, ceramic, old-style hollow match holder, 5¾" L....**$75.00**

Autographs

'Philography' is an extremely popular hobby, one that is very diversified. Autographs of sports figures, movie stars, entertainers, and politicians from our lifetime may bring several hundred dollars, depending on rarity and application, while John Adams' simple signature on a document from 1800, for instance, might bring thousands. A signature on a card or cut from a letter or document is the least valuable type of autograph. A handwritten letter is generally the most valuable, since in addition to the signature you get the message as well. Depending upon what it reveals about the personality who penned it, content can be very important and can make a major difference in value.

Many times a polite request accompanied by an SASE to a famous person will result in receipt of a signed photo or a short handwritten note that might in several years be worth a tidy sum!

Obviously as new collectors enter the field, the law of supply and demand will drive the prices for autographs upward, especially when the personality is deceased. There are forgeries around, so before you decide to invest in expensive autographs, get to know your dealers.

Over the years many celebrities in all fields have periodically employed secretaries to sign their letters and photos. They have also sent out photos with preprinted or rubber stamped signatures as time doesn't always permit them to personally respond to fan mail. With today's advanced printing, even many long-time collectors have been fooled with a mechanically produced signature.

Advisors: Don and Anne Kier (See Directory, Autographs)

Newspaper: *Autograph Times*
2303 N 44th St., #225, Phoenix, AZ 85008
602-947-3112 or fax: 602-947-8363

Allen, Woody; signed color photo, 8x10"+matt...........**$20.00**
Anderson, Richard D; signed color photo, 8x10"+matt..**$18.00**
Baldwin, Alec; signed color photo, 8x10"+matt **$38.00**
Basinger, Kim; signed color photo, 8x10"+matt **$50.00**
Blanc, Mel; signed color photo at desk w/Warner Bros cartoon characters, 8x10" **$70.00**
Bono (U2), signed color photo, 8x20"+matt................**$75.00**
Brown, Jim; signed color photo, 8x10"+matt..............**$35.00**
Cain, Dean; signed color photo, 8x10"+matt..............**$25.00**
Carey, Mariah; signed color photo, 8x10"+matt **$75.00**
Chan, Jackie; signed color photo, 8x10".....................**$35.00**
Cobain, Kurt; signed color photo, 8x10"+matt **$145.00**
Cox, Courtney; signed color photo, 8x10"..................**$40.00**
Cruise, Tom; signed color photo, 8x10"+matt **$85.00**
Cybill, signed color photo of 5 cast members, 8x10" ..**$140.00**

Dean, James; signed and inscribed black and white photo, early 1950s, 3½x2½", $2,800.00.

DeNiro, Robert; signed color photo, 8x10"................$80.00
Duchovny, David; signed color photo, 8x10" $50.00
Dylan, Bob; signed color photo, 8x10"+matt $200.00
Elton, John; signed color photo, 8x10"+matt...............$85.00
Estevez, Emilio; signed color photo, 8x10".................$15.00
Foreman, George; signed color photo, 8x10"+matt $45.00
Frasier, signed color photo of 5 cast members, 8x10" ..$175.00
Ghost & the Darkness, signed color photo by Kilmer &
   Douglas, 8x10"+matt...$85.00
Graham, Heather; signed color photo, 8x10" $50.00
Griffey, Ken, Jr; signed baseball bat $140.00
Henie, Sonja; signed black & white photo, 7x9" $175.00
Hoffman, Dustin; signed color photo, 8x10"+matt.....$50.00
Hunter, Rachel; signed color photo, 8x10" $30.00
Ireland, Kathy; signed Sports Illustrated magazine, 25th
   Anniversary issue..$55.00
Jewel, signed Pieces of You album............................$40.00
Jolson, Al; inscribed & signed black & white photo,
   5x7"...$175.00
Kilmer, Val; signed color photo, 8x10".......................$38.00
Lee, Christopher; signed color photo, 8x10"+matt......$35.00
Lewis, Daniel Day; signed color photo, 8x10"+matt ...$55.00
Lucas, George; signed color photo, 8x10"+matt........$125.00
Mantle, Mickey; signed color photo, 20x16"...............$75.00
Montana, Ashley; signed Sports Illustrated magazine,
   February 1991..$50.00

Montana, Joe; signature on Wheaties box (never assembled), framed, 16x22½", $110.00.

Mulgrew, Kate; signed color photo, 8x10"+matt $40.00
Nicholson, Jack; signed color photo, 8x10".................$60.00
O'Donnell, Chris; signed color photo, 8x10"..............$40.00
Parker, Sara Jessica; signed color photo, 8x10"...........$40.00
Petty, Tom; signed color photo, 8x10"+matt $75.00
Prince, signed color photo, 8x10"+matt.....................$275.00
Russell, Kurt; signed color photo, 8x10" $50.00
Seagal, Steven; signed color photo, 8x10"+matt.........$20.00
Simon & Garfunkel, color photo signed by both, 8x10" ..$125.00
Snipes, Wesley; signed color photo, 8x10"+matt.........$40.00
Springsteen, Bruce; signed color photo, 8x10"+matt ..$150.00
Starr, Ringo; signed drumskin....................................$200.00

Stewart, James; signed black & white photo, 4x5" $35.00
Stowe, Madeline; signed color photo, 8x10" $38.00
Third Rock From the Sun, signed color photo of 4 cast mem-
   bers, 8x10"..$140.00
Turner, Kathleen; signed color photo, 8x10"+matt $35.00
Van Halen Band, signed Guitar magazine, April
   1985 ....$150.00
Weissmuller, Johnny; signed Tarzan poster, mounted on
   foam-cor, 24x30" $195.00
Williams, Robin; signed color photo, 8x10"................$50.00

Nixon, Richard; signed and inscribed Congressional Breakfast program, 1969 (as president), $250.00.

Automobilia

Automobilia remains a specialized field, attracting antique collectors and old car buffs alike. It is a field that encompasses auto-related advertising and accessories like hood ornaments, gear shift and steering wheel knobs, sales brochures, and catalogs. Memorabilia from the high-performance, sporty automobiles of the sixties is very popular with baby boomers. Unusual items have been setting auction records as the market for automobilia heats up. Note: Badges vary according to gold content — 10k or sterling silver examples are higher than average. Dealership booklets (Ford, Chevy, etc.) generally run about $2.00 to $3.00 per page, and because many reproductions are available, very few owner's manuals sell for more than $10.00. See also License Plates; Tire Ashtrays.

Advisor: Leonard Needham (See Directory, Automobilia)

Bank, Buick Fireball Eight/Best Buick Yet, white & red globe,
   5", EX+..$110.00
Bank, Chevrolet The Symbol of Savings For 27 Years, tin
   globe, Chein, 5", EX+ $60.00
Banner, Chevrolet Task Force Trucks/New 1956...On Display,
   cloth, close-up of front of truck, white & yellow, 33x91",
   VG...$70.00

Banner, Weed Chains/Heap Smart Driver!, heavy paper, trapper in coonskin cap looking at tire tracks in snow, 29x60", EX **$90.00**

Calendar, Chevrolet Motor Cars, 1920, paper litho, framed, 33½x20", EX+ **$80.00**

Change purse, leather cap shape w/nickel-plated brass bill & bottom embossed w/touring car, Aug 1910, 2½" dia, EX **$120.00**

Clock, Cadillac, square desk-type light up w/numbers around Cadillac emblem, ca 1960, 9x10", NM....**$200.00**

Clock, Dodge Brothers, metal face w/wood frame, winged logo in center, black numbers, early, 15x15", nonworking o/w EX..**$250.00**

Clock, Ford, glass and metal, lights up, 18x18", VG, $750.00.

Clock, Jeep The 2-Car Cars/Great For Work Or Play, clock at left of changing picture, red & white, 19x32", EX........**$275.00**

Clock, Pontiac, plastic neon, round red & white Indian head logo, red numbers, 19" dia, VG..**$375.00**

Clock, Pontiac Service, plastic, white lettering on blue border around numbered face, 15" dia, EX..**$350.00**

Compact mirror, Dodge Brothers Coupe, name below image of auto against sky blue ground shading into yellow, 2" dia, EX..**$360.00**

Desk accessory, GMC truck in bronze-plated white metal on beveled base marked Camden Motor Truck Co..., 3x4x7", EX..**$100.00**

Display, Buick, wooden cabinet w/color combinations for the 1960 Buick, drawer holds fabric, 16x21", G+ **$200.00**

Display, Pontiac, wire figural Indian head logo on wire circle attached to wire base, ca 1930s, 20x47", M..**$275.00**

Display rack, Greyhound Bus literature, 4-tiered, blue-painted wood w/gold trademark dog on front, 7x15x4", EX **$200.00**

Hood ornament, Packard's Goddess of Speed mascot, chrome-plated, ca 1932-37, EX **$170.00**

Jigsaw puzzle, Dodge Brothers New Eight Sedan/Six Sedan, 2-sided, car against farm scene/cityscape, ca 1932, 9x16", EX **$125.00**

Lamp shade, Chevrolet, plastic stained-glass look, multicolored, 15" dia, VG..**$250.00**

License plate attachment, Chrysler/It Pays To Buy a Fine Car, tin, black top hat, gloves & cane on red oval, 6x9", VG+..**$275.00**

License plate attachment, Ford/Let's Take It Easy, metal emblem w/reflective paint showing cartoon cop, 4x7", EX..**$20.00**

Lighter, Buick, silver-tone pressed-tin car shape w/white rubber wheels, Occupied Japan, late 1940s, 5", EX, very rare..**$350.00**

Lighter, Chevrolet School Bus, gold-tone metal w/image of school bus on porcelain inlay, 1½x2", EX..........**$25.00**

Magazine, Motor Magazine's Annual, October, 1939, cover art by Radchaugh, VG..**$30.00**

Magazine, *TACH*, monthly publication of American Hot Rod Association, March 1967, $20.00. (Photo courtesy Jim and Nancy Schaut)

Map, Greyhound route, dated November 1, 1934, 20x31", EX **$30.00**

Matchbooks, Chevrolet, Dealers (1953-1967), M, ea...**$11.00**

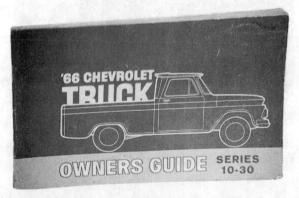

Owner's guide, '66 Chevy Truck, Series 10-30, $10.00.

Paperweight, Chalmers Motor Co, brass w/embossed images & lettering, 2¼x3½", EX..**$120.00**

Paperweight, OIM Transport Corp, cast-metal semi truck, red & orange w/black base, 2x1½x5", EX **$125.00**

Picnic set, Ford, set of 4 graniteware dishes, silverware marked Ford, metal thermos, shakers & food box in case, VG **$275.00**

Pin, Chevrolet Corvette Owner, metal, round w/crossed-flag logo in center, 1955-56, NM..**$260.00**

Plate, Ford, building in center w/name on rim, Shenango China, 6", EX..**$150.00**

Pocketknife, Chevrolet, blue bow-tie logo on cream plastic casing, 3½", EX..**$40.00**

Pocketknife, Ford, blue script logo on red plastic casing, 3½", EX..**$60.00**

Postcard, Nash Ambassador 600, Here's That Sensational New Nash — In The Lowest Price Field!, pictures auto, NM **$20.00**

Poster, Ford/1939 Baseball All-Stars, dealers' names flank logo above illustrated ball game, photos & stats, 32x17", EX+ **$650.00**

Salt & pepper shakers, Greyhound Bus, metal bus shapes, EX, pr...**$100.00**

Sign, Auto License Lock, cardboard, Foil the Thief With... above busy street scene, text below, wood frame, 26x18", VG **$385.00**

Sign, Chevrolet Sales & Service For Economical Transportation, porcelain, white lettering on blue, 2-sided, 28x40", NM...**$650.00**

Sign, Chevrolet/Over The Years/America's First Choice, red, white & blue molded plastic light-up emblem, 24x28", VG **$130.00**

Sign, DeSoto/Authorized Dealer/Top Value, diecut metal emblem w/2-color ground, 16x36", VG **$235.00**

Sign, Edsel Service, arrow-shaped light-up w/plastic inserts on stainless steel housing, 2-sided, 36x72x14", M ...**$1,200.00**

Sign, Oldsmobile Service, porcelain, round w/name on blue band around sleek globe emblem, 2-sided, 60" dia, EX+ **$850.00**

Sign, Pontiac, neon, logo above name, red & yellow, 24x42", EX **$375.00**

Sign, Pontiac/Master Salesman, molded emblem, sleek Indian logo, black & red on gold-tone, 36x39", EX+ **$375.00**

Sign, The New Willys Cars... on blue band above multiple images of cars around center car, paper, 27x41", VG **$150.00**

Table, Chrysler/Plymouth/Dodge/DeSoto, wood, fold-down top inlayed w/car carrier over map, 26x26", VG .**$330.00**

Thermometer, Buick Motor Cars, porcelain, white on dark blue w/white border, 27x7", NM **$350.00**

Thermometer, Chevrolet Corvair/OK, tin, red, white & black on white, vertical, EX..**$225.00**

Thermometer, Mack Trucks, round dial type w/logo on white tin face, glass front, VG+ **$200.00**

Watch fob, Cadillac, sterling silver emblem w/black inlayed ducks opposite red & white design, black fabric strap, NM **$200.00**

Watch fob, Ford, metal oval emblem w/blue cloisonne, silver-tone trim, 1x2", EX+ **$50.00**

Autumn Leaf Dinnerware

A familiar dinnerware pattern to just about all of us, Autumn Leaf was designed by Hall China for the Jewel Tea Company who offered it to their customers as premiums. In fact, some people erroneously refer to the pattern as 'Jewel Tea.' First made in 1933, it continued in production until 1978. Pieces with this date in the backstamp are from the overstock that was in the company's warehouse when production was suspended. There are matching pitchers, tumblers, and stemware all made by the Libbey Glass Company, and a set of enameled cookware that came out in 1979. You'll find blankets, tablecloths, metal canisters, clocks, playing cards, and many other items designed around the Autumn Leaf pattern. All are collectible.

Since 1984 the Hall company has been making special items for the National Autumn Leaf Collectors Club. These pieces are designated as such by the 'Club' marking that is accompanied by the date of issue. Limited edition items (also by Hall) are being sold by China Specialties, a company in Ohio; but once you become familiar with the old pieces, these are easy to identify, since the molds have been redesigned or were not previously used for Autumn Leaf production.

For further study, we recommend *The Collector's Encyclopedia of Hall China* by Margaret and Kenn Whitmyer. For information on company products, see Jewel Tea.

Advisor: Gwynneth M. Harrison (See Directory, Autumn Leaf)

Club: National Autumn Leaf Collectors' Club
Gwynneth Harrison
P.O. Box 1, Mira Loma, CA 91752-0001; 909-685-5434
E-mail: morgan99@pe.net

Newsletter: *Autumn Leaf*
Bill Swanson, Editor
807 Roaring Springs Dr.
Allen, TX 75002-2112; 972-727-5527

Baker, cake; Mary Dunbar, Heatflow, glass, 1½-qt.....**$65.00**

Baker, French; two-pint, 6½", from $150.00 to $175.00.

Baker, French; 3-pt, 1936-76.......................................**$20.00**
Baker, souffle; 1966-76, 4⅛" **$12.00**
Baker, souffle; 1978, 4½" **$50.00**
Bean pot, 2-handled, 1960-76....................................**$250.00**
Blanket, Vellux, Autumn Leaf color, 1979+, full sz ...**$175.00**
Blanket, Vellux, Autumn Leaf color, 1979+, king sz ..**$220.00**
Bottle, Jim Beam, broken seal...................................**$110.00**

Bottle, Jim Beam, w/stand $130.00
Bowl, cream soup; 1950-76.......................................$35.00
Bowl, fruit; 1936-76, 5½" $6.00
Bowl, mixing; New Metal, 1980+, 3-pc set..............$275.00
Bowl, mixing; 1933-76, 3-pc set $65.00
Bowl, soup; Melmac...$20.00
Bowl, vegetable; Melmac, oval.................................$50.00
Bowl, vegetable; oval, divided, 1957-76...................$125.00

Bowl, vegetable; oval, with lid, $75.00.

Bowl, vegetable; round, 9" $150.00
Bowl, vegetable; Royal Glasbake, milk white, divided...$125.00
Box, oatmeal..$100.00
Butter dish, regular, ruffled top, 1961-76, ¼-lb.........$250.00
Butter dish, regular, 1959-60, 1-lb $500.00
Butter dish, wings top, 1961+, ¼-lb.......................$1,800.00
Cake plate, on metal stand, 1958-69 ....$225.00
Cake plate, 1937-76..$28.00
Cake safe, side motif, 1950-53 ....$50.00
Can, cleanser, EX..$1,200.00
Candle holder, Club, 1989, pr..................................$250.00
Candlesticks, metal, Douglas, pr $100.00
Canister, metal, square, 1959+, 4-pc set..................$350.00
Canister, metal w/ivory plastic lid $10.00
Casserole, Club, w/lid...$150.00
Casserole, Mary Dunbar, Heatflow, clear glass, w/lid, oval, 2-qt..$125.00
Casserole, round, w/lid, 1935-76, 2-qt $45.00
Casserole, Royal Glasbake, milk white, w/lid, oval....$90.00

Clock, electric, ca 1950s – 60s, 9½" diameter, from $400.00 to $550.00.

Clock, salesman award, 1980....................................$400.00
Coaster, metal, sm, 3⅛" $8.00
Coffee dispenser, 1941 ....$400.00
Coffeepot, electric percolator, 1957-69.....................$350.00
Coffeepot, Jewel's Best, 30-cup................................$600.00
Coffeepot, Rayed, 1937-49, 9-cup.............................$45.00
Cooker, Mary Dunbar, waterless, metal $75.00
Cookie jar, Tootsie, Rayed, 1936-39 ....$300.00
Cookware, New Metal, 7-pc set $650.00
Creamer & sugar bowl, Melmac.................................$40.00
Creamer & sugar bowl, Rayed, 1930s style, 1934-40 ..$80.00
Cup, coffee; Jewel's Best..$30.00
Cup, St Denis...$30.00
Cup, tea; regular, Ruffled-D, 1936-76 ....$6.00
Custard cup, Radiance, 1936-76................................$10.00
Drip jar, w/lid...$20.00
Dripper, metal for coffeepot $25.00
Dutch oven, metal & porcelain, w/lid, 1979+, 5-qt.....$175.00
Flatware, silverplate, ea place pc $35.00
Flatware, silverplate, ea serving pc $100.00
Flatware, stainless steel, ea place pc $30.00
Flatware, stainless steel, ea serving pc.....................$60.00
Fondue, complete set, 1980+ $200.00
Fork, pickle; Jewel Tea...$75.00
Goblet, gold & frost on clear, footed, Libbey, 6½-oz.$65.00
Gravy boat, 1940-76...$30.00
Hot pad, round, metal back, 1937+, 7¼".....................$20.00
Hot pad, round, red or green back, 1946+, 7¼"........$20.00
Jug, Baby Ball, Club $95.00
Jug, ball; #3, 1938-76...$40.00
Jug, utility; Rayed, 1937-76......................................$25.00
Loaf pan, Mary Dunbar $85.00
Meat chopper, jewel on handle................................$450.00
Mug, conic, 1966-76...$65.00
Mug, Irish coffee, from $125 to...............................$150.00
Mustard, condiment set, 3-pc, 1938-39 ....$100.00
Place mats, set of 8, MIB...$325.00
Plate, dinner; Melmac, 10" $20.00
Plate, pie; Mary Dunbar, Heatflow, clear glass, from $75 to $125.00
Plate, salad; Melmac, 7"...$20.00
Plate, 1938-76, 9" $12.00
Plate, 7¼" $10.00
Platter, oval, 1938-76, 13½" $28.00
Platter, oval, 1942-76, 9" $25.00
Saucepan, w/lid, 1979+, 2-qt...................................$100.00
Saucepan, w/warmer base, Douglas, 1960-62..........$500.00
Saucer, regular, Ruffled-D, 1936-76............................$3.00
Saucer, St Denis...$8.00
Scales, Jewel's Family $200.00
Shelf liner, paper, 1945+, 108" $50.00
Sifter, metal...$400.00
Skillet, metal & porcelain, 1979+, 9½".....................$125.00
Spray, No-Dust..$50.00
Stack set, 1951-76, 4-pc $125.00
Tablecloth, muslin, 56x81".......................................$300.00
Tablecloth, plastic, 54", 62" or 72", ea $150.00

Tea for 2 set, Club	$175.00
Teakettle, metal & porcelain, 1979+	$250.00
Teapot, Aladdin, 1942-76	$70.00
Teapot, donut, Club	$125.00
Teapot, French, Club	$95.00
Teapot, New York, Club, 1984	$600.00
Teapot, Newport, 1978	$200.00
Teapot, Rayed, long spout, 1978	$200.00
Teapot, Solo, Club	$100.00
Thermos, picnic jug, 1941+	$375.00
Tidbit, 2-tier, 1954-69	$100.00
Tin, cocoa; paper label	$70.00
Tin, coffee; paper label	$100.00
Tin, fruitcake; white	$10.00
Towel, tea; 16x33"	$60.00
Toy, Jewel Van, Tonka, brown, 1954	$425.00
Toy, Jewel's Skipper Squeak	$70.00
Toy, Jewel's Truck, orange	$195.00
Toy, Jewel's Truck, semi-trailer, white	$375.00
Trash can, red, 1951	$400.00
Tray, coffee service, oval, 18¾"	$100.00
Tray, red	$100.00
Tray, wood & glass	$100.00
Tumbler, Brockway, 1975-76, 16-oz	$45.00
Tumbler, Brockway, 1975-76, 9-oz	$45.00
Tumbler, gold & frost on clear, Libbey, 10-oz	$65.00
Tumbler, juice; frosted, Libbey, 3¾"	$35.00
Vase, bud; Club	$40.00
Vase, bud; sm or regular decal, 1940	$225.00
Warmer, round, 1956-60	$160.00

Salt and pepper shakers, Casper, $30.00 for the pair; Range shakers, $30.00 for the pair.

Barbie Doll and Her Friends

Barbie doll was first introduced in 1959, and soon Mattel found themselves producing not only dolls but tiny garments, fashion accessories, houses, cars, horses, books, and games as well. Today's Barbie doll collectors want them all. Though the early Barbie dolls are very hard to find, there are many of her successors still around. The trend today is toward Barbie doll exclusives — Holiday Barbie dolls and Bob Mackie Barbie dolls are all very 'hot' items. So are special-event Barbie dolls.

When buying the older dolls, you'll need to do a lot of studying and comparisons to learn to distinguish one Barbie doll from another, but this is the key to making sound buys and good investments. Remember, though, collectors are sticklers concerning condition; compared to a doll mint in box, they'll often give an additional 20% if that box has never been opened (or as collectors say 'never removed from box,' indicated in our lines by 'NRFB')! As a general rule, a mint-in-the-box doll is worth from 50% to 100% more than one mint, no box. The same doll, played with and in only good condition, is worth half as much (or less than that). If you want a good source for study, refer to one of these fine books: *A Decade of Barbie Dolls and Collectibles, 1981 – 1991,* by Beth Summers; *The Wonder of Barbie* and *The World of Barbie Dolls* by Paris and Susan Manos; *The Collector's Encyclopedia of Barbie Dolls and Collectibles* by Sibyl DeWein and Joan Ashabraner; *Barbie Doll Fashion, Vol I and Vol II,* by Sarah Sink Eames; *Barbie Exclusives, Books I and II,* by Margo Rana; *The Barbie Doll Boom, 1986 – 1995,* and *Collector's Encyclopedia of Barbie Doll Exclusives and More* by J. Michael Augustyniak; *The Barbie Years, 1959 to 1995,* by Patrick C. Olds; *The Story of Barbie* by Kitturah Westenhouser; *Barbie, The First 30 Years, 1959 Through 1989,* by Stefanie Deutsch; *Collector's Guide to Barbie Doll Paper Dolls* by Lorraine Mieszala; and *Schroeder's Collectible Toys, Antique to Modern* (Collector Books).

Dolls

Allan, 1963, painted red hair, straight legs, MIB	$125.00
Barbie, #1, 1958-59, blond hair, MIB	$9,950.00
Barbie, #2, brunette hair, MIB	$8,500.00
Barbie, #3, 1960, brunette hair, MIB	$2,250.00
Barbie, #4, 1960, blond hair, MIB	$1,100.00
Barbie, #5, 1961, red hair, MIB	$1,300.00
Barbie, #6, brunette hair, original swimsuit, NM	$350.00
Barbie, American Girl, 1964, blond hair, original swimsuit, NM	$550.00

Barbie, Angel Lights, Christmas tree topper, lights up, 1993, M, $100.00. (Photo courtesy Lee Garmon)

Barbie, Anniversary Star, 1992, Wal-Mart 30th Anniversary, MIB $45.00

Barbie, Back to School, 1992, MIB.............................$30.00

Barbie, Ballerina on Tour, 1976, MIB.......................$100.00

Barbie, Bubble-Cut, 1961, blond hair or brunette hair, MIB..$500.00

Barbie, Bubble-Cut, 1961, red hair, MIB..................$600.00

Barbie, Busy Gal, 1994, NRFB $75.00

Barbie, Chinese, 1993, Dolls of the World, NRFB......$45.00

Barbie, Cinderella, 1996, Children's Collector Series, NRFB $35.00

Barbie, Country Looks, 1992, MIB.............................$30.00

Barbie, Doctor, 1987, NRFB $35.00

Barbie, Dramatic New Living, 1970, blond or red hair, NRFB $350.00

Barbie, Egyptian Queen, 1993, Great Eras, NRFB.....$175.00

Barbie, Empress Bride, 1992, Bob Mackie, MIB $1,195.00

Barbie, English, 1991, Dolls of the World, NRFB........$75.00

Barbie, Evening Sparkle, 1990, Hills Dept Store, MIB ..$45.00

Barbie, Fashion Photo, 1977, MIB $85.00

Barbie, Feelin' Groovy, 1986, MIB $175.00

Barbie, Golden Greetings, 1989, FAO Schwarz, MIB..$275.00

Barbie, Hawaiian, 1975, MIB $85.00

Barbie, Holiday, 1988, NRFB, minimum value.......$1,000.00

Barbie, Holiday, 1989, NRFB $300.00

Barbie, Holiday, 1990, NRFB $300.00

Barbie, Holiday, 1991, NRFB $300.00

Barbie, Holiday, 1992, NRFB $200.00

Barbie, Holiday, 1993, NRFB $200.00

Barbie, Holiday, 1994, NRFB $200.00

Barbie, Holiday, 1995, NRFB $75.00

Barbie, Holiday, 1996, NRFB $50.00

Barbie, Hot Looks, 1991, MIB.....................................$35.00

Barbie, India, 1981, Dolls of the World, NRFB $150.00

Barbie, Japanese, 1984, Dolls of the World, NRFB ...$150.00

Barbie, Kenyan, 1993, Dolls of the World, NRFB $35.00

Barbie, Lavender Surprise, 1989, MIB $50.00

Barbie, Little Bo Peep, Children's Classic Series, NRFB .$125.00

Barbie, Live Action, 1971, original outfit, NM $150.00

Barbie, Magic Moves (Black), 1985, NRFB $35.00

Barbie, Malibu, 1971, MIP $85.00

Barbie, Midnight Gala, 1994, Classique Collection, NRFB ...$95.00

Barbie, Moonlight Rose, 1991, NRFB $40.00

Barbie, Night Sensation, 1991, FAO Schwarz, MIB ...$150.00

Barbie, Olympic Gymnast, 1995, NRFB $75.00

Barbie, Parisienne, 1980, Dolls of the World, MIB ...$200.00

Barbie, Picnic Pretty, 1992, Osco, NRFB.....................$30.00

Barbie, Pink Jubilee, 1987, Wal-Mart, MIB..................$85.00

Barbie, Ponytail, 1961, blond hair, original swimsuit, VG....$285.00

Barbie, Pretty in Purple (Black), 1992, NRFB..............$50.00

Barbie, Quick Curl Miss America, 1972, MIB $125.00

Barbie, Regal Reflections, 1992, Spiegel, NRFB........$350.00

Barbie, Satin Nights, 1992, MIB..................................$65.00

Barbie, Savvy Shopper, 1994, Bloomingdales, NMIB..$85.00

Barbie, Scarlett O'Hara, 1994, Hollywood Legends Series, red dress, NRFB $75.00

Barbie, Sleeping Beauty, 1992, NRFB $35.00

Barbie, Snow Princess, 1994, Seasons Series, NRFB.$135.00

Barbie, Standard, 1970, blond hair, MIB...................$700.00

Barbie, Starlight Splendor (Black), Bob Mackie, second in the series, M, $500.00. (NRFB, $900.00.) (Photo courtesy Lee Garmon)

Barbie, Swirl Ponytail, 1964, red hair, original swimsuit, NM $450.00

Barbie, Talking, 1968, blond or brunette hair, original swimsuit, NM, ea $175.00

Barbie, Twist 'N Turn, 1967, black hair, original outfit, NM $325.00

Barbie, Walk Lively, 1972, NRFB...............................$300.00

Barbie, Winter Fantasy, 1990, FAO Schwarz, NRFB..$300.00

Brad, Talking, 1971, M...$125.00

Brad, 1969, bendable legs, NRFB..............................$175.00

Cara, Deluxe Quick Curl, 1976, MIB...........................$65.00

Christie, Talking, 1968, original swimsuit, EX $150.00

Fluff, Living, 1971, NRFB, minimum value...............$175.00

Francie, Hair Happenin's, 1970, original outfit, EX...$150.00

Francie, 1966, blond hair, bendable legs, original swimsuit, NM $200.00

Jamie, Walking, brunette hair, original outfit, NM.....$275.00

Kelly, Yellowstone, 1973, NRFB $450.00

Ken, Free Movin', 1975, NRFB..................................$100.00

Ken, Mod Hair, 1972, NRFB......................................$115.00

Ken, Perfume Giving; NFRB, $28.00; Whitney, Perfume Pretty, hard to find, NRFB, $70.00. (Photo courtesy J. Michael Agustyniak)

Ken, Prince Charming, 1991, NRFB.............................$35.00
Ken, Rhett Butler, 1994, Holywood Legends Series, NRFB $75.00
Ken, Sun Valley, 1973, NRFB................................$125.00
Ken, The Beast, 1991, NRFB..................................$35.00
Midge, 1963, blond hair, straight legs, MIB..............$150.00
PJ, Live Action, 1971, original outfit, VG.................$125.00
Ricky, 1965, MIB..$175.00
Skipper, Cool Tops, MIB..$35.00
Skipper, Living, 1970, MIB...................................$125.00
Skipper, Quick Curl, 1973-75, MIB..........................$75.00
Skipper, 1965, red hair, bendable legs, original swimsuit, NM $100.00
Skooter, Funtime, 1976, NRFB, minimum value........$200.00
Skooter, 1965, blond hair, bendable legs, MIB..........$225.00
Stacey, Twint 'N Turn, 1968, blond hair, original swimsuit, NM $300.00
Stacie, Toontown, 1993, MIB...................................$40.00
Steffie, Busy Talking, 1972, original outfit, NM..........$275.00
Tiff, Pose 'N Play, 1972, NRFB, minimum value.......$500.00
Todd, 1965, NRFB..$225.00
Tuttie, 1966, brunette hair, dressed in Cookin' Goodies, EX $50.00
Whitney, Jewel Secrets, 1986, NRFB $100.00

Accessories

Case, 1963, blue or black, from $20.00 to $35.00; red or white, from $30.00 to $45.00.

Case, Barbie, Francie, Casey & Tutti, hard plastic, 1966, NM, minimum value......................................$100.00
Case, Barbie & Skipper Vanity Trunk, vinyl, 1965, rare, NM, minimum value...$250.00
Case, Ken Rally Days, teal, 1962, EX $20.00
Case, Pink & Pretty Barbie, vinyl w/metal closure, 1982, M $10.00
Case, Tutti's Playhouse, 1965, M $150.00
Case, Tutti & Chris Patio Picnic Case, NM.............$100.00
Furniture, Go-Together Swing, 1964, complete, M ...$100.00
Furniture, Superstar Barbie Piano Set, 1989, complete, MIB $25.00
Furniture, Suzy Goose Vanity, 1963, complete, EX.....$35.00

Furniture & Francie's House, 1966, complete, EX.......$75.00
Furniture & Barbie & Ken Theater, 1964, complete, NMIB.$600.00
Furniture & Barbie Country Living House, 1973-77, complete, EX...$75.00
Furniture & Barbie Dream House, 1st edition, 1961, complete, NM...$150.00
Furniture & Cool Tops Skipper T-Shirt Shop, 1989, complete, MIB $20.00
Furniture & Tutti's Ice Cream Stand, 1965, rare, NM$300.00
Outfit, Barbie, Baby Doll Pinks, #3403-1, complete, M ..$45.00
Outfit, Barbie, Beauty & the Beast Dinner Fashion, #3152, 1992, MIP..$30.00
Outfit, Barbie, Bride's Dream, #947-2, complete, EX..$85.00
Outfit, Barbie, Campus Sweetheart, #1616-0, complete, M...$600.00
Outfit, Barbie, Cheerleader Set, #7278, 1990, NRFP....$10.00
Outfit, Barbie, Cinderella's Ballgown, #1275, 1991, NRFB $30.00
Outfit, Barbie, Dreamy Blues, #1456-0, complete, M..$65.00
Outfit, Barbie, Golden Girl, #911-1, complete, NM.....$70.00
Outfit, Barbie, Holland, #823-2, complete, NM.........$125.00

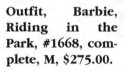

Outfit, Barbie, Riding in the Park, #1668, complete, M, $275.00.

Outfit, Barbie, Silken Flame, #977-0, complete, NM...$75.00
Outfit, Barbie, Tennis Anyone, #941-0, complete, NM..$45.00
Outfit, Barbie, White Delight, Designer Originals #3799, NRFP $20.00
Outfit, Francie, Altogether, #1242-0, complete, NM..$125.00
Outfit, Francie, Gad Abouts, #1250-0, complete, NM ..$150.00
Outfit, Francie, Mini Chex, #1209-0, complete, NM....$75.00
Outfit, Francie, Two for the Ball, #1232, complete, VG..$125.00
Outfit, Ken, American Airlines Captain, #779-1, complete, M $225.00
Outfit, Ken, Campus Hero, #770, complete, VG.........$35.00
Outfit, Ken, Country Clubbin', #1400, NRFB.............$175.00
Outfit, Ken, Dandy Lines, Designer Originals #3797, 1981, NRFB $20.00
Outfit, Ken, Day-To-Night, several variations, 1984, MIP, ea $15.00
Outfit, Ken, Doctor, #793, VG $45.00
Outfit, Ken, Going Bowling, #1403-0, complete, NM .$25.00
Outfit, Ken, Graduation, #795, NRFB....................$75.00

Outfit, Ken, King Arthur, #773, NRFB, $325.00.

Outfit, Ken, Masquerade, #794-0, complete, M **$65.00**
Outfit, Ricky, Sunday Suit, #1503, complete, NM........**$35.00**
Outfit, Skipper, Beachy Peachy, #1938, NRFB, minimum value **$175.00**
Outfit, Skipper, Best Buy Fashion Pak, #7771, NRFP, minimum value..**$35.00**
Outfit, Skipper, Chill Chasers, #1926, 1966, complete, M ...**$50.00**
Outfit, Skipper, Daisy Crazy, #1732, 1970, NRFB **$75.00**
Outfit, Skipper, Flower Power, #3373, 1972, MIP........**$45.00**
Outfit, Skipper, Fun Runners, #3372, complete, M **$55.00**
Outfit, Skipper, Town Toggs, #1922, 1965, complete, M...**$75.00**
Outfit, Skipper & Fluff, Action Fashion, MOC, minimum value **$75.00**
Outfit, Skipper & Fluff, Some Shoes Fashion Pak, 1971, MIP **$50.00**
Outfit, Skipper & Skooter, Shoe Parade Fashion Pak, 1965, MOC...**$95.00**
Outfit, Todd, Plaid Lad, #8595, NRFB **$75.00**
Outfit, Tutti, Flower Girl, #3615, complete, NM........**$125.00**
Outfit, Tutti, Kinderparty, #7983, minimum value **$150.00**
Outfit, Tutti, Ship Shape, #3602, complete, NM **$15.00**

Vehicle, 1957 Chevy, aqua, 1989, first edition, MIB, $150.00.

Vehicle, Barbie Goin' Boating, Sears Exclusive, 1973, NM..**$50.00**

Vehicle, Barbie's, Jeep, 1987, MIB..............................**$15.00**
Vehicle, Barbie's Motor Bike, 1983, MIB....................**$35.00**
Vehicle, Cinderella's Wedding Carriage & Horse, 1991, MIB **$55.00**
Vehicle, Ken's Hot Rod, Irwin, 1961, NM **$165.00**
Vehicle, Skipper's Beach Buggy, Irwin, 1964, rare, MIB, minimum value **$500.00**
Vehicle, Ten Speeder, 1973, MIB................................**$25.00**

Gift Sets

Barbie's Sparkling Pink Gift Set #1011 (1963 booklet), MIB, $500.00.

Barbie & Kelly Gardening Fun, 1996, NRFB **$45.00**
Beach Fun Barbie & Ken, 1993, complete, MIB **$35.00**
Birthday Beauties, Tutti, #3617, 1968, NRFB............**$175.00**
Cinderella Gift Pak, Disney Classics, 1992, NRFB.....**$125.00**
Clown Around, Tutti, #3606, 1967, complete, M.........**$65.00**
Denim Fun Barbie, Ken & Skipper, 1989, NRFB.........**$60.00**
Dressing Fun Barbie, 1993, complete, MIB **$55.00**
Francie Rise & Shine, 1971, NRFB, minimum value ..**$1,000.00**
Island Fun Barbie & Ken, 1993, complete, MIB.........**$35.00**
PJ Swingin' in Silver, Sears, 1970, complete, MIB.....**$800.00**
Skipper on Wheels, 1965, complete, MIB **$600.00**
Twirly Curls Barbie, 1982, NRFB................................**$60.00**
Wedding Party Midge, 1990, NRFB **$150.00**

Miscellaneous

Binder, Barbie & Skipper in School Days, vinyl w/pink background, rare, NM, minimum value......................**$150.00**
Book, Barbie's New York Summer, Random House, 1962, EX...**$25.00**
Box, Ken, 1961, EX..**$50.00**
Box, Ponytail Barbie, 1962, G....................................**$65.00**
China Dinner Set, Barbie, Chilton Globe Inc, 1989, 16 pcs, NRFB...**$30.00**
Comic Books, Barbie, Marvel Comics, 1991, several issues, M, ea **$3.00**
Diary, My Very Own Diary By Barbie, Western Publishing, 1985, NM...**$5.00**

Embroidery Set, Barbie, Ken & Midge, 1963, complete, MIB, from $200 to...**$250.00**

Embroidery Set, Skipper, Standard Toycraft, 1965, complete, rare, MIB, minimum value **$200.00**

Headphones, Barbie, built-in radio w/volume switch, Nasta/Mattel, 1984, M **$35.00**

Paper dolls, New 'N Groovy PJ, Whitman #1981, 1970, uncut, M **$50.00**

Polly Pocket, Barbie, 1994, M...**$12.00**

Poster, Dream Room Barbie, w/space for name, 1989, M ..**$5.00**

Scrapbook, Swirl Ponytail Barbie, 1964, NM **$65.00**

Wallet, red vinyl, 1962, NM $55.00.

Wallet, Skipper wearing masquerade, blue or yellow vinyl, rare, NM, ea from $55 to.......................................**$65.00**

World of Barbie Play Fun Box, Whitman, 1972, complete, NMIB, from $25.00 to $35.00.

Barware

From the decade of the '90s, the cocktail shaker has emerged as a hot new collectible. These micro skyscrapers are now being saved for the enjoyment of future generations, much like the 1930s buildings saved from destruction by landmarks preservation committees of today.

Cocktail shakers — the words just conjure up visions of glamour and elegance. Seven hard shakes over your right shoulder and you can travel back in time, back to the glamor of Hollywood movie sets with Fred Astaire and Ginger Rogers and luxurious hotel lounges with gleaming chrome; back to the world of F. Scott Fitzgerald and *The Great Gatsby*; or watch *The Thin Man* movie showing William Powell instruct a bartender on the proper way to shake a martini — the reveries are endless.

An original American art form, cocktail shakers reflect the changing nature of various styles of art, design, and architecture of the era between WWI and WWII. We see the graceful lines of Art Nouveau in the early '20s being replaced by the rage for jagged geometric modern design. The geometric cubism of Picasso that influenced so many designers of the '20s was replaced with the craze for streamline design of '30s. Cocktail shakers of the early '30s were taking the shape of the new deity of American architecture, the skyscraper, thus giving the appearance of movement and speed in a slow economy.

Cocktail shakers served to penetrate the gloom of depression, ready to propel us into the future of prosperity like some Buck Rogers rocket ship — both perfect symbols of generative power, of our propulsion into better times ahead.

Cocktail shakers and architecture took on the aerodynamically sleek industrial design of the automobile and airship. It was as Norman Bel Geddes said: 'a quest for speed.' All sharp edges and corners were rounded off. This trend was the theme of the day, as even the sharp notes of jazz turned into swing.

Cocktail shakers have all the classic qualifications of a premium collectible. They are easily found at auctions, antique and secondhand shops, flea markets, and sales. They can be had in all price ranges. They require little study to identify one manufacturer or period from another, and lastly they are not easily reproduced.

The sleek streamline cocktail shakers of modern design are valued by collectors of today. Those made by Revere, Chase, and Manning Bowman have taken the lead in this race. Also commanding high prices are those shakers of unusual design such as penguins, zeppelins, dumbbells, bowling pins, town crier bells, airplanes, even ladies' legs. They're all out there, waiting to be found, waiting to be recalled to life, to hear the clank of ice cubes, and to again become the symbol of elegance.

For more information we recommend *Vintage Bar Ware, An Identification and Value Guide*, by Stephen Visakay (Collector Books).

Advisor: Steve Visakay (See Directory, Barware)

Cocktail cup, blue glass on stepped chrome base, 3½x2¼" **$20.00**

Cocktail cup, rooster head & tail feathers on 3¼" dia bowl, stemmed, 1930s-40s, 3½" **$250.00**

Cocktail cups, green or white Catalin w/chrome stems, stamped NUDAWN USA, ca 1930, 6¾", ea....................**$10.00**

Cocktail shaker, black onyx w/silk-screen recipes, ca 1930s, 12" **$195.00**

Cocktail shaker, chrome w/walnut-colored Catalin handle, 12¾"..**$38.00**

Cocktail shaker, clown or jingle bell, 3 chrome balls surmounted by a wooden handle, 4 bells on top ball, ca 1935, 14x5"..**$250.00**

Cocktail shaker, glass, painted rooster motif w/yellow background, silver-plated top, stamped Mappin & Webb, 1930s, 10"...**$250.00**

Cocktail shaker, leather over wood, painted & lacquered, metal insert, French, 1930s, 11¾x3⅛"..............**$300.00**

Cocktail shaker, nickle-plated, 12-sided, stamped Jos Heinrichs, Paris & New York, Pat February 22, 1910, 12¾"...**$175.00**

Cocktail shaker, ribbed glass, painted horizontal black bands, Czechoslovakia, 1930s.................................**$110.00**

Cocktail shaker, rooster's head & breast in silver plate over brass, clear bottom, brass strainer insert, 1920s, 10⅞"..**$750.00**

Cocktail shaker, ruby glass w/fighting cocks in applied sterling silver, chrome top, 1930s, party size, 12"....**$295.00**

Cocktail shaker, silver-plated, penguin form, beak spout, feet form base, ca 1936, 12"....................................**$900.00**

Cocktail shaker, The Tippler, West Bend Aluminum Co., ca 1934, 11", from $45.00 to $65.00; add $10.00 for recipe booklet. (Photo courtesy Stephen Visakay)

Cocktail tumbler, White Cloud **$125.00**

Glass, hand-hammered silver-plated rooster head & tail feathers w/cut glass cone insert **$125.00**

Ice bucket, aluminum w/plastic trim, stamped Imperator, ca 1930s, 9½x9" **$35.00**

Ice bucket, chrome w/Bakelite trim & porcelain liner, stamped Keystone Ware, ca 1930s, 10½x6¼".......**$75.00**

Ice bucket, penguin form, ca 1941, 8x8"..................**$25.00**

Ice chopper, Ice-O-Matic, metal & plastic, ca 1940, 9" ...**$40.00**

Ice tongs, nickle-plated, ca 1928, 7½x1" **$45.00**

Mixer, chrome w/jade Catalin mounts, K128, ca 1928, 52-oz, 10¾"...**$250.00**

Mixer, chrome w/red enameled cast-iron base, electric, Stevens, Pat 4-19-33, 12¾" **$250.00**

Mixer, outboard motor, metal & plastic, battery-operated, 6" L **$65.00**

Mixer, Yo-Yo Cocktail Mixer, plastic & metal w/yo-yo in middle for mixing, Alabe Crafts, 7¼" **$45.00**

Pitcher, martini; Gorham Gift Ware paper label, gold lacquer finish, ca 1950, 11"..**$45.00**

Pitcher, martini; stainless steel, walnut handle, stamped Italy, 9¼"...**$45.00**

Sign, cardboard, novelty gin bottle, Bath Tub Gin, Aged in Porcelain, dated 1932, 11¾x4⅝" **$45.00**

Soda syphon, Shipstones Nottingham w/etched star design, English, ca 1930s, 12¾"...**$45.00**

Soda syphon, Soda King Syphon, chrome w/enameled top, red, black or blue, Walter Kidder Sales Co, 10", ea **$195.00**

Swizzle stick, Bottoms-Up, plastic, 6⅛" **$12.00**

Traveling bar, nickle-plated, cocktail shaker form, stamped Germany, 9 pcs, ca 1928, 8" **$95.00**

Traveling bar, nickle-plated, shaker form, 2 decanters/shaker/4 cups/juicer/funnel, stamped Germany, 1930s, 13¾".**$250.00**

Tray, blue-green & black metal w/red rooster on weather vane design, ca 1940s-50s, 9x14"..........................**$20.00**

Tray, canape; 5 O'Clock #813, satin chromium over brass, designed to nest, Norman Bel Geddes, ca 1935, 6¾x4⅝"...**$10.00**

Tray, glass & wood, peacock design, ca 1930s, 11x18" ...**$45.00**

Ice bucket, anodized aluminum, on three-leg base, 10x8", from $35.00 to $55.00. (Photo courtesy Steve Visakay)

Baseball Cards

Collecting memorabilia from all kinds of sports events has been a popular hobby for years. Baseball has long been known as the 'national pastime' with literally millions of fans who avidly follow the sport at every level from 'sand lot' to the major leagues. So it only follows that many collectors find baseball cards a worthwhile investment. Hundreds have been printed, and many are worth less that 20¢ apiece, but some of the better cards bring staggering prices, as you'll see in our listings.

If you're totally unfamiliar with cards, you'll need to know how to determine the various manufacturers. 1)

Bowman: All are copyrighted Bowman or B.G.H.L.I. except a few from the fifties that are marked '...in the series of Baseball Picture Cards.' 2) Donruss: All are marked with the Donruss logo on the front. 3) Fleer: From 1981 to 1984, the Fleer name is on the backs of the cards; after 1985 it was also on the front. 4) Score & Sportflics: Score written on the front, Sportflics on back of each year. 5) Topps: 1951 cards are baseball game pieces with red or blue backs (no other identification). After that, either Topps or T.G.C. appears somewhere on the card. 6) Upper Deck: Marked front and back with Upper Deck logo and hologram.

Learn to judge the condition of your card, since its condition is a very important factor when it comes to making an accurate evaluation. Superstars' and Hall of Famers' cards are most likely to appreciate, and the colored photo cards from the thirties are good investments as well. Buy modern cards by the set while they're inexpensive. Who knows what they may be worth in years to come. Any of today's rookies may be the next Babe Ruth!

Though baseball cards have cooled off considerably from their heyday of a few years ago, many are holding their values well. Prices listed below are from a recent cataloged auction.

Brooks Robinson, Topps, 1957, EX..................$80.00
Brooks Robinson, Topps, 1967, EX+..................$70.00
Gaylord Perry, Topps, 1966, EX $20.00
Hank Aaron, Topps, 1954, EX..................$375.00

Hank Aaron, Topps, 1955, EX/M, $125.00.

Hank Aaron, Topps, 1956, NM+..................$175.00
Jackie Robinson, Topps, 1956, NM..................$45.00
Jim Bunning, Topps, 1967, NM+ $75.00
Jim Palmer, Topps, 1966, NM $30.00
Johnny Bates, Ramly #T204, 1909, VG..................$60.00
Mark McGuire, Topps Rookie Card, 1985, NM+ $135.00
Mickey Mantle, Topps, 1956, VG $230.00
Mickey Mantle, Topps, 1957, EX..................$185.00
Mickey Mantle, Topps, 1959, NM (off-center)..........$150.00
Mickey Mantle, Topps, 1960, EX+ $100.00
Mickey Mantle, Topps, 1961, EX+ $135.00
Mickey Mantle, Topps, 1962, EX+ $115.00
Mickey Mantle, Topps, 1963, NM..................$290.00
Mickey Mantle, Topps, 1964, EX $65.00

Mickey Mantle, Topps All-Star, 1959, EX $95.00
Mickey Mantle & Yogi Berra, Power Hitters, Topps, 1957, NM (off-center) $125.00
Nolan Ryan, Topps, 1969, VG+ $50.00
Nolan Ryan, Topps, 1970, EX..................$60.00
Nolan Ryan & Jerry Koosman, Topps Rookie Stars, 1968, NM $605.00
Phil Rizzuto, Bowman, 1948, EX $70.00
Reggie Jackson, Topps, 1969, EX+ $85.00
Roberto Clemente, Topps, 1955, EX $485.00
Roberto Clemente, Topps, 1957, NM $75.00
Roberto Clemente, Topps, 1961, NM+ $140.00
Roberto Clemente, Topps, 1968, EX+ $110.00
Roger Maris, Topps, 1961, NM..................$80.00
Roger Maris, Topps, 1962, EX+..................$60.00
Roy Campanella, Bowman, 1949, EX-..................$115.00
Roy Campanella, Topps, 1959, NM $30.00
Sandy Koufax, Topps, 1955, EX $210.00
Set, Topps, 1979, complete, 726 cards, EX+-NM.........$60.00
Set, Topps, 1980, complete, 726 cards, NM..................$25.00
Ted Williams, Topps, 1955, EX..................$100.00
Ted Williams, Topps, 1956, NM..................$85.00
Ted Williams, Topps, 1957, EX..................$100.00

Bauer Pottery

Undoubtedly the most easily recognized product of the Bauer Pottery Company who operated from 1909 until 1962 in Los Angeles, California, was their colorful Ring dinnerware (made from 1932 until sometime in the early '60s). They made other lines of dinnerware that are collectible as well, although by no means as easily found. Bauer also made a line of Gardenware vases and flowerpots for the florist trade.

In the lines of Ring and Plain ware, pricing depends to some extent on color. Use the low end of our range of values for light brown, Chinese yellow, orange-red, jade green, red-brown, olive green, light blue, turquoise, and gray; the high-end colors are delph blue, ivory, dusky burgundy, cobalt, chartreuse, papaya, and burgundy. Black is 50% higher than the high end; to evaluate white, double the high side. An in-depth study of colors and values may be found in *The Collector's Encyclopedia of California Pottery, Second Edition,* and *Collector's Encyclopedia of Bauer Pottery,* both by Jack Chipman.

Advisor: Jack Chipman (see Directory, California Pottery)

Brusche Al Fresco, bowl, vegetable; yellow, round, 7½"..$24.00
Brusche Al Fresco, plate, bread & butter; pink, 6" $6.00
Brusche Al Fresco, sugar bowl, gray, w/lid.................$20.00
Brusche Contempo, bowl, soup/cereal; pumpkin, deep, 5¼"..................$15.00
Brusche Contempo, mug, pumpkin, 8-oz..................$12.00
Brusche Contempo, pitcher, Indian brown, 1-pt.........$30.00
Cal-Art, pitcher, vase; matt yellow, 10" $120.00
Cal-Art, vase, horn of plenty; matt blue, 6½"...........$45.00

Gardenware, basket, hanging; orange-red, 8" $225.00
Gardenware, jardiniere, Biltmore; Delph blue, 12" ...$225.00
Gardenware, pot, pinnacle; olive green, 10" $85.00
Gardenware, pot, strawberry; burgundy, 8-cup, 9" ...$185.00
Gardenware, pot saucer, black, 8", minimum value ...$80.00
Hi-Fire, rose bowl, Monterey blue, 4" $55.00
Hi-Fire, vase (stock), olive green, 9" $100.00
La Linda, bowl, cereal; burgundy, 6" $25.00
La Linda, gravy boat, green $25.00
La Linda, platter, matt yellow, oval, 12" $30.00
Mission Moderne, plate, bread & butter; gray, 6½" $8.00
Mission Moderne, sugar bowl, chartreuse/brown, w/lid $27.50
Monterey, bowl, fruit; yellow, 3-legged, 9", from $45 to $65.00
Monterey, bowl, vegetable; yellow, oval, 10", from $55 to .$80.00
Monterey Moderne, ashtray, speckled cocoa brown ..$15.00
Monterey Moderne, bowl, pumpkin; matt pink, med,
    5x8" $80.00
Monterey Moderne, vase, green, #505, 8" $50.00
Ring, batter bowl, 2-qt, from $85 to...........................$125.00
Ring, bowl, mixing; #18, from $45 to $65.00
Ring, bowl, mixing; black, #24, from $35 to $50.00
Ring, bowl, mixing; yellow, #18, from $45 to $65.00
Ring, bowl, nappy; #9, from $65 to $95.00
Ring, bowl, vegetable; yellow, oval, 8", from $85 to ..$125.00
Ring, butter dish, oblong, ¼-lb, from $175 to...........$250.00
Ring, coffeepot, drip; from $300 to............................$400.00

Ring, eight-cup covered coffee server with handle, from $65.00 to $95.00.

Ring, creamer, yellow, restyled, from $20 to $30.00
Ring, mug, barrel shape, from $100 to $150.00
Ring, nappy, red, #9, from $65 to $95.00
Ring, pitcher, original shape, 2-qt, from $85 to $125.00
Ring, plate, salad; 7½", from $30 to $45.00
Ring, platter, green, oval, 9", from $30 to...................$45.00
Ring, platter, oval, 9", from $30 to $45.00
Ring, sugar shaker, from $200 to................................$300.00
Ring, teapot, red, 2-cup, from $75 to..........................$100.00
Ring, teapot, 2-cup, from $75 to $100.00

Beanie Babies

Who can account for this latest phenomenon that some liken to the Cabbage Patch doll craze we saw many years ago! The appeal of these stuffed creatures is disarming to both children and adults, and excited collectors are eager to scoop up each new-found treasure. There is much to be learned about Beanie Babies. For instance, there are different tag styles, and each indicates date of issue:

#1, Swing tag: single heart-shaped tag (only on first-generation tush tag Beanies dated 1993) (Photos courtesy Amy Hopper)

#2, Swing tag: heart-shaped; folded, with information inside; narrow lettering (Photos courtesy Amy Hopper)

#3, Swing tag: heart-shaped; folded, with information inside; wider lettering (Photos courtesy Amy Hopper)

#4, Swing tag: heart-shaped; folded, with information inside; wider lettering with no gold outline around the 'ty'; yellow star on front; first tag to include a poem and birthdate (Photos courtesy Amy Hopper)

#5, Swing tag: heart-shaped; folded, with information inside; different font on front and inside; birth month spelled out, no style number listed, website listed (Photos courtesy Amy Hopper)

For Beanies with a #1, #2, or #3 tag, add $30.00 to $50.00 to the prices suggested below.

On August 31, 1999, the Ty company posted an announcement on its website stating that on December 31, 1999, at 11:59 p.m. CST, all Beanie Babies would be retired, and production of the Beanie Baby line would end. This caused quite an uproar with collectors, and resulted in many pleas, through letters and e-mail, to the company's founder, Ty Warner. On December 23, 1999, Ty Warner posted another announcement on the Ty website that the Beanie Babies were officially retired on that date, and that on December 24 there would be yet another global announcement. On Christmas Eve, collectors learned from Ty Warner that a worldwide vote would begin on December 31, and last until January 2, 2000, whereby collectors could vote yes or no to continue production of the Beanie Babies. The final result: 91% voted "yes" and 9% voted "no." Thus, the Beanie Babies were continued. The next edition of *Garage Sale* will include listings for the Beanie Babies of 2000.

Advisor: Amy Hopper (See Directory, Beanie Babies)

Ally, alligator, #4032 ....**$50.00**
Almond, beige bear, #4246, from $6 to **$10.00**
Amber, gold tabby cat, #4243, from $6 to **$10.00**
Ants, anteater, #4195, from $10 to.....................**$15.00**
BB, birthday bear, #4253, from $20 to.................**$40.00**
Baldy, eagle, #4074...**$20.00**
Batty, pink bat, #4035, from $10 to.....................**$15.00**
Batty, tie-dyed bat, #4035, from $15 to................**$20.00**
Beak, kiwi bird, #4211, from $6 to.......................**$10.00**
Bernie, St Bernard, #4109, from $10 to................**$15.00**
Bessie, brown cow, #4009 ....**$60.00**
Blackie, black bear, #4011, from $10 to................**$20.00**
Blizzard, white tiger, #4163.................................**$20.00**
Bones, brown dog, #4001 ....**$15.00**
Bongo, brown monkey w/matching body & tail color, #4067, from $40 to......................................**$75.00**
Bongo, brown monkey w/matching paws & face, #4067, from $15 to..**$20.00**
Britannia, British bear, #4601, Ty UK exclusive, from $130 to...**$165.00**
Bronty, blue brontosaurus, #4085, minimum value ..**$750.00**

Brownie, brown bear, #4010, w/hang tag, minimum value...**$2,000.00**
Bruno, terrier, #4183, from $10 to **$15.00**
Bubbles, yellow & black fish, #4078.....................**$135.00**
Bucky, beaver, #4016...**$35.00**
Bumble, bee, #4045, minimum value **$350.00**
Butch, bull terrier, #4227, from $6 to **$10.00**
Canyon, cougar, #4212, from $6 to **$10.00**
Caw, black crow, #4071, from $450 to **$600.00**
Cheeks, baboon, #4250, from $6 to **$10.00**
Chilly, polar bear, #4012, minimum value..............**$1,000.00**
Chip, calico cat, #4121, from $10 to.....................**$15.00**
Chipper, chipmunk, #4259, from $6 to **$10.00**
Chocolate, moose, #4015, from $10 to.....................**$15.00**

Chops, cream lamb with black face, #4019, $150.00; Teenie Beanie Baby, from $15.00 to $25.00. (Photo courtesy Amy Hopper)

Claude, tie-dyed crab, #4083, from $10 to...................**$15.00**
Clubby, bear, Beanie Babies Official Club gold member exclusive (mail order only), from $30 to **$45.00**
Clubby II, Beanie Babies Official Club, Platinum Kit exclusive (mail order only), from $25 to.............**$40.00**
Congo, gorilla, #4160, from $10 to.....................**$15.00**
Coral, tie-dyed fish, #4079, minimum value.............**$150.00**
Crunch, shark, #4130, from $10 to **$15.00**
Cubbie, brown bear, #4010...................................**$35.00**
Curly, brown bear, #4052, from $15 to.....................**$25.00**
Daisy, black & white cow, #4006, from $10 to...........**$15.00**
Derby, horse, 1st issue, fine yarn mane & tail, #4008, minimum value..**$2,000.00**
Derby, horse, 2nd issue, brown, coarse mane & tail, #4008, from $25 to.......................................**$30.00**
Derby, horse, 3rd issue, coarse mane & tail, white star on forehead, #4008, from $15 to.................**$20.00**
Derby, horse, 4th issue, fine hair mane & tail, #4008, from $10 to...**$15.00**
Digger, orange crab, #4027, minimum value............**$450.00**
Digger, red crab, #4027, minimum value.................**$85.00**
Doby, doberman, #4110, from $10 to.........................**$15.00**
Doodle, tie-dyed rooster, #4171...........................**$35.00**
Dotty, dalmatian, #4100, from $10 to.....................**$15.00**
Early, robin, #4190, from $6 to...........................**$10.00**
Ears, brown rabbit, #4018 ....**$20.00**
Echo, dolphin, #4180...**$20.00**
Eggbert, baby chick, #4232, from $10 to.....................**$15.00**

Erin, Irish bear, #4186, from $15 to........................**$25.00**
Eucalyptus, koala, #4240, from $6 to **$10.00**
Ewey, lamb, #4219, from $10 to...........................**$15.00**
Fetch, golden retriever, #4189, from $10 to.........**$15.00**
Flash, dolphin, #4021 ....**$100.00**
Fleece, white lamb w/cream face, #4125, from $10 to ...**$15.00**
Flitter, butterfly, #4255, from $10 to..................**$20.00**
Flip, white cat, #4012 ....**$35.00**
Floppity, lavender bunny, #4118.........................**$25.00**

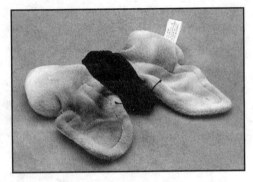

Flutter, tie-dyed butterfly, #4043, minimum value, $700.00. (Photo courtesy Amy Hopper)

Fortune, panda bear, #4196, from $10 to.............**$15.00**
Freckles, leopard, #4066, from $10 to.................**$15.00**
Fuzz, bear, #4237, from $6 to **$10.00**
Garcia, tie-dyed bear, #4051, from $150 to **$225.00**
Germania, German bear, #4236, Ty German exclusive, from $125 to..**$175.00**
Gigi, poodle, #4191, from $6 to **$10.00**
Glory, American bear, #4188, from $25 to............**$40.00**
Goatee, mountain goat, #4235, from $6 to..........**$10.00**
Gobbles, turkey, #4034, from $10 to...................**$15.00**
Goldie, goldfish, #4023..**$40.00**
Goochy, jellyfish, #4230, from $6 to...................**$10.00**
Gracie, swan, #4126, from $10 to........................**$15.00**
Groovy, bear, #4256, from $10 to........................**$15.00**
Grunt, red razorback pig, #4092.......................**$120.00**
Halo, angel bear, #4208, from $10 to..................**$15.00**
Happy, gray hippopotamus, #4061, 1st issue, minimum value **$375.00**
Happy, lavender hippopotamus, #4061, 2nd issue.....**$25.00**

Humphrey, camel, #4060, minimum value, $1,500.00. (Photo courtesy Amy Hopper)

Hippie, tie-dyed bunny, #4218, from $10 to **$15.00**
Hippity, mint green bunny, #4119....................**$25.00**
Hissy, snake, #4185, from $10 to.......................**$15.00**
Honks, goose, #4258, from $6 to **$10.00**
Hoot, owl, #4073 ....**$40.00**
Hope, praying bear, #4213, from $6 to.................**$15.00**
Hoppity, pink bunny, #4117...............................**$25.00**
Iggy, iguana, #4038, all issues retired, from $10 to **$15.00**
Inch, worm w/felt antennae, #4044, minimum value..**$100.00**
Inch, worm w/yarn antennae, #4044 ....**$20.00**
Inky, 1st issue, tan octopus, no mouth, #4028, minimum value **$500.00**
Inky, 2nd issue, tan octopus w/mouth, #4028, minimum value **$450.00**
Inky, 3rd issue, pink octopus, #4028, from $20 to **$30.00**
Jabber, parrot, #4197, from $6 to.............................**$10.00**
Jake, mallard duck, #4199, from $6 to **$10.00**
Jolly, walrus, #4082...**$20.00**
Kicks, soccer bear, #4229, from $6 to **$15.00**
Kiwi, toucan, #4070, minimum value.....................**$130.00**
Knuckles, pig, #4247, from $6 to **$10.00**
Kuku, cockatoo, #4192, from $6 to.........................**$10.00**
Lefty, donkey w/American flag, #4086, minimum value..**$200.00**
Legs, frog, #4020...**$25.00**
Libearty, white bear w/American Flag, #4057, from $300 to **$350.00**
Lips, fish, #4254, from $10 to **$20.00**
Lizzy, 1st issue, tie-dyed lizard, #4033, minimum value..**$700.00**
Lizzy, 2nd issue, blue lizard, #4033, from $15 to.......**$30.00**
Loosy, Canadian goose, #4206, from $6 to.................**$10.00**
Lucky, 1st issue, ladybug w/7 glued spots, #4040, minimum value **$125.00**
Lucky, 2nd issue, ladybug w/21 spots, #4040, minimum value...**$300.00**
Lucky, 3rd issue, ladybug w/11 spots, #4040, from $15 to **$30.00**

Luke, lab puppy, #4214, from $6.00 to $10.00. (Photo courtesy Amy Hopper)

Mac, cardinal, #4225, from $6 to **$10.00**
Magic, winged dragon, #4088, from $35 to.................**$50.00**
Manny, manatee, #4081, minimum value **$115.00**

Maple, Canadian bear, #4600, Ty Canadian exclusive, from $125 to................$200.00

Mel, koala bear, #4162, from $10 to................$15.00

Millennium, bear, #4226, from $10.00 to $20.00. (Photo courtesy Amy Hopper)

Mooch, spider monkey, #4224, from $6 to................$10.00

Mystic, unicorn, 1st issue, fine yarn mane & tail, #4007, minimum value................$200.00

Mystic, unicorn, 2nd issue, coarse yarn mane & brown horn, #4007, from $25 to................$35.00

Mystic, unicorn, 3rd issue, iridescent horn, #4007, from $15 to................$25.00

Mystic, unicorn, 4th issue, rainbow mane, #4007, from $10 to................$15.00

Nana, monkey, #4067, 1st issue of Bongo, w/hang tag, minimum value................$3,000.00

Nanook, husky dog, #4104, from $10 to................$15.00

Neon, sea horse, #4239, from $6 to................$10.00

Nibbler, rabbit, #4216, from $10 to................$15.00

Nibbly, rabbit, #4217, from $10 to................$15.00

Nip, cat, 1st issue, gold w/white tummy, #4003, minimum value................$300.00

Nip, cat, 2nd issue, all gold, #4003, minimum value..$650.00

Nip, cat, 3rd issue, gold w/white paws, #4003, from $15 to................$25.00

Nuts, squirrel, #4114, from $10 to................$15.00

Osito, Mexican bear, #4244, sold in US, from $10 to .$20.00

Patti, platypus, 1st issue, maroon, #4025, minimum value................$350.00

Patti, platypus, 2nd issue, purple, #4025, from $20 to..$30.00

Paul, walrus, #4248, from $6 to................$10.00

Peace Bear, tie-dyed w/embroidered Peace sign, #4053, from $15 to................$20.00

Peanut, light blue elephant, #4062................$20.00

Peanut, royal blue elephant, #4062, manufacturing mistake, minimum value................$3,000.00

Pecan, gold bear, #4251, from $6 to................$10.00

Peking, panda bear, #4013, minimum value............$900.00

Pinchers, lobster, #4026, from $15 to................$25.00

Pinky, flamingo, #4072, from $10 to................$15.00

Pouch, kangaroo, #4161, from $10 to................$15.00

Pounce, brown cat, #4122, from $10 to................$15.00

Prance, gray cat, #4123, from $10 to................$15.00

Prickles, hedgehog, #4220, from $6 to................$10.00

Princess, purple bear commemorating Diana, Princess of Wales, #4300................$30.00

Puffer, puffin, #4181, from $10 to................$15.00

Pugsly, pug dog, #4106, from $10 to................$15.00

Pumkin', pumpkin, #4205, from $25 to................$35.00

Punchers (1st issue of Pinchers), lobster, #4026, w/hang tag, minimum value................$1,800.00

Quackers, duck, #4024, wingless, 1st issue, minimum value, $1,000.00; with wings, 2nd issue, from $20.00 to $30.00. (Photo courtesy Amy Hopper)

Radar, black bat, #4091, minimum value................$110.00

Rainbow, chameleon, #4037, all issues retired, from $10 to................$15.00

Rex, tyrannosaurus, #4086, minimum value............$650.00

Righty, gray elephant w/American flag, #4085, minimum value................$200.00

Ringo, raccoon, #4014, from $10 to................$15.00

Roam, buffalo, #4209, from $6 to................$10.00

Roary, lion, #4069, from $10 to................$15.00

Rocket, blue jay, #4202, from $6 to................$10.00

Rover, red dog, #4101, from $25 to................$30.00

Sammy, tie-dyed bear, #4215, from $6 to................$10.00

Santa, #4203, from $25 to................$40.00

Scaly, lizard, #4263, from $6 to................$10.00

Scat, cat, #4231, from $6 to................$10.00

Schweetheart, orangutan, #4252, from $6 to............$10.00

Scoop, pelican, #4107, from $10 to................$15.00

Scorch, dragon, #4210, from $6 to................$10.00

Scottie, Scottish terrier, #4102, from $15 to................$25.00

Seamore, white seal, #4029, minimum value............$85.00

Seaweed, otter, #4080, from $10 to................$20.00

Sheets, ghost, #4260, from $15 to................$20.00

Silver, gray tabby cat, #4242, from $6 to................$10.00

Slippery, seal, #4222, from $6 to................$10.00

Slither, snake, #4031, minimum value................$800.00

Slowpoke, sloth, #4261, from $6 to................$10.00

Sly, fox w/brown belly, 1st issue, #4115, minimum value................$100.00

Sly, fox w/white belly, 2nd issue, #4115, from $10 to..$15.00

Smoochy, frog, #4039, from $10 to................$15.00

Snip, Siamese cat, #4120, from $10 to................$15.00

Snort, red bull w/cream feet, #4002, from $10 to.......**$15.00**
Snowball, snowman, #4201, from $30 to....................**$45.00**
Spangle, American bear, #4245, from $10 to.............**$20.00**
Sparky, dalmatian, #4100, minimum value...............**$100.00**
Speedy, turtle, #4030, from $30 to **$35.00**
Spike, rhinoceros, #4060, from $10 to **$15.00**
Spinner, spider, #4036, from $10 to.........................**$15.00**
Splash, whale, #4022..**$100.00**
Spooky, ghost, #4090 ....**$35.00**
Spot, dog, 1st issue, no spot on back, #4000, minimum
　　value..**$1,000.00**
Spot, dog, 2nd issue, black spot on back, #4000........**$50.00**
Spunky, cocker spaniel, #4184, from $10 to **$15.00**
Squealer, pig, #4005..**$25.00**
Steg, stegosaurus, #4087, minimum value **$700.00**
Stilts, stork, #4221, from $10 to **$15.00**
Sting, stingray, #4077, minimum value **$130.00**
Stinger, scorpion, #4193, from $10 to.......................**$15.00**
Stinky, skunk, #4017, from $10 to **$15.00**
Stretch, ostrich, #4182, from $10 to.........................**$15.00**
Stripes, tiger, 1st issue, gold color w/thin black stripes, #4065,
　　minimum value...**$250.00**
Stripes, tiger, 2nd issue, caramel color w/wide stripes,
　　#4065...**$20.00**
Strut, rooster, #4171, from $10 to **$15.00**
Swirly, snail, #4249, from $6 to **$10.00**
Tabasco, red bull w/red feet, #4002, minimum value ..**$130.00**
Tank, armadillo, 1st issue, 7 lines & no shell, #4031, mini-
　　mum value **$110.00**
Tank, armadillo, 2nd issue, 9 lines & no shell, #4031, mini-
　　mum value **$130.00**
Tank, armadillo, 3rd issue (9 lines w/shell), #4031, from $55
　　to **$80.00**
Teddy, brown bear, #4050, old face **$2,000.00**
Teddy, brown bear, #4050, new face, from $75 to.....**$115.00**
Teddy, cranberry bear, #4052, old face **$1,200.00**
Teddy, cranberry bear, #4052, new face................**$1,200.00**
Teddy, jade bear, #4057, old face **$1,200.00**
Teddy, jade bear, #4057, new face **$1,200.00**
Teddy, magenta bear, #4056, old face **$1,200.00**
Teddy, magenta bear, #4056, new face **$1,200.00**
Teddy, teal bear, #4051, old face **$1,200.00**
Teddy, teal bear, #4051, new face **$1,200.00**
Teddy, violet bear, #4055, old face **$1,200.00**
Teddy, violet bear, #4055, new face **$1,200.00**
The End, black bear, #4265, from $25 to....................**$30.00**
Tiny, chihuahua, #4234, from $6 to **$10.00**
Tiptoe, mouse, #4241, from $6 to **$10.00**
Tracker, basset hound, #4198, from $6 to...................**$10.00**
Tuffy, terrier, #4108, from $10 to.............................**$15.00**
Tusk, walrus, #4076, minimum value **$100.00**
Twigs, giraffe, #4068, from $15 to............................**$20.00**
Ty #1 bear (December 1998), only 253 made & issued to Ty
　　sales reps, new face red bear w/#1 on chest, minimum
　　value...**$8,500.00**
Ty Employee Billionaire bear (1998), new face brown bear
　　w/dollar sign on chest, minimum value..........**$1,600.00**

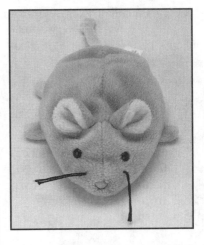

Trap, mouse, #4042, minimum value, $900.00. (Photo courtesy Amy Hopper)

Ty Employee Christmas Bear (1997), Teddy new face violet,
　　minimum value..**$1,800.00**
Ty 2K, bear, #4262, from $15 to **$30.00**
Valentina, magenta bear w/white heart, #4233, from $6
　　to **$10.00**
Valentino, white bear w/red heart, #4058...................**$20.00**
Velvet, black panther, #4064 ....**$35.00**
Waddle, penguin, #4075..**$25.00**
Wallace, bear, #4264, from $15 to **$30.00**
Waves, whale, #4084 ....**$20.00**
Web, spider, #4041, minimum value **$700.00**
Weenie, daschund, #4013 ....**$30.00**
Whisper, deer, #4194, from $6 to **$10.00**
Wise, 1998 graduation owl, #4194, from $15 to.........**$30.00**
Wiser, 1999 graduation owl, #4238, from $10 to........**$20.00**
Wrinkles, bull dog, #4103, from $10 to.....................**$15.00**
Zero, holiday penguin, #4207, from $20 to.................**$25.00**
Ziggy, zebra, #4063..**$20.00**
Zip, cat, 1st issue, black w/white tummy, #4004, minimum
　　value **$250.00**
Zip, cat, 2nd issue, all black, #4004, minimum value.**$700.00**
Zip, cat, 3rd issue, black w/white paws, #4004 ....**$35.00**
1997 Holiday Teddy, bear, #4200, from $35 to **$50.00**
1998 Holiday Teddy, bear, #4204, from $30 to **$50.00**
1999 Holiday Teddy, bear, #4257, from $15 to **$30.00**
1999 Signature Bear, #4228, from $10 to **$20.00**

Beanie Buddies

　　This line is of special interest to Beanie Babies collectors, since these animals are larger versions of the Beanie Babies. Currently there are 45.

Amber, cat, #9341, from $20 to **$30.00**
Beak, kiwi, #9301, retired, from $25 to **$30.00**
Bongo, monkey, #9312, from $10 to..........................**$20.00**
Britannia, British bear, UK exclusive, #9601, ...**$50.00**
Bubbles, fish, #9323, retired, from $10 to..................**$20.00**
Chilly, bear, #9317, retired, from $10 to **$20.00**
Chip, calico cat, #9318, from $10 to..........................**$20.00**
Clubby, bear, Beanie Babies Official Club Gold Member
　　exclusive (mail order only), #9990, from $15 to ..**$30.00**

Clubby II, bear, Beanie Babies Official Club Platinum Member exclusive (mail order only), #9991, from $15 to ...**$30.00**

Erin, Irish bear, #9309, retired, from $20 to................**$30.00**

Fetch, golden retriever, #9338, from $10 to................**$20.00**

Fuzz, bear, #9328, from $10 to................**$25.00**

Gobbles, turkey, #9333, from $10 to................**$20.00**

Halo, angel bear, 39337, from $20 to................**$30.00**

Hippity, mint green bunny, #9324, from $10 to........**$15.00**

Hope, praying bear, #9327, from $10 to................**$20.00**

Humphrey, camel, #9307, from $10 to................**$15.00**

Inch, worm, #9331, from $15 to................**$25.00**

Jabber, parrot, #9326, from $10 to................**$15.00**

Jake, mallard duck, #9304, from $10 to................**$15.00**

Maple, Canadian bear, Canada exclusive, #9600........**$50.00**

Millennium, bear, #9325, retired, from $20 to............**$35.00**

Patti, platypus, #9320, retired, from $15 to................**$25.00**

Peace, bear, #9335, from $25 to................**$40.00**

Peanut, royal blue elephant, #9300, from $15 to.......**$30.00**

Peking, panda, #9310, from $10 to................**$20.00**

Pinky, flamingo, #9316, from $10 to................**$15.00**

Princess, bear, #9329, from $20 to................**$40.00**

Pumkin', pumpkin, #9332, retired, from $10 to.........**$20.00**

Quackers, duck, #9302, retired, from $15 to..............**$25.00**

Rover, dog, #9305, from $10 to................**$20.00**

Schweetheart, orangutan, #9330, from $15 to................**$25.00**

Silver, cat, #9340, from $10 to................**$15.00**

Slither, snake, #9339, from $15 to................**$25.00**

Smoochy, frog, #9315, retired, from $10 to................**$15.00**

Snort, bull, #9311, from $10 to................**$15.00**

Snowboy, snowboy, #9342, from $20 to................**$30.00**

Spangle, American bear, #9336, from $30 to..............**$40.00**

Spinner, spider, #9334, from $10 to................**$15.00**

Squealer, pig, #9313, retired, from $10 to................**$20.00**

Stretch, ostrich, #9303, from $10 to................**$15.00**

Teddy, cranberry bear, #9306, retired, from $20 to.....**$40.00**

Tracker, basset hound, #9319, retired, from $10 to.....**$20.00**

Twigs, giraffe, #9308, retired, from $125 to..............**$160.00**

Waddle, penguin, #9314, from $10 to................**$15.00**

McDonald's® Happy Meal Teenie Beanie Babies

The Teenie Beanie Babies debuted in April 1997 at McDonald's restaurants across the country. The result was the most successful Happy Meal promotion in the history of McDonald's. The toys were quickly snatched up by collectors, causing the promotion to last only one week instead of the planned five-week period. To date there have been three Teenie Beanie promotions, one annually in 1997, 1998, and 1999.

1997, Chocolate, moose, from $20 to................**$30.00**

1997, Chops, lamb, from $15 to................**$25.00**

1997, Goldie, goldfish, from $15 to................**$20.00**

1997, Lizz, lizard, 1997, from $10 to................**$15.00**

1997, Patti, platypus, from $20 to................**$30.00**

1997, Pinky, flamingo, from $20 to................**$30.00**

1997, Quacks, duck, from $10 to................**$15.00**

1997, Seamore, seal, from $15 to................**$20.00**

1997, Snort, bull, $15 to................**$20.00**

1997, Speedy, turtle, from $15 to................**$20.00**

1998, Bones, dog, from $5 to................**$8.00**

1998, Bongo, monkey, from $10 to................**$15.00**

1998, Doby, doberman, from $10 to................**$15.00**

1998, Happy, hippo, from $5 to................**$7.00**

1998, Inch, worm, from $5 to................**$7.00**

1998, Mel, koala, from $5 to................**$7.00**

1998, Peanut, elephant, from $5 to................**$8.00**

1998, Pinchers, lobster, from $5 to................**$7.00**

1998, Scoop, pelican, from $5 to................**$7.00**

1998, Twigs, giraffe, from $8 to................**$12.00**

1998, Waddle, penguin, from $5 to................**$8.00**

1998, Zip, cat, from $8 to................**$10.00**

1999, Antsy, anteater, from $2 to................**$4.00**

1999, Chip, calico cat, from $2 to................**$4.00**

1999, Claude, crab, from $2 to................**$4.00**

1999, Freckles, leopard, from $2 to................**$4.00**

1999, Iggy, iguana, from $2 to................**$4.00**

1999, 'Nook, husky, from $2 to................**$4.00**

1999, Nuts, squirrel, from $2 to................**$4.00**

1999, Rocket, blue jay, from $2 to................**$4.00**

1999, Smoochy, frog, from $2 to................**$4.00**

1999, Spunky, cocker spaniel, from $2 to................**$4.00**

1999, Stretchy, ostrich, from $2 to................**$4.00**

1999, Strut, rooster, from $2 to................**$4.00**

International Bears

These were offered at McDonald's directly after the 1999 Teenie Beanie Babies.

Brittania, British bear, from $5 to................**$7.00**

Erin, Irish bear, from $5 to................**$7.00**

Glory, American bear, from $5 to................**$7.00**

Maple, Canadian bear, from $5 to................**$7.00**

Beatles Collectibles

Possibly triggered by John Lennon's death in 1980, Beatles fans (recognizing that their dreams of the band ever reuniting were gone along with him) began to collect vintage memorabilia of all types. Recently some of the original Beatles material has sold at auction with high-dollar results. Handwritten song lyrics, Lennon's autographed high school textbook, and even the legal agreement that was drafted at the time the group disbanded are among the one-of-a-kind multi-thousand dollar sales recorded.

Unless you plan on attending sales of this caliber, you'll be more apt to find the commercially produced memorabilia that literally flooded the market during the '60s and beyond when the Fab Four from Liverpool made their unprecedented impact on the entertainment world. A word about their 45 rpm records: they sold in such mass quantities that unless the record is a 'promotional' (made to send to radio stations or for jukebox distribution), they have very little value. Once a record has lost much of its original gloss due to wear and handling, becomes scratched, or has writing on the label, its value is minimal. Even in near-mint condition, $4.00 to $6.00 is plenty to pay for a 45 rpm (much less if it's worn), unless the original picture sleeve is present. (An exception is the white-labeled Swan recording of 'She Loves You/I'll Get You'.) A Beatles picture sleeve is usually valued at $30.00 to $40.00, except for the rare 'Can't Buy Me Love,' which is worth ten times that amount. (Beware of reproductions!) Albums of any top recording star or group from the '50s and '60s are becoming very collectible, and the Beatles are among the most popular. Just be very critical of condition! An album must be in at least excellent condition to bring a decent price. For more information, we recommend *The Beatles, Second Edition,* by Barbara Crawford, Hollis Lamon, and Michael Stern (Collector Books).

See also Celebrity Dolls; Magazines; Movie Posters; Records; Sheet Music.

Advisor: Bojo/Bob Gottuso (See Directory, Character and Personality Collectibles)

Newsletter: *Beatlefan*
P.O. Box 33515, Decatur, GA 30033; Send SASE for information.

Ashtray, white china w/black head images & names, square w/concave sides, EX+ $250.00
Balloon, various colors w/group shot in black, United Industries, MIP, sealed (package reads Blow Up!...Fab Beatle...) $150.00
Book, Hard Day's Night, 1st edition, 1964, softcover, G..$10.00
Bookmark, Yellow Submarine, w/Old Fred or Apple Bonker, multicolored cardboard, 9"....................................$10.00
Brooch, gold-tone banjo w/mop-top figures, movable beaded eyes, painted hair & strings, EX.......................$65.00

Button, flasher, G, $30.00; EX/M, $35.00. (Photo courtesy Barbara Crawford, Hollis Lamon, and Michael Stern)

Bulletin board, Yellow Submarine, group photo, 17½x23", EX (original wrapping)................................$140.00
Cake decorations, The Swingers, MIP......................$175.00
Calendar card, 1964-65, plastic-coated w/various images, Louis F Dow Co, NM, ea..................................$25.00

Christmas stocking, net stocking contains plastic toys, games & Beatles pictures, 27", unopened, M.................$125.00
Comb, plastic, Lido Toys, 14½", NM (Beware of reproductions)..$225.00
Concert booklet, black & white photos w/multicolored photo cover, 1965, 12x12", EX.............................$30.00

Costume figures of Ringo Starr and George Harrison, original tags and display stands, EX, 22" $65.00 each. (Photo courtesy June Moon)

Cup, plastic, close-up portrait of group w/names lettered on white w/white rim, 1960s, NM (Beware of reproductions)..$90.00
Dolls, inflatable cartoon images, set of 4, EX $130.00
Figures, cartoon series, hand-painted resin, set of 4, 1985, 6", NM $150.00
Flasher rings, set of 4, EX (Beware of reproductions)..$80.00
Game, Hullabaloo, 1965, VG (VG box)......................$75.00
Guitar, Four Pop by Mastro, red & pink 4-string w/faces & autographs, complete, 21", EX.............................$450.00
Harmonica, Hohner, 1964, MOC $600.00
Headband, allover head shots & signatures in black on blue, Dame, 1964, EX $85.00
Key chain, Yellow Submarine, plastic, Pride Creations, EX $65.00
Mobile, cardboard popouts, Sunshine Art Studios, unused, MIP..$140.00
Mug, plastic w/paper portrait insert, 4", EX (reproduction) $20.00
Nodders, composition, w/signatures on gold base, Carmascots, 1964, set of 4, 8", EX (EX box) ...$1,000.00
Nodders, composition, w/signatures on gold base, Carmascots, 1968, set of 4, 8", EX (no box).......$500.00
Notebook binder, The Beatles lettered above group photo & signatures, white (colors are higher), 3-ring or 2-ring, NM $150.00
Pennant, We Luv You Beatles, white felt w/red lettering & musical notes, George & Ringo lettered in red hearts, VG $150.00

Photo album, Sgt Pepper's Lonely Hearts Club Band, sm,
EX $400.00
Pin-back button, I Love the Beatles, white w/red line encir-
cling blue lettering, M $25.00

**Plate, bamboo, 12",
G, $120.00; EX/M,
$145.00. (Photo
courtesy Barbara
Crawford, Hollis
Lamon, and
Michael Stern)**

Portraits, sketched head images w/signatures, MIP
(header marked The Beatles Portraits/Suitable For
Framing) $110.00
Poster, black & white photos of ea Beatle on pink back-
ground, Dell, #2, 1960s, 18x52" (folds to magazine size),
NM $30.00
Program, 1964 US tour, 24 pages, EX $35.00
Purse, colorful image of John on silky material, gold metal
clasp, Canadian, 1970s, EX $35.00
Record carrier, Disk-Go-Case, plastic w/group photo, brown,
round, EX $400.00
Record carrier, Disk-Go-Case, plastic w/group photo,
round, any color other than brown, EX, ea from $175
to $225.00
Scarf, triangular w/tie strings, white w/red graphics & trim,
M $90.00
Scrapbook, color photos on front & back, Whitman, unused,
11x13", EX $75.00
Sign, Yeah! Yeah! Yeah! — Beatles Stamps Are Here!, orange
paper w/color pics of 5 different stamps, 1960s, 3x19",
NM $45.00
Stationery, Yellow Submarine, 4 sheets (1 w/ea member) &
matching envelopes, 1968, EX..............................$20.00
Stick-ons, Yellow Submarine, 'Beatles,' Dal Manufacturing
Corp, 1968, NMIP...$80.00
Travel bag, white cloth w/blue photo head images surround-
ed by red lettering w/musical graphics, M.........$200.00
Tray, 4 colored portraits w/musical notes & stars on rim,
made in Great Britain, 13x13", VG (Beware of reproduc-
tions)...$50.00
Tumbler, plastic w/multicolored paper insert of group &
lips under rim, original issue, VG (Beware of reproduc-
tions)...$85.00
Wallet, plastic w/group photo on front, New Jersey tourist
map on back, gold trim, NM $250.00
Watercolor set, Yellow Submarine, Craft Master, complete,
MIB $145.00

Beatnik Collectibles

The 'Beats,' later called 'Beatniks,' consisted of artists, writers, and others disillusioned with Establishment mores and
values. The Beatniks were noncomformists, Bohemian free-
thinkers who energetically expressed their disdain for society
from 1950 to 1962. From a collector's point of view, the most
highly regarded Beat authors are Allen Ginsberg, Lawrence
Ferlinghetti, and Jack Kerouac. Books, records, posters, pam-
phlets, leaflets, and other items associated with them are very
desirable. Although in their day they were characterized by the
media as a 'Maynard G. Krebs' (of Dobie Gillis TV fame),
today the contributions they made to American literature and
the continuation of Bohemianism are recognized for their
importance and significance in American culture.

Values are for examples in excellent to near-mint condition.

Advisor: Richard Synchef (See Directory, Beatnik and Hippie
Collectibles)

Beatnik kit, w/beret, cigarette holder & beard, 1950s, 12x11"
package $60.00
Book, H Is for Heroin, Hulburd, Doubleday & Co, NY,
1952, hardbound in dust jacket, 1st edition, teenager's
story $90.00
Book, The Beat Generation & the Angry Young Men,
Feldman & Gartenberg, Dell, NY, 1959 (significant
anthology) $120.00
Book, The Essential Lenny Bruce, Cohen, Douglas, NY, 1960,
hardbound in dust jacket, 1st edition $125.00
Booklet, Berlin, Lawrence Ferlinghetti, Golden Mountain
Press, 1961, 8-page, poetry................................$120.00
Booklet, Prospectus for Naked Lunch, William
Burroughs, Grove Press, 1962, 16-page promotional,
very scarce..$175.00
Booklet, The Nova Convention, November 30/December 2,
1978, NY, 12-page program, Burroughs, etc, rare..$150.00
Cigarette holder, Beatnik, black plastic, 12", mounted on
cardboard display card, 1950s $50.00
Handbill, poetry reading, Rexroth, Ginsberg, Ferlinghetti,
Kandel, U of Santa Barbara Gym, April 18, 1970..$500.00

**Handbill, *The Beard*,
M. McClure's contro-
versial award-winning
play, Premier March
31, 1965, pink, 11x7",
$400.00. (Photo cour-
tesy Richard Synchef)**

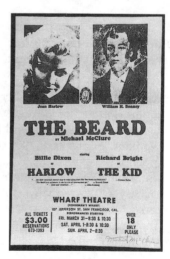

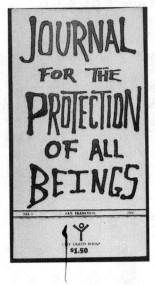

Magazine, *Journal for Protection of All Beings*, #1, City Lights Books, San Francisco, early Ferlinghetti, Snyder, and Ginsberg, 1961, $200.00. (Photo courtesy Richard Synchef)

Magazine, Life, September 21, 1959, Squaresville vs Beatsville..**$50.00**

Magazine, Startling Detective, March 1961, My Life As a Beatnik cover story...**$75.00**

Magazine, The Second Coming, March, 1962, NY, Burrough's chapter from Nova Express, scarce.....................**$150.00**

Paperback, Beatville, USA, George Mandel, Avon, NY, 1961 (humorous look at Beat life)..............................**$60.00**

Paperback, Naked Lunch, William Burroughs, Grove Press, NY, 1962, 1st US edition of landmark book.......**$400.00**

Paperback, Planet News, 1961-67, Allen Ginsberg, City Lights Books, San Francisco, 1968, Pocket Poet Series #23 ....**$200.00**

Paperback, Tristessa, Jack Kerouac, Avon, NY, 1960, paperback original **$125.00**

Pin-back buttons, celluloid: neon orange and blue, 1½", VG+, $20.00; blue and white, 1¼", VG, $20.00.

Poster, poetry reading, Ginsberg, Ferlinghetti, McClure, Di prima, UC Berkeley, August 19, 1971, 9x14"......**$250.00**

Record, Kaddish, Allen Ginsberg, monaural LP, Atlantic Verbum Series #4001, 1965 (Ginsberg reads entire classic poem) **$150.00**

Record, Lenny Bruce - American, Lenny Bruce, monaural AP, Fanasy #7011, red vinyl, 1961...........................**$125.00**

Record, Poetry for the Beat Generation, Jack Kerouac, monaural AP, Hanover Records (Kerouac reads, Steve Allen at piano) **$500.00**

Record, San Francisco Poets, monaural LP, Hanover M5001, 1959 (includes Rexroth, Ginsberg, Whalen, Ferlinghetti, others) **$200.00**

Record, The Beatniks, 45 rpm movie promotional tie-in, 1960, scarce...**$150.00**

Beatrix Potter

Since 1902 when *The Tale of Peter Rabbit* was published by Fredrick Warne & Company, generations have enjoyed the adventures of Beatrix Potter's characters. Beswick issued ten characters in 1947 that included Peter Rabbit, Benjamin Bunny, Squirrel Nutkin, Jemima Puddleduck, Timmy Tiptoes, Tom Kitten, Mrs. Tittlemouse, Mrs. Tiggywinkle, Little Pig Robinson, and Samuel Whiskers. The line grew until it included figures from other stories. Duchess (P1355) was issued in 1955 with two feet that were easily broken. Later issues featured the Duchess on a base and holding a pie. This was the first figure to be discontinued in 1967. Color variations on pieces indicate issue dates as do the different backstamps that were used. Backstamps have changed several times since the first figures were issued. There are three basic styles: Beswick brown, Beswick gold, and Royal Albert — with many variations on each of these. Unless stated otherwise, figures listed here are Beswick brown.

Advisor: Nicki Budin (See Directory, Beatrix Potter)

Amiable Guinea Pig, B3..**$300.00**
And This Little Pig Had None, B6.............................**$55.00**
Aunt Petitoes, B3 ....**$55.00**
Aunt Petitoes, B6 ....**$75.00**
Benjamin Bunny, bank, B6..**$45.00**
Benjamin Bunny, ears out, 3B..................................**$195.00**
Benjamin Bunny, head turned, 3B...........................**$115.00**
Benjamin Bunny, 3B...**$55.00**
Benjamin Bunny/Peter Rabbit, B3.........................**$125.00**
Benjamin Wakes Up, B6...**$55.00**
Cecily Parsley, B6 ....**$65.00**
Cecily Parsley, 3A **$95.00**
Chippy Hackee, C3..**$75.00**
Christmas Stocking, B6...**$250.00**
Cottontail, B6..**$45.00**
Cottontail, 3B..**$45.00**
Cousin Ribby, B3 ....**$55.00**
Cousin Ribby, B6 ....**$50.00**
Diggory Diggory Delvet, 3B **$50.00**
Flopsy, Mopsy, Cottontail, 2B.................................**$195.00**
Foxy Whiskered Gentleman, 3B................................**$75.00**
Gentleman Mouse Made Bow, B6..............................**$65.00**
Goody & Timmy Tiptoes, B6....................................**$150.00**
Goody Tiptoes, B3...**$60.00**
Hunca Munca, C3 ....**$65.00**
Hunca Munca, 2B gold **$175.00**
Hunca Munca, 3B **$65.00**
Hunca Munca Spills Beads, B6..................................**$65.00**

Jemima Puddleduck, B3 .... **$55.00**
Jemima Puddleduck, lg, gold B8 .... **$95.00**
Jemima Puddleduck, sm, gold B10 .... **$50.00**
Jemima Puddleduck, 2B **$160.00**
Jemima Puddleduck/Nest, B3 .... **$65.00**
Jemima Puddleduck/Nest, B6 .... **$45.00**
John Joiner, B6 .... **$55.00**
Johnny Townmouse, B3 .... **$55.00**
Johnny Townmouse w/Bag, B6 .... **$150.00**
Lady Mouse Made Curtsy, B6 .... **$45.00**
Little Pig Robinson, B3 .... **$45.00**
Little Pig Robinson, B6 .... **$45.00**
Little Pig Robinson Spying, B6 .... **$125.00**
Miss Dormouse, B6 .... **$85.00**
Miss Moppet, 3B **$55.00**
Mittens & Moppet, B6 .... **$185.00**
Mother Ladybird, B6 .... **$115.00**
Mr Alderman Ptolemy, 6B **$65.00**
Mr Benjamin Bunny, 3B **$40.00**
Mr Benjamin Bunny/Peter Rabbit, B3 .... **$75.00**
Mr Benjamin Bunny/Peter Rabbit, B6 .... **$75.00**
Mr Drake Puddleduck, B3 .... **$50.00**
Mr Jackson, B3 .... **$55.00**
Mr Jackson, B6 .... **$65.00**
Mr Jeremy Fisher, B3 .... **$65.00**
Mr Jeremy Fisher, C3 .... **$70.00**
Mr Jeremy Fisher Digging, B4 .... **$195.00**
Mr Tod, B6 .... **$150.00**
Mrs Flopsy Bunny, B3 .... **$65.00**
Mrs Rabbit, umbrella out, 2B **$450.00**
Mrs Rabbit, 3B **$60.00**
Mrs Rabbit w/Bunnies, 3B **$85.00**
Mrs Rabbit w/Peter, B6 .... **$65.00**
Mrs Tiggywinkle, B3 .... **$55.00**
Mrs Tiggywinkle Washing, Beswick/Ware **$125.00**
Mrs Tittlemouse, 3C **$45.00**
No More Twists, B6 .... **$55.00**
Old Mr Bouncer, B6 .... **$55.00**
Old Mr Bouncer, C3 .... **$85.00**
Old Mr Brown, B3 .... **$60.00**
Old Woman in Shoe, B3 .... **$45.00**
Old Woman in Shoe Knitting, B3 .... **$95.00**
Old Woman in Shoe Knitting, B6 .... **$45.00**
Peter in Gooseberry Net, 6B **$75.00**
Peter Rabbit, B10 .... **$50.00**
Peter Rabbit, jug **$125.00**
Peter Rabbit, 1st version, 3B **$95.00**
Pickles, 3A **$450.00**
Pigling Bland, B3 .... **$50.00**
Poorly Peter Rabbit, B3 .... **$75.00**
Poorly Peter Rabbit, B6 .... **$65.00**
Rebecca Puddleduck, B3 .... **$40.00**
Ribby, 3A **$75.00**
Ribby, 3B **$65.00**
Ribby & Patty Pan, B6 .... **$45.00**
Sally Henny Penny, B3 .... **$75.00**
Samuel Whiskers, B3 .... **$45.00**

Sir Isaac Newton, 3B **$450.00**

Susan, ca 1983, 4", $225.00. (Photo courtesy Marbena Fyke)

Tabitha Twitchit, B3 .... **$75.00**
Tabitha Twitchit, B6 .... **$40.00**
Tabitha Twitchit/Miss Moppet, B6 .... **$150.00**
Tabitha Twitchit/Miss Moppet, 3B **$175.00**
Thomasina Tittlemouse, 3B **$110.00**
Timmy Tiptoes, 3B **$65.00**
Timmy Willie, B3 .... **$45.00**
Timmy Willie, B6 .... **$65.00**
Timmy Willie Sleeping, 3C **$150.00**
Tom Kitten, B10 .... **$50.00**
Tom Kitten, B4 .... **$75.00**
Tom Kitten, 1st version, 3B **$85.00**

Tom Kitten With Butterfly, ca 1989, 3½", $185.00. (Photo courtesy Marbena Fyke)

Tom Thumb, B3 .... **$85.00**
Tom Thumb, B6 .... **$55.00**
Tommy Brock, 2nd version, lg patch, 3B **$65.00**

Beer Cans

In January of 1935 the Continental Can Co. approached a New Jersey brewery with the novel idea of selling beer in cans. After years of research, Continental had perfected a plastic coating for the inside of the can which prevented the beer from contacting and adversely reacting to metal. Consumers liked the idea, and throw-away beer cans soon replaced returnable bottles as the most popular container in which to purchase beer.

The first beer can was a steel flat top which actually bore a picture of the newly invented 'can opener' and instructions on how to use it. Because most breweries were not equipped to fill a flat can, a 'cone top' was invented to facilitate passage through the bottle filler. By the 1950s the cone top was obsolete. Ten years later, can companies introduced a 'tab top' can which made the can opener unnecessary. Aluminum cans and cans ranging in size from 6-ounce to one-gallon were popularized during the 1960s.

Beer can collecting reached its heyday during the 1970s. Thousands of collectors bought, drank, and saved cans throughout America. Unfortunately, the number of collectors receded, creating a huge supply of cans with minimal demand. There are many valuable beer cans today — however, they pre-date 1970. A post-1970 can worth more than a few dollars is rare.

Values are based on cans in conditions as stated. A can with flaws — rust, fading, or scratches — may still have value; however, it is generally much less than its excellent condition counterpart.

Advisor: Dan Andrews (See Directory, Beer Cans and Breweriana)

Newsletter: *Beer Cans and Brewery Collectibles*
Beer Can Collectors of America
747 Merus Ct., Fenton, MO 63026-2092
Phone or fax: 314-343-6486; e-mail: bcca@bcca.com; http://www.bcca.com. Subscription: $30 per year for US residents; includes 6 issues and right to attend national CANvention®

Barbarossa Beer, Red Top Brewing Co., Cincinnati, OH, cone top, $100.00. (Photo courtesy Dan Andrews)

Altes Lager Beer, Tivoli Brewing/Detroit, crowntainer, IRTP, 12-oz, EX $45.00

American Beer, Eastern Brewing/Hammonton, pull tab, bottom opened, 12-oz, NM $10.00

Ballantine XXX Ale, Ballantine Brewing/Newark, flat top, 12-oz, NM $25.00

Belair Beer, Horlacher Brewing/Allentown, flat top, bottom opened, 12-oz, EX+ $40.00

Berghoff 1887 Beer, Berghoff Brewing/Ft Wayne, IRTP, cone top, 12-oz, EX+ $40.00

Beverwyck Cream Ale, Beverwyck Brewing/Albany, IRTP, cone top, 12-oz, NM+ $65.00

Blatz Old Heidelberg Beer, Blatz Brewing/Milwaukee, IRTP, cone top, 12-oz, NM- $75.00

Breidt's Pilsner Beer, P Breidt Brewing/Elizabeth, IRTP, cone top, 12-oz, NM- $100.00

Canadian Ace Bock Beer, Canadian Ace Brewing/Chicago, flat top (opened), 12-oz, NM+ $50.00

Cardinal Premium Beer, Standard Brewing/Scranton, cone top, 12-oz, NM $90.00

Champagne Velvet Beer, Terre Haute Brewing/Terre Haute, cone top, 12-oz, EX+ $35.00

Copper Club Beer, A Hass Brewing/Hancock, cone top, 12-oz, EX+ $80.00

Country Club Beer, MK Goetz Brewing/St Joseph, cone top, 12-oz, EX+ $40.00

Dart Premium Beer, Eastern Brewing/Hammonton, pull tab, bottom opened, 12-oz, EX+ $10.00

Dawson Diamond Ale, Dawson's Brewing/New Bedford, zip tab, bottom opened, 1956, 12-oz, NM+ $25.00

Dawson's Ale, Dawson's Brewing/New Bedford, IRTP, cone top, 12-oz, EX- $60.00

Dawson's Master Ale, Dawson's Brewing/New Bedford, IRTP, cone top, 12-oz, NM- $75.00

E&B Special Beer, Ekhardt & Becker Brewing/Detroit, IRTP, cone top, 12-oz, NM $65.00

Eastside Beer, Los Angeles Brewing/Los Angeles, IRTP, cone top, 12-oz, NM- $55.00

Edelweiss, S Edelweiss Brewing/Chicago, IRTP, cone top, 12-oz, EX $30.00

Fergenspan Light Beer, C Fergenspan Brewing/Newark, IRTP, flat top, 12-oz, NM+ $100.00

Fergenspan XXX Amber Ale, C Fergenspan Brewing/Newark, IRTP, flat top, 12-oz, NM+ $70.00

Fountain Brew Beer, Fountain Brewing/Fountain City, new cone top, 12-oz, EX $90.00

Fox Deluxe Beer, Peter Fox Brewing/Chicago, IRTP, instructional, 12-oz, EX $55.00

Fox Head Malt Liquor, Fox Head Brewing/Waukesha, flat top, 12-oz, EX $40.00

GEM Premium Beer, F&S Brewing/Shamokin, flat top, 12-oz, EX $20.00

Gibbons Beer, Lion Inc/Wilkes-Barre, cone top, 12-oz, EX .$45.00

Gipps Amberlin Beer, Gipps Brewing/Peoria, cone top, 12-oz, EX+ $30.00

Gluek's Beer, Gluek Brewing/Minneapolis, IRTP, crowntainer, 12-oz, EX+ $70.00

Gold Star Beer, Hoff-Brau Brewing/Ft Wayne, IRTP, cone top, 12-oz, EX $55.00

Grain Belt Beer, Minneapolis Brewing/Minneapolis, cone top, 12-oz, NM **$45.00**

Grand Union Beer, Eastern Brewing/Hammonton, pull tab, 12-oz, NM **$5.00**

Haffenreffer Lager Beer, Haffenreffer & Company/Boston, pull tab, bottom opened, 12-oz, NM....................**$20.00**

Heileman's Beer, G Heileman Brewing/Lacrosse, Permis Dist #7-U-729, flat bottom, cone top, 12-oz, EX **$120.00**

Hull's Cream Ale, Hull Brewing/New Haven, flat top, 12-oz, EX+ **$40.00**

Keglet Beer, Esslinger Inc/Philadelphia, flat top, 12-oz, EX+..**$45.00**

Kentucky Malt Liquor, Oertel Brewing/Louisville, flat top, PA taxed lid, 12-oz, EX **$20.00**

Krueger Cream Ale, G Krueger Brewing/Newark, IRTP, flat top, AL taxed lip, instructional, 12-oz, NM **$95.00**

Oertel's 92 Beer, Oertel Brewing/Louisville, IRTP, crowntainer, 12-oz, EX+..**$35.00**

Old Crown Ale, Centlivre Brewing/Ft Wayne, IRTP, instructional, flat top, bottom opened, OH tax stamp, 12-oz, EX **$25.00**

Old German Beer, Queen City Brewing/Cumberland, cone top, 12-oz, EX **$30.00**

Old Topper Snappy Ale, Rochester Brewing/Rochester, IRTP, cone top, 12-oz, EX..**$50.00**

Ortlieb's Beer, HF Ortlieb Brewing/Philadelphia, cone top, 12-oz, EX **$40.00**

Noch-Eins Pale Beer, M, $275.00; Rhinelander Export Beer, M, $60.00; Yuengling Beer, M, $85.00.

Schmidt's Ale, C Schmidt & Sons/Philadelphia, cone top, IRTP, 12-oz, EX+ **$45.00**

Schmidt's Beer, C Scmidt & Sons/Philadelphia, cone top, IRTP, 12-oz, EX+ **$80.00**

Stoney's Pilsner Beer, Jones Brewing/Smithton, cone top, 12-oz, NM **$75.00**

Thorobred Malt Liquor, Oertel Brewing/Louisville, U-tab, GA tax stamp, EX+ **$50.00**

Weber Waukesha Beer, Weber Waukesha/Waukesha, cone top, 12-oz, EX+ **$80.00**

Wooden Shoe Lager Beer, Wooden Shoe Brewing/Minster, IRTP, cone top, 12-oz, NM **$60.00**

Pabst Blue Ribbon, flat top, VG, $30.00.

Bells

Bell collectors claim that bells rank second only to the wheel as being useful to mankind. Down through the ages bells have awakened people in the morning, called them to meals and prayers, and readied them to retire at night. We have heard them called rising bells, Angelus Bells (for deaths), noon bells, Town Crier bells (for important announcements), and curfew bells. Souvenir bells are often the first type collected, with interest spreading to other contemporaries, then on to old, more valuable bells. As far as limited edition bells are concerned, the fewer made per bell, the better. (For example a bell made in an edition of 25,000 will not appreciate as much as one from an edition of 5,000.)

For further information we recommend *World of Bells #5*, *Bell Tidings*, *Lure of Bells*, *Collectible Bells*, *More Bell Lore*, *Bells Now and Long Ago*, and *Legendary Bells*, all by Dorothy Malone Anthony.

Advisor: Dorothy Malone Anthony (See Directory, Bells)

Newsletter: *The Bell Tower*
The American Bell Association
P.O. Box 19443, Indianapolis, IN 46219

Aunt Agnes (mate to Uncle Toby), ceramic, rare, 3", $50.00. (Photo courtesy Dorothy Malone Anthony)

Beer mug, heavy glass w/bicycle bell, 6" $18.00
Berlin Annual Christmas, West Germany, 3⅜" $15.00
Bermuda carriage, double-chimed, 5" dia $65.00
Bing & Grondahl Christmas, 1974-78, 5", ea $35.00
Chintz china, English Summertime, 4¼" $70.00

Cut overlay glass, Murano, Italy, 7", $35.00. (Photo Courtesy Dorothy Malone Anthony)

Danbury Mint, Bicentenial, porcelain..........................$25.00
Fenton, Patriots Bell, blue...$75.00
Fenton, Patriots Bell, white or red, ea $45.00
Freedem bell, Gorham, wooden handle, 10" $25.00
Glen Jones, crystal, Christmas series, 6", ea $24.00
Glen Jones, crystal, Praying Angel, 6"..........................$24.00

Griffin handle, brass, copy of Italian bell, 5", $30.00. (Photo description Dorothy Malone Anthony)

Hammerslay, annuals, 1971-74, 6", ea..........................$22.00
Hammerslay, bicentennials, 6", ea.................................$25.00
Hummelwerk, glass, Christmas series, 7", ea..............$90.00
Jan Hagara, doll bells, 6", ea $55.00
Kaiser, porcelain, Christmas, West Germany, 1976 .....$25.00
Noritake, Christmas series, 3¼", ea $20.00
Reuge, Bicentennial, Christmas Musical series, 3 in series, ea $30.00
Roman, Way to Emmaus, porcelain................................$12.00

Senacca, Bicentennial, glass, in holder, 4½"...............$50.00
Spiegel, Dick bride dolls, 5", ea $35.00
US Holidays, Reed & Barton, silver, set of 12, 5", ea .$28.00
Veneto Flair, Children series, Rivershore, 7", ea.........$45.00

Bicycle Collectibles

Some collectible bicycles have increased in value. Prices have reached levels at auction never imagined just three years ago. Here are examples of prices realized: Phillips (London) – $160,000.00; Sotheby's (Chicago) – $106,000.00; Copake (New York state) – about $33,000.00. Generally these are most unusual in style or have exceptional provenance. Before selling bikes which seem unusual in structure, contact someone in the 'know.' Do **not** repaint your bike to get more from a collector — it usually devaluates the bike by 50%.

Historically, the bicycle is directly responsible for many of the innovations in automobiles, airplanes, and motorcycles. To mention a few of these traceable developments, consider the pneumatic tire, the automotive differential, and advanced gearing. The bicycle can even be linked to social changes such as the emancipation of women.

Since many of the collectibles cross over from category to category, items that fall into one field can be even more desirable in another. An example of this is photographic images. These images can be worth much more to the cycling collector who owns the type of bike or bikes depicted in the image than a collector who just collects old photographs.

The hobby itself generally splits into three areas: those collecting pre-1910, those devoted to the development of the classic, and a smaller group who covet lightweight racing machines. Of course, there are always those who collect 'all' and those who are specialists in a particular area.

Nowadays you might see collections of paper ephemera, accessories, watches, photographica, the actual bikes and trikes, rare and unusual parts, cycling radios, prints, and so much more.

Bikes from the 1950s can dramatically exceed the prices of those from the 1880s or 1890s. Much of this has to do with nostalgia, the affluence of the baby boomers, design, and mechanical achievement.

Advisor: Lorne Shields (See Directory, Bicycles and Tricycles)

Collectors' Bicycles

Columbia, Highwheel or Pennyfarthing, Expert, 52" front wheel w/nameplate, brake mechanism missing, 1880s, VG $1,700.00
Columbia Five Star, man's, spring front fork, original paint, headlight & chrome mud guards, 1953, VG.......$650.00
Dixie Flyer-Pained 26" Balloon, man's, complete & all original w/lamp, rear carrier, etc, 1939, VG $2,200.00
Elgin Bluebird 26" Balloon, man's, original overall w/fender mascot, ca 1936, EX $4,000.00

JC Higgins, boy's 24", w/kick stand, front torpedo light & New Departure coaster brake, VG $150.00

Lizbell, man's gear-driven (chainless) bike, 1897, restored, $5,000.00. (Photo courtesy Mel Short)

Monarch 'Silver King,' 26", hex tube, replacement components, 1946 ....$500.00

Pierce Co, man's, made in Buffalo NY, shaft drive w/spring leaf front form, wood rims (bent), as found...$1,500.00

Pierce Pneumatic Safety, lady's, made in Buffalo NY, good saddle & wood rims, ca 1898, VG original.........$500.00

Raleigh Chopper, 20", 16" front wheel, 3-speed, red line tires, ca 1973, EX $250.00

Rollfast, American Flyer (man's), spring front fork, original black tires, light & carrier, 1940, well used/all there $400.00

Rudge Highwheeler, 52" front wheel, brake mechanism, complete w/nameplate, EX......................................$2,600.00

Schwinn Black Phantom, man's 26", balloon tires, original paint, rear carrier, tank & front shock fork, 1952, EX $1,700.00

Schwinn Fastback Stingray, 20", Coaster, orange w/white-wall tires, ca 1975, G $400.00

Schwinn Panther, man's, head lamp & rear carrier, front fork suspension, original, 1950, EX......................$1,500.00

Shelby Air Flow, 'Flying Cloud,' boy's, 1938, used but all there, VG..$3,500.00

Shelby 'Flying Cloud' (man's), original lamp & rear carrier, 1947 ....$600.00

Star Safety, ratchet pump, rear-lever drive, solid tires, 1889, restored, $8,000.00. (Photo courtesy Mel Short)

Victor, man's, Pneumatic Safety, tall frame, original, 1890s, unrestored, G $400.00

Victor/Overman Wheel Co Cross Frame, man's, lg pedals/saddle, missing hardware/leather, 1888...................$1,000.00

Western Flyer, man's tank bike, all original w/tank, mud guards & rear carrier, 1948, G $400.00

Westfield 50th Anniversary model, lady's 26", balloon tires, w/stand & headlight, ca 1937, EX......................$250.00

Used Bicycles

Adult tricycle, 24x1.75 wheels, big saddle, 1980s/90s, G...$125.00

GT BMX, 20", alloy rims w/number plate, pad set, 1980s, VG $75.00

Huffy 24" Mountain Bike, boy's, 6-speed derailer, gum wall tires, padded seat, 1980s, G $50.00

Murray 20" Mountain Bike, boy's, coaster brakes, 1990s, VG $30.00

Nishiki 27" 10-speed Racer, gum tires, Sun Tour gears, alloy rims & brakes, needs a bike shop tune-up $50.00

Raleigh Racer Superbe, 26x1⅜", 3-speed, w/fenders & chain guard, 1960s, VG $80.00

Royce Union, boy's or girl's 16" BMX style, colorful, air tires, 1990s, G running order $25.00

Sun Cycle 26" Cruiser, man's or lady's, big saddle, white-wall tires $75.00

Trek 26" Mountain Bike, alloy rims, cranks & derailers, 1990s, VG (needs a tune-up) $250.00

Miscellaneous

Bell, Highwheel era, dome top, narrow handlebar mount, Fine $400.00

Bell, Mickey Mouse, chrome, rotary action, Made in Germany, approximately 1¾" $5.00

Bell, Victorian w/embossed design, 1895-1920, VG ...$20.00

BMX number plate, hard, 1970s, needs new ties..........$5.00

BMX pad set, top tube, handlebar & stem, 3-pc, VG ...$3.00

BMX ½" aluminum pedals, platform type, Taiwan, pr, VG.$4.00

Carrier, automobile; holds 2 bikes, strap to trunk for support, 1990s, buy w/caution unless VG $15.00

Carrier, front; zinc plated, about 16x10x10", 1950-80s, G ..$5.00

Carrier, rear; chrome, tubular, w/spring clamp, 1960s-70s, VG $5.00

Carrier, rear; JC Higgins, stamped, w/supports, painted, 1950s, G $40.00

Carrier bag, nylon front, w/2 straps, about 12x7x10", G ..$2.00

Carrier bags, heavy quality pr for mounting over back wheels, VG $20.00

Catalog/flyer, Schwinn, fold-out w/actors & actresses, 1950s, EX...$50.00

Cup, cyclist, collapsible, embossed w/couple on tandem, 1897, VG...$25.00

Cyclometer, American Waltham Watch, enamel dial, 1900s, 3" dia $125.00

Cyclometer, Matex, Japan, w/mounting bracket & spoke attachment, 27"..$1.00

Grips, horse head at ends, matched pr, 1950s, EX **$12.00**
Grips, plastic w/finger-hold bottom, VG......................**$1.00**
Head badge, Columbia, 1940s, EX **$10.00**
Head badge, Harley-Davidson, raised, ca 1910, worn but VG...**$250.00**
Headlamp, Delta for Schwinn, torpedo style, front fender mount, 1950s...**$40.00**
Headlamp, Monark, aerodynamic style, pedestal front fender mount, 1950s, VG..**$200.00**
Headlamp & horn combination, chromed, Made in Hong Kong, 1960-70s, EX...**$5.00**
Headlight, carbide, nickle plated, solar, cracked lens, wear to surface, ca 1910 ....**$60.00**
Helmet, rather than buy used, we recommend a new approved model w/proper sizing from your local bike or specialty shop
Horn, Seiss, handlebar mount w/top plunger, Klaxton type, white paint, 1930s, VG...**$75.00**
Horn, 9" bulb, chrome plated, handlebar mount, 1-trumpet, 1950-1980s, from $2 to **$4.00**
Kickstand, 26" mountain bike, rear axle mount, plated..**$2.50**
Kickstand, 27" alloy racer, fits behind crank, w/top plate & bolt, VG..**$2.50**
License plate, Side Path, Suffolk County, New York, figural, 1899, EX..**$75.00**
License plate, Wisconsin, 1969, G **$7.50**
License plate, Wyoming, 1953, G **$8.50**
Light set, Sears, chrome plated, w/generator & taillight, 1960s-70s, EXIB...**$15.00**
Lock, sm hoop shape, 'sprocket' type, cast, nickel plated, 1890s, missing key, EX..**$30.00**
Lock, 10" long shackel type, 1940s, w/1 key, VG.........**$6.00**
Lock, 18" plastic-coated cable & 2 keys, 1950s-80s, VG .**$1.00**
Mirror, 4" round w/rear reflector, chrome plated, 1960s, VG..**$2.00**
Model, 1/6 scale, Schwinn Apple Krate, 1 of 10,000 limited edition, 1980, MIB..**$60.00**
Model, 1:10 scale, antique high-wheel bicycle, MIB...**$10.00**
Mud flaps, Skull & Crossbones, pr, sm & lg, 1960s-70s, MIP .**$10.00**
Mug, Crown Devon, Daisy Bell Tandem bike theme, music box base, Made in England, 5", EX....................**$150.00**
Owner's manual, Huffy, 1950s, MIP...........................**$15.00**
Owner's manual, Raleigh, 1970s, VG **$2.00**
Photo, balloon bicycles w/adults, 1940s, 4x5", EX **$10.00**
Photo, family w/boy & his new balloon bike at Christmas, 1950s, EX..**$10.00**
Photo, high-wheel bicycle & man, 1880s, 2½x4"........**$50.00**
Postcard, comic, multicolor, 1920s, VG.........................**$3.00**
Postcard, Florida Boardwalk, 1930s, EX.......................**$.50**
Pump, hand-operated, w/connector, painted or chrome, 1950-80, 18", VG..**$2.50**
Pump, 16", foot-held, red paint, braided hose & hardwood handle, folding foot base, working **$7.00**
Radio & horn combination, 5½x3½" bracket mount to handlebars, used but working **$10.00**
Radio for bike, Charlie the Tuna, novelty transistor, working, 1973 ....**$25.00**

Reflector, 1½", red glass (not plastic), screw back, EX.**$3.00**
Reflector, 4" wide for banana saddle, chrome rim, 1960-70s, VG...**$5.00**
Reflector kit, 4-pc: 1 for front (white), 1 for rear (red) and 2 for wheels, plastic w/fittings, 1980-90s **$3.00**
Repair kit, Firestone, tin w/bicycle graphics, complete, 1940s, EX..**$15.00**
Repair kit, Goodyear, round cardboard w/serrated top, incomplete contents, 1960s, VG **$7.00**
Saddle, Banana, w/standard chromed support bar, glitter & ribbed saddle, 1970s, VG...**$30.00**
Saddle, for lady's touring bike, mattress style, nylon top w/gel inside, VG...**$7.00**
Saddle, for man's touring bike, mattress style, plastic top, black, 1960, used but still EX..............................**$4.00**
Saddle, racing pattern for 10-speed bike, plastic top, black, 11" long, used but no rips, VG...............................**$3.00**
Salt & pepper set, done as trike w/toothpick in front, plated metal w/glass bottles, Taiwan, 1980s, 3-pc, EX......**$7.00**
Siren, Persons Majestic, chain bull, fork mount, round, internal revolving, chrome, 1950s, EX **$60.00**
Siren, 3-sound, Cycle 27, battery-operated electric, 1980s, working...**$5.00**
Speedometer, Schwinn, mounts to handlebar, w/all wheel, fork & handlebar fittings, 1940s...........................**$60.00**
Speedometer, Stewart Warner, black plastic, mounts to the handlebar, 1960s, 26", VG.................................**$25.00**
Tire, 20x1.75", black, foreign, VG................................**$3.00**
Tire, 20x2.125", Goodyear, black, for Crate/Highriser .**$15.00**
Tire, 24x1.75", black & gum side, for junior mountain bike, foreign, EX..**$5.00**
Tire, 26x1⅜", black, foreign, VG..................................**$3.00**
Tire, 26x2.00", for mountain bike, black, Kenda, knobby, EX...**$5.00**
Tire, 26x2.125", white-wall, foreign made, ca 1980 ......**$5.00**
Tool bag, leather seat mount, plain, w/2 wrenches, repair kit & tire levers, 1950s, 5x6", VG+ **$15.00**
Tool bag, vinyl seat mount w/1 reflector, 1970s, 11x8", EX..**$5.00**
Tool kit, leather, w/repair kit & wrench, 1950s-70s, 6x3½", VG...**$7.00**
Trailer for children, Winchester, nylon intact, wheels sound, holds 2 children, 1980-90s **$75.00**
Wheel, front; 26" mountain bike, steel rim, heavy spokes w/tire & tube, EX..**$12.00**
Wheels, 20" BMX, alloy Mongoose, working rear hub & all fittings, 1980s, pr..**$50.00**

Black Americana

There are many avenues one might pursue in the broad field of Black Americana and many reasons that might entice one to become a collector. For the more serious, there are documents such as bills of sale for slaves, broadsides, and other historical artifacts. But by and far, most collectors enjoy attractive advertising pieces, novelties and kitchenware items, toys and dolls, and Black celebrity memorabilia.

It's estimated that there are at least 50,000 collectors around the country today that specialize in this field. There are large auctions devoted entirely to the sale of Black Americana. The items they feature may be as common as a homemade potholder or a magazine or as rare as a Lux Dixie Boy clock or a Mammy cookie jar that might go for several thousand dollars. In fact, many of the cookie jars have become so valuable that they're being reproduced; so are salt and pepper shakers, so beware.

For further study, we recommend *Black Collectibles Sold in America* by P.J. Gibbs.

See also Advertising, Aunt Jemima; Condiment Sets; Cookie Jars; Postcards; Salt and Pepper Shakers; Sheet Music; String Holders.

Advisor: Judy Posner (See Directory, Black Americana)

Activity book, Sambo's Circus, by Bill Woddon, Sambo's Restaurant premium, early 1960s, 11x8½", M.......**$50.00**
Ashtray, multicolored bobbin'-head boy on copper-colored tin bowl opposite double rest, marked Made in Japan, 4¼", EX.................**$200.00**
Bank, bisque baby w/nodding head leaning against alligator marked Florida, Kenmar, Japan, 1950s, 6", NM..**$125.00**
Bell, girl kneeling in prayer in white gown w/pink & gold trim, eyes closed, red lips, ceramic, 1940s, EX.....**$60.00**
Book, Charlotte Steiner's Story-Book Theatre, Little Black Sambo w/5 other story books, 1944, EX............**$225.00**
Book, Little Black Sambo, Whitman Top-Top Tales, 1961, illustrated by Violet La Mont, EX......................**$90.00**
Book, Little Brown Koko, 1940 1st edition, hardcover, 96 pages, 11x8", EX......................**$90.00**
Book, Rufty Tufty Flies High, Heinemann Publishing, illustrated by Ruth Ainsworth, 1959, EX.....................**$70.00**
Book, Watermelon Pete, by Elizabeth Gordon, 1937 edition, illustrated by Clara Powers Wilson, hardcover, 7x5", EX **$90.00**
Boot scraper, cast iron, Black man sitting atop arch holding 2 side brushes on oval fluted bowl base, 13x10", EX.................**$225.00**
Brochure cover, Le Jazz-Band, paper litho, orange & black drawing of lively band on white, framed, 17x21", VG **$45.00**
Cigarette box, wooden box w/2 painted male figures that face ea other when lid is opened by lever, 6¼", VG **$150.00**
Cookbook, Rebecca's Cookbook, privately published by Rebecca West, 1942, 9x6", M **$135.00**
Dexterity puzzle, Sambo, blue plastic head figure w/exaggerated features, Fun Inc, 1950s, MIP..................**$65.00**
Dice toy, carved wood, ivory eyes pop in & out, hat unscrews to hold dice, Kobe, 3¾", NM.............**$200.00**
Doll, golliwog boy, stuffed cloth w/glued-on oilcloth features, red-striped pants, yellow shirt, blue jacket, 16", EX................**$100.00**
Doll, Kewpie, jointed shoulders, w/diaper, Noma Toys, catalog #1347, 11", EX (EX box)..............**$375.00**

Doll, Mammy, stuffed cloth w/yarn hair, bandanna, dress w/apron, painted features, Georgene (?), 14½", EX..**$185.00**
Doll, pickaninny, inflatable plastic w/flasher eyes, yellow skirt & hair bow, 1950s, 10", EX..........................**$35.00**
Doll, pickaninny, stuffed cloth w/yarn hair, plaid dress, unmarked, 1940s-50s, 12", EX.............................**$125.00**
Doll, topsy-turvy, Chocolate & Vanilla, molded faces w/painted features, Eugene Doll & Novelty Corp, WWII era, 12", M....................**$400.00**
Doll kit, Sambo, Bucilla Needlework, 1950s, complete ..**$95.00**
Figure, painted-brass Black man lying on stomach in nightclothes cooking over open fire, 7½", EX...........**$120.00**
Flower holder, sm girl standing beside ear of corn, ceramic, yellow, green & red, 1950, 5", EX.......................**$75.00**
Game, Double Push-Up Pinball, cardboard back w/metal catchalls, glass front, wood frame, 18x12", VG..**$110.00**
Jack-in-the-Box, golliwog jumps out, Germany, 1950s, 7", EX+.............................**$250.00**
Lobby card, Little Rascals, Fishy Tales, Monogram Pictures, 1951, framed, 11x14", EX **$50.00**

Marionette, plastic clown with painted features, ca 1945 – 55, 12", MIB, from $125.00 to $175.00. (Photo courtesy P.J. Gibbs)

Match holder, Black boy standing next to basket on beveled base, painted pewter, 3¼", EX+ **$170.00**
Nodder, native figure, papier-mache, Woolworth, 1940s, 5", EX **$125.00**
Paper dolls, Betty & Billy, Whitman, 1955, NM **$125.00**
Pencil sharpener, minstrel playing accordion, painted metal, Occupied Japan, 2¼", EX+ **$225.00**
Plate, Sambo's Restaurant, heavy china, light blue graphics on white, Jackson China, 1950s, 8" dia, VG **$70.00**
Pocket mirror, round celluloid photo image of 2 Black women, w/swinging metal handle, 3½", EX **$55.00**
Postcard, RCA Victor promotion featuring Duke Ellington as Victor's Celebrated Jazz Composer-Pianist, 1940s, EX....................**$25.00**
Poster, Louis Satchmo Armstrong, L'Ambassadeur Du Jazz Bruxelles, red & black on white, 1958, 21x14", EX..................**$125.00**

Pull toy, Snowflakes & Swipes, Black boy walking dog w/toothache on 4-wheeled platform, litho tin, 7½", EX...**$350.00**

Puppet, Jambo the Jiver Marionette, wood w/cloth clothes, fiber hair, Talent Products, 1948, 14", VG...........**$225.00**

Puppet, Tonga from the Congo Marionette, painted wood & plastic, string skirt, Talent Products, 1948, 14", VG.**$225.00**

Puzzle, cardboard frame-tray, pictures Jumbo w/umbrella & Mumbo putting on Sambo's jacket, USA, 1945, M.**$75.00**

Record, Little Black Sambo, RCA Victor Y333, 1947, 78 rpm, 2 in album, EX, from $50 to **$125.00**

Record, Little Brave Sambo, Peter Pan, 1950, EX (EX sleeve) **$65.00**

Record, Vogue picture; Basin Street Blues, 78 rpm, shows riverboat scene w/dapper couple & banjo player, 10" dia, EX **$125.00**

Record album, Uncle Remus Stories, RCA Victor, 78 rpm, 2 records w/illustrated cover, 1940s, EX.................**$110.00**

Salt & pepper shakers, bellhop, wood, black skin tone, red lips & hats, googly eyes, 1949, 2", EX, pr.............**$60.00**

Salt & pepper shakers, maid & chef, dark brown skin tones, side-glance googly eyes on chef, glossy, Japan, 1950s, 2", pr...**$60.00**

Scouring pad holder, Mammy's head w/bandanna & neck scarf, ceramic, ink-stamped Coventry Made in USA, 1940s, EX...**$110.00**

Sheet music, Blue Boogie, by John W Schaum, 1946, EX....**$65.00**

Sheet music, The Cotton Club Presents — Mania, red, white & brown stylized graphics, 1931, EX **$50.00**

Shopping pegboard, wood, shows puzzled Mammy saying 'Reckon Ah Needs...' above 2 rows of items, 1940s, 8¼x6", EX...**$90.00**

Stacking blocks, features Sambo & Tiger, 1940s, set of 5, EX...**$125.00**

Tablecloth, white cloth w/embroidered image of girl lying on stomach & saying Wednesday Ah Is Lazy, 1930s, 37", NM **$95.00**

Talking book, *Little Black Sambo* (musical radio script), G, 10½", **$65.00**.

Teapot & stacking creamer set, cold-painted Black faces on oval shapes, Thames, Japan, 1930s, 8½", EX **$75.00**

Thermometer, baby peeking from behind thermometer, pressed wood, Multi Products, 1949, 5½", EX......**$65.00**

Tile, Currier & Ives, Low Water in the Mississippi, ceramic, Black scene w/banjo player, 6" dia w/9½" square frame, EX...**$125.00**

Towel, handmade applique of Mammy w/watermelons & embroidered fruit, 1930s, EX **$60.00**

Towel rack, cast-iron image of Johnny Griffin flanked by leaves & scrollwork on 5-hook bar, worn gold finish, 7x13", VG **$210.00**

Tray, litho tin, center shows 2 Black children ready for bed on turquoise ground, black rim, rounded corners, 6x9", EX...**$275.00**

Wall plaque, man wearing straw hat, chalkware, yellow, brown & blue, 1950, 6", EX, from $55 to **$65.00**

Wall plaque, mini cast-iron skillet w/embossed painted profile image of Mammy, New Orleans, 1930s, 4", EX..**$70.00**

Water sprinkler, painted-metal figure of Black man holding hose attached to metal ground spike, 36", VG...**$335.00**

Black Cats

Kitchenware, bookends, vases, and many other items designed as black cats were made in Japan during the 1950s and exported to the United States where they were sold by various distributors who often specified certain characteristics they wanted in their own line of cats. Common to all these lines were the red clay used in their production and the medium used in their decoration — their features were applied over the glaze with 'cold (unfired) paint.' The most collectible is a line marked (or labeled) Shafford. Shafford cats are plump and pleasant looking. They have green eyes with black pupils; white eyeliner, eyelashes, and whiskers; and red bow ties. The same design with yellow eyes was marketed by Royal, and another fairly easy-to-find 'breed' is a line by Wales with yellow eyes and gold whiskers. You'll find various other labels as well. Some collectors buy only Shafford, while others like them all.

When you evaluate your black cats, be critical of their paint. Even though no chips or cracks are present, if half of the paint is missing, you have a half-price item. Remember this when using the following values which are given for cats with near-mint to mint paint.

Advisor: Doug Dezso (See Directory, Candy Containers)

Ashtray, flat face, Shafford, hard to find size, 3¾"......**$45.00**

Ashtray, flat face, Shafford, 4¾" **$18.00**

Ashtray, head shape, not Shafford, several variations, ea, from $12 to...**$15.00**

Ashtray, head shape w/open mouth, Shafford, 3" **$22.00**

Bank, seated cat w/coin slot in top of head, Shafford, from $225 to...**$275.00**

Bank, upright cat, Shafford-like features, marked Tommy, 2-part, from $150 to...**$175.00**

Cigarette lighter, Shafford, 5½" **$175.00**

Cigarette lighter, sm cat stands on book by table lamp..**$65.00**

Condiment set, upright cats, yellow eyes, 2 bottles & pr of matching shakers in wireware stand, row arrangement **$95.00**

Condiment set, two joined heads, J&M bows, w/intact spoons, Shafford, $95.00.

Condiment set, 2 joined heads, yellow eyes (not Shafford) **$65.00**
Cookie jar, cat's head, fierce expression, yellow eyes, brown-black glaze, heavy red clay, lg, rare **$250.00**
Cookie jar, lg head cat, Shafford, from $80 to **$100.00**
Creamer & sugar bowl, cat-head lids are salt & pepper shakers, yellow eyes variation, 5⅜" **$50.00**
Creamer & sugar bowl, Shafford **$45.00**
Cruet, slender form, gold collar & tie, tail handle **$12.00**
Cruet, upright cat w/yellow eyes, open mouth, paw spout **$30.00**
Cruets, oil & vinegar; cojoined cats, Royal Sealy, 1-pc (or similar examples w/heavier yellow-eyed cats), 7¼"..**$40.00**
Cruets, upright cats, she w/V eyes for vinegar, he w/O eyes for oil, Shafford, pr, from $60 to **$75.00**
Decanter, long cat w/red fish in his mouth as stopper...**$60.00**
Decanter, upright cat holds bottle w/cork stopper, Shafford **$50.00**
Decanter set, upright cat, yellow eyes, +6 plain wines .**$35.00**
Decanter set, upright cat, yellow eyes, +6 wines w/cat faces **$50.00**
Demitasse pot, tail handle, bow finial, Shafford, 7½"..**$165.00**
Desk caddy, pen forms tail, spring body holds letters, 6½" **$8.00**

Egg cup, Shafford, 3", from $95.00 to $125.00.

Grease jar, sm cat head, Shafford, scarce, from $95 to ..**$110.00**
Ice bucket, cylindrical w/embossed yellow-eyed cat face, 2 sizes, ea **$75.00**
Measuring cups, 4 sizes on wooden wall-mount rack w/painted cat face, Shafford, rare, from $350 to **$400.00**

Mugs, Shafford, 4" (hard to find), from $70.00 to $80.00; 3½", $55.00; 3½", cat handle lower on body, hard to find, $95.00.

Paperweight, cat's head on stepped chrome base, open mouth, yellow eyes, rare..**$75.00**
Pincushion, cushion on cat's back, tongue measure ..**$25.00**
Pitcher, milk; seated upright cat, ear forms spout, tail handle, Shafford, 6", or 6½", ea **$150.00**
Pitcher, squatting cat, pour through mouth, Shafford, rare, 5", 14½" circumference **$90.00**
Pitcher, squatting cat, pour through mouth, Shafford, scarce, 4½", 13" circumference........................**$75.00**
Pitcher, squatting cat, pour through mouth, Shafford, very rare, 5½", 17" circumference..............................**$250.00**
Planter, cat & kitten in a hat, Shafford-like paint........**$30.00**
Planter, cat sits on knitted boot w/gold drawstring, Shafford-like paint, Elvin, 4¼x4½" **$30.00**
Planter, upright cat, Shafford-like paint, Napco label, 6" **$20.00**
Pot holder caddy, 'teapot' cat, 3 hooks, Shafford, from $170 to..**$195.00**
Salad set, spoon & fork, funnel, 1-pc oil & vinegar cruet & salt & pepper shakers on wooden wall-mount shield-shape rack, Royal Sealy..**$200.00**
Salt & pepper shakers, long crouching cat, shaker in ea end, Shafford, 10"..**$165.00**
Salt & pepper shakers, range size; upright cats, Shafford, scarce, 5" **$65.00**
Salt & pepper shakers, round-bodied 'teapot' cat, Shafford, pr, from $125 to..**$140.00**
Salt & pepper shakers, seated, blue eyes, Enesco label, 5¾", pr..**$15.00**
Salt & pepper shakers, upright cats, Shafford, 3¾" (watch for slightly smaller set as well), pr **$25.00**
Spice set, triangle, 3 rounded tiers of shakers, 8 in all, in wooden wall-mount triangular rack, Stafford, very rare **$450.00**
Spice set, 4 upright cat shakers hook onto bottom of wireware cat-face rack, Shafford, rare........................**$450.00**
Spice set, 6 square shakers in wooden frame, Shafford....**$175.00**
Spice set, 6 square shakers in wooden frame, yellow eyes..**$125.00**

Stacking tea set, mamma pot w/kitty creamer & sugar bowl, yellow eyes..**$80.00**

Stacking tea set, 3 cats w/red collar, w/gold ball, yellow eyes, 3-pc...**$80.00**

Sugar bowl/planter, sitting cat, red bow w/gold bell, Shafford-like paint, Elvin, 4"..............................**$25.00**

Teapot, bulbous body, head lid, green eyes, lg, Shafford, 7"..**$75.00**

Teapot, bulbous body, head lid, green eyes, Shafford, med size, from $40 to..**$45.00**

Teapot, bulbous body, head lid, green eyes, Shafford, sm, 4 - 4½"..**$30.00**

Teapot, cat face w/double spout, Shafford, scarce, 5", from $200 to...**$250.00**

Teapot, cat's face, yellow hat, blue & white eyes, pink ears, lg, from $40 to...**$50.00**

Teapot, crouching cat, paw up to right ear is spout, green jeweled eyes, 8½" L..**$80.00**

Teapot, panther-like appearance, gold eyes, sm.........**$20.00**

Teapot, upright, slender cat (not ball-shaped), lift-off head, Shafford, rare, 8"..**$250.00**

Teapot, upright cat w/paw spout, yellow eyes & red bow, Wales, 8¼"...**$60.00**

Teapot, yellow eyes, 1-cup...**$30.00**

Teapot, yellow-eyed cat face embossed on front of standard bulbous teapot shape, wire bale...........................**$60.00**

Thermometer, cat w/yellow eyes stands w/paw on round thermometer face..**$30.00**

Toothpick holder, cat on vase atop book, Occupied Japan..**$12.00**

Tray, flat face, wicker handle, Shafford, rare, lg.......**$185.00**

Utensil (fork, spoon or strainer), wood handle, Shafford, scarce, ea..**$125.00**

Utensil rack, flat-backed cat w/3 slots for utensils, cat only..**$125.00**

Wall pocket, flat-backed 'teapot' cat, Shafford, from $125 to...**$150.00**

Wine, embossed cat's face, green eyes, Shafford, sm..**$75.00**

Blair Dinnerware

American dinnerware has been a popular field of collecting for several years, and the uniquely styled lines of Blair Ceramics are very appealing, though not often seen except in the Midwest (and it's there that prices are the strongest). Blair was located in Ozark, Missouri, manufacturing dinnerware only from the mid-'40s until the early '50s. Gay Plaid, recognized by its squared-off shapes and brush-stroke design (in lime, brown, and dark green on white), is the pattern you'll find most often. Several other lines were made as well. You'll be able to recognize all of them easily enough, since most pieces (except for the smaller items) are marked.

Bowl, fruit/cereal; Gay Plaid, square, from $8 to.......**$10.00**
Bowl, onion soup; Bamboo, rope handle, w/lid........**$22.00**
Bowl, sauce; Gay Plaid, double spout, handled.........**$16.00**

Bowl, serving; Autumn Leaf..**$12.50**
Bowl, vegetable; Bird, divided, rectangular w/tab handles **$32.50**
Celery dish, Bird, from $20 to **$25.00**
Coffee server, Bamboo, rope handle, from $40 to......**$50.00**
Cruet, Bird, cone form w/ring handle **$27.50**
Cup & saucer, Autumn Leaf......................................**$12.00**
Cup & saucer, Bamboo, rope handle.........................**$12.00**
Mug, Gay Plaid **$18.00**
Pitcher, utility; Gay Plaid, bulbous body, smooth curved handle, sm...**$15.00**
Pitcher, water; Gay Plaid, rope handle, ice lip...........**$45.00**
Plate, dinner; Bamboo, rectangular...........................**$12.50**
Plate, dinner; Bird, square **$17.50**
Platter, Yellow Plaid, 3-compartment **$27.50**
Salt & pepper shakers, Bird, pr **$16.00**
Sugar bowl, Gay Plaid, rope handle, w/lid.................**$17.50**

Tumbler, Gay Plaid, from $12.00 to $15.00.

Blue Danube

A modern-day interpretation of the early Meissen Blue Onion pattern, Blue Danube is an extensive line of quality dinnerware that has been produced in Japan since the early 1950s and distributed by Lipper International of Wallingford, Connecticut. It is said that the original design was inspired by a pattern created during the Yuan Dynasty (1260 – 1368) in China. This variation is attributed to the German artist Kandleva. The flowers depicted in this blue-on-white dinnerware represent the ancient Chinese symbols of good fortune and happiness. The original design, with some variations, made its way to Eastern Europe where it has been produced for about two hundred years. It is regarded today as one of the world's most famous patterns.

At least one hundred twenty-five items have at one time or another been made available by the Lipper company, making it the most complete line of dinnerware now available in the United States. Collectors tend to pay higher prices for items with the earlier banner mark (1951 to 1976), and reticulated (openweave) pieces bring a premium. Unusual serving or decorative items generally command high prices as well.

The more common items that are still being produced usually sell for less than retail on the secondary market.

The banner logo includes the words 'Reg US Pat Off' along with the pattern name. In 1976 the logo was redesigned and the pattern name within a rectangular box with an 'R' in circle to the right of it was adopted. Very similar lines of dinnerware have been produced by other companies, but these two marks are the indication of genuine Lipper Blue Danube. Among the copycats you may encounter are Mascot and Vienna Woods — there are probably others.

Advisor: Lori Simnionie (See the Directory, Blue Danube)

Bell **$25.00**
Biscuit jar, 9" **$50.00**
Bone dish/side salad, crescent shape, banner mark, 9", from $18 to **$22.00**
Bowl, cereal; banner mark, 6" **$12.00**

Candy dish with lid, from $50.00 to $60.00. (From the collection of Elaine France)

Bowl, cream soup; from $18.00 to $22.00; Saucer, from $8.00 to $11.00. (From the collection of Elaine France)

Bowl, cream soup; w/lid, from $30 to **$35.00**
Bowl, dessert; 5½", from $7 to **$10.00**
Bowl, divided vegetable; 11x7½" **$50.00**
Bowl, lattice edge, 9", from $50 to **$60.00**
Bowl, low pedestal skirted base, shaped rim, banner mark, 2x9x12" **$70.00**
Bowl, soup; 8½" **$15.00**
Bowl, vegetable; oval, 10" L, from $25 to **$35.00**
Bowl, vegetable; 3¼x10" **$45.00**
Bowl, vegetable; 9", from $25 to **$35.00**
Bowl, wedding; w/lid, footed, square, 8½x5", from $50 to **$60.00**
Box, white lacquer ware, gold label w/rectangular logo, 2¼x4½" **$30.00**
Butter dish, round, 8½" **$80.00**
Butter dish, stick type, ¼-lb, from $25 to **$35.00**
Cache pot, w/handles, 8x8" **$45.00**
Cake pedestal, lattice edge, rectangular mark, 5x10" .**$70.00**
Cake pedestal, 4x10" **$50.00**
Candlesticks, 6½", pr, from $40 to **$50.00**

Casserole, individual; banner mark, 6" across handles.**$35.00**
Casserole, 5½x10½" (across handles) **$65.00**
Chamber stick, Old Fashioned, 4x6" dia **$25.00**
Cheese board, wooden, w/6" dia tile & glass dome, from $25 to **$35.00**
Chop plate, 12" dia **$40.00**
Coasters, set of 4, from $25 to **$35.00**
Coffee mug, 3⅛", set of 4, from $50 to **$60.00**
Coffeepot, embossed applied spout, ornate handle, 7½", from $55 to **$65.00**
Condiment bowl, 2½" deep, w/saucer, 6¾" **$25.00**
Creamer, bulbous, 3½" **$16.00**
Creamer, ovoid shape, 3½" **$15.00**
Creamer & sugar bowl, 'y' handles, bulbous, 4¾", 3½", from $35 to **$40.00**
Cup & saucer, 'y' handle, from $7 to **$9.00**
Cup & saucer, angle handle, scalloped rims, from $6 to.**$8.00**
Cup & saucer, demitasse **$10.00**
Cup & saucer, farmer's; 4x5" (across handle), from $15 to...**$20.00**
Cup & saucer, Irish coffee; cylindrical cup, from $12 to **$16.00**
Cutting board, 14x9½", +stainless steel knife **$30.00**
Dish, leaf shape, 5¾x4" **$20.00**
Egg cup, double, 3¾", from $12 to **$15.00**
Ginger jar, 5" **$30.00**
Goblet, clear glass w/Blue Danube design, 7¼", set of 12...**$60.00**
Gravy boat, double spout, w/undertray, 3½x6", from $35 to **$40.00**
Gravy boat, 6⅜x9¾", from $65 to **$75.00**
Hurricane lamp, glass mushroom globe **$75.00**
Ice cream scoop, cutting blade, no mark **$50.00**
Inkstand, 2 lidded inserts, shaped base, banner mark, 9" L **$300.00**
Napkins, Sunnyweave, set of 4, from $25 to **$30.00**
Pitcher, bulbous w/flared spout, fancy handle, 5¼", from $25 to **$30.00**
Pitcher, bulbous w/flared spout, fancy handle, 6¼"...**$40.00**
Pitcher, milk; 'y' handle, 5¼", from $25 to **$30.00**
Plate, lattice rim, 8" **$15.00**
Plate, triangular, 9¾" L **$50.00**

Plate, 10¼", from $10 to..**$15.00**
Plate, 8¼", from $8 to **$11.00**
Platter, 12x8½", from $30 to **$40.00**
Platter, 14x10", from $55 to.......................................**$65.00**
Salt & pepper shakers, dome top w/bud finial, bulbous bottom, 5", pr **$35.00**
Salt & pepper shakers, 5 holes in salt, 3 in pepper, 5", pr.**$25.00**
Salt box, wooden lid, 4¾x4¾" **$50.00**
Snack plate & cup **$25.00**
Soup ladle, from $35 to..**$45.00**
Soup tureen, w/lid, from $135 to...............................**$150.00**
Spooner, 4¾x4" **$50.00**
Sugar bowl w/lid, ovoid shape, 5", from $18 to.........**$25.00**
Tablecloth, 50x70", +4 napkins...................................**$95.00**
Tazza, attached pedestal foot, banner mark, 4½x15", from $85 to **$95.00**
Tea tile/trivet, 6", from $18 to....................................**$25.00**
Teakettle, enamel, wood handle w/fold-down metal sides, 9x9½" **$25.00**
Teapot, 'y' handle, 6½", from $50 to............................**$60.00**
Temple jar, 10½" **$60.00**
Tidbit tray, 2-tier **$35.00**
Tidbit tray, 3-tier **$40.00**
Tray, fluted shell shape w/rolled end, sm...................**$45.00**
Undertray, for soup tureen **$45.00**
Vase, scalloped top, embossed design under rim, round foot, wide body, no mark, 6" **$20.00**

Blue Garland

During the 1960s and '70s, this dinnerware was offered as premiums through grocery stores. Its ornate handles, platinum trim and the scalloped rims on the flat items and the bases of the hollow ware pieces when combined with the 'Haviland' backstamp suggested to most supermarket shoppers that they were getting high quality dinnerware for very little. And indeed the line was of good quality, but the company that produced it had no connection at all to the famous Haviland company of Limoges, France, who produced fine china there for almost one hundred years. The mark is Johann Haviland, taken from the name of the founding company that later became Philip Rosenthal and Co. This was a German manufacturer who produced chinaware for export to the United States from the mid-1930s until well into the '80s. Today's dinnerware collectors find the delicate wreath-like blue flowers and the lovely shapes very appealing.

Bell, from $50 to...**$60.00**
Beverage sever (teapot/coffeepot), w/lid, 11", from $60 to...**$70.00**
Bowl, fruit; 5⅛" dia, from $4.50 to..............................**$6.00**
Bowl, oval, 10¾" L **$65.00**
Bowl, soup; 7⅝", from $9 to **$12.00**
Bowl, vegetable; 8½" dia, from $25 to **$35.00**
Butter dish, ¼-lb, from $45 to **$55.00**
Candlesticks, 3½x4", pr, from $75 to **$85.00**

Caserole, with lid, 12" wide, from $50.00 to $60.00.

Chamberstick, metal candle cup & handle, 6" dia **$75.00**
Coaster/butter pat, 3¾" dia, from $9 to.......................**$12.00**
Creamer, from $10 to..**$14.00**
Cup & saucer, flat, from $5 to **$8.00**
Cup & saucer, footed, from $9 to.................................**$12.00**
Gravy boat, w/attached underplate, from $30 to........**$40.00**
Plate, bread & butter; 6¼", from $3 to........................**$4.00**
Plate, dinner; 10", from $8 to.......................................**$10.00**
Plate, salad; 7¾" dia, from $7 to **$9.00**
Platter, 13", from $22 to...**$28.00**
Platter, 14½", from $30 to **$40.00**
Platter, 15½", from $45 to **$50.00**
Salt & pepper shakers, 4¼", pr, from $32 to..............**$38.00**
Sugar bowl, w/lid, from $15 to **$18.00**
Teakettle, porcelain w/stainless steel lid....................**$25.00**
Teapot, 7", from $55 to...**$65.00**
Tidbit tray, 1-tier...**$45.00**
Tidbit tray, 3-tier...**$90.00**

Blue Ridge Dinnerware

Blue Ridge has long been popular with collectors, and prices are already well established, but that's not to say there aren't a few good buys left around. There are! It was made by a company called Southern Potteries, who operated in Erwin, Tennessee, from sometime in the latter '30s until the mid-'50s. They made many hundreds of patterns, all hand decorated. Some collectors prefer to match up patterns, while others like to mix them together for a more eclectic table setting.

One of the patterns most popular with collectors (and one of the most costly) is called French Peasant. It's very much like Quimper with simple depictions of a little peasant man with his staff and a lady. But they also made many lovely floral patterns, and it's around these where most of the buying and selling activity is centered. You'll find roosters, plaids, and simple textured designs, and in addition to the dinnerware, some vases and novelty items as well.

Very few pieces of dinnerware are marked except for the 'china' or porcelain pieces which usually are. Watch for a similar type of ware often confused with Blue Ridge that is sometimes (though not always) marked Italy.

The values suggested below are for the better patterns. To evaluate the French Peasant line, double these figures; for the simple plaids and textures, deduct 25% to 50%, depending on their appeal.

If you'd like to learn more, we recommend *The Collector's Encyclopedia of Blue Ridge Dinnerware, Identification and Values*, by Betty and Bill Newbound.

Advisors: Bill and Betty Newbound (See Directory, Dinnerware)

Newsletter: *National Blue Ridge Newsletter*
Norma Lilly
144 Highland Dr., Blountsville, TN 37617

Ashtray, individual, from $20 to **$25.00**
Baking dish, divided, 8x13", from $25 to **$30.00**
Bowl, cereal/soup; 6", from $20 to **$25.00**
Bowl, flat soup; from $22 to **$25.00**
Bowl, fruit; 5¼", from $7 to **$9.00**
Bowl, mixing; lg, from $25 to **$30.00**
Bowl, mixing; med, from $20 to **$25.00**
Bowl, mixing; sm, from $15 to **$20.00**
Bowl, salad; 10½", from $70 to **$75.00**
Bowl, vegetable; divided, oval, 9", from $24 to **$27.00**
Bowl, vegetable; oval, 9", from $28 to **$35.00**
Bowl, vegetable; 8" dia, from $20 to **$25.00**
Butter dish, from $40 to **$45.00**
Cake lifter, from $30 to **$35.00**
Carafe, w/lid, from $100 to **$125.00**
Casserole, w/lid, from $50 to **$55.00**
Chocolate pot, from $250 to **$275.00**
Coffeepot, ovoid shape, from $125 to **$150.00**
Creamer, pedestal, from $55 to **$65.00**
Creamer, regular, from $15 to **$18.00**

Creamer and sugar bowl, Verna, footed, 3¾", $120.00.

Cup, dessert; glass, from $10 to **$12.00**
Cup & saucer, demitasse; from $40 to **$45.00**
Cup & saucer, jumbo, from $55 to **$65.00**
Custard cup, from $15 to **$18.00**
Egg cup, double, from $25 to **$30.00**
Gravy boat, from $25 to **$30.00**
Jug, batter; w/lid, from $85 to **$95.00**
Jug, syrup; w/lid, from $90 to **$95.00**
Pie baker, from $30 to **$35.00**

Pitcher, Alice, china, 6", from $150 to **$175.00**
Pitcher, Betsy, china, from $180 to **$195.00**
Pitcher, Charm House, from $200 to **$225.00**
Pitcher, Jane, from $120 to **$125.00**

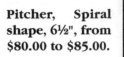
Pitcher, Spiral shape, 6½", from $80.00 to $85.00.

Plate, child's; from $120 to **$125.00**
Plate, Christmas Doorway, from $85 to **$90.00**
Plate, dinner; 10½", from $25 to **$30.00**
Plate, dinner; 9¼", from $20 to **$25.00**
Plate, divided, from $35 to **$45.00**
Plate, party; w/cup well & cup, from $40 to **$45.00**
Plate, Specialty, 11", from $125 to **$130.00**
Plate, Square Dance, 14", from $225 to **$250.00**
Plate, Still Life, 8½", from $30 to **$35.00**
Plate, Thanksgiving Turkey, from $80 to **$85.00**
Plate, 11½", from $45 to **$50.00**
Plate, 6", from $6 to **$8.00**
Plate, 8x8", from $18 to **$22.00**
Platter, 12½", from $22 to **$25.00**
Ramekin, w/lid, 5", from $25 to **$30.00**
Relish, Charm House, from $150 to **$160.00**
Relish, Palisades, from $50 to **$60.00**
Salad fork, from $45 to **$50.00**
Salad spoon, from $45 to **$50.00**
Salt & pepper shakers, Apple, 1¾", pr, from $25 to **$30.00**
Salt & pepper shakers, Blossom Top, pr, from $50 to **$55.00**
Salt & pepper shakers, Charm House, pr, from $125 to **$150.00**
Salt & pepper shakers, footed, tall, pr, from $80 to **$85.00**
Salt & pepper shakers, Good Housekeeping, pr, from $90 to **$95.00**
Salt & pepper shakers, Mallards, pr, from $325 to **$350.00**
Sconce, wall; from $75 to **$85.00**
Sherbet, from $25 to **$30.00**
Sugar, Rope Handle, w/lid, from $20 to **$25.00**
Sugar bowl, Colonial, open, sm, from $18 to **$22.00**
Sugar bowl, Woodcrest, w/lid, from $25 to **$30.00**
Tea tile, 3", from $40 to **$45.00**
Teapot, Charm House, from $275 to **$300.00**
Teapot, Colonial, from $125 to **$135.00**
Teapot, Good Housekeeping, from $175 to **$180.00**

Teapot, Palisades, from $95 to **$110.00**
Teapot, Snub Nose, from $180 to.............................**$190.00**

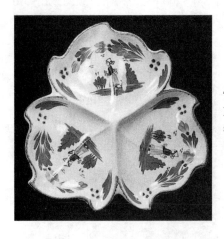

Tray, snack; French Peasant, Martha shape, 11½", from $300.00 to $325.00.

Tray, snack; Martha, from $155 to..............................**$165.00**
Tray, tidbit; 2-tier, from $25 to.....................................**$30.00**
Tray, tidbit; 3-tier, from $40 to.....................................**$45.00**
Tumbler, juice; glass, from $12 to **$15.00**
Vase, boot, 8", from $95 to **$110.00**
Vase, bud; from $150 to...**$160.00**

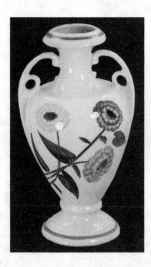

Vase, handled, 7½", from $90.00 to $95.00.

Vase, ruffled top, 9½", from $110 to..........................**$125.00**

Blue Willow Dinnerware

Blue Willow dinnerware has been made since the 1700s, first by English potters, then Japanese, and finally American companies as well. Tinware, glassware, even paper 'go-withs' have been produced over the years — some fairly recently, due to on-going demand. It was originally copied from the early blue and white wares made in Nanking and Canton in China. Once in awhile you'll see some pieces in black, pink, red, or even multicolor.

Obviously the most expensive will be the early English wares, easily identified by their backstamps. You'll be most likely to find pieces made by Royal or Homer Laughlin, and even though comparatively recent, they're still collectible, and their prices are very affordable.

For further study we recommend *Blue Willow Identification and Value Guide* by Mary Frank Gaston.

See also Homer Laughlin; Royal China.

Advisor: Mary Frank Gaston (See Directory, Dinnerware)

Newsletter: *American Willow Report*
Lisa Kay Henze, Editor
P.O. Box 900, Oakridge, OR 97463. Bimonthly newsletter, subscription: $15 per year, out of country add $5 per year

Newsletter: *The Willow Word*
Mary Berndt, Publisher
P.O. Box 13382, Arlington, TX 76094; Send SASE for information about subscriptions and the International Willow Collector's Convention

Ashtray, fish figural, marked Japan, 5" L, from $25 to ..**$30.00**
Bank, 3 stacked pigs, marked Japan, 7", from $65 to...**$75.00**
Batter jug, frosted glass, w/plastic lid, Hazel Atlas Glass Co, 9", from $75 to **$85.00**
Biscuit jar, Two Temples II pattern, Traditional border, w/lid & cane handle, marked Adderley, 4½", from $175 to...**$200.00**
Bone dish, crescent shape, marked Bourne & Leigh (EB & JEL) (English), 6¼" L, from $45 to........................**$55.00**
Bowl, console; glass w/etched Traditional pattern in green enamel, marked Cambridge Glass, 3½x11" dia, from $225 to..**$275.00**

Bowl, cream soup; 5¾", with 7" underplate, no mark, $35.00.

Bowl, muffin; w/lid, English, 3½x9" dia, from $150 to...**$175.00**
Bowl, pedestal base, marked John Tams Ltd (English), 5x9¼", from $130 to...**$160.00**
Bowl, rice; Two Temples II reversed pattern, marked Ridgway, 3x5¼", from $30 to **$35.00**
Bowl, soup/cereal; scalloped rim, Flow Blue Willow, marked Doulton, 7½", from $100 to................................**$120.00**
Bowl, undecorated pedestal foot, marked Holland, 4x7½", from $120 to...**$140.00**

Bowl, vegetable; beaded outer rim, marked Aynsley & Co (English), 9¼" dia, from $55 to **$65.00**

Bowl, vegetable; pink, marked Japan, 9¾" dia, from $25 to...**$35.00**

Bowl, vegetable; pink, scalloped edge, interior pattern, w/lid, marked Allerton (English), 6x12", from $260 to **$285.00**

Bowl, vegetable; Variant pattern decals, w/lid, marked Limoges China (American), 11x8½", from $55 to ..**$65.00**

Candle holder, square base & top, marked Doulton, 7½", pr, from $400 to..**$500.00**

Casserole baker, tab handled, square, marked Heritage Mint Ltd, 7" L **$15.00**

Chamberstick, scalloped edge, gold trim, marked Gibson & Sons (English), 5" dia, from $150 to **$175.00**

Cheese dish, w/lid, marked Wiltshaw & Robinson (English) **$225.00**

Clock, Traditional pattern w/pictorial border, 8-Day, German works, tin, from $150 to.....................................**$165.00**

Coaster, advertisement for Yorkshire Relish, unmarked English, 4" dia, from $35 to **$45.00**

Coffeepot, graniteware, unmarked, 6½", from $90 to..**$110.00**

Compote, footed, marked Shenango China, 3x6" dia, from $50 to..**$60.00**

Creamer, individual; scalloped edge, marked England, 2", from $40 to...**$45.00**

Creamer & sugar bowl, gold trim, unmarked Japanese, 3½", pr, from $50 to...**$60.00**

Cup, cream soup; Canton pattern, 2-handled, marked Wood & Son (English), 3", from $20 to **$25.00**

Cup, handleless, marked Pountney & Co (English), 3½" dia, from $75 to...**$85.00**

Cup, punch; Two Temples II pattern, Butterfly border, pedestal foot, unmarked English, 3", from $55 to **$65.00**

Cup & saucer, demitasse; marked Japan, 2½", from $14 to .**$18.00**

Cup & saucer, handleless, pink, unmarked, from $90 to ...**$100.00**

Dish, baking; Two Temples II Simplified pattern, line border, American, 3x8" dia, from $25 to............................**$30.00**

Drainer, meat; unmarked English, 6x6", from $100 to ..**$120.00**

Egg cup, double; Two Temples II pattern reversed, Butterfly border, unmarked, 3½", from $30 to.....................**$40.00**

Flatware, stainless steel w/plastic handle, Japanese, 4-pc place setting, from $45 to **$55.00**

Gravy boat w/attached underplate, scalloped edge, marked Allerton (English), 7½" L, from $150 to **$165.00**

Lamp, oil style w/glass shade, electric, marked Made in Japan, 7½", from $45 to **$55.00**

Mug, Farmer's Cup, heavy, marked Japan, 4", from $35 to **$40.00**

Planter, cat figural, marked Lipper & Mann Inc, 9¼", from $275 to...**$300.00**

Plate, grill; Traditional center & border patterns, marked Made in Japan, 10½" dia, from $20 to **$25.00**

Plate, Traditional center & border patterns, 10-sided panelled edge, Mulberry Willow, 9" dia, from $55 to **$65.00**

Plate, Turner center pattern, Scroll & Flower border, marked Ideal (American), 11" dia, from $20 to.................**$25.00**

Platter, Traditional center & border patterns, green, marked John Steventon & Sons (English), 8¾"x11", from $75 to...**$100.00**

Platter, Traditional center & border patterns, marked William & Samuel Edge (English), 14x11¼".....................**$250.00**

Spice set, 5 individual canisters, green tin w/blue tops & holder, Spanish names for spices, 3½", from $60 to **$75.00**

Spoon rack, rolling-pin style w/open planter pocket, 3 attached spoon hooks, unmarked Japanese, 9½" L, from $75 to...**$85.00**

Tea set, child's; plastic, Ideal Toys, 16-pc, MIB, from $80 to **$100.00**

Teakettle, enameled metal, Blue Willow Pantry Collection, marked Heritage Mint Ltd, Taiwan.......................**$30.00**

Teapot, Pictorial border, Traditional pattern, marked Myott Son & Co (English), 8", from $120 to **$140.00**

Teapot, Two Temples pattern on body, Butterfly border, unmarked, 3¼", 2-cup, from $50 to.....................**$60.00**

Tumbler, blue graphics, unmarked Jeannette Glass, ca 1949, 4", from $15 to...**$20.00**

Tumbler, clear glass w/wide band decoration, 5", from $16 to...**$20.00**

Tumbler, juice; ceramic, unmarked Japan, from $25 to ..**$30.00**

Pitcher, marked Japan, 6", $65.00.

Bookends

You'll find bookends in various types of material and designs. The more inventive their modeling, the higher the price. Also consider the material. Cast-iron examples, especially if in original polychrome paint, are bringing very high prices right now. Brass and copper are good as well, though elements of design may override the factor of materials altogether. If they are signed by the designer or marked by the manufacturer, you can about triple the price. Those with a decidedly Art Deco appearance are often good sellers. See *Collector's Guide to Bookends* by Louis Kuritzky (Collector Books) for more information.

Advisor: Louis Kuritzky (See Directory, Bookends)

American Legion, bronze, ca 1939, 8", pr..................**$115.00**

Angelus, iron, Hubley, 1925, 5½", $65.00 for the pair. (Photo courtesy Louis Kuritzky)

Appeal to the Great Spirit, Indian on horseback, gray metal, ca 1926, 7¼", pr..**$195.00**
Around the Globe, gray metal, K&O, ca 1930, 5¾", pr ..**$100.00**
Basket Case, bronze clad, ca 1930, 5½", pr **$125.00**
Best Foot Forward, cast gray metal, ca 1930, 5", pr.**$125.00**
Burro, iron, Hubley #492, ca 1925, 4", pr..................**$150.00**
Cape Cod Fisherman, iron, CT Foundry, 1928, 5½", pr..**$65.00**
Catwalk, aluminum, ca 1970, 3½", pr **$25.00**
Crane, in flight, gray metal, Dodge, ca 1946, 6¾", pr...**$75.00**
Crusaders, iron, Hubley #300, ca 1926, 5½", pr.........**$75.00**
Floral design, brass, ca 1925, 6" **$50.00**
Florentine, wood, ca 1985, 5¾", pr **$15.00**
Gladiators, bronze on marble base, ca 1932, 7¾", pr..**$600.00**
Goldfish, pottery, Rookwood, 1992, 4½", pr...............**$85.00**
Lincoln's Cabin, iron, Judd, ca 1925, 3¾", pr.............**$50.00**
Madrigal, gray metal w/bronze, 1925, 4½", pr...........**$75.00**
Nude on Book, iron, ca 1929, 8", pr.........................**$160.00**
Nude on Sphinx, bronze clad, ca 1925, 6", pr **$175.00**
Orphans, 2 puppies snuggle, iron, #272, ca 1923, 4½", pr **$100.00**
Polo Player, iron, Littco, ca 1928, 5½", pr **$85.00**
Ready for Flight, Cambridge Glass, ca 1940, 5½", pr..**$160.00**
Robin & Marian, gray metal on polished stone base, ca 1924, 7", pr..**$295.00**
Roses, leather, ca 1930, 5", pr....................................**$40.00**

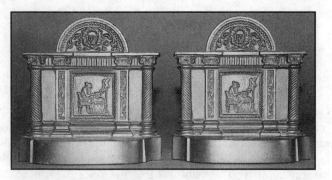

Spinning Scene, iron, 4⅜", $50.00. (Photo courtesy Louis Kuritzky)

Student Monk, gray metal, K&O, 1926, 7", pr...........**$150.00**
Tapestry Dancer, iron, ca 1925, 7¼", pr **$175.00**

The Hunter & His Dog, iron, Hubley #423, ca 1925, 6¼", pr..**$450.00**
The Mill, iron, Verona, ca 1925, 6¾", pr.....................**$60.00**
Thespian, iron, #140, ca 1925, 5½", pr **$115.00**

Books

Books have always fueled the mind's imagination. Before television lured us out of the library into the TV room, everyone enjoyed reading the latest novels. Western, horror, and science fiction themes are still popular to this day — especially those by such authors as Louis L'Amour, Steven King, and Ray Bradbury, to name but a few. Edgar Rice Burrough's Tarzan series and Frank L. Baum's Wizard of Oz books are regarded as classics among today's collectors. A first edition of a popular author's first book (especially if it's signed) is avidly sought after, so is a book that 'ties in' with a movie or television program.

Dick and Jane readers are fast becoming collectible. If you went to first grade sometime during the 1930s until the mid-1970s, you probably read about their adventures. These books were used all over the United States and in military base schools over the entire world. They were published here as well as in Canada, the Philippine Islands, Australia, and New Zealand; there were special editions for the Roman Catholic parochial schools and the Seventh Day Adventists', and even today they're in use in some Mennonite and Amish schools.

On the whole, ex-library copies and book club issues (unless they are limited editions) have very low resale values.

Besides the references in the subcategory narratives that follow, for further study we also recommend *Old Book Value Guide; Collector's Guide to Children's Books, 1850 to 1950, Vols I and II,* by Diane McClure Jones and Rosemary Jones; and *Whitman Juvenile Books* by David and Virginia Brown. All are published by Collector Books.

Magazine: *AB Bookman's Weekly*
P.O. Box AB, Clifton, NJ 07015; 201-772-0020 or fax: 201-772-9281. Sample copies: $10.

Big Little Books

The Whitman Publishing Company started it all in 1933 when they published a book whose format was entirely different than any other's. It was very small, easily held in a child's hand, but over an inch in thickness. There was a cartoon-like drawing on the right-hand page, and the text was printed on the left. The idea was so well accepted that very soon other publishers — Saalfield, Van Wiseman, Lynn, World Syndicate, and Goldsmith — cashed in on the idea as well. The first Big Little Book hero was Dick Tracy, but soon every radio cowboy, cartoon character, lawman, and space explorer was immortalized in his own adventure series.

When it became apparent that the pre-teen of the '50s preferred the comic-book format, Big Little Books were finally phased out; but many were saved in boxes and stored in attics, so there's still a wonderful supply of them around. You need to watch condition carefully when you're buying or selling. For further information we recommend *Big Little Books, A Collector's Reference and Value Guide*, by Larry Jacobs (Collector Books).

Newsletter: *Big Little Times*
Big Little Book Collectors Club of America
Larry Lowery
P.O. Box 1242, Danville, CA 94526; 415-837-2086

Alice in Wonderland, Whitman #759, EX.....................**$55.00**
Andy Panda & Tiny Tom, Whitman #1425, 1944, EX.**$40.00**
Blondie in Hot Water, Whitman #1410, NM **$45.00**
Buccaneers, Whitman #1646, 1958, VG **$15.00**
Buck Jones in The Fighting Code, Whitman, 1934, EX.**$40.00**
Bugs Bunny & His Pals, Whitman #1496, EX.............**$50.00**
Convoy Patrol, Whitman #1469, 1942, NM **$40.00**
Cowboy Stories, Whitman #724, NM...........................**$60.00**

Detective Dick Tracy and the Spider Gang, **Whitman #1446, EX, $75.00.**

Dick Tracy Out West, Whitman #723, VG **$95.00**
Donald Duck Up in the Air, Whitman #1486, NM **$55.00**

Flash Gordon on the Planet Mongo, **EX/NM, $95.00.**

Flint Roper & the Six Gun Showdown, Whitman #1467, EX...**$30.00**
G-Man in Action, Saalfield #1173, 1940, VG...............**$30.00**
Gang Busters in Action, Whitman #1451, 1938, VG ...**$35.00**
Green Hornet Returns, Whitman #1496, 1941, NM...**$145.00**
Jungle Jim, Whitman, #1138, 1936, NM **$75.00**
Lone Ranger & the Silver Bullets, Whitman #1499, EX+ **$60.00**
Mickey Mouse & the Stolen Jewels, Whitman #1464, NM .**$75.00**
Nancy & Sluggo, Whitman #1400, EX.........................**$75.00**
Our Gang on the March, Whitman #1451, 1942, NM .**$65.00**

Return of Tarzan, Whitman #1102, 1938, EX+.............**$75.00**
Silver Streak, Whitman #1155, 1935, VG.....................**$40.00**
Spike Kelly of the Commandos, Whitman #1467, NM.**$45.00**
Tarzan & the Ant Men, Whitman #1444, NM..............**$75.00**
Tom Mix in Hoard of Montezuma, Whitman, 1937, NM...**$35.00**
Tom Mix in Stranger From the South, Whitman, 426 pages, NM **$35.00**
Two-Gun Montana, Whitman #1104, VG.....................**$25.00**
Wash Tubbs in Pandemonia, Whitman #751, EX........**$45.00**
Zane Grey's Tex Thorn Comes Out of the West, Whitman #1440, EX...**$30.00**

Children's Miscellaneous Books

Above the Blue, Bruce Publishing, 1958, EX................**$9.00**
Adventure Rare & Magical, Phyllis Fenner, Pitz illustrations, Knopf, 1st edition, 1945, EX **$15.00**
Anderson's Fairy Tales, Hans Christian Anderson, translated by Lucas & Paull, Grosset & Dunlap, cloth cover, 1945, EX...**$15.00**
Bear's Surprise Party, Eager Reader, #809, 1st edition, EX **$8.00**
Black Beauty, Anna Sewell, paper-on-boards cover w/wraparound illustrations, Eichenberg illustrations, ca 1947, EX...**$20.00**
Black Beauty, Anna Sewell, Whitman Classics, 1955, EX...**$8.00**
Blue Willow, Doris Gates, Lantz illustrations, Viking, 1940, EX...**$35.00**
Book of Food, Josephine Van Dolzen Pease, Grosset & Dunlap, 1938, EX...**$12.00**
Buddy the Taxi, Eleanor Corwin, Rand McNally Elf Books, #564, 1958, EX **$10.00**
Buffalo Bill, Shannon Garst, Fox black & white illustrations, Messner, 1948, EX...**$10.00**
Call of the Wild, Jack London, Whitman Classics, 1970, EX...**$4.00**
Christopher Bunny, Golden Story Book, #3, 1949, EX.**$15.00**
Country Bunny & the Little Gold Shoes, Heyward DuBose, Flack illustrations, Houghton, 1939, EX................**$35.00**
Deputy Dawg & the Space Man, Wonder Books, 1961, full-color art, hardcover, NM **$15.00**
Donna Parker, A Spring To Remember; Marcia Martin, Whitman Adventure, 1960, EX.................................**$6.00**
Famous American Ships, Golden Library of Knowledge, #7703, A edition, EX...**$6.50**
Flip & the Cows, Morgan Dennis, Viking, 1942, 63 pages, EX...**$20.00**
Green Ginger Jar, Clara Ingram Judson, Brown illustrations, cover illustration, Houghton, 1949, EX **$15.00**
Gulliver's Travels, Jonathan Swift, wraparound cover illustration by Watson, Grosset & Dunlap, 1947, ca 1947, EX ...**$20.00**
Henry Huggins, Beverly Cleary, Darling illustrations, 1950, 1st edition, 155 pages, EX...**$35.00**
Hungry Moon, Patricia Ross, Merida color illustrations, Knopf, 1946, oversize, 74 pages, EX.....................**$20.00**
Jamba the Elephant, Theodore J Waldeck, Wiese illustrations, Viking, 1942, EX...**$15.00**

Johnny Longfoot, Catherine Basterman, Bobbs Merrill, black & white illustrations by Chappell, 1947, EX **$25.00**

King Is Born, diecut, Bonnie Book, #4005, 1954, EX.**$12.00**

King Philip the Indian Chief, Esther HT Averill, 1950, EX..**$15.00**

Koos the Hottentot, Josef Marais, Stahlhut illustrations Knopf, 1945, 196 pages, EX **$20.00**

Lester's Creation (Critter Country), Happy Days Book, #3455, 1987, EX...**$3.00**

Little King, Otto Soglow, John Martins' House, 1945, oversize, 29 pages, EX **$40.00**

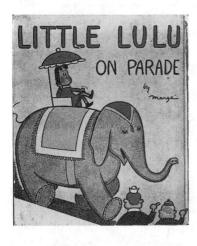

Little Lulu, by Marge (Marjorie Henderson Buell), Curtis, 1935, VG, $50.00. (Photo courtesy Diane McClure Jones and Rosemary Jones)

Little Women, Louisa May Alcott, Grosset & Dunlap, paper-on-boards cover, 8 color plates, ca 1947, EX **$20.00**

Lupe Goes to School, Esther Brann, black & white illustrations, Macmillan, 1930, EX.....................................**$15.00**

Merry Adventures of Robin Hood, Howard Pyle, black & white illustrations, 8 color plates, Grosset & Dunlap, ca 1947, EX..**$20.00**

Mickey Mouse Crusoe, Whitman, 1936, softcover, VG .**$40.00**

Mickey Mouse in Ye Olden Days, pop-up, Blue Ribbon Press, 1934, G **$110.00**

Mike Mulligan & His Steam Shovel, 1939 Weekly Reader Edition, EX...**$15.00**

Monkey w/a Notion, Glenn Blough, DeCuir black & white illustrations, Holt, 1946, 88 pages, EX.....**$15.00**

Mrs Polly's Party, Winifred Bromhall, pictorial cover, Knops, 1949, oversize, EX.....................................**$20.00**

New Home for Snowball, Eager Reader, #800, 1st edition, EX...**$5.00**

Noddy Goes to Toyland, by Enid Blyton, Sampson London, small size, EX, $35.00. (Photo courtesy Diane McClure Jones and Rosemary Jones)

Pepper Moon, Esther Wood, Bannon illustrations, Longmans, 1940, EX...**$20.00**

Peter Gets His Wish, Bonnie Book, #4032, 1947, w/dust jacket, EX **$45.00**

Pirates in the Deep Green Sea, Eric Linklater, Reeves illustrations, map end papers, London, 1949, EX...........**$15.00**

Prince Valiant/Companions in Adventure, Nostaglia Press, 1974, w/dust jacket, NM..**$25.00**

Rabbit Hill, Robert Lawson (author & illustrator), NY, 1944, EX...**$45.00**

Rooster Crows, Maude & Miska Pertersham (author/illustrators), Macmillan, 1945, 1st edition, EX.................**$65.00**

Sawdust in His Shoes, Eloise Jarvis McGraw, Coward McCann, 1950, EX...**$15.00**

Seven Bear Skins, Erick Berry, Winston, black & white illustrations, 1948, 275 pages, EX.............................**$15.00**

Seventeenth Summer, Maureen Daly, Dodd, 1942, 1st edition, EX...**$35.00**

Spoodles, Jolly Book, #201, 1952, EX **$7.00**

Tall Book of Fairy Tales, Eleanor Vance, black & white Sharp illustrations, Harper, 1947, 5x11", EX **$40.00**

Tangletown Tale, Read-Along-With-Me Story Book, Bonnie Books, 1966, EX...**$10.00**

Terry & the Pirates, Milton Caniff (author & illustrator), NY, 1946, EX...**$35.00**

Thimble Theatre Starring Popeye, Big Big Book, Whitman, 1935, hardbound, 318 pages, EX..........................**$65.00**

Treasures Long Hidden, Arthur Chrisman, Yap illustrations, Dutton, 1st edition, 1941, 302 pages, EX.............**$15.00**

TV Pals, Little Owl Book, #101, EX..............................**$5.00**

Twenty-One Balloons, William Pene Du Bois (author & illustrator), Viking, 1947, EX...**$35.00**

Two Jungle Books, Rudyard Kipling, paste-on picture on cover, Garden City, 1950 edition, EX....................**$20.00**

Walter the Lazy Mouse, Marjorie Flack (author & illustrator), Doubleday, 1941, oversize, EX..............................**$30.00**

Whitey's Sunday Horse, Glen Rounds (author & illustrator), Grosset, 1942, EX...**$15.00**

Yogi Bear & the Colorado River, Modern Promotions, #39018, EX...**$3.00**

Your Friend the Policeman, Miss Frances Ding Dong School Book, #200, EX **$8.00**

Juvenile Series Books

Ameliaranne Keeps Shop, Constance Heward, Pearce illustrations, London & McKay, 1928, EX **$30.00**

Augustus & the Mountains, Henderson Le Grand, Bobbs Merril, 1941, oversize, about 130 pages, EX.........**$25.00**

Baseball Joe at Yale, Lester Chadwick, Cupples & Leon, 1920s, EX...**$15.00**

Betty Gordon at Boarding School, Alice B Emerson, Cupples & Leon, 1930s, sm, EX **$10.00**

Bewitched, the Opposite Uncle; William Johnson, Whitman Authorized TV Edition, 1970, EX...........................**$20.00**

Blondie & Dagwood's Snapshot Clue, black & white illustrations, Whitman Authorized Editions, 1940s, EX ...**$15.00**

Blue Ridge Billy (Regional Stories), Lois Lenski (author & illustrator), Lippincott, 1946, EX **$20.00**

Bobbsey Twins at the Seashore, Laura Lee Hope, Whitman, 1954, EX **$6.00**

Boy's King Arthur, Sidney Lanier, Scribner Classics, Wyeth color plates, 1947 edition, EX..................... **$50.00**

Boys of Bellwood School, Frank V Webster, Cupples & Leon, 1920s, EX **$15.00**

Clue in the Patchwork Quilt (Judy Bolton), Margaret Sutton, Grosset & Dunlap, 1930s, EX **$10.00**

Clue of the Leaning Chimney (Nancy Drew), Carolyn Keene, black & white illustrations, plain cloth cover, 1949, EX **$20.00**

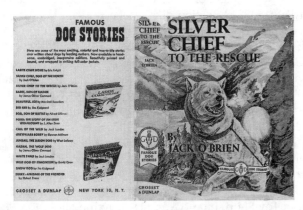

Famous Dog Stories Series, various authors, Grosset & Dunlap, ca 1940s, with illustrated dust jacket, $20.00 (without, $7.00). (Photo courtesy Diane McClure Jones and Rosemary Jones)

Five Little Peppers & How They Grew, Margaret Sidney, Whitman Fiction for Young People, 1955, EX........ **$6.00**

Gene Autry & the Ghost Riders, Lewis B Patton, Whitman Authorized Edition, 1955, EX **$20.00**

Ghost at the Waterfall (Vicki Barr), Helen Wells, Grosset, 1930s, EX **$15.00**

Ginny Gordon & the Lending Library, Julie Campbell, Whitman Mystery, 1971, EX **$4.00**

Girl Scouts' Canoe Trip, Edith Lavell, 1930s, EX **$10.00**

Grace Harlowe's First Year at Overton College, Jessie Graham Flower, cloth cover, Altemus, 1915, EX................. **$10.00**

Hardy Boys, Mystery of the Flying Express, FW Dixon, Grosset & Dunlap, 1920s, EX **$15.00**

Kim Aldrich, Miscalculated Risk; Jinny McDonnell, Whitman, 1972, EX **$4.00**

Little Women, Louisa May Alcott, Whitman Classics, 1955, EX **$5.00**

Lucky Bucky in Oz, John R Neill (author & illustrator), cloth cover, 1942, EX **$55.00**

Meg, The Ghost of Hidden Springs; Holly Beth Walker, Whitman #1530, 1970, EX **$5.00**

Motor Boys on the Atlantic, Clarence Yung, illustrations, Cupples & Leon, 1920s, EX **$15.00**

Mystery of the Brass Bound Box (Rick & Ruddy), Howard Garis, McLoughlin, 1930s, 256 pages, EX **$30.00**

Mystery of the Locked Room, Carolyn Keene, Dana Girls Mystery Series, Grosset, 1930s, EX **$10.00**

Outdoor Girls in the Air, Laura Lee Hope, Whitman, 1933, EX **$10.00**

Outdoor Girls on a Hike, Laura Lee Hope, Whitman Books for Girls, 1939, EX **$15.00**

Radio Boys at the Sending Station, Allen Chapman, Grosset & Dunlap, 1910s, EX **$10.00**

Raggedy Ann Helps Grandpa Hoppergrass, McLoughlin Westfield Classic, black & white & color illustrations, EX **$40.00**

Raggedy Ann in the Magic Book, Johnny Gruelle, Justin & Worth Gruelle illustrations, 1939, EX.....................**$40.00**

Robinson Crusoe, Whitman Classics, 1930s, EX..........**$10.00**

Roy Rogers & the Enchanted Canyon, Jim Rivers, Whitman Authorized Edition, 1954, EX **$25.00**

Rushton Boys at Treasure Cove, Spencer Davenport, Whitman Adventures for Boys, 1916, EX.............**$10.00**

Ruth Fielding Homeware Bound, Alice B Emerson, Cupples & Leon, 1920s, sm **$15.00**

Secret Sky Express (Slim Tyler Air Stories), Richard Stone, Cupples & Leon, 1920s, EX **$15.00**

Story of Dr Doolittle, Hugh Lofting (author & illustrators), Lippincott, 1948 edition, EX **$15.00**

Timber Trail Riders, Long Trail North; Michael Murray, Whitman, 1963, EX **$8.00**

Tom Slade at Temple Camp, Percy K Fitzhugh, Whitman, 1917, EX **$20.00**

Triplets Become Good Neighbors, Bertha Moore, Eerdmans, 1940s, EX **$15.00**

Trixie Belden & the Black Jacket Mystery, Kathryn Kenny, Whitman, 1961, EX **$12.00**

Walt Disney's Annette, Sierra Summer; Doris Schroeder, Whitman Authorized Edition, 1960, EX.................**$10.00**

Walton Boys in High Country, Hal Burton, Whitman Boy's Adventure Series, 1960, EX **$5.00**

Little Golden Books

Everyone has had a few of these books in their lifetime; some we've read to our own children so many times that we still know them word for word, and today they're appearing in antique malls and shops everywhere. The first were printed in 1942. These are recognizable by their blue paper spines (later ones had gold foil). Until the early 1970s, they were numbered consecutively; after that they were unnumbered.

First editions of the titles having a 25¢ or 29¢ cover price can be identified by either a notation on the first or second pages, or a letter on the bottom right corner of the last page (A for 1, B for 2, etc.). If these are absent, you probably have a first edition.

Condition is extremely important. To qualify as mint, these books must look just as good as they looked the day they were purchased. Naturally, having been used by children, many show signs of wear. If your book is only lightly soiled, the cover has no tears or scrapes, the inside pages have only small creases or folded corners, and the spine is still strong, it will be worth about half as much as one in mint condition. A missing cover makes it worthless. Additional damage would of course lessen the value even more.

A series number containing an 'A' refers to an activity book, while a 'D' number identifies a Disney story.

For more information we recommend *Collecting Little Golden Books* by Steve Santi (who provided us with our narrative material).

Advisor: Ilene Kayne (See Directory, Books)

Aladdin - The Magic Carpet Ride, #107-92, A edition, EX...**$6.00**
Alice in Wonderland, Disney, #103-1, 14th edition, EX ..**$2.00**
Baby's Day Out, #113-01, A Edition, EX......................**$15.00**
Bert's Hall of Fame, #321, 4th edition, EX....................**$2.00**

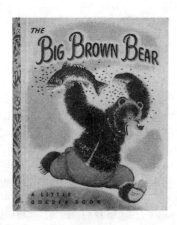

The Big Brown Bear, #89, 1949, NM, $15.00.

Bongo, #D9, E edition, EX.................................**$10.00**
Book of God's Gifts, #112, 4th edition, EX....................**$6.00**
Bugs Bunny at the Easter Party, #183, A edition, EX .**$12.00**
Bugs Bunny Birthday, #98, A edition, EX.....................**$14.00**
Chitty-Chitty Bang-Bang, #581, 4th edition, EX............**$7.00**
Christmas Carols, #26, B edition, EX...........................**$12.00**
Corky Hiccups, #503, 2nd edition, EX **$7.00**
Counting Rhymes, #361, B edition, EX **$3.00**
Donald Duck & Santa Claus, Mickey Mouse Club, #D27, C
    (1st) edition, EX..**$18.00**
Donald Duck & the One Bear, Disney, #102-3, 4th edition,
    EX..**$3.00**
Donald Duck Christmas Tree, #D39, D edition, EX......**$9.00**
Donald Duck in Disneyland, #D44, A edition, EX......**$12.00**
Fire Engines (Fisher-Price edition), #310-88, A edition,
    EX **$12.00**
Five Little Firemen, #301, P (N is 1st) edition, EX **$7.00**
Fly High, #597, 1st edition, EX.................................**$10.00**
Forest Hotel, #350, 6th edition, EX............................**$2.00**
Heidi, #358, A edition, EX..**$8.00**
Horses, #459, B edition, EX **$8.00**
Large & Growly Bear, #510, 3rd edition, EX **$6.00**
Little Golden Cut-Out Christmas Manger, #176, A edition,
    EX..**$14.00**
Little Golden Picture Dictionary, #90, A edition, EX...**$15.00**
Little Lulu, #476, 2nd edition, EX **$16.00**
Lively Little Rabbit, blue binding, #15, 5th edition, EX.**$18.00**

Madeline, #186, A edition, EX **$20.00**
Manni the Donkey, #D75, A edition, EX **$10.00**
Mary Poppins, #D113, A edition, EX............................**$12.00**
Merry Shipwreck, #170, A edition, VG......................**$12.00**
Mickey Mouse & Pluto Pup, #D76, 18th edition (E is 1st),
    EX...**$4.00**
Mother Goose, blue spine, war edition, 24-page, #4, 2nd edi-
    tion, EX..**$20.00**
My Christmas Treasury, #144, 1st edition, EX...............**$6.00**
My First Counting Book, #434, F edition, EX **$4.00**
New Baby, #291, 5th edition, EX................................**$6.00**
New Friends for the Saggy Baggy Elephant, #131, 2nd edi-
    tion, EX...**$6.00**
Oscar's New Neighbor, #109-67, A edition, EX.............**$5.00**
Our Flag, #388, A edition, EX.....................................**$8.00**
Peter & the Wolf, no gold spine, #D5, I edition, EX....**$8.00**
Pick Up Sticks, #461, A edition, EX...........................**$16.00**
Pinocchio, Mickey Mouse Club Book, #D8, N (1st) edition,
    EX...**$20.00**
Pokey Little Puppy's First Christmas, Big Golden Book,
    #10395, 6th edition, EX **$10.00**
Riddles, Riddles, #490, A edition, EX **$12.00**
Road Runner, #122, 6th edition, EX **$2.00**
Robin Hood, #D126, 1st edition, EX **$12.00**
Rudolph the Red-Nosed Reindeer, #331, A edition, EX ..**$10.00**
Sailor Dog, #156, unknown edition, EX.....................**$12.00**
Santa's Toy Shop, blue cover, #D16, 16th edition, EX..**$8.00**
Scamp, #D63, E edition, EX..**$8.00**
Shy Little Kitten, blue cover, #494, C (1st) edition, EX.**$9.00**
Tale of Peter Rabbit, illustrated by Adriana Saviozzi, #307-10,
    MCMXCII, EX...**$5.00**
Three Bears, #47, 38th edition, EX.............................**$8.00**
Thumbelina, #300-55, A edition, EX............................**$3.00**
Tom & Jerry's Party, #235, 5th edition **$8.00**
Topsy Turvy Circus, #161, A edition, G.......................**$5.00**
We Help Mommy, #305-42, S edition, EX....................**$5.00**
Where Did the Baby Go?, #116, 5th edition, EX..........**$3.00**
Wild Animal Babies, #332, 8th edition **$8.00**
Wild Kingdom, #151, 1st edition, EX **$10.00**
Willie Found a Wallet, #205-56, B edition, EX............**$6.00**
Winnie the Pooh - A Tight Squeeze, #10859, 22nd edition,
    EX...**$5.00**
Woody Woodpecker Drawing Fun for Beginners, #372, A edi-
    tion, EX...**$17.00**

Movie and TV Tie-Ins

Circus Boy, War on Wheels; Dorothea J Snow, Whitman
    Authorized TV Edition, 1958, EX.......................**$25.00**
Combat! The Counterattack; Franklin M Davis Jr, Whitman
    Authorized TV Adventure, 1964, EX **$15.00**
Dr Kildare Assigned to Trouble, Robert C Ackworth,
    Whitman Authorized TV Adventure, 1963, EX.....**$12.00**
Dragnet Case Stories, Richard Deming, Whitman Authorized
    TV Edition, 1957, EX..**$20.00**
Fury & the Mystery at Trapper's Hole, Troy Nesbit, Whitman
    Authorized TV Edition, 1959, EX.......................**$18.00**

Gilligan's Island, William Johnston, Whitman Authorized TV Edition, 1966, EX **$18.00**

Green Hornet in the Case of the Disappearing Doctor, Whitman, 1966, VG..**$25.00**

Gunsmoke, Showdown on Front Street; Paul S Newman, Whitman Authorized TV Adventure, 1969, EX **$15.00**

Have Gun Will Travel, Barlow Meyers, Whitman Authorized TV Edition, EX **$25.00**

High Chaparral, The Apache Way; Steve Frazee, Whitman Authorized TV Edition, 1969, EX.........................**$15.00**

I Spy, Message From Moscow; Brandon Keith, Whitman Authorized TV Edition, 1966, EX...........................**$25.00**

Janet Lennon, Adventure at Two Rivers; Barlow Meyers, Whitman Authorized TV Adventure, 1961, EX **$12.00**

Land of the Giants, Flight of Fear; Carl Henry Rathjen, Whitman Authorized TV Adventure, EX **$20.00**

Land of the Giants, Pyramid #1846, 1968, paperback, EX..**$15.00**

Land of the Giants, The Hot Spot; Pyramid #1921, 1968, EX...**$15.00**

Leave It to Beaver, Cole Fannin, Whitman Authorized TV Adventure, 1962, EX...**$30.00**

Man From UNCLE, Affair of the Gunrunner's Gold; Whitman Authorized TV Adventure, 1967, EX **$12.00**

Mod Squad, The Assignment: The Arranger; Richard Deming, Whitman Authorized TV Adventure, 1969, EX **$12.00**

Monkees, Who's Got the Button; William Johnston, Whitman Authorized TV Adventure, 1968, EX **$25.00**

Real McCoys & Danger at the Ranch, Cole Fannin, Whitman Authorized TV Adventure, 1961, EX **$15.00**

Rifleman, Cole Fannin, Whitman Authorized TV Adventure, 1959, EX..**$20.00**

Voyage to the Bottom of the Sea, Raymond F Jones, Whitman Authorized TV Adventure, 1965, EX **$20.00**

Walt Disney's Zorro, Steve Frazee, Whitman Authorized TV Edition, 1958, EX **$25.00**

Bonanza, Killer Lion, #1568, Steve Frazee, published by Whitman, 212 pages, $18.00. (Photo courtesy David and Virginia Brown)

Bottle Openers

A figural bottle opener is one where the cap lifter is an actual feature of the subject being portrayed — for instance,

the bill of a pelican or the mouth of a four-eyed man. Most are made of painted cast iron or aluminum; others were chrome or brass plated. Some of the major bottle-opener producers were Wilton, John Wright, L&L, and Gadzik. They have been reproduced, so beware of any examples with 'new' paint. Condition of the paint is an important consideration when it comes to evaluating a vintage opener.

For more information, read *Figural Bottle Openers, Identification Guide*, by the Figural Bottle Opener Collectors. Number codes in our descriptions correspond with their book.

Advisor: Charlie Reynolds (See Directory, Bottle Openers)

Club: Figural Bottle Opener Collectors
Linda Fitzsimmons
9697 Gwynn Park Dr., Ellicott City, MD 21043; 301-465-9296

Newsletter: *Just for Openers*
John Stanley
3712 Sunningdale Way, Durham, NC 27707-5684; 919-419-1546. Quarterly newsletter covers all types of bottle openers and corkscrews

Alligator, F-136, cast iron, VG.......................................**$70.00**

Alligator & boy, F-134, Wilton Products, VG+ **$175.00**

Amish boy, F-31, painted cast iron, rare, 1953, 4x2" ..**$225.00**

Billy goat, F-74, painted cast iron, J Wright, from $150 to **$180.00**

Bulldog head, F-425, cast iron, ca 1900, 4x3¾x1½", NM..**$75.00**

Canada goose, F-105, cast iron, multicolored paint, Wilton Products, EX...**$80.00**

Clown head, F-417, cast iron, EX original paint, wall mount, from $75.00 to $90.00.

Cocker spaniel, F-80, brown & white, EX.................**$120.00**

Cowboy w/guitar, F-27, aluminum, M **$15.00**

Dachshund, F-83, brass **$50.00**

Donkey, F-60, cast iron, paint traces...........................**$20.00**

Elephant, F-49, cast iron, pink paint, J Wright, EX **$65.00**

False teeth, F-420. painted cast iron, common, 2⅜x3⅜"...**$75.00**

Fish, F-162, pot metal, no paint...................................**$20.00**

Flamingo, F-120, cast iron, hollow, Wilton Products, EX, from $100 to...**$135.00**

Foundryman, F-29, painted cast iron, J Wright, EX.....**$95.00**

Jimmy Carter, 1975, M **$55.00**

Lobster, F-167, cast iron, EX paint.............................$32.00
Negro w/smooth pupils, F-402c, brass......................$45.00
Nude native girl kneeling, zinc, 1950s.....................$35.00
Old Snifter, 1933 ....$160.00
Palm tree, F-21, brass $25.00
Parrot, F-108, long blue tail, painted cast iron, J Wright,
    5¼"...$65.00
Parrot, F-112, Wilton Products, sm, VG $65.00
Peacock, F-103, brass $55.00
Pelican, F-129, cast iron, EX paint...........................$75.00
Sailor, F-17, painted cast iron, 1950s, 3¾", EX..........$100.00
Salted pretzel, F-230 ....$50.00
Sea gull, F-123, cast iron, worn paint, Wright, VG......$65.00
Setter, F-79, cast iron, EX multicolored paint $80.00
Shovel, F-221, brass..$20.00
Signpost Drunk, F-11, cast iron, VG paint..................$18.00
Skunk, F-92, cast iron, original black & white paint, J
    Wright $165.00

Boyd Crystal Art Glass

After the Degenhart glass studio closed (see the Degenhart section for information), it was bought out by the Boyd family, who added many of their own designs to the molds they acquired from the Degenharts and other defunct glasshouses. They are located in Cambridge, Ohio, and the glass they've been pressing in the more than 350 colors they've developed since they opened in 1978 is marked with their 'B in diamond' logo. All the work is done by hand, and each piece is made in a selected color in limited amounts — a production run lasts only about eight weeks or less. Items in satin glass or an exceptional slag are especially collectible, so are those with hand-painted details.

Note: An 'R' in the following lines indicates an item that has been retired.

Advisor: Joyce Pringle (See Directory, Boyd)

Club: Boyd's Art Glass Collectors Guild
P.O. Box 52, Hatboro, PA 19040-0052

Airplane, Mirage...$11.00
Angel, Green Bouquet..$18.50
Angel, Vaseline Carnival..$22.00
Artie Penguin, Chocolate..$12.00
Artie Penguin, Classic Black......................................$15.00
Artie Penguin, Rosie Pink...$9.00
Bow Slipper, Aqua Diamond $8.75
Bow Slipper, Avocado $8.50
Bunny Salt, Mountain Haze $17.50
Bunny Salt, Peacock Blue $8.50
Candy the Carousel Horse, Bernard Boyd Black $15.00
Candy the Carousel Horse, Chocolate Carnival..........$11.00
Candy the Carousel Horse, Purple Frost.....................$8.00
Cat Slipper, Rosewood $10.00
Cat Slipper, Rosie Pink...$9.50

Chick Salt, Antique White $115.00
Chick Salt, Nutmeg Carnival.....................................$9.50
Chick Salt, Thanksgiving $15.00
Eli & Sarah, Chocolate...$12.00
Eli & Sarah, Tangy Lime...$11.00
Elizabeth, Alpine Blue (R)...$8.50
Elizabeth, Cashmire Pink (R) $15.00
Fuzzy Bear, Capri Blue (R)..$9.00
Fuzzy Bear, Oxford Gray, (R).....................................$10.00
JB Scotty, Daffodil (R)..$35.00
JB Scotty, Mirage (R)..$12.00
JB Scotty, Mountain Haze (R).....................................$32.00
JB Scotty, Mulberry Mist (R)......................................$80.00
JB Scotty, Spring Surprise (R).....................................$85.00
Jeremy Frog, Chocolate (R).......................................$10.00
Jeremy Frog, Pacifica (R)..$9.25
Lil Luck the Unicorn, Classic Black Carnival (R).........$15.00
Lil Luck the Unicorn, Sunkist Carnival (R)...................$9.00
Louise, Alpine Blue, hand painted.............................$26.00
Louise, Ice Green..$80.00
Louise, Persimmon..$25.00
Melissa, Peacock Blue $8.00
Nancy Doll, Pacifica Green $9.25
Nancy Doll, Vaseline..$13.50
Skippy Dog, Cornsilk..$6.00
Skippy Dog, Pippin Green...$8.00
Taffy the Carousel Horse, Spring Surprise.................$18.00
Taffy the Carousel Horse, Vaseline Carnival..............$28.50
Tucker Car, Cobalt Carnival $18.00
Tucker Car, Peach...$12.50
Willie the Mouse, Buckeye..$9.50
Willie the Mouse, Pale Orchid...................................$8.25
Zack the Elephant, Bermuda Slag $45.00
Zack the Elephant, Ebony...$40.00
Zack the Elephant, Sandpipper $15.00

Boyds Bears and Friends

In 1992 Gary Lowenthal began designing cold-cast sculptural interpretations of his now-famous Bears, Tabbies, Moose, etc. These sculptures are extraordinary in detail and highly sought after by collectors. For more information, color photos, and an extensive listing of current values, we recommend *Rosie's Secondary Market Price Guide to Boyd's Bears and Friends* by Rosie Wells.

Values are given for examples in mint condition and retaining their original boxes.

Advisor: Rosie Wells (See Directory, Boyd's Bears)

Bearstone, 1993, Neville, 2E/2002 ....$81.00
Bearstone, 1994, Elliot & the Tree, 2E/2241.............$135.00
Bearstone, 1994, Justina & M Harrison, 1E/2015........$90.00
Bearstone, 1994, Sebastian's Prayer, 1E/2227 ....$95.00
Bearstone, 1995, Wilson, 1E/2261 ....$55.00
Bearstone, 1996, Emma the Witchy Bear, 1E/2770 .....$57.00

Bearstone, 1997, Maynard & Melvin, 2E/27720 ....**$40.00**
Bearstone, 1997, Stonewall, 1E/228302 ....**$40.00**
Dollstone, 1996, Annie, 1E/3599 ....**$45.00**
Dollstone, 1996, Patricia w/Molly, 2E/3501 ....**$48.00**
Dollstone, 1996, Rebecca w/Elliot, 1E/3509 ....**$58.00**
Dollstone, 1997, Edmund w/Shelly, Pem Ed/3527 ......**$70.00**
Dollstone, 1997, Laura w/Jane, 1E/3522 ....**$48.00**
Folkstone, 1994, Chilly & Son, 1E/2811 ....**$70.00**
Folkstone, 1994, Nikki, 1E/2801 ....**$63.00**
Folkstone, 1995, Beatrice, 2E/2836 ....**$34.00**
Folkstone, 1996, Elmo Tex Beefcake, 1E/2853 ....**$45.00**
Folkstone, 1997, Krystal Isinglass, 1E/28206 ....**$46.00**

Brastoff, Sascha

Sascha Brastoff was flamboyant, talented, and a man of many facets. He had already found a niche in sculpting when he joined the Army's Air force in 1942 and became involved in costume and scenery design, performing, drawing war bond posters, and creating Christmas displays and murals. He emulated Carmen Miranda and became involved with many movies, hob-nobbing with the movie stars along the way.

In 1947 Sascha realized his dream of producing ceramics when he opened a small operation in West Los Angeles, California. In 1953 Nelson Rockefeller and several other business men adept at mass production techniques joined forces with Sascha and built a pottery on Olympic Boulevard in Los Angeles.

Over his lifetime Sascha worked in such mediums as resins, oils, enamels, and textiles. He designed jewelry, dinnerware, and later he created holograms.

Sascha designed hand-painted china with names such as Allegro, Night Song, and Roman Coin. A pottery dinnerware line called Surf Ballet was made in pink, blue, or yellow and dipped in real gold or platinum to produce a marbleized swirl effect. Rooftops, Merbaby, and Star Steed are three of his artware patterns that are popular today.

Sascha's talents enabled him to flourish with each decade, moving with ease from one to the other and successfully changing motifs, mediums, and designs as was warranted. He created a Western line that was popular in the late 1940s and early 1950s, and just before the poodle craze hit in the 1950s, he had the foresight to introduce his poodle line. The same was true for smoking accessories.

Sascha's involvement in any artistic field was never superficial. His creations were all marked with some form of his name. In 1940 pieces at the Clay Club were signed with a full signature or 'Sascha'; costume designs at 20th Century Fox (1946 – 47) were signed 'Sascha'; war bonds and posters were also signed 'Sascha' or 'Pvt.' or Sgt. Brastoff.' By 1947 he had turned to commercial production and hired other artists to hand decorate his designs. 'Sascha B' became the standard mark — usually placed on the front, lower left or right, with no underside mark or logo. When he opened his new studio in 1953, a chanticleer, the name Sascha Brastoff

(be careful not to confuse this mark with the full signature), California, U.S.A., the copyright symbol, and a hand-written style number, all in gold, were used on the bottom with 'Sascha B.' on the front or topside of the item.

When Brastoff left his company in 1962, a handwritten 'R' in a circle (registered trademark symbol), 'Sascha B,' and a handwritten style number came into use. The chanticleer may be found with this mark. Brastoff died on February 4, 1993. For additional information consult *The Collector's Encyclopedia of Sascha Brastoff* by Steve Conti, A. DeWayne Bethany, and Bill Seay. Another source of information is *The Collector's Encyclopedia of California Pottery (Second Edition)* by Jack Chipman. Both are available from Collector Books.

Advisor: Susan Cox (See Directory, California Pottery)

Ashtray, Americana line, girl w/flowers, #056A, 7" **$70.00**
Ashtray, artichoke shape, enamel, 5½" **$30.00**
Ashtray, Minos design, hooded, 8" **$125.00**
Ashtray, Mosaics line, fish shape, 17" **$225.00**
Ashtray, Star Steed, 4x5" **$45.00**
Bowl, ballerina, 3-footed, 2¼x10" **$150.00**
Bowl, cereal; Night Song porcelain, 6" **$35.00**
Candle holder, shell shape, white foam finish, lg **$200.00**
Canister, tea; w/lid, #C43, 13" **$300.00**
Cigarette box, Star Steed **$65.00**
Cigarette holder, pipe shape, Abstract #080 ....**$125.00**
Coffeepot, Jewel Bird line, long handle, 15" **$220.00**
Cup & saucer, Surf Ballet, silver & pink on white **$25.00**
Dish, Alaska line, polar bear, square, 3½" **$40.00**
Dish, Alaska line, seal half out of water, footed, oblong, 2¼x7½" **$65.00**
Dish, fruit pattern, early, low, square, 11¼" **$100.00**
Dish, lady at beach, whimsical, free-form fish shape, footed, full signature, 10" **$850.00**
Figurine, horse, platinum on matt pink, ca 1957, 10½" ..**$250.00**
Figurine, Merbaby, white foam finish **$350.00**

Figurine, rooster, textured and shaded thick gold leaf glaze, full signature, 17", $800.00.

Gravy boat, Smoke Tree earthenware, w/underplate .**$80.00**
Obelisk w/lid, Abstract Originals, full signature, 21" ..**$975.00**
Patio lamp/candle holder, abstract face in gold, 9½" .**$150.00**
Plate, dinner; Winrock porcelain, 11" **$45.00**
Plate, salad; Night Song porcelain, 9" **$35.00**
Sculpture, horse head, satin-matt crackle, wood base,
    7½"...**$400.00**
Server, Rooftops line, free-form, 13" **$75.00**
Teapot, black w/gold leaves, 8¼x12" **$150.00**

Tray, horse, presentation piece dated 1950, signed Sascha B, 11x11", $185.00.

Vase, Abstract Originals line, straight sides, 9" **$100.00**
Vase, Alaska line, Eskimo, 13½"................................**$325.00**
Vase, chalice shape, abstract in gold, 6" **$85.00**
Vase, floral; Abstract Originals line, colored bands, 20"..**$250.00**
Vase, Star Steed, 9½" **$100.00**
Vase/planter, Rooftops line, free-form, 5½x7½"..........**$90.00**
Wall mask, African native, 9½"..................................**$550.00**

Brayton Laguna

Durlin E. Brayton founded this pottery in Laguna Beach, California, in 1927. His marriage to Ellen (Webb) Webster Grieve brought two extraordinary talents together, and they became not only husband and wife but business partners as well. At one point the company employed more than 125 workers and 20 designers. But when imports flooded the country after World War II, they found themselves struggling to stay afloat. Eventually, they (as well as many other small California companies) could no longer compete, and the business ceased operations in 1968.

Many marks were used throughout Brayton's history, and some of them are significant to various lines. For example, the very early hand-turned pieces made from 1927 to 1930 were incised 'Laguna Pottery' in Durlin Brayton's handwriting. These items include vases, ashtrays, and dinnerware. Though made in limited quantities, they are beginning to attract collector interest. Brayton's artware line called Calasia has become very collectible just over the past several months. It is decorated in relief with feather-like designs and spheres that resemble children's marbles. It was made in Tropical Fern or Asian White, but the green is far more plentiful. Its finish is smooth and pleasing to the touch.

In any of Brayton's lines, the wallhanging items are hard to find. Wallhanging items such as the Blackamoors can command values as high as $500.00. Webton Ware wallhangings are becoming popular as they remind one of 'country' which is highly collectible today. One of their most popular lines is the Children's series, created by Lietta J. Dodd. Generally, if supply exceeds demand, prices remain low, but even though these figures seem to be abundant, their prices are relatively high and became so over a comparatively short period. Both white and pink clays were used, and there were several in the line — some of them posing in playful positions and all of them wearing clothing with colorful eye-appealing glazes. The name of each child is included with the mark along with the copyright symbol and 'Brayton Pottery.' Look carefully for the mark, which is sometimes faint or obscure. Paper labels were sometimes used as well.

Carole Safholm designed sculptures for Brayton including Indian and Peruvian pieces such as voodoo figures, matadors, drummers, elephants, and so forth. Her pieces are well received today. Blackamoors are also popular. Ruth Peabody was responsible for this line, which though limited is a favorite among collectors. Andy Anderson created the Hillbilly series (his most notable being the prized shotgun wedding group) as well as the purple bull, cow, and calf, which are even more desirable than the wedding group when found in other colors. Webton Ware is inexpensive and is now attracting considerable interest. It depicts men and women planting trees, flowers, etc., and other scenes of farmlands and the people involved. Usually these pieces have a white body decorated with various pastels including blue, green, and pink.

Webb Brayton died in 1948, and Durlin died just three years later.

For further study, read *The Collector's Encyclopedia of California Pottery (Second Edition)* by Jack Chipman (Collector Books).

Advisor: Susan Cox (See Directory, California Pottery)

Candy jar, chicken shape, sm.....................................**$225.00**
Chamberstick, red, handmade, 3¼" **$250.00**
Chess piece, Castle, 1946, 10½" **$200.00**
Cookie jar, chicken shape, 10" **$400.00**
Cookie jar, Christina, Swedish maid, ca 1941, 11" **$550.00**
Cookie jar, Mammy, hand-decorated, being reproduced,
    value for marked original **$1,200.00**
Figurine, abstract man w/cat, satin-matt black, ca 1957,
    21"..**$600.00**
Figurine, African native drummer, stained bisque & white
    crackle glaze, 1950s, 10½" **$125.00**
Figurine, bear seated, front legs apart, 1950s, 3½" **$75.00**
Figurine, cat, recumbent, head up, 4½x6½" **$85.00**
Figurine, cow, w/sticker, caramel glaze w/black accents,
    8x6" **$400.00**
Figurine, Dutch boy & girl, pr...................................**$250.00**
Figurine, elephant, woodtone & white crackle, ca 1957,
    13½" **$200.00**

Figurine, Eric & Inga, Swedish boy & girl, pr $300.00

Figurine, Ferdinand the Bull, Walt Disney series, paper label, 7½x8".................................**$500.00**

Figurine, fighting pirates, dark brown-stained bisque w/colored & crackle glazes, ca 1956, pr **$650.00**

Figurine, Gay Nineties Series, bar scene, 9x8½", $145.00.

Figurine, gent in top hat & cigar store Indian, ca 1940, 9½" **$850.00**

Figurine, Gepetto, Walt Disney series, 8" **$800.00**

Figurine, head & shoulders sculpture in matt black or white, 12x13", minimum value.......................................**$600.00**

Figurine, Jiminy Cricket, Walt Disney series, 3" **$600.00**

Figurine, lady in pink underclothes, on phone beside chair, early 1940s, 9½"...**$250.00**

Figurine, Little Boy Blue **$275.00**

Figurine, Little Red Riding Hood **$275.00**

Figurine, Lovers in Cab, w/coachman, Gay Ninties series, ca 1941, 7½x11"..**$350.00**

Figurine, Maestro, at piano w/sm vase attached & chanteuse (singer), 3-pc set, minimum value **$1,500.00**

Figurine, Mexican man, yellow poncho, w/sombrero, 9" ..**$250.00**

Figurine, Mexican peasant couple, textured bisque w/high glaze, 12½"...**$225.00**

Figurine, monkey male & female, white crackle w/stained bisque faces, 13", pr **$650.00**

Figurine, mule, w/yoke, 7¼x10" **$250.00**

Figurine, Pedro, Mexican boy w/yellow sombrero, scarf across shoulder, 6½"...**$200.00**

Figurine, Pinocchio, Walt Disney series, 6" **$500.00**

Figurine, pirate sitting on treasure chest, 9" **$450.00**

Figurine, Pluto, howling, Walt Disney series, 6" **$180.00**

Figurine, Pluto, sniffing ground, Walt Disney series, 3¼x6" **$150.00**

Figurine, quail, turquoise, beige, black speckles, 12" ..**$135.00**

Figurine, Rosita, Mexican girl w/flower basket, 5½" .**$100.00**

Figurine, Sambo & Petunia, Black boy & girl, pr **$600.00**

Figurine, St Bernard, stands w/head turned, late 1930s..**$200.00**

Figurine, toucan, polychrome high glaze, 9"............**$200.00**

Figurine, toucan, woodtone w/high glaze, 9" **$125.00**

Figurine, voodoo drummer, stained bisque, crackle glass & slip decoration, 13"..**$450.00**

Flower holder, sea horse w/sm pot at back, white, turquoise, pink, blue, 9" **$200.00**

Flower holder, Swedish woman, ca 1939, 11½" **$350.00**

Flowerpot, dark purple, 5½"....................................**$95.00**

Pitcher, blue, 5"...**$250.00**

Plate, eggplant glaze, handmade, early, 9"................**$125.00**

Salt & pepper shakers, Chef & Jemima, ca 1945, pr.**$150.00**

Tile, blue, fanciful trees, blue, black & yellow w/purple background, square, 6½" **$400.00**

Tile, Mexican man sleeping, cacti & tree nearby, square, 6½" **$450.00**

Tile, white & yellow mushrooms on blue background, square, 4½" **$300.00**

Vase, bud; blue w/entwined snake, 8" **$400.00**

Vase, waisted neck, bulbous body, yellow, 5½".......**$250.00**

Wall hanging, man standing, arms over head, Webton Ware mark, 13" **$275.00**

Breweriana

Breweriana refers to items produced by breweries which are intended for immediate use and discard, such as beer cans and bottles, as well as countless items designed for long-term use while promoting a particular brand. Desirable collectibles include metal, cardboard, and neon signs; serving trays; glassware; tap handles; mirrors; coasters; and other paper goods.

Breweriana is generally divided into two broad categories: pre- and postprohibition. Preprohibition breweries were numerous and distributed advertising trays, calendars, etched glassware, and other items. Because American breweries were founded by European brewmasters, preprohibition advertising often depicted themes from that region. Brewery scenes, pretty women, and children were also common.

Competition was intense among the breweries that survived prohibition. The introduction of canned beer in 1935, the postwar technology boom, and the advent of television in the late 1940s produced countless new ways to advertise beer. Moving signs, can openers, enameled glasses, and neon are prolific examples of postprohibition breweriana.

A better understanding of the development of the product as well as advertising practices of companies helps in evaluating the variety of breweriana items that may be found. For example, 'chalks' are figural advertising pieces which were made for display in taverns or wherever beer was sold. Popular in the 1940s and '50s, they were painted and glazed to resemble carnival prizes. Breweries realized in addition to food shopping, women generally assumed the role of cook — what better way to persuade women to buy a particular beer than a cookbook? Before the advent of the bottle cap in the early 1900s, beer bottles were sealed with a porcelain stopper or cork. Opening a corked bottle required a corkscrew which often had a brewery logo.

Prior to the advent of refrigeration, beer was often served at room temperature. A mug or glass was often half warm beer and half foam. A 1" by 8" flat piece of plastic was used to scrape foam from the glass. These foam scrapers came in various colors and bore the logo of the beer on tap.

Before prohibition, beer logos were applied to glassware by etching the glass with acid. These etched glasses often had ornate designs that included a replica of the actual brewery or a bust of the brewery's founder. After prohibition, enameling became popular and glasses were generally 'painted' with less ornate designs. Mugs featuring beer advertising date back to the 1800s in America; preprohibition versions were generally made of pottery or glass. Ceramic mugs became popular after prohibition and remain widely produced today.

Tap handles are a prominent way to advertise a particular brand wherever tap beer is sold. Unlike today's ornate handles, 'ball knobs' were prominent prior to the 1960s. They were about the size of a billiard ball with a flat face that featured a colorful beer logo.

The books we recommend for this area of collecting are *World of Beer Memorabilia* by Herb and Helen Haydock; *Vintage Bar Ware* by Stephen Visakay; and *Huxford's Collectible Advertising*. (All are published by Collector Books.)

See also Bar Ware; Beer Cans.

Advisor: Dan Andrews (See Directory, Breweriana)

Club: Beer Can Collectors of America
747 Merus Ct., Fenton, MO 63026
Annual dues: $27; although the club's roots are in beer can collecting, this organization offers a bimonthly breweriana magazine featuring many regional events and sponsors an annual convention; http://www.bcca.com

Ashtray, Ortels, plaster, 8", EX, $40.00; Bank, Lone Star, plaster, VG, $35.00.

Ashtray, Anheuser-Busch, brass emblem w/red-enameled A-&-eagle logo in relief, VG+ $60.00
Bank, Erin Brew Standard Beer, chalkware barrel shape w/black bands, gold lettering, EX, 8x6" dia $20.00
Beer pail, Anheuser-Busch, straight-sided porcelain metal w/bale handle, white A-&-eagle decal, 1930s (?), 4", VG+ $220.00
Blimp, Genesee Beer, Good Beer, blow-up, 1970s, 14x30", NM $25.00

Book, Schlitz Brewing Company, Quality Control Story, 1940s, 20-page, EX...$10.00
Cash register mount, Grain Belt Beer, lighted, early 1970s, 15x7x5", NM $25.00
Cash register mount, Schlitz Beer, rotating globe w/clock, lighted, plastic w/metal base, 14x10x7", NM........$55.00
Charger, Budweiser, Say When, couple pouring beer into chafing dish, 1930s, 16" dia, VG.........................$200.00
Clock, Budweiser, wristwatch shape w/Bud Man telling time w/arms, face about 9" dia, EX..............................$75.00
Clock, Budweiser King of Beers, plastic light-up pocket watch shape, 17x12x4", NM................................$100.00
Clock, Pabst Blue Ribbon, brown plastic grandfather style w/Roman numerals, Good Old Time Beer..., 1960s, 20x12", EX $50.00
Clock, Schmidt's Light Beer, Lucite tips rotate colors, 1960s, 14x4", EX+ $40.00
Clock, Walter's Beer, wood-tone barrel shape w/black lettering & gold trim, 12", EX...$75.00

Decanter, Hamms, ceramic, 1973, $30.00. (Photo courtesy Dan Andrews)

Display, Anheuser-Busch, chalkware, waiter w/white shirt, black pants & yellow apron, medal around neck, 20", EX...$190.00
Display, Bud Man figurine, hard foam w/2 capes & string, 19", NM...$165.00
Display, Goebel, chalkware, colorful rooster holding top hat & facing bottle on beveled base, EX....................$85.00
Display, Hanley Export Beer, chalkware, hand holding bottle, 1940s, 14x6", EX+..................................$140.00
Display, Pabst.../At Popular Prices, metal bartender figure balancing 4 mugs on arm, w/bottle, 1970s, 15x14", EX $85.00
Display, Rolling Rock Premium Beer, chalkware horse rearing up on rocks w/raised lettering, 1950s, 11", EX $50.00
Display, Schlitz, chalkware, Bart holding bottle, 1950s, 18", VG+ $35.00
Display, Schmidt's of Philadelphia Beer — Ale, cast metal barrel & bartender figure w/2 mugs on base, 1950s, 8", EX...$35.00
Display sign, Hamm's, molded plastic Hamm's Bear leaning on beer can, 12½x9", NM $30.00

Foam scraper holder, Crown Premium Lager Beer, plastic, 1950s, EX+ $25.00

Foam scraper holder, Piel's Beer, 2 cast-metal elves wrapped around keg on beveled base, multicolored, 1940s, 6x9", G $75.00

Foam scraper holder, Rheingold Extra Dry Lager Beer, plastic, 1950s, 11x3x5", EX $30.00

Knife/corkscrew, Anheuser-Busch, embossed, EX $75.00

Lamp, hanging; Seagram's Extra Dry Gin, plastic w/tin frame, lighted, w/mounting bracket, 12x6" $30.00

Light globe, Anheuser-Busch on Draught, milk glass, round w/flat sides, A-&-eagle logo decal, 8" dia, VG+ .$230.00

Light-up display, Draft-Brewed Blatz Now at Local Prices..., molded plastic can & bottle men at keg, 1960s, 19x20", VG $165.00

Light-up display, Hamm's/Refreshing As the Land of Sky Blue Waters, gold-framed lake scene on base, 1950s, 8x11", VG $150.00

Light-up display figure, Spuds MacKenzie, vinyl, NM .$150.00

Lighter, Schlitz Beer can shape, 1960s, 5", EX $15.00

Lights, hanging; Schlitz on Draft, plastic, 1970s, 8x12", pr .$65.00

Menu cover, National Premium Beer, 1960s, 9x11½", unused $5.00

Menu holder, Budweiser/Makes Our Good Food Taste Even Better, framed image of waiter on heavy paper, 1950s, EX $6.00

Mug, Budweiser Clydesdale, Ceramarte, 1984, 8", NM ..$20.00

Mug, Hamms, Octoberfest, ceramic, 1973, 8", EX $15.00

Paperweight, Schlitz, glass, round & beveled w/encased brewery scene, VG $100.00

Print, Anheuser-Busch, Westward Ho, framed, EX ...$200.00

Salt & pepper shakers, Blatz Beer, mini bottles, pr $20.00

Salt & pepper shakers, Bud Man, Ceramarte, EX, pr.$200.00

Salt & pepper shakers, Falstaff Beer, mini bottles, 1950s, pr $21.00

Sign, Ballantine Draught Beer, pressed wood, dated 1951, 10x14", EX $25.00

Sign, Budweiser King of Beers/Preferred Everywhere, tin/cardboard stand-up, glass on modern design, 17x15", VG+ $80.00

Sign, Burgermeister Beer, for displaying prices, lighted, plastic, 1965, 5x12x24", NM $25.00

Sign, Drewry's Old Stock Ale, composition, round w/lettering on red band around Mounty w/horse, 1940s, 13½", VG $75.00

Sign, Genny Genny Genny Beer & Light, lighted w/clock, plastic, early 1990s, 21x11x3", EX+ $15.00

Sign, light-up, Schmidt's Cold Beer/Take One Beautiful Beer Home, shows frosty mug in snow, metal, 1960s, 29x12", EX $30.00

Sign, neon; Anheuser-Busch/St Louis/Beer lettered on aluminum frame around Budweiser in neon lettering, 9x28", NM $300.00

Sign, neon; Bud Dry, plastic-encased neon letters atop housing marked Cold Filtered Draft, red & blue, 23", EX $40.00

Sign, neon; Schlitz, plastic globe shape, 1970s, 19x20", NM $165.00

Sign, Old Style Beer, lighted, plastic, 1970s, 17x11x5", NM+ $50.00

Sign, Piel's Real Draft Beer, tin on cardboard, self-standing, 1970s, 14x17", NM $10.00

Sign, plaque, composition, Schlitz/No Bitterness/Just the Kiss of Hops, bottle & hops on wood-grain, 17x11", VG+ $50.00

Sign, Rheingold Extra Dry Lager Beer, 1960s Miss Rheingold Candidate, lighted, plastic, 3x14x18", EX $25.00

Sign, Rolling Rock Premium Beer, Chateaugay, KY Derby Winner, 1963, pressed wood, 11x14", EX+ $40.00

Sign, Schmidt's of Philadelphia, lighted, plastic on metal frame, early 1960s, 20x13x4", NM $45.00

Sign, wall plaque; Budweiser King of Beers, lighted, early 1960s, 14x19", NM+ $55.00

Sign, Walter's Family Beer, multicolored, w/string hanger, cardboard, 7x12", NM+ $40.00

Sign, Wiedemann Fine Beer, 3-D, lighted, plastic, 1960s, 15x10", NM $25.00

Stein, Anheuser-Busch, ceramic, by Gertz, 1988, 8", NMIB $60.00

Tap handle, Holihan's Light Ale, plastic, 1960s, NM $6.00

Tap knob, Bud Man figure w/arms up as if flying, vinyl, NM $20.00

Thermometer, Ortlieb's Famous Beer, tin on cardboard, 1960s, NM $60.00

Tip tray, Budweiser King of Beers, red & white w/red lettering & logo, 1950s, 4x6", EX $15.00

Tip tray, Miller High Life the Champagne of Bottle Beer, red, yellow & white w/black trim, ornate border, 1952, 4x6", EX $15.00

Towel rack, backbar, 10 folding wire arms attached to molded composition piece w/bartender & bottles, 1950s, 6x10", VG $30.00

Tray, allegorical scene w/A-&-eagle logo, decorative rim, 11x13" oval, VG $130.00

Tray, Budweiser/Ask Your Customers To Make the Test..., waiter & tray, deep rim, 13" dia, VG+ $90.00

Tray, Buffalo Co-Operative Brewing Co Beer/Ale/Porter, 2 bottles on draped ground, gold trim on deep rim, round, EX+ $100.00

Tray, National Bohemian Salutes the Tall Ships, 1976, 16½", NM $15.00

Tray, Pabst Blue Ribbon Beer, ribbon surrounded by barley & hops, 1990s, 15" dia, EX+ $12.00

Tray, The Stag Brewery, pre-prohibition factory scene, reproduction, 1976, 16½" dia, EX+ $22.00

Sign, Miller High Life, embossed rim, red emblem in center, 20x24", EX, $100.00.

Breyer Horses

Breyer horses have been popular children's playthings since they were introduced in 1952, and you'll see several at any large flea market. Garage sales are good sources as well. The earlier horses had a glossy finish, but after 1968 a matt finish came into use. You'll find smaller domestic animals too. They are evaluated by condition, rarity, and desirability; some of the better examples may be worth a minimum of $150.00. Our values are for average condition; examples in mint condition are worth from 10% to 15% more.

For more information and listings, see *Schroeder's Collectible Toys, Antique to Modern* (Collector Books); and *Breyer Animal Collector's Guide, Second Edition,* by Felicia Browell. Our advisor is the author of several articles for *The Model Horse Gazette* and *Western Horseman* magazine on model collecting, values, and care.

Advisor: Carol Karbowiak Gilbert (See Directory, Breyer Horses)

Action Stock Horse Foal, chestnut leopard appaloosa, 1989-93, Traditional scale **$15.00**
Arabian Foal, gray, 1973-82, Classic scale....................**$18.00**
Arabian Stallion, dapple gray, 1975-76, Stablemate scale.**$33.00**
Arabian Stallion, Desert Arabian Family, bay, 1992-94, Classic scale **$13.00**
Balking Mule, bay/chestnut, 1968-73, Traditional scale .**$120.00**
Belgian, smoke, 1965-71, Traditional scale **$80.00**
Black Beauty, black, 1979-88, Traditional scale **$26.00**
Bucking Bronco, black, 1966-73, 1975-76, Classic scale .**$42.00**
Buckshot, Hickock, blue roan pinto, 1995, Traditional scale..**$28.00**
Clydesdale, chestnut, 1984-88, Little Bit scale **$12.00**
Clydesdale Foal, chestnut, 1969-89, Traditional scale .**$13.00**
Clydesdale Stallion, Laddie II, black pinto, 1996-current, Traditional scale **$22.00**
Draft Horse, dark or light sorrel, 1976-87, Stablemate scale **$10.00**
El Pastor, Tobe, Rocky Mountain Horse, chocolate sorrel, 1995-96, Traditional scale **$21.00**
Family Arabian Mare, bay, 1967-74, Traditional scale.**$24.00**
Family Arabian Stallion, Realto, light gray, 1996, Traditional scale **$20.00**
Fighting Stallion, alabaster, 1961-64, Traditional scale...**$92.00**
Five Gaitor, Project Universe, chestnut pinto, 1987-89, Traditional scale **$33.00**
Foundation Stallion, Lakota Pony, alabaster w/blue markings, 1992, Traditional scale **$37.00**
Fury Prancer, palomino, 1956-63, Traditional scale **$70.00**
Hanoverian, Gifted, bay, 1994, Traditional scale.........**$52.00**
Indian Pony, buckskin, 1970-72, Traditional scale....**$165.00**
John Henry, dark bay, 1988-90, Traditional scale **$30.00**
Jumping Horse, Starlight, dark bay, 1994, Traditional scale **$37.00**
Lady Phase, Night Deck, Black Horse Ranch, black, 1992, Traditional scale **$38.00**
Lady Roxanna, Cinnamon, bay appaloosa, 1996, Traditional scale **$21.00**

Lipizzan Stallion, alabaster, 1975-80, Classic scale **$30.00**

Master Crafter Mantlepiece clock decorated with Western horse, minimum value, $75.00. (This product was abandoned when the clock company returned the horse mold in lieu of payment. The company then went on to manufacture Breyer Animal Creations.) (Photo courtesy Carol Karbowiak Gilbert)

Midnight Sun, Tennesse Walker, High Flyer, chestnut pinto, 1995-96, Traditional scale **$22.00**
Morgan, Lippitt Pegasus, red bay, 1994-95, Traditional scale **$25.00**
Morgan Mare, chestnut, 1976, Stablemate scale **$30.00**
Morganglanz, Samsung Woodstock, Westphalian, chestnut, 1996-current, Traditional scale **$20.00**
Mustang, Black Horse Ranch, palomino, 1988, Traditional scale **$80.00**
Pacer, Dan Patch, red bay, 1990, Traditional scale **$40.00**
Phar Lap, Hobo, buckskin, 1991-92, Traditional scale.**$26.00**
Polo Pony, bay, 1976-82, molded woodgrain base, Classic scale **$45.00**
Porcelain Shire, black, 1993, limited edition of 2,500, Traditional scale **$165.00**
Proud Arabian Foal, alabaster, 1956-60, Traditional scale...**$26.00**
Proud Arabian Stallion, mahogany bay, 1971-80, Traditional scale **$30.00**
Quarter Horse Gelding, buckskin, 1961-80, Traditional scale **$31.00**
Quarter Horse Stallion, Appaloosa, black appaloosa, 1985-88, Little Bit scale **$11.00**
Quarter Horse Stallion, chestnut, 1976, Stablemate scale ..**$30.00**
Race Horse, Derby Winner, chestnut, 1954-66/67, Traditional scale **$80.00**
Rearing Stallion, bay, 1965-80, Classic scale **$20.00**
Running Foal, Little Bub, red bay, 1994-95, Traditional scale **$15.00**
Running Mare, smoke/charcoal, 1961-70, Traditional scale **$42.00**
Running Stallion, Sky Blue Unicorn, turquoise blue, 1985, Traditional scale **$64.00**
San Domingo, Black Gold, black, 1985, Traditional scale..**$95.00**
Seabiscuit, bay, 1976-90, Stablemate scale...................**$10.00**
Secretariat, chestnut, 1987-95, Traditional scale **$21.00**
Shetland Pony, alabaster, 1960-72, Traditional scale...**$26.00**
Stock Horse Foal, American Buckskin Stock Horse Foal, buckskin, Traditional scale **$20.00**
Stock Horse Mare, Appy Mare, red roan/leopard appaloosa, 1991-92, Traditional scale **$26.00**

Stormy, Marguerite Henry's Stormy, chestnut pinto, 1977-current, Traditional scale **$10.00**

Stud Spider, black appaloosa, 1978-89, Traditional scale ..**$30.00**

Swaps, chestnut, 1975-90, Classic scale **$18.00**

Thoroughbred Mare, chestnut, 1975-87, Stablemate scale **$10.00**

Western Horse, Tic Toc, alabaster, 1992-94, Traditional scale **$25.00**

Western Pony, Black Beauty, black, 1956-63, Traditional scale **$60.00**

Wood-grain foal, #909, 6½", $75.00.

Other Animals

Basset Hound, matt dark brown, 1966-68 ....**$68.00**
Bear, matt brown, 1967-71 ....**$45.00**
Bear Cub, matt brown, 1967-71 ....**$25.00**
Bighorn Ram, matt tan & white, 1969-80 ....**$82.00**
Boxer, 1958-74, several color variations, ea **$40.00**
Charolais Bull, matt alabaster, 1975-95 ....**$25.00**
Guernsey Cow, tan & white pinto pattern, 1972-73 ...**$62.00**
Hampshire Hog, matt black & white, 1980 ....**$112.00**
Jasper the Market Hog, matt white & gray, 1974-present...**$12.50**
Kitten, black & white, 1995-96 ....**$20.00**
Poodle, woodgrain, 1961-64 ....**$295.00**
Pronghorn Antelope, matt brown & white, 1971-76.**$115.00**

British Royal Commemoratives

While seasoned collectors may prefer the older pieces using circa 1840 (Queen Victoria's reign) as their starting point, even present-day souvenirs make a good inexpensive beginning collection. Ceramic items, glassware, metalware, and paper goods have been issued on the occasion of weddings, royal tours, birthdays, christenings, and many other celebrations. Food tins are fairly easy to find, and range in price from about $30.00 to around $75.00 for those made since the 1950s.

We've all seen that items related to Princess Diana have appreciated rapidly since her untimely and tragic demise, and in fact collections are being built exclusively from memorabilia marketed both before and after her death. For more information, we recommend *British Royal Commemoratives* by Audrey Zeder.

Advisor: Audrey Zeder (See Directory, British Royalty Commemoratives)

Album, Royal Family by Panini, completely filled, 1984..**$50.00**

Bank, Charles & Diana 1981 wedding portrait, blue, Adams, round, 3" **$50.00**

Bank, Prince William 1984 birthday, multicolor decoration, Aynsley, round **$55.00**

Beaker, wedding; Charles & Diana, glass, multicolored portrait, 4⅝" **$25.00**

Beer mat, pub; Elizabeth II, 1977, cardboard, 4x4" **$5.00**

Bell, Andrew & Sarah 1986 wedding, Westminister Abbey, brown decoration, wood handle **$45.00**

Bell, Charles & Diana 1981 wedding, black & white portrait, multicolored decoration, Sadler **$50.00**

Book, The Queen & Princess Anna, Lisa Sheridan, 1959, hardback **$25.00**

Booklet, Princess Margaret's Wedding Day, Pitkins, 1960 ..**$15.00**

Booklet, The Royal Wedding Official Souvenir, 1981 wedding, Pitkins...**$30.00**

Bottle, beer; Charles & Diana 1981 wedding, George Gale & Company, empty...**$25.00**

Bumper sticker, Charles & Diana wedding, black portrait, multicolored decoration.....................................**$6.00**

Cards, tribute; Diana, boxed set, 1997, 3½x2½" **$20.00**

Cup & saucer, Princess Diana memorial, multicolored portrait/decoration...**$40.00**

Decanter, Charles & Diana 1981 wedding, white ceramic, multicolored portrait/decoration, cork top **$45.00**

Dish, memorial; Princess Diana, iridescent glass, 3½" ..**$30.00**

Jewelry, Elizabeth II coronation, crown-shaped earrings on commemorative card **$25.00**

Magazine, Woman, Charles & Diana Italian tour, 6/15/85 ....**$20.00**

Medallion, Charles & Diana wedding, relief portrait, gilded, velvet case, 1¾" **$50.00**

Medallion, Princess Diana 1997 memorial, relief portrait, cupro-nickel **$35.00**

Mug, Charles & Diana 1981 engagement, black portrait, blue decoration, stoneware **$55.00**

Mug, Charles & Diana 1981 wedding, black portrait in red heart frame, stoneware.......................................**$25.00**

Mug, Prince Henry 1984 birthday, multicolored decoration, miniature, 1½" **$35.00**

Mug, Princess Diana 1997 memorial, black portrait/decoration, LE 125, stoneware **$45.00**

Newspaper, Princess Diana memorial, The Sun, 9/1/97.**$20.00**

Novelty, Charles & Diana wedding purse mirror, multicolored portrait in wedding clothes....................................**$20.00**

Photograph, Princess Elizabeth & Margaret, black & white, 7½x6" **$50.00**

Plate, Charles & Diana 1981 wedding, multicolored portrait, relief design rim, 9½" **$65.00**

Plate, Charles & Diana 1981 wedding, multicolored portrait/decoration, green border, 8½" **$45.00**

Plate, Princess Anne 1973 wedding, blue jasper, Wedgwood, 4½" **$60.00**

Plate, Princess Diana 1987 memorial, black portrait/decoration, LE 125, 7½"...$45.00

Plate, Queen Elizabeth Coronation, #1609, 9", $40.00.

Postcard, George V at front WWI, multicolored, Daily Mail, unused $15.00

Postcard, Princess Diana 1997 memorial, multicolored portrait, WPL, boxed set of 12 ....$25.00

Scrapbook, Queen Elizabeth II coronation, commemorative cover, newspaper clippings.....................................$50.00

Spoon, King George VI, relief portrait/decoration, 4¼"..$30.00

Spoon, loving; Charles & Diana wedding, brass, relief decoration, 9½"...$45.00

Tin, Charles & Diana wedding, pastel multicolored portrait/decoration, Jameson, round, 9x2½" $45.00

Tin, Queen Elizabeth Coronation, full-face portrait, 7", $25.00.

Towel, wedding; Charles & Diana, light blue border, multicolored portrait/decoration, cotton........................$35.00

Tray, Charles & Diana wedding, multicolored portrait/decoration, light blue border, 19x12"............................$55.00

Trinket box, Charles & Diana wedding, heart shape, 2¼x1¾" $30.00

Bubble Bath Containers

There's no hotter area of collecting today than items from the '50s through the '70s that are reminiscent of early kids' TV shows and hit movies, and bubble bath containers fill the bill. Most of these were made in the 1960s. The Colgate-Palmolive Company produced the majority of them — they're the ones marked 'Soaky' — and these seem to be the most collectible. Each character's name is right on the bottle. Other companies followed suit; Purex also made a line, so did Avon. Be sure to check for paint loss, and look carefully for cracks in the brittle plastic heads of the Soakies. Our values are for examples in excellent to near mint condition.

For more information, we recommend *Schroeder's Collectible Toys, Antique to Modern*, and *Collector's Guide to Bubble Bath Containers* by Greg Moore and Joe Pizzo. (Both are published by Collector Books.)

Advisors: Matt and Lisa Adams (See Directory, Bubble Bath Containers)

Baloo (Jungle Book), Soaky slip-over, 1966, NM........$20.00

Batman, Soaky, 1966, NM $55.00

Batmobile, Avon, 1979, NM $25.00

Big Bird, w/towel around shoulders, Grosvenor (England), 1996, NM $25.00

Brutus (Popeye), Soaky, 1965, NM...............................$45.00

Bugs Bunny, in purple robe w/carrot, Centura (Canada), 1994, NM $30.00

Butterfly Princess Barbie, Kid Care, 1995, NM $10.00

Darth Vader (Star Wars), Cliro (England), 1978, NM...$60.00

Dick Tracy, Soaky, 1965, NM...$55.00

Dino & Pebbles (Flintstones), Cosrich, 1994, NM.......$15.00

Dinosuds, deLagar (Canada), riding skateboard, 1990, NM $10.00

ET, Avon, 1984, NM...$10.00

Flipper riding a wave, Kid Care, 1996, NM, from $8 to..$10.00

Frankenstein, Soaky, 1963, EX......................................$90.00

Genie (Aladdin), Damascar (Italy), 1996, NM $35.00

GI Joe Canteen, DuCair Bioescence, 1987, NM $10.00

GI Joe Drill Instructor, DuCair Bioescence, 1980s, NM..$10.00

Holly Hobbie, Benjamin Ansehl, 1980s, NM $10.00

Huckleberry Hound, Purex, 1960s, 10", NM................$30.00

Incredible Hulk, Benjamin Ansehl, 1990, NM $25.00

Jack Skellington (Nightmare Before Christmas), behind coffin, Centura (Canada), 1994, NM $20.00

Jungle Land Boat, Top Care (Canada), 1995, NM $15.00

Little Orphan Annie, Lander, 1977, NM, $30.00.

Marshall Bravestarr, DuCair Bioescence, 1986, NM.....**$25.00**
Matchbox Road Grader, Grosvenor (England), 1994, NM..**$35.00**
Michelangelo (Ninja Turtle), Kid Care, 1991, NM.........**$8.00**
Mickey Mouse Bandleader, Soaky, 1960s, NM **$30.00**
Popeye, Soaky, 1977, NM **$40.00**
Power Ranger (Red), Kid Care, 1994, M **$8.00**
Ricochet Rabbit, Purex, movable arms, 1964, NM **$40.00**
Robin, Kid Care, 1995, NM **$10.00**
RoboCop, Cosway, 1990, NM **$10.00**
Rocky the Flying Squirrel (Bullwinkle), Soaky, 1962, NM...**$25.00**
Rugby player, Boots Co (England), musical, 1995, NM.**$30.00**
R2-D2 (Star Wars), Omni, 1981, NM..............................**$20.00**

Secret Squirrel, Purex, 1966, NM, $80.00.

Simba (Lion King), Kid Care, 1996, NM.........................**$8.00**
Skeletor (Masters of the Universe), DuCair Bioescence, 1985,
   NM, from $15 to...**$20.00**
Spider-Man, Soaky, 1977, NM.......................................**$45.00**
Superman, Avon, w/cape, 1978, NM............................**$20.00**
Sylvester & Tweety, Minnetonka, 1996, NM **$8.00**
Tennessee Tuxedo, Soaky, 1965, NM...........................**$30.00**
Tinkerbell, Tinkerbell Inc, 1997, NM **$10.00**
Woodsy Owl, Lander, 1970s, NM, from $50 to............**$60.00**

Yogi Bear, Purex, 1960s, $30.00.

Cake Toppers

We owe the availability of these delicate collectibles to all brides who kept them as mementoes of their wedding day.

The earliest bridal pairs from before the turn of the century were made of sugar and usually disintegrated quickly. Then came finely detailed couples carved from wood. These were usually secured to plaster bases and stood together in front of a plaster 'Good Luck' horseshoe.

Sturdier bisque porcelain molds were imported from Germany in the 1920s and 1930s. American molds, made mostly of chalkware and plaster, started appearing during that time as well. In the late 1930s and into the 1940s, celluloid figures were popular, reflecting the 'kewpie' influence of the day. In the 1950s plastic toppers became commonplace and remained so into the 1960s and '70s. The 1980s saw a return to bisque porcelain, and by the '80s and '90s, fine china from some of the world's best-known factories was used to produce exquisite bridal couples. These are meant to be displayed and do not require special treatment to preserve them from the ravages of time and air pollution.

The history of fashion can often be traced and dated through cake toppers. On brides, bustles, dropped waistlines, flapper dresses, empire waists, and various hem lengths are evident. On the groom can be seen cut-away coats, spats, tuxedos, single- and double-breasted suits, and white dinner jackets — not to mention handlebar mustaches and long sideburns!

Even the flowers, lace, and other trim can assist in dating a topper. Cloth flowers and leaves were used for many years, and earlier toppers used lilies-of-the-valley almost exclusively.

During WWII, many cake-topper grooms appeared in military dress representing all branches of the service, and most were accompanied by a 48-star paper flag. These tiny flags were usually suspended from the flower arbor, but some were on little wooden 'flag poles' anchored into the base.

American companies such as Wilton, California Novelty, and Coast Novelty produced many toppers; they sometimes dated them as well. Other toppers might be stamped or incised simply 'Germany,' 'Japan,' 'Canada,' or 'Italy.'

The true cake topper consists of a bride and groom, anchored to or part of a flat, usually round platform which serves to make the entire piece extremely stable for resting atop a soft, frosted cake. They should not be confused with bride and groom doll sets. While some smaller dolls could and did serve as toppers, they were usually too unstable to stay upright on a cake. Cake toppers never do double-duty as play items.

Expect to find these miniatures in all stages of completeness. Some will still have every bead and flower intact. Others may have lost all trim with only the bridal pair remaining.

Advisor: Jeannie Greenfield (See Directory, Cake Toppers)

1900s couple, carved wood figures on plaster stand..**$50.00**
1920s couple, single mold, poured lead.....................**$45.00**
1920s porcelain couple (3½") standing on cardboard
   'steps' w/bow overhead, silver leaves & floral trim on
   bower **$45.00**

1940s couple, plaster/chalkware combination.............**$25.00**
1940s couple standing in front of 3 lg bells, all plastic .**$30.00**
1950s (early) couple, chalkware.................................**$20.00**
1950s (early) couple, chalkware/plaster combination, flower
   bower w/pale peach-colored roses......................**$25.00**

Art Deco era, chalkware with shiny finish, gown and base are one piece, 6", $40.00. (Photo courtesy Jeannie Greenfield)

Calculators

It is difficult to picture the days when a basic four-function calculator cost hundreds of dollars, especially when today you get one free by simply filling out a credit application. Yet when they initially arrived on the market in 1971, the first of these electronic marvels cost from $300.00 to $400.00. All this for a calculator that could do no more than add, subtract, multiply, and divide.

Even at that price there was an uproar by consumers as calculating finally became convenient. No longer did you need to use a large mechanical monster adding machine or a slide rule with all of its complexity. You could even put away your pencil and paper for those tough numbers you couldn't 'do' in your head.

With prices initially so high and the profit potential so promising, several hundred companies jumped onto the calculator bandwagon. Some made their own; many purchased them from other (often overseas) manufacturers, just adding their own nameplate. Since the product was so new to the world, most of the calculators had some very different and interesting body styles.

Due to the competitive nature of all those new entries to the market, prices dropped quickly. A year and a half later, prices started to fall below $100.00 — a magic number that caused a boom in consumer demand. As even more calculators became available and electronics improved, prices continued to drop, eventually forcing many high-cost makers (who could not compete) out of business. By 1978 the number of major calculator companies could be counted on both hands. Fortunately calculators are still available at almost every garage sale or flea market for a mere pittance — usually 25¢ to $3.00.

For more information refer to *A Guide to HP Handheld Calculators and Computers* by Wlodek Mier-Jedrzejowicz, *Collector's Guide to Pocket Calculators* by Guy Ball and Bruce Flamm (both published by Wilson/Barnett), and *Personal Computers and Pocket Calculators* by Dr. Thomas Haddock.

Note: Due to limited line length, we have used these abbreviations: flr — fluorescent; fct — function.

Advisor: Guy D. Ball (See Directory, Calculators)

Club: International Association of Calculator Collectors
14561 Livingston St., Tustin, CA 92781-0345
Fax/phone: 714-730-6140; e-mail: mrcalc@usa.net
Membership includes subscription to newsletter *The International Calculator Collector*

Related Web Sites: http://www.oldcalcs.com and http://vintageelectronics.home.att.net

Adler, #60, 4-fct, green LED, 4-AA replaceable battery pack, Japan, 4x6" **$50.00**
APF, Mark #82, 4-fct, %, red LED, 9V battery, Japan, 2½x5¼".**$25.00**
Berkey, #4030, science-fct, flr, 4-AA battery, USA, 3½x6¾"..**$55.00**
Busicom, #60DA, 4-fct, tube, 2-AA batteries, Japan, 1973, 4x7" **$110.00**
Busicom, 120-LE, 4-fct, from $150 to **$250.00**
Candle, #800N, 4-fct, %, square root, green flr, 2-AA batteries, Korea, 3x5½" **$70.00**
Casio, #FX-15, science-fct, blue flr, 4-AA batteries, Japan, 3½x7½" **$45.00**
Commodore, #9R-23, 4-fct, memory, %, sealed battery, green flr, Japan, 3x5½" **$45.00**
Concept, #24, 4-fct, memory, square root, green flr, 2-AA sealed batteries, Japan, 3x5¾" **$40.00**
Craig, #4518, 4-fct, memory, %, purple LED, 9V battery, 2½x4½" **$60.00**
Elite, 4-fct, memory, %, green flr, 4-AA batteries, 3½x6" .**$65.00**
Hanimex, #BCM-30, 4-fct, memory, %, red LED, 9V battery, Hong Kong, 2¾x5" **$25.00**
Hewlett Packard, HP-01, calculator watch, from $700 to ..**$1,000.00**
Imperial, #90K, 4-fct, %, green flr, 4-AA batteries, Japan, 4¾x2¾" **$50.00**
Kovac, #SM-858M, 4-fct, memory, %, square root, green flr, 4-AA batteries, ca 1974, Japan, 3¾x6¼" **$70.00**
Lloyd's, #320, 4-fct, %, square root, 4-AA batteries, Japan, 3½x5½"..**$25.00**
Melcor, #380, 4-fct, memory, %, red LED, 9V battery, USA, 3x6" **$55.00**
Monroe-Litton, #30, 4-fct, %, red LED, sealed battery, ca 1973, USA, 3½x6" **$50.00**
National Semiconductor, Scientist, science-fct, memory, exponent, red LED, sealed battery, Hong Kong, 3x6" ...**$45.00**
Omron, #86, 4-fct, %, sign changer, flr, 2-AA batteries, Japan, 3x5¼" **$45.00**
Plustron, #308, 4-fct, red LED, 9V battery, gray body w/round blue & white keys, 3x4"..................................**$50.00**

Radio Shack, #EC-3005, 4-fct, memory, %, square root, parentheses, green flr, 4-AA batteries, Hong Kong, 3¼x8".......**$25.00**

RFT, #MR-201, 4-fct, sealed battery, East Germany, 3x6" ..**$70.00**

Santron, #300SR, science-fct, 14 digit red LED, 3-AA batteries, black case, 3¼x6" **$55.00**

Sanyo, #ICC-810, 4-fct, flr, sealed battery, Japan, 3½x6"......**$50.00**

Silver Reed, #SR104, science-fct, flr, sealed battery, Japan **$60.00**

Sovrin, #908, 4-fct, memory, %, red LED, 9V battery, Singapore, 2¾x5¼" **$70.00**

Teal, #110PD, 4-fct, printer, flr, sealed battery, 3½x8¾" .**$25.00**

Texas Instruments, #TI-1000, 4-fct, %, sign changer, red LED, 9V battery, USA, 3x5¾" **$15.00**

Toko, Mini 8, 4-fct, flr, 4-AA batteries, Japan, 3½x6"..**$30.00**

Unicom, #102, 4-fct, red LED, 9V battery, Mexico, 3x6"..**$40.00**

Unisonic, #154IL, 4-fct, memory, %, red LED, 9V battery, Hong Kong, ca 1973, 3x5¼" **$20.00**

Universal, #202, 4-fct, memory, %, red LED, 9V battery, 2¾x4½" **$25.00**

California Potteries

This is a sampling of the work of several potteries and artists who operated in California from the 1940s to the 1960s. Today good examples are among the most highly collectible pottery items on the market. As you begin to observe their products, you will see a certain style emerge. Figural pieces account for a large percentage of their work, and very often their glazes tended toward beautiful pastels, more vivid than the norm and often used in striking combinations. Some of the more renowned companies are listed elsewhere in this book.

For more information we recommend *The Collector's Encyclopedia of California Pottery, Second Edition,* by Jack Chipman.

See also Sascha Brastoff; Brayton, Laguna; Cleminson Pottery; Cookie Jars; Kay Finch; Brad Keeler; Howard Pierce; Hedi Schoop; Twin Winton; and Weilware.

Adams, Matthew; ashtray, husky, #061, 13x10"...........**$40.00**

Adams, Matthew; bowl, Eskimo child on green & white, #099b, 2½x7½x6½" **$35.00**

Adams, Matthew; bowl, iceberg on lid, #158, 4x6½" .**$75.00**

Adams, Matthew; bowl, walrus on yellow to white, free-form boat shape, 3-footed, 3¾x6" **$55.00**

Adams, Matthew; box, bear & spruce trees on light blue, #188, w/lid, 7¾" L **$70.00**

Adams, Matthew; creamer & sugar bowl, walrus, 5" .**$125.00**

Adams, Matthew; ice bucket, seal, 6½x5½" **$85.00**

Adams, Matthew; spoon rest, walrus on light blue, #176, 9¾" L **$30.00**

Adams, Matthew; tray, seal on ice floe, square, 15x11"..**$85.00**

Adams, Matthew; vase, bear on yellow, oval rim, #126, 7x4½" **$65.00**

Adams, Matthew; vase, glacier on black & white w/gold accents, irregular top, #126, 9" **$50.00**

Adams, Matthew; vase, seals & brown splashes, cylindrical, #127, 18" **$150.00**

Adams, Matthew; vase, walrus on green & white, tumbler shape, #143a, 4x3½" **$25.00**

Bellaire, Marc; ashtray, Mardi Gras, 2 abstract figures, mauve, black & blue on charcoal textured ground, 8¾x9" ..**$100.00**

Bellaire, Marc; bowl, brown sponging on white w/stylized snowflake design, oval, 6½x4½" **$30.00**

Bellaire, Marc; bowl, Jamaican theme, boat shape, 12" L.**$95.00**

Bellaire, Marc; bowl, Jamaican theme, free-form, 16" L, from $120 to..**$145.00**

Bellaire, Marc; box, Luau, 2x4½x3¾" **$50.00**

Bellaire, Marc; figurine, buffalo, brown & black sponging on white, 9½" L **$465.00**

Bellaire, Marc; figurine, island man, seated on keg, bent over bongo drums, 8½" **$400.00**

Bellaire, Marc; fruit dish, 3 pears, yellow & green on white, oblong w/button feet **$65.00**

Bellaire, Marc; platter, island fisherman w/nets, 16" dia...**$150.00**

Bellaire, Marc; vase, leafy spray, white outlines on charcoal, pedestal base, 9" **$68.00**

Boru, Sorcha; cup, 3 dinosaur handles **$75.00**

Boru, Sorcha; salt & pepper shakers, elephants, pr..**$95.00**

Boru, Sorcha; sugar shaker, lady figural, 6"..............**$110.00**

Boru, Sorcha; vase, applied flowers & leaves, 8"........**$85.00**

Brock of California, carafe, Forever Yours.................**$30.00**

Brock of California, cup & saucer, rural scene.............**$6.00**

Brock of California, double egg cup, farm scene, 3¼"..**$10.00**

Brock of California, plate, dinner; milkmaid & cow, 9"..**$15.00**

Brock of California, plate, farm scene, 11" **$8.50**

Brock of California, plate, farm scene, 6½".................**$6.00**

Brock of California, plate, haywagon on path to red barn, 11" **$9.00**

Brock of California, platter, Country Modern, rooster on fence, 13¾"..**$14.00**

Brock of California, salt & pepper shakers, farmhouse & rooster, yellow & dark green, 2⅝", pr **$25.00**

Brock of California, salt & pepper shakers, red barn on milk can shape, 3½", pr..**$12.00**

Brock of California, sugar bowl, Country Meadow, w/lid **$12.00**

Brock of California, tray, farm scene w/haystacks, 11¾x4½".**$15.00**

Brock of California, vase, potbellied stove shape, yellow & green..**$15.00**

DeForest of California, garlic holder, comical man's head, lid is hat, 5" **$25.00**

DeForest of California, tray, pig head shape, Go Ahead..., 13x13", from $30 to **$45.00**

DeForest of California, wall plaques, fish pr, he in black bowler hat, she w/gold bow, 5¾", 4¾", pr..........**$40.00**

Freeman-McFarlin, figurine, bunny, marked Anthony, 11"..**$45.00**

Freeman-McFarlin, figurine, cat, gold, marked Anthony, 5½" **$60.00**

Freeman-McFarlin, figurine, eagle, brown w/gold overglaze, bluish head, 12½" **$60.00**

Freeman-McFarlin, figurine, fox, thin white glaze, #145, 9" **$80.00**

Freeman-McFarlin, figurine, frog, 4½x7x8".................**$42.00**

Freeman-McFarlin, figurine, goldfish, white w/gray accents, 'glass' eyes, 13x8" **$55.00**

Freeman-McFarlin, figurine, mermaid holding shell, planter behind, pink bisque body w/high-gloss tail, 7¾" L.**$40.00**

Freeman-McFarlin, figurine, Persian cat, gold, excellent detailing, marked Anthony, #175, 8½" **$65.00**

Freeman-McFarlin, figurine, Siamese cat, to hang on rim of fishbowl **$45.00**

Freeman-McFarlin, planter, mouse w/exaggerated ears, taupe bisque, #410, 10" L **$30.00**

Freeman-McFarlin, reclining cat, designed by Kay Finch, gold leaf, #832, $250.00. (Photo courtesy Frick, Frick, and Martinez)

Freeman-McFarlin, plaques, kissing fish, dated 1959, 7½x7¾", pr...**$85.00**

Gilner, figurine, pixie, 3x2" **$35.00**

Gilner, figurines, kissing boy & girl shelf sitters, 4¼", pr **$65.00**

Gilner, planter, chartreuse pixie on green log, 8" L.**$15.00**

Gilner, planter, maroon pixie sits on branch of tree stump, 5" **$22.00**

Gilner, planter, turquoise boat shape w/gold-trimmed pink pixie sitting on end, 5½" L......................**$35.00**

Gilner, tray, dark green pixie sitting inside chartreuse leaf, 3x6" **$40.00**

Gilner, vase, 2 pixies sitting on rim, hat shape, 4x7" .**$30.00**

Gilner, wall pocket, red pixie on bunch of green grapes, 5½" **$45.00**

Gilner, wall pocket, yellow pumpkin w/red pixie sitting in arched recess, 8x6" **$55.00**

Hagen-Renaker, figurine, basset hound, glossy, 1954, 6¼" **$50.00**

Hagen-Renaker, figurine, Drafter, horse, #459, 2¾"....**$80.00**

Hagen-Renaker, figurine, fawn waking, #32, 1½".......**$12.00**

Hagen-Renaker, figurine, Spooky Dalmatian, 6" **$95.00**

Hagen-Renaker, figurine, Starlite, white cat, 1958-75, 6½" **$40.00**

Kaye of Hollywood, bust, head & neck of lady holding flower, applied bow under chin, 10½", EX........**$200.00**

Kaye of Hollywood, figurine, lady in long green coat holding muff at waist, #314, 9x9" **$40.00**

Kindell, Dorothy; figurine, Balinese dancer, 7½"......**$165.00**

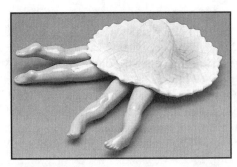

Kindell, Dorothy; ashtray, Beachcombers, 11", from $125.00 to $150.00. (Photo courtesy Jack Chipman)

Kindell, Dorothy; figurine, male Balinese dancer, kneeling, ornate headdress, 14"............................**$300.00**

Kindell, Dorothy; head vase, Burmese male, pearl lustre w/multicolors & gold, 13½"..............................**$350.00**

Kindell, Dorothy; head vase, island lady w/lg gold earrings, eyes closed, hair in updo, 5¼" **$80.00**

Kindell, Dorothy; mugs, lady in strapless gown progresses to various stages of undress, set of 6 ....**$250.00**

Kindell, Dorothy; pitcher, water; handle is nude......**$435.00**

Kindell, Dorothy; salt & pepper shakers, handles are nudes, pr..**$50.00**

Manely, Jean; figurine, blond lady in long dress w/cape-like collar, holds muff at waist, 8¼" **$60.00**

Manley, Jean; figurine, lady in green skirt & jacket w/pink flowers, peach muff & bonnet, 6" **$48.00**

McCulloch, Stewart; figurine, rooster, white, 10".........**$45.00**

Modglins, figurine, chick, marked #15, 4" **$27.00**

Pacific, bowl, salad; white, footed, #314, 13" **$95.00**

Pacific, bowl, yellow (scarce color), 5".........................**$30.00**

Pacific, coffeepot, Apache Red, 3 rings at rim, angle handle, #41, 10"..**$200.00**

Pacific, cup & saucer, demitasse; Hostessware, white gloss...**$38.00**

Pacific, cup & saucer, tiger lilies, hand painted **$30.00**

Pacific, figurine, stylized madonna, white matt, #902, 8"..**$90.00**

Pacific, flowerpot, delphinium blue, horizontal rings, 5½x6¾"...**$65.00**

Pacific, flowerpot/vase, Hostessware, yellow (scarce color), 5x6" **$50.00**

Pacific, goblet, red-orange, ring style 5½" **$70.00**

Pacific, plate, flower, blue on white shading to blue at rim, bulb-painted, 10½" **$130.00**

Pacific, plate, grill; Hostessware, Apache Red, NM.....**$28.00**

Pacific, plate, tiger lilies in center & around rim, hand painted, 9¾" **$52.00**

Pacific, tray, white gloss, #330, rectangular, 9¾" L **$30.00**

Pacific, vase, leaf mold, fan shape, #300D, 4"............**$45.00**

Simmons, Robert; figurine, Bernie, St Bernard pup, #7, 4½" **$18.00**

Simmons, Robert; figurine, boxer dog, 7x10"..............**$35.00**

Simmons, Robert; figurine, bulldog, 5¼" L **$35.00**

Simmons, Robert; figurine, Champ, standing Great Dane, #113, 6x6" **$90.00**

Simmons, Robert; figurine, collie dog, 4¾x7" **$35.00**

Simmons, Robert; figurine, doe & fawn, 5x7" **$25.00**
Wallace China, bowl, chili; Rodeo...................**$65.00**
Wallace China, bowl, serving; Boots & Saddle, oval...**$250.00**
Wallace China, cup & saucer, El Rancho **$40.00**
Wallace China, plate, child's; Rodeo **$165.00**
Wallace China, plate, dinner; Rodeo **$85.00**
Wallace China, plate, Little Buckaroo **$150.00**
Wallace China, platter, Chuck Wagon, 12"...............**$75.00**
Wallace China, salt & pepper shakers, Rodeo, pr.....**$125.00**
Wallace China, sugar bowl w/lid, Boots & Saddle ...**$125.00**
West Coast Pottery, bowl, console; lavender & turquoise blue
    mottling, #617, 13" L.................**$18.00**
West Coast Pottery, figure vase, peasant girl w/basket on hip,
    5½".................................**$30.00**
West Coast Pottery, vase, rose & turquoise, #430, 8½"..**$30.00**
West Coast Pottery, vase, sea foam, Art Moderne shape,
    5¾"..............................**$20.00**
West Coast Pottery, vase, white & green, #28, 10½"..**$26.00**
West Coast Pottery, wall pocket, grapes & leaves, 10½"
    L.....................................**$32.00**
Will-George, candle holders, lily design, pr..............**$120.00**
Will-George, container, horse shape, separates mid-body,
    speckled glaze, 8½x7"...................**$60.00**
Will-George, figurine, child-like artist & model, ca 1939,
    set.................................**$200.00**
Will-George, figurine, cockatoo, pink, late 1940s, sm ..**$85.00**
Will-George, figurine, cockatoo, pink, lg, 12" **$165.00**
Will-George, figurine, cocker spaniel, black,
    7½x9½"....................................**$225.00**
Will-George, figurine, dachshund, ca 1945, 6½x9"...**$200.00**
Will-George, figurine, Faith, girl w/pigtails, on footstool,
    10"..**$150.00**
Will-George, figurine, flamingo, female, head down,
    6½"...................................**$150.00**
Will-George, figurine, flamingo, female, head in wing,
    10"......................................**$200.00**
Will-George, figurine, flamingo, male, ca 1945, 11½"...**$200.00**
Will-George, figurine, flamingo, male, head up, 9½" .**$150.00**
Will-George, figurine, flamingo, pink, wings spread, 15½",
    minimum value...........................**$275.00**
Will-George, figurine, giraffe, female, 13" **$130.00**
Will-George, figurine, giraffe, male, 14½" **$150.00**
Will-George, figurine, macaw, red, on tree trunk, w/2
    flower openings, 14½" **$165.00**
Will-George, figurine, Polynesian female, seated, 5½" ..**$80.00**
Will-George, figurine, Polynesian female, standing,
    7½".....................................**$100.00**
Will-George, figurine, sm bird on branch, paper label,
    2x5".....................................**$60.00**
Will-George, figurine, young Pan, w/attendant forest crea-
    tures, 7"................................**$85.00**
Will-George, flower bowl, gondola shape, w/detachable,
    Chinese boy oarsman, 20" **$175.00**
Will-George, flower bowl, low, 15" L............**$60.00**
Will-George, glass, wine/cordial; rooster-shaped ceramic
    base, 5"...................................**$50.00**
Will-George, vase, pillow; Chinese girl seated in front...**$85.00**

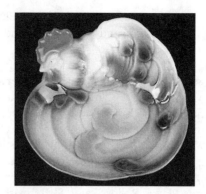

Will-George, rooster tray, small, $60.00. (Photo courtesy Jack Chipman)

Winfield, bowl, vegetable; Dragon Flower, w/lid, 14½"
    L **$35.00**
Winfield, charger, turquoise w/white at rim, 13" **$40.00**
Winfield, coffeepot, Dragon Flower, 8"......................**$75.00**
Winfield, platter, Dragon Flower, 14½"......................**$25.00**
Winfield, vase, violet pink to light pink, pale pink interior,
    5"......................................**$50.00**
Yona, decanter, clown figural, cold-painted, 13".........**$65.00**
Yona, figure vase, girl in blue bonnet w/rose trim, #47,
    7"......................................**$30.00**
Yona, figurine, angel carrying dog in her arms, gold trim,
    5" **$30.00**
Yona, figurine, medieval ladies, in gold-trimmed attire, facing
    pr, 10".................................**$135.00**
Yona, figurine, Oriental man & woman, #15/#16, 9", pr...**$50.00**
Yona, figurine, Siamese dancers, light green & white mottled
    clothing, much gold, 12", 14", pr.......**$115.00**
Yona, figurine, Victorian man & lady, lime green attire
    w/gold accents, 7½", pr **$55.00**
Yona, napkin holder, red & white striped, chef standing
    behind, Country Club #8751 ....**$90.00**
Yona, pill jar, plump lady, hair is lid, Shafford label, c
    1960 ....**$45.00**
Yona, pretzel jar, red & white striped, Country Club
    #8741...................................**$150.00**
Yona, salt & pepper shakers, clowns (Salty & Peppy), 1957,
    MIB, pr.................................**$40.00**
Yona, wall pocket, clown pulling cart, multicolored, c 1957,
    marked Shafford, 6".....................**$75.00**

California Raisins

Since they starred in their first TV commercial in 1986, the California Raisins have attained stardom through movies, tapes, videos, and magazine ads. Today we see them everywhere on the secondary market — PVC figures, radios, banks, posters — and they're very collectible. The PVC figures were introduced in 1987. Originally there were four, all issued for retail sales — a singer, two conga dancers, and a saxophone player. Before the year was out, Hardee's, the fast-food chain, came out with the same characters, though on a slightly smaller scale. A fifth character, Blue Surfboard (horizontal), was created, and three 5½" Bendees with flat pancake-style bodies appeared.

In 1988 the ranks had grown to twenty-one: Blue Surfboard (vertical), Red Guitar, Lady Dancer, Blue/Green Sunglasses, Guy Winking, Candy Cane, Santa Raisin, Bass Player, Drummer, Tambourine Lady (there were two styles), Lady Valentine, Boy Singer, Girl Singer, Hip Guitar Player, Sax Player with Beret, and four Graduates (styled like the original four, but on yellow pedestals and wearing graduation caps). And Hardee's issued an additional six: Blue Guitar, Trumpet Player, Roller Skater, Skateboard, Boom Box, and Yellow Surfboard.

Still eight more characters came out in 1989: Male in Beach Chair, Green Trunks with Surfboard, Hula Skirt, Girl Sitting on Sand, Piano Player, AC, Mom, and Michael Raisin. They made two movies and thereafter were joined by their fruit and vegetable friends, Rudy Bagaman, Lick Broccoli, Banana White, Leonard Limabean, and Cecil Thyme. Hardee's added four more characters in 1991: Anita Break, Alotta Style, Buster, and Benny.

All Raisins are dated with these exceptions: those issued in 1989 (only the Beach Scene characters are dated, and they're actually dated 1988) and those issued by Hardee's in 1991.

For more information we recommend *Schroeder's Collectible Toys, Antique to Modern* (Collector Books).

Applause, Captain Toonz, w/blue boom box, yellow glasses & sneakers, Hardee's Second Promotion, 1988, sm, M **$3.00**

Applause, FF String, w/blue guitar & orange sneakers, Hardee's Second Promotion, 1988, sm, M **$3.00**

Applause, Michael Raisin (Jackson), w/silver microphone & studded belt, Special Edition, 1989, M **$20.00**

Applause, Rollin' Rollo, w/roller skates, yellow sneakers & hat marked H, Hardee's Second Promotion, 1988, sm, M **$3.00**

Applause, SB Stuntz, w/yellow skateboard & blue sneakers, Hardee's Second Promotion, 1988, sm, M **$3.00**

Applause, Trumpy Trunote, w/trumpet & blue sneakers, Hardee's Second Promotion, 1988, sm, M **$3.00**

Applause, Waves Weaver I, w/yellow surfboard connected to foot, Hardee's Second Promotion, 1988, sm, M **$4.00**

Applause, Waves Weaver II, w/yellow surfboard not connected to foot, Hardee's Second Promotion, 1988, sm, M **$6.00**

Applause-Claymation, Banana White, yellow dress, Meet the Raisins First Edition, 1989, M **$20.00**

Applause-Claymation, Lick Broccoli, green & black w/red & orange guitar, Meet the Raisins First Edition, 1989, M...**$20.00**

Applause-Claymation, Rudy Bagaman, w/cigar, purple shirt & flipflops, Meet the Raisins First Edition, 1989, M ..**$20.00**

CALRAB, Blue Surfboard, board connected to foot, Unknown Production, 1988, M...**$35.00**

CALRAB, Blue Surfboard, board in right hand, not connected to foot, Unknown Production, 1987, M...........**$50.00**

CALRAB, Guitar, red guitar, First Commercial Issue, 1988, M **$8.00**

CALRAB, Hands, left hand points up, right hand points down, Post Raisin Bran Issue, 1987, M...................**$4.00**

CALRAB, Hands, pointing up w/thumbs on head, First Key Chains, 1987, M..**$5.00**

CALRAB, Hands, pointing up w/thumbs on head, Hardee's First Promotion, 1987, sm, M **$3.00**

CALRAB, Microphone, right hand in fist w/microphone in left, Post Raisin Brand Issue, 1987, M **$6.00**

CALRAB, Microphone, right hand points up w/microphone in left, Hardee's First Promotion, 1987, sm, M **$3.00**

CALRAB, Microphone, right hand points up w/microphone in left, First Key Chains, 1987, M............................**$7.00**

CALRAB, Santa, red cap & green sneakers, Christmas Issue, 1988, M **$9.00**

CALRAB, Saxophone, gold sax, no hat, First Key Chains, 1987, M **$5.00**

CALRAB, Saxophone, gold sax, no hat, Hardee's First Promotion, 1987, sm, M **$3.00**

CALRAB, Saxophone, inside of sax painted red, Post Raisin Bran Issue, 1987, M **$4.00**

CALRAB, Singer, microphone in left hand not connected to face, First Commercial Issue, 1988, M **$6.00**

CALRAB, Sunglasses, holding candy cane, green glasses, red sneakers, Christmas Issue, 1988, M **$9.00**

CALRAB, Sunglasses, index finger touching face, First Key Chains, 1987, M..**$5.00**

CALRAB, Sunglasses, index finger touching face, orange glasses, Hardee's First Promotion, 1987, M.............**$3.00**

CALRAB, Sunglasses, right hand points up, left hand points down, orange glasses, Post Raisin Bran Issue, 1987, M **$4.00**

CALRAB, Sunglasses II, eyes not visible, aqua glasses & sneakers, First Commercial Issue, 1988, M **$6.00**

CALRAB, Sunglasses II, eyes visible, aqua glasses & sneakers, First Commercial Issue, 1988, M............................**$25.00**

CALRAB, Winky, in hitchhiking pose & winking, First Commercial Issue, 1988, M **$6.00**

CALRAB-Applause, AC, 'Gimme 5' pose, tall pompadour & red sneakers, Meet the Raisins Second Edition, 1989, M..**$150.00**

CALRAB-Applause, Alotta Stile, w/purple boom box, pink boots, Hardee's Fourth Promotion, 1991, sm, MIP..**$12.00**

CALRAB-Applause, Anita Break, shopping w/Hardee's bag, Hardee's Fourth Promotion, 1991, sm, M **$12.00**

CALRAB-Applause, Bass Player, w/gray slippers, Second Commercial Issue, 1988, M **$8.00**

CALRAB-Applause, Benny, w/bowling ball, orange sunglasses, Hardee's Fourth Promotion, 1991, sm, MIP **$20.00**

CALRAB-Applause, Boy in Beach Chair, orange glasses, brown base, Beach Theme Edition, 1988, M........**$15.00**

Calrab-Applause, Boy w/Surfboard, purple board, brown base, Beach Theme Edition, 1988, M...................**$15.00**

CALRAB-Applause, Cecil Thyme (Carrot), Meet the Raisins Second Promotion, 1989, M................................**$175.00**

CALRAB-Applause, Drummer, black hat w/yellow feather, Second Commercial Issue, 1988, M **$8.00**

CALRAB-Applause, Girl w/Boom Box, purple glasses, green shoes, brown base, Beach Theme Edition, 1988, M ..**$15.00**

CALRAB-Applause, Girl with Tambourine, green shoes and bracelet, tambourine held down, Special Raisin Club Issue, marked 1988, $12.00. (Photo courtesy Larry DeAngelo)

CALRAB-Applause, Girl w/Tambourine (Ms Delicious), yellow shoes, Second Commercial Issue, 1988, M....**$15.00**

CALRAB-Applause, Hands, Graduate w/both hands pointing up & thumbs on head, Graduate Key Chains, 1988, M **$85.00**

CALRAB-Applause, Hip Band Guitarist (Hendrix), w/headband & yellow guitar, Third Commercial Issue, 1988, M.**$22.00**

CALRAB-Applause, Hip Band Guitarist (Hendrix), w/headband & yellow guitar, Second Key Chains, 1988, sm, M **$65.00**

CALRAB-Applause, Hula Girl, yellow shoes & bracelet, green skirt, Beach Theme Edition, 1988, M **$15.00**

CALRAB-Applause, Lenny Lima Beans, purple suit, Meet the Raisins Second Promotion, 1989, M **$125.00**

CALRAB-Applause, Microphone (female), yellow shoes & bracelet, Third Commercial Edition, 1988, M.....**$9.00**

CALRAB-Applause, Microphone (female), yellow shoes & bracelet, Second Key Chains, 1988, sm, M **$45.00**

CALRAB-Applause, Microphone (male), left hand extended w/open palm, Third Commercial Issue, 1988, M ...**$9.00**

CALRAB-Applause, Microphone (male), left hand extended w/open palm, Second Key Chains, 1988, sm, M..**$45.00**

CALRAB-Applause, Mom, yellow hair, pink apron, Meet the Raisins Second Promotion, 1989, M **$125.00**

CALRAB-Applause, Piano, blue piano, red hair, green sneakers, Meet the Raisins First Edition, 1989, M **$35.00**

CALRAB-Applause, Saxophone, black beret, blue eyelids, Third Commercial Issue, 1988, M **$15.00**

CALRAB-Applause, Saxophone, Graduate w/gold sax, no hat, Graduate Key Chain, 1988, M **$85.00**

CALRAB-Applause, Singer (female), reddish purple shoes & bracelet, Second Commercial Issue, 1988, M.....**$12.00**

CALRAB-Applause, Sunglasses, Graduate w/index finger touching face, orange glasses, Graduate Key Chains, 1988, M **$85.00**

CALRAB-Applause, Valentine, Be Mine, girl holding heart, Special Lover's Issue, 1988, M.....**$8.00**

CALRAB-Applause, Valentine, I'm Yours, boy holding heart, Special Lover's Issue, 1988, M.....**$8.00**

CALRAB-Claymation, Sunglasses/Singer/Hands/Saxophone or Graduate on yellow base, Post Raisin Bran, 1988, ea, from $45 to.....**$65.00**

Miscellaneous

AM-FM radio, Nasta, posable arms and legs, MIB, from $150.00 to $175.00. (Photo courtesy Larry DeAngelo)

Balloon, Congo line, 1987, M **$12.00**
Belt, lead singer w/mike on buckle, 1987, EX.....**$15.00**
Book, Birthday Boo Boo, 1988, EX.....**$10.00**
Bubble Bath, Rockin' Raisin, 24-oz, M.....**$4.00**
Cap, 1988, EX.....**$5.00**
Coloring Book, Sports Crazy, 1988, EX.....**$5.00**
Costume, Collegeville, 1988, MIB.....**$10.00**
Game, California Raisin board game, MIB.....**$25.00**
Mugs, Christmas Issue, 1988, set of 4, MIB **$60.00**
Party invitations, M.....**$15.00**
Pin-back button, California Raisins on Ice, 1988-89 Ice Capades, Applause.....**$8.00**
Postcard, Claymation/Will Vinton, 1988, M.....**$5.00**
Poster, California Raisin Band, 22x28", M **$8.00**
Sticker album, Diamond Publishing, 1988, M.....**$15.00**
Sunshield, Congo Line, 1988, EX.....**$10.00**
Video, Hip To Be Fit, M.....**$18.00**
Wallet, yellow plastic, 1988, EX.....**$20.00**
Wind-up toy, figure w/right hand up & orange glasses, 1987, MIB.....**$8.00**
Wind-up toy, w/left hand up & right hand down, plastic, 1987, MIB.....**$8.00**
Wristwatch, Official Fan Club, w/3 different bands, Nelsonic, 1987, MIB **$50.00**

Camark Pottery

Camark Pottery was manufactured in CAMden, ARKansas, from 1927 to the early 1960s. The pottery was founded by Samuel J. 'Jack' Carnes, a native of east-central Ohio familiar with Ohio's fame for pottery production. Camark's first wares were made from Arkansas clays shipped by Carnes to John B. Lessell in Ohio in early to mid-1926. Lessell was one of the associates responsible for the early art pottery. These wares consisted of Lessell's lustre and iridescent finishes based on similar ideas he pioneered earlier at Weller and other potteries. The variations made for Camark included versions of Weller's Marengo, LaSa, and Lamar. These 1926 pieces were signed only with the 'Lessell' signature. When Camark began operations in the spring of 1927, the company had many talented, experienced workers including Lessell's wife and stepdaughter (Lessell himself died unexpectedly in December 1926), the Sebaugh family, Frank Long, Alfred Tetzschner, and Boris Trifonoff. This group produced a wide range of art pottery finished in glazes of many types, including lustre and iridescent (signed LeCamark), Modernistic/Futuristic, crackles, and combination glaze effects such as drips. Art pottery manufacture continued until the early 1930s when emphasis changed to industrial castware (molded wares) with single-color, primarily matt glazes.

In the 1940s Camark introduced its Hand Painted line by Ernst Lechner. This line included the popular Iris, Rose, and Tulip patterns. Concurrent with the Hand Painted Series (which was made until the early 1950s), Camark continued mass production of industrial castware — simple, sometimes nondescript pottery and novelty items with primarily glossy pastel glazes — until the early 1960s.

Some of Camark's designs and glazes are easily confused with those of other companies. For instance, Lessell decorated and signed a line in his lustre and iridescent finishes using porcelain (not pottery) blanks purchased from the Fraunfelter China Company. Camark produced a variety of combination glazes including the popular drip glazes (green over pink and green over mustard/brown) closely resembling Muncie's — but Muncie's clay is generally white while Camark used a cream-colored clay for its drip-glaze pieces. Muncie's are marked with a letter/number combination, and the bottoms are usually smeared with the base color. Camark's bottoms have a more uniform color application.

For more information, we recommend the *Collector's Guide to Camark Pottery* by David Edwin Gifford, Arkansas pottery historian and author of *Collector's Encyclopedia of Niloak Pottery*. (Both books are published by Collector Books.)

Advisor: Tony Freyaldenhoven (See Directory, Camark)

Artware

Ashtray, brown stipple, early circular mold mark 400, 2", from $30 to..**$40.00**
Basket, Orange Green Overflow, 1st block letter, 6"..**$80.00**
Bowl, Delphinium Blue, embossed design, scalloped rim, unmarked, 3½", from $40 to..................................**$50.00**
Figurine, frog, Sea Green, unmarked, 4x3" **$80.00**
Lamp, LeCamark Old English, Rose, signed LeCamark, 8"..**$500.00**
Pitcher, dark blue w/multicolor bird handle, gold Arkansas ink stamp, 6½", from $160 to **$180.00**
Vase, Autumn, 1st block letter, 6¼" **$80.00**
Vase, bright yellow, shouldered, ink stamp, 4½", from $20 to...**$30.00**

Vase, Celestial Blue w/black overflow, cylindrical, Arkansas die stamp, 10¾", from $250 to **$300.00**
Vase, gray & blue mottled, unmarked, 4", from $30 to...**$40.00**
Vase, light blue, stick neck, unmarked, 4", from $10 to .**$20.00**
Vase, Old English Rose, signed LeCamark, 8", from $800 to **$1,000.00**
Vase, Platinum Blue, stick neck, unmarked, 5", from $10 to...**$20.00**
Vase, Sandpaper, gold Arkansas ink stamp, 4½" **$120.00**

Vases, dark blue matt, 7½", no mark, from $35.00 to $40.00; 3¼", mold mark USA, from $10.00 to $20.00; 7¾", no mark, from $40.00 to $60.00. (Photo courtesy David Gifford)

Water jug, brown stipple, ball form, gold Arkansas stamp, 6¾", from $180 to..**$200.00**

Hand-Painted Ware

Basket, Morning Glory, #805MG, 9¾" **$125.00**
Candlesticks, Iris, #269R, 5¼" **$35.00**
Console bowl, Full-Blown Tulip, #574D, 5¼"..........**$250.00**
Ewer, Morning Glory, #800R, 14" **$225.00**
Vase, Iris, pillow form, #846R, 7" **$125.00**
Vase, Morning Glory, majolica, #831K, 8¼" **$125.00**
Vase, Rose, urn form w/tab handles, #573D, 9½" **$100.00**
Wall pocket, Rose, cup & saucer, unmarked, 7½" **$80.00**

Industrial Castware

Bowl, leaf & grape design, #160, 14"..........................**$25.00**
Hand vase, #867, 5¾"..**$40.00**
Pitcher, swirl design, #237, miniature, 3" **$15.00**
TV lamp, prancing horse w/Nor-So 22k gold decoration, 3567TV, 9"...**$75.00**
Vase, Arts & Crafts style, w/handles, #303, 3" **$30.00**
Vase, embossed morning glory design, #548, 7¾"......**$45.00**
Vase, tornado shape, #539, 7"......................................**$40.00**

Cambridge Glassware

If you're looking for a 'safe' place to put your investment dollars, Cambridge glass is one of your better options. But as with any commodity, in order to make a good investment, knowledge of the product and its market is required. There are two books we would recommend for your study, *Colors in Cambridge Glass,* put out by the National Cambridge Collectors Club, and *The Collector's Encyclopedia of Elegant Glass* by Gene Florence.

The Cambridge Glass Company (located in Cambridge, Ohio) made fine quality glassware from just after the turn of the century until 1958. They made thousands of different items in hundreds of various patterns and colors. Values hinge on rarity of shape and color. Of the various marks they used, the 'C in triangle' is the most common. In addition to their tableware, they also produced flower frogs representing ladies and children and models of animals and birds that are very valuable today. To learn more about them, you'll want to read *Animals and Figural Flower Frogs of the Depression Era* by Lee Garmon and Dick Spencer (Collector Books).

Advisor: Debbie Maggard (See Directory, Elegant Glassware)

Newsletter: *The Cambridge Crystal Ball*
National Cambridge Collectors, Inc.
P.O. Box 416, Cambridge, OH 43725-0416.
Dues: $17 for individual member and $3 for associate member of same household

Apple Blossom, crystal, bowl, finger; w/underplate, #3130 ....**$30.00**
Apple Blossom, crystal, bowl, 4-footed, 12" **$40.00**
Apple Blossom, crystal, plate, sandwich; tab handled, 11½" **$22.00**

Apple Blossom, green, four-part relish with center handle, 9" diameter, $90.00.

Apple Blossom, pink or green, bowl, 2-handled, 10".**$85.00**
Apple Blossom, pink or green, candlestick, keyhole; 2-light **$37.50**
Apple Blossom, pink or green, stem, tall sherbet; #3135, 6-oz..**$20.00**
Apple Blossom, yellow or amber, bowl, bonbon; 2-handled, 5½" **$25.00**
Apple Blossom, yellow or amber, bowl, 13" **$60.00**
Apple Blossom, yellow or amber, stem, low sherbet; #3130, 6-oz..**$15.00**
Apple Blossom, yellow or amber, tumbler, #3025, 12-oz..**$32.50**

Candlelight, crystal, bowl, flared, 4-footed, #3400/4, 12" ..**$70.00**
Candlelight, crystal, candle, 2-light, #3900/72, 6"........**$45.00**
Candlelight, crystal, nut cup, 4-footed, #3400/71, 3" ..**$65.00**
Candlelight, crystal, plate, 4-toed, #3900/26, 12" **$60.00**
Candlelight, crystal, relish, divided, 2-handled, #3900/124, 7" **$40.00**
Candlelight, crystal, stem, low sherbet; #3111, 7-oz ...**$17.50**
Candlelight, crystal, stem, wine; #3111, 2½" **$60.00**
Candlelight, crystal, vase, globe shape, #1309, 5".......**$55.00**
Caprice, blue or pink, bowl, belled, 4-footed, #62, 12½"...**$90.00**
Caprice, blue or pink, candlestick, #67, 2½", ea.........**$32.50**
Caprice, blue or pink, celery & relish, 3-part, #124, 8½".**$45.00**
Caprice, blue or pink, plate, cabaret; 4-footed, #33, 14"..**$85.00**
Caprice, blue or pink, stem, water; blown, #300, 9-oz..**$38.00**
Caprice, blue or pink, vase, crimped top, #345, 5½"..**$210.00**
Caprice, crystal, bowl, 4-footed, square, #58, 10" **$35.00**
Caprice, crystal, comport, low footed, #130, 6" **$22.00**
Caprice, crystal, nut dish, #93, 2½" **$22.00**
Caprice, crystal, stem, low sherbet; #4, 5-oz **$25.00**
Caprice, crystal, tumbler, table; flat, #310, 10-oz.........**$25.00**
Caprice, crystal, vase, #243, 8½" **$110.00**
Caprice, crystal, vase, ball shape, #240, 9¼"............**$140.00**
Chantilly, crystal, bowl, flared, 4-footed, 10".............**$40.00**

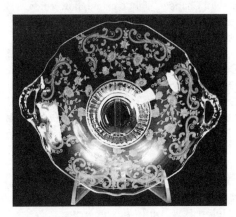

Chantilly, crystal, bowl, open handles, 9", $45.00.

Chantilly, crystal, lamp, hurricane; candlestick base.**$120.00**
Chantilly, crystal, pitcher, ball shape.........................**$120.00**
Chantilly, crystal, plate, 4-footed, 13".........................**$30.00**
Chantilly, crystal, stem, low oyster cocktail; #3625, 4½-oz..**$16.00**
Chantilly, crystal, stem, tall sherbet; #3600, 7-oz.........**$17.50**
Chantilly, crystal, tumbler, juice; footed, #3625, 5-oz .**$15.00**
Cleo, blue, bowl, relish; 2-part **$40.00**
Cleo, blue, comport, tall, #3115, 7" **$85.00**
Cleo, blue, plate, luncheon; Decagon, 8½" **$30.00**
Cleo, blue, sugar bowl, footed **$30.00**
Cleo, pink, green, yellow or amber, bowl, cranberry; 6½" **$30.00**
Cleo, pink, green, yellow or amber, bowl, 2-handled, Decagon, 10" **$40.00**
Cleo, pink, green, yellow or amber, pitcher, #38, 3-pt.**$195.00**
Cleo, pink, green, yellow or amber, salt dip, 1½" **$75.00**
Cleo, pink, green, yellow or amber, vase, 5½" **$75.00**

Decagon, pastel colors, bowl, bonbon; 2-handled, 5½" ..**$10.00**
Decagon, pastel colors, bowl, relish; 2-part, 9"..........**$25.00**
Decagon, pastel colors, plate, bread & butter; 6¼" **$3.00**
Decagon, pastel colors, tray, pickle; 9".....................**$20.00**
Decagon, red or blue, basket, 2-handled, upturned sides, 7"...**$25.00**
Decagon, red or blue, bowl, cereal; belled, 6" **$25.00**
Decagon, red or blue, bowl, relish; 2-part, 11"..........**$32.00**
Decagon, red or blue, ice bucket.............................**$65.00**
Decagon, red or blue, stem, high sherbet; 6-oz..........**$22.00**
Diane, crystal, bowl, berry; 5"................................**$20.00**
Diane, crystal, bowl, relish; 2-part, 7" **$22.00**
Diane, crystal, mayonnaise, divided, w/ladle & liner .**$45.00**
Diane, crystal, plate, 2-handled, 13½" **$35.00**
Diane, crystal, tumbler, 13-oz.................................**$32.00**
Elaine, crystal, bowl, bonbon; 2-handled, 5¼"............**$15.00**
Elaine, crystal, bowl, celery & relish; 3-part, 9" **$35.00**
Elaine, crystal, bowl, ear handle, 4-footed, oval, 12"..**$47.50**
Elaine, crystal, plate, footed, 2-handled, 8" **$18.00**
Elaine, crystal, stem, cocktail; #3500, 3-oz................**$24.00**
Elaine, crystal, stem, cordial; #1402, 1-oz..................**$60.00**
Elaine, crystal, stem, goblet; #3104, 9-oz..................**$125.00**
Elaine, crystal, vase, footed, 8".................................**$60.00**
Figurine, Bashful Charlotte, light emerald, flower frog, 11½"..**$350.00**
Figurine, Bashful Charlotte, pink, flower frog, 6" **$225.00**
Figurine, bird on stump, green, flower frog, 5¼" **$325.00**
Figurine, bridge hound, emerald................................**$50.00**
Figurine, Draped Lady, crystal frost, flower frog, 13¼".......**$175.00**
Figurine, Draped Lady, Dianthus frost, flower frog, 8½" **$140.00**
Figurine, Draped Lady, light emerald, flower frog, 8½"......**$225.00**
Figurine, Draped Lady, Moonlight Blue, flower frog, 8½"..**$475.00**
Figurine, Draped Lady, pink frost, flower frog, 8½"..**$150.00**
Figurine, Draped Lady, yellow, flower frog, 8½"......**$190.00**
Figurine, frog, crystal satin....................................**$25.00**
Figurine, Mandolin Lady, crystal, flower frog...........**$250.00**
Figurine, Mandolin Lady, green, bent back, flower frog, 9".**$425.00**
Figurine, Melon Boy, pink, flower frog....................**$425.00**
Figurine, Rose Lady, crystal satin, flower frog, tall base, 9¾"...**$225.00**
Figurine, Rose Lady, dark amber, flower frog, tall base, 9¾"...**$275.00**
Figurine, Rose Lady, light pink, flower frog, 8½" **$175.00**
Figurine, swan, dark green, style #3, 8½" **$175.00**
Figurine, swan, ebony, 12½"...................................**$300.00**
Figurine, swan, milk glass, candlestick, 4½", ea **$175.00**
Figurine, swan, milk glass, 3"...................................**$60.00**
Figurine, Two Kids, amber, flower frog, oval base, 9¼"..**$325.00**
Figurine, Two Kids, crystal, flower frog, 9¼"............**$200.00**
Gloria, crystal, bowl, bonbon; footed, 5½" **$15.00**
Gloria, crystal, bowl, cream soup; w/square saucer...**$22.00**
Gloria, crystal, plate, 2-handled, 6" **$9.00**
Gloria, crystal, saucer, after dinner; round..................**$8.00**
Gloria, crystal, tumbler, footed, #3130, 5-oz...............**$25.00**
Gloria, green, pink or yellow, basket, sides up, 2-handled, 6"...**$35.00**
Gloria, green, pink or yellow, bowl, fruit; 2-handled, 11"...**$75.00**

Gloria, green, pink or yellow, cup, round or square .**$27.00**
Gloria, green, pink or yellow, icer, w/insert **$90.00**
Gloria, green, pink or yellow, plate, sandwich; tab handled, 11½"...**$40.00**
Gloria, green, pink or yellow, salt & pepper shaker, short, pr...**$75.00**
Gloria, green, pink or yellow, sugar bowl, footed **$18.00**
Imperial Hunt Scene, colors, creamer, flat..................**$35.00**
Imperial Hunt Scene, colors, stem, claret; #3085, 4½-oz...**$67.50**
Imperial Hunt Scene, colors, tumbler, footed, #3085, 2½-oz...**$45.00**
Imperial Hunt Scene, crystal, bowl, cereal; 6"............**$15.00**
Imperial Hunt Scene, crystal, tumbler, flat, #1402, 5-oz...**$20.00**
Mt Vernon, amber or crystal, ashtray, #68, 4".............**$12.00**
Mt Vernon, amber or crystal, bowl, shallow cupped, #61, 11½"...**$30.00**
Mt Vernon, amber or crystal, bowl, toilet; square, #18, 7-oz...**$65.00**
Mt Vernon, amber or crystal, box, w/lid, round, #16, 3" .**$30.00**
Mt Vernon, amber or crystal, cologne, w/stopper, #1340, 2½-oz...**$37.50**
Mt Vernon, amber or crystal, mayonnaise, divided, w/2 spoons, #107...**$25.00**
Mt Vernon, amber or crystal, plate, finger bowl liner; #23...**$4.00**
Mt Vernon, amber or crystal, relish, 3-part, #200, 11".**$25.00**
Mt Vernon, amber or crystal, sugar bowl, footed, #8.**$10.00**
Mt Vernon, amber or crystal, vase, #42, 5".................**$15.00**
Mt Vernon, amber or crystal, vase, footed, #54, 7" **$35.00**
Portia, crystal, bowl, finger; w/liner, #3124 ....**$40.00**
Portia, crystal, bowl, flared, 4-footed, 10"..................**$40.00**
Portia, crystal, cocktail icer, 2-pt..............................**$65.00**
Portia, crystal, cup, round.......................................**$15.00**
Portia, crystal, mayonnaise, w/ladle & liner...............**$40.00**
Portia, crystal, plate, dinner; 10½"...........................**$65.00**
Portia, crystal, stem, cocktail; #3126, 3-oz **$17.50**
Portia, crystal, stem, goblet; #3126, 9-oz....................**$20.00**
Portia, crystal, stem, wine; #3124, 3-oz......................**$30.00**
Portia, crystal, tumbler, water; #3126, 10-oz...............**$15.00**
Portia, crystal, vase, flower; 11"................................**$65.00**
Rosalie, amber, creamer, footed................................**$12.00**
Rosalie, amber, plate, bread & butter; 6¾"...................**$5.00**
Rosalie, amber, plate, dinner; 9½"..............................**$35.00**
Rosalie, blue, pink or green, bowl, fruit; 5½" **$18.00**
Rosalie, blue, pink or green, bowl, 11".......................**$55.00**
Rosalie, blue, pink or green, salt dip, footed, 1½" **$60.00**
Rose Point, crystal, ashtray, oval, #3500/131, 4½" **$65.00**
Rose Point, crystal, bowl, bonbon; 2-handled, #3400/1180, 5½"...**$35.00**
Rose Point, crystal, bowl, cream soup; w/liner, #3400 .**$165.00**
Rose Point, crystal, bowl, nut; 4-footed, #3400/71, 3" ..**$700.00**
Rose Point, crystal, bowl, 2-handled, #3400/1185.......**$70.00**
Rose Point, crystal, candelabrum, 3-light, #1338.........**$65.00**
Rose Point, crystal, celery, #3400/652, 12"..................**$47.50**
Rose Point, crystal, coaster, #1628, 3½" **$55.00**
Rose Point, crystal, comport, blown, #3500/101, 5⅜"..**$65.00**
Rose Point, crystal, grapefruit, w/liner, #187............**$115.00**
Rose Point, crystal, pitcher, #3900/115, 76-oz **$195.00**

Rose Point, crystal, plate, 2-handled, #3400/1181, 6" .**$20.00**
Rose Point, crystal, relish, 2-part, #3400/90, 6" **$32.50**
Rose Point, crystal, relish, 4-part, 2-handled, #3500/87, 10" **$60.00**
Rose Point, crystal, stem, cocktail; #3106, 3-oz **$35.00**
Rose Point, crystal, sugar bowl, #3500/14 ....**$20.00**
Rose Point, crystal, tumbler, juice; low foot, #3500, 5-oz **$40.00**
Rose Point, crystal, vase, bud; #1528, 10"....................**$80.00**
Rose Point, crystal, vase, footed, #6004, 5" **$50.00**
Valencia, crystal, bowl, handled, #3500/49, 5" **$18.00**
Valencia, crystal, creamer, individual, #3500/15 ....**$20.00**
Valencia, crystal, relish, 3-part, #3500/69, 6½" **$25.00**
Valencia, crystal, relish, 4-part, #3500/65, 10" **$35.00**
Valencia, crystal, stem, claret; #3500, 4½-oz...............**$45.00**
Valencia, crystal, sugar bowl, #3500/14 ....**$15.00**
Valencia, crystal, tumbler, footed, #3500, 5-oz **$15.00**
Wildflower, crystal, bowl, relish; 3-part, 3-handled, #3400/91, 8" **$25.00**
Wildflower, crystal, creamer, #3900/41........................**$15.00**
Wildflower, crystal, pitcher, #3900/115, 76-oz...........**$175.00**

Wildflower, crystal, salt and pepper shakers, pair: flat, $37.50, footed, $40.00; Creamer and sugar bowl, individual; $40.00 for the set.

Wildflower, crystal, stem, cordial; #3121, 1-oz **$57.50**
Wildflower, crystal, vase, flower; footed, #6004, 6" **$40.00**
Wildflower, crystal, vase, pedestal footed, #1299, 11" .**$75.00**

Cameras

Camera collecting as an investment or hobby continues to grow in popularity, as evidenced by the interest shown in current publications and at numerous camera shows that emphasize both user and classic collectible types.

Buying at garage sales, flea markets, auctions, or estate sales are ways to add to collections, although it is rare to find an expensive classic camera offered through these outlets. However, buying at such sales to resell to dealers or collectors can be profitable if one is careful to buy quality items, not common cameras that sell for very little at best, especially when they show wear. A very old camera is not necessarily valuable, as value depends on availability and quality. Knowing how to check out a camera or to judge quality will pay off when building a collection.

There are many distinct types of cameras to consider: large format (such as Graflex and large view cameras), medium format, early folding and box styles, 35mm single-lens-reflex (SLR), 35mm range finders, twin-lens-reflex (TLR), miniature or sub-miniature, novelty, and other types — including the more recent 'point-and-shoot' styles, Polaroids, and movie cameras. Though there is a growing interest in certain types, we would caution you against buying common Polaroids and movie cameras for resale, as there is very little market for them at this time. Most pre-1900 cameras will be found in large-format view camera or studio camera types. From the 1920s to the '30s, folding and box-type cameras were produced, which today make good collector items. Most have fairly low values because they were made in vast numbers. Many of the more expensive classics were manufactured in the 1930 – 1955 period and include primarily the range-finder type of camera and those with the first built-in meters. The most prized of these are of German or Japanese manufacture, valued because of their innovative designs and great optics. The key to collecting these types of cameras is to find a mint-condition item or one still in the original box. In camera collecting, quality is the most important aspect.

This updated listing includes only a few of the various categories and models of cameras from the many thousands available and gives current average retail prices for working models with average wear. Note that cameras in mint condition or like new with their original boxes may be valued much higher, while very worn examples with defects (scratches, dents, torn covers, poor optics, nonworking meters or range finders) would be valued far less. A dealer, when buying for resale, will pay only a percentage of these values, as he must consider his expenses for refurbishing, cleaning, etc. Again, remember that quality is the key to value, and prices on some cameras vary widely according to condition. Typical collector favorites are old Alpa, Contax, Nikon, Canon or Leica rangefinders, Rolleiflex TLR's, some Zeiss-Ikon models, Exakta, and certain Voigtlander models. For information about these makes as well as models by Anthony and Conley (early view cameras), please consult the advisor.

Advisor: C.E. Cataldo (See Directory, Cameras)

Agfa, Billy, early 1930s...**$15.00**
Agfa, Isolette **$20.00**
Agfa, Karat 3.5, 1940 ....**$35.00**
Aires, 35III, 1958..**$35.00**

Aires 35 III L, 35mm, 1957, $65.00. (Photo courtesy C.E. Cataldo)

Ansco, Memar, 1956-59 ....$25.00
Ansco, Speedex, Standard, 1950................................$15.00
Ansco, Super Speedex, 75/3.5 lens, 1953-58.............$150.00
Argoflex Seventy-Five, TLS, 1949-58.......................$7.00
Argus A2F, 1939-41 ....$20.00
Argus C3, black brick type, 1940-50.........................$10.00
Argus C4, 50 2.8 lens w/flash $25.00
Asahi Pentax, original, 1957.....................................$200.00
Asahitflex I, 1st Japanese SLR..................................$500.00
Baldi, by Balda-Werk, Germany, 1930s.....................$30.00
Bolsey, B2 ....$20.00
Braun Paxette I, 1952..$30.00
Canon A-1 ....$185.00
Canon AE-1 ....$90.00
Canon AE-1P $155.00
Canon F-1..$225.00
Canon IIB, 1949-52 ....$250.00
Canon III $300.00
Canon III, 1951-53 ....$225.00
Canon S-II, Seiki Kogaku, 1946-47 ....$800.00
Canon S-11, 1947-49 ....$375.00
Canon 7, 1961-64 ....$300.00
Ciroflex, TLR, 1940s..$30.00
Compass Camera, 1938, from $1,000 to $1,300.00
Contax II or III, 1936-42, from $300 to.....................$450.00
Contessa 35, 1950-55, from $110 to $150.00
Detrola Model D, Detroit Corp, 1938-40...................$20.00
Eastman Folding Brownie Six-20...............................$12.00
Eastman Kodak-35, 1940-51......................................$25.00
Eastman Premo, many models available, any $30.00
Edinex, by Wirgin..$40.00
Exakta II, 1949-50..$130.00
Exakta VX, 1951...$80.00
Fed 1, USSR, postwar, from $50 to...........................$75.00
Fed 1, USSR, prewar, from $150 to $250.00
Fujica AX-3...$90.00
Fujica AX-5...$125.00
Fujica ST-701..$70.00
Graflex Pacemaker Crown Graphic, various sizes $135.00
Graflex Speed Graphic, various sizes, ea, from $120 to .$150.00
Hasselglad 1000F, 1952-57, from $500 to..................$700.00

**Japanese 'Hit' camera, subminiature novel-
ty, many variations and names, from $15.00
to $30.00. (Photo courtesy C.E. Cataldo)**

Kodak Baby Brownie, Bakelite................................$10.00
Kodak Bantam, Art Deco design, 1935-38.................$35.00
Kodak Box Brownie 2A..$7.00
Kodak Box Hawkeye No 2A.......................................$8.00
Kodak Hawkeye, plastic...$8.00
Kodak Medalist, 1941-48, from $140 to $200.00
Kodak No 1 Folding Pocket.......................................$20.00
Kodak No 3A Folding Pocket $30.00
Kodak Retina I $50.00
Kodak Retina II $65.00
Kodak Retina IIa $90.00
Kodak Retina IIIc, from $150 to................................$180.00
Kodak Retina IIIC, from $350 to $500.00
Kodak Retinette, various models, from $30 to $45.00
Kodak Signet 35...$20.00
Kodak View, early 1900s, from $150 to.....................$175.00
Kodak 35, w/range finder, 1940-51 ....$25.00
Konica Autoreflex TC, various models, from $60 to...$90.00
Konica Autoreflex T4 ....$135.00
Konica FS-1 ....$85.00
Konica III, 1956-59 ....$120.00
Leica II, from $250 to $450.00
Leica IID, 1932-38, from $250 to $400.00
Leica IIIa, 35mm, 1935-50, from $250 to $350.00
Leica IIIc, from $200 to $300.00
Leica IIIf, 1950-56, from $300 to $500.00
Leica M3, 1954-66, from $700 to $1,000.00
Mamiya-Sekor 500TL, 1966 ....$25.00
Mamiyaflex 1, TLR, 1951...$140.00
Mercury Model II, CX, 1945......................................$40.00
Minolta Autocord, TLR $100.00
Minolta HiMatic Series, various models, from $15 to..$20.00
Minolta SR-7...$50.00
Minolta SRT 101...$75.00
Minolta SRT 202...$90.00
Minolta XD-11, 1977..$175.00
Minolta XE-5...$180.00
Minolta XG-1..$60.00
Minolta X700..$145.00
Minolta 35, early models, 1947-50, from $300 to......$500.00
Minolta-16, miniature, various models, from $15 to ...$25.00
Minox B (Spy Camera)..$125.00
Miranda Automex II, 1963...$70.00
Nikkormat FTN...$135.00
Nikon EM $65.00
Nikon F, various finders & meters, from $150 to......$250.00
Nikon FA, from $230 to..$280.00
Nikon FG, from $120 to $135.00
Nikon FM, from $150 to $195.00
Nikon S, 1951-54, from $350 to.................................$550.00
Nikon S2, 1954-58, from $300 to $500.00
Nikon S3, 1958-60, from $600 to...............................$1,200.00
Olympus CM-2..$150.00
Olympus OM-1 ....$120.00
Olympus OM-10..$60.00
Olympus Pen EE, compact half frame $35.00
Olympus Pen F, compact half frame SLR, from $150 to...$200.00

Olympus 35IV, 1949-53 ....**$50.00**
Pax-M3, 1957, from $30 to..................................**$50.00**
Pentax K-1000, from $90 to...............................**$120.00**
Pentax ME **$75.00**
Pentax Spotmatic, many models, from $50 to..........**$125.00**
Perfex Speed Candid, 35mm, Bakelite body, ca 1938 ...**$70.00**
Petri FT, FT1000 or FT-EE, ea..............................**$70.00**
Petri 7, 1961, from $15 to **$20.00**
Plaubel-Makina II, 1933-39...................................**$200.00**
Polaroid, most models, from $5 to......................**$10.00**
Polaroid, SX-70, from $30 to...............................**$50.00**
Polaroid, 110, 110A or 110B Pathfinder, ea, from $30 to.....**$50.00**
Polaroid, 180, 185, 190, 195, ea, from $150 to..........**$300.00**
Praktica FX, 1952-57 ....**$40.00**
Praktica Super TL, 1968-74..................................**$50.00**
Realist Stereo, 3.5 lens...**$110.00**
Regula, King, various models, fixed lens.................**$25.00**
Regula, King, w/interchangeable lenses **$80.00**
Ricoh Diacord L, TLR, built-in meter, 1958.................**$70.00**
Ricoh KR-30 ....**$100.00**
Rolleicord II, 1936-50, from $70 to.......................**$90.00**
Rolleiflex Automat, 1937 ....**$125.00**
Rolleiflex 3.5E, 1956-59, from $200 to **$300.00**
Samoca 35, 1950s...**$25.00**
Seroco 4x5, Folding Plate, Sears, 1901, from $90 to.**$125.00**
Tessina, miniature, chrome, from $300 to **$500.00**
Tessina, miniature, colors, from $500 to..................**$700.00**
Topcon Super D, 1963-74 ....**$135.00**

Topcon Super Dm, 1963-75, SLR 35 mm, $150.00. (Photo courtesy C.E. Cataldo)

Topcon Uni **$40.00**
Tower 45 (Sears), w/Nikkor Lens............................**$200.00**
Tower 50 (Sears), w/Cassar lens.............................**$18.00**
Unives, Universal Camera Co, 1935-39 ....**$25.00**
Voigtlander Bessa, various folding models, 1931-49 ...**$25.00**
Voigtlander Bessa, w/range finder, 1936..................**$140.00**
Voigtlander Brilliant, TLR, metal body version, 1933 ..**$50.00**
Voigtlander Vitessa L, 1954 ....**$175.00**
Voigtlander Vito II, 1950.......................................**$50.00**
Yashica A, TLR **$45.00**
Yashica Electro 35, 1966.......................................**$25.00**
Yashica FX-1, 1975...**$50.00**
Yashica FX-70..**$70.00**

Yashicamat 124G, TLR, from $180 to **$200.00**
Zeiss Baldur Box Tengor, Frontar lens, ca 1935, from $35 to..**$50.00**
Zeiss-Ikon Box Tengor 43/2, 1934-38 ....**$40.00**
Zeiss-Ikon Juwell (275/11), 1927-39.......................**$500.00**
Zeiss-Ikon Nettar, folding roll film, various sizes........**$30.00**
Zeiss-Ikon Super Ikonta B (532 16), 1937-56............**$160.00**
Zenit E, USSR **$35.00**
Zorki 4, USSR..**$70.00**

Candlewick Glassware

This is a beautifully simple, very diverse line of glassware made by the Imperial Glass Company of Bellaire, Ohio, from 1936 to 1982. (The factory closed in 1984.) From all explored written material found so far, it is known that Mr. Earl W. Newton brought back a piece of the French Cannonball pattern upon returning from a trip. The first Candlewick mold was derived using that piece of glass as a reference. As for the name Candlewick, it was introduced at a Wheeling, West Virginia, centennial celebration in August of 1936, appearing on a brochure promoting the crafting of 'Candlewick Quilts.'

Imperial did cuttings on Candlewick; several major patterns are Floral, Valley Lily, Starlight, Princess, DuBarry, and Dots. Remember, these are *cuts* and should not be confused with etchings. (Cuts that were left unpolished were called Gray Cut — an example of this is the Dot cut.) The most popular Candlewick etching was Rose of Sharon (Wild Rose). All cutting was done on a wheel, while etching utilized etching paper and acid. Many collectors confuse these two processes. Imperial also used gold, silver, platinum, and hand painting to decorate Candlewick, and they made several items in colors.

With over 740 pieces in all, Imperial's Candlewick line was one of the leading tableware patterns in the country. Due to its popularity with collectors today, it is still number one and has the distinction of being the only single line of glassware ever to have had two books written about it, a national newsletter, and over fifteen collector clubs across the USA devoted to it exclusively.

There are reproductions on the market today — some are coming in from foreign countries. Look-alikes are often mistakenly labeled Candlewick, so if you're going to collect this pattern, you need to be well informed. Most collectors use the company mold numbers to help identify all the variations and sizes. The *Imperial Glass Encyclopedia, Vol. 1*, has a very good chapter on Candlewick. Also reference *Candlewick, The Jewel of Imperial*, by Mary Wetzel-Tomalka; and *Elegant Glassware of the Depression Era* by Gene Florence (Collector Books).

Advisor: Joan Cimini (See Directory, Imperial Glass)

Newsletter: *The Candlewick Collector* (Quarterly)
Virginia R. Scott, Editor
Subscriptions, $7.00 direct to
Connie Doll
6534 South Ave., Holland, OH 43528; 419-866-6350
e-mail: CWCollector@AOL.com

Ashtray, heart, #400/172, 4½" **$10.00**
Ashtray, round, #400/19, 2¾" **$9.00**
Ashtray, square, #400/653, 5¾" **$45.00**
Basket, handled, #400/73/0, 11" **$225.00**
Bowl, #400/13F, 10" **$45.00**
Bowl, butter/jam; 3-part, #400/262, 10½" **$180.00**
Bowl, cream soup; #400/50, 5" **$65.00**

Bowl, cream soup; #400/50, and 8" plate with seat, from $75.00 to $80.00 for the set.

Bowl, cupped edge, #400/75F, 10" **$45.00**
Bowl, finger; footed, #3400 ....**$30.00**
Bowl, float; 1¼" deep, #400/101, 13" **$160.00**
Bowl, fruit; #400/3F, 6" **$12.00**
Bowl, handled, #400/113B, 12" **$160.00**
Bowl, heart, #400/53H, 5½" **$25.00**
Bowl, lily, 4-footed, #400/74J, 7" **$185.00**
Bowl, nappy, 4-footed, #400/74B, 8½" **$75.00**
Bowl, relish; 2-handled, oval, #400/217, 10" **$40.00**
Bowl, round, #400/10F, 9" **$45.00**
Butter & jam set, #400/204, 5-pc **$350.00**
Calender desk; 1947 ....**$200.00**
Candle holder, flower, #400/40F, 6" dia **$30.00**
Candle holder, mushroom, #400/86 ....**$35.00**
Candle holder, w/fingerhold, #400/81, 3½" **$50.00**
Candle holder, 3-toed, #400/207, 4½" **$80.00**
Candy box, w/lid, #400/259, 7" **$130.00**
Cigarette box, w/lid, #400/134 ....**$40.00**
Clock, 4" dia **$400.00**
Cocktail, seafood; w/beaded foot, #400/190 ....**$65.00**
Compote, arched tri-stem, #400/220, 5" **$80.00**
Compote, fruit; footed, crimped, #400/103C, 10" **$165.00**
Creamer, domed foot, #400/18 ....**$125.00**
Cup, punch; #400/211 ....**$30.00**
Ice tub, #400/63, 5½" deep, 8" dia **$100.00**
Jar tower, 3-section, #400/655 ....**$425.00**
Mirror, standing, 4½" dia **$115.00**
Oil, bulbous bottom, #400/274, 4-oz **$45.00**
Oil, etched Oil, w/stopper, #400/121 ....**$60.00**
Pitcher, beaded handle, #400/16, 16-oz **$200.00**
Pitcher, plain, #400/419, 40-oz **$45.00**
Plate, dinner; #400/10D, 10½" **$37.50**
Plate, oval, #400/169, 8" **$30.00**
Plate, salad; #400/3D, 7" **$8.00**
Plate, salad; #400/5D, 8½" **$10.00**
Plate, torte; cupped edge, #400/75V, 12½" **$35.00**
Plate, torte; flat edge, #400/20D, 17" **$55.00**

Plate, w/indent, oval, #400/98, 9" **$15.00**
Plate, 2-handled, #400/42D, 5½" **$10.00**
Plate, upturned handles, #400/113D, 14" **$45.00**
Punch set, bowl on base, 12 cups & ladle, 15-pc, #400/20 ....**$245.00**
Salt dip, #400/61, 2" **$11.00**
Salt spoon, w/ribbed bowl, #4000 ....**$11.00**
Saucer, tea or coffee; #400/35 or #400/37, ea **$3.00**
Stem, champagne/sherbet; #3800, 4-oz **$30.00**
Stem, cordial; #400/190, 1-oz **$90.00**
Stem, oyster cocktail; #3400, 4-oz **$16.00**
Stem, parfait; #3400, 6-oz **$55.00**
Stem, sherbet; #400/190, 5-oz **$14.00**
Sugar bowl, beaded handle, flat, #400/126 ....**$40.00**
Tidbit set, #400/2701, 2-pc **$75.00**
Tray, condiment; #400/148, 5¼x9¼" **$225.00**
Tumbler, #3800, 12-oz **$30.00**
Tumbler, cocktail; #400/18, 3½-oz **$45.00**
Tumbler, footed, #3400, 10-oz **$20.00**
Tumbler, low sherbet; #400/19, 5-oz **$15.00**
Tumbler, water; #400/18, 9-oz **$45.00**
Vase, bead footed, flared rim, #400/21, 8½" **$225.00**
Vase, fan; #400/287F, 6" **$45.00**
Vase, footed, #400/193, 10" **$300.00**
Vase, ivy bowl; #400/74J, 7" **$175.00**
Vase, rose bowl; footed, #400/132, 7½" **$425.00**

Pitcher, #400/24, 80-ounce, $150.00; Tumbler, #400/19, 5¼", 12-oz, $18.00.

Candy Containers

Most of us can recall buying these glass toys as a child, since they were made well into the 1960s. We were fascinated by the variety of their shapes then, just as collectors are today. Looking back, it couldn't have been we were buying them for the candy, though perhaps as a child those tiny sugary balls flavored more with the coloring agent than anything else were enough to satisfy our 'sweet tooth.'

Glass candy containers have been around since our country's centennial celebration in 1876 when the first two, the Liberty Bell and the Independence Hall, were introduced. Since then they have been made in hundreds of styles, and some of them have become very expensive. The leading manufacturers were in the East — Westmoreland, Victory Glass, J.H. Millstein, Crosetti, L.E. Smith, Jack Stough, T.H. Stough, and West Bros. made perhaps 90% of them — and collectors report finding many in the Pennsylvania area. Most are clear, but you'll find them in various other colors as well.

If you're going to deal in candy containers, you'll need a book that will show you all the variations available. A very comprehensive book, *Collector's Guide to Candy Containers* by Douglas M. Dezso, J. Leon Poirier and Rose D. Poirier, was released early in 1998. D&P numbers in our listings refer to that book. Published by Collector Books, it is a must for beginners as well as seasoned collectors. Other references are *The Compleat American Glass Candy Containers Handbook* by Eilkelberner and Agadjaninian (revised by Adele Bowden) and Jenny Long's *Album of Candy Containers, Vol. 1 and Vol. 2*, published in 1978 – 83, now out of print.

Because of their popularity and considerable worth, many of the original containers have been reproduced. Beware of any questionable glassware that has a slick or oily touch. Among those that have been produced are Amber Pistol, Auto, Carpet Sweeper, Chicken on Nest, Display Case, Dog, Drum Mug, Fire Engine, Independence Hall, Jackie Coogan, Kewpie, Mail Box, Mantel Clock, Mule and Waterwagon, Peter Rabbit, Piano, Rabbit Pushing Wheelbarrow, Rocking Horse, Safe, Santa, Santa's Boot, Station Wagon, and Uncle Sam's Hat. Others are possible.

Our values are given for candy containers that are undamaged, in good original paint, and complete (with all original parts and closure). Repaired or repainted containers are worth much less.

See also Christmas; Easter; Halloween.

Advisor: Doug Dezso (See Directory, Candy Containers)

Club/Newsletter: *The Candy Gram*
Candy Container Collectors of America
Joyce L. Doyle
P.O. Box 426, North Reading, MA 01864-0426

Army bomber, D&P #76, ca 1944 ....$50.00
Bulldog, round base, Victory Glass, D&P #18, ca 1930....$100.00
Bus, w/screw-on closure, D&P #153 ....$400.00
Cannon, 2-wheel mount #1, D&P #384, ca 1929-30 .$450.00
Car, streamliner, tin-wheeled, 4-door, Victory Glass, D&P #181 ....$160.00
Charlie Chaplin, by straight barrel, LE Smith, D&P #196, ca 1920s...$600.00
Condiment set, Rainbow Candy, D&P #297, ca 1907 .$60.00
Fire Engine, Fire Department #99, Victory Glass, D&P #252, ca 1944, from $100 to.........................$135.00
Jack-O-Lantern, slant eyes, D&P #265 ....$225.00
Lamp, Kerosene; w/swizzle stick, D&P #333 ....$50.00
Lamp, plastic, cork closure, D&P #340, ca 1950 ....$75.00
Lantern, K600, D&P #355, ca 1912...........................$25.00
Lanterns, 2 hanging on anchor, D&P #370, ca 1920...$30.00
Limousine, West Bros, D&P #169, ca 1913...............$100.00
Locomotive, American Type #23, D&P #489, clear...$175.00

Locomotive, no couplers, D&P #517.........................$200.00
Locomotive, Single Window #888, D&P #500, ca 1940 ..$60.00

Motorcycle, Man On; #466, 5" L, from $500.00 to $600.00. (Photo courtesy Doug Dezso, J. Leon Poirier, and Rose D. Poirier)

Mug, Victory Glass, D&P #434, ca 1938.......................$25.00
Nurser, waisted, D&P #125, ca 1962 ....$30.00
Piano, clear, D&P #460, clear, ca 1920.......................$250.00
Rabbit, crouching, D&P #54 ....$125.00
Racer, plastic, D&P #472 ....$35.00
Revolver, Victory Glass, blown, D&P #404.................$35.00
Santa Claus, Sears, D&P #283, ca 1967 ....$20.00
Scottie, D&P #35, ca 1946...$35.00
Soldier, Doughboy, D&P #209.....................................$300.00
Submarine, George Borgfeldt, D&P #104, ca 1915 ...$600.00
Swing, porch; metal, candy bag tied w/ribbon to seat, D&P #315, ca 1933-36 ....$250.00
Tank, man in turret, D&P #412, ca 1942, from $40 to..$50.00
Telephone, Lynne, sunken dial, D&P #232, ca 1947, from $50 to $60.00
Telephone, Pewter Top #1, D&P #236.......................$150.00
Top, Eagle Glass & Manufacturing, D&P #442, ca 1908 .$125.00
Village School House, metal flag, D&P #143.............$175.00
Wheelbarrow, D&P #531...$100.00
Windmill, plastic bank, D&P #536, ca 1950................$75.00

Cape Cod by Avon

You can't walk through any flea market or mall now without seeing a good supply of this lovely ruby red glassware. It was made by Wheaton Glass Co. and sold by Avon from the 1970s until it was discontinued in 1997, after a gradual phasing-out process that lasted for approximately two years. The small cruet and tall candlesticks, for instance, were filled originally with one or the other of their fragrances, the wine and water goblets were filled with scented candle wax, and the dessert bowl with guest soap. Many 'campaigns' featured accessory tableware items such as plates, cake stands, and a water pitcher. Though still plentiful, dealers tell us that interest in this glassware is on the increase, and we expect values to climb as supplies diminish.

Advisor: Debbie Coe (See Directory, Cape Cod)

Bell, Hostess; marked Christmas 1979, 6½"................**$22.50**

Bell, hostess; unmarked, 1979-80, 6½" **$17.50**

Bowl, dessert; 1978-90, 5" **$14.50**

Bowl, rimmed soup; 1991, 7½" **$20.00**

Bowl, vegetable; marked Centennial Edition 1886-1986, 8¾" **$38.00**

Bowl, vegetable; unmarked, 1986-90, 8¾" **$24.50**

Box, heart form, w/lid, 1989-90, 4" wide **$18.00**

Butter dish, w/lid, 1983-84, ¼-lb, 7" L........................**$22.50**

Cake knife, red plastic handle, wedge-shaped blade, Regent Sheffield, 1981-84, 8" **$18.00**

Candle holder, hurricane-type w/clear chimney, 1985, 13" **$38.00**

Candlestick, 1975-80, 8¾", ea...................................**$12.50**

Candlestick, 1983-84, 2½", ea....................................**$9.75**

Candy dish, 1987-90, 3½x6" dia **$19.50**

Christmas ornament, 6-sided, marked Christmas 1990, 3¼" **$10.00**

Cruet, oil; w/stopper, 1975-80, 5-oz **$12.50**

Cup & saucer, 15th anniversary, marked 1975-1990 on cup, 7-oz **$24.50**

Cup & saucer, 1990-93, 7-oz **$19.50**

Decanter, w/stopper, 1977-80, 16-oz, 10½" **$20.00**

Goblet, champagne; 1991, 8-oz, 5¼" **$12.50**

Goblet, claret; 1992, 5-oz, 5¼".....................................**$9.50**

Goblet, water; 1976-90, 9-oz **$12.50**

Mug, pedestal foot, 1982-84, 6-oz, 5" **$12.50**

Napkin ring, 1989-90, 1¾" dia **$9.50**

Pie plate, server, 1992-93, 10¾" dia **$24.50**

Pitcher, water; footed, 1984-85, 60-oz **$50.00**

Plate, bread & butter; 1992-93, 5½" **$7.50**

Plate, cake; pedestal foot, 1991, 3½x10¾" dia...........**$50.00**

Plate, dessert; 1980-90, 7½"..**$9.50**

Plate, dinner; 1982-90, 11" **$22.50**

Platter, oval, 1986, 13" **$38.00**

Relish, rectangular, 2-part, 1985-86, 9½".....................**$19.50**

Sauce boat, footed, 1988, 8" L **$25.00**

Tidbit tray, 2-tiered (7" & 10" dia), 1987, 9¾" **$49.50**

Sugar bowl, footed, 1980 – 83, $12.50; salt and pepper shakers, 1978 – 80, per pair: unmarked, $10.00, marked May 1978, $17.00; creamer, footed, 1981 – 84, 4", $12.50.

Tumbler, straight-sided, footed, 1988, 8-oz, 3⅜"...........**$9.50**

Tumbler, straight-sided, 1990, 12-oz, 5½"....................**$12.50**

Vase, footed, 1985, 8" **$20.00**

Wine goblet, 1977-80, 3-oz, 4½"..................................**$2.50**

Cardinal China Company

This was the name of a distributing company who had their merchandise made to order and sold it through a chain of showrooms and outlet stores in several states from the late 1940s through the 1950s. (Although they made some of their own pottery early on, we have yet to find out just what they themselves produced.) They used their company name to mark cookie jars (some of which were made by the American Bisque Company), novelty wares and kitchen items, many of which you'll see as you make your flea market rounds. *The Collector's Encyclopedia of Cookie Jars* by Joyce and Fred Roerig (Collector Books) shows a page of their jars, and more can be seen in *American Bisque* by Mary Jane Giacomini (Schiffer).

See also Cookie Jars.

Celery tray, celery stalk shape, 11¾" L **$8.50**

Cup, cowboy hat form **$6.00**

Dresser dish, Doxie-dog...**$18.00**

Egg dish, rooster & flowers on white, 1 lg (for eating) & 2 sm (to hold eggs) indents, 6¼" dia **$10.00**

Egg plate, rosters on white, 12 indents, 9" dia, from $12 to **$15.00**

Gravy separator/server, green, 2½x8x6½" **$8.00**

Measuring spoon holder, cottage w/peaked roof, applied thermometer **$15.00**

Measuring spoon holder, Measure Boy.......................**$20.00**

Measuring spoon holder, flowerpot shape, basketweave base, with spoons, $15.00; spoon rest, single flower, $6.00; salt and pepper shakers, Chinese man and lady, green and yellow, $22.00 for the pair.

Spoon rest, double sunflower form, from $8 to..........**$10.00**

String holder, nest w/chicken figural, from $20 to **$25.00**

Carnival Chalkware

From about 1910 until sometime in the '50s, winners of carnival games everywhere in the United States were awarded chalkware figures of Kewpie dolls, the Lone Ranger, Hula girls, comic characters, etc. The assortment was vast and varied. The earliest were made of plaster with a pink cast. They ranged in size from about 5" up to 16".

They were easily chipped, so when it came time for the carnival to pick up and move on, they had to be carefully wrapped and packed away, a time consuming, tedious chore. When stuffed animals became available, concessionists found that they could simply throw them into a box without fear of damage, and so ended an era.

Today the most valuable of these statues are those modeled after Disney characters, movie stars, and comic book heroes.

Chalkware figures are featured in *The Carnival Chalk Prize, Vols I and II*, and *A Price Guide to Chalkware/Plaster Carnival Prizes*, all written by Thomas G. Morris. Along with photos, descriptions and values, Mr. Morris has also included a fascinating history of carnival life in America.

Advisor: Tom Morris (See Directory, Carnival Chalkware)

Air Raid Warden, holding US flag, ca 1940s, 14" **$95.00**
Alice the Goon, from Popeye cartoon, ca 1930-40, 6".**$95.00**
Apache dancer, hands in pockets, tilted hat, ca 1935-45, 13" **$65.00**
Bathing beauty, ca 1940, 9x7" **$65.00**
Black boy, eating watermelon, marked By Buelah, ca 1930-40, 7½" **$95.00**
Boy & dog, marked Pals, ca 1935-45, 10x9" **$45.00**
Child, kneeling, crossed arms, nude, ca 1920-30, 6" ..**$40.00**
Child, yawning, sitting on knees, ca 1920-30, 6" **$45.00**
Chinaman, marked Chinky, ca 1920-30, 9½" **$110.00**

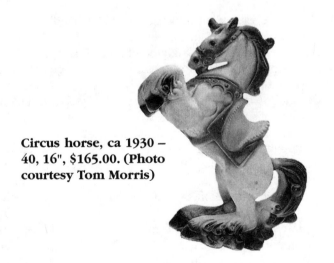

Circus horse, ca 1930 – 40, 16", $165.00. (Photo courtesy Tom Morris)

Dog, sits begging, front marked Have a Heart, back marked 1920, 6½"..**$35.00**
Donald Duck, head bank, Disney, ca 1940-50, 10½" ..**$80.00**
Fan dancer, ashtray, ca 1940, 10½" **$95.00**
Girl, kewpie type, hand-painted & air brushed, jointed arms, mohair wig, crepe paper dress, ca 1920s, 12"....**$185.00**
Girl, sits winking, hand painted, sticker marked Winkie 1919, 6" **$65.00**
Girl w/Homburg type hat, hands in pockets, ca 1930-40, 13½"..**$95.00**

Girl w/sombrero, ca 1930, 14".....................................**$85.00**
Horace the Horse, Disney, marked, ca 1930-40, 11" ..**$60.00**
Indian, ashtray, sitting w/bowl between crossed legs, ca 1930-40, 6"..**$20.00**
Indian, incense burner, ca 1930-40, 4½"......................**$15.00**
Indian, w/drum, marked KC Art Statuary, ca 1940-50, 13"...**$60.00**
Jackie Coogan, hands in suspenders, pink chalk, marked My Boy, 1930s, 17" **$250.00**
Lady, posing, lying on side, hand painted, ca 1920s, 3½x7"...**$135.00**
Little mail boy, ca 1935-45, 7".....................................**$30.00**
Little paper boy, ca 1935-45, 7"...................................**$30.00**
Mae West, as sailor girl, marked WM Rainwater 1936, 14"...**$145.00**
Maggie & Jiggs, Maggie w/rolling pin, Armistice printed on base, ca 1925-40, 11½"..........................**$265.00**
Nora, Maggie & Jigg's daughter, ca 1930-40, 9" **$95.00**
Nude, w/feather, ca 1930-40, 12" **$125.00**
Penguin, w/top hat, glass eyes, ca 1935-45, 7¼"........**$50.00**
Pluto, sitting, ca 1930-40, 6"..**$65.00**
Popeye, smoking pipe, holding can of spinach, ca 1930-40, 21"...**$185.00**
Sailor girl, Jenkin's style, marked Copyright 1934, 14".**$85.00**
Shriner, kewpie type, marked Portland 1920 on base, 10½" **$115.00**

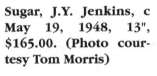

Sugar, J.Y. Jenkins, c May 19, 1948, 13", $165.00. (Photo courtesy Tom Morris)

Three Little Pigs, flat back, 5x5½"................................**$25.00**
Uncle Scrooge, standing w/money bag, ca 1940-50, 8"..**$50.00**
US Sailor, arms folded, ca 1935-45, 13" **$95.00**
US Soldier, kewpie type, jointed arms, ca WWI era.**$165.00**

Cat Collectibles

Cat collectibles continue to grow in popularity as cats continue to dominate the world of household pets. Cat memorabilia can be found in almost all categories, and this allows for collections to grow rapidly! Most cat lovers/collectors are attracted to all items and to all breeds, though some do specialize. Popular categories include Siamese, black cats, Kitty

Cucumber, Kliban, cookie jars, teapots, books, plates, post-cards, and Louis Wain.

Because cats are found throughout the field of collectibles and antiques, there is some 'crossover' competition among collectors. For example: Chessie, the C&O Railroad cat, is collected by railroad and advertising buffs; Felix the Cat, board games, puppets, and Steiff cats are sought by toy collectors. A Weller cat complements a Weller pottery collection just as a Royal Doulton Flambe cat fits into a Flambe porcelain collection.

Since about 1970 the array and quality of cat items have made the hobby explode. And, looking back, the first half of the twentieth century offered a somewhat limited selection of cats — there were those from the later Victorian era, Louis Wain cats, Felix the Cat, the postcard rage, and the kitchen-item black cats of the 1950s. But prior to 1890, cat items were few and far between, so a true antique cat (100-years old or more) is scarce, much sought after, and when found in mint condition, pricey. Examples of such early items would be original fine art, porcelains, and bronzes.

There are several 'cat' books available on today's market; if you want to see great photos representing various aspects of 'cat' collecting, you'll enjoy *Cat Collectibles* by Pauline Flick, *Antique Cats for Collectors* by Katharine Morrison McClinton, *American Cat-alogue* by Bruce Johnson, *The Cat Made Me Buy It* and *The Black Cat Made Me Buy It*, both by Muncaster and Yanow, and *Collectible Cats, Book II,* by Marbena Fyke.

See also Black Cats; Character Collectibles; Cookie Jars; Holt Howard; Lefton.

Advisor: Marilyn Dipboye (See Directory, Cat Collectibles)

Club/Newsletter: Cat Collectors, *Cat Talk*
Marilyn Dipboye, President
33161 Wendy Dr., Sterling Hts., MI 48310; 810-264-0285.
Subscription $20 per year US or $27 Canada. Also conventions.

Bookends, antique white, compo, Universal Statuary Corp Original Sculpture B/W Marlotta **$50.00**
Dish, gold w/brown flowers, pottery, Los Angeles Potteries CA USA, 7¼x6¼" **$15.00**
Doorstop, pink cat w/red hearts & blue bow, metal, American Folkart paper label, 10½" **$8.00**

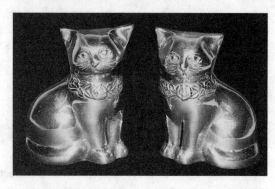

Figurines, brass, Made in Korea on paper label, 4¾", $12.00 for the pair. (Photo courtesy Marilyn Dipboye)

Figurine, brass cat on marble base, 10" tall, 7" square base **$150.00**
Figurine, brown cat w/pink ball, cold-cast porcelain, Made in Italy, 3" **$35.00**
Figurine, cat, green, pottery, no marks, 8x6¾" **$85.00**
Figurine, cat stalking, brass, 9½" **$44.00**
Figurine, orange striped tabby, closed eyes, ceramic, 16"...**$80.00**
Figurine, red tabby Persian, ceramic, Shafford, 1967, 10" ...**$45.00**
Figurine, Siamese, cream & black, Made in Japan label, 5¼" **$12.00**
Figurine, standing cat, white w/multicolored floral wreath around neck, marked Italy, 8½" **$65.00**
Matchbox holder, cat on top, metal, 2¼x1½x3" **$50.00**

Perfume bottle, Max Factor Sophisti-Cat, holds 1-oz. bottle of Golden Woods, plastic dome, M, $25.00. (Photo courtesy Marilyn Dipboye)

Pitcher, wine; elbow cut out for spout, tail is handle, marked WMF Germany, 8" **$30.00**
Planter, cat, cream w/pink & green florals, pottery, 4".**$7.00**
Salt & pepper shakers, royal blue w/pink & green floral, applied pink flowers at neck, 2¼" **$10.50**
Snow globe, musical, yellow tabby atop globe, 2 kittens w/ball of yarn inside, plays White Christmas, Silvestri, 7", MIB **$50.00**
Teapot, light gray cat in Victorian dress w/yellow overskirt, carrying a fan-shaped purse & bouquet of flowers (spout) **$30.00**
Thermometer, white metal cat on base, hammered aluminum, 5¼" **$40.00**
Toy, gray & white stuffed cat, meows & moves front paws, battery-operated **$24.00**
Toy, yellow tabby w/wire tail, tin, roll-over, key wind, orig box, 5" **$20.00**
Tray, sleeping cat shaped, blue & cream, pottery, signed Sautler 76, 9½" **$22.00**

Character Cats

Cat in the Hat, ornament, hand-painted resin, 4½" **$18.00**
Cat in the Hat, pocket watch, figural, lights up, swivel clip attachment, Art Watch International, M in collector's tin..**$35.00**

Cat in the Hat, trinket box, porcelain, 4"......................**$27.00**

Cheshire Cat, suncatcher, Wonderland Miniature series, Glassmasters Inc, oval, 4¾" **$35.00**

Chessie, candy jar, Sea Green Satin, embossed image, Fenton, limited edition, 8", EX **$46.00**

Chessie, pin-back, Chesapeake & Ohio Railway, Whitehead-Hogg, Newark, NJ, EX..**$16.50**

Chessie, playing cards, B&O Chessie System Railroad, full deck, MIB (unopened) **$30.00**

Felix the Cat, button sew-on cards, buttons, yarn & cards on diecut figural, 1959, 7¼x11", EX..........................**$50.00**

Felix the Cat, cookie jar, black & white, Clay Art, 9½", M **$32.00**

Felix the Cat, doll, plush, velvet eyes, marked Applause 1988, 20", EX **$8.00**

Felix the Cat, pin, carrying sign reading If You Can Read This, You're Too Darn Close, black & red enamel, 1¼", EX **$27.00**

Felix the Cat, pin-back, Act Weird And Make Them Wonder, 1¼", M **$8.00**

Felix the Cat, pin-back, winking w/thumb up, 1" dia ..**$8.00**

Felix the Cat, Rummy Card Game, Built Rite Toys, Felix w/top hat & cane next to puppy on box, EX......**$30.00**

Felix the Cat, slide-tile puzzle, EX (G original card) ..**$30.00**

Figaro, pin, dancing, cloisonne..**$8.00**

Garfield, bib, image of Garfield riding in sleigh, MOC...**$2.00**

Garfield, bookends, pushing against wall, Enesco, pr, from $150 to..**$175.00**

Garfield, books, United Features Publications, 1981-84, ea **$10.00**

Garfield, Christmas ornament, Hallmark, 1992, 2½" ...**$10.00**

Garfield, Danbury Mint figurines, 6 different scenes, ea..**$35.00**

Garfield, clock, Sunbeam #89230, Assembled in China, 6½", EX, $55.00.

Garfield, Danbury Mint plate, Dreams Can Take You Anywhere **$25.00**

Garfield, Danbury Mint plate, I Deny Everything **$25.00**

Garfield, doll, Souvenir of Colorado, 9½" **$25.00**

Garfield, doll, talker, Mattel, 1983, 10", EX................**$45.00**

Garfield, figure, Garfield as Santa, vinyl, 6", EX.........**$25.00**

Garfield, jack-in-the-box, Pop Goes the Odie, MIB....**$30.00**

Garfield, pin dish, 4" **$10.00**

Garfield, play money, MIP **$3.00**

Garfield, salt & pepper shakers, Garfield Santa heads, Enesco, 1993, pr..**$15.00**

Garfield, shoe lace holders **$5.00**

Garfield, Talking Telephone, says 10 different things...**$40.00**

Garfield, trinket box, Be My Valentine, ceramic, Enesco....**$30.00**

Garfield, trivet, cartoon w/Garfield at table eating, 9x4¾".**$10.00**

Garfield, yo-yo **$10.00**

Kitty Cucumber, Ellie, green & white striped nightgown & sleeping hat, holding red candle, 1985, Schmid sticker, EX........**$45.00**

Kitty Cucumber, Ginger, in pale blue bridesmaid dress w/bouquet of flowers & hankerchief, 1989, EX...**$18.50**

Kitty Cucumber, Ginger, Loves Me Loves Me Not, Victorian Garden Party Series, sits on bench, EXIB (w/display card)..**$25.00**

Kitty Cucumber, Ginger in clown suit riding unicycle, EXIB (w/original pamphlet) **$40.00**

Kitty Cucumber, in basket of hearts & flowers, music box plays Love Me Tender, 1987-88, 5¼" **$38.00**

Kitty Cucumber, ornament, Kitty & snowman, #333-106, 3-D, 1987, 3¼", EX..**$90.00**

Kitty Cucumber, Priscilla & Buster, Christmas Waltz, #31242, 1992, MIB **$30.00**

Kliban, bank, wearing red sneakers, 1979, 6½".........**$85.00**

Kliban, beach towel, Shower Cat, sits in the rain w/umbrella, ca 1980s, 35x58", EX..**$45.00**

Kliban, candy jar, Sigma, 10", $85.00.

Kliban, cookie jar, playing guitar, Sigma, from $165 to .**$180.00**

Kliban, creamer, mouth spout, tail handle, Sigma **$85.00**

Kliban, doll, Hula Fat Cat, in grass skirt & lei, plush, w/Kliban tag & Hawaii crazy shirt tag, plush, 10", EX.........**$55.00**

Kliban, mug, I Love LA, MIB **$8.00**

Kliban, pillow, pattern of tiny black cats on white on reverse side, 22" L, M **$22.00**

Kliban, pillow, stuffed figure, 22"................................**$22.00**

Kliban, rubber stamp, Holding Tight, 2 cats cuddle w/tails together, heart overhead, NM **$35.00**

Kliban, sugar bowl, top of head forms lid, Sigma **$75.00**

Kliban, teapot, in airplane, Sigma #246, from $325 to ..**$375.00**

Kliban, teapot, in tuxedo, from $175 to **$285.00**

Kliban, wastebasket, 12"..**$22.50**

Cat-Tail Dinnerware

Cat-Tail was a dinnerware pattern popular during the late '20s until sometime in the '40s. So popular, in fact, that ovenware, glassware, tinware, even a kitchen table was made to coordinate with it. The dinnerware was made primarily by Universal Potteries of Cambridge, Ohio, though a catalog from Hall China circa 1927 shows a three-piece coffee service, and others may have produced it as well. It was sold for years by Sears Roebuck and Company, and some items bear a mark that includes their name.

The pattern is unmistakable: a cluster of red cattails (usually six, sometimes one or two) with black stems on creamy white. Shapes certainly vary; Universal used at least three of their standard mold designs, Camwood, Old Holland, Laurella, and possibly others. Some Cat-Tail pieces are marked Wheelock on the bottom. (Wheelock was a department store in Peoria, Illinois.)

If you're trying to decorate a '40s vintage kitchen, no other design could afford you more to work with. To see many of the pieces that are available and to learn more about the line, read *The Collector's Encyclopedia of American Dinnerware* by Jo Cunningham (Collector Books).

Advisors: Barbara and Ken Brooks (See Directory, Dinnerware)

Bean pot, 2 handles	$35.00
Bowl, footed, 9½"	$20.00
Bowl, mixing; 7"	$15.00
Bowl, mixing; 8"	$23.00
Bowl, soup; 8"	$15.00
Bowl, straight sides, 4¼"	$8.00
Bowl, straight sides, 6¼"	$12.00
Bowl, sunken knob lid, 2-qt, 8¼"	$30.00
Bowl, 6¼"	$10.00
Butter dish, 1-lb	$50.00
Butter dish, ¼-lb	$48.00
Casserole, tab handle, 7½"	$34.00
Coffeepot, electric	$150.00
Cookie jar, from $100 to	$135.00
Creamer	$20.00
Cup, from $20 to	$25.00
Custard cup	$9.00
Fork	$35.00
Gravy boat, from $18 to	$25.00
Gravy liner, from $15 to	$25.00
Jug, ball; ceramic-topped cork stopper	$37.50
Jug, batter	$75.00
Jug, canteen	$38.00
Jug, syrup	$75.00
Jug, 1-qt, 6"	$25.00
Leftover, 4" dia	$12.00
Leftover, 6" dia	$25.00
Pie baker, 10"	$30.00
Pitcher, barrel shape, w/reamer, from $150 to	$175.00
Plate, chop	$35.00
Plate, grill	$30.00
Plate, square, 7¼"	$7.00
Plate, 10"	$15.00
Platter, oval, 11½", from $15 to	$20.00
Platter, oval, 13½"	$30.00
Platter, round, tab handle, 11"	$30.00
Salt & pepper shakers, pr, from $15 to	$20.00
Saucer, from $3 to	$6.00

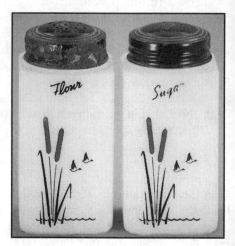

Shakers, Flour or Sugar, white glass with metal tops, 4¼", from $25.00 to $35.00 each. (Photo courtesy Barbara and Ken Brooks)

Shakers, Salt or Pepper, glass, made by Tipp, ea, from $25 to	$35.00
Spoon	$35.00
Sugar bowl, w/lid, from $20 to	$25.00
Teapot, 6-cup, from $42.50 to	$50.00
Tray, for batter set	$75.00
Tumbler, iced tea; glass, from $45 to	$50.00
Tumbler, marked Universal Potteries, scarce, from $65 to	$70.00
Tumbler, water; glass	$35.00

Catalin Napkin Rings

Plastic (Catalin) napkin rings topped with heads of cartoon characters, animals, and birds are very collectible, especially examples in red and orange; blue is also good, and other colors can be found as well.

Band, lathe turned, amber, red or green, 1¾"	$10.00
Band, plain, amber, red or green, 2", ea	$8.00
Band, plain, colors, 2", set of 6, MIB	$40.00
Camel, inlaid eye rod	$72.00
Chicken, no inlaid eyes	$30.00
Donald Duck, w/decal, from $65 to	$80.00
Duck, no inlaid eyes	$30.00
Elephant, ball on head	$35.00
Elephant, inlaid eye rod	$40.00
Elephant, no ball on head	$30.00
Fish, no inlaid eyes	$30.00
Mickey Mouse, w/decal, from $70 to	$85.00
Rabbit, inlaid eye rod	$40.00
Rabbit, no inlaid eyes	$30.00

Rocking horse, inlaid eye rod.....................................$72.00
Schnauzer dog, no inlaid eyes.................................$30.00

Scottie dog, no eye rod, $40.00, with inlaid eye rod, $50.00. (Photo courtesy Candace Sten Davis and Patricia Baugh)

Ceramic Arts Studio

American-made figurines are very popular now, and these are certainly among the best. They have a distinctive look you'll soon learn to identify with confidence, even if you happen to pick up an unmarked piece. They were first designed in the '40s and sold well until the company closed in 1955. (After that, the new owner took the molds to Japan and produced them over there for a short time.) The company's principal designer was Betty Harrington, who modeled the figures and knicknacks that so many have grown to love. In addition to the company's marks (there were at least seven, possibly more), many of the later pieces she designed carry their assigned names on the bottom as well.

The company also produced a line of metal items to accessorize the figurines. These were designed by Liberace's stepmother, Zona, who was also Betty's personal friend and art director of the figurine line.

Though prices continue to climb, once in a while one of many unmarked bargains can be found, but first you must familiarize yourself with your subject!

Advisors: BA Wellman and John Canfield
(See Directory, Ceramic Arts Studio)
e-mail: bawellman@net1plus.com

Catalog Reprints: BA Wellman and John Canfield
P.O. Box 673, Westminster, MA 01473-1435

Newsletter/Club: CAS Collectors Association
CAS Collector quarterly newsletter
P.O. Box 46, Madison, WI 53701; 608-241-9138
Newsletter $15; Annual membership, $15. Inventory record and price guide listing 800+ works, $12 postage paid.

Accessory, garden shelf, metal, for Mary Contrary, 4x12".**$95.00**
Accessory, park bench, wood, 1¾x2"..........................**$50.00**
Accessory, sofa, metal, for Maurice & Michelle, from $60 to...**$80.00**
Accessory, spider web, corner; metal, for Miss Muffet, 4"...**$95.00**
Accessory, window, metal, for religious figure, either style...**$75.00**

Ashtray, hippo, 3½"...$165.00
Figurine, accordion boy, 5".....................................$80.00
Figurine, Adonis, 9"..$275.00
Figurine, angel, praying boy, 3¼"...............................$80.00
Figurine, angel w/star, standing, 5½"...........................$80.00
Figurine, angels, Blessing, hand down, 5¾"......................$90.00
Figurine, Autumn Andy, 5", from $85 to...........................$95.00
Figurine, Bali-Gong, crouched, 5½"..............................$95.00
Figurine, Bashful girl, 4½".....................................$90.00
Figurine, bass violin boy, 5"...................................$75.00
Figurine, Billy, boxer (dog), sprawling, 2" L...................$95.00
Figurine, Black baby, Bobby, 3¼"................................$265.00
Figurine, bunny, 1¾"...$50.00
Figurine, bunny mother, snuggle, 4½"............................$50.00
Figurine, cellist man, 6½".....................................$295.00

Figurine, Cinderella and Prince Charming, green, $175.00 for the pair.

Figurine, circus dog, 2½".......................................$50.00
Figurine, collie pup sleeping, 2¼"..............................$45.00
Figurine, Colonial man, 6½".....................................$65.00
Figurine, cow, snuggle, 5½"....................................$120.00
Figurine, duckling, 2¼"...$75.00
Figurine, Egyptian woman, 9½"..................................$325.00
Figurine, Encore man, 8½"......................................$135.00
Figurine, fawn, 4¼"...$50.00
Figurine, fish, head up or w/straight tail, pr.................$95.00
Figurine, Frisky the colt, 3¾".................................$125.00
Figurine, Frisky the lamb, plain, 3¾"...........................$50.00
Figurine, horse, mother, 4¼"...................................$125.00
Figurine, Inky & Dinky, skunks, 2¼", pr, from $65 to.$85.00
Figurine, Katrinka, chubby, 6¼".................................$95.00
Figurine, kitten w/ball, 2".....................................$45.00
Figurine, kitten washing, 2"....................................$45.00
Figurine, leopards, fighting, pr, from $250 to.................$295.00
Figurine, lion & lioness, 5" L, 6½", pr........................$450.00
Figurine, Little Miss Muffet #2, 4".............................$80.00
Figurine, Lu-Tang (man), 6".....................................$60.00
Figurine, Minnehaha, standing, 6½".............................$165.00
Figurine, Mr Monkey, scratching, 4".............................$95.00
Figurine, Our Lady of Fatima, 9"...............................$195.00
Figurine, Palomino colt, 5¾"...................................$150.00
Figurine, Paul Bunyan, 4½"......................................$75.00
Figurine, Pepita, Pan-American, 4½".............................$45.00

Figurine, Pied Piper, early & rare, 6¼" **$195.00**
Figurine, Pioneer Suzie w/broom accessory, 5" **$65.00**
Figurine, Polish boy & girl, 6½", 6½", pr **$120.00**
Figurine, pomeranians, sitting & standing, pr **$125.00**
Figurine, Rebekah, 10" **$165.00**
Figurine, Rep the elephant, 4½" **$125.00**
Figurine, Rhumba woman, 7" **$85.00**
Figurine, rooster, stylized, 7" **$135.00**
Figurine, saxophone boy, 5" **$75.00**
Figurine, seal on rock, 2-pc, very rare, set................**$450.00**
Figurine, shepherd & shepherdess, 8½", pr **$275.00**
Figurine, Smi-Li & Mo-Pi, 6", pr..................................**$60.00**
Figurine, Spaniel pup, 2"...**$50.00**

Figurines, sultan and harem girls, $225.00 for the set.

Figurine, Swedish Dance couple, 7", pr **$395.00**
Figurine, Tembino the baby elephant, 2½" **$150.00**
Figurine, tiger, stylized, 5" L **$225.00**
Figurine, tortoise w/cane, standing, 2¼" **$95.00**
Figurine, Water man & woman, 11½", pr **$495.00**
Figurine, Wendy, 5¼" **$95.00**
Figurine, White baby, Woody, 3¼" **$165.00**
Head vase, Becky, 5¼" **$165.00**
Head vase, Sven, 6"...**$175.00**
Jug, rose; 3" **$45.00**
Jug/pitcher, Toby, 2¾" **$65.00**
Lamp, Bali-Lao **$400.00**
Lamp, Lester Lutist..**$450.00**
Mug, Barber Shop Quartet, 3½" **$150.00**
Planter, bamboo, 2½" **$35.00**
Plaque, Arabesque, 9¼" **$70.00**
Plaque, Black-a-moor, 4¾"..**$295.00**
Plaque, cockatoos, A & B, 7½", pr **$165.00**
Plaque, Columbine & Harlequin, 8", pr **$225.00**
Plaque, Comedy & Tragedy masks, 5", pr.................**$165.00**
Plaque, Jack & the metal beanstalk, 6½", set............**$165.00**
Plaque, Lotus lantern woman, 8"..................................**$95.00**
Plaque, Shadow Dancers, A &B, pr **$185.00**
Salt & pepper shakers, bear & cub, brown, snuggle type, pr,
  from $65 to...**$90.00**
Salt & pepper shakers, clown & dog, snuggle, pr....**$235.00**
Salt & pepper shakers, cocks fighting, pr, from $70 to..**$80.00**
Salt & pepper shakers, Dutch boy & girl, 4", pr **$50.00**
Salt & pepper shakers, fish on tail, pr **$75.00**

Salt & pepper shakers, fox & goose, pr **$225.00**
Salt & pepper shakers, frog & toadstool, pr, from $75 to ..**$95.00**
Salt & pepper shakers, girl kneeling in chair, pr **$95.00**
Salt & pepper shakers, mouse & cheese, snuggle, 2", 3",
  pr..**$65.00**
Salt & pepper shakers, Mr & Mrs Penguin, pr, from $80
  to **$100.00**
Salt & pepper shakers, Peek & Boo, Siamese cats, snuggle,
  pr..**$185.00**
Salt & pepper shakers, Sabu & elephant, snuggle, 2¾", pr...**$265.00**
Salt & pepper shakers, sea horse & seaweed, snuggle, 3½",
  pr..**$185.00**
Salt & pepper shakers, Suzette the poodle & pillow, pr..**$250.00**
Salt & pepper shakers, Wee Chinese girl & boy, 3", pr ..**$35.00**
Salt & pepper shakers, Wee Pigs, pr **$95.00**
Salt & pepper shakers, Wee Scottish boy & girl, pr...**$80.00**
Salt & pepper shakers, Wee Swedish boy & girl, pr...**$75.00**
Shelf sitter, Balinese boy & girl, 5½", pr...................**$295.00**
Shelf sitter, boy w/dog & girl w/cat, 4¼", pr...........**$145.00**
Shelf sitter, canary, 5" **$65.00**
Shelf sitter, cowboy & cowgirl, 4¾", pr...................**$165.00**
Shelf sitter, Dutch boy & girl, 4½", pr......................**$65.00**
Shelf sitter, En Pos & En Repos, ballerinas, pr.........**$195.00**
Shelf sitter, farm girl & farm boy fishing w/pole & fish, pr.**$195.00**
Shelf sitter, Fluffy & Tuffy the cats, 7", pr **$185.00**
Shelf sitter, Mexican girl & boy, pr **$195.00**
Shelf sitter, Michelle & Maurice, pr **$165.00**
Shelf sitter, Pete & Polly parrots, 7½", pr **$195.00**
Shelf sitter, Pierrot & Pierette, 6½", pr......................**$185.00**
Teapot, grapes, 2" **$75.00**
Vase, flying ducks relief, round, 2" **$45.00**

Cereal Boxes and Premiums

Yes, cereal boxes — your eyes aren't deceiving you. But think about it. Cereal boxes from even the '60s have to be extremely scarce. The ones that are bringing the big bucks today are those with a well-known character emblazoned across the front. Am I starting to make more sense to you? Good. Now, say the experts, is the time to look ahead into the future of your cereal box collection. They recommend going to your neighborhood supermarket to inspect the shelves in the cereal aisle today! Choose the ones with Batman, Quisp, Ninja Turtles, or some other '90s' phenomenon. Take them home and (unless you have mice) display them unopened, or empty them out and fold them up along the seam lines. If you want only the old boxes, you'll probably have to find an old long-abandoned grocery store or pay prices somewhere around those in our listings when one comes up for sale.

Store displays and advertising posters, in-box prizes or 'send-a-ways,' coupons with pictures of boxes, and shelf signs and cards are also part of this field of interest.

Our values are based on examples in mint condition. If you want to learn more about this field of collecting, we recommend *Toys of the Sixties* by Bill Bruegman; *Cereal Box*

Bonanza, The 1950s, ID and Values, and *Cereal Boxes and Prizes, 1960s* , both by Scott Bruce.

See also Advertising Characters; Toys, Rings.

Advisor: Scott Bruce (See Directory, Advertising)

Newsletter: *FLAKE, The Breakfast Nostalgia Magazine*
P.O. Box 481
Cambridge, MA 02140; 617-492-5004

Boxes

Alpha Bits, Ruff & Reddy cutout & Fury adventure kit, Post, 1960, 8½"...**$200.00**
Apple Jacks, color comics & bully-buster card game, Kellogg, 1966, 9"...**$225.00**
Cap'n Crunch, bo'sun whistle, Quaker Oats, 1964, 9½"....**$200.00**
Cap'n Crunch's Peanut Butter Crunch, free action figure promo, game on back, 1986, flat, EX.................**$22.00**
Cocoa Krispies, recipes, Kellogg, 1960, 9¾" **$150.00**
Corn Chex, checkerboard squarecrow doll, Ralston, 1966-67, 11¼"..**$95.00**

Corn Flakes, Canadian, 1960, 12½", from $100.00 to $150.00; Yogi Bear mug, from $10.00 to $15.00. (Photo courtesy Scott Bruce)

Corn Flakes, Hey Yogi Bear record, Kellogg, 1964, 9¾"..**$100.00**
Corn Flakes w/Instant Bananas, Pronto Banana Man, introductory, Kellogg, 1965, 9"...................................**$225.00**
Country Corn Flakes w/Rice, scarecrow, General Mills, 1963, 9½"...**$45.00**
Froot Loops, Batman periscope, Kellogg, 1966, 10".**$400.00**
Frosted Sugar Stars, hillbilly goat, famous folklore folks, Kellogg, 1965, 9"..**$150.00**
Honey Wheats, Howdy Doody rings, Nabisco, 1960, 9½"...**$200.00**
Jets, go-carting boys picnic cutout, General Mills, 1961, 9½"...**$125.00**
Jets, Tooter-tune toys, General Mills, 1960, 9½" **$150.00**
Maypo, Marky Maypo shirt offer, Maltex, 1961, 7" ...**$200.00**

OKs, Big Otis catapult game, Kellogg, 1960, 11¼"...**$225.00**
Quake, comic book, Quaker Oats, 1966, 10½".........**$750.00**

Quaker Puffed Rice box with Sgt. Preston Klondike land offer, 1955, 9", $150.00; Sgt. Preston's Klondike prospector pouch, chamois cloth, 1955, 4½", $45.00. (Photo courtesy Scott Bruce)

Raisin Bran, Batman printing press, Kellogg, 8" **$300.00**
Rice Honeys, Buffalo Bee, Mary Poppins pop-up, Nabisco, 1964, 9½"...**$200.00**
Rice Krispies, Dennis the Menace cereal spoon & free fruit offer, Kellogg, 1961, 8½"...................................**$125.00**
Spoon Size Shreaded Wheat, totem pole head, Nabisco, 1961, 7¾"...**$65.00**
Sugar Coated Corn Flakes, Cornelius, Bugs Bunny Magic Water Paint book, Post, 1961, 11" **$150.00**
Sugar Crisp, Dandy-style bear, pick-up sticks, Post, 1964, 9" **$75.00**
Sugar Pops, Fort Tomahawk playset offer, Kellogg, 1963, 9¾"...**$125.00**
Sugar Pops, Sugar Pops Pete, Mark Wilson's trick, Kellogg, 1961, 9¾"...**$125.00**
Sugar Sparkled Flakes, genie boy, action football player kit offer, Post, 1963, 10½" **$125.00**
Top 3, introductory (3 sheep), Post, 1960, 10"..........**$125.00**
Trix, Corvair contest/Impala model, General Mills, 1960, 9½"...**$150.00**
Twinkles, grab-bag flap, General Mills, 1963, 9½" ...**$175.00**
Wackies, introductory, General Mills, 1965, 9½".......**$250.00**
Wheaties, Bob Richards raw wheat commercial, General Mills, 1966, 12¼"...**$45.00**
40% Bran Flakes, Plymouth Fury contest, Post, 1960, 11"..**$125.00**

Premiums

Bank, Tony the Tiger, Kellogg, 1968, 8¾" **$75.00**
Book, adventure; Quake, Quaker Oats, 1968, 8¼x11".**$100.00**
Book, joke; Homer & Jethro's Confucius Say, Kellogg, 1964, 7¼x5"..**$25.00**
Buttons, rub-on transfers, Archies, Post, 1969, 5x6" sheet, ea **$75.00**
Cards, Dr Dolittle, Post, 1967, 2½x3¾" (in box).........**$50.00**

Coins, picture; Monkees, Kellogg, 1967, 1¼" dia, ea..**$45.00**

Comic book, Yogi's Birthday, Kellogg, 1962, 10¼x7¼"..**$35.00**

Compass, Cap'n Crunch, Quaker Oats, 1966, 8½"......**$75.00**

Critter cards, Linus's, Post, 1964, 2¼x3¾" (in box) **$50.00**

Dwarf (Snow White) walkers w/tunnel (cutout), Nabisco, 1967, 2¼", ea..**$30.00**

Finger puppet, Huckleberry Hound, Kellogg, 1960....**$15.00**

Flicker rings, 6 different Howdy Doody characters, Nabisco Rice Honeys cereal, NM+, ea.................................**$28.00**

Model, Russian Tu-104 jet, Post, 1960, 8½"................**$60.00**

Model, 1960 Impala, General Mills, 1960, 8"............**$175.00**

Models, 1961 Thunderbird, Post, 3¼"..........................**$20.00**

Periscope, Batman; Kellogg, 1966, expands from 11" to 21"..**$75.00**

Puzzle, jig-jag; Smakin' Brothers, Kellogg, cutout, 1966, 5¾x5½"...**$7.00**

Records, Banana Splits, Kellogg, 1968, in 7x7" square sleeve, ea **$85.00**

Rings, flicker; Monkees, Kellogg, 1967, ¾", ea **$45.00**

Roy Rogers plastic cup, Quaker Oats Co., 1950, 4", $25.00. (Photo courtesy Scott Bruce)

Sponge, Twinkles the Elephant, General Mills, 1960-61, 4¼x3¼"..**$50.00**

Stampets printing set, Huckleberry Hound, Kellogg, 1961, 4½"..**$45.00**

Toy, So-Hi rickshaw, plastic, Post, 1963, 2½"..............**$45.00**

Toy, stuffed; Toucan Sam, cloth, Kellogg, 1964, 8".....**$45.00**

Toy, Woody Woodpecker swimmer, Kellogg, 1967, 7½" .**$100.00**

Toys, Yogi or Huckleberry Hound, stuffed, Kellogg, 1960, 18", ea..**$45.00**

Train, crazy; Cocoa Puff Kids, General Mills, locomotive & 3 cars, 1959-61, 12" L...**$100.00**

Wiggle picture, Sherman & Peabody, Wheat Hearts, General Mills, 1960, 6 different views, 1x1¼"....................**$15.00**

Character and Promotional Drinking Glasses

In any household, especially those with children, I would venture to say, you should find a few of these glasses. Put out by fast-food restaurant chains or by a company promoting a product, they have for years been commonplace. But now, instead of glass, the giveaways are nearly always plastic. If a glass is offered at all, you'll usually have to pay 99¢ for it.

Some are worth more than others. Among the common ones are Camp Snoopy, B.C. Ice Age, Garfield, McDonald's, Smurfs, and Coca-Cola. The better glasses are those with super heroes, characters from Star Trek and '30s movies such as 'Wizard of Oz,' sports personalities, and cartoon characters by Walter Lantz and Walt Disney. Some of these carry a copyright date, and that's all it is. It's not the date of manufacture.

Many collectors are having a good time looking for these glasses. If you want to learn more about them, we recommend *Tomart's Price Guide to Character and Promotional Drinking Glasses* by Carol Markowski, and *Collectible Drinking Glasses, Identification and Values*, by our advisors Mark Chase and Michael Kelly (Collector Books).

There are some terms used in the descriptions that may be confusing. 'Brockway' style refers to a thick, heavy glass that tapers in from top to bottom. 'Federal' style, on the other hand, is thinner, and the top and bottom diameters are the same.

Advisors: Mark Chase and Michael Kelly (See Directory, Character and Promotional Drinking Glasses)

Newsletter: *Collector Glass News*
P.O. Box 308
Slippery Rock, PA 16057; 724-946-2838; fax: 724-946-9012 or e-mail: cgn@glassnews.com; www.glassnews.com

Al Capp Characters, Brockway, 1975, 16-oz, footed, Mammy, Pappy, Sadie, Lil' Abner, or Daisy Mae, ea, from $40 to............**$80.00**

Animal Crackers, Chicago Tribune/NT News Syndicate, 1978, Lyle Dodo, Gnu, Lana, Eugene, ea, from $7 to....**$10.00**

Animal Crackers, Chicago Tribune/NY News Syndicate, 1978, Louis, scarce, from $25 to **$35.00**

Apollo Series, Marathon Oil, ea, from $3 to...................**$5.00**

Arby's, Bicentennial Cartoon Character Series, 1976, 10 different, 6", ea, from $20 to **$30.00**

Archies, Welch's, 1971, 6 different w/many variations, ea ..**$3.00**

Archies, Welch's, 1973, 6 different w/many variations, ea ..**$3.00**

Battlestar Galactica, Universal Studios, 1979, 4 different, ea, from $7 to..**$10.00**

Burger Chef, Burger Chef & Jeff, Now We're Glassified!, from $15 to **$25.00**

Burger Chef, Endangered Species Collector's Series, 1978, Tiger, Orang-Utan, Bald Eagle, ea, from $5 to **$7.00**

Burger Chef, Friendly Monster Series, 1977, 6 different, ea, from $20 to..**$35.00**

Burger King, Dallas Cowboys, Dr Pepper, 6 different, ea, from $7 to..**$15.00**

Burger King, Have It Your Way 1776-1976 Series, 1976, 4 different, ea, from $4 to...**$6.00**

Currier & Ives, Arby's, 1975-76, 4 different, titled, ea, from $3 to **$5.00**

Dick Tracy, 1940s, frosted, 8 different characters, 3" or 5", ea, from $50 to...**$75.00**

Disney Characters, 1936, Mickey, Minnie, Donald, Pluto, Clarabelle, Horace, F Bunny, 4¼" or 4¾", ea, from $40 to **$75.00**

Disney Characters, 1990, frosted tumblers, Mickey, Minnie, Donald, Daisy, Goofy, or Scrooge face images, ea, from $5 to **$8.00**

Disney Collector Series, Burger King, 1994, multicolored images on clear plastic, 8 different, MIB, ea **$3.00**

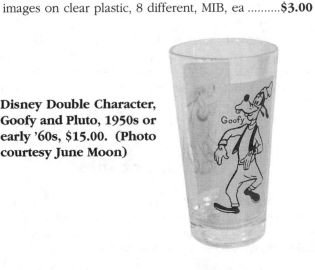

Disney Double Character, Goofy and Pluto, 1950s or early '60s, $15.00. (Photo courtesy June Moon)

Disney's All-Star Parade, 1939, 10 different, ea, from $40 to **$75.00**

Domino's Pizza, Avoid the Noid, 1988, 4 different, ea .**$7.00**

Elsie the Cow, Borden, Elsie & family in 1976 Bicentennial parade, red, white & blue graphics, from $5 to **$7.00**

ET, Pepsi/MCA Home Video, 1988, 6 different, ea, from $15 to **$25.00**

Flintstone Kids, Pizza Hut, 1986, 4 different, ea, from $2 to **$4.00**

Flintstones, Welch's, 1962 (6 different), 1963 (2 different), 1964 (6 different), ea, from $8 to **$12.00**

Goonies, Godfather's Pizza/Warner Bros, 1985, 4 different, ea, from $4 to **$8.00**

Hanna-Barbera, Pepsi/Brockway, 1977, Yogi/Huck, Josie/Pussycats, Mumbly, Scooby, Flintstones, Dynomutt, ea, from $20 to **$35.00**

Hanna-Barbera, 1960s, jam glass w/Flintstones, Yogi Bear, Quick Draw, Cindy Bear, Huck, rare, ea, from $75 to **$110.00**

Happy Days, Dr Pepper/Pizza Hut, 1977, Ralph, Joanie, Potsie, ea, from $8 to **$12.00**

Harvey Cartoon Characters, Pepsi, 1970s, action pose, Casper, Baby Huey, Wendy, Hot Stuff, ea, from $8 to **$15.00**

Harvey Cartoon Characters, Pepsi, 1970s, static pose, Richie Rich, from $15 to **$25.00**

Harvey Cartoon Characters, Pepsi, 1970s, static pose, Sad Sack, scarce, from $25 to **$35.00**

Howdy Doody, Welch's/Kagran, 1950s, 6 different, embossed bottom, ea, from $15 to **$20.00**

Indiana Jones & the Temple of Doom, 7-Up (w/4 different co-sponsors), 1984, set of 4, ea, from $8 to **$15.00**

James Bond 007, 1985, 4 different, ea, from $10 to ...**$15.00**

Jungle Book, Canadian, three from a set of six, from $35.00 to $50.00 each. (Photo courtesy Collector Glass News)

Jungle Book, Disney/Pepsi, 1970s, Mowgli, unmarked, from $40 to **$50.00**

Keebler, Soft Batch Cookies, 1984, 4 different, ea, from $7 to **$10.00**

King Kong, Coca-Cola, Dino De Laurentis Corp, 1976, from $5 to **$8.00**

Leonardo TTV, Collector Series, Pepsi, Underdog, Sweet Polly, Simon Bar Sinister, 5", ea, from $8 to.........**$15.00**

Looney Tunes/Warner Bros, Arby's, 1988, Adventures Series, footed, Bugs, Daffy, Porky, Sylvester, ea, from $35 to **$45.00**

Looney Tunes/Warner Bros, Pepsi, 1973, Bugs, Daffy, Porky, Sylvester, Tweety, Road Runner, 16-oz, ea, from $5 to **$12.00**

Looney Tunes/Warner Bros, Pepsi Collector's Series, 1979, round bottom, 6 different, ea, $7 to....................**$10.00**

Looney Tunes/Warner Bros, Welch's, 1976-77, 8 different, names around bottom, ea, from $5 to **$7.00**

Mark Twain Country Series, Burger King, 1985, 4 different, ea, from $8 to **$10.00**

Masters of the Universe, Mattel, 1983, Teels, He-Man, Skeletor, Man-at-Arms, ea, from $5 to...................**$10.00**

McDonald's, Camp Snoopy, 1983, white plastic, Lucy or Snoopy, ea, from $5 to..**$8.00**

McDonald's, McDonaldland Collector Series, 1970s, 6 different, ea **$4.00**

MGM Collector Series, Pepsi, 1975, Tom, Jerry, Tuffy, Barney, Droopy, or Spike, ea, from $10 to **$15.00**

Mickey Mouse, Happy Birthday, Pepsi, 1978, Daisy & Donald, from $12 to **$15.00**

Mickey Mouse, Happy Birthday, Pepsi, 1978, Mickey, Minnie, Donald, Goofy, Pluto, Uncle Scrooge, ea, from $6 to..**$10.00**

Mickey Mouse, Mickey's Christmas Carol, Coca-Cola, 1982, 3 different, ea **$10.00**

NFL, Mobil Oil, helmets on colored bands, Colts, Oilers, Steelers, Cowboys, rocks w/flat bottom, ea, from $2 to **$4.00**

NFL, Mobil Oil, helmets on white bands, Redskins, Bills, Steelers, Eagles, Buccaneers, footed rocks, ea, from $3 to **$5.00**

Norman Rockwell, Summer Scenes, Arby's, 1987, 4 different, tall, ea, from $3 to **$5.00**

PAT Ward, Pepsi, late 1970s, static pose, Boris & Natasha, 6", from $20 to..**$25.00**

Peanuts Characters, Kraft, 1988, Snoopy in pool, Lucy on swing, Snoopy on surfboard, Charlie Brown flying kite, ea..**$2.00**

Peanuts Characters, Snoopy Sport Series, Dolly Madison Bakery, 4 different, ea, from $4 to **$6.00**

Pepsi, Night Before Christmas, 1982-83, 4 different, ea, from $4 to..**$6.00**

Pepsi, Twelve Days of Christmas, 1976, ea, from $1 to.**$3.00**

Pocahontas, Burger King, 1995, 4 different, MIB, ea **$3.00**

Sleeping Beauty, American, late 1950s, 6 different, ea, from $15 to **$20.00**

Snow White & the Seven Dwarfs, Bosco, 1938, ea, from $25 to **$45.00**

Star Trek, Dr Pepper, 1976, 4 different, ea, from $20 to ..**$25.00**

Star Wars Trilogy: Empire Strikes Back, Burger King/Coca-Cola, 1980, ea, from $7 to......................................**$10.00**

Star Wars Trilogy: Star Wars, Burger King/Coca-Cola, 1977, 4 different, ea, from $12 to **$15.00**

Sunday Funnies, 1976, O Annie, Smilin' Jack, Moon Mullins, Gasoline Alley, Terry & Pirates, Brenda Starr, ea, from $8 to..**$15.00**

Super Heroes, Marvel/Federal, 1978, Captain America, Hulk, Spider-Man, Thor, ea, $100 to..........................**$150.00**

Super Heroes, Marvel/7-Eleven, 1977, Captain America, Fantastic Four, Howard the Duck, Thor, ea..........**$20.00**

Super Heroes, Marvel/7-Eleven/Federal, 1977, Amazing Spider-Man, from $30 to..................................**$45.00**

Super Heroes (Moon) Series, Pepsi/DC Comics, 1976, Green Arrow, from $20 to **$30.00**

Super Heroes (Moon) Series, Pepsi/NPP, 1976, Riddler, Green Lantern, Joker, Penguin, ea, from $20 to **$40.00**

Super Heroes (Moon) Series, Pepsi/DC Comics or NPP, 1976, Supergirl or Wonder Woman, $15.00 each.

Universal Monsters, Universal, Frankenstein, Mummy, Wolfman, Creature From the Black Lagoon, tapered, ea, from $50 to..**$75.00**

Universal Monsters, Universal, 1980, Frankenstein, Mummy, Mutant, Wolfman, Dracula, Creature, footed, ea, from $75 to..**$125.00**

Walter Lantz, Pepsi, 1970s, Woody Woodpecker, from $10 to..**$20.00**

Wendy's, Clara Pella, w/phrase or w/o phrase, ea, from $4 to..**$6.00**

Western Heroes, Annie Oakley, Buffalo Bill, Wild Bill Hickok, Wyatt Earp, ea, from $8 to.................**$12.00**

Winnie the Pooh, Sears/WDP, 1970s, 4 different, ea from $15 to..**$25.00**

Wizard of Oz, Coca-Cola/Krystal, 1989, 50th Anniversary Series, 6 different, ea, from $10 to.....................**$15.00**

Ziggy, 7-Up Collector Series, 4 different, ea, from $4 to **$7.00**

Character Banks

Since the invention of money there have been banks, and saving it has always been considered a virtue. What better way to entice children to save than to give them a bank styled after the likeness of one of their favorite characters! Always a popular collectible, mechanical and still banks have been made of nearly any conceivable material. Cast-iron and tin banks are often worth thousands of dollars. The ones listed here were made in the past fifty years or so, when ceramics and plastics were the materials of choice. Still, some of the higher-end examples can be quite pricey! (You can assume that all the banks we've listed here are ceramic, unless another type of material is mentioned in the description line.)

For more information see *Collector's Guide to Banks* by Jim and Beverly Mangus; several are shown in *The Collector's Encyclopedia of Cookie Jars* (there are three in the series) by Fred and Joyce Roerig. All of these books are published by Collector Books.

See also Advertising Character Collectibles; American Bisque; Cowboy Collectibles; MAD Collectibles; Star Trek; Star Wars.

Advisor: Robin Stine (See Directory, Cleminson)

Andy Panda, litho tin book shape, EX.......................**$125.00**

Batman, ceramic, w/hands on hips, NPPI, 1966, NM.**$90.00**

Batman, vinyl, Transogram, 1966, 20", VG **$45.00**

Bionic Woman, plastic, figure on pile of rocks, Animals Plus, 1970, NM **$45.00**

Bozo the Clown, plastic, 1972, lg, NM.......................**$35.00**

Bugs Bunny, ceramic, figure w/present, Warner Bros, 1981, EX..**$50.00**

Bugs Bunny, painted metal, figure w/carrot leaning on tree trunk, 6", EX...**$135.00**

Casper the Friendly Ghost, ceramic, NM...................**$200.00**

Chipmunks, Alvin, plastic, NM **$12.00**

Elmer Fudd, metal, figure beside tree stump, Metal Moss Mfg, 6", NM (NM box) **$250.00**

Elmo in Train, Enesco, marked 1993 c Jim Henson Productions, Inc., 5¾", from $45.00 to $50.00. (Photo courtesy Beverly and Jim Mangus)

Flintstones, Barney & Bamm-Bamm, hard plastic, Homecraft, 13", M...**$75.00**

Flintstones, Fred, Pebbles & Bamm-Bamm on tin-can shape, Kanley, 1988, NM...**$30.00**

Flintstones, Fred standing by rock, plastic, 1973, EX..**$30.00**

Flintstones, Pebbles, plastic, Transogram, 1960s, EX..**$45.00**

Flintstones, Wilma w/Pebbles, plastic, NM.................**$30.00**

Flipper, plastic, 1960s, 17½", NM **$45.00**

Garfield, in rabbit suit sitting on egg, Enesco, 1978, NM..**$40.00**

Garfield, w/knife & fork, Enesco, NM **$35.00**

Incredible Hulk, plastic bust, Renzi, 1979, 15", NM....**$25.00**

King Kong, painted plaster, Universal Statuary, 1952, 11", M **$100.00**

King Kong, plastic, 17", NM...**$35.00**

Laurel & Hardy, Laurel, plastic, Play Pal, 1972, 14", NM..**$65.00**

Little Lulu, plastic, Play Pal Plastics, 7½", NM.............**$50.00**

Little Red Riding Hood, ceramic, NAPCo, NM **$125.00**

London Tour Bus, designed exclusively for the Warner Bros. Studio Store TM & c 1995 WB Made in China, from $50.00 to $60.00. (Photo courtesy Fred and Joyce Roerig)

Marilyn Monroe, vinyl, in Seven Year Itch dress on base marked Funtime Savings, China, 1960s, 12", MIB **$175.00**

Peanuts, Lucy at desk, ceramic, NM............................**$30.00**

Peanuts, Snoopy, chalkware, Lego, 1950s, 8", VG **$45.00**

Peanuts, Snoopy on rainbow, composition, NM.........**$25.00**

Planet of the Apes, General Ursus, plastic, Apac Products, 1967, 18", NM...**$30.00**

Popeye, plastic, NM..**$30.00**

Raggedy Ann, ceramic, seated w/puppy, yarn hair, Pussy Willow Creations/Bobbs-Merrill, 1981, 6", M........**$25.00**

Raggedy Ann & Andy, papier-mache, Determined/Bobbs-Merrill, 1971, 6", M **$25.00**

Sesame Street, Big Bird on toy box, ceramic, NM **$20.00**

Sesame Street, Big Bird w/egg, composition, NM.......**$20.00**

Sesame Street, Ernie on train, ceramic, NM.................**$20.00**

Skeletor, plastic, HG Toys, 1984, 6", MOC...................**$30.00**

Spider-Man, plastic bust, Renzi, 1979, 15", EX **$25.00**

Superman, composition, Enesco, 1987, MIB **$85.00**

Superman, plastic, NPPI, 1974, NM..............................**$55.00**

Teenage Mutant Ninja Turtles, Leonardo, Taiwan, NM..**$25.00**

Uncle Wiggily, litho tin, Chein, 5", NM.....................**$350.00**

Wizard of Oz, Dorothy, handpainted, w/original tag, Arnart Imports, 1960s, 7", NMIB **$825.00**

Wizard of Oz, Scarecrow, handpainted, w/original tag, Arnart Imports, 1960s, 7", NMIB **$100.00**

Wizard of Oz, Tin Woodsman, handpainted, w/original tag, Arnart Imports, 1960s, 7", MIB **$135.00**

Character Clocks and Watches

There is growing interest in the comic character clocks and watches produced from about 1930 into the '50s and beyond. They're in rather short supply simply because they were made for children to wear (and play with). They were cheaply made with pin-lever movements, not worth an expensive repair job, and many were simply thrown away. The original packaging that today may be worth more than the watch itself was usually ripped apart by an excited child and promptly relegated to the wastebasket.

Condition is very important in assessing value. Unless a watch is in like-new condition, it is not mint. Rust, fading, scratching, or wear of any kind will sharply lessen its value, and the same is true of the box itself. Good, excellent, and mint watches can be evaluated on a scale of one to five, with excellent being a three, good a one, and mint a five. In other words, a watch worth $25.00 in good condition would be worth five times that amount if it were mint ($125.00). Beware of dealers who substitute a generic watch box for the original. Remember that these too were designed to appeal to children and (99% of the time) were printed with colorful graphics.

Some of these watches have been reproduced, so be on guard. For more information, we recommend *Comic Character Clocks and Watches* by Howard S. Brenner, and *Schroeder's Collectible Toys, Antique to Modern* (Collector Books).

See also Advertising and Promotional Wristwatches.

Advisor: Howard Brenner (See Directory, Character Clocks and Watches)

Clocks

Bambi Wall Clock, yellow plastic w/image of Bambi & friends in forest, battery-operated, 11x11", NM **$65.00**

Bozo Alarm Clock, Larry Harmon/French, Bozo on face, round, rare, 1960s, EX..**$150.00**

Bugs Bunny Alarm Clock, Ingraham USA, 4½", EX, $150.00.

Bugs Bunny Travel Alarm Clock, Seth Thomas, Bugs image w/glow-in-the-dark hands, blue case, 1970, M **$65.00**

Cinderella Alarm Clock, Scene of Cinderella leaving slipper on steps, Bradley/Japan, 3" dia, scarce, MIB......**$125.00**

Cinderella Wall Clock, red metal w/image of Cinderella trying on slipper, Phinney Walker, 1970s, 8" dia, NM.......**$65.00**

Disneyland Alarm Clock, musical analog, image of Mickey as band leader w/parade of characters, Bradley, EX..**$125.00**

Donald Duck Alarm Clock, blue-painted metal case & base, Donald's hands keep time, Bayard, 1930s, 5" dia, NM..**$250.00**

Flintstones Alarm Clock, ceramic figure of Fred w/dial in center, Sheffield, 1960s, 8½", EX....................**$185.00**

Goofy Wall Clock, blue plastic w/full-color image of Goofy pointing time, Welby by Elgin, 1970s, 8" dia, NM..**$65.00**

Howdy Doody & Clarabelle Alarm Clock, Howdy & Clarabelle figures at right & bottom, Janex, 1974, EX **$85.00**

Mickey Mouse Wall Clock, green metal alarm-clock shape w/Mickey's face, red hands, Hamilton, 1970s, 10" dia, EX..**$75.00**

Mighty Mouse Alarm Clock, orange case w/yellow bells, image of Mighty Mouse pointing time, 1960s, NM..............**$85.00**

Minnie Mouse Alarm Clock, Minnie in purple dress, double bell, purple-painted metal case, Bradley, 1976, M..........**$100.00**

Peanuts Alarm Clock, Charlie Brown & Snoopy sleeping next to round dial, Janex, 1974, EX, from $30 to........**$45.00**

Pinnochio Alarm Clock, various characters beside numbers surround Pinocchio, Bayard/France, 1967, EX...**$250.00**

Planters, Plaque style w/image of Mr Peanut & It's Always Time for...1906, battery-operated, Bayard, 1978, 5", MIB **$100.00**

Raggedy Ann & Andy Talking Alarm Clock, round dial above relief images of Raggedy Ann & Andy, Equity, NM..**$35.00**

Sesame Street Talking Alarm Clock, round dial in building w/Big Bird reading to Ernie & Oscar the Grouch, 11", EX **$35.00**

Smokey the Bear Alarm Clock, image & Prevent Forest Fires on face, white case w/blue bells, Bradley, 1950s, 7", NMIB...**$150.00**

Tweety Bird Talking Alarm Clock, battery-operated, Janex, 1978, EX...**$75.00**

Underdog Alarm Clock, Underdog's hands keep time, yellow plastic octagonal case, Germany, 1970s, 3", NM..**$195.00**

Winnie the Pooh Alarm Clock, Sunbeam, 1980s, MIB..**$75.00**

Woody Woodpecker, Alarm Clock, nodding Woody w/spatula at Cafe tree, round white case, Westclox, 5½", EX **$175.00**

Pocket Watches

Dan Dare, space scene w/spaceship & gun ticking off seconds, Ingersoll/Great Britain, 1950s, MIB...........**$800.00**

Hopalong Cassidy, black dial w/white numbers surround bust image of Hopalong, chrome case, unmarked, 1950s, 2" dia, EX...**$100.00**

James Bond 007 Spy Watch, w/secret lenses, Gilbert, EXIB..**$300.00**

Mickey Mouse, full-figure Mickey on face, tin case, Bradley, 1960s, 2" dia, MIB.................................**$155.00**

Three Stooges, Moe pulling Curly's tooth w/pliers, nickel-plated case, mk FTTC, 2" dia, EX.....................**$100.00**

Wristwatches

Alice in Wonderland, blue & white w/blue leather band, w/figurine of Alice, US Time, 1950s, EX+ (EX+ box)...**$135.00**

Archie, Archie's head revolves as it ticks, red band, Rouan, 1960s, NM..**$100.00**

Batman, batwings keep time on round face encased in black plastic wings, no band, Marcel, 1966, EX..........**$200.00**

Big Jim, figure in red shorts w/arms as hands, Big Jim in blue & red lettering, black vinyl band, Bradley, 1973, NM..**$150.00**

Bozo the Clown, Bozo on face, replaced red band, Bradley, 1960s, EX..**$75.00**

Bozo the Clown, face pictures Bozo & name in red lettering, red vinyl band, 1960s, EX.....................................**$45.00**

Casper the Ghost, Casper flies over mountains on blue dial, white vinyl band, Bradley, 1960s, NM................**$150.00**

Cool cat, full-figure image, replaced band, Sheffield, 1960s, VG..**$50.00**

Dale Evans, round horseshoe image, rectangular gold-tone case, tan leather strap, Bradley, 1950s, EXIB **$275.00**

Davy Crockett, Davy holding rifle, green plastic waterproof case, brown band, Disney, 1950s, EX.................**$75.00**

Dennis the Menace, blue-trimmed face w/image of Dennis & Ruff, replaced band, 1960s, EX..........................**$75.00**

Donald Duck, 50th Anniversary Registered Edition, battery-operated, Bradley, 1985, complete w/paperwork, MIB **$150.00**

Dukes of Hazzard, stainless steel band, LCD Quartz, Unisonic, 1981, MIB.......................................**$35.00**

Elmer Fudd, Elmer in hunting outfit, white vinyl band, Sheffield, 1960s, NMIB **$150.00**

Flintstones, close-up image of Fred & Pebbles, replaced red band, Bradley, 1960s, NM.................................**$65.00**

Girl From UNCLE Secret Agent, pink face w/black numbers & line drawing, white grid design w/white lettering, 1960s, EX...**$65.00**

Hazel, bust image of lady in uniform, 1971, NM........**$65.00**

Howdy Doody Watch, Ideal, blue leather band, MIB, $500.00.

Character Collectibles

Any popular personality, whether factual or fictional, has been promoted through the retail market to some degree. Depending on the extent of their fame, we may be deluged with this merchandise for weeks, months, even years. It's no wonder, then, that the secondary market abounds with these items or that there is such wide-spread collector demand for them today. There are rarities in any field, but for the beginning collector, many nice items are readily available at prices most can afford. Disney characters, Western heroes, TV and movie personalities, super heroes, comic book characters, and sports greats are the most sought after.

For more information, we recommend *Character Toys and Collectibles* by David Longest; *Toys of the Sixties* and *Superhero Collectibles: A Pictorial Price Guide,* both by Bill Bruegman; *Collector's Guide to TV Memorabilia, 1960s and 1970s,* by Greg Davis and Bill Morgan; and *Howdy Doody* by Jack Koch. *Schroeder's Collectible Toys, Antique to Modern,* published by Collector Books contains an extensive listing of character collectibles with current market values.

See also Advertising Characters; Beatles Collectibles; Bubble Bath Containers; California Raisins; Character and Promotional Drinking Glasses; Character Watches; Coloring Books; Cookie Jars; Cowboy Character Collectibles; Disney Collectibles; Dolls, Celebrity; Elvis Presley Memorabilia; Movie Stars Posters; Paper Dolls; Pez Candy Containers; Pin-Back Buttons; Puzzles; Rock 'n Roll Memorabilia; Shirley Temple; Star Trek; Star Wars; Toys; Vandor.

Note: Our listings are often organized by the leading character with which they're associated (for example, Pokey is in the listings that begin Gumby) or the title of the production in which they appear. (Mr. T. is with A-Team listings.)

Club: Barbara Eden's Official Fan Club
P.O. Box 556
Sherman Oaks, CA 91403; 818-761-0267

Lassie, image of Lassie sitting, white w/name in blue, 1960s, NM $75.00

Man From UNCLE, line drawing of Napolean talking on communicator, replaced band, 1966, EX.....................$75.00

Mickey Mouse, Mickey on face, red band, US Time, 1958, complete w/plastic Mickey figure, EXIB.............$200.00

Mickey Mouse, 50th Anniversary, image w/lg arms as hands, round chrome base, black lizard strap, Bradley, NMIB..$85.00

Miss Piggy, image of Miss Piggy w/animated hearts, digital, Timex, 1982, MIB..$65.00

Nightmare Before Christmas, features Lock, Shock & Barrel, Timex, MIB..$175.00

Porky Pig, image of Porky tipping his hat, blue band, Sheffield, 1960s, NMIB $150.00

Raggedy Ann, image of Raggedy w/arms as hands, replaced band, Bobbs-Merrill, 1971, EX $50.00

Rocketeer, digital, metal w/plastic band, Hope, 1991, NMOC $35.00

Rudolph the Red-Nosed Reindeer, rectangular chrome case, red vinyl strap, USA, EX..$75.00

Rudoph the Red Nosed Reindeer, rectangular face pictures Rudolph, original red band, 1940s, nonworking o/w EX $85.00

Space Mouse, black & white image on face, red strap, Webster, 1960s, MIB..$65.00

Superman, color image of Superman, brown leather band, EX $85.00

Tom Corbett Space Cadet, shows Tom & rocket ship w/red lightning bolt hands, original band w/space design, EX...$125.00

Tweety Bird, image of Tweety w/lg arms, red chrome case, red leather strap, Topolino/Swiss, EXIB $50.00

Woody from Toy Story, limited edition of 7,500, Fossil, complete w/certificate, plaque & round tin case, M $125.00

Zorro, chrome case, black leather strap w/silver stamped designs, w/display hat, US Time, EXIB $400.00

Alvin & the Chipmunks, kite, Roalex, 1960s, MIP $65.00

Alvin & the Chipmunks, Stuff & Lace Set, w/3 padded vinyl dolls, w/yarn, needle & instructions, Hasbro, 1950s-60s, NMIB...$85.00

Archie, pick-up sticks, Ja-Ru, 1986, MOC $10.00

Archies, pocket puzzle, Jaymar, 1960s, MOC $25.00

Aristocats, Colorforms, 1960s, NM (EX box) $38.00

Banana Splits, harmonica, Larami, 1973, MOC............$45.00

Banana Splits, tambourine, Larami, 1973, MIP $40.00

Batman, banner, Batman Vs the Riddler, white cloth w/colorful image, 1966, 27", EX.......................................$100.00

Batman, bicycle siren, Supersonic, yellow, red & blue plastic, battery-operated, Empire, 1978, M (EX box)........$35.00

Batman, bop bag, Batman & Robin on front, inflatable vinyl, Arco, 1981, 48", M (EX box) $35.00

Batman, bowl, white w/Joker image, Melmac, 1966, 5", EX.$15.00

Batman, charm bracelet, w/6 brass charms, 1966, EX (EX card)..$75.00

Batman, doll, stuffed cloth w/vinyl face, 1960s, 16", VG.**$75.00**

Batman, flashlight, plastic figure, Nasta, 1981, 4", MOC...**$15.00**

Batman, hand puppet, vinyl head w/blue cloth body, Ideal, 1966, M (VG bag w/header) **$65.00**

Batman, lamp, Vanity Fair Industries, plastic, 7½" wide with expandable arm for light, EX, from $130.00 to $150.00.

Batman, lamp base, Joker figure, ceramic, Price, 1978, 6" figure, EX **$45.00**

Batman, mask, sturdy black plastic, 1960s, EX **$25.00**

Batman, mug, clear plastic w/colorful paper insert of Batman characters, 1966, 4", VG **$15.00**

Batman, notebook binder, 3-ring, shows Batman w/wings spread on yellow vinyl, 1966, 12x11", EX+ **$85.00**

Batman, paint set, Super Heroes, Craft Master, 1984, MIB (sealed) **$15.00**

Batman, paint-by-number set, Hasbro, 1966, unused, MIB **$45.00**

Batman, pencil case, yellow vinyl zippered pouch w/Batman & Robin on the front, 1977, 6x9", EX....................**$15.00**

Batman, pin, flat bat shape, 1966, M (EX card) **$45.00**

Batman, pin, raised bat shape, 1966, M (no card)......**$25.00**

Batman, pin, Zonk! lettering w/purple border, 1966, M (EX card)...**$45.00**

Batman, print set, w/6 character rubber stamps, pad & instructions, 1966, VG (w/original mailer box) **$65.00**

Batman, program, w/photos & information on the Batman TV show featuring Adam West in & out of costume, 1966, 13x10", NM **$45.00**

Batman, slide-tile puzzle, red plastic, American Publishing Co, 1977, MOC...**$25.00**

Batman, sunglasses, bat style w/official green & red bat sticker on 1 side of frame, 1966, EX **$100.00**

Batman, tie, Boys Ready-Knot clip-on, Omega, 1966, 11", NMIB...**$100.00**

Batman & Robin, cup, white w/graphics, Melmac, 1966, 4", EX...**$15.00**

Batman & Robin, latch hook rug kits, Batman or Robin, 1970s, 12x12", MIB (sealed), ea..........................**$25.00**

Batman & Robin, marker pens, pictures Batman or Robin, 1980, MIP...**$15.00**

Batman & Robin, puffy stickers, Super Heroes, set of 8, Our Way, 1981, MOC **$15.00**

Batman & Robin, stickers, Charter Member — Batman & Robin Society, uncut sheet w/4 3½" dia stickers, 1966, EX...**$35.00**

Beany & Cecil, Cartoon Kit, Colorforms, 1960s, complete, EX (worn box), from $100 to **$125.00**

Betty Boop, ashtray, china figural Betty & Bimbo, 1930s, EX...**$75.00**

Betty Boop, doll blanket, c Max Fleisher Studio, 1930s, NM **$70.00**

Betty Boop, figure, chalkware, 14", NM **$275.00**

Betty Boop, figure, jointed wood, Jaymar, 1930s, 4", M...**$100.00**

Betty Boop, rub-on decals, 2 cards, 1930s, M.............**$25.00**

Beverly Hillbillies, car, Ideal, 1960s, plastic, EX........**$400.00**

Beverly Hillbillies, Cartoon Kit, Colorforms, 1963, MIB.**$75.00**

Big Al, doll, plush & vinyl, EX **$30.00**

Bionic Woman, Play-Doh Action Playset, Kenner, 1977, NMIB...**$25.00**

Bionic Woman, tattoos & stickers, 8 stickers & 25 tattoos, Kenner, 1976, complete, MIP.............................**$20.00**

Blippy, jack-in-the-box, Mattel, M, from $100 to **$150.00**

Blondie & Dagwood, blocks, paper litho on wood, change positions for various expressions, Gaston, 1950s, VG (G box) **$25.00**

Blondie & Dagwood, dexterity puzzle, paper litho under glass w/red metal case, 1940s, 5x3", EX **$25.00**

Bozo the Clown, Decal Decorator Kit, Meyercord, 1950s, unused, EX (EX box)......................................**$40.00**

Brady Bunch, Brain Twisters, Larami, 1973, MOC......**$25.00**

Brady Bunch, Fan Club Kit, Tiger Beat, 1972, complete, MIB, from $150 to...**$200.00**

Brenda Starr, doll, complete w/pink shoes, 2 bobby pins, instruction booklet & stand, Madame Alexander, 1960s, 12", MIB...**$400.00**

Brothers Grimm, school kit, Hasbro, 1962, NMOC.....**$50.00**

Buck Rogers, Colorforms Adventure Set, 1979, MIB...**$30.00**

Bugs Bunny, bookends, 1970, EX, pr **$20.00**

Bugs Bunny, Cartoon-O-Graph, NM (VG box) **$15.00**

Bugs Bunny, doll, stuffed, Mighty Star, 18", NM **$15.00**

Bugs Bunny, gumball dispenser, w/carrot on tree trunk, mini, MOC..**$10.00**

Bugs Bunny, jack-in-the-box, Mattel, 1970s, VG.........**$15.00**

Bugs Bunny, planter, ceramic, 1950s, M **$35.00**

Bugs Bunny, poster, I Want You, Bugs as Uncle Sam w/pals, 22x16", EX **$5.00**

Bugs Bunny, soap, 1930s, MIB **$45.00**

Captain America, bath puppet, MIP **$40.00**

Captain America, bicycle license plate, litho tin, Marx, 1967, NM **$50.00**

Captain America, black-light poster, Third Eye, 1971, 21x33", NM **$30.00**

Captain America, kite, full-color image, Pressman, 1966, MIP..**$50.00**

Captain Kangaroo, TV Eras-O-Board Set, Hasbro, 1956, complete, M (VG box) **$30.00**

Captain Marvel, key chain, plastic w/Captain Marvel & Jr on front, ...Captain Marvel Club on back, 1940s, EX...**$75.00**

Captain Marvel, portrait picture, color full-figure w/facsimile inscription, Whiz Comics promo at bottom, 10x7", EX+ **$110.00**

Care Bears, phonograph, 1983, MIB (sealed)...........**$125.00**

Casper the Friendly Ghost, jewelry set, 10-pc, AAI Inc, 1995, MOC..**$15.00**

Casper the Friendly Ghost, toss-up balloon, floats through air & lands on feet, Pioneer Rubber, 1950s, 36", MOC......**$70.00**

Charlie Chaplin, figure, celluloid, Germany, 3", VG ...**$65.00**

Charlie Chaplin, figure, celluloid, jointed arms, Japan, 10", NM **$1,500.00**

Charlie McCarthy, figure, wood, jointed, Jaymar, 1939, 5½", rare, NM...**$675.00**

Charlie's Angels, backpack, vinyl w/group photo on top flap, Travel Toys, 1977, M, from $65 to........................**$75.00**

Charlie's Angels, magic slate, Whitman, 1977, M, from $25 to..**$30.00**

CHiPs, bicycle siren, 1970s, EX **$20.00**

CHiPs, sunglasses, Fleetwood, 1977, MOC................**$15.00**

Cool Cat, poster, 1968, M...**$10.00**

Daffy Duck, candle holder, painted bisque, 1980, M .**$35.00**

Daffy Duck, doll, stuffed plush, Mighty Star, 1971, 19", NM...**$25.00**

Dennis the Menace, night light, $30.00; record, 78 rpm, $10.00; Margret hand puppet, $25.00. (Photo courtesy Cindy Sabulis)

Deputy Dawg, doll, stuffed body w/vinyl head, red vest & black hat, Ideal, 1960s, 14", EX **$100.00**

Dick Tracy, Crimestoppers Set, Larami, 1967, NMIP...**$40.00**

Dick Tracy, figure, Bonnie Braids, plastic, Charmore, 1951, 1¼", MOC...**$50.00**

Dick Tracy, flashlight, black & red w/etched image of Tracy on side, 1950s, pocket-size, NMIB **$75.00**

Dick Tracy, magnifying glass, Larami, 1979, MOC......**$20.00**

Dick Tracy, Secret Service Phone, Lan-Dee, 1930s, VG ..**$100.00**

Dick Tracy, TV Watch, Ja-Ru, NMOC **$20.00**

Ding Dong School, record player, RCA, 1950s, EX+...**$200.00**

Ding Dong School, scrapbook, Whitman, 1950s, VG .**$40.00**

Dr Dolittle, jack-in-the-box, plays 'The Bear Went Over the Mountain,' Giraffe, 1967, NM................................**$40.00**

Dr Dolittle, medical playset, Hasbro, NM **$75.00**

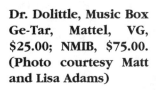

Dr. Dolittle, Music Box Ge-Tar, Mattel, VG, $25.00; NMIB, $75.00. (Photo courtesy Matt and Lisa Adams)

Dr Dolittle, periscope, Bar-Zim, NMIP **$30.00**

Dr Dolittle, Stitch-A-Story, Hasbro, NMIP **$25.00**

Dr Seuss, doll, Cat in the Hat, stuffed plush, Coleco, 1983, MIB **$150.00**

Dr Seuss, doll, Horton the Elephant, stuffed plush, Coleco, 1983, EX...**$50.00**

Dr Seuss, doll, Thidwick the Big Hearted Moose, stuffed plush, Coleco, 1983, 16", NM.............................**$90.00**

Dr Seuss, riding toy, Cat in the Hat, Coleco, 1983, NM..**$75.00**

Dr Seuss, ring, Cat in the Hat, gold-tone metal w/head view, NM...**$5.00**

Dracula, doll, talker, stuffed cloth, Commonwealth Toy & Novelty Co, NMIB...**$100.00**

Dukes of Hazzard, Colorforms, 1981, NM (NM box) .**$30.00**

Dukes of Hazzard, TV tray, pictures the General Lee w/Bo, Luke & Daisy, 1981, 13x17", EX **$25.00**

Elmer Fudd, mask, cardboard, Warner Bros, NM, from $60 to.**$90.00**

Elmer Fudd, pistol/flashlight, EX................................**$15.00**

Elmer Fudd, pull toy, Elmer in fire chief's car, paper litho on wood, EX...**$300.00**

Emmett Kelly, doll, vinyl w/cloth outfit, 1960s, 13", EX....**$50.00**

Emmett Kelly Circus, Colorforms, 1960, complete, NMIB.**$40.00**

ET, figure, talker, 1982, 7", MIB **$60.00**

ET, photo album, M (sealed) **$12.00**

ET, Spaceship Launcher, push buttons & ET pops out, LJN, 1982, MOC...**$35.00**

Fall Guy, truck, motorized break-apart type, Fleetwood, 1981, MOC...**$6.00**

Family Affair, Buffy Make-Up & Hairstyling Set, Amsco, 1971, MIB **$50.00**

Family Affair, Cartoon Kit, Colorforms, 1970, MIB......**$35.00**

Family Affair, doll, Buffy w/Mrs Beasley doll, talker, Mattel, 1967, VG+...**$55.00**

Family Affair, doll, Mrs Beasley, rag-type w/red or blue dress, Mattel, 1968, 10", EX..**$15.00**

Fat Albert & the Cosby Kids, figures, Rudy, Bill, or Bucky, Tedro Enterprises, 1982, MOC, ea **$30.00**

Flash Gordon, Colorforms Adventure Set, 1980, MIB.**$35.00**

Flash Gordon, slide-tile puzzle, Defenders of Earth, Ja-Ru, 1985, MOC..**$18.00**

Flash Gordon, space outfit, Esquire Novelty, 1950s, complete, EXIB **$425.00**

Flip Wilson/Geraldine, talking doll, stuffed cloth, c 1970, non-working, EX, $20.00.

Flintstones, Baby Pebbles Cave House, Ideal, 1964, M..**$175.00**

Flintstones, bubble pipe, Bamm-Bamm, 1960s, 8", EX **$20.00**

Flintstones, flashlight, Fred, 1876, M **$8.00**

Flintstones, Flintstone Circus, complete w/7 figures & 8 pcs of circus equipment, Kohner, 1960s, NMIB **$85.00**

Flintstones, gumball machine, plastic head figure of Fred, Hasbro, 1968, 8", EX...**$50.00**

Flintstones, Paint 'em Pals, Craftmaster, 1978, MIB (sealed) **$25.00**

Flintstones, pillow, Fred, 1970s, M **$15.00**

Flintstones, Play Fun Set, Whitman, 1965, complete, EXIB **$65.00**

Flintstones, squeak toy, Barney, vinyl, 1960, M **$15.00**

Flipper, jack-in-the-box, litho tin, Mattel, 1966, NM .**$150.00**

Flipper, squirt gun, plastic figure, 1960s, MIC.............**$40.00**

Flipper, ukelele, Mattel, 1968, MIP **$100.00**

Freddy Kreuger, doll, talker, Matchbox, 18", NRFB **$50.00**

G-Man, Police Set, Pressman, complete, rare, EXIB .**$250.00**

G-Man, Signal Lite, litho metal, 7", EX.......................**$175.00**

Gilligan's Island, baseball cap, stitched logo, American Needle, 1994, EX...**$10.00**

Gilligan's Island, doll, Gilligan, vinyl w/molded clothes, Turner, 9", M **$20.00**

Gilligan's Island, note pad, Gilligan & Skipper on glossy cover, 1960s, unused, M **$75.00**

Goose Bumps, rings, set of 4, MOC...........................**$35.00**

Green Hornet, balloon, Black Beauty, 1966, MIP **$100.00**

Green Hornet, flasher ring, silver-tone plastic, changes from Green Hornet to Kato, Vari-Vue, 1960s, NM........**$70.00**

Green Hornet, Thingmaker Mold, Mattel, 1966, complete, MOC..**$225.00**

Green Hornet, walkie-talkies, 2-way electromagnetic, green plastic, Remco, 1966, 9", MIB **$400.00**

Gremlins, Colorforms Deluxe Set, MIB........................**$65.00**

Gremlins, doll, Gizmo, plush, Quiron, 1984, 14", rare, MIB..**$150.00**

Gremlins II, magic slate, Golden, 1990, EX.................**$8.00**

Gulliver's Travels, doll, King Little, wood & composition w/orginal decal, Ideal, 12", EX...........................**$575.00**

Gulliver's Travels, doll, Prince David, composition w/cloth cape & tights, Ideal, 1939, 11", EX.....................**$350.00**

Gumby, doll, stuffed cloth, w/guitar & headband, Applause, 1989, 6", NM...**$10.00**

Gumby, sunglasses, MOC **$20.00**

Gumby & Pokey, Adventure Costumes, cowboy, astronaut or fireman, Lakeside, 1965, MOC, ea.......................**$20.00**

Gumby & Pokey, Colorforms, 1988, MIB **$10.00**

Gumby & Pokey, figure, Pokey, bendable, Lakeside, 1965, MOC..**$55.00**

Gumby & Pokey, figures, bendable rubber, Jesco, 1980s, MOC, ea, from $10 to...**$15.00**

Gumby & Pokey, paint set, rare, NM.........................**$200.00**

Hair Bear Bunch, doll, Bubi Bear, stuffed, Sutton, 1971, rare, NM **$50.00**

Happy Days, Colorforms, Fonzie, unused, EXIB **$30.00**

Happy Days, guitar, Fonzie, 1976, MIB (sealed).........**$75.00**

Hardy Boys, poster put-ons, Shawn Cassidy or Parker Stevenson, 1970, NM, ea **$6.00**

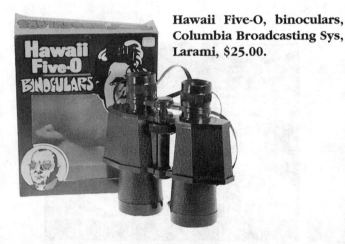

Hawaii Five-O, binoculars, Columbia Broadcasting Sys, Larami, $25.00.

Howdy Doody, Bee-Nee Kit, 1950s, NMIB..................**$65.00**

Howdy Doody, bib/apron, blue & white vinyl in the shape of Howdy w/dangling arms & bells attached, sm, EX **$125.00**

Howdy Doody, bread label album, American History, Wonder Bread, 1950s, 8 pages, unused, 8x8", NM..............**$75.00**

Howdy Doody, bread label poster, w/circus graphics & Wonder Bread ad on back, complete w/16 labels, 1950s, 14x12", VG...**$65.00**

Howdy Doody, coloring set, complete w/cards, colored pencils, etc, Kagran, 14x14", EX **$150.00**

Howdy Doody, Cookie-Go-Round cookie tin, color litho of all characters on merry-go-round, 1950s, 18", EX **$150.00**

Howdy Doody, embroidery kit, complete, M **$100.00**

Howdy Doody, Flip-A-Ring, Flub-A-Dub, 1950, MIP..**$45.00**

Howdy Doody, night light, glass head of Howdy, Leco Electric Mfg, 1950s, 1x2", NM (EX box).............**$200.00**

Howdy Doody, plate, ceramic, pictures Howdy as cowboy, 1950s, 9", EX **$65.00**

Howdy Doody, Play TV Stage, 6 different character & accessory pieces cut from Blue Bonnet Margarine boxes, 1950s, EX+...**$40.00**

Howdy Doody, slide-tile puzzle, Howdy Doody & His Famous TV Friends, Roalex, 1950s, EX...............**$125.00**

Howdy Doody, soda fountain hat, Howdy Says 'Welch's — My Favorite,' white paper w/purple & red art, 1950s, 4x8", EX...**$100.00**

Howdy Doody, swim ring, inflatable plastic, red & blue litho on yellow, Ideal, 1950s, appears unused, NM ...**$110.00**

Howdy Doody, wall lamp shade, translucent w/yellow, blue & red graphics of characters & balloons, 1950s, 4x9x7", EX **$200.00**

Howdy Doody, washcloth mitt, Clarabell litho on terry cloth, Bernard Ulmann Co, 1950s, 8½x7", EX+ **$45.00**

Huckleberry Hound, doll, plush & vinyl, Knickerbocker, 20", EX..**$55.00**

Huckleberry Hound, ring, plastic, EX **$50.00**

Huckleberry Hound, TV Pals Paint Kit, MIB (sealed).**$60.00**

I Dream of Jeanie, magic slate, Rand McNally, 1975, NM...**$65.00**

Incredible Hulk, paint-by-number set, Hasbro, 1982, unused, MIB **$30.00**

Incredible Hulk, push-&-go toy, plastic, 1979, 7", EX...**$25.00**

Incredible Hulk, wastebasket, litho metal, EX...........**$45.00**

James Bond, attache case, MPC, 1964, complete, VG+ .**$550.00**

James Bond, exploding coin, silver coin explodes w/cap, embossed w/Bond on top, Coibel, 1980s, MOC..**$15.00**

James Bond, pencil case, black zippered vinyl w/James Bond 007 target logo on front, 1960s, 4x8", EX..........**$100.00**

Joan Palooka, doll, latex w/vinyl head, jointed, Ideal, 1953, 14", NM, minimum value...............................**$85.00**

Josie & the Pussycats, jewlery set, Larami, 1973, MOC...**$30.00**

Junior G-Men, fingerprint set, Hale-Nass Corp, early 1940s, complete, EX (G box) **$200.00**

Justice League of America, paint-by-number set, Hasbro, 1967, complete, EXIB **$150.00**

King Kong, Panoramic Play Set, Colorforms, 1976, complete, EX (EX box) **$25.00**

Knight Rider, Colorforms Adventure Set, 1982, MIB...**$35.00**

Knight Rider, Self-Inking Stamp Set, Larami, 1982, complete, MOC...**$30.00**

Land of the Lost, Cosmic Signal, Larami, 1975, MOC .**$20.00**

Land of the Lost, Safari Shooter, Larami, 1975, MOC..**$25.00**

Lassie, doll, stuffed plush w/vinyl face, glass eyes, Knickerbocker, 1960s, 12", VG **$15.00**

Laugh-In, Electric Drawing Set, Lakeside, 1969, EX (VG box) **$100.00**

Laurel & Hardy, Fuzzy Felt Playset, Standard Toykraft, 1962, complete, NMIB **$75.00**

Laverne & Shirley, Secretary Set, Harmony, 1977, MOC..**$35.00**

Leave It to Beaver, baseball cap, Beaver, stitched graphics, American Needle, 1994, EX.................................**$10.00**

Li'l Abner, mug, ceramic, profile on side, 1968, NM...**$12.00**

Li'l Abner, plate, china, Al Capp Enterprises, 1968, M..**$20.00**

Li'l Abner & Daisy Mae, bookends, painted plaster, 9" & 6", NM, pr...**$85.00**

Little House on the Prairie, Colorforms, 1978, MIB **$35.00**

Little Lulu, crossword puzzle book, Whitman, 1974, unused, M...**$45.00**

Little Lulu, doll, stuffed cloth w/red dress & yarn hair, 1944, 15", scarce, EX **$200.00**

Little Orphan Annie, Clothes Pins, Transogram, 1930s, NMIP, $125.00. (Photo courtesy Dunbar Gallery)

Little Orphan Annie, slide whistle, brass w/Sandy's head at top, 1930s premium, EX.................................**$45.00**

Little Orphan Annie, tea set, ceramic, Germany, 12-pc, M..**$150.00**

Little Orphan Annie & Sandy, figures, painted plastic, Annie in red dress, 1950s, 1½" & 1", EX, pr...................**$65.00**

Little Orphan Annie & Sandy, figures, wood, jointed limbs, Jaymar, 5", EX, pr **$165.00**

Looney Tunes, Cartoon-O-Graph Sketch Board, Warner Bros, 1950s, complete, EXIB.................................**$125.00**

Looney Tunes, Cartoon-O-Matic Molding & Coloring Set, Warners Bros, complete, EXIB, from $100 to.....**$150.00**

M*A*S*H, helicopter, Durham, 1975, unused, EXIB **$90.00**

Magilla Gorilla, doll, bendable felt body w/vinyl head, complete w/felt accessories, Ideal, 1960s, 8", EX........**$85.00**

Magilla Gorilla, squeeze toy, vinyl w/hand-painted features, Screen Gems/Spain, 1967, 8", NM.....................**$125.00**

Man From UNCLE, Secret Print Putty, Colorforms, 1965, complete, NMOC...**$80.00**

Marvel Super Heroes, checkers set, 1976, MIP (sealed) .**$45.00**

Marvel Super Heroes, light-up drawing desk, Lakeside, 1977, complete, EXIB **$40.00**

Marvel Super Heroes, New Super Heroes Sparkle Paints, Kenner, 1967, unused, MIB.................................**$75.00**

Marvel Super Heroes, pillow, inflatable plastic w/color image of Thor, Marvel Comics, 1968, 12x12", MIP.......**$100.00**

Masters of the Universe, He-man Superblobo, inflatable vinyl, Unique, 1984, expands to 7 ft, MIP.....................**$20.00**

Masters of the Universe, Magnetix Playset, American Publishing, 1985, MIP (sealed) **$25.00**

Max Headdroom, Fingertronic Puppet, Bendy Toys, 1987, 6", MIB...**$20.00**

Mighty Mouse, magic slate, Lowe, 1950s, NM...........**$50.00**

Mighty Mouse, squeeze toy, painted vinyl figure w/red felt cape, Terrytoons, 1950s, 10", EX+ **$75.00**

Moon Mullins, ventriloquist dummy, heavy stock paper punchout, Pure Oil Co premium, 1938, 20x11", unused, EX **$65.00**

Moon Mullins & Kayo, figures, wood w/jointed limbs, Jaymar, 5½" & 4", EX, pr...**$200.00**

Mork & Mindy, gumball machine, Mork figure sits on top, Hasbro, 1980, EX **$25.00**

Mork & Mindy, Shrinky Dinks, Colorforms, 1979, MIB (sealed) **$25.00**

Mother Goose, dishes, plastic, 26 pcs, Ideal, 1940s, MIB..**$150.00**

Mother Goose, jack-in-the-box, plays 'Mother Goose' song, NM **$25.00**

Mr Fantastic, flashlight, 1978, miniature, NMOC **$45.00**

Mr. Magoo, hand puppet, cloth and vinyl, 1962, EX, $35.00. (Photo courtesy June Moon)

Mr Magoo, playing cards, double pack in plastic casing, 1960s, NM...**$15.00**

Munsters, Colorforms, complete, 1965, EX.................**$60.00**

Munsters, flasher ring, Lily w/name, 1965, EX **$18.00**

Muppet Babies, doll, Kermit or Miss Piggy, Hasbro, 1985, 12", MIB, ea **$35.00**

Muppets, doll, Kermit the Frog, stuffed, Fisher-Price, 1976, 18", VG **$25.00**

Muppets, doll, Miss Piggy, foam-stuffed body w/vinyl head, rooted hair, purple dress, Fisher-Price, 1980, 14", EX **$20.00**

Mushmouth, doll, bendable felt body w/vinyl head, red felt vest, original tag on leg, Ideal, 1960s, 8", EX.....**$120.00**

Mutt & Jeff, drum, litho tin, Converse, 8" dia, EX.....**$200.00**

New Zoo Review, doll, Charlie Owl, w/tag, Rushton Co, 1971, EX...**$75.00**

New Zoo Review, doll, Freddie, stuffed plush, Kamar, 1977, EX..**$30.00**

Partridge Family, bulletin board, red cork w/music staff & logo in white, 1970s, 18x24", EX............................**$75.00**

Patty Duke, Charm Jewelry Set, complete w/jewelry box & charms, Standard Toykraft, 1963, NMIB...............**$75.00**

Peanuts, Colorforms, How's the Weather Lucy, EX (EX box) **$30.00**

Peanuts, Colorforms, Peanuts Preschool, VG (VG box) .**$25.00**

Peanuts, dish, Snoopy lying on back on lid, ceramic, Determined, 1977, 7½x4", NM.......................**$150.00**

Peanuts, doll, Charlie Brown, vinyl, 1950s, 9", VG **$75.00**

Peanuts, doll, Linus, vinyl, in red shirt w/hand out, Hungerford, 8", MIP..**$75.00**

Peanuts, doll, Lucy, stuffed printed-cloth pillow type, 1963, NM **$40.00**

Peanuts, doll, Snoopy, stuffed printed-cloth pillow type, VG+...**$35.00**

Peanuts, doll, Woodstock as Santa, plush, Applause, 9", MIP...**$20.00**

Peanuts, guitar, crank action, Mattel, NM **$50.00**

Peanuts, poster, Support the Olympics, paper, Springbok (sold by Hallmark), 1971, NM......................**$20.00**

Peanuts, tea set, Chein, complete, MIB **$50.00**

Phantom, poster, advertising DC Comic Books w/lg Phantom image, 1984, 22x14", NM...................................**$25.00**

Phantom, press kit, colorful folder comes w/Handbook of Production Information & 6 8x10" black & white photos, 1996, M...**$25.00**

Phantom, slide-tile puzzle, Super Heroes, Ja-ru, 1985, 4x5", MOC..**$25.00**

Phantom of the Opera, slide-tile puzzle, Defenders of the Earth, Ja-Ru, 1985, MOC..................................**$25.00**

Pink Panther, Silly Putty, Ja-Ru, 1980, MOC **$10.00**

Pinky Lee, paint set, Gabriel, 1950s, 12x16", complete, EX (NM box)..**$75.00**

Pinky Lee, party packet, 1950s, complete, M (NM mailer)..**$100.00**

Planet of the Apes, Colorforms Adventure Set, 1967, EXIB..**$30.00**

Pogo, figures, vinyl, set of 6, Proctor & Gamble premiums, 1969, 5", EX..**$85.00**

Popeye, Bubble Set, Transogram, 1935, complete, MIB .**$125.00**

Popeye, doll, Bluto, rubber w/painted details, Italy/KFS, 1940s-50s, 8", NMIP...................................**$125.00**

Popeye, doll, Popeye, stuffed cloth w/vinyl head, Play-By-Play, M...**$15.00**

Popeye, flasher ring, silver-tone plastic, switches from Popeye to his buck-toothed nephew, Vari-Vue, 1960s, NM..**$30.00**

Popeye, Pencil-By-Number Set, 1959, unused, MIB ...**$35.00**

Popeye, Spinach Can Music Box, working, missing pipe, otherwise EX, $125.00. (Photo courtesy June Moon)

Popeye, Stitch-A-Story, Hasbro, 1967, MOC **$55.00**

Porky Pig, bubble gum machine, plastic figure, Banko Matic, 1970s, 9½", EXIB **$25.00**

Porky Pig, figure, chalkware, 1930s, 7", EX...............**$75.00**

Prince Valiant, figure, pressed wood on base, 1942, 6", NM...$200.00

Punky Brewster, doll, Galoob, 1984, 18", NRFB.........$40.00

Raggedy, Colorforms, Pop-Up Tea Party, complete, MIB.$30.00

Raggedy Andy, bulletin board, diecut, Manton Cork Corp, 23", MIP...$30.00

Raggedy Ann, Busy Apron, Whitman/Bobbs-Merrill, 1969, MIB...$35.00

Raggedy Ann, jewelry box, plays Raindrops Keep Falling on My Head, Burham/Bobbs-Merrill, 1972, M, from $25 to...$30.00

Raggedy Ann, jump rope, plastic handles, Hallmark/Bobbs-Merrill, MIP...$22.00

Raggedy Ann & Andy, bank, seated, papier-mache, Determined/Bobbs-Merrill, 1971, 6", M.................$25.00

Raggedy Ann & Andy, beanbag chair, full-color image on white, Bobbs-Merrill, 1975, rare, M.....................$50.00

Raggedy Ann & Andy, ceramic figures, Lefton, NM, ea..$25.00

Raggedy Ann & Andy, tea set, plastic & metal, Wolverine/Bobbs-Merrill, 1978, 26-pc, MIB.........$50.00

Ripcord, magic slate, Lowe, 1963, unused, NM.........$40.00

Road Runner, figure, PVC, Shell Gas premium, MIP.....$3.00

Robin Hood, iron-on patch, Bondex fabric, Johnson & Johnson, 1956, 3x3", MOC.................................$25.00

Rocky & Bullwinkle, blackboard, diecut figure atop, Frolic Toys, 1970s, 12x16", VG...................................$50.00

Rocky & Bullwinkle, dish set, features Bullwinkle, Melmac, EX...$65.00

Rocky & Bullwinkle, figure set, Rocky, Natasha & Boris, bendable, 1991, MOC.......................................$20.00

Rocky & Bullwinkle, spelling & counting board, Larami, 1969, MOC...$28.00

Rocky & Bullwinkle, telescope, features Bullwinkle, Larami, 1970s, MOC...$10.00

Rootie Kazootie, hand puppet, cloth body w/painted vinyl head, RK Inc, 1953, 10", EX.............................$30.00

Scooby Doo, gumball machine, clear plastic head w/yellow base, Hasbro, EX...$25.00

Scooby Doo, necklace, King's Island, MOC...............$30.00

Scooby Doo, rubber stamp, 1982, MOC....................$10.00

Sesame Street, doll, Big Bird, talks w/tape player, Ideal, 25", VG...$55.00

Sesame Street, doll, Cookie Monster, stuffed plush w/ping-pong ball eyes, Hasbro, 1970s, 12", VG...............$15.00

Sesame Street, piano, Cookie Monster's eyes twirl when played, Gabriel, 1976, 9½", EX..........................$15.00

Shadow, ink blotter, cardboard, features Shadow figure w/corner ad promo for Blue Coal sponsor, late 1930s-40s, 4x9", EX...$45.00

Simpsons, chalk, Bart, 3-D sculptured & colored, Noteworthy, MOC...$10.00

Simpsons, doll, Bubble Blowin' Lisa, complete w/4-oz bottle of bubble solution, Mattel, 10½", MIB.................$50.00

Simpsons, doll, Really Rude Bart, w/2 noisemakers, Mattel, 18", MIB...$50.00

Simpsons, doll, Sweet Suckin' Maggie, sucks pacifier, Mattel, 18", MIB...$60.00

Simpsons, figure, any character, PVC, ea w/5 interchangeable balloons, Mattel, MOC, ea, from $20 to...............$25.00

Simpsons, flashlight, 3-D figure of Bart in green shirt on side of red flashlight, Happiness Express, MOC.........$12.00

Simpsons, frisbee, white w/image of Radical Dude, Betras Plastics, M...$5.00

Simpsons, pinball game, plastic, Ja-Ru, MIP...............$10.00

Simpsons, poster book, Button-Up, complete w/8 tear-out posters, NM...$8.00

Six Million Dollar Man, fan club kit, 1970s, NM.........$85.00

Smurfs, barrettes, 1982, set of 2, MIP.......................$3.00

Smurfs, calendar, M, from $20 to...........................$35.00

Smurfs, clip-on figures, Papa Smurf, set of 4, Applause, 1991, MOC...$10.00

Smurfs, doll, Smurfette, stuffed, 1981, 8", EX............$10.00

Smurfs, figure, pewter, M, from $15 to.....................$35.00

Smurfs, figure, porcelain, Wallace-Berrie, ea, from $15 to..$20.00

Smurfs, figure, PVC, USA issue, M, ea, from $3 to.......$4.50

Smurfs, fire truck, diecast, Ertl, EX...........................$5.00

Smurfs, greeting card, Hallmark, M, from $5 to...........$8.00

Smurfs, jack-in-the-box, plastic, 1982, VG................$45.00

Smurfs, mushroom cottage, MIB..............................$50.00

Smurfs, pencil case, w/Smurfette, M..........................$3.00

Smurfs, playsets, Super Super, different editions, MIB, ea, from $25 to...$200.00

Smurfs, punching balloons, set of 6 w/various characters, NM...$15.00

Smurfs, record player, 1982, EX..............................$20.00

Smurfs, sewing cards, MIB (sealed)..........................$25.00

Smurfs, Space Traveler toy, 1978, MOC....................$25.00

Smurfs, toothbrush & cup set, MIB...........................$25.00

Smurfs, zipper pull, Brainy or Smurfette, hard plastic w/clip, 2½", ea..$5.00

Sneaky Pete, Magic Show, Remco, complete, 1950s, VG..$125.00

Snuffy Smith, charm, full figure, silver finish, EX.......$18.00

Soupy Sales, doll, vinyl w/real hair, WMC, 1960s, 5", EX.$45.00

Space Kidettes, magic slate, Watkins, 1968, M...........$35.00

Spider-Man, doll, Energized Spider-Man, Remco, 11", EX (G box)...$40.00

Spider-Man, poster, glossy, Hudson Pharmaceutical Corp, 1975, 30x20", EX...$50.00

Spider-Man, Spider-Man & the Marvel Heroes Rub 'N Play Magic Transfer Set, Colorforms, 1978, complete, MIB..$50.00

Spider-Man, wallet, brown plastic w/image on yellow circle, 1978, NM...$18.00

Starsky & Hutch, handcuffs & wallet, Fleetwood, 1976, MOC...$25.00

Starsky & Hutch, walkie-talkies, Mettoy, 1970s, MIB..$75.00

Super Friends, party cutouts, 1978, 11", MIP.............$15.00

Super Heroes, checker set, w/12 cardboard Super Heroes & 12 Villians on plastic bases, Hasbro, 1976, MIB (sealed).$45.00

Super Heroes, postcard book, various characters, Marv IV Press, 1981, M...$15.00

Super Powers, poster, Super Powers Collection, pictures all the characters, 1984, 24x17", M (w/mailer).........$65.00

Superman, Cartoonist Stamp Set, 1966, complete, MOC..**$75.00**

Superman, doll, talker, stuffed cloth, Mego, 1970s, 24", EX..**$45.00**

Superman, fan club kit, Gold Member..., complete, 1980, NM (w/mailer) **$100.00**

Superman, gym bag, yellow & blue vinyl w/image & logo, DC Comics, 1971, 9x12", NM..............................**$50.00**

Superman, Kryptonite Rock, DC Comics, 1978, glows in the dark, MIB, from $20.00 to $30.00. (Photo courtesy June Moon)

Superman, ornament, vinyl figure, Presents, 1989, 3", MIB **$25.00**

Superman, playsuit, complete w/Superman's Buddy comic book, Funtime Playwear, 1954, EXIB, from $400 to **$500.00**

Superman, playsuit, w/shirt, pants, cape & leather belt, Ben Cooper, 1950s, EX+ (EX+ box)............................**$100.00**

Superman, Thingmaker Accessory Kit, Mattel, 1960s, complete, MOC **$85.00**

Superman, Tricky Trapeze, plastic, Kohner, 1960s, 3" figure on 6" trapeze, EX.......................................**$65.00**

Superman, wallet, yellow vinyl w/color graphics, w/magic pad & pencil, etc, 1966, NM **$85.00**

Sylvester the Cat, hand puppet, ca 1950, EX..............**$15.00**

Tasmanian Devil, doll, stuffed, Mighty Star, 12", NM..**$30.00**

Tasmanian Devil, figure, on motorcycle, diecast, Ertl, 1989, MOC..**$25.00**

Three Stooges, figure set, w/tags & stands, Applause, 1988, 14", M **$140.00**

Three Stooges, Slap-Stick-On, Colorforms, 1959, MIB ..**$300.00**

Tom & Jerry, checkers game, Ja-Ru, 1990, MOC.........**$10.00**

Tom & Jerry, hand puppet, cloth & vinyl, 1952, EX...**$25.00**

Tom & Jerry, Music Maker, litho tin, plays theme song, Mattel, 1960s, NM **$75.00**

Toonerville Trolley, figure set, Katrinka, Skipper, Mickey McGuire & Trolley, bisque, 2" to 3", NM............**$300.00**

Tweety Bird, doll, Chatter Chum, Mattel, 1976, MIB ..**$50.00**

Uncle Wiggily, doll, stuffed cloth w/original clothes, Georgene, 20", NM **$550.00**

Uncle Wiggly, figure, bisque, 4", EX..........................**$18.00**

Universal Monsters, iron-on transfers, set of 6, 1964, M (NM T-shirt shaped card) **$190.00**

Universal Monsters, Stick 'N Lift Monsters Kit, American Publishing, 1980s, MIB (sealed)............................**$65.00**

Wally Walrus, planter, ceramic figure in baseball catcher's uniform giving signals to pitcher, 1958, 4½", EX.**$50.00**

Welcome Back Kotter, jump rope, MSS, 1977, MIP.....**$35.00**

Welcome Back Kotter, record case, color photos on both sides, Komack/Walper, 1976, EX **$90.00**

Where's Waldo, figure set, PVC, set of 5, Applause, M.**$12.00**

Wile E Coyote, finger puppet, Dakin, 1970s, MIP **$20.00**

Wizard of Oz, dolls, Dorothy, Cowardly Lion or Wizard, stuffed cloth w/vinyl heads, Artistic Toy Co, 1962, 14", EX, ea **$65.00**

Wizard of Oz, jack-in-the-box, Scarecrow, plays Hail Hail the Gangs All Here, 1967, NM **$50.00**

Wizard of Oz, Magic Kit, Fun Inc, 1960s, complete, NMIB..**$50.00**

Wizard of Oz, sunglasses, Scarecrow, yellow plastic, Multi-Kids/Lowes, 1989, MOC..**$20.00**

Wizard of Oz, toy watch, Scarecrow & Tin Woodsman, red fabric band, Occupied Japan, 1940s, M **$50.00**

Wizard of Oz, trinket box, ruby slipper, Presents, 1989, MIB **$15.00**

Wizard of Oz, valentine, diecut cardboard w/image of Scarecrow, American Colortype Co/Licenses by Lowe's, 1940, 5x3", NM...**$100.00**

Wolfman, flashlight key chain, Basci Fun, 1995, MOC.**$12.00**

Wonder Woman, Magnetic Maze Chase Game, plastic, Nasta, 1980, MOC...**$35.00**

Wonder Woman, slide-tile puzzle, 1978, EX...............**$30.00**

Woody Woodpecker, harmonica, plastic figure, early, 6", EX...**$30.00**

Woody Woodpecker, kazoo, red plastic figure, Linden, 1960s, 7", EX...**$25.00**

Yogi Bear, bubble pipe, red plastic figure, Hanna-Barbera, 1960s, NM..**$25.00**

Yogi Bear, camera, plastic, 1960s, M **$90.00**

Yogi Bear, doll, Knickerbocker, EX..............................**$50.00**

Yogi Bear, doll, pillow-type w/bells inside, 1977, 15", NM **$25.00**

Yogi Bear, pencil box, silver-tone metal w/colorful image, Kanley/Australia, 1980s, unused, NM....................**$25.00**

Yogi Bear, Wipe-Off Coloring Cloth, Hanna-Barbera, 1960s, MIP, from $25 to **$35.00**

Yogi Bear & Friends, wastebasket, tin litho featuring Hanna-Barbera characters, 1960s, 13", VG.......................**$65.00**

Yosemite Sam, hand puppet, toothpaste premium, M.**$12.00**

Christmas Collectibles

Christmas is nearly everybody's favorite holiday, and it's a season when we all seem to want to get back to time-honored traditions. The stuffing and fruit cakes are made like Grandma always made them, we go caroling and sing the old songs that were written two hundred years ago, and the same Santa that brought gifts to the children in a time long forgotten still comes to our house and yours every Christmas Eve.

So for reasons of nostalgia, there are thousands of collectors interested in Christmas memorabilia. Some early Santa figures are rare and may be very expensive, especially when dressed in a color other than red. Blown glass ornaments and Christmas tree bulbs were made in shapes of fruits and vegetables, houses, Disney characters, animals, and birds. There are Dresden ornaments and candy containers from Germany, some of which were made prior to the 1870s, that have been lovingly preserved and handed down from generation to generation. They were made of cardboard that sparkled with gold and silver trim.

Artificial trees made of feathers were produced as early as 1850 and as late as 1950. Some were white, others blue, though most were green, and some had red berries or clips to hold candles. There were little bottle-brush trees, trees with cellophane needles, and trees from the '60s made of aluminum.

Collectible Christmas items are not necessarily old, expensive, or hard to find. Things produced in your lifetime have value as well. To learn more about this field, we recommend *Christmas Ornaments, Lights and Decorations, Vols. I, II, and III,* by George Johnson (Collector Books).

Candy container, ball, cardboard covered w/foil, opens in center, US, 2" dia, from $5 to.................................**$8.00**
Candy container, bell, paper w/scrap decoration, US, 1930s, 5½", from $25 to.................................**$35.00**
Candy container, cornucopia, cardboard, much decor, 12", from $75 to.................................**$95.00**
Candy container, heart, cardboard covered w/red paper w/angel print, separates at sides, 1¾-6", from $45 to.............**$90.00**
Candy container, horse prancing, Dresden, gold or silver, double, 3½".................................**$170.00**
Candy container, lady's high-heeled boot, cardboard covered w/satin & gold foil, 1950s, 5½", from $35 to.......**$45.00**
Candy container, Santa boots, papier-mache w/fabric or net bag at top, Germany, Japan or US, 3-4", from $10 to.................................**$15.00**
Candy container, slipper, cardboard w/fabric covering, Dresden trim, 2¾-3¾", ea.................................**$165.00**

Candy containers: Snowman playing accordion, 5", $25.00; Snowball with Santa figure, Made in Western Germany, 3¾", $25.00. (Photo courtesy Margaret and Kenn Whitmyer)

Candy container, turkey (roasted), papier-mache, 3-10", from $45 to.................................**$85.00**
Decoration, Santa head wall display, papier-mache relief image w/paper eye inserts, glitter highlighting on hat, 17", EX.**$135.00**
Kugel, orange, mold blown ball shape w/embossed dimples, unsilvered, 1991, 3" dia, from $50 to.................**$60.00**
Light bulb, angelfish, multicolored on milk glass, short/wide, Japan, 2", from $50 to.................................**$60.00**
Light bulb, bear, multicolored on milk glass, Japan, ca 1950, 2¾", from $75 to.................................**$80.00**
Light bulb, bubble light, C-7 vase, old, ea, from $2 to..**$70.00**
Light bulb, bulldog on ball, multicolored on clear, Japan, ca 1925, 2¼", from $15 to.................................**$20.00**
Light bulb, cat, clear glass, 1 paw raised, Japan, ca 1925, 2½", from $10 to.................................**$15.00**
Light bulb, cat sitting on bow, multicolored on clear, Japan, from $30 to.................................**$35.00**
Light bulb, clown, multicolored on clear, exhaust tip, from $60 to.................................**$70.00**
Light bulb, dog in polo outfit, milk glass, Japan, ca 1950, 2¾", from $25 to.................................**$35.00**
Light bulb, Dutch boy, multicolored on milk glass, Japan, 1950s, 3", from $75 to.................................**$85.00**
Light bulb, ear of corn, milk glass, individual kernels & lg leaves, Japan, 4", from $20 to.................................**$30.00**
Light bulb, flapper girl, multicolored on milk glass, Japan, 1950s, 2¾", from $55 to.................................**$65.00**
Light bulb, frog, clear or milk glass, US or Japan, ca 1925-55, 2¼", from $10 to.................................**$15.00**
Light bulb, Joey, clown head, multicolored on clear, Japan, 2", from $25 to.................................**$35.00**
Light bulb, lion, sitting, brown & black on clear, from $150 to.................................**$175.00**
Light bulb, lion w/tennis racket, milk glass, tennis clothes, Japan, 1935 & 1955, 2¾", from $20 to.................**$30.00**
Light bulb, log cabin, milk glass, Japan, 1950s, 2", from $10 to.................................**$15.00**
Light bulb, Mother Goose, multicolored on milk glass, Paramount, 2¾", from $15 to.................................**$25.00**
Light bulb, owl in vest & top hat, multicolored on milk glass, Japan, 2¼".................................**$100.00**
Light bulb, peacock, milk glass, double-sided, Japan, 1950s, 2¼", from $40 to.................................**$50.00**
Light bulb, pig playing tuba, multicolored on milk glass, Japan, 2½", from $175 to.................................**$200.00**
Light bulb, puppy on ball, multicolored on milk glass, Japan, 2¼", from $25 to.................................**$35.00**
Light bulb, rose, pink on clear, Watt, ca 1920, 1½", from $20 to.................................**$25.00**
Light bulb, Santa w/arms in sleeves, multicolored on clear, exhaust tip, 3", from $115 to.................................**$130.00**
Light bulb, snowman skier, multicolored on clear, Japan, 2¼", from $100 to.................................**$125.00**
Light bulb, songbird, milk or clear glass, common type w/folded wings, Japan, 1920-55, 3¼", from $10 to..........**$15.00**
Light bulb, St Nicholas, multicolored on milk glass, Japan, 1925-50, 2¾", from $25 to.................................**$35.00**

Light bulb, strawberry, red on clear, from $15 to **$20.00**

Light bulb, wolf head, multicolored on milk glass, Japan, 2¾", from $55 to **$65.00**

Lights, Noma, ca 1940s, EXIB, $45.00. (Photo courtesy Margaret and Kenn Whitmyer)

Ornament, angel, tin w/filigree wings, 3-D, detailed filigree, West Germany, 3", from $3 to....................................**$6.00**

Ornament, angel, wax over compo or papier-mache, standard type, 3"-4", ea **$65.00**

Ornament, angel head w/lg wings, mold-blown, Italy, 1950s, 2½", from $30 to **$40.00**

Ornament, apple, free-blown, covered in crushed glass, 2"..**$30.00**

Ornament, apples & grapes in basket, mold-blown, Germany, 1980, 2½", from $25 to **$35.00**

Ornament, Austrian passenger ship, mold-blown, 2 smokestacks, 6 portholes, 1970s, 2¾", from $12 to.......**$15.00**

Ornament, ball or sphere, free-blown, ¾-8" dia, made in many countries, commonly found, from .01 up to...........**$10.00**

Ornament, banjo, mold- & free-blown, wire strings, 1991, 4". from $30 to...**$40.00**

Ornament, Barney Google head, mold-blown, 2¼", from $275 to..**$300.00**

Ornament, bell, spun cotton covered in crushed glass, Germany or Japan, 1¾-3½", from $10 to **$20.00**

Ornament, bell w/embossed church, mold-blown, 1½", from $20 to..**$30.00**

Ornament, bird, mold-blown w/spun-glass crest, clip-on, 1991, 3½", from $15 to.......................................**$20.00**

Ornament, bird on pine cone, mold-blown, Germany, 1990s, 3", from $35 to **$45.00**

Ornament, boat, Sebnitz, foil over cardboard, 3 masts, scrap rider, 4½"...**$135.00**

Ornament, camel, Dresden, natural, double-sided, standard standing type w/1 hump, common, 2", from $40 to.**$60.00**

Ornament, candle, free-blown, tubluar w/pencil-point style flame, silvered, common, 3½", from $2 to.............**$3.00**

Ornament, carousel, mold-blown, embossed animals, 6-paneled roof, Germany, 1980s, 2½-3", from $35 to ...**$45.00**

Ornament, cat sleeping in shoe, bow at toe, mold-blown, 1960-70 reissue, 3½", from $40 to........................**$55.00**

Ornament, church, mold-blown, centered steeple, Czechoslovakia, 1975, 3", from $15 to **$25.00**

Ornament, cockatiel, mold-blown, Germany, from 3-4", common, ea from $20 to...**$30.00**

Ornament, daisy, mold-blown, on geometric form, Germany or Austria, made many years, 1-3", from $3 to....**$15.00**

Ornament, daisy on a heart, mold-blown, 2¼", from $8 to.**$12.00**

Ornament, dog (begging) w/basket, mold-blown, nicely molded fur, Germany, 1970s, 5", from $150 to ..**$175.00**

Ornament, dog in a bag (cocker spaniel), My Darling embossed on bag, mold-blown, Germany, 1970s, 3½", from $40 to..**$50.00**

Ornament, duck, mold-blown, standing, wings at side, bumpy body, bill on chest, Germany, 1970s, 3", from $25 to **$30.00**

Ornament, Dutch girl head, mold-blown, Czechoslovakia, 1950s & 1980s, 2", from $80 to............................**$90.00**

Ornament, fish, embossed details, mold-blown w/spun-glass tail, Japan or Germany, 1950s-90s, 2-3", from $15 to........**$25.00**

Ornament, flower basket, free-blown, Germany, Czechoslovakia or Austria, commonly found, 4-5", from $35 to...**$60.00**

Ornament, frog on leaf, mold-blown, Germany, 1991, 2½", from $35 to..**$50.00**

Ornament, glass beaded flat shape, Germany, Czechoslovakia, or Japan, 2-6", from $2 to.............**$8.00**

Ornament, grapes embossed on egg shape, mold-blown, Corning, long production, 1½", from $2 to **$3.00**

Ornament, ice cream cone, free-blown, 4", from $5 to ..**$10.00**

Ornament, icicle, looped & folded wire, Germany & US, 5½", from $1 to...**$2.00**

Ornament, Japanese bird, free-blown, ball form, 1950s, fairly common, from $2 to...**$6.00**

Ornament, lighthouse, mold-blown, 6-sided, 1950s-60s, 3", from $35 to..**$35.00**

Ornament, owl, cat & bulldog heads, 3-sided, mold-blown, Germany, 1980s, 2½", from $150 to...................**$175.00**

Ornament, owl on leaf, mold-blown, Germany, 1970s, 3x2¼", from $75 to..**$85.00**

Ornament, peach, mold-blown, unsilvered w/fabric leaves, fairly common, 2½-3", from $15 to **$25.00**

Ornament, peacock, mold-blown, fanned feathers (turkeylike in appearance), post-WWII, Germany, 3¾", from $35 to **$45.00**

Ornament, pickle, mold-blown, resembles Heinz pickle, unsilvered, 1985, 3½-3¾", from $75 to.................**$90.00**

Ornament, purse w/embossed roses, mold-blown, Germany, 1970s-80s, 2¼", from $40 to................................**$50.00**

Ornament, rooster embossed on oval, mold-blown, Germany, 1930s, common, 2", from $10 to.........**$15.00**

Ornament, rosette, foil light-reflector type w/center hole for light bulb, Germany, 2-3" dia, from $3 to...............**$5.00**

Ornament, rosette, spun glass, foil flower on tinsel burst w/Santa head & holly, 4" dia, from $35 to...........**$40.00**

Ornament, Santa (double-faced) head, mold-blown, flowing beard, 1970s, 2¾", from $70 to............................**$90.00**

Ornament, Santa in airplane, mold-blown w/tinsel wire wings & propeller, 1950s up until recently, 3", from $20 to **$25.00**

Ornament, stork, mold- & free-blown, spun-glass tail, clip-on holder, Germany, common, 3", from $30 to.........**$40.00**

Ornament, strawberry, mold-blown, 1¾-2¼", from $10 to...................**$20.00**

Ornament, swan w/indents, free-blown, sizes vary, made many years, common, from $10 to **$15.00**

Ornament, telephone, mold-blown, square base, pyramidal shape, paper dial, 1950s & 1990s, 1¾", from $40 to.**$50.00**

Ornaments, Bradford, unbreakable plastic, eight bells and balls in addition to tree topper, MIB, from $25.00 to $30.00. (Photo courtesy George Johnson)

Stocking, printed felt, from 1920s onward, from $15 to ..**$30.00**

Tinsel roping, gold, silver, red, green or purple, Germany or US, up to 18-ft L, from $5 to...................................**$8.00**

Cigarette Lighters

Collectors of tobacciana tell us that cigarette lighters are definitely hot! Look for novel designs (figurals, Deco styling, and so forth), unusual mechanisms (flint and fuel, flint and gas, battery, etc.), those made by companies now defunct, advertising lighters, and quality lighters made by Ronson, Dunhill, Evans, Colibri, and Zippo. For more information we recommend *Collector's Guide to Cigarette Lighters, Vols. I and II,* by James Flanagan (Collector Books).

Newsletter: *On the Lighter Side*
Judith Sanders
Route 3, 136 Circle Dr.
Quitman, TX 75783; 903-763-2795; SASE for information

Advertising, Bosch of Germany, spark plug form, chromium & paint, ca 1975, ⅞x3¼".......................................**$30.00**

Advertising, Camel, red, white letters, black camel, Zippo, ca 1993, w/gift box, 1½x2¼"............................**$35.00**

Advertising, Coca-Cola bottle, plastic, ca 1953, 2½x¾" dia..**$30.00**

Advertising, Dodge Trucks, oil drum form, red Bakelite, ca 1940s, 3"...**$30.00**

Advertising, Lucky Strike, table model, painted chromium, Japan, ca 1950s, 3x4⅜"....................................**$30.00**

Advertising, Swedish Chicago Line, ship form, chromium & white paint, Sarome, ca 1960s, 3¼x1⅛" **$30.00**

Advertising, Willie the Kool Penguin, table model, painted metal, ca 1930s, 4x1½" dia **$110.00**

Art Deco, Electro-Match, black plastic w/gold trim, Korex Co, ca 1950s, 4½" dia...**$25.00**

ASR, lighter/letter opener, metal, plastic grips on handle, ca 1950s, 2¾x9⅞"..**$35.00**

Aurora, lighter/flashlight, chromium & leather, ca 1960, 2½x2"...**$30.00**

Evans, lighter/case, chromium, ca 1950s, 3¼x5¾" **$80.00**

Evans, lighter/case, chromium & black enamel, ca 1930s, 2½x4¼"..**$50.00**

Figural, Aladdin-type lamp, table model, silverplate, Evans, ca 1950s, 4¼x3"...**$45.00**

Figural, apple, gold-tone brass, table model, Evans, ca 1950s, 3x2¼" dia **$45.00**

Figural, boxing glove, butane, German, ca 1990, 1⅜x2⅝"..**$25.00**

Figural, bust of knight, chromium, tortoise-colored cigarette box base, Negbaur, ca 1950s, 4x4⅛"....................**$50.00**

Figural, cowboy boot, embossed roses, silverplated, Occupied Japan, ca 1950, 3½x3".........................**$70.00**

Figural, dinosaur, table model, butane, chromium, Japan, ca 1988, 4x4¾"...**$30.00**

Figural, double-barrel pistol, chromium, Made in Japan, early '80s, 5½" L, from $15.00 to $25.00.

Figural, double barrel shotgun, table model, butane, ca 1980s, 20½x3" **$50.00**

Figural, elephant, brass, made in Austria, Pat April 2, 1912, 3½x3"..**$100.00**

Figural, engine, chromium & plastic, touch-tip style, Remier Co Ltd, ca 1947, 5¼x3½" **$150.00**

Figural, fire extinguisher, butane, German, ca 1990, 1x3"..**$25.00**

Figural, flintlock Derringer, table model w/plastic stand, 1968, 5¾x3"..**$30.00**

Figural, gas pump, metal, Occupied Japan, ca 1949, 1¼x3½"..**$80.00**

Figural, hand grenade, chromium, butane, PGL, ca 1960, 2¼x4¼"...**$30.00**

Figural, horse, table model, ceramic, Japan, ca 1955, 5½x 5½"" **$25.00**

Figural, knight, chromium on plastic base, lighter in helmet, Thorens, ca 1940s, 3x6⅞" **$45.00**

Figural, lighthouse, table, silverplated, Occupied Japan, ca 1948, 4¼x1½" dia **$75.00**

Figural, lion, silverplated, ca 1935, 1¾x2⅜" **$70.00**

Figural, megaphone, butane, German, ca 1990, 2x2⅞" .**$25.00**

Figural, piano, chromium & plastic, table model, Occupied Japan, ca 1948, 2⅝x3¼" **$125.00**

Figural, pistol, chromium w/black plastic grips, Japan, ca 1950s, 2x1½" **$25.00**

Figural, potbellied stove, brass, ca 1950s, ½x3¼" **$20.00**

Figural, rocket ship, table model, chromium, Occupied Japan, ca 1948, 3x1" **$100.00**

Figural, rose, table model, chromium, ca 1960s, 2½x1⅝" dia **$35.00**

Figural, saxophone, butane, German, ca 1990, 2x3½" ..**$25.00**

Figural, seated camel, painted metal, lift-arm type, ca 1930s, 4¾x2½" **$40.00**

Figural, slot machine, table, batteries & butane, ca 1960s, 6x6¾" **$45.00**

Figural, smoking pipe, brass, table model, Occupied Japan, ca 1948, 4½x2¾" **$70.00**

Figural, Statue of Liberty, table model, batteries & butane, 1950s, 3½x7½" **$100.00**

Figural, swan, table model, chromium, Japan, 1960s, 3¾x3" **$20.00**

Figural, telegraph, table model, plastic, brass & wood, battery & butane, Japan, ca 1950s, 6x3¾" **$50.00**

Figural, Thompson machine gun, table model, chromium, ca 1988, 11¼x3¾" **$60.00**

Figural, ticker tape, table model, plastic & glass, Japan, ca 1950s, 5¼x3¼" dia..**$50.00**

Perky, lift-arm type, chromium w/painted Japanese scene, ca 1950s, ¾x⅞" **$40.00**

Ronson, Diana, table model, silverplated, ca 1950s, 2¾x2½" **$30.00**

Ronson, lighter/case, Mastercase, chromium & black enamel, ca 1933, 2½x4¾" **$50.00**

Ronson, Mayfair, table model, silverplated, ca 1936, 1⅝x3" **$25.00**

Ronson, Wedgwood-style, green, table model, ca 1962, 2⅛x2¾" **$60.00**

Scripto, Vu-Lighter, clear plastic & chromium, w/tin box & instructions, ca 1950s, 1½x2¾" **$40.00**

Cleminson Pottery

One of the several small potteries that operated in California during the middle of the century, Cleminson was a family-operated enterprise that made kitchenware, decorative items, and novelties that are beginning to attract a considerable amount of interest. At the height of their productivity, they employed 150 workers, so as you make your rounds, you'll be very likely to see a piece or two offered for sale just about anywhere you go. Prices are not high; this may be a 'sleeper.'

They marked their ware fairly consistently with a circular ink stamp that contains the name 'Cleminson.' But even if you find an unmarked piece, with just a little experience you'll easily be able to recognize their very distinctive glaze colors. They're all strong, yet grayed-down, dusty tones. They made a line of bird-shaped tableware items that they marketed as 'Distlefink' and several plaques and wall pockets that are decorated with mottoes and Pennsylvania Dutch-type hearts and flowers.

In Jack Chipman's *The Collector's Encyclopedia of California Pottery, Second Edition,* you'll find a chapter devoted to Cleminson Pottery. Roerig's *The Collector's Encyclopedia of Cookie Jars* has additional information. (Both of these books are published by Collector Books.)

See also Clothes Sprinkler Bottles; Cookie Jars.

Advisor: Robin Stine (See Directory, California Pottery)

Ashtray, fruit, footed, 10" **$35.00**

Bobby pin holder, Bobbie Guard, w/hat as lid, 4½" ..**$50.00**

Bread tray, Distlefink, 12½" **$35.00**

Butter dish, Distlefink, w/lid..**$50.00**

Cleanser shaker, Katrina, hand-decorated, 6¼" **$30.00**

Egg cup, from $30 to..**$35.00**

Gravy bowl, Distlefink, w/ladle, 5½" **$50.00**

Jar, Chinese man, white w/black hat, w/lid **$60.00**

Pie bird, chicken, white w/multicolored trim, 4½", from $25 to..**$40.00**

Pitcher, Distlefink line, 9½", from $50.00 to $60.00.

Plate, crowing rooster decoration, 9½"......................**$30.00**

Plate, hand-painted fruit or flowers, ca 1948, 7½", ea, from $15 to..**$25.00**

Razor blade bank, Gay Blade, 4" **$40.00**

Salt & pepper shakers, artist w/palette, 6¼", pr **$75.00**

Spoon rest, floral decoration, 8½"................................**$25.00**

String holder, wall hanging, house shape, 6½"..........**$75.00**

Toothpick holder, butler, 4½" **$50.00**

Tray, Galagray; 12" **$25.00**

Wall decoration, kettle shape, w/verse, detachable handle, 9" **$25.00**

Wall pocket, Antoine, chef's head, 7¼" **$75.00**

Wall pocket, fireplace bellows shape, 10½" **$40.00**

Wall pocket, kettle shape, w/verse, 7¼".....................**$30.00**
Wall pocket, key shape, 7¼" **$35.00**
Wall pocket, little house on top of the world, 8"........**$50.00**

Wall pocket, long johns, 8", from $25.00 to $35.00.

Clothes Sprinkler Bottles

With the invention of the iron, clothes were sprinkled with water, rolled up to distribute the dampness, and pressed. This created steam when ironing, which helped to remove wrinkles. The earliest bottles were made of hand-blown clear glass. Ceramic figurals were introduced in the 1920s; these had a metal sprinkler cap with a rubber cork. Later versions had a true cork with an aluminum cap. More recent examples contain a plastic cap. A 'wetter-downer' bottle had no cap but contained a hole in the top to distribute water to larger items such as sheets and tablecloths. These were filled through a large opening in the bottom and plugged with a cork. Some 'wetter-downers' are mistaken for shakers and vice versa. In the end, with the invention of more sophisticated irons that produced their own steam (and later had their own sprayers), the sprinkler bottle was relegated to the attic or, worse yet, the trash can.

The variety of subjects depicted by figural sprinkler bottles runs from cute animals to laundry helpers and people who did the ironing. Because of their whimsical nature, their scarcity and desirability as collectibles, we have seen a rapid rise in the cost of these bottles over the last couple of years.

See also Kitchen Prayer Ladies.

Advisor: Ellen Bercovici (See Directory, Clothes Sprinkler Bottles)

Cat, marble eyes, cereamic, American Bisque, from $195 to **$250.00**
Cat, variety of designs & colors, homemade ceramic, from $100 to..**$150.00**
Chinese man, Sprinkle Plenty, white, green & brown, holding iron, ceramic, from $175 to **$225.00**
Chinese man, Sprinkle Plenty, yellow & green, ceramic, Cardinal China Co, from $20 to..................**$30.00**

Chinese man, towel over arm, from $175 to.............**$250.00**
Chinese man, variety of designs & color, handmade ceramic, from $50 to..**$150.00**
Chinese man, white & aqua, ceramic, Cleminson, from $30 to..**$40.00**
Chinese man, white & aqua w/paper shirt tag, ceramic, Cleminson, from $75 to..................................**$100.00**

Clothespin, face with stenciled eyes and airbrushed cheeks and lips, from $200.00 to $250.00. (Photo courtesy Ellen Bercovici)

Clothespin, hand decorated, ceramic, from $150 to .**$200.00**
Clothespin, red, yellow & green plastic, from $20 to.**$40.00**
Dearie Is Weary, ceramic, Enesco, from $250 to **$350.00**
Dutch boy, green & white ceramic, from $175 to **$250.00**
Dutch girl, white w/green & pink trim, wetter-downer, ceramic, from $175 to **$250.00**
Elephant, pink & gray, ceramic, from $50 to **$75.00**
Elephant, trunk forms handle, ceramic, American Bisque, from $400 to..**$600.00**
Elephant, white & pink w/shamrock on tummy, ceramic, from $100 to..**$150.00**
Emperor, variety of designs & colors, handmade ceramic, from $150 to..**$200.00**
Iron, blue flowers, ceramic, from $100 to **$150.00**
Iron, green ivy, ceramic, from $50 to **$75.00**
Iron, green plastic, from $25 to..................................**$45.00**
Iron, lady ironing, ceramic, from $45 to.....................**$75.00**
Iron, man & woman farmer, ceramic, from $200 to .**$275.00**
Iron, souvenir of Aquarena Springs, San Marcos TX, ceramic, from $200 to...**$300.00**
Iron, souvenir of Florida, pink flamingo, ceramic, from $250 to..**$325.00**
Iron, souvenir of Wonder Cave, ceramic, from $250 to.**$300.00**
Mammy, ceramic, possibly Pfaltzgraff, from $250 to ..**$350.00**
Mary Maid, all colors, plastic, Reliance, from $15 to..**$35.00**
Mary Poppins, ceramic, Cleminson, from $250 to **$350.00**
Myrtle, ceramic, Pfaltzgraff, from $250 to.................**$350.00**
Peasant woman, w/laundry poem on label, from $200 to...**$300.00**

Poodle, gray & pink or white, ceramic, from $200 to ..**$300.00**
Queen or King, ceramic, Tilso, Japan, from $100 to ..**$125.00**
Rooster, green, tan & red detailing over white, ceramic, from
$125 to..**$200.00**

Clothing and Accessories

Watch a 'golden oldie' movie, and you can't help admiring the clothes — what style, what glamour, what fun! Due in part to the popularity of old movie classics and great new movies with retro themes, there's a growing fascination with the fabulous styles of the past — and there's no better way to step into the romance and glamour of those eras than with an exciting piece of vintage clothing!

'OOOhhh, it don't mean a thing, if it ain't got that S-W-I-N-G!' In 1935, Benny Goodman, 'King of Swing,' ushered in the swing era from Los Angeles' Polmar Ballroom. After playing two standard sets, he switched to swing, and the crowd went crazy! Swing's the 'in' thing in vintage clothing this year, and swing dance devotees are looking for the sassy styles of the late '30s through the mid-40s to wear 'clubbing.' Swing era gals' clothing featured short full or pleated skirts, wide padded shoulders, and natural waistlines. Guys, check out those wild, wide ties that were worn with 'gangster-look' zoot suits!

Clothes of the 1940s though the 1970s are not as delicate as their Victorian and Edwardian counterparts; they're easier to find and much more affordable! Remember, the more indicative of its period, the more desirable the item. Look for pieces with glitz and glamour — also young, trendy pieces that were expensive to begin with. Look for designer pieces and designer look-alikes. Although famous designer labels are hard to find, you may be lucky enough to run across one! American designers like Adrian, Claire McMardell, Charles James, Mainboucher, Hattie Carnegie, Norell, Pauline Trigere, and Mollie Parnis came to the fore during World War II. The '50s were the decade of Christian Dior; others included Balenciaga, Balmain, Chanel, Jacques Heim, Nona Ricci, Ann Fogarty, Oleg Cassini, and Adele Simpson. In the '60s and '70s, Mary Quant, Betsey Johnson, Givenchy, Yves St. Laurent, Oscar de la Renta, Galanos, Pierre Cardin, Rudi Gernreich, Paco Rabanne, Courreges, Arnold Scassi, Geoffrey Beene, Emilio Pucci, Zandra Rhodes, and Jessica McClintock (Gunne Sax) were some of the names that made fasion headlines.

Pucci, Lilli Ann of Calfornia, Eisenberg, and Adele Simpson designs contine to be especially sought after. Enid Colins imaginative bags are popular, but prices are lower than last year's. Look for lingerie — '30s and '40s lace/hook corsets, and '50s pointy 'bullet' bras (like the ones in the Old Maidenform Dream ads). For both men and women, '70s disco platform shoes (the wilder, the better), cowboy shirts and jackets, also fringed 'hippie' items. For men, look for bowling shirts, '50s 'Kramer' shirts, and '40s and '50s wild ties, especially those by Salvadore Dali.

Levi jeans and jackets made circa 1971 and before have a cult following, especially in Japan. Among the most sought-after denim Levi items are jeans with a capitol 'E' on a *red* tab or back pocket. The small 'e' jeans are also collectible; these were made during the late 1960s and until 1970 (with two rows of single stitching inside the back pocket). Worth watching for as well are the 'red line' styles of the '80s (these have double-stitched back pockets). Other characteristics to look for in vintage Levis are visible rivets inside the jeans and single pockets and silver-colored buttons on jackets with vertical pleats. From the same era, Lee, Wrangler, Bluebell, J.C. Penney, Oxhide, Big Yanks, James Dean, Doublewear, and Big Smith denims are collectible as well.

As with any collectible, condition is of the utmost importance. 'Deadstock' is a term that refers to a top-grade item that has never been worn or washed and still has its original tags. Number 1 grade must have no holes larger than a pinhole. A torn belt loop is permissible if no hole is created. There may be a few light stains and light fading. The crotch area must have no visible wear and the crotch seam must have no holes. And lastly, the item must not have been altered. Values in the listing here are for items in number 1 grade. There are also other grades for items that have more defects.

While some collectors buy with the intent of preserving their clothing and simply enjoy having it, many buy it to wear. If you do wear it, be very careful how you clean it. Fabrics may become fragile with age.

For more information, refer to *Vintage Hats and Bonnets, 1770 – 1970, Identifications and Values,* by Sue Langley, *Collector's Guide to Vintage Fashions* by Kristina Harris, and *Antique and Vintage Clothing, 1850 to 1940,* by Diane Snyder-Haug (all from Collector Books); *Vintage Fashions for Women, the 1950s & '60s,* by Kristina Harris, and *Clothing and Accessories From the '40s, '50s and '60s* by Jan Lindenberger (both from Schiffer); *Vintage Denim* by David Little; *Shoes* by Linda O'Keefe; *Plastic Handbags* by Kate E. Dooner; *Fit To Be Tied, Vintage Ties of the '40s and Early '50s,* by Rod Dyer and Ron Spark; and *The Hawaiian Shirt* by H. Thomas Steele. For more information about denim clothing and vintage footwear see *How To Identify Vintage Apparel for Fun and Profit,* available from Flying Deuce Auction & Antiques (see Auction Houses).

Prices are a compilation of shows, shops, and Internet auctions. They are retail values and apply to items in excellent condition. Note: Extraordinary items bring extraordinary prices!

Clothing in the following illustrations are from the collection of Sue Downing; photography by John Dowling, copyright 1999.

Advisors: Sue Langley, Clothing; Teresa Clawson, Vintage Denim (See Directory, Clothing and Accessories)

Newsletter: *Costume Society of America*
55 Edgewater Dr., P.O. Box 73
Earleville, MD 21919
Phone: 410-275-1691 or fax: 410-275-8936
www.costumesocietyamerica.com

Newsletter: *The Vintage Connection*
904 North 65 Street
Springfield, OR 97478-7021

1940s Women's Day Wear

Dress, Broadway motif print.........................$145.00
Dress, multicolor 'hands' printed on rayon...............$135.00
Dress, orchids printed on rayon..................$60.00
Dress, snails printed on rayon.........................$65.00
Halter top, green-checked printed cotton...................$20.00
House dress, cotton print w/rickrack trim...................$24.00
Playsuit, printed cotton, 1-pc, short legs.................$25.00
Slacks, gray wool gabardine $45.00
Suit, burgundy wool.........................$145.00
Suit, Lilli Ann, navy w/eyelet-trimmed jacket...........$250.00
Suit, New Look, black wool, late '40s.......................$110.00
Suit, New Look, Eisenberg Original, gray gabardine.$125.00
Suit, New Look, gray rayon faille $62.00
Suit, pink wool gabardine.........................$115.00
Suit blouse, white rayon..........................$15.00
Tennis shorts, cotton twill, pleated, wide legs...........$32.00

1940s Women's Coats and Jackets

Coat, Pauline Trigere, wool tweed w/fitted waist.....$300.00
Coat, red wool, fitted $65.00
Coat, swing style, beige wool..........................$115.00
Coat, swing style, black velvet, ¾-length $80.00
Jacket, black wool w/braid trim..................$75.00
Jacket, tan wool, plain but nicely tailored..................$35.00
Mink neckpiece w/head & tails..................$24.00

1940s Women's Evening Wear

Cocktail dress, sequins, peplum, knee length, from $75
   to $95.00
Dinner dress, cotton floral, long w/bustle back........$165.00
Dinner gown, purple rayon crepe w/beaded neckline.$200.00
Evening coat w/hood, black rayon velvet, long.......$125.00
Gown, black rayon crepe w/sequin trim, long........$145.00

Swing-era sequinned dress for 'clubbing,' from $75.00 to $95.00.

1940s Women's Intimate Apparel/Lounge Wear

Bra, peach rayon satin, marked Miss America on label..$6.00
Corset, peach color, long, back-laced.........................$20.00

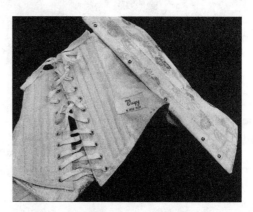

Corset, 'Waspy,' for Dior's wasp-waisted new-look fashions, $25.00.

Dress & jacket, Hawaiian print, Made in Hawaii......$125.00
Lounging pajamas, Hawaiian print on rayon, wide legs..$95.00
Lounging robe, purple satin w/quilted & embroidered collar
   & cuffs $130.00
Nightie, rayon satin floral print..........................$45.00
Nightie, sheer black silk w/strategic decorations........$75.00
Panties, peach rayon, wide-leg step-ins......................$10.00
Panties, rayon satin, See No Evil print, glow-in-the-dark zip-
   per w/figural 3-monkeys pull $55.00
Robe, butterfly print on cotton seersucker, long........$55.00
Slip, peach rayon satin $8.00

1940s Women's Accessories

Fedora, yellow Casablanca style..................$85.00
Gloves, gauntlet style, brown cotton $15.00
Gloves, long evening mitts, jeweled black velvet.....$125.00
Hanky, cat w/rhinestone eyes child's $14.00
Hat, black w/purple snood back, platter style...........$45.00
Hat, green felt petals, doll style..................$60.00
Hat, red felt, wide brim..........................$150.00
Hat, straw w/flowers & veil, toy style, sm...................$35.00
Hat, topper, black straw w/lg red 'wing' & back-tied
   veil $55.00
Hat, w/wimple (scarf across chin) $115.00
Purse, alligator bag, Cuba $75.00
Purse, clutch style, red plastic squares......................$30.00
Purse, evening clutch style, pearls $30.00
Purse, fine floral needlepoint..........................$45.00
Purse, rayon ribbed cord, plastic zipper ornament.....$35.00
Purse, Whiting & Davis, clutch style, silver w/rhinestone
   clasp..........................$50.00
Scarf, hats printed on silk $15.00
Shoes, alligator pumps, plain..........................$50.00
Shoes, alligator sling-backs w/'Minnie ear' clips........$75.00
Shoes, gold satin evening slippers $35.00

Shoes, '40s swing-era studded green suede, from $75.00 to $150.00; '50s – '60s stillettos, $25.00; '60s square-toed faille with beaded lion heads, from $55.00 to $75.00; and '70s disco three-tone gunmetal oxfords, from $95.00 to $125.00.

1950s Women's Day Wear

Bathing suit, cotton plaid	$25.00
Bathing suit, gold lamè	$55.00
Blouse, sleeveless, cotton	$10.00
Circle skirt, flocked floral trim & sequins	$45.00
Circle skirt, masques printed on fabric	$35.00
Cowboy shirt, cowboy on bucking bronco on back	$45.00
Lounging dress, cotton w/printed Paris scenes	$35.00
Sheath skirt, pink wool flannel	$25.00
Shirtwaist dress, pink cotton gingham	$45.00
Suit, tweed w/mink collar	$55.00
Sundress, printed fabric w/hats, full skirt	$25.00

1950s Women's Coats and Sweaters

Coat, Lilli Ann, pink wool, full skirt	$275.00
Coat, wool Pendleton plaid, ¾-length	$25.00
Mexican jacket, red felt w/cowboy scene & laced edge	$40.00
Sweater, beaded cardigan style, from $35 to	$85.00
Sweater, beige cashmere w/fur collar	$85.00
Sweater set (shell & cardigan), purple orlon	$35.00

1950s Women's Evening Wear

Ball gown, strapless, velvet & net w/sequin trim, long	$300.00
Coat, swing style, navy silk faille, mid-calf length	$55.00
Cocktail dress, red velvet, bateau neckline, full skirt	$125.00
Cocktail dress, strapless, black lace, full skirt	$45.00
Dress, rhinestone & pearl velvet top, taffeta circle skirt	$75.00
Gown, chartreuse chiffon w/spaghetti straps	$150.00
Prom dress, strapless, red net w/white lace top	$25.00
Suzy Wong Chinese dress, short & tight, from $35 to	$95.00

1950s Women's Intimate Apparel/Lounge Wear

Bra, Locket, strapless & boned, pointed 'Wonder Woman' look	$15.00
Bra, pointy 'bullet' style	$12.00

Crinoline, hoop skirt	$15.00
Crinoline, net, Florele label	$20.00
Pajamas, baby doll, pink cotton print	$8.00
Robe, aqua chenille, long	$40.00

1950s Women's Accessories

Collar, detachable, gold jeweled, from India	$15.00
Collar, detachable, white cotton pique	$6.00
Gloves, white cotton, short, from $5 to	$10.00
Hat, black felt w/red poinsettia trim, sm	$32.00
Hat, green velvet w/strawberries, Emme label	$22.00
Hat, jeweled w/pearls & rhinestones, sm	$75.00
Hat, mink, sm	$22.00
Hat, pink velvet w/ostrich feather trim, sm	$55.00

Hat, profile style, red plaid cellophane straw, $25.00.

Hat, straw trimmed w/cherries, sm	$45.00
Hat, wide brim, fine straw	$110.00
Hat, wide brim, velvet-edged w/maribou	$125.00
Pop-it beads, plastic	$5.00
Purse, evening clutch style, velvet w/gold India embroidery	$35.00
Purse, Lucite, gold & black, Dorset Rex 5th Ave	$130.00
Purse, Lucite, gray marbleized	$85.00
Purse, Lucite, red marbleized, Wilardy, rare	$700.00
Purse, Lucite, shiny black, Rialto	$250.00
Purse, Lucite/hard plastic, from $25 to	$700.00
Purse, velvet bag, jeweled & sequined poodle	$85.00
Purse, whimsical: poodles, etc, from $45 to	$85.00
Purse, wooden box style w/decoupage designs, from $35 to	$55.00
Scarf/kerchief, floral print on silk	$15.00
Scarf/kerchief, Moulin Rouge scene printed on silk	$75.00
Shoes, black suede ballet-style flats	$22.00
Shoes, Lucite Cinderella heels, from $25 to	$55.00
Shoes, saddle style	$20.00
Swimcap, decorated w/flowers	$22.00

1960s – 70s Women's Day Wear and Coats

Blouse, Emilio Pucci, Saks 5th Ave, 1970s	$110.00

Caftan, flamingo print, 1960s $18.00
Coat, acid green polka-dot polyester, 1960s...............$35.00
Coat dress, Adele Simpson, faux leopard, 1960s $125.00
Coat dress, Galanos couture, black wool knit $325.00
Coat dress, yellow polka-dots, Twiggy label...............$55.00
Dress, Emilio Pucci, silk w/crystal bead tie, 1970s ...$225.00
Dress, Emilio Pucci, silk w/matching sash, 1970s.....$125.00
Dress, Gunne Sax (Jessica McClintock), calico print, 1970s $45.00
Dress, paper, in original package, 1960s $22.00
Halter dress, paisley print on tricot, long skirt...........$25.00
Jacket, Emilio Pucci, Saks 5th Ave, 1970s $85.00
Mini dress, Oleg Cassini, orange polyester, 1960s $75.00
Mini dress, paper, quilted metallic blue, 1960s $45.00

1960s – 70s Women's Evening Wear

Blouse, Emilio Pucci, Saks 5th Ave, 1970s $110.00
Coat, black, sequinned, long $150.00
Cocktail ensemble: short dress & coat, beaded $125.00
Cocktail mini dress, white w/allover beading $55.00
Culotte dress, white polyester, long w/wide legs $65.00
Evening suit, Emilio Pucci, wool, 2-pc, 1970s...........$125.00
Mini dress, white crepe w/rhinestone zippers on neck & sleeves $65.00

Pants suit, bell-bottom pants, satin disco style, 1960s – 70s, $75.00.

Sheath dress, Ann Fogarty, brown velvet, long skirt ..$85.00
Sheath dress & coat, white brocade w/poppies $150.00
Sheath gown, red satin, plain w/good tailoring, long skirt $45.00
Top, sequinned & beaded knit, sleeveless $45.00

1960s – 70s Women's Accessories

Go-go boots, green vinyl, 1960s.................................$40.00
Go-go boots, snakeskin, late 1960s............................$85.00
Hat, bubble toque, Jack McConnell, feathered, 1960s ..$125.00
Hat, net whimsey, Sally Victor, w/hatbox...................$24.00

Hat, pillbox, red velvet w/gold India embroidery, 1960s..$45.00
Hat, toque, pink metallic brocade, 1960s $12.00
Purse, clear plastic over embroidered jeweled print...$22.00
Purse, Enid Collins, from $40 to $75.00
Purse, Hippie bag, long fringed suede, shoulder strap..$12.00
Purse, Judith Leiber, gold & rhinestones $550.00
Purse, Magazine...$45.00
Purse, silver faux leather w/plastic handles, lg $12.00

1940s – 70s Men's Wear

Bomber jacket, leather, souvenir, reversible..............$500.00
Bomber jacket, leather, souvenir, 1940s-60s, from $75 to..$500.00
Bowling shirt, Pepsi, red, 1950s $55.00
Bowling shirt, teal blue, decorated, 1950s..................$35.00
Bowling shirt, 1950s, from $25 to $75.00
Cowboy shirt, royal flush yoke, 1950s $42.00
Hawaiian shirt, print by Frank MacIntosh, silk, Hookano label, from $600 to $800.00
Hawaiian shirt, rayon or cotton print, 1940s-50s, from $55 to...$150.00
Hawaiian shirt, red print, 100% cotton, Made in Hawaii .$150.00
Jacket, gabardine, zip front, 1950s, from $45 to $400.00
Leisure suit, polyester, bell-bottom pants, 1960s.........$55.00
Shirt, disco style, photo scenes, 1970s, from $20 to ...$55.00
Shirt, Kramer style, pink gabardine w/black checks, 1950s $45.00
Shirt, photographic disco style $20.00
Shoes, disco platform style, brown leather-look vinyl..$24.00
Shoes, psychedelic disco platform style, 3-color vinyl..$80.00

Skinny tie from the '50s, from $8.00 to $12.00; Dali's 'Birth of Knowledge,' from $125.00 to $200.00; swing-era tie with 'Girlie,' from $75.00 to $150.00; swing-era Zoot suit tie with wolf, from $150.00 to $200.00; swing-era geometric style, from $20.00 to $35.00; pink and black '50s style, from $15.00 to $25.00.

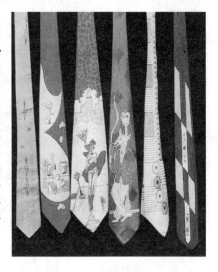

Smoking jacket, blue corduroy w/rust satin trim, 1940s.$45.00
Tie, hand-painted sailfish...$30.00
Tie, Salvador Dali, Soaring Wall, EX $250.00

Vintage Denim

Jacket, Lee, cowboy on button, from $900 to........$1,500.00
Jacket, Lee, red & gold tag, from $600 to $800.00
Jacket, Lee, 1960s-70s, from $70 to $100.00

Jacket, Levi, 1st edition, 1 pocket w/flap & pleated front, from $600 to...**$700.00**

Jacket, Levi, 2nd edition, 2 pockets w/flaps & pleated front, from $500 to...**$600.00**

Jacket, Levi, 3rd edition, 2 pocket, w/Big E tag on left pocket, inside pocket, unpleated front, from $100 to.**$200.00**

Jacket, Levi, 4th edition, 2 pockets, red tag w/sm e on left pocket, inside pocket, unpleated front................................**$50.00**

Jacket, Levi, two-pocket, red tab with small 'e,' ca 1970s, $50.00.

Jacket, Wrangler Rodeo, from $1,000 to.................**$1,500.00**

Jeans, Lee, 1960s, from $130 to.................................**$160.00**

Jeans, Lee, 1970s, from $50 to.....................................**$70.00**

Jeans, Levi, Double XX, buckle backs, from $2,000 to..**$3,000.00**

Jeans, Levi, Double XX, Every Garment Guaranteed tag, from $800 to..**$1,500.00**

Jeans, Levi, Double XX, leather tag, from $600 to....**$700.00**

Jeans, Levi, red lines, double stitched, 31" waist or smaller, from $20 to...**$40.00**

Jeans, Levi, red lines, double stitched, 32" to 38" waist, from $60 to...**$80.00**

Jeans, Levi, red lines, single stitched, 31" waist or smaller, from $20 to...**$40.00**

Jeans, Levi, red lines, single stitched, 32" to 38" waist, from $200 to...**$250.00**

Jeans, Levi, red lines, single stitched, 39" to 44" waist, from $60 to...**$200.00**

Jeans, Wrangler, Bluebell, 1950s, from $200 to.........**$400.00**

Jeans, Wrangler, Bluebell, 1960s, from $100 to.........**$200.00**

Coca-Cola Collectibles

Coca-Cola was introduced to the public in 1886. Immediately an advertising campaign began that over the years and continuing to the present day has literally saturated our lives with a never-ending variety of items. Some of the earlier calendars and trays have been known to bring prices well into the four figures. Because of these heady prices and the extremely widespread collector demand for good Coke items, reproductions are everywhere, so beware! Some of the

items that have been reproduced are pocket mirrors (from 1905, 1906, 1908 – 11, 1916, and 1920), trays (from 1899, 1910, 1913 – 14, 1917, 1920, 1923, 1926, 1934, and 1937), tip trays (from 1907, 1909, 1910, 1913 – 14, 1917, and 1920), knives, cartons, bottles, clocks, and trade cards. In recent years, these items have been produced and marketed: an 8" brass 'button,' a 27" brass bottle-shaped thermometer, cast-iron toys, bottle-shaped door pulls, Yes Girl posters, a 12" 'button' sign (with one round hole), a rectangular paperweight, a 1949-style cooler radio, and there are others. Look for a date line.

In addition to reproductions, 'fantasy' items have also been made, the difference being that a 'fantasy' never existed as an original. Don't be deceived. Belt buckles are 'fantasies.' So are glass doorknobs with an etched trademark, bottle-shaped knives, pocketknives (supposedly from the 1933 World's Fair), a metal letter opener stamped 'Coca-Cola 5¢,' a cardboard sign with the 1911 lady with fur (9" x 11"), and celluloid vanity pieces (a mirror, brush, etc.).

When the company celebrated its 100th anniversary in 1986, many 'centennial' items were issued. They all carry the '100th Anniversary' logo. Many of them are collectible in their own right, and some are already expensive.

If you'd really like to study this subject, we recommend these books: *Huxford's Collectible Advertising* by Sharon and Bob Huxford; *Collectible Coca-Cola Toy Trucks* by Gael de Courtivron; *B.J. Summers' Guide to Coca-Cola, Second Edition,* by B.J. Summers; and *Coca-Cola Commemorative Bottles,* by Bob and Debra Henrich (all from Collector Books); *Collector's Guide to Coca-Cola Items, Vols I* and *II,* by Al Wilson; and *Petretti's Coca-Cola Collectibles Price Guide* by Allan Petretti.

Advisor: Craig and Donna Stifter (See Directory, Soda Pop Collectibles)

Club: Coca-Cola Collectors Club International
P.O. Box 49166
Atlanta, GA 30359. Annual dues: $25

Apron, cloth bib-type, Pause/Refresh!/Drink C-C Ice Cold/In Bottles, shows tilted bottle on white, EX............**$115.00**

Blotter, 1936, 50th Anniversary/1886-1936, EX+..........**$25.00**

Blotter, 1940, The Greatest Pause on Earth, clown w/bottle, EX+ **$45.00**

Blotter, 1955, Friendliest Drink on Earth, hand-held bottle over image on Earth, NM+..................................**$15.00**

Bookends, brass bottle shapes, 1963, 8", NM, pr......**$325.00**

Bottle caddy for shopping cart, Enjoy Coca-Cola While You Shop/Place Bottle Here, white-on-red sign w/2 wire holders, EX..**$75.00**

Bottle carrier, aluminum, wire handle, Delicious & Refreshing, w/6 bottles, 1950s, VG+...................**$175.00**

Bottle carrier, wood, wing logos, wire handle w/wood grip, no dividers, 1930s-40s, NM.............................**$100.00**

Bottle opener, flat metal bottle shape, 1950s, EX+.....**$22.00**

Calendar, 1936, 50th Anniversary, complete, M........**$900.00**

Calendar, 1941, complete, VG.................................**$200.00**

Calendar, 1950, complete, EX+................................**$240.00**

Calendar, 1957, complete, NM+..................................$175.00

Clock, Drink C-C in Bottles on red dot on round bubble-glass front w/thin metal frame, reverse-painted, 1950s, NM+ **$600.00**

Clock, Things Go Better w/Coke & Drink C-C button, green numbers, metal frame, 1960s, 13x16", EX...........**$250.00**

Dispenser, footed wooden barrel painted red w/chrome bands, 2 spigots, 15-gal, 1950s, 28", VG+...........**$375.00**

Display bottle, green glass w/cap, 1960s, 20", NM+...**$90.00**

Display, window; cardboard diecut, 3-D soda fountain scene, 1950s, 24x36", $400.00. (Photo courtesy Craig and Donna Stifter)

Doll, Buddy Lee in C-C uniform w/hat, composition, 1950s, EX+ **$750.00**

Doll, Frozen C-C mascot, stuffed striped cloth, 1960s, NM+...**$145.00**

Door plate, embossed tin, Drink C-C, bottle in center on white ground w/red, yellow & green border, 1930s, 13", EX **$425.00**

Door push bar, porcelain, Pause.../Drink C-C/...Refresh, white on red, EX **$350.00**

Fan, cardboard w/wooden handle, Quality Carries On, shows hand-held bottles bursting through paper, 1950s, G+ **$50.00**

Game, NFL Football Game, ca 1964, NM **$15.00**

Game, Tic-Tac-Toe, EXIB..**$165.00**

Games (both Milton Bradley): set, ca 1940s, $115.00; Bingo, 1940s, $65.00. (Photo courtesy Craig and Donna Stifter)

Lighter, bottle shape, Bakelite, 1950s, 2½", NM..........**$30.00**

Lighter, flip top, 75th Anniversary, contour logo, M...**$40.00**

Matchbook cover, Season's Greetings/Drink C-C on button logo, shows Santa w/bottle, NM..........................**$35.00**

Menu board, cardboard, C-C/Sign of Good Taste, bottles in lower corners, wood-tone border, 1959, 28x19", EX+ **$200.00**

Menu board, plastic light-up, Good w/Food, fishtail logo flanked by menu slots, 19x49", EX.....................**$200.00**

Menu board, tin, Enjoy C-C/Things Go Better w/Coke, red dot on white above green board, white border, 28x20", EX..**$85.00**

Picnic cooler, 6-pack, red metal w/side opener, grip handle on lid w/larger carrying handle, 1950s, NM.......**$475.00**

Pillow, race-car shape, stuffed print cloth w/other advertising & #16, 'Goodyear' tires, 1970s, 15", NM **$100.00**

Playing cards, C-C Adds Life to...Everything Nice, 1976, MIB (sealed) **$30.00**

Playing cards, Coke Refreshes You Best, bowling girl, 1961, EX+..**$60.00**

Pocket mirror, C-C/Memos/59th Anniversary, 1936, EX+...**$120.00**

Pretzel bowl, aluminum, round w/3 cast bottles, 8" dia, EX+...**$225.00**

Radio, red plastic cooler form, Drink C-C Ice Cold, 1950s, VG+...**$450.00**

Record, Let's Go Go Go for the Three in a Row, 45-rpm, 1966, EX+ **$20.00**

Record holder, Hi-Fi Club, red vinyl w/black handle holds 45s, 9x7½", NM...**$55.00**

School kit, Real Pals, complete, 1930s, unused, VG.**$150.00**

Sign, cardboard, Come Over for Coke, girl at party table, green wooden frame, 1947, 21x37", EX.............**$275.00**

Sign, cardboard, 1940s, 29x50", $775.00. (Photo courtesy Craig and Donna Stifter)

Sign, cardboard, Enjoy That Refreshing New Feeling, bongo couple w/bottles, aluminum frame, 1960s, 39x22", VG..**$50.00**

Sign, cardboard, Have a Coke, cheerleader w/megaphone & bottle, 1946, 20x36", EX+ **$400.00**

Sign, cardboard, Hello Refreshment, girl leaving pool to enjoy a bottle of Coke, 1942, 20x36", EX...........**$425.00**

Sign, cardboard, Hospitality, 2 couples at open refrigerator, gold frame, 1948, 27x16", EX...................**$385.00**

Sign, cardboard, Join the Friendly Circle, party around picnic cooler, gold frame, 1954, horizontal, EX............**$400.00**

Sign, cardboard, Now! For Coke, trapeze artist reaching for bottle of Coke, gold frame, 1959, 20x36", VG....**$300.00**

Sign, cardboard, Play Refreshed, cowgirl, 1951, 20x36", G+...**$375.00**

Sign, cardboard, Things Go Better w/Coke, girl on phone, gold frame, 1960s, 27x16", VG+ **$200.00**

Sign, cardboard, Things Go Better w/Coke, guy helping girl skater after fall, aluminum frame, 1960s, 24x40", VG...**$160.00**

Sign, cardboard, Yes, bathing beauty eyeing hand-held bottle on white background, gold border, 1946, horizontal, VG **$300.00**

Sign, cardboard cutout, C-C/Delicious & Refreshing, 6-pack & wicker picnic basket displaying food, 32x40", VG+ **$175.00**

Sign, cardboard cutout, Extra Bright Refreshment, Santa standing by lamppost, easel back, 1958, 28x15", M **$325.00**

Sign, cardboard cutout, Serve Cold, shows Old Man Winter w/lg bottle & 6-pack, 1953, 21x16", NM...........**$225.00**

Sign, cardboard hanger, Drink C-C 5¢, orange & white on red, 2-sided, 1940s-50s, 6½" dia, EX+ **$75.00**

Sign, cardboard trolley, Yes, sunbather eyeing hand-held bottle & disk logo on white, 1946, 11x28", EX+ **$750.00**

Sign, celluloid, Pause/Go Refreshed, full glass shown in center on red background w/gold border, 9" dia, G **$200.00**

Sign, diecut metal policeman, Slow School Zone, 1950s, VG...**$1,500.00**

Sign, diecut wood, Kay Displays, Stop for a Pause/Drink C-C/Go Refreshed, policeman directing traffic, 1940s, EX **$3,500.00**

Sign, light-up counter-top w/square clock, 1950s, 9x20", EX...**$475.00**

Sign, light-up disk on rotating base, Shop Refreshed above Drink C-C In Bottles on red arrow, yellow base, 1950s, NM **$950.00**

Sign, paper, The Pause That Refreshes, lady in red dress seated holding bottle & glass, 1940s, 20x18", EX.....**$135.00**

Sign, porcelain, bottle shape, 1950s, 12", VG+ **$150.00**

Sign, porcelain, bottle shape, 1950s, 16", NM **$275.00**

Sign, porcelain, Drink C-C In Bottles, white lettering on red, curved ends, 1950s, 16x44", EX..........................**$125.00**

Sign, porcelain, Drink C-C/Sold Here Ice Cold, white & yellow on red, yellow & green border, 1930s, 12x32", VG+...**$425.00**

Sign, porcelain button, Drink C-C, red, 1950s, 24", NM+ .**$375.00**

Sign, tin, Drink C-C, white lettering on red field pointing to bottle on white, 1950s, 12x32", VG+...................**$125.00**

Sign, tin, Drink C-C in Bottles/D&R, white & yellow phrase on red right of bottle on white, green border, 10x28", VG+...**$675.00**

Sign, tin, Enjoy That Refreshing New Feeling, fishtail logo (vertical) above bottle, green border, 1963, 54x18", EX+ **$250.00**

Sign, tin, Enjoy That Refreshing New Feeling Ice Cold/phrase left of bottle, 1963, 20x28", NM+........................**$275.00**

Sign, tin, Sign of Good Taste, diecut yellow ribbon banner w/phrase in red, 10x42", EX..................................**$75.00**

Sign, tin, Things Go Better w/Coke, phrase, Drink C-C disk logo & bottle on white, raised rim, 1960s, 54x18", NM..**$325.00**

Sign, tin button w/flat arrow, Drink C-C on red w/silver arrow, 1950s, 16", NM+.......................................**$700.00**

Standee, cardboard cutout, Wayne Gretsky in hockey gear w/Coke bottle, life-size, NM+ **$75.00**

Syrup jug, glass w/paper label showing paper cup & Coke glass, 1960s, EX...**$20.00**

Thermometer, dial, Things Go Better w/Coke, white, 1964, 12" dia, EX+...**$250.00**

Thermometer, plastic, Drink C-C, orange & white, 1960s, 18", EX...**$30.00**

Thermometer, tin, gold bottle on red panel, 1936, 16", EX **$275.00**

Tie clip, 5-Year, gold & enameled bar, NM **$75.00**

Tip tray, 1920, EX+...**$260.00**

Tire rack display sign, tin, 1960s, $650.00. (Photo courtesy Craig and Donna Stifter)

Toy truck, Buddy L, tractor-trailer w/clear plastic cab top & steel red & white trailer, #5270J, 1980s, 14", NM+ .**$40.00**

Toy truck, Budgie, diecast delivery w/divided open bay, orange w/orange hubs, 1950s, 5", EX+..............**$120.00**

Toy truck, Marx, delivery w/stake bed, tin, yellow w/red & blue trim, Sprite Boy logo, #1088, 1956, 18¾", EX.........**$350.00**

Toy truck, Marx, plastic delivery w/6 plastic cases, 1956, EX+ (EX box) **$475.00**

Toy truck, Matchbox, delivery w/even load, diecast, yellow w/red trim, #37, 1950s-60s, 2¼", NMIB **$115.00**

Toy truck, Sanyo, Route Truck for C-C, tin, yellow & white w/red trim, 1960s, 12½", EXIB **$450.00**

Tray, 1930, Bathing Beauty, EX................................**$425.00**

Tray, 1933, Francis Dee, 10½x13", NM.....................**$700.00**

Tray, 1937, Running Girl, 10½x13", NM $425.00
Tray, 1938, Girl in Yellow Seated, 13x11", EX..........$275.00
Tray, 1939, Springboard Girl, 10½x13", EX..............$285.00

Tray, 1941, Ice Skater, NM, $325.00.

Tray, 1942, Roadster, 10½x13", NM+ $425.00
Tray, 1950s, Girl w/Wind in Hair, solid background, 10½x13", NM $175.00
Tray, 1953-60, Menu Girl, 13x11", NM+.....................$65.00
Tray, 1957, Umbrella Girl, 10½x13", M......................$375.00
Vienna art plates, any except topless girl, w/frames, VG-EX, from $400 to..$575.00
Watch, 100th Anniversary, round gold-tone face w/black leather strap, NM..$120.00

Coloring and Activity Books

Coloring and activity books representing familiar movie and TV stars of the 1950s and '60s are fun to collect, though naturally unused examples are hard to find. Condition is very important, of course, so learn to judge their values accordingly. Unused books are worth as much as 50% to 75% more than one only partially colored.

Addams Family Paint Book, Saalfield, 1965, unused, EX...$100.00
Adventures of Batman Coloring Book, Whitman, 1966, few pages colored, NM..$30.00
Amazing Spider-Man Sticker Book, Whitman, 1976, unused, EX..$20.00
Atom Ant Coloring Book, Watkins-Strathmore, 1965, unused, EX..$25.00
Bambi Paint Book, WDP, 1941, unused, EX...............$65.00
Banana Splits Coloring Book, Whitman, 1969, several pages colored, EX..$25.00
Batman Color-By-Number Book, Whitman, 1966, oversized, unused, M..$35.00
Beatles Coloring Book, Saafield, 1964, unused, NM.$100.00
Beverly Hillbillies Punch-Out Book, Whitman, 1960s, unused, EX..$85.00
Bewitched Activity Book, Treasure, 1965, unused, EX.$20.00

Bionic Woman Activity Book, Grosset & Dunlap, 1976, unused, EX..$10.00
Bionic Woman Coloring Book, Treasure Books, 1976, unused, NM..$30.00
Black Hole Coloring Book, Whitman, 1979, unused, NM...$10.00
Bonzana Coloring Book, Artcraft, 1960, unused, M....$50.00
Brady Bunch Coloring Book, Whitman, 1974, unused, EX..$45.00
Bullwinkle Coloring Book, General Mills premium, 1963, unused, EX..$30.00
Captain America Coloring Book, Whitman, 1966, unused, NM..$25.00
Centurians Coloring Book, Golden, 1986, unused, M...$10.00
CHiPs Coloring & Activity Book, Waldman, 1983, unused, NM..$15.00
Curiosity Shop Punch-Out Book, Artcraft, 1971, unused, EX..$35.00
Disneyland Sticker Fun Book, Whitman, 1967, unused, M..$45.00
Donnie & Marie Coloring Book, Whitman, 1977, unused, EX..$10.00
Donnie & Marie Sticker Book, Whitman, 1977, unused, EX..$15.00
Dr Dolittle & His Animals Coloring Book, 1967, few pages colored, EX..$10.00
Dudley Do-Right Coloring Book, Whitman, 1972, few pages colored, EX..$15.00
Dune Activity Book, EX $7.00
Elizabeth Taylor Coloring Book, Whitman, 1952, few pages colored, EX..$35.00
F-Troop Coloring Book, Saalfield, 1967, unused, NM...$55.00
Family Affair Coloring Book, Whitman, 1968, unused, NM..$25.00

Flash Gordon Coloring Book, A. McWilliams, King Features, 1952, M, $75.00.

Flintstones Sticker Fun, Whitman, 1966, unused, M ...$35.00
Fonzie Coloring Book, Treasure Books, 1976, unused, M..$25.00
Frankenstein Jr Sticker Book, Whitman, 1967, unused, NM..$35.00
Garrison's Gorillas Coloring Book, Whitman, 1968, unused, EX..$45.00

Gilligan's Island Coloring Book, Whitman, 1965, unused, EX $35.00

Green Hornet Coloring Book, Whitman, 1966, unused, M...$75.00

Hanna-Barbera's Amazing Chan & the Chan Clan Sticker Book, 1973, M..........................$40.00

Hot Wheels Sticker Book, 1985, unused, EX................$8.00

HR Pufnstuf Press-Out Book, Whitman/Sid & Marty Kroft, 1970, 16 pages, unused, M...................$65.00

Huckleberry Hound Coloring Book, Whitman #1134, 1963, few pages colored, EX $10.00

Incredible Hulk Sticker Book, Whitman, 1979, unused, M...$25.00

Jabber Jaw & the Rustlers Read & Color Book, Rand McNally, 1977, unused, EX.....................$20.00

Johnny Lightning Sticker Book, Whitman, 1970, unused, NM...$20.00

Julia Coloring Book, Saalfield, 1968, unused, EX........$25.00

Land of the Lost Coloring Book, Whitman, 1975, unused, NM $35.00

Laverne & Shirley Coloring Book, Playmore, 1983, unused, NM $20.00

Little Lulu Coloring Book, Whitman, 1973, unused, NM..$65.00

Man From UNCLE Coloring Book, Watkins Strathmore, 1965, unused, EX $55.00

Mighty Mouse Sticker Book, Whitman, 1967, unused, NM..$50.00

Mork's Book of Orkian Fun Activity Book, Wonder Books, 1979, unused, EX.................................$20.00

Mrs. Beasley Coloring Book, Whitman, #1648, 1974, EX/NM, from $15.00 to $20.00. (Photo courtesy Greg Davis and Bill Morgan)

My Three Sons Coloring Book, Whitman, 1967, unused, NM...$45.00

Nanny & the Professor Coloring Book, Saalfield, 1971, unused, EX..$25.00

Partridge Family Coloring Book, Saalfield, 1971, unused, EX..$25.00

Pebbles & Bamm-Bamm Coloring Book, Whitman, 1964, unused, NM..$25.00

Planet of the Apes Coloring Book, Artcraft, 1975, unused, EX $16.00

Raggedy Ann & Andy Dot-to-Dot Book, Whitman, 1978, unused, EX..$10.00

Raggedy Ann's Trace 'n' Rub Book, Random House, 1987, unused, EX...$5.00

Rocketeer Sticker Book, Western Publishing, 1991, unused, M...$5.00

Sabrina Coloring Book, Whitman, 1971, few pages colored, VG..$10.00

Six Million Dollar Man Activity Book, Saalfield, 1975, unused, M...$25.00

Smokey the Bear Coloring Book, Whitman, 1969, unused, M...$45.00

Space Ghost Coloring Book, Whitman, 1965, unused, NM $30.00

Star Trek Coloring Book, Saalfield, 1968, unused, NM ...$35.00

Steve Canyon's Interceptor Station Punch-Out Book, Golden, 1959, unused, NM.................................$45.00

Superboy Coloring Book, Whitman, 1967, unused, M..$50.00

Superman Color-By-Number, Whitman #1409, 1966, unused, M...$50.00

Superman Coloring Book, Whitman #1157, 1964, M..$45.00

Tarzan Punch-Out Book, Whitman, 1967, unused, NM..$45.00

Tennessee Tuxedo Coloring Book, 1969, M................$20.00

That Girl Coloring Book, Saafield, #4539, 1970s, EX/NM, from $20.00 to $25.00. (Photo courtesy Greg Davis and Bill Morgan)

The Shadow Coloring Book, Saafield, 1974, unused, NM..$20.00

Universal Monsters Mark & See Book, w/4 monster cards, NM..$5.00

V Coloring Book, Cliveden Press/England, 1985, unused, NM $45.00

Waltons Sticker Book, Whitman, 1975, unused, EX....$25.00

Wild Kingdom Coloring Book, few pages colored, EX ..$6.00

Winnie the Pooh & Friends Punch-Out Book, Golden, 1983, unused, NM...$15.00

Wonder Woman Faces the Menace of the Mole Men Coloring Book, Whitman, 1975, unused, NM $15.00

Wonderbug Down Mexico Way Coloring Book, Whitman, 1978, unused $15.00

101 Dalmatians Coloring Book, Whitman, 1960, unused, EX $25.00

Comic Books

Though just about everyone can remember having stacks and stacks of comic books as a child, few of us ever saved them for more than a few months. At 10¢ a copy, new ones quickly replaced the old, well-read ones. We'd trade them with our friends, but very soon, out they went. If we didn't throw them away, Mother did. So even though they were printed in huge amounts, few survive, and today they're very desirable collectibles.

Factors that make a comic book valuable are condition (as with all paper collectibles, extremely important), content, and rarity, but not necessarily age. In fact, comics printed between 1950 and the late 1970s are most in demand by collectors who prefer those they had as children to the earlier comics. They look for issues where the hero is first introduced, and they insist on quality. Condition is first and foremost when it comes to assessing worth. Compared to a book in excellent condition, a mint issue might bring six to eight times more, while one in only good condition would be worth less than half the price. We've listed some of the more collectible (and expensive) comics, but many are worth very little. You'll really need to check your bookstore for a good reference book before you actively get involved in the comic book market.

Abbott & Costello, Charlton Comics #11 ....$16.00
Adventures of Cyclops & Phoenix, Marvel #1 ....$5.00
Adventures of the Planet of the Apes, Marvel Comic Group #1 ....$4.00
Akira, Marvel Comics #3...$8.00
Al Capp's Wolf Gal, #2, 1952, VG+ $55.00
Alexander the Great, Dell Four-Color #688, VG+ $17.00
Andy Panda, Dell Four-Color #25/1, VG+ $175.00
Animal World, Dell Four-Color #713, VG+ $16.00
Annie Oakley, Dell #6, VG+ $30.00
Annie Oakley, Gold Key #1, VG+ $15.00
Around the World in Eighty Days, Dell Four-Color #784, VG $14.00
Atlantis the Lost Continent, Dell Four-Color #1188, G..$12.00
Avengers, Gold Key #1, 1968, EX..................................$45.00
Avengers, Marvel #4, 1963, He Lives Again!, Captain America cover, EX $445.00
Bat Masterson, #6, EX..$25.00
Bat Masterson, Dell Four-Color #1013, 1959, EX $35.00

Batman, DC Comics #4, NM, $3,000.00. (Photo courtesy Bill Bruegman)

Beany & Cecil, Dell Four-Color #570, VG $45.00
Ben Bowie & His Mountain Men, #11, EX $21.00
Ben Casey, Dell #1, 1962, photo cover, EX................$15.00
Bewitched, #1, VG..$9.00
Big Town, #14, G+ $16.00
Blazing West, #10, VG $8.00
Bonanza, #207, 1962, EX...$60.00
Bozo, Dell Four-Color #508, G $12.00
Brave One, Dell Four-Color #773, VG $10.00
Buccaneers, Dell Four-Color #800, VG+ $17.00
Bugs Bunny, Dell Four-Color #164, VG.......................$30.00
Bugs Bunny, Dell Four-Color #432, VG.......................$11.00
Bugs Bunny, Dell Four-Color #88, G+ $37.00
Burke's Law, #3, VG..$8.00
Casper the Friendly Ghost, #18, VG............................$18.00
Charlie McCarthy, #6, VG+...$19.00
Cheyenne, Dell #16, 1960, EX $15.00
Christmas & Archie, Archie Comics #1, 1974, EX.......$10.00
Christmas in Disneyland, #1, EX..................................$90.00
Colt .45, #4, VG+ $26.00
Colt .45, Dell #5, 1960, EX...$20.00
Conan the Barbarian, Marvel Treasury #4, 1975, oversized, NM..$8.00
Cowboy in Africa, #1, VG+ $9.00
Daisy Duck's Diary, #659, EX+.....................................$15.00
Dark Shadows, Gold Keys #5. 1970, NM.....................$50.00

David Cassidy, Charlton, 1972, EX, from $10.00 to $15.00 each. (Photo courtesy Greg Davis and Bill Morgan)

David Cassidy, Charlton #1, 1972, photo cover, NM ..$18.00
Dick Tracy, Dell #4, NM $100.00
Doctor Solar, #5, VG+ $15.00
Donald Duck, Dell Four-Color #62, 1945, NM.......$1,200.00
Donald in Mathmagic Land, #1198, VG $12.00
Durango Kid, #28, NM $15.00
Fantastic Voyage, Gold Key #2, 1969, EX....................$10.00
Felix the Cat, Dell #18, 1953, VG $10.00
Flash, Why?, DC Comics, 1965, NM, from $30 to $40.00
Flintstones, Gold Key #33, VG+ $6.00
Garrison's Gorillas, Dell #3, 1968, photo cover, EX....$10.00
Gidget, Dell #1, 1966, photo cover, VG......................$25.00
Goodbye Mr Chips, Movie Comics #10346-006, VG $8.00
Gorgo, #4, G+ $14.00
Great Family Cat, Dell Four-Color #750, VG $13.00

Great Locomotive Chase, Dell Four-Color #712, Fess Parker cover, EX $20.00
Green Lantern, DC Comics #7, 1960, NM.................$200.00
Hand of Zorro, Dell Four-Color #574, 1954, EX $40.00
Hardy Boys, Dell Four-Color #760, 1956, photo cover, EX $25.00
Helen of Troy, Dell Four-Color #684, G+ $13.00
House of Secrets, Dell #50, EX.....................................$38.00
Howdy Doody, Dell #15, 1952, EX $25.00
Howdy Doody, Dell Four-Color #811, G+ $17.00
Invaders, #1, G+ $16.00
Johnny Mack Brown, Dell Four-Color #645, EX $28.00
Josie & the Pussycats, Archie #6, 1964, EX.................$15.00
Journey Into Mystery, Dell #116, VG $15.00
Kidnapped, Dell Four-Color #1101, G+ $9.00
Konga, #2, VG+ $26.00
Lash Larue, #5, G+...$65.00
Lassie, #20, VG+ $12.00
Lassie's Forest Ranger Handbook, 1967, NM.............$45.00
Last Hunt, Dell Four-Color #678, VG+ $22.00
Little Lulu Christmas Diary, Gold Key #166, 1963, EX...$40.00
Lost World, Dell Four-Color #1145, G+.........................$24.00
Marge's Little Lulu, Dell #42, 1951, VG $20.00
Mod Squad, Dell #5, 1970, NM....................................$10.00
My Little Margie, Dell #27, EX $11.00
Nick Fury Agent of Shield, Marvel Comics, EX..........$15.00
Orion of the New Gods, DC Comics #3, NM $10.00
Our Gang, Dell #20, G $15.00
Partridge Family in Keith's Hero Image, #16, 1973, EX.$25.00
Pinocchio, Dell #252, 1949 movie version, VG $20.00
Popeye, Dell #48, 1959, EX...$12.00
Rawhide Kid, Dell #34, VG $12.00
Real Screen Comics, #1, VG...$65.00
Red Mask, #42, G+ $30.00
Restless Gun, #1045, EX..$55.00
Richie Rich, #23, VG $15.00
Rin-Tin-Tin, #8, EX $15.00
Rudolph the Red-Nosed Reindeer, DC Comics, 1952, EX..$25.00
Ruff & Reddy, #7, EX...$35.00
Sergeant Preston of the Yukon, #18, NM....................$35.00
Sleeping Beauty, #984, 1959, NM $90.00
Snow White, Dell Four-Color #382, 1944, EX+ $45.00
Space Busters, #2, 1952, EX.......................................$175.00
Space Ghost, Gold Key #1, 1960s, VG.........................$45.00
Spooky Spooktown, #1, G+ $16.00
Steve Canton, Dell Four-Color #841, 1955, NM...........$35.00
Superman's Pal Jimmy Olsen, Dell #32, EX.................$30.00
Tales of the Unexpected, #74, EX $25.00
Tarzan's Jungle Annual, Dell Giant #4, 1955, EX.......$25.00
Tex Morgan, #9, VG+...$36.00
Tex Ritter, #1, G+..$100.00
Tex Ritter Western, Fawcett/Charlton #33, EX............$20.00
Three Musketeers, 1st Series #8, VG $20.00
Three Stooges, Dell #1170, 1961, VG $20.00
Tom & Jerry, #62, VG $10.00
Tom Corbett Space Cadet, #9, EX $50.00
Tomahawk, #1, VG+...$295.00

Top Cat, #8, VG+ $12.00
Twilight Zone, #1288, EX...$25.00
Two-Gun Kid, #2, VG $60.00
Untouchables, Dell #207, EX $40.00
Wagon Train, #10, VG+..$27.00
Walt Disney's Merry Christmas, Dell Giant #39, NM...$190.00
Wild Bill Elliott, #16, VG+..$20.00
Will Rogers, #5, G+...$46.00
Wings of Eagles, Dell #790, VG....................................$30.00
Wonder Woman, DC Comics #52, EX............................$25.00
Woody Woodpecker, #1, 1947, EX $90.00
Wyatt Earp, #12, VG+...$23.00
Young Eagle, #8, VG+...$24.00
Zane Grey's Stories of the West, #270, VG $15.00
Zorro, Dell #13, 1961, EX+ $35.00

Tales To Astonish, Marvel Comics, NM, $50.00. (Photo courtesy Bill Bruegman)

Compacts and Purse Accessories

When 'liberated' women entered the work force after WWI, cosmetics, previously frowned upon, became more acceptable, and as as result the market was engulfed with compacts of all types and designs. Some went so far as to incorporate timepieces, cigarette compartments, coin holders, and money clips. All types of materials were used — mother-of-pearl, petit-point, cloisonne, celluloid, and leather among them. There were figural compacts, those with wonderful Art Deco designs, souvenir compacts, and some with advertising messages.

Carryalls were popular from the 1930s to the 1950s. They were made by compact manufacturers and were usually carried with evening wear. They contained compartments for powder, rouge, and lipstick, often held a comb and mirror, and some were designed with a space for cigarettes and a lighter. Other features might have included a timepiece, a tissue holder, a place for coins or stamps, and some even had music boxes. In addition to these, solid perfumes and lipsticks are becoming increasingly popular as well.

For further study, we recommend *Vintage Ladies' Compacts, Vintage Vanity Bags and Purses*, and *Vintage and*

Contemporary Purse Accessories, all by Roselyn Gerson; and *Collector's Encyclopedia of Compacts, Carryalls, and Face Powder Boxes, Volumes I and II*, by Laura Mueller.

Advisor: Roselyn Gerson (See Directory, Compacts)

Newsletter The Compacts Collector Chronicle
Powder Puff
P.O. Box 40
Lynbrook, NY 11563. Subscription: $25 (4 issues, USA or Canada) per year

Carryalls

Elgin, Caryette, black faille w/abalone lid panels, exterior lipstick opener, back pocket & comb, 2¼x3½x1" .**$115.00**

Elgin American, Lucite tortoise-shell case w/gold-tone trim & accessories, 2⅝x8½x1⅜", from $300 to **$350.00**

Evans, black satin pouch w/gold-thread florets, gold-tone fittings, no case ID, 4½" dia w/2½" dia case, from $150 to...**$175.00**

Evans, red snakeskin, rigid handle, padded case w/gold-tone frame, double access, 3⅛x5½x1", from $125 to...**$150.00**

Evans, Sunburst silver-tone case w/lattice lid & emerald-cut rhinestones, gold-tone interior, case signed, 3⅛x5½x1" **$85.00**

Jeanne Bernard, black suede canopic jar shape w/rhinestone accented bowknots, braid wrist cord, Effiel Tower label, 7" **$185.00**

Terri, white metal, oval luggage case, faux black leather with 'chrome' bands, comb, lipstick, mirror, 2¼x3¾x1".**$160.00**

Unmarked, copper enameled case plates w/Zodiac, gold-tone fittings, coin purse, comb, powder, mirrors, 3⅛x5¼x¾" **$160.00**

Unmarked, gold-tone, mesh strap, double access, powder, lipstick, coin purse & comb, money clip, glued mirror, 5½x3" **$135.00**

Unmarked, mother-of-pearl w/rhinestones & gilt scrolls, snake chain, bottom hinge, powder, coin purse, lipstick, 5x3x¾" **$85.00**

Unmarked, white metal w/padded red leather double-access case, exterior lipstick w/red tassel, leather lined, 3x5x⅝" **$160.00**

Unmarked Wadsworth, white Bakelite w/gold-tone frame & panels, beveled mirror, link handle, 6¼x3¼x1¼", from $75 ....**$90.00**

Volupte, black suede w/gold-tone lipstick, comb clip, etc; framed mirror, narrow handles, Swinglok, 3¼x4¼x1" **$80.00**

Volupte, champleve enamel Persian horses & tendrils on gold-tone signed case, coin purse w/lipstick & comb, 4¾x6x⅝" **$335.00**

Volupte, gold-tone 'matchstick shade' lid motif, 3 faux sapphires on attached plate, chain handle, 3⅛x4¼x1" **$85.00**

Volupte, yellow linen-like lid enamel w/floral bands in black faille carrier, taffeta coin purse, bottom hinge, 3x5x½" **$185.00**

Zell, Round Towner, Portmanteau, red leather w/gold-tone interior, cloisonne compact lid plate, signed, 3¼x4x1" **$85.00**

Compacts

Deere, gold-tone w/embossed logo, signed lid, framed mirror, 1½" dia, from $35 to.....................**$50.00**

Dorette, snakeskin, no ID, glued mirror, 3¼" square, from $75 to.....................**$100.00**

Elgin American, hammered gold-tone square w/rhinestone Christmas bell in center, red stone movable clapper, 2¾", from $60 to.....................**$100.00**

Evans, Statue of Liberty, gold-tone statue on blue enamel, gold-tone accents, 2½" square, from $125 to.....**$150.00**

Fillwik Co, Art Deco silver-tone stepped pyramid shape, black & red panels, 1¾x1½", from $75 to..........**$100.00**

French, gold-tone w/green enamel lid, shaped as hand mirror, from $100 to.....................**$125.00**

Harriet Hubbard Ayers, white metal w/center initial logo on striped ground, 1½" dia, from $15 to.....................**$20.00**

Marinello, pink enamel disk in 5-sided gold-tone case, Art Deco bust depicted on puff, signed, 1½x⅜", from $25 to **$35.00**

Mavco, plexiglas, yellow translucent faceted case, signed Eleanor Hamlin, 4" dia, from $75 to **$90.00**

Paul D Newton, peach enameled case w/gold-tone frame, Peggy Newton lid logo, 1⅝" dia, from $10 to......**$15.00**

Pigmalion, gold-tone grand piano-shaped compacts, collapsible legs, 2¼x2¾x1½", from $350.00 to $400.00 each. (Photo courtesy Roselyn Gerson/Photographer Alvin Gerson)

Revell, Soubrette, plastic tortoise-shell case, glued mirror, 5" dia, from $75 to **$100.00**

Richard Hudnut, gold-tone w/tiny embossed stars, case signed Three Flowers, 1½" dia, from $25 to **$35.00**

Schidkraut, cloisonne enamel on gold-tone w/Follies Bergere poster art decor, 2¾x2½", from $50 to **$70.00**

Trio-ette, plastic w/embossed rose, stick handle contains lipstick, 2¾" dia, 4¼" L, minimum value **$125.00**

Unmarked, Aloha USS Idaho w/ship on gold-tone rectangular case, 3x2⅜x⅜", from $175 to.........................**$200.00**

Unmarked, Buick Eight logo in center, silver-tone w/maroon enamel band about perimeter, 3" dia, from $70 to ..**$85.00**

Unmarked, gold-tone oblong w/2 concentric circles superimposed over black & gold quadrants, 2¾x1½", from $75 to ..**$100.00**

Unmarked, Lucite, 3-sided top, semicircle bottom, apricot w/gold-tone filigree & faux sapphire, 4½x4", from $150 to **$175.00**

Unmarked, round silver-tone case w/Art Deco geometric panels of yellow & black enamel, 2" dia, from $50 to **$75.00**

Unmarked, silver-tone w/plastic disks depicting musicians in relief, 2¼" dia, from $50 to **$75.00**

Unmarked, sterling compact charm, basketweave exterior, 2½" dia, from $25 to...**$50.00**

Unmarked, wood, blond cushion case w/stenciled initial on lid, 4½" dia, from $100 to **$125.00**

Zanadu, gold-tone Art Deco/Art Moderne case shaped to conform to orange & black curving elements, 1½x3½", $100 to...**$125.00**

Lipsticks

Atomette, gold-tone w/embossed & applied owl having rinestone eyes & body, 3 rows of rhinestones on mirrored lid, 2¼" **$65.00**

Barbara Gould, copper-tone w/ribbed clear Lucite base, 2¼", from $15 to...**$25.00**

Bourjois, Evening in Paris, silver-tone ¾" cap w/dancers etc, blue metal bottom, 1¾", from $15 to.....................**$25.00**

Coty, gold-tone, 1½", from $15 to...............................**$20.00**

Coty, gold-tone tube w/green enamel stripes, 2½", from $45 to...**$55.00**

Elizabeth Arden, gold-tone tube w/pearls & rhinestones on dome lid, row of Es at lower rim, 2½", from $20 to.............**$30.00**

Hazel Bishop, gold-tone tube flares toward bottom, ball finial, 3", from $25 to...**$35.00**

Helena Rubenstein, Cracker Jack, black with gold 'mesh' design, shaped tube w/central gold ribbed band, 2¾", from $30 ....**$40.00**

Helena Rubinstein, Stay Long, ribbed gold-tone tube w/prong-set cabachon stone on top, 2⅜", from $10 to...**$15.00**

Jennifer Cosmetics, red & black marbleized plastic, gold-tone bow in center, from $15 to **$25.00**

Lucien Lelong, leopard print cover w/gold-tone accents, 2¼", from $45 to...**$65.00**

Mary Dunhill, white enamel on silver-tone, domed lid w/red, clear & green rhinestones, 2", from $25 to...........**$40.00**

Max Factor, oval case holds lipstick & mirror, mother-of-pearl lid, 2¼x1", from $25 to **$35.00**

Mexican, papier-mache doll head atop tube painted as torso, 3⅝", from $45 to...**$65.00**

Polly Bergen, brushed gold-tone w/jewel-set turtle on lid, 3", in original box, from $10 to.................................**$20.00**

Revlon, blue & red plastic w/white lettering, 2¼", from $15 to...**$25.00**

Revlon, gold-tone w/ball point pen, 4¾", from $35 to..**$55.00**

Richard Hudnut, Du Barry, gold-tone tube w/square Lucite base, square rhinestone on lid, 2½", from $25 to ..**$35.00**

Richard Hudnut, gold-tone w/engraved stripes, 2⅝", from $55 to...**$65.00**

Rich On Inc., plastic tubes with various patterns, 2¾", from $10.00 to $20.00 each. (Photo courtesy Roselyn Gerson/Photographer Alvin Gerson)

Schiaparelli, Schiap Atomic, hot pink, white & silver plastic tube, 2¼", w/original box, from $35 to **$50.00**

Unmarked, gold-tone tube w/filigree, pearls & rhinestones in graceful arrangement on lid, 2¼", from $45 to **$60.00**

Unmarked, square tube painted w/textured white enamel & 3-color rose spray, mirror in back panel, 2", from $35 to **$55.00**

Unmarked, sterling w/lg faceted amethyst stone on lid, larger than normal in circumference, 2¼", from $100 to.**$125.00**

Unmarked, tube attached to 2" dia mirror case, black poodle on pearlized lid, from $45 to **$65.00**

Volupte, gold-tone w/enameled Persian motif, 2", from $25 to **$35.00**

Weisner of Miami, allover pearls w/2 rows of aurora borealis accents, 2¼", from $45 to **$65.00**

Mirrors

Avon, clear plastic scrolling frame around oval mirror holds perfume, plastic gold-tone handle, 6½x3", from $15 to.**$25.00**

Carolee, card symbols, red & black inlays in round gold-tone case, 2¼" dia, 1995...**$25.00**

Enameled, blue w/pink rose, faux jade handle, decorative gold-tone framing, 5¾x2", from $15 to................**$25.00**

Filigree gold-tone w/lg pink cabachon centering sm stones, 3 sm stones in handle, 3¾x1½", from $30 to.......**$40.00**

Florenza, gold-tone w/antique white finish, embossed Nouveau motif, 3⅞x2", from $20 to......................**$30.00**

Limoges enamel courting scene signed Fragonard, colored stones set in handle, beveled, 4x2½", from $25 to..**$30.00**

Lucite w/embedded silver squares, square gold-tone frame, 4⅛x2½", from $20 to.......................................**$35.00**

Mosaic flowers in handle & banding mirror, elaborate gold-tone filigree, Italy, 5¼x2½", from $35 to.............**$45.00**

Petit-point roses, multicolor on black, gold-tone framing, 2¾x5", from $20 to.......................................**$30.00**

Plastic, pearl-like w/gold lines & rhinestone-set squares & arcs on swinging 'lid' w/corner hinge, 2⅝", from $30 to...**$50.00**

Plastic 'gold-tone' centered w/Colonial couple transfer on white plastic disk, 2½x4½", from $15 to **$20.00**

Portrait under glass dome, wide engraved silver-tone border, ornate openwork handle, beveled, Denmark, 4½x2½", from $25 to.......................................**$35.00**

Silver, hand-engraved scrolls, comb concealed in handle, coral cabochon thumb piece, 4¾x2¾", from $55 to **$75.00**

Silver-tone w/engine-turned wide & narrow stripes, 1¾x3¼", from $20 to.......................................**$35.00**

Sterling shield shape, engine-turned stripes, monogram on rectangular plaque, beveled, 4x1¾", from $75 to........**$90.00**

Stratton, black enamel gold-tone mirror with flowers, folding handle, England, 2½" diameter, from $20.00 to $30.00. (Photo courtesy Roselyn Gerson/Photographer Alvin Gerson)

Stratton Birthday Collection, white enameled mirror/compact w/month & flower, 1995, 2¼" square **$35.00**

Swivel gold-tone oval w/engine-turned stripes & central rectangle, embossed handle acts as stand, 2¼x2", from $25 to.......................................**$35.00**

Symbols of Twelve Tribes of Israel on gold-tone, menorah in center, enameled, framed mirror retainer, 5½x2¾" ..**$45.00**

Zodiac sign on black disk set in gold-tone, 5x2½", from $15 to.......................................**$25.00**

Solid Perfumes

Avon, daisy in white enamel on gold-tone, brushed gold-tone center, wear as pin, 2½" dia, from $15 to **$20.00**

Avon, gold-tone grand piano, 1½x1", from $40 to **$50.00**

Avon, gold-tone mandolin, 2¼x1", from $30 to..........**$40.00**

Avon, gold-tone ring set w/pearls in square recesses, ⅞x1½", from $15 to.......................................**$25.00**

Coty, gold-tone case designed as 8-petal flower, blue cabochon in center, 1½" dia, in original fitted box, from $30 to.....**$40.00**

Coty, silver-tone egg, screw-off top, 1x1½", from $20 to..**$30.00**

Estee Lauder, Fantastic Voyage Balloon, gold-tone & enameled hot-air balloon, 1995, 1½x2¼" **$85.00**

Estee Lauder, gold-tone pocket watch w/black Roman numeral hour markers, 1⅜" dia, from $20 to.......**$25.00**

Estee Lauder, Golden Chains, heart-shaped gold-stone case wrapped w/embossed & studded chains, 1994, 1½x1½".......................................**$45.00**

Estee Lauder, portrait disk centers oblong gold-tone case w/scrollwork motif, 3⅞x1", from $25 to...............**$35.00**

Fuller Brush, gold-tone fish w/blue set-in eyes, 1¾x1¾", from $25 to.......................................**$35.00**

Guy Laroche, gold-tone shell shape, 2½x2½", from $30 to **$40.00**

Houbigant, white plastic heart w/pink bow, 2⅜x2½", from $25 to.......................................**$35.00**

Lancome, orange translucent lid designed as pyramid centered w/faceted square crystal, 1995, 1⅜x1" **$50.00**

Mary Chess, elongated octagon case set w/carved green stone suspended from ornate gold-tone key brooch, 1½x1⅛".......................................**$45.00**

Mary Chess, oval gold-tone pendant set w/rhinestones in embossed latticework, 1¾x1¼", from $75 to **$90.00**

Max Factor, faux jade disk w/gold-tone love-knot strap, wear as pendant, 2¼" dia, from $25 to **$35.00**

Molinard, red sphere decorated w/painted yellow flowers on black base, ⅞" dia, from $35 to **$45.00**

Payot, oval case w/embossed stylized swan on ribbed background, 1⅝x⅞", from $35 to **$45.00**

Revlon, gold-tone pendant with embossed scrolls & flowers set w/red cabochon in center, 2x2", from $35 to.**$45.00**

Revlon, portrait disk centers black enameled gold-framed octagon, 1¾", from $30 to **$40.00**

Unmarked, brushed silver-tone 3-cherry cluster, leaves set w/red stones, 1⅝x1¼", from $35 to.....................**$45.00**

Unmarked, gold-tone feather-textured swan w/green stone eyes, 1½x1¾", from $40 to **$50.00**

Unmarked, gold-tone ring set w/sm turquoise cabochons, more on shank, ⅞", from $15 to **$25.00**

Vanda, gold-tone owl w/green stone eyes, 1¾x1⅛", from $40 to **$50.00**

Viviane Woodward, gold-tone blue enameled purse, 2x1½", from $45 to.......................................**$65.00**

Condiment Sets

Whimsical styling make these sets a lot of fun to collect. Any species of animal, plant, bird, or mammal that ever existed and many that never did or ever will are represented, so an extensive collection is possible, and prices are still reasonable. These sets are usually comprised of a pair of salt and pepper shakers and a small mustard pot with spoon on a tray. Technically, the set must include a mustard pot to be considered a condiment set. Some never had a tray — but virtually all Japanese sets did. Others were figurals that were made in three parts. Though you'll find some with other backstamps, by and far the majority of these were made in Japan. (Ours are of generic Japanese origin unless a specific company is noted in our descriptions.) For more information, we recommend *Collector's Guide to Made in Japan Ceramics, Books I, II, and III,* by Carole Bess White; *Salt and Pepper Shakers, Vols I through IV,* by Helene Guarnaccia; and *Collector's Encyclopedia of Salt and Pepper Shakers, Figural and Novelty,* by Melva Davern. Note: without the matching ceramic spoon, prices on condiment sets should be 25% to 40% less than values listed here. See also Black Americana.

Advisor: Carole Bess White (See Directory, Japan Ceramics)

Airplane w/shakers & pot, white opal lustre w/gold trim, Sarsaparilla Deco Designs label/Japan, 1981, 7½" L..**$30.00**

Art Deco set, rounded geometric forms on oblong tray w/multicolored glossy Deco leaf motif................**$25.00**

Beehive set, white w/vine design & bee finials, 3-pc, Occupied Japan, marked w/K in circle................**$22.50**

Beer barrels and brewmeister, post-WWI Japan, 5¾" long, from $18.00 to $25.00. (Photo courtesy Carole Bess White)

Bird & grain motif on shakers, pot & 4½" round tray, brown on matt yellow w/blue lustre trim, Japan.............**$45.00**

Birds (2) on a log, white w/yellow beaks facing each other & looking up on light brown log, w/spoon, Japan, 4½".......................................**$40.00**

Birds (3) on round tray, tan, blue & green lustre shakers & pot, red beaks, Japan, 6" dia **$77.00**

Black woman w/3 pumpkins, multicolored, England.**$55.00**

Bulldog sitting upright w/2 basket shakers on arms, tan dog pot w/red collar, green basket shakers **$25.00**

Castle w/black cat finial, cream w/blue, orange, red & black trim, 3¾"...**$135.00**

Cherry blossoms, blue lustre w/white blossoms & black branches on shakers, pot & 7" 3-part tray w/handles, gold trim..**$52.00**

Cherry blossoms, tan lustre w/white blossoms & black branches on shakers & pot w/5" round tray, Japan...........**$40.00**

Cow resting, 3-part w/head & tail shakers & center pot, light brown airbrushing, England..................................**$45.00**

Dachshund set, brown gloss, salt head, pepper torso, mustard pot rear & tail spoon, Victoria Ceramics Japan **$35.00**

Dogs (3) in a basket, brown & black mother & 2 puppies in yellow basket, yellow basket, glossy, 3-pc...........**$30.00**

Dogs on round base, tan lustre w/red trim on rounded ears, black accented features, white round base, Japan, 4".............**$75.00**

Donkey set, 2 white cruets & shakers w/colorful floral motif hanging from brown donkey, glossy, Japan, 7¼" ..**$25.00**

Dutch couple & pot on heart-shaped tray, red & green plaid on cream, gold trim, Japan, 3"............................**$135.00**

Elephants, sitting (connected) side by side w/lg center elephant as pot & 2 smaller elephant-head shakers on bodies..**$50.00**

Fish w/pot & shakers, mother-of-pearl lustre w/side decal, gold trim, England **$50.00**

Flower buds on leaf tray w/handle, ball-shaped shakers & pot w/butterfly finial, multicolored lustre, 3" **$50.00**

Hen & chicks on straw nest, multicolored glossy.......**$30.00**

House shakers & pot on oval tray w/2 end handles, multi-colored lustre, Noritake..**$50.00**

Old Mother Goose set, goose, old woman & house on marked tray, multicolored.....................................**$45.00**

Peasant girl w/flower baskets on round tray, blue & green w/multicolored flowers, glossy, Japan, 3¾" **$150.00**

Penguins, 3 hanging from penguin holder, multicolored, glossy, Japan, 7"..**$55.00**

Pineapples w/happy & sad faces, cojoined horseradish & mustard pots w/green center handle, 4"..............**$45.00**

Rabbit, ears are salt & pepper shakers, w/spoon, blue & tan lustre, Japan, 4½"...**$50.00**

Rabbits (3) on base, center rabbit w/1 ear up & 1 ear down, end rabbits w/ears down, tan lustre, marked Germany, 3¾"...**$55.00**

Scenic motif, shakers & pot on 5¼" cloverleaf tray w/insert holes, multicolored lustre, Japan **$65.00**

Scottie dogs (3) on tray, red dogs w/black trim on cloverleaf-shaped tray, 4" **$75.00**

Swan w/3 birds on back, multicolored lustre w/black outline trim, Japan, 4¾" **$58.00**

Tomatoes (3) on green 6¼" L rectangular tray, w/spoon, Occupied Japan back stamp **$35.00**

Cookbooks and Recipe Leaflets

If you've ever read a nineteenth-century cookbook, no doubt you've been amused by the quaint way the measurements were given. Butter the size of an egg, a handful of flour, a pinch of this or that — sounds like a much more time-efficient method, doesn't it? They'd sometimes give household tips or some folk remedies, and it's these antiquated methods and ideas that endear those old cookbooks to collectors, although examples from this era are not easily found.

Cookbooks from the early twentieth century are scarce too, but even those that were printed thirty and forty years ago are well worth collecting. Food and appliance companies often published their own, and these appeal to advertising buffs and cookbook collectors alike, especially if they illustrate pre-1970s kitchen appliances. Some were diecut to represent the product, perhaps a pickle or a slice of bread. Cookbooks that focus on unusual topics and those that have ethnic or regional recipes are appealing as well, and once in awhile you'll find one endorsed by a movie star or some other well-known personality.

Perhaps no single event in the 1950s attracted more favorable attention for the Pillsbury Flour Company than the one first staged in 1949. Early in the year, company officials took the proposal to its advertising agency. Together they came up with a plan that would become an American institution — the Pillsbury Bake-Off Contest. On December 12, 1949, in the grand ballroom of the Waldorf Astoria Hotel in New York City, ninety-seven women and three men were standing nervously over one hundred ranges ready to compete for $100,000.00 in cash prizes. Philip Pillsbury, Eleanor Roosevelt, and Art Linkletter presented the awards to the winners. The Duke and Duchess of Windsor were in attendance as guests. The bake-offs have been held each year since that time.

Betty Crocker, the ultimate, eternal and supreme house-wife was fabricated by the Washburn Crosby Company, who in 1928 became part of the merger that was General Mills, Inc. She was introduced to the public in 1917 via the *Gold Medal Flour Cook Book*, an 8½" x 11" soft-cover book that was published twice in 1917. Betty appeared in the second printing. She soon became a most believable entity complete with radio voice, signature, and a black and white composite drawing for advertising purposes. Hundreds of Betty Crocker/General Mills cookbooks and advertising booklets have been printed over the years, many displaying Betty's portrait, which has been modified from time to time to keep her hairstyle and clothing attune with current fashions. Today there are many collectors who vie for not only the cookbooks but package inserts, magazine ads, and any other material where Betty's likeness appears.

For further study, we recommend *A Guide to Collecting Cookbooks* by Colonel Bob Allen, and *Price Guide to Cookbooks and Recipe Leaflets* by Linda Dickinson. (Both are published by Collector Books.) Our values are based on cookbooks in excellent condition.

Advisor: Bob Allen (See Directory, Cookbooks)

Club/Newsletter: *Cookbook Gossip*
Cookbook Collectors Club of America, Inc.
Bob and Jo Ellen Allen
P.O. Box 56
St. James, MO 65559

Newsletter: *The Cookbook Collector's Exchange*
Sue Erwin
P.O. Box 32369
San Jose, CA 95152-2369

Adjustable Diet Cookbook, Suzy Chapin, 1967, hardcover, 346 pages, EX..**$10.00**
All American Cookbook — Favorite Recipes of Famous Persons, 1954, paperback, EX...................................**$6.00**
Amy Vanderbilt Success Casserole Cookery, Charlotte Adams, 1966, hardcover, EX...................................**$15.00**
Anheuser-Busch's How To Cook w/Budweiser, 1952, paper-back, 34 pages, EX...................................**$30.00**
Art & Secrets & Secrets of Chinese Cookery, La Choy Food Products, 1942, 15 pages, EX...................................**$15.00**
Art of Fine Baking, Paula Beck, 1961, hardcover, 320 pages, EX..**$15.00**
Art of Salad Making, Carol Traux, 1968, hardcover, EX..**$12.50**
Best in Cookery in the Middle West, Grace Grosvenor Clark, Doubleday, 1956, hardcover, EX **$20.00**

Better Homes & Gardens Casserole Cook Book, 1968, hard-cover, 160 pages, EX..**$7.50**
Better Homes & Gardens Holiday Cook Book, 1959, 1961, 160 pages, EX..**$12.50**
Better Homes & Gardens Jiffy Cooking, 1967, hardcover, EX..**$7.50**
Better Homes & Gardens Meals in Minutes, hardcover, 62 pages, EX..**$12.50**
Better Homes & Gardens Pies & Cakes, 1966, hardcover, 96 pages, EX..**$10.00**
Better Homes & Gardens So Good Luncheons for Bridge & Other Occasions, 1942, 31 pages, EX **$12.50**
Betty Crocker Cookbook, 1959, hardcover, EX...........**$25.00**
Betty Crocker Dinner for Two, 1st edition, 1958, hardcover, 207 pages, EX..**$6.00**
Betty Crocker Microwave Cookbook, 1981, hardcover, 288 pages..**$10.00**
Big Boy Barbecue Book, Tested Recipe Institute, 1956, 1957, EX..**$10.00**
Blender Cookbook, Seranne & Garden, New York, 1961, hardcover, EX..**$10.00**
Blueberry Hill Menu Cookbook, Elsie Masterson, 1963, hard-cover, 374 pages, EX **$20.00**
Book of Cookies, No 2, 1958, 68 pages, EX **$10.00**
Brunches & Coffees, Marion Courteny, 1969, hardcov-er, EX..**$15.00**
Cake & Food Decorating, Welcolite, 1956, hardcover, EX..**$20.00**
Calumet's Reliable Recipes, 11th edition, paperback, EX..**$8.50**
Campbell's Cooking w/Soup, 1965, spiral-bound, 200 pages, EX..**$10.00**
Campbell's Great Restaurant Cook Book, Doris Townsend, Rutledge Books, 1969, hardcover, 160 pages **$15.00**
Come for Cocktails Stay for Supper, Marian Burres & Lois Levine, 1970, hardcover, EX................................**$10.00**
Come to Our Barbecue — Taylor Wine Cook Book, 1958, EX **$10.00**
Cranberry Dishes That Children Love, 1950, EX.........**$10.00**
Cross Creek Cookery, Marjorie Kinman Rawlings, 1st edition, 1942, hardcover, 254 pages, EX........................**$35.00**
Culinary Arts Institute, Entertaining Six or Eight — 143 Delectable Recipes for Delicious Foods, No 116, 1956, 68 pages..**$6.00**
Culinary Arts Institute, The Salad Book — 400 Delicious Recipes, 2 wooden covers w/4 plastic rings, 48 pages, EX..**$8.00**
Culinary Arts Institute, 250 Ways To Prepare Poultry & Game Birds, No 4, 1st printing, 48 pages, EX...................**$8.00**
Culinary Arts Institute Low Calorie Recipes, 1955, paperback, 68 pages, EX..**$3.00**
Dinah Shore Cook Book, 1973, 386 pages, EX.............**$8.00**
Dinners That Wait: A Cook Book, Betty Wason, 1954, hard-cover, 216 pages, EX **$25.00**
Dutch Cook Book, Heller, 1953, hardcover, EX.........**$20.00**
Eat Italian Once a Week, Vernon Jarratt, 1967, hardcover, EX..**$15.00**

Family Circle Dessert & Fruit Cook Book, 1st edition, 1954, hardcover, 144 pages, EX......................................**$20.00**

Fannie Farmer Cookbook, revised by Wilma Lord Perkins, 11th edition/12th print, 1959, 1964, 1965, hardcover, 624 pages......................................**$15.00**

Frito Recipes & Menus for All Occasions, Frito Co, 1947, paperback, 31 pages, EX......................................**$3.00**

General Foods Kitchens Cook Book, by the women of General Foods Kitchens, 1959, hardcover, 436 pages, EX......................................**$20.00**

Good Housekeeping's Around the World Cook Book, Consolidated Book Publishers, 1958, hardcover, EX..**$20.00**

Good Housekeeping's Book of Cookies, No 2, 68 pages, EX......................................**$8.00**

Good Housekeeping's Meat Cook Book, No 9, 68 pages, EX......................................**$8.00**

Grandma's Cooking, Allan Keller, 1956, hardcover, EX.**$20.00**

Heinz Magic of Food Show From the Theatre of Food — Festival of Gas Pavilion, New York World's Fair, 1964-65, 28 pages......................................**$8.00**

Holiday Party Casseroles, Edna Beileyson, Peter Pauper Press, 1956, hardcover, 60 pages, EX..................**$15.00**

Hungarian Cookery Book, K Grudel, 1958, 114 pages, EX......................................**$48.00**

Ice Cream, H Walden, 1983, hardcover, 160 pages, EX..**$13.00**

Ida Bailey Allen's Money-Saving Cook Book, 1st edition, 1940, hardcover, 481 pages, EX......................................**$35.00**

Indiana Farmers Guide New Cookbook, Huntington, Indiana, paperback, EX......................................**$12.50**

Irvin Cobb's Own Recipe Book, 1936, leaflet, 51 pages, EX......................................**$5.00**

It's a Picnic, Nancy Fair McIntyre, 1969, hardcover, 150 pages, EX......................................**$15.00**

It's Easy To Be a Gourmet w/Peanuts...., Oklahoma Peanut Commission, 1964, 29 pages, EX......................................**$8.00**

Jack Bailey's What's Cookin', World Publishers, 1st edition, 1949, hardcover, 187 pages, EX......................................**$30.00**

Jell-O, Desert Magic, 1944, 6th printing, 26 pages, EX.**$8.00**

Jell-O, Jack & Mary's Jell-O Recipe Book, 1937, paperback, EX......................................**$35.00**

Jell-O, What Mrs Dewy Did w/the New Jell-O, 1933, leaflet, 23 pages, EX......................................**$10.00**

Kate Smith Cook Book, Kate Smith, 1958, hardcover, EX......................................**$25.00**

Kraft, Cheese & Ways To Serve It, 32 pages, EX.......**$20.00**

Kraft Cookery — Salads, Desserts, Main Dishes, Sandwiches, pamphlet, 12 pages, EX......................................**$5.00**

Kroger, Ways To Save Sugar, Jean Allen, 1940s, WWII flyer, EX......................................**$12.50**

Larkin Housewives Cook Book, The Larkin Co (mail-order products for the home), EX......................................**$20.00**

Libby's Evaporated Milk Recipes, can-shaped leaflet, EX......................................**$6.00**

LL Bean Game & Fish Cookbook, A Cameron, 1983, hardcover, 475 pages, EX......................................**$12.00**

Low-Fat Cookery, Evelyn Stead & Gloria Warren, 1959, hardcover, EX......................................**$15.00**

Magic Chef Cooking, America Stove, 1937, hardcover, 200 pages, EX......................................**$10.00**

Margaret Mitchell's Magic (Meat & Poultry Cooking), 1951, hardcover, EX......................................**$20.00**

Margaret Rudkin Pepperidge Farm Cookbook, 1963, 450 pages, EX......................................**$20.00**

Martha Washington Cookbook, M Kimball, 1940, EX.**$10.00**

Modern Cook Book & Kitchen Guide for the Busy Woman, Mabel Claire, 1932, hardcover, EX......................................**$35.00**

Modern Family Cookbook, M Given, 1942, 938 pages, EX......................................**$12.00**

Modern French Culinary Art, Pelaprat, 1st edition, 1966, EX......................................**$25.00**

Murder on the Menu, Jeanine Larmoth & Charlotte Turgeon, 1972, hardcover, 268 pages, EX......................................**$10.00**

Outdoor Picture Cook Book, 1954, hardcover, EX.....**$20.00**

Paula Peck's Art of Good Cooking, 1961, hardcover, EX..**$15.00**

Pillbury Bake-Off Cookie Favorites, 1969, paperback, 64 pages, EX......................................**$4.00**

Pillsbury Silver Anniversary Bake-Off, 1974, paperback, 92 pages, EX......................................**$5.00**

Pillsbury's Best of the Bake-Off Collection, 1959, EX.**$38.00**

Pillsbury's Diamond Anniversary Recipes, 1944, paperback, EX......................................**$8.00**

Pillsbury's Grand National Recipe & Baking Contest, 1950s, Nos 3 through 10, ea, from $15 to......................................**$18.00**

Pillsbury's 100 Prize Winning Recipes, 3rd Grand National, 1953, from $15 to......................................**$18.00**

Practical Candy Making, Porter, 1930, hardcover, EX.**$30.00**

Pyrex Prize Recipes, Corning Glass Works, 1953, hardcover, EX......................................**$20.00**

Quaker Recipes, Woman's Auxiliary, North Carolina, 1954, paperback, 198 pages, EX......................................**$8.00**

Quality Grocer, March, 1931, paperback, 24 pages, EX.**$11.00**

Ralston Purina, Breakfast Around the World, ca 1940, $12.50. (Photo courtesy Bob Allen)

Recipes From the Kitchens of West Virginia, 1969, hardcover, EX......................................**$15.00**

Rodale Herb Book, W Hylton, 1974, hardcover, 633 pages, EX......................................**$8.00**

Royal Baking Powder, 1942, leaflet, EX.....................**$7.00**

Royal Cream of Tarter Cook Book, 1944, paperback, 64 pages, EX...**$6.00**

Royal Pudding, Ginger Rogers, 1940, EX...................**$12.50**

Simple New England Cookery, Edna Beilenson, 1962, hardcover, 62 pages, EX.................................**$10.00**

Stillmeadow Cookbook, G Taber, 1965, hardcover, 335 pages, EX...**$42.00**

Sun-Maid, Downright Delicious Sun-Maid Raisin Recipes, 1949, $12.50. (Photo courtesy Bob Allen)

Teenager's Menu Cookbook, Charlotte Adams, 1969, hardcover, EX **$15.00**

Tested Tasties, Naylor, 1967, hardcover, EX................**$15.00**

Texas Cookbook, Mary Faulk, Koock Bros Pub, 1st edition, 1965, hardcover, 499 pages, EX.........................**$15.00**

The 5 Minute Dessert, Marie Buynon Roy, 1961, hardcover, EX...**$10.00**

Thoughts for Buffets, William Barass, 1954, hardcover, EX **$20.00**

Time-Life Recipes, any 1969 paperback publication, EX, ea **$6.00**

Towle's Log Cabin Syrup, set of 24 recipe cards, EX .**$35.00**

Treasury of Outdoor Cooking, James Beard, 1960, hardcover, EX..**$15.00**

Twelve Days of Christmas Cookbook, Suzanne Huntley, 1965, hardcover, EX...............................**$15.00**

Victory Garden Cook Book, M Morash, 1982, paperback, 371 pages, EX..**$18.00**

Virginia Cookery, Velma Moeschlein, 1930, hardcover, EX **$35.00**

Weight Watchers Cook Book, Jean Nidetch, Hearthside Press, 1st edition, 1966, hardcover, 288 pages, EX.........**$10.00**

Who Says We Can't Cook, Women's National Press Club, 1955, hardcover, EX...............................**$20.00**

Williamsburg Art of Cookery, Helen Bullock, 3rd edition, 1942, hardcover, EX......................................**$20.00**

Woman's Day Encyclopedia of Cookery, 1965, hardcover binder to hold 12 softcover publications, EX.......**$15.00**

Woman's Home Companion Cook Book, intro by Dorothy Kirk, 1946, hardcover, EX....................................**$25.00**

Working Girls Must Eat, Hazel Young, 1938, hardcover, EX **$35.00**

You Can Cook for One, Louise Pickoff, 1966, EX **$15.00**

10,000 Snacks, Brown, 1948, hardcover, 593 pages, EX ..**$10.00**

Cookie Cutters

In recent years, cookie cutters have come into their own as worthy kitchen collectibles. Prices on many have risen astronomically, but a practiced eye can still sort out a good bargain. Advertising cutters and product premiums, especially in plastic, can still be found without too much effort. Aluminum cutters with painted wood handles are usually worth several dollars each, if in good condition. Red and green are the usual handle colors, but other colors are more highly prized by many. Hallmark plastic cookie cutters, especially those with painted backs, are always worth considering, if in good condition.

Be wary of modern tin cutters being sold for antique. Many present-day tinsmiths chemically antique their cutters, especially if done in a primitive style. These are often sold by others as 'very old.' Look closely because most tinsmiths today sign and date these cutters.

Molds, instead of cutting the cookie out, impressed a design into the dough. To learn more about both types (and many other old kitchenware gadgets as well), we recommend *300 Years of Kitchen Collectibles* by Linda Campbell Franklin and *Kitchen Antiques, 1790 to 1940*, by Kathryn McNerney. Also read *The Cookie Shaper's Bible* by Phyllis Wetherill and our advisor, Rosemary Henry.

Advisor: Rosemary Henry (See Directory, Cookie Cutters)

Newsletter: *Cookies*
Rosemary Henry
9610 Greenview Ln.
Manassas, VA 20109-3320
Subscription: $12.00 per year for 6 issues

Newsletter: *Cookie Crumbs*
Cookie Cutter Collectors Club
Ruth Capper
1167 Teal Rd. SW
Dellroy, OH 44620; 216-735-2839 or 202-966-0869

Acorn, brown or golden, hard plastic, eyelet, Hallmark, 1976, 4" **$7.50**

Angel w/lute, blue, soft plastic, Hallmark, 1979 ....**$6.00**

Bell, aluminum w/green wood handle **$4.00**

Betsy McCall, aluminum, marked McCall, 1971, NYC/Hong Kong, 8"...**$50.00**

Buffalo, tin w/strap handle, 1930s, 3x4" **$20.00**

Butterfly, Martha Stewart, in original tin, M................**$25.00**

Cat, copper, marked Cape Cod, 8x6", EX....................**$45.00**

Cat, sitting, tin, embossed Davis Baking Powder, 3¼" .**$25.00**

Cupid w/heart, pink, soft plastic, eyelet, Hallmark, 1981, 4¼"...**$3.00**

Elephant, metal w/green wood handle, 3½x3" **$25.00**

Elsie the Cow, daisy w/face in center, yellow plastic, 2 handles, 2¾" dia $35.00

Female symbol, dark green plastic outline, $4.00. (Photo courtesy Rosemary Henry)

Flag, aluminum w/red wood handle, 4" L...................$15.00

Football helmet, red, soft plastic, eyelet, Hallmark, 1978, 4"...$10.00

Football w/Cowboys logo in center, gray, Hallmark, 1995 ....$5.00

Garfield & Odie, plastic, Wilton, 1978, set of 4, MOC..$20.00

Ghost, white, soft plastic, Hallmark, 1983, 4"...............$4.50

Gingerbread policeman, aluminum, ca 1950s $12.50

Gumby, green plastic outline silhouette, Domino Sugar premium, 5½"..$25.00

Heart w/hearts in red, soft plastic, eyelet, Hallmark, 1980-81, 3"...$6.00

Heart w/Love Ya, red, lavender, yellow & pink, hard plastic, Hallmark, 1977, 2¾" $9.50

Ice cream cone w/smiley face, orange, soft plastic, eyelet, Hallmark, 1980 ....$24.50

Indian, metal, Germany #2833, 5½x2⅜", EX..............$45.00

Jack Frost Sugar elf, white plastic with impression lines, $2.00. (Photo courtesy Rosemary Henry)

Kermit w/shamrock, green, soft plastic, eyelet, Hallmark, 1982, 3½"...$2.50

Mickey Mouse head, side view, red, hard plastic, eyelet, Hallmark, 1979, 3"...$5.00

Monster Rock, light green, soft plastic, eyelet, Hallmark, 1978, 3½"...$5.00

My Little Pony, pink plastic, Hasbro-Bradley, 1985, 3½x4"..$10.00

Pioneer seed corn emblem, white plastic, 3x2".........$18.00

Pony, tin, early, 3½x2¾"...$22.00

Rabbit, Formay advertising, 6" $25.00

Ringling Bros, Bake & Decorate set, includes 12 animals, clowns etc, Chilton, 1979, MIB............................$40.00

Robin Hood characters, flour premiums, various colors, plastic, set of 8, from $40 to...$50.00

Roller type, tin on wooden pastry roller type base, cuts entire piece of dough at once, 26" L $22.00

Rudolph Red Nosed Reindeer, plastic, Domar Corp, MOC $30.00

Santa Claus w/pack, aluminum w/green wood handle, 3½"...$15.00

Scottie dog, aluminum w/red wooden handle, ca 1940s $18.00

Scottie dog, aluminum w/strap handle, sm $6.00

Shaper, butterfly, hard plastic, Hallmark, 1986-87.........$6.50

Shaper, Christmas tree, green, soft plastic, Hallmark, 1981 & 1984-85..$3.00

Shaper, dinosaur, yellow, Hallmark, 1987.....................$5.00

Shaper, gingerbread boy, brown, Hallmark, 1992.........$4.50

Shaper, graduation cap, Royal Blue, Hallmark, 1997..$10.00

Shaper, hippopotamus, lavender, Hallmark, 1988.........$5.00

Shaper, Indian girl, gold tab, Hallmark, 1990-91 ....$5.00

Shaper, pumpkin, orange, soft plastic, Hallmark, 1985-87 ..$3.50

Shaper, rocking horse, green, Hallmark, 1986-87.........$5.00

Shaper, snowman, white, soft plastic, Hallmark, 1984-87, 4½"...$3.50

Shaper, tulip w/leaves, hard plastic, Hallmark, 1986-87 .$6.50

Simpsons, in box w/cookie mix, MIB........................$10.00

Squirrel, tin, 4½x3¾"...$25.00

Star, tin w/strap handle, 2¾" $12.00

Sunbonnet Sue, tin, handmade ca 1930, 5½".............$12.00

Teddy bear, lg handle embossed w/Nordstrom, Martha Stewart, 7x6", MIB $60.00

Tinypotamus, light blue, hard plastic, eyelet, Hallmark, 1977, 3½"...$8.50

Turkey, brown, soft plastic, Hallmark, 1984.................$3.00

Winnie-the-Pooh, orange w/honey pot, hard plastic, Walt Disney Production, Hallmark, 1979........................$8.50

Witch holding broom, orange, soft plastic, eyelet, Hallmark, 1979, 4"..$10.50

Witch on broom, black, eyelet, Hallmark, 1981, 4½" ...$3.50

12 Days of Christmas, plastic, Aluminum Specialty, Chilton, 3-D, 1978, set $20.00

Cookie Jars

This is an area that for years saw an explosion of interest that resulted in some very high prices. Though the market has leveled off to a large extent, rare cookie jars sell for literally thousands of dollars. Even a common jar from a good manufacturer will fall into the $40.00 to $100.00 price range. At the top of the list are the Black-theme jars, then come the cartoon characters such as Popeye, Howdy Doody, or the Flintstones — in fact, any kind of a figural jar from an American pottery is collectible.

The American Bisque company was one of the largest producers of these jars from 1930 until the 1970s. Many of their jars have no marks at all; those that do are simply marked 'USA,' sometimes with a mold number. But their air-brushed colors are easy to spot, and collectors look for the molded-in wedge-shaped pads on their bases — these say 'American Bisque' to cookie jar buffs about as clearly as if they were marked.

The Brush Pottery (Ohio, 1946 – 71) made cookie jars that were decorated with the airbrush in many of the same colors used by American Bisque. These jars are strongly holding their values, and the rare ones continue to climb in price. McCoy was probably the leader in cookie-jar production. Even some of their very late jars bring high prices. Abingdon, Shawnee, and Red Wing all manufactured cookie jars, and there are a lot of wonderful jars by many other companies. Joyce and Fred Roerig's books *The Collector's Encyclopedia of Cookie Jars*, Vols. I, II, and III, cover them all beautifully, and you won't want to miss Ermagene Westfall's *An Illustrated Value Guide to Cookie Jars II*, another wonderful reference. All are published by Collector Books.

Warning! The marketplace abounds with reproductions these days. Roger Jensen of Rockwood, Tennessee, is making a line of cookie jars as well as planters, salt and pepper shakers, and many other items which for years he marked McCoy. Because the 'real' McCoys never registered their trademark, he was able to receive federal approval to begin using this mark in 1992. Though he added '#93' to some of his pieces, the vast majority of his wares are undated. He used old molds, and novice collectors are being fooled into buying the new for 'old' prices. Here are some of his reproductions that you should be aware of: McCoy Mammy, Mammy With Cauliflower, Clown Bust, Dalmatians, Indian Head, Touring Car and Rocking Horse; Hull Little Red Riding Hood; Pearl China Mammy; and the Mosaic Tile Mammy. Within the past couple of years, though, one of the last owners of the McCoy Pottery Company was able to make a successful appeal to end what they regarded as the fradulent use of their mark (it seems that they at last had it registered), so some of the later Jensen reproductions have been marked 'Brush-McCoy' (though this mark was never used on an authentic cookie jar) and 'B.J. Hull.' Besides these forgeries, several Brush jars have been reproduced as well (see Roerig's books for more information), and there are others. Some reproductions are being made in Taiwan and China, however er there are also jars being reproduced here in the states.

Cookie jars from California are getting their fair share of attention right now, and then some! We've included several from companies such as Brayton Laguna, Treasure Craft, Vallona Starr, and Twin Winton. Westfield's and Roerig's

books have information on all of these. Advisor Mike Ellis is the author of *Collector's Guide to Don Winton Designs* (Collector Books); and another of our advisors, Bernice Stamper, has written *Vallona Starr Ceramics*, which we're sure you will enjoy.

Advisors: April Tvorak, Enesco (see Directory, Figural Ceramics); Susan Cox, Brayton Laguna (see Directory, California Pottery); Pat and Ann Duncan, Holt Howard (See Directory, Holt Howard); Rick Spencer, Shawnee (See Directory, Shawnee); Mike Ellis, Twin Winton (See Directory, Twin Winton); Bernice Stamper, Vallona Star (See Directory, Vallona Star); Lois Wildman, Vandor (See Directory, Vandor).

Newsletter: *Cookie Jarrin' With Joyce*
R.R. 2, Box 504
Walterboro, SC 29488

A Little Company, Bella (dancer), 1995, 12"..............**$150.00**
A Little Company, Dolphin Boy, 1994, 11"...............**$180.00**
A Little Company, Santa Fe Railroad Station, 1993, 8".**$160.00**
A Little Company, Secret Girls, 1997, 12" **$190.00**
Abingdon, Baby, Black, #561 ....**$300.00**
Abingdon, Choo Choo, #651 ....**$150.00**
Abingdon, Clock, #653 ....**$100.00**
Abingdon, Daisy Jar, marked Abingdon USA #677.....**$50.00**
Abingdon, Fat Boy, marked Abingdon USA #495, 1941 ..**$250.00**
Abingdon, Hippo, w/yellow daisy, marked Abingdon USA #549 ....**$235.00**
Abingdon, Hobby Horse, #602.................................**$185.00**
Abingdon, Humpty Dumpty, decorated, #663..........**$250.00**
Abingdon, Jack-in-the Box, marked Abingdon USA #611, 1947, from $275 to..**$325.00**
Abingdon, Little Bo Peep, marked #694, from $250 to...**$275.00**

Abingdon, Little Girl, #693, from $60.00 to $75.00. (Photo courtesy Ermagene Westfall)

Abingdon, Little Miss Muffet, marked Abingdon USA #622, 1949 ....**$225.00**
Abingdon, Little Old Lady, brown, marked Abingdon USA #471 ....**$215.00**
Abingdon, Little Old Lady, plaid apron, marked Abingdon USA #471, Dec B **$300.00**

Abingdon, Miss Muffet, #622 ....**$200.00**

Abingdon, Money Bag, marked Abingdon USA #588, 1947 ....**$75.00**

Abingdon, Mother Goose, marked Abingdon USA #695, from $275 to..**$350.00**

Abingdon, Pineapple, marked Abingdon USA #664, 1949...**$95.00**

Abingdon, Three Bears Jar, marked Abingdon USA #696, from $90 to..**$100.00**

Abingdon, Wigwam, marked Abingdon USA #665, 1949, minimum value **$300.00**

Abingdon, Windmill, marked Abingdon USA #678, 1949, from $175 to..**$185.00**

Advertising, Archway Van, 5¾x10"............................**$16.00**

Advertising, Betty Crocker, red spoon logo & stripes on white jar **$90.00**

Advertising, Big Boy (1956 replica), 1997, 16"..........**$200.00**

Advertising, Chips Ahoy! Jar, blue lettering w/red trim on white, unmarked **$45.00**

Advertising, Chuck E Cheese, 20th Anniversary, K&L Enterprises, 1997......................................**$110.00**

Advertising, Coca-Cola Six Pack, Enesco, 1996...........**$65.00**

Advertising, Hard Rock Hotel Bear, 1997 ....**$36.00**

Advertising, Katy the Korn Top Pig, Bartlow Bros Inc Korn Top, Haeger USA **$110.00**

Advertising, Keebler Hollow Tree **$40.00**

Advertising, Keebler Sandies Jar, red & white graphics w/elf on white **$80.00**

Advertising, Mrs Fields Chocolate Chip, Niccum **$175.00**

Advertising, PH Max Jar, Pfaltzgraff USA 506, 3½-qt..**$50.00**

Advertising, Pillsbury Best All Purpose Flour Sack, 1993..**$65.00**

Advertising, Planet Hollywood Globe......................**$30.00**

Advertising, Quaker Grain Drops Canister, Weiss, 1981..**$225.00**

Advertising, Sprout (Green Giant), 1988.....................**$95.00**

Advertising, Stack of Oreo Cookies, Nabisco Classics Collection..**$30.00**

American Bisque, Basket O' Cookies, airbrushed, marked USA, 1958 ....**$60.00**

American Bisque, Boy Pig, airbrushed, unmarked **$90.00**

American Bisque, Chalkboard Hobo (Musn't Forget), marked USA **$375.00**

American Bisque, Churn, #CJ-756 ....**$35.00**

American Bisque, Cookie Truck, marked USA, found in 2 sizes **$75.00**

American Bisque, Davy Crockett (against forest), marked USA..**$750.00**

American Bisque, Davy Crockett (figural), marked USA ...**$375.00**

American Bisque, French Poodle, #CJ751 ....**$125.00**

American Bisque, Gift Box, marked USA, 1958 ....**$225.00**

American Bisque, Grandma #CJ-752, from $125 to ..**$150.00**

American Bisque, Hen & Chick, marked USA, 9".....**$150.00**

American Bisque, Jack-in-the Box, #CJ-753...............**$150.00**

American Bisque, Lady Pig, #CJ-755 ....**$90.00**

American Bisque, Recipe Jar, #CJ-563 ....**$110.00**

American Bisque, Rocket Ship (Cookies Out of this World), marked USA......................................**$325.00**

American Bisque, Rubbles House, marked USA, 9½"...**$750.00**

American Bisque, Schoolhouse (After School Cookies), marked USA 741 ....**$70.00**

American Bisque, Sitting Horse, marked USA, rare, 11½", from $1,100.00 to $1,250.00. (Photo courtesy Mary Jane Giacomini)

American Bisque, Teakettle, colonial couple embossed on side...**$50.00**

American Bisque, Treasure Chest, #CJ-562.................**$175.00**

American Bisque, Umbrella Kids (Sweethearts), marked USA 739 ....**$325.00**

American Bisque/Disney, Babes in Toyland, soldier standing guard at gate **$375.00**

American Bisque/Hanna-Barbera, Yogi Bear............**$475.00**

Brayton Laguna, Grandma w/Wedding Band, from $500 to **$600.00**

Brayton Laguna, Granny, yellow & brown w/white apron **$350.00**

Brayton Laguna, Maid (Black), marked w/black stamp, 12½", minimum value..............................**$1,500.00**

Brayton Laguna, Mammy, yellow w/white apron, minimum value **$900.00**

Brayton Laguna, Provincial Lady, 13".......................**$375.00**

Brush, Antique Touring Car, minimum value............**$700.00**

Brush, Boy w/Baloons, minimum value.....................**$850.00**

Brush, Cinderella Pumpkin, #W32, from $200 to......**$275.00**

Brush, Circus Horse, gr...**$950.00**

Brush, Clown, yellow pants.......................................**$250.00**

Brush, Clown Bust, #W49, minimum value..............**$325.00**

Brush, Cookie House, #W31.......................................**$125.00**

Brush, Covered Wagon, dog finial, #W30, minimum value **$550.00**

Brush, Cow w/Cat on Back, brown, #W10 ....**$125.00**

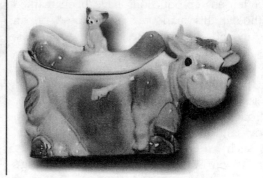

Brush, Cow With Cat on His Back, purple, W10, minimum value, $1,000.00.

Brush, Davy Crockett, no gold, marked USA............$300.00
Brush, Dog & Basket...$250.00
Brush, Donkey w/Cart, ears up, #W33, minimum value...$800.00
Brush, Donkey w/Cart, gray, ears down, #W33.......$400.00
Brush, Elephant w/Ice Cream Cone.........................$500.00
Brush, Elephant w/Monkey on Back, minimum value.$5,000.00
Brush, Fish, #W52...$500.00
Brush, Formal Pig, green hat & coat........................$300.00
Brush, Gas Lamp, #K1..$75.00
Brush, Granny, pk apron, bl dots on skirt...............$325.00
Brush, Granny, plain skirt, minimum value..............$400.00
Brush, Happy Bunny, white, #W25............................$225.00
Brush, Hen on Basket, unmarked..............................$125.00
Brush, Hillbilly Frog, minimum value....................$4,500.00
Brush, Hillbilly Frog, reissue (may or may not be marked Re-
    issue by JD)..$150.00
Brush, Hippo w/Monkey on Back, #W27, from $750 to...$850.00
Brush, Humpty Dumpty, #W29, w/black peaked hat, eyes,
    nose, belt & shoes, from $250 to.......................$350.00
Brush, Humpty Dumpty, w/beany & bow tie...........$275.00
Brush, Little Angel...$800.00
Brush, Little Boy Blue, #K24 Brush USA, lg.............$800.00
Brush, Little Boy Blue, gold trim, #K25, sm.............$700.00
Brush, Little Girl, #017...$550.00
Brush, Little Red Riding Hood, gold trim, marked, lg, mini-
    mum value..$850.00
Brush, Little Red Riding Hood, no gold, #K24 USA,
    sm..$550.00
Brush, Night Owl..$125.00
Brush, Old Clock, #W10...$165.00
Brush, Old Shoe, #W23..$125.00
Brush, Panda, #W21..$250.00
Brush, Peter, Peter Pumpkin Eater, #W24...............$300.00
Brush, Peter Pan, gold trim, lg.................................$800.00
Brush, Peter Pan, sm..$550.00
Brush, Puppy Police..$585.00
Brush, Raggedy Ann, #W16, from $475 to...............$525.00
Brush, Sitting Pig, #W37, from $400 to....................$450.00
Brush, Smiling Bear, #W46...$350.00
Brush, Squirrel on Log, #W26....................................$100.00
Brush, Squirrel w/Top Hat, black coat & hat...........$275.00
Brush, Squirrel w/Top Hat, green coat.....................$250.00
Brush, Stylized Owl..$350.00
Brush, Stylized Siamese, #W41, from $400 to..........$500.00
Brush, Teddy Bear, feet apart...................................$250.00
Brush, Teddy Bear, feet together..............................$200.00
Brush, Treasure Chest, #W28.....................................$150.00
Califorina Originals, Yellow Taxi...............................$175.00
California Originals, Beaver, #2625...........................$35.00
California Originals, Clown on Elephant, #896.........$45.00
California Originals, Cookie Safe (cat atop lid), #2630...$45.00
California Originals, Frog w/Bow Tie, #2645...........$45.00
California Originals, Santa Claus, #871.....................$275.00
California Originals/DC Comics, Superman in Phone Booth,
    marked USA 846, 1978..$600.00
California Originals/DC Comics, Wonder Woman Cookie
    Bank, USA 847, 1978, 14"....................................$1,100.00

California Originals/Disney, Donald Duck Leaning on
    Pumpkin, sepia wash on white, marked Walt Disney
    Productions 805...$325.00
California Originals/Disney, Eeyore, #901................$600.00
California Originals/Disney, Tigger, #902.................$275.00
California Originals/Disney, Winnie the Pooh, #900..$200.00
California Originals/Muppets Inc, Big Bird on Nest, #971..$50.00
California Originals/Muppets Inc, Cookie Monster, #970....$55.00
California Originals/Muppets Inc, Ernie & Bert Fine Cookies,
    #977, scarce...$425.00
California Originals/Muppets Inc, Oscar the Grouch,
    #970...$90.00
Cardinal, Castle, #307..$175.00
Cardinal, Clown Crying (I Want Some Cookies), #302.$125.00
Cardinal, Cookie Kate, #301......................................$125.00
Cardinal, Garage (Free Parking For Cookies), #306....$85.00

Cardinal, Old Fashioned Wall Telephone, #311 USA, $80.00. (Photo courtesy Ermagene Westfall)

Carol Gifford, Watermelon Sammy, 1987, $160.00. (Photo courtesy Pat and Ann Duncan)

Certified International, Barney Rubble..........................$55.00
Certified International, Dino & Pebbles.......................$55.00
Certified International, Flintstone House.....................$55.00
Certified International, Fred Flintstone.......................$55.00
Clay Art, Baking Time Mammy, 1995...........................$35.00
Clay Art, Black Jazz Player, 1995.................................$35.00
Clay Art, Cabbage Bunny, 1992...................................$45.00
Clay Art, Catfish, white or black, 1990........................$45.00
Clay Art, Catnap, 1991...$45.00

Clay Art, Dog Bone, 1991 ....$45.00
Clay Art, Humpty Dumpty, 1991 ....$125.00
Clay Art, Road Hog, 1995............................$50.00
Clay Art, Wizard of Oz, 1990.......................$150.00

Cleminson, Card King, from $500.00 to $550.00. (Photo courtesy Ermagene Westfall)

Cleminson, Cookstove.................................$175.00
Cleminson, Pig..$275.00
Cleminson, Potbellied Stove, 9".................$225.00
Danawares/Disney, Donald Duck Jar, w/hat finial, multicolor on white $125.00
Danawares/Disney, Goofy, from $90 to $125.00
Danawares/Disney, Winnie the Pooh Treehouse........$95.00
DeForest of California, Barrel, #5538 ....$30.00
DeForest of California, Beans Pig, 1959 .....$125.00
DeForest of California, Clown $175.00
DeForest of California, Cocky (Dandee Rooster)......$350.00
DeForest of California, Cookie Gem, brown..............$40.00
DeForest of California, Cookie King, minimum value ..$800.00
DeForest of California, Goodies Pig.............$125.00
DeForest of California, Henny (Dandee Hen)...........$225.00
DeForest of California, Owl, #5537 ....$35.00
DeForest of California, Poodle, 1960 ....$50.00
DeForest of California, Puppy, #5515 ....$55.00
DeForest of California, Ranger Bear, #5523.................$45.00
Department 56, Beehive................................$35.00
Department 56, Bowl of Cherries..................$50.00
Department 56, Cowboy in Silhouette, 10½" $110.00
Department 56, Fishing Creel Basket............$65.00
Department 56, Mirage Cactus.....................$65.00
Department 56, Short Order Toaster..............$60.00
Department 56, Vegetable Cottage, #1001, from $60 to..$75.00
Department 56, Witch, from $150 to.........................$200.00
Doranne of California, Catsup Bottle, #CJ-68 ....$40.00
Doranne of California, Cookie Cola, #CJ-67 ....$45.00
Doranne of California, Cow on Moon, #J-2..............$375.00
Doranne of California, Cow w/Milk Can, #CJ-107 ......$60.00
Doranne of California, Doctor, #CJ-130 ....$275.00
Doranne of California, Donkey, #CJ-108 ....$60.00
Doranne of California, Elephant, #16............$70.00
Doranne of California, Fish, #J-9 ....$45.00

Doranne of California, Hen, #CJ-100............$45.00
Doranne of California, Jack Rabbit, 13" $50.00
Doranne of California, Mother Goose, #CJ-16..........$175.00
Doranne of California, Opossum, brown....................$50.00
Doranne of California, Peanut, #CJ-18 ....$35.00
Doranne of California, School Bus, #CJ-120 ....$175.00
Enesco, Bear Pull Toy, 1996 ....$60.00
Enesco, Bulldog, in green sweater & red collar..........$60.00
Enesco, Clown Head, #E-5835.....................$150.00
Enesco, Mary's Moo Moo, dressed cow w/milk bottle, 1993 ....$50.00
Enesco, Mother in Kitchen (Kitchen Prayer Lady), pink, 9½" $395.00
Enesco, Owl (Who's Eating Owl Cookies), 1997, 8¼" .$30.00
Enesco, Sweet Pickles Alligator, 1981, from $150 to...$175.00
Enesco/Disney, Mickey Mouse Bust in Santa Hat.......$70.00
Enesco/Disney, Mickey Mouse Cookie Time Clock, marked WDE-219 ....$450.00
Enesco/Disney, Mickey Mouse Head, in straw hat marked Cookies $70.00
Fitz & Floyd, Angel's Christmas $65.00
Fitz & Floyd, Autumn Woods Rabbit............$90.00
Fitz & Floyd, Bacon & Eggs Hog $95.00
Fitz & Floyd, Bloomers $110.00
Fitz & Floyd, Christmas Quilt Santa in Chair, from $100 to...$150.00
Fitz & Floyd, Christmas Quilt Stocking......................$125.00
Fitz & Floyd, Christmas Wreath Santa, from $150 to ..$190.00

Fitz & Floyd, Cindella Fairy Godmother, $125.00. (Photo courtesy Pat and Ann Duncan)

Fitz & Floyd, Coq Du Village (rooster).....................$125.00
Fitz & Floyd, Dinosaur Holding Sack of Cookies, from $75 to...$135.00
Fitz & Floyd, Domesticat, from $65 to $95.00
Fitz & Floyd, Father Christmas Sleigh $200.00
Fitz & Floyd, Haunted House, from $85 to $150.00
Fitz & Floyd, Heidi Holstein.........................$90.00
Fitz & Floyd, Herb Garden Rabbit.............................$90.00
Fitz & Floyd, Hermoine Heifer $85.00
Fitz & Floyd, Hippo Limpix, from $50 to ...$85.00

Fitz & Floyd, Holiday Cat......................................**$130.00**

Fitz & Floyd, Kerchief Cat w/Fish, from $65 to **$95.00**

Fitz & Floyd, Kris Kringle Santa & Tree..................**$240.00**

Fitz & Floyd, Leap Frog, from $60 to **$90.00**

Fitz & Floyd, Mother Goose, from $150 to................**$200.00**

Fitz & Floyd, Mother Rabbit, from $80 to.................**$120.00**

Fitz & Floyd, Night Before Christmas.......................**$225.00**

Fitz & Floyd, Nutcracker Sweets Sugar Plum Castle, from $115 to **$175.00**

Fitz & Floyd, Old MacDonald's County Fair.............**$100.00**

Fitz & Floyd, Old World Santa, from $125 to...........**$165.00**

Fitz & Floyd, Peter the Great, from $65 to **$85.00**

Fitz & Floyd, Plaid Teddy, from $85 to....................**$140.00**

Fitz & Floyd, Prunella Pig, from $85 to **$110.00**

Fitz & Floyd, Queen of Hearts **$125.00**

Fitz & Floyd, Raccoon, from $75 to **$100.00**

Fitz & Floyd, Rio Rita, from $70 to **$125.00**

Fitz & Floyd, Rose Terrace Rabbit **$90.00**

Fitz & Floyd, Santa's Toy Factory **$85.00**

Fitz & Floyd, Sheriff, from $250 to **$300.00**

Fitz & Floyd, Southwest Santa, from $500 to **$575.00**

Fitz & Floyd, Sugar Plum Christmas Santa..................**$90.00**

Fitz & Floyd, Summer Berry Patch (lamb), from $50 to ..**$75.00**

Fitz & Floyd, Victorian House, from $165 to............**$200.00**

Fitz & Floyd, Wanda Witch......................................**$210.00**

Flambro, Emmett Kelly Jr on Barrel, from $475 to ...**$700.00**

Fredericksburg Art Pottery, Cow on Moon, marked J 2 USA **$250.00**

Fredericksburg Art Pottery, Dove, marked FAPCo USA ..**$30.00**

Fredericksburg Art Pottery, Windmill, marked FAPCo ..**$50.00**

Goebel, Lion's Head, wearing crown, 1983.................**$80.00**

Goebel, Parrot's Head, wearing blue beanie.............**$80.00**

Guisewite Studio, Cathy (So Many Cookies So Little Time), 1995, 8½" **$80.00**

Hallmark, Christmas Bear, from $35 to **$60.00**

Hallmark, Maxine Sitting w/Dog, from $60 to **$100.00**

Hallmark, Shirt Tales Ricky Raccoon Cookie Bandit, from $225 to **$300.00**

Happy Memories, Hopalong Cassidy, 15½" **$315.00**

Happy Memories, Scarlett O'Hara, in green drapery dress, 14¾"...**$300.00**

Harry James, Homer Simpson in Chair, 1990, minimum value **$450.00**

Harry James/Enesco, Garfield, 1981..........................**$125.00**

Harry James/Molly Houswares, Garfield w/Cookie, 1981 ...**$325.00**

Harry James/Turner Entertainment, Tom & Jerry, 10"...**$225.00**

Harry James/Turner Entertainment, Tom & Jerry, 7" **$200.00**

Hearth & Home (H&HD), Bird House.........................**$40.00**

Hearth & Home (H&HD), Carousel Horse **$55.00**

Hearth & Home (H&HD), Cheetah **$55.00**

Hearth & Home (H&HD), Giraffe **$50.00**

Hearth & Home (H&HD), Stagecoach, from $45 to....**$75.00**

Hearth & Home (H&HD), Sundance Kid, from $50 to ..**$100.00**

Hirsch, Beehive, 19½" **$175.00**

Hirsch, Cookie Planet..**$85.00**

Hirsch, For the Team Basketball **$125.00**

Hirsch, Gingerbread House...**$60.00**

Hirsch, Hobby Horse, 1956.....................................**$200.00**

Hirsch, Lot'sa Goodies! Chef...................................**$275.00**

Hirsch, Mamma Rabbit, marked WH '58....................**$40.00**

Hirsch, Peck O' Cookies Rooster.............................**$225.00**

Hirsch, Treasure Chest, all brown, marked WH '58....**$70.00**

Hirsch, Wall Phone...**$110.00**

Hull, Barefoot Boy, blue pants & red hat................**$425.00**

Hull, Little Red Riding Hood, closed basket, minimum value **$360.00**

Hull, Little Red Riding Hood, open basket...............**$350.00**

Hull, Little Red Riding Hood, open basket, red shoes..**$850.00**

Hull, Little Red Riding Hood, poinsettia.................**$1,050.00**

Hull, Little Red Riding Hood, red spray w/gold bows, red shoes..**$950.00**

Hull, Little Red Riding Hood, stars on apron, minimum value **$675.00**

Hull, Little Red Riding Hood, white.......................**$200.00**

Japan, Alice's Adventures in Wonderland, house w/Alice's head coming out of roof & legs out front door, from $75 to **$95.00**

Japan, Cookie Time Clock w/Mouse Finial, blue w/multicolored trim...**$20.00**

Japan, Cookies Can w/Racoon & Ladybugs **$20.00**

Japan, Grandma, If All Else Fails Ask Grandma lettered on hat, orange..**$20.00**

Japan, Hippo Fisherman **$35.00**

Japan, Horse Doctor..**$35.00**

Japan, Majorette Head, multicolored.........................**$25.00**

Japan, Pear w/Smiling Face, marked 6 C 30 ....**$30.00**

Japan, Pig Chef, white upper body w/multicolored accents, blue pants w/black belt **$30.00**

Japan, Professor Owl, w/scroll marked Cookies, brown.**$20.00**

Japan, Rag Doll (Raggedy Ann type), pink w/white pinafore, orange hair...**$30.00**

Japan, Tom & Jerry Cookies, brown jar w/cookies embossed allover, Tom finial & Jerry on side w/colorful lettering..**$325.00**

JC Miller, Sister Ruth (Black Choir Singer)..................**$50.00**

K&L Enterprises, Mother's Wonder (buffalo)............**$110.00**

Lark Creations, 1948 Tucker Sedan, 1997.................**$150.00**

Lefton, Bluebird, #289, 7¼", from $200.00 to $275.00. (Photo courtesy Loretta DeLozier)

Lefton, Dutch Girl, #2366................................$225.00
Lefton, French Girl, #1174, 9".........................$300.00
Lefton, Girl, #397, 8⅜"..................................$225.00
Lefton, Green Holly..$70.00
Lefton, Miss Priss, blue cat head $135.00
Leisuramics/Disney, Mickey Mouse Club House......$175.00
MacMillan, Raggedy Ann or Raggedy Andy, 1993, ea ..$95.00
Maddux of California, Bear, #2101 ....$75.00

Maddox, Beatrix Potter/ Shopping Rabbit, from $150.00 to $175.00. (Photo courtesy Ermagene Westfall)

Maddux of California, Clown, very lg, from $325 to ..$395.00
Maddux of California, Humpty Dumpty, #2113 ....$300.00
Maddux of California, Queen, #2104, from $125 to .$140.00
Maddux of California, Raggedy Ann, #2108, from $250
   to $300.00
Maddux of California, Scottie............................$75.00
Maddux of California, Strawberry.......................$35.00
Maddux of California, Walrus $65.00
McCoy, Animal Crackers Jar w/Clown Finial, marked USA,
   1960, from $85 to $100.00
McCoy, Apollo Age, minimum value......................$1,000.00
McCoy, Apple, airbrushed blush, 1950-64 ....$50.00
McCoy, Apple, 1967.......................................$60.00
McCoy, Asparagus Bunch, unmarked, 1977-79 ....$50.00
McCoy, Astronauts, from $750 to $850.00
McCoy, Bamboo Cylinder w/Ball Finial, brown, marked #188
   209L McCoy USA..$60.00
McCoy, Bananas, from $135 to...........................$150.00
McCoy, Barnum's Animals, from $350 to $400.00
McCoy, Barrel, Cookies sign on lid.....................$125.00
McCoy, Basket of Eggs....................................$40.00
McCoy, Basket of Potatoes...............................$40.00
McCoy, Bear, cookie in vest, no 'Cookies', from $75 to ...$85.00
McCoy, Bear, cookie in vest, w/'Cookies'...............$85.00
McCoy, Bear & Beehive, marked #143 USA...............$45.00
McCoy, Bear Hugging Cookie Barrel, marked #142 USA,
   1978, from $75 to.....................................$95.00
McCoy, Betsy Baker, from $250 to.......................$300.00
McCoy, Black Kettle, w/immovable bail, hand-painted flow-
   ers $40.00
McCoy, Blue Willow Pitcher, #202 McCoy USA, 1973-75 ...$50.00
McCoy, Bobby Baker, #183, original.....................$65.00

McCoy, Boy on Baseball, from $250 to $300.00
McCoy, Boy on Football, marked #222 McCoy USA, 1983,
   from $245 to..$275.00
McCoy, Bugs Bunny, cylinder, from $165 to............$200.00
McCoy, Burlap Bag, red bird on lid, from $50 to $70.00
McCoy, Burlap Cookie Sack, marked #207 McCoy USA,
   1985 ....$40.00
McCoy, Caboose, from $200 to $250.00
McCoy, Canister w/Strawberries & Flowers, red, green &
   white on white, marked McCoy USA...................$40.00
McCoy, Cat on Coal Scuttle $250.00

McCoy, Chairman of the Board, $550.00.

McCoy, Chef, bust $110.00
McCoy, Chilly Willy $50.00

McCoy, Chipmunk, $125.00.

McCoy, Christmas Tree, minimum value $800.00
McCoy, Chuck Wagon Coffeepot, brown & white, marked
   #186 McCoy USA, 1974-75 ....$60.00
McCoy, Churn, 2 bands...................................$35.00
McCoy, Churn, 3 bands, wood-grain, unmarked, 1961 .$250.00
McCoy, Circus Horse, black..............................$250.00
McCoy, Clown Bust $75.00
McCoy, Clown in Barrel, blue, yellow or green..........$85.00
McCoy, Clyde Dog, from $200 to.........................$250.00
McCoy, Coalby Cat, from $325 to $375.00

McCoy, Coca-Cola Can..$100.00

McCoy, Coca-Cola Jug..$85.00

McCoy, Coffee Grinder...$45.00

McCoy, Coffee Mug...$45.00

McCoy, Colonial Fireplace $85.00

McCoy, Concave Jar w/Lilies, black gloss, marked USA, mid 1930s $40.00

McCoy, Cook Stove, white w/gold trim, marked McCoy USA, 1961-69 ....$35.00

McCoy, Cookie Bank, 1961..$165.00

McCoy, Cookie Barrel w/Sign, brown wood-grain, marked #146 McCoy USA, 1969-72, from $35 to $45.00

McCoy, Cookie Bell, unmarked, 1953-66....................$50.00

McCoy, Cookie Box, marked USA, 1963 ....$150.00

McCoy, Cookie Boy...$225.00

McCoy, Cookie Cabin..$80.00

McCoy, Cookie Jug, double loop $35.00

McCoy, Cookie Jug, single loop, 2-tone green rope...$35.00

McCoy, Cookie Jug, w/cork stopper, brown & white..$40.00

McCoy, Cookie Log, squirrel finial, from $35 to $45.00

McCoy, Cookie Mug $45.00

McCoy, Cookie Safe...$65.00

McCoy, Cookstove, black or white................................$35.00

McCoy, Corn, row of standing ears, yellow or white, 1977 ....$85.00

McCoy, Corn, single ear, yellow...................................$175.00

McCoy, Covered Wagon..$95.00

McCoy, Cylinder, cobalt blue, marked USA #28.........$40.00

McCoy, Cylinder, Flower Panels, modern motif, yellow, marked, #254 McCoy USA, 1970-71......................$40.00

McCoy, Cylinder, mustard w/green drip glaze, marked USA #28 ....$45.00

McCoy, Cylinder, w/red flowers $45.00

McCoy, Cylinder w/Cat, white w/black trim, marked McCoy USA $225.00

McCoy, Cylinder w/Two Puppies, marked McCoy USA ...$200.00

McCoy, Dalmatians in Rocking Chair, from $345 to .$375.00

McCoy, Davy Crockett..$600.00

McCoy, Dog in Doghouse w/Bird on Top, unmarked, 1983 ....$250.00

McCoy, Dog on Basketweave, from $75 to $90.00

McCoy, Drum, red $90.00

McCoy, Duck on Basketweave, from $75 to $90.00

McCoy, Duck w/Leaf in Bill, yellow w/red bill, 1964, from $65 to...$85.00

McCoy, Dutch Boy..$45.00

McCoy, Dutch Treat Barn..$50.00

McCoy, Eagle on Basket, from $35 to...........................$50.00

McCoy, Early American Chest (Chiffoniere) $85.00

McCoy, Elephant w/Split Trunk, rare, minimum value..$300.00

McCoy, Elephant w/Whole Trunk, unmarked, 1953.$200.00

McCoy, Engine, black...$175.00

Mccoy, Flowerpot, plastic flower on top...................$500.00

McCoy, Forbidden Fruit, from $65 to..........................$90.00

McCoy, Fortune Cookies, marked McCoy USA, 1965-68...$65.00

McCoy, Freddie the Gleep, #189, original, minimum value $500.00

McCoy, Friendship 7...$200.00

McCoy, Frontier Family Jar (Cookies), unmarked, 1964-71 ....$55.00

McCoy, Fruit in Bushel Basket, from $65 to..............$80.00

McCoy, Garbage Can, marked #350.............................$35.00

McCoy, Gingerbread Boy on Ribbed Cylinder, marked USA, 1961..$75.00

McCoy, Globe, from $300 to $375.00

McCoy, Gookie Goose, marked USA, 1986................$40.00

McCoy, Grandfather Clock, black or brown...............$90.00

McCoy, Grandma w/Eyes Closed & Hands Folded, red & yellow w/white apron, marked, USA, 1972-73, from $90 to...$120.00

McCoy, Hamm's Bear...$225.00

McCoy, Happy Face $80.00

McCoy, Hen on Basket, white......................................$85.00

McCoy, Hen on Nest, marked USA, 1958-59, from $85 to...$95.00

McCoy, Hobby Horse, from $125 to $150.00

McCoy, Hobnail (Ball-Shaped), unmarked, 1940 .....$100.00

McCoy, Hobnail (Heart-Shaped), unmarked, 1940, from $400 to...$500.00

McCoy, Hocus Rabbit $45.00

McCoy, Honey Bear, Rustic glaze, from $65 to..........$80.00

McCoy, Hot Air Balloon..$40.00

McCoy, Hound Dog, head down, 1977........................$35.00

McCoy, Ice Cream Cone...$45.00

McCoy, Indian, brown..$350.00

McCoy, Indian, majolica...$400.00

McCoy, Jack-O'-Lantern $600.00

McCoy, Kangaroo, blue...$300.00

McCoy, Kangaroo, McCoy USA 1965, original $425.00

McCoy, Keebler Tree House, from $50 to $70.00

McCoy, Kettle, bronze, 1961..$40.00

McCoy, Kissing Penguins, from $100 to $125.00

McCoy, Kitten on Basketweave, from $75..................$90.00

McCoy, Kitten on Coal Bucket, black & brown, marked #219 McCoy USA, 1983 ....$225.00

McCoy, Kittens (2) on Low Basket, minimum value ..$600.00

McCoy, Kittens on Ball of Yarn....................................$85.00

McCoy, Koala Bear $85.00

McCoy, Kookie Kettle, black $35.00

McCoy, Lamb on Basketweave, from $75 to $90.00

McCoy, Liberty Bell $75.00

McCoy, Little Clown $75.00

McCoy, Lollipops $80.00

McCoy, Lunch Bucket, marked #377 USA $35.00

McCoy, Mac Dog...$95.00

McCoy, Mammy, Cookies on base, white..................$150.00

McCoy, Mammy w/Cauliflower, good paint, minimum value..$1,100.00

McCoy, Milk Can, Spirit of '76....................................$45.00

McCoy, Milk Can w/Gingham Flowers, marked #333 USA..$40.00

McCoy, Milk Can w/Liberty Bell, marked USA #154, from $75 to...$100.00

McCoy, Mother Goose..$175.00

McCoy, Mouse Head, w/'Mickey Mouse' ears, yellow, 1978...**$40.00**

McCoy, Mouse on Clock....................................**$40.00**

McCoy, Mr & Mrs Owl, from $75 to.................**$90.00**

McCoy, Nibble Kettle, black, marked McCoy USA, 1960-77...**$60.00**

McCoy, Nursery, decal of Humpty Dumpty, from $70 to.**$80.00**

McCoy, Oaken Bucket, from $25 to.................**$30.00**

McCoy, Orange..**$55.00**

McCoy, Panda Bear w/Swirl Cookie, marked #141 USA, 1978...**$200.00**

McCoy, Pear, 1952...**$85.00**

McCoy, Pears on Basketweave..........................**$70.00**

McCoy, Penguin w/Cookie Sign on Chest, white w/black & red trim or solid white, marked McCoy, 1940-43, from $175 to...**$200.00**

McCoy, Pepper, yellow or green.......................**$40.00**

McCoy, Picnic Basket, from $65 to **$75.00**

McCoy, Pig, winking...**$300.00**

McCoy, Pineapple, marked McCoy USA, 1956-57.......**$80.00**

McCoy, Pineapple, Modern, from $75 to.........**$90.00**

McCoy, Pirate's Chest, from $125 to **$145.00**

McCoy, Popeye, cylinder **$200.00**

McCoy, Potbelly Stove, black.............................**$35.00**

McCoy, Puppy, w/sign.......................................**$60.00**

McCoy, Raggedy Ann.......................................**$110.00**

McCoy, Red Barn With Cow in Door, minimum value, $350.00. (Photo courtesy Ermagene Westfall)

McCoy, Rooster, white, 1970-74.......................**$60.00**

McCoy, Rooster, 1955-57, from $75 to **$95.00**

McCoy, Sad Clown...**$85.00**

McCoy, Snoopy on Doghouse, marked United Features Syndicate, from $175 to..............**$200.00**

McCoy, Snow Bear, from $65 to.......................**$75.00**

McCoy, Soccer Ball, whistle finial, unmarked, 1978, minimum value..........................**$1,500.00**

McCoy, Strawberry, 1955-57.............................**$65.00**

McCoy, Strawberry, 1971-75.............................**$45.00**

McCoy, Stump w/Frog, marked #216 McCoy USA, 1972..**$80.00**

McCoy, Stump w/Monkey, marked #253 McCoy USA (1970), from $50 to...**$60.00**

McCoy, Stump w/Mushroom, marked #214 McCoy USA (1972)...**$40.00**

McCoy, Stump w/Rabbit, marked McCoy USA, 1971..**$50.00**

McCoy, Teapot (Cookies), metallic brown, marked McCoy USA, 1972...**$60.00**

McCoy, Tepee, slant top...................................**$350.00**

McCoy, Tepee, straight top...............................**$300.00**

McCoy, Timmy Tortoise.....................................**$45.00**

McCoy, Tomato..**$60.00**

McCoy, Touring Car, from $85 to....................**$100.00**

McCoy, Traffic Light..**$50.00**

McCoy, Tudor Cookie House **$125.00**

McCoy, Turkey, green & brown, marked McCoy, 1945..**$325.00**

McCoy, Turkey, multicolored, marked McCoy USA, 1960..**$250.00**

McCoy, Uncle Sam's Hat, unmarked, 1973, from $650 to..**$750.00**

McCoy, Upside Down Bear, panda **$50.00**

McCoy, WC Fields...**$200.00**

McCoy, Wedding Jar, from $70 to **$90.00**

McCoy, Windmill, from $85 to **$100.00**

McCoy, Wishing Well...**$40.00**

McCoy, Woodsy Owl, from $250 to.................**$300.00**

McCoy, Wren House, side lid............................**$175.00**

McCoy, Yosemite Sam, cylinder, from $150 to.........**$200.00**

McMe Productions, Allie Rebecca w/Baby Buggy, 14" ...**$125.00**

McMe Productions, Cathy, 1994 ....**$150.00**

McMe Productions, Dale Evans, 1994 ....**$160.00**

McMe Productions, Roy Rogers Bust, 1994 ....**$160.00**

McMe Productions, Roy Rogers on Trigger, 1995 ....**$225.00**

Metlox, Acorn w/Woodpecker Finial, stained finish.**$375.00**

Metlox, Apple, red w/brown & green stem **$65.00**

Metlox, Ballerina Bear......................................**$125.00**

Metlox, Basset Hound, minimum value............**$650.00**

Metlox, Bear on Roller Skates...........................**$150.00**

Metlox, Beaver w/Bouquet of Daisies **$200.00**

Metlox, Brownie Scout Head, 9⅛", minimum value.**$750.00**

Metlox, Calf's Head, says Moo, from $300 to...........**$375.00**

Metlox, Candy Girl, $350.00. (Photo courtesy Ermagene Westfall)

Metlox, Clown, white w/black trim...........................**$200.00**

Metlox, Cookie Girl, color glazed...............................**$80.00**

Metlox, Cow (Yellow) w/Floral Collar & Butterfly on Back, blue, from $350 to...**$375.00**

Metlox, Daisy Topiary **$75.00**

Metlox, Dinosaur (Dina), blue, 1987.......................**$150.00**

Metlox, Dinosaur (Mona), yellow, 1987.....................**$175.00**

Metlox, Dinosaur (Rex), aqua, 1987..........................**$175.00**

Metlox, Drummer Boy, 2½-qt, minimum value **$500.00**

Metlox, Duck (Sir Francis Drake), white w/yellow bill & feet, green grass..**$50.00**

Metlox, Flamingo, minimum value.............................**$750.00**

Metlox, Frog (Prince)w/Single Daisy, green w/white collar & yellow tie...**$250.00**

Metlox, Gingerbread, bisque, 3½-qt..........................**$125.00**

Metlox, Gingham Dog, blue **$225.00**

Metlox, Grapes, purple w/green leaf lid, from $200 to....**$250.00**

Metlox, Hippo (Bubbles) w/Water Lily on Back, yellow, minimum value **$350.00**

Metlox, Humpty Dumpty, seated w/feet **$275.00**

Metlox, Jolly Chef, 11¼" **$400.00**

Metlox, Kangaroo w/Baby, minimum value..........**$1,000.00**

Metlox, Koala Bear **$125.00**

Metlox, Lamb, says Baa...**$125.00**

Metlox, Lamb w/Floral Collar **$325.00**

Metlox, Lion, yellow..**$175.00**

Metlox, Little Red Riding Hood, minimum value...**$1,250.00**

Metlox, Noah's Ark, color glazed **$175.00**

Metlox, Nun w/Plate of Cookies, white w/blue trim, minimum value **$1,000.00**

Metlox, Orange w/Blossom Finial **$65.00**

Metlox, Owls on Stump, bisque **$50.00**

Metlox, Panda Bear, no lollipop...............................**$100.00**

Metlox, Parrot on Stump, green, minimum value **$350.00**

Metlox, Pine Cone w/Baby Bluebird Finial, brown stain ...**$75.00**

Metlox, Pineapple..**$75.00**

Metlox, Pinocchio Head, 10¾" **$400.00**

Metlox, Pretzel Barrel **$125.00**

Metlox, Rabbit on Cabbage.......................................**$150.00**

Metlox, Raccoon Cookie Bandit w/Apples, color glazed ..**$150.00**

Metlox, Rag Doll (Boy) **$200.00**

Metlox, Rag Doll (Girl)...**$175.00**

Metlox, Rose Bud, light pink w/green leaves **$425.00**

Metlox, Scottie Dog, black..**$125.00**

Metlox, Spaceship w/Alien (Greetings Earth People), minimum value **$1,000.00**

Metlox, Strawberry, 9½"..**$70.00**

Metlox, Teddy Bear w/Cookie, light tan in blue sweater...**$45.00**

Metlox, Whale w/Duck Finial, white, from $300 to..**$350.00**

North American Ceramics, Airplane, w/movable propellers..**$625.00**

North American Ceramics, Corvette, #ACC J9, 1986.**$150.00**

North American Ceramics, Double-Decker Bus **$375.00**

Omnibus, Alley Cat w/Bowling Ball **$40.00**

Omnibus, Chili Cow..**$70.00**

Omnibus, Clover Hill Dairy Cow **$120.00**

Omnibus, Cowboy Cats...**$50.00**

Omnibus, French Country Hen **$65.00**

Omnibus, Garden Party...**$55.00**

Omnibus, German Santa **$75.00**

Omnibus, Hot Rod, from $85 to................................**$110.00**

Omnibus, Pig Driving Car (Road Hog), from $50 to ..**$85.00**

Omnibus, Rabbit on Cabbage......................................**$60.00**

Omnibus, Village Carolers..**$65.00**

Red Wing, Bob White, unmarked, from $100 to.......**$135.00**

Red Wing, Carousel, unmarked, from $900 to **$950.00**

Red Wing, Chef Pierre, blue, unmarked....................**$195.00**

Red Wing, Chef Pierre, pink, marked **$400.00**

Red Wing, Dutch Girl, yellow w/brown trim, marked, from $175 to..**$200.00**

Red Wing, Friar Tuck, green, marked........................**$300.00**

Red Wing, Grapes, green, marked, from $250 to **$275.00**

Red Wing, King of Tarts, multicolored, marked........**$975.00**

Red Wing, King of Tarts, pink w/blue trim, marked....**$1,000.00**

Red Wing, Peasant Design on Barrel Shape, brown w/painted-on colors **$275.00**

Red Wing, Pineapple, yellow **$200.00**

Regal, Chef (French), #54-192 ....**$375.00**

Regal, Clown w/Cookie, green collar, marked...........**$675.00**

Regal, Davy Crockett, marked **$550.00**

Regal, Diaper Pin Pig, #404 ....**$795.00**

Regal, Fisherman/Whaler, gold trim, unmarked........**$650.00**

Regal, Goldilocks, marked **$375.00**

Regal, Hobby Horse, #706 ....**$250.00**

Regal, Little Miss Muffet, #705 ....**$385.00**

Regal, Majorette Head **$675.00**

Regal, Oriental Lady w/Baskets, unmarked...............**$600.00**

Regal, Poodle (Fi Fi), marked....................................**$650.00**

Regal, Quaker Oats, marked.......................................**$125.00**

Regal, Toby Cookies, unmarked.................................**$750.00**

Robinson-Ransbottom, Chef w/Bowl & Spoon, heavy gold trim, #411 ....**$225.00**

Robinson-Ransbottom, Dutch Boy, white, blue & yellow w/black trim, unmarked..**$275.00**

Robinson-Ransbottom, Jocko the Monkey.................**$375.00**

Robinson-Ransbottom, Ol' King Cole, multicolored w/black pipe & mug...**$425.00**

Robinson-Ransbottom, Peter Peter Pumpkin Eater, marked...**$275.00**

Robinson-Ransbottom, Pig Sheriff, #363 ....**$125.00**

Robinson-Ransbottom, Pig Sheriff, heavy gold trim, #363..**$175.00**

Robinson-Ransbottom, Whale With Hat, $550.00. (Photo courtesy Ermagene Westfall)

Schmid/Disney, 101 Dalmatians (musical), from $100 to..**$165.00**

Shawnee, Cooky, white w/floral decals lg painted tulip & gold trim, marked USA...**$300.00**

Shawnee, Corn King, marked Shawnee #66 ....**$300.00**

161

Shawnee, Cottage, marked USA #6........................$1,350.00

Shawnee, Drum Major, gold trim, marked USA 10, minimum value $500.00

Shawnee, Drum Major, no gold, from $325.00 to $375.00. (Photo courtesy Joyce and Fred Roerig)

Shawnee, Dutch Boy, marked Great Northern USA #1025 ....$325.00

Shawnee, Dutch Girl, white w/brown hair, blue trim, marked, #1026..$300.00

Shawnee, Elephant (Jumbo), sitting upright, white w/yellow neck bow, marked USA #6 ....$125.00

Shawnee, Elephant (Lucky), sitting upright, decals & gold trim, marked USA $825.00

Shawnee, Fern Ware, yellow, marked USA $85.00

Shawnee, Fruit Basket, marked Shawnee 84............$225.00

Shawnee, Happy, w/patches on pants, gold buttons & trim, marked USA $375.00

Shawnee, Happy, white w/floral decals, blue & gold trim, marked USA $300.00

Shawnee, Jack, cold-painted, marked USA..............$125.00

Shawnee, Jill, cold-painted, marked USA $125.00

Shawnee, Jo-Jo the Clown, gold trimmed, marked Shawnee USA 12, minimum value $500.00

Shawnee, Jug, blue, marked USA............................$95.00

Shawnee, Little Chef Hexagon Jar, white w/multicolored & gold trim, marked USA....................................$225.00

Shawnee, Muggsy, decals & gold trim, marked Pat Muggsy USA $875.00

Shawnee, Muggsy, plain white w/blue trim, marked USA..$425.00

Shawnee, Owl Winking, hand-decorated & gold trim, marked USA $300.00

Shawnee, Owl Winking, white w/trimmed face & neck, marked USA $150.00

Shawnee, Puss 'n Boots, decals & gold trim, marked Pat Puss 'n Boots USA......................................$625.00

Shawnee, Sailor Boy, white w/cold-painted black trim, marked USA $125.00

Shawnee, Sailor Boy, yellow hair & gold neck tie, marked GOB & USA $725.00

Shawnee, Smiley the Pig, clover blooms, marked Pat Smiley USA..$500.00

Shawnee, Smiley the Pig, tulips, gold trim, marked USA..$475.00

Shawnee, Smiley the Pig, white w/blue neck scarf, black hooves & buttons, marked USA $300.00

Shawnee, Winnie the Pig, brown coat w/green collar, marked USA #61..$425.00

Shawnee, Winnie the Pig, clover blooms, marked Winnie USA $475.00

Shawnee (New), Billy in Dad's Sheriff Uniform........$175.00

Shawnee (New), Farmer Pig....................................$175.00

Shawnee (New), Sowly Pig......................................$175.00

Sierra Vista, Clown Jack-in-the-box, from $125.00 to $150.00. (Photo courtesy Joyce and Fred Roerig)

Sierra Vista, Elephant, blue w/white, black & yellow plaid vest..$150.00

Sierra Vista, Elephant Seated Looking Up, gray & white w/maroon ears......................................$125.00

Sierra Vista, Poodle Sitting Upright, gray & white w/pink bow..$200.00

Sierra Vista, Rooster, brown matt stain $50.00

Sierra Vista, Spaceship, matt brown, unmarked........$425.00

Sierra Vista, Stagecoach..$375.00

Sierra Vista, Train, happy face on front $95.00

Sigma, Agatha $200.00

Sigma, Beaver Fireman..$275.00

Sigma, Circus Fat Lady $200.00

Sigma, Circus Ringmaster $75.00

Sigma, Circus Strong Man $70.00

Sigma, Cubs Bear..$150.00

Sigma, Elephant w/Ball & Glove............................$150.00

Sigma, Fat Cat, in pink dress w/red dots $325.00

Sigma, Fat Cat, in tuxedo, minimum value $450.00

Sigma, Hortense..$175.00

Sigma, Kermit the Frog in TV................................$425.00

Sigma, Millicent..$250.00

Sigma, Panda Chef..$95.00

Sigma, Popcorn Vendor, minimum value $450.00

Sigma, Rag Doll..$225.00

Sigma, Santa w/Bag of Goodies $95.00

Sigma, Senorita $350.00

Sigma, Snowman $125.00

Sigma, Victoria $255.00

Sigma, Wind in the Willows, 1981 ....**$150.00**
Treasure Craft, Baseball...**$50.00**
Treasure Craft, Ben Franklin w/Liberty Bell, from $175
    to **$275.00**
Treasure Craft, Bowling Ball.......................................**$45.00**
Treasure Craft, Cookie Balloon...................................**$40.00**
Treasure Craft, Cowardly Lion **$300.00**
Treasure Craft, Dorothy & Toto.................................**$375.00**
Treasure Craft, Droopy Dog (I'm So Happy) **$375.00**
Treasure Craft, Football **$50.00**
Treasure Craft, Grandpa Munster **$275.00**
Treasure Craft, Herman Munster **$275.00**
Treasure Craft, Hobby Horse.......................................**$50.00**
Treasure Craft, Hobby Horse, plaid...........................**$55.00**
Treasure Craft, King Kong **$275.00**
Treasure Craft, Policeman Bear **$40.00**
Treasure Craft, Seymour J Snailsworth......................**$425.00**
Treasure Craft/Disney, Aladdin Genie Seated Holding Magic
    Lamp **$80.00**
Treasure Craft/Disney, Buzz Lightyear, from $185 to .**$240.00**
Treasure Craft/Disney, Donald Duck, seated w/arms fold-
    ed **$60.00**
Treasure Craft/Disney, Dopey (Snow White) **$50.00**
Treasure Craft/Disney, Goofy, seated Indian style......**$60.00**
Treasure Craft/Disney, Simba (Lion King) **$95.00**
Treasure Craft/Henson, Fozzie Bear...........................**$50.00**
Treasure Craft/Henson, Kermit the Frog, serenading
    w/banjo...**$75.00**
Treasure Craft/Henson, Miss Piggy, seated in glamorous
    pose **$50.00**
Treasure Craft/Henson, Miss Piggy on Column Jar.....**$75.00**
Twin Winton, Church..**$600.00**
Twin Winton, Cookie Elf, green, 8½x12" **$65.00**
Twin Winton, Cow, gray w/neck bell & bow in tail ..**$75.00**
Twin Winton, Cowboy Rabbit, Collector Series, fully paint-
    ed..**$225.00**
Twin Winton, Dutch Girl, Collector Series, fully painted ..**$200.00**
Twin Winton, Goose, in bonnet & shawl, Collector Series,
    fully painted, 1961 ....**$225.00**
Twin Winton, Happy Bull, gray w/floral ring around
    neck...**$90.00**
Twin Winton, Hobby Horse, Collector Series, fully paint-
    ed **$300.00**
Twin Winton, Lamb (For Good Little Lambs Only), Collector
    Series, fully painted...**$175.00**
Twin Winton, Lion & Lamb, wood stain w/white-painted
    lamb, painted features...**$500.00**
Twin Winton, Mouse, seated in sailor outfit, Collector Series,
    fully painted...**$175.00**
Twin Winton, Pear w/Worm, wood stain w/painted
    detail, avocado green, pineapple yellow, orange or
    red, ea **$300.00**
Twin Winton, Pirate Fox, Collector Series, fully painted, from
    $225 to...**$250.00**
Twin Winton, Pirate Fox, wood stain **$75.00**
Twin Winton, Police Bear, Collector Series, fully paint-
    ed **$125.00**

Twin Winton, Professor Owl, Collector Series, fully painted, $125.00. (Photo courtesy Ermagene Westfall)

Twin Winton, Ranger Bear, Collector Series, fully paint-
    ed **$125.00**
Twin Winton, Rooster, Collector Series, fully painted...**$125.00**
Ungemach, School House, marked CJ 7 USA **$150.00**
USA Demand Marketing, Big Bird, Bert & Ernie, multicol-
    ored **$45.00**
USA Pottery By JD, Nancy (head)............................**$150.00**
USA Pottery By JD, Nancy (seated) **$200.00**

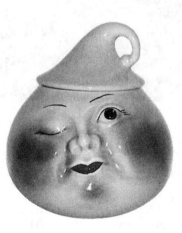

Vallona Starr, Winkie, original colors: pink and yellow with blush (beware of other colors), from $600.00 to $900.00. (Photo courtesy Bernice Stamper)

Vandor, Baseball **$55.00**
Vandor, Beethoven Piano...**$65.00**
Vandor, Betty Boop Head w/Top Hat, from $150 to ..**$200.00**
Vandor, Cowboy, stamped **$60.00**
Vandor, Crocagator **$75.00**
Vandor, Curious George on Rocketship......................**$60.00**
Vandor, Fred Flinstone Standing, from $150 to.........**$195.00**
Vandor, Frog Head, from $200 to................................**$275.00**
Vandor, Greatful Dead Bus, from $100 to **$130.00**
Vandor, Harley-Davidson Engine.................................**$55.00**
Vandor, Honeymooners Bus, from $120 to **$150.00**
Vandor, I Love Lucy Characters in Car, minimum value....**$150.00**
Vandor, Lamp **$35.00**
Vandor, Mona Lisa **$55.00**
Vandor, Pedal Car, from $35 to...................................**$50.00**
Vandor, Popeye, from $420 to.....................................**$500.00**
Vandor, Pull Toy Bear **$50.00**

Vandor, Toaster **$125.00**
Viacom, Real Monsters Garbage Can **$36.00**
Viacom, Tommy Pickles (Rugrats) **$40.00**
Wade, Brew Gaffer, 8⅜" **$150.00**
Wade, Peasant Woman w/Tray of Cookies, 1991, 10½"..**$110.00**
Warner Bros, Animaniacs, 1994 .... **$110.00**
Warner Bros, Bugs Bunny Bust w/Carrot **$45.00**
Warner Bros, Bugs Bunny Head (tall ears), Six Flags exclu-
    sive, 1994 .... **$35.00**
Warner Bros, Daffy Duck as Baseball Player **$45.00**
Warner Bros, Looney Tunes Garden Shop **$50.00**
Warner Bros, Michael Jordan Bust w/Bugs Bunny (Space
    Jam), 11" **$100.00**
Warner Bros, Pinky & the Brain, 1996, 12½" **$75.00**
Warner Bros, Porky Pig in TV, 1995, 10½" **$65.00**
Warner Bros, Taz, NFL Series, 1994, ea **$55.00**
Warner Bros, Yosemite Sam, 1993 .... **$50.00**

Vandor, Howdy Doody in Bumper Car, minimum value, $325.00. (Photo courtesy Ermagene Westfall)

Coors Rosebud Dinnerware

Golden, Colorado, was the site for both the Coors Brewing Company and the Coors Porcelain Company, each founded by the same man, Adolph Coors. The pottery's inception was in 1910, and in the early years they manufactured various ceramic products such as industrial needs, dinnerware, vases, and figurines; but their most famous line and the one we want to tell you about is 'Rosebud.'

The Rosebud 'Cook 'n Serve' line was introduced in 1934. It's very easy to spot, and after you've once seen a piece, you'll be able to recognize it instantly. It was made in solid colors — rose, blue, green, yellow, ivory, and orange. The rosebud and leaves are embossed and handpainted in contrasting colors. There are nearly fifty different pieces to collect, and bargains can still be found; but prices are accelerating, due to increased collector interest. For more information we recommend *Coors Rosebud Pottery* by Robert Schneider and *Collector's Encyclopedia of Colorado Pottery, Identification and Values,* by Carol and Jim Carlton.

Note: Yellow and white tends to craze and stain. Our prices are for pieces with minimal crazing and no staining. To evaluate pieces in blue, add 10% to the prices below; add 15% for items in ivory.

Advisor: Rick Spencer (See Directory, Regal China)

Newsletter: *Coors Pottery Newsletter*
Robert Schneider
3808 Carr Pl. N
Seattle, WA 98103-8126

Bean pot, lg. **$68.00**
Bowl, cream soup; 4" **$38.00**
Bowl, mixing; no rosebud, 6" **$35.00**
Bowl, mixing; no rosebud, 9" **$55.00**
Bowl, pudding; tab handles, 5" **$42.00**
Casserole, straight-sided, 8", w/lid **$75.00**
Casserole, triple service; w/lid, 2-pt **$64.00**
Creamer, from $32 to **$44.00**
Cup & saucer, from $42 to **$48.00**
Custard **$27.00**

Dutch casserole, sm, $72.00.

Egg cup **$54.00**
French casserole, 7½", w/lid **$90.00**
Honey pot, no spoon, w/lid, from $150 to **$180.00**
Jar, utility; no rosebud, rope handle, w/lid, 2½-pt **$90.00**
Loaf pan, from $42 to **$55.00**
Pie plate, from $38 to **$50.00**
Plate, 10" **$40.00**
Plate, 9¼" **$34.00**
Platter, 9x12", from $42 to **$48.00**
Ramekin, 4¼" **$40.00**
Salt & pepper shakers, sm individual size, pr **$75.00**
Salt & pepper shakers, straight, range size, pr **$70.00**
Salt & pepper shakers, tapered, range size, pr **$65.00**
Shirred egg dish, 6½" **$42.00**
Sugar shaker **$80.00**
Teapot, 2-cup, rare, from $145 to **$175.00**
Teapot, 6-cup, from $160 to **$185.00**
Tumbler, footed or handled, from $105 to **$130.00**

Cottage Ware

Made by several companies, cottage ware is a line of ceramic table and kitchen accessories, each piece styled as a cozy cottage with a thatched roof. At least four English potteries made the ware, and you'll find pieces marked 'Japan' as well as 'Occupied Japan.' From Japan you'll also find pieces styled as windmills and water wheels, though the quality is inferior. The better pieces are marked 'Price Brothers' and 'Occupied Japan.' They're compatible in coloring as well as in styling, and values run about the same. Items marked simply 'Japan' are worth considerably less.

Bank, English, 5" L **$85.00**
Bell, English (Price), rare, from $125 to **$150.00**
Bowl, salad; English **$65.00**
Butter dish, English...**$60.00**
Butter pat, embossed cottage, rectangular, Occupied Japan...**$17.50**
Chocolate pot, English **$135.00**

Condiment set, two shakers and mustard on leaf tray, Price Brothers, $75.00.

Condiment set, 2 shakers & mustard on tray, Occupied Japan...**$45.00**
Condiment set, 2 shakers & mustard pot on tray, row arrangement, 7¾"...**$45.00**
Condiment set, 3-part cottage on shaped tray w/applied bush, English, 4½"...**$75.00**
Cookie jar, lid w/dormer & chimney, English, 5½x4½x5", minimum value **$125.00**
Cookie jar, pink, brown & green, square, Japan, 8½x5½"..**$65.00**
Cookie jar, rectangular w/wicker handle, English or Occupied Japan..**$85.00**
Cookie jar, windmill, wicker handle, English (Price), rare, 5", minimum value **$135.00**
Cookie jar/canister, cylindrical, English, 8½x5".........**$125.00**
Cookie jar/canister, cylindrical, English, 8x3¾".........**$200.00**
Creamer, windmill, Occupied Japan, 2⅝"...................**$25.00**
Creamer & sugar bowl, English, 2½x4½" **$45.00**
Cup & saucer, English, 2½", 4½"................................**$45.00**
Demitasse pot, English **$100.00**
Dish w/cover, Occupied Japan, sm............................**$35.00**
Egg cups, 4 on 6½" square tray, English **$60.00**
Gravy boat & tray, English, rare, lg **$250.00**
Grease jar, Occupied Japan.......................................**$35.00**

Marmalade, English..**$40.00**
Mug, Price Bros..**$50.00**
Pin tray, English, 4" dia **$20.00**
Pitcher, water; English...**$150.00**
Salt & pepper shakers, windmill, Occupied Japan, pr..**$20.00**
Sugar bowl, windmill, w/lid, Occupied Japan, 3⅞"....**$25.00**
Sugar box, for cubes, English, 5¾" L **$45.00**
Tea set, child's, Japan, serves 4 ....**$150.00**
Teapot, English or Occupied Japan, 5".......................**$45.00**
Teapot, English or Occupied Japan, 6½".....................**$70.00**
Toast rack, English, from $65 to **$75.00**
Tumbler, Occupied Japan, 3½"...................................**$10.00**

Creamer and sugar bowl on 8" tray, Occupied Japan, $65.00.

Cow Creamers

Cow creamers (and milk pitchers) have been around since before the nineteenth century, but, of course, those are rare. But by the early 1900s, they were becoming quite commonplace. In many of these older ones, the cow was standing on a platform (base) and very often had a lid. Not all cows on platforms are old, however, but it is a good indication of age. Examples from before WWII often were produced in England, Germany, and Japan.

Over the last fifty years there has been a slow revival of interest in these little cream dispensers, including the plastic Moo cows, made by Whirley Industries, U.S.A, that were used in cafes during the '50s. With the current popularity of anything cow-shaped, manufacturers have expanded the concept, and some creamers now are made with matching sugar bowls. If you want to collect only vintage examples, nowadays you'll have to check closely to make sure they're not new.

Advisor: Shirley Green (See Directory, Cow Creamers)

Advertising, Dogpatch USA, white w/blue, Japan, 3½x4"..**$22.50**
Advertising, iridescent white, Worthing Parade, foreign, 4½x6"..**$28.00**
Advertising, Jell-O, multicolored, 5x6½"....................**$175.00**
Arthur Wood, ironstone, w/sailboat on side, England, 5½x7"...**$85.00**
Borden Co, Elsie on side, mark on bottom, white w/gold trim, 5x7" **$55.00**

Burleigh, lazy cow, blue & white, on base, 5x6½".....$60.00
C Cooke, w/suckling calf on platform, w/lid, 5x6½".$225.00

Calico, Burleigh, Staffordshire, England, ca 1975, 7" L, from $65.00 to $75.00. (Photo courtesy Shirley Green)

China, Blue Onion design, blue & white, sitting cow, 4x3½"..$20.00
Czech, marigold iridescent, reclining cow on base, 5½x7"..$55.00
Delft, blue & white w/windmill on side bell, Holland, 4x6½"..$22.00
Goebel, full bee mark, brown & white, 4x6"..............$35.00
Holstein, black & white, K403 on bottom, 4½x8"......$48.00

Hummel, full bee mark, Germany, 1960s, 4x6", from $35.00 to $45.00. (Photo courtesy Shirley Green)

Jackfield-type, red clay, w/lid, 19th century, on platform, 5½x7"..$175.00
Japan, luster, creamer & sugar bowl, Texas longhorn, w/lid, 5x6½"..$125.00
Kenmar, pink w/bell, Japan, 5x6½"..........................$30.00
Lefton, creamer & sugar bowl, tan w/white markings, 4x5½"..$42.00
McMaster, pottery, creamer & sugar bowl set, 4x6"....$37.00
Occupied Japan, green & tan, lg body, 6x5"..............$65.00
Staffordshire, chintz, multicolored, w/lid, on platform, 5½x7"..$135.00
Straucht Frae the Coo, white w/gold, Germany, 6x5½".$47.50
TG Green, reclining, tan, England, 4x6"....................$37.00
Unmarked, purple & white w/yellow horns, 3-pc set, 4x4½"..$17.50
Unmarked, white porcelain, for child's tea set, 1½x2".$15.00
Whirley, plastic, upright Moo Cow, 5x3"....................$15.00

Cowboy Character Collectibles

When we come across what is now termed cowboy character toys and memorabilia, it rekindles warm memories of childhood days for those of us who once 'rode the range' (often our backyards) with these gallant heroes. Today we can really appreciate them for the positive role models they were. They sat tall in the saddle; reminded us never to tell an un-truth; to respect 'women-folk' as well as our elders, animal life, our flag, our country, and our teachers; to eat all the cereal placed before us in order to build strong bodies; to worship God; and have (above all else) strong values that couldn't be compromised. They were Gene, Roy, and Tex, along with a couple of dozen other names, who rode beautiful steeds such as Champion, Trigger, and White Flash.

They rode into a final sunset on the silver screen only to return and ride into our homes via television in the 1950s. The next decade found us caught up in more western adventures such as Bonanza, Wagon Train, The Rifleman, and many others. These set the stage for a second wave of toys, games, and western outfits.

Annie Oakley was one of only a couple of cowgirls in the corral; Wild Bill Elliott used to drawl, 'I'm a peaceable man'; Ben Cartwright, Adam, Hoss, and Little Joe provided us with thrills and laughter. Some of the earliest collectibles are represented by Roy's and Gene's 1920s predecessors — Buck Jones, Hoot Gibson, Tom Mix, and Ken Maynard. There were so many others, all of whom were very real to us in the 1930s – '60s, just as their memories and values remain very real to us today.

Remember that few items of cowboy memorabilia have survived to the present in mint condition. When found, mint or near-mint items bring hefty prices, and they continue to escalate every year. Our values are for examples in good to very good condition.

For more information we recommend these books: *Roy Rogers, Singing Cowboy Stars, Silver Screen Cowboys, Hollywood Cowboy Heroes*, and *Western Comics: A Comprehensive Reference*, all by Robert W. Phillips. Other books include: *Collector's Guide to Hopalong Cassidy Memorabilia* by Joseph J. Caro, *Collector's Reference & Value Guide to The Lone Ranger* by Lee Felbinger, *W.F. Cody Buffalo Bill* by James W. Wojtowicz, and *Hake's Guide to Cowboy Character Collectibles* by Ted Hake.

See also Toys, Guns; Toys, Rings.

Advisor: Robert W. Phillips, Phillips Archives (See Directory, Character and Personality Collectibles)

Club/Newsletter: The Old Cowboy Picture Show
George F. Coan
PO Box 66
Camden, SC 29020; 803-432-9643

Club/Newsletter: Cowboy Collector
Joseph J. Caro, Publisher
P.O. Box 7486
Long Beach, CA 90807

Club/Newsletter: Hopalong Cassidy Fan Club International
and *Hopalong Cassidy Newsletter*
Laura Bates, Editor
6310 Friendship Dr.
New Concord, OH 4362-9708; 614-826-4850

Newsletter: *Gene Autry Star Telegram*
Gene Autry Development Association
Chamber of Commerce
P.O. Box 158, Gene Autry, OK 73436

Newsletter: *The Lone Ranger Silver Bullet*
P.O. Box 553
Forks, WA 98331; 206-327-3726

Annie Oakley, outfit, red blouse & fringed skirt w/silkscreened image of Annie on pockets, Pla-Master, 1950, NMIB..**$200.00**
Bat Masterson, cane, plastic w/chrome cover, 1958, NM..**$35.00**
Bat Masterson, wallet, Croyder, 1950s, NMIB..............**$75.00**
Bonanza, cup, features Adam, lithographed tin, 3½" dia, EX **$30.00**
Bonanza, record, cardboard, 'This Is a Musical Message From Ben Cartwright,' Chevy promotion, 1960s, NM (w/mailer)..**$50.00**
Bonanza, Stardust Touch of Velvet Art, Hasbro, complete, NMIB...**$85.00**
Bonanza, sweatshirt, white cotton w/portraits, logo & map, Norwich, 1960-63, rare, VG **$150.00**
Cisco Kid, hobbyhorse, vinyl w/wood handle, VG **$50.00**
Daniel Boone, Fess Parker Boone Pak, Standard Plastics/American Traditions Co, 1964, EX+ **$150.00**
Daniel Boone, Fess Parker Cartoon Kit, Colorforms, 1964, complete, MIB...**$35.00**
Davy Crockett, belt, elastic w/punch-out stand-up photo, England, NMOC **$65.00**
Davy Crockett, boots, leather w/yellow lettering on suede fringe, Davy pictured on side, 1950s, EX **$250.00**
Davy Crockett, charm bracelet, gold-colored metal w/7 charms, 1950s, NM...**$35.00**
Davy Crockett, guitar, fiberboard w/decal, complete w/pick & songbook, Peter Puppet/Walt Disney Productions, 25", EXIB..**$200.00**
Davy Crockett, hobbyhorse, wood w/heavy bouncing springs, 23x33", EX..**$175.00**
Davy Crockett, notebook binder, 3-ring, brown w/Davy on front, not Disney, 1950s, EX **$45.00**
Davy Crockett, shoe rack, yellow vinyl w/brown trim & images, 1950s, 12x26", EX......................................**$65.00**
Davy Crockett, sunglasses, white plastic w/rifles & image of Davy, green lenses, 1950s, EX..............................**$65.00**
Davy Crockett, vest, Davy w/musket on front & Davy fighting bear on back, brown vinyl w/fringe, 1950s, EX...**$100.00**
Davy Crockett, wallet, brown vinyl w/profile view of Davy in imitation fur cap, 1955, NMIB..........................**$100.00**
Gabby Hayes, sheriff's set, 1950s, MOC, from $75 to...**$100.00**
Gabby Hayes, target set, EXIB................................**$195.00**

Gene Autry, Adventure Story Trail Map, for display Schafer's Bread labels, 1950s, 22x17", EX..........................**$110.00**

Gene Autry, guitar, Emenee, ca 1950, tan plastic with embossed image of Gene and western scenes, 31", M (EX+ box), $225.00.

Gunsmoke, pencil case, features Matt Dillon, blue cardboard, Hasbro, 1961, 4x9", EX................................**$30.00**
Hoot Gibson, shirt, boy's, plaid w/Universal Jewel Ranch felt patch on pocket, 1930s, VG+ **$150.00**
Hopalong Cassidy, barette, silver-tone metal w/emb image of Hoppy, unmarked, NM....................................**$25.00**
Hopalong Cassidy, binoculars, metal & plastic w/paper decals, marked Sports Glass Chicago, EX...........**$165.00**
Hopalong Cassidy, film, Danger Trail, 16mm, Castle Films, 1950s, NM...**$30.00**
Hopalong Cassidy, money clip, silver w/photo flanked by name, marked USA, 2", NM...............................**$95.00**
Hopalong Cassidy, pen, bust image at top w/western symbols & name in white rope design, Parklite-Parker, 1950s, NM **$150.00**
Hopalong Cassidy, pennant, felt w/image of Hoppy on Topper w/name lettered in rope effect, 1950s, 27", EX **$95.00**
Hopalong Cassidy, picture frame, Your Pal Hopalong Cassidy, white cardboard w/green & black graphics, 1950s, 9x7", EX..**$65.00**
Hopalong Cassidy, poster, Compliments of New Sunny Spread, black & white image of Hoppy & Topper, 1950s, 22x17", NM...**$65.00**

Hopalong Cassidy, spurs, NM, $200.00.

Johnny Ringo, hand puppet, cloth body w/painted vinyl head & felt hands, Tops in Toys/Zane Grey, 1959-60, 10", EX+ **$50.00**

Lone Ranger, Action Arcade, 1975, NMIB, from $100 to **$125.00**

Lone Ranger, ballpoint pen, bust image of Lone Ranger on top w/name in white raised lettering, 1950s, 6", EX **$125.00**

Lone Ranger, bank, vinyl boot-shape w/cartoon artwork of Lone Ranger on Silver, British, 1960s, EX **$50.00**

Lone Ranger, binoculars, red & black plastic w/decals, red vinyl strap, 1950, EX, from $100 to **$125.00**

Lone Ranger, Cartoon Kit, Colorforms, 1966, complete, NMIB **$45.00**

Lone Ranger, crayons, 1953, complete, NM (NM tin box), from $75 to...**$100.00**

Lone Ranger, figure, chalkware w/glitter highlights, 1940s, 16", NM, from $75 to......................................**$100.00**

Lone Ranger, hat, green felt w/green repeated images of Lone Ranger, Tonto & name on yellow band, 1950s, EX..**$65.00**

Lone Ranger, horseshoe set, rubber, Gardner Games, 1950, complete, NMIB, from $175 to **$125.00**

Lone Ranger, magic slate, cardboard w/lift-up erasable film sheet, Whitman, 1978, EX, from $55 to **$75.00**

Lone Ranger, party horn, lithographed tin, 1950, EX..**$25.00**

Lone Ranger, pencil sharpener, silver bullet shape w/red & white Merita Bread decal on front, 1940s, NM.....**$65.00**

Lone Ranger, sleeping bag, image of Lone Ranger & Tonto, 1975, NM, from $75 to **$125.00**

Lone Ranger, telescope, 1946, NMIB, from $150 to..**$200.00**

Maverick, TV Eras-O-Picture Book, Hasbro, 1959, MIB (sealed) **$100.00**

Pancho, photo, black & white, Pancho on horse, Don't Miss the Cisco Kid & Pancho..., Butter-Nut promo, 1950s, 8x10", EX..**$25.00**

Range Rider, chair, wood folding-type w/image on black fabric back, white fringe on bottom, 1956, rare, 24", EX..**$75.00**

Red Ryder, token, target design on 1 side & Red Ryder embossed on the other, Daisy premium, 1938, 2", EX **$25.00**

Rin-Tin-Tin, outfit, Corporal Rusty 101st Cavalry, complete, Pla-Master, 1955, scarce, EXIB **$150.00**

Roy Rogers, bank, boot on horseshoe-shaped base, detailed metal w/copper lustre, 5", EX....................**$75.00**

Roy Rogers, banner, green felt w/white image & lettering, 1950s, 28", EX **$185.00**

Roy Rogers, Cowboy & Indian Kit, Colorforms, complete, NMIB..**$150.00**

Roy Rogers, doll, plastic w/fringed leather pants, green checked shirt, vest & hat, 1950s, 7", EX **$125.00**

Roy Rogers, flashlight, red & white plastic, Bantam, 1974, complete w/Trail Guide pamphlet, 3", NM........**$165.00**

Roy Rogers, gloves, w/Sears tag, M **$150.00**

Roy Rogers, mug, plastic head shape w/name on hat, Quaker Oats premium, 4", EX..............................**$25.00**

Roy Rogers, outfit, Merit Playsuits, 1950s, complete, NMIB **$350.00**

Roy Rogers, pencil box, brown wood-grain cardboard w/Roy & Trigger on lid, w/2 drawers & tray, 1950s, 2x9x5", EX..**$100.00**

Roy Rogers, scarf, color litho on silk fabric w/images of Roy & Trigger, 1950s, 22x22", EX+................................**$55.00**

Roy Rogers, scarf and cowboy hat slide set, #N367/USA, EX+ (EX box), $400.00.

Roy Rogers, wallet, embossed lettering on brown leather w/multicolored image, 1950s, NMIB...................**$150.00**

Sky King, Spy Detecto Writer, silver w/brass dial & backing, w/built-in magnifier & rubber stamp, 1950s premium, 2", EX..**$65.00**

Tales of Wells Fargo, coloring set, Transogram, 1959, complete, NMIB **$65.00**

Tom Mix, badge, Captain Ralston Straight Shooter, silver-tone w/hanging spur, 1940s, EX+ **$95.00**

Tom Mix, belt w/buckle, white plastic w/red check & cowboy design, brass buckle w/image & secret compartment, 1930s, EX..**$125.00**

Tom Mix, magnifier & compass, glow-in-the-dark plastic w/yellow fold-out magnifying glass, 1930s, EX....**$45.00**

Tom Mix, whistle ring, brass w/silver slide whistle, 1940s, EX **$65.00**

Wild Bill Hickok, Marshal Badge, Leslie-Henry, 1950s, 2", EX (w/5x4" card) **$100.00**

Wild Bill Hickok, Western Bunkhouse Kit, complete, Vornado, 1950s, MIB..**$65.00**

Wild Bill Hickok & Jingles, sign, cardboard, 'Try Our Brand Pardner...Dan-Dee Potato Chips...,' 1950s, 12x10", VG..**$175.00**

Wyatt Earp, guitar, 24", EX..**$125.00**

Wyatt Earp, spurs, plastic, Selcol, NMOC **$50.00**

Zorro, bolo tie, round slide w/image of Zorro, Westminster, 1950s, 1½" dia, MOC..**$50.00**

Zorro, charm bracelet, painted brass w/picture, figure, fan, castle, gun & foil, 1950s, NMIB **$100.00**

Zorro, hat & mask, M..**$100.00**

Zorro, key chain, flasher, WDP, 1966, EX....................**$35.00**

Zorro, pinwheel, wood pole w/plastic 8-point star, rings as it spins, 1950s, rare, EX **$150.00**

Zorro, TV Promotion Kit, box only, red cardboard w/silhouette image of Zorro & Disney's Zorro logo, 1950s, 13x14x4", EX..**$200.00**

Cracker Jack Toys

In 1869 Frederick Rueckheim left Hamburg, Germany, bound for Chicago, where he planned to work on a farm for his uncle. But farm life did not appeal to Mr. Rueckheim, and after the Chicago fire, he moved there and helped clear the debris. With another man whose popcorn and confectionary business had been destroyed in the fire, Mr. Rueckheim started a business with one molasses kettle and one hand popper. The following year, Mr. Rueckheim bought out his original partner and sent for his brother, Louis. The two brothers formed Rueckheim & Bro. and quickly prospered as they continued expanding their confectionary line to include new products. It was not until 1896 that the first lot of Cracker Jack was produced — and then only as an adjunct to their growing line. Cracker Jack was sold in bulk form until 1899 when H.G. Eckstein, an old friend, invented the wax-sealed package, which allowed them to ship it further and thus sell it more easily. Demand for Cracker Jack soared, and it quickly became the main product of the factory. Today millions of boxes are produced — each with a prize in every box.

The idea of prizes came along during the time of bulk packaging; it was devised as a method to stimulate sales. Later, as the wax-sealed package was introduced, a prize was given (more or less) with each package. Next, the prize was added into the package, but still not every package received a prize. It was not until the 1920s that 'a prize in every package' became a reality. Initially, the prizes were put in with the confection, but the company feared this might pose a problem, should it inadvertently be mistaken for the popcorn. To avoid this, the prize was put in a separate compartment and, finally, into its own protective wrapper. Hundreds of prizes have been used over the years, and it is still true today that there is 'a prize in every package.' Prizes have ranged from the practical girl's bracelet and pencils to tricks, games, disguises, and stick-anywhere patches. To learn more about the subject, you'll want to read *Cracker Jack Toys, The Complete Unofficial Guide for Collectors*, and *Cracker Jack, The Unauthorized Guide to Advertising Collectibles*, both by our advisor, Larry White.

Advisor: Larry White (See Directory, Cracker Jack)

Airplane, lithographed tin, orange w/black & red circles...**$45.00**
Airplane, tin, green & yellow...**$55.00**
Airplane card, paper, multicolored, marked CJR-2, miniature, 6 different, ea **$2.00**
Alphabet animals, plastic, marked Nosco, various colors, ea...**$4.00**
Alphabet charms, plastic, marked CJ Co, various colors, ea...**$4.00**
Animal charms, lion, rabbit, camel, fox, horse, etc, pot metal, various colors, unmarked, ea..................................**$5.00**
Badge, Smitty, plastic **$42.00**
Banjo, lithographed tin..................................**$47.00**
Bike sticker, paper w/bike wheel on cover, various colors, ID 1380, 10 different, ea **$5.00**

Book, Baby Bears, paper, CJ box on back, 12 different, ea **$170.00**
Bookmark, spaniel, bulldog, collie or Scottie, lithographed tin, ea..**$14.00**
Circus animals, lithographed tin, 5 different, ea **$135.00**
Clicker, Frog Chirper, black on green.....................**$30.00**
Clicker/screamer, metal.....................................**$40.00**
Coin, plastic, red..**$5.00**
Dexterity puzzle, Cow Jumped Over the Moon, celluloid on paper, CJ box on back **$80.00**
Dexterity puzzle, Gee Cracker Jack Is Good.............**$125.00**
Figure, baseball player, plastic, gray or blue, marked CJ Co, ea...**$20.00**
Figure, boy, girl, soldier, Santa, etc, ceramic, marked Japan, ea...**$18.00**
Figure, skunk, squirrel, fish, etc, plastic, 1950, EX, ea..**$10.00**
Game, Monkey Ring Toss, paper, red & green, 1940, EX..**$30.00**
Garage, lithographed tin **$78.00**
Halloween mask, paper, orange, black & red, 5 different, ea **$22.00**
Horse & wagon, lithographed tin w/Cracker Jack & Angelus boxes, red, white & blue.....................................**$65.00**
Indian headdress, Me For Cracker Jack **$230.00**
Invisible magic picture, image of man fishing, What Will He Catch?..**$12.00**
Jigsaw puzzle, paper, several different, ea **$10.00**
Magic picture, image of man holding hoop, Who's Jumping Thru!..., plastic...**$10.00**
Magic square, hidden pictures, paper, several different, ea..**$4.00**
Magnifying glass, plastic, various edge designs, unmarked, ea **$3.00**
Minute movie, Cloudcrest Creations, paper, orange & black on white, 12 different, ea.....................................**$20.00**
Palm puzzle, image of 2 cats, marked Germany.........**$45.00**
Palm puzzle, kangaroo, elephant, etc, plastic bubble on paper, multicolored, ea.....................................**$7.00**
Pencil, wood, red lettering on white......................**$7.00**
Pencil stencils, B Series 13, paper, multicolored, 20 different, ea **$10.00**
Picture panorama, circus, barnyard animals, etc, paper, EX, ea **$10.00**
Pin, Pied Piper, metal.......................................**$65.00**
Pin, Victorian lady on paper insert...........................**$90.00**
Pipe, dog's head, ceramic, red, pink & blue, Japan ...**$10.00**
Pocket clip, whale, dog, Sailor Jack, etc, various colors, ea **$2.00**
Put-together prize, plastic, several different, unmarked, ea **$10.00**
Puzzle, Last Round-Up, paper, red & green, 1940, EX .**$30.00**
Razz Zooka whistle, paper, red & white....................**$50.00**
Riddle book, Cracker Jack w/jester, paper **$45.00**
Riddle card, paper, CJ box on front, riddles on back.**$20.00**
Ring, wheel, heart or other faux stone, pot metal, unmarked, ea **$12.00**
Shuffle game, paper, red, green & black....................**$26.00**
Sled, metal w/silver finish.................................**$18.00**

Slide card, Cracker Jack, fireman, pear, owl, cat, etc, paper, ea $95.00

Slide card, Cracker Jack Movies, paper, yellow front .$120.00

Spinner game, Cracker Jack Golf $90.00

Squirt gun, early...$90.00

Stand-up, circus theme w/popcorn vendor & 2 acrobats, plastic, various colors, unmarked, ea $3.00

Stand-up, Herby...$80.00

Sticker, glow-in-the-dark, black on yellow, 1970, EX ...$4.00

Tilt card, magician, elephant, pirate, etc, plastic & paper, 1950, EX, ea...$8.00

Tools, hammer, saw, pipe wrench, etc, plastic, various colors, unmarked, ea $4.00

Top, Always on Top, red, white & blue, w/Cracker Jack prize box $55.00

Train, engine, coal tender, boxcar, tanker & caboose, plastic, EX..$10.00

Train, Lone Eagle Flyer, lithographed tin, 4 different, ea .$120.00

Tray, lithographed tin w/Cracker Jack box, red & white on blue $95.00

Trick mustache, paper, red or black, 1940, EX, ea $20.00

Typewriter, lithographed tin $95.00

Visor, marked Cracker Jack, paper, green $125.00

Wheel walker, elephant, police dog, pig, etc, unmarked, ea $28.00

Zodiac coin, plastic, various colors, ea $8.00

First row: metal Man-in-the-Moon plate, $95.00; metal patriotic whistle, $85.00; plastic astronaut, $10.00. Second row: Cracker Jack Air Corp stud, $95.00. Third row: plastic and paper rising moon palm puzzle, $85.00; metal Mary Lu Quick Delivery truck, $78.00; plastic invisible magic picture, $9.00. (Photo courtesy Mary and Larry White)

Crackle Glass

At the height of productivity from the 1930s through the 1970s, nearly five hundred companies created crackle glass. As pieces stayed in production for several years, dating an item may be difficult. Some colors, such as ruby red, ambe-

rina, cobalt, and cranberry, were more expensive to produce. Smoke gray was made for a short time, and because quantities are scarce, prices tend to be higher than on some of the other colors, amethyst, green, and amber included. Crackle glass is still being produced today by the Blenko Glass Company, and it is being imported from Taiwan and China as well. For further information on other glass companies and values we recommend *Crackle Glass, Identification and Value Guide, Book I and Book II,* by Stan and Arlene Weitman (Collector Books).

Advisors: Stan and Arlene Weitman (See Directory, Crackle Glass)

Apple, cobalt, Blenko, 1950s – 60s, 4½", from $50.00 to $75.00. (Photo courtesy Stan and Arlene Weitman)

Basket, topaz w/crystal handle, Pilgrim, 1960s, 4¾" ..$65.00

Bowl, light blue, scalloped, Blenko, 1960s, 5½x2½"..$50.00

Bowl, ruby, heart shape, yellow handle, Rainbow, 1950-60s, 3¼x2¾"...$70.00

Creamer, blue, drop-over handle, Rainbow, 1957-87, 3"...$40.00

Cruet, blue, pulled-back handle, Pilgrim, 1949-69, 6¾"..$75.00

Cruet, orange, pulled back handle, Rainbow, 1940s-60s, 6¾" $75.00

Decanter, amber, straight sides, ball stopper, Czechoslovakian, 1920s, 7" $135.00

Decanter, blue, bent neck, drop-over handle, Blenko, late 1940s, 11½"...$135.00

Decanter, blue, ruffled rim, Blenko, 1940s-50s, 10¾" ...$110.00

Decanter, captain's; green, Blenko, 1965, 13¾" $165.00

Decanter, captain's; ruby, Pilgrim, 1949-69, 10x8" $215.00

Decanter, crystal, bulbous body, ball stopper, Bonita, 1931-53, 6¼"...$90.00

Decanter, topaz, Rainbow, 1953, 11" $110.00

Hat, turquoise, Blenko, 1950s-60s, 3".........................$65.00

Patio light, topaz, Viking, 1944-60, 3x5" $45.00

Pitcher, amberina, pulled-back handle, Hamon, 1940s-66, 4½"...$50.00

Pitcher, amberina, ribbed drop-over handle, Pilgrim, 1949-69, 3½"...$45.00

Pitcher, blue, crystal handle, Rainbow, 1940-60s, 6"..$65.00

Pitcher, blue green, drop-over handle, Rainbow, 1950s, 5¼"...$50.00

Pitcher, butterscotch, crystal drop-over handle, Heritage, paper label, 5"...$75.00

Pitcher, chartreuse, drop-over handle, Pilgrim, 1960s, 6½" **$65.00**

Pitcher, crystal, amber drop-over handle, Hamon, 1960s, 5¼" **$50.00**

Pitcher, crystal, blue drop-over handle, blue twist down from rim, Blenko, 1960s, 12¾" **$130.00**

Pitcher, emerald green, crystal drop-over handle, Bischoff, 1950s, 8" **$80.00**

Pitcher, emerald green, pointed stopper, ruffled rim, Rainbow, 1940s-60s, 12".....................................**$165.00**

Pitcher, green, pulled-back handle, Rainbow, 1940s-60s, 9¼" **$85.00**

Pitcher, ruby, yellow drop-over handle, Blenko, 1960s, 5½" **$55.00**

Pitcher, tangerine/amberina, drop-over handle, Blenko, 1973, 10" **$95.00**

Pitcher, vaseline yellow, pulled-back handle, Rainbow, 1940s-60s, 4"....................................**$45.00**

Tumbler, crystal w/green snake, European, 1920s, 8" ..**$80.00**

Tumbler, ruby, pinched, Bischoff, 1950s, 3½".............**$55.00**

Vase, amethyst, Hamon, 1940s-50s, 9½" **$125.00**

Vase, blue, Blenko, 1960s, 5½"....................................**$55.00**

Vase, cobalt blue, 1940s, 4"..**$75.00**

Vase, green, ruffled rim, Jamestown, 1959-68, 5"........**$45.00**

Vase, green w/crystal foot, 13" **$175.00**

Vase, orange, ruffled rim, Rainbow, 1940s-60s, 5" **$50.00**

Vase, orange, scalloped, footed, Blenko, 1940s-50s, 7"...**$130.00**

Vase, penguin shape; blue gray, polished pontil, 6½" **$115.00**

Vase, tangerine/amberina, Blenko, 1950s, 8"..............**$85.00**

Pitcher, amberina, pulled back handle, Kanawha, 1957 – 70s, 5¼", from $60.00 to $65.00. (Original labels increase values.) (Photo courtesy Stan and Arlene Weitman)

Cuff Links

Many people regard cuff links as the ideal collectible. Cuff links are very available; they can be found at almost every garage sale, flea market, thrift store, and antique shop. Cuff links can also be very affordable. Collectors take pride in showing off great looking examples which they bought for only a dollar or two. Some of these cuff links turn out to be worth a lot more! The possibility of such 'finds' is one of the many joys of cuff link collecting, but it's educational as well fun for the whole family. In use for centuries as cuff fasteners and an item of fashion, cuff links have always mimicked the art of their period.

It is easy to display a cuff link collection. Their small size is convenient for curio cabinets, shadow boxes, wall framing, and shelf arrangements. Storing a cuff link collection is simple. Entire collections can often be stored on a closet shelf or in a dresser drawer. Some cuff-linking families devote weekend days to garage sales and flea markets. Often individual family members have their own areas of specialization. These include antique, modern, large, small, fraternal, advertising themes, metal, wood, glass, etc. Some collectors even specialize in 'singles' — they enjoy the art form and the search for the mate. It's no wonder that cuff links are one of the fastest-growing collectibles in the world.

Advisor: Gene Klompus (See Directory, Cuff Links)

Club: The National Cuff Link Society

Newsletter: *The Link*
Gene Klompus, President
P.O. Box 5700
Vernon Hills, IL 60010
Phone or fax: 847-816-0035
e-mail: Genek@cufflink.com

Dice (removable), made in Austria (marked), ca 1960, American Toggle closure, ca 1960, EX, $75.00. (Photo courtesy Gene Klompus)

Antique, gold-plated base metal, Florentine pattern, loop prong closure, ca 1880, ¾" square, G.................**$150.00**

Art Deco triangle w/sm pearl in center, double-sided, American Toggle closure, ca 1940, EX..................**$75.00**

Baseball glove w/ball in 'mitt position,' figural, gold-colored base metal, ca 1935, good condition.....................**$95.00**

Bill Clinton, American Eagle raised in center against blue background, beaded border, MIB **$495.00**

Bowling pin & ball, 14k gold (8 grams), American Toggle closure, ca 1975, M..**$250.00**

Camp David, Presidential Eagle on blue background, Presidental Retreat, Camp David around white edge, clear cover...**$250.00**

Century of Progress, including original Marshall Field & Co souvenir box, rare **$175.00**

Comedy/Tragedy 'masks,' base metal, gold color, round lever closure, ca 1895, ½" faces, VG **$100.00**

Dachshund dog, brown & white enamel, double-sided, chain connector, ca 1920, VG **$125.00**

Domino motif, black & white, rectangular, vinyl, toggle closure, ca 1955, good condition (minor scratches on 1) **$30.00**

Enamel, octagon shape, blue & black, double-sided, ca 1960, M **$85.00**

Enamel, purple & black, double-sided, round, ca 1960, M **$85.00**

Grecian head w/Grecian Key relief, metal base, silver color, double-sided w/chain connector closure, ca 1905, ¾" dia **$100.00**

Horse head, gold-plated base metal, blue celluloid surround horsehead inset, loop prong closure, ca 1883, ¾" square, G **$250.00**

Indian head pennies, relief removed, copper alloy, American Toggle closure, hand carved, ca 1950, ¾" dia......**$45.00**

Jade (faux), oval faces in base metal filigree surround, wraparound closure, Destino brand, ca 1955, ¾" L, ornate box..**$45.00**

Lovebirds motif, porcelain, multicolored enamel w/gold leaf surround, flat disc closure, ca 1920, VG **$95.00**

Marilyn Monroe, red oval, centerfold pose from 1st Playboy Magazine **$100.00**

Peace sign, base metal, silver color, was rallying symbol for 1960s-era peace movement, ca 1960, ¾" dia........**$50.00**

Photographs, 1 male face, 1 female face, 14k gold, beaded surround, ca 1910, ¾", EX **$175.00**

Pierre Cardin, cultured pearls in gold-colored star setting, ca 1960 ....**$45.00**

Pistol motif, six-shooters to scale, silver color, ca 1950 ..**$75.00**

Precious, 14k (15.7 grams), ea contains a beveled arch rectangular carnelian stone w/hand-engraved edge, ca 1965..**$700.00**

Presidental Helicopter HMX-1, die-struck Presidental Eagle surrounded by Presidental Helicopter Squadron HMX-1, MIB **$150.00**

Ronald Reagan, Seal of the President of the United States, flat, Reagan's name on top of original blue box........**$245.00**

Scroll theme, gold-plated base metal, prong closure, ca 1875, EX, $100.00. (Photo courtesy Gene Klompus)

Snappers, state initials, ca 1920, M, ea..........................**$40.00**

Star design, gold plate, rare hinged closure, modified square shape, ca 1885, ¾"..**$75.00**

Sunburst design, gold filled, ea w/synthetic amethyst w/open back, oval, ca 1950, ¾x½", sm scratch on 1 ....**$50.00**

Thunderbird, sterling silver, black wings & body, inscribed back, ca 1950, 1x½"..**$80.00**

US Navy Anchors, base metal, silver color, double-sided w/flat chain closure, ca 1950, ½" square..............**$75.00**

Utensils, 1 fork & 1 knife, mother-of-pearl handles, ca 1955 .**$45.00**

Watch, 1 working watch, 1 a complimentary design, rectangular, metal base, gold color, brushed finish, ca 1955, ¾x1"..**$135.00**

Wedgwood, black w/white horse jumping over bar, gold filled, w/tie tack, ca 1955..**$225.00**

Wedgwood, Gemini or Sagittarius sign, ca 1955, ea **$150.00**

Wraparounds, faux gemstone, different colors, ca 1965, ea **$35.00**

Accessories

Tie bar, Marilyn Monroe, green oval, centerfold pose from 1st Playboy Magazine, ca 1960 ....**$75.00**

Tie bar, Piercers, appears to pierce tie, sword or arrow, ca 1949, ea **$15.00**

Czechoslovakian Glass and Ceramics

Established as a country in 1918, Czechoslovakia is rich in the natural resources needed for production of glassware as well as pottery. Over the years it has produced vast amounts of both. Anywhere you go, from flea markets to fine antique shops, you'll find several examples of their lovely pressed and cut glass scent bottles, Deco vases, lamps, kitchenware, tableware, and figurines.

More than thirty-five marks have been recorded; some are ink stamped, some etched, and some molded in. Paper labels have also been used. *Czechoslovakian Glass and Collectibles* by Diane and Dale Barta and Helen M. Rose, and *Made in Czechoslovakia* by Ruth Forsythe are two books we highly recommend for further study. (Both are published by Collector Books.)

Club: Czechoslovakian Collectors Guild International
P.O. Box 901395
Kansas City, MO 64190

Ceramics

Basket, floral, blue & yellow, Eichwald Majolica, 7½"..**$185.00**

Box, red flower w/green leaves on pale yellow, rectangular, 3x6", from $40 to **$45.00**

Candy basket, lustreware flower form w/applied orange handle, 4¼" **$25.00**

Covered dish, duck figural, multicolor (muted colors), 4¼", from $40 to...**$45.00**

Creamer, cow figural, white w/orange lustre tail, 3" ..**$48.00**

Creamer, pearlescent lustreware w/green rim & handle, slightly inverted cylinder, 3¾", from $20 to........**$25.00**

Creamer, pink lustreware top & handle, green lustreware bottom divided by black band, 3¼", from $35 to **$40.00**

Creamer, swan figural, white w/orange & black details, w/lid, 3¼", from $50 to...**$55.00**

Dinnerware, Sylvia pattern, 8-place set w/serving pieces ..**$415.00**

Figurine, cat, white w/pink details, 5", from $40 to ...**$45.00**

Figurine, colt standing w/stiff legs, short tail up, 5½", from $45 to **$50.00**

Flower holder, bird on stump figural, multicolor on green base, 4½", from $35 to **$40.00**

Mustard pot, pansies on white w/black trim, black loop finial, 3½", from $45 to..**$50.00**

Napkin ring, girl figural, 4" **$27.50**

Pitcher, chicken figural, red & white w/black beak spout, 7½", from $50 to...**$55.00**

Pitcher, milk; painted to resemble wood grain w/knothole, shades of brown w/black band at rim, 5¾".........**$45.00**

Pitcher, pancake batter; poppies w/green vining leaves on white, orange trim, Erphila, from $50 to **$55.00**

Plate, Tartan plaid, brown, light green, tan, red & black, Erphila mark, from $25 to...................................**$30.00**

Sprinkling can, floral garland on white, 4½"...............**$35.00**

Vase, classical ladies pull Cupid in wagon reserve on blue, trumpet neck, 3¾", from $25 to **$30.00**

Vase, pearlescent blue mottle, slightly bulbous, 8", from $45 to..**$50.00**

Vase, varigated pastels w/glossy finish, bulbous w/sm handles, 4¾", from $45 to...**$50.00**

Wall pocket, bird among apples, 4¾".............................**$50.00**

Watering can, 2 swans in water on white, 5¼", from $45 to..**$50.00**

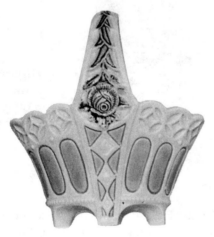

Basket, yellow with green oval panels and red rose, 6", from $40.00 to $45.00. (Photo courtesy Dale and Diane Barta and Helen M. Rose)

Glassware

Bowl, white cased w/fluted crystal rim, 3", from $40 to..**$45.00**

Box, powder; red cased w/coralene flower design, 3½" dia, from $40 to...**$50.00**

Candlestick, multicolored mottle in autumn tones, wide foot, 3"...**$55.00**

Candy basket, black w/silver mica, blue interior, jet handle, 8"...**$350.00**

Candy basket, mottled red & yellow, crystal straight-top handle, 8½"...**$125.00**

Candy bowl, green & white w/green aventurine, cased, 3 black buttressed feet, 4½", from $45 to...............**$50.00**

Champagne glass, cranberry w/swirled ribs, crystal stem, 6", from $40 to..**$45.00**

Compote, orange cased w/applied jet feet, 5¾" dia, from $80 to...**$90.00**

Decanter, amber w/embossed rings, flat stopper, 9" ..**$95.00**

Perfume bottle, amber cut to clear, atomizer, 8½"....**$200.00**

Perfume bottle, crystal stepped shape w/frosted lovebirds stopper, 4⅜"...**$165.00**

Perfume bottle, topaz shouldered shape, shield-shaped stopper, 5½"...**$160.00**

Pitcher, orange & green segments, clear handle, 12½" ...**$250.00**

Pitcher, smoke color w/applied jet handle & red threading at top half, inverted cone form, 6", from $80 to **$90.00**

Pitcher, yellow & red mottle w/applied cobalt handle & rim, 3 spouts (unusual), 4", from $70 to.....................**$75.00**

Salt & pepper shakers, crystal waffle weave, 3½", pr, from $25 to...**$30.00**

Salt & pepper shakers, cut crystal, 2", pr, from $20 to .**$25.00**

Vase, black amethyst, bottle neck w/flared rim, slightly bulbous, 6", from $30 to...**$35.00**

Vase, black amethyst w/silver overlay decor, slim, 6⅛", from $95 to...**$100.00**

Vase, blue w/cream & pink flecks, cobalt overlay, cobalt pedestal foot, 9½", from $125 to........................**$130.00**

Vase, bud; blue varigated, cased, 8½", from $60 to....**$65.00**

Vase, bud; pink w/wide swirled ribs & applied white threading, globular w/bottle neck, 5¼", from $30 to.....**$35.00**

Vase, cream w/mottled red & yellow base, fluted rim, slim, 9", from $60 to...**$65.00**

Vase, crystal w/red spiral threading, cylindrical, 8¼"..**$150.00**

Vase, exotic bird hand painted on black, silver rim, classic shape, 7¼"...**$145.00**

Vase, green cased w/jet serpentine, slim inverted cylinder, 6½", from $50 to..**$60.00**

Vase, light pink w/cobalt overlay streak on body, red & blue mottled base, ruffled rim, 9¼", from $150 to **$160.00**

Vase, orange cased, jack-in-the-pulpit form, 7", from $45 to **$50.00**

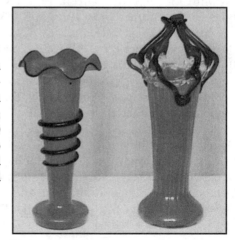

Vases, red with black applications, 8¼", from $90.00 to $95.00; 10½", from $95.00 to $100.00. (Photo courtesy Dale and Diane Barta and Helen M. Rose)

Vase, orange w/black serpentine, inverted cylinder, 8" ..**$90.00**

Vase, pale blue opaque w/embossed swirl design, flared rim, footed, 6", from $40 to **$45.00**

Vase, pink w/hand-painted scenic decor, slim shouldered form, 7½"..**$85.00**

Vase, red & yellow mottle w/applied blue rigaree, bulbous w/short flared rim, 5½", from $80 to **$90.00**

Vase, yellow & white mottle, w/metal flower arranger, 4¼" **$75.00**

Vase, yellow cased w/applied black serpentine trim, gourd form, 9", from $45 to **$50.00**

Dakin

Dakin has been in the toy-making business since the 1950s and has made several lines of stuffed and vinyl dolls and animals. But the Dakins that collectors are most interested in today are the licensed characters and advertising figures made from 1968 through the '70s. Originally there were seven Warner Brothers characters, each with a hard plastic body and a soft vinyl head, all under 10" tall. The line was very successful and eventually expanded to include more than fifty cartoon characters and several more that were advertising related. In addition to the figures, there are banks that were made in two sizes. Some Dakins are quite scarce and may sell for over $100.00 (a few even higher), though most will be in the $30.00 to $60.00 range. Dakin is now owned by Applause, Inc.

Condition is very important, and if you find one still in the original box, add about 50% to its value. Figures in the colorful 'Cartoon Theatre' boxes command higher prices than those that came in a clear plastic bag or package (MIP). More Dakins are listed in *Schroeder's Collectible Toys, Antique to Modern*, published by Collector Books.

Advisor: Jim Rash (See Directory, Dakins)

Baby Puss, Hanna-Barbera, 1971, EX+ **$100.00**

Bamm-Bamm, Hanna-Barbera, w/club, 1970, EX **$35.00**

Bay View, bank, 1976, EX+ **$30.00**

Bob's Big Boy, missing hamburger o/w VG **$80.00**

Bozo the Clown, Larry Harmon, 1974, EX...................**$35.00**

Bugs Bunny, Warner Bros, 1976, MIB (TV Cartoon Theater box) **$40.00**

Bugs Bunny, Warner Bros, 1978, MIB (Fun Farm bag) .**$20.00**

Bull Dog, Dream Pets, EX..**$15.00**

Christian Bros Brandy, St Bernard, 1982, VG **$30.00**

Cool Cat, Warner Bros, w/beret, 1970, EX+ **$40.00**

Daffy Duck, Warner Bros, 1976, MIB (TV Cartoon Theater box) **$40.00**

Deputy Dawg, Terrytoons, 1977, EX............................**$40.00**

Dewey Duck, Disney, straight or bent legs, EX..........**$40.00**

Donald Duck, Disney, 1960s, straight or bent legs, EX ..**$20.00**

Dumbo, Disney, 1960s, cloth collar, MIB **$25.00**

Elmer Fudd, Warner Bros, 1968, tuxedo, EX...............**$30.00**

Foghorn Leghorn, Warner Bros, 1970, EX+ **$75.00**

Freddie Fast, 1976, M **$100.00**

Goofy, Disney, 1960s, EX...**$20.00**

Goofy Gram, Dog, You're Top Dog, EX.......................**$20.00**

Goofy Gram, Kangaroo, World's Greatest Mom!, EX ..**$20.00**

Hokey Wolf, 1971, EX, $250.00. (Photo courtesy Jim Rash)

Huckleberry Hound, Hanna-Barbera, 1970, EX+ **$75.00**

Jack-in-the-Box, bank, 1971, EX...................................**$25.00**

Kangaroo, Dream Pets, EX...**$15.00**

Kernal Renk, American Seeds, 1970, rare, EX+.........**$350.00**

Louie Duck, Disney, straight or bent legs, EX **$30.00**

Merlin the Magic Mouse, Warner Bros, 1970, EX+......**$25.00**

Mickey Mouse, Disney, 1960s, cloth clothes, EX **$20.00**

Midnight Mouse, Dream Pets, w/original tag, EX.......**$15.00**

Mighty Mouse, Terrytoons, 1978, EX, $100.00. (Photo courtesy Jim Rash)

Minnie Mouse, Disney, 1960s, cloth clothes, EX.........**$20.00**

Monkey on a Barrel, bank, 1971, EX **$25.00**

Olive Oyl, King Features, 1976, MIB (TV Cartoon Theater box) **$40.00**

Opus, 1982, cloth, w/tag, 12", EX **$15.00**

Pepe Le Peu, Warner Bros, 1971, EX **$55.00**

Pink Panther, Mirisch-Frelong, 1976, MIB (TV Cartoon Theater box)..**$50.00**

Popeye, King Features, 1974, cloth clothes, MIP **$50.00**

Porky Pig, Warner Bros, 1968, EX+.............................**$30.00**

Quasar Robot, bank, 1975, NM **$150.00**

Road Runner, Warner Bros, 1968, EX+ **$30.00**

Rocky Squirrel, Jay Ward, 1976, MIB (TV Cartoon Theater box)..**$60.00**
Sambo's Boy, 1974, EX+ **$75.00**
Sambo's Tiger, 1974, EX+...**$125.00**
Scooby Doo, Hanna-Barbera, 1980, EX **$75.00**
Seal on a Box, bank, 1971, EX...................................**$25.00**
Second Banana, Warner Bros, 1970, EX **$35.00**
Smokey Bear, 1974, MIP **$20.00**
Smokey Bear, 1976, MIB (TV Cartoon Theater box) ..**$30.00**
Speedy Gonzales, Warner Bros, MIB (TV Cartoon Theater box) **$50.00**
Stan Laurel, Larry Harmon, 1974, EX+ **$30.00**
Swee' Pea, beanbag doll, King Features, 1974, VG **$20.00**
Sylvester, Warner Bros, 1968, EX+..............................**$20.00**
Sylvester, Warner Bros, 1978, MIP (Fun Farm bag) **$20.00**
Tiger in a Cage, bank, 1971, EX.................................**$25.00**
Tweety Bird, Warner Bros, 1966, EX+..........................**$20.00**
Tweety Bird, Warner Bros, 1976, MIB (TV Cartoon Theater box) **$40.00**
Wile E Coyote, bank, 1971, EX...................................**$30.00**
Wile E Coyote, Warner Bros, 1968, MIB **$30.00**
Woodsey Owl, 1974, MIP..**$60.00**
Yosemite Sam, Warner Bros, 1968, MIB.......................**$40.00**

Decanters

The first company to make figural ceramic decanters was the James Beam Distilling Company. Until mid-1992 they produced hundreds of varieties in their own US-based china factory. They first issued their bottles in the mid-'50s, and over the course of the next twenty-five years, more than twenty other companies followed their example. Among the more prominent of these were Brooks, Hoffman, Lionstone, McCormick, Old Commonwealth, Ski Country, and Wild Turkey. In 1975, Beam introduced the 'Wheel Series,' cars, trains, and fire engines with wheels that actually revolved. The popularity of this series resulted in a heightened interest in decanter collecting.

There are various sizes. The smallest (called miniatures) hold two ounces, and there are some that hold a gallon! A full decanter is worth no more than an empty one, and the absence of the tax stamp doesn't lower its value either. Just be sure that all the labels are intact and that there are no cracks or chips. You might want to empty your decanters as a safety precaution (many collectors do) rather than risk the possibility of the inner glaze breaking down and allowing the contents to leak into the porous ceramic body.

All of the decanters we've listed are fifths unless we've specified 'miniature' within the description.

See also Elvis Presley Collectibles.

Advisor: Art and Judy Turner, Homestead Collectibles (See Directory, Decanters)

Newsletter: *Beam Around the World*
International Association of Jim Beam Bottle and Specialties Clubs
Shirley Sumbles, Executive Administrator
2015 Burlington Ave., Kewanee, IL 61443; 309-853-3370

Newsletter: *The Ski Country Collector*
1224 Washington Ave., Golden, CO 80401

Beam, Centennial Series, Statue of Liberty 1976 ....**$20.00**
Beam, Convention Series, #15 Las Vegas Showgirl, brunette **$30.00**
Beam, Convention Series, #19 Kansas City................**$45.00**
Beam, Convention Series, #9 Houston Cowboy, beige .**$30.00**
Beam, Organization Series, Ducks Unlimited #05, Canvasback Drake, 1979 ....**$45.00**
Beam, Organization Series, Ducks Unlimited #07, Green-winged Teal, 1981..**$40.00**
Beam, Organization Series, Ducks Unlimited #15, Black Duck, 1989 ....**$95.00**
Beam, Organization Series, Phi Sigma Kappa **$24.00**

Beam, Organization Series, Telephone #3, 1928 Cradle style, $25.00.

Beam, People Series, Hannah Dustin...........................**$40.00**
Beam, Regal China Series, Christmas Tree w/paperweight...**$140.00**
Beam, Regal China Series, Tobacco Festival...............**$17.00**

Beam, Sports Series, Baseball, $25.00.

Beam, Sports Series, PGA **$20.00**
Beam, State Series, Colorado **$25.00**
Beam, State Series, New Jersey, gray **$30.00**
Beam, Wheel Series, Bass Boat **$40.00**
Beam, Wheel Series, Circus Wagon............................**$25.00**

Beam, Wheel Series, Duesenberg Convertible, dark blue .$125.00

Beam, Wheel Series, Ernie's Flower Cart $25.00

Beam, Wheel Series, Space Shuttle $65.00

Beam, Wheel Series, Tractor Trailer, beige or white...$50.00

Beam, Wheel Series, Train (Casey Jones), Bumpers, 2-pc...$10.00

Beam, Wheel Series, Train (General), Caboose, gray .$75.00

Beam, Wheel Series, Train (Grant), Caboose, red.......$75.00

Beam, Wheel Series, Train (Grant), Dining Car $85.00

Beam, Wheel Series, Train (Grant), Observation Car .$65.00

Beam, Wheel Series, Train (Turner), Boxcar, yellow ..$125.00

Beam, Wheel Series, Train (Turner), Locomotive $125.00

Beam, Wheel Series, Train (Turner), Lumber Car $65.00

Beam, Wheel Series, Volkswagen, blue or red...........$75.00

Beam, Wheel Series, 1903 Ford Model A, black $50.00

Beam, Wheel Series, 1903 Oldsmobile $45.00

Beam, Wheel Series, 1914 Stutz, yellow or gray $50.00

Beam, Wheel Series, 1929 Ford Phaeton $70.00

Beam, Wheel Series, 1929 Ford Woodie Wagon $75.00

Beam, Wheel Series, 1930 Ford Paddy Wagon $165.00

Beam, Wheel Series, 1934 Ford Roadster, PA, cream .$125.00

Beam, Wheel Series, 1935 Ford Police Tow Truck $75.00

Beam, Wheel Series, 1955 Chevy Corvette, copper $95.00

Beam, Wheel Series, 1956 Ford T-Bird, black $95.00

Beam, Wheel Series, 1957 Chevy, black $95.00

Beam, Wheel Series, 1957 Chevy, red $95.00

Beam, Wheel Series, 1957 Chevy Convertible, black..$80.00

Beam, Wheel Series, 1957 Chevy Convertible, cream..$125.00

Beam, Wheel Series, 1957 Chevy Corvette, black.......$70.00

Beam, Wheel Series, 1957 Chevy Corvette, copper..$125.00

Beam, Wheel Series, 1957 Chevy Hot Rod, yellow.....$95.00

Beam, Wheel Series, 1959 Cadillac, light green $125.00

Beam, Wheel Series, 1963 Chevy Corvette, NY, blue .$95.00

Beam, Wheel Series, 1963 Chevy Corvette, red $90.00

Beam, Wheel Series, 1964 Ford Mustang, black $150.00

Beam, Wheel Series, 1968 Chevy Corvette, green $175.00

Beam, Wheel Series, 1968 Chevy Corvette, yellow...$175.00

Beam, Wheel Series, 1969 Chevy Camaro, green $175.00

Beam, Wheel Series, 1969 Chevy Camaro Convertible, silver..$125.00

Beam, Wheel Series, 1970 Dodge Challenger, blue..$180.00

Beam, Wheel Series, 1970 Dodge Hot Rod, lime......$125.00

Beam, Wheel Series, 1974 Mercedes, blue $50.00

Beam, Wheel Series, 1974 Mercedes, mocha $50.00

Beam, Wheel Series, 1974 Mercedes, white $65.00

Beam, Wheel Series, 1978 Chevy Corvette, red $65.00

Beam, Wheel Series, 1984 Chevy Corvette, black......$95.00

Beam, Wheel Series, 1984 Chevy Corvette, gold $95.00

Beam, Wheel Series, 1986 Chevy Corvette, PA, red....$95.00

Double Springs, Cadillac, 1913 ....$38.00

Double Springs, Cord, 1937 ....$35.00

Double Springs, Peasant, boy or girl, ea.....................$5.00

Double Springs, Stutz Bearcat, 1919..........................$40.00

Ezra Brooks, Automobile & Transportation Series, Ford Mustang, Indy Pace Car...$50.00

Ezra Brooks, Automobile & Transportation Series, 1978 Corvette, Pace Car $50.00

Ezra Brooks, Basketball Player $18.00

Ezra Brooks, Charolais Bull $15.00

Ezra Brooks, Elephant, Big Bertha $20.00

Ezra Brooks, Goldpanner..$8.00

Ezra Brooks, Grandfather Clock $10.00

Ezra Brooks, Jester...$10.00

Ezra Brooks, Kitten on Pillow......................................$12.00

Famous Firsts, Hurdy Gurdy $18.00

Famous Firsts, Racer, Marmon Wasp $75.00

Famous Firsts, Renault Racer #3A................................$65.00

Famous Firsts, Spirit of St Louis, lg............................$150.00

Famous Firsts, Spirit of St Louis, miniature.................$50.00

Famous Firsts, Telephone Johnny Reb........................$35.00

Hoffman, Aesop's Fables, 6 different, ea $25.00

Hoffman, Betsy Ross...$50.00

Hoffman, College Series, Helmet, Nebraska...............$45.00

Hoffman, College Series, Mascot, LSU, Running or Passing.$40.00

Hoffman, Indy 500 Commemorative, 1972 ....$30.00

Hoffman, Mr Lucky Series, Mr Cobbler......................$29.00

Hoffman, Mr Lucky Series, Mr Cobbler, miniature......$15.00

Hoffman, Mr Lucky Series, Mr Harpist........................$25.00

Hoffman, Mr Lucky Series, Mr Photographer, miniature.$18.00

Hoffman, Mr Lucky Series, Mr Sandman.....................$25.00

Hoffman, Wildlife Series, Falcon & Rabbit $65.00

Hoffman, Wildlife Series, Panda $65.00

Kontinental, Editor...$35.00

Kontinental, Editor, miniature $20.00

Kontinental, Gandy Dancer...$25.00

Kontinental, Lumberjack...$25.00

Kontinental, Medicine Man $50.00

Kontinental, Saddle Maker $35.00

Lionstone, Annie Oakley $20.00

Lionstone, Buccaneer $25.00

Lionstone, Falcon...$25.00

Lionstone, Fireman #1, red hat.................................$100.00

Lionstone, Judge Roy Bean..$22.00

Lionstone, Lonely Luke $25.00

Lionstone, Molly Brown $20.00

Lionstone, Quail...$25.00

Lionstone, Sodbuster $20.00

Lionstone, Woodhawk...$25.00

McCormick, Bicentennial Series, Ben Franklin............$25.00

McCormick, Bicentennial Series, Ben Franklin, miniature..$18.00

McCormick, Bicentennial Series, Betsy Ross...............$28.00

McCormick, Bicentennial Series, Thomas Jefferson, miniature $18.00

McCormick, Edison, Thomas $25.00

McCormick, Elvis, See Elvis Presley category

McCormick, Ford, Henry...$30.00

McCormick, Gunfighters, 8 different, miniature, ea $25.00

McCormick, Lindbergh, Charles; miniature.................$18.00

McCormick, Missouri, China $10.00

McCormick, Pocahontas $50.00

McCormick, Stowger Telephone..................................$35.00

McCormick, Twain, Mark $30.00

Old Commonwealth, Boot, Western............................$25.00

Old Commonwealth, Coal Miner #3, w/Lump of Coal, miniature $20.00

Old Commonwealth, Leprechaun, Irish Minstrel, 1982.**$35.00**
Old Commonwealth, Lumberjack.................................**$30.00**
Old Commonwealth, Volunteer #5, miniature.............**$30.00**
Old Commonwealth, Volunteer #6........................**$75.00**
Old Fitzgerald, 'Hook'em Horns'................................**$20.00**
Old Fitzgerald, Irish Charm, 1977.............................**$22.00**
Old Fitzgerald, Old Ironsides.....................................**$5.00**
Old Fitzgerald, Sons of Ireland, 1969.......................**$15.00**
Old Fitzgerald, Venetian..**$4.00**
Pacesetter, Ahrens Fox, gold.............................**$250.00**
Pacesetter, Ahrens Fox, white & red........................**$125.00**
Pacesetter, Mack, white & red.............................**$150.00**
Ski Country, Antelope, Pronghorn **$60.00**
Ski Country, Badger Family **$55.00**
Ski Country, Badger Family, miniature **$28.00**
Ski Country, Chicadees...**$70.00**
Ski Country, Chicadees, miniature............................**$35.00**
Ski Country, Duck, King Eider.................................**$35.00**
Ski Country, Duck, King Eider, miniature...................**$35.00**
Ski Country, Ducks Unlimited, Oldsquaw, miniature .**$35.00**
Ski Country, Hawk Eagle **$150.00**
Ski Country, Hawk Eagle, miniature **$75.00**
Ski Country, Kangaroo, miniature **$125.00**
Ski Country, Lion on Drum....................................**$48.00**
Ski Country, Lion on Drum, miniature.......................**$26.00**
Ski Country, Peacock **$100.00**
Ski Country, Ringmaster **$35.00**
Ski Country, Ringmaster, miniature **$25.00**
Ski Country, US Ski Team **$35.00**
Ski Country, US Ski Team, miniature **$16.00**
Ski Country, Woodpecker, miniature........................**$35.00**
Wade, Tetley Tea Moneybox Truck...........................**$45.00**
Wild Turkey, Crystal, Baccarat..................................**$225.00**
Wild Turkey, Mack Truck.......................................**$28.00**
Wild Turkey, Series I, #6...**$25.00**

Wild Turkey, Series II, Lore #1, 1979, $25.00.

Wild Turkey, Series II, Lore #3 ....**$45.00**
Wild Turkey, Series III, #12, Turkey & Skunks **$95.00**
Wild Turkey, Series III, #12, Turkey & Skunks, miniature .**$45.00**
Wild Turkey, Series III, #2, Turkey & Bobcat, miniature .**$45.00**
Wild Turkey, Series III, #5, Turkey & Raccoon **$95.00**
Wild Turkey, Series III, #5, Turkey & Raccoon, miniature .**$45.00**

Wild Turkey, Series III, #8, Turkey & Owl...............**$100.00**
Wild Turkey, Series III, #8, Turkey & Owl, miniature .**$50.00**

Degenhart

John and Elizabeth Degenhart owned and operated the Crystal Art Glass Factory in Cambridge, Ohio. From 1947 until John died in 1964, they produced some fine glassware. John was well known for his superior paperweights, but the glassware that collectors love today was made after '64, when Elizabeth restructured the company, creating many lovely moulds and scores of colors. She hired Zack Boyd, who had previously worked for Cambridge Glass, and between the two of them, they developed almost 150 unique and original color formulas.

Complying with provisions she had made before her death, close personal friends at Island Mould and Machine Company in Wheeling, West Virginia, took Elizabeth's moulds and removed the familiar 'D in heart' trademark from them. She had requested that ten of her moulds be donated to the Degenhart Museum, where they remain today. Zack Boyd eventually bought the Degenhart factory and acquired the remaining moulds. He has added his own logo to them and is continuing to press glass very similar to Mrs. Degenhart's.

For more information, we recommend *Degenhart Glass and Paperweights* by Gene Florence, published by the Degenhart Paperweight and Glass Museum, Inc., Cambridge, Ohio.

Club: Friends of Degenhart
Degenhart Paperweight and Glass Museum
P.O. Box 186, Cambridge, OH 43725; Individual membership: $5 per year; membership includes newsletter, *Heartbeat*, a quarterly publication and free admission to the museum

Baby (Hobo) Shoe Toothpick Holder, Caramel **$15.00**
Baby (Hobo) Shoe Toothpick Holder, Mint Green **$12.00**
Baby (Hobo) Shoe Toothpick Holder, Pearl Gray **$20.00**
Baby (Hobo) Shoe Toothpick Holder, Vaseline **$12.00**
Basket Toothpick Holder, Opalescent.........................**$20.00**
Beaded Oval Toothpick Holder, Amberina...................**$25.00**
Beaded Oval Toothpick Holder, Bloody Mary **$45.00**
Beaded Oval Toothpick Holder, Heather **$20.00**
Beaded Oval Toothpick Holder, Mulberry...................**$20.00**
Beaded Oval Toothpick Holder, Pigeon Blood...........**$35.00**
Bicentennial Bell, Angel Blue **$12.00**
Bicentennial Bell, Cobalt...**$15.00**
Bicentennial Bell, Heliotrope....................................**$30.00**
Bicentennial Bell, Mauve...**$12.00**
Bicentennial Bell, Opalescent **$12.00**
Bicentennial Bell, Rose Marie **$12.00**
Bird Salt & Pepper Shakers, Aqua..............................**$35.00**
Bird Salt & Pepper Shakers, Baby Green....................**$45.00**
Bird Salt & Pepper Shakers, Ivory..............................**$45.00**
Bird Salt & Pepper Shakers, Teal...............................**$25.00**
Bird Salt w/Cherry, Burnt Amber **$20.00**
Bird Salt w/Cherry, Champagne **$20.00**

Bird Salt w/Cherry, Forest Green $15.00
Bird Salt w/Cherry, Spring Green $15.00
Bird Toothpick Holder, Canary $15.00
Bird Toothpick Holder, Taffeta $25.00
Bow Slipper, Blue Marble Slag $25.00
Bow Slipper, Marigold $25.00
Bow Slipper, Royal Blue $20.00
Buzz Saw Wine, Bluebell $40.00
Buzz Saw Wine, Opal White $25.00
Buzz Saw Wine, Taffeta $40.00
Chick Covered Dish, Bloody Mary, 2" $50.00
Chick Covered Dish, Gold, 2" $20.00
Chick Covered Dish, Red, 2" $35.00
Coaster, Peach Blo $10.00
Colonial Drape Toothpick Holder, Aqua $20.00
Colonial Drape Toothpick Holder, Sunset $20.00
Daisy & Button Creamer & Sugar, Custard $90.00
Daisy & Button Salt, Dichromatic $15.00
Daisy & Button Salt, Sapphire $12.00
Daisy & Button Salt, Sunset $15.00
Daisy & Button Toothpick Holder, Heliotrope $35.00
Daisy & Button Toothpick Holder, Off White $15.00
Daisy & Button Toothpick Holder, Topaz $25.00
Elephant Head Toothpick Holder, Holly Green $25.00
Forget-Me-Not Toothpick Holder, Amethyst $15.00
Forget-Me-Not Toothpick Holder, Baby Green Slag ...$30.00
Forget-Me-Not Toothpick Holder, Brown $15.00
Forget-Me-Not Toothpick Holder, Champagne $15.00
Forget-Me-Not Toothpick Holder, Crystal & Cobalt Slag ..$20.00
Forget-Me-Not Toothpick Holder, End of Blizzard $15.00
Forget-Me-Not Toothpick Holder, Honey $15.00
Forget-Me-Not Toothpick Holder, Jade $30.00
Forget-Me-Not Toothpick Holder, Old Lavender $20.00
Forget-Me-Not Toothpick Holder, Pine Green $25.00
Forget-Me-Not Toothpick Holder, Snow White $15.00
Forget-Me-Not Toothpick Holder, White $15.00
Gypsy Pot Toothpick Holder, Aqua $20.00
Gypsy Pot Toothpick Holder, Cobalt $20.00
Gypsy Pot Toothpick Holder, Holly Green $25.00
Gypsy Pot Toothpick Holder, Persimmon $25.00
Hand, Blue Jay $15.00
Hand, Fog $20.00
Hand, Ruby $6.00
Hand, Willow Blue $10.00

Heart & Lyre Cup Plate, Emerald Green, $15.00.

Heart & Lyre Cup Plate, Aqua $12.00
Heart & Lyre Cup Plate, Elizabeth's Lime Ice $12.00
Heart & Lyre Cup Plate, Pine Green $12.00
Heart Jewel Box, Antique Blue $25.00
Heart Jewel Box, Blue Marble Slag $45.00
Heart Jewel Box, Delft Blue $25.00
Heart Jewel Box, Lavender Green Slag $40.00
Heart Toothpick Holder, Bittersweet Slag $45.00
Heart Toothpick Holder, Blue & White Slag $25.00
Heart Toothpick Holder, Forest Green $15.00
Heart Toothpick Holder, Maverick $35.00
Heart Toothpick Holder, Sapphire $15.00

Heart Toothpick, White Opalescent, $18.00.

Hen Covered Dish, April Green, 3" $30.00
Hen Covered Dish, Canary, 3" $25.00
Hen Covered Dish, Green, 5" $50.00
Hen Covered Dish, Jade, 3" $25.00
Hen Covered Dish, Persimmon, 3" $25.00
Hen Covered Dish, Ruby, 5" $90.00
High Boot, Emerald Green $25.00
High Boot, Jade $40.00
Kat Slipper, Cambridge Pink $25.00
Lamb Covered Dish, Apple Green, 5" $65.00
Lamb Covered Dish, Lemon Custard, 5" $75.00
Lamb Covered Dish, Milk White, 5" $50.00
Mini Pitcher, Heatherbloom $25.00
Mini Slipper w/out Sole, Gray Slag $40.00
Mini Slipper w/Sole, Milk Blue $35.00
Owl, Bittersweet $75.00
Owl, Blue Fire, clear $40.00
Owl, Caramel $75.00
Owl, Cobalt $35.00
Owl, Crown Tuscan Slag $50.00
Owl, Dirty Sally $60.00
Owl, Frosty Jade $45.00
Owl, Jabe's Amber $65.00
Owl, Light Amethyst $30.00
Owl, Lime Sherbet $35.00
Owl, Misty Blue $45.00
Owl, Nile Green Opal $50.00
Owl, Royal Violet $50.00

Owl, Smoke...$50.00
Owl, Tiger...$40.00
Owl, Willow Green.......................................$50.00
Pooch, Bernard Boyd's Ebony.........................$35.00
Pooch, Blue Marble Slag................................$20.00
Pooch, Caramel Custard Slag..........................$35.00
Pooch, Cobalt..$15.00
Pooch, Dapple Gray.....................................$15.00
Pooch, Dark Amethyst..................................$15.00
Pooch, Fawn...$15.00
Pooch, Henry's Blue.....................................$25.00
Pooch, Ivory...$25.00
Pooch, Lavender Slag...................................$40.00
Pooch, Orchid...$25.00
Pooch, Powder Blue Slag...............................$45.00
Pooch, Toffee..$20.00
Pottie Salt, Bluebell.....................................$15.00
Pottie Salt, Green..$6.00
Priscilla Doll, April Green..............................$125.00
Priscilla Doll, Periwinkle...............................$95.00
Priscilla Doll, Vaseline.................................$110.00
Robin Covered Dish, Cambridge Pink, 5"............$65.00

Roller Skate, Light Sapphire, early plain edge, $35.00.

Roller Skate (Skate Shoe), Gold......................$40.00
Seal of Ohio, Peach Blo................................$12.00
Star & Dew Drop Salt, Amberina......................$25.00
Star & Dew Drop Salt, Crown Tuscan................$20.00
Star & Dew Drop Salt, Topaz..........................$20.00
Stork & Peacock Child's Mug, Bluebell...............$25.00
Stork & Peacock Child's Mug, Chocolate Slag......$50.00
Stork & Peacock Child's Mug, Mint Green...........$20.00
Stork & Peacock Child's Mug, Pine Green...........$25.00
Texas Boot, Baby Green Slag..........................$25.00
Texas Creamer & Sugar, Crystal......................$40.00
Tomahawk, Custard Maverick..........................$75.00
Turkey Covered Dish, Bluebell, 5"....................$65.00
Turkey Covered Dish, Daffodil, 5"....................$70.00
Turkey Covered Dish, Green Marble, 5"..............$80.00
Turkey Covered Dish, Milk Blue, 5"...................$60.00
Turkey Covered Dish, Tomato, 5"....................$125.00

Wildflower Candle Holder, Cobalt.....................$25.00
Wildflower Candy Dish, Apple Green.................$35.00
Wildflower Candy Dish, Emerald Green..............$25.00
Wildflower Candy Dish, Pink...........................$25.00

deLee Art Pottery

Jimmie Lee Adair Kohl founded her company in 1937, and it continued to operate until 1958. She was the inspiration, artist, and owner of the company for the 21 years it was in business. The name deLee means 'of or by Lee' and is taken from the French language. She trained as an artist at the San Diego Art Institute and UCLA where she also earned an art education degree. She taught art and ceramics at Belmont High School in Los Angeles while getting her ceramic business started. On September 9, 1999, at the age of 93, Jimmie Lee died after having lived a long and wonderfully creative life.

The deLee line included children, adults, animals, birds, and specialty items such as cookie jars, banks, wall pockets, and several licensed Walter Lantz characters. Skunks were a favorite subject, and more of her pieces were modeled as skunks than any other single animal. Her figurines are distinctive in their design, charm, and excellent hand painting; when carefully studied, they can be easily recognized. Jimmie Lee modeled almost all the pieces — more than 350 in all.

The beautiful deLee colors were mixed by her and remained essentially the same for 20 years. The same figurine may be found painted in different colors and patterns. Figurines were sold wholesale only. Buyers could select from a catalog or visit the deLee booth in New York and Los Angeles Gift Marts. All figurines left the factory with name and logo stickers. The round Art Deco logo sticker is silver with the words 'deLee Art, California, Hand Decorated.' Many of the figures are incised 'deLee Art' on the bottom.

The factory was located in Los Angeles during its twenty-one years of production and in Cuernavaca, Mexico, for four years during WWII. Production continued until 1958, when Japanese copies of her figures caused sales to decline. For further study we recommend *deLee Art* by Joanne and Ralph Schaefer and John Humphries.

Advisors: Joanne and Ralph Schaefer (See Directory, deLee)

Ashtray, skunk match holder in tail, 5" dia, from $45 to ..$60.00
Bank, Money Bunny, rabbit w/purse, pink clay, from $90 to...$125.00
Bank, Stinkie, skunk, unmarked, 7".........................$20.00
Candle holder, Twinkle or Star, ea, from $25 to.........$35.00
Figurine, Andy Pandy, incised deLee Art 40, A Walter Lantz Creation, round label on base, from $75 to.......$100.00
Figurine, Angel, praying pose w/sm wings on back, incised deLee Art 1944, E painter's mark, 6½"..................$20.00
Figurine, boy in swimming trunks, seated w/right foot on left knee, 4", from $85 to..$125.00

Figurine, Buddy, boy w/basket planter on shoulder, painted open eyes, unmarked, 7", from $45 to **$60.00**

Figurine, Carol, angel w/song book, incised deLee Art, 4½" **$48.00**

Figurine, Corny, standing w/fish on line in left hand & 2 fish on lines over right shoulder, 5¼", from $85 to ..**$125.00**

Figurine, Danny, tipping bowler hat, incised deLee Art 1947, 9", from $35 to **$50.00**

Figurine, Flipper, seal, incised deLee Art USA, very hard to find, 4½" **$150.00**

Figurine, girl kneeling in prayer, incised deLee Art 39 USA, 3", from $65 to **$85.00**

Figurine, Grunt & Groan, pigs seated & standing, incised deLee Art 42 USA, pr, from $75 to **$100.00**

Figurine, Hank, boy in top hat & vest, incised deLee Art 1943, 7½", from $30 to **$40.00**

Figurine, Hank, boy leans on planter w/legs crossed, several color variations, deLee Art 1943, 7½", from $30 to..**$40.00**

Figurine, Hattie, girl in long skirt w/fan & planter, 7½", from $30 to **$45.00**

Figurine, June, girl seated w/open book, 4", from $65 to..**$85.00**

Figurine, Katrina, Dutch girl w/hands on hips, open planter apron, marked deLee Art Hollywood 1944, 6½"..**$35.00**

Figurine, Kitty, cat sitting w/painted closed eyes, floral decor, 4", from $35 to **$45.00**

Figurine, Lassie, black Scottie, scarce, 4" **$150.00**

Figurine, Leilani, Hawaiian girl seated, applied lei, w/name label, 9", from $150 to...**$175.00**

Figurine, Lorenzo, boy carries lg bowl of flowers on head, matches Maria, 10½", from $90 to......................**$125.00**

Figurine, Lou, girl in waisted long dress & bonnet, side pocket planters, 7", from $35 to **$50.00**

Figurine, Lucky, pink elephant w/floral decor............**$75.00**

Figurine, Mandy, Black child, mauve, blue & white plaid dress, round silver label, rare, 6"........................**$118.00**

Figurine, Maria, girl holding open planter skirt, pink tone, round sticker on base, 7½", from $25 to **$35.00**

Figurine, Mickey, kitten playing w/ball, 4", from $45 to..**$60.00**

Figurine, Miss Muffet, seated in wide hoop skirt w/spider & bowl, 5", from $90 to **$125.00**

Figurine, Mr & Mrs Skunk, planter at back or in hat, 6", pr, from $70 to..**$85.00**

Figurine, Mr Chips, chipmunk w/lg acorn planter, incised deLee Art 1940, 4½", from $25 to........................**$35.00**

Figurine, Nina, girl holding open planter skirt, incised deLee Art 1940, 7"...**$20.00**

Figurine, Oswald the Rabbit, w/tag, Copyright Walter Lantz, from $80 to...**$100.00**

Figurine, Panchita, girl holding open planter skirt, incised deLee Art LA 44, 7", from $30 to...........................**$45.00**

Figurine, Patsy, girl w/long skirt holds umbrella at front & basket planter under right arm, 7", from $35 to...**$45.00**

Figurine, Pedro, Mexican boy strumming guitar, incised deLee Art Hollywood USA 44, E painter's mark, 8"...........**$52.00**

Figurine, Pedro & Panchita, adult Cuban couple, Pedro playing drums, Panchita dancing, 13" & 7½", pr, from $150 to...**$200.00**

Figurine, Rags, English Sheepdog, w/foil name sticker, 4", from $35 to..**$45.00**

Figurine, Sally, girl holding chick, incised Sally (cursive) deLee Art 1938, 6½" **$38.00**

Figurine, Siamese, sitting tall w/tail curled to front, airbrushed, incised mark, 12", from $75 to............**$125.00**

Figurine, Siamese dancer, green & black clothing, incised deLee Art copyright, 13", from $75 to.................**$100.00**

Figurine, Song, Oriental girl w/stepped planter at back, incised 1948 deLee Art, 9", from $50 to...............**$60.00**

Figurine, The Thinker, boy sitting w/legs crossed, 2¾", from $65 to..**$85.00**

Figurine, Tops, giraffe, 7½", from $50.00 to $65.00. (Photo courtesy Joanne and Ralph Schaefer)

Figurine, Whitey, white lamb, standing, 4", from $30 to..**$40.00**

Figurine, Yard Bird, soldier at attention w/rifle at left side & salute, 6", from $40 to **$60.00**

Figurines, Chesty & Nutsy, squirrels, Chesty incised deLee Art USA, Nutsy unmarked, 3½", pr, from $60 to........**$70.00**

Flower frog, girl atop rounded base, from $90.00 to $125.00. (Photo courtesy Joanne and Ralph Schaefer)

Head vase, Bobby Pin Up, lady w/locket, 3½", from $60 to **$90.00**

Match holder, DeStinker, skunk figural, wall mount, from $20 to **$35.00**

Salt & pepper shakers, Sniffy & Snuffy, skunks, 4", pr, from $35 to...**$45.00**

Depression Glass

Since the early '60s, this has been a very active area of collecting. Interest is still very strong, and although values have long been established, except for some of the rarer items, Depression glass is still relatively inexpensive. Some of the patterns and colors that were entirely avoided by the early wave of collectors are now becoming popular, and it's very easy to reassemble a nice table setting of one of these lines today.

Most of this glass was manufactured during the Depression years. It was inexpensive, mass-produced, and available in a wide assortment of colors. The same type of glassware was still being made to some extent during the '50s and '60s, and today the term 'Depression glass' has been expanded to include the later patterns as well.

Some things have been reproduced, and the slight variation in patterns and colors can be very difficult to detect. For instance, the Sharon butter dish has been reissued in original colors of pink and green (as well as others that were not original); and several pieces of Cherry Blossom, Madrid, Avocado, Mayfair, and Miss America have also been reproduced. Some pieces you'll see in antique malls and flea markets today have been recently made in dark uncharacteristic carnival colors, which, of course, are easy to spot.

For further study, Gene Florence has written several informative books on the subject, and we recommend them all: *The Pocket Guide to Depression Glass, The Collector's Encyclopedia of Depression Glass,* and *Very Rare Glassware of the Depression Years* (Collector Books).

Publication: *Depression Glass Daze*
Teri Steel, Editor/Publisher
Box 57, Otisville, MI 48463; 810-631-4593
The nation's marketplace for glass, china, and pottery

Adam, ashtray, green, 4½" $25.00
Adam, bowl, pink, w/lid, 9" $65.00
Adam, bowl, pink, 6¾" $26.00
Adam, butter dish, pink, w/lid $80.00
Adam, candy jar, green, w/lid, 2½" $100.00
Adam, creamer, pink $20.00
Adam, cup, green $23.00
Adam, pitcher, pink, 32-oz, 8" $40.00
Adam, plate, salad; pink or green, square, 7¾" $15.00
Adam, tumbler, green, 4½" $28.00
Adam, tumbler, iced tea; pink, 5½" $75.00
American Pioneer, bowl, crystal or pink, w/lid, 8¾".$125.00
American Pioneer, candlesticks, green, 6½", pr........$125.00
American Pioneer, candy jar, crystal or pink, w/lid, 1-lb.$100.00
American Pioneer, creamer, crystal or pink, 2¾" $25.00
American Pioneer, cup, green.......................................$12.00
American Pioneer, goblet, cocktail; amber, 3½-oz, 4" ..$40.00
American Pioneer, goblet, water; green, 8-oz, 6"........$58.00
American Pioneer, lamp, crystal or pink, ball shape, round, 5½" $150.00
American Pioneer, mayonnaise, green, 4¼" $90.00

American Pioneer, pitcher, urn; crystal or pink, w/lid, 5"...$175.00
American Pioneer, plate, crystal or pink, 6" $12.50
American Pioneer, plate, green, 8" $12.00
American Pioneer, sherbet, green, 4¾".......................$37.50
American Pioneer, sugar bowl, crystal or pink, 3½"...$20.00
American Pioneer, tumbler, green, 8-oz, 4" $50.00
American Pioneer, vase, crystal or pink, 4 styles, 7" .$100.00
American Sweetheart, bowl, cereal; cremax, 6" $10.00
American Sweetheart, bowl, cereal; pink, 6"...............$17.00
American Sweetheart, bowl, soup; smoke & other trims, 9½" $135.00
American Sweetheart, creamer, blue, footed.............$175.00
American Sweetheart, cup, monax...............................$10.00
American Sweetheart, plate, bread & butter; smoke & other trims, 6"...$20.00
American Sweetheart, plate, dinner; pink, 9¾"...........$40.00
American Sweetheart, plate, salad; blue, 8"...............$115.00
American Sweetheart, plate, salver; red, 12" $185.00
American Sweetheart, platter, smoke & other trims, oval, 13"..$225.00
American Sweetheart, saucer, pink...............................$4.00
American Sweetheart, sherbet, smoke & other trims, footed, 4¼"..$100.00
American Sweetheart, sugar bowl, red, open foot....$150.00
Aunt Polly, bowl, berry; green or iridescent, lg, 7⅞" .$20.00
Aunt Polly, bowl, green or iridescent, 2x4¾"..............$15.00
Aunt Polly, butter dish, blue, w/lid............................$225.00
Aunt Polly, candy jar, blue, footed, 2-handled...........$45.00
Aunt Polly, candy jar, green or iridescent, 2-handled, w/lid $75.00
Aunt Polly, plate, sherbet; blue, 6"..............................$14.00
Aunt Polly, sherbet, green or iridescent.....................$10.00
Aunt Polly, sugar bowl, blue $30.00
Aunt Polly, vase, green or iridescent, footed, 6½"......$30.00
Aurora, cup, cobalt or pink $15.00
Aurora, plate, cobalt or pink, 6½"...............................$12.00
Aurora, tumbler, cobalt or pink, 10-oz, 4¾"...............$25.00
Avocado, bowl, green, 3¼x9½".................................$175.00
Avocado, bowl, preserve; pink, handle, 7½" $30.00
Avocado, bowl, relish; crystal, footed, 6"....................$9.00
Avocado, creamer, pink, footed...................................$30.00
Avocado, plate, cake; green, 2-handled, 10¼" $55.00
Avocado, sugar bowl, crystal, footed $12.00
Beaded Block, bowl, amber, round, unflared, 6¾" ...$14.00
Beaded Block, bowl, canary yellow, fluted edges, round, 7½"...$35.00
Beaded Block, bowl, celery; pink, 8¼" $18.00
Beaded Block, bowl, green, round, deep, 6"...............$15.00
Beaded Block, bowl, ice blue, square, 5½" $24.00
Beaded Block, plate, red, square, 7¾"........................$12.00
Beaded Block, sugar bowl, milk white.......................$30.00
Block Optic, bowl, berry; green, lg, 8½".....................$25.00
Block Optic, bowl, pink, 1⅜x4¼"...............................$11.00
Block Optic, candlesticks, pink, 1¾", pr....................$75.00
Block Optic, comport, mayonnaise; pink, 4"..............$90.00
Block Optic, goblet, cocktail; green, 4" $37.00
Block Optic, green, plate, 12¾" $30.00

Block Optic, pitcher, green, 54-oz, 8½"........................**$60.00**
Block Optic, plate, luncheon; yellow, 8".....................**$5.00**
Block Optic, plate, sherbet; yellow, 6"..........................**$3.00**
Block Optic, saucer, green, w/cup ring, 5¾"............**$10.00**
Block Optic, tumbler, green, flat, 9½-oz, 3¾"...........**$15.00**
Block Optic, tumbler, pink, footed, 3-oz, 3¼"............**$28.00**
Block Optic, tumbler, yellow, flat, 12-oz, 4⅞"...........**$25.00**
Block Optic, whiskey, green, 2-oz, 2¼"....................**$30.00**
Bowknot, bowl, cereal; green, 5½"..........................**$22.50**
Bowknot, cup, green..**$8.00**
Bowknot, tumbler, footed, 10-oz, 5"........................**$22.50**
Cameo, bowl, console; pink, 3-leg, 11"....................**$70.00**
Cameo, bowl, sauce; crystal, 4¼"...............................**$6.00**
Cameo, bowl, soup; pink, rimmed, 9"....................**$135.00**
Cameo, butter dish, green, w/lid.............................**$235.00**
Cameo, candy jar, yellow, low, w/lid, 4"................**$110.00**
Cameo, comport, mayonnaise; pink, 5"..................**$195.00**
Cameo, creamer, green, 4¼".....................................**$28.00**
Cameo, cup, crystal, 2 styles......................................**$5.50**
Cameo, domino tray, green, 7", w/3" indentation **$150.00**
Cameo, pitcher, juice; green, 36-oz, 6".....................**$60.00**
Cameo, plate, dinner; yellow, 9½"..............................**$9.00**
Cameo, plate, sherbet; crystal, 6"...............................**$2.00**
Cameo, platter, yellow, w/closed handles, 12"...........**$40.00**
Cameo, sherbet, pink, blown, 3⅛"............................**$75.00**
Cameo, tumbler, water; green, 9-oz, 4"....................**$26.00**
Cameo, tumbler, yellow, footed, 9-oz, 5"..................**$16.00**
Cherry Blossom, bowl, berry; delphite, 4¾"..............**$15.00**
Cherry Blossom, bowl, berry; green, round, 8½".......**$48.00**
Cherry Blossom, butter dish bottom, green.................**$25.00**
Cherry Blossom, creamer, delphite............................**$20.00**

Cherry Blossom, cup, green, $22.00; saucer, $5.00.

Cherry Blossom, cup, pink **$20.00**
Cherry Blossom, pitcher, green, allover pattern, scalloped
   bottom, 36-oz, 6¾"...**$65.00**
Cherry Blossom, plate, grill; green, 10" **$125.00**
Cherry Blossom, plate, sherbet; delphite, 6" **$10.00**
Cherry Blossom, saucer, green....................................**$5.00**
Cherry Blossom, tray, sandwich; delphite, 10½"........**$22.00**
Cherry Blossom, tumbler, green, allover pattern, scalloped
   foot, 8-oz, 4½" **$40.00**
Cherry Blossom, tumbler, green, pattern at top, flat, 9-oz,
   4¼"...**$24.00**
Cherry Blossom, tumbler, pink, allover pattern, footed, 4-oz,
   3¾"...**$17.00**

Cherryberry, bowl, crystal, 2x6¼" **$50.00**
Cherryberry, butter dish, iridescent, w/lid.................**$145.00**
Cherryberry, comport, green, 5¾"............................**$25.00**
Cherryberry, creamer, crystal, lg, 4⅝".....................**$15.00**
Cherryberry, pickle dish, pink, oval, 8¼".................**$18.00**
Cherryberry, plate, sherbet; crystal, 6" **$6.00**
Cherryberry, sherbet, pink...**$10.00**
Cherryberry, sugar bowl, iridescent, open, sm...........**$12.00**
Chinex Classic, bowl, soup; browntone, 7¾".............**$12.50**
Chinex Classic, bowl, vegetable; decal decorated, 9".**$25.00**
Chinex Classic, butter dish, castle decal, w/lid.........**$150.00**
Chinex Classic, creamer, plain ivory..........................**$5.50**
Chinex Classic, cup, browntone **$4.50**
Chinex Classic, plate, dinner; castle decal, 9¾".........**$20.00**
Chinex Classic, plate, sherbet; decal decorated, 6¼"....**$3.50**
Chinex Classic, saucer, decal decorated......................**$4.00**
Circle, bowl, green or pink, 5¼"...............................**$10.00**
Circle, bowl, green or pink, 8"..................................**$18.00**
Circle, cup, green or pink, 2 styles **$5.00**
Circle, goblet, water; green or pink, 8-oz..................**$11.00**
Circle, plate, luncheon; green or pink, 8¼"................**$4.00**
Circle, tumbler, juice; green or pink, 4-oz, 3½" **$8.00**
Circle saucer, green or pink, w/cup ring....................**$2.50**
Cloverleaf, ashtray, black, match holder in center, 4"...**$65.00**
Cloverleaf, bowl, dessert; yellow, 4".........................**$27.50**
Cloverleaf, bowl, salad; green, deep, 7" **$55.00**
Cloverleaf, cup, pink **$7.00**
Cloverleaf, plate, grill; yellow, 10¼" **$25.00**
Cloverleaf, saucer, black..**$6.00**
Cloverleaf, tumbler, green, flat, flared, 10-oz, 3¾"......**$40.00**
Colonial, bowl, berry; crystal, lg, 9" **$25.00**
Colonial, bowl, berry; pink, 4½"................................**$16.00**
Colonial, bowl, cream soup; green, 4½" **$70.00**
Colonial, bowl, vegetable; pink, oval, 10" **$35.00**
Colonial, butter dish bottom, green **$32.50**
Colonial, pitcher, milk/cream; crystal, 16-oz, 5"..........**$20.00**
Colonial, plate, grill; crystal, 10"..............................**$15.00**
Colonial, plate, sherbet; green, 6" **$8.00**
Colonial, saucer/plate, sherbet; pink..........................**$6.00**
Colonial, sherbet, crystal, 3⅜"...................................**$7.00**
Colonial, stem, water; crystal, 8½-oz, 5¾".................**$22.00**
Colonial, tumbler, green, footed, 10-oz, 5¼"..............**$47.00**
Colonial, tumbler, green, 11-oz, 5⅛".........................**$42.00**
Colonial, tumbler, juice; pink, 5-oz, 3"......................**$20.00**
Colonial Block, bowl, pink, 4"....................................**$6.50**
Colonial Block, butter dish, green, w/lid....................**$45.00**
Colonial Block, creamer, white **$7.00**
Colonial Block, goblet, pink.......................................**$12.50**
Colonial Block, sugar bowl lid, green.........................**$12.00**
Colonial Fluted, bowl, berry; green, 4" **$7.50**
Colonial Fluted, cup, green..**$5.00**
Colonial Fluted, plate, sherbet; green, 6" **$2.50**
Colonial Fluted, sherbet, green....................................**$6.00**
Columbia, bowl, soup; crystal, low, 8" **$22.00**
Columbia, butter dish, crystal, w/lid..........................**$20.00**
Columbia, cup, pink...**$25.00**
Columbia, saucer, crystal...**$3.50**

Coronation, bowl, berry; Royal Ruby, handled, 4¼" **$7.00**
Coronation, bowl, nappy; pink, handled, 6½" **$6.00**
Coronation, cup, Royal Ruby...**$6.50**
Coronation, plate, luncheon; Royal Ruby, 8½" **$10.00**
Coronation, sherbet, green..**$75.00**
Cremax, bowl, cereal; 5¾" **$3.50**
Cremax, bowl, soup; blue, 7¾" **$7.00**
Cremax, creamer, decal decorated................................**$8.00**
Cremax, cup, blue, castle decal......................................**$7.50**
Cremax, plate, bread & butter; 6¼" **$2.00**
Cremax, plate, sandwich; blue, 11½" **$5.50**
Cremax, saucer, decal decorated **$3.50**
Cube, butter dish, green, w/lid.....................................**$65.00**
Cube, candy jar, pink, w/lid, 6½" **$30.00**
Cube, coaster, green, 3¼" **$7.50**
Cube, creamer, pink, 3½"..**$6.00**
Cube, plate, sherbet; green, 6".......................................**$4.00**
Cube, powder jar, pink, w/lid, 3-leg..............................**$27.50**
Cube, saucer, green **$2.50**
Diamond Quilted, bowl, blue, crimped edge, 7"........**$18.00**
Diamond Quilted, bowl, cereal; pink, 5"......................**$7.50**
Diamond Quilted, cake salver, green, tall, 10" dia......**$60.00**
Diamond Quilted, candlesticks, black, 2 styles, pr **$50.00**
Diamond Quilted, creamer, blue **$17.50**
Diamond Quilted, goblet, champagne; pink, 9-oz, 6" ..**$11.00**
Diamond Quilted, goblet, cordial; green, 1-oz............**$12.00**
Diamond Quilted, mayonnaise set: ladle, plate, & comport;
 black **$56.00**
Diamond Quilted, plate, luncheon; blue, 8"...............**$12.00**
Diamond Quilted, plate, sandwich; green, 14"...........**$15.00**
Diamond Quilted, saucer, pink **$3.00**
Diamond Quilted, tumbler, iced tea; green, 12-oz........**$9.00**
Diamond Quilted, whiskey, pink, 1½-oz.......................**$8.00**
Diana, bowl, amber, scalloped edge, 12" **$20.00**
Diana, bowl, cereal; crystal, 5" **$6.00**
Diana, bowl, salad; pink, 9"...**$20.00**
Diana, coaster, pink, 3½"..**$7.00**
Diana, creamer, crystal, oval **$5.00**
Diana, plate, bread & butter; pink, 6"...........................**$4.00**
Diana, plate, sandwich; amber, 11¾"...........................**$10.00**
Diana, saucer, pink **$5.00**
Diana, sugar bowl, crystal, open, oval..........................**$5.00**
Dogwood, creamer, green, flat, thin, 2½".....................**$47.50**
Dogwood, cup, cremax, thick **$40.00**
Dogwood, cup, pink, thin...**$16.00**
Dogwood, plate, bread & butter; monax, 6" **$21.00**
Dogwood, plate, cake; pink, heavy solid foot, 13"..**$145.00**
Dogwood, plate, grill; green, border design only, 10½" ...**$25.00**
Dogwood, saucer, cremax...**$20.00**
Dogwood, sugar bowl, pink, footed, thick, 3¼".........**$18.00**
Dogwood, tumbler, green, decorated, 11-oz, 4¾" **$100.00**
Doric, bowl, berry; green, 4½"......................................**$10.00**
Doric, bowl, cereal; pink, 5½".......................................**$75.00**
Doric, bowl, green, 2-handled, 9" **$20.00**
Doric, butter dish bottom, pink....................................**$25.00**
Doric, coaster, green, 3"..**$18.00**
Doric, cup, pink..**$9.00**

Doric, plate, cake; green, 3-leg, 10" **$22.50**
Doric, plate, dinner; pink, 8"...**$16.00**
Doric, plate, sherbet; green, 6"......................................**$5.00**
Doric, relish tray, green, 4x4".......................................**$10.00**
Doric, saucer, pink...**$3.50**
Doric, sugar bowl, green **$12.50**
Doric, tumbler, green, 9-oz, 4½"..................................**$110.00**
Doric, tumbler, pink, footed, 12-oz, 5" **$80.00**
Doric & Pansy, bowl, berry; pink, 4½".......................**$10.00**
Doric & Pansy, bowl, green, handled, 9" **$35.00**

Doric and Pansy, plate, ultramarine, 9", $35.00. (Photo courtesy Gene Florence)

Doric & Pansy, saucer, pink..**$4.00**
English Hobnail, ashtray, pink, square, 4½"...............**$25.00**
English Hobnail, bottle, toilet; turquoise, 5-oz...........**$50.00**
English Hobnail, bowl, ice blue, rolled edge, 11"......**$80.00**
English Hobnail, bowl, nappy; pink, round, 6½" **$20.00**
English Hobnail, bowl, pickle, pink, 8" **$30.00**
English Hobnail, candy dish, green, 3-footed **$55.00**
English Hobnail, cigarette jar, turquoise, round, w/lid .**$60.00**
English Hobnail, cup, pink..**$18.00**
English Hobnail, marmalade, pink, w/lid...................**$40.00**
English Hobnail, plate, green, round, 6½" **$10.00**
English Hobnail, plate, pink, round, 8½"....................**$12.50**
English Hobnail, saucer, turquoise, round...................**$5.00**
English Hobnail, stem, sherbet; ice blue, footed, square,
 high..**$35.00**
English Hobnail, tumbler, ice tea; pink, 10-oz **$25.00**
English Hobnail, vase (straw jar), pink, 10" **$95.00**
Floral, bowl, berry; pink, 4"..**$20.00**
Floral, bowl, salad; green, 7½"......................................**$24.00**
Floral, butter dish bottom, pink...................................**$25.00**
Floral, canister, coffee, tea, cereal or sugar; jade-ite, 5¼",
 ea..**$95.00**
Floral, cup, green...**$14.00**
Floral, pitcher, pink, cone shape, footed, 32-oz, 8" **$35.00**
Floral, plate, dinner; green, 9" **$18.00**
Floral, refrigerator dish, delphite, w/lid, square, 5" **$95.00**
Floral, sherbet, delphite..**$85.00**
Floral, tray, green, closed handles, square, 6"............**$20.00**
Floral, tumbler, juice; pink, footed, 5-oz, 4"..............**$18.00**
Floral & Diamond Band, bowl, berry; green, lg, 8"....**$15.00**
Floral & Diamond Band, bowl, nappy; pink, handled, 5¾"..**$12.00**
Floral & Diamond Band, creamer, green, sm.............**$11.00**

Floral and Diamond Band, pitcher, green, $125.00. (Photo courtesy Gene Florence)

Floral & Diamond Band, sherbet, green **$8.00**

Floral & Diamond Band, tumbler, iced tea; pink, 5" ..**$40.00**

Floral & Diamond Band, tumbler, water; green, 4" **$25.00**

Florentine No 1, bowl, cereal; pink, 6" **$30.00**

Florentine No 1, bowl, vegetable; green, oval, w/lid, 9½" ..**$55.00**

Florentine No 1, butter dish, yellow, w/lid **$160.00**

Florentine No 1, creamer, crystal..............................**$9.50**

Florentine No 1, plate, grill; green, 10" **$12.00**

Florentine No 1, plate, sherbet; green, 6" **$6.00**

Florentine No 1, saucer, yellow **$4.00**

Florentine No 1, tumbler, green, footed, 4-oz, 3¼" **$16.00**

Florentine No 1, tumbler, pink, ribbed, 9-oz, 4" **$22.00**

Florentine No 2, bowl, berry; crystal, 4½"..................**$12.00**

Florentine No 2, bowl, berry; yellow, 8" **$35.00**

Florentine No 2, bowl, cream soup; pink, 4¾" **$16.00**

Florentine No 2, bowl, green, flat, 9"..........................**$27.50**

Florentine No 2, butter dish lid, yellow......................**$80.00**

Florentine No 2, comport, pink, ruffled, 3½" **$15.00**

Florentine No 2, creamer, yellow **$10.00**

Florentine No 2, pitcher, green, 76-oz, 8¼" **$110.00**

Florentine No 2, pitcher, yellow, cone foot, 28-oz, 7½" .**$30.00**

Florentine No 2, plate, dinner; green 10" **$15.00**

Florentine No 2, plate, grill; yellow, 10¼"..................**$14.00**

Florentine No 2, plate, sherbet; crystal, 6"..................**$4.00**

Florentine No 2, relish dish, pink, plain or 3-part, 10", ea **$25.00**

Florentine No 2, sherbet, yellow, footed **$11.00**

Florentine No 2, tumbler, crystal, footed, 9-oz, 4½" ...**$27.50**

Florentine No 2, tumbler, green, blown, 12-oz, 5"......**$20.00**

Florentine No 2, tumbler, iced tea; yellow, 12-oz, 5" .**$50.00**

Florentine No 2, tumbler, juice; pink, 5-oz, 3⅜"........**$12.00**

Flower Garden w/Butterflies, bowl, orange; black, footed, 11"...**$225.00**

Flower Garden w/Butterflies, candy jar, blue, cone-shaped, w/lid, 7½"..**$175.00**

Flower Garden w/Butterflies, comport, black, footed, 7"..**$175.00**

Flower Garden w/Butterflies, comport, canary yellow, 4¼x4¾"..**$50.00**

Flower Garden w/Butterflies, comport, green, 3" (fits 10" plate)..**$23.00**

Flower Garden w/Butterflies, creamer, blue-green **$70.00**

Flower Garden w/Butterflies, plate, amber, indent for 3" comport **$32.00**

Flower Garden w/Butterflies, plate, blue, 7" **$30.00**

Flower Garden w/Butterflies, sugar bowl, pink..........**$75.00**

Fortune, bowl, berry; pink, 4" **$7.00**

Fortune, bowl, salad/berry; crystal, 7¾" **$18.00**

Fortune, plate, sherbet; pink, 6" **$3.00**

Fortune, tumbler, water; crystal, 9-oz, 4" **$11.00**

Fruits, bowl, berry; green, 5" **$30.00**

Fruits, cup, pink..**$7.00**

Fruits, saucer, pink..**$4.00**

Fruits, sherbet, green **$9.00**

Fruits, tumbler, juice; green, 3½".................................**$60.00**

Fruits, tumbler, pink, combination of fruits, 4" **$20.00**

Georgian, bowl, green, deep, 6½"................................**$65.00**

Georgian, butter dish, green, w/lid..............................**$85.00**

Georgian, creamer, green, footed, 3" **$12.00**

Georgian, hot plate, green, center design, 5"..............**$47.50**

Georgian, plate, luncheon; green, 8"............................**$9.00**

Georgian, saucer, green..**$12.00**

Georgian, sugar bowl, green, footed, w/lid, 3"..........**$50.00**

Georgian, tumbler, green, flat, 12-oz, 5¼".................**$135.00**

Hex Optic, bowl, berry; pink, ruffled, 4¼"..................**$5.50**

Hex Optic, bowl, mixing; green, 8¼"..........................**$17.50**

Hex Optic, cup, green, 2 styles of handles, ea **$4.50**

Hex Optic, plate, sherbet; pink, 6".............................**$2.50**

Hex Optic, platter, green, round, 11"..........................**$14.00**

Hex Optic, salt & pepper shakers, pink, pr **$27.50**

Hex Optic, saucer, green..**$2.50**

Hobnail, bowl, salad; crystal, 7" **$4.50**

Hobnail, creamer, crystal, footed................................**$3.50**

Hobnail, goblet, water; crystal, 10-oz..........................**$7.00**

Hobnail, plate, sherbet; pink, 6"..................................**$2.00**

Hobnail, saucer/sherbet plate, pink **$2.00**

Hobnail, sugar bowl, crystal, footed **$4.00**

Hobnail, tumbler, juice; crystal, 5-oz..........................**$4.00**

Homespun, bowl, cereal; pink, closed handles, 5".....**$27.50**

Homespun, creamer, crystal, footed............................**$10.00**

Homespun, plate, dinner; pink, 9¼"..........................**$16.00**

Homespun, tumbler, iced tea; crystal, 12½-oz, 5⅜" ...**$30.00**

Homespun, tumbler, pink, band at top, 9-oz, 4¼" **$20.00**

Homespun, tumbler, pink, footed, 5-oz, 4" **$7.00**

Homespun, tumbler, pink, straight sides, 7-oz, 3⅞"...**$20.00**

Indiana Custard, bowl, berry; ivory, 5½"....................**$10.00**

Indiana Custard, plate, bread & butter; ivory, 5¾" **$6.50**

Indiana Custard, plate, luncheon; ivory, 8⅞" **$18.00**

Indiana Custard, sugar bowl, ivory **$12.00**

Iris, bowl, berry; crystal, beaded edge, 8" **$85.00**

Iris, bowl, fruit; iridescent, ruffled, 11½" **$14.00**

iris, bowl, sauce; iridescent, ruffled, 5"......................**$27.50**

Iris, butter dish bottom, crystal..................................**$13.50**

Iris, candlesticks, iridescent, pr..................................**$45.00**

Iris, goblet, cocktail; crystal, 4-oz, 4½" **$27.50**

Iris, pitcher, iridescent, footed, 9½" **$40.00**

Iris, plate, sherbet; crystal, 5½"..................................**$15.00**

Iris, saucer, iridescent **$11.00**

Iris, sugar bowl, crystal, w/lid **$23.00**

Iris, tumbler, crystal, footed, 6"..................................**$18.00**

Iris, vase, green, 9" **$195.00**

Jubilee, bowl, fruit; yellow, flat, 11½" $195.00
Jubilee, plate, luncheon; pink, 8¾" $27.50
Jubilee, stem, cocktail; yellow, 4-oz, 4¾" $75.00
Jubilee, tray, cake; pink, 2-handled, 11" $65.00
Jubilee, tray, sandwich; yellow, center-handled, 11" ..$210.00
Lace Edge, bowl, salad; pink, ribbed, 7¾" $50.00
Lace Edge, butter dish bottom, pink, 7¾" $27.50

Lace Edge, candy jar, pink, $50.00.

Lace Edge, fish bowl, crystal, 136-oz $30.00
Lace Edge, plate, luncheon; pink, 8¼" $23.00
Lace Edge, plate, relish; pink, 3-part, 10½" $25.00
Lace Edge, plate, salad; pink, 7¼" $25.00
Lace Edge, saucer, pink...$11.00
Laced Edge, basket bowl, opalescent $225.00
Laced Edge, bowl, opalescent, 5½" $37.50
Laced Edge, bowl, soup; opalescent, 7" $80.00
Laced Edge, creamer, opalescent...............................$40.00
Laced Edge, plate, salad; opalescent, 8" $32.00
Laced Edge, tidbit, opalescent, 2-tiered, 8" & 10" plates ..$100.00
Lake Como, creamer, white, footed $32.50
Lake Como, cup, St Denis; white $30.00
Lake Como, salt & pepper shakers, white, pr............$42.50
Lake Como, sugar bowl, white, footed.......................$32.50
Laurel, bowl, blue, 3-leg, 10½".................................$65.00
Laurel, bowl, vegetable; blue, oval, 9¾"...................$50.00
Laurel, bowl, white, 3-leg, 6".....................................$12.50
Laurel, candlestick, ivory, 4", pr $35.00
Laurel, creamer, jade green, tall................................$12.00
Laurel, plate, dinner; ivory, 9⅛"...............................$13.00
Laurel, plate, sherbet; white opalescent, 6" $5.00
Laurel, saucer, ivory...$3.00
Laurel, sherbet/champagne, jade green, 5"..................$45.00
Laurel, sugar bowl, ivory, tall $11.00
Lincoln Inn, bowl, amethyst, crimped, 6" $8.50
Lincoln Inn, bowl, finger; red....................................$20.00
Lincoln Inn, candy dish, black, footed, oval $20.00
Lincoln Inn, goblet, water; cobalt blue......................$27.00
Lincoln Inn, plate, green, 8".......................................$7.50
Lincoln Inn, saucer, red...$5.00
Lincoln Inn, tumbler, cobalt blue, footed, 5-oz..........$30.00
Lincoln Inn, tumbler, juice; green opalescent, flat, 4-oz ..$9.50
Lincoln Inn, tumbler, pink, footed, 12-oz...................$19.00

Lorain, bowl, salad; crystal, 7¼"..............................$45.00
Lorain, creamer, green, footed..................................$16.00
Lorain, cup, yellow...$15.00
Lorain, plate, luncheon; crystal, 8⅜" $17.50
Lorain, plate, sherbet; yellow, 5½"...........................$11.00
Lorain, platter, yellow, 11½"......................................$45.00
Lorain, saucer, green..$4.50
Lorain, sugar bowl, yellow, footed............................$25.00
Madrid, bowl, console; pink, low, 11".......................$11.00
Madrid, bowl, cream soup; amber, 4¾".....................$16.00
Madrid, bowl, soup; green, 7"...................................$16.00
Madrid, bowl, vegetable; green, oval, 10" $20.00
Madrid, candlesticks, amber, 2¼", pr $22.00
Madrid, creamer, green, footed.................................$11.00
Madrid, cup, blue $16.00
Madrid, hot dish coaster, amber $40.00
Madrid, pitcher, blue, square, 60-oz, 8".....................$160.00
Madrid, pitcher, green, 80-oz, 8½"............................$200.00
Madrid, plate, dinner; green, 10½"............................$40.00
Madrid, plate, sherbet; amber, 6".............................$4.00
Madrid, platter, amber, oval, 11½"............................$15.00
Madrid, tumbler, amber, 9-oz, 4¼"...........................$15.00
Madrid, tumbler, green, footed, 5-oz, 4"...................$40.00
Manhattan, ashtray, crystal, round, 4" $11.00
Manhattan, bowl, berry; pink, w/handles, 5⅜".........$20.00
Manhattan, bowl, crystal, closed handles, 8".............$22.00
Manhattan, candy dish, pink, 3-leg $12.00
Manhattan, pitcher, crystal, tilted, 80-oz $45.00
Manhattan, plate, saucer/sherbet; crystal $7.00
Manhattan, relish tray, pink, w/inserts, 14" $85.00
Manhattan, salt & pepper shakers, pink, square, 2", pr ..$45.00
Manhattan, tumbler, pink, footed, 10-oz...................$17.00
Mayfair (Open Rose), bowl, cereal; blue, 5½"...........$50.00
Mayfair (Open Rose), bowl, pink, low, flat, 11¾" $57.50
Mayfair (Open Rose), bowl, vegetable; yellow, oval, 9½"..$135.00

Mayfair, candy dish, blue, $315.00. (Photo courtesy Gene Florence)

Mayfair (Open Rose), cup, pink $18.00
Mayfair (Open Rose), goblet, cocktail; green, 3-oz, 4".$395.00
Mayfair (Open Rose), pitcher, blue, 37-oz, 6" $165.00
Mayfair (Open Rose), plate, cake; blue, footed, 10"...$72.50

Mayfair (Open Rose), plate, cake; pink, w/handles ...**$50.00**

Mayfair (Open Rose), plate, sherbet; pink, round, 6½".**$12.50**

Mayfair (Open Rose), plate, yellow, 5¾"....................**$90.00**

Mayfair (Open Rose), platter, pink, open handles, oval, 12".**$30.00**

Mayfair (Open Rose), relish tray, green, no partitions, 8⅜" **$295.00**

Mayfair (Open Rose), sherbet, pink, flat, 2¼"...........**$195.00**

Mayfair (Open Rose), tumbler, water; pink, 9-oz, 4¼" ..**$30.00**

Mayfair (Open Rose), tumbler, yellow, footed, 10-oz, 5¼" **$180.00**

Mayfair Federal, bowl, cereal; green, 6" **$20.00**

Mayfair Federal, bowl, sauce; crystal, 5" **$6.50**

Mayfair Federal, bowl, vegetable; crystal, oval, 10" **$18.00**

Mayfair Federal, cup, amber **$9.00**

Mayfair Federal, saucer, green **$4.00**

Mayfair Federal, sugar bowl, green, footed.................**$16.00**

Miss America, bowl, cereal; crystal, 6¼"....................**$10.00**

Miss America, bowl, fruit; pink, straight sides, deep, 8¾"..**$80.00**

Miss America, butter dish lid, pink **$600.00**

Miss America, candy jar, crystal, w/lid, 11½" **$60.00**

Miss America, comport, crystal, 5".............................**$14.00**

Miss America, goblet, wine; Royal Ruby, 3-oz, 3¾" .**$295.00**

Miss America, pitcher, pink, 65-oz, 8"......................**$135.00**

Miss America, plate, dinner; pink, 10¼" **$30.00**

Miss America, plate, sherbet; crystal, 5¾".....................**$6.00**

Miss America, saucer, Royal Ruby **$65.00**

Miss America, sugar bowl, crystal................................**$8.00**

Miss America, tumbler, water; crystal, 10-oz, 4½".......**$15.00**

Moderntone, bowl, berry; amethyst, lg, 8¾" **$40.00**

Moderntone, bowl, berry; cobalt, 5" **$26.00**

Moderntone, bowl, cereal; amethyst, 6½" **$75.00**

Moderntone, custard/cup, amethyst, handleless **$14.00**

Moderntone, plate, salad; cobalt, 6¾"........................**$12.50**

Moderntone, plate, sandwich; amethyst, 10½"............**$40.00**

Moderntone, platter, cobalt, oval, 12" **$77.50**

Moderntone, saucer, amethyst **$4.00**

Moderntone, tumbler, amethyst, 5-oz..........................**$32.00**

Moderntone, tumbler, cobalt, 9-oz **$37.50**

Moderntone, whiskey, cobalt, 1½-oz...........................**$42.50**

Moondrops, bowl, pickle; colors other than red & blue, 7½" **$14.00**

Moondrops, bowl, vegetable; red, oval, 9¾"...............**$45.00**

Moondrops, butter dish, blue, w/lid..........................**$450.00**

Moondrops, candlesticks, colors other than blue or red, sherbet style, 4½", pr..**$20.00**

Moondrops, candlesticks, red, metal stem, 8½", pr **$40.00**

Moondrops, decanter, blue, med, 8½"........................**$70.00**

Moondrops, goblet, wine; colors other than blue or red, 4-oz, 4"...**$13.00**

Moondrops, goblet, wine; red, metal stem, 3-oz, 5⅛"..**$16.00**

Moondrops, mug, colors other than blue or red, 12-oz, 5⅛" **$23.00**

Moondrops, plate, blue, 5⅞".......................................**$11.00**

Moondrops, plate, sandwich; red, 2-handled, 14".......**$60.00**

Moondrops, sherbet, colors other than blue or red, 4½" ..**$16.00**

Moondrops, tumbler, colors other than blue or red, 7-oz, 4⅜" **$10.00**

Moondrops, tumbler, red, 12-oz, 5⅛" **$30.00**

Mt Pleasant, bowl, black, footed, scalloped, 1¾" **$30.00**

Mt Pleasant, bowl, fruit; amethyst, footed, square, 4⅞" **$20.00**

Mt Pleasant, bowl, green, 3-footed, rolled out edge, 7" .**$16.00**

Mt Pleasant, bowl, rose; pink, 4" opening..................**$18.00**

Mt Pleasant, candlestick, cobalt, single, pr **$30.00**

Mt Pleasant, cup, pink..**$9.50**

Mt Pleasant, plate, amethyst, 2-handled, scalloped, 7" .**$15.00**

Mt Pleasant, plate, cake; black, 2-handled, 10½"........**$30.00**

Mt Pleasant, plate, green, square or scalloped, 8" **$10.00**

Mt Pleasant, salt & pepper shakers, green, 2 styles....**$24.00**

Mt Pleasant, sugar bowl, cobalt..................................**$18.00**

New Century, bowl, cream soup; green, 4¾" **$20.00**

New Century, creamer, crystal....................................**$8.50**

New Century, pitcher, green, w/ or w/out ice lip, 80-oz, 8"...**$40.00**

New Century, plate, dinner; crystal, 10" **$18.00**

New Century, plate, sherbet; green, 6" **$3.50**

New Century, salt & pepper shakers, crystal, pr.........**$35.00**

New Century, saucer, pink..**$7.50**

New Century, tumbler, cobalt, 9-oz, 4¼" **$18.00**

New Century, tumbler, green, footed, 5-oz, 4"............**$20.00**

Newport, bowl, berry; cobalt, 4¾"..............................**$20.00**

Newport, bowl, cream soup; amethyst, 4¾" **$18.00**

Newport, cup, amethyst..**$10.00**

Newport, plate, sherbet; cobalt, 5⅞".............................**$7.00**

Newport, platter, amethyst, oval, 11¾".......................**$40.00**

Newport, saucer, amethyst **$5.00**

Newport, sherbet, amethyst **$13.00**

No 610 Pyramid, bowl, berry; crystal, 4¾"................**$11.00**

No 610 Pyramid, bowl, green, oval, handled, 9½" **$35.00**

No 610 Pyramid, bowl, master berry; pink, 8½".........**$30.00**

No 610 Pyramid, bowl, pickle; yellow, 5¾x9½".........**$55.00**

No 610 Pyramid, creamer, green **$30.00**

No 610 Pyramid, sugar bowl, crystal..........................**$17.50**

No 610 Pyramid, tumbler, yellow, footed, 2 styles, 8-oz...**$70.00**

No 612 Horseshoe, bowl, berry; yellow, lg, 9½" **$50.00**

No 612 Horseshoe, bowl, cereal; yellow, 6½" **$30.00**

No 612 Horseshoe, bowl, salad; green, 7½" **$25.00**

No 612 Horseshoe, butter dish, green, w/lid............**$800.00**

No 612 Horseshoe, cup, yellow **$13.00**

No 612 Horseshoe, plate, sherbet; green, 6" **$8.00**

No 612 Horseshoe, saucer, green **$5.00**

No 612 Horseshoe, tumbler, yellow, footed, 9-oz.......**$25.00**

No 616 Vernon, creamer, green, footed......................**$25.00**

No 616 Vernon, saucer, yellow.....................................**$4.00**

No 616 Vernon, tumbler, crystal, footed, 5".................**$15.00**

No 618 Pineapple & Floral, bowl, vegetable; crystal, oval, 10"...**$25.00**

No 618 Pineapple & Floral, comport, red, diamond-shape...**$8.00**

No 618 Pineapple & Floral, cup, crystal **$11.00**

No 618 Pineapple & Floral, plate, sandwich; crystal, 11½" **$17.50**

No 618 Pineapple & Floral, sherbet, amber, footed....**$18.00**

Normandie, bowl, cereal; amber, 6½".........................**$28.00**

Normandie, bowl, vegetable; pink, oval, 10" $37.50
Normandie, plate, dinner; pink, 11".........................$115.00

Normandie, plate, grill; iridescent, 11", $9.00; sherbet, $7.00; bowl, cereal, 6½", $8.50; cup, $6.00; saucer, $3.00. (Photo courtesy Gene Florence)

Normandie, plate, salad; amber, 7¾" $8.50
Normandie, platter, iridescent, 11¾"........................$12.00
Normandie, tumbler, iced tea; pink, 12-oz, 5" $110.00
Normandie, tumbler, juice; amber, 5-oz, 4" $32.00
Old Cafe, bowl, crystal, tab handles, 4½"...................$6.00
Old Cafe, bowl, Royal Ruby, closed handles, 9".........$16.00
Old Cafe, candy dish, pink, tab handles, low, 8" $12.00
Old Cafe, cup, Royal Ruby...$9.00
Old Cafe, olive dish, crystal, oblong, 6"......................$7.00
Old Cafe, pitcher, pink, 80-oz $125.00
Old Cafe, sherbet, crystal, low footed $12.00
Old Cafe, tumbler, juice; Royal Ruby, 3" $14.00
Old Cafe, vase, pink, 7¼"...$20.00
Old English, candy dish, green, flat, w/lid................$50.00
Old English, compote, amber, 2-handled, 6⅜x3½" $22.50
Old English, creamer, pink $17.50
Old English, plate, green, indent for compote............$20.00
Old English, vase, amber, footed, 12" $60.00
Ovide, bowl, berry; decorated white, 4¾"...................$7.00
Ovide, candy dish, green, w/lid $22.00
Ovide, creamer, black...$6.50
Ovide, plate, dinner; decorated white, 9"..................$20.00
Ovide, saucer, Art Deco $18.00
Oyster & Pearl, bowl, crystal, heart-shaped, handled, 5¼"...$12.00
Oyster & Pearl, bowl, fruit; Royal Ruby, deep, 10½" .$55.00

Oyster and Pearl, candleholder, pink, 3½", $10.00; relish dish, 10¼", $12.00; bowl, handled, $15.00. (Photo courtesy Gene Florence)

Parrot, bowl, berry; green, lg, 8" $95.00
Parrot, bowl, soup; amber, 7" $35.00
Parrot, cup, green...$40.00
Parrot, plate, grill; amber, square, 10½"....................$30.00
Parrot, plate, grill; green, round, 10½" $32.00
Parrot, saucer, green...$15.00
Parrot, sugar bowl, amber..$50.00

Parrot, sugar bowl, green, $40.00.

Parrot, tumbler, amber, heavy, footed, 5¾".............$125.00
Patrician, bowl, berry; amber, 5" $12.50
Patrician, bowl, vegetable; pink, oval, 10".................$25.00
Patrician, jam dish, pink...$30.00
Patrician, plate, grill; green, 10½" $15.00
Patrician, plate, luncheon; pink, 9".............................$10.00
Patrician, plate, sherbet; crystal, 6"...........................$10.00
Patrician, platter, crystal, oval, 11½".........................$30.00
Patrician, sherbet, pink..$14.00
Patrician, tumbler, green, 9-oz, 4¼"..........................$25.00
Patrick, bowl, fruit; yellow, handled, 9" $135.00
Patrick, creamer, yellow $37.50
Patrick, goblet, juice; pink, 6-oz, 4¾" $80.00
Patrick, plate, luncheon; pink, 8" $45.00
Patrick, plate, sherbet; yellow, 7" $12.00
Patrick, saucer, yellow..$12.00
Patrick, tray, yellow, 2-handled, 11".........................$60.00
Petalware, bowl, cereal; monax plain, 5¾" $8.00
Petalware, bowl, cream soup; pink, 4½" $12.50
Petalware, creamer, crystal, footed $3.00
Petalware, plate, dinner; crystal, 9" $4.00
Petalware, plate, salver; pink, 12" $11.00
Petalware, plate, sherbet; red trim floral, 6" $20.00
Petalware, saucer, cream soup liner; monax plain......$18.00
Petalware, sherbet, monax floral, low footed, 4½".....$12.00
Primo, bowl, green, 4½"...$18.00
Primo, bowl, yellow, 3-footed, 11"............................$30.00
Primo, coaster/astray, green......................................$8.00
Primo, plate, yellow, 6¼"...$10.00
Primo, saucer, green $3.00
Primo, tumbler, green, 9-oz, 5¾"...............................$22.00
Princess, bowl, cereal/oatmeal; green, 5" $35.00
Princess, bowl, vegetable; pink, oval, 10" $28.00
Princess, creamer, green, oval $14.00
Princess, pitcher, pink, 60-oz, 8" $55.00
Princess, plate, salad; apricot, 8" $15.00
Princess, plate, sandwich; green, handled, 10¼" $16.00
Princess, platter, pink, closed handles, 12"................$25.00

Princess, salt & pepper shakers, topaz, pr..................$85.00
Princess, sherbet, green, footed..................................$24.00
Princess, tumbler, iced tea; apricot, 13-oz, 5¼" $30.00
Princess, vase, green, 8"..$35.00
Queen Mary, ashtray, pink, oval, 2x3¾".....................$5.00
Queen Mary, bowl, berry; crystal, lg, 8¾" $10.00
Queen Mary, bowl, crystal, 2-handled, 5½" $5.50
Queen Mary, cigarette jar, crystal, oval, 2x3"..............$5.50
Queen Mary, cup, pink, lg...$7.00
Queen Mary, plate, salad; crystal, 8¾".......................$5.50
Queen Mary, plate, sandwich; pink, 12"......................$16.00
Queen Mary, relish tray, crystal, 4-part, 14" $12.00
Queen Mary, sherbet, pink, footed $9.00
Raindrops, bowl, fruit; green, 4½" $6.00
Raindrops, creamer, green..$7.50
Raindrops, saucer, green $2.00
Raindrops, tumbler, green, 14-oz, 5⅜".......................$12.00
Raindrops, tumbler, green, 4-oz, 3"............................$5.00
Raindrops, whiskey, green, 1-oz, 1⅞"..........................$7.00
Ribbon, bowl, berry; black, lg, 8" $35.00
Ribbon, bowl, cereal; green, 5" $35.00
Ribbon, cup, green $5.00
Ribbon, plate, luncheon; green, 8"..............................$5.00
Ribbon, saucer, green $2.50
Ring, bowl, berry; crystal w/decoration, 5" $6.00
Ring, butter/ice tub, crystal.......................................$22.00
Ring, creamer, green, footed..$6.00
Ring, goblet, cocktail; crystal, 3½-oz, 3¾"..................$11.00
Ring, pitcher, crystal w/decoration, 60-oz, 8"..............$25.00
Ring, plate, crystal, off-center ring.............................$5.00
Ring, saucer, crystal $1.50
Ring, sherbet, green, footed, 4¾" $9.00
Ring, tumbler, crystal, 12-oz, 5⅛"...............................$7.00
Ring, tumbler, water; crystal, footed, 5½"....................$6.00
Rock Crystal, bowl, colors other than red or crystal, scalloped
   edge, 5"..$24.00
Rock Crystal, bowl, red, center handle, 8½".............$225.00
Rock Crystal, bowl, relish; colors other than red or crystal, 2-
   part, 11½"...$50.00
Rock Crystal, bowl, salad; red, scalloped, 8".............$75.00
Rock Crystal, candelabra, colors other than red or crystal, 2-
   light, pr...$105.00
Rock Crystal, comport, crystal, 7"..............................$35.00
Rock Crystal, cup, colors other than red or crystal, 7-oz.$27.50
Rock Crystal, jelly jar, red, scalloped edge, footed, 5"..$52.50
Rock Crystal, pitcher, crystal, ½-gal, 7½" $110.00
Rock Crystal, plate, red, scalloped edge, 10½" $65.00
Rock Crystal, salt dip, crystal....................................$40.00
Rock Crystal, spooner, crystal....................................$45.00
Rock Crystal, stem, cocktail; colors other than red or crystal,
   footed, 3½-oz...................................$21.00
Rock Crystal, sundae, red, low foot, 6-oz..................$35.00
Rock Crystal, tumbler, crystal, concave or straight sides, 9-
   oz..$18.00
Rose Cameo, plate, salad; green, 7"...........................$12.00
Rose Cameo, tumbler, green, footed, 2 styles, 5".......$22.00
Rosemary, bowl, cream soup; amber, 5" $17.00

Rosemary, bowl, vegetable; green, oval, 10"..............$27.50
Rosemary, cup, pink..$10.00
Rosemary, plate, grill; green $15.00
Rosemary, plate, salad; amber, 6¾"............................$5.50
Rosemary, saucer, pink..$6.00
Rosemary, sugar bowl, green, footed..........................$12.50
Roulette, bowl, fruit; pink, 9" $15.00
Roulette, plate, sandwich; crystal, 12".......................$11.00
Roulette, sherbet, green...$5.50
Roulette, tumbler, iced tea; pink, 12-oz, 5⅛".............$30.00
Roulette, tumbler, water; crystal, 9-oz, 4⅛"...............$13.00
Round Robin, domino tray, green...............................$37.50
Round Robin, plate, sandwich; iridescent, 12" $7.00
Round Robin, sherbet, iridescent................................$6.00
Roxana, bowl, berry; yellow, 5" $11.00
Roxana, sherbet, yellow, footed $12.00
Royal Lace, bowl, cream soup; crystal, 4¾" $12.00
Royal Lace, bowl, green, rolled edge, 3-leg, 10".......$125.00

Royal Lace, creamer, blue, $57.50; sugar bowl, $35.00, sugar lid, $195.00.

Royal Lace, pitcher, crystal, w/lip, 68-oz, 8"..............$50.00
Royal Lace, pitcher, green, straight sides, 48-oz........$115.00
Royal lace, plate, sherbet; pink, 6"..............................$8.00
Royal Lace, salt & pepper shakers, green, pr...........$125.00
Royal Lace, sherbet, blue, in metal holder $40.00
Royal Ruby, bowl, berry; Old Cafe, 3¾"......................$7.00
Royal Ruby, bowl, Old Cafe, closed handled, 8" $16.00
Royal Ruby, bowl, Sandwich, scalloped, 5¼" $20.00
Royal Ruby, cup, Coronation $6.50
Royal Ruby, goblet, ball stem.....................................$10.00
Royal Ruby, mint dish, Old Cafe, low, 8" $16.00
Royal Ruby, puff box, crystal w/ruby lid, 4⅝".............$9.00
S Pattern, creamer, crystal, thick or thin $6.00
S Pattern, plate, cake; amber, heavy, 13"...................$75.00
S Pattern, plate, dinner; yellow, 9¼"...........................$9.00
S Pattern, plate, sherbet; monax, 6" $8.00
Sandwich, basket, amber, 10".....................................$35.00
Sandwich, bowl, console; pink, 9"..............................$40.00
Sandwich, candlesticks, crystal, 3½", pr....................$16.00
Sandwich, cup, teal blue...$8.50
Sandwich, plate, sandwich; red, 13"..........................$35.00
Sandwich, saucer, red..$7.50
Sandwich, tumbler, water; crystal, footed, 8-oz...........$9.00

Sandwich (Indiana), plate, dinner; crystal, 10½", $8.00. (Photo courtesy Gene Florence)

Sharon, bowl, cream soup; amber, 5" $28.00
Sharon, bowl, flat soup; pink, 7¾x1⅞" $55.00
Sharon, bowl, fruit; green, 10½" $42.50
Sharon, plate, cake; pink, footed, 11½" $42.50
Sharon, plate, salad; amber, 7½" $15.00
Sharon, salt & pepper shakers, green, pr $70.00
Sharon, sugar bowl, pink $14.00
Sharon, tumbler, amber, thin, 12-oz, 5¼" $52.00
Ships, ice bowl, blue/white $35.00
Ships, saucer, blue/white $17.00
Sierra, bowl, berry; green, lg, 8½" $32.00
Sierra, cup, pink $12.00
Sierra, pitcher, green, 32-oz, 6½" $130.00
Sierra, saucer, green $8.00
Spiral, bowl, berry; green, lg, 8" $12.50
Spiral, plate, luncheon; green, 8" $3.50
Spiral, saucer, green $2.00
Starlight, bowl, salad; crystal, 11½" $25.00
Starlight, plate, bread & butter; white, 8½" $5.00
Starlight, relish dish, white $15.00
Starlight, sherbet, crystal $15.00
Strawberry, bowl, salad; crystal, 6½" $15.00
Strawberry, butter dish, pink, w/lid $195.00
Strawberry, creamer, iridescent, sm $12.00
Strawberry, olive dish, green, handled, 5" $17.00
Strawberry, plate, salad; crystal, 7½" $12.00
Strawberry, sugar bowl, pink, open, sm $20.00
Sunburst, bowl, crystal, 11" $22.00
Sunburst, plate, dinner; crystal, 9¼" $20.00
Sunburst, saucer, crystal $2.00
Sunburst, sugar bowl, crystal $9.00
Sunflower, cup, green $15.00
Sunflower, plate, cake; pink, 3-leg, 10" $15.00
Sunflower, sugar bowl, pink $18.00
Swirl, bowl, console; pink, footed, 10½" $20.00
Swirl, butter dish bottom, ultramarine $40.00
Swirl, candle holder, delphite, single branch, pr $125.00
Swirl, plate, dinner; delphite, 9¼" $12.00
Swirl, plate, pink, 7¼" $8.00
Swirl, vase, pink, ruffled, footed, 6½" $18.00
Tea Room, bowl, banana split; green, footed, 7½" $85.00
Tea Room, creamer, amber, footed, 4½" $75.00
Tea Room, ice bucket, pink $52.50

Tea Room, plate, luncheon; pink, 8¼" $30.00
Tea Room, sherbet, green, flared edge, low $30.00
Tea Room, sugar bowl, pink, flat, w/lid....................$160.00
Tea Room, tumbler, green, footed, 12-oz....................$65.00
Tea Room, vase, green, ruffled edge, 11"..................$250.00
Tea Room, vase, pink, straight sides, 11"..................$150.00
Thistle, bowl, cereal; pink, 5½".................................$22.50
Thistle, plate, cake; green, heavy, 13" $175.00
Tulip, creamer, amethyst..$20.00
Tulip, ice tub, crystal, 3x4⅞".....................................$65.00
Tulip, plate, blue, 6"...$10.00
Tulip, tumbler, whiskey; green...................................$20.00
Twisted Optic, bowl, cream soup; pink, 4¾".............$11.00
Twisted Optic, bowl, green, 4¼x11½".......................$22.50
Twisted Optic, candy jar, amber, footed, w/lid, tall....$40.00
Twisted Optic, candy jar, canary yellow, flat, flanged edge,
   w/lid $70.00
Twisted Optic, comport, pink.....................................$18.00
Twisted Optic, cup, blue...$10.00
Twisted Optic, plate, canary yellow, oval w/indent,
   7½x9"...$9.00
Twisted Optic, sandwich server, pink, open center han-
   dle $20.00
Twisted Optic, sherbet, blue.......................................$10.00
Twisted Optic, tumbler, green, 12-oz, 5¼" $8.00
US Swirl, bowl, berry; green, 4⅜" $5.50
US Swirl, bowl, pink, oval, 2¾x8¼" $40.00
US Swirl, butter dish bottom, green...........................$100.00
US Swirl, plate, salad; green, 7"...................................$7.00
US Swirl, sherbet, green, 3¼" $4.50
US Swirl, tumbler, pink, 12-oz, 4¾" $15.00
Victory, bowl, cereal; amber, 6½" $11.00
Victory, bowl, console; black, 12" $65.00
Victory, comport, pink, 6¾x6" $15.00
Victory, saucer, amber $4.00
Vitrock, bowl, berry; white, 4"....................................$4.50
Vitrock, creamer, white, oval $5.00
Vitrock, plate, dinner; white, 10".................................$8.50
Vitrock, plate, luncheon; white, 8¾"............................$4.50
Vitrock, saucer, white..$2.50
Waterford, bowl, berry; crystal, 4¾"............................$6.50
Waterford, bowl, berry; pink, lg, 8¼"..........................$25.00
Waterford, butter dish lid, crystal $19.00
Waterford, cup, pink...$15.00
Waterford, plate, sandwich; pink, 13¾".......................$27.50
Waterford, plate, sherbet; crystal, 6"............................$3.00
Waterford, sherbet, pink, footed.................................$15.00
Waterford, tumbler, juice; pink, Miss America style, 5-oz,
   3½"...$95.00
Windsor, bowl, pink, boat shape, 7x11¾"...................$35.00
Windsor, bowl, vegetable; green, oval, 9½".................$27.50
Windsor, creamer, pink...$12.50
Windsor, cup, green..$12.50
Windsor, platter, pink, oval, 11½"...............................$20.00
Windsor, saucer, ice blue $15.00
Windsor, tray, crystal, w/handles, square, 4".................$5.00
Windsor, tumbler, green, 5-oz, 3¼"............................$35.00

Disney

The largest and most popular area in character collectibles is without doubt Disneyana. There are clubs, newsletters, and special shows that are centered around this hobby. Every aspect of the retail market has been thoroughly saturated with Disney-related merchandise over the years, and today collectors are able to find many good examples at garage sales and flea markets.

Disney memorabilia from the late '20s and '30s was marked either 'Walt E. Disney' or 'Walt Disney Enterprises.' After about 1940 the name was changed to 'Walt Disney Productions.' This mark was in use until 1984 when the 'Walt Disney Company' mark was introduced, and this last mark has remained in use up to the present time. Some of the earlier items have become very expensive, though many are still within the reach of the average collector.

During the '30s, Mickey Mouse, Donald Duck, Snow White and the Seven Dwarfs, and the Three Little Pigs (along with all their friends and cohorts) dominated the Disney scene. The last of the '30s' characters was Pinocchio, and some 'purists' prefer to stop their collections with him.

The '40s and '50s brought many new characters with them — Alice in Wonderland, Bambi, Dumbo, Lady and the Tramp, and Peter Pan were some of the major personalities featured in Disney's films of this era.

Even today, thanks to the re-releases of many of the old movies and the popularity of Disney's vacation 'kingdoms,' toy stores and department stores alike are full of quality items with the potential of soon becoming collectibles.

If you'd like to learn more about this fascinating field, we recommend *Stern's Guide to Disney Collectibles, First and Second Series*, by Michael Stern; *The Collector's Encyclopedia of Disneyana* by Michael Stern and David Longest; *Character Toys and Collectibles* and *Toys, Antique and Collectible*, both by David Longest; and *Schroeder's Collectible Toys, Antique to Modern*. All are published by Collector Books.

See also Character and Promotional Drinking Glasses; Character Banks; Character Watches; Cowboy Character Memorabilia; Dolls, Mattel; Games; Pin-Back Buttons; Puzzles; Salt and Pepper Shakers; Toys; Valentines.

Note: In the following listings, many of the characters have been sorted by the name of the feature film in which they appeared.

Advisor: Judy Posner (See Directory, Character and Personality Collectibles)

Aladdin, doll, Genie, stuffed cloth w/vinyl head, Mattel, 1992, 11", MIB..**$25.00**
Aladdin, doll, Genie or Prince Ali, Applause, vinyl w/cloth clothes, 10", MIB, ea..............................**$15.00**
Aladdin, doll, Jasmine, stuffed cloth w/vinyl head, Mattel, 1993, 14", MIB.................................**$20.00**
Aladdin, figures, any character, Mattel, 5", MOC, ea...**$10.00**
Alice in Wonderland, Stitch-A-Story, Hasbro, 1969, complete, NMIB..**$25.00**

Alice in Wonderland, Tea Time Dishes, embossed plastic, Plasco, 11-pc set, EXIB.........................**$75.00**
Bambi, figurine, Flower, ceramic, American Pottery, 1930s, 4"...**$75.00**
Bambi, figurine, Thumper, ceramic, American Pottery, 1930s, 4", NM...................................**$75.00**
Beauty & the Beast, doll, Beast, plush w/cloth clothes, Mattel, 1993, NMIB.............................**$30.00**
Black Hole, Golden Book of Things To Do, 1979, complete & unused, NM................................**$20.00**
Cinderella, wastebasket, metal, tells story w/graphics, 1950s, 19x10" dia, EX............................**$50.00**
Disneyland, Character Play World, fold-away, unused, MIB...**$125.00**
Disneyland, scrapbook, Whitman, 1955, softcover, unused, EX...**$50.00**
Disneyland, tray, metal, black & yellow map of California w/Disneyland location & character graphics, 1950s, 11" dia, NM...**$85.00**
Disneyland, Walt Disney's Guide to Disneyland, 1955 (year it opened — later issues are less), EX, from $150 to.**$200.00**
Disneyland, xylophone, w/music stand, Original Concert Grand, MIB.......................................**$135.00**
Donald Duck, bank, ceramic, Donald figure waving, Japan, 1960s, 6", from $50.............................**$75.00**
Donald Duck, bank, ceramic, Donald in tent, Japan, 5", EX...**$50.00**
Donald Duck, Doctor Kit, WDP, 1940s, EXIB..........**$125.00**
Donald Duck, doll, Dancing Donald, stuffed cloth w/vinyl head, squeeze hands for action, Hasbro, 1977, 18", EX...**$35.00**
Donald Duck, figure, bisque, head turned right, long bill, Japan, 1930s, 2", EX................................**$65.00**
Donald Duck, figure, celluloid, jointed limbs, Japan/WD, 3½", M...**$140.00**

Donald Duck, Magic Slate, NM, $25.00. (Photo courtesy June Moon)

Donald Duck, nodder figure, plastic, Marx, 1960s, 2", EX+...**$45.00**

Donald Duck, paint box, litho tin w/image of Donald painting on lid, Transogram, 1948, NM......................$65.00

Donald Duck, plate, Birthday, 1934, Wise Hen, ceramic, 6¼", MIB $85.00

Donald Duck, soap figure, Lightfoot Shultz Co, EX+ (NM box) $65.00

Donald Duck, sweeper, litho wood, Ohio Art/DE, EX ..$125.00

Donald Duck, Whirl-A-Tune Music Maker, Ideal, 1965, NMIB...$80.00

Ducktales, Colorforms, 1986, EXIB $10.00

Dumbo the Elephant, doll, composition w/cloth ears, Cameo Products, 1941, 8", EX $300.00

Ferdinand the Bull, doll, painted composition, Ideal, 9", VG+ $200.00

Goofy, figure, bisque, Japan, 1930s, 2", EX.................$75.00

Goofy, nodder figure, plastic, Marx, 1960s, 2¾", EX+ ..$45.00

Goofy, Weebles figure, 1973, EX.................................$15.00

Hunchback of Notre Dame, dolls, Quasimodo, Phoebus, Frollo, or Esmarelda, vinyl, Applause, 1996, 9", MIB, ea $12.00

Hunchback of Notre Dame, figure set, PVC, Applause, 1996, set of 6, 3", M..$20.00

Lady & the Tramp, figure, Peg, Hagen-Renaker, 1950s, 2", NM..$165.00

Lady & the Tramp, wallet, red vinyl, WDP, 1950s, from $30 to $40.00

Lion King, Colorforms, 1994, EXIB...............................$6.00

Mary Poppins, spoon, silver-plated, figure of Mary Poppins at top of handle, 1964, M......................................$20.00

Mickey Mouse, bank, Mickey waving, ceramic, Japan, 1960s, 6", M, from $50 ....$75.00

Mickey Mouse, birthday candle holders, ceramic w/embossed image of Mickey, set of 5, Cypress Novelty, 1930s, 1", MIB $150.00

Mickey Mouse, blotter, Post-O Cereal advertising for Mickey's silver-plated spoon w/name embossed on handle, 1930s, EX...$20.00

Mickey Mouse, Dance-A-Tune, Jaymar, M (EX box), $125.00.

Mickey Mouse, doll, Posie, Ideal, 1950s, EXIB...........$45.00

Mickey Mouse, figure, bisque, arms at side, Japan, 1930s, 2", VG..$75.00

Mickey Mouse, figure, bisque, waving, Japan, 1930s, 1½", EX $65.00

Mickey Mouse, figurines, bisque, as musicians, MIB, from $400.00 to $500.00. (Photo courtesy Dunbar Gallery)

Mickey Mouse, gumball machine, plastic head on round stepped base, Hasbro, EX.....................................$15.00

Mickey Mouse, Jumpkins figure, plastic, Mickey dances on string, Kohner, 1960s, 5", MOC $55.00

Mickey Mouse, mask, black litho on white molded mesh canvas, early rat-like image, 1930s, NM....................$125.00

Mickey Mouse, nodder figure, plastic, Marx, 1960s, 2", EX+...$45.00

Mickey Mouse, party horn, wood & paper, Marks Bros, 1930s, 7", EX+..$145.00

Mickey Mouse, Pin the Tail on Mickey Party Game, Marks Bros, complete, EXIB $125.00

Mickey Mouse, planter, Mickey pushing cart, ceramic, D Brechner Co, 1960s, 5", EX+ $65.00

Mickey Mouse, recipe scrapbook, color images of Mickey, Minnie & Pluto, 3 pages for bread labels, 1930s, EX (w/envelope)...$95.00

Mickey Mouse, rocker board, facing left, 1950s, EX, from $150.00 to $200.00. (Photo courtesy Dunbar Gallery)

Mickey Mouse, Rub 'N' Play Magic Transfer Set, Colorforms, 1978, unused, MIB...$30.00

Mickey Mouse, soap figure, Lightfoot Shultz Co, 1930s, NMIB $145.00

Mickey Mouse, sweeper, litho tin & wood, Ohio Art, 1930s, EX $225.00

Mickey Mouse & Donald Duck, drum, tin & paper, WDE, 1930s, EX...$350.00

Mickey Mouse & Donald Duck, magic slate, 1951, EX...**$25.00**

Mickey Mouse & Minnie, blotter, Blue Sunoco advertising, featured a married Mickey & Minnie in car, 1939, EX **$20.00**

Mickey Mouse & Minnie, figures, bisque, standing w/hands on hips, Japan, 1930s, 5", EX+, pr......................**$385.00**

Mickey Mouse & Minnie, party horn, litho cardboard, Marks Bros/WDE, 1935, 7", EX......................................**$165.00**

Mickey Mouse & Minnie, playhouse, litho cardboard w/Mickey & Minnie peering out windows, Andrews, 1934, EX **$225.00**

Mickey Mouse & Minnie, scrapbook, #640, 1936, complete, unused, VG **$85.00**

Mickey Mouse & Minnie, tambourine, image of Minnie watching Mickey juggle, Noble Cooley/WDE, EX.........**$300.00**

Mickey Mouse & Minnie, wall plaques, painted wood cut-out figures w/nephew, 3-pc set, WD, 1930s, 10" & 6", EX+ **$250.00**

Mickey Mouse Club, Build-Up Blocks, Eldon, 1950s, complete, M (NM tower-like box) **$30.00**

Mickey Mouse Club, Mouskartooner, Mattel, 1950s, EXIB...**$65.00**

Mickey Mouse Club, washcloth, features the Mousketeers, EX **$15.00**

Minnie Mouse, bank, Minnie in house, composition, WDP/Japan......................................**$50.00**

Minnie Mouse, coffee mug, lg image of Minnie brushing her hair w/mirror in hand, Patriot China, 1930s, EX+ ..**$95.00**

Minnie Mouse, doll, stuffed cloth w/leather-type shoes, Gund, 1940s, 18", scarce, VG **$280.00**

Minnie Mouse, doll, wooden swivel body w/flexible limbs, decals on body & shoe, WD, 7", NM...............**$275.00**

Nightmare Before Christmas, figure, Jack as Santa, Hasbro, 1993, MOC......................................**$70.00**

Nightmare Before Christmas, figures: Lock, Shock, and Barrel, Hasbro, 1993, 5", MIB, $125.00. (Photo courtesy June Moon)

Nightmare Before Christmas, figures in coffins, 14" Jack & Sally figures in 17" coffins, Japan, MIB, pr.........**$370.00**

Pagemaster, doll, Richard, plush, Applause, 1994, 11", M ...**$15.00**

Pagemaster, key chains, PVC, Applause, 1994, set of 5, MOC......................................**$10.00**

Peter Pan, hatbox, imitation green leather on cardboard w/flocked image of Peter Pan & Tinker Bell, Ne Evel, 1950s, NM......................................**$175.00**

Peter Pan, Television Studio, cardboard, Admiral TV premium, 1952, M **$165.00**

Pinocchico, Color Box, Transogram, 1940s, complete, EXIB **$50.00**

Pinocchio, clicker, 1950s, yellow plastic head, NM **$20.00**

Pinocchio, cup, Jiminy Cricket, plastic figural head w/flicker eyes, 1950s, 4", NM+ **$30.00**

Pinocchio, doll, Jiminy Cricket, jointed wood, Ideal, 1930s, 8", EX **$500.00**

Pinocchio, mask, Figaro, paper, Gillette Razor Blades premium, 1939, EX **$35.00**

Pinocchio, Puppet Show, complete w/stage & 8 characters, Whitman, EXIB **$125.00**

Pinocchio, tie, dark blue w/2" embroidered image of Pinocchio & his name, WDP, 1940s, 24", EX+......**$65.00**

Pluto, bank, sitting upright, ceramic, Japan, 1960s, 6", M, from $50 to......................................**$75.00**

Pluto, nodder figure, plastic, Marx, 1960s, 1¾", EX+..**$45.00**

Pluto, Peppy Puppet, miniature plastic marionette, Kohner, MOC......................................**$55.00**

Pluto, Playful Pluto pull toy, wood, Jaymar, 1950s, 8", EX......................................**$300.00**

Rocketeer, beach towel, 2 designs, promo for AMC Theatres, NM, ea **$30.00**

Rocketeer, Poster Pen Set, Rose Art #1921, 1991, complete, MOC, from $20 to......................................**$30.00**

Rocketeer, roll-along figures, PVC, set of 3, Applause, 1990, M......................................**$15.00**

Rocketeer, wallet, Pyramid Handbag Co, M................**$40.00**

Seed packets, ca 1970s, from $10.00 to $15.00 each. (Photo courtesy Dunbar Gallery)

Sleeping Beauty, Colorforms Dress-Up Kit, WDP, 1959, incomplete, EXIB **$45.00**

Sleeping Beauty, Disneykins, Sleeping Beauty or Prince Charming, 2nd series, 1960s, EX, ea **$45.00**

Sleeping Beauty, ring, silver plastic w/blue plastic shield, removable sword, 1950s, EX................**$45.00**

Sleeping Beauty, ring, silver-tone plastic w/blue plastic 'Truth-Virtue' shield & sm removable silver sword, 1950s, EX......................................**$45.00**

Sleeping Beauty, sewing set, Transogram, unused, EX...**$65.00**

Snow White & the Seven Dwarfs, Dance 'N Play Deluxe Gift Set, Mattel, 1993, MIB......................................**$45.00**

Snow White & the Seven Dwarfs, Disneykins, any character, 1st series, 1960s, EX, ea **$10.00**

Snow White & the Seven Dwarfs, dolls, Snow White, Storybook Small-Talk, Mattel 1970, MIB **$125.00**

Snow White & the Seven Dwarfs, fan card, features all 8 characters on royal blue background, 1930s, VG........**$75.00**

Snow White & the Seven Dwarfs, figures, any character, bisque, Japan, 1930s, 3", ea, from $50 to **$60.00**

Snow White & the Seven Dwarfs, perfume, Kerk Guild/WDE, 1938, 6", EXIB......................**$150.00**

Snow White & the Seven Dwarfs, picture cards, die-punched cardboard, NBC Bread premium, 1950s, set of 3, 7x6", NM+ **$50.00**

Snow White and the Seven Dwarfs, Talking Telephone, Hasbro, 1967, M (VG box), $225.00. (Photo courtesy June Moon)

Snow White & the Seven Dwarfs, toothpick holder, Sneezy figure, porcelain, Maw Co, England, 1930s, 4", rare, NM **$275.00**

Snow White & the Seven Dwarfs, watering can, litho tin, Ohio Art, 1930s, 8", EX **$200.00**

Snow White & the Seven Dwarfs, writing tablet, colorful cover, White & Wyckoff/WD Entertainment, 1932, 9x5½", VG+ **$65.00**

Space Jam, figure set, set of 3, Playmates, 1996, MIB .**$30.00**

Sword in the Stone, ring, blue or pink plastic, premium, 1970s, EX, ea....................**$12.00**

Three Little Pigs, figure set, bisque, 3 pigs w/musical instruments & Big Bad Wolf, Japan, 3½", NM............**$140.00**

Three Little Pigs, washing machine, litho tin, complete w/wringer & pedestal, Chein, 8" **$350.00**

Three Little Pigs top, metal w/lithoed characters, NM, minimum value **$200.00**

Toy Story, Colorforms, 1993, complete, MIB............**$15.00**

Toy Story, figures, Buzz Lightyear or Woody, PVC, 3", MOC, ea....................**$6.00**

Toy Story, pull toy, Slinky Dog, MIB **$20.00**

Who Framed Roger Rabbit, doll, Roger Rabbit, inflatable vinyl, LJN, 1987, 36", NM **$12.00**

Who Framed Roger Rabbit, Wacky heads hand puppet, Roger Rabbit, Applause, NM....................**$15.00**

Winnie the Pooh, doll, Tigger, stuffed plush, Sears, 1970s, EX **$35.00**

101 Dalmatians, Corporate Christmas card, opens to view of 101 Dalmatians, w/1961 calendar, NM....................**$75.00**

Dog Collectibles

Dog lovers appreciate the many items, old and new, that are modeled after or decorated with their favorite breeds. They pursue, some avidly, all with dedication, specific items for a particular accumulation or a range of objects, from matchbook covers to bronzes.

Perhaps the Scottish Terrier is one of the most highly sought-out breeds of dogs among collectors; at any rate, Scottie devotees are more organized than most. Both the Aberdeen and West Highland Terriers were used commercially; often the two are found together in things such as magnets, Black & White Scotch Whiskey advertisements, jewelry, and playing cards, for instance. They became a favorite of the advertising world in the 1930s and 1940s, partly as a result of the public popularity of President Roosevelt's dog, Fala. For information on Scottish Terriers see *A Treasury of Scottie Dog Collectibles, Identification and Values, Books I* and *II*, by Candace Sten Davis and Patricia Baugh (Collector Books).

Poodles were the breed of the 1950s, and today items from those years are cherished collectibles. Trendsetter teeny-boppers wore poodle skirts, and the 5-&-10¢ stores were full of pink poodle figurines with 'coleslaw' fur. For a look back at these years, we recommend *Poodle Collectibles of the '50s and '60s* by Elaine Butler (L-W Books).

Many of the earlier collectibles are especially prized, making them expensive and difficult to find. Prices listed here may vary as they are dependent on supply and demand, location, and dealer assessment.

Advisor: Elaine Butler, Poodles (See Directory, Poodle Collectibles)

Club: Heart of America Scottish Terrier Club
Ms. Nancy McGray
507 Kurzweil
Raymore, MD 64083

Newsletter: *Canine Collectibles Quarterly*
Patty Shedlow, Editor
736 N Western Ave., Ste. 314
Lake Forest, IL 60045; Subscription: $28 per year

Brittany Spaniel, print, Scent Savy, Randy McGovern, limited edition, 6¾x10¼"....................**$30.00**

Bull Terrier, plate, Staffordshire, 4¼" dia....................**$13.00**

Chinese Bulldog, butter pat, face form, no mark, 2¾" dia, VG....................**$15.00**

Cocker Spaniel pup, plate, porcelain, 22k gold rim, 4¼" dia, EX....................**$30.00**

German Shepherd, figurine, sitting, Lenox, 1994, 7", MIB....................**$40.00**

Pekingese, The Book On; Queenie Verity-Steele, hardback, 1949, VG....................**$40.00**

Poodle, bookends, red clay, marked Japan, pr, from $10 to....................**$15.00**

Poodle, figurine, black Poodle w/green hat on skis, marked Japan, from $15 to....................**$20.00**

Poodle, figurine, ceramic, stamped Relpo 2030, from $15 to $20.00

Poodle, figurine, Poodle fireman at hydrant w/hose, unmarked, from $15 to......$20.00

Poodle, huggies, stamped #E-1795, paper label reads Inarco Japan, pr, from $15 to $20.00

Poodle, pin, gold-tone w/rhinestones, unmarked, from $10 to $15.00

Poodle, purse, labeled Princess Charming by Atlas Hollywood Fla., from $20.00 to $25.00. (Photo courtesy Elaine Butler)

Poodle, Yvonne, by Hagen-Renaker, paper label on back, from $35 to $40.00

Retriever, figurine, dressed in postman's uniform, Regency Fine Arts, 4½", MIB $32.00

Scottie, ashtray, copper, Scottie in center, 4 rests, ca 1940s, 3x3" square, from $5 to $15.00

Scottie, bowl, cereal; white w/red Scotties, Hazel Atlas Co, ca 1930s, 5", from $22 to $55.00

Scottie, cocktail shaker, clear w/white Scotties & red checked ring, metal lid, Bartlett Collins Glass Company, 8" .$60.00

Scottie, compact, red enameled metal w/metal Scottie in center, ca 1940s, 2¼x⅜", from $30 to $50.00

Scottie, figurine, composition, ca 1930s, 2x1x2", from $10 to $20.00

Scottie, figurine, milk glass, white w/red collar, LE Smith, 2½x6x5", from $35 to $50.00

Scottie, gong, hangs from tree w/yellow Scottie holding mallet in mouth, wood & metal, ca 1930s, 5", from $35 to $40.00

Scottie, nutcracker, wood, mouth cracks nut, Johann Weith Gmb H Germany, 1990s, 3x4½x7¾", from $60 to ..$80.00

Scottie, salt & pepper shakers, silver-colored metal, ca 1940s, 2x3", pr, from $25 to $40.00

Scottie, storage jar, clear glass w/black Scottie in painted-on red bow, red plastic lid, 1990s, 3x7", from $2 to ...$5.00

Scottie, stuffed, vinyl, ca 1950s, 6x8x9", from $20 to ..$40.00

Scottie, tray, reverse painting on glass w/wood frame, Bartlett Collins Glass Company, ca 1940s, 11x19", from $30 to $45.00

Scottie, wall plaque, black Scottie face, ceramic, ca 1940-50s, 4x2½", from $10 to $20.00

Welsh Corgi, advertisement, Friskies, 1958, 10x13½", EX $17.50

Yorkies (2), plate, China Collectors, Staffordshire, 4¼" dia $13.00

Scottie, paperweight, cast iron, Hamilton Foundry, 2½x3½", $35.00.

Dollhouse Furniture

Some of the mass-produced dollhouse furniture you're apt to see on the market today was made by Renwal and Acme during the '40s and Ideal in the 1960s. All three of these companies used hard plastic for their furniture lines and imprinted most pieces with their names. Strombecker furniture was made of wood, and although it was not marked, it has a certain recognizable style to it. Remember that if you're lucky enough to find it complete in the original box, you'll want to preserve the carton as well.

Advisor: Judith Mosholder (See Directory, Dollhouse Furniture)

Acme, stroller, pink w/blue or white wheels, ea $6.00

Acme, swing, red, green & yellow $20.00

Allied, vanity, pink $3.00

Best, rocking horse, pink $12.00

Blue Box, chair, kitchen; avocado $2.00

Blue Box, vanity, tan w/heart-shaped mirror $3.00

Donna Lee, stove, white $6.00

Endeavor, refrigerator w/opening door, ivory $5.00

Endeavor, stove, ivory $5.00

Fisher-Price, dinette, #251, complete $5.00

Fisher-Price, dollhouse family, #265, w/mom, dad & 2 daughters, M $10.00

Fisher-Price, music room, #258, complete $8.00

Grand Rapids, dresser w/mirror, stained wood $20.00

Grand Rapids, hutch, stained wood $20.00

Ideal, chair, living room; blue or pink, ea $15.00

Ideal, doll, baby; w/diaper $10.00

Ideal, fireplace, brown w/cream base $35.00

Ideal, hamper, blue $6.00

Ideal, lamp, floor; brown w/white shade $25.00

Ideal, lamp, table; brown w/white shade $20.00

Ideal, Petite Princess, dressing table set, complete $28.00

Ideal, potty chair, blue $15.00

Ideal, sofa, green $20.00

Ideal, table, tilt-top; brown $45.00

Ideal, vanity, marbleized maroon...............................$15.00
Ideal Petite Princess, buffet, complete $25.00

Ideal Petite Princess, Fantasy Furniture, Royal Dressing Table, MIB, $28.00.

Ideal Petite Princess, Little Princess bed, blue $40.00
Ideal Petite Princess, sofa, brocade...........................$25.00
Ideal Petite Princess, table, dining room $15.00
Ideal Petite Princess, tea cart, w/rollers, complete $25.00
Ideal Young Decorator, chair, dining room; marbleized
    maroon w/yellow seat...$10.00
Ideal Young Decorator, hutch, dining room; marbelized
    maroon $25.00
Irwin, dust pan, blue, orange or yellow, ea $4.00
Irwin, garden set, MOC...$75.00
Irwin, tray, light blue $3.00
Jaydon, buffet, reddish brown $4.00
Jaydon, chair, dining room; reddish brown swirl..........$2.00
Jaydon, chest of drawers, reddish brown swirl.............$6.00
Kilgore, chair, bedroom; cast iron, green $40.00
Kilgore, potty chair, cast iron, blue $60.00
Kilgore, sink, bathroom; cast iron, blue......................$50.00
Kilgore, sink, kitchen; cast iron, tan..........................$75.00
Marx, buffet, maroon or brown swirl, hard plastic, ea.$3.00
Marx, dining room set, brown, soft plastic, 7-pc $20.00
Marx, dining room set, brown swirl, hard plastic, 7-pc..$30.00
Marx, nightstand, yellow hard plastic...........................$5.00
Marx, sink, kitchen; yellow or ivory, soft plastic, ea $3.00
Marx, sofa, red or yellow, soft plastic, ea...................$3.00
Marx, sofa, yellow or red, hard plastic, ea $5.00
Marx, table, coffee; light green, hard plastic $10.00
Marx, TV/phonograph, red, soft plastic $3.00
Marx Little Hostess, piano & bench, MIB $35.00
Marx Little Hostess, vanity, ivory...............................$10.00
Mattel Littles, armoire $8.00
Mattel Littles, bed w/cover & pillow, MIB..................$15.00
Mattel Littles, chair, living room................................$4.00
Mattel Littles, doll, Belinda; w/chairs & pop-up room setting,
    MIB $25.00
Mattel Littles, dresser & lamp, MIB $12.00
Mattel Littles, sofa $8.00
Plasco, bathroom set, 5-pc w/floor plan, MIB $65.00
Plasco, chair, dining room; brown w/striped paper seat
    cover $4.00

Plasco, dining room set, 8-pc, MIB $55.00
Plasco, sink, bathroom; pink or turquoise, ea.............$4.00
Plasco, table, kitchen; light blue................................$5.00
Plasco, vanity w/mirror, pink......................................$5.00
Renwal, bathinette, blue, no decal $8.00
Renwal, bathinette, pink, w/decal.............................$15.00
Renwal, bed, brown w/ivory spread.............................$8.00
Renwal, buffet w/opening drawer, brown.....................$8.00
Renwal, carpet sweeper $85.00
Renwal, chair, barrel; dark red w/brown base...........$12.00
Renwal, chair, teacher's; blue $18.00
Renwal, clock, kitchen; ivory or red, ea.....................$20.00
Renwal, desk, student's; red, brown, or yellow, ea....$12.00
Renwal, doll, baby..$10.00
Renwal, doll, father; blue suit, metal rivets $30.00
Renwal, doll, nurse...$40.00
Renwal, ironing board & iron, pink or blue, ea $22.00
Renwal, lamp, floor; red w/ivory shade $15.00
Renwal, potty chair, blue w/decal.............................$12.00

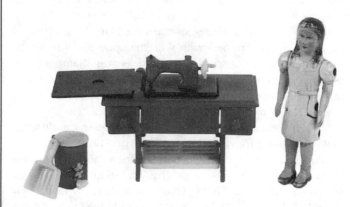

Renwal, sister #41, $25.00; sewing machine #89, $30.00; garbage can and dust pan, #64, $25.00. (Photo courtesy Judith Mosholder)

Renwal, stove, light turquoise, nonopening door.......$12.00
Renwal, table, folding; copper...................................$18.00
Renwal, telephone, yellow w/red $22.00
Renwal, toydee, blue or pink, ea $6.00
Renwal, washing machine, blue or pink w/bear decal, ea..$30.00
Strombecker, chair, living room; aqua $10.00
Strombecker, toilet, yellow, ivory, or aqua, ea...........$10.00
Superior, chair, dining room; yellow...........................$3.00
Superior, tub, yellow or red, ea..................................$5.00
Superior, washing machine, white...............................$5.00
Tomy Smaller Homes, bar, kitchen $12.00
Tomy Smaller Homes, chair, kitchen..........................$3.00
Tomy Smaller Homes, kitchen sink w/dishwasher, 2
    racks...$12.00
Tomy Smaller Homes, stove w/hood...........................$15.00
Tootsietoy, chair, dining room; brown or ivory, ea $7.00
Tootsietoy, rocker, gold or ivory wicker-style w/cushion...$22.00
Tootsietoy, table, living room; gold $20.00
Wolverine, bed w/headboard $12.00
Wolverine, dresser w/mirror $10.00

Dolls

Doll collecting is one of the most popular hobbies in the United States. Since many of the antique dolls are so expensive, modern dolls have come into their own and can be had at prices within the range of most budgets. Today's thrift-shop owners know the extent of 'doll mania,' though, so you'll seldom find a bargain there. But if you're willing to spend the time, garage sales can be a good source for your doll buying. Granted most will be in a 'well loved' condition, but as long as they're priced right, many can be re-dressed, rewigged, and cleaned up. Swap meets and flea markets may sometimes yield a good example or two, often at lower-than-book prices.

Modern dolls, those from 1935 to the present, are made of rubber, composition, magic skin, synthetic rubber, and many types of plastic. Most of these materials do not stand up well to age, so be objective when you buy, especially if you're buying with an eye to the future. Doll repair is an art best left to professionals, but if yours is only dirty, you can probably do it yourself. If you need to clean a composition doll, do it very carefully. Use only baby oil and follow up with a soft dry cloth to remove any residue. Most types of wigs can be shampooed with wig shampoo and lukewarm water. Be careful not to matt the hair as you shampoo, and follow up with hair conditioner or fabric softener. Comb gently and set while wet, using small soft rubber or metal curlers. Never use a curling iron or heated rollers.

In our listings, unless a condition is noted in the descriptions, values are for dolls in excellent condition.

For further study, we recommend these books: *Madame Alexander Dolls, 1965 – 1990*, by Pat Smith; *Doll Values, Antique to Modern, Third Editon*, and *Modern Collectible Dolls, Vols I, II, and III*, by Patsy Moyer; *Black Dolls: 1820 – 1991* and *Black Dolls, Book II*, by Myla Perkins; *Chatty Cathy Dolls* by Kathy and Don Lewis; *Collector's Guide to Ideal Dolls* by Judith Izen; *Collector's Guide to Tammy* by Cindy Sabulis and Susan Weglewski; *Little Kiddles, An Identification Guide*, by Paris Langford (which includes other dolls as well); and *Collector's Encyclopedia of Vogue Dolls* by Judith Izen and Carol J. Stover. All these references are published by Collector Books.

See also Barbie and Friends; Shirley Temple; Toys (Action Figures and GI Joe); Trolls.

Magazine: *Doll Castle News*
37 Belvidere Ave., P.O. Box 247
Washington, NJ 07882
908-689-7042 or fax: 908-689-6320

Magazine: *Doll Castle News*
P.O. Box 247, Washington, NJ 07882

Newsletter: Doll Collectors of America
30 Norwood Ave., Rockport, MA 01966-1730

Newsletter: *Doll Investment Newsletter*
P.O. Box 1982, Centerville, MA 02632

Newsletter: *Doll News*
United Federation of Doll Clubs
P.O. Box 14146, Parkville, MO 64152

Newsletter: *Modern Doll Club Journal*
Jeanne Niswonger
305 W Beacon Rd., Lakeland, FL 33803

Annalee

Barbara 'Annalee' Davis' was born in Concord, New Hampshire, on February, 11, 1915. She started dabbling at dollmaking at an early age, often giving her creations to friends. She married Charles 'Chip' Thorndike in 1941 and moved to Meredith, New Hampshire, where they started a chicken farm and sold used auto parts. By the early 1950s, with the chicken farm failing, Annalee started crafting her dolls on the kitchen table to help make ends meet. She designed her dolls by looking into the mirror, drawing faces as she saw them, and making the clothes from scraps of material.

The dolls she developed are made of wool felt with 'hand-painted' features and flexible wire frameworks. The earlier dolls from the 1950s had a long white red-embroidered tag with no date. From 1959 to 1964, the tags stayed the same except there was a date in the upper right-hand corner. From 1965 to 1970, this same tag was folded in half and sewn into the seam of the doll. In 1970 a transition period began. The company changed its tag to a satiny white tag with a date preceded by a copyright symbol in the upper right-hand corner. In 1975 they made another change to a long white cotton strip with a copyright date. In 1982 the white tag was folded over, making it shorter. Many people mistake the copyright date as the date the doll was made — not so! It wasn't until 1986 that they finally began to date the tags with the year of manufacture, making it much easier for collectors to identify their dolls. Besides the red-lettered white Annalee tags, numerous others were used in the 1990s, but all reflect the year the doll was actually made.

For many years the company held a June auction on the premises; this practice has been discontinued. The auction has been moved to Wayne Mock's Auction Hall in Chocorua, New Hampshire. None of the dolls at this auction will be signed. Annalee's signature can increase a doll's value by as much as $300.00, sometimes more, but at this time she is not signing *any* dolls. Only Chuck (her son) and Karen Thorndike are now signing them.

Remember, these dolls are made of wool felt. To protect them, store them with moth balls, and avoid exposing them to too much sunlight, since they will fade. Our advisor has been a collector for fifteen years and a secondary market dealer since 1988. Most of these dolls have been in her collection at one time or another. She recommends 'If you like it, buy it, love it, treat it with care, and you'll have it to enjoy for many years to come.'

Our values are suggested for dolls in very good to excellent condition, not personally autographed by Annalee herself.

Advisor: Jane Holt (See Directory, Dolls)

Newsletter: *The Collector*
Annalee Doll Society
P.O. Box 1137, 50 Reservoir Rd., Meredith, NH 03253-1137
1-800-433-6557

1972, choir girl, blond w/lace collar, 10"	**$95.00**
1972, elephant head pick	**$100.00**
1972, elf, red w/black hair, 10"	**$60.00**
1975, Christmas stocking, red & white stripe, 22"	**$100.00**
1976, colonial girl head pick	**$100.00**
1977, boy tennis mouse, 7"	**$50.00**
1977, Easter Parade, girl or boy bunny, ea	**$80.00**
1977, Jack Frost, 22"	**$75.00**
1978, clown w/green polka dots, 10"	**$85.00**
1978, mouse nurse w/needle, 7"	**$60.00**
1978, scarecrow, 10"	**$95.00**
1979, disco mouse, 7"	**$60.00**
1979, Goin' Fishing mouse, 7"	**$55.00**
1979, mouse swimmer w/inner tube, 7"	**$60.00**
1980, angel tree topper, 7"	**$35.00**
1980, boy on raft, 10"	**$125.00**

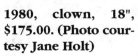
1980, clown, 18", $175.00. (Photo courtesy Jane Holt)

1980, mouse jogger, 7"	**$30.00**
1980, mouse skater, pink outfit, 7"	**$50.00**
1980, reindeer, 36"	**$150.00**
1981, Christmas monkey, w/bag, 7"	**$100.00**
1981, clown w/orange polka dots, 18"	**$135.00**
1981, woodchopper, 7"	**$40.00**
1982, cat w/mouse & mistletoe, 18"	**$95.00**
1982, dragon w/boy, 5"	**$200.00**
1982, girl bunny pick	**$40.00**
1982, girl mouse graduate, 7"	**$35.00**
1982, mouse cheerleader, 7"	**$60.00**
1982, skunk boy & girl, 12", pr	**$350.00**
1983, drummer boy	**$40.00**
1983, pilot duck, 5"	**$40.00**
1983, snowman, 18"	**$60.00**
1984, boy fishing, 7"	**$55.00**

1984, boy w/kite, 7"	**$55.00**
1984, clown w/orange polka dots	**$65.00**
1984, girl w/basket, 7"	**$55.00**
1984, man or woman caroller, 10", ea	**$40.00**
1984, monk w/jug, 16"	**$95.00**
1984, mouse bowler, 7"	**$65.00**
1984, mouse dentist, 7"	**$60.00**
1984, Robin Hood, 10"	**$400.00**
1985, boy hockey player, 7"	**$55.00**
1985, boy w/sled, 12"	**$65.00**
1985, bride & groom, 10"	**$150.00**
1985, Christmas stocking w/mouse, 22"	**$50.00**
1985, clown head ornament	**$40.00**
1985, girl bunny w/flowerpot, 7"	**$30.00**
1985, mouse witch, 7"	**$35.00**
1985, naughty angel, 7"	**$40.00**
1986, angel head ornament	**$30.00**
1986, drummer boy, 7"	**$30.00**
1986, duck w/raincoat, 5"	**$45.00**
1986, elf skier, green w/red skis, 10"	**$45.00**
1986, skier ornament	**$30.00**
1986, unicorn, w/plaque, 10"	**$95.00**
1986, valentine girl, logo w/pin, 7"	**$175.00**
1987, baby mouse w/bottle, 7"	**$35.00**
1987, bunny mobile w/carrot, 7"	**$125.00**
1987, Christmas goose, 10"	**$30.00**
1987, clown, pastel blue & pink, 10"	**$50.00**
1987, elf, brown, green or orange, 10", ea	**$35.00**
1987, elf, red, white or green, 10", ea	**$25.00**
1987, heart mobile w/5" cupid	**$100.00**
1988, Christmas morning kid, 5"	**$30.00**
1988, elf, red, 30"	**$55.00**
1988, Huck Finn, 10"	**$150.00**
1988, mouse w/candy cane, 7"	**$25.00**
1988, mouse w/presents, 7"	**$25.00**
1988, raincoat kid, logo w/pin, 7"	**$100.00**
1988, Santa bear, 10"	**$45.00**
1988, Sherlock Holmes, 10"	**$200.00**
1989, angel tree topper, gold w/star, 12"	**$50.00**
1989, bunny artist, blue, 18"	**$75.00**
1989, Christmas kid, logo w/pin, 7"	**$90.00**
1989, duck on sled, 7"	**$40.00**
1989, Easter girl duck, 5"	**$20.00**
1989, mouse business man, 7"	**$30.00**
1989, mouse knitting, 7"	**$30.00**
1989, polar bear, w/plaque, 7"	**$95.00**
1990, angel w/wings & instruments, 12"	**$60.00**
1990, bear w/snowball, 10"	**$45.00**
1990, clown kid, logo w/pin, 7"	**$80.00**
1990, deer head w/Santa hat ornament	**$20.00**
1990, Friar Tuck mouse, 7"	**$45.00**
1990, Maid Marion mouse, 7"	**$45.00**
1990, PJ kid, 18"	**$50.00**
1990, Robin Hood mouse, 7"	**$45.00**
1990, Santa ornament	**$20.00**
1991, Desert Storm mouse, 7"	**$45.00**
1991, Earth Day mouse, 7"	**$45.00**

1991, mouse baker, 7" $30.00
1991, reading kid, logo w/pin, 7"..............................$75.00
1991, video mouse, 7" $40.00
1992, angel, 5"..$30.00
1992, back-to-school kid, logo w/pin, 7"....................$60.00
1992, flower pick, pink $10.00
1992, flower pick, yellow...$10.00
1992, mouse w/wedge of cheese, 7" $30.00
1993, boy baseball pitcher, 10"..................................$50.00
1993, dove, white w/blue ribbon, 7" $35.00
1993, Flood Relief mouse, 7" $45.00
1993, ice-cream kid, logo, w/pin, 7" $50.00
1993, mouse fireman, 7"...$45.00
1993, New Year's baby, 7" $40.00
1993, Santa on toboggan, 10" $100.00
1994, boy soccer player, 10" $45.00
1994, fishing Santa ornament.....................................$35.00
1994, marble kid, 7"...$35.00
1994, snowman head ornament $25.00
1996, Disney bear, 10"...$200.00
1996, Indian boy or girl, 3", ea...................................$22.00
1996, mouse w/cheese, 3" $25.00
1996, nurse mouse, 3" $24.00
1996, Santa w/gift, ornament, 5" $20.00
1996, teacher, 3"..$22.00
1997, Two for Tea, logo, 7" $30.00

Betsy McCall

The tiny 8" Betsy McCall doll was manufactured by the American Character Doll Company from 1957 through 1963. She was made from high-quality hard plastic with a bisque-like finish and hand-painted features. Betsy came in four hair colors — tosca, red, blond, and brunette. She had blue sleep eyes, molded lashes, a winsome smile, and a fully jointed body with bendable knees. On her back there is an identification circle which reads McCall Corp. The basic doll wore a sheer chemise, white taffeta panties, nylon socks, and Mary Jane-style shoes and could be purchased for $2.25.

There were two different materials used for tiny Betsy's hair. The first was a soft mohair sewn into fine mesh. Later the rubber skullcap was rooted with saran which was more suitable for washing and combing.

Betsy McCall had an extensive wardrobe with nearly one hundred outfits, each of which could be purchased separately. They were made from wonderful fabrics such as velvet, taffeta, felt, and even real mink. Each ensemble came with the appropriate footwear and was priced under $3.00. Since none of Betsy's clothing was tagged, it is often difficult to identify other than by its square snap closures (although these were used by other companies as well).

Betsy McCall is a highly collectible doll today but is still fairly easy to find at doll shows. The prices remain reasonable for this beautiful clothes horse and her many accessories. For further information we recommend *Betsy McCall, A Collector's Guide*, by Marci Van Ausdall.

Advisor: Marci Van Ausdall (See Directory, Dolls)

Newsletter: *Betsy's Fan Club*
Marci Van Ausdall
P.O. Box 946, Quincy, CA 95971
e-mail: dreams707@aol.com
Subscription $16.00 per year or send $4 for sample copy.

Doll, American Character, Birthday Party outfit, 8", from $150.00 to $175.00. (Photo courtesy Marci Van Ausdall)

Doll, American Character, in Playtime outfit, 14", EX ..$250.00
Doll, American Character, in Town & Country Outfit, 8", M .$175.00
Doll, American Character, original outfit, jointed, 29", MIB $250.00
Doll, Ideal, all original, 14", M $225.00
Doll, starter kit #9300, blond hair w/side part, complete, EX (worn card), minimum value.............................$225.00
Doll, TV Time, #9153, all original, M........................$150.00
Doll, Uneeda, all original, 11½", EX $45.00
Outfit, April Showers, complete, EX $45.00
Outfit, Bar-B-Que, MOC..$75.00
Outfit, fur stole & muff, MIB $150.00
Outfit, Prom Time Formal, blue, EX $50.00
Outfit, Sunday Best, 1957, complete, EX....................$100.00
Outfit, Zoo Time, complete, VG....................................$50.00
Pattern, McCall's #2247, uncut $25.00
Toy calendar, Betsy McCall's & Sandy McCall's Everyday Calendar, Milton Bradley, EXIB $25.00

Celebrity Dolls

Celebrity and character dolls have been widely collected for many years, but they've lately shown a significant increase in demand. Except for rarer examples, most of these dolls are still fairly easy to find at doll shows, toy auctions, and flea markets, and the majority are priced under $100.00. These are the dolls that bring back memories of childhood TV shows, popular songs, favorite movies, and familiar characters. Mego, Mattel, Remco, and Hasbro are among the largest manufacturers.

Condition is a very important worth-assessing factor, and if the doll is still in the original box, so much the better!

Should the box be unopened (NRFB), the value is further enhanced. Using mint as a standard, add 50% for the same doll mint in the box and 75% if it has never been taken out. On the other hand, dolls in only good or poorer condition drop at a rapid pace.

See also Elvis Presley Memorabilia.

Advisor: Henri Yunes (See Directory, Dolls)

Alan Alda (as Hawkeye from M*A*S*H), Woolworth, 1976, 8½", MOC..**$30.00**

Angie Dickenson (Police Woman), Horsman, 1976, 9", MIB...**$60.00**

Barbara Eden (from I Dream of Jeanie), Remco, 1972, 6½", MIB (sealed)...**$100.00**

Bobby Orr, Regal, 1975, 12", rare, MOC..................**$800.00**

Brooke Shields, LJN, 1982, 1st issue, 11½", NRFB, $50.00. (Photo courtesy Martin and Carolyn Berens)

Carol Channing (from Hello Dolly), Nasco Dolls, 1962, 11½", rare, MIB...**$350.00**

Cher, 1st edition, pink dress, Mego, 1976, 12", MIB (sealed orange box)..**$70.00**

Clark Gable (as Rhett Butler from Gone With the Wind), 1st edition, World Dolls, 1980, 12", MIB (sealed) **$65.00**

Debbie Boone, Mattel, 1978, 11", MIB........................**$50.00**

Desi Arnez (as Ricky Ricardo from I Love Lucy), Applause, 1988, 17", MIB..**$50.00**

Diana Ross (from The Supremes), Ideal, 1969, 19", MIB (sealed)..**$150.00**

Dolly Parton, 1st edition, red jumpsuit, Eegee, 1980, 12", MIB (sealed)..**$65.00**

Donnie & Marie Osmond, Mattel, 1976, 12", M (VG single box) **$65.00**

Elizabeth Montgomery (as Samantha from Bewitched), Ideal, 1965, 12", rare, MIB.............................**$600.00**

Elizabeth Taylor, 3 different outfits, World Doll, 1989, 11½", MIB, ea **$65.00**

Farrah Fawcett (as Jill from Charlie's Angels), jumpsuit & scarf, Hasbro, 1977, 8½", MIB **$40.00**

Fred Gwynne (as Herman Munster), plush body w/vinyl head, Presents, 1990, 12", MIB..............**$35.00**

Grace Kelly (from The Swan or Mogambo), Tristar, 1982, 11½", MIB...**$125.00**

Harrison Ford (as Indiana Jones), Kenner, 1982, 12", MIB..**$200.00**

Jimmy Walker (as JJ from Good Times), Shindana, 1974, 15", MIB **$50.00**

John Travolta (On Stage...Superstar), Chemtoy, 1977, 12", MIB (sealed).......................................**$125.00**

John Wayne, Great Legends series, Spirit of the West outfit, Effanbee, 1981, 17", MIB.........**$125.00**

Julie Andrews (Mary Poppins), 1st edition, Horsman, 1964, 12", MIB...**$125.00**

Julie Andrews (Mary Poppins), 2nd edition, Horsman, 1973, 11", MIB...**$75.00**

Karen Mulder (Top Models Collection), Hasbro, 1995, 11½", rare, MIB...**$100.00**

Kate Jackson, (as Sabrina from Charlie's Angels), jumpsuit & scarf, Hasbro, 1977, 8½", MOC.....**$40.00**

KISS, Ace Frehley, Gene Simmons, Paul Stanley or Peter Cris, Mego, 12", MIB (sealed), ea...............**$125.00**

Laurel & Hardy, cloth bodies w/vinyl heads, Knickerbocker, 1960, 9½", MIB, ea **$65.00**

Linda Carter (Wonder Woman), 2nd issue, Mego, 1977, 12", MIB (no photo).....................................**$90.00**

Lucille Ball (from I Love Lucy), cloth, 1952, 26", rare, MIB (sealed)..**$800.00**

Macaully Caulkin (from Home Alone), screams, THQ Inc, 1989, MIB **$25.00**

Marie Osmond, Mattel, 1976, 11", MIB **$50.00**

Marylin Monroe, issued in 4 different outfits, Tristar, 1982, 16", MIB (sealed), ea **$60.00**

Marylin Monroe, issued in 6 different outfits, DSI, 1993, 11½", MIB (sealed), ea................................**$60.00**

Marylin Monroe, issued in 8 different outfits, Tristar, 1982, 11½", MIB (sealed), ea................................**$100.00**

MC Hammer, purple outfit, Mattel, 1991, 11½", MIB..**$70.00**

Michael Jackson, issued in 4 different outfits, LJN, 1984, 11½", MIB (sealed), ea **$70.00**

Mr T, 1st edition, bib overalls, 1983, 12", MIB............**$60.00**

Mr T, 2nd edtion, vest & jeans, talker, 1983, 12", MIB..**$75.00**

Muhammad Ali, Mego, 1976, 9¼", MOC....................**$55.00**

New Kids on the Block, 1st edition, Hangin' Loose, 5 different dolls, 1990, 12", MIB, ea...............**$40.00**

New Kids on the Block, 2nd edition, In Concert, 5 different dolls, 1990, 12", MIB, ea....................**$50.00**

OJ Simpson, Deluxe Set, w/several outfits & accessories, Shindana, 1975, 9½", MIB.................**$250.00**

OJ Simpson, in football uniform, Shindana, 1975, 9½", MIB **$125.00**

Pam Dawber (from Mork & Mindy), Mattel, 1979, 8½", MIB **$50.00**

Parker Stevenson (as Frank from The Hardy Boys), Kenner, 1978, MIB (sealed)..................................**$50.00**

Princess Diana, pink dress, Danbury Mint, 1985, 15", MIB **$110.00**

Princess Diana, silver dress, Goldberger, 1982, 11½", MIB (sealed)..**$350.00**

Princess Diana, wedding gown, Goldberger, 1982, 11½", MIB (sealed)..**$450.00**

Princess Diana, wedding gown, Peggy Nesbet/England, 1984, 8", M **$100.00**

Redd Fox, cloth, talker, Shindana, 1977, MIB..............**$45.00**

Rex Harrison (as Dr Dolittle), cloth body w/vinyl head, talker, Mattel, 1969, 24", MIB......................................**$130.00**

Richard Anderson (as Richard Goldman from Six Million Dollar Man), Kenner, 1976, 12", MIB **$45.00**

Richard Chamberlin (Dr Kildare), Bing Crosby Productions, 1962, rare, MIB **$350.00**

Robin Williams (from Mork & Mindy), cloth body, talker, Mattel, 16", MIB..**$50.00**

Selena, Arm Enterprise, 1996, 11½", MIB **$45.00**

Susan Dey (as Laurie from Partridge Family), Remco, 1973, 16", rare, MIB **$250.00**

Suzanne Sommers (as Chrissy from Three's Company), Mego, 1975, 12½", MIB **$85.00**

Sylvester Stalone (from Over the Top), Lewco Toys, 1986, 20", MIB (sealed) **$35.00**

Tatum O'Neal (from International Velvet), Kenner, 1979, 11½", MIB..**$85.00**

Three Stooges, set of 3, Collins, 1982, 13", MOC......**$140.00**

Toni Tenille (from Captain & Tenille), Mego, 1977, 12½", MIB **$60.00**

Vanilla Ice, issued in 3 different outfits, THQ Inc, 1991, 12", MIB (sealed), ea..**$50.00**

Vanna White, wedding dress, limited edition, Totsy Toys, 1990, rare, MIB **$125.00**

Wayne Gretsky, The Great Gretsky/Le Magnifique, Mattel, 1982, 11½", MIB **$150.00**

Yvonne de Carlo (as Lily Munster), Remco, 1964, MIB ..**$150.00**

Chatty Cathy and Other Mattel Talkers

One of the largest manufacturers of modern dolls is the Mattel company, the maker of the famous Barbie doll. But besides Barbie doll, there are many other types of Mattel's dolls that have their own devotees, and we've tried to list a sampling of several of their more collectible lines.

Next to Barbie doll, the all-time favorite doll was Mattel's Chatty Cathy. She was first made in the 1960s, in blond and brunette variations, and much of her success can be attributed to that fact that she could talk! By pulling the string on her back, she could respond with eleven different phrases. The line was expanded and soon included Chatty Baby, Tiny Chatty Baby and Tiny Chatty Brother (the twins), Charmin' Chatty, and finally Singin' Chatty. They all sold successfully for five years, and although Mattel reintroduced the line in 1969 (smaller and with a restyled face), it was not well received. For more information we recommend *Chatty Cathy Dolls, An Identification & Value Guide,* by our advisors, Kathy and Don Lewis.

In 1960 Mattel introduced their first line of talking dolls. They decided to take the talking doll's success even further by introducing a new line — cartoon characters that the young TV viewers were already familiar with.

Below you will find a list of the more popular dolls and animals available. Most MIB (mint-in-box) toys found today are mute, but this should not detract from the listed price. If the doll still talks, you may consider adding a few more dollars to the price.

Advisors: Kathy and Don Lewis (See Directory, Dolls)

Animal Yacker, Bernie Bernard, MIB **$250.00**

Animal Yacker, Bernie Bernard, played with, nontalking...**$125.00**

Animal Yacker, Chester O' Chimp, MIB....................**$375.00**

Animal Yacker, Chester O' Chimp, played with, nontalking..**$125.00**

Animal Yacker, Crackers the Talking Plush Parrot, MIB (sealed)..**$450.00**

Animal Yacker, Crackers the Talking Plush Parrot, played with, nontalking..**$150.00**

Animal Yacker, Larry the Talking Plush Lion, MIB ...**$325.00**

Animal Yacker, Larry the Talking Plush Lion, played with, nontalking..**$85.00**

Baby First Step, MIB..**$225.00**

Baby First Step, played with, nontalking..................**$110.00**

Baby Say 'n See, MIB..**$200.00**

Baby Say 'n See, played with, nontalking **$95.00**

Baby Secret, MIB..**$175.00**

Baby Secret, played with, nontalking........................**$75.00**

Baby Small Talk, MIB..**$125.00**

Baby Small Talk, played with, nontalking **$65.00**

Black Chatty Baby, MIB..**$650.00**

Black Chatty Cathy, pageboy-style hair, MIB.........**$1,200.00**

Black Chatty Cathy, w/pigtails, MIB (sealed).........**$2,000.00**

Black Drowsy, MIB..**$175.00**

Black Drowsy, played with, nontalking......................**$95.00**

Black Tiny Chatty Baby, M **$650.00**

Bozo the Clown, MIB..**$300.00**

Bozo the Clown, played with, nontalking **$75.00**

Bozo the Clown hand puppet, played with, nontalking .**$75.00**

Bozo the Clown hand puppet, 1965, MIB................**$190.00**

Bozo the Clown hand puppet, 1965 or 1967, MIB (sealed) **$300.00**

Buffy & Mrs Beasley, MIB (sealed), from $225 to **$250.00**

Buffy & Mrs Beasley, played with, nontalking........**$100.00**

Bugs Bunny, played with, nontalking, 1962..............**$75.00**

Bugs Bunny, 1962, MIB **$300.00**

Bugs Bunny hand puppet, MIB....................................**$225.00**

Bugs Bunny hand puppet, played with, nontalking...**$95.00**

Casper the Friendly Ghost, played with, nontalking, 15" ..**$140.00**

Casper the Friendly Ghost, 15", MIB (sealed) **$450.00**

Cat in the Hat, rag & plush, MIB **$375.00**

Cat in the Hat, rag & plush, played with, nontalking..**$200.00**

Cecil the Seasick Serpent, MIB **$250.00**

Cecil the Seasick Serpent, MIB (sealed)....................**$325.00**

Cecil the Seasick Serpent, played with, nontalking ..**$200.00**

Charmin' Chatty, auburn or blond hair, blue eyes, record, MIB, ea **$250.00**

Chatty Baby, brunette hair, red pinafore over white romper, MIB **$250.00**

Chatty Baby, early, blond hair, blue eyes, ring around speaker, MIB **$300.00**

Chatty Baby, early, brunette hair, brown eyes, MIB.**$300.00**

Chatty Baby, open speaker, blond hair, blue eyes, MIB ..**$250.00**

Chatty Baby, open speaker, brunette hair, blue eyes, MIB **$250.00**

Chatty Baby, open speaker, brunette hair, brown eyes, MIB **$375.00**

Chatty Cathy, 1960, MIB, $250.00. (Photo courtesy Kathy and Don Lewis)

Chatty Cathy, later issue, open speaker grille, 1964, played with, nontalking...................................**$850.00**

Chatty Cathy, Patent Pending, 1960, MIB..............**$1,200.00**

Chatty Cathy, porcelain, 1980, MIB **$750.00**

Chatty Cathy, 1970, MIB......................................**$80.00**

Dr Dolittle, MIB **$250.00**

Dr Dolittle, played with, nontalking.......................**$75.00**

Dr Dolittle hand puppet, MIB **$285.00**

Dr Dolittle hand puppet, played with, nontalking ...**$110.00**

Drowsy, MIB **$125.00**

Drowsy, played with, nontalking **$50.00**

Herman Munster hand puppet, MIB **$350.00**

Herman Munster hand puppet, played with, nontalking..**$175.00**

King Kong & Bobby Bond, rag & plush, MIB **$350.00**

King Kong & Bobby Bond, rag & plush, played with, nontalking **$150.00**

King Kong & Bobby Bond hand puppet, MIB..........**$350.00**

King Kong & Bobby Bond hand puppet, played with, nontalking **$175.00**

Larry Lion hand puppet, MIB **$225.00**

Larry Lion hand puppet, played with, nontalking **$85.00**

Linus the Lionhearted, MIB...................................**$150.00**

Linus the Lionhearted, played with, nontalking..........**$75.00**

Maurice Monkey, MIB (sealed)...............................**$250.00**

Maurice Monkey, played with, nontalking **$95.00**

Monkees finger puppet, MIB...................................**$350.00**

Monkees finger puppet, played with, nontalking.....**$150.00**

Mother Goose, rag & plush, MIB **$220.00**

Mother Goose, rag & plush, played with, nontalking...**$55.00**

Mrs Beasley, rag & plush, MIB (sealed) **$225.00**

Mrs Beasley, rag & plush, played with, nontalking..**$100.00**

Off To See the Wizard finger puppet, MIB **$250.00**

Off To See the Wizard finger puppet, played with, nontalking...**$150.00**

Patootie, rag & plush, MIB **$350.00**

Patootie, rag & plush, played with, nontalking.........**$150.00**

Porky Pig, MIB...**$225.00**

Scooba-Doo, played with, nontalking......................**$100.00**

Shrinkin' Violette, MIB (sealed), minimum value......**$200.00**

Shrinkin' Violette, played with, nontalking **$125.00**

Singin' Chatty, blond or brunette hair, MIB, ea **$250.00**

Sister Belle the Talking Doll, MIB **$300.00**

Sister Belle the Talking Doll, played with, nontalking..**$75.00**

Storybook Small-Talk, Cinderella, MIB **$250.00**

Storybook Small-Talk, Cinderella, played with, nontalking **$55.00**

Storybook Small-Talk, Goldilocks, MIB **$250.00**

Storybook Small-Talk, Goldilocks, nontalking............**$55.00**

Storybook Small-Talk, Little Bo Peep, MIB................**$250.00**

Storybook Small-Talk, Little Bo Peep, played with, nontalking **$75.00**

Storybook Small-Talk, Snow White, MIB...................**$250.00**

Storybook Small-Talk, Snow White, played with, nontalking **$45.00**

Talk Up, Casper, MIB **$70.00**

Talk Up, Casper, played with, nontalking **$25.00**

Talk Up, Funny Talk, played with, nontalking............**$25.00**

Talk Up, Mickey Mouse, MIB.................................**$125.00**

Talk Up, Mickey Mouse, played with, nontalking **$25.00**

Talk Up, Silly Talk, MIB **$45.00**

Talk Up, Tweety Bird, MIB.....................................**$75.00**

Talk Up, Tweety Bird, played with, nontalking..........**$25.00**

Tatters, MIB (sealed) **$200.00**

Tatters, played with, nontalking **$75.00**

Teachy Keen, MIB **$200.00**

Timey Tell, 1968, MIB, $125.00. (Photo courtesy Kathy and Don Lewis)

Timey Tell, played with, nontalking $45.00
Tiny Chatty Baby, blond hair, blue eyes, 1963, MIB
    (sealed) $250.00
Tiny Chatty Baby, brunette hair, blue eyes, MIB $350.00
Tiny Chatty Baby, brunette hair, brown eyes, MIB...$375.00
Tom & Jerry, rag & plush, MIB (sealed)....................$275.00
Tom & Jerry, rag & plush, played with, nontalking .$125.00

Dawn Dolls by Topper

Made by Deluxe Topper in the 1970s, this 6" fashion doll was part of a series sold as the Dawn Model Agency. They're becoming highly collectible, especially when mint in the box. They were issued already dressed in clothes of the highest style, or you could buy additional outfits, many complete with matching shoes and accessories.

Advisor: Dawn Parrish (See Directory, Dolls)

Case, Dawn, pink w/stars & clouds, NM.....................$10.00
Colorforms, Dawn & Angie dolls, MIB $50.00
Dawn's Apartment, complete w/furniture, MIB $50.00
Doll, Dancing Angie, MIB (sealed) $30.00
Doll, Dancing Dale, MIB (sealed) $50.00
Doll, Dancing Dawn, MIB (sealed) $30.00
Doll, Dancing Gary, MIB (sealed).............................$40.00
Doll, Dancing Glory, MIB (sealed)............................$30.00
Doll, Dancing Jessica, MIB (sealed)..........................$30.00
Doll, Dancing Ron, MIB (sealed) $40.00
Doll, Dancing Van, MIB (sealed)...............................$50.00

Doll, Daphne, Dawn Model Agency, green and silver dress, NRFB, $75.00. (Photo courtesy Pat Smith)

Doll, Dawn Head to Toe, pink & silver dress, MIB (sealed).$90.00
Doll, Dawn Majorette, MIB (sealed)...........................$75.00
Doll, Gary, MIB (sealed) $30.00
Doll, Jessica, MIB (sealed) $30.00
Doll, Kevin, MIB (sealed)...$30.00
Doll, Kip Majorette, MIB (sealed)..............................$45.00

Doll, Longlocks, MIB (sealed) $30.00
Doll, Ron, MIB (sealed)..$30.00
Outfit, Bell Bottom Bounce, #0717, pants & top, EX....$8.00
Outfit, Black Tie 'n Tux, #8393, MIB (sealed)............$65.00
Outfit, Bouffant Bubble, #0711, dress & wrap, M.........$8.00
Outfit, Bride, MIP...$25.00
Outfit, City Slicker, #0720, coat, hat & boots, M $8.00
Outfit, Fuchsia Flash, #0612, MIB (sealed) $35.00
Outfit, Green Fling, #8113, MIB.................................$25.00
Outfit, Green Slink, dress only, EX $5.00
Outfit, Party Puffery, #0712, dress, M..........................$8.00
Outfit, Wedding Belle Dream, NRFB...........................$30.00
Outfit, What a Racket, #8116, MIB $25.00

Holly Hobbie

In the late 1960s a young homemaker and mother, Holly Hobbie, approached the American Greeting Company with some charming country-styled drawings of children as proposed designs for greeting cards. Her concepts were well received by the company, and since that time thousands of Holly Holly items have been produced. Nearly all are marked HH, H. Hobbie, or Holly Hobbie.

Advisor: Donna Stultz (See Directory, Dolls)

Newsletter: *Holly Hobbie Collectors Gazette*
c/o Donna Stultz
1455 Otterdale Mill Rd.
Taneytown, MD 21787-3032; 410-775-2570
Subscription: $25 per year for 6 issues; includes free 50-word ad per issue

Creative Craft Plaque Set, 1972, MIB (sealed)............$20.00
Doll, Country Fun Holly Hobbie, 1989, 16", NRFB.....$25.00
Doll, Grandma Holly, cloth, Knickerbocker, 14", MIB..$20.00
Doll, Grandma Holly, cloth, Knickerbocker, 24", MIB..$30.00
Doll, Holly Hobbie, Heather, Amy or Carrie, cloth,
    Knickerbocker, 6", MIB, ea $10.00
Doll, Holly Hobbie, Heather, Amy or Carrie, cloth,
    Knickerbocker, 9", MIB, ea $15.00
Doll, Holly Hobbie, Heather, Amy or Carrie, cloth,
    Knickerbocker, 16", MIB, ea $25.00
Doll, Holly Hobbie, Heather, Amy, or Carrie, cloth,
    Knickerbocker, 27", MIB, ea $35.00
Doll, Holly Hobbie, Heather, Amy or Carrie, cloth,
    Knickerbocker, 33", MIB, ea $45.00
Doll, Holly Hobbie, scented, clear ornament around neck,
    1988, 18", NRFB $40.00
Doll, Holly Hobbie Bicentennial, cloth, Knickerbocker, 12",
    MIB $30.00
Doll, Holly Hobbie Day 'N Night, cloth, Knickerbocker, 14",
    MIB $20.00
Doll, Holly Hobbie Dream Along, Holly Hobby, Amy, or
    Carrie, cloth, Knickerbocker, 9", MIB, ea.............$15.00
Doll, Holly Hobbie Dream Along, Holly Hobbie, Amy, or
    Carrie, Knickerbocker, cloth, 12", MIB, ea...........$20.00

Doll, Holly Hobbie Talker, cloth, 4 sayings, 16", MIB ..**$30.00**
Doll, Little Girl Holly, cloth, Knickerbocker, 1980, 15",
   MIB **$30.00**
Doll, Robby, cloth, Knickerbocker, 1981, 16", MIB.....**$30.00**
Doll, Robby, cloth, Knickerbocker, 9", MIB................**$20.00**
Doll Making Kit, Heather, complete, EX....................**$25.00**

Dollhouse, M, $300.00. (Photo courtesy Helen McCale)

Sewing Machine, plastic & metal, battery-operated, Durham,
   1975, 5x9", EX..**$40.00**
Sing-Along Electric Parlor Players, Vanity Fair, 1970s, com-
   plete, scarce, NMIB...**$45.00**

Ideal Dolls

The Ideal Toy Company made many popular dolls such as Shirley Temple, Betsy Wetsy, Miss Revlon, Toni, and Patti Playpal. Ideal's doll production was so enormous that since 1907 over 700 different dolls have been 'brought to life,' made from materials such as composition, latex rubber, hard plastic, and vinyl.

Since Ideal dolls were mass produced, most are still accessible and affordable. Collectors often find these dolls at garage sales and flea markets. However, some Ideal dolls are highly desirable and command high prices — into the thousands of dollars. These sought-after dolls include the Samantha doll, variations of the Shirley Temple doll, certain dolls in the Patti Playpal family, and some Captain Action dolls.

The listing given here is only a sampling of Ideal dolls made from 1907 to 1989. This listing reports current, realistic selling prices at doll shows and through mail order. Please remember these values are for dolls in excellent condition with original clothing.

For more information please refer to *Collector's Guide to Ideal Dolls: Identification and Values, Second Edition,* by Judith Izen (Collector Books).

See also Advertising Characters; Shirley Temple; and Dolls' subcategories: Betsy McCall, Celebrity Dolls, and Tammy.

Advisor: Judith Izen (See Directory, Dolls)

Club: Ideal Collectors Club
Judith Izen
P.O. Box 623, Lexington, MA 02173
Subscription: $20 per year for 4 issues; includes free wanted/for sale ads in each issue

Baby Beautiful, 1938 ....**$150.00**
Baby Coos, 1959, 21"...**$85.00**
Baby Giggles, 1968, 15" **$60.00**
Betsy Wetsy, 1954-56, curly caracul wig, 13½" **$135.00**
Betsy Wetsy, 1954-56, painted hair, 20" **$170.00**
Betsy Wetsy, 1960-62, rooted hair, 16" **$60.00**
Betsy Wetsy (Little), 1957, rooted hair, 8", MIB..........**$55.00**
Betsy Wetsy (Tearie), 1968, 11½" **$45.00**
Bonnie Play Pal, 1959, 24" **$350.00**
Bonny Braids, 1953, walker, 13½" **$150.00**
Bride, 1939-44, 15" **$150.00**
Cream Puff, 1959-62, 19-24".....................................**$150.00**
Crissy (Beautiful), 1969, hair-to-floor version, 17½" .**$100.00**
Crissy (Talky), 1971, English, 17½" **$65.00**
Cuddles, 1928-40, 22" **$150.00**
Deanna Durbin, 1938-41, 21"....................................**$520.00**
Ducky, 1932-39, 15"...**$80.00**
Harriet Hubbard Ayer, 1953, 18" **$250.00**
Honeyball, 1967, 9½" **$35.00**
Honeybunch, 1956-57, 15-23".....................................**$85.00**
Little Miss Revlon, 1958-59, 10½", from $100 to **$125.00**
Miss Revlon, 1959, bent knees **$275.00**
Miss Revlon, 1959, walker, 18" **$250.00**

**Miss Revlon, 20", MIB, $500.00.**

Patti Partridge, 1971......................................**$85.00**
Plassie, 1942, 16" **$125.00**
Play 'n Jane, 1971, 15"....................................**$45.00**
Playtex Dryper Baby, 1959, 21"......................**$200.00**
Playtex Dryper Baby, 1959, 23".......................**$225.00**
Posie, 1967, 18"..**$55.00**
Russian Boy, 1939, 13" **$100.00**
Sara Ann, 1951, 15" **$175.00**

Saucy Walker, 1951-55, 22" **$195.00**
Saucy Walker, 1960-61, 28" **$200.00**
Saucy Walker (Big Sister), 1954, 25" **$300.00**
Saucy Walker Boy, 1953, 22" **$250.00**
Snoozie, 1933, 16" **$150.00**
Soldier, early 1940s, 13" **$150.00**
Suzette (also Lifetime or Idenite), 1936, 12" **$150.00**
Suzy Play Pal, 1959-60, 28" **$400.00**
Talking Tot (also called Talkytot), 1950, unmarked, 22" ..**$100.00**
Thumbelina (In-a-Minute!), 1971, 9" **$70.00**
Thumbelina (Newborn), 1968-72, 9" **$60.00**
Timmy Tumbles, 1977, 16½" **$35.00**
Timmy Tumbles (Black), 1977, 16½" **$50.00**
Tippy Tumbles, 1977, 16½" **$35.00**
Tippy Tumbles (Black), 1977, 16½" **$40.00**
Toddler, 1940, 17" & 20" **$150.00**
Toddler Thumbelina, 1969-71, on rocking horse, 9",
    MIB **$85.00**
Twinkle Eyes, 1957-60, 25" **$105.00**

Jem

The glamorous life of Jem mesmerized little girls who watched her Saturday morning cartoons, and she was a natural as a fashion doll. Hasbro saw the potential in 1985 when they introduced the Jem line of 12" dolls representing her, the rock stars from Jem's musical group, the Holograms, and other members of the cast, including the only boy, Rio, Jem's road manager and Jerrica's boyfriend. Each doll was poseable, jointed at the waist, head, and wrists, so that they could be positioned at will with their musical instruments and other accessory items. Their clothing, their makeup, and their hairdos were wonderfully exotic, and their faces were beautifully modeled. The Jem line was discontinued in 1987 after being on the market for only two years.

Aja, blue hair, complete w/accessories, MIB **$40.00**
Clash, straight purple hair, complete, MIB **$40.00**
Danse, pink & blond hair, invents dance routines, MIB ..**$40.00**
Jem, Flash 'N Sizzle, complete w/accessories, MIB, from $40
    to **$50.00**
Jem, Roll 'N Curl, 12", MIB (sealed), from $40 to **$50.00**
Jem/Jerrica, Glitter & Gold, w/accessories, MIB, from $50
    to **$75.00**
Jetta, black hair w/silver streaks, complete, MIB **$40.00**
Pizzaz from Misfits, chartreuse hair, complete, MIB ... **$40.00**
Raya, pink hair, complete, MIB **$40.00**
Rio, Glitter & Gold, complete, MIB, from $50 to **$75.00**
Roxy, blond hair, complete, MIB **$40.00**
Shana from Holograms Band, purple hair, complete, EX,
    from $30 to **$40.00**
Starlight Girl, Ashley (blond curls), Krissie (brown curls &
    dark skin, or Banee (long black hair), +stand, 11", MIB,
    ea **$25.00**
Stormer from Misfits, curly blue hair, complete, MIB .**$40.00**
Synergy from Holograms, all purple doll, complete, MIB..**$45.00**
Video from Holograms, complete, MIB **$30.00**

Kimber, red hair, MIB, $40.00. (Photo courtesy Pat Smith)

Liddle Kiddles

These tiny little dolls ranging from ¾" to 4" tall were made by Mattel from 1966 until 1979. They all had poseable bodies and rooted hair that could be restyled, and they came with accessories of many types. Some represented storybook characters, some were flowers in perfume bottles, some were made to be worn as jewelry, and there were even spacemen 'Kiddles.'

Serious collectors prefer examples that are still in their original packaging and will often pay a minimum of 30% (to as much as 100%) over the price of a doll in excellent condition with all her original accessories. A doll whose accessories are missing is worth from 65% to 70% less. For more information, we recommend *Liddle Kiddles* by Paris Langford and *Schroeder's Collectible Toys, Antique to Modern* (both published by Collector Books).

Advisor: Dawn Parrish (See Directory, Dolls)

Club: Liddle Kiddle Klub
Laura Miller
3639 Fourth Ave., La Crescenta, CA 91214

Cinderiddle, MIP, $100.00.

Apple Blossom Kologne, #3707, MIP......................**$60.00**
Baby Rockaway, #3819, MIP..............................**$150.00**
Cookin' Kiddle, #3846, complete, M....................**$150.00**
Freezy Sliddle, #3516, complete, M......................**$65.00**
Heart Ring Kiddle, #3744, MIP **$50.00**
Howard Biff Boodle, #3502, complete, M **$75.00**

Kiddle Komedy Theatre, missing boy, EX, $50.00. (Photo courtesy Martin and Carolyn Berens)

Lady Lace, #A3840, MIP **$85.00**
Launa Locket, #3680, complete, M......................**$35.00**
Lenore Limousine, #3643, complete, M................**$85.00**
Liddle Biddle Peep, #3544, complete, M **$125.00**
Liddle Kiddles Kastle, #3522, M..........................**$55.00**
Liddle Kiddles Ranch House, #3524, M **$30.00**
Lilac Locket, #3540, MIP....................................**$75.00**
Lolli-Mint, #3658, MIP......................................**$75.00**
Millie Middle, #3509, complete, M....................**$125.00**
Miss Mouse, #3638, MIP....................................**$95.00**
Pink Funny Bunny, #3532, MIP..........................**$100.00**
Romeo & Juliet, #3782, MIP..............................**$200.00**
Santa Kiddle, #3595, MIP **$60.00**
Sizzly Friddle, #3513, complete, M......................**$75.00**
Snap-Happy Living Room, #5173, NMIP................**$20.00**
Sweet Pea Kologne, #3705, MIP..........................**$60.00**
Teresa Touring Car, #3644, complete, M................**$75.00**
Vanilla Lilly, #2819, MIP **$25.00**
Windy Fliddle, #3514, complete, M......................**$85.00**

Littlechap Family

Accessories, Family Room, Bedroom or Dr John's Office,
    complete, EX, ea..**$125.00**
Carrying case..**$25.00**
Doll, Dr John, MIB (sealed)................................**$60.00**
Doll, Judy, MIB (sealed)....................................**$65.00**
Doll, Libby, MIB (sealed)..................................**$45.00**
Doll, Lisa, MIB (sealed)....................................**$60.00**
Outfit, Dr John, MIB (sealed), from $30 to..........**$50.00**
Outfit, Judy, MIB (sealed), from $35 to **$75.00**
Outfit, Libby, MIB (sealed), from $35 to..............**$50.00**
Outfit, Lisa, MIB (sealed), from $35 to................**$75.00**

Nancy Ann Storybook Dolls

This company was in business as early as as 1936, producing painted bisque dolls with mohair wigs and painted eyes. Later they made hard plastic 8" Muffie and Miss Nancy Ann Style Show dolls. Debby (11") and Lori Ann (7½") had vinyl heads and hard plastic bodies. In the 1950s and '60s, they produced a 10½" Miss Nancy Ann and Little Miss Nancy Ann, vinyl high-heeled fashion-type dolls. For information we recommend *Modern Collectible Dolls* by Patsy Moyer.

Boy Blue, painted bisque, w/brochure, gold foil wrist tag &
    blue-dot box, 8" **$35.00**
Debut #75 (Commencement Series), hard plastic, w/wrist tag
    & box, 5" **$75.00**
Lassie Fair #178, painted bisque, w/gold wrist tag & box,
    5" **$50.00**
Lucy Locket, painted bisque, w/original locket, 5"...**$275.00**

Muffie, nonwalker, all original, 8", $175.00.

Muffie walker, hard plastic, molded lashes & brows, 1954,
    8"..**$150.00**
Nancy Ann, vinyl, dress w/black bodice & full red skirt
    w/white polka-dots, high heels, w/tag, 10½".......**$85.00**
Nancy Ann (Style Show), hard plastic, in ball gown, w/gold
    hand tag, 17"..**$800.00**
Nancy Ann Sweet & Lovely #2403 (Style Show), hard plastic,
    nonwalker, w/wrist booklet, 17" **$600.00**
New Moon #305 (Operetta Series), hard plastic, painted eyes,
    w/tag & box, 5" **$125.00**
Portuguese, painted bisque, jointed legs, wrist tag, 5" .**$325.00**

Raggedy Ann and Andy

Raggedy Ann dolls have been made since the early part of the twentieth century, and over the years many companies have produced their own versions. They were created originally by Johnny Gruelle, and though these early dolls are practically nonexistent, they're easily identified by the mark, 'Patented Sept. 7, 1915.' P.F. Volland made them from 1920 to 1934; theirs were very similar in appearance to the originals.

The Mollye Doll Outfitters were the first to print the now-familiar red heart on her chest, and they added a black outline around her nose. These dolls carry the handwritten inscription 'Raggedy Ann and Andy Doll/Manufactured by Mollye Doll Outfitters.' Georgene Averill made them ca 1938 to 1950, sewing their label into the seam of the dolls. Knickerbocker dolls (1963 to 1982) also carry a company label. The Applause Toy Company made these dolls for two years in the early 1980s, and they were finally taken over by Hasbro, the current producer, in 1983.

Our values are for dolls in mint condition, or nearly so. If your doll has been played with but is still in good condition with a few minor flaws (as most are), you'll need deduct about 75% from these prices. Refer to *The World of Raggedy Ann Collectibles* by Kim Avery, and *Doll Values, Antique to Modern,* by Patsy Moyer (Collector Books).

Advisor: Kim Avery

Applause, 7", Ann & Andy, musical, w/rotating heads, 1986, ea **$55.00**
Applause, 12", Ann & Andy (Awake/Asleep), ea **$30.00**
Applause, 15½", Ann & Andy puppets, 1987, ea **$50.00**
Applause, 16", Ann & Andy (70th Anniversary), 1988, ea..**$32.00**
Applause, 17", Ann & Andy (Sleepytime), ea..............**$35.00**
Applause, 19", Ann & Andy (75th Anniversary), 1st limited edition, made to look like Georgene dolls, 1992, MIB, pr **$135.00**
Applause, 25", Andy, 1986 ....**$50.00**
Applause/Knickerbocker, 12", Andy, 1986...................**$25.00**
Applause/Knickerbocker, 12", Ann (Christmas), 1981...**$55.00**
Bobbs-Merrill, 30", Ann ventriloquist doll, 1973..........**$95.00**

Bobbs-Merrill, Wamsutta Fabrics, 20", from $25.00 to $30.00 each. (Photo courtesy Kim Avery)

Bobbs-Merrill/Hallmark, 6", Ann & Andy, 1974, ea **$25.00**
Bobbs-Merrill/Knickerbocker, 3½", Ann & Andy (Mini Dolls), #9628, 1973, (pr in single box).............................**$30.00**
Bobbs-Merrill/Nasco, 9", Ann & Andy, plastic, fully jointed, 1975, ea **$20.00**
Bobbs-Merrill/Nasco, 24", Ann & Andy, plastic, 1972, ea **$40.00**
Georgene Novelties, 12½", Ann (Awake/Asleep), 1940-45..**$325.00**

Georgene Novelties, 15", Ann & Andy, 1946-63, ea ...**$95.00**
Georgene Novelties, 19", Ann, black-outlined nose, 1938-45..**$350.00**
Georgene Novelties, 19", Ann & Andy, 1946-63, ea .**$125.00**
Georgene Novelties, 22", Ann, feet same material as dress, 1945-48 ....**$250.00**
Georgene Novelties, 22", Ann & Andy, 1946-63, ea .**$145.00**
Georgene Novelties, 30", Ann & Andy, 1946-63, ea.**$275.00**
Knickerbocker, 7", Ann & Andy (Embraceables), #9216, Taiwan, 1973, M (pr in single box)......................**$30.00**
Knickerbocker, 9", Ann & Andy, bendable, cloth over wire, Japan, late 1960s, ea................................**$30.00**
Knickerbocker, 10", Ann & Andy (hand puppets), cloth, Taiwan, 1973, MIP, ea..................................**$25.00**
Knickerbocker, 15", Andy (Musical), plays 'Rock-a-bye Baby,' Hong Kong...**$55.00**

Knickerbocker, 15", Andy, Hong Kong, MIB, from $75.00 to $80.00. (Photo courtesy Kim Avery)

Knickerbocker, 15", Ann (Musical), plays 'Rock-a-bye Baby' or 'Pop Goes the Weasel,' Hong Kong, ea **$40.00**
Knickerbocker, 15", Ann & Andy, Taiwan, 1976-78, ea.**$30.00**
Knickerbocker, 15", Ann & Andy (Bedtime), plastic or iron-on eyes, Taiwan, ea...............................**$25.00**
Knickerbocker, 19", Ann & Andy, Hong Kong, mid to late 1960s, ea...**$55.00**
Knickerbocker, 19", Ann & Andy, pull-string talkers, Taiwan **$75.00**
Knickerbocker, 20", Ann & Andy (Teach & Dress), shiny black shoes, Hong Kong, 1960s, ea **$55.00**
Knickerbocker, 25", Ann & Andy, Taiwan, 1976-78, ea.**$65.00**
Knickerbocker, 31", Ann & Andy, Taiwan, ea.............**$85.00**
Knickerbocker, 38", Andy (Musical), elastic straps on feet for dancing, Hong Kong.................................**$235.00**
Knickerbocker, 38", Ann (Musical), elastic straps on feet for dancing, 2-tone hair, Hong Kong.......................**$275.00**
Knickerbocker/Hallmark, 6", Ann & Andy, MIP, ea....**$20.00**
Playskool, 12", Ann & Andy (Special Holiday Edition), 1990, M (pr in single box)..............................**$40.00**
Reliable Toy Co/Canada, 19", Ann & Andy, ea.........**$195.00**

Strawberry Shortcake and Friends

Strawberry Shortcake came on the market with a bang around 1980. The line included everything to attract small girls — swimsuits, bed linens, blankets, anklets, underclothing, coats, shoes, sleeping bags, dolls and accessories, games, and many other delightful items. Strawberry Shortcake and her friends were short lived, lasting only until the mid-1980s.

Advisor: Geneva Addy (See Directory, Dolls)

Newsletter: *Berry-Bits*
Strawberry Shortcake Collector's Club
Peggy Jimenez
1409 72nd St., N Bergen, NJ 07047

Big Berry Trolly, 1982, EX **$40.00**
Doll, Almond Tea, 6", MIB.................................**$25.00**
Doll, Angel Cake, 6", MIB...................................**$25.00**
Doll, Apple Dumpling, MIB................................**$25.00**
Doll, Apricot, 15", NM...**$35.00**

Doll, Baby Butter Cookie and Jelly Bear, EX, $12.00 for the set. (Photo courtesy Pat Smith)

Doll, Baby Needs a Name, 15", NM.....................**$35.00**
Doll, Berry Baby Orange Blossom, 6", MIB **$35.00**
Doll, Cafe Ole, 6", MIB **$35.00**
Doll, Cherry Cuddler, 6", MIB.........................**$25.00**
Doll, Mint Tulip, 6", MIB....................................**$25.00**
Doll, Raspberry Tart, 6", MIB............................**$25.00**
Doll, Strawberry Shortcake, 12", NRFB **$45.00**
Doll, Strawberry Shortcake, 15", NM...................**$35.00**
Dollhouse, M...**$125.00**
Dollhouse furniture, attic, 6-pc, rare, M...............**$140.00**
Dollhouse furniture, bathroom, 5-pc, rare, M **$65.00**
Dollhouse furniture, bedroom, 7-pc, rare, M **$90.00**
Dollhouse furniture, kitchen, 11-pc, rare, M **$100.00**
Dollhouse furniture, living room, 6-pc, rare, M **$85.00**
Figure, Almond Tea w/Marza Panda, PVC, 1", MOC ..**$10.00**
Figure, Lemon Meringue w/Frappo, PVC, 1", MOC....**$10.00**
Figure, Lime Chiffon w/Balloons, PVC, 1", MOC........**$10.00**

Figure, Merry Berry Worm, MIB **$25.00**
Figure, Mint Tulip w/March Mallard, PVC, MOC **$10.00**
Figure, Purple Pieman w/Berry Bird, poseable, MIB..**$35.00**
Figure, Raspberry Tart w/Bowl of Berries, MOC **$10.00**
Figure, Raspberry Tart w/Rhubarb, PVC, 1", MOC.....**$10.00**
Figure, Sour Grapes w/Dregs, Strawberryland Miniatures, MIP, from $15 to **$20.00**
Storybook Play Case, M...**$35.00**
Stroller, Coleco, 1981, M **$85.00**
Telephone, figural, battery-operated, M.......................**$85.00**

Dolls, Baby Lemon and Baby Lime Chiffon, EX, $12.00 each; aboard Flutter Bit Butterfly, 1982, EX, $15.00. (Photo courtesy Pat Smith)

Tammy and Friends

In 1962 the Ideal Novelty and Toy Company introduced their teenage Tammy doll. Slightly pudgy and not quite as sophisticated-looking as some of the teen fashion dolls on the market at the time, Tammy's innocent charm captivated consumers. Her extensive wardrobe and numerous accessories added to her popularity with children. Tammy had a car, a house, and her own catamaran. In addition, a large number of companies obtained licenses to issue products using the 'Tammy' name. Everything from paper dolls to nurses' kits were made with Tammy's image on them. Her success was not confined to the United States; she was also successful in Canada and several other European countries. See *Collector's Guide to Tammy, the Ideal Teen,* by Cindy Sabulis and Susan Weglewski (published by Collector Books) for more information.

Advisor: Cindy Sabulis (See Directory, Dolls)

Accessory Pak, #9181-80, MIP **$20.00**
Accessory Pak, #9233-8, NRFB **$25.00**
Case, Dodi, green, EX **$30.00**
Case, Misty & Tammy, hatbox style, EX **$40.00**
Doll, Bud, MIB, minimum value **$500.00**
Doll, Grown-Up Tammy, MIB **$75.00**
Doll, Pepper, MIB..**$65.00**
Doll, Pepper (trimmer body & smaller face), MIB......**$75.00**

Doll, Pos'n Misty & Her Telephone Booth, MIB.......**$125.00**
Doll, Pos'n Salty, MIB.................................**$125.00**
Doll, Pos'n Tammy & Her Telephone Booth, MIB ...**$100.00**
Doll, Tammy's Dad, MIB.............................**$65.00**
Doll, Tammy's Mom, MIB **$70.00**
Doll, Ted, MIB **$65.00**
Outfit, Dad & Ted, pajamas & slippers, #9456-5, MIP ..**$20.00**
Outfit, Pepper, Birthday Party, #9326-0, complete, MIP.**$45.00**
Outfit, Tammy, Beauty Queen, #9769-4 or #9947-3, MIP.**$80.00**
Outfit, Tammy's Mom, Nighty Mite, #9415-1, MIP **$30.00**
Pepper's Treehouse, MIB............................**$150.00**
Tammy & Ted Catamaran, MIB **$200.00**
Tammy's Bed, Dresser & Chair, MIB.................**$85.00**
Tammy's Car, MIB....................................**$75.00**
Tammy's Ideal House, M, minimum value.............**$100.00**
Tammy's Jukebox, M..................................**$50.00**

Doll, Dodi, MIB, $75.00. (Photo courtesy Pat Smith)

Tressy

Tressy was American Character's answer to Barbie doll. This 11½" fashion doll was made from 1963 to 1967. Tressy had a unique feature — her hair 'grew' by pushing a button on her stomach. She and her little sister, Cricket, had numerous fashions and accessories.

Advisor: Cindy Sabulis (See Directory, Dolls)

Apartment, M **$150.00**
Beauty Salon, M..**$125.00**
Case, Cricket, M **$30.00**
Case, Tressy, M **$25.00**
Doll, Pre-Teen Tressy, M..............................**$75.00**
Doll, Tressy, MIB **$90.00**
Doll, Tressy in Miss America Character Outfit, NM.....**$65.00**
Doll, Tressy w/Magic Makeup Face, M.................**$25.00**
Doll Clothes Pattern, M **$10.00**
Gift Paks w/Doll & Clothing, NRFB, ea, minimum value..**$100.00**
Hair Accessory Paks, NRFB, ea.........................**$20.00**
Hair Dryer, M **$40.00**

Hair or Cosmetic Accessory Kits, M, ea, minimum value .**$50.00**
Millinery, M **$150.00**
Outfits, NRFB, ea, minimum value.....................**$65.00**
Outfits (Budjet), MIB, ea **$30.00**

Doll, Tressy (with growing hair), Regal Toy Ltd. of Canada, box labeled in French and English, ca 1964, 11½", MIB, $125.00. (Photo courtesy Patsy Moyer and Debby Davis)

Uneeda Doll Co., Inc.

The Uneeda Doll Company was located in New York City and began making composition dolls about 1917. Later a transition was made to plastics and vinyl. Listings here are for dolls that are mint in their original boxes.

Baby Dollikins, vinyl head w/hard plastic body, jointed elbows, wrists & knees, 1960, 21" **$45.00**
Baby Trix, vinyl & hard plastic, 1965, 19" **$30.00**
Bareskin Baby, vinyl & hard plastic, 1968, 12½" **$20.00**
Blabby, vinyl & hard plastic, ca 1962, 14" **$28.00**
Coquette, Black, vinyl & hard plastic, ca 1963, 16" **$36.00**
Coquette, vinyl & hard plastic, ca 1963, 16".................**$28.00**
Dollikins, vinyl & hard plastic, multi-jointed, 1960s, 20" **$50.00**
Dollikins, vinyl & hard plastic, multi-jointed & poseable, marked Uneeda Doll Co/MCMLXIX (1969) on head, 11"...**$35.00**
Fairy Princess, vinyl & hard plastic, 1961, 32"...........**$110.00**
Freckles, ventriloquist doll, vinyl head & hands, rooted hair, cotton-stuffed cloth body, 1973, 30".....................**$70.00**
Freckles, vinyl & hard plastic, 1960, 32"...................**$100.00**
Jennifer, vinyl w/painted features, rooted side-parted hair, hard plastic teen body, mod clothing, 1973, 18"..**$25.00**
Maggie Meg, vinyl & plastic, rooted hair that grows, sleep eyes, 16" **$25.00**
Pir-thilla, vinyl w/rooted hair, sleep eyes, blows up balloons, 1958, 12½"..**$12.00**
Pollyanna, vinyl & plastic, 1960, 11" **$35.00**
Pollyanna, vinyl & plastic, 1960, 17" **$55.00**
Pollyanna, vinyl & plastic, 1960, 35".........................**$150.00**
Purty, vinyl & plastic w/painted features, long rooted hair, 1973, 11" **$25.00**

Serenade, vinyl & hard plastic, rooted blond hair, blue sleep eyes, speaker in tummy, w/phonograph & records, 1962, 21" **$55.00**

Suzette (Carol Bent), vinyl & plastic, 12" **$65.00**

Stella Walker, sleep eyes, ca 1960, marked U on head, 34", $95.00. (Photo courtesy Patsy Moyer)

Door Knockers

Though many of the door knockers you'll see on the market today are of the painted cast-iron variety (similar in design to doorstop figures), they're also found in brass and other metals. Most are modeled as people, animals and birds; and baskets of flowers are common. All items listed are cast iron unless noted otherwise. Prices shown are suggested for examples without damage and in excellent original paint.

Advisor: Craig Dinner (See Directory, Doorstops)

Buster Brown & Tige, cream shirt & pants, cream dog w/black spots, #200, 4¾x2" **$500.00**

Butterfly, black, green, yellow & pink, under pink rose, cream & purple backplate, 3½x2½" **$225.00**

Cardinal, red feathers w/black highlights on light brown branch, black & yellow berries, cream & green backplate, 5x3" **$285.00**

Cardinal, yellow & brown (female) on light brown branch, black & yellow berries, cream & green backplate, 5x3" **$285.00**

Castle, cream w/3 flags, blue sky, green trees, gold band, white oval backplate, 4x3" **$265.00**

Cottage, white w/peak & 2 chimneys, red roof, dark green trees behind cottage, cream oval backplate, 3½x2½" **$485.00**

Dancing Cupid, brown hair, white wings, 3 red roses, purple scarf on blue, cream oval background, Hubley #618, 3x4¼" **$625.00**

Dog, brown, at entrance to cream doghouse, pink dish in front of dog, dark brown backplate, 4x3" **$850.00**

Flower basket, deep basket w/blue bow, yellow & blue flowers w/2 pink roses, cream oval backplate, 4x3" ..**$65.00**

Flower basket, yellow ribbon on white basket, pink & blue flowers w/green leaves, yellow & white backplate, 4x2½" **$95.00**

Flowers in a basket, yellow, pink & blue flowers, white backplate, 4x2" **$85.00**

Ivy basket, light & dark green ivy in yellow basket, white backplate, 4½x2½" **$135.00**

Laundry Mammy, red and white bandana, red and yellow shirt, brown basket on head, knocking causes breasts to move, 7x4⅜", $1,750.00. (Photo courtesy Craig Dinner)

Morning Glory, purple-blue single flower w/1 bud, green leaves as backplate, 3x3" **$325.00**

Owl, yellow, light & dark brown & white feathers, black eyes & highlights on face, cream & green backplate, 4¾x3" **$250.00**

Parrot, faces right, on brown branch, multicolor feathers, green leaves, cream & green backplate, 4¾x2¾" **$100.00**

Peacock, blue, green yellow & black feathers outstretched, black bird, white backplate, 3x3" **$625.00**

Rooster, holding branch, red comb & waddle, red, yellow & brown feathers, cream & green oval backplate, 4½x3" **$250.00**

Roses, pink & cream w/green leaves, brown stems, cream oval backplate, signed Hubley #626, 3x4" **$325.00**

Ship, gold waves & ship w/highlights, oval backplate w/blue waves, 4x2¾" **$250.00**

Snow owl, mostly white feathers, black eyes & highlights on face, cream & green backplate, 4¾x3" **$275.00**

Spider on web, gray web w/black strings, orange, black & yellow spider, yellow, black & brown fly, 3½x1⅞" **$775.00**

Woodpecker, red head w/black & white feathers, tree backplate, brown & green leaves w/pink flowers, 3¾x2½" **$135.00**

Doorstops

There are three important factors to consider when buying doorstops — rarity, desirability, and condition. Desirability is often a more important issue than rarity, especially if the doorstop is well designed and detailed. Subject matter often overlaps into other areas, and if they appeal to collectors of Black Americana and advertising, for instance, this tends to drive prices upward. Most doorstops are made of painted cast iron, and value is directly related to the condition of the paint. If there is little paint left or if the figure has been repainted or is rusty, unless the price has been significantly reduced, pass it by.

Be aware that Hubley, one of the largest doorstop manufacturers, sold many of their molds to the John Wright Company who makes them today. Watch for seams that do not fit properly, grainy texture, and too-bright paint.

The doorstops we've listed here are all of the painted cast-iron variety unless another type of material is mentioned in the description. Values are suggested for original examples in near-mint condition and paint and should be sharply reduced if heavy wear is apparent. Recent auctions report even higher prices realized for examples in pristine condition. For further information, we recommend *Doorstops, Identification and Values*, by Jeanne Bertoia.

Club: Doorstop Collectors of America
Jeanne Bertoia
2413 Madison Ave.
Vineland, NJ 08630; 609-692-4092
Membership $20.00 per year, includes 2 *Doorstoppers* newsletters and convention. Send 2-stamp SASE for sample

Basket of Kittens, M Rosenstein, C 1932, 10x7" **$425.00**
Basket of Tulips, Hubley, 13x9", from $275 to **$350.00**
Bellhop, blue uniform, #1244, 8⅞x4⅝" **$300.00**
Bird Dog, w/bird in mouth, on base, National Foundry, 6x11¾" **$225.00**

Black Man on Cotton Bale, 7¾x6⅞", EX, minimum value, $1,200.00; Organ Grinder, two-sided, 10x5¾", NM, from $500.00 to $600.00.

Bloodhound, drooping face, full-figured, 6¾x4¼" ...**$250.00**
Bobby Blake, black shorts, blue shirt, w/teddy bear, Hubley #46, 9½x5¼" **$475.00**
Boxer, brown, full-figured, Hubley, 8½x9" **$350.00**
Castle, winding road leads to castle at top, 8x5¼", from $275 to **$350.00**
Cinderella Carriage, 9¾x19", from $150 to **$225.00**
Clown, multicolored clothes, sitting, rubber knobs on back, marked cJo, 8x3½" **$550.00**
Colonial Dame, pink dress, blue shawl, multicolored hat, Hubley #37, 8x4½" **$250.00**
Colonial Woman, white dress & hat w/black purse in hand, Littco Products, 10¼x5¾" **$175.00**
Covered Wagon, Hubley, #375, 5⅛x9½", from $125 to ..**$200.00**
Doberman Pinscher, full-figured, Hubley, 8x8½" **$400.00**
Doll on Base, rose-colored dress, full-figured, solid, 5½x4⅞" **$125.00**
Drum Major, red jacket & hat, cream pants, w/baton, full-figured, solid, 13½x6½" **$425.00**
Dutch Girl, carries 2 water buckets w/shoulder yoke, marked cJo, #1255, 7⅛x5¾" **$325.00**
Dutch Girl w/Big Shoes, dark blue dress w/white apron & hat, on base, 9¾x9¼" **$400.00**
Elephant w/out Tree, head reared back, National Foundry #9, 10x9⅞" **$225.00**

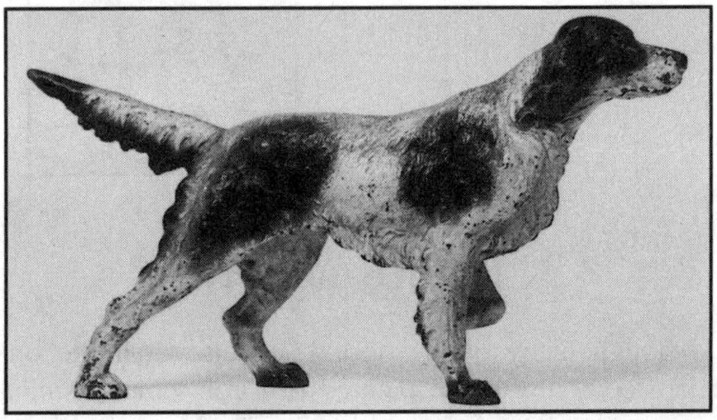

English Setter, 9½x15", EX original paint, $250.00.

Fireplace, Eastern Specialty Co, #G1, 6¼x8", from $225 to **$275.00**
French Bulldog, sitting, looking right, full-figured, Hubley/National Foundry/others, 7⅝x6¾" **$175.00**
Geisha Girl, in dark kimono, holding fan, full-figured, Hubley, 10¼x3½" **$500.00**
Grapes & Leaves, Albany Foundry, 7¾x6½", from $125 to **$175.00**
Huckleberry Finn, blue overalls, yellow hat, w/walking stick & bucket, Littco Products, 12½x9½" **$600.00**
Hunchback Cat, full-figured, Hubley/others, 10⅝x7½" ..**$150.00**
Jill, pearl dress & hat w/white apron, carrying bucket, Hubley #226, 8¾x5¼" **$450.00**
Maiden, blue hat & dress w/white borders, w/flower basket, 8⅞x3¾" **$400.00**
Olive Picker, man & burro w/2 lg olive baskets, on base, #207, 7¾x8¾" **$650.00**
Pelican on Dock, Albany Foundry #113, 8x7¼" **$300.00**
Peter Rabbit, standing, eating carrot, Hubley #96, 9½x4¾" **$425.00**
Pirate w/Sword, red shirt, white pants, pistol in green waist belt, black shoulder strap, on base, 12x5¾" **$450.00**
Popeye, full-figured, Hubley, 9x4½", minimum value **$750.00**
Puss in Boots, white kitten in red boot, 8¼x5¾" **$450.00**
Scottish Highlander, w/spear, on base, 15½x13" **$300.00**

Senorita, yellow dress, green shawl, holding flower basket, 11¼x7" **$325.00**
Southern Belle, blue dress w/hat in hand, National Foundry #72, 11¼x6" **$175.00**
St Bernard, reclining, full-figured, Hubley, 3½x10½" ... **$375.00**
Uncle Sam, dress in red, white & blue, 12x5½", minimum value **$750.00**
White Cockatoo, on base, Albany/National Foundry, #82, 11¾x5¼" **$175.00**
Windmill, National Foundry, #10 Cape Cod, 6¾x6⅞", from $100 to **$125.00**
Woman Holding Flowers, red dress, white bonnet, 8½x4¾" **$175.00**
Woman in Ruffled Dress, holding white fan, blue dress w/black ribbon bows, full-figured, 6¼x4¾" **$200.00**

Duncan and Miller Glassware

Although the roots of the company can be traced back as far as 1865 when George Duncan went into business in Pittsburgh, Pennsylvania, the majority of the glassware that collectors are interested in was produced during the twentieth century. The firm became known as Duncan and Miller in 1900. They were bought out by the United States Glass Company who continued to produce many of the same designs through a separate operation which they called the Duncan and Miller Division.

In addition to crystal, they made some of their wares in a wide assortment of colors including ruby, milk glass, some opalescent glass, and a black opaque glass they called Ebony. Some of their pieces were decorated by cutting or etching. They also made a line of animals and bird figures. For information on these, see *Glass Animals of the Depression Era* by Lee Garmon and Dick Spencer (Collector Books).

Advisor: Roselle Schleifman (See Directory, Elegant Glass)

Canterbury, pitcher, crystal, 64-ounce, $225.00. (Photo courtesy Gene Florence)

Canterbury, ashtray, crystal, club shape, 4½" **$14.00**
Canterbury, basket, crystal, crimped, w/handles, 3½" . **$35.00**
Canterbury, bowl, crystal, flared, 8x2½" **$17.50**
Canterbury, bowl, crystal, oval, handled, 4½x4¾x4¾" .. **$20.00**
Canterbury, bowl, crystal, oval, 8½x5" **$27.50**
Canterbury, bowl, rose; crystal, 6" **$20.00**
Canterbury, cake plate, crystal, 14" **$35.00**
Canterbury, candlestick, crystal, 6", ea **$25.00**
Canterbury, comport, crystal, high, 6x5½" **$20.00**
Canterbury, stem, wine; crystal, #5115, 3½-oz, 6" **$25.00**
Canterbury, tumbler, juice; crystal, flat, 5-oz, 3¾" **$8.00**
Canterbury, vase, crystal, cloverleaf shape, 4" **$15.00**
Canterbury, vase, flower arranger; crystal, 7" **$45.00**
Caribbean, bowl, blue, 8½" **$70.00**
Caribbean, bowl, finger; crystal, 4½" **$15.00**
Caribbean, bowl, flower; crystal, oval, handled, 10¾" . **$35.00**
Caribbean, cigarette holder, blue, stack ashtray top ... **$80.00**
Caribbean, cup, punch; crystal **$8.00**
Caribbean, mustard, blue, w/slotted lid, 4" **$65.00**
Caribbean, plate, salad liner; blue, rolled edge, 12" ... **$60.00**
Caribbean, plate, soup liner; crystal, rolled edge, 7¼" . **$6.00**
Caribbean, relish, crystal, oblong, 4-part, 9½" **$40.00**
Caribbean, saucer, blue **$8.00**
Caribbean, stem, champagne; crystal, footed, ball stem, 6-oz, 4" **$15.00**
Caribbean, tray, mint; blue, handled, divided, 6¼" **$30.00**
Caribbean, vase, crystal, footed, ruffled edge, 5¾" **$24.00**
Figurine, Bird of Paradise, crystal **$700.00**
Figurine, donkey, crystal **$120.00**
Figurine, dove, crystal, head down, 11½" L **$175.00**
Figurine, duck, cigarette box, red, 6" **$170.00**
Figurine, Fat Goose, pale blue **$210.00**
Figurine, heron, crystal satin, 7" **$120.00**
Figurine, swan, blue opalescent, W&F, spread wings, 10x12½" **$245.00**
Figurine, swan, chartreuse, open back, 7" **$45.00**
Figurine, swan, crystal, open back, 10½" **$45.00**
Figurine, swan, crystal, open back, 7" **$45.00**
Figurine, swan, crystal, solid, 3" **$25.00**
Figurine, swan, crystal, solid, 5" **$30.00**
Figurine, swan, crystal, solid, 7" **$75.00**
Figurine, swan, dark green, open back, 10½" **$65.00**
Figurine, swan, milk glass w/red neck, 10½" **$450.00**
Figurine, swan, red, open back, 7½" **$60.00**
Figurine, swordfish, crystal **$275.00**
Figurine, Sylvan swan, crystal, 12" **$85.00**
Figurine, Sylvan swan, yellow opalescent, 7½" **$140.00**
Figurine, Tropical Fish, candle holder, crystal, 5½", ea.. **$500.00**
First Love, ashtray, crystal, #30, 6½x4¼" **$33.00**
First Love, bowl, crystal, footed, flared rim, #111, 10x3¾" **$55.00**
First Love, candle holder, crystal, 1-light, #111, 3" **$25.00**
First Love, cigarette box, crystal, w/lid, #30, 4½x3½" . **$35.00**
First Love, creamer, crystal, #115, 7-oz, 3¾" **$15.00**
First Love, mustard, crystal, w/lid & underplate **$60.00**
First Love, plate, crystal, #115, 7½" **$18.00**
First Love, plate, dinner; crystal, #115, 11¼" **$60.00**
First Love, salt & pepper shakers, crystal, #115, pr **$40.00**
First Love, sugar bowl, crystal, #115, 7-oz, 3" **$14.00**
First Love, tumbler, sham; crystal, #5200, 10-oz, 4¾" . **$37.50**

First Love, vase, crystal, footed, #506, 8" $90.00

Sandwich, ashtray, crystal, square, 2¾" $8.00

Sandwich, basket, crystal, oval, w/loop handle, 10"...$175.00

Sandwich, bowl, crystal, handled, 5½" $15.00

Sandwich, bowl, salad; crystal, deep, 10" $72.50

Sandwich, candlestick, crystal, 1-light, 4" $14.00

Sandwich, candy box, crystal, square, 6" $375.00

Sandwich, candy comport, crystal, low footed, crimped, 3¼" $20.00

Sandwich, epergne, garden; crystal, 9" $125.00

Sandwich, plate, torte; crystal, 12"..............................$45.00

Sandwich, salt & pepper shakers, crystal, w/metal lids, 2½", pr..$18.00

Sandwich, stem, parfait; crystal, footed, 4-oz, 5¼" $30.00

Sandwich, tray, fruit epergne; crystal, 12"...................$52.00

Spiral Flutes, bowl, bouillon; amber, green or pink, 3¾" $15.00

Spiral Flutes, bowl, lily pond; amber, green or pink, 10½" $40.00

Spiral Flutes, bowl, nappy; amber, green or pink, handled, 6"...$22.00

Spiral Flutes, candle holder, amber, green or pink, 9½" $75.00

Spiral Flutes, comport, amber, green or pink, low footed, flared, 9" $55.00

Spiral Flutes, mug, amber, green or pink, handled, 9-oz, 7"...$35.00

Spiral Flutes, plate, salad; amber, green or pink, 7½" ..$4.00

Spiral Flutes, platter, amber, green or pink, 11".........$35.00

Spiral Flutes, stem, wine; amber, green or pink, 3½-oz, 3¾"..$17.50

Spiral Flutes, tumbler, amber, green or pink, flat, 8-oz, 4¼" $30.00

Tear Drop, ashtray, crystal, 5"...$8.00

Tear Drop, bowl, fruit nappy; crystal, 6" $6.00

Tear Drop, bowl, salad; crystal, 12" $40.00

Tear Drop, candy box, crystal, w/lid, 2-handled, 2-part, 7"..$55.00

Tear Drop, creamer, crystal, 3-oz...................................$5.00

Tear Drop, ice bucket, crystal, 5½" $65.00

Tear Drop, olive dish, crystal, 2-part, 6" $15.00

Tear Drop, plate, crystal, 4-handled, 13" $25.00

Tear Drop, relish, crystal, 3-handled, 3-part, 9" $30.00

Tear Drop, saucer, crystal, 6" $1.50

Tear Drop, stem, claret; crystal, 4-oz, 5½"..................$17.50

Tear Drop, tray, crystal, center handle, for cruets, 7¾" .$12.50

Tear Drop, tumbler, crystal, footed, 9-oz, 4½" $8.00

Terrace, ashtray, crystal or amber, square, 4¾"...........$22.00

Terrace, candle holder, cobalt or red, 1-light, 3".........$65.00

Terrace, creamer, crystal or amber, 10-oz, 3" $18.00

Terrace, plate, cobalt or red, 7½"..................................$35.00

Terrace, plate, sandwich; crystal or amber, handled, 11" $40.00

Terrace, relish, crystal or amber, handled, 4-part, 12" ..$40.00

Terrace, stem, wine; crystal or amber, #5111½, 3-oz, 5¼" $32.50

Terrace, tumbler, cobalt or red $45.00

Viking boat, 12", from $175.00 to $225.00.

Egg Cups

Egg cups were once commonplace kitchen articles that were often put to daily use. These small egg holders were commonly made in a variety of shapes from ceramics, glass, metals, minerals, treen, and plastic. They were used as early as ancient Rome and were very common on Victorian tables. Many were styled like whimsical animals or made in other shapes that would specifically appeal to children. Some were commemorative or sold as souvenirs. Still others were part of extensive china or silver services.

Recent trends in US dietary patterns have caused egg cups to follow butter pats and salt dishes into relative obscurity. Yet today in other parts of the world, especially Europe, many people still eat soft-boiled eggs as part of their daily ritual, so the larger china companies in those locations continue to produce egg cups.

Though many are inexpensive, some are very pricey. Sought-after categories (or cross-collectibles) include Art Deco, Art Pottery, Black Memorabilia, Chintz, Golliwoggs, Majolica, Personalities, Pre-Victorian, Railroad, and Steamship. Single egg cups with pedestal bases are the most common, but shapes vary to include buckets, doubles, figurals, hoops, and sets of many types.

Pocillovists, as egg cup collectors are known, are increasing in numbers every day. For more extensive listings we recommend *Egg Cups: An Illustrated History and Price Guide,* by Brenda C. Blake (Antique Publications); and *Schroeder's Antiques Price Guide* (Collector Books).

Advisor: Brenda C. Blake (See Directory, Egg Cups)

Newsletter: *Egg Cup Collector's Corner*
Dr. Joan George, Editor
67 Stevens Ave., Old Bridge, NJ 08857
Subscription $20 per year for 4 issues; sample copies available at $5 each

Antique car, figural, yellow, 1940s $30.00

Bakelite, single, mottled, British NB Ware $8.00

Donald Duck pushing wheelbarrow, Japanese lustreware, 1940s, 3" $175.00
Duck, yellow, figural, Royal Art Pottery $20.00
Dumbo the Elephant pulling cart, Japanese lustreware, 1940s, 2½" $250.00
Glass, single, purple slag w/vertical ribs, scalloped rim ..$75.00
Jade-ite, double..$35.00

Japan, orange lustre cup with multicolor bunnies, 3", either style, from $15.00 to $20.00. (Photo courtesy Carole Bess White)

Little Bay Beach Hotel, single, brown logo w/gilt......$16.00
Little Bo Peep, single, yellow, Keele St Pottery $25.00
Mickey Mouse w/sombrero in his hand standing beside cup, Japan, 1930s, 2¾" $200.00
Milk glass, duck figure, Deco, Opalex, 1930s $12.00
Nescafe, single, red, Carlton Ware, 1980s..................$25.00
Peasant, single, female, hand-painted Quimper..........$60.00
Pirate, figural, black eye patch, 1980s........................$14.00
Queen Elizabeth, single, 70th Birthday, Coronet, 1996..$15.00

Royal Doulton, Lowestoft Bouquet, double, 3½", $20.00.

Santa Claus, figural, applied nose & mustache $20.00
Smiley face, single, rubber..$8.00
Spratling, single, silver, footed, 1930s $115.00
Weetman Cinderella Ware, baby blue w/embossed image of Gus the mouse, 1950s, 2¼" $65.00

Egg Timers

Egg timers are comprised of a little glass tube (pinched in the center and filled with sand) attached to a figural base, usually between 3" and 5" in height. They're all the rage today among collectors. Most figural egg timers reached their heyday in the 1940s. However, Germany produced many beautiful and detailed timers much earlier. Japan followed suit by copying many German designs. Today, one may find timers from the United Kingdom as well as many foreign ports. The variety of subjects represented by these timers is endless. Included are scores of objects, animals, characters from fiction, and people in occupational or recreational activities. Timers have been made in many materials including bisque, china, ceramic, chalkware, cast iron, tin, brass, wood, and plastic.

Although they were originated to time a three-minute egg, some were also used to limit the duration spent on telephone calls as a cost-saving measure. Frequently a timer is designed to look like a telephone, or a phone is depicted on it.

Since the glass tubes were made of thin, fine glass, they were easily broken. You may recognize a timer masquerading as a figurine by the empty hole that once held the tube. Do not pass up a good timer just because the glass is missing. These can be easily replaced by purchasing a cheap egg timer with a glass tube at your local grocery story.

Listings are for timers in excellent to mint condition with their glass tubes attached.

Advisor: Ellen Bercovici (See Directory, Egg Timers)

Boy with large red bow, ceramic, German, from $85.00 to $100.00. (Photo courtesy Ellen Bercovici)

Bear dressed as chef w/towel over arm, ceramic, Japan, 4" $65.00
Bellhop, green, ceramic, Japan, 4½"..........................$60.00
Bellhop on phone, ceramic, Japan, 3" $40.00
Black chef sitting w/right hand raised holding timer, ceramic, many sizes & shadings, German, from $95 to.....$120.00
Black chef standing w/frying pan, chalk, Japan.......$125.00
Black chef standing w/lg fish, timer in fish's mouth, ceramic, Japan, 4¾"..$125.00
Boy, Mexican playing guitar, ceramic, German, 3½"..$65.00

Boy skiing, ceramic, German, 3" **$65.00**

Boy stands on head (plastic) which fills w/sand, ceramic, Cooley Lilley sticker, 3¾" **$50.00**

Boy w/black cap stands & holds black bird, ceramic, unmarked, 3½" **$65.00**

Boy w/black cloak & cane, ceramic, German, 3¾" **$65.00**

Boy w/red cap stands & holds different glass tubes in both hands, wooden, unmarked, 4½" **$35.00**

Cat standing by base of grandfather clock, ceramic, German, 4¾" **$65.00**

Cat w/ribbon at neck, ceramic, marked Germany **$85.00**

Chef holding plate w/hole to hold timer which removes to change, ceramic, Japan, 3¾" **$50.00**

Chef in white on blue base holding spoon, ceramic, German, 4" **$60.00**

Chef in yellow pants, white jacket, blue trim, holds platter of food, ceramic, Japan, 3½" **$50.00**

Chef standing in blue w/white apron, towel over right arm, timer in jug under left, ceramic, Japan, 4½" **$50.00**

Chef winking, white clothes, timer in back, turn upside down to tip sand, ceramic, 4" **$50.00**

Chicken, wings hold tube, ceramic, German, 2¾" **$50.00**

Chicken on nest, green plastic, England, 2½" **$30.00**

Chimney sweep carrying ladder, ceramic, German, 3¼" ..**$85.00**

Clown on phone, standing, yellow suit, ceramic, Japan, 3¾" **$65.00**

Clown sitting w/legs to side, timer in right hand, ceramic, German, 3¼" **$85.00**

Colonial lady w/bonnet, variety of dresses & colors, ceramic, German, 3¾" **$65.00**

Colonial man in knickers, ruffled shirt, waistcoat hides hat, ceramic, Japan, 4¾" **$65.00**

Dutch boy kneeling, ceramic, Japan, 2½" **$40.00**

Dutch boy standing, ceramic, German, 3½" **$65.00**

Dutch girl on phone, standing, blue & white, ceramic, Japan, 3¾" **$50.00**

Dutch girl w/flowers, walking, chalkware, unmarked, 4½" **$65.00**

Geisha, ceramic, German, 4½" **$85.00**

Goebel, double, chefs, man & woman, ceramic, German, 4" **$100.00**

Goebel, double, Mr Pickwick, green, ceramic, German, 4"..**$150.00**

Goebel, double, rabbits, various color combinations, ceramic, German, 4½" **$100.00**

Goebel, double, roosters, various color combinations, ceramic, German, 4" **$100.00**

Goebel, single chimney sweep, ceramic, German, 4¼"..**$70.00**

Goebel, single Friar Tuck, ceramic, German, 4" **$70.00**

Golliwog, bisque, English, 4½" **$200.00**

Kitten w/ball of yarn, chalkware **$50.00**

Leprechaun, shamrock on base, brass, Ireland, 3¼" ..**$40.00**

Lighthouse, blue, cream & orange lustre, ceramic, German, 4½" **$85.00**

Mammy, tin, lithographed picture of her cooking, pot holder hooks, unmarked, 7¾" **$150.00**

Mouse, yellow & green, chalkware, Josef Originals, Japan, 1970s, 3¼" **$35.00**

Newspaper boy, ceramic, Japan, 3¾" **$65.00**

Parlor maid w/cat, ceramic, Japan, 4" **$65.00**

Penguin, chalkware, England, 3¾" **$50.00**

Pixie, ceramic, Enesco, Japan, 5½" **$40.00**

Sailor, blue, ceramic, German, 4" **$65.00**

Sailor w/sailboat, ceramic, German, 4" **$85.00**

Santa Claus w/present, ceramic, Sonsco, Japan, 5½" ..**$75.00**

Scotsman w/bagpipes, plastic, England, 4½" **$50.00**

Sea gull, ceramic w/lustre finish, German **$95.00**

Sultan, Japan, 3½" **$75.00**

Telephone, black glaze on clay, Japan, 2" **$35.00**

Telephone, candlestick type on base w/cup for timer, wooden, Cornwall Wood Prod, So Paris ME **$25.00**

Veggie man or woman, bisque, Japan, 4½" **$85.00**

Welsh woman, ceramic, German, 4½" **$85.00**

Windmill w/dog on base, Japan, 3¾" **$85.00**

Kitchen Maid with measuring spoons, ceramic, DAVAR, from $100.00 to $125.00. (Photo courtesy Ellen Bercovici)

Elvis Presley Memorabilia

Since he burst upon the '50s scene wailing 'Heartbreak Hotel,' Elvis has been the undisputed 'King of Rock 'n Roll.' The fans that stood outside his dressing room for hours on end, screamed themselves hoarse as he sang, or simply danced till they dropped to his music are grown-up collectors today. Many of their children remember his comeback performances, and I'd venture to say that even their grandchildren know Elvis on a first-name basis.

There has never been a promotion in the realm of entertainment to equal the manufacture and sale of Elvis merchandise. By the latter part of 1956, there were already hundreds of items that appeared in every department store, drugstore, specialty shop, and music store in the country. There were bubble gum cards, pin-back buttons, handkerchiefs, dolls, guitars, billfolds, photograph albums, and scores of other items. You could even buy sideburns from a coin-operated machine. Look for the mark 'Elvis Presley Enterprises' (along with a 1956 or 1957 copyright date); you'll know you've found a gold mine. Items that carry the 'Boxcar' mark are from 1974 to 1977, when Elvis's legendary manager, Colonel Tom Parker, promoted another line of merchandise to augment their incomes during the declining years. Upon his death in 1977 and until 1981, the trademark became 'Boxcar Enterprises, Inc., Lic. by Factors ETC. Bear, DE.' The 'Elvis Presley Enterprises, Inc.' trademark reverted back to Graceland in 1982, which re-opened to the public in 1983.

Due to the very nature of his career, paper items are usually a large part of any 'Elvis' collection. He appeared on the cover of countless magazines. These along with ticket stubs, movie posters, lobby cards, and photographs of all types are sought after today, especially those from before the mid-'60s.

Though you sometimes see Elvis 45s with $10.00 to $15.00 price tags, unless the record is in near mint to mint condition, this is just not realistic, since they sold in such volume. In fact, the picture sleeve itself (if it's in good condition) will be worth more than the record. The exceptions are, of course, the early Sun label records (he cut five in all) that collectors often pay in excess of $500.00 for. In fact, a near-mint copy of 'That's All Right' (his very first Sun recording) realized $2,800.00 at an auction held a couple of years ago! And some of the colored vinyls, promotional records, and EPs and LPs with covers and jackets in excellent condition are certainly worth researching further. For instance, though his *Moody Blue* album with the blue vinyl record can often be had for under $25.00 (depending on condition), if you find one of the rare ones with the black record you can figure on about ten times that amount! For a thorough listing of his records as well as the sleeves, refer to *Official Price Guide to Elvis Presley Records and Memorabilia* by Jerry Osborne.

For more general information and an emphasis on the early items, refer to *Elvis Collectibles* and *Best of Elvis Collectibles* by Rosalind Cranor, P.O. Box 859, Blacksburg, VA 24063 ($19.95+$1.75 postage each volume).

Special thanks to Art and Judy Turner, Homestead Collectibles (see Directory, Decanters) for providing information on decanters. See also Magazines; Movie Posters; Pinback Buttons; Records.

Advisor: Lee Garmon (See Directory, Elvis Presley)

Autograph book, Elvis Presley Enterprises, 1956, EX, from $400 to...**$500.00**
Belt buckle, commemorative, bust, singing into microphone w/1935-1977, First Edition Commemorative, bronze, 3¼x2½"...**$25.00**
Bracelet, die-cut ELVIS on gold-colored metal, 1970s, EX.**$8.00**
Bracelet, dog tag, Elvis Presley Enterprises, 1950s, EX..**$150.00**
Coin, commemorative; issued by Republic of Marchall Island in 1993, cupronickel, legal tender, M.................**$30.00**
Decanter, McCormick, 1978, Elvis '77, plays Love Me Tender, 750 ml...**$125.00**
Decanter, McCormick, 1978, Elvis Bust, no music box, 750 ml..**$75.00**
Decanter, McCormick, 1979, Elvis '55, plays Loving You, 750 ml...**$125.00**
Decanter, McCormick, 1979, Elvis '77 Mini, plays Love Me Tender, 50 ml......................................**$55.00**

Decanter, McCormick, 1979, Elvis Gold, plays My Way, 750 ml...**$175.00**
Decanter, McCormick, 1980, Elvis '55 Mini, plays Loving You, 50 ml...**$65.00**
Decanter, McCormick, 1980, Elvis '68, plays Can't Help Falling in Love, 750 ml...........................**$125.00**
Decanter, McCormick, 1980, Elvis Silver, plays How Great Thou Art, 750 ml..........................**$175.00**
Decanter, McCormick, 1981, Aloha Elvis, plays Blue Hawaii, 750 ml...**$150.00**
Decanter, McCormick, 1981, Elvis '68 Mini, plays Can't Help Falling in Love, 50 ml.........................**$55.00**
Decanter, McCormick, 1981, Elvis Designer I White (Joy), plays Are You Lonesome Tonight, 750 ml.........**$150.00**
Decanter, McCormick, 1982, Aloha Elvis Mini, plays Blue Hawaii, 50 ml...**$175.00**
Decanter, McCormick, 1982, Elvis Designer II White (Love), plays It's Now or Never, 750 ml..................**$125.00**
Decanter, McCormick, 1982, Elvis Karate, plays Don't Be Cruel, 750 ml...**$350.00**
Decanter, McCormick, 1983, Elvis Designer III White (Reverence), plays Crying in the Chapel, 750 ml.**$250.00**
Decanter, McCormick, 1983, Elvis Gold Mini, plays My Way, 50 ml...**$125.00**
Decanter, McCormick, 1983, Elvis Silver Mini, plays How Great Thou Art, 50 ml............................**$95.00**
Decanter, McCormick, 1983, Sgt Elvis, plays GI Blues, 750 ml.**$295.00**
Decanter, McCormick, 1984, Elvis & Rising Sun, Plays Green, Green Grass of Home, 750 ml...........**$495.00**
Decanter, McCormick, 1984, Elvis Designer I Gold, plays Are You Lonesome Tonight, 750 ml..............**$175.00**
Decanter, McCormick, 1984, Elvis Designer II Gold, plays It's Now or Never, 750 ml.....................**$195.00**
Decanter, McCormick, 1984, Elvis Karate Mini, plays Don't Be Cruel, 50 ml.................................**$125.00**
Decanter, McCormick, 1984, Elvis on Stage, plays Can't Help Falling in Love, 50 ml (decanter only)...........**$195.00**
Decanter, McCormick, 1984, Elvis w/Stage, 50 ml (complete w/seperate stage designed to hold decanter) **$450.00**
Decanter, McCormick, 1984, Elvis 50th Anniversary, plays I Want You, I Need You, I Love You, 750 ml.......**$495.00**
Decanter, McCormick, 1984, Sgt Elvis Mini, plays GI Blues, 50 ml...**$95.00**
Decanter, McCormick, 1985, Elvis Designer I White Mini, plays Are You Lonesome Tonight, 50 ml.....**$125.00**
Decanter, McCormick, 1985, Elvis Designer III Gold, plays Crying in the Chapel, 750 ml...............**$250.00**
Decanter, McCormick, 1985, Elvis Teddy Bear, plays Let Me Be Your Teddy Bear, 750 ml **$695.00**
Decanter, McCormick, 1986, Elvis & Gates of Graceland, plays Welcome to My World, 750 ml.........**$150.00**
Decanter, McCormick, 1986, Elvis & Rising Sun Mini, plays Green, Green Grass of Home, 50 ml........**$250.00**
Decanter, McCormick, 1986, Elvis Designer I Gold Mini, plays Are You Lonesome Tonight, 50 ml.......**$150.00**
Decanter, McCormick, 1986, Elvis Designer I Silver Mini, Plays Are You Lonesome Tonight, 50 ml......**$135.00**

Decanter, McCormick, 1986, Elvis Hound Dog, plays Hound Dog, 750 ml **$695.00**

Decanter, McCormick, 1986, Elvis Season's greetings, plays White Christmas, 375 ml **$195.00**

Decanter, McCormick, 1986, Elvis Teddy Bear Mini, plays Let Me Be Your Teddy Bear, 50 ml **$295.00**

Decanter, McCormick, 1986, Elvis 50th Anniversary Mini, plays I Want You, I Need You, I Love You, 50 ml **$250.00**

Decanter, McCormick, 1987, Elvis Memories, cassette player base, lighted top, extremely rare, 750 ml, from $1,000 to **$1,200.00**

Doll, Elvis Hound Dog, stuffed plush w/'Elvis' lettered on white neck ribbon, Smile Toy Co, NM **$250.00**

Elongated penny, Elvis Presley-1935-1977-The King, picture of Elvis looking down, dotted border, M...............**$8.00**

Fan club kit, w/button, membership card & letter, 1956, EX..**$400.00**

Flasher ring, 1957, EX...**$50.00**

Frisbee, yellow and blue plastic, M, $20.00. (Photo courtesy Lee Garmon)

Game, The Elvis Trivia Game, by Classic, #14,471 of 25,000 limited edition, MIP (sealed)...................................**$20.00**

Guitar, w/litho face & raised plastic signature, original strings, braid cord & tuner, Selcol, 32", EX+ (EX+ box) **$500.00**

Lighter, Zippo Slim Line, Aloha Elvis on front, w/signature & '50 Years w/Elvis,' from $75 to **$100.00**

Menu, from show at Sahara Tahoe, designed to look like a record, folds, mid-1970s **$55.00**

Necklace, dog tag, Elvis Presley Enterprises, 1958, from $150 to..**$175.00**

Necklace, Love Me Tender, Elvis Presley Enterprises, 1956, from $175 to..**$225.00**

Nipper, plush dog, white w/brown ears, Elvis's signature embroidered on back, gold hang tag, 14" **$50.00**

Pennant, I Love Elvis, red w/white letters, stars & hearts, ca 1960s, 12x30", new old stock, MIP (sealed) **$45.00**

Perfume, Teddy Bear, Elvis Presley Enterprises, 1957, lg, unused, MIB..**$250.00**

Perfume, Teddy Bear, Elvis Presley Enterprises, 1957, sm, unused, MIB..**$35.00**

Pin-back, Don't Be Cruel, white w/broken red heart, 1950s, 1", EX..**$25.00**

Pin-back, Jailhouse Rock, a gold album w/portrait & signature in middle, 3x3", EX..**$15.00**

Plate, Remembering Elvis, colored rhinestone accents, artist Nate Gorgio, Bradford Exchange #77G, w/certificate **$40.00**

Plate, 1968 Comeback Special, Delphi, #1, M **$55.00**

Postcard, Italy, $10.00. (Photo courtesy Rosalind Cranor)

Recipe book, Are You Hungry Tonight–Elvis's Favorite Recipes, Bluewood Books, hardback, 1992, 64 pages, 9x11", VG **$12.00**

Record case, Elvis Presley Enterprises, 1956 ....**$500.00**

Rubber stamp, Takin' Care of Business **$20.00**

Sheet music, All Shook Up, EX..................................**$25.00**

Sheet music, Don't Ask Me Why, EX..........................**$25.00**

Sheet music, Good Luck Charm, EX............................**$20.00**

Sheet music, Kentucky Rain, EX.................................**$25.00**

Sheet music, Love Me Tender, WW Fosdick & George R Paulton, photo cover, 1956 ....**$25.00**

Sheet music, She Thinks I Still Care, EX.....................**$20.00**

Sheet music, The Girl I Never Loved, EX....................**$25.00**

Thermometer, Some Like It Cool, shows Elvis in white w/guitar & microphone, 36"...**$80.00**

Ticket stub, Indiana State University, September 16, 1977, full, unused, NM+ **$20.00**

Tie tac, Elvis playing guitar & singing, metal & enamel, AGB Inc of Atlanta, 1987, 1¼ x ¾" **$8.00**

Trading cards, The Cards of His Life, first series of The Elvis Collection, MIB (sealed)..**$15.00**

Wine, Always Elvis, Collector Series #1, poem by Col. Tom on back, 1978, Factors, Boxcar Enterprises, from $100.00 to $125.00; 1993 first vintage Cabernet Sauvigon, sold for $22.50 at date of issue. (Photo courtesy Lee Garmon)

Erich Stauffer Figurines

From a distance, these child-like figures closely resemble Hummel figurines. They're marked 'Designed by Erich Stauffer' in blue script, often with a pair of crossed arrows or a crown. They always carry a number, generally with the letter S or U before it. As an added bonus, you may find a paper label bearing the title of the featured subject. Arnart Imports Inc imported Erich Stauffer figurines from Japan from the late 1950s through the 1980s. Some of these pieces may be found with original Arnart blue and gold stickers.

Figurines range in size from 4½" up to 12" tall. The most common is the single figure, but some may have two or three children on a single base. The most interesting are those that include accessories or animals to complete their theme. Note that Arnart Imports also made a similar line, but those pieces are smaller and not of the same quality. As a rule, figures marked Erich Stauffer and Arnart Imports would be valued at $3.00 to $5.00 per inch in height, sometimes a bit more if the accessories are unique and if stickers and tags are present.

Advisor: Joan Oates (See Directory, Erich Stauffer Figurines)

#S8517, Country Outing, boy, kneeling, holding closed umbrella in hand, 5"....................................$22.00
#S8543, Junior Doctor, boy holding boy doll, headband & mirror on doctor's head, 7"....................................$30.00

#S8588, Junior Nurse, 7", $30.00; #U8588, Junior Doctor, 7", $30.00. (Photo courtesy Joan Oates)

#U8542, Backyard Products, boy chef on fence, dog below, 5¼"....................................$21.00
#U8543, Photo Play, boy holding camera on its stand, head is bent & arm outstretched, 6¼"....................................$25.00
#U8543, Photo Play, girl sitting, reading a book w/her legs crossed, 6¼"....................................$22.00
#55/1057, Pet Time, boy brushing his dog who is sitting on a stool, 5"....................................$15.00
#55/1556, Dancing Time, boy & girl, dancing side by side, 5½"....................................$20.00

#55/645, Dancing Time, 2 girls dancing, hands on hips, side by side, 5½"....................................$30.00
#8268, Farm Chores, boy holding up a ladder, goose by his feet, 5½"....................................$20.00
#8268, Farm Chores, girl carring basket of grapes, goose at her feet, 5"....................................$20.00
#8268, Farm Chores, girl holding teapot, bird on fence...$21.00
#8316, Spring Time, nun w/basket over 1 arm, closed umbrella over other arm, fence at back, 5¼".......$30.00
#8326, Champion Collie, collie sitting, chain around neck has title, 6½"....................................$20.00
#8326, Champion Shepherd, shepherd sitting, chain around neck has title, 7"....................................$22.00
#8336, God's Children, girl sitting beside a post w/Virgin Mary image inside, goose beside her, 4⅞"..........$30.00
#8336, God's Children, girl squatting beside post w/Virgin Mary image inside, feeding pet goose, 4¾".........$30.00
#8515, Young Folks, boy sitting, holding orange sprinkling can on his knees, 6¼"....................................$23.00
#8515, Young Folks, girl sitting, holding a spade in her lap, 6¼"....................................$20.00
#8543, girl sitting, reading a book w/her legs crossed, 6¼"....................................$22.00
#8543, Music Time, boy sitting playing violin, wearing bowler hat, 6"....................................$18.00
#8543, Music Time, girl sitting playing accordion, 4".$15.00

Eye Winker

Designed along the lines of an early pressed glass pattern by Dalzell, Gilmore and Leighton, Eye Winker was one of several attractive glassware assortments featured in the catalogs of L. G. Wright during the '60s and '70s. The line was extensive and made in several colors: amber, blue, green, crystal, and red. It was probably pressed by Fostoria, Fenton, and Westmoreland, since we know these are the companies that made Moon and Star for Wright, who was not a glass manufacturer but simply a distributing company. Red and green are the most desirable colors and are priced higher than the others we mentioned. The values given here are for red and green, deduct about 20% for examples in clear, amber, or light blue.

Advisor: Sophia Talbert (See Directory, Eye Winker)

Ashtray, allover pattern, 4½" dia $25.00
Bowl, 4 toes, 2½x5" $28.00
Butter dish, allover pattern, 4½" dia lid, 6" base, from $65 to $75.00
Candy dish, all over pattern, disk foot, w/lid, 5¼x5½".$45.00
Candy dish, oval, 4-toed, 5x3½"....................................$30.00
Celery or relish, ruffled rim, oblong, 9½x5", from $40 to...$45.00
Compote, allover pattern except for plain flared rim, patterned lid, 10½x6"+finial $75.00
Compote, allover pattern except for plain flared rim & foot, patterned lid, 7x5", w/lid $60.00

Compote, allover pattern except for plain flared rim & foot, 7x7" $35.00

Compote, jelly; patterned lid, plain foot & rim, 4¼x3½" $45.00

Compote, ruffled rim, plain foot, 4-sided, 7x6"..........$45.00

Compote, ruffled rim, 4-sided, 6x10" $60.00

Creamer & sugar bowl, allover pattern, disk foot, sm, 3¼"..$45.00

Fairy lamp, allover pattern, disk foot, 2-pc, from $50 to .$60.00

Goblet, plain rim & foot, 6¼" $32.00

Marmalade, w/lid, 5¼x4" $45.00

Pitcher, ruffled rim, plain foot, 1-qt, from $70 to........$85.00

Pitcher, 28-oz, 7¾", minimum value $50.00

Salt and pepper shakers, allover pattern with metal lids, 3¾", $25.00 for the pair. (From the collection of Sophia Talbert)

Salt cellar, allover pattern, ruffled rim, 1¾" $12.00

Sherbet, plain rim & foot, 4½"......................................$25.00

Toothpick holder, allover pattern, ruffled rim, 2¼" $12.00

Tumbler, 8-oz, from $30 to $35.00

Vase, ruffled rim, 3-sided, 3-toed, 7¾", from $50 to...$60.00

Vase, three-footed, scalloped, 6", from $50.00 to $60.00. (From the collection of Sophia Talbert)

Fast-Food Collectibles

Since the late 1970s, fast-food chains have been catering to their very young customers through their kiddie meals. The toys tucked in each box or bag have made a much longer-lasting impression on the kids than any meal could. Today it's not just kids but adults (sometimes entire families) who are clamoring for them. They're after not only the kiddie meal toys but also boxes, promotional signs used by the restaurant, the promotional items themselves (such as Christmas ornaments you can buy for 99¢, collector plates, glass tumblers, or stuffed animals), or the 'under 3' (safe for children under 3) toys their toddler customers are given on request.

There have been three kinds of promotions: 1) national — every restaurant in the country offering the same item, 2) regional, and 3) test market. While, for instance, a test market box might be worth $20.00, a regional box might be $10.00, and a national, $1.00. Supply dictates price.

To be most valuable, a toy must be in the original package, just as it was issued by the restaurant. Beware of dealers trying to 'repackage' toys in plain plastic bags. Most original bags were printed or contained an insert card. Vacuform containers were quickly discarded, dictating a premium price of $10.00 minimum. Toys without the original packaging are worth only about one-half to two-thirds as much as those mint in package, which are the values we give in our listings.

Toys representing popular Disney characters draw cross-collectors, so do Star Trek, My Little Pony, and Barbie toys. It's not always the early items that are the most collectible, because some of them may have been issued in such vast amounts that there is an oversupply of them today. At the same time, a toy only a year or so old that might have been quickly withdrawn due to a problem with its design will already be one the collector will pay a good price to get.

If you'd like to learn more about fast-food collectibles, we recommend *Tomart's Price Guide to Kid's Meal Collectibles* by Ken Clee; *The Illustrated Collector's Guide to McDonald's® Happy Meal® Boxes, Premiums and Promotions©*, *McDonald's® Happy Meal Toys in the USA*, *McDonald's® Happy Meal Toys Around the World*, and *Illustrated Collector's Guide to McDonald's® McCAPS*, all by Joyce and Terry Losonsky; *McDonald's® Collectibles* by Gary Henriques and Audre Du Vall; and *Schroeder's Collectible Toys, Antique to Modern* (Collector Books).

See also California Raisins.

Note: Unless noted otherwise, values are given for MIP items (when applicable).

Club: McDonald's® Collector Club
1153 S Lee St., Ste. 200
Des Plaines, IL 60016
Membership: $15 per year for individual or out of state, $7 for juniors, or $20 per family or International members; includes annual dated lapel pin, quarterly newsletter, and annual members directory; send LSASE for club information, chapter list, and publication list
http://www.concentric.net/~Gabrielc/McDclub2.htm

Newsletter: *Sunshine Express* (monthly)
and club's Sunshine Chapter
Bill and Pat Poe founders and current officers

220 Dominica Circle E.
Niceville, FL 32578-4085
850-897-4163; fax: 850-897-2606
e-mail: McPoes@aol.com
Club membership: as per above; annual show in February in central FL area

Newsletter: *Collecting Tips*
Meredith Williams
Box 633, Joplin, MO 64802. Send SASE for information.

Arby's, Barbar's squirters, $2.00 each; Barbar's racers, $3.00 each.

Arby's, Barbar's World Tour, stampers, 1991, ea **$3.00**
Arby's, Looney Tunes Characters, 1988, standing, ea ...**$5.00**
Arby's, Looney Tunes Fun Fingers, 1989, ea **$5.00**
Arby's, Snow Domes, 1995, Yogi or Snagglepuss, ea ...**$5.00**
Burger King, Action Figures, 1991, ea...........................**$3.00**
Burger King, Aladdin Hidden Treasures, 1994, ea **$2.00**
Burger King, Beauty & the Beast, 1991, 4 different, ea **$4.00**
Burger King, Beetlejuice, 1990, 6 different, ea **$2.00**
Burger King, Capitol Critters, 1992, 4 different, ea **$2.00**
Burger King, Dino Crawlers, 1994, 5 different, ea **$2.00**
Burger King, Go-Go Gadget Gizmos, 1991, 4 different, ea..**$3.00**
Burger King, Goof Troop Bowlers, 1992, 4 different, ea ..**$3.00**
Burger King, Hunchback of Notre Dame, 1996, 8 different, ea **$4.00**
Burger King, Kid Transporters, 1990, 6 different, ea.....**$2.00**
Burger King, Lion King, 1995, finger puppets, 6 different, ea **$3.00**
Burger King, McGruff Cares for You, 4 different song book & tape sets, ea..**$6.00**
Burger King, Oliver & Co, 1996, 5 different, ea **$3.00**
Burger King, Pinocchio Summer Inflatables, 1992, 5 different, ea...**$4.00**
Burger King, Rodney Reindeer & Friends, 1986, 4 different, ea..**$5.00**
Burger King, Super Powers, door shield.......................**$8.00**
Burger King, Toy Story, 1995, Action-Wing Buzz..........**$6.00**
Burger King, World Travel Adventure Kit, 1991, 4 different, ea...**$5.00**
Dairy Queen, Alvin & the Chipmunks Music Makers, 1994, 4 different, ea **$5.00**
Dairy Queen, Radio Flyer, 1991, miniature wagon **$5.00**
Dairy Queen, Rock-A-Doodle, 1991, 6 different, ea **$7.00**
Denny's, Adventure Seekers Activity Packet, 1993, ea..**$2.00**

Denny's, Flintstones Fun Squirters, 1991, 5 different, ea ..**$4.00**
Denny's, Jetson's Go Back to School, 1992, 4 different, ea **$3.00**
Dominos Pizza, Donnie Domino, 1989, 4" **$6.00**
Dominos Pizza, Keep the Noid Out, 1987, 3 different, ea ...**$5.00**
Hardee's, Apollo 13 Spaceship, 1995, 3-pc set............**$12.00**
Hardee's, Camp California, 1994, 4 different, ea...........**$3.00**
Hardee's, Dinobend Buddies, 1994, 4 different, ea.......**$3.00**
Hardee's, Fender-Bender 500 Racers, 1990, 5 different, ea **$3.00**
Hardee's, Funmeal Pack, 1990, 6 different, ea **$3.00**
Hardee's, Homeward Bound II, 1996, 5 different, ea ...**$3.00**
Hardee's, Kazoo Crew Sailors, 1991, 4 different, ea **$3.00**
Hardee's, Marvel Super Heroes in Vehicles, 1990, 4 different, ea...**$3.00**
Hardee's, Pound Puppies, 1986, plush, 4 different, ea.**$5.00**
Hardee's, Tattoads, 1995, 4 different, ea **$3.00**
Hardee's, Waldo & Friends Holiday Ornaments, 1991, 3 different, ea..**$4.00**
Jack-in-the Box, Bendable Buddies, 1975, 4 different, ea ..**$10.00**
Jack-in-the-Box, Star Trek Generations, 1994, 6 different, ea...**$5.00**
Long John Silver's, Berenstain Bears Book, 1995, 4 different, ea...**$3.00**
Long John Silver's, Free Willy II, 1995, 5 different, ea .**$4.00**
Long John Silver's, Map Activities, 1991, 3 different, ea ..**$4.00**
McDonald's, Airport, 1986, Ronald McDonald seaplane ..**$5.00**
McDonald's, Amazing Wildlife, 1995, ea.......................**$2.00**
McDonald's, Barbie/Hot Wheels, 1993, Barbie, any except under age 3, ea **$3.00**
McDonald's, Barbie/Hot Wheels, 1993, Barbie, under age 3, Rose Bride **$4.00**
McDonald's, Barbie/Hot Wheels, 1993, Hot Wheels, any except under age 3, ea...............................**$3.00**
McDonald's, Barbie/Hot Wheels, 1993, Hot Wheels, under age 3, Hammer & Wrench, ea................**$4.00**
McDonald's, Barbie/Mini Streex, 1991, Barbie, any except under age 3, ea...**$3.00**
McDonald's, Batman (animated), 1993, any except under age 3, ea **$3.00**
McDonald's, Batman (animated), 1993, under age 3, Batman..**$4.00**
McDonald's, Beanie Babies, 1996, any except Pinky Flamingo, from $8 to..**$15.00**
McDonald's, Beanie Babies, 1996, Pinky Flamingo, from $15 to **$25.00**
McDonald's, Bedtime, 1989, wash mitt, blue foam.......**$5.00**
McDonald's, Chip 'N Dale Rescue Rangers, 1989, 4 different, ea..**$4.00**
McDonald's, Crazy Creatures w/Popoids, 1985, 4 different, ea..**$5.00**
McDonald's, Ducktails II, 1988, launch pad in airport..**$5.00**
McDonald's, Feeling Good, 1985, soap dish, Grimace .**$5.00**
McDonald's, Ghostbusters, 1987, pencil case, Containment Chamber **$5.00**
McDonald's, Happy Birthday 15 Years, 1994, Muppet Babies #11 train pc **$8.00**

McDonald's, Happy Meal box, Circus Wagon, 1979, five in the series, from $25.00 to $40.00. (Photo courtesy Terry and Joyce Losonsky)

McDonald's, Lego Building Set, 1986, helicopter or airplane, ea...**$3.00**

McDonald's, Little Golden Book, 1982, 5 different, ea.**$3.00**

McDonald's, McDonaldland Band, 1986, Ronald harmonica...**$5.00**

McDonald's, Movables, 1988, any except Ronald, ea ...**$8.00**

McDonald's, Peanuts, 1990, any except under age 3, ea..**$3.00**

McDonald's, Peanuts, 1990, under age 3, Charlie Brown egg basket or Snoopy's potato sack, ea **$5.00**

McDonald's, School Days, 1984, eraser, Birdie or Grimace, ea **$3.00**

McDonald's, Stomper Mini 4x4, 1986, 15 different, ea .**$8.00**

McDonald's, Super Mario Brothers, 1990, any except under age 3, ea **$3.00**

McDonald's, Super Mario Brothers, 1990, under age 3, Super Mario...**$4.00**

McDonald's, Totally Toy Holiday, under age 3, ea from $4 to **$5.00**

McDonald's, Totally Toy Holiday, 1995, any except under age 3, ea from $3 to **$4.00**

McDonald's, Winter Worlds, 1983, Grimace or Hamburglar ornament, ea **$6.00**

McDonald's, 101 Dalmatians, 1991, 4 different, ea **$4.00**

Pizza Hut, Air Garfield, parachute, 1993......................**$8.00**

Pizza Hut, Beauty & the Beast, 1992, hand puppets, 4 different, ea **$4.00**

Pizza Hut, Land Before Time, 1988, hand puppet, Cara, Littlefoot, Spike, or Duckie, ea **$5.00**

Pizza Hut, Land Before Time, 1988, hand puppet, Sharptooth **$8.00**

Pizza Hut, Pagemaster, 1994, 4 different, ea.................**$4.00**

Sonic, Airtoads, 6 different, ea.......................................**$4.00**

Sonic, Brown Bag Bowlers, 1994, 4 different, ea..........**$5.00**

Sonic, Go Wild Balls, 1995, 4 different, ea....................**$3.00**

Sonic, Wacky Sackers, 1994, set of 6 ....**$20.00**

Subway, Bobby's World, 1995, 4 different, ea...............**$4.00**

Subway, Cone Heads, 1993, 4 different, ea...................**$4.00**

Subway, Inspector Gadget, 1994, 4 different, ea...........**$4.00**

Subway, Monkey Trouble, 1994, 5 different, ea............**$3.00**

Subway, Save the Wildlife, 1995, 4 different, ea...........**$3.00**

Taco Bell, Hugga Bunch, 1984, Fluffer, Gigglet, or Tuggins, plush, ea **$8.00**

Taco Bell, The Tick, 1995, finger puppet, Arthur Wall Climber or Thrakkorzog, ea **$4.00**

Taco Bell, The Tick, 1996, Arthur w/wings or Sewer Urchin, ea..**$4.00**

Wendy's, Alf Tales, 1990, 6 different, ea **$2.00**

Wendy's, Cybercycles, 1994, 4 different, ea..................**$3.00**

Wendy's, Fast Food Racers, 1990, 6 different, ea **$3.00**

Wendy's, Furskins Bears, 1986, 4 different, plush, ea...**$6.00**

Wendy's, Glofriends, 1989, 9 different, ea **$2.00**

Wendy's, Jetsons Space Vehicles, 1989, 6 different, ea.**$5.00**

Wendy's, Jetsons: The Movie, 1990, 5 different, ea.......**$3.00**

Wendy's, Rocket Writers, 1992, 4 different, ea **$2.00**

Wendy's, World Wild Life, 1988, books, 4 different, ea ..**$4.00**

Wendy's, Yogi Bear & Friends, 1990, 6 different, ea.....**$3.00**

White Castle, Fat Albert & the Cosby Kids, 1990, 4 different, ea **$10.00**

White Castle, Holiday Huggables, 1990, 3 different, ea..**$6.00**

Fenton Glass

Located in Williamstown, West Virginia, the Fenton company is still producing glassware just as they have since the early part of the century. Nearly all fine department stores and gift shops carry an extensive line of their beautiful products, many of which rival examples of finest antique glassware. The fact that even some of their fairly recent glassware has collectible value attests to its fine quality.

Over the years they have made many lovely colors in scores of lines, several of which are very extensive. Paper labels were used exclusively until 1970. Since then some pieces have been made with a stamped-in logo.

Numbers in the descriptions correspond with catalog numbers used by the company. Collectors use them as a means of identification as to shape and size. If you'd like to learn more about the subject, we recommend *Fenton Glass, The Second Twenty-Five Years,* and *Fenton Glass, The Third Twenty-Five Years,* by William Heacock; *Fenton Glass, The 1980s,* by James Measell; and *Fenton Art Glass, 1907 to 1939,* and *Fenton Art Glass Patterns, 1939 to 1980,* both by Margaret and Kenn Whitmyer.

Advisor: Ferill J. Rice (See Directory, Fenton Glass)

Club: Fenton Art Glass Collectors of America, Inc.
P.O. Box 384
Williamstown, WV 26187

Club: Pacific Northwest Fenton Association
P.O. Box 881
Tillamook, OR 97141, 503-842-4815; Subscription: $20 per year; includes quarterly informational newsletter

Baskets

Aurora, Antique Rose, #7630AF, 1989, 7".....................$45.00
Aurora, Colonial Amber, #7638CA............................$20.00
Aurora, Copper Rose, #7630KP $65.00
Blue Dogwood on Cameo Satin, basketweave, #9334BD..$45.00
Blue Ridge, #2635BI, special 80th anniversary assortment, 1985 ....$95.00
Country Cranberry, daisy basket, #2534CC, 7" $72.00
Country Scene, #7237LT..$65.00
Daisies on Cameo Satin, #7237CD, 7" $42.00
Diamond Optic, Cranberry Opalescent, #1739CR, 7"..$85.00
Faberge, Crystal Velvet, #9431VE, mini, 1981-82........$24.00
Federal Blue, #G1636FB.......................................$28.00
Iris Collection on Bone White, #7539IN, 7½"...........$50.00
Jacqueline, Country Cranberry, #9434CC, 1989.........$75.00
Mountain Reflections, #7437MV..............................$85.00
Pink Dogwood on Burmese Satin, #7535PD, 7½" $95.00

Poppy, rose satin, 9", $65.00.

Priscilla, Salem Blue, #9036SR, 12".........................$60.00
Provincial Bouquet, hand painted, #7635FS, square...$42.00
Strawberries on French Opalescent, basketweave, #9334SF, 7".........................$48.00
Sunset on Cameo Satin, #7437SS, 7¼".....................$67.00
Velva Rose, panelled, #9432VR, 11" $75.00
Vintage on Cameo Satin, #7534VI, 7".......................$40.00

Bells

Barnyard Buddies, lamb, #V1774V4, 1985.................$24.00
Beauty, Periwinkle Blue, #9665PW $22.00
Bow & Drape, Salem Blue, #9266SR, 4½" $15.00
Budweiser Clydesdales, #7564XA, 1983......................$60.00
Chocolate Roses on Cameo Satin, basketweave, #9462DR......................$36.00
Christmas, musical, plays Joy to the World, w/Christmas message, #7669VZ, 1988........................$55.00
Christmas Faith, #7667XS, 1986 ....$65.00
Clown on Custard Satin, Childhood Treasures Series, #1760CL, petite.........................$22.00

Cross (handle), Teal Royale, #9761OC.....................$24.00
Daisies on Cameo Satin, basketweave, #9462CD........$36.00
Down by the Station, #7564TT.................................$45.00
Frisky Pup, Childhood Treasures Series, #1760PN, petite.$22.00
Frosted Asters on Blue Satin, #1760FA, mini $20.00
Gentle Fawn on Custard Satin, Mother's Day Series, #7564FN, 1981 ....$50.00
Heart's Desire, Christmas Fantasy Series, #7667WP, 1985-86 ....$50.00
Iris Collection on Bone White, #7564IN $36.00
Jacob's Ladder, Botanical assortment, #7668 ....$32.00
Jade Green, #7564JA...$36.00
Nativity, Florentine Blue, #9463FT $50.00
New Sheffield, Peaches 'n Cream, #6665UO $28.00
Pink Velvet, girl, #9662VP $26.00
Smoke & Cinders on White Satin, Designer Series, #7667TL, rare......................$90.00
Strawberries on French Opalescent, basketweave, #9462SF $40.00
Sunset on Cameo Satin, #7564SS............................$35.00
Templebells, Lilac, #9560LX...................................$25.00
The Farm, #7564F8..$45.00
Velva Blue, star crimped, #7462VB $42.00
Wisteria, hand painted, Connoisseur Collection, #7666ZW, 1988 ....$85.00

Carnival Glass

Note: Carnival glass items listed here were made after 1970.

Bell, Famous Women, Ruby Carnival, Connoisseur Collection, #9163UR, 1984....................$65.00
Bowl, rose; Aqua Opal Carnival, #8454IO, 5" $65.00
Coaster, for Australian Carnival Glass Enthusiasts.......$20.00
Comport, Pinwheel, Teal Marigold, #8227OI...............$26.00
Epergne, Teal Marigold, #4801OI, 4-pc $150.00
Figurine, fox, Cobalt Marigold Carnival, #5226NK......$28.00
Lamp, student; Wild Rose & Bowknot, Aqua Opal Carnival, #2805IO, 20".........................$275.00
Pitcher, Plytec, Cobalt Marigold Carnival, #9461NK, 1987, 32-oz.........................$45.00
Pitcher, Sunburst, Cobalt Marigold Carnival, #8667NK, 1985.........................$35.00
Pitcher, water; Lily, Teal Marigold, #8464OI, 36-oz.....$50.00
Plate, Garden of Eden, Cobalt Marigold Carnival, #9614NK, 1985, 8".........................$35.00
Spitton, Atlantis, Peach Opalescent Carnival, #5150PI..$50.00
Toothpick, Cactus, Red Sunset Carnival, #3495RN......$28.00
Trinket box, Floral, Red Carnival, #9384RN, w/lid......$35.00
Vase, daffodil; Red Carnival, #9752RN $50.00
Vase, swung; Cactus, Red Sunset Carnival, #3483RN, 9"..$75.00

Crests

Apple Blossom, bowl, relish; heart-shaped, #7333, from $65 to.........................$75.00
Apple Blossom, vase, #7254, 4½", from $25 to..........$35.00

Aqua, basket, handled, #1924, 5", from $45 to **$55.00**
Aqua, bonbon, flared, oval, #36, 4½", from $10 to **$12.00**
Aqua, bowl, double crimped, #1522, 10", from $65 to..**$75.00**
Aqua, cake plate, footed, #680, 13", from $75 to........**$85.00**
Aqua, candle holder, #1523, from $60 to...................**$75.00**
Aqua, creamer, aqua handle, #1924, from $40 to **$50.00**
Aqua, nut dish, footed, #680, from $20 to..................**$30.00**
Aqua, saucer, #680, 5½" dia, from $10 to..................**$12.00**
Aqua, sugar bowl, #680, 3", from $30 to **$35.00**
Aqua, vase, double crimped, #36, 6¼", from $22 to ..**$28.00**
Black, basket, crimped, #7336, 6½", from $100 to ...**$125.00**
Black, plate, #7219, 6", from $10 to **$12.00**
Black, relish, heart shape, #7333, from $45 to **$60.00**
Black, vase, fan form, #7356, 6¼", from $28 to **$32.00**
Black Rose, vase, #7256, 6", from $65 to...................**$85.00**
Blue, bonbon, #7428, 8", from $35 to.......................**$45.00**
Blue, comport, footed, #7429, from $40 to.................**$50.00**
Crystal, basket, cone shape, #36, 8", from $75 to **$95.00**
Crystal, bowl, flared, #203, 8½", from $30 to............**$40.00**
Crystal, candle holder, #192, from $40 to **$45.00**
Crystal, puff box, #192-A, from $20 to......................**$25.00**
Crystal, vase, double crimped, #192, 6", from $35 to.**$40.00**
Emerald, basket, #7236, 5"..................................**$78.00**
Emerald, bowl, dessert; shallow, #7222 ....**$20.00**
Emerald, cake plate, low ftd, #5813.........................**$100.00**
Emerald, comport, double crimped, footed.................**$38.00**
Emerald, mayonnaise set, crystal ladle, #7203, 3-pc...**$60.00**
Emerald, pitcher, beaded melon, #7116, 6" handle.....**$55.00**
Emerald, plate, #7210, 10".....................................**$40.00**
Emerald, sherbet, footed, #7226 ....**$22.50**
Emerald, sugar bowl, clear reeded handles, #7231.....**$35.00**
Emerald, tidbit, 2-tiered, 5½".................................**$65.00**
Gold, basket, cone-shape, footed, #36, 4½", from $40
   to...**$60.00**
Gold, candle holder, cornucopia, #951, from $35 to..**$45.00**
Gold, plate, #681, 9", from $15 to **$18.00**
Ivory, bowl, finger; #202, from $18 to **$22.00**
Ivory, rose bowl, #204, from $25 to..........................**$30.00**
Peach, basket, handled, #192, 7", from $40 to **$50.00**
Peach, bowl, double crimped, #192, 10½", from $60
   to...**$65.00**
Peach, jug, handled, #192, 8", from $35 to.................**$40.00**
Peach, rose bowl, #204, from $25 to **$30.00**
Peach, vanity set, #192-A, 3-pc, from $135 to...........**$145.00**
Peach, vase, cornucopia, #1523, from $50 to.............**$65.00**
Rose, bowl, #1522, 10", from $75 to **$85.00**
Rose, plate, #680, 12", from $55 to **$65.00**
Rose, saucer, #680, 5½", from $5 to..........................**$8.00**
Silver, ashtray, Violets in the Snow decor, #7377, from $35
   to...**$40.00**
Silver, bonbon, #7428, 8" **$12.00**
Silver, bonbon, Yellow Rose decor, #7225, 5½", from, $15
   to...**$20.00**
Silver, bowl, dessert; deep, #7221 ....**$32.50**
Silver, bowl, relish; heart-shape, Violets in the Snow decor,
   #7333, from $40 to...**$45.00**
Silver, bowl, soup; #680, 5½" **$35.00**

Silver Crest, cake stand, #7213, 5x13", $50.00.

Silver, candle holder, bulbous base, #1523................**$15.00**
Silver, candy box, #7280 ....**$70.00**
Silver, candy box, Violets in the Snow decor, #7484, from $35
   to...**$40.00**
Silver, creamer, ruffled top.....................................**$50.00**
Silver, mayonnaise set, #7203, 3-pc **$45.00**
Silver, plate, #7211, 12½"......................................**$40.00**
Silver, relish, divided, #7334 ....**$32.50**
Silver, sherbet, #7226 ....**$10.00**
Silver, sugar bowl, ruffled top **$45.00**
Silver, tidbit, Violets in the Snow decor, 2-tiered, #7294, from
   $25 to **$30.00**
Silver, tidbit, 2-tiered, ruffled bowl, #7394................**$75.00**
Silver, vase, #7450, 10" **$115.00**
Silver, vase, bulbous base, #186, 8"..........................**$40.00**
Silver, vase, Violets in the Snow decor, #7258, 8", from $35
   to...**$40.00**
Snow, bowl, amber, #1522, 11", from $30 to **$40.00**
Snow, vase, blue, #194, 8", from $45 to **$55.00**
Snow, vase, dark green, #3005, 7½", from $80 to **$85.00**

Figurals and Novelties

Alley cat, Amethyst Carnival, 11"..............................**$125.00**
Angel praying, Opal Satin w/blue highlights, #5114AB,
   1985...**$24.00**
Bear, black, sitting on font......................................**$38.00**
Bear cub, Provincial Bouquet, hand painted, #5151FS.**$28.00**
Bird, Copper Rose, #5249KP, open back **$32.00**
Boot, Love Bouquet, #9590WQ, 1986.......................**$24.00**
Boot, Pink Blossom on Custard Satin, #9590PY.........**$18.00**
Boy, black, praying...**$12.00**
Boy & girl, Crystal Frost, pr **$35.00**
Bunny, Jade Green, #5162JA...................................**$32.00**
Bunny, pale yellow...**$20.00**
Butterfly, Periwinkle Blue, #5171PW, on stand...........**$24.00**
Cardinal head, ruby, 6½" **$125.00**
Cat, Strawberries on French Opalescent, #5165SF **$32.00**
Desert Storm Schwarz Bear, special order, #5151,
   w/American flag, 1991......................................**$35.00**
Doll, Almost Heaven Blue Slag, #5228 ....**$42.00**
Duckling, Strawberries on French Opalescent, #5169SF.**$30.00**
Elephant, flower bowl, black satin, 6½x9"...................**$400.00**

Elephant, whiskey bottle, Periwinkle, 8" **$450.00**
Fish, red w/amberina tail & fins, 2½" **$55.00**
Fish, vase, milk glass w/black tail & eyes, 7" **$425.00**
Frog, Daisies on Cameo Satin, #5166CD.................**$28.00**
Happiness bird, Daisies on Cameo Satin, #5197CD....**$36.00**
Happiness bird, red, 6½" **$35.00**
Happiness bird, Salem Blue, #5197SR.................**$24.00**
Hen, Roselene **$85.00**
Hen on nest, Dusty Rose, #5186DK.................**$20.00**
Iceberg, Misty Morn, hand painted, #8741MM **$28.00**
Lion, Blue Royale, #5241KK, 1990.................**$25.00**
Mallard, drake; Natural Animals, #5147NM.................**$24.00**
Mouse, brown, Natural Animals, #5148NJ **$20.00**
Mouse, French Opalescent, #5148FO, 1986.................**$28.00**
Owl, Jade Green, #5168JA.................**$32.00**
Panda, Natural Animals, #5151PJ.................**$24.00**
Rabbit, paperweight, Rosalene **$75.00**
Santa in Chimney, Opal Carnival, hand painted, #5235DS..**$36.00**
Scottie dog, crystal, #5214CY, 1986 ....**$17.00**

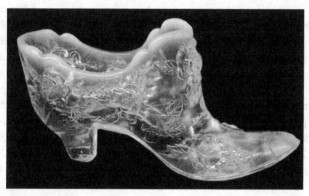

Shoe, embossed roses, green opalescent, #1995, from $30.00 to $40.00.

Spaniel, recumbent, Natural Animals, #5159SP **$26.00**
Squirrel, Meadow Blooms on Opal Satin, #5215JU, 1986 .**$28.00**
Swan, Provincial Blue Opalescent, #5127OO, open back..**$16.00**
Whale, Berries & Blossoms on Opal Satin, #5152RK..**$28.00**

Hobnail

Banana stand, Plum Opalescent, deep color, crimped, #3720PO, 1984 ....**$100.00**
Bonbon, milk glass, #3937MI, 2-handled.................**$16.00**
Bowl, Topaz Opalescent, 10".................**$150.00**
Candle bowl, Ebony, #3872BK, 1968-74.................**$17.00**
Cookie jar, milk glass, #3680MI, w/lid.................**$60.00**
Cruet, Pink Opalescent, Fenton's Collectors Extravaganza, #A3863UP, w/stopper.................**$95.00**
Epergne, jack in the pulpit; Pink Opalescent, Fenton's Collectors Extravaganza, #A3701UO, 10".................**$195.00**
Epergne, Turquoise, #389, mini, 4-pc.................**$55.00**
Fairy light, Plum Opalescent, deep color, #3804PO, 3-pc, 1984.................**$225.00**
Jug, Cranberry Opalescent, 80-oz.................**$285.00**

Kettle, milk glass, #3990.................**$15.00**
Novelty, boot, milk glass, #3992MI, 1981-82, 4".........**$14.00**
Nut dish, Ebony, #3633BK, oval.................**$14.00**
Pitcher, milk glass, #3660MI.................**$26.00**
Punch bowl, Green Opalescent, Connoisseur Collection, #3712GO, w/base, 1985.................**$650.00**
Punch cup, Green Opalescent, Connoisseur Collection, #3847GO, ea.................**$24.00**
Vase, Blue Opalescent, #389, 5½".................**$32.00**
Vase, Colonial Amber, #3952CA.................**$9.00**
Vase, Cranberry Opalescent, #3850, double crimped, 5"...**$65.00**
Vase, French Opalescent, #3958, 8".................**$65.00**
Vase, milk glass, #3954, 7".................**$25.00**

Vase, milk glass, 10½", $47.50.

Vase, Plum Opal, #3750, 6".................**$45.00**
Water set, Pink Opalescent, Fenton's Collectors Extravaganza, pitcher & 6 tumblers, #A3908UO.................**$250.00**

Lamps

Coin Dot, Country Cranberry, #1400CC, 20" **$275.00**
Colonial, scenic oil well, hammered, #7204OW, rare, 16"..**$325.00**
Cross (handle), Crystal Velvet, #9761VE, 1989 ....**$24.00**
Fairy, All Is Calm, Christmas Classics Series, #7300AC, 1981 ....**$60.00**
Fairy, Mountain Reflections, #7300MV, 2-pc.................**$75.00**
Fairy, Nativity, Florentine Brown, #9401FL.................**$62.00**
Fairy, Pink Dogwood on Burmese Satin, #7501PD, 3-pc..**$125.00**
Fairy, Velva Rose, beaded, #8405VR **$50.00**
French Provincial, Butterflies & Bamboo, hand painted, #7507YB, 25½".................**$525.00**
Hurricane candle, Holly Berry, decorated, #8376HL...**$38.00**
Hurricane candle, Teal Royale, #8376OC.................**$24.00**
Oil candle, Periwinkle, Artisan Series Geometrics, #8809EP, 6¼".................**$120.00**
Princess, Chickadee, hand painted, #7504CQ, 19"....**$325.00**
Student, A Bluebird in Snowfall, #7209NB, rare, 21" ..**$375.00**
Student, Country Scene, #7209LT, 21".................**$395.00**
Student, Pastel Violets, #9308VC, 23".................**$225.00**

Student, Strawberries on French Opalescent, basketweave, #9305SF, 20" **$295.00**

Pancake lamp, light pink with cut decor, #G-70, $250.00. (Photo courtesy Ferril J. Rice)

Louise Piper Decorated Pieces

Ashtray, Decorated Violets (Violets in the Snow), #7377DV, 1970 ....**$35.00**

Basket, Plain Burmese, #7437BR, med, 1970-72 ....**$95.00**

Bonbon, Bluebells on Hobnail, #3926BB, 1971-72, 6" ..**$25.00**

Candy box, Rose Burmese, #7284RB, w/lid, 1973-74 .**$200.00**

Pitcher, Leaf Decorated Burmese, #7461BD, 1970-72 .**$65.00**

Vase, Decorated Burmese, #7457DB, 5" **$75.00**

Plates

Anticipation, Christmas Fantasy Series, #7418AI, 1983, 8" ..**$65.00**

Downy Woodpecker — Chiseled Song, Bird of Winter Series, #7418BL **$75.00**

Harvest, Currier & Ives Series, #8417TN, 1981 ....**$35.00**

Lighthouse Point on Custard Satin, Designer Series, #7418LT, 1983, rare, 8" **$95.00**

Majestic Flight on White Satin, Designer Series, #7618EE, 1984, rare **$90.00**

Nativity, Antique Green, #9412 ....**$38.00**

Nature's Awakening on Custard Satin, Mother's Day Series, #7418NA, 8" **$55.00**

Statue of Liberty, Designer Series, sand carved in crystal, #8011LE, 9" **$65.00**

Sunset on Cameo Satin, #7418SS, 8" **$45.00**

Miscellaneous

Bonbon, Butterfly, Iridescent Plum Opalescent, made for Fenton Art Glass Collectors of America, 1982-83 .**$45.00**

Bottle, Blue Dogwood on Cameo Satin, handled, #7363BD **$75.00**

Bowl, Cased Jade Opaline, #7727AG, 14" **$100.00**

Candle holder, Almost Heaven Blue Slag, #3674, pr ..**$54.00**

Candle holders, Forget-Me-Not Blue, Flower Band, #6370KL, pr..**$24.00**

Candy, Paneled Daisy, Shell Pink, #9185PE, w/lid, 1982 ..**$32.00**

Candy box, Blue Burmese Satin, Connoisseur Collection, #9394UE, w/lid, 3-pc, rare, 1984 ....**$125.00**

Candy box, Chocolate Roses on Cameo Satin, w/lid, #7484DR **$37.00**

Candy box, Wave Crest, hand-painted Cranberry, Connoisseur Collection, #6080ZX, w/lid, 1988 ...**$125.00**

Cane, twisted, milk glass, ruby & crystal, 1984 ....**$50.00**

Clock, A Chickadee Ballet on Opal Satin, Birds of Winter Series, #8600BD, rare, 1988..**$85.00**

Clock, alarm; Country Scene, #8600LT..........................**$90.00**

Clock, alarm; Lilac, #8691LX **$80.00**

Clock, Log Cabin, #8600LC **$85.00**

Comport, Empress, Holly Berry, decorated, #9229HL.**$37.00**

Cruet, Drapery Optic, Cranberry Opalescent, #2095CR, w/stopper **$95.00**

Cruet, Vasa Murrhina, Connoisseur Collection, #6462IM, 1983..**$125.00**

Goblet, Heritage Green, #G1645HG..........................**$18.00**

Ivy ball, Silver Poppies on Ebony, #7522PE..........**$30.00**

Jewel box, Blue Roses on Custard Satin, #9589BQ, oval ...**$24.00**

Mug, Prayer Children, girl, Crystal Velvet, #9649VE, 1984..**$24.00**

Nut dish, Forget-Me-Not Blue, Flower Band, #6321 ...**$12.00**

Ornament, ruby, 8-pointed star, #1714RU, 1982 ....**$15.00**

Pitcher, Coin Dot; Country Cranberry, #1432CC, 32-oz .**$65.00**

Pitcher, Sandwich, Lilac, #9666LX, 1990 ....**$36.00**

Pitcher, Sculptured Ice Optics, #8560AY, 70-oz...........**$50.00**

Ring holder, Fine Cut & Block, Dusty Rose, #9120DK .**$7.00**

Salt & pepper shakers, Amethyst, #G1606AY, pr.........**$20.00**

Sugar shaker, Candleglow, #G1692YL..........................**$32.00**

Temple jar, Down by the Station, #7488TT **$45.00**

Temple jar, Silver Poppies on Ebony, #7588PE...........**$75.00**

Tobacco jar, Grape & Cable, Almost Heaven Blue Slag, #9188, w/lid..**$75.00**

Toothpick holder, Love Bouquet, #9592WQ, 1986 .....**$28.00**

Trinket box, Valencia, Provincial Blue Opalescent, #8304OO, w/lid **$24.00**

Vase, bud; Peaches 'n Cream, #6650UO, 6"................**$20.00**

Vase, Copper Rose, #8817KP, 8½" **$80.00**

Vase, Country Cranberry, #8551CC, 1982, cylinder, 10½" ...**$65.00**

Vase, Cranberry Swirl opalescent, 5¾", $95.00.

Vase, feather; Country Cranberry, #2050CC, 6½" **$52.00**
Vase, Pastel Violets, #7254VC, 4½"..............................**$28.00**
Vase, Rose, Artisan Series Geometrics, #8802ER, oval, 12"...**$150.00**
Vase, Sophisticated Ladies, sand carved, #7655SX, 1982, spherical, 10"...**$150.00**
Vase, tulip bud; Cranberry Opaline, #7373KH **$42.00**
Vase, Wheat, Periwinkle Blue Overlay, #5858OP, 1985 ..**$40.00**

Fiesta

You still can find Fiesta, but it's hard to get a bargain. Since it was discontinued in 1973, it has literally exploded onto the collectibles scene, and even at today's prices, new collectors continue to join the ranks of the veterans.

Fiesta is a line of solid-color dinnerware made by the Homer Laughlin China Company of Newell, West Virginia. It was introduced in 1936 and was immediately accepted by the American public. The line was varied. There were more than fifty items offered, and the color assortment included red (orange-red), cobalt, light green, and yellow. Within a short time, ivory and turquoise were added. (All these are referred to as 'original colors.')

As tastes changed during the production years, old colors were retired and new ones added. The colors collectors refer to as '50s colors are dark green, rose, chartreuse, and gray, and today these are very desirable. Medium green was introduced in 1959 at a time when some of the old standard shapes were being discontinued. Today, medium green pieces are the most expensive. Most pieces are marked. Plates were ink stamped, and molded pieces usually had an indented mark.

In 1986 Homer Laughlin reintroduced Fiesta, but in colors different than the old line: white, black, cobalt, rose (bright pink), and apricot. Many of the pieces had been restyled, and the only problem collectors have had with the new colors is with the cobalt. But if you'll compare it with the old, you'll see that it is darker. Turquoise, periwinkle blue, yellow, and Seamist green were added next, and though the turquoise is close, it is a little greener than the original. Lilac and persimmon were later made for sale exclusively through Bloomingdale's department stores. Production was limited on lilac (not every item was made in it), and now that it's been discontinued, collectors are already clamoring for it, often paying several times the original price. Sapphire blue, a color approximating the old cobalt, was new a couple of years ago; it's also a Bloomingdale's exclusive, and the selection is limited. Probably another 'instant collectible' in the making! Chartreuse was next; it's a little more vivid than the chartreuse of the '50s. The last color to be added was gray.

Items that have not been restyled are being made from the original molds. This means that you may find pieces with the old mark in the new colors (since the mark is an integral part of the mold). When an item has been restyled, new molds had to be created, and these will have the new mark. So will any piece marked with the ink stamp. The new ink mark is a script 'FIESTA' (all letters upper case), while the old is 'Fiesta.' Compare a few, the difference is obvious. Just don't be fooled into thinking you've found a rare cobalt juice pitcher or individual sugar and creamer set; they weren't made in the old line.

For further information, we recommend *The Collector's Encyclopedia of Fiesta, Eighth Edition,* by Sharon and Bob Huxford.

Note: The term 'original colors' in the following listings refers to light green, yellow, and turquoise, with the exception of the items followed by the asterisk. Those items in turquoise are valued in the range of red, cobalt, and ivory. (Red, cobalt, and ivory are also 'original' colors, but because of high collector demand have been elevated to the next price point.)

Newsletter: *Fiesta Club of America*
P.O. Box 15383, Loves Park, IL 61132-5383

Newsletter: *Fiesta Collector's Quarterly*
China Specialties, Inc.
Box 471, Valley City, OH 44280. $12 (4 issues) per year

Ashtray, '50s colors...**$88.00**
Ashtray, original colors..**$47.00**
Ashtray, red, cobalt or ivory **$60.00**
Bowl, covered onion soup; cobalt or ivory..............**$725.00**
Bowl, covered onion soup; red....................................**$750.00**
Bowl, covered onion soup; turquoise, minimum value ..**$8,000.00**
Bowl, covered onion soup; yellow or light green....**$600.00**
Bowl, cream soup; '50s colors.....................................**$72.00**
Bowl, cream soup; med green, minimum value....**$4,000.00**
Bowl, cream soup; original colors...............................**$42.00**
Bowl, cream soup; red, cobalt or ivory **$60.00**
Bowl, dessert; '50s colors, 6" **$52.00**
Bowl, dessert; med green, 6"......................................**$475.00**
Bowl, dessert; original colors, 6"................................**$38.00**
Bowl, dessert; red, cobalt or ivory, 6" **$52.00**
Bowl, footed salad; original colors * **$300.00**
Bowl, footed salad; red, cobalt or ivory **$350.00**
Bowl, fruit; '50s colors, 4¾"...**$40.00**
Bowl, fruit; '50s colors, 5½"..**$40.00**
Bowl, fruit; med green, 4¾"..**$485.00**
Bowl, fruit; med green, 5½"...**$75.00**
Bowl, fruit; original colors, 4¾"...................................**$28.00**
Bowl, fruit; original colors, 5½"...................................**$28.00**
Bowl, fruit; original colors, 11¾" * **$300.00**
Bowl, fruit; red, cobalt or ivory, 11¾" **$300.00**
Bowl, fruit; red, cobalt or ivory, 4¾" **$35.00**
Bowl, fruit; red, cobalt or ivory, 5½" **$35.00**
Bowl, individual salad; med green, 7½"....................**$105.00**
Bowl, individual salad; red, turquoise or yellow, 7½"..**$85.00**
Bowl, nappy; '50s colors, 8½" **$65.00**
Bowl, nappy; med green, 8½".....................................**$140.00**
Bowl, nappy; original colors, 8½" * **$40.00**
Bowl, nappy; original colors, 9½" * **$52.00**
Bowl, nappy; red, cobalt or ivory, 8½" **$60.00**
Bowl, nappy; red, cobalt or ivory, 9½" **$65.00**

Bowl, Tom & Jerry; ivory w/gold letters $260.00
Bowl, unlisted salad; red, cobalt or ivory $500.00
Bowl, unlisted salad; yellow $105.00
Candle holders, bulb; original colors, pr * $95.00
Candle holders, bulb; red, cobalt or ivory, pr $130.00
Candle holders, tripod; original colors, pr * $465.00
Candle holders, tripod; red, cobalt or ivory, pr $600.00
Carafe, original colors * $250.00
Carafe, red, cobalt or ivory $300.00
Casserole, '50s colors $300.00
Casserole, French; standard colors other than yellow, minimum value $650.00
Casserole, French; yellow $300.00
Casserole, med green $725.00
Casserole, original colors $150.00
Casserole, red, cobalt or ivory $200.00
Coffeepot, '50s colors $350.00
Coffeepot, demitasse; original colors * $340.00
Coffeepot, demitasse; red, cobalt or ivory $435.00
Coffeepot, original colors $195.00
Coffeepot, red, cobalt or ivory $245.00
Compote, original colors, 12" * $148.00
Compote, red, cobalt or ivory, 12" $185.00
Compote, sweets; original colors * $75.00
Creamer, individual; red $250.00
Creamer, individual; turquoise or cobalt $345.00
Creamer, individual; yellow $70.00
Creamer, regular; '50s colors $40.00
Creamer, regular; med green $80.00
Creamer, regular; original colors $22.00
Creamer, regular; red, cobalt or ivory $35.00
Creamer, stick handled, original colors * $45.00
Creamer, stick handled, red, cobalt or ivory $70.00
Cup, demitasse; '50s colors $350.00
Cup, demitasse; original colors $65.00
Cup, demitasse; red, cobalt or ivory $75.00
Cup, see teacup
Egg cup, '50s colors $160.00
Egg cup, original colors $58.00
Egg cup, red, cobalt or ivory $70.00
Lid, for mixing bowl #1-#3, any color, minimum value. $785.00
Lid, for mixing bowl #4, any color, minimum value... $1,000.00
Marmalade, original colors * $230.00
Marmalade, red, cobalt or ivory $285.00
Mixing bowl #1, original colors * $170.00
Mixing bowl #1, red, cobalt or ivory $225.00
Mixing bowl #2, original colors * $110.00
Mixing bowl #2, red, cobalt or ivory $125.00
Mixing bowl #3, original colors * $120.00
Mixing bowl #3, red, cobalt or ivory $130.00
Mixing bowl #4, original colors * $130.00
Mixing bowl #4, red, cobalt or ivory $155.00
Mixing bowl #5, original colors * $155.00
Mixing bowl #5, red, cobalt or ivory $185.00
Mixing bowl #6, original colors * $200.00
Mixing bowl #6, red, cobalt or ivory $265.00
Mixing bowl #7, original colors * $280.00

Mixing bowl, #7, cobalt, M, $350.00.

Mixing bowl #7, red or ivory $350.00
Mug, Tom & Jerry; '50s colors $100.00
Mug, Tom & Jerry; ivory w/gold letters $65.00
Mug, Tom & Jerry; original colors $60.00
Mug, Tom & Jerry; red, cobalt or ivory $85.00
Mustard, original colors * $200.00
Mustard, red, cobalt or ivory $250.00
Pitcher, disk juice; gray, minimum value $2,500.00
Pitcher, disk juice; Harlequin yellow $62.00
Pitcher, disk juice; red $450.00
Pitcher, disk juice; yellow $45.00
Pitcher, disk water; '50s colors $275.00
Pitcher, disk water; med green, minimum value ... $1,150.00
Pitcher, disk water; original colors $125.00
Pitcher, disk water; red, cobalt or ivory $165.00
Pitcher, ice; original colors * $140.00
Pitcher, ice; red, cobalt or ivory $160.00
Pitcher, jug, 2-pt; '50s colors $150.00
Pitcher, jug, 2-pt; original colors $90.00
Pitcher, jug, 2-pt; red, cobalt or ivory $120.00
Plate, '50s colors, 6" $9.00
Plate, '50s colors, 7" $13.00
Plate, '50s colors, 9" $22.00
Plate, '50s colors, 10" $52.00
Plate, cake; original colors * $750.00
Plate, cake; red, cobalt or ivory $885.00
Plate, calendar; 1954 or 1955, 10" $45.00
Plate, calendar; 1955, 9" $50.00
Plate, chop; '50s colors, 13" $100.00
Plate, chop; '50s colors, 15" $115.00
Plate, chop; med green, 13" $275.00
Plate, chop; original colors, 13" $35.00
Plate, chop; original colors, 15" $48.00
Plate, chop; red, cobalt or ivory, 13" $55.00
Plate, chop; red, cobalt or ivory, 15" $75.00
Plate, compartment; '50s colors, 10½" $75.00
Plate, compartment; green or yellow, 12" $50.00
Plate, compartment; original colors, 10½" $40.00
Plate, compartment; red, cobalt or ivory, 10½" $40.00
Plate, compartment; red, cobalt or ivory, 12" $60.00
Plate, deep; '50s colors $55.00

Plate, deep; med green..................................$120.00
Plate, deep; original colors.........................$40.00
Plate, deep; red, cobalt or ivory.................$60.00
Plate, med green, 6"....................................$20.00
Plate, med green, 7"....................................$32.00
Plate, med green, 9"....................................$45.00
Plate, med green, 10"..................................$110.00
Plate, original colors, 6"..............................$5.00
Plate, original colors, 7"..............................$9.00
Plate, original colors, 9"..............................$12.00
Plate, original colors, 10"............................$32.00
Plate, red, cobalt or ivory, 6".......................$7.00
Plate, red, cobalt or ivory, 7"......................$10.00
Plate, red, cobalt or ivory, 9"......................$18.00
Plate, red, cobalt or ivory, 10"....................$40.00
Platter, '50s colors......................................$58.00
Platter, med green.......................................$140.00
Platter, original colors................................$35.00
Platter, red, cobalt or ivory........................$45.00
Relish tray, gold decor, complete, minimum value...$250.00
Relish tray base, original colors *................$65.00
Relish tray base, red, cobalt or ivory..........$85.00
Relish tray center insert, original colors *.....$42.00
Relish tray center insert, red, cobalt or ivory.....$55.00
Relish tray side insert, original colors *.......$40.00
Relish tray side insert, red, cobalt or ivory.....$48.00
Salt & pepper shakers, '50s colors, pr.........$45.00
Salt & pepper shakers, med green, pr.........$140.00
Salt & pepper shakers, original colors, pr.....$22.00
Salt & pepper shakers, red, cobalt or ivory, pr.....$30.00
Sauce boat, '50s colors................................$78.00
Sauce boat, med green................................$155.00
Sauce boat, original colors..........................$45.00
Sauce boat, red, cobalt or ivory..................$75.00
Saucer, demitasse; '50s colors....................$95.00
Saucer, demitasse; original colors...............$18.00
Saucer, demitasse; red, cobalt or ivory.......$22.00
Saucer, '50s colors.....................................$6.00
Saucer, med green......................................$12.00
Saucer, original colors................................$4.00
Saucer, red, cobalt or ivory.........................$5.00
Sugar bowl, individual; turquoise................$350.00
Sugar bowl, individual; yellow....................$120.00
Sugar bowl, w/lid, '50s colors, 3¼x3½".....$72.00
Sugar bowl, w/lid, med green, 3¼x3½".....$160.00
Sugar bowl, w/lid, original colors, 3¼x3½".....$45.00
Sugar bowl, w/lid, red, cobalt or ivory, 3¼x3½".....$55.00
Syrup, original colors *...............................$325.00
Syrup, red, cobalt or ivory..........................$400.00
Teacup, '50s colors.....................................$38.00
Teacup, med green......................................$58.00
Teacup, original colors................................$25.00
Teacup, red, cobalt or ivory........................$35.00
Teapot, lg; original colors *........................$185.00
Teapot, lg; red, cobalt or ivory....................$220.00
Teapot, med; med green, minimum value.....$1,000.00
Teapot, med; original colors........................$160.00

Teapot, medium; '50s colors, $325.00.

Teapot, med; red, cobalt or ivory...............$200.00
Tray, figure-8; cobalt..................................$90.00
Tray, figure-8; turquoise or yellow..............$350.00
Tray, utility; original colors *.....................$38.00
Tray, utility; red, cobalt or ivory.................$42.00
Tumbler, juice; chartreuse, Harlequin yellow or dark green...$460.00
Tumbler, juice; original colors....................$40.00
Tumbler, juice; red, cobalt or ivory.............$45.00
Tumbler, juice; rose....................................$65.00
Tumbler, water; original colors *................$60.00
Tumbler, water; red, cobalt or ivory............$85.00
Vase, bud; original colors *........................$80.00
Vase, bud; red, cobalt or ivory....................$110.00
Vase, original colors, 8" *..........................$600.00
Vase, original colors, 10" *.........................$750.00
Vase, original colors, 12" *.........................$1,000.00
Vase, red, cobalt or ivory, 8".......................$700.00
Vase, red, cobalt or ivory, 10".....................$850.00
Vase, red, cobalt or ivory, 12", minimum value.....$1,200.00

Vase, turquoise, 8", $700.00.

Kitchen Kraft

Bowl, mixing; light green or yellow, 6".....$65.00
Bowl, mixing; light green or yellow, 8".....$82.00

Bowl, mixing; light green or yellow, 10".....................$100.00
Bowl, mixing; red or cobalt, 6" $75.00
Bowl, mixing; red or cobalt, 8" $92.00
Bowl, mixing; red or cobalt, 10" $120.00
Cake plate, light green or yellow $55.00
Cake plate, red or cobalt......................................$65.00
Cake server, light green or yellow $130.00
Cake server, red or cobalt....................................$140.00
Casserole, individual; light green or yellow $140.00
Casserole, individual; red or cobalt.......................$155.00
Casserole, light green or yellow, 7½".......................$85.00
Casserole, light green or yellow, 8½" $100.00
Casserole, red or cobalt, 7½" $90.00
Casserole, red or cobalt, 8½" $110.00
Covered jar, lg; light green or yellow $300.00
Covered jar, lg; red or cobalt $320.00
Covered jar, med; light green $260.00
Covered jar, med; red or cobalt.............................$280.00

Covered jar, medium; yellow, $260.00.

Covered jar, sm; light green or yellow.......................$270.00
Covered jar, sm; red or cobalt $290.00
Covered jug, light green or yellow $250.00
Covered jug, red or cobalt...................................$275.00
Fork, light green or yellow...................................$100.00
Fork, red or cobalt $125.00
Metal frame for platter.......................................$26.00
Pie plate, light green or yellow, 9"..........................$40.00
Pie plate, light green or yellow, 10"........................$40.00
Pie plate, red or cobalt, 9" $45.00
Pie plate, red or cobalt, 10" $45.00
Pie plate, spruce green $290.00
Platter, light green or yellow $68.00
Platter, red or cobalt..$78.00
Platter, spruce green...$350.00
Salt & pepper shakers, light green or yellow, pr........$95.00
Salt & pepper shakers, red or cobalt, pr $105.00
Spoon, light green or yellow $100.00
Spoon, red or cobalt $125.00
Stacking refrigerator lid, ivory $205.00
Stacking refrigerator lid, light green or yellow...........$70.00
Stacking refrigerator lid, red or cobalt.....................$80.00

Stacking refrigerator unit, ivory $195.00
Stacking refrigerator unit, light green or yellow $45.00
Stacking refrigerator unit, red or cobalt......................$55.00

Finch, Kay

Wonderful ceramic figurines signed by artist-decorator Kay Finch are among the many that were produced in California during the middle of the century. She modeled her line of animals and birds with much expression and favored soft color combinations often with vibrant pastel accents. Some of her models were quite large, but generally they range in size from 12" down to a tiny 2". She made several animal 'family groups' and some human subjects as well. After her death a few years ago, prices for her work began to climb.

She used a variety of marks and labels, and though most pieces are marked, some of the smaller animals are not; but you should be able to recognize her work with ease, once you've seen a few marked pieces.

For more information, we recommend *Kay Finch Ceramics, Her Enchanted World,* by Mike Nickel and Cindy Horvath (Schiffer); *Collectible Kay Finch* by Richard Martinez, Devin Frick, and Jean Frick; and *The Collector's Encyclopedia of California Pottery, Second Edition,* by Jack Chipman (both by Collector Books).

Advisors: Mike Nickel and Cindy Horvath (See Directory, Kay Finch)

Bank, pig, Sassy, looking up, #166, 3¾x4" $175.00
Box, Easter egg; floral decoration, 9x8"....................$175.00
Figurine, American Indian Family, Indian Brave, Indian Squaw & Papoose, #205, #206, #207, 6¾", 6½" & 3½", set......$500.00
Figurine, angel, #114a, #114b, or #114c, ea $50.00
Figurine, bear, Mama; #4907, 9" $600.00

Figurine, bear, Sleepy, 4½", $275.00.

Figurine, bear, Tubby, sitting, #4847, 4¼" $250.00
Figurine, bird, Mr & Mrs; #454, #453, 4½", 3", pr.....$225.00
Figurine, bull, matt white glaze, #6211, 6½" $300.00

Figurine, Burro, Prospector's; white & gray w/pink in ears, #475, 10" $850.00

Figurine, camel, w/ or w/out saddle, #464, 5", ea....$450.00

Figurine, cat, Ambrosia; #155, 10½", minimum value..$700.00

Figurine, cat, Jezebel, #179, 6" $225.00

Figurine, cat, long eared; matt glaze, #5925, 5¾" $175.00

Figurine, cherub head, #212, 2¼" $85.00

Figurine, Chinese boy, #4629, 6¾"...........................$125.00

Figurine, choir boy, kneeling, #211, 5½"....................$75.00

Figurine, cockatoo, #5401, 15"..................................$750.00

Figurine, Court Prince, #451, 11"...............................$200.00

Figurine, dog, Afghan, sitting, #5553, 5¼"................$550.00

Figurine, dog, Beggar, #5262, 8"................................$600.00

Figurine, dog, Pekingese; #154, 14" L $550.00

Figurine, dog, pups, Yorky; #170 & #171, pr $650.00

Figurine, dog, Vicki, pink & white w/gold accents, #455, 11"...$1,000.00

Figurine, dog, Windblown Afghan, pewter-like glaze, #5757, 6x6"...$450.00

Figurine, Dog Show Boxer, #5025, 5x5" $400.00

Figurine, Dog Show Maltese, #5833, 2½" $300.00

Figurine, Duck, Mama; #472, 4¼" $300.00

Figurine, ducks, Peep & Jeep; #178a & #178b, 3", pr..$100.00

Figurine, elephant, Mumbo, sitting, #4804, 4½"........$225.00

Figurine, elephant, Peanuts; #191, 8½"......................$350.00

Figurine, Godey couple, #122, 9½", pr.......................$200.00

Figurine, guppy, #173, 2½" L $125.00

Figurine, hippo, eating tropical flower or wearing a bow, polka dots optional, #5019, 5¾", ea....................$600.00

Figurine, lamb, Prancing Lamb, white or pink, #168, 10½"...$900.00

Figurine, Littlest Angel, #4803, 2½"...........................$175.00

Figurine, Mermaid, Sirens of the Sea series, #161, 6½" ...$550.00

Figurine, monkey, Happy, sitting, #4903, 11", minimum value $1,000.00

Figurine, owl, Hoot; #187, 8½" $195.00

Figurine, owl, Toot; #188, 5¾"....................................$100.00

Figurine, Pajama Girl, #5002, 5½"..............................$225.00

Figurine, Pekingese, 14" long, $550.00.

Figurine, pheasant, 3 colors of blue iridescent glazes, #5300, 10"..$550.00

Figurine, pig, Porky, #5055, 2¾x3" $275.00

Figurine, pig, Smiley, clover-decorated version, #165, 6x7½"..$375.00

Figurine, pig, Winkie, #185, 3¾x4" $125.00

Figurine, quail, Mama; blue, #5984, 7" $450.00

Figurine, rabbit, Mama; #120, 4x4" $175.00

Figurine, rooster & hen, Butch & Biddy; #177 & #178, he: 8½", pr..$200.00

Figurine, Scandie Boy (#127) & Girl (#126), both 5¼", pr.$250.00

Figurine, Squirrels, Papa, Mama; #108A, B & C, 3½", pr....$175.00

Fountain, Bird Bath w/Bird, #5388, 6"........................$150.00

Planter, Baby Block w/bear, 6½" $100.00

Plate, Rooster Cocktail; hand painted, #5409, 6¾" ...$125.00

Shaker, cat, Puss, gray & white or pink & white w/colored collar, #4616, 6"..$425.00

Vase, South Sea Girl, #4912, 8¾".................................$200.00

Wall plaque, butterfly, #5720, 14"...............................$225.00

Wall plaque, sea horse, blue w/gold accents, #5788, 16" $250.00

Fire-King

This is an area of collecting interest that you can enjoy without having to mortgage the home place. In fact, you'll be able to pick it up for a song, if you keep your eyes peeled at garage sales and swap meets.

Fire-King was a trade name of the Anchor Hocking Glass Company, located in Lancaster, Ohio. As its name indicates, this type of glassware is strong enough to stand up to high oven temperatures without breakage. From the early '40s until the mid-'70s, they produced kitchenware, dinnerware, and restaurant ware in a variety of colors. (We'll deal with Jade-ite, the most collectible of these colors later on in the book.) Blues are always popular with collectors, and Anchor Hocking made two, turquoise blue and Azur-ite (light sky blue). They also made pink, forest green, ruby red (popular in the Bubble pattern), gold-trimmed lines, and some with fired-on colors. During the late '60s they made Soreno in avocado green to tie in with home-decorating trends.

Bubble (made from the '30s through the '60s) was produced in just about every color Anchor Hocking ever made. You may also hear this pattern referred to as Provincial or Bullseye.

Alice was a mid-'40s to '50s line. It was made in Jade-ite and a white that was sometimes trimmed with blue or red. Cups and saucers were given away in boxes of Mother's Oats, but plates had to be purchased (so they're scarce today).

In the early '50s, they produced a 'laurel leaf' design in peach and 'Gray Laurel' lustres (the gray is scarce), followed later in the decade and into the '60s with several lines of white glass decorated with decals — Honeysuckle, Fleurette, Primrose, and Game Bird, to name only a few.

Anchor Hocking made ovenware in many the same colors and designs as their dinnerware. Their most extensive line (and one that is very popular today) was made in sapphire blue, clear glass with a blue tint, in a pattern called Philbe. Most pieces are still very reasonable, but some are already worth in excess of $50.00, so now is the time to start your collection. These are the antiques of the future! If you'd like to study more about Anchor Hocking and Fire-King, we recommend *Anchor Hocking's Fire-King & More* and *Collectible Glassware of the 40s, 50s, and 60s* by Gene Florence. See also Jade-ite; Kitchen Collectibles.

Newsletter: *The '50s Flea!!!*
April and Larry Tvorak
P.O. Box 94
Warren Center, PA 18851
Subscription: $5 per year for 1 yearly postwar glass newsletter; includes free 30-word classified ad

Alice, white with blue trim, plate, 9½", $30.00; cup, $12.00; saucer, $6.00. (Photo courtesy Gene Florence)

Alice, plate, white w/red trim, 9½"	**$30.00**
Anniversary Rose, bowl, chili; white w/decal, 5"	**$12.00**
Anniversary Rose, creamer, white w/decal	**$10.00**
Anniversary Rose, cup, snack; white w/decal, 5-oz	**$5.00**
Anniversary Rose, cup, white w/decal, 8-oz	**$7.50**
Anniversary Rose, plate, dinner; white w/decal, 10"	**$12.00**
Blue Mosaic, bowl, dessert; white w/decal, 4⅝"	**$6.00**
Blue Mosaic, creamer, white w/decal	**$8.00**

Blue Mosaic, cup, $4.00; saucer, $2.00; plate, 10", $8.00; bowl, 8", $15.00; plate, 7⅜", $6.00. (Photo courtesy Gene Florence)

Blue Mosaic, sugar bowl, white w/decal, w/lid	**$13.00**
Bubble, bowl, cereal; Forest Green, 5¼"	**$18.00**
Bubble, bowl, fruit; white, 4½"	**$4.50**
Bubble, plate, dinner; crystal or iridescent, 9⅜"	**$6.00**
Bubble, plate, dinner; Ruby Red	**$24.00**
Bubble, sugar bowl, Sapphire Blue	**$25.00**
Charm/Square, bowl, dessert; Azur-ite, 4¾"	**$5.00**
Charm/Square, bowl, salad; Forest Green, 7⅜"	**$14.00**
Charm/Square, plate, dinner; Forest Green, 9¼""	**$30.00**
Charm/Square, plate, luncheon; Royal Ruby, 8⅜"	**$9.00**
Fish Scale, bowl, cereal; ivory, deep, 5½"	**$12.00**
Fish Scale, cup, ivory w/blue trim, 8-oz	**$20.00**
Fish Scale, platter, ivory w/red trim, 11¾"	**$45.00**
Fleurette, bowl, soup plate; 6⅝"	**$6.00**
Fleurette, plate, salad; white w/decal, 7⅜"	**$3.50**
Fleurette, platter, white w/decal, 9x12"	**$13.00**
Fleurette, tray, snack; white w/decal, 11x6"	**$2.50**
Forget Me Not, bowl, soup plate; white w/decal, 6⅝"	**$18.00**
Forget Me Not, custard, white w/decal	**$6.00**
Forget Me Not, platter, white w/decal, 9x12"	**$20.00**
Game Bird, bowl, dessert; white w/decal, 4⅝"	**$4.25**
Game Bird, plate, salad; white w/decal, 7⅜"	**$4.00**
Game Bird, platter, white w/decal, 12x9"	**$20.00**
Game Bird, tumbler, iced tea; white w/decal, 11-oz	**$9.00**
Gray Laurel, bowl, soup plate; 7⅝"	**$8.00**
Gray Laurel, bowl, vegetable; 8¼"	**$12.00**
Gray Laurel, creamer, footed	**$5.00**
Gray Laurel, plate, salad; 7⅜"	**$4.00**
Gray Laurel, plate, serving; 11"	**$16.00**
Gray Laurel, sugar bowl, footed	**$5.00**
Harvest, bowl, vegetable; white w/decal, 8¼"	**$15.00**
Harvest, plate, dinner; white w/decal, 10"	**$6.00**
Harvest, sugar bowl, white w/decal, w/lid	**$12.00**
Hobnail, cookie jar, milk white, w/lid	**$25.00**
Hobnail, jardiniere, coral, green or yellow, 5½"	**$10.00**
Hobnail, vase, milk white, 9½"	**$10.00**
Homestead, bowl, dessert; white w/decal, 4⅝"	**$5.00**
Homestead, plate, dinner; white w/decal, 10"	**$8.00**
Honeysuckle, cup, white w/decal, 8-oz	**$4.00**
Honeysuckle, tumbler, juice; white w/decal, 5-oz	**$7.00**
Jane Ray, bowl, cereal; ivory or white, 5⅞"	**$7.50**
Jane Ray, bowl, flat soup; ivory or white, 9"	**$35.00**
Jane Ray, cup, demitasse; Peach Lustre	**$15.00**
Jane Ray, plate, salad; ivory or white, 7¾"	**$7.00**
Jane Ray, platter, ivory or white, 9x12"	**$14.00**
Jane Ray, sugar bowl, ivory or white, w/lid	**$9.00**
Lace Edge, bowl, milk white or Azur-ite, footed, 11"	**$15.00**
Lace Edge, plate, salad; milk white or Azur-ite, Kansas Centennial, 8¼"	**$15.00**
Meadow Green, bowl, cereal; white w/decal, 5"	**$3.00**
Meadow Green, cake dish, white w/decal, round, 9"	**$6.50**
Meadow Green, casserole, white w/decal, w/lid, 2-qt	**$9.00**
Meadow Green, dish, utility; 2-qt	**$7.00**
Meadow Green, pan, loaf; 5x9"	**$6.50**
Meadow Green, platter, 12x9"	**$8.00**
Oven Glass, baker, ivory, round, 1-qt	**$6.00**
Oven Glass, bowl, measuring; Sapphire Blue, 16-oz	**$25.00**

Oven Glass, casserole, Sapphire Blue, knob handle lid, 2-qt **$22.00**
Oven Glass, nurser, Sapphire Blue, 8-oz **$30.00**
Oven Glass, pan, loaf; ivory, deep, 9⅛x5⅛" **$13.50**
Oven Glass, pan, utility; ivory, 10½x2" deep **$15.00**
Oven Glass, roaster, Sapphire Blue, 10⅜" **$75.00**
Peach Lustre, bowl, dessert; 4⅞" **$3.00**
Peach Lustre, bowl, vegetable; 8¼" **$9.50**
Peach Lustre, creamer, footed **$3.50**
Peach Lustre, cup, 8-oz **$3.50**
Peach Lustre, plate, dinner; 9⅛" **$4.00**
Peach Lustre, plate, salad; 7⅜" **$3.00**
Peach Lustre, sugar bowl, footed **$3.50**
Philbe, bowl, cereal; crystal, 5½" **$18.00**
Philbe, creamer, pink or green, footed, 3¼" **$135.00**
Philbe, plate, salver; crystal, 10½" **$40.00**
Philbe, plate, sherbet; blue, 6" **$95.00**
Philbe, tumbler, iced tea; pink or green, footed, 15-oz, 6½" **$85.00**
Philbe, tumbler, juice; blue, footed, 3½" **$175.00**
Primrose, casserole, white w/decal, knob lid, 1½-qt..**$12.00**

Primrose, gravy boat, $125.00. (Photo courtesy Gene Florence)

Primrose, pan, baking; white w/decal, w/lid, 5x9" **$15.00**
Primrose, pan, cake; white w/decal, round, 8" **$9.00**
Primrose, plate, bread & butter; white w/decal, 6¼"....**$3.00**
Primrose, plate, dinner; white w/decal, 9⅛" **$5.00**
Primrose, tumbler, water; crystal, 9-oz **$6.50**
Swirl, bowl, cereal; Golden Shell, 6⅜" **$2.50**
Swirl, bowl, fruit/dessert; Anchorwhite, ivory or white, 7¼" **$2.50**
Swirl, bowl, soup plate; Golden Anniversary, 7⅝" **$3.00**
Swirl, bowl, vegetable; Lustre Shell, 8½" **$9.00**
Swirl, creamer, pink, flat **$8.00**
Swirl, cup, Azur-ite or Sunrise, 8-oz **$5.50**
Swirl, plate, serving; Azur-ite or Sunrise, 11" **$17.50**
Swirl, plate, serving; Lustre Shell, 11" **$11.00**
Swirl, platter, Anchorwhite, ivory or white, 12x9".....**$6.00**
Swirl, platter, Golden Shell, 9½x13" **$9.00**
Swirl, sugar bowl, Golden Anniversary, open handles, footed **$3.50**
Swirl, sugar bowl, pink, tab handles, flat **$7.00**
Turquoise Blue, ashtray, 4⅝" **$10.00**

Turquoise Blue, bowl, berry; 4½" **$6.00**
Turquoise Blue, bowl, mixing; round, 3-qt **$16.00**
Turquoise Blue, bowl, mixing; tear shape, 1-qt..........**$18.00**
Turquoise Blue, bowl, mixing; tear shape, 3-qt..........**$30.00**
Turquoise Blue, bowl, soup/salad; 6⅝" **$15.00**
Turquoise Blue, cup **$4.00**
Turquoise Blue, mug, 8-oz...**$10.00**
Turquoise Blue, plate, w/cup indent, 9" **$6.00**
Turquoise Blue, plate, 10" **$28.00**
Turquoise Blue, sugar bowl..**$6.00**
Wheat, bowl, soup plate; white w/decal, 6⅝" **$7.00**
Wheat, casserole, white w/decal, knob lid, 1½-qt........**$9.50**
Wheat, pan, baking; white w/decal, w/lid, 5x9".........**$15.00**
Wheat, tray, snack; white w/decal, rectangular, 11x6" .**$3.50**

Fishbowl Ornaments

Prior to World War II, every dime store had its bowl of small goldfish. Nearby were stacks of goldfish bowls — small, medium, and large. Accompanying them were displays of ceramic ornaments for these bowls, many in the shape of Oriental pagodas or European-style castles. The fish died, the owners lost interest, and the glass containers along with their charming ornaments were either thrown out or relegated to the attic. In addition to pagodas and castles, other ornaments included bridges, lighthouses, colonnades, mermaids, and fish. Note that figurals such as mermaids are difficult to find.

Many fishbowl ornaments were produced in Japan between 1921 and 1941, and again after 1947. The older Japanese items often show clean, crisp mold designs with visible detail of the item's features. Others were made in Germany and some by potteries in the United States. Aquarium pieces made in America are not common. Those produced in recent years are usually of Chinese origin and are more crude, less colorful, and less detailed in appearance. In general, the more detail and more colorful, the older the piece. A few more examples are shown in *Collector's Guide to Made in Japan Ceramics* by Carole Bess White (Collector Books).

Advisor: Carole Bess White (See Directory, Japan Ceramics)

Bathing beauty on turtle, red, tan & green on white, 2½", from $20 to...**$30.00**
Boy riding dolphin on wave, multicolored matt glazes, 3¾", from $20 to..**$30.00**
Castle towers w/3 arches, tan lustre towers w/red arches on green & white rocks, 5¼" **$22.00**
Castle w/arch, multicolored, 2½" or 3½", ea..............**$20.00**
Colonade w/palm tree, green, blue & white, 3¾x4" ..**$20.00**
Coral w/deep sea diver, orange glossy glaze w/black image of diver, 3½"...**$20.00**
Diver holding dagger, white suit & helmet, blue gloves, brown boots & black airpack, 4¾" **$22.00**
Doorway, stone entry w/open aqua wood-look door, 2" ..**$15.00**
Fish riding waves, 2 white fish on cobalt waves, 3½x3"....**$22.00**

Lighthouse, orange, yellow & brown, 2x2½" **$16.00**
Lighthouse, tan, black, brown & green, 6½x4" **$26.00**
Mermaid on sea horse, white, green & orange glossy glazes, 3¼", from $20 to **$30.00**
Mermaid on 2 seashells, multicolored matt glazes, 3½", from $30 to **$40.00**

Mermaid on snail, 4", from $35.00 to $45.00. (Photo courtesy Carole Bess White)

Nude on starfish, bisque, 4½", from $40 to **$50.00**
Oriental building w/foundation archway, resembles Noah's Ark w/foundation & double stairway forming archway, 2½" **$18.00**
Pagoda, triple roof, blue, green & maroon, 5½x3¼"..**$20.00**

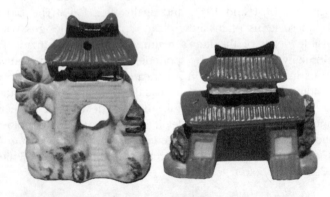

Pagodas, 3½" and 3¼", from $15.00 to $20.00 each. (Photo courtesy Carole Bess White)

Sign on tree trunk, No Fishing, brown, black & white, 2½x4" **$12.00**
Torii gate, multicolored glossy glazes, 3¾" **$22.00**

Fisher-Price

Probably no other toy manufacturer is as well known among kids of today as Fisher-Price. Since the 1930s they've produced wonderful toys made of wood covered with vividly lithographed paper. Plastic parts weren't used until 1949, and this can sometimes help you date your finds.

These toys were made for play, so very few older examples have survived in condition good enough to attract collectors. Watch for missing parts and avoid those that are dirty. Edge wear and some paint dulling is normal and to be expected. Our values are for toys with minimum signs of such wear.

For more information we recommend *Fisher-Price Toys, A Pictorial Price Guide to the More Popular Toys,* by Brad Cassity (available from the author); *Modern Toys, American Toys, 1930 – 1980,* by Linda Baker; *Fisher-Price, A Historical, Rarity Value Guide,* by John J. Murray and Bruce R. Fox (Books Americana); and *Schroeder's Collectible Toys, Antique to Modern,* published by Collector Books.

Advisor: Brad Cassity (See Directory, Toys)

Club: Fisher-Price Collector's Club
Jeanne Kennedy
1442 N Ogden, Mesa, AZ 85205; Monthly newsletter with information and ads; send SASE for more information

Museum: Toy Town Museum
636 Girard Ave., PO Box 238, East Aurora, NY 14052; Monday through Saturday, 10 – 4

Adventure People & Their TV Action Team, #309, 1977-78, complete **$50.00**
Adventure People Construction Workers, #352, 1976-79, complete **$15.00**
Adventure Sport Plane, #306, 1975-80............................**$8.00**
Big Bill Pelican, #794, 1961, w/cardboard fish............**$85.00**
Bouncing Buggy, #122, 1974-79, 6 wheels **$5.00**
Bouncy Racer, #8, 1960...**$40.00**
Bucky Burro, #166, 1955...**$250.00**
Bunny Engine, #703, 1954 ....**$100.00**
Buzzy Bee, #325, 1950, 1st version, dark yellow & black w/wooden wheels & antennae tips.......................**$40.00**
Cackling Hen, #123, 1966-68, red litho......................**$40.00**
Chick Basket Cart, #302, 1957 ....**$40.00**
Chubby Cub, #164, 1969-72 ....**$20.00**
Creative Block Wagon, #161, 1961-64, 18 building blocks & 6 wooden dowels fit into pull-along wagon **$75.00**
Creative Coaster, #987, 1964-81, MIB.........................**$50.00**
Doggy Racer, #7, 1942...**$200.00**
Dr Doodle, #100, 1st Fisher-Price limited edition of 5,000, 1995 ....**$125.00**
Ducky Flip Flap, #715, 1964-65 ....**$65.00**
Ferry Boat, #932, 1979-80, complete...........................**$45.00**
Fisher-Price Tractor, #629, 1962-68.............................**$30.00**
Frisky Frog, #154, 1971-83, squeeze plastic bulb & frog jumps...**$25.00**
Gabby Duck, #190, 1939..**$350.00**
Hot Dog Wagon, #445, 1940..**$250.00**
Humpty Dumpty Truck, #145, 1963-64 & Easter 1965..**$40.00**
Jenny Doll, #201, 1974-78 ....**$50.00**
Jiffy Dump Truck, #156, 1971-73, squeeze bulb & dump moves **$25.00**

Jolly Jalopy, #724, 1965-78......................**$15.00**
Katie Kangaroo, #158, 1976-77, squeeze bulb & she hops..................................**$25.00**
Kicking Donkey, #175, 1937......................**$450.00**
Leo the Drummer, #480, 1952 ....**$225.00**
Little People Main Street, #2500, 1986-90, complete...**$50.00**
Little People Playground, #2525, 1986-90, complete...**$15.00**
McDonald's Restaurant, #2552, 1990, 1st version, complete **$75.00**
Merry Mousewife, #662, 1962 ....**$50.00**
Milk Wagon, #131, 1964-72, truck w/bottle carrier **$50.00**
Music Box Bear, #450, 1981-83, Schubert's Cradle Song..**$15.00**

Music Box Lacing Shoe, #991, 1964, $50.00. (Photo courtesy Brad Cassity)

Music Box TV, #114, 1967-83, plays London Bridge & Row Row Row Your Boat **$5.00**
Natalie Doll, #202, 1974-78 ....**$25.00**
Oscar the Grouch, #177, 1977-84 ....**$20.00**
Perky Penguin, #786, 1973-75.....................**$20.00**
Piggy Bank, #166, 1981-82, plastic **$15.00**
Play Family Airport, #996, 1972-76, 1st version, complete..............................**$75.00**
Play Family Animal Circus, #135, 1974-76, complete..**$60.00**
Play Family Car & Camper, #992, 1980-84, complete .**$35.00**
Play Family Castle, #993, 1974-77, 1st version, complete ..**$100.00**
Play Family Fun Jet, #183, 1970, 1st version **$25.00**
Play Family Houseboat, #985, 1972-76, complete.......**$45.00**

Play Family Sesame Street, #938, $70.00. (Photo courtesy Brad Cassity)

Play Family Sesame Street Clubhouse, #937, 1977-79, complete..........................**$75.00**
Play Pull-Along Lacing Shoe, #146, 1970-75, w/6 figures..**$50.00**
Pull-A-Tune Pony Music Box, #190, 1969-72..............**$10.00**
Roly Raccoon, #172, 1980-82, waddles from side to side .**$10.00**
Safety School Bus, #983, 1959, w/6 figures, Fisher-Price Club logo..................................**$250.00**
Stake Truck, #649, 1960 ....**$50.00**
Super Jet, #415, 1952................................**$225.00**
Tailspin Tabby Pop-Up, #600, 1947 ....**$250.00**

Teddy Bear Xylophone, #752, 1948, $325.00. (Photo courtesy Brad Cassity)

Timmy Turtle, #150, 1953-55 & Easter 1956, green shell .**$100.00**
Tip-Toe Turtle, #773, 1962, vinyl tail **$15.00**
Tote-A-Tune Radio, #795, 1984-91, Toyland.................**$5.00**
Tuggy Tooter, #139, 1967-73.......................**$40.00**
Tumble Tower Game, #118, 1972-75, w/10 marbles ..**$10.00**
TV Radio, #158, 1967, Little Boy Blue **$50.00**
Woofy Wowser, #700, 1940.......................**$400.00**
Ziggy Zilo, #734, 1958-59...........................**$75.00**

Fishing Lures

There have been literally thousands of lures made since the turn of the century. Some have bordered on the ridiculous, and some have turned out to be just as good as the manufacturers claimed. In lieu of buying outright from a dealer, try some of the older stores in your area — you just might turn up a good old lure. Go through any old tackle boxes that might be around, and when the water level is low, check out the river banks.

If you have to limit your collection, you might want to concentrate just on wooden lures, or you might decide to try to locate one of every lure made by a particular company. Whatever you decide, try to find examples with good original paint and hardware. Though many lures are still very reasonable, we have included some of the more expensive examples as well to give you an indication of the type you'll want to fully research if you think you've found a similar model. For such information, we recommend *Fishing Lure Collectibles* by Dudley Murphy and Rick Edmisten; *The Fishing Lure*

Collector's Bible by R.L. Streater with Rick Edmisten and Dudley Murphy; and *Collector's Guide to Creek Chub Lures and Collectibles* by Harold E. Smith, M.D. All are published by Collector Books.

Advisor: Dave Hoover (See Directory, Fishing Lures)

Club: NFLCC Tackle Collectors
HC 3, Box 4012
Reeds Spring, MO 65737
Send SASE for more information about membership and their publications: *The National Fishing Lure Collector's Club Magazine* and *The NFLCC Gazette*.

Arbogast, Jitterbug, black scaling on silver, red eyes, EX..**$55.00**

Arbogast, Twin Liz, white w/red nose, MIB (plastic top) **$75.00**

Christianson, Fly Rod Brown Trout, single hook, M (w/wooden slide-top box) **$60.00**

Christianson, Fly Rod Rainbow Trout, single hook in tail, 2½", M (w/wooden slide-top box)........................**$55.00**

Creek Chub, Beetle, black w/red wings, black bead eyes, EX **$225.00**

Creek Chub, Bomber, Perch, painted eyes, mid-size, VG+.**$30.00**

Creek Chub, Darter, frog spot, MIB (plastic top)........**$25.00**

Creek Chub, Deepster, gray sucker finish, painted eyes, EX **$55.00**

Creek Chub, Deluxe Wag Tail, goldfish, glass eyes, double-line tie, VG+..**$195.00**

Creek Chub, Ding Bat, perch, glass eyes, brown tails, old non-reinforced lip, EX....................................**$65.00**

Creek Chub, Ding Bat, pike, wire leader, VG+...........**$25.00**

Creek Chub, Fly Rod Ding Bat, white w/red head & white tails, EX (2-pc True to Nature box).....................**$250.00**

Creek Chub, Fly Rod Plunker Bass Bug, gray w/white wings, VG (2-pc True to Nature box)............................**$125.00**

Creek Chub, Giant Jointed Pike #800, tack eyes, 1 pointer, EXIB..**$95.00**

Creek Chub, Husky Musky, hand-painted gills, glass eyes, early, VG **$125.00**

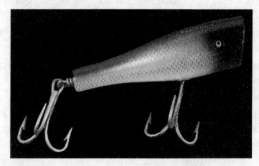

Creek Chub, Husky Plunker, #5804, Golden Shiner, wooden, from $80.00 to $120.00. (Photo courtesy Harold E. Smith M.D.)

Creek Chub, Injured Minnow #1600, glass eyes, VG .**$195.00**

Creek Chub, Jointed Midget Pike, rainbow fire, glass eyes, VG..**$75.00**

Creek Chub, Jointed Pike #2631, rainbow fire, glass eyes, EXIB..**$135.00**

Creek Chub, Jointed Striper Pike #6807, pale mullet, glass eyes, EX-..**$85.00**

Creek Chub, Kingfish Pike, tiger stripe, glass eyes, VG-.**$250.00**

Creek Chub, Pickerel Pikie #2600, yellow tail w/flitter head, glass eyes, lg body, EX (w/2-pc box & catalog).**$250.00**

Creek Chub, Plunker, white scales, glass eyes, VG+.**$125.00**

Creek Chub, Pop & Dunk, white w/red head, glass eyes, EX+ **$45.00**

Creek Chub, Snook Pikie #2618, blue flash, glass eyes, EX+ (w/2-pc box)..**$225.00**

Creek Chub, Tarpon Pike, silver flash, glass eyes, 2 lg single hooks, VG **$235.00**

Creek Chub, Wiggle Diver #1841, yellow w/red head, MIB (plastic top)..**$275.00**

Creek Chub, Wiggler #100, perch, glass eyes, EX **$75.00**

Creek Chub, Wiggler #200, perch, glass eyes, VG+....**$65.00**

Evans, Undertaker, yellowed white body w/red head, tack eyes, EX **$60.00**

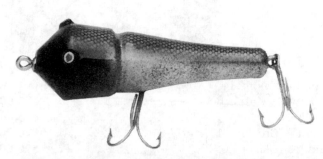

Garland Brothers, Cork-Head Minnow, ca 1936, 3¾", from $60.00 to $90.00. (Photo courtesy Dudley Murphy and Rick Edmisten)

Heddon, #100, shiner scale, glass eyes, lg, VG.........**$175.00**

Heddon, #210, white w/red head, glass eyes, sm, EX..**$85.00**

Heddon, Baby Crab Spook, white w/red tail, red bead eyes, spinner on nose, 2-pc, VG+..................................**$55.00**

Heddon, Baby Crab Wiggler, full color, glass eyes, VG..**$65.00**

Heddon, Baby Gamefisher, white w/red nose & tail, lg, EX **$110.00**

Heddon, Baby Vamp #7400, white w/red tail, red around glass eyes, lg, EX-..**$65.00**

Heddon, Crazy Crawler #2100, black w/white head & wings, red center eye, sm, EX......................................**$70.00**

Heddon, Deluxe Basser, white w/red gills, red around glass eyes, wire break-away rig, EX..........................**$125.00**

Heddon, Flap-Tail, silver flash, glass eyes, 2-pc, VG..**$45.00**

Heddon, Hi-Tail, frog spots, EX **$65.00**

Heddon, King Zig Wag #8350, shiner scales, painted eyes, string tie, EX..**$35.00**

Heddon, Meadow Mouse, white w/black stripes & red around bead eyes, lg, EXIB..............................**$150.00**

Heddon, Punkinseed, black shore w/copper eyes, tiny, EX+ $115.00

Heddon, River Runt, perch, glass eyes, 2-pc, EX......$145.00

Heddon, Stingaree, white shore, EX+ $65.00

Heddon, Weedless Widow, luny frog finish, EX.......$185.00

Heddon, Wounded Spook, black shore, MIB (plastic top) $95.00

Heddon, Zig-Wag, shiner scales, glass eyes, lg, EX..$145.00

Jaminson, Fly Rod Coaxer Floating Bass Fly, black w/black tail, EX+ $125.00

Jaminson, Fly Rod Coaxer Floating Trout, white w/red heather, EX+..$125.00

Jaminson, Fly Rod Goof Ball, yellow w/yellow tail feathers & trim, EX+..$40.00

Pflueger, Five-Hook Neverfail Minnow, white w/red & green spots, glass eyes, hand-painted gills, VG............$145.00

Pflueger, Globe #3750, natural pike scales w/red head, 5¼", EXIB $125.00

Pflueger, Wizzard, luminous w/red lightning stripe & trim, glass eyes, 3", EX......................................$145.00

Shur-Luk, Fly Rod Minnow, black w/yellow head, side hooked, EX- $20.00

South Bend, Dart-Oreno #945YP, yellow perch, tack eyes, VG+ (w/2-pc box) $25.00

South Bend, Fin-Dingo, orange scales w/black spots, MIB $125.00

South Bend, Jointed Explorer #G2920, fire lacquer red & yellow, clear eyes, MIB (plastic lid)..........................$55.00

Wright & McGill, Flapper Crab, green w/red stripes, glass eyes, EX...$225.00

Wright & McGill, Fly Rod Bass Bug, red w/black head, yellow glass eyes, VG $65.00

Wright & McGill, Fly Rod Nature Faker, red w/red wings, black bead glass eyes, EX+..................................$85.00

Fitz & Floyd

If you've ever visited a Fitz & Floyd outlet store, you know why collectors find this company's products so exciting. Steven Speilberg has nothing on their designers when it comes to imagination. Much of their production is related to holidays, and they've especially outdone themselves with their Christmas lines. But there are wonderful themes taken from nature featuring foxes, deer, birds, or rabbits, and others that are outrageously and deliberately humorous. Not only is the concept outstanding, so is quality.

Prices for Fitz & Floyd are on the rise due to the uncertainty of the company's future. See also Cookie Jars.

Bank, Cheshire Cat $65.00

Cake stand, Holly Christmas, 4x10" dia $120.00

Candy jar, Santa & Reindeer in Rolls Royce $135.00

Clock, Fox & the Hounds, battery operated, 6x5" $50.00

Creamer & sugar bowl, spring flowers on white basketweave..$36.00

Dish, bunch of light gray asparagus w/pink bow, w/lid, 6¾x4" $22.00

Dish, shell shape, white w/yellow interior, 3 shell feet, 8x8x5" $32.50

Egg holders, chicks, set of 8, 2½x1½" $30.00

Mug, English Garden Bunnies $25.00

Mug, pumpkin face w/figural vulture handle, from $50 to $75.00

Mug, School Days Bunnies, bunny swings on branch that makes handle, 4" $25.00

Pitcher, fish design w/shell base, 9"...........................$38.00

Pitcher, sailor's bookshelf, intricate detailing, 5x8", MIB..$18.00

Plate, Alice in Wonderland's A Mad Tea Party, edition of 5,000, MIB $35.00

Plate, canape; Mayfair Bunnies, MIB..........................$29.00

Plate, canape; rooster, Coq du Village collection........$60.00

Plate, salad; Chaises II, gold trim, 8¼", MIB $20.00

Plates, salad; marked Kalahari, w/zebra, giraffe, elephant & tiger, set of 4, 8", M...$50.00

Salt & pepper shakers, ceramic, he holding ear of corn, she holding pumpkin, glossy, pr..................................$30.00

Salt & pepper shakers, mice, pr $22.50

Salt & pepper shakers, mice dressed w/bonnets, pr ..$22.00

Teapot, purple & white iris on front w/lilies of the valley on back, 10¼x8"..$24.00

Teapot, Santa Car, candy cane handle, from $100 to .$125.00

Teapot, School Days Bunnies, mother's head is lid, student's hat is spout, apron ties make handle, 9", MIB $48.00

Teapot, Snowman, broom across belly, wearing red hat, from $50 to..$75.00

Teapot, White House, Collector Series, edition of 5,000, 6" $85.00

Bank, Dracula, 6½", $135.00. (Photo courtesy Jim and Beverly Mangus)

Florence Ceramics

During the '40s, Florence Ward began modeling tiny ceramic children as a hobby at her home in Pasadena, California. She was so happy with the results that she expanded, hired decorators, and moved into a larger building where for two decades she produced the lovely line of figurines, wall plaques, busts, etc., that have become so popular today. The 'Florence Collection' featured authentically detailed models of such couples as Louis XV and Madame Pompadour, Pinkie and Blue Boy, and Rhett and Scarlett. Nearly all of the Florence figures have names which are written on their bases.

Many figures are decorated with 22k gold and lace. Real lace was cut to fit, dipped in a liquid material called slip, and fired. During the firing it burned away, leaving only hardened ceramic lace trim. The amount of lace work that was used is one of the factors that needs to be considered when evaluating a 'Florence.' Size is another. Though most of the figures you'll find today are singles, a few were made as groups, and once in awhile you'll find a lady seated on a divan. The more complex, the more expensive.

There are Florence figurines that are very rare and unusual, i.e., Mark Anthony, Cleopatra, Story Hour, Grandmother and I, Carmen, Dear Ruth, Spring and Fall Reverie, Clocks, and many others. These may be found with a high price; however, there are bargains still to be had.

Our wide range of values reflects the amounts of detailing and lace work present. If you'd like to learn more about the subject, we recommend *The Collector's Encyclopedia of California Pottery, Second Edition,* by Jack Chipman; and *The Florence Collectibles, An Era of Elegance,* by Doug Foland.

Advisors: Doug Foland and Jerry Kline (See Directory, Florence Ceramics)

Artware, Baltimore Orioles, adult & 2 young on branch, from $400 to..**$450.00**
Artware, Diane powder box, from $375 to **$400.00**
Artware, Dresden picture frame, 5x7", from $110 to..**$120.00**
Artware, high-button shoe, from $100 to **$125.00**
Artware, owl, wings slightly open, on tree trunk base, from $400 to..**$450.00**
Artware, vase, bud; 6¾", from $90 to **$100.00**
Ballerina, lace trim, gold, 7", minimum value, from $375 to **$400.00**
Birthday Girl, 9", from $350 to **$850.00**
Bowl, shell; for Merrymaids, 3¼x15¾", from $275 to..**$300.00**
Bud & Dot, young boy & girl in western clothes, she w/doll, 7½", ea, from $500 to...**$550.00**
Cockatoo, on branch, #W24, 13¼", from $400 to.....**$450.00**
Cynthia, lace & fur, gold, 9¼" **$750.00**
Dealer sign, lady holding sign, w/gold, 6¼x5", from $650 to..**$700.00**
Diana, powder box, 6¼"...**$400.00**
Dog Ford Bank, black & white, Scripto era, single dog, from $75 to...**$85.00**
Dog Ford Bank, black & white, Scripto era, double dog, from $90 to...**$110.00**
Don, white tuxedo jacket & black pants, 9½", from $325 to..**$350.00**
Fern, wall pocket, w/gold, 7", from $175 to **$200.00**
Gibson Girl, painted mark, 11", from $350 to...........**$375.00**
Grandmother & I, from $2,500 to **$3,000.00**
Irene, white dress w/gold, Godey.............................**$70.00**

Jerry, flower holder, man in white playing bass viola, from $180 to..**$190.00**
John Alden, gray, white & black, 9¼", from $250 to.**$275.00**
Joy, flower holder, white dress w/blue trim, w/harp, from $180 to..**$190.00**
Judy, white prom dress w/floral, 8¾", from $400 to .**$450.00**
Karlo, Oriental lady, w/fan, 14", from $400 to..........**$450.00**
Kay, fur trim w/gold, 6"...**$100.00**
Lady Diana, red & white dress, flowers in hair, 10", from $750 to..**$800.00**
Linda Lou, red or teal, 7¾", from $160 to **$400.00**

Louis XVI, 11", and Marie Antoinette, 11", $750.00 for the pair.

Marianne, orange dress, holds hat at waist, 8¾", from $500 to..**$550.00**
Martin, red coat, w/cane, 10½", from $375 to **$400.00**
Merrymaids, Rosie, Jane or Betty, 7", 7", 4½", ea, from $200 to..**$225.00**
Mikado, Oriental man, 14", from $400 to **$450.00**
Mockingbird (single bird), attached flowers on base, #W4, 5¼", from $275 to..**$300.00**
Patsy, stands by stone wall, 6", from $50 to...............**$60.00**
Priscilla & John Alden, pr **$600.00**

Rosemarie (child), pink dress, 7", from $350.00 to $375.00.

Sandy & Blondie, boy & girl in blue swimsuits, both 7½", pr, from $850 to..**$900.00**

Scarlet & Rhett, no hand away, 8¾", 9", pr..............**$550.00**
Shirley, no hand away, 8"......................................**$225.00**
Stephen, lace, gold, 8¾", from $400 to....................**$450.00**
Susie, little girl in bonnet, white floral dress, 5½"....**$175.00**
Suzanna, lace, gold, 8¾", from $375 to...................**$400.00**
Taka, Oriental lady, w/parasol, 13", from $400 to....**$450.00**
Vase, shell, pink & gray lustre, 6x6½", from $90 to .**$100.00**

Victor, 10", $325.00 to $350.00.

Victoria, on attached divan, ribbons, roses & lace trim
w/gold, 7x8¼", from $475 to.............................**$500.00**
Violet, wall pocket, w/gold, 7", from $175 to..........**$200.00**

Flower Frogs

Nearly every pottery company and glasshouse in America produced their share of figural flower frogs, and many were imported from Japan as well. They were probably most popular from about 1910 through the 1940s, coinciding not only with the heyday of American glass and ceramics, but with the gracious, much less hectic style of living the times allowed. Way before a silk flower or styrofoam block was ever dreamed of there were fresh cut flowers on many a dining room sideboard or table, arranged in shallow console bowls with matching frogs such as we've described in the following lines. See also specific pottery and glass companies.

Advisor: Nada Sue Knauss (See Directory, Flower Frogs)

Bird, orange lustre bird on blue lustre base, 2½"........**$8.00**
Bird angled downward on stump, shades of green w/red
crest, pointed beak, glossy, 7¼"...........................**$25.00**
Bird on forked stump, black & white face & breast, orange
beak, tan lustre stump, Japan, 4½"......................**$28.00**
Bird on rock-like base, green, brown & black, brown base,
Japan, 6"...**$15.00**
Bird on stump, majolica style, green w/yellow breast & sm
pink beak, brown stump, glossy glazes, 4½", from $30
to...**$45.00**

Bird on stump, yellow w/turquoise wings & pink breast, blue
stump, Japan, 4"..**$15.00**
Bird on stump w/lg flower & leaves, majolica style, shades
of green & gray w/red breast, matt finish, 4", from $30
to...**$45.00**
Bird on 2-branch perch w/holes around base, lustre finish,
Japan, 2¾"...**$18.00**
Bird w/head down & pointed beak on rooted stump,
majolica style, glossy blue w/natural stump, 5¾",
from $40 to...**$50.00**
Birds, row of 3, blue lustre w/yellow breasts, orange &
white faces, on blue lustre branch base, Japan,
4x3¾x2"...**$25.00**
Birds on stump, orange crests w/lavender breasts,
orange lustre base, inscribed Niagara Falls, Canada,
Japan, 6"...**$15.00**
Bluebird on branch, lilac breast, yellow beak, yellow, green
& red flower on orange lustre base, Japan, 3".....**$15.00**

Butterfly, German, 4", $85.00. (Photo courtesy Nada Sue Knauss)

Crab in bowl, glossy purple, 7½" round footed bowl, Japan,
from $60 to...**$70.00**
Ducks (2) calling on gold lustre mound, Japan, 5" **$25.00**

Fish, Jamieson's, Capistrano, Calif. (with maple leaf), 6½", in matching bowl, from $45.00 to $55.00. (Photo courtesy Nada Sue Knauss)

Flower bud on logs, yellow & blue w/lg green leaves, blue lustre logs, Japan, 2½"..**$18.00**

Frog, blue lustre w/yellow belly, front legs on pink flower, orange lustre base, hand painted, Japan, 3x3", from $15 to..**$20.00**

Frog in bowl, leaves & flowers w/blue & gold lustre finish, Japan, 6"...**$25.00**

Frog singing & playing mandolin on stump in bowl w/berries & leaves, green, yellow & red w/tan lustre, 5", from $45 to..**$55.00**

House & trees on rocky base w/steps, majolica style, red, yellow, blue & green w/brown base, semi-gloss, 4", from $30 to..**$45.00**

Lady dancing in attached scalloped bowl, white w/hint of yellow on sides, 6½x5", from $15 to **$25.00**

Lotus bud cupped in 2 rings of green petals, glossy, Japan, 4½"...**$18.00**

Owl on stump, majolica style, blue & white w/touch of rust on breast, brown stump, glossy, 6", from $40 to .**$50.00**

Parrot on stump w/lg tulip, majolica style, purple & blue bird & tulip, green stump & leaves, 4¼" **$18.00**

Pelican, yellow lustre body, orange glossy wings & crest, blue lustre stump, Japan, 3".................................**$12.00**

Pelican on logs, yellow w/burgundy beak & legs, orange tinted & black wings, turquoise logs, Japan **$15.00**

Pelican on rocky ledge, majolica style, Japan, 6½" **$24.00**

Penguins (2) on icy base, blue lustre w/pale yellow breasts, pearl lustre base, Japan, 4¾" **$25.00**

Scarf dancer in attached scalloped bowl, Yankoware, 1920s, 7½"..**$20.00**

Scarf dancer on base, Deco style, lime green, 9", from $15 to **$25.00**

Scarf dancer on oval base, nude, semi-matt white, 6½", from $15 to...**$25.00**

Turtle on rock, glossy terra-cotta finish, Rushmore Pottery, 3½"...**$35.00**

Water lily leaf, dark green, old, 1½x4x4" **$22.50**

Water lily on irregular square base, orange & yellow w/green leaves on sides, Japan, 2½x3¼x2¼", from $10 to .**$12.00**

Woodpecker on multi-branch stump, blue, white, black & gold, Japan, 6"...**$30.00**

Fostoria

This was one of the major glassware producers of the twentieth century. They were located first in Fostoria, Ohio, but by the 1890s had moved to Moundsville, West Virginia. By the late '30s, they were recognized as the largest producers of handmade glass in the world. Their glassware is plentiful today and, considering its quality, not terribly expensive.

Though the company went out of business in the mid-'80s, the Lancaster Colony Company continues to use some of the old molds — herein is the problem. The ever-popular American and Coin Glass patterns are currently in production, and even experts have trouble distinguishing the old from the new. Before you invest in either line, talk to deal-

ers. Ask them to show you some of their old pieces. Most will be happy to help out a novice collector. Read *Elegant Glassware of the Depression Era* by Gene Florence; *Fostoria Glassware, 1887 – 1982,* by Frances Bones; *Fostoria, An Identification and Value Guide, Books I and II,* by Ann Kerr; and *Fostoria Stemware, The Crystal for America*, by Milbra Long and Emily Seate.

You'll be seeing a lot of inferior 'American' at flea markets and (sadly) antique malls. It's often priced as though it is American, but in fact it is not. It's been produced since the 1950s by Indiana Glass who calls it 'Whitehall.' Watch for pitchers with only two mold lines, they're everywhere. (Fostoria's had three.) Remember that Fostoria was handmade, so their pieces were fire polished. This means that if the piece you're examining has sharp, noticeable mold lines, be leery. There are other differences to watch for as well. Fostoria's footed pieces were designed with a 'toe,' while Whitehall feet have a squared peg-like appearance. The rays are sharper and narrower on the genuine Fostoria pieces, and the glass itself has more sparkle and life. And if it weren't complicated enough, the Home Interior Company sells 'American'-like vases, covered bowls, and a footed candy dish that were produced in a foreign country, but at least they've marked theirs.

Coin Glass was originally produced in crystal, red, blue, emerald green, olive green, and amber. It's being reproduced today in crystal, green (darker than the original), blue (a lighter hue), and red. Though the green and blue are 'off' enough to be pretty obvious, the red is very close. Beware. Here are some (probably not all) of the items currently in production: bowl, 8" diameter; bowl, 9" oval; candlesticks, 4½"; candy jar with lid, 6¼"; creamer and sugar bowl; footed comport; wedding bowl, 8¼". Know your dealer!

Numbers included in our descriptions were company-assigned stock numbers that collectors use as a means to distinguish variations in stems and shapes.

Advisor: Debbie Maggard (See Directory, Elegant Glassware)

Newsletter/Club: *Facets of Fostoria*
Fostoria Glass Society of America
P.O. Box 826, Moundsville, WV 26041
Membership: $12.50 per year

American, crystal, basket with reed handle, 9" across, $115.00.

American, crystal, appetizer, w/6 inserts, 10½"..........**$250.00**
American, crystal, bottle, cordial; w/stopper, 9-oz, 7¼"...**$90.00**
American, crystal, bowl, almond; oval, 3¾" **$18.00**
American, crystal, bowl, boat shape, 12" **$17.50**
American, crystal, bowl, tri-cornered, handled, 5" **$12.00**
American, crystal, candy box, w/lid, pedestal foot.....**$37.50**
American, crystal, creamer, tea; #2056½, 3-oz, 2⅜"......**$9.00**
American, crystal, hat (sm ashtray), 2⅛".................**$16.00**
American, crystal, mayonnaise, divided..................**$15.00**
American, crystal, picture frame **$15.00**
American, crystal, saucer..**$3.00**
American, crystal, sugar bowl, w/lid, 2-handled........**$20.00**
American, crystal, tray, muffin; 2 upturned sides, 10" .**$30.00**
American, crystal, tumbler, juice; footed, #2056, 5-oz,
 4¾"..**$12.00**
American, crystal, vase, straight sides, 10"................**$90.00**
Baroque, blue, bowl, handled, 4 styles, 4"................**$22.50**
Baroque, blue, plate, 6" **$10.00**
Baroque, crystal, ashtray **$7.50**
Baroque, crystal, candle, 8-lustre, 7¾"....................**$50.00**
Baroque, crystal, tumbler, cocktail; footed, 3½-oz, 3" .**$10.00**
Baroque, yellow, bowl, 2-part, 6½".........................**$20.00**
Baroque, yellow, platter, oval, 12" **$45.00**
Baroque, yellow, tumbler, tea; 14-oz, 5¾" **$55.00**

Buttercup, crystal, pitcher, 8½", $265.00.

Buttercup, crystal, plate, cracker; #2364, 11¼"...........**$30.00**
Buttercup, crystal, vase, #2614, 10"..........................**$135.00**
Camelia, crystal, ice bucket......................................**$75.00**
Camelia, crystal, mustard, w/spoon & lid....................**$35.00**
Century, crystal, butter dish, w/lid, ¼-lb **$35.00**
Century, crystal, pitcher, 16-oz, 6⅛"..........................**$50.00**
Century, crystal, plate, torte; 14".............................**$30.00**
Chintz, crystal, dinner bell......................................**$125.00**
Chintz, crystal, plate, luncheon; #2496, 8½"...............**$21.00**
Chintz, crystal, stem, cocktail; #6026, 4-oz, 5"...........**$24.00**
Chintz, crystal, vase, #4108, 5"................................**$95.00**
Coin, amber, ashtray, center coin, #1372/119, 7½".....**$20.00**
Coin, amber, bowl, footed, #1372/199, 8½" **$60.00**
Coin, amber, lamp, coach or patio; #1372/461 ....**$50.00**
Coin, amber, pitcher, #1372/453, 32-oz....................**$55.00**
Coin, amber, sugar bowl, w/lid, #1372/673................**$35.00**

Coin, amber, cake stand, $100.00.

Coin, blue, bowl, round, #1372/179, 8" **$50.00**
Coin, blue, candle holder, #1372/316, 4½", pr............**$50.00**
Coin, blue, candy box, w/lid, #1372/354, 4⅛"............**$60.00**
Coin, blue, lamp, coach; oil, #1372/320, 13½"..........**$195.00**
Coin, blue, salt & pepper shakers, chrome tops, #1372/652,
 3¼", pr...**$65.00**
Coin, crystal, bowl, wedding; w/lid, #1372/162..........**$55.00**
Coin, crystal, condiment set, #1372/737, 4-pc..........**$135.00**
Coin, crystal, cup, punch; #1372/615 ....**$32.00**
Coin, crystal, nappy, #1372/495, 4½".......................**$22.00**
Coin, crystal, sugar bowl, w/lid, #1372/673 ....**$25.00**
Coin, crystal, tumbler, iced tea/high ball; #1372/64, 12-oz,
 5⅛"..**$37.50**
Coin, green, ashtray, #1372/123, 5"..........................**$30.00**
Coin, green, cruet, w/stopper, #1372/531, 7-oz........**$160.00**
Coin, green, sugar bowl, w/lid, #1372/673.................**$65.00**
Coin, olive, cigarette urn, footed, #1372/381, 3⅜"......**$20.00**
Coin, olive, cruet, #1372/680 ....**$15.00**
Coin, olive, nappy, handled, #1372/499, 5⅜" **$18.00**
Coin, olive, pitcher, #1372/453, 32-oz, 6⅜"................**$55.00**
Coin, olive, tumbler, iced tea; #1372/58, 14-oz..........**$40.00**
Colony, crystal, bowl, fruit; 10" **$35.00**
Colony, crystal, bowl, round, 4¼" **$7.00**
Colony, crystal, candlestick, 9" **$30.00**
Colony, crystal, plate, bread & butter; 6"....................**$4.00**
Corsage, crystal, candlestick, #2535, 5½"..................**$35.00**
Corsage, crystal, relish tray, 4-part, #2419 ....**$42.50**
Fairfax, amber, bowl, fruit; 5" **$6.00**
Fairfax, amber, cup, flat...**$4.00**
Fairfax, amber, plate, bread; oval, 12" **$25.00**
Fairfax, amber, sugar bowl, tea **$8.00**
Fairfax, green or topaz, celery dish, 11½"..................**$16.00**
Fairfax, rose, blue or orchid, baker, oval, 10½"..........**$40.00**
Fairfax, rose, blue or orchid, mayonnaise liner, 7" **$6.00**
Fairfax, rose, blue or orchid, plate, salad; 7½"..............**$5.00**
Heather, crystal, bowl, flared, 8" **$32.50**
Heather, crystal, platter, 12" **$85.00**
Heather, crystal, vase, bud; 6".................................**$30.00**
Hermitage, amber, green or topaz, tumbler, footed, #2449, 2-
 oz, 2½"..**$8.00**
Hermitage, blue, plate, #2449½, 6" **$8.00**
Hermitage, blue, tumbler, #2449½, 9-oz, 4¾" **$15.00**
Hermitage, crystal, saucer, #2449..............................**$2.00**

Hermitage, wisteria, #2449, 2-part, 6" $25.00

Jamestown, amber or brown, bowl, dessert; #2719/421, 4½" **$8.50**

Jamestown, amethyst, crystal or green, plate, #2719/550, 8"..$16.00

Jenny Lind, milk glass, cologne flask and stopper, ca 1953 – 65, 10¾", from $85.00 to $90.00. (Photo courtesy Lee Garmon)

Jenny Lind, milk glass, glove box, 10x4½", from $60 to..**$65.00**

Jenny Lind, milk glass, handkerchief box w/lid, 5¼x2⅛", from $40 to..$50.00

Jenny Lind, milk glass, pin tray, from $25 to $30.00

June, crystal, bowl, mint; 3-footed, 4½"...................$10.00

June, crystal, plate, salad; 7½" $5.00

June, pink or blue, candlestick, 2" $30.00

June, pink or blue, whipped cream bowl $20.00

June, yellow, creamer, footed..............................$17.50

June, yellow, relish, 3-part, 8½" $35.00

Kashmir, blue, bowl, soup; 7"...............................$65.00

Kashmir, blue, plate, luncheon; 9" $12.00

Kashmir, blue, sandwich tray with center handle, $40.00. (Photo courtesy Gene Florence)

Kashmir, yellow or green, ashtray...............................$25.00

Kashmir, yellow or green, candlestick, 3"....................$20.00

Kashmir, yellow or green, stem, oyster cocktail; 4½-oz..$16.00

Lido, crystal, plate, cracker; 11"................................$22.50

Mayflower, crystal, creamer, #2560............................$12.00

Mayflower, crystal, salt & pepper shakers, pr............**$65.00**

Meadow Rose, crystal, bowl, handled, 10½".............**$55.00**

Meadow Rose, crystal, sauce dish, 6½x5¼".............**$125.00**

Navarre, crystal, candlestick, #2496, 4"....................$22.00

Navarre, crystal, creamer, individual, #2496 ....$17.50

Navarre, crystal, plate, salad; #2440, 7½"..................$15.00

Navarre, crystal, saucer, #2440..................................$5.00

New Garland, amber or topaz, bowl, 12"...................$50.00

New Garland, amber or topaz, plate, 6" $4.00

New Garland, amber or topaz, sauce bowl liner.......$15.00

New Garland, amber or topaz, sugar bowl, footed $15.00

New Garland, rose, bowl, finger; footed, #6002 ....$18.00

New Garland, rose, vase, 8"....................................$50.00

Romance, crystal, bowl, baked apple; #2364, 6".........$15.00

Romance, crystal, vase, #4121, 5"............................$40.00

Royal, amber or green, bowl, soup; #2350, 7¾".........$25.00

Royal, amber or green, plate, bread & butter; #2350, 6".....**$3.00**

Royal, amber or green, server, center handle, #2287, 11".$25.00

Seville, amber, bowl, low foot, #2315, 7" $16.00

Seville, amber, comport, #2350, 8" $27.50

Seville, amber, grapefruit, blown, #945½..................$40.00

Seville, green, bowl, flared, deep, #2297, 12" $32.50

Seville, green, plate, dinner; #2350, sm, 9½"..............$13.50

Seville, green, tumbler, footed, #5084, 9-oz................$16.50

Trojan, rose, bowl, lemon; #2375 ....$18.00

Trojan, rose, plate, bread & butter; #2375, 6"...............$6.00

Trojan, rose, tumbler, footed, #5009, 9-oz, 5¼" $22.50

Trojan, topaz, goblet, claret; #5009, 4-oz, 6" $90.00

Trojan, topaz, saucer, after dinner; #2375 ....$10.00

Versailles, blue, plate, cake; 2-handled, #2375, 10".....$45.00

Versailles, pink or green, finger bowl, w/6" liner, #869/2283...$40.00

Versailles, pink or green, goblet, cocktail; #5098 or #5099, 3-oz, 5¼", ea $25.00

Versailles, pink or green, mayonnaise ladle $30.00

Versailles, pink or green, whipped cream pail, #2378.$15.00

Versailles, yellow, salt & pepper shaker, footed, #2375, pr $95.00

Vesper, amber, bowl, flared, #2375, 10½"...................$35.00

Vesper, amber, egg cup, #2350................................$40.00

Vesper, blue, comport, 6".......................................$50.00

Vesper, blue, plate, center handle, #2287, 11"............$55.00

Vesper, blue, tumbler, footed, #5100, 12-oz $60.00

Vesper, green, plate, salad; #2350, 7½".......................$6.00

Vesper, green, sauce boat, w/liner, #2350 ....$135.00

Figurines and Novelties

Cat, light blue, 3¾"..$35.00

Chanticleer, crystal..$215.00

Deer, blue, sitting or standing $55.00

Deer, Silver Mist, sitting or standing, ea $40.00

Duck, mama, amber frost, #2632/404, 4"...................$35.00

Duck w/3 ducklings, amber, set................................$50.00

Duckling, crystal, walking (+)..................................$20.00

Eagle, bookend, Silver Mist, ea $150.00

Horse, bookend, crystal, 7¾", ea	$45.00
Madonna & Child, Silver Mist, 13½"	$300.00
Mermaid, crystal, 11½"	$125.00
Pelican, crystal	$60.00
Sea horse, bookend, crystal, 8", ea	$125.00
Squirrel, amber, running	$45.00

Franciscan Dinnerware

Franciscan is a trade name of Gladding McBean, used on their dinnerware lines from the mid-'30s until it closed its Los Angeles-based plant in 1984. They were the first to market 'starter sets' (four-place settings), a practice that today is commonplace.

Two of their earliest lines were El Patio (simply styled, made in bright solid colors) and Coronado (with swirled borders and pastel glazes). In the late '30s, they made the first of many hand-painted dinnerware lines. Some of the best known are Apple, Desert Rose, and Ivy. From 1941 to 1977, Masterpiece (true porcelain) china was produced in more than 170 patterns.

Many marks were used, most included the Franciscan name. An 'F' in a square with 'Made in U.S.A.' below it dates from 1938, and a double-line script 'F' was used in more recent years.

For further information, we recommend *The Collector's Encyclopedia of California Pottery, Second Edition,* by Jack Chipman.

Note: To evaluate maroon items in El Patio and Coronado, add 10% to 20% to suggested prices.

Advisors: Mick and Lorna Chase, Fiesta Plus (See Directory, Dinnerware)

Apple, ashtray, oval	$137.50
Apple, bowl, cereal; 6"	$15.00
Apple, bowl, fruit	$12.00
Apple, bowl, mixing; med	$125.00
Apple, bowl, rimmed soup	$28.00
Apple, bowl, salad; 10"	$145.00
Apple, bowl, straight sides, lg	$65.00
Apple, bowl, vegetable; divided	$45.00
Apple, bowl, vegetable; 9"	$45.00
Apple, box, cigarette	$150.00
Apple, box, round	$250.00
Apple, candle holders, pr	$137.00
Apple, casserole, 1½-qt	$145.00
Apple, coffeepot	$145.00
Apple, compote	$75.00
Apple, creamer, individual	$45.00
Apple, cup, tall	$45.00
Apple, cup & saucer, demitasse	$60.00
Apple, egg cup	$38.00
Apple, gravy boat	$35.00
Apple, mug, 7-oz	$35.00
Apple, piggy bank	$275.00
Apple, pitcher, milk	$95.00

Apple, pitcher, water; 2½-qt	$145.00
Apple, plate, 9½"	$22.00
Apple, platter, 14"	$45.00
Apple, teapot	$165.00
Apple, tumbler, 10-oz	$50.00
Coronado, bowl, cereal	$18.00
Coronado, bowl, vegetable; serving, round, 8½"	$22.50
Coronado, creamer, from $12 to	$15.00
Coronado, cup & saucer, jumbo, from $28 to	$35.00
Coronado, gravy boat, w/attached plate, from $28 to	$40.00
Coronado, plate, 6½"	$6.00
Coronado, plate, 8½", from $12 to	$15.00
Coronado, platter, 13", from $30 to	$45.00
Coronado, teapot, from $65 to	$95.00
Desert Rose, ashtray, oval	$125.00
Desert Rose, bell, Danbury Mint	$125.00
Desert Rose, bowl, bouillon; w/lid	$325.00
Desert Rose, bowl, cereal; 6"	$12.00
Desert Rose, bowl, fruit	$8.00
Desert Rose, bowl, soup; footed	$32.00
Desert Rose, bowl, vegetable; 9"	$40.00
Desert Rose, box, egg	$195.00
Desert Rose, butter dish	$45.00
Desert Rose, candle holders, pr	$125.00
Desert Rose, casserole, 2½-qt; no established value	
Desert Rose, coffeepot	$125.00
Desert Rose, cookie jar	$295.00
Desert Rose, cup & saucer, demitasse	$55.00
Desert Rose, gravy boat	$32.00
Desert Rose, napkin ring	$65.00
Desert Rose, pitcher, syrup	$75.00
Desert Rose, plate, chop; 12"	$75.00
Desert Rose, plate, 10½"	$18.00
Desert Rose, plate, 6½"	$6.00
Desert Rose, platter, 14"	$65.00
Desert Rose, salt shaker & pepper mill, pr	$295.00
Desert Rose, sugar bowl, individual	$125.00
Desert Rose, tea canister	$225.00
Desert Rose, teapot	$125.00
Desert Rose, tile, square	$65.00

Desert Rose, tray, Long and Narrow, $495.00. (Photo courtesy Mick and Lorna Chase)

Desert Rose, tumbler, juice; 6-oz	$50.00
El Patio, bowl, cereal; from $15 to	$20.00
El Patio, bowl, salad; 3-qt, from $50 to	$65.00

El Patio, bowl, vegetable; oval, 10½", from $22 to.....**$30.00**
El Patio, cup, from $8 to...**$10.00**
El Patio, cup & saucer, demitasse; from $28 to..........**$45.00**
El Patio, plate, 10½", from $20 to **$25.00**
El Patio, relish, handled, from $50 to **$65.00**
El Patio, sugar bowl, w/lid, redesigned **$25.00**
El Patio, sugar bowl, w/lid, regular..........................**$18.00**
Forget-Me-Not, bowl, fruit..**$12.00**
Forget-Me-Not, bowl, soup/cereal.............................**$18.00**
Forget-Me-Not, bowl, vegetable; 9".........................**$65.00**
Forget-Me-Not, plate, 8½"..**$18.00**
Forget-Me-Not, platter, 14"..**$95.00**
Ivy, coffeepot...**$175.00**
Ivy, plate, 10½"...**$30.00**
Ivy, plate, 8½"...**$25.00**
Ivy, sherbet..**$35.00**
Ivy, teapot **$295.00**
Ivy, tumbler, 10-oz...**$65.00**
Meadow Rose, bowl, rimmed soup.............................**$32.00**
Meadow Rose, bowl, vegetable; 8" **$32.00**
Meadow Rose, butter dish **$65.00**
Meadow Rose, plate, chop; 12" **$75.00**
Meadow Rose, plate, 9½"...**$20.00**
Meadow Rose, sherbet **$25.00**
Meadow Rose, teapot..**$195.00**
Meadow Rose, tumbler, 10-oz **$32.00**

October, platter, 14", $50.00; creamer, $18.00; sugar bowl, $25.00.

Poppy, bowl, fruit..**$40.00**
Poppy, butter dish..**$175.00**
Poppy, cup & saucer..**$35.00**
Poppy, plate, 10½" **$45.00**
Poppy, salt & pepper shakers, pr............................**$125.00**
Starburst, ashtray, oval, lg..**$50.00**
Starburst, bowl, fruit..**$15.00**
Starburst, bowl, salad; individual..............................**$25.00**
Starburst, bowl, soup...**$15.00**
Starburst, butter dish...**$55.00**
Starburst, candlesticks, pr, from $175 to...................**$200.00**
Starburst, child's plate, 3-part...................................**$35.00**

Starburst, coffeepot...**$150.00**
Starburst, creamer, from $10 to................................**$20.00**

Starburst, gravy boat with attached tray, $35.00; ladle, from $25.00 to $45.00.

Starburst, pepper grinder, from $150 to....................**$175.00**
Starburst, pitcher, 7½", from $50 to............................**$75.00**
Starburst, plate, chop; from $55 to............................**$65.00**
Starburst, plate, 6½", from $5 to..................................**$6.00**
Starburst, sugar bowl, w/lid.......................................**$20.00**
Starburst, teapot...**$145.00**
Starburst, TV tray, from $75 to **$100.00**

Frankoma

After graduating from the Chicago Art Institute in 1927, John Nathaniel Frank was offered the monumental task of creating the first Ceramic Art Department at the University of Oklahoma. He taught ceramics in that department until 1936, unaware of the legacy he would someday leave behind.

In 1933 while still teaching art, Mr. Frank and Grace Lee Bowman Frank, whom he had married in 1928, purchased a tiny building in Norman and began making pottery. They marked these creations 'Frank Potteries' and then 'Frankoma Potteries.' Pieces with these marks are hard to find, but they are more plentiful than those marked 'First Kiln, Sapulpa 6/7/38.' This mark was utilized after the Franks moved to Sapulpa in February 1938. There they built a new plant and fired their first pieces (probably less than 100 items) on 6/7/38, hence the mark.

The Frank family endured many hardships, but faith in their pottery never faltered. A fire destroyed the plant in November 1938, but it was quickly rebuilt. There was another devastating fire in 1983; once again, the operation was rebuilt.

Grace Lee Frank worked beside her husband throughout the years and was a talented designer in her own right, creating many limited edition Madonna plates, birds, Christmas cards, etc. She passed away in 1996.

In 1990 the I.R.S. stepped in because of past due taxes, but by filing Chapter 11, Joniece, the Franks' daughter and a talented ceramic designer who had been president of the company since John's death in 1973, was able to remain in control and continue the operation. Mr. Richard Bernstein purchased Frankoma in 1990, and the business is still operating. Joniece Frank was retained to design limited edition items.

High on collectors' lists are items that carry the 'Pot and Leopard' mark, which was used from 1934 through November 1938, the time of the first fire.

Just as valued are the pieces in ivory, Rosetone, and Rose Rud. In the past year, turquoise has also become quite desirable, and Peach Glow is slowly becoming a popular glaze color as well. John Frank experimented continually and created unusual combinations that have never been duplicated. The use of Rutile in some of the early glazes helped create eye-pleasing colors that enhanced the relief designs.

Even Frankoma catalogs, postcards, and other paper memorabilia are collectible. They are filled with sculptures, miniatures, advertising, jewelry, limited editions, and dinnerware.

It is difficult to have a conversation about Frankoma pottery without discussing Gracetone Pottery. Synar Ceramics, a company in Muskogee, Oklahoma, was purchased by the Franks in 1959. They continued to produce the Synar line from the white clay on hand there until supplies were exhausted. After that, the name was changed to Gracetone Pottery in honor of Grace Lee Frank. Frankoma's standard clay as well as some of its products became part of the Gracetone line. Many of those products which were serving both companies were marked with the stock number and an 'F' to distinguish one company from the other. The glazes used in Gracetone's production were aqua, Pink Champagne, Cinnamon, and black, known as Gunmetal. John Frank had Mr. Taylor, a long-time friend and associate, manage Gracetone; when he decided to discontinue Gracetone's operation in 1962, Mr. Taylor purchased the company, and it remained in operation until 1967. The sole dinnerware line Mr. Frank created for Gracetone was called 'Orbit,' and it is sought by Frankoma collectors today. At the present time, it is hard to find.

If you'd like to learn more, we recommend *Frankoma Pottery, Value Guide and More,* by Susan Cox; and *Frankoma and Other Oklahoma Potteries* by Phyllis and Tom Bess.

Advisor: Susan Cox (See Directory, Frankoma)

Club/Newsletter: Frankoma Family Collectors Association
c/o Nancy Littrell
P.O. Box 32571, Oklahoma City, OK 73123-0771
Membership dues: $25; includes newsletter and annual convention

Ashtray, arrowhead, Turquoise, Red clay, 1953, #453, 7" .**$15.00**
Ashtrays, Dutch shoes, Clay Blue, 1958, #466, 6", pr (right & left)..**$75.00**
Baker, Mayan Aztec, Prairie Green, Ada clay, 1949, #7U, individual **$30.00**
Bookend, mountain girl, Prairie Green, 1939, #425, 5¾", ea **$250.00**
Bookend, sea horse, Prairie Green, pot mark, #426, 5", ea **$450.00**
Bookends, boot, Prairie Green, Ada clay, 1951, #433, 7", pr..**$90.00**

Bookends, Charger Horse, Black Onyx, #420, $225.00; #111, $150.00.

Bowl, centerpiece; Prairie Green, Ada clay, 1942, #219, 18"..**$80.00**
Bowl, oblong, Prairie Green, Ada clay, 1955, #45, 12".**$40.00**
Bowl, Tiki God, Prairie Green, #T6 ....**$100.00**
Candelabrum, Ivory, 1934-42, #306..........................**$110.00**
Candle holder, Aladdin lamp, White Sand, 1968, #309, 8½"..**$75.00**
Catalog, company, 1936, 20 pages, Norman #425 seated figure...**$60.00**
Catalog, company, 1953, back dated July 1, 1953, front: color postcard of Donna & Joniece Frank.....................**$45.00**
Catalog, company, 1973, Grace Lee & John Frank on cover...**$25.00**
Christmas card, ashtray, Prairie Green, 1959, #467 .....**$75.00**
Christmas card, bowl, Clay Blue, 1954, #511 ....**$80.00**
Christmas card, bowl, Peach Glow, 1964, #477 ....**$75.00**
Christmas card, pitcher, Desert Gold, 1949, #551 ....**$80.00**
Creamer, wagon wheel, Prairie Green, Ada clay, 1942, #94A **$14.00**
Figurine, bull, Silver Sage, 1942, #166, 2" **$95.00**
Figurine, charging tiger, iridescent black, 1934, #103, 13",...**$550.00**
Figurine, circus horse, Ivory, Ada Clay, #138, 4½" ...**$125.00**
Figurine, coyote pup, Prairie Green, 1934, #105, 7¾" ..**$550.00**
Figurine, English Setter, Fawn Brown, Ada Clay, 1942, #141, 5½"..**$275.00**
Figurine, Fan Dancer, w/matching platter (#5P), Prairie Green, 1934, #113, 8½"..**$475.00**
Figurine, Indian Chief, Prairie Green, Ada clay, 1938, #142, 8"..**$150.00**
Figurine, prancing colt, Prairie Green, Ada clay, #117, 8" ..**$900.00**
Figurine, walking ocelot, Ivory, #104, 10½" **$400.00**
Flower frog, fish (2) on base, Prairie Green, #404 ...**$550.00**
Flower holder, duck, Sky Blue, 1942, #184, 3¾" **$200.00**
Jar, carved, Jade Green, 1934, 6"................................**$45.00**
Jug, juice; Royal Blue, w/stopper, 1936, #90, 1-qt **$75.00**
Jug, Texas Centennial 1936, Ivory, pot mark, 5".......**$100.00**
Jug, Uncle Slug, Osage Brown, 1942, #10, 2¼" **$20.00**
Match cover, w/out matches, G-...................................**$8.00**
Mug, barrel, Prairie Green, 1950, #97M, 14-oz............**$20.00**
Mug, Donkey, Carter-Mondale, Rosetone, 1977.........**$35.00**

Mug, Elephant, white, 1968 ....**$125.00**
Mug & plate, child's; Mouse, Robin Egg Blue, 1983, #257 ..**$25.00**
Paperweight, turtle, Prairie Green, 1971, #170, 4½" ...**$10.00**
Pitcher, Guernsey; Desert Gold, 1940-65, #93, w/lid, 5½"...**$45.00**
Pitcher, snail, Old Gold, 1942, #558, miniature, 2" **$20.00**
Postcards of Frankoma family, factory or showroom, ea.**$15.00**
Salt & pepper shakers, bull, Silver Sage, 1942, #166H, 2",
   pr **$130.00**
Salt & pepper shakers, puma, White Sand, 1942, #165H, 3",
   pr **$100.00**
Teacup, Desert Gold, 1942, #92C, 6-oz........................**$30.00**
Toothbrush holder, Flame, 1980, #401 ....**$20.00**
Trivet, Eagle, Desert Gold, 1966-67, #2TR **$50.00**
Vase, bottle; Chinese Red, 1934, #14, 9" **$300.00**

**Vase, bottle; with
base, #V15, 1983,
3,000 made, $65.00.**

Vase, cross, Prairie Green, 1955-61, #804, 6½" **$55.00**
Vase, fan; shell shape, Desert Gold, Ada clay, 1942, #54,
   6" **$40.00**
Vase, pod; Prairie Green, 1964, #237, 7".....................**$20.00**
Vase, ram's head, Jade, 1934, #74, 9¼"......................**$185.00**
Wall plaque, Indian mask, Ivory, 1934, #135, 3¾"......**$45.00**
Wall pocket, bird handle, Prairie Green, Ada clay, 1942,
   5" **$100.00**
Wall pocket, ram's head, Prairie Green, Ada clay, 1942, #193,
   6" **$100.00**
Wall pocket, wagon wheel, Desert Gold, Ada clay, #94Y,
   7" **$50.00**

Furniture

   A piece of furniture can often be difficult to date, since
many seventeenth- and eighteenth-century styles have been
reproduced. Even a piece made early in the twentieth century now has enough age on it that it may be impossible for
a novice to distinguish it from the antique. Sometimes cabi-
netmakers may have trouble identifying specific types of
wood, since so much variation can occur within the same
species; so although it is usually helpful to try to determine

what kind of wood a piece has been made of, results are
sometimes inconclusive. Construction methods are usually
the best clues. Watch for evidence of twentieth-century tools
— automatic routers, lathes, carvers, and spray guns.

   For further information we recommend *Antique Oak
Furniture* by Conover Hill; *Collector's Guide to Oak
Furniture* by Jennifer George; *Heywood-Wakefield Modern
Furniture* by Steven Rouland and Roger Rouland; *Collector's
Encyclopedia of American Furniture, Vols I and II,* and
Furniture of the Depression Era, both by Robert and Harriett
Swedberg; and *American Oak Furniture* by Katherine
McNerney. All are published by Collector Books.

Bed, pencil-post style, birch w/pine headboard, refinished,
   83x74x38" **$275.00**
Bedroom set, waterfall type w/bleached mahogany veneer, bed,
   dressing table, bench, chest of drawers, 4-pc set.....**$575.00**
Book case, oak, single door, 4-shelf, applied wing decor on
   back rail, 50x29x10" **$425.00**
Bookcase, oak, 5 stacking sections, 47x34x12".........**$795.00**
Bookcase/desk, oak w/applied decor on drop front & back
   rail, 66x39x13"..**$995.00**
Cedar chest, walnut & orientalwood V-matched veneered
   waterfall, 1940s, 25x45x19"...................................**$245.00**
Chair, arm; Oak Mission style, restored upholstry, refinished,
   38" **$145.00**
Chair, arm; Windsor, bamboo style w/cut-down spindle
   back, splayed base, 34"...**$125.00**
Chair, captain's; oak w/hand-hold in back rail, spindle-back
   w/continuous arms, 31x22"...................................**$220.00**

**Chair, open-arm
tub stye; Heywood-
Wakefield, Lady's
Club Chair, M 568
C, ca 1951 – 58, EX,
$150.00. (Photo
courtesy Steve
Rouland and Roger
Rouland)**

Chair, side; arrow back, plank seat, EX old finish, 32" ..**$110.00**
Chair, side; bird's-eye maple, pressed cane seat, 32"..**$165.00**
Chair, side; elm, pressed back w/spindles, cane seat,
   40"..**$80.00**
Chair, side; half-spindle 2-slat back, dark finish, 33" ..**$95.00**
Chair, side; vase splat, plank seat, dark finish, 33", 4 for..**$450.00**
Chair, side; 2-slat back w/ball finials, replaced rush seat,
   34"..**$155.00**
Chair, side; 4 graduated-slat ladderback, rush seat, 41",
   pr **$165.00**

Chair, Windsor, armless w/bow back, 34"...............**$600.00**

Chair, Windsor, armless w/rod back, dark finish, 36"...**$285.00**

Chest, Heywood-Wakefield, blond birch, 5-drawer, 44x38", EX **$300.00**

Chest, Heywood-Wakefield, Catalina, 4-drawer, champagne finish, 43x32x19", from $100 to **$200.00**

Chest, oak, 3 graduated drawers, original brasses, 32x40x18" **$465.00**

Chifferobe, Oriental V-matched and walnut veneer w/cedar-lined section on left, 1940s, 62x34x19"................**$295.00**

China buffet, oak w/convex glass mirror at back, claw feet, 52x46x19" **$595.00**

China cabinet, Oak Mission style, leaded glass in top panels, 65x32x16" **$650.00**

China cabinet, Shop of the Crafters, original finish, paper label, 64x43", $4,750.00.

Cupboard, corner; newly painted pine, 9-panel door over flat-panel double doors, 78x40x18"..................**$1,395.00**

Cupboard, corner; pine, 1-pane double doors over flat panel double doors, dark finish, 72x39x23" **$1,500.00**

Cupboard, pine; single pane double doors over drawer over double doors, refinished, 69x39x16"................**$1,500.00**

Curio cabinet, oak, lg glass door, 3-shelf, gallery, 48x23x11½" **$160.00**

Desk, ribbon mahogany & maple, fall front, 1920s, 40x33x18" **$450.00**

Dresser, Heywood-Wakefield, Encore, pin tray in top drawer, 4 graduated drawers, plate glass mirror, from $325 to ..**$650.00**

Dresser, oak, carved facade, swivel mirror, pressed/carved decor..**$500.00**

Love seat, Heywood-Wakefield, designed by WJ Carr, upholstered w/2 cushions, 44" between arms, from $500 to..**$1,000.00**

Ottoman, multi-banded rattan w/vinyl cushion, Fifties Modern, 12x23x23" **$200.00**

Rocker, armchair; comb back, arrow spindles, old repaint, 44" **$550.00**

Rocker, oak, armless, pressed back w/6 spindles, cane seat, 36" **$145.00**

Shelves, hardwood, 3 step-back shelves w/turned posts, varnish, hanging, 21x23" **$60.00**

Table, cocktail; Fifties Modern, 48" dia glass top on bent aluminum base..**$250.00**

Table, coffee; mahogany Queen Anne style, cabriole legs, 48x18x16+10" drop leaves **$275.00**

Table, corner; hard rock maple, Heywood-Wakefield, 1950s, 22x32x32" **$155.00**

Table, dining; Arts & Crafts, quarter-sawn oak veneer, 48" dia...**$750.00**

Table, oak, gate legs, old finish, 37x28x24" **$350.00**

Table, oak extension type w/pedestal base, 4 paw feet, 30x42" dia...**$695.00**

Table, occasional; Willet, 2 drawers below shelf, on casters, 1950s, 27x23x20", pr.......................................**$695.00**

Washstand/commode, oak w/attached bar rack, 54x32x17" **$550.00**

Games

Games from the 1870s to the 1970s and beyond are fun to collect. Many of the earlier games are beautifully lithographed. Some of their boxes were designed by well-known artists and illustrators, and many times these old games are appreciated more for their artwork than for their entertainment value. Some represent a historical event or a specific era in the social development of our country. Characters from the early days of radio, television, and movies have been featured in hundreds of games designed for children and adults alike.

If you're going to collect games, be sure that they're reasonably clean, free of water damage, and complete. Most have playing instructions printed inside the lid or on a separate piece of paper that include an inventory list. Check the contents, and remember that the condition of the box is very important too.

If you'd like to learn more about games, we recommend *Toys, Antique and Collectible*, by David Longest; *Board Games of the '50s, '60s & '70s* by Stephanie Lane; *Baby Boomer Games* by Rick Polizzi; and *Schroeder's Collectible Toys, Antique to Modern*.

Club: American Game Collectors Association
49 Brooks Ave., Lewiston, ME 04240

Newsletter: *Game Times*
Joe Angiolillo
4628 Barlow Dr., Bartlesville, OK 74006

$64,000 Dollar Question Jr Edition, Lowell, 1956, EXIB .**$40.00**

A-Team, Parker Bros, #00089, EXIB **$20.00**

Alien, Kenner, 1979, EXIB...**$50.00**

Amazing Spider-Man & the Fantastic Four, Milton Bradley, 1977, EXIB..**$50.00**

Angela Cartwright's Buttons & Bows, Transogram, 1960, EXIB..**$50.00**

Aquaman & the Justice League of America, Hasbro, 1967, NM (EX box) $200.00

Astro Launch, Ohio Art, 1963, EXIB................$75.00

Batman (Animated Series), 3-D board game, Parker Bros, EXIB $20.00

Batman & Robin Target, Hasbro, 1966, MIB $200.00

Beat the Clock, Lowell, 1954, EXIB.....................$40.00

Beverly Hillbillies, Standard Toykraft, 1963, NMIB $75.00

Black Beauty, Transogram, 1957, EXIB.......................$60.00

Brady Bunch, Whitman, 1973, MIB $85.00

Buccaneers, Transogram, 1957, EXIB.......................$45.00

Bullwinkle Hide & Seek, Milton Bradley, 1961, NM (EX box)..$50.00

Captain America, Milton Bradley, 1966, MIB.............$100.00

Captain Video, Milton Bradley, EXIB $125.00

Car 54 Where Are You?, Allison, 1963, EXIB $250.00

Charlie's Angels, Milton Bradley, 1977, MIB (sealed) .$35.00

Chase Back, Milton Bradley, 1962, MIB (sealed) $25.00

Chubby Checker's Limbo, Wham-O, 1961, EXIB $65.00

Cinderella, Parker Bros, 1964, EXIB..........................$50.00

Concentration, Milton Bradley, 1959, 1st Edition, EXIB.$45.00

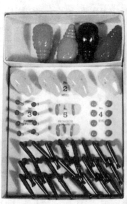

Cootie, W.H. Schaper Mfg. Co., 1950s, MIB, $45.00. (Photo courtesy June Moon)

Dark Shadows, Milton Bradley, 1969, NMIB $65.00

Dating Game, Hasbro, 1967, EXIB $45.00

Doctor Dolittle Marble Maze, Hasbro, 1967, EXIB......$40.00

Dr Kildare, Ideal, 1962, unused, NMIB $60.00

Dragnet, Transogram, 1955, NMIB $65.00

Dragnet Dart Target, Knickerbocker, 1955, EX (G+ box)..$55.00

Dukes of Hazzard, Ideal, 1981, EXIB.........................$25.00

Electra Woman & Dyna Girl, Ideal, 1977, EXIB $60.00

Emergency, Milton Bradley, 1973, EXIB $22.00

Fall Guy, Milton Bradley, EXIB.................................$22.00

Family Ties, Applestreet, 1986, EXIB $30.00

Flintstones Big Game Hunt, Whitman, 1962, NMIB....$80.00

Flintstones Stoneage, Transogram, 1961, EXIB............$40.00

Flipper Flips, Mattel, 1965, EXIB $50.00

Flying Nun, Milton Bradley, 1968, NMIB.....................$150.00

GI Joe Combat Infantry Game, NMIB $25.00

Gilligan's Island, Game Gems/T Cohn, 1965, EXIB..$225.00

Great Grape Ape, Milton Bradley, 1975, NMIB..........$60.00

Groucho's TV Quiz, Pressman, 1954, EXIB.................$75.00

Gunsmoke, Lowell, 1959, EXIB $70.00

Have Gun Will Travel, Parker Bros, 1959, EXIB $75.00

Howdy Doody Adventure Game, Milton Bradley, 1950s, EXIB...$125.00

Hunt for Red October, 1988, EXIB.............................$30.00

I Dream of Jeanie, Milton Bradley, 1965, NMIB........$100.00

James Bond Secret Agent, Milton Bradley, 1964, EXIB..$30.00

Jeopardy, Milton Bradley, 1972, 10th edition, NMIB ..$25.00

Jetsons Fun Pad, Milton Bradley, 1963, EXIB, from $75 to...$100.00

King Kong, Milton Bradley, 1966, EXIB......................$25.00

Kreskin's ESP, Milton Bradley, EXIB..........................$15.00

Land of the Lost, Milton Bradley, 1975, EXIB $25.00

Laverne & Shirley, MIB (sealed)................................$25.00

Let's Make a Deal, Ideal, 1964, EXIB $22.00

Lost in Space 3-D Game, Remco, 1966, EXIB...........$225.00

M*A*S*H Trivia Game, Golden, 1984, EXIB...............$25.00

Marvel Super Heroes Card Game, Milton Bradley, 1978, MIB $40.00

McHale's Navy, Transogram, 1962, EXIB.....................$45.00

Melvin Pervis' G-Men Detective Game, Parker Bros, 1930s, NMIB...$250.00

Merv Griffin's Word for Word, Mattel, 1963, M (EX box)..$25.00

Mickey Mantle Big 6 Sports, Gardner, 1950s, VG (VG box)..$150.00

Mickey Mouse Rollem Game, Marks Bros, incomplete o/w EX (no box) $275.00

Mighty Mouse, Parker Bros, 1964, NMIB.....................$75.00

Mork & Mindy, Parker Bros, 1979, MIB (sealed) $30.00

Mr Ed, Parker Bros, 1960s, EXIB $75.00

Mr Novak, Transogram, 1963, unused, EXIB...............$50.00

Murder She Wrote, Warren, VG (VG box)...................$20.00

Orbit, Parker Brothers, NM, $85.00. (Photo courtesy June Moon)

Outer Limits, Milton Bradley, 1964, unused, MIB $350.00

Overland Trail, Transogram, 1960, EXIB.....................$65.00

Patty Duke, Milton Bradley, 1963, EXIB.....................$50.00

Peter Gunn Detective, Lowell, 1960, EXIB $45.00

Pirate Plunder, All-Fair, VG (VG box)........................$50.00

Planet of the Apes, Milton Bradley, 1967, EXIB..........$70.00

PT Boat 109, Ideal, 1963, VG (G box) $35.00

Rich Uncle, Parker Bros, 1959, EXIB..........................$40.00

Rin-Tin-Tin, Transogram, EX (G box) $10.00

Rock 'Em Sock 'Em Robots, Marx, 1966, EXIB..........$135.00

Safari Tiger Wind-Up Dart Game, Japan, 1950s, Shoot Me & I'll Growl, makes growl sound when target is hit, EXIB..**$75.00**

Scooby Doo Where Are You?, Milton Bradley, 1973, EXIB..**$30.00**

Shenanigans, Milton Bradley, 1964, EXIB...................**$50.00**

Sinking the Titanic, Ideal, 1976, EXIB.......................**$35.00**

Smurf Game, Milton Bradley, 1981, EXIB...................**$30.00**

Space Pilot, Cadaco, 1951, EXIB................................**$75.00**

Tales of Wells Fargo, Milton Bradley, 1959, NMIB......**$80.00**

That Girl, Remco, 1969, EXIB....................................**$70.00**

Three Stooges Fun House, Lowell, 1959, EXIB.........**$200.00**

Tin Can Alley, Ideal, 1976, EXIB................................**$50.00**

Top Cop, Cadaco, 1961, EXIB....................................**$45.00**

Truth or Consequences, Gabriel, 1955, EXIB.............**$50.00**

Video Village, Milton Bradley, 1960, NMIB.................**$35.00**

Walt Disney's Fantasyland, Parker Bros, 1950s, MIB ..**$50.00**

Waltons, Milton Bradley, 1974, EXIB..........................**$30.00**

Wanted Dead or Alive, Lowell, 1959, EXIB...............**$100.00**

Wendy the Good Little Witch, Milton Bradley, 1966, EXIB..**$165.00**

Woody Woodpecker Ring Toss Game, 1958, MIB **$100.00**

Yogi Bear, Milton Bradley, #4107, 1971, EXIB............**$15.00**

You Bet Your Life, Lowell, 1955, unused, M (VG+ box)...**$95.00**

Zorro, Whitman, 1965, NMIB....................................**$75.00**

Gas Station Collectibles

Items used and/or sold by gas stations are included in this very specialized area of advertising collectibles. Those with an interest in this field tend to specialize in memorabilia from a specific gas station like Texaco or Signal. This is a very regional market, with items from small companies that are no longer in business bringing the best prices. For instance, memorabilia decorated with Gulf's distinctive 'orange ball' logo may sell more readily in Pittsburgh than in Los Angeles. Gas station giveaways like plastic gas pump salt and pepper sets and license plate attachments are gaining in popularity with collectors. If you're interested in learning more about these types of collectibles, we recommend *Huxford's Collectible Advertising* by Sharon and Bob Huxford, and *Gas Station Memorabilia* by B.J. Summers and Wayne Priddy, both published by Collector Books.

See also Ashtrays; Automobilia.

Newsletter: *Petroleum Collectors Monthly*
Scott Benjamin and Wayne Henderson, Publishers
411 Forest St., LaGrange, OH 44050; 216-355-6608
Subscription: $29.95 per year (Samples: $5).

Ashtray, Mobil, bronzed-plated cast metal w/winged horse figure above 5-point emblem dish, 6x6x7", EX+......**$350.00**

Ashtray, Texaco, bronze-look metal w/2 Scottie dogs at end of tray w/oval well (no glass insert), 1930s, 5x3x6", EX **$375.00**

Badge, Esso Service, cloisonne on nickel, oval emblem atop name plate, 1½x2", VG+.....................................**$130.00**

Bank, Esso tiger figure, hard rubber, 8", NM, from $35 to **$45.00**

Bank, Save At Your Esso Dealer, clear plastic footed oval shape, 4x6", EX...**$25.00**

Bank, Shell, yellow plastic shell shape w/red embossed lettering, 4", EX...**$175.00**

Banner, Oilzum Motor Oil, Escape To No Wear! (script) next to triangle logo w/Oilzum Man, 1950s, 26x12", M **$500.00**

Banner, Texaco Presents Eddie Canter/I Love To Spend Each Sunday w/You, head image on cloth, 35x56", G+ .**$60.00**

Blotter, Gulf Gasoline, There Is More Power In That Good.../From The Orange Pump, shows attendant pumping gas, 4x6", EX..................................**$65.00**

Blotter, Texaco Motor Oil, Under The Rack & Strain Of Racing Wise Drivers Use..., pit crew working on racer, 3x6", EX...**$110.00**

Calendar, Goodyear, 1935, shows bear surprising fisherman, artist Hy Hintermeister, complete w/cover sheet, 21x12", NM **$25.00**

Calendar, Mobilgas, 1953, Along The Magnolia Trail, 23x13", complete, EX...**$50.00**

Calendar, Sealed Power Piston Ring Sets, 1952, paper, Ring Champ, Beagle dog watching 2 boys boxing, 34x16", NM **$40.00**

Can, White Rose Cup Grease No 2, 1-lb, yellow w/trademark image, VG..**$25.00**

Catalog, Firestone Auto Supplies, Spring/Summer, 1944, 53 pages, EX...**$25.00**

Chalkboard, Sinclair H-C Products, dealer's name arched above round H-C logo on green board w/chalk ledge, 24x12", EX+...**$135.00**

Chart, Mobilubrication Disc Chart, posterboard, 1942, 26x42", VG...**$900.00**

Chart, Sinclair Law Of Lubrication/Recommendation For Trucks..., w/Dino logo, red, white & black, 2-sided, 12x16", EX..**$165.00**

Clock, Ask For Quaker State Motor Oil, square plastic light-up, green on white, 16x16", MIB **$90.00**

Dinnerware, Mobil, white china w/red winged horse in center, swirled border, 16-pc set w/plates, cups & saucers, M...**$520.00**

Display rack, Quaker State Motor Oil, tin sign hangs above 2-tiered wire rack, 39x22", EX **$470.00**

Display rack, Sunoco, wire, holds 8 glass bottles w/painted labels & metal screw-on pouring nozzles, 18", VG+...........**$415.00**

Display stand, Whiz Service Center, metal, 4-shelf slant top on box-shaped base, sign atop, graphics on green, 54", VG...**$300.00**

Drinking glasses, North Star Oil, clear glass w/red, white & blue logo, set of 6, 5", MIB...................................**$45.00**

Fan, Skelly, cardboard w/3 bell-shaped foldouts, gas station scene w/traffic, VG..**$220.00**

Game, Gulf, Travel Bingo, 1951, EX **$5.00**

Hat, Mobiloil, cloth service type w/winged horse logo in blue & white on red, M **$150.00**

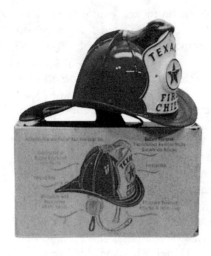

Helmet, Fire Chief's, plastic with battery-operated microphone and speaker, NMIB, $220.00.

Helmet, Texaco Fire Chief, red plastic, station premium, EX+ **$65.00**

Jigsaw puzzle, Foiled By Essolube, by Dr Seuss, 11x17", EX **$65.00**

Jigsaw puzzle, image of Jimmy Doolitte flying Shell Lightning plane over airfield, multicolored, 10x14", NM **$340.00**

Lamp, Texaco, Tiffiny-style shade w/logos repeated on white panels, plastic & metal, electric, 18x9" dia, M....**$280.00**

Lighter, Buy At The Esso Sign, metal tube w/rounded ends, red, blue & cream, 2", EX **$40.00**

Lighter, Texaco, silver-tone metal w/round gold star logo, 2", EX **$160.00**

Mirror/paperweight, Socony Motor Oils, celluloid, scene w/Socony billboard on country road, 3½" dia, EX.**$160.00**

Mug, Mobiloil, white ceramic w/red Gargoyle logo & 2 blue stripes around rim, early, NM **$140.00**

Oil can, Husky Motor Oil, 1-qt, blue or yellow, EX, ea **$550.00**

Oil can, Oilzum, ½-gal, elongated w/spout right of center grip handle, orange & black, fits under auto seat, 3x13", NM **$600.00**

Ornament, Happy the Esso Drop figure w/arms & legs spread, oval logo on chest, multicolored, 3½", EX..............**$85.00**

Pen holder, Shell, plastic, holds 3 pens, red advertising on yellow, EX...**$120.00**

Pennant, Firestone, orange-on-blue felt, 8x28", EX.....**$45.00**

Pin-back button, Standard Red Crown Superfuel/More Live Power Per Gallon, w/tiger logo, red, white & blue, 4" dia, EX **$110.00**

Plaque, Gulf, embossed brass, Honor/Award honoring a Gulf Service Station for 3% Motor Oil Sales.../Spring 1938, 9", EX...**$85.00**

Playing cards, Kelly Springfield Tires, shows Lotta Miles framed by tire, complete, EX (original box).......**$200.00**

Pocket mirror, Socony Motor Gasoline/Standard Oil, w/shield logo, red, white & blue, 3½" dia, NM...**$75.00**

Pocketknife, Esso, medal modern-shape gas pump (no globe), 2½", EX...**$100.00**

Pocketknife w/scissors, Shell, metal w/engraved lettering & logo, Mileage Is Our Business, 2½", EX **$50.00**

Pump sign, Mobilgas, porcelain 5-point emblem w/red winged horse logo above black name on white, 13x13", VG .**$100.00**

Pump sign, Shell, red porcelain shell shape w/orange lettering outlined in black, black-trimmed edge, 12", EX.....**$600.00**

Rack sign, Royal Triton Motor Oil/America's Finest Motor Oil!, porcelain, can above blue lettering on white, 14" dia, EX...**$325.00**

Restroom key tags, Texaco, hexagonal, marked Men/Ladies, black & red on white, 5½", NM+ **$165.00**

Salt and pepper shakers, DX Boron, red plastic with paper labels, 3", $75.00 for the pair.

Salt & pepper shakers, Esso/Esso Extra gas pumps, plastic, EX, pr...**$40.00**

Salt & pepper shakers, Firestone US Rubber, tire shapes, EX, pr...**$65.00**

Sign, Esso, diecut Esso Drop Girl atop sign, red, yellow, blue & white, 16x7", EX **$250.00**

Sign, Fisk Tires/Tubes/Service Station, metal, image of Fisk Boy w/reflective lettering on yellow, 30x14", VG+........**$425.00**

Sign, Havoline Waxfree Oil/Indian Refining Co, porcelain flange, bull's-eye atop panel, red, white & blue, 20x24", EX **$650.00**

Sign, Humble/Restroom, porcelain, The Next User Of This Restroom..., 9x7", NM+...**$375.00**

Sign, Install Sealed Power Piston Rings..., tin w/arched top, red nude logo on yellow dot on blue ground, 35x22", EX+ **$200.00**

Sign, Phillips 66, porcelain shield, black & orange w/white edge trim, 29", EX...**$500.00**

Sign, Stabilized Quaker State Motor Oil, paper, The Right Change...For Summer Driving, bust of old lady, 34x58", EX+ **$100.00**

Sign, That Good Powerine Gas, porcelain, white emblem w/phrase on red ground, black trim, 2-sided, 20x28", EX+ **$185.00**

Sign, White Rose Gasoline, porcelain, shows boy holding sign, multicolor on white w/black border, 12" dia, EX **$325.00**

Sign, Whiz Gear Grease/Service Station, porcelain, w/triangle symbol, framed, 24x36", EX...**$650.00**

Soap tin, Whiz Soap/Davies Young Soap Co, Free Sample/Enter Whiz-Exit Dirt, slip lid, 1¼x1½" dia, EX **$35.00**

Standee, Texaco, diecut cardboard figure of Eddie Canter holding sign reading I'll Be w/You..., 1930s, 64", EX....**$575.00**
Suggestion box, Socony-Vacuum Suggestion System, wood & pressed board, w/Pegasus logo, Win A Cash Award, 18", VG...**$135.00**

Tank sign, Mobiloil A, porcelain, two-sided, 9", EX+, $275.00; can, one-quart, VG+, $150.00.

Thermometer, ShellZone Anti-Freeze, metal, yellow on red, NMIB...**$250.00**
Thermometer, Texaco, tin lollipop sign, white, 22", EX+..**$300.00**
Thread container/thimble, metal cylinder w/thimble on end, blue advertising on orange center, 2", EX..........**$300.00**
Winterfront, Shell, diecut cardboard, Quick Starting! above logo, Shell lettered down sides, red on yellow, 13x21", EX+ **$60.00**

Gay Fad Glassware

What started out as a home-based 'one-woman' operation in the late 1930s within only a few years had grown into a substantial company requiring much larger facilities and a staff of decorators. The company, dubbed Gay Fad by her husband, was founded by Fran Taylor. Originally they decorated kitchenware items but later found instant success with the glassware they created, most of which utilized frosted backgrounds and multicolored designs such as tulips, state themes, Christmas motifs, etc. Some pieces were decorated with 22-karat gold and sterling silver. In addition to the frosted glass which collectors quickly learn to associate with this company, they also became famous for their 'bentware' — quirky cocktail glasses whose stems were actually bent.

Some of their more collectible lines are 'Beau Brummel' — martini glasses with straight or bent stems featuring a funny-faced drinker wearing a plaid bow tie; 'Gay Nineties' — various designs such as can-can girls and singing bartenders; '48 States' — maps with highlighted places of interest; 'Rich Man, Poor Man' (or Beggar Man, Thief, etc.); 'Bartender' (self-explanatory); 'Currier & Ives' — made to coordinate with the line by Royal China; 'Zombies' — extra tall and slim with various designs including roses, giraffes, and flamingos; and the sterling silver- and 22-karat gold-trimmed glassware.

Until you learn to spot it a mile away (which you soon will), look for an interlocking 'G' and 'F' or 'Gay Fad,' the latter mark indicating pieces from the late 1950s to the early 1960s. The glassware itself has the feel of satin and is of very good quality. It can be distinguished from other manufacturers' wares simply by checking the bottom — Gay Fad's are frosted; generally other manufacturers' are not. Hand-painted details are another good clue. (You may find similar glassware signed 'Briard'; this is not Gay Fad.)

This Ohio-based company was sold in 1963 and closed altogether in 1965. Be careful of condition. If the frosting has darkened or the paint is worn or faded, it's best to wait for a better example.

Advisor: Donna S. McGrady (See the Directory, Gay Fad)

Juice pitcher, Ada Orange, frosted, 36-ounce, $30.00. (Photo courtesy Donna McGrady)

Ashtray, Trout Flies, clear..**$5.00**
Bent tray, Phoenix Bird, clear, signed Gay Fad, 13¾" dia..**$15.00**
Bent tray, Stylized Cats, clear, signed Gay Fad, 11½" dia...**$14.00**
Bent trays, classic design, paper label, 2 square trays in metal frame...**$22.00**
Beverage set, Colonial Homestead, frosted, 85-oz pitcher & 6 12-oz tumblers...**$60.00**
Beverage set, magnolia, clear, 86-oz pitcher & 6 13-oz tumblers **$45.00**
Beverage set, Red Hibiscus, frosted, 86-oz ball pitcher & 6 13-oz round-bottom tumblers **$80.00**
Bowl, mixing; Poinsettia, red w/green leaves on ivory Swirl, Anchor Hocking, 8" **$25.00**
Canister set, Red Rose, red lids, white interior, 3-pc ..**$55.00**
Casserole, tulips (rosemaling) on lid, clear, 2-qt, w/black wire rack...**$20.00**
Chip n' Dip, Horace the Horse w/cart, knife tail, 3 bowls, double old-fashion glass as head, signed Gay Fad.......**$60.00**
Cocktail set, Poodle, metal frame 'body' w/martini mixer, double old-fashion glass as head & 4 5-oz glasses, signed **$60.00**
Cocktail set, The Last Hurdle (fox hunt scenes), 32-oz shaker & 6 4-oz tumblers..**$58.00**
Cocktail shaker, Ballerina Shoes, red metal screw-top lid, frosted, 32-oz, 7"...**$18.00**
Cocktail shaker, full-figure ballerina, frosted, 28-oz, 9"..**$35.00**

Cruet set, Oil & Vinegar, Cherry, clear..........................$15.00

Decanter set, Gay '90s, Scotch, Rye, Gin & Bourbon, frosted or white inside **$80.00**

Goblet, Bow Pete, Hoffman Beer, 16-oz.....................**$12.00**

Ice tub, Gay '90s, frosted **$16.00**

Juice set, Tommy Tomato, frosted, 36-oz pitcher & 6 4-oz tumblers..**$45.00**

Loaf pan, Apple, red & yellow w/green leaves on ivory, Anchor Hocking..**$25.00**

Luncheon set, Cattails, square plate, cup & saucer, tumbler, clear, 1 complete place setting, 4-pc....................**$18.00**

Luncheon set, Fantasia Hawaiian Flower, 1 place setting (square plate, cup & saucer)............................**$15.00**

Martini mixer, 'A Jug of Wine...,' w/glass stirring rod, clear, signed Gay Fad, 10⅝".....................................**$16.00**

Mix-A-Salad set, Ivy, 22-oz shaker w/plastic top, garlic press, measuring spoon, recipe book, MIB.....................**$70.00**

Mug, Notre Dame, frosted, 16-oz **$15.00**

Mug set, Here's How in a different language on ea mug, frosted, 12-pc **$72.00**

Pilsner set, Gay 90s, portraits: Mama, Papa, Victoria, Rupert, Aunt Aggie, Uncle Bertie, Gramps & Horace, frosted, 8-pc **$90.00**

Pitcher, Currier & Ives, blue & white, frosted, 86-oz..**$50.00**

Pitcher, martini; cardinal & pine sprig, frosted, w/glass stirrer, 42-oz **$35.00**

Pitcher, Rosemaling (tulips), white inside, 32-oz **$28.00**

Punch set, turquoise veiling, bowl & 8 cups in metal frame **$65.00**

Range set, Rooster, salt, pepper, sugar & flour shakers, frosted w/red metal lids, 8-oz, 4-pc **$36.00**

Refrigerator container, Distlefink on ivory, Anchor Hocking, w/lid, 4x8"...**$35.00**

Salad set, Fruits, frosted, lg bowl, 2 cruets, salt & pepper shakers..**$50.00**

Salad set, Outlined Fruits, lg bowl, 2 cruets, salt & pepper shakers, frosted, 5-pc...**$65.00**

Salt & pepper shakers, Morning Glory, frosted w/red plastic tops, pr **$12.00**

Stem, bent cocktail, Beau Brummel, clear, signed Gay Fad, 3½-oz **$12.00**

Stem, bent cocktail, Souvenir of My Bender, frosted, 3-oz **$11.00**

Tea & toast, Magnolia, square plate w/cup indent & cup, clear **$11.00**

Tom & Jerry set, Christmas bells, milk white, marked GF, bowl & 6 cups...**$70.00**

Tumbler, Derby Winner Citation, frosted, 1948, 14-oz..**$50.00**

Tumbler, grouse, brown, aqua & gold on clear, signed Gay Fad, 10-oz **$8.00**

Tumbler, Hors D'oeuvres, clear, 14-oz **$8.00**

Tumbler, Kentucky state map (1 of 48), pink, yellow or lime, frosted, marked GF, 10-oz **$5.00**

Tumbler, Oregon State Map on pink picket fence, clear, marked GF..**$5.00**

Tumbler, Pegasus, gold & pink on black, 12-oz **$8.00**

Tumbler, Say When, frosted, 4-oz **$5.00**

Tumbler, Zombie, flamingo, frosted, marked GF, 14-oz .**$15.00**

Tumbler, Zombie, giraffe, frosted, marked GF, 14-oz.**$15.00**

Tumbler set, Famous Fighters (John L Sullivan & the others), frosted, 16-oz, 8-pc..**$85.00**

Tumbler set, Game Birds & Animals, clear, 12-oz, 8-pc, MIB **$75.00**

Tumbler set, Sports Cars, white interior, 12-oz, 8-pc..**$45.00**

Tumblers, angels preparing for Christmas, frosted, 12-oz, set of 8...**$72.00**

Tumblers, Dickens Christmas Carol characters, frosted, 12-oz, set of 8..**$65.00**

Tumblers, French Poodle, clear, 17-oz, set of 8 in original box **$96.00**

Tumblers, Ohio Presidents, frosted, 12-oz, set of 8....**$60.00**

Tumblers, Rich Man, Poor Man (nursery rhyme), frosted, marked GF, 16-oz, set of 8...................................**$95.00**

Vanity set, butterflies in meadow, pink inside, 5-pc...**$60.00**

Vase, Red Poppy, clear, footed, 10" **$22.00**

Waffle set, Blue Willow, 48-oz waffle batter jug & 11½-oz syrup jug, frosted, pr.....................................**$65.00**

Waffle set, Little Black Sambo, frosted, 48-oz waffle batter jug, 11½-oz syrup jug................................**$200.00**

Waffle set, Peach Blossoms, 48-oz waffle batter jug & 11½-oz syrup jug, frosted, pr.....................................**$32.00**

Waffle set, Red Poppy, frosted, 48-oz waffle batter jug, 11½-oz syrup jug **$24.00**

Wine set, Grapes, decanter & 4 2½-oz stemmed wines, clear, 5-pc..**$35.00**

Tumbler, Merry Christmas From Gay Fad, from $10.00 to $12.00. (Photo courtesy Donna McGrady)

Geisha Girl China

The late nineteenth century saw a rise in the popularity of Oriental wares in the US and Europe. Japan rose to meet the demands of this flourishing ceramics marketplace with a flurry of growth in potteries and decorating centers. These created items for export which would appeal to Western tastes and integrate into Western dining and decorating cultures, which were distinct from those of Japan. One example of the wares introduced into this marketplace was Geisha Girl porcelain.

Hundreds of different patterns and manufacturers' marks have been uncovered on Geisha Girl porcelain tea and dinnerware sets, dresser accessories, decorative items, etc., which were produced well into the twentieth century. They all share in common colorful decorations featuring kimono-clad ladies and children involved in everyday activities. These scenes are set against a backdrop of lush flora, distinctive Japanese architecture and majestic landscapes. Most Geisha Girl porcelain designs were laid on by means of a stencil, generally red or black. This appears as an outline on the ceramic body. Details are then completed by hand-painted washes in a myriad of colors. A minority of the wares were wholly hand painted.

Most Geisha Girl porcelain has a colorful border or edging with handles, finials, spouts, and feet similarly adorned. The most common border color is red which can range from orange to red-orange to a deep brick red. Among the earliest border colors were red, maroon, cobalt blue, light (apple) green, and Nile green. Pine green, blue-green, and turquoise made their appearance circa 1917, and a light cobalt or Delft blue appeared around 1920. Other colors (e.g. tan, yellow, brown, and gold) can also be found. Borders were often enhanced with gilded lace or floral decoration. The use of gold for this purpose diminished somewhat around 1910 to 1915 when some decorators used economic initiative (fewer firings required) to move the gold to just inside the border or replace the gold with white or yellow enamels. Wares with both border styles continued to be produced into the twentieth century. Exquisite examples with multicolor borders as well as ornate rims decorated with florals and geometrics can also be found.

Due to the number of different producers, the quality of Geisha ware ranges from crude to finely detailed. Geisha Girl porcelain was sold in sets and open stock in outlets ranging from the five-and-ten to fancy department stores. It was creatively used for store premiums, containers for store products, fair souvenirs, and resort memorabilia. The fineness of detailing, amount of gold highlights, border color, scarcity of form and, of course, condition all play a role in establishing the market value of a given item. Some patterns are scarcer than others, but most Geisha ware collectors seem not to focus on particular patterns.

The heyday of Geisha Girl porcelain was from 1910 through the 1930s. Production continued until the World War II era. During the 'Occupied' period, a small amount of wholly hand-painted examples were made, often with a black and gold border. The Oriental import stores and catalogs from the 1960s and 1970s featured some examples of Geisha Girl porcelain, many of which were produced in Hong Kong. These are recognized by the very white porcelain, sparse detail coloring, and lack of gold decoration. The 1990s has seen a resurgence of reproductions with a faux Nippon mark. These items are supposed to represent high quality Geisha ware, but in reality they are a blur of Geisha and Satsuma-style characteristics. They are too busy in design, too heavily enameled, and bear poor resemblance to items that rightfully carry Noritake's green M-in-Wreath Nippon

mark. Once you've been introduced to a few of these reproductions, you'll be able to recognize them easily.

Note: Colors mentioned in the following listings refer to borders.

Advisor: Elyce Litts (See Directory, Geisha Girl China)

Ashtray, Temple A, multicolored, spade shaped.........**$25.00**
Bonbon, Parasol C, red-orange w/gold, scalloped, fluted, 5½"..**$15.00**
Bowl, individual berry; Rivers Edge, green, orange & gold.**$20.00**
Bowl, nut; Basket A, dark apple green, 9-lobed, 3-footed, master, 6"...**$30.00**
Box, Barden Bench B, red sides, 6-sided, 6"..............**$35.00**
Box, manicure (trinket); Rokkasen, red-orange **$25.00**
Box, trinket; Koto, club shaped...............................**$28.00**
Chamberstick, Courtesan Precessional **$60.00**
Cocoa pot, Battledore, yellow green, ewer shaped, 9"..**$85.00**
Cocoa pot, Garden Bench J, multicolored, fluted.....**$100.00**
Creamer, Geisha in Sampan B, cobalt blue **$7.00**
Creamer, Porch, red-orange, modern **$5.00**
Creamer & sugar bowl, Mother & Son B, red-orange w/gold **$30.00**
Cup, sake; Geisha Face, yellow-green w/gold trim **$10.00**
Cup & saucer, after-dinner; Bamboo Trellis, red-orange w/gold buds...**$10.00**
Cup & saucer, cocoa; Small Sounds of Summer, red..**$20.00**
Cup & saucer, tea; Bamboo Tree, dark green.............**$12.00**
Demitasse pot, Fan Dance A, ornate hand-painted background, pattern in reverse **$85.00**
Dish, Prayer Ribbon, apple green w/gold, footed, oblong.**$32.00**
Eggcup, double; Cherry Blossom Ikebana, red..........**$15.00**
Hair receiver, Fan Silhouette of Hoo Bird, wavy cobalt blue w/gold, red between gold waves, lg **$32.00**
Hair reciever, grass green, melon ribbed....................**$20.00**
Jardiniere, miniature on pedestal, Cloud B, red w/gold border...**$150.00**
Mustard jar, Gardening, cobalt blue, scalloped, w/spoon..**$25.00**
Napkin ring, Rivers Edge, red, triangular....................**$35.00**
Nut cup, Lesson, cobalt blue w/gold, footed, individual..**$4.00**
Nut cup, red-orange, individual.................................**$3.00**

Pancake server, So Big, Kutani, $145.00. (Photo courtesy Elyce Litts)

Pin tray, Duck Watching B, pine green w/white, uneven edge, sm $14.00

Pitcher, Garden Bench K, red, 5" $18.00

Plate, Bird Cage, red-orange w/gold, 6" $10.00

Plate, Flute & Koto, blue-green w/gold buds, 7" $16.00

Plate, Greeting Grandma, red w/gold, swirl fluted, scalloped edge, 8½" $25.00

Plate, Lantern B, cobalt blue w/gold, 6" $12.00

Plate, Picnic A, red w/gold, 9½" $28.00

Plate, Temple B, gold border, 6⅛" $14.00

Plate, Water Boy, pine green, 7" $14.00

Platter, Garden Bench F, red w/gold, floral edge, double foot rim, Kutani, 12x8" $75.00

Potpourri jar, Garden Bench B, red, 5½" $27.00

Powder jar, Carp A: Watching the Carp, deep brownish red w/gold $26.00

Powder jar, Chrysanthemum Garden, wavy red w/gold lacing beneath, pattern on lid & body, melon ribbed $25.00

Powder jar, Garden Bench E, geometric red, mint green & gold, Kutani, oversize..$45.00

Puff box, Field Laborers, red w/gold..........................$10.00

Ring tree, Temple A, Nippon.......................................$75.00

Salt & pepper shakers, Parasol F, red-orange, 3-footed, pr $20.00

Salt & pepper shakers, To the Teahouse, red w/gold, pr ..$28.00

Salt dish, Cloud A, red-orange w/flowers....................$14.00

Salt dish, Temple A, red w/gold, bowl shaped, Nippon .$18.00

Sugar bowl, Boat Festival, pale cobalt blue $15.00

Teacup & saucer, w/geisha lithophane, turquoise border, Made in Japan..$15.00

Teapot, Cloud B, red-orange w/yellow, melon ribbed ...$30.00

Teapot, Mother & Son C, gold, floral finial $75.00

Teapot, Pointing D, red w/gold lacing, squat $35.00

Toothpick holder, much gold and coralene, cobalt border, Made in Japan by Kato, $40.00. (Photo courtesy Elyce Litts)

Vase, Parasol C: Parasol, deep red, milk bottle shape, 2 handles, 6½" $25.00

GI Joe

The first GI Joe was introduced by Hasbro in 1964. He was 12" tall, and you could buy him with blond, auburn, black, or brown hair in four basic variations: Action Sailor, Action Marine, Action Soldier, and Action Pilot. There was also a Black doll as well as representatives of many other nations. By 1967 GI Joe could talk, all the better to converse with the female who was first issued that year. The Adventure Team series (1970 – 1976) included Black Adventurer, Talking Astronaut, Sea Adventurer, Talking Team Commander, Land Adventurer, and several variations. At this point, their hands were made of rubber, making it easier for them to grasp the many guns, tools, and other accessories that Hasbro had devised. Playsets, vehicles, and clothing completed the package, and there were kid-size items designed specifically for the kids themselves. The 12" dolls were discontinued by 1976.

Brought out by popular demand, Hasbro's 3¾" GI Joes hit the market in 1982. Needless to say, they were very well accepted. In fact, these smaller GI Joes are thought to be the most successful line of action figures ever made. Loose figures (those removed from the original packaging) are very common, and even if you can locate the accessories that they came out with, most are worth only about $3.00 to $10.00. It's the mint-in-package items that most interest collectors, and they pay a huge premium for the package. There's an extensive line of accessories that goes with the smaller line as well. Many more are listed in *Schroeder's Collectible Toys, Antique to Modern,* and *Collector's Guide to Dolls in Uniform* by Joseph Bourgeois, both published by Collector Books.

Note: A/M was used in the description lines as an abbreviation for Action Man.

12" Figures and Accessories

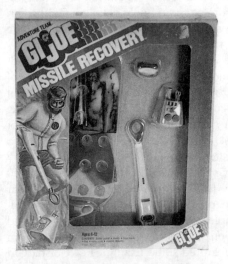

Accessory, Missile Recovery, MIB, $40.00.

Accessory, Action Flame Thrower, A/M, green, w/helmet sticker, MOC..$60.00

Accessory, Action Windboat Backpack, w/instructions, EX $35.00

Accessory, Air Force Air Vest, #7809, MOC (sealed)...$125.00

Accessory, Army Poncho, green, EX..........................$20.00

Accessory, Astro Locker, EX $200.00

Accessory, British Commando Equipment, #8304, MOC..$250.00

Accessory, Combat Mess Kit, #7509, complete, MOC.**$70.00**
Accessory, Crash Crew Set, #7820, complete, MIB ...**$260.00**
Accessory, Demolition Set, complete, M (EX box) ...**$250.00**
Accessory, Footlocker, green, w/tray, EX **$20.00**
Accessory, German Stormtrooper Equipment, #8300, complete, MOC **$265.00**
Accessory, Mae West Life Vest, yellow cloth, EX **$100.00**
Accessory, Marine Pup Tent, EX.................................**$35.00**
Accessory, Medic Shoulder Bag, EX...........................**$30.00**
Accessory, Military Police Duffle Bag, #7523, MOC....**$60.00**
Accessory, Mine Detection Set, A/M, complete, MIB..**$150.00**
Accessory, Pursuit Craft Pilot, A/M, complete, MIP ..**$100.00**
Accessory, Scramble Pilot Air Vest & Accessories, MOC ..**$100.00**
Accessory, Shore Patrol Billy Club, white, EX.............**$10.00**
Accessory, Ski Patrol Jacket & Pants, EX **$40.00**
Accessory, Super Joe Sonic Scanner, #7538, complete, NMIB **$50.00**
Figure, Action Marine, complete, MIB **$325.00**
Figure, Action Pilot, complete, EX+ **$125.00**
Figure, Action Soldier, 30th Anniversary, 1994, NRFB .**$100.00**
Figure, Adventure Team Air Adventurer, complete, NM ..**$100.00**
Figure, Adventure Team Talking Commander, complete, NM (EX box) **$275.00**
Figure, Adventure Team Talking Man of Action, complete, EX+ **$100.00**
Figure, Air Security, complete, rare, NM **$1,000.00**
Figure, Airborne Military Police, Kay Bee Toys, NRFB.**$75.00**
Figure, Battle of the Bulge, Toys-R-Us, NRFB **$65.00**
Figure, Combat Soldier, A/M, complete, MIB...........**$100.00**
Figure, German Stormtrooper, complete, VG...........**$350.00**
Figure, Home for the Holiday (Black), Wal-Mart, NRFB.**$70.00**
Figure, Japanese Imperial Soldier, complete, M........**$625.00**
Figure, LSO, complete, EX, from $200 to **$250.00**

Figure, Man of Action, Kung Fu hands, MIB, $325.00.

Figure, Sea Adventurer, hard hands, complete, EXIB.**$265.00**
Figure, Space Ranger Captain, A/M, complete, MIB.**$100.00**
Figure, Space Ranger Patroller, A/M, complete, MIB..**$90.00**
Figure, Tank Commander, complete, EX...................**$450.00**

Vehicle, Action Pack Turbo Copter, MIB (sealed).......**$50.00**
Vehicle, Action Pilot Space Capsule, complete, MIB...**$250.00**
Vehicle, Adventure Team Sandstorm Jeep, green, EXIB...**$275.00**
Vehicle, Fire Engine, A/M, MIP.................................**$75.00**
Vehicle, Iron Knight Tank, #9031, EXIB **$250.00**
Vehicle, Jet Helicopter, complete, EXIB....................**$400.00**
Vehicle, Sea Wolf Submarine, EX (VG box) **$265.00**
Vehicle, Space Capsule, Sears Exclusive, MIB..........**$400.00**
Vehicle, Team Vehicle, yellow ATV, VG (G box)........**$85.00**

3¾" Figures and Accessories

Figure, Red Star Oktober Guard, MIP, $10.00.

Accessory, Action Force SAS Parachutist Attack, MIP.**$35.00**
Accessory, Arctic Blast, 1988, EX................................**$12.00**
Accessory, Armadillo Mini Tank, 1984, EX **$8.00**
Accessory, Battle Copter, w/Ace figure, MIB..............**$20.00**
Accessory, Battlefield Robot Tri-Blaster, 1988, NRFB..**$30.00**
Accessory, Cobra Emperor w/Air Chariot, 1986, NRFB.**$60.00**
Accessory, Cobra Wolf w/Ice Viper, 1985, NM...........**$20.00**
Accessory, Condor Z25, 1989, w/instructions, EX......**$25.00**
Accessory, Falcon Glider w/Grunt, complete, EX.....**$100.00**
Accessory, Jet Pack JUMP & Platform, 1982, MIP (Canadian) **$50.00**
Accessory, Machine Gun, 1983, EX..............................**$5.00**
Accessory, Mauler MBT Tank, 1985, NRFB..................**$80.00**
Accessory, Mobile Missile System, complete, EX........**$45.00**
Accessory, Motorized Battle Wagon, 1991, MIP **$35.00**
Accessory, Polar Battle Gear, 1983 mail-in, MIP **$10.00**
Accessory, Q Force Battle Gear, MIP **$5.00**
Accessory, Snow Cat w/Frostbite, 1984, complete, EX..**$25.00**
Accessory, Whirlwind Twin Battle Gun, 1983, EX......**$20.00**
Figure, Ace, 1983, MOC **$25.00**
Figure, Airborne, 1983, MOC....................................**$50.00**
Figure, Astro Viper, 1988, w/accessories & ID card, EX **$6.00**
Figure, Bazooka, 1983-85, MOC **$35.00**
Figure, Beachhead, 1983-85, MOC **$30.00**
Figure, Buzzer, 1985, MOC **$35.00**
Figure, Clutch, 1988, MOC.......................................**$18.00**

Figure, Cobra Commander, 1983, MOC $125.00
Figure, Cobra Soldier, 1983, MOC $60.00
Figure, Deep Six, 1989, MOC $14.00
Figure, Dojo, 1992, MOC $10.00
Figure, Dreadnok, 1985, MOC $35.00
Figure, Duke, 1985, MOC $100.00
Figure, Eels, 1985, MOC...$52.00
Figure, Flash, 1982, w/accessories, EX......................$20.00
Figure, Gyro Viper, 1987, w/accessories, EX.............$10.00
Figure, Iceberg, 1983-85, MOC $32.00
Figure, Leatherneck, 1983-85, MOC $25.00
Figure, Mainframe, 1986, MOC...................................$32.00
Figure, Maverick, 1988, MOC......................................$27.00
Figure, Mutt & Junkyard, 1984, MOC........................$50.00
Figure, Ozone, 1993, MOC...$5.00
Figure, Raptor, 1987, MOC..$20.00
Figure, Recondo, 1989, MOC.......................................$40.00
Figure, Road Pig, 1988, MOC......................................$20.00
Figure, Sci-Fi, 1991, MOC..$15.00
Figure, Sergeant Savage, 1995, MOC..........................$6.00
Figure, Shockwave, 1988, MOC...................................$22.00
Figure, T'Jbang, 1992, MOC...$10.00
Figure, Tiger Force Tiger Shark, 1988, MOC.............$18.00
Figure, Wild Bill, 1992, MOC......................................$10.00
Figure, Zandar, 1983-85, MOC....................................$25.00

Glass Knives

Popular during the Depression years, glass knives were made in many of the same colors as the glass dinnerware of the era — pink, green, light blue, crystal, and more rarely, amber or white (originally called opal). Some were hand painted with flowers or fruit. The earliest boxes had poems printed on their tops explaining the knife's qualities in the pre-stainless steel days: 'No metal to tarnish when cutting your fruit, and so it is certain this glass knife will suit.' Eventually, a tissue flyer was packed with each knife, which elaborated even more on the knife's usefulness. 'It is keen as a razor, ideal for slicing tomatoes, oranges, lemons, grapefruit and especially constructed for separating the meaty parts of grapefruit from its rind...' Boxes add interest by helping identify distributors as well as commercial names of the knives.

When originally sold, the blades were ground to a sharp cutting edge, but due to everyday usage, the blades eventually became nicked. Collectors will accept reground, resharpened blades as long as the original shape has been maintained.

Documented US glass companies that made glass knives are the Akro Agate Co., Cameron Glass Corp., Houze Glass Corp., Imperial Glass Corp., Jeannette Glass Co., and Westmoreland Glass Co.

Internet final-auction bid prices indicate what a person is willing to pay to add a new or different piece to a personal collection and may not necessarily reflect any value given in a price guide.

Advisor: Michele A. Rosewitz (See Directory, Glass Knives)

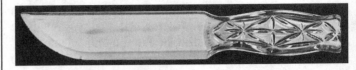

Aer-Flo (Grid), pink, 7½", $90.00.

BK Co/ESP 12-14-20, crystal, hand-painted handle, 9" ..**$35.00**
BK Co/ESP 12-14-20, green, hand-painted handle, 9" ..**$60.00**
Cryst-o-lite (3 Flowers), crystal, 8½" **$10.00**
Dur-X, 3-leaf, blue, 8½" or 9"....................................**$40.00**
Dur-X, 3-leaf, crystal, 8½" or 9"................................**$15.00**
Dur-X, 3-leaf, green, 8½" or 9"..................................**$40.00**
Dur-X, 3-leaf, pink, 8½" or 9"....................................**$40.00**
Dur-X, 5-leaf, blue, 9"...**$45.00**
Dur-X, 5-leaf, crystal, 9"...**$25.00**
Dur-X, 5-leaf, green, 9"...**$45.00**
Dur-X, 5-leaf, pink, 9"...**$45.00**
Imperial Candlewick, crystal, 8½" **$500.00**
Steel-ite, crystal, 8½"...**$35.00**
Steel-ite, green, 8½"...**$75.00**
Steel-ite, pink, 8½"...**$70.00**
Stonex, amber, 8½"...**$250.00**
Stonex, crystal, 8½"...**$40.00**
Stonex, green, 8½"...**$80.00**
Stonex, opal, 8½"...**$350.00**
Thumbguard, crystal, hand-painted handle, 9"............**$35.00**
Vitex (Star & Diamond), blue, 8½" or 9"...................**$30.00**
Vitex (Star & Diamond), crystal, 8½" or 9".................**$15.00**
Vitex (Star & Diamond), pink, 8½" or 9"...................**$30.00**

Golden Foliage

In 1935 Libbey Glass was purchased by Owens-Illinois but continued to operate under the Libbey Glass name. After World War II, the company turned to making tableware and still does today. Golden Foliage is just one of the many patterns made during the 1950s. It is a line of crystal glassware with a satin band that features a golden maple leaf as well as other varieties. The satin band is trimmed in gold, above and below. Since this gold seems to have easily worn off, be careful to find mint pieces for your collection. This pattern was made in silver as well.

Advisor: Debbie Coe (See Directory, Cape Cod)

Drink set, includes 6 jiggers & brass-finished caddy ..**$35.00**
Drink set, includes 8 tumblers (9-oz), ice tub & brass-finished
caddy **$50.00**
Drink set, includes 8 tumblers (9-oz) & brass-finished
caddy..**$36.00**
Goblet, cocktail; 4-oz...**$5.00**
Goblet, cordial; 1-oz **$8.50**
Goblet, pilsner; 11-oz **$8.50**

Goblet, sherbet; 6½-oz...**$4.50**
Goblet, water; 9-oz..**$6.50**
Ice tub, in metal 3-footed frame............................**$19.50**
Pitcher, 5¼", w/metal frame **$12.50**
Salad dressing set, includes 3 bowls (4") & brass-finished
   caddy **$19.50**
Tumbler, beverage; 12½-oz.................................**$8.50**
Tumbler, cooler; 14-oz.......................................**$9.50**
Tumbler, jigger; 2-oz...**$7.00**
Tumbler, juice; 6-oz..**$5.00**
Tumbler, old fashion; 9-oz.................................**$4.50**
Tumbler, water; 10-oz.......................................**$6.50**

Creamer and sugar bowl, $15.00 for the set.

Granite Ware

Though it really wasn't as durable as its name suggests, there's still a lot of granite ware around today, though much of it is now in collections. You may even be able to find a bargain. The popularity of the 'country' look in home decorating and the exposure it's had in some of the leading decorating magazines has caused granite ware prices, especially on rare items, to soar in recent years.

It's made from a variety of metals coated with enameling of various colors, some solid, others swirled. It's color, form, and, of course, condition that dictates value. Swirls of cobalt and white, purple and white, green and white, and brown and white are unusual, but even solid gray items such as a hanging salt box or a chamberstick can be expensive, because pieces like those are rare. Decorated examples are uncommon — so are children's pieces and salesman's samples.

For further information, we recommend *The Collector's Encyclopedia of Granite Ware, Colors, Shapes, and Values,* by Helen Greguire (Collector Books).

Asparagus boiler, lg gray mottle, Extra Agate..., 11" L,
   G+ **$235.00**
Bean pot, blue solid w/black, white interior, handles, w/lid,
   7¾x5¾", NM **$125.00**
Bread pan, aqua/white mottle w/cobalt, Granite Steel Ware,
   10¾", G+ **$295.00**
Bread pan, green & white lg swirl w/black, envelope ends,
   10" L, G+ **$285.00**

Bucket, green & white lg swirl w/cobalt, w/matching lid,
   5¼", M **$525.00**
Canister, white w/dark blue trim & lettering, 7½x5", M.**$85.00**
Chamber pot, blue & white mottle, w/matching lid, Lisk,
   6½x9½", G+ **$240.00**
Coffee biggin, red & white med mottle w/red, 4-pc, 9¼x5¼",
   NM **$595.00**
Coffee boiler, blue & white lg mottle w/black, bail handle,
   12x9⅝", NM....................................**$265.00**
Coffee boiler, brown & white lg mottle w/brown, Elite..., 11",
   G+ **$325.00**

Coffee boiler, red and white large swirl, white interior and cobalt trim, seamed body, riveted construction, very rare, $2,100.00. (Photo courtesy Helen Greguire)

Coffee carrier, pink & white lg swirl w/cobalt, 7¼x4⅞",
   G+ **$325.00**
Coffeepot, shaded blue w/black, ring handle on lid, 9¼x6",
   G+ **$295.00**
Coffepot, blue & white wavy mottle w/black, seamed,
   9¼x5¾", NM **$375.00**
Creamer, 4-color lg swirl w/red, white interior, seamless,
   5½", NM **$750.00**
Cup & saucer, roses & violets on white w/gold & black, 2",
   3⅞", G+ **$95.00**
Dinner bucket, floral on blue w/black, Stuart, 3-pc,
   7⅜x9x6½", NM **$695.00**
Double boiler, green & white lg swirl w/cobalt, Emerald
   Ware, NM....................................**$575.00**
Dustpan, gray lg mottle, Haberman's label, 14x12¾", G+..**$795.00**
Fish kettle/poacher, cobalt solid, white interior, insert, 20" L,
   G+ **$95.00**
Fry pan, white solid w/black, white interior, ca 1960, 9⅜"
   dia, G+....................................**$30.00**
Fudge pan, lavender-cobalt & white lg swirl w/cobalt, 9½" L,
   G+ **$195.00**
Funnel, blue & white lg swirl w/cobalt, Blue Diamond Ware,
   4x5⅝", NM....................................**$575.00**
Funnel, green & white lg swirl w/cobalt, Emerald Ware,
   4x5¾", NM....................................**$595.00**
Kettle, gray lg mottle, seamless, bail handle, 7x15¾", G+.**$145.00**
Milk can, brown & white lg swirl w/black, white interior,
   seamless, 9½", NM....................................**$895.00**

Milk can, dark blue & white med relish w/cobalt & black, 9", NM **$295.00**

Milk can, shaded green, Shamrock Ware, 9¼x5", G+ ...**$325.00**

Muffin pan, dark plum w/gray & white lg mottle, 8-cup, 14", G- **$265.00**

Mug, cow & flower scene, blue & white, 1980s, 2⅞x3⅝", M **$20.00**

Mug, fruits on green to white w/cobalt, ca 1980, 7¾", G+ **$65.00**

Mug, red & white lg mottle w/black, ca 1960, 3x3⅜", NM **$40.00**

Mug, white solid, hinged lid, marked Germany, 4⅛x3½", M **$85.00**

Pie plate, brown & blue-gray lg mottle interior/exterior, 7¾", G+ **$65.00**

Pie plate, green & white lg swirl w/cobalt, white interior, Emerald Ware, 9", NM **$110.00**

Pitcher, molasses; blue checks on white w/cobalt, marked...Depose, G+ **$285.00**

Plate, light blue & white med swirl ea side, 10", G+ ..**$95.00**

Platter, fruit & berries on white w/brown, Corona, 16x13", M **$95.00**

Pudding pan, white w/cobalt, No 1 label, eyelet, 1½x7", M **$35.00**

Roaster, black w/red med mottle interior/exterior, oval, 2-pc, 15" L, G+ **$125.00**

Roaster, red with blue trim, 14" long (plus handles), NM, $110.00. (Photo courtesy Helen Greguire)

Saucepan, blue & white lg mottle, blue-gray interior, lipped, 5¾" dia, G+ **$75.00**

Soup ladle, red & white lg swirl (old) w/cobalt, 15½", NM **$1,250.00**

Spoon, blue & white lg mottle w/black handle, 13", G+ ..**$110.00**

Strainer, yellow solid w/black, Made in Poland 46, 4x7½", G **$35.00**

Tea steeper, dark green & white lg mottle w/cobalt, w/lid, 4⅞", NM **$595.00**

Tea strainer, gray med mottle, perforated bottom, 4" dia, NM **$85.00**

Teakettle, green & white lg swirl, seamless, Emerald Ware, 6x5¼", M **$850.00**

Teakettle, light blue & white lg swirl w/black, ca 1940, 5x5½", G+ **$165.00**

Teapot, blue/white/brown chicken-wire w/black, Duchess Ware, 8x5⅛", G+ **$595.00**

Teapot, cobalt w/white speckled interior/exterior, 1920s, 8¼", G+ **$110.00**

Teapot, gray lg mottle, label: Cream City...Milwaukee USA, 8x5½" **$235.00**

Teapot, green & white lg swirl w/cobalt, Emerald Ware, 9⅛", NM **$850.00**

Teapot, white & light blue lg swirl w/black, seamless, 9x5½", G+ **$255.00**

Tray, gray lg mottle, L&G Mfg Co, 13⅜x9½", NM **$135.00**

Tube cake mold, light blue & white lg swirl w/black, 8-sided, 8" dia, G+ **$285.00**

Tumbler, brown & white lg swirl w/brown, white interior, 3½x3¼", NM **$325.00**

Wash pitcher & bowl, brown & white med relish w/cobalt, 8⅜", 10", G+ **$395.00**

Griswold Cast-Iron Cooking Ware

Late in the 1800s, the Griswold company introduced a line of cast-iron cooking ware that was eventually distributed on a large scale nationwide. Today's collectors appreciate the variety of skillets, cornstick pans, Dutch ovens, and griddles available to them, and many still enjoy using them to cook with.

Several marks have been used; most contain the Griswold name, though some were marked simply 'Erie.'

If you intend to use your cast iron, you can clean it safely by using any commercial oven cleaner. (Be sure to re-season it before you cook in it.) A badly pitted, rusty piece may leave you with no other recourse than to remove what rust you can with a wire brush, paint the surface black, and find an alternate use for it around the house. For instance, you might use a kettle to hold a large floor plant or some magazines. A small griddle or skillet would be attractive as part of a wall display in a country kitchen. It should be noted that prices are given for pieces in excellent condition. Items that are cracked, chipped, pitted, or warped are worth substantially less or nothing at all, depending on rarity.

Advisors: Grant Windsor (See Directory, Griswold)

Crispy cornstick pan, #262, miniature, 4x8½", $65.00. (Buyer beware! This piece is heavily reproduced with reproductions outnumbering the genuine Griswold pans ten to one.)

Bowl, patty: marked block logo+Patty Bowl+#871, ca 1930s, 7½x3⅛" deep **$100.00**
Bread pan, marked Erie No 22 on handles, ca 1910-20, 13⅜x7⅜" **$55.00**
Cake mold, rabbit form, marked Griswold Mfg Co, Erie PA (on loop), 862 & 863, chrome, ca 1940s-50s, 10x11x4" **$275.00**
Casserole, #91, oval, block logo, EPU, loop handle on lid, 1940s **$300.00**
Danish cake pan (aebleskiver), diamond logo, ca 1905, 9½" dia **$200.00**
Fluter, w/fixed handle, marked, nickel or iron, ca 1880s.. **$500.00**
French roll pan, #11, wide band **$70.00**
Gas heater, #100, marked Griswold logo, #100 on base, black w/nickel trim, ca 1910-20 .... **$200.00**
Gem pan, marked #1, 940, 11 cups, iron, 1890-1910, 11½x11⅞" **$100.00**
Griddle, #12, block logo, bailed, round **$75.00**
Griddle, #7, handled, slant Erie logo, 8½" dia **$35.00**
Ice shave, #1, marked Griswold Mfg Co, Erie PA USA, tinned finish, 1900-20 .... **$100.00**
Kettle, bulge; #8, marked Erie, iron, 1890 .... **$75.00**
Lemon squeezer, #6, marked 367, tinned iron, ca 1910, 10½" **$85.00**
Loaf pan, #877 .... **$400.00**
Plett pan, slant logo, ca 1919, 9½" dia **$75.00**
Post box, #2, marked Griswold Mfg Co, Erie PA USA, 347 & 348 (cover), ca 1920s-40s **$150.00**
Pot, rimmed; #8, marked Erie Pat'd Mar 10 '91, ca 1905 l, ca 1905 .... **$60.00**
Sad iron, marked Griswold Erie, early 1900s, 4-lb, 5½-lb or 6-lb, ea **$85.00**
Skillet, #3, square **$175.00**
Skillet, #8, Erie B, 1870s-1900 .... **$35.00**
Skillet, #14, slant logo EPU, 1919-29 .... **$900.00**
Skillet, egg; #53, square **$35.00**
Spoon, basting; stamped logo, ca 1910 .... **$50.00**
Trivet, oval roaster; #3, marked **$175.00**
Turk head pan, marked 953, Griswold Erie PA USA, iron, 11 cups, ca 1930-50s, 10⅜x7⅛" **$550.00**
Vienna roll pan, #6, marked NOG & 958 .... **$100.00**
Waffle iron, #11, The American Waffle Iron, Pat'd May 14 & 21 1901, wood handles, ball hinge, high base, ca 1910 .... **$90.00**
Waffle iron, #7 & 8, Selden Griswold Mfg Co, Erie PA, The American Pat June 29 1880, button hinge, 1880s. **$200.00**
Wax ladle, marked Erie 964, ca 1890-1910, 7¾" L **$90.00**

Gurley Candle Company

Gurley candles were cute little wax figures designed to celebrate holidays and special occasions. They are all marked Gurley on the bottom. They were made so well and had so much great detail that people decided to keep them year after year to decorate with instead of burning them. Woolworth's and other five-and-dime stores sold them from about 1940 until the '70s. They're still plentiful today and inexpensive.

Tavern Novelty Candles were actually owned by Gurley. They were similar to the Gurley candles but not quite as detailed. All are marked Tavern on the bottom. Prices listed here are for unburned candles with no fading.

Advisor: Debbie Coe (See Directory, Cape Cod)

Christmas, angel, marked Gurley, 3" **$3.50**
Christmas, angel, marked Gurley, 5" **$8.50**
Christmas, baby angel on half moon, marked Gurley, 2½" **$10.00**
Christmas, Black caroler man w/red clothes, 3" **$6.00**
Christmas, blue grotto w/star, angel & baby, 4½" **$10.00**
Christmas, caroler man w/red clothes, 7" **$8.50**
Christmas, caroler set: lamppost, girl & boy carolers w/song books, cello player, in package **$28.50**

Christmas, church with three green trees against starry night background, packaged set, $24.50. (Photo courtesy Debbie Coe)

Christmas, green candelabra w/red candle, 5" **$7.50**
Christmas, grotto w/shepherd & sheep **$10.00**
Christmas, lamppost, yellow cap & garland, 5½" **$3.50**
Christmas, reindeer, marked Tavern, 3½" **$2.50**
Christmas, Rudolph w/red nose, 3" **$2.50**
Christmas, Santa, 6¼" **$12.00**
Christmas, Santa sitting on present on sled, 3" **$12.50**
Christmas, snowman running w/red hat, 3" **$8.50**
Christmas, snowman w/red pipe & green hat, 5" **$5.00**
Christmas, white church w/choir boy inside, 6" **$9.00**
Christmas, 3" deer standing in front of candle, 5" **$6.50**
Easter, pink birdhouse w/yellow bird, 3" **$7.50**
Easter, pink egg w/bunny inside, 3" **$10.00**
Easter, pink egg w/squirrel inside, 3" **$12.00**
Easter, pink winking rabbit w/carrot, 3¼" **$3.50**
Easter, white lily w/blue lip & green candle, 3" **$4.00**
Halloween, black cat (4") w/orange candlestick beside it. **$15.00**
Halloween, black owl on orange stump, 3½" **$2.50**
Halloween, pumpkin w/black cat, 2½" **$7.00**
Halloween, skeleton, 8½" **$24.00**
Halloween, white ghost, 4½" **$5.00**
Halloween, witch, black, 8" **$18.50**

Halloween, witch w/black cape, 3½" **$7.50**

Halloween, 4" cut-out orange owl w/7½" black candle
    behind it **$20.00**

Other Holidays, birthday boy, marked Tavern, 3" **$3.50**

Other Holidays, bride & groom, 4½", ea **$9.50**

Other Holidays, Eskimo & igloo, marked Tavern, 2-pc ..**$8.50**

Other Holidays, Western girl or boy, 3", ea..................**$8.50**

Thanksgiving, acorns & leaves, 3½".............................**$6.50**

Thanksgiving, gold sailing ship, 7½" **$10.00**

Thanksgiving, male Indian w/red clothes, 5"..............**$12.00**

Thanksgiving, Pilgrim girl or boy, 2½", ea **$4.50**

Thanksgiving, turkey, 2½"...**$2.50**

Hadley, M. A.

Since 1940, the M.A. Hadley Pottery (Louisville, Tennessee) has been producing handmade dinnerware and decorative items painted freehand in a folky style with barn-yard animals, baskets, whales, and sailing ships in a soft pastel palette of predominately blues and greens. Each piece is signed by hand with the first two initials and last name of artist-turned-potter Mary Alice Hadley, who has personally created each design. Some items may carry an amusing message in the bottom — for instance, 'Please Fill Me' in a canister or 'The End' in a coffee cup! Examples of this ware are beginning to turn up on the secondary market, and it's being snapped up not only by collectors who have to 'have it all' but by those who enjoy adding a decorative touch to a country-style room with only a few pieces of this unique pottery. Horses and pigs seem to be popular subject matter; unusual pieces and the older, heavier examples command the higher prices.

Advisor: Susan Fritz

Baking dish, whale & ship, 4¾x10½" **$45.00**

Cache pot, pig, 6x8" **$45.00**

Canister, 'Drippings' and scrollwork, 'Please Fill Me' in bottom, ca 1970s, 5x6½", $50.00. (Photo courtesy Susan Fritz)

Canisters, lg w/pig, med w/cow, sm w/horse, 'The End'
    inside ea, 3-pc set, from $150 to **$180.00**

Clock, duck, made from plate, 9¼" **$50.00**

Cup and saucer, pig...**$15.00**

Flower frog, quail, brown & cream, 3¾x7"..................**$40.00**

Gravy boat, cow, 3"...**$50.00**

Pitcher, cow, 2-qt, 8"..**$55.00**

Pitcher, horse, 'Whoa' in bottom, 8"...........................**$65.00**

Pitcher, snowman, w/2 mugs, Mr & Mrs Claus, 5¼", 4", set ...**$40.00**

Plate, dinner; skier, 11"..**$20.00**

Plate, farmer, 9"..**$10.00**

Plate, salad; horse, kidney shape **$30.00**

Platter, basket, oval, 9¼" **$55.00**

Platter, horse, oval, 14x9x1½"....................................**$60.00**

Syrup pitcher, w/lid...**$30.00**

Teapot, basket, 6-cup..**$45.00**

Teapot, lamb, 6-cup, 6" **$50.00**

Hall China Company

Hall China is still in production in East Liverpool, Ohio, where they have been located since around the turn of the century. They have produced literally hundreds of lines of kitchen and dinnerware items for both home and commercial use. Many of these have become very collectible.

They're especially famous for their teapots, some of which were shaped like automobiles, basketballs, doughnuts, etc. Each teapot was made in an assortment of colors, often trimmed in gold. Many were decaled to match their dinnerware lines. Some are quite rare, and collecting them all would be a real challenge.

During the 1950s, Eva Zeisel designed dinnerware shapes with a streamlined, ultra-modern look. Her lines, Classic and Century, were used with various decals as the basis for several of Hall's dinnerware patterns. She also designed kitchenware lines with the same modern styling. They were called Casual Living and Tri-Tone. All her designs are very popular with today's collectors, especially those with an interest in the movement referred to as '50s modern.

Although some of the old kitchenware shapes and teapots are being produced today, you'll be able to tell them from the old pieces by the backstamp. To identify these new issues, Hall marks them with the shaped rectangular 'Hall' trademark they've used since the early 1970s.

For more information, we recommend *The Collector's Encyclopedia of Hall China* by Margaret and Kenn Whitmyer.

Newsletter: *Hall China Collector's Club Newsletter*
P.O. Box 360488, Cleveland, OH 44136

Acacia, bowl, Radiance, 6"..**$16.00**

Acacia, custard, Radiance..**$11.00**

Acacia, jug, Radiance, #3 or #4....................................**$55.00**

Arizona, bowl, celery; Tomorrow's Classic, oval........**$15.00**

Arizona, egg cup, Tomorrow's Classic **$27.00**

Arizona, plate, Tomorrow's Classic, 8" **$4.50**

Arizona, vase, Tomorrow's Classic **$27.00**

Beauty, bowl, salad; 12"..**$40.00**

Blue Blossom, creamer, morning set...........................**$45.00**

Blue Blossom, jug, ball; #4 ....**$145.00**

Blue Blossom, shirred egg dish $65.00
Blue Blossom, teapot, New York $255.00
Blue Bouquet, bowl, cereal; D-style, 6" $13.00
Blue Bouquet, bowl, vegetable; round, D-style, 9¼" . $32.00
Blue Bouquet, gravy boat, D-style $30.00

Blue Bouquet, jug, Radiance #3, from $70.00 to $80.00. (Photo courtesy Margaret and Kenn Whitmyer)

Blue Bouquet, platter, oval, D-style, 11¼" $24.00
Blue Bouquet, saucer, D-style $2.50
Blue Bouquet, teapot, Boston, 6-cup $175.00
Blue Crocus, bowl, straight sides, 6" $18.00
Blue Crocus, bowl, Thick Rim, 8½" $27.00
Blue Floral, bowl, 6¼" $12.00
Blue Floral, casserole $30.00
Blue Garden, bowl, Thick Rim, 7½" $25.00
Blue Garden, jug, ball; #1 .... $95.00
Blue Garden, leftover, loop handle $95.00
Blue Willow, ashtray $10.00
Blue Willow, bowl, finger; 4" $27.00
Bouquet, bowl, baker; Tomorrow's Classic, open, 11-oz.. $18.00
Bouquet, bowl, cereal; Tomorrow's Classic, 6" $8.50

Bouquet, celery tray, Eva Zeisel design, 12", $18.00.

Bouquet, onion soup, Tomorrow's Classic, w/lid $35.00
Bouquet, plate, Tomorrow's Classic, 6" $3.00
Buckingham, bowl, baker; Tomorrow's Classic, open, 11-oz $16.00
Buckingham, bowl, fruit, Tomorrow's Classic, 5¾" $6.50
Buckingham, gravy boat, Tomorrow's Classic $25.00
Buckingham, plate, Tomorrow's Classic, 11" $12.00
Buckingham, vinegar bottle, Tomorrow's Classic $35.00
Cactus, coffeepot, Viking Drip-O-lator $35.00
Cactus, sugar bowl, New York, w/lid $30.00

Cameo Rose, bowl, cream soup; 5" $85.00

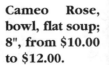

Cameo Rose, bowl, flat soup; 8", from $10.00 to $12.00.

Cameo Rose, bowl, vegetable; round, 9" $22.00
Cameo Rose, gravy boat, w/underplate $32.00
Cameo Rose, plate, 8" $8.50
Cameo Rose, platter, oval, 15½" $25.00
Cameo Rose, teapot, 8-cup $60.00
Caprice, bowl, salad; Tomorrow's Classic, lg, 14½" $21.00
Caprice, butter dish, Tomorrow's Classic $75.00
Caprice, candlestick, Tomorrow's Classic, 4½" $22.00
Caprice, platter, Tomorrow's Classic, 12¼" $18.00
Carrot/Golden Carrot, bowl, Five Band, 7¼" $22.00
Carrot/Golden Carrot, custard, #351½ $15.00
Christmas Tree & Holly, bowl, oval $30.00
Christmas Tree & Holly, coffeepot $225.00
Christmas Tree & Holly, mug, Irish coffee; 3-oz $22.00
Christmas Tree & Holly, saucer $4.00
Clover (Pink), bowl, Thick Rim, 7½" $16.00
Clover (Pink), casserole, Radiance $150.00
Clover/Golden Clover, bowl, Radiance, 10" $37.00
Clover/Golden Clover, stack set $125.00
Crocus, bowl, fruit; D-style, 5½" $7.00
Crocus, cake safe, metal $35.00
Crocus, coffeepot, Five Band $60.00
Crocus, drip jar, open, #1188 .... $40.00
Crocus, leftover, square $70.00
Crocus, plate, D-style, 6" $6.00
Crocus, saucer, D-style $2.50
Crocus, teapot, New York, 6-cup $135.00
Eggshell, baker, Plaid or Swag, fish shaped, 13½" $55.00
Eggshell, bowl, salad; Dot, 9¾" $25.00
Eggshell, cocotte, Dot, handled, 4" $18.00
Eggshell, mug, Tom & Jerry; Dot $11.00
Eggshell, mustard, Plaid or Swag $37.00
Fantasy, ashtray, Tomorrow's Classic $6.00
Fantasy, casserole, Sundial, #4 .... $37.00
Fantasy, casserole, Tomorrow's Classic, 1¼-qt $25.00
Fantasy, custard, Thick Rim $20.00
Fantasy, gravy boat, Tomorrow's Classic $25.00
Fantasy, jug, ball; #2 .... $125.00
Fantasy, saucer, Tomorrow's Classic $2.00

Fern, ashtray, Century $6.00
Fern, bowl, vegetable; divided, Century....................$20.00
Fern, ladle, Century $10.00
Five Band, bowl, batter; red or cobalt........................$55.00
Five Band, bowl, colors other than red or cobalt, 6" .$10.00
Five Band, casserole, red or cobalt, 8"....................$35.00
Five Band, syrup, red or cobalt.............................$65.00
Flamingo, casserole, Radiance $42.00
Flamingo, salt & pepper shakers, handled, pr $44.00
Flareware, bowl, Gold Lace, 6"..............................$7.00
Flareware, casserole, Heather Rose, 2-qt $27.00
Flareware, coffee urn, Radial, 15-cup $22.00
Flareware, cookie jar, Autumn Leaf........................$19.00
Floral Lattice, coffeepot, Viking Drip-O-lator $40.00
Floral Lattice, onion soup, individual....................$35.00
French Flower, creamer, Bellevue $20.00
Frost Flowers, bowl, fruit; Tomorrow's Classic, 5¾".....$5.00
Frost Flowers, coffeepot, Tomorrow's Classic, 6-cup..$90.00
Frost Flowers, jug, Tomorrow's Classic, 1¼-qt...........$28.00
Frost Flowers, salt & pepper shakers, pr $18.00
Game Bird, bowl, Thick Rim, china, 6" $14.00
Game Bird, casserole, china $30.00
Game Bird, mug, coffee; china..............................$12.00
Game Bird, plate, E-style, 6½"............................$10.00
Game Bird, sugar bowl, E-style, w/lid....................$25.00
Gold Label, jug, Rayed $14.00
Golden Glo, baking shell, 4"................................$6.00
Golden Glo, mug, #343......................................$12.00
Harlequin, bowl, cereal; Tomorrow's Classic, 6"..........$8.00
Harlequin, candlestick, Tomorrow's Classic, 8"..........$30.00
Harlequin, creamer, AD; Tomorrow's Classic $10.00
Harlequin, ladle, Tomorrow's Classic......................$13.00
Heather Rose, bowl, Flare-shape, 7¾"....................$12.00
Heather Rose, jug, Rayed....................................$14.00
Heather Rose, plate, 9¼"....................................$7.50
Heather Rose, saucer $2.00
Heather Rose, teapot, London................................$25.00
Holiday, bowl, coupe soup; Tomorrow's Classic, 9" ..$11.00
Holiday, casserole, Tomorrow's Classic, 1¼-qt $25.00
Holiday, marmite, Tomorrow's Classic, w/lid.............$27.00
Homewood, bowl, flat soup; D-style, 8½" $10.00
Homewood, bowl, Radiance, 6" $11.00
Homewood, creamer, Art Deco..............................$25.00
Homewood, sugar bowl, Art Deco..........................$30.00
Lyric/Mulberry, bowl, fruit; Tomorrow's Classic, 5¾"...$5.00
Lyric/Mulberry, egg cup, Tomorrow's Classic.............$25.00
Lyric/Mulberry, onion soup, Tomorrow's Classic, w/lid.$30.00
Lyric/Mulberry, vase, Tomorrow's Classic.................$27.00
Meadow Flower, casserole, Radiance........................$40.00
Meadow Flower, drip jar, #1188, open $35.00
Medallion, bowl, colors other than Lettuce or ivory, #6, 10" $30.00
Medallion, bowl, Lettuce, #2, 5¼"........................$10.00
Medallion, salt & pepper shakers, ivory, pr $24.00
Medallion, snack set, Lettuce $55.00
Morning Glory, bowl, straight sides, 5" $20.00
Morning Glory, bowl, Thick Rim, 8½"....................$18.00

Morning Glory, custard, straight sides, 3½"................$13.00
Mums, bowl, round, D-style, 9¼"............................$27.00
Mums, casserole, Medallion $37.00
Mums, coffeepot, Terrace....................................$70.00
Mums, custard, Radiance....................................$12.00
Mums, jug, Simplicity $140.00
Mums, platter, oval, D-style, 13¼"........................$25.00
Mums, pretzel jar $120.00
No 488, bowl, fruit; D-style, 5½"..........................$7.50
No 488, bowl, salad; 9"......................................$25.00
No 488, bowl, Thin Rim, 8½"..............................$42.00
No 488, creamer, Meltdown................................$32.00
No 488, drip jar, Medallion, w/lid $30.00
No 488, jug, Rayed $35.00
No 488, plate, D-style, 9"..................................$16.00
No 488, shirred egg dish....................................$35.00
Orange Poppy, baker, French; fluted........................$18.00
Orange Poppy, bowl, Radiance, 7½"........................$18.00
Orange Poppy, casserole, oval, 13"........................$90.00
Orange Poppy, creamer, Great American....................$18.00
Orange Poppy, cup, C-style..................................$16.00
Orange Poppy, jug, Radiance, #5............................$27.00
Orange Poppy, pie baker....................................$32.00
Orange Poppy, platter, oval, C-style, 13¼"................$30.00
Orange Poppy, salt & pepper shakers, handled, pr ...$32.00
Orange Poppy, sifter, metal..................................$45.00
Orange Poppy, spoon $70.00
Orange Poppy, teapot, Melody $260.00
Pastel Morning Glory, bean pot, New England, #4 .$110.00
Pastel Morning Glory, bowl, oval, D-style.................$25.00
Pastel Morning Glory, cup, St Denis........................$35.00
Pastel Morning Glory, pie baker............................$30.00
Pastel Morning Glory, plate, D-style, 6" $4.50
Pastel Morning Glory, platter, D-style, 13¼" $25.00
Pastel Morning Glory, tea tile $60.00
Peach Blossom, ashtray, Tomorrow's Classic $8.00
Peach Blossom, plate, Tomorrow's Classic, 6".............$5.00
Peach Blossom, saucer, Tomorrow's Classic................$2.50
Pert, bowl, Cadet, straight sides, 9"........................$14.00
Pert, casserole, Chinese Red, tab handles..................$30.00
Pert, jug, Chinese Red, 5"..................................$18.00
Pert, salt & pepper shakers, Cadet, pr $10.00
Pinecone, bowl, celery; Tomorrow's Classic, oval $17.00
Pinecone, jug, Tomorrow's Classic, 1¼-qt..................$25.00
Pinecone, plate, E-style, 6"..................................$4.00
Pinecone, saucer, Tomorrow's Classic......................$2.00
Primrose, cup, E-style..$7.50
Primrose, pie baker, E-style $22.00
Primrose, plate, E-style, 10"................................$8.00
Primrose, platter, E-style, oval, 13¼"......................$18.00
Radiance, bowl, red or cobalt, #6, 10"....................$27.00
Radiance, canister, ivory, 2-qt..............................$20.00
Radiance, casserole, colors other than red, cobalt or ivory $30.00
Radiance, stack set, red or cobalt..........................$115.00
Red Poppy, bowl, cereal; D-style, 6"......................$14.00
Red Poppy, bowl, Radiance, 9"............................$18.00

Red Poppy, coffee dispenser, metal..........................$30.00
Red Poppy, creamer, Modern $15.00
Red Poppy, cup, D-style..$13.00
Red Poppy, gravy boat, D-style.............................$30.00
Red Poppy, jug, ball; #3.......................................$60.00
Red Poppy, jug, milk/syrup; Daniel, 4" $47.00
Red Poppy, mixer cover, plastic..........................$27.00
Red Poppy, plate, D-style, 9".................................$11.00
Red Poppy, platter, D-style, 11¼"........................$22.00
Red Poppy, recipe box, metal $35.00
Red Poppy, salt & pepper shakers, Teardrop, pr........$36.00
Red Poppy, sugar bowl, Daniel, w/lid....................$25.00

Red Poppy, teapot, New York style, from $85.00 to $110.00.

Red Poppy, waste can, metal, oval, 12½"..................$40.00
Ribbed, baker, russet or red, vertical ribs, 2- or 3-qt..$16.00
Ribbed, bowl, salad; colors other than russet or red, 9"..$14.00
Ribbed, casserole, colors other than russet or red, 8"..$16.00
Ribbed, casserole, russet or red, side handle.............$50.00
Ribbed, ramekin, russet or red, scalloped, 4-oz..........$6.50
Rose Parade, baker, French; fluted..........................$32.00
Rose Parade, creamer, Pert $16.00
Rose Parade, custard, straight sides........................$15.00
Rose Parade, jug, Pert, 5"......................................$25.00
Rose White, bean pot, tab handles $70.00
Royal Rose, bowl, salad; 9"....................................$30.00
Royal Rose, casserole, Thick Rim............................$32.00
Royal Rose, teapot, French $95.00
Rx, casserole...$25.00
Rx, gravy boat, w/underplate $20.00
Sear's Arlington, bowl, cereal; E-style, 6¼" $5.50
Sear's Arlington, creamer, E-style...........................$9.00
Sear's Arlington, plate, E-style, 10".........................$6.00
Sear's Arlington, plate, E-style, 6½".........................$2.50
Sear's Fairfax, creamer..$8.00
Sear's Fairfax, saucer..$2.00
Sear's Fairfax, sugar bowl, w/lid $12.00
Sear's Monticello, bowl, cereal; E-style, 6¼" $7.00
Sear's Monticello, pickle dish, E-style, 9".................$6.00
Sear's Monticello, platter, oval, E-style, 11¼" $13.00
Sear's Mount Vernon, bowl, cereal; E-style, 6¼"........$8.00
Sear's Mount Vernon, casserole, E-style, w/lid...........$32.00

Sear's Mount Vernon, plate, E-style, 8"....................$4.00
Sear's Richmond/Brown-Eyed Susan, bowl, fruit; 5¼" .$4.50
Sear's Richmond/Brown-Eyed Susan, plate, 7¼"..........$5.00
Serenade, bowl, fruit; D-style, 5½".........................$5.50
Serenade, bowl, Radiance, 7½".............................$12.00
Serenade, bowl, salad; 9".....................................$16.00
Serenade, creamer, Art Deco $18.00
Serenade, pie baker...$27.00
Serenade, plate, D-style, 6" $4.00
Serenade, platter, D-style, 13¼"............................$22.00
Serenade, sugar bowl, Modern, w/lid......................$15.00
Shaggy Tulip, canister, Radiance $140.00
Shaggy Tulip, salt & pepper shakers, Radiance Novelty, pr..$74.00
Silhouette, bowl, cereal; D-style, 6".......................$16.00
Silhouette, bowl, flared, 3⅝".................................$12.00
Silhouette, bread box $75.00
Silhouette, casserole, Medallion............................$40.00
Silhouette, clock, electric......................................$75.00
Silhouette, creamer, Modern $15.00
Silhouette, drip jar, Medallion, w/lid......................$28.00
Silhouette, leftover, rectangular $55.00
Silhouette, match safe...$40.00
Silhouette, pitcher, crystal, Federal.......................$120.00
Silhouette, pretzel jar...$125.00
Silhouette, salt & pepper shakers, handled, pr.........$100.00
Silhouette, saucer, D-style $2.00
Silhouette, silverware box......................................$65.00
Silhouette, teapot, New York................................$250.00
Silhouette, wax paper dispenser.............................$55.00
Spring, bowl, coupe soup; Tomorrow's Classic, 9".....$10.00
Spring, candlestick, Tomorrow's Classic, 4½"............$20.00
Spring, ladle, Tomorrow's Classic...........................$12.00
Springtime, bowl, fruit; D-style, 5½".........................$5.50
Springtime, bowl, oval, D-style................................$22.00
Springtime, bowl, salad; 9" $14.00
Springtime, casserole, Thick Rim............................$27.00
Springtime, jug, Radiance, #6.................................$25.00
Springtime, plate, D-style, 8¼"................................$6.00
Springtime, sugar bowl, Modern, w/lid.....................$18.00
Stonewall, bowl, Radiance, 7½" $19.00
Stonewall, jug, Radiance, #6, w/lid $85.00
Stonewall, leftover, square.....................................$70.00
Sundial, casserole, red or cobalt, #4, 8".....................$27.00
Sundial, coffeepot, colors other than red or cobalt, individual $40.00
Sundial, creamer, red or cobalt..............................$11.00
Sunglow, bowl, fruit; Century, 5¾" $4.50
Sunglow, plate, Century, 6"....................................$3.50
Sunglow, relish, Century, 4-part $22.00
Tulip, bowl, flat soup; D-style, 8½" $18.00
Tulip, bowl, Radiance, 7½".....................................$14.00
Tulip, coffeepot, Perk..$60.00
Tulip, gravy boat, D-style.......................................$27.00
Tulip, saucer, St Denis..$9.00
Tulip, tidbit, 3-tiered, D-style..................................$55.00
Tulip, waffle iron, metal..$85.00

Wild Poppy, creamer, Hollywood $30.00
Wild Poppy, leftover, square................................$85.00
Wild Poppy, tea tile, 6" $60.00
Wildfire, bowl, fruit; D-style, 5½" $6.00
Wildfire, bowl, straight sides.............................$22.00
Wildfire, coffee dispenser, metal.........................$22.00
Wildfire, coffeepot, S-lid................................$55.00
Wildfire, plate, D-style, 6" $4.00
Wildfire, salt & pepper shakers, Teardrop, pr...........$28.00
Yellow Rose, bowl, flat soup; D-style, 8½" $15.00
Yellow Rose, bowl, Radiance, 6" $12.00
Yellow Rose, coffeepot, Dome $35.00
Yellow Rose, onion soup $32.00
Yellow Rose, plate, D-style, 8¼" $7.00
Yellow Rose, saucer, D-style $2.00
Yellow Rose, sugar bowl, Norse, w/lid....................$25.00

Airflow, cobalt and gold 'special,' from $45.00 to $55.00.

Teapots

Aladdin, green w/gold, 6-cup...............................$85.00
Albany, turquoise w/gold, 6-cup...........................$45.00
Basketball, maroon, 6-cup $625.00
Bellvue, Stock Brown or Stock Green, 4-cup.............$15.00
Donut, colors other than red or cobalt..................$295.00
French Flower, French....................................$45.00
Game Bird, Grape, Thorley, china $140.00
Game Bird, Windshield, china............................$165.00
Gold Label, Aladdin, Swag................................$95.00
Medallion, Lettuce, 64-oz $90.00
Moderne, Marine Blue w/gold, 6-cup $45.00
Mums, New York $150.00
Nautilus, pink, 6-cup....................................$250.00
Parade, yellow w/gold, 6-cup.............................$45.00
Pert, Chinese Red, 6-cup.................................$40.00
Radiance, ivory, 6-cup...................................$65.00
Sani-Grid, Canary, 6-cup.................................$45.00
Spring, Tomorrow's Classic, 6-cup $80.00
Surfside, Canary w/gold, 6-cup $100.00
Windshield, turquoise w/gold, 6-cup......................$65.00

Hallmark

Since the early 1970s when Hallmark first introduced their glass ball and yarn doll ornaments, many lines and themes have been developed to the delight of collectors. Many early ornaments are now valued at several times their original price. This is especially true of the first one issued in a particular series. For instance, Betsy Clark's first edition issued in 1973 has a value today of $125.00 (MIB).

If you'd like to learn more about them, we recommend *The Secondary Price Guide to Hallmark Ornaments* by Rosie Wells.

Our values are for ornaments that are mint and in their original boxes.

Advisor: The Baggage Car (See Directory, Hallmark)

Newsletter: The Baggage Car
3100 Justin Dr., Ste. B
Des Moines, IA 50322; 515-270-9080 or fax 515-223-1398
Includes show and company information along with current listing

Acorn Wreath, QXM5686, miniature, 1990..................$12.00
Baby's First Christmas, QXM514-5, miniature 1993.....$12.00
Barbie, Enchanted Evening, QX16541, 1996...............$30.00
Batman, QX5853, 1994....................................$30.00
Batmobile, QX5739, 1995.................................$30.00
Beauty of Friendship, QX303-4, 1980 ....$65.00
Betsy Clark, Home for Christmas, QX2776, 1986.......$35.00

Betsy Clark Series, 3¼" ball, 1978, MIB, from $50.00 to $60.00.

Bringing Home the Tree, QLX7249, 1991 ....$60.00
Brother, QX554-2, 1993...................................$15.00
Bugs Bunny, QX5019, 1995 ....$20.00
Cherry Jubilee, QX4532, 1989 ....$20.00
Christmas Crocodile, QX4373, 1989 ....$25.00
Circling the Globe, QLX7124, 1988 ....$45.00
Colors of Christmas, Star of Bethleham, QX352-7, 1979.$85.00
Cookie Mouse, QX454-6, 1982 ....$60.00
Country Showtime, QLX7416, 1994 ....$45.00
Doggy in Stocking, QX474-2, 1985 ....$40.00
Elf Marionette, QX593-1, 1992 ....$25.00

Elves, XHD 103-5, 1973.....................................**$99.00**
Fifty Years Together, QX443-7, 1987 ....**$25.00**
Fishing Party, Walrus, QK1037, Showcase, 1995.........**$32.00**
Friends of Joy, QXM5764, acrylic, miniature, 1988 .....**$10.00**
Godchild, QX587-5, 1993 ....**$23.00**
Granddaughter, QX243-1, 1984.............................**$30.00**
Grandmother, QX267-6, 1978 ....**$50.00**
Here Comes Santa, Santa's Express, QX143-4, 1980.**$275.00**
Holiday Heirloom, QX485-7, 1st edition, 1987............**$25.00**
Holiday Wildlife, Cardinals, QX313-3, 1st edition, 1982..**$375.00**
Jingle Bell Band, QX5783, 1994................................**$30.00**

Keepsake Miniature, The Kringles, 1989, first edition, MIB, $35.00.

Kringle Moon, QX4951, 1988.................................**$35.00**
Noah's Ark, QX4867, 1991 ....**$50.00**
Norman Rockwell, QX111-1, Santa on ea side, 1974....**$95.00**
Nostalgia, Rocking Horse, QX128-1, 1975 ....**$175.00**
Old-Fashioned Christmas, QX217-9, 1983....................**$35.00**
Peppermint Mouse, QX401-5, 1981 ....**$37.50**
Shutterbug, Ladybug w/Camera, QXM4212, miniature, 1997 ....**$14.00**
Snoopy, QLX7277, 1995 ....**$50.00**
Snoopy & Friends Panorama Ball, QX154-1, 2nd edition, 1980 ....**$175.00**
Statue of Liberty, QX3843, acrylic, dated 1986............**$26.00**
Swan, QX4642, 1989...**$20.00**
Twirl-About, QX193-5, Della Robia Wreath, 1977.....**$135.00**
Winnie the Pooh, Kanga & Roo, QX5617, 1991..........**$50.00**
Wizard of Oz, Emerald City, QLX7475, 1996...............**$65.00**

Halloween

Halloween is now the second biggest money-making holiday of the year, and more candy is sold at this time than for any other holiday. Folk artists are making new items to satisfy the demands of collectors and celebrators that can't get enough of the old items. Over one hundred years of celebrating this magical holiday has built a social history strata by strata, and wonderful and exciting finds can be made in all periods! From one dollar to thousands, there is something to excite collectors in every price range, with new col-

lectibles being born every year. For further information we recommend *Collectible Halloween, More Halloween Collectibles* (a third volume is available as well), *Salem Witchcraft and Souvenirs,* and *Anthropomorphic Beings of Halloween* (all published by Schiffer); also see *Around Swanzey* (Arcadia). The author of these books is Pamela E. Apkarian-Russell (Halloween Queen), a freelancer who also writes an ephemera column for *Unravel the Gavel.*

Note: The letters JOL in our listings is an abbreviation used for jack-o'-lantern.

Advisor: Pamela E. Apkarian-Russell (See Directory, Halloween)

Newsletter: *Trick or Treat Trader*
P.O. Box 499, Winchester, NH 03470; 603-239-8875
e-mail: halloweenqueen@cheshire.net
Subscription: $15 per year for 4 quarterly issues

Bank, haunted house w/Bugs, Sylvester, etc, hard plastic, Russell Stover **$12.00**
Bank, skull, PVC, from Disney movie 'Hook' **$12.00**
Bank, Snoopy on JOL, hard plastic, Whitman's Candy..**$15.00**
Bean bag Santa, Nightmare Before Christmas **$55.00**
Book, Bogie, Dennison, 1922, some staining, fair to good...**$85.00**
Book, Creepy Halloween Celebrations, Paine Publishing Co, 1926, 151 pages **$65.00**
Book, Goosebumps, Abominable Snowman of Pasadena..**$4.00**
Book, Goosebumps, Monster Blood II.........................**$4.00**
Book, Goosebumps, Piano Lessons Can Be Murder.....**$4.00**
Book, Goosebumps, Return of the Mummy....................**$4.00**
Book, Holidays Remembered, Leisure Arts Inc, ca 1994, 96 pages...**$20.00**
Book, Realness of Witchcraft, Monroe Aurand Jr, pre-zip code, 32 pages **$20.00**
Candle, haunted house, hollow, Capri Candle Co, 6" ..**$25.00**
Candle holder, witch face, blown glass, 4¾" **$250.00**
Candy container, black cat w/wiggly eyes, composition ..**$500.00**
Candy container, JOL, glass, 4".................................**$95.00**
Candy container, JOL fishermen (1 lg & 1 sm) atop, composition **$300.00**
Candy container, JOL on stick, paper & cardboard **$20.00**
Candy container, plum face w/hat, paperboard w/wooden horn nose **$450.00**
Candy container, 2 nodders (skeleton & goblin veggie being) sitting on log, composition, 3½" **$500.00**
Cards, fortune telling; Gypsy Witch, in box **$4.00**
Clock, elf on JOL face, Beistle, 12" **$95.00**
Coffeepot, JOL man, china, Made in Germany, miniature...**$350.00**
Coin-op fortune-telling machine, The Wizard, painted aluminum **$3,500.00**
Cup & saucer, expresso (or cocoa); for NY restaurant, Bavaria, 1932..**$45.00**
Decoration, JOL face, cardboard, Beistle **$8.00**
Decoration, witch flying on broom, diecut, German, lg.**$125.00**

Figure, boy dressed in orange carrying JOL, on wheels, plastic, Rosen, RI $150.00

Figure, dancing Charlie Brown in vampire costume ..$25.00

Figure, dancing Lucy in witch costume $25.00

Figure, dancing Snoopy w/light-up crystal ball..........$25.00

Figure, girl dressed in orange & black carrying JOL, on wheels, plastic, Rosen $150.00

Figure, owl, solid orange, celluloid, reproduction $5.00

Figure, owl on tree stump, squirrel inside, celluloid ..$150.00

Figure, pirate w/corn body & JOL head, celluloid ...$200.00

Figure, Snoopy as vampire w/gravestone, sunglasses, yellow fangs & cape, plastic, Russell Stover $8.00

Figure, Snoopy in JOL costume carrying flashlight & yellow 'trick or treat' sack, sunglasses, plastic, Russel Stover $8.00

Figure, Snoopy w/green mummy wrapping says 'boo' & carries orange 'trick or treat' case, plastic, Russell Stover $8.00

Figure, witch driving auto w/cat on running board, celluloid, Viscoloid Co...$350.00

Figure, witch in rocket, black w/orange wheels, hard plastic, 5½" L $275.00

Figure, witch on rocket, orange w/black wheels, hard plastic, 5¾" L $300.00

Figure, witch pulling cart w/ghost passenger, celluloid, Viscoloid Co...$250.00

Folk art, Corn Goddess, papier-mache, by Virginia Betourne $125.00

Folk art, Halloween box totem, hand-carved papier-mache, 7-pc, by Rick Conant...$400.00

Folk art, lamp shade w/fortune-telling motif, hand painted by Rebecca Venable...$400.00

Folk art, pomegranite man w/JOL head & cat lantern, by Virginia Betourne...$90.00

Forks, knives & spoons, orange & black PVC, contemporary, unopened bag $3.00

Game, Ask Zandar, Milton Bradley, 1992 ....$30.00

Game, fortune telling; Black Cat, Parker Bros, 1897...$80.00

Game, fortune telling; Finger of Fate, Colorforms, 1971.$45.00

Game, fortune telling; Marja Fortune Teller, 1930.......$45.00

Game, Ouija board, Fuld, 1919.....................................$20.00

Game, punchboard; Coo Coo Fortune Teller, 1925 ....$15.00

Greeting card, scarecrow sitting, leaning on JOL, w/cat on his knees, Rustcraft #5953, 1940s....................................$8.00

Hat, moon face & JOL on black side, cat & JOL on orange side, felt $25.00

Horn, cardboard w/Halloween designs.......................$20.00

Horn, cardboard w/wood JOL head.............................$55.00

Horn, cardboard w/wood mouthpiece & handle that is attached to rachet mechanism inside, Marks Bros, 1931, both pcs $25.00

Horn, cardboard w/wood tip inserted through wood-rimmed paper-faced drum, German......................................$75.00

Horn, devil w/horns, composition w/wood mouthpiece, German..$300.00

Horn, paper coil blows out, lg, w/cat face & sm blower .$12.00

Horn, paper coil blows out, wood mouthpiece, sm.....$4.00

House, A&W, Nightmare Before Christmas, cardboard, NBC...$600.00

Lantern, cat JOL, cardboard, double-sided: 1 mean & 1 sweet face (beware of reproduction)............................$125.00

Lantern, full-body cat, pulp $200.00

Lantern, watermelon w/glass nose, 3½"...................$450.00

Magazine, Halloween Frolics, contains music............$45.00

Magazine, Ladies' Home Journal, Oct 1919, article: New Halloween Frolics..... & illustrations on page 63....$9.00

Mask, Bat Man, rubber, over-the-head type $45.00

Mask, gauze, multicolored, ca 1940-50 ....$3.00

Mask (Max Headroom, Kreschev, Jimmy Carter, Nixon, Reagan, witch, etc), plastic, ea $12.00

Mug, Relax I'm Just Here for the Cake, Happy Birthday, Grim Reaper holding a cupcake.......................................$5.00

Neckties, mini set of 3, ea 4½" L, 1 red w/black cat, 1 navy blue w/JOL, & 1 white w/witch on broom $50.00

Neon sign, jack-o'-lantern, $400.00. (Photo courtesy Pamela Apkarian-Russell)

Noise maker, cardboard w/paper inserts & metal strikers, German $12.00

Noise maker, paper label over wood w/metal ratchet workings, Safe Toy No 20, Made in USA, 1918 ....$35.00

Noise maker, quadruple ratchet, wood w/cardboard JOL face, German..$85.00

Noise maker, single ratchet, wood w/composition skeleton head, hinged jar...$75.00

Noise maker, single ratchet (wood body), composition JOL head, early...$125.00

Noise maker, tin clicker, owl & cats in tree under moon face $20.00

Noise maker, triple ratchet, wood & cardboard, witch, German $85.00

Noise maker, triple ratchet, wood w/composition cat & JOL man rider (w/crepe-covered body)....................$175.00

Party plates, cats, JOL & fence, Reed's, 8", unopened pack..$25.00

Pitcher, Grandpa Munster, Fitz & Floyd, +4 mugs $400.00

Place card, 3 JOLs & 3 black cats................................$8.00

Poster, Unicef, w/Mighty Mouse.............................$250.00

Puzzle, black cat dressed in orange clothes, diecut, USA, 1926 ....$45.00

Rattle, double-faced; celluloid Viscaloid bean & JOL, 4½" $200.00

Rattle, plastic witch on wood stick, pebbles inside produce noise **$95.00**

Rattle, skeleton, cardboard, Merri-Lee **$25.00**

Rattle, wood w/paper cat face, crepe ruffle on top simulates fan effect.................................**$95.00**

Rattle, wood w/paper JOL face, sm pebbles inside produce noise, German...........................**$75.00**

Skeleton, papier-mache in wood coffin, life-size......**$600.00**

Soda mug, Nightmare Before Christmas, PVC, from theatre.................................**$45.00**

Sunglasses, Nightmare Before Christmas **$20.00**

Tambourine, paper w/wood frame, cat, Japan **$100.00**

Toy, coffin (Daffy Duck-Enstein, Bugs Mummy or Count Taz), hard plastic, plays theme from Hitchcock, Russell Stover, ea **$12.00**

Voodoo table, table tapping & tilting game, wood & cardboard, 1939.................................**$75.00**

Poster, Unicef, $125.00. (Photo courtesy Pamela Apkarian-Russell)

Harker Pottery

Harker was one of the oldest potteries in the country. Their history can be traced back to the 1840s. In the '30s, a new plant was built in Chester, West Virginia, and the company began manufacturing kitchen and dinnerware lines, eventually employing as many as three hundred workers.

Several of these lines are popular with collectors today. One of the most easily recognized is Cameoware. It is usually found in pink or blue decorated with white silhouettes of flowers, though other designs were made as well. Colonial Lady, Red Apple, Amy, Mallow, and Pansy are some of their better-known lines that are fairly easy to find and reassemble into sets.

If you'd like to learn more about Harker, we recommend *The Collector's Encyclopedia of American Dinnerware* by Jo Cunningham, and *The Collector's Guide to Harker Pottery* by Neva Colbert, both published by Collector Books.

Amy, creamer.................................**$10.00**
Amy, platter, meat.................................**$30.00**

Amy, scoop **$50.00**
Amy, sugar bowl.................................**$10.00**
Amy, 3-bowl stack set, w/lid **$42.00**
Autumn Leaf, plate, 9" **$9.00**
Becky, bowl, utility.................................**$25.00**
Birds & Flowers, plate, utility; 12".................................**$25.00**
Blue Blossoms, pitcher, Regal.................................**$25.00**
Boyce, pitcher, Regal, w/gold trim handle **$45.00**
Cameo Rose, platter, meat **$25.00**
Cameo Rose, salad spoon, yellow.................................**$30.00**
Cameo Shellware, cup & saucer.................................**$14.00**

Cameo Shellware, plate, 9½", $14.00.

Cherry, salt & pepper shakers, utility; pr....................**$20.00**
Cherry Trim, plate, w/cup indent **$3.00**
Colonial Lady, baker/casserole, individual **$6.00**
Colonial Lady, cookie jar, w/lid.................................**$42.00**
Colonial Lady, pitcher, syrup **$25.00**
Colonial Lady, salt & pepper shakers, table size, ea ..**$14.00**
Cottage, plate, 8¼".................................**$8.00**
Countryside, server.................................**$25.00**
Deco-Dahlia, ashtray **$12.00**
Deco-Dahlia, plate, utility; 12".................................**$25.00**

Deco Dahlia, six custard cups in wireware holder, cups: $6.00 each; holder: $8.00.

Enchantment, creamer.................................**$10.00**
English Countryside, custard, individual **$6.00**
Heritage, sugar bowl, w/lid **$12.00**
Ivy Vine, plate, 8" **$6.00**

Ivy Vine, saucer $10.00
Leaf, bowl, Swirl $5.00
Leaf, coffee server, Swirl $37.00
Old Vintage, bowl, flat soup; Royal Gadroon, 8"........$10.00
Old Vintage, creamer, Royal Gadroon $10.00
Old Vintage, platter, Royal Gadroon, 13½" $20.00
Old Vintage, sugar bowl, Royal Gadroon, w/lid.........$14.00
Pastel Tulip, bowl, utility; 10"...................................$35.00
Pastel Tulip, plate, cake; 11".....................................$27.00
Patè sur Patè, saucer...$3.00
Petit Point Rose I, cake server....................................$27.00
Petit Point Rose I or II, rolling pin...........................$130.00
Petit Point Rose II, cake server...................................$27.00
Poppy, bowl, florist $50.00
Red Apple II, plate, hot...$35.00
Red Apple II, sugar bowl, w/lid..................................$15.00
Rose Spray, bowl, tab handled....................................$10.00
Rose Spray, cup & saucer..$14.00
Rose Spray, plate, dinner; 10".....................................$12.00
Royal Rose, cake server $25.00
Ruffled Tulip, pitcher, Arches, w/lid $35.00
Shellridge, sugar bowl, w/lid......................................$12.00
White Rose, pepper shaker..$14.00

Hartland Plastics, Inc.

The Hartland company was located in Hartland, Wisconsin, where during the '50s and '60s they made several lines of plastic figures: Western and Historic Horsemen, Miniature Western Series, and the Hartland Sport Series of Famous Baseball Stars. Football and bowling figures and religious statues were made as well. The plastic, virgin acetate, was very durable and the figures were hand painted with careful attention to detail. They're often marked.

Though prices have come down from their high of a few years ago, rare figures and horses are still in high demand. Dealers using this guide should take these factors into consideration when pricing their items: values listed here are for the figure, horse (unless noted gunfighter), hat, guns, and all other accessories for that particular figure in near-mint condition with no rubs and all original parts. All parts were made exclusively for a special figure, so a hat is not just a hat — each one belongs to a specific figure! Many people do not realize this, and it is important for the collector to be knowledgeable. An excellent source of information is *Hartland Horses and Riders* by Gail Fitch. In our listings for sports figures, mint to near-mint condition values are for figures that are white or near-white in color; excellent values are for those that are off-white or cream-colored.

See also *Schroeder's Collectible Toys, Antique to Modern* (Collector Books).

Advisor: James Watson, Sports Figures (See Directory, Hartland); Judy and Kerry Irvin, Western Figures (See Directory, Hartland)

Sports Figures

Babe Ruth, NM/M, from $175 to $200.00
Dick Groat, EX, from $800 to................................$1,000.00
Dick Groat, NM/M, from $1,200 to.......................$1,500.00
Don Drysdale, EX, from $275 to $300.00
Don Drysdale, NM/M, from $325 to $400.00
Duke Snider, EX, from $300 to $325.00
Duke Snider, M, from $500 to $600.00
Eddie Mathews, NM/M, from $125 to $150.00
Ernie Banks, EX, from $200 to $225.00
Ernie Banks, NM/M, from $250 to $350.00
Harmon Killebrew, NM/M, from $400 to..................$500.00
Henry Aaron, EX, from $150 to $175.00
Henry Aaron, NM/M, from $200 to $250.00
Little Leaguer, 6", EX, from $100 to $125.00
Little Leaguer, 6", NM/M, from $200 to $250.00
Louie Aparacio, EX, from $200 to $225.00
Louie Aparacio, NM/M, from $250 to $350.00
Mickey Mantle, NM/M, from $250 to $350.00
Minor Leaguer, 4", EX, from $50 to...........................$75.00
Minor Leaguer, 4", NM/M, from $100 to $125.00
Nellie Fox, NM/M, from $200 to $250.00
Rocky Colavito, NM/M, from $600 to $700.00
Roger Maris, EX, from $300 to $350.00
Roger Maris, NM/M, from $350 to...........................$400.00
Stan Musial, EX, from $150 to $175.00
Stan Musial, NM/M, from $200 to............................$250.00
Ted Williams, NM/M, from $225 to.........................$300.00
Warren Spahn, NM/M, from $150 to $175.00
Willie Mays, EX, from $150 to $200.00
Willie Mays, NM/M, from $225 to $250.00
Yogi Berra, w/mask, EX, from $150 to $175.00
Yogi Berra, w/mask, NM/M, from $175 to $250.00
Yogi Berra, w/out mask, NM/M, from $150 to.........$175.00

Horsemen and Gunfighters

Paladin, NMIB, $350.00. (Photo courtesy Kerry and Judy's Toys)

Alkine Ike, NM...$150.00
Bill Longley, NM..$600.00

Brave Eagle, NMIB $300.00
Bret Maverick, standing gunfighter, NM $150.00
Bret Maverick, w/gray horse, rare, NM....................$700.00
Cheyenne, miniature series, NM............................$75.00
Chief Thunderbird, rare shield, NM $150.00
Chris Colt, standing gunfighter, NM $150.00
Dale Evans, blue version, rare, NM........................$400.00
Dale Evans, purple version, NM............................$300.00
General Custer, NMIB...$200.00
General Custer, reproduction flag, NM $150.00
General George Washington, NMIB.........................$175.00
General Robert E Lee, NMIB $175.00
Jim Bowie, w/tag, NM...$250.00
Lone Ranger, rearing, NMIB.................................$300.00
Matt Dillon, w/tag, NMIB....................................$275.00
Rebel, miniature series, reproduction hat, NM..........$100.00
Rifleman, NMIB..$350.00
Ronald MacKenzie, NM.....................................$1,200.00
Roy Rogers, semi-rearing, rare, NMIB.....................$350.00
Roy Rogers, walking, NMIB..................................$250.00
Seth Adams, NM $275.00
Sgt Lance O'Rourke, NMIB $250.00
Sgt Preston, reproduction flag, NM $750.00
Tonto, miniature series, NM.................................$75.00
Warpaint Thunderbird, w/shield, NMIB....................$350.00
Wyatt Earp, standing gunfighter, NM $200.00

Head Vases

These are fun to collect, and prices are still reasonable. You've seen them at flea markets — heads of ladies, children, clowns, even some men and a religious figure now and then. A few look very much like famous people — there's a Jackie Onassis vase by Inarco that leaves no doubt as to who it's supposed to represent!

They were mainly imported from Japan, although a few were made by American companies and sold to florist shops to be filled with flower arrangements. So if there's an old flower shop in your neighborhood, you might start your search with their storerooms.

If you'd like to learn more about them, we recommend *Head Vases, Identification and Values*, by Kathleen Cole (Collector Books).

Newsletter: *Head Hunters Newsletter*
Maddy Gordon
P.O. Box 83H, Scarsdale, NY 10583, 914-472-0200
Subscription: $24 per year for 4 issues; also holds convention

Baby, Enesco, #E0491, hooded head turned w/eyes open, pink chubby cheeks, 5"....................................$40.00
Baby, Enesco, #2185, w/telephone, ruffled bonnet, pearl necklace, 5" $45.00
Baby, Relpo, #2010, looking straight, blond, blue & white cap w/bill, blue bodice w/white collar, 7" $70.00
Baby, Relpo, #2013, blond hair, pink & white scalloped bonnet, pink bodice w/white scalloped collar, 6"......$50.00

Baby, unmarked, #TP-2118, looking up, fat cheeks, blond ponytails w/pink bows, pink & white bodice, 6".$50.00
Boy fireman, Inarco (paper label), holding hose nozzle, looking up, red & black, 5" $75.00
Boy Indian, Inarco, #E3155, chief's headdress, eyes closed, blond hair, 5½" $40.00
Boy soldier, Inarco, #E3250, eyes closed, black hat & shoulders, red & white trim, 6" $50.00
Christmas girl, Inarco, #E1274, white hooded cape w/red flower, brown hair, 3¾" $45.00
Christmas girl, Napco, #CX2348B, holding present to cheek, eyes looking up, mouth open, red & white, black trim, 5½"...$75.00
Clown, Napcoware, #1988, bald top w/light brown side hair, blue-shadow eyes looking up, green neck bow w/white dots, 5"..$45.00
Clown, unmarked, #7576, yellow hair, mouth & ruffled collar, black smiley eyes, white top hat w/black band, 7"...$48.00
Clown, unmarked, tall red cone hat w/white ball tassel, white face black & red details, red & white ruffled collar, 7"..$40.00
Colonial lady, Relpo, #K1335, white banana curls, open eyes, double row of ruffles & bow on bodice, 8" $350.00
Geisha girl, unmarked, #3237, black hair w/white headband, light blue top w/stand-up collar, gold trim, 7½"..$85.00
Girl, Inarco, #E2965, blond pigtails, eyes glancing up, yellow headscarf & bodice, gold trim, 7"..........................$58.00
Girl, Inarco, #E2520, auburn hair, eyes open, yellow hat & bodice, green trim, 6½".................................$50.00
Girl, Japan, holding gift, looking up, blond, pink speckled hat & bodice w/white flowers & collar, gold trim, 5½".$50.00
Girl, Japan, ponytail (w/bow) draped over shoulder, heavy dark shadow on eyelids (open), pearl earring, 7" $175.00
Girl, Nancy Pew, #2262, long hair, yellow mod hat w/bow above bill, yellow bodice w/neck scarf, pearl earrings, 5½"..$75.00
Girl, Reliable Glassware, #K679C, waving, eyes glancing sideways, blond pigtails, green hat & bodice, 6".$45.00
Girl, unmarked, winking, blond w/blue daisy hat, white neck w w/blue dots, 5" $45.00
Girl, unmarked, winking, holding plumed fan, blond, black hat w/white plumes, yellow earrings, 6" $75.00
Girl graduate, unmarked, #609, eyes glancing sideways, open mouth, blond hair w/side bow, white & pink trim, 5¼"..$40.00
Lady, Inarco, #E1066, blond, black hat w/white band, black bodice w/pink rose on white bow, gold trim, earrings, 4½"..$65.00
Lady, Inarco, #E190/M, hand to chin, blond upswept hair, black hat w/gold-trimmed white bow, black bodice, pearls, 5"..$50.00
Lady, Inarco, #E2966, brown frosted upswept hair, black scalloped bodice, 4-strand pearl necklace & earrings, 11"..$450.00
Lady, Japan (paper label), hand at temple, upswept hair, black hat & bodice w/gold trim, pearl jewelry, 5½"........$35.00

Lady, Napcoware, #C569, hand (w/black sleeve) to face, blond upswept hair, black flat hat w/row of cut-out circles, 5" **$50.00**

Lady, Orion (paper label), head tilted up, eyes closed, hat w/front rim, white collar w/gold trim, earrings, 6½" .**$45.00**

Lady, Parma, #A219, frosted hair w/side flip, eyes open, green bodice w/bows at shoulders, pearl necklace, 8½"...**$300.00**

Lady, Rubens, #497M, blond w/gold-trimmed rose in hair, white leaf bodice w/gold & pearl trim, pearl necklace, 6½"...**$60.00**

Lady, Rubens, #499B, blond upswept hair w/ponytail, straw hat & bodice w/blue flowers trimmed w/gold & pearls, 6"..**$70.00**

Lady, unmarked, #A602, blond, black hat w/white flowers, black bodice w/white stand-up collar, gold-painted jewelry, 7" **$100.00**

Lady, unmarked, head bowed, yellow hair, white skin, black flat hat & white scalloped open-front bodice, glossy, 6"...**$45.00**

Lady, unmarked, head turned, brown flip, lg pink bow on top of head, pink bodice, pearl necklace & earrings, 7½"..**$300.00**

Lady, unmarked, praying hands, light brown hair, green & white hooded cape w/pink floral design, gold trim, 6" **$45.00**

Lady, VCAGO, blond upswept hair, pink & white flat hat, pink bodice w/white stand-up collar, earrings, 5¼" **$45.00**

Madonna & child, unmarked, blue & white w/gold trim, baby w/red hair, both w/rosy cheeks, 6" **$38.00**

Majorette, unmarked, blond w/eyes open & wide open-mouth smile, pink & white w/gold trim, rare, 6".............**$150.00**

Nun, Napco (paper label), praying hands, black & white, 5½"..**$28.00**

Teenage girl, Inarco, #E2967, blond flip, eyes open, blue head band & bodice, 5½" **$65.00**

Teenage girl, Napcoware, #C8493, long hair, eyes open, yellow head band w/bow, yellow bodice w/white collar, 5½"..**$65.00**

Teenage girl, unmarked, blond pig tails, eyes open, sunglasses on top of head, pink lips, 7½" **$350.00**

Inarco, #E3143, 7½" and United Import (on paper label), 7½", $250.00 each. (Photo courtesy Kathleen Cole)

Heisey Glass

From just before the turn of the century until 1957, the Heisey Glass Company of Newark, Ohio, was one of the largest, most successful manufacturers of quality tableware in the world. Though the market is well established, many pieces are still reasonably priced; and if you're drawn to the lovely patterns and colors that Heisey made, you're investment should be sound.

After 1901 much of their glassware was marked with their familiar trademark, the 'Diamond H' (an H in a diamond) or a paper label. Blown pieces are often marked on the stem instead of the bowl or foot.

Numbers in the listings are catalog reference numbers assigned by the company to indicate variations in shape or stem style. Collectors use them, especially when they buy and sell by mail, for the same purpose. Many catalog pages (showing these numbers) are contained in *The Collector's Encyclopedia of Heisey Glass* by Neila Bredehoft. This book and *Elegant Glassware of the Depression Era* by Gene Florence are both excellent references for further study. If you're especially interested in the many varieties of glass animals Heisey produced, you'll want to get *Glass Animals and Flower Frogs of the Depression Era* by Lee Garmon and Dick Spencer. All are published by Collector Books.

Newsletter: *The Heisey News*
Heisey Collectors of America
169 W Church St., Newark, OH 43055; 612-345-2932

Cabochon, crystal, bowl, cereal; #1951, 7" **$6.00**
Cabochon, crystal, tumbler, pressed, #1951, 12-oz **$12.50**
Charter Oak, crystal, bowl, finger; #3362 ....**$10.00**

Charter Oak, crystal, goblet, high foot, #3362, 8-ounce, $35.00. (Photo courtesy Gene Florence)

Charter Oak, green, plate, luncheon/salad; Acorn & Leaves, #1246, 7" **$17.50**
Charter Oak, Hawthorne, stem, oyster cocktail; low foot, #3362, 3½-oz..**$40.00**
Charter Oak, Marigold, tumbler, flat, #3362, 10-oz **$30.00**
Charter Oak, pink, plate, salad; Acorn & Leaves, #1246..**$10.00**

Chintz, crystal, bowl, jelly; footed, 2-handled, 6".........**$17.00**
Chintz, crystal, saucer...**$3.00**
Chintz, yellow, plate, bread & butter; square, 6"........**$15.00**
Chintz, yellow, tumbler, juice; footed, #3389, 5-oz.....**$22.00**
Crystolite, crystal, bonbon, shell shape, 7"..................**$22.00**
Crystolite, crystal, candle block, 1-light, square **$20.00**
Crystolite, crystal, mayonnaise ladle............................**$12.00**
Crystolite, crystal, salt & pepper shakers, pr **$45.00**
Crystolite, crystal, urn, flower; 7" **$75.00**
Empress, cobalt, plate, 8"..**$70.00**
Empress, green, creamer, dolphin foot.....................**$45.00**
Empress, green, plate, square, 7".................................**$17.00**
Empress, orchid, plate, sandwich; 2-handled, 12" **$180.00**
Empress, pink, bowl, nappy; 4½" **$25.00**
Empress, pink, tray, celery; 13" **$30.00**

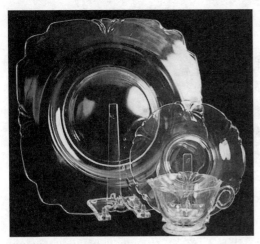

Empress, Sahara, dinner plate, square, 10", $100.00; cup, $30.00, saucer, $10.00.

Empress, yellow, bowl, floral; rolled edge, 9".............**$42.00**
Greek Key, crystal, bowl, nappy; shallow, 6" **$30.00**
Greek Key, crystal, cup, punch; 4½-oz **$20.00**
Greek Key, crystal, plate, 8"..**$70.00**
Greek Key, crystal, tumbler, water; 5½-oz **$50.00**
Greek Key, crystal, water bottle **$210.00**
Ipswich, crystal, creamer...**$35.00**
Ipswich, green, tumbler, soda; footed, 12-oz **$95.00**
Ipswich, pink, plate, square, 7".....................................**$60.00**
Ipswich, yellow, sherbet, footed, knob in stem, 4-oz...**$30.00**
Lariat, crystal, bowl, nut; individual, 4".......................**$32.00**
Lariat, crystal, candlestick, individual, 1-light **$30.00**
Lariat, crystal, plate, finger bowl liner; 6" **$8.00**
Lariat, crystal, stem, wine; blown, 2½-oz **$25.00**
Lariat, crystal, tumbler, juice; footed, 5-oz.................**$22.00**
Lodestar, Dawn, bowl, mayonnaise; 5".........................**$85.00**
Lodestar, Dawn, relish, 3-part, 7½" **$60.00**
Minuet, crystal, bowl, pickle & olive; 13"....................**$45.00**
Minuet, crystal, bowl, salad dressing; 6½"...................**$35.00**
Minuet, crystal, comport, #5010, 5½".........................**$40.00**
Minuet, crystal, plate, torte; Toujours, #1511, 14" **$60.00**
Minuet, crystal, tumbler, water; low foot, #5010, 9-oz..**$35.00**
New Era, crystal, pilsner, 8-oz **$25.00**

New Era, crystal, tumbler, soda; footed, 5-oz............**$15.00**
Octagon, crystal, bowl, nut; 2-handled, individual **$10.00**
Octagon, green, plate, cream soup liner.......................**$9.00**
Octagon, orchid, saucer, after dinner......................**$12.00**
Octagon, pink, bowl, flat soup; 9"...............................**$15.00**
Octagon, yellow, creamer, hotel................................**$30.00**
Old Colony, yellow, bowl, 3-handled, 9" **$90.00**
Old Colony, yellow, grapefruit, 6"...............................**$30.00**
Old Colony, yellow, plate, round, 7" **$20.00**
Old Colony, yellow, stem, wine; #3380, 2½-oz **$35.00**
Old Colony, yellow, tray, celery; 10" **$30.00**
Old Colony, yellow, tumbler, tea; footed, #3380, 12-oz .**$22.00**
Old Sandwich, crystal, bowl, floral; footed, oval, 12".**$35.00**
Old Sandwich, green, tumbler, 10-oz...........................**$45.00**

Old Sandwich, Moongleam (green), popcorn bowl, $125.00; pitcher, $185.00. (Photo courtesy Gene Florence)

Old Sandwich, pink, sundae, 6-oz **$30.00**
Old Sandwich, yellow, pilsner, 10-oz...........................**$37.00**
Orchid, crystal, bowl, crimped, 10"..............................**$72.50**
Orchid, crystal, bowl, nappy; Queen Ann, 4½".........**$37.50**
Orchid, crystal, candlestick, Trident, 2-light, 5"...........**$55.00**
Orchid, crystal, creamer, footed...................................**$35.00**
Orchid, crystal, plate, salad; 7".....................................**$22.00**
Orchid, crystal, plate, sandwich; Waverly, 15" **$75.00**
Orchid, crystal, stem, sherbet; #5022 or #5025, 6-oz ..**$25.00**
Orchid, crystal, vase, fan shape, footed, 7" **$90.00**
Plantation, crystal, bowl, celery; 13" **$70.00**
Plantation, crystal, bowl, honey; footed, cupped, 6½" ..**$75.00**
Plantation, crystal, comport, 5" **$50.00**
Plantation, crystal, plate, salad; 7" **$25.00**
Plantation, crystal, stem, pressed or blown, 10-oz, ea.**$50.00**
Pleat & Panel, crystal, bowl, grapefruit/cereal; 6½"......**$5.00**
Pleat & Panel, green, stem, saucer champagne; 5-oz.**$18.00**
Pleat & Panel, pink, plate, bouillon underliner; 6¾" **$8.00**
Provincial, crystal, bowl, nappy; 4½" **$15.00**
Provincial, crystal, tumbler, iced tea; flat, 13".............**$20.00**
Provincial, Limelight Green, plate, luncheon; 8".........**$50.00**
Queen Ann, crystal, bottle, oil; 4-oz **$40.00**
Queen Ann, crystal, bowl, floral; rolled edge, 9"........**$25.00**
Queen Ann, crystal, cup..**$15.00**
Queen Ann, crystal, vase, flared, 8" **$55.00**
Ridgeleigh, crystal, ashtray, round..............................**$14.00**
Ridgeleigh, crystal, bowl, floral; 10" **$45.00**
Ridgeleigh, crystal, bowl, lemon; w/lid, 5".................**$65.00**

Ridgeleigh, crystal, cigarette holder, round $14.00
Ridgeleigh, crystal, mustard, w/lid $80.00
Ridgeleigh, crystal, plate, salver; 14" $50.00
Ridgeleigh, crystal, stem, cocktail; blown, 3½-oz $35.00
Ridgeleigh, crystal, vase, cupped top, #2 individual...$45.00
Rose, crystal, bowl, jelly; Waverly, footed, 6½" $45.00
Rose, crystal, candlestick, 1-light, #112 ....$45.00
Rose, crystal, cigarette holder, #4035 ....$125.00
Rose, crystal, creamer, Waverly, individual................$40.00
Rose, crystal, plate, sandwich; Waverly, 11" $60.00
Saturn, crystal, ashtray $10.00
Saturn, crystal, bowl, celery; 10" $15.00
Saturn, crystal, pitcher, juice $40.00
Saturn, crystal, tumbler, juice; 5-oz.........................$8.00
Saturn, Zircon or Limelight Green, bowl, finger $65.00
Saturn, Zircon or Limelight Green, creamer $180.00
Saturn, Zircon or Limelight Green, saucer................$30.00
Stanhope, crystal, creamer, 2-handled, w/ or w/out round
    knobs $45.00
Stanhope, crystal, stem, cocktail; #4083, 3½-oz $20.00
Twist, crystal, bonbon, individual $15.00
Twist, green, mayonnaise, #1252½ $45.00
Twist, marigold, sugar bowl, footed $60.00
Twist, pink, bowl, floral; 9" $40.00
Victorian, crystal, decanter, w/stopper, 32-oz............$70.00
Victorian, crystal, tumbler, old-fashion; 8-oz $35.00
Waverly, crystal, bowl, relish; round, 4-part, 9" $25.00
Waverly, crystal, candle epergnette, 5".....................$15.00
Waverly, crystal, candy box, w/bow tie knob, 6" $45.00
Waverly, crystal, honey dish, footed, 6½" $50.00

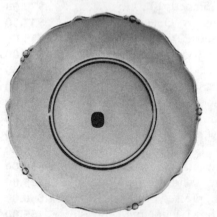

Waverly, crystal, plate, 10½", $50.00. (Photo courtesy Gene Florence)

Waverly, crystal, vase, violet; 3½" $60.00
Yeoman, green, salver, low footed, 12" $70.00
Yeoman, Marigold, sugar bowl, w/lid........................$40.00
Yeoman, pink, bowl, berry; 2-handled, 8½" $22.00
Yeoman, yellow, grapefruit, footed...........................$24.00

Figurals and Novelties

Airedale, crystal..$650.00
Chick, crystal, head down or up, ea..........................$100.00
Colt, amber, kicking $650.00

Colt, amber, standing...$550.00
Colt, cobalt, rearing...$1,500.00
Colt, cobalt, standing $1,200.00
Colt, crystal, standing $100.00
Doe head, bookend, crystal, 6¼", ea.......................$850.00
Donkey, crystal $295.00
Duck, ashtray, Flamingo $400.00
Duck, flower block, crystal $140.00
Elephant, amber, sm..$1,600.00
Elephant, crystal, sm...$225.00
Filly, crystal, head forward $1,100.00

Fish, bowl, 9", $525.00.

Frog, cheese plate, Flamingo, #1210.........................$145.00
Gazelle, crystal, 10¾"...$1,500.00
Goose, crystal, wings down.....................................$450.00
Goose, crystal, wings up...$110.00
Horse head, bookend, crystal frost, ea $140.00
Horse head, stopper, crystal, 4½"............................$160.00
Irish setter, ashtray, Moongleam $55.00
Kingfisher, flower block, Moongleam $250.00
Mallard, crystal, wings half $200.00
Piglet, crystal, sitting...$100.00
Plug horse, cobalt...$1,200.00
Plug horse, crystal $160.00
Rabbit mother, crystal, 4½x5½"...........................$1,000.00
Rooster, amber, 5⅜" $2,500.00
Rooster, Fighting; crystal frost, 7½x5½".................$200.00
Rooster head, stopper, crystal, 4½" $45.00
Sea horse, cocktail, crystal $160.00
Show horse, crystal $1,250.00
Sparrow, crystal $120.00
Swan, master nut, crystal, #1503.............................$45.00

Hippie Collectibles

The 'Hippies' perpetuated the 'Beatnik' genre of rebellious, free-thinking, Bohemian nonconformity during the decade of the 1960s. Young people created a 'counterculture' with their own style of clothing, attitudes, music, politics, and behavior. They created new forms of art, theatre, and political activism. The center of this movement was the Haight-Ashbury district of San Francisco. The youth culture culminated there in 1967 in the 'Summer of Love.' Woodstock, in August 1969, attracted at least 400,000 people. Political activism against the Viet Nam War was intense and widespread. Posters, books, records, handbills, and other items from that era are highly collectible because of their uniqueness to this time period.

Advisor: Richard Synchef (See Directory, Beatnik and Hippie Collectibles)

Admission ticket, Woodstock Music & Art Fair, Globe Ticket Co, August 1969, 1-day or 3-day ticket, from $100 to..**$125.00**

Book, Black Panthers Speak, Philip Foner editor, JB Lippincott Co, NY, 1970, Newton, Cleaver, Seale, Hampton, others...**$150.00**

Book, Day After Superman Died, Ken Kesey, Northridge Co, Lord John Press, 1980, death of Neal Cassidy, very scarce...**$450.00**

Book, Flashbacks, Timothy Leary, Boston, JP Tarcher, Inc, 1983, Leary's autobiography **$125.00**

Book, Hell's Angels, Hunter S Thompson, NY, Random House, 1967, 1st book by originator of 'Gonzo journalism' **$400.00**

Book, Quotations From Chairman Mao Tse-Tung, Foreign Language Press, Peking, 1966, 'The Little Red Book' **$375.00**

Book, Trips: Rock Life in the Sixties, Ellen Sander, NY, Charles Scribner's Sons, 1973, account of '60s music scene..**$80.00**

Book, We Are Everywhere, Jerry Rubin, NY, Harper & Row, 1971, Yippie leader's classic scenario of the 1960s............**$175.00**

Book, Weed: Adventures of a Dope Smuggler, Jerry Kamstra, NY, Harper & Row, 1974, Beat poet turned smuggler's exploits **$100.00**

Book, With the Weathermen, Susan Stern, NY, Doubleday & Co, 1975 (personal journal of a revolutionary woman)...**$80.00**

Bumper sticker, Join the Conspiracy, Chicago 7 Defense Fund, red, 1969, 9x3", very scarce **$150.00**

Bumper sticker, RFK in '68, black letters on red, 3x12", scarce..**$125.00**

Comic, underground, Arcade, Comics Review, No 1, Spring, 1975, SF, Mint Print, Crumb cover, Spiegleman/Griffith editors...**$150.00**

Comic, underground, Conspiracy Capers, The Conspiracy, K Cleaver & S Sontag, 1959, proceeds for Chicago 8, rare...**$300.00**

Comic, underground, Yellow Dog, #5 (of 12), SF, Apex Novelties, 1970..**$125.00**

Comic, underground, Young Lust, #2, The Print Mint, Berkeley, CA, 1971, B Grifith, J Greene, others, etc, classic...**$100.00**

Figurine, Hippie man w/sign: Fight Hate!, Napcoware, 1970, 6"...**$90.00**

Handbill, Blushing Peony, artist unknown, pink, for store in Haight-Ashbury during 1967 'Summer of Love,' 8½x11" **$75.00**

Handbill, Human Be-In, Gathering of Tribes, Mouse, Kelley, Bowen (artists), Bindweed Press, January 14, 1967, 8½x11"...**$750.00**

Handbill, Magic Mountain Music Festival, June 3-4, 1967, Marin Co, CA, artist unknown, 10x5", 'Summer of Love' event **$500.00**

Handbill, Poetry Is Revolution, benefit reading for John Sinclair of White Panther Party, artist unknown, Jan 25, 1971 ....**$400.00**

Handbill, rock concert, Avalon Ballroom, SF, W Wilson artist, May 6-7, 1966, w/Daily Flash/Rising Sons (Family Dog #7)..**$1,300.00**

Handbill, YIPPIE!, Youth International party, August 1968, before National Democratic Convention, 8½x11" ..**$600.00**

Handbill, Zenefit, Zen Mountain Center Benefit, November 13, 1966, Marin County, California (significant event with Grateful Dead, many others), 8x6", $700.00. (Photo courtesy Richard Synchef)

Jigsaw puzzle, Life, Peter Max artist, Schisgall, NY, 1970, 500 pieces, 5½x7½"....................................**$120.00**

Jigsaw puzzle, Richard Nixon/Spiro Agnew, NY, Puzzle Factory, 1970, 2-sided, 22x15" **$100.00**

Magazine, Avant Garde, R Ginsburg editor, NY, March 1968, Issue 2, Marilyn Monroe issue, Bert Stern photos..**$225.00**

Magazine, CAW!, Students for a Democratic Society, February 1968, 1st issue, very rare...................................**$250.00**

Magazine, Cheetah, Peter Max cover, December, 1967, counterculture articles...**$80.00**

Magazine, Life, May 25, 1970, Tragedy at Kent State..**$50.00**

Magazine, Newsweek, March 2, 1970, Verdict in Chicago, Judge Hoffman & Chicago on cover......................**$50.00**

Magazine, Ramparts, March, 1967, Social History of Hippies, re: Haight-Ashbury, important **$100.00**

Magazine, Saturday Evening Post, November 2, 1968, Bob Dylan & Pop Scene, Dylan on cover **$50.00**

Map, Haight-Ashbury: San Francisco Hippieville Guide & Map, WT Samhill, Sausilito CA, 1967, folding style **$80.00**

Newspaper, Berkeley Barb, November 14, 1969, Vol 9, #19, Moritorium issue **$40.00**

Newspaper, Black Panther, September 8, 1971, Vol 7, #4, Massacre at Attica, Oakland CA, 16x12" **$150.00**

Newspaper, Guerilla, January 1967, Artist's Workshop Press, Detroit MI, 1st issue w/very important writers...**$250.00**

Newspaper, Los Angeles Free Press, May 20, 1966, #96..**$75.00**

Newspaper, Patriot, March 21, 1970, NY, 1st issue, Patriot Party publication by poor white leftists, very rare...........**$250.00**

Newspaper, Rat, Subterranean News, September 6, 1968, NY, weekly major newspaper **$45.00**

Newspaper, San Francisco Oracle, #5, Human Be-In Issue, January, 1967, THE underground newspaper to have..**$500.00**

Newspaper, Yipster Times, Youth International party, Vol 1, 1971, NY...**$250.00**

Paperback, Age of Rock, Jonathan Eisen editor, NY, Vintage, 1969, essays from 1967-68....................................**$80.00**

Paperback, Goliath, David Harris, NY, Avon, 1970, written while in prison by leader of anti-draft movement.**$75.00**

Paperback, Jefferson Airplane & San Francisco Sound, RJ Gleason (SF Chronical music editor), NY, Ballantine, 1969 ....**$100.00**

Paperback, Making of Counter Culture, T Roszak, NY, Anchor Books, 1969, author coined term counterculture...**$100.00**

Paperback, Prophetic Minority, Jack Newfield, NY, Signet, 1967, overview of student protest by award-winning writer..**$75.00**

Paperback, Revolutionary Nonviolence, D Delinger, NY, Anchor Books, 1972, essays on the Chicago 7.....**$80.00**

Paperback, Telling It Like It Was, Chicago Riots, Ginsberg, Mailer, Burroughs, Wicker, etc, NY, Signet, 1969.**$80.00**

Paperback, The LSD Story, John Cashman, Greenwich CT, Fawcett, 1966, early presentation of history of LSD ..**$100.00**

Pin-back button, Be Leary of LSD, black letters on red, ca 1969, 1½"...**$80.00**

Pin-back button, Boycott Lettuce, black letters on maroon, ca 1968, 1½"..**$80.00**

Pin-back button, Dump Johnson in 1968, blue letters on white, 1¼", rare **$100.00**

Pin-back button, Eugene McCarthy for President, various issues, from $20 to **$120.00**

Pin-back button, Free Speech Movement, Berkeley CA, white letters on blue, 1964, 1", Genesis of student protest....**$200.00**

Pin-back button, Out Now, Nov 6 Demonstrate Against the War, National Peace Action Coalition, 1971, 1¾" ...**$75.00**

Pin-back button, Stop the Draft, white letters on red, ca 1969, 2"...**$60.00**

Poster, Bobby Hutton Murdered by Oakland Pigs, Black Panther Party, Oakland CA, April 1968, 18x23", scarce **$600.00**

Poster, Clean-In, Spring Mobilization for Haight Ashbury Neighborhood, Victor Moscoso artist, 1967, 20x14".**$200.00**

Poster, Dick Gregory for President, Peace & Freedom Party, 1968, 29x22", rare **$500.00**

Poster, Human Be-In, Gathering of the Tribes, January 14, 1967, Kelly, Mouse, Bowen, Bindweed Press, primary '60s poster..**$750.00**

Poster, Out Now, Stop the Bombing, March Against the War, Student Mobilization Committee, Berkeley CA, 1970, 22x14"...**$100.00**

Poster, Stand for McCarthy, Rally Sacramento, August 10, white on blue, 23x18"......................................**$125.00**

Program, Woodstock Music & Art Fair, August, 1969, 52-page, 8½x11", very rare...**$750.00**

Program, Woodstock: The Movie, Warner Bros, 48-page, 1970 ....**$125.00**

Record, Abbie Hoffman, Wake Up America, NY, Big Toe, LP, 1969 ....**$250.00**

Record, Can You Pass the Acid Test?, K Kesey & Merry Pranksters, Sound City Productions, very rare ...**$550.00**

Record, Is Freedom Academic?, KPFA-Pacifica Foundation, 1964, Berkeley CA, Free Speech Movement documentary **$250.00**

Record, LSD, Battle for the Mind, Supreme Recordings, M-113, Glendale CA, LP, critical of LSD **$175.00**

Record, Murder at Kent State University, Pete Hamill, narrated by Rosco, Flying Dutchman Records, LP, 1970.....**$175.00**

Record, Rod McKuen Takes a San Francisco Hippie Trip, Tradition/Everest Records, LP, 1969.....................**$60.00**

Record, Timothy Leary, LSD, NY, Pixie Records, 1966, very scarce **$200.00**

Record, Wit of Senator Eugene McCarthy, McCarthy for President Committee, LP, 1968.........................**$75.00**

Sticker, various peace signs, Atomic Energy Group, 1967 .**$10.00**

Poster, *Blushing Peony*, Victor Moscoso art, Haight Street store ad, 1967, 14x20", $100.00. (Photo courtesy Richard Synchef)

Holt Howard

Here's one of today's newest collectibles, and dealers from all over the country tell us interest is on the increase! Now's the time to pick up the kitchenware (cruets, salt and peppers, condiments, etc.), novelty banks, ashtrays, and planters marked Holt Howard. They're not only marked but dated as well; you'll find production dates from the 1950s through the '70s. (Beware of unmarked copy-cat lines!) There's a wide variety of items and decorative themes; those you're most likely to find will be from the rooster (done in golden brown, yellow, and orange), white cat (called Kozy Kitten), and Christmas lines. Not as easily found, the Pixies are by far the most collectible of all, and even though the market for the more common Holt Howard items may have leveled off (and is perhaps cooling just a bit), collectors are still hot after Pixies! Internet auctions may be affecting this market right now with the 'more supply, less demand' principal (more exposure therefore lower prices), but rather than let all this cause us to jump to premature conclusions, we think it best to maintain the suggested values we gave you last year.

Advisors: Pat and Ann Duncan (See Directory, Holt Howard)

Christmas

Angel, cardboard cone body covered w/pink feathers, ceramic head, from $20 to **$30.00**
Ashtray, Santa, med **$25.00**
Bell, holly decoration **$20.00**
Candle holder, angel figural, pr..**$35.00**
Candle holder, Santa & train w/tree cart attached by chain, dated 1959, 3½x7" **$80.00**
Candle holder, Santa w/climbing mouse, pr **$35.00**
Candle holder, 3 carolers w/song book, holder ea side, 4½" **$60.00**
Candle holders, girl in red attire carrying stack of presents, pr **$80.00**
Candle holders, kneeling camels, jeweled red fabric saddle blankets & gilt harness, pr **$35.00**
Candle huggers, figural snowman, pr, from $20 to **$25.00**
Candlestick, Santa handle **$25.00**
Candlestick, sleeping mouse under ruffled coverlet at side, gold trim on ring handle & rim **$25.00**
Candlestick, winking Santa head as candle cup on red saucer base, white handle...**$20.00**
Candy container, w/pop-up Santa, 4¼" **$50.00**
Demitasse pot, inverted fluting, flared cylinder, white matt w/applied holly & berries, from $50 to **$65.00**
Dish, Christmas tree form, divided, 13⅞" **$25.00**
Dish, Christmas tree form, 9⅞".....................................**$15.00**
Dish, Santa head w/scalloped beard as bowl **$25.00**
Head vase, girl w/holly headband, stylized features & heart mouth, pearl earrings, holly trim collar at base, 1949, 4" **$140.00**
Hurricane lamp, Santa figural w/candle holder in hat inside glass chimney, red trim & ring handle, from $25 to............**$35.00**
Hurricane lamp, standing bird w/tree cap to hold candle inside glass chimney, sponged gold trim, from $25 to.......**$35.00**
Mug, Christmas tree w/Santa handle.............................**$10.00**
Mug, winking Santa, mini..**$5.00**
Pitcher, juice; winking Santa, naturalistic molding, +6 sm mugs **$95.00**
Pitcher, juice; winking Santa, stylized fan-like beard, +6 mugs **$95.00**
Planter, candy cane..**$20.00**
Planter, stylized deer head w/antlers, red nose **$25.00**

Salt & pepper shakers, Christmas tree w/Santa, pr.....**$25.00**
Salt & pepper shakers, full-figured Santa, S or P on tummy, pr..**$30.00**
Salt & pepper shakers, holly girl holds lg poinsettia w/P or S at center, holly bow in hair, pr, from $15 to **$20.00**
Salt & pepper shakers, Santa & Rudolph in bed, 3-pc .**$55.00**
Salt & pepper shakers, Santa's head is salt, stacks on pepper body, from $30 to..**$40.00**
Salt & pepper shakers, stylized deer, 1 buck & 1 doe, pr..**$30.00**
Salt & pepper shakers, 2 stacked gift boxes, 'Merry Xmas on top, pr..**$15.00**
Votive candle holder, Santa, dated 1968, 3"................**$20.00**

Santa cookie/candy jar, three-piece, hard to find, $250.00. (Photo courtesy Pat and Ann Duncan)

Kozy Kitten

Ashtray, cat on square plaid base, 4 corner rests, from $60 to **$75.00**
Bud vase, cat in plaid cap & neckerchief, from $65 to .**$75.00**
Butter dish, cats peeking out on side, ¼-lb, rare **$150.00**
Cookie jar, head form, from $40 to............................**$50.00**
Cottage cheese keeper, cat knob on lid **$100.00**
Creamer & sugar bowl, stackable..............................**$195.00**
Letter holder, cat w/coiled wire back **$75.00**
Memo finder, full-bodied cat, legs cradle note pad..**$125.00**
Powdered cleanser shaker, full-bodied lady cat wearing apron, w/broom..**$150.00**
Salt & pepper shakers, cat's head, pr.........................**$30.00**
Salt & pepper shakers, tall cats, pr............................**$40.00**
Salt & pepper shakers, 4 individual cat heads, stacked on upright dowel, from $90 to................................**$120.00**
Sewing box, figural cat w/tape-measure tongue on lid..**$100.00**
Spice set, stacking **$175.00**
Spice shaker, cat head w/loop atop for hanging, 2½x3" ..**$35.00**
String holder, head only...**$95.00**
Sugar shaker, cat in apron carries sack lettered Pour, shaker holes in hat, side pour spout formed by sack, rare............**$145.00**
Tape measure, cat on cushion.....................................**$85.00**
Wall pocket, cat's head...**$95.00**

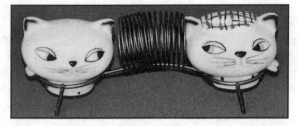

Salt and pepper shakers, head forms, in wireware napkin holder frame, from $50.00 to $75.00. (Photo courtesy Pat and Ann Duncan)

Pixie Ware

Ashtray, 4½" L..$250.00
Candlesticks, pr...$55.00
Cherries jar, flat head finial on lid, w/cherry pick or spoon.$150.00
Chili sauce, rare, minimum value................................$300.00
Cocktail olives, winking green head finial on lid.....$150.00
Creamer...$55.00
Cruets, oil & vinegar, Sally & Sam, pr, minimum value ..$200.00
Decanter, Devil Brew, striped base, 10½", rare, minimum value..$200.00
Decanter, flat-head stopper w/300 Proof & red rose, minimum value..$200.00
Decanter, winking head stopper w/Whiskey, minimum value..$200.00
Dish, flat-head handle w/crossed eyes & pickle nose, green stripes, minimum value.......................................$100.00
French dressing bottle, minimum value.....................$200.00
Honey, very rare, minimum value.............................$300.00

Hors d'oeuvre, head on body pierced for toothpicks, minimum value, $200.00; salt and pepper shakers, $25.00 for the pair. (Photo courtesy Pat and Ann Duncan)

Instant coffee jar, brown-skinned blond head finial, hard to find, minimum value...$250.00
Italian dressing bottle, minimum value.....................$300.00
Jam & jelly jar, flat-head finial on lid..........................$75.00
Ketchup jar, orange tomato-like head finial on lid.....$75.00

Mayonnaise jar, winking head finial on lid, minimum value..$250.00
Mustard jar, yellow head finial on lid, from $45 to....$75.00
Olive jar, winking green head finial on lid.................$95.00
Onion jar, flat onion-head finial on lid, 1958..............$95.00
Russian dressing bottle, minimum value...................$300.00
Salt & pepper shakers, gourd form, pointed beak & 'eye' suggests bird-like appearance, stripes, no pixie, pr..$30.00
Salt & pepper shakers, Salty & Peppy, attached flat head w/painted wood handle, pr................................$65.00
Spice set, stacking..$150.00
Sugar bowl, Lil' Sugar w/spoon & pixie lid, +cream crock, pr...$150.00
Towel hook, flat head w/sm loop hanger, rare, minimum value..$200.00

Ponytail Girl

Candle holder, from $50.00 to $60.00. (Photo courtesy Pat and Ann Duncan)

Lipstick holder, from $60 to....................................$75.00
Salt & pepper shakers, pr...................................$45.00
Tray, double; 2 joined flower cups, girl between.......$65.00

Rooster

Bowl, cereal; 6"...$25.00
Butter dish, embossed rooster, ¼-lb......................$50.00
Chocolate pot, tall & narrow w/flaring sides, embossed rooster on front...$95.00
Coffeepot, electric..$100.00
Coffeepot, embossed rooster...............................$100.00
Cookie jar, embossed rooster...............................$200.00
Creamer & sugar bowl, embossed rooster, pr.............$75.00
Cup & saucer..$25.00
Dish, figural rooster w/open-body receptacle...........$30.00
Egg cup, double; figural rooster...........................$40.00
Jam & jelly jar, embossed rooster.........................$75.00
Ketchup jar, embossed rooster.............................$75.00
Mug, embossed rooster (3 sizes), ea......................$20.00
Mustard jar, embossed rooster on front, w/lid..........$75.00
Napkin holder..$40.00

Pitcher, syrup; embossed rooster on front, tail handle .**$40.00**
Pitcher, water; flaring sides, tail handle, tall...............**$60.00**
Plate, embossed rooster, 8½"...**$25.00**
Platter, embossed rooster, oval **$35.00**
Salt & pepper shakers, embossed rooster, pr.............**$10.00**
Salt & pepper shakers, figural rooster, tall, pr, from $25
    to..**$30.00**
Spoon rest, figural rooster, from $30 to **$35.00**
Tray, facing left **$25.00**
Trivet, tile w/rooster in iron framework **$50.00**
Vase, bud; figural rooster, from $30 to.......................**$35.00**

Cigarette holder, wooden, $150.00; recipe box, wooden, $100.00; pitcher, cylindrical, no handle, $60.00. (Photo courtesy Pat and Ann Duncan)

Miscellaneous

Ash receiver, comical man in yellow shirt & blue pants, open-
    ing & cigarette rests in stomach, from $100 to....**$125.00**
Ash receiver, fisherman w/hat, dated 1961, 5½".........**$80.00**
Ashtray, lady w/bottle **$110.00**
Ashtray/coaster, mouse...**$25.00**
Atomizer, kneeling nude child w/pink bow in hair in recess
    on side of flared white bottle **$75.00**
Bank, Coin Clown, bobbing head, from $150 to......**$185.00**
Bank, Dandy Lion, bobbing head, from $140 to **$160.00**
Bank, pig w/florals & blue trim, well for scissors in tail ..**$125.00**
Bookends, eagle w/uplifted wings, pr......................**$150.00**
Candle holder, baby chick, from $20 to **$25.00**
Candle holder, boy on shoe **$22.00**
Candle holder, kneeling girl, 2-light............................**$20.00**
Candle holders, Happy Birthday, figural baby w/real safety
    pins, 3½", pr...**$45.00**
Card holder, gray-haired grandmother, glasses sliding off
    nose, indent in hat...**$25.00**
Cocktail shaker, bartender theme, +4 tumblers...........**$75.00**
Creamer & sugar bowl, fruit cold painted on heavy pottery,
    marked Holt Howard Italy **$40.00**
Desk accessory, spread-winged eagle figure on marble base,
    holds 1 pen...**$100.00**
Desk set, figural chickens in white, gold & brown, sharpen-
    er, pencil holder & pen holder, 3-pc set..............**$95.00**
Ice cream toppings, 2 covered containers & 2 pitchers mod-
    eled like layer cakes, 4-pc set................................**$75.00**

Jam 'n Jelly jar, yellow w/red lettering on white band, dome
    lid w/handle, wood-handle spoon **$50.00**
Match holder, pink mouse w/cane, unmarked, 6"......**$48.00**
Merry Cocktail Mice, hors d'oeuvre (hole in tail for toothpick),
    hangs on rim of glass tumbler, set of 5, MIB **$135.00**
Mug, Nursery Rhymes, footed, verse printed in wide graphic
    band...**$25.00**
Napkin ring, sm white, yellow & green bird atop white ring,
    dated 1958, 1" dia...**$110.00**
Note pad holder, 3-dimensional lady's hand.............**$45.00**

Onions, Cherries, and Olives, butler head, minimum value, $200.00 each. (Photo courtesy Pat and Ann Duncan)

Paper clip, painted square faces w/black back clip, rare,
    pr **$50.00**
Pitcher, blue forals on white, 1964-65, +4 mugs, 5-pc..**$75.00**
Plant feeder, bird form **$35.00**
Planter, mother deer & fawn, white w/gold bow, from $25 to..**$35.00**
Plate, Rake 'N Spade, MIB **$20.00**
Playing card holder, on base w/3-dimensional bust of granny
    holding playing cards, from $45 to **$55.00**
Salt & papper shakers, Rock 'N Roll kids, heads on springs,
    pr **$150.00**
Salt & pepper shaker, bunnies in wicker baskets, pr .**$45.00**
Salt & pepper shaker, tomatoes, pr...............................**$15.00**
Salt & pepper shakers, bride & groom, pr **$30.00**
Salt & pepper shakers, chick figural w/yellow topknot, beak
    & feet, original tag marked Li'l Bo Peep, pr.........**$50.00**
Salt & pepper shakers, mice in wicker baskets, pr.....**$35.00**
Salt & pepper shakers, New York Thruway souvenir, stylized
    girls w/wings marked Li'l Pepper & Li'l Salt, red & white,
    pr...**$25.00**
Salt & pepper shakers, pink mouse w/red bow, dated 1958,
    4¼", pr..**$40.00**
Snack set, tomato cup & lettuce leaf plate, 1962........**$25.00**
Soup tureen, fruit cold painted on heavy pottery, marked
    Holt Howard Italy, lg, +6 mugs...........................**$150.00**
Soup tureen, tomato form, lg, from $85 to **$100.00**
Tape dispenser, pelican...**$130.00**
Tape dispenser, stylized poodle w/red neck band & pencil
    sharpener...**$50.00**
Votive candle holder, pig, pastel, dated 1958, 5½".....**$45.00**
Wall pocket, embossed pheasant, marked Holt Howard 1958,
    rare, minimum value **$150.00**

Homer Laughlin China Co.

Since well before the turn of the century, the Homer Laughlin China Company of Newell, West Virginia, has been turning out dinnerware and kitchenware lines in hundreds of styles and patterns. Most of their pieces are marked either 'HLC' or 'Homer Laughlin.' As styles changed over the years, they designed several basic dinnerware shapes that they used as a basis for literally hundreds of different patterns simply by applying various decals and glaze treatments. A few of their most popular lines are represented below. If you find pieces stamped with a name like Virginia Rose, Rhythm, or Nautalis, don't assume it to be the pattern name; it's the shape name. Virginia Rose, for instance, was decorated with many different decals. If you have some you're trying to sell through a mail or a phone contact, it would be a good idea to send the prospective buyer a zerox copy of the pattern.

For further information see *The Collector's Encyclopedia of Homer Laughlin Pottery* and *American Dinnerware, 1880s to 1920s*, both by Joanne Jasper. *The Collector's Encyclopedia of Fiesta* by Sharon and Bob Huxford has photographs and prices of several of the more collectible lines such as listed here.

See also Fiesta.

Newsletter: *The Laughlin Eagle* (published quarterly)
c/o Richard Racheter
1270 63rd Terrace South, St. Petersburg, FL 33705

Amberstone

Ashtray, rare	$30.00
Bowl, vegetable; from $12 to	$16.00
Casserole, from $50 to	$55.00
Creamer, from $6.50 to	$7.50
Cup & saucer, black decoration	$7.00
Pie plate, black decoration	$40.00
Platter, black decoration, oval, from $12 to	$16.00
Sugar bowl, w/lid	$8.50
Tea server	$53.00

Americana

Bowl, cream soup, from $60 to	$75.00
Bowl, vegetable; oval, 8½", from $20 to	$25.00
Creamer	$15.00
Cup & saucer	$15.00
Egg cup	$16.00
Platter, 15", from $50 to	$55.00
Sauce boat	$24.00
Sauce boat stand, from $45 to	$60.00
Sugar bowl, w/lid, from $18 to	$25.00
Teapot	$80.00

Blue Willow

Bowl, flat soup; 8"	$15.00
Bowl, serving; oval or round	$30.00
Bowl, 5"	$6.00
Casserole, w/lid	$45.00
Creamer	$18.00
Egg cup	$25.00
Plate, 6¼"	$8.00
Plate, 7¼"	$10.00
Plate, 9¼"	$15.00
Plate, 9¾"	$18.00
Platter, 11"	$20.00
Platter, 13"	$30.00
Sauceboat	$30.00
Sugar bowl, w/lid	$20.00
Teacup	$10.00
Teapot	$60.00

Dogwood

Plate, 10", from $12.00 to $15.00; cup and saucer, $12.00; fruit bowl, $8.00.

Bowl, mixing; KK, gold trim, 10½", from $35 to	$45.00
Bowl, vegetable; gold trim, oval, 9½", from $20 to	$25.00
Plate, gold trim, 8", scarce, from $12 to	$15.00
Platter, gold trim, 13½", from $25 to	$35.00
Sauce boat, gold trim	$20.00
Sugar bowl, w/lid, gold trim	$12.00

Embossed Line

Ashtray, from $30 to	$40.00
Bean pot, w/decal, 4¼x5½"	$18.00
Bowl, mixing; 7¼", from $12 to	$15.00
Bowl, soup; tab-handled, 7"	$10.00
Casserole, w/decals, 8½"	$45.00
Casserole, 10", from $32 to	$38.00
Casserole, 7½", from $20 to	$25.00
Cup, 3¾", rare	$18.00
Oval baker, w/decal, 8½"	$18.00
Plate, 7", from $5 to	$7.00

Epicure

Bowl, fruit; from $18 to	$22.00

Bowl, nappy; 8¾"..........	**$35.00**
Bowl, vegetable; w/lid..........	**$75.00**
Casserole, individual, from $75 to..........	**$80.00**
Ladle, 5½", from $45 to..........	**$50.00**
Plate, 10", from $30 to..........	**$35.00**
Plate, 6½"..........	**$9.00**
Platter, lg, from $28 to..........	**$32.00**
Sugar bowl, w/lid..........	**$30.00**

Harlequin

Note: The high range of values should be used to price maroon, dark green, gray, and spruce green; chartreuse, rose, red, light green, and mauve blue will run about 10% less. The low range is for evaluating turquoise and yellow. Prices for medium green Harlequin are soaring; we would suggest that you at least double the high side of the high range when evaluating this very rare color.

Ashtray, basketweave, high..........	**$58.00**
Bowl, cream soup; high, from $25 to..........	**$30.00**
Bowl, nappy; high, 9"..........	**$40.00**
Bowl, oval baker; high, from $35 to..........	**$40.00**
Butter dish, low, ½-lb..........	**$115.00**
Candle holders, low, pr, from $220 to..........	**$240.00**
Creamer, regular, low..........	**$14.00**
Cup, demitasse; low, from $38 to..........	**$42.00**
Egg cup, double, low..........	**$20.00**
Egg cup, single, high, from $30 to..........	**$35.00**
Nut dish, basketweave, low..........	**$13.00**
Plate, deep; high..........	**$30.00**
Plate, low, 10"..........	**$24.00**
Platter, high, 11", from $20 to..........	**$25.00**
Platter, med green, 13"..........	**$250.00**
Sauce boat, high, from $30 to..........	**$35.00**

Service water pitcher, low range: from $65.00 to $75.00; high range: from $85.00 to $100.00.

Sugar bowl, w/lid, high, from $28 to..........	**$32.00**
Syrup, red or yellow..........	**$175.00**

Jubilee

Bowl, fruit..........	**$5.00**
Bowl, mixing; KK, 10", from $120 to..........	**$140.00**

Casserole, from $35 to..........	**$40.00**
Creamer..........	**$6.00**
Egg cup..........	**$9.00**
Plate, 10"..........	**$9.00**
Plate, 7"..........	**$4.00**
Platter, 13"..........	**$12.00**
Sauce boat..........	**$12.00**
Teapot..........	**$45.00**

Kitchen Kraft; Oven Serve

Bowl, mixing; 6"..........	**$22.00**
Casserole, individual..........	**$55.00**
Casserole, 8½"..........	**$40.00**
Platter..........	**$40.00**
Salt & pepper shakers, pr..........	**$40.00**

Mexican Decaled Lines

Use the values below to evaluate Hacienda, Mexicana, and Conchita on Century shapes and Max-I-Cana on Yellowstone. Kitchen Kraft items will be designated KK within the line.

Hacienda, creamer, from $15.00 to $20.00; sugar bowl, from $28.00 to $32.00.

Bowl, fruit; 5"..........	**$14.00**
Bowl, lug soup; 4½", from $35 to..........	**$40.00**
Bowl, mixing; KK, 10"..........	**$45.00**
Bowl, mixing; KK, 8"..........	**$40.00**
Butter dish, ½-lb, from $125 to..........	**$140.00**
Casserole, individual, KK..........	**$95.00**
Cup & saucer, from $18 to..........	**$22.00**
Jar, w/lid, KK, lg..........	**$160.00**
Pie plate, KK, from $30 to..........	**$35.00**
Plate, 6"..........	**$7.00**
Plate, 9", from $18 to..........	**$22.00**
Platter, square well, 15"..........	**$50.00**
Salt & pepper shakers, KK, pr..........	**$55.00**
Spoon, KK, from $65 to..........	**$70.00**
Tumbler, fired-on design, 6-oz..........	**$13.00**
Underplate, KK, 6", rare, from $40 to..........	**$45.00**

Priscilla

Bowl, fruit; gold trim, KK, 9½", scarce, from $32 to..	**$38.00**

Cake plate, gold trim, KK, 11", from $20 to **$25.00**
Casserole, gold trim, KK, round, 8½", from $35 to.....**$40.00**
Coffeepot, gold trim, KK...**$80.00**
Pitcher, water; gold trim, KK, from $30 to..................**$35.00**
Plate, gold trim, 10"...**$15.00**
Platter, gold trim, 13½", from $25 to...........................**$30.00**
Sauce boat, gold trim, from $20 to..............................**$25.00**
Teapot, Republic, gold trim, rare.................................**$85.00**

Rhythm

Bowl, fruit; 5½"...**$6.00**
Bowl, mixing; KK, 10", from $125 to.........................**$145.00**
Bowl, salad; lg, from $45 to..**$55.00**
Cup & saucer, after dinner; scarce, from $150 to **$200.00**
Plate, 10"..**$13.00**
Plate, 8", very rare..**$18.00**
Platter, 13½"..**$16.00**
Salt & pepper shakers, pr **$12.00**
Suger bowl, w/lid, from $12 to **$16.00**

Riviera

Riviera, juice pitcher, yellow, from $110.00 to $120.00; juice tumblers, from $48.00 to $52.00.

Bowl, fruit; 5½"..**$12.00**
Bowl, oatmeal; 6", from $35 to.....................................**$40.00**
Butter dish, ¼-lb, from $125 to **$135.00**
Cup & saucer, demitasse; from $70 to **$80.00**
Pitcher, juice; mauve blue..**$200.00**
Plate, 6"...**$8.00**
Platter, 15", from $50 to..**$60.00**
Salt & pepper shakers, pr, from $15 to........................**$20.00**
Sugar bowl, w/lid, from $15 to **$20.00**
Tidbit, 2-tiered, from $70 to..**$75.00**

Serenade

Bowl, nappy; 9" **$25.00**
Casserole, from $65 to..**$75.00**
Plate, chop **$30.00**
Plate, 10", from $15 to...**$20.00**

Plate, 7"...**$7.00**
Sugar bowl, w/lid, from $15 to **$20.00**
Teapot...**$100.00**

Virginia Rose

Bowl, fruit; 5½", from $5 to...**$8.00**
Bowl, mixing; KK, 10", from $35 to..............................**$45.00**
Bowl, oatmeal; 6"..**$12.00**
Butter dish, ½-lb...**$105.00**
Cake plate, KK, scarce, from $60 to...............................**$70.00**
Egg cup...**$85.00**
Pitcher, milk; 5"...**$40.00**
Plate, 8", scarce, from $15 to..**$18.00**
Platter, 15½", from $40 to **$50.00**
Sauce boat..**$25.00**

Wells Art Glaze

Bowl, cream soup, from $22 to..**$28.00**
Casserole, from $62 to..**$68.00**
Coffeepot, individual..**$120.00**
Cup & saucer, from $15 to...**$20.00**
Plate, chop; w/handles, from $20 to..............................**$25.00**
Plate, square, 6", from $12 to **$15.00**
Plate, 10", from $20 to...**$25.00**
Platter, oval, 13½", from $25 to **$30.00**
Syrup, w/decals, from $50 to...**$60.00**
Teapot..**$90.00**

Horton Ceramics

In 1946 Mr. and Mrs. Horace Horton began to formulate plans for a pottery to be based in Eastland, Texas. Mrs. Geri Horton designed most all wares which were sold to florists, department stores, and gift shops. The line consisted of ash-trays, contemporary planters and vases, novelty items, western-designed dinnerware, casual outdoor food service pieces, and jardinieres. Numbers and letters found in listings given here refer to the mold numbers which appear on the bottom of each piece.

Advisor: Darlene Nossaman (See Directory, Horton Ceramics)

Ashtray, black & orange or turquoise & yellow, #159, 5x7½"...**$6.00**
Ashtray, horseshoe shape, brown & white...................**$7.00**
Ashtray, smoking pipe, brown, 10x5" **$6.00**
Ashtray, #S8 shell shape, deep blue with pink or gray with white **$8.00**
Bean pot, dark green with lime or yellow with lime, #BP, 3"..**$10.00**
Pitcher, yellow w/brown or dark green w/lime, #P5, 6" .**$12.00**
Planter, black, pink, green or white, #97, 9x4" **$7.00**
Planter, bowling ball & pin, black & white, 8"............**$8.00**

Planter, dog, from $10.00 to $12.00. (Photo courtesy Darlene Nossaman)

Planter, Little League ball, white, 3½x4" **$8.00**
Planter, novelty, antelope head, natural, #AH, 15" **$18.00**
Planter, novelty, cradle, pink or blue, 6x9" **$8.00**
Planter, novelty, donkey, brown, 10x10" **$12.00**
Planter, novelty, owl, 2-tone brown, #O1...................**$10.00**
Planter, novelty, penguin, black & white, #P1 ....**$14.00**
Planter, novelty, rabbit, white or natural, #R1, 6x7" ...**$12.00**
Planter, novelty, skunk, black & white, #S1, 6½" **$12.00**
Vase, cedar-type bowl, turquoise & white or plum & white, #B63, 6x3" **$18.00**
Vase, cone shape in metal black spiral stand, white or pink, 8" **$15.00**
Vase, gingerbread man, various colors, 6"..................**$16.00**
Vase, refrigerator style, white, pink, black or green, 9x5" **$12.00**

Hull

Hull has a look of its own. Many lines were made in soft, pastel matt glazes and modeled with flowers and ribbons, and as a result, they have a very feminine appeal.

The company operated in Crooksville (near Zanesville), Ohio, from just after the turn of the century until they closed in 1985. From the '30s until the plant was destroyed by fire in 1950, they preferred the soft matt glazes so popular with today's collectors, though a few high gloss lines were made as well. When the plant was rebuilt, modern equipment was installed which they soon found did not lend itself to the duplication of the matt glazes, so they began to concentrate on the production of glossy wares, novelties, and figurines.

During the '40s and '50s, they produced a line of kitchenware items modeled after Little Red Riding Hood. Original pieces are expensive today and most are reproduced by persons other than Hull. (See also Little Red Riding Hood.)

Hull's Mirror Brown dinnerware line made from 1960 until they closed in 1985 was very successful for them and was made in large quantities. Its glossy brown glaze was enhanced with a band of ivory foam, and today's collectors are finding its rich colors and basic, strong shapes just as

attractive now as they were back then. In addition to table service, there are novelty trays shaped like gingerbread men and fish, canisters and cookie jars, covered casseroles with ducks and hens as lids, vases, ashtrays, and mixing bowls. It's easy to find, and though you may have to pay 'near book' prices at co-ops and antique malls, bargains are out there. It may be marked Hull, Crooksville, O; HPCo; or Crestone.

If you'd like to learn more about this subject, we recommend *The Collector's Encyclopedia of Hull Pottery* and *Ultimate Encyclopedia of Hull Pottery*, both by Brenda Roberts; and *Collector's Guide to Hull Pottery, The Dinnerware Lines*, by Barbara Loveless Gick-Burke.

Advisor: Brenda Roberts (See Directory, Hull)

Ashtray, Butterfly, heart shape, #B3, 7", from $30 to..**$45.00**
Ashtray, Parchment & Pine, #S-14, 14", from $125 to..**$165.00**
Basket, Magnolia, matt pink, scalloped rim, #10, 10½", from $350 to..**$400.00**
Basket, Mardi Gras/Granada, yellow shading to cream & pink, #65, 8", from $135 to **$170.00**
Bell, blue shading to cream & green, yellow flowers, unmarked, 6½", from $255 to............................**$325.00**

Bell, Sunglow, 6½", $150.00.

Bowl, console; Ebb Tide, shell form on leaf base, #E-12, 15¾", from $145 to...**$195.00**
Bowl, console; Magnolia, matt pink shading to cream, ring handles, #26, 12", from $175 to..........................**$200.00**
Bowl, console; Wildflower, pink shading to cream, scalloped rim, ring handles, #70, 12", from $375 to **$475.00**
Bowl, fruit; light green w/yellow & cream interior, scalloped edge, footed, #159, 10½", from $30 to..................**$45.00**
Bowl, mixing; Cinderella Kitchenware (Blossom), #20, 9½", from $40 to...**$65.00**
Bowl, Open Rose, pink shading to cream, scalloped rim, tab handles, low, #113, 7", from $135 to **$175.00**
Bowl, Orchid, blue, low, #312, 7", from $165 to......**$200.00**
Candle holder, Calla Lily, green shading to pink, unmarked, 2¼", from $95 to..**$125.00**
Candle holder, Iris, pink shading to green, handled, #411, 5", from $120 to..**$145.00**

Candle holder, Magnolia, glossy, pink flowers on cream, #H-24, 4", from $40 to................................**$60.00**

Candle holder, Woodland, matt yellow shading to cream & green, ring handle, #W30, 3½", from $130 to **$165.00**

Cornucopia, Dogwood, yellow shading to cream & green, #522, 4¾", from $95 to..**$125.00**

Cornucopia, Rosella, scalloped rim, #R-13, 8½", from $115 to..**$160.00**

Creamer, Ebb Tide, shell form w/ring handle, #E-15, 4", from $75 to..**$100.00**

Ewer, Calla Lily, pink shading to blue, #506, 10", from $380 to..**$480.00**

Ewer, Ebb Tide, #E-10, 14", $180.00. (Photo courtesy Brenda Roberts)

Figurine, rabbit, light blue, unmarked, 5½", from $30 to..**$40.00**

Flowerpot w/saucer, Bow-Knot, pink shading to cream & green, #B-6, 6½", from $225 to **$275.00**

Flowerpot w/saucer, Sueno Tulip, yellow shading to blue, #116-33, 4¼", from $135 to..................................**$165.00**

Grease jar, Heritageware, light blue w/white lid, tab handles, #A-3, 5¾", from $25 to..**$35.00**

Jardiniere, Bow-Knot, pink shading to cream & green, bow-shaped handles, #B-18, 5¾", from $200 to.........**$260.00**

Jardiniere, Water Lily, pink shading to cream, tab handles, #L-23, 5½", from $110 to.......................................**$155.00**

Jardiniere, Woodland, matt, scalloped rim, sm ring handles, #W7, 5½", from $165 to **$225.00**

Leaf dish, cream, #86, 10", from $20 to **$30.00**

Leaf dish, white, 3 sections, #31, 8¾", from $15 to **$20.00**

Pitcher, Cinderella Kitchenware (Bouquet), #22, 64-oz, from $150 to..**$175.00**

Pitcher, Heritageware, yellow, triangular handle, #A-6, 7", from $35 to..**$45.00**

Pitcher, Sunglow, yellow w/pink flowers, #52, 24-oz, from $40 to..**$60.00**

Planter, dog w/yarn, #88, 5½x8", from $30 to **$35.00**

Planter, goose, #411, 12½", from $50 to.....................**$80.00**

Planter, lamb, cream w/blue neck ribbon, #965, 8", from $30 to..**$45.00**

Planter, lovebirds, maroon, black & cream, #93, 6", from $40 to..**$60.00**

Planter, shell form, cream, #203, 5½", from $30 to.....**$40.00**

Planter, teddy bear in front of basket planter, #811, 7", from $30 to..**$45.00**

Rose bowl, Iris, cream, tab handles, #412, 7", from $170 to **$210.00**

Salt & pepper shakers, Cinderella Kitchenware (Bouquet), 3½", pr, from $25 to..**$40.00**

Sugar bowl, Magnolia, glossy, blue flowers on cream, handled, w/lid, #H-22, 3¾", from $40 to...................**$60.00**

Teapot, Bow-Knot, pink shading to cream & blue, #B-20, 6", from $375 to..**$500.00**

Vase, Bow-Knot 6½", $175.00.

Vase, Early Art, turquoise, tab handles, 4½", from $60 to.**$80.00**

Vase, leaf form, yellow & green, #100, 9", from $30 to.....**$40.00**

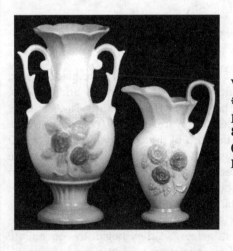

Vase, Open Rose, #124-12, $350.00; pitcher, #115-8½", $300.00. (Photo courtesy Brenda Roberts)

Vase, Open Rose, pink shading to cream, fan form w/scalloped rim & handles, #108, 8½", from $195 to..**$240.00**

Vase, Open Rose, swan figure, pink shading to cream, #135, 6¼", from $165 to...**$195.00**

Vase, Poppy, green shading to cream & pink, bulbous w/sm angle handles, footed, #607, 6½", from $145 to...**$175.00**

Vase, Serenade, hat form, #S4, 5¼", from $60 to........**$80.00**

Vase, Sueno Tulip, pink shading to blue, ring handles, #110-33, 6", from $130 to...**$150.00**

Vase, Sueno Tulip, pink shading to blue, ring handles, #110-33, 6", from $130 to.................................**$150.00**

Vase, Water Lily, cream shading to pink, bulbous w/fancy ear-type handles, scalloped rim, #L-16, 12½", from $355 to.................................**$455.00**

Vase, Wildflower, yellow shading to cream & pink, scalloped rim, ornate ring handles, #W-14, 10½", from $200 to.................................**$275.00**

Wall pocket, Bow-Knot, iron shape, blue shading to cream & pink, unmarked, 6¼", from $300 to.................**$385.00**

Wall pocket, Bow-Knot, whisk broom, blue shading to cream & pink, #B-27, 8", from $265 to.........................**$300.00**

Wall pocket, goose, dark green, maroon & cream, #67, 6½", from $50 to.................................**$70.00**

Wall pocket, mandolin, Mayfair, #84, 7", from $35 to.**$45.00**

Wall pocket, Rosella, heart form, #R-10, 6½", from $150 to.................................**$180.00**

Wall pocket, Sunglow, cup & saucer, #80, 6¼", from $100 to.................................**$125.00**

Window box, Royal Imperial, pink & white mottle, scalloped edge, #82, 12½", from $25 to.................................**$35.00**

Dinnerware

Avocado, casserole, French handle, individual, w/lid, 12-oz.................................**$7.00**

Avocado, coffee cup (mug), 9-oz.................................**$5.00**

Avocado, gravy boat, w/tray.................................**$60.00**

Avocado, plate, dinner; 10¼".................................**$8.00**

Country Belle, bowl, serving; oval.................................**$26.00**

Country Belle, bowl, 10".................................**$35.00**

Country Belle, cookie jar.................................**$85.00**

Country Belle, creamer & sugar bowl.................................**$45.00**

Country Belle, plate, salad.................................**$8.00**

Country Belle, skillet.................................**$60.00**

Country Squire, baker/casserole, 3-pt.................................**$30.00**

Country Squire, bowl, mixing; 5¼".................................**$15.00**

Country Squire, plate, dinner; 10¼".................................**$9.00**

Country Squire, teapot, 5-cup.................................**$30.00**

Crestone, baker, turquoise.................................**$18.00**

Crestone, creamer, turquoise, 8-oz.................................**$18.00**

Crestone, gravy boat & saucer, turquoise, 10-oz.........**$32.00**

Crestone, plate, dessert; turquoise, 7½".................................**$7.00**

Crestone, steak plate, oval, 11¾x9".................................**$35.00**

Gingerbread, Depot cookie jar.................................**$250.00**

Gingerbread, Train Engine, brown.................................**$500.00**

Gingerbread Man, coaster, sand, 5x5".................................**$30.00**

Gingerbread Man, server, brown, 10x10".................................**$45.00**

Heartland, bowl, soup/salad; heart stencil, 12-oz.........**$9.00**

Heartland, cheese server, heart stencil.................................**$18.00**

Heartland, creamer, heart stencil.................................**$18.00**

Heartland, pitcher, heart stencil, 66-oz.................................**$80.00**

Heartland, platter, heart stancil, oval.................................**$35.00**

Mirror Almond, baker, square, 3-pt.................................**$20.00**

Mirror Almond, bowl, divided vegetable; 10⅞x7⅞".....**$18.00**

Mirror Almond, bowl, fruit.................................**$5.00**

Mirror Almond, bowl, soup/salad; 6½".................................**$7.00**

Mirror Almond, creamer, 8-oz.................................**$14.00**

Mirror Almond, custard cup, 6-oz.................................**$6.00**

Mirror Almond, French casserole, open.................................**$7.00**

Mirror Almond, jug, 2-qt.................................**$36.00**

Mirror Almond, mug, 9-oz.................................**$6.00**

Mirror Almond, plate, dinner; 10¼".................................**$10.00**

Mirror Almond, plate, luncheon; 9⅜".................................**$7.00**

Mirror Almond, snack set.................................**$22.50**

Mirror Almond, stein.................................**$7.00**

Mirror Almond, sugar bowl, 12-oz.................................**$14.00**

Mirror Brown, ashtray, w/deer imprint, #563, 8".......**$22.00**

Mirror Brown, bake 'n serve dish, #573.................................**$10.00**

Mirror Brown, bake 'n serve dish, oval, #574, 16-oz..**$11.00**

Mirror Brown, bake 'n serve dish, round, #589, 6½".**$10.00**

Mirror Brown, baker, rectangular, #534, 7-pt.............**$26.00**

Mirror Brown, baker, rectangular, #567.................................**$35.00**

Mirror Brown, baker, square, #568, 3-pt.................................**$12.00**

Mirror Brown, baker with chicken cover, #560, 11½x13½", $225.00. (Photo courtesy Brenda Roberts)

Mirror Brown, baker, w/rooster imprint, #558, 3" deep..**$95.00**

Mirror Brown, bean pot, w/lid, #524, individual, 12-oz.**$7.00**

Mirror Brown, bean pot, w/lid, 1-qt.................................**$40.00**

Mirror Brown, beer stein, #526, 16-oz.................................**$12.00**

Mirror Brown, bowl, fruit; #503, 5¼".................................**$5.00**

Mirror Brown, bowl, fruit; #533, 6".................................**$8.00**

Mirror Brown, bowl, mixing; #536, 6".................................**$8.00**

Mirror Brown, bowl, mixing; #537, 7".................................**$15.00**

Mirror Brown, bowl, mixing; #538, 8".................................**$16.00**

Mirror Brown, bowl, onion soup; #535, 12-oz, w/lid...**$9.00**

Mirror Brown, bowl, salad; w/rooster imprint, oval, #508 ..**$70.00**

Mirror Brown, bowl, soup/salad; #569, 6½".................................**$8.00**

Mirror Brown, bud vase, 9".................................**$30.00**

Mirror Brown, butter dish, #561, ¼-lb.................................**$15.00**

Mirror Brown, canister set, #556/#557/#558/#559, hard to find in mint condition, 4-pc.................................**$450.00**

Mirror Brown, carafe, #505, 2-cup.................................**$40.00**

Mirror Brown, casserole, open, #543, 2-pt, 7x11".........**$8.00**

Mirror Brown, casserole, oval, w/chicken lid, 2-qt.....**$60.00**

Mirror Brown, casserole, oval, w/lid, #544, 2-pt.........**$20.00**

Mirror Brown, casserole, oval, w/lid, 2-qt.................................**$30.00**

Mirror Brown, casserole, round, w/lid, #314...............**$14.00**

Mirror Brown, casserole, w/duck lid, #5770, 2-qt.......**$75.00**

Mirror Brown, casserole, w/lid, #507, 32-oz................**$25.00**

Mirror Brown, cheese shaker, #582.............................**$36.00**

Mirror Brown, chip 'n dip, #586, 2-pc, 12x11".........**$135.00**

Mirror Brown, chip 'n dip leaf, #521, 15"..................**$30.00**

Mirror Brown, chip 'n dip leaf, #591, 9x12¼"..........**$35.00**

Mirror Brown, coffee cup, #597, 7-oz.........................**$4.00**

Mirror Brown, coffee cup/mug, #502, 9-oz.................**$5.00**

Mirror Brown, coffeepot, #522, 8-cup.........................**$35.00**

Mirror Brown, cookie jar, #523...................................**$30.00**

Mirror Brown, corn-serving dish, #573, 9" L...............**$40.00**

Mirror Brown, custard cup, #576, 6-oz........................**$4.00**

Mirror Brown, Dutch oven, #565, 2-pc........................**$35.00**

Mirror Brown, fish platter, 11".....................................**$80.00**

Mirror Brown, French casserole, #513, individual, open, 9-oz...**$5.00**

Mirror Brown, French casserole, #979, 3-pt, w/lid & warmer, 3-pc...**$90.00**

Mirror Brown, French casserole, stick handle, #562, w/lid, 9-oz...**$7.00**

Mirror Brown, garlic cellar, #3505, 13-oz...................**$20.00**

Mirror Brown, gravy boat, #511...................................**$26.00**

Mirror Brown, gravy boat underplate, #512................**$10.00**

MIrror Brown, ice jug, #514, 2-qt................................**$26.00**

Mirror Brown, jam/mustard jar, #551, 12-oz...............**$10.00**

Mirror Brown, jug, #525, 2-pt......................................**$17.00**

Mirror Brown, jug, water; #509, 80-pz.........................**$30.00**

Mirror Brown, leaf dish, #590, 7¼x4¼"......................**$9.00**

Mirror Brown, leaf serve-all, #540, 7½x12"................**$28.00**

Mirror Brown, mug, #302, 1980s, 10-oz......................**$5.00**

Mirror Brown, mug, Continental; #571, 10-oz or 12-oz, ea...**$20.00**

Mirror Brown, oil cruet, #584 ....**$32.00**

Mirror Brown, pie plate, #566, 9½"..............................**$20.00**

Mirror Brown, plate, dinner; #500, 10¼" **$7.00**

Mirror Brown, plate, salad; #501, 6½"..........................**$5.00**

Mirror Brown, plate, steak; oval, #641, 9x11⅞" **$16.00**

Mirror Brown, quiche dish, #508.................................**$65.00**

Mirror Brown, ramekin, #600, 1980s, 2½-oz...............**$5.00**

Mirror Brown, roaster, rectangular, w/lid, #535, 7-pt..**$60.00**

Mirror Brown, salad server, rectangular, #583, 6½x11"..**$22.00**

Mirror Brown, salt & pepper shakers, 3¼", pr, from $15 to **$15.00**

Mirror Brown, salt & pepper shakers, mushroom form, #587/588, 3¾", pr...**$15.00**

Mirror Brown, sauce bowl for chip 'n dip, #584.........**$35.00**

Mirror Brown, saucer, #598, 6".....................................**$3.00**

Mirror Brown, server, w/handle, #873H **$50.00**

Mirror Brown, serving dish, scalloped, #517...............**$40.00**

Mirror Brown, skillet, #595 ....**$40.00**

Mirror Brown, snack set, tray #554 & mug #553........**$15.00**

Mirror Brown, spoon rest, #594, 6¾".........................**$45.00**

Mirror Brown, stein, jumbo; #572, 32-oz....................**$22.00**

Mirror Brown, tidbit tray, 2-tier, #592.........................**$50.00**

Mirror Brown, tray for chip 'n dip set, #584 ....**$50.00**

Mirror Brown, vegetable dish, divided, #542, 7x10⅞"..**$14.00**

Mirror Brown, vinegar cruet, #585 ....**$32.00**

Provincial, bake dish, 3-pt...**$22.00**

Provincial, bean pot, w/lid, individual, 12-oz **$18.00**

Provincial, bowl, mixing; 5¼".......................................**$12.00**

Provincial, plate, salad; 6½"...**$11.00**

Provincial, salt & pepper shakers, w/corks, 3¾", pr..**$24.00**

Rainbow, plate, luncheon (colors); 8½"........................**$9.00**

Rainbow, saucer (colors), 5½".......................................**$4.00**

Rainbow, tidbit, all colors, 2-tier **$32.00**

Rainbow, tray for snack set, butterscotch **$5.00**

Ridge, bowl, gray or sand, 2½x5½"..............................**$6.00**

Ridge, creamer, gray or sand, 8-oz.............................**$10.00**

Ridge, plate, dinner; gray or sand, 10¼" **$12.00**

Ridge, tray, gray or sand, 7x9½"..................................**$22.00**

Ring, coffee cup, brown..**$7.00**

Ring, coffeepot, brown..**$125.00**

Ring, cookie jar, brown...**$75.00**

Ring, creamer & sugar bowl, brown **$30.00**

Ring, custard cup, brown..**$8.00**

Ring, pitcher, brown, 36-oz...**$50.00**

Ring, pitcher, brown, 66-oz...**$65.00**

Ring, plate, salad; brown..**$7.00**

Tangerine, bean pot, 2-qt..**$28.00**

Tangerine, bud vase, Imperial, 9".................................**$18.00**

Tangerine, butter dish, ¼-lb..**$22.00**

Tangerine, chip 'n dip leaf, 15x10½" **$35.00**

Tangerine, creamer or jug, 8-oz **$12.00**

Tangerine, pie plate, 9¼" dia.......................................**$22.00**

Tangerine, plate, salad; 6½"...**$5.00**

Imperial Glass

Organized in 1901 in Bellaire, Ohio, the Imperial Glass Company made carnival glass, stretch glass, a line called NuCut (made in imitation of cut glass), and a limited amount of art glass within the first decade of the century. In the mid-'30s, they designed one of their most famous patterns (and one of their most popular with today's collectors), Candlewick. Within a few years, milk glass had become their leading product.

During the '50s they reintroduced their NuCut line in crystal as well as colors, marketing it as 'Collector's Crystal.' In the late '50s they bought molds from both Heisey and Cambridge. Most of the glassware they reissued from these old molds was marked 'IG,' one letter superimposed over the other. When Imperial was bought by Lenox in 1973, an 'L' was added to the mark. The ALIG logo was added in 1981 when the company was purchased by Arthur Lorch. In 1982 the factory was sold to Robert Stahl of Minneapolis. Chapter 11 bankruptcy was filled in October that year. A plant resurgence continued production. Many Heisey by Imperial animals done in color were made at this time. A new mark, the NI for New Imperial, was used on a few items. In November of 1984 the plant closed forever and the assets were sold at liquidation. This was the end of the 'Big I.'

Numbers in the listings were assigned by the company and appeared on their catalog pages. They were used to indicate differences in shapes and stems, for instance. Collectors still use them.

For more information on Imperial we recommend *Imperial Glass* by Margaret and Douglas Archer; *Elegant Glassware of the Depression Era* by Gene Florence; *Imperial Carnival Glass* by Carl O. Burns; and *Imperial Glass Encyclopedia, Vol I, A – Cane,* and *Vol II, Cane to M,* edited by James Measell. To research Imperial's glass animals, refer to *Glass Animals of the Depression Years* by Lee Garmon and Dick Spencer.

See also Candlewick.

Note: To determine values for Cape Cod in colors, add 100% to prices suggested for crystal for Ritz Blue and Ruby; Amber, Antique Blue, Azalea, Evergreen, Verde, black, and milk glass are 50% higher than crystal.

Advisor: Joan Cimini (See Directory, Imperial)

Club: National Imperial Glass Collectors' Society, Inc. P.O. Box 534, Bellaire, OH 43906. Dues: $15 per year (+$1 for each additional member of household), quarterly newsletter: *Glasszette,* convention every June

Ashtray, #150, purple slag, 5" **$50.00**
Ashtray, Cape Cod, crystal, #160/134/1, 4".................**$14.00**
Ashtray, heart shape, #294, ruby slag, 4½".................**$25.00**
Baked Apple, Traditional, crystal.........................**$8.00**
Basket, Cape Cod, crystal, handled, #160/40, 11" ...**$125.00**
Basket, Crocheted Crystal, 12" **$60.00**
Basket, Crocheted Crystal, 6".........................**$27.50**
Bottle, cologne; Early American Hobnail, pink...........**$45.00**
Bottle, condiment, Cape Cod, crystal, #160/224, 6-oz .**$65.00**
Bottle, ketchup, Cape Cod, crystal, #160/237, 14-oz ..**$210.00**
Bowl, Cape Cod, crystal, footed, #160/137B, 10"........**$75.00**
Bowl, Cape Cod, crystal, oval, #160/124, 11".............**$80.00**
Bowl, Cape Cod, crystal, oval, #160/131B, 12" **$80.00**
Bowl, Cape Cod, crystal, tab handled, #160/199, 6½"..**$25.00**
Bowl, Cape Cod, crystal, 2-handled, #160/145B, 9½"...**$37.50**
Bowl, Cape Cod, crystal, 2-handled, #160/62B, 7½" ..**$27.50**
Bowl, console; Cape Cod, crystal, #160/75L, 13" **$42.50**
Bowl, console; Crocheted Crystal, 12" **$30.00**
Bowl, dessert; Cape Cod, crystal, tab handled, #160/197, 4½".........................**$25.00**
Bowl, Diamond Quilt, black, crimped, 7"....................**$20.00**
Bowl, finger; Cape Cod, crystal, #1602, 4" **$12.00**
Bowl, fruit; Cape Cod, crystal, #160/23B, 5½" **$10.00**
Bowl, fruit; Cape Cod, crystal, #160/3F, 6" **$10.00**
Bowl, grape; crimped, ruby slag, #47C, 1969, 9" **$75.00**
Bowl, heart; Cape Cod, crystal, handled, #160/40H, 6"..**$20.00**
Bowl, Hobnail, #641, purple slag, 8½" **$95.00**
Bowl, Katy, green opalescent, #749B, 9"...................**$125.00**
Bowl, Rose, jade slag, #62C, 9" **$80.00**
Bowl, salad; Cape Cod, crystal, #1608B, 11" **$40.00**
Butter dish, Cape Cod, crystal, w/lid, #160/161, ¼-lb ..**$45.00**

Cake stand, Cape Cod, crystal, #160/103D, 11" **$80.00**
Cake stand, Cape Cod, crystal, footed, #160/67D, 10½"..**$55.00**
Cake stand, Crocheted Crystal, footed, 12"..................**$45.00**
Candle holder, Cape Cod, crystal, #160/81, 4" **$25.00**
Candle holder, Cape Cod, crystal, Aladdin style, #160/90, 5"..**$75.00**
Candle holder, centerpiece; Cape Cod, crystal, #160/48C, 6" **$75.00**
Candle holder, Crocheted Crystal, 6" L **$20.00**
Candle holders Dolphin, #779, caramel slag, 5", pr....**$80.00**
Celery, Cape Cod, crystal, oval, #160/105, 8"............**$35.00**
Celery tray, Huckabee, pink, oval, 8¼" **$32.50**
Cigarette holder, Cape Cod, crystal, footed, #1602 .....**$12.50**
Coaster, Cape Cod, crystal, flat, #160/1R, 4½"..............**$9.00**
Coaster, Cape Cod, crystal, w/spoon rest, #160/76.....**$10.00**
Comport, Cape Cod, crystal, #160/45, 6" **$25.00**
Comport, Cape Cod, crystal, #160/48B, 7"..................**$35.00**
Comport, Cape Cod, crystal, w/lid, footed, #160/140, 6"..**$75.00**
Compote, #431C, ruby slag, crimped, footed, 6½" **$55.00**
Cookie jar, Cape Cod, crystal, wicker handle, w/lid, #160/195, 6½" **$100.00**
Cordial, Decorated Western Apple, crystal, #176, 2-oz ..**$20.00**
Covered box, dog, #822, purple slag.........................**$185.00**
Covered box, rooster, #158, jade slag........................**$190.00**
Covered box, squirrel, #821, purple slag, 5½"..........**$180.00**
Covered dish, duck on nest, #146, jade slag, 4½" **$65.00**
Creamer, Beaded Block, crystal................................**$20.00**
Creamer, Cape Cod, crystal, #160/30............................**$8.00**
Cruet, Cape Cod, crystal, w/stopper, #160/70, 5-oz....**$25.00**
Cup, coffee; Cape Cod, crystal, #160/37.......................**$7.00**
Cup & saucer, Pillar Flutes, light blue.........................**$25.00**
Decanter, cask #1, Antique Blue **$55.00**
Decanter, rye; Cape Cod, crystal, #160/260.................**$80.00**
Egg cup, Cape Cod, crystal, #160/225 ....**$32.50**

Epergne, Cape Cod, #160/196, 12", $200.00.

Figurine, Asiatic pheasant, amber **$425.00**
Figurine, bull, amber, very rare.................................**$725.00**
Figurine, colt, amber, standing **$125.00**
Figurine, colt, caramel slag, balking.........................**$140.00**
Figurine, colt, Sunshine Yellow, standing...................**$75.00**
Figurine, dog, Airedale, caramel slag........................**$115.00**

Figurine, donkey, Meadow Green carnival.................$55.00
Figurine, elephant, Meadow Green carnival, #674, med...$60.00
Figurine, flying mare, amber, ALIG mark...............$1,350.00
Figurine, gazelle, black, 11"..............................$350.00
Figurine, giraffe, amber, ALIG mark, extremely rare ..$350.00
Figurine, mallard, Horizon Blue, wings down, HCA, 4½" .$35.00
Figurine, piglet, amber, standing $40.00
Figurine, piglet, ruby, standing...........................$35.00
Figurine, ring-necked pheasant, amber, marked NI..$300.00
Figurine, rooster, amber $375.00
Figurine, Scottie, milk glass, 3½".........................$45.00
Figurine, standing colt, ultra blue, #12/3, 5" $40.00
Figurine, wood duck, caramel slag $45.00
Figurine/bookend, fish, amber (crystal or frosted), rare, ea .$175.00
Figurine/paperweight, tiger, caramel slag.................$150.00
Figurine/paperweight, tiger, jade green, 8" L $75.00
Goblet, Chroma, burgundy, #123 ....$30.00
Gravy bowl, Cape Cod, crystal, #160/202, 18-oz $65.00
Icer, Cape Cod, crystal, bowl, 2 inserts, #160/53/3, 3-pc ..$50.00

Jar, owl, Horizon Blue, #800, two-piece, from $50.00 to $65.00.

Jar, pokal; Cape Cod, crystal, #160/128, 11"................$85.00
Jar, vanity; Reeded (Spun), pink, #701, 7⅝"...............$45.00
Ladle, mayonnaise; Cape Cod, crystal, #160/135 ....$10.00
Ladle, mayonnaise; Crocheted Crystal.........................$5.00
Lamp, hurricane; Cape Cod, crystal, bowl-like base, #1604, 2-pc $115.00
Mayonnaise, Cape Cod, crystal, #160/52H, 3-pc set ...$37.50
Mug, Cape Cod, crystal, handled, #160/188, 12-oz.....$45.00
Nappy, poppy; #478, jade slag, handled, 5½".............$55.00
Nut dish, Cape Cod, crystal, handled, #160/184, 4"...$30.00
Pitcher, Cape Cod, crystal, #160/24, 2-qt $80.00
Pitcher, Cape Cod, crystal, ice lip, #160/19, 40-oz......$75.00
Pitcher, Dew Drop, opalescent, #624, 56-oz...............$65.00
Pitcher, jade slag, #104, 3" miniature $45.00
Plate, bread & butter; Cape Cod, crystal, #160/1D, 6½" ..$8.00
Plate, bread; Cape Cod, crystal, #160/222, 12½".........$70.00
Plate, Cape Cod, crystal, center-handled tray, #160/149D, 8" $50.00
Plate, Cape Cod, crystal, cupped, #160/20V, 16".........$60.00
Plate, Cape Cod, crystal, 2-handled, #160/62D, 9½"...$40.00
Plate, Crocheted Crystal, 14" $25.00

Plate, Katy, blue opalescent, 6" $20.00
Plate, salad; Cape Cod, crystal, #160/5D, 8" $9.00
Plate, salad; Crocheted Crystal, 8" $7.50
Plate, torte; Cape Cod, crystal, #1608F, 13" $37.50
Puff box, Cape Cod, crystal, w/lid, #1601 ....$45.00
Relish, Cape Cod, crystal, oval, 3-part, #160/55, 9½" .$35.00
Relish, Crocheted Crystal, 3-pt, 11½" $25.00
Salad dressing, Cape Cod, crystal, w/handle & spout, #160/208, 6-oz..$55.00
Salt & pepper shakers, Cape Cod, crystal, #160/109, square, pr..$20.00
Salt & pepper shakers, Cape Cod, crystal, footed, #160/116, pr..$20.00
Salt dip, ruby slag, #61, 4-footed..............................$16.00
Saucer, tea; Cape Cod, crystal, #160/35 ....$4.00
Sherbet, Huckabee, pink, footed..............................$30.00
Spoon, Cape Cod, crystal, #701..............................$15.00
Stem, cocktail; Cape Cod, crystal, #1602, 3½-oz...........$8.00
Stem, goblet; Cape Cod, crystal, #160, magnum, 14-oz..$35.00
Stem, luncheon; Cape Cod, crystal, 9-oz $10.00
Stem, parfait; Cape Cod, crsytal, #1602, 6-oz $12.00
Stem, sherbet; Crocheted Crystal, 6-oz.......................$10.00
Sugar bowl, Cape Cod, crystal, #160/30 ....$8.00
Toothpick holder, ruby slag, #1, 1969-77....................$25.00
Tray, Cape Cod, crystal, for creamer & sugar bowl, #160/29..$18.00
Tumbler, #552, caramel slag, 11-oz.........................$80.00
Tumbler, Cape Cod, crystal, #160, 16-oz....................$35.00
Tumbler, iced tea; Crocheted Crystal, footed, 12-oz...$15.00
Tumbler, juice; Cape Cod, crystal, footed, #1602, 6-oz.$9.00
Tumbler, tea; Cape Cod, crystal, footed, #1600, 12-oz .$19.00
Tumbler, water; Cape Cod, crystal, footed, #1602, 10-oz..$10.00
Vase, #965, caramel slag, footed, 9½"........................$120.00
Vase, bud; Free-Hand, hearts & vines, light green on opalescent, 8½" $350.00
Vase, Cape Cod, crystal, footed, #160/22, 7½"............$40.00
Vase, Cape Cod, crystal, footed, #160/28, 8½"............$42.50
Vase, flip; Cape Cod, crystal, #1603, 11"....................$165.00
Vase, Free-Hand, gold w/pink & orange iridescent, ovoid, 10" $350.00
Vase, Katy, blue opalescent, #743B, 5¼" $45.00
Vase, Loganberry, milk glass, crimped, #356, 10" $35.00
Vase, Reeded (Spun), red, 9" $75.00

Crocheted Crystal, sugar bowl, $18.00; pedestal bowl, $30.00; mayonaise bowl, $12.50; underplate, $7.50; compote, $40.00; creamer, $18.00. (Photo courtesy Gene Florence)

Indiana Glass

From 1972 until 1978, Indiana Glass Company produced a line of iridescent 'new carnival' glass, much of which was embossed with grape clusters and detailed leaves in a line they called Harvest. It was made in blue, gold, and lime, and was evidently a good seller for them, judging from the amount around today. They also produced a line of 'press cut' iridescent glass called Heritage, which they made in amethyst and Sunset (amberina). Collectors always seem to gravitate toward lustre-coated glassware, whether it's old or recently made, and there seems to be a significant amount of interest in this line.

There was also a series of four Bicentennial Commemorative plates made in blue and gold carnival: American Eagle, Independence Hall, Liberty Bell, and Spirit of '76. They're valued at $12.00 for the gold and $15.00 for the blue, except for the American Eagle plate, which is worth from $12.00 to $15.00 regardless of color.

This glass is a little difficult to evaluate, since you see it in malls and at flea markets with such a wide range of 'asking' prices. On one hand, you'll have sellers who themselves are not exactly sure what it is they have but since it's 'carnival' assume it should be fairly pricey. On the other hand, you have those who've just 'cleaned house' and want to get rid of it. They may have bought it new themselves and know it's not very old and wasn't expensive to start with. This is what you'll be up against if you decide you want to collect it.

In addition to the iridescent glass lines, Indiana produced colored glass baskets, vases, etc., as well as a line called Ruby Band Diamond Point, a clear diamond-faceted pattern with a wide ruby-flashed rim band. We've listed some of the latter below; our values are for examples with the ruby-flashing in excellent condition.

Over the last ten years, the collectibles market has changed. Nowadays, some shows' criteria regarding the merchandise they allow to be displayed is 'if it's no longer available on the retail market, it's OK.' I suspect that this attitude will become more and more widespread. At any rate, this is one of the newest interests at the flea market/antique mall level, and if you can buy it right (and like its looks), now is the time!

See also King's Crown; Tiara.

Bicentennial Commemorative plate, American Eagle, made in blue as well as gold carnival, either color, from $12.00 to $15.00 each.

Iridescent Amethyst Carnival Glass (Heritage)

Basket, footed, 9x5x7"...$35.00
Butter dish, 5x7½" dia, from $25 to...........................$35.00
Candle holder, 5½", ea, from $22 to.........................$30.00
Center bowl, 4¾x8½", from $30 to.............................$40.00
Goblet, 8-oz...$17.50
Pitcher, 8¼", from $40 to..$50.00
Punch set, 10" bowl & pedestal, 8 cups, & ladle, 11-pc.$125.00
Swung vase, slender & footed w/irregular rim, 11x3"...$30.00

Iridescent Blue Carnival Glass

Basket, Canterbury, waffled pattern, flared sides drawn in at handle, 11x8x12"..$45.00
Basket, Monticello, allover faceted embossed diamonds, square, 7x6"...$35.00
Butter dish, Harvest, embossed grapes, ¼-lb, 8" L, from $20 to...$25.00
Candy box, Harvest, embossed grapes w/lace edge, w/lid, 6½"..$30.00
Candy box, Princess, diamond-point bands, pointed faceted finial, 6x6" dia, from $20 to.............................$25.00
Canister/Candy jar, Harvest, embossed grapes, 7"......$30.00
Canister/Cookie jar, Harvest, embossed grapes, 9".....$45.00
Canister/Snack jar, Harvest, embossed grapes, 8".......$35.00
Center bowl, Harvest, embossed grapes w/paneled sides, 4-footed, 4½x8½x12", from $25 to.........................$35.00
Cooler (iced tea tumbler), Harvest, embossed grapes, 14-oz, set of 4, from $32 to...$40.00
Creamer & sugar bowl on tray, Harvest, embossed grapes, 3-pc, from $25 to..$30.00
Egg/Hors d'oeuvre tray, sectioned w/off-side holder for 8 eggs, 12¾" dia, from $25 to.................................$35.00
Garland bowl (comport), paneled, 7½x8½" dia.........$35.00
Goblet, Harvest, embossed grapes, 9-oz, set of 4, from $25 to.$30.00
Hen on nest, from $10 to...$15.00
Pitcher, Harvest, embossed grapes, 10½", from $40 to..$50.00
Plate, Bicentennial; American Eagle, from $12 to.......$15.00
Plate, hostess; Canterbury, allover diamond facets, flared crimped rim, 10", from $25 to.............................$35.00
Punch set, Princess, 26-pc, from $75 to......................$95.00
Tidbit, allover embossed diamond points, shallow w/flared sides, 6½", from $12 to.......................................$18.00
Wedding bowl (sm compote), Thumbprint, footed, 5x5", from $15 to...$22.00

Iridescent Gold Carnival Glass

Basket, Canterbury, waffle pattern, flaring sides drawn in at handle terminals, 9½x11x8½", from $35 to..........$40.00
Basket, Monticello, lg faceted allover diamonds, square, 7x6"...$25.00
Candy box, Harvest, embossed grapes, lace edge, footed, 6½x5¾"...$20.00
Candy dish, Harvest, embossed grapes, lace edge, footed, 6½"...$20.00

Canister/Candy jar, Harvest, embossed grapes, 7" **$25.00**
Canister/Cookie jar, Harvest, embossed grapes, 9" **$35.00**
Canister/Snack jar, Harvest, embossed grapes, 8" **$30.00**
Center bowl, Harvest, oval w/embossed grapes & paneled sides, 4½x8½x12", from $15 to **$20.00**
Console set, wide naturalistic leaves form sides, 9" bowl w/pr 4½" bowl-type candle holders, 3-pc **$30.00**
Cooler (iced tea tumbler), Harvest, 14-oz, from $8 to ..**$10.00**
Egg relish plate, 11", from $18 to **$25.00**
Goblet, Harvest, embossed grapes, 9-oz **$12.00**
Hen on nest, 5½", from $10 to **$15.00**

Pitcher, Harvest, embossed grapes, 10½", from $35.00 to $45.00; tumbler, iced tea (cooler), 5½", set of four, from $35.00 to $40.00.

Plate, hostess; diamond embossing, shallow w/crimped & flared sides, 10", from $12 to **$18.00**
Punch set, Princess, 6-qt bowl w/12 cups, 12 hooks & ladle, 26-pc, from $75 to **$95.00**
Relish tray, Vintage, 6 sections, 9x12¾", from $15 to.**$20.00**
Salad set, Vintage, embossed fruit, apple-shaped rim w/applied stem, 13", w/fork & spoon, 3-pc, from $18 to.........**$25.00**
Wedding bowl, Harvest, embossed grapes, pedestal foot, 8½x8", from $25 to **$35.00**
Wedding bowl (sm compote), 5x5", from $9 to.........**$12.00**

Iridescent Lime Carnival Glass

Candy box, Harvest, embossed grapes w/lace edge, w/lid, 6½" **$25.00**
Canister/Candy jar, Harvest, embossed grapes, 7" **$25.00**
Canister/Cookie jar, Harvest, embossed grapes, 9" **$35.00**
Canister/Snack jar, Harvest, embossed grapes, 8" **$30.00**
Center bowl, Harvest, embossed grapes, paneled sides, 4-footed, 4½x8½x12", from $25 to **$30.00**
Compote, Harvest, embossed grapes, 7x6", from $20 to ..**$30.00**
Console set, Harvest, embossed grapes, 10" comport w/compote-shaped candle holders, 3-pc **$45.00**
Cooler (iced tea tumbler), Harvest, embossed grapes, 14-oz, from $8 to...**$10.00**
Creamer & sugar bowl on tray, Harvest, embossed grapes, 3-pc, from $20 to **$25.00**
Egg/Relish tray, 12¾", from $18 to **$25.00**
Goblet, Harvest, embossed grapes, 9-oz, from $8 to ..**$10.00**

Hen on nest, from $10 to..**$15.00**
Pitcher, Harvest, embossed grapes, 10½", from $28 to .**$35.00**
Plate, hostess; allover diamond points, flared crimped sides, 10", from $15 to **$20.00**
Punch set, Princess, 26-pc, from $75 to.....................**$95.00**
Salad set, Vintage, embossed fruit, apple-shaped rim w/applied stem, 13", w/fork & spoon, 3-pc, from $35 to **$45.00**
Snack set, Harvest, embossed grapes, 4 cups & 4 plates, 8-pc, from $25 to **$35.00**

Iridescent Sunset (Amberina) Carnival Glass (Heritage)

Basket, footed, 9x5x7", from $40 to **$50.00**
Basket, squared, 9½x7½", from $50 to **$60.00**
Bowl, crimped, 3¾x10", from $40 to **$50.00**
Butter dish, 5x7½" dia, from $35 to **$45.00**
Cake stand, 7x14" dia, from $55 to **$65.00**
Center bowl, 4¾x8½", from $40 to **$50.00**
Creamer & sugar bowl **$45.00**
Dessert set, 8½" bowl, 12" plate, 2-pc, from $60 to ...**$75.00**
Goblet, 8-oz, from $15 to..**$20.00**
Pitcher, 7¼", from $50 to **$65.00**
Pitcher, 8¼", from $60 to **$75.00**
Plate, rim w/4 lg & 4 sm opposing lobes, 2x14", from $50 to...**$60.00**
Punch set, 10" bowl, pedestal, 8 cups, & ladle, 11-pc..**$150.00**
Rose bowl, 6½x6½", from $30 to................................**$40.00**
Sauce set, 4½" bowl, 5½" plate, w/spoon, 3-pc, from $30 to...**$35.00**
Swung vase, slender, footed, w/irregular rim, 11x3", from $25 to...**$35.00**
Tumbler, 3½", from $12 to...**$15.00**

Patterns

Canterbury, basket, waffle pattern, Lime, Sunset, or Horizon Blue, 5½x12", from $35 to **$55.00**
Monticello, basket, lg faceted diamonds overall, Lemon, Lime, Sunset, or Horizon Blue, square, 7x6", from $25 to **$35.00**
Monticello, basket, lg faceted diamonds overall, Lemon, Lime, Sunset, or Horizon Blue, 8¾x10½", from $35 to **$45.00**
Monticello, candy box, lg faceted overall diamonds, w/lid, Lemon, Lime, Sunset, or Horizon Blue, 5¼x6", from $20 to **$25.00**
Ruby Band Diamond Point, chip & dip set, 13" dia, from $18 to...**$25.00**
Ruby Band Diamond Point, comport, 14½" dia, from $15 to...**$20.00**
Ruby Band Diamond Point, cooler (iced tea tumbler), 15-oz, from $8 to...**$10.00**
Ruby Band Diamond Point, creamer & sugar bowl, 4½", from $12 to..**$15.00**
Ruby Band Diamond Point, creamer & sugar bowl, 4¾", on 6x9" tray, from $15 to **$22.00**

Ruby Band Diamond Point, goblet, 12-oz, from $9 to .**$12.00**

Ruby Band Diamond Point, On-the-Rocks, 9-oz, from $8 to **$10.00**

Ruby Band Diamond Point, pitcher, 8", from $15 to ..**$20.00**

Ruby Band Diamond Point, plate, hostess; 12", from $12 to...**$18.00**

Ruby Band Diamond Point, relish tray, 1-part, 12" dia, from $15 to...**$20.00**

Ruby Band Diamond Point, salt & pepper shakers, 4", pr, from $15 to...**$20.00**

Ruby Band Diamond Point, butter dish, from $20.00 to $28.00.

Indianapolis 500 Racing Collectibles

You don't have to be a Hoosier to know that unless the weather interfers, this famous 500-mile race is held in Indianapolis every Memorial day and has been since 1911. Collectors of Indy memorabilia have a plethora of race-related items to draw from and can zero in on one area or many, enabling them to build extensive and interesting collections. Some of the special areas of interest they pursue are autographs, photographs, or other memorabilia related to the drivers; pit badges; race programs and yearbooks; books and magazines; decanters and souvenir tumblers; and model race cars.

Advisor: Eric Jungnickel (See Directory, Indy 500 Memorabilia)

Ashtray, ceramic, round, 3 rests on straight edge, 74th/May 27, 1990, red & black on white, 4½" dia.............**$13.00**

Ashtray, dark glass w/race scene, car & IMS logo, 3½" dia **$10.00**

Ashtray, Indianapolis Motor Speedway '500,' white ceramic w/gold trim & winged wheel logo.......................**$20.00**

Bank, metal, #32 Haroun's Marmon Wasp, '11 Indy Winner, stamped w/sponsoring bank, 7"............................**$50.00**

Bobbin' head doll, driver in helmet standing w/blue shirt, Indianapolis 500 in gold on chest.....................**$300.00**

Cigarette lighter, silver w/IMS logo on front, track scene, state of Indiana on back, Zippo **$25.00**

Decal, IMS/USAC logo, dated 1960............................**$12.00**

Decal, water-dip style, shows IMS Main Gate & period car, 1960s...**$15.00**

Decanter, Al Unser's Johnny Lightning race car, blue w/gold, #2 ....**$75.00**

Decanter, black w/winged wheel logo on front, JW Dant, 1969 ....**$25.00**

Decanter, Mario Andretti, red #9 car, Old Mr Boston.**$50.00**

Decanter, May 30th 1970, yellow race car on front, winged wheel logo on back, Jim Beam, 1970 ....**$15.00**

Flag, black & white checks, Indianapolis Speedway, #1 car shown **$10.00**

Game, Champion Spark Plugs Auto Race, premium, 1934, M **$75.00**

Lunch box, Auto Race Magazine Game Kit, w/thermos, playing pieces & spinner, 1967, M **$125.00**

Magazine, Sports Illustrated, June 5, 1978, Unser's 3rd cover, NM **$12.00**

Magazine, Sports Illustrated, May 26, 1956, Bob Sweikert cover, M..**$30.00**

Model, '64 Mustang Indy Pace Car, Monogram, 1995, complete **$10.00**

Model, Kraco Special March 88C, AMT, 1989, MIB (sealed)...**$25.00**

Pamphlet, Why I Became a Race Car Driver, by Wilbur Shaw, Firestone Tires, 1940..**$10.00**

Pennant, Souvenir of Indianapolis Speedway, maroon felt w/white lettering & graphics, 29½", EX+ **$160.00**

Pennant, Souvenir of Indianapolis Speedway, red w/IMS logo, 500 mile race, crossed flags & race car on left, 1950s..**$75.00**

Pennant, Speedway Ind, green felt w/white lettering & early race car graphics, 26½", NM..............................**$175.00**

Pillow sham, Souvenir of Indianapolis Speedway, pink silk w/race scene...**$30.00**

Pinball game, 500 Mile Speedway Game, pictures race scene, w/spinner & bell, Wolverine Toy Company, 22", EX.**$25.00**

Pit badge, 1950, bronze **$150.00**

Pit badge, 1952, bronze, Firestone Tire **$125.00**

Pit badge, 1956, silver, IMS Main Gate........................**$90.00**

Pit badge, 1960, bronze, Champion Spark Plug..........**$50.00**

Pit badge, 1969, bronze, salutes movie 'Winning'.......**$75.00**

Pit badge, 1978, bronze, STP **$50.00**

Pit badge, 1982, silver, Camero **$65.00**

Pit badge, 1991, bronze, Dodge **$50.00**

Poster, Champion Spark Plug dealer's, pictures Donohue, Parsons & others...**$20.00**

Program, 1925, scored...**$350.00**

Program, 1930, soiled, loose pages............................**$200.00**

Program, 1937, EX **$150.00**

Program, 1940, M..**$100.00**

Program, 1955, NM **$50.00**

Program, 1961, 50th Anniversary, M **$35.00**

Program, 1977-80s, any, EX **$10.00**

Record, Great Moments From the Indy 500 (1911-1974), 33⅓ rpm, narrated by Sid Collins, M...................**$20.00**

Salt & pepper shakers, smoke glass w/wood handles, depicts IMS logo, IMS Main Gate, race car, 4½", pr **$25.00**

Seat cushion, Indianapolis 500 Speedway, black & white checks w/1970s race car $25.00

Ticket, 1929, w/rain check, shows race scene w/pagoda, NM $100.00

Ticket, 1946, 31st International Sweepstakes, VG.......$40.00

Ticket, 1955, w/rain check, shows previous year's winner, Bill Vukovich, M $40.00

Ticket, 1962, w/rain check, shows previous year's winner AJ Foyt, M..$30.00

Ticket, 1973, shows previous year's winner, Rick Mears .$10.00

Ticket, 1991, VIP Suite, unused....................................$15.00

Tie bar & cuff links, Parnelli Jones in helmet, gold filled, 3-pc $35.00

Tumbler, 1967, Parnelli Jones, 5½", from $9.00 to $12.00.

Tumbler, IMS logo, 1953 ....$25.00

Tumbler, IMS logo on front, winners listed on back, Tony Hulman facsimile signature, 1968.........................$20.00

Watch fob, shows 1911 winner, Marmon Wasp, souvenir of 1930s, $125.00. (Photo courtesy Jim and Nancy Schaut)

Yearbook, 1947, Floyd Clymer, features Mauri Rose...$30.00

Yearbook, 1961, Floyd Clymer, Foyt's 1st win $50.00

Yearbook, 1972, Carl Hugness, 1st annual Hugness...$75.00

Yearbook, 1982, Carl Hugness, Johncock cover..........$30.00

Italian Glass

Throughout the century, the island of Murano has been recognized as one of the major glassmaking centers of the world. Companies including Venini, Barovier, Aureliano Toso, Barvini, Vistosi, AVEM, Cenedese, Cappellin, Seguso, and Archimede Seguso have produced very fine art glass, examples of which today often bring several thousand dollars on the secondary market — superior examples much more. Such items are rarely seen at the garage sale and flea market level, but what you will be seeing are the more generic glass clowns, birds, ashtrays, and animals, generally referred to simply as Murano glass. Their values are determined by the techniques used in their making more than size alone. For instance, an item with gold inclusions, controlled bubbles, fused glass patches, or layers of colors is more desirable than one that has none of these elements, even though it may be larger. For more information concerning the specific companies mentioned above, see *Schroeder's Antiques Price Guide* (Collector Books).

Ashtray, clear w/multicolored splotches & w/silver mica, 6¼x6¼" $23.50

Ashtray, clown, white face w/red features, blue body & black feet, 4x5"...$50.00

Ashtray, white milk glass w/green interior, metal rim, 1¼x5" $12.00

Bottle, lg duck is stopper (green to amber), on black bottle base, Luxards 1969 on base, 12½" $70.00

Bowl, alternating stripes of filigree & latticinio, 4-corner rim w/points alternately up & down, 8" L $150.00

Bowl, amberina, free-form w/rim pulled into several long spikes, 13" $30.00

Bowl, amethyst w/internal bubbles, lobed petal rim, 9½" $50.00

Bowl, asymetrical design in turquoise & white w/silver flecks, 6" $25.00

Bowl, floriform; coral, 2 elongated downward curving petals, 8" $25.00

Bowl, ice blue swirl w/aventurine over white opaque, pulled clear handles, free-form, 11" L..............................$25.00

Bowl, magenta rim shading to clear, turquoise base, lg applied ring hdls, internal gold flecks, 17" L......$200.00

Bowl, spiral colors of mottled green, brown & butterscotch w/silver foil cased over white ground, free-form, 9"..........$35.00

Bowl, turquoise shading to coral, free-form, 9" $35.00

Bowl, white opaque cased w/spiral of apple green & aventurine, free-form, 11" $25.00

Bowl, white w/patches of orange & aventurine, pinched & fluted rim, 9" $30.00

Candle holder, clear & red w/gold mica, decorated w/bubbles, 2½x3" $38.00

Candle holder, votive; 6-petal flower form, blues & greens, 5½x4" $15.00

Compote, bird form, white & adventurine encased in apple green, clear aventurine fluted base, 11"................$85.00

Cornucopia, crystal w/emerald green shading, free-form on high pedestal base, 15½" $65.00

Figurine, bear, clear w/rusty red inside, 4½" $25.00

Figurine, bird, cobalt blue w/light blue tail, face & body, gilt flecks on base, 8x6"..$48.00

Figurine, bird, magenta to amber w/lg scrolled tails on arched pedestal base in clear w/gold flecks, 12", pr.........**$150.00**

Figurine, bird, mottled blue & white w/adventurine & controlled bubbles, clear base w/internal aventurine, 8".............**$60.00**

Figurine, cat (sitting upright), magenta aventurine encased in white opalescent w/controlled bubbles, 7"........**$110.00**

Figurine, clown, bowl form, electric blue body w/aventurine, white face & hands, black feet & hat, 7½"...........**$60.00**

Figurine, clown, bowl form, red cased in white w/silver foil, white collar, yellow hair, applied features, 7"......**$60.00**

Figurine, clown, bowl form w/rolled sides, spirals of mottled brown, blue, green, amber & yellow w/silver flecks, 8½"..**$80.00**

Figurine, clown, 11", from $100.00 to $125.00.

Figurine, deer, amber, blue & silver foil encased in crystal, attributed to Seguso, 9"...**$90.00**

Figurine, dolphin, clear w/internal cobalt stripe, on lg freeform pedestal, 12½...**$80.00**

Figurine, duck, magenta encased in clear, clear swirled-rib base, 11"..**$50.00**

Figurine, duck, red w/silver mica & yellow beak, 8½".**$50.00**

Figurine, fish, clear w/red & black inside, 8¾x8".......**$75.00**

Figurine, fish, clear w/spring green inside, 4½x4"......**$20.00**

Figurine, fish, green encased in crystal w/light blue tint on base w/opal center, 12"..**$50.00**

Figurine, fish, red, purple & white in clear, amber fins & base, Genuine Venetia, 12"....................................**$60.00**

Figurine, flamenco dancer, gold flecks & ice blue trim & ornamentation on bell-shaped foot, 9"..............**$115.00**

Figurine, garden snail, clear w/ocean blue, 5x5"........**$32.00**

Figurine, gold fish, clear w/front half encasing red, back w/foil, clear fins on gray base, 9", pr.................**$200.00**

Figurine, goldfish, electric blue & silver foil on white, yellow fins, 4-finned pulled rib base w/blue interior, 13"..**$170.00**

Figurine, horse, rearing, clear w/2 shades of blue, Campanella Glass, 9½"..**$32.00**

Figurine, manta ray, smooth glass w/purple inside, outlined in white w/clear edges, 2¼x5½"...........................**$55.00**

Figurine, parrot, clear w/green swirls around body, gold feathers on head, perched on brown tree w/gold flecks, 13".**$185.00**

Figurine, penguin (upright), amber area w/bubbles encased in clear, 13"..**$40.00**

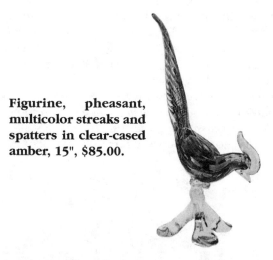

Figurine, pheasant, multicolor streaks and spatters in clear-cased amber, 15", $85.00.

Figurine, rooster, clear & amber w/green inside upper torso & tail, 13¼"...**$80.00**

Figurine, seal, clear w/plum blended w/cobalt blue inside, 4x3½"...**$25.00**

Figurine, snail, clear w/amber inside shell, signed Seguso AV, 7½x5"...**$180.00**

Figurine, swan, purple w/silver flake mica, 8½", from $65 to..**$75.00**

Figurines, doves, blue w/gold flakes inside, 5½x3¾", pr..**$60.00**

Figurines, females, red outfits w/clear trim, internal gold flecks, swirled-rib base w/gold flecks, 11", pr ...**$600.00**

Flower, green, blue, white & pink petals, twisted green stem, 5x6½"...**$30.00**

Necklace, 100 millefiori beads on 60" strand, hand-knotted, EX...**$25.00**

Paperweight, apple shape, light blue w/amber interior, 4" dia...**$55.00**

Perfume bottle, shell motif, orange over green w/gold dividing colors, green shell stopper, 5¾"......................**$40.00**

Rolling pin, green w/white & red stripes, 17" L.........**$50.00**

Straw holder, purple w/graduated rings at base, w/lid, 11"..**$45.00**

Vase, blue w/controlled bubbles, flared rim, green handles from rim to shoulder, 7"....................................**$30.00**

Vase, bud; clear w/turquoise, gold & white vertical ribbons, bulbous bottom, 6¾"...**$45.00**

Vase, floriform; pulled petal tips in cobalt shading to ice blue, 10½"..**$45.00**

Vase, ruby red over white opaque, rim w/3 lg petals, body tapers to tri-corner clear base, 11".......................**$60.00**

Jade-ite Glassware

For the past few years, Jade-ite has been one of the fastest-moving types of collectible glassware on the market. It was produced by several companies from the 1940s through 1965. Many of Anchor Hocking's Fire-King lines were available in the soft opaque green Jade-ite, and Jeannette Glass as well as McKee produced their own versions.

It was always very inexpensive glass, and it was made in abundance. Dinnerware for the home as well as restaurants and a vast array of kitchenware items literally flooded the country for many years. Though a few rare pieces have become fairly expensive, most are still reasonably priced, and there are still bargains to be had.

For more information we recommend *Anchor Hocking's Fire-King & More, Kitchen Glassware of the Depression Years,* and *Collectible Glassware of the 40s, 50s, and 60s,* all written by Gene Florence and published by Collector Books.

Ashtray, 4½" $30.00

Batter bowl, Fire-King, ¾" rim at top, 4x9½" from spout to handle, from $20.00 to $25.00.

Bonbon, straight rim, diamond bottom, 6" $35.00
Bowl, beaded edge, Fire-King, 6" $10.00
Bowl, beater; metal beater, Jeannette $30.00
Bowl, bonbon; diamond pattern, ruffled rim, Fire-King, 6½" $35.00
Bowl, breakfast; Restaurant Ware, Fire-King, 10-oz $24.00
Bowl, bulb; ruffled top, 6¾" $20.00
Bowl, cereal; Anchor Hocking, 16-oz $45.00
Bowl, cereal; flanged rim, G305, Restaurant Ware, Fire-King, 8-oz $16.00
Bowl, cereal; Shell, Fire-King, 6⅜" $18.00
Bowl, dessert; Charm, Fire-King, 4¾" $10.00
Bowl, dessert; Jane Ray, Fire-King, 4⅞" $7.00
Bowl, dessert; Sheaves of Wheat, Fire-King, 4½" $35.00
Bowl, flat soup; Restaurant Ware, Fire-King, 9¼" $55.00
Bowl, flat soup; 1700 Line, Fire-King, 7½" $35.00
Bowl, fruit; Restaurant Ware, Fire-King, 4¾" $7.50
Bowl, horizontal ribs, Jeannette, 9¾" $40.00
Bowl, mixing; Colonial Kitchen, Fire-King, 6" $40.00
Bowl, mixing; Colonial Kitchen, Fire-King, 7¼" $45.00
Bowl, mixing; Colonial Kitchen, Fire-King, 8¾" $50.00
Bowl, mixing; Ribbed, Fire-King, 7½" $30.00
Bowl, mixing; Splash Proof, Anchor Hocking, 8½" $65.00
Bowl, mixing; Swedish Modern, Anchor Hocking, 6" .$80.00
Bowl, mixing; Swirl, Fire-King, 6" $12.50
Bowl, mixing; Swirl, Fire-King, 9" $20.00

Bowl, mixing; vertical ribs, 4¾" $35.00
Bowl, mixing; w/decal flowers, 1-qt, 6¾" $110.00
Bowl, oatmeal; Jane Ray, Fire-King, 5⅞" $14.00
Bowl, ruffled rim, diamond bottom, 6½" $35.00
Bowl, soup plate; Jane Ray, Fire-King, 7⅝" $16.00
Bowl, soup plate; Shell, Fire-King, 7⅝" $22.00
Bowl, soup; Charm, Fire-King, 6" $23.00
Bowl, vegetable; Jane Ray, Fire-King, 8¼" $18.00
Bowl, vegetable; Shell, oval, Fire-King, 8½" $125.00
Bowl, vegetable; Three Bands, Fire-King, 8¼" $40.00
Bowl, vertical ribs, Jeannette, 8" $20.00
Butter dish, ribbed w/ribbed crystal lid, Anchor Hoching, ¼-lb $100.00
Butter dish, w/plain crystal lid, Anchor Hocking, ¼-lb .$75.00
Cactus pot, square w/ribbed sides, Anchor Hocking, 2¼x2½" $15.00
Cactus pot, 2¼x2½" $15.00
Candy dish, maple leaf shape......................................$15.00
Candy dish, Sea Shell, Fire-King, sm $16.00
Canister, round, black lettering, screw-on lid, Jeannette, 40-oz $95.00

Canister, square, Jeannette, 48-ounce, $70.00.

Creamer, Charm $18.00
Creamer, Jane Ray, Fire-King $7.50
Creamer, Shell, footed, Fire-King................................$12.00
Cup, Alice, Fire-King $5.00
Cup, extra heavy, G299, Restaurant Ware, Fire-King, 7-oz..$9.00
Cup, narrow rim, Restaurant Ware, 7-oz.....................$10.00
Cup, Shell, Fire-King, 8-oz $8.00
Cup, tapered sides, Restaurant Ware, Fire-King, 7-oz.$20.00
Cup & saucer, Charm, Fire-King.................................$12.50
Cup & saucer, demitasse; Jane Ray, Fire-King............$65.00
Cup & saucer, Jane Ray, Fire-King $7.00
Drippings jar, McKee, 4x5", from $75 to....................$85.00
Egg cup, plain, Anchor Hocking, 4", from $28 to......$32.00
Flowerpot, scalloped top, 3¼".....................................$15.00
Grease jar, horizontal rings, screw-on lid, Fire-King...$45.00
Jewel box, embossed design on lid, Anchor Hocking..$40.00
Mug, chocolate; Fire-King, Restaurant Ware, slim, 6-oz..$18.00
Mug, coffee; Philbe, Fire-King, 8-oz..........................$75.00
Mug, coffee; Restaurant Ware, Fire-King, 7-oz $7.00
Mug, Tom & Jerry, McKee $25.00

Pitcher, ball shape, Anchor Hocking, 80-oz **$300.00**
Pitcher, measuring; sunflower bottom, Jeannette, 2-cup..**$18.00**
Pitcher, milk; Beaded & Bar, Anchor Hocking, 20-oz..**$125.00**
Pitcher, reamer; light, Jeannette, 2-cup **$35.00**
Plate, child's, divided, Fire-King, 7½" **$150.00**
Plate, dinner; Alice, Fire-King, 9½" **$25.00**
Plate, dinner; Jane Ray, Fire-King, 9⅛" **$9.00**
Plate, dinner; Sheaves of Wheat, Fire-King, 9"............**$45.00**
Plate, dinner; 1700 Line, Fire-King, 9⅛" **$20.00**
Plate, luncheon; Charm, Fire-King, 8⅜".......................**$12.00**
Plate, pie; Fire-King, 9" **$125.00**
Plate, salad; Charm, Fire-King, 6⅝" **$15.00**
Plate, salad; Restaurant Ware, Fire-King, 6¾" **$7.00**
Plate, salad; Shell, Fire-King, 7¼" **$10.00**
Plate, 5-part, G311, Restaurant Ware, Fire-King, 9⅝"..**$25.00**
Platter, Charm, Fire-King, 11x8".....................................**$35.00**
Platter, Restaurant Ware, Fire-King, 11½" **$26.00**
Platter, Restaurant Ware, Fire-King, 9½" **$30.00**
Platter, Shell, Fire-King, oval, 13" **$45.00**
Reamer, light, Jeannette, lg **$30.00**
Refrigerator container, clear lid, Anchor Hocking, 4x4"..**$35.00**
Refrigerator container, Philbe, w/Jade-ite lid, Fire-King,
    5⅛x9½"...**$50.00**
Refrigerator dish, embossed floral lid, Jeannette, 10x5"..**$75.00**
Salt & pepper shakers, horizontal rings, Fire-King, range size,
    pr...**$45.00**
Saucer, Alice, Fire-King...**$2.00**
Saucer, demitasse; Restaurant Ware, Fire-King **$35.00**
Saucer, Sheaves of Wheat, Fire-King...........................**$10.00**
Sugar bowl, Charm, Fire-King.......................................**$18.00**
Sugar bowl, Jane Ray, Fire-King, w/lid.........................**$18.00**
Sugar bowl, Shell, Fire-King, no lid **$12.00**
Sugar bowl lid, Shell, Fire-King....................................**$25.00**

Swirl, dinner plate, $40.00; cup, $20.00; saucer, $10.00. (Photo courtesy Gene Florence)

Tumbler, Jeannette, 12-oz **$22.00**
Vase, Deco style w/scalloped rim & handles, Anchor
    Hocking, 5¼" **$12.00**
Vase, tab handled, Anchor Hocking, 7¾" **$50.00**

Japan Ceramics

This category is narrowed down to the inexpensive novelty items produced in Japan from 1921 to 1941 and again from 1947 until the present. Though Japanese ceramics marked Nippon, Noritake, and Occupied Japan have long been collected, some of the newest fun-type collectibles on today's market are the figural ashtrays, pincushions, wall pockets, toothbrush holders, etc., that are marked 'Made in Japan' or simply 'Japan.' In her books called *Collector's Guide to Made in Japan Ceramics* (there are three in series), Carole Bess White explains the pitfalls you will encounter when you try to determine production dates. Collectors refer to anything produced before WWII as 'old' and anything made after 1952 as 'new.' Backstamps are inconsistent as to wording and color, and styles are eclectic. Generally, items with applied devices are old, and they are heavier and thicker. Often they were more colorful than the newer items, since fewer colors mean less expense to the manufacturer. Lustre glazes are usually indicative of older pieces, especially the deep solid colors. When lustre was used after the war, it was often mottled with contrasting hues and was usually thinner.

Imaginative styling and strong colors are what give these Japanese ceramics their charm, and they also are factors to consider when you make your purchases. You'll find all you need to know to be a wise shopper in the books we've recommended.

See also Blue Willow; Cat Collectibles; Condiment Sets; Flower Frogs; Geisha Girl; Holt Howard; Kreiss; Lamps; Lefton; Napkin Dolls; Occupied Japan Collectibles; Powder Boxes; Toothbrush Holders; Wall Pockets.

Advisor: Carole Bess White (See Directory, Japan Ceramics)

Newsletter *Made in Japan Info Letter*
Carole Bess White
P.O. Box 819
Portland, OR 97207; fax: 503-281-2817; e-mail: CBESSW@aol.com.
Send SASE for information; no appraisals given.

Ashtray, prewar, from $75.00 to $125.00. (Photo courtesy Carole Bess White)

Ashtray, Art Deco style w/hands clasping match holder above tray, white lustre w/floral motif, 5"...........**$55.00**

Ashtray, Art Deco-style cat in tan lustre on straight-sided rim of yellow tray w/white lustre center, 2¼" **$25.00**

Ashtray, clown w/banjo seated on triangular tray, multicolored glossy glazes, 3¼" **$30.00**

Ashtray, fish shape in multicolored lustre & glossy glazes, set of 4, 5", ea **$15.00**

Astray, dog & turtle on rim w/wood-look box, glossy green, 2¾" **$15.00**

Astray, dog & water barrel on seesaw, white lustre w/multicolored glossy trim, 3" **$15.00**

Astray, frog in smoking jacket lying on stomach in lily pond, multicolored semigloss, 5" **$18.00**

Basket, embossed flower band around middle of scalloped woven design in blue glossy glaze, 4" **$12.00**

Basket, Majolica style w/yellow embossed flowers on blue basketweave, green leaf handle, 7" **$65.00**

Basket, 3-footed w/brightly colored bird-&-flower motif on white, blue lustre ornate handle & feet, tan center, 5½" **$25.00**

Biscuit barrel, allover tiny rose design on white w/blue & green trim, glossy, woven handle, 5½" **$48.00**

Biscuit barrel, Majolica-style tree trunk w/red, blue & yellow blossoms on black branches, glossy, 5½" **$48.00**

Biscuit barrel, white basketweave w/rose finial, woven handle, glossy, 6¼" **$48.00**

Biscuit barrel, wood-textured w/red berries & green leaves, woven handle, semigloss, 6½" **$48.00**

Bowl, country cottage scene on cream w/black rim, reed handle, glossy, 7¼" **$10.00**

Bowl, country scene w/path leading to Tudor house, multicolored w/orange sky, irregular scalloped rim w/gold trim, 7" **$50.00**

Bowl, lotus blossom shape in multicolored lustre glazes, 4¾" dia **$10.00**

Cache pot, Art Deco style w/green & white stripes on fluted sides, fluted rim, decorated underplate, glossy, 3¼". **$20.00**

Cache pot, Dutch boy carring water buckets on shoulders by well, multicolored lustre, 4¼" **$15.00**

Cache pot/vase, Majolica-style Dutch girl next to pot w/floral motif on basketweave, pedestal base, glossy, 5½" .**$25.00**

Candlesticks, butterfly motif on short flared cups w/loop handles, bright multicolored lustre glazes, 4" dia bottoms, pr **$30.00**

Candlesticks, flower blossom cups in semigloss pink & yellow on handled bases in blue & tan lustre, 4" dia bases, pr.. **$30.00**

Cigarette box, lady holding skirt in tan lustre on blue lustre box w/red & white border trim, gold corner feet, 4½" L.. **$75.00**

Cigarette box, scenic motif w/swan on lake near cottage, tan lustre trim, 4", ... **$30.00**

Cigarette holder, clown figure w/4 stacking ashtrays as collar, bright glossy colors, complete........................ **$50.00**

Cigarette holder, onion dome w/crescent moon atop ball finial, orange & cream stripes w/floral motif, glossy, 7" **$65.00**

Creamer & sugar bowl w/tray, angular w/colorful floral motif on white w/blue trim, gold finial, tan lustre tray, 6½" **$75.00**

Decanter, elephant wearing crown & howdah holding 4 ceramic glasses w/handles, red blanket marked Whiskey, gold trim, 8"...................................**$20.00**

Egg separator, chicken form in multicolored glazes, script lettering on chest, 4"...**$25.00**

Figurine, bellhop w/2 suitcases looking up, multicolored porcelain finish, 5"...**$20.00**

Figurine, birds (2) on tree branches looking at each other, 2 pink blossoms w/green leaves, 4"........................**$18.00**

Figurine, cat sitting & meowing, tan w/glossy white glaze overcoat, 8" **$30.00**

Figurine, colonial lady in white dress w/pink & blue floral decor holding flower in hand, gold trim, 7"........**$30.00**

Figurine, fishing boy w/bare feet seated on rock, wooden pole w/ceramic fish on string, glossy, 4¾"...........**$35.00**

Figurine, nude bathing beauty lying on stomach, white glossy glaze, 4" L **$25.00**

Figurine, pixie sitting on butterfly w/flower pedestal, multicolored, glossy, 3½" **$25.00**

Figurine, pixie w/accordion, bisque w/matt colors, 4¾".**$20.00**

Flower bowl, circle of birds in multicolored lustre on white, 5¾" **$35.00**

Flower bowl, circle of swans in tan & blue lustre, 6¼" .**$35.00**

Flower bowl, Majolica style w/multicolored embossed flowers on textured dark background, handled, 8½" **$25.00**

Flower frog, bird on a branch, multicolored lustre & glossy glazes, 7½" **$30.00**

Hatpin holder/bud vase, amber lustre on handled vessel w/lg blue flower & leaves on top, 4¾" **$20.00**

Humidor, bust figure of colonial man w/pipe, opening in head for dampened sponge, orange & blue lustre, 6" **$85.00**

Incense burner, bisque, seated man, 3½", $30.00. (Photo courtesy Carole Bess White)

Incense burner, Egyptian woman lying outstretched on stomach holding duck bowl, gold lustre w/red & blue trim, 9¾" L..**$40.00**

Incense burner, geisha girl & dog w/bowl, multicolored lustre & glossy glazes, 4¾" **$40.00**

Jardiniere, multicolored bird & flower motif on yellow center w/flowers on black top band, glossy, 7¼"...........**$40.00**

Lamp, Satsuma-style figure of geisha girl in rickshaw pulled by male figure on rectangular base, multicolored, 8" ...**$40.00**

Lemon server, square w/Mexican motif, multicolored scene on white w/red trim, 5½" **$25.00**

Lemon server, square w/white bird handle & center bordered w/flowers, orange rim trimmed in white, glossy, 6".**$25.00**

Marmalade/jam pot, tulip form w/black silhouette scene of 3 figures, trees & pond on tan lustre, w/liner plate, 6½" **$85.00**

Mayonnaise set, ovoid w/lg colorful floral motif inside bowl, rim of underplate & spoon bowl on green, brown rim, 7¼"..**$35.00**

Nut set, lg blue flower petal design w/black center & trim, glossy, 5-pc, 5" bowl **$35.00**

Paperweight, figure of sleeping Mexican in multicolored glossy glazes, 5½"..**$20.00**

Pincushion, Black child in white tux & top hat sitting w/legs spread, red cushion atop hat, blue bow tie, 2¾".**$50.00**

Pincushion, black mark, lustre glazes, 3", $38.00. (Photo courtesy Carole Bess White)

Pincushion, camel resting w/basket on back, tan lustre, 2" **$18.00**

Pincushion, Satsuma-style gnome in multicolors on pig in tan lustre, 2½" **$18.00**

Pincushion, Scottie dog w/head turned, glossy gray & white, 2½" **$20.00**

Pitcher, Art Deco style w/orange handle on irregular vessel w/floral motif on blue & green textured ground, 7¾"........**$45.00**

Pitcher, cat figure glancing sideways, white w/brown spots, pink cheeks, blue neck ribbon, black handle, glossy, 3½" **$20.00**

Pitcher & mug set, green wood-textured barrel shape w/black bands, 5-pc, 8½" **$25.00**

Planter, Art Deco style w/irregular angular shape, purple & green geometric design on white w/tan trim, glossy, 4¼"...**$20.00**

Plaque, Art Deco lady's head in white porcelain w/short yellow curly hair & green hat, 4½" **$30.00**

Plaques, monkey, bear or horse head forms in whimsical depictions, multicolored glossy glazes, 5½", ea ...**$15.00**

Plate, country lake scene w/swan & cottage in the distance, multicolored lustre w/orange sky, 8¼" dia..........**$20.00**

Pomander, figural bird in multicolored glossy glazes hanging from blue ribbon, 4½"....................................**$25.00**

Relish dish, round 3-part w/scalloped edge, allover floral motif on embossed wedding-ring design, rattan handle, 8¼"..**$18.00**

Salt box, embossed cherubs w/garlands of fruit, multicolors on cream, wooden lid, 5½" **$50.00**

Spice set, Chef (multicolor) on white, set of 6 shakers, NM **$55.00**

Spice set, potbelly stove, shakers w/wood & pottery spoon & fork, marked...**$45.00**

Spice set, rooster (multicolor) on white, figural shakers hang from neck on rack along w/3 spoons, NM **$110.00**

Spice set, rooster (multicolor) on white, set of 6 shakers, NM **$32.00**

Spice set, rooster (multicolor) on white, set of 6 shakers in wooden cabinet, EX **$46.00**

Spice set, rooster & hen, shakers on top of 2 drawers, marked, NM..**$55.00**

Spice set, strawberries on white, 4 shakers & wood holders for spoons, NM **$26.00**

Spice set, Victorian couple on white, set of 5 shakers .**$18.00**

Teapot, Art Deco style w/cottage & lake scene on square shape w/canted corners, multicolored lustre, 7"..**$35.00**

Teapot, elephant figure w/trunk up & tusks, tan lustre w/colorful blanket, rattan handle, 5¾"...........................**$45.00**

Teapot, Quimper style w/figural scene & decoration in shades of brown, blue & green on cream, scalloped rim, footed, 7"..**$45.00**

Toast rack, 4 spacers & center handle on rectangular base, blue & tan lustre, 5½" L **$25.00**

Vase, Art Deco triangular shape w/colorful floral motif, multicolored lustre & glossy glazes, 7".......................**$50.00**

Vase, Art Deco 3-part graduating cylinders encircled by molded ring in bright glossy blue, 7¾" **$20.00**

Vase, fish form w/mouth wide open, tail flipped up, white glossy glaze, 3½" **$10.00**

Vase, Majolica style w/3 birds facing out forming vessel on 2-step base, multicolored glossy glazes, 7¼"..........**$85.00**

Vase, Satsuma-style urn w/butterfly motif on multicolored patterned background w/gold trim, 5".................**$25.00**

Vase, watering can form w/multicolored country cottage scene on white w/red trim, 5¼"..........................**$15.00**

Jewel Tea Company

At the turn of the century, there was stiff competition among door-to-door tea-and-coffee companies, and most of them tried to snag the customer by doling out coupons that could eventually be traded in for premiums. But the thing that set the Jewel Tea people apart from the others was that their premiums were awarded to the customer first, then 'earned' through the purchases that followed. This set the tone of their business dealings which obviously contributed to their success, and very soon in addition to the basic products they started out with, the company entered the food-manufacturing field. They eventually became one of the country's largest retailers. Today their products, containers, premiums, and advertising ephemera are all very collectible.

Advisors: Bill and Judy Vroman (See Directory, Jewel Tea)

Baking Powder, Jewel, cylindrical tin w/script logo & white lettering, 1950s-60s, 1-lb, from $20 to **$30.00**

Cake decorator set, late 1940s, from $50 to **$65.00**

Candy, Jewel Mints, round green tin, 1920s, 1-lb, from $30 to **$40.00**

Candy, Jewel Tea Spiced Jelly Drops, orange box w/orange & white lettering, from $20 to **$30.00**

Cereal, Jewel Quick Oats, cylindrical box w/white & orange lettering, from $40 to..**$50.00**

Cocoa, Jewel or Jewel Tea, various boxes, ea, from $25 to **$45.00**

Coffee, one-pound tins: Private brand, from $18.00 to $30.00; Royal brand, from $20.00 to $35.00. (Photo courtesy Bill and Judy Vroman)

Coffee, Jewel Blend, orange & gold w/white lettering & logo, paper label **$40.00**

Coffee, Jewel Private Blend, brown w/white lettering, 1-lb, from $15 to...**$25.00**

Coffee, Jewel Special Blend, brown stripes on white, white & orange lettering on brown circle, 2-lb, from $15 to...**$25.00**

Coffee, Royal Jewel, yellow w/brown & white, 1-lb, from $20 to **$35.00**

Coffee, West Coast, orange & brown w/white lettering, bell at top center, 1960s, 2-lb, from $25 to.............**$35.00**

Dishes, Melmac, 8 place settings, from $150 to........**$170.00**

Extract, Jewel Imitation, Vanilla, brown box w/orange & white lettering, 1960s, 4-oz, from $20 to **$30.00**

Extract, Jewel Lemon, orange, blue & white, 1916-19, from $40 to **$50.00**

Flour sifter, litho metal, EX......................................**$485.00**

Garmet bag, 1950s, MIP, from $25 to.......................**$30.00**

Laundry, Daintflakes, pink & blue box marked Soft Feathery Flakes of Pure Mild Soap, from $25 to **$30.00**

Laundry, Daybreak Laundry Set, from $15 to.............**$20.00**

Laundry, Grano Granulated Soap, blue & white box marked Made For General Cleaning, 2-lb, from $25 to.....**$30.00**

Laundry, Pure Gloss Starch, teal & white box, from $25 to...**$30.00**

Malted milk mixer, Jewel-T, from $40 to **$50.00**

Mix, Jewel Sunbrite Mix, Mason jar w/paper label & metal screw lid, 1960s, 26-oz, from $15 to **$25.00**

Mix, Jewel Tea Coconut Dessert, round tan tin w/brown & white logo & lettering, 1930s, 14-oz, from $30 to.**$40.00**

Mix, Jewel Tea Devil's Food Cake Flour, 1920s, 10-oz, from $30 to...**$40.00**

Mix, Jewel Tea Prepared Tapioca, tall square orange & brown striped tin w/logo & brown lettering, 1930s, from $25 to...**$35.00**

Mixer, Mary Dunbar, electric w/stand, bowl & original hang tag, white...**$100.00**

Mixer, Mary Dunbar, hand-held style w/stand, 1940, from $40 to **$50.00**

Napkins, paper w/printed pattern, box of 200 ....**$25.00**

Nuts, Jewel Mixed Nuts, round brown-striped tin w/orange & brown lettering, 1960s, 1-lb, from $15 to **$20.00**

Peanut butter, one-pound glass jar, ca 1930s, from $30.00 to $40.00. (Photo courtesy Bill and Judy Vroman)

Pickle fork, Jewel-T, from $20 to................................**$25.00**

Razor blades, Jewel-T..**$5.00**

Salesman's award, Ephraim Coffee cup w/saucer, 1939, 1-qt (given to top 400 salesmen), from $175 to........**$350.00**

Scales, Jewel-T, from $45 to...**$55.00**

Sweeper, Jewel, gold lettering on black, 1930s-40s, from $80 to...**$100.00**

Sweeper, Jewel Little Bissell, from $40 to...................**$50.00**

Sweeper, Jewel Suction Sweeper, early 1900s, lg **$150.00**

Sweeper, Jewel Suction Sweeper, tan lettering on dark tan, 1930s-40s, from $60 to **$100.00**

Tea bags, Jewel Tea, box w/dragon logo, gold & brown, 1948...**$65.00**

Tumblers, insulated; Jewel, box marked Set of Six, Keeps Drinks Hot or Cold, from $20 to **$30.00**

Tea, Orange Pekoe and Pekoe, from $20.00 to $25.00. (Photo courtesy Bill and Judy Vroman)

Jewelry

Today's costume jewelry collectors may range from nine to ninety and have tastes as varied as their ages, but one thing they all have in common is their love of these distinctive items of jewelry, some originally purchased at the corner five-&-dimes, others from department stores and boutiques.

Costume jewelry became popular, simply because it was easily affordable for all women. Today jewelry made before 1954 is considered to be 'antique,' while the term 'collectible' jewelry generally refers to those pieces made after that time. In 1954 costume jewelry was federally recognized as an American art form, and the copyright law was passed to protect the artists' designs. The copyright mark (c in a circle) found on the back of a piece identifies a post-1954 'collectible.'

Quality should always be the primary consideration when shopping for these treasures. Remember that pieces with colored rhinestones bring the higher prices. (Note: a 'rhinestone' is a clear, foil-backed, leaded glass crystal — unless it is a 'colored rhinestone' — while a 'stone' is not foiled.) A complete set (called a parure) increases in value by 20% over the total of its components. Check for a manufacturer's mark, since a signed piece is worth 20% more than one of comparable quality, but not signed. Some of the best designers are Miriam Haskell, Eisenberg, Trifari, Hollycraft, and Joseff.

Early plastic pieces (Lucite, Bakelite, and celluloid, for example) are very collectible. Some Lucite is used in combination with wood, and the figural designs are especially desirable.

There are several excellent reference books available if you'd like more information. Lillian Baker has written several: *Art Nouveau and Art Deco Jewelry; Twentieth Century Fashionable Plastic Jewelry; 50 Years of Collectible Fashion Jewelry;* and *100 Years of Collectible Jewelry.* Books by other authors include *Collectible Costume Jewelry* by Fred Rezazadeh; *Collector's Encyclopedia of Hairwork Jewelry* by C. Jeanenne Bell, G.G.; and Video Books *Hidden Treasures Series* by Christie Romero and Marcia Brown. Look for *Unsigned Beauties of Costume Jewelry* by Marcia "Sparkles" Brown, available through Collector Books by the spring of 2000.

Advisors: Marcia Brown (See Directory, Jewelry)

Club/Newsletter: *Vintage Fashion and Costume Jewelry Newsletter Club*
P.O. Box 265, Glen Oaks, NY 11004

Bracelet, celluloid cuff style w/laminated lace inserts, 1950-70, from $145 to **$165.00**
Bracelet, Ciner, black Bakelite & gilded brass links, 1950s, from $135 to...**$150.00**
Bracelet, Coro, aurora borealis stones on gold-plated links w/Art Moderne influence, 1950s, from $25 to......**$35.00**
Bracelet, Eisenberg, rhinestones & rhodium, individual links, flexible, 1960s, from $110 to...............................**$125.00**

Bracelet, Eisenberg Ice, rhinestones & rhodium, special patented clasp, 1940s, from $95 to **$125.00**
Bracelet, Karu, gold-plated metal w/ivory enameling in floral openwork design, 2" W, from $90 to..................**$125.00**
Bracelet, Napier, gold-plated flexible mesh w/faux jade stone at clasp, 1950s, from $45 to **$55.00**
Bracelet, Nettie Rosenstein, pave-set rhinestones on gold-tone, 1950s, from $95 to **$125.00**
Bracelet, red aurora borealis & clear rhinestones on gold-plated scroll design, 1950s, 1" W, safety catch, from $45 to **$70.00**

Bracelet, Schiaparelli, pink iridescent rhinestones and pearls, hinged, from $225.00 to $265.00.

Bracelet, Trifari, molded turquoise plastic flowers w/clear rhinestones on gold-plated swirls, 1950s, 1" W, from $75 to **$95.00**
Bracelet, Trifari, pear-cut white iridescent plastic stones on silver-tone metal, 1960s, from $50 to **$75.00**
Bracelet, unmarked, apple green Venetian glass beads & rhinestones (all prong set), 1950s, from $75 to..**$105.00**
Bracelet, unmarked, clear thermoplastic w/channel or pave-set rhinestones, clasped cuff style, 1991, from $275 to **$300.00**
Bracelet, unmarked, ivory Bakelite w/geometric carvings, 1" W, from $150 to **$250.00**
Bracelet, unmarked, red deeply carved Bakelite bangle, 1" W, from $175 to...**$250.00**
Bracelet, unmarked, 7 strands of brown glass beads w/brown simulated pearls, fancy clasp, 1950s, from $75 to **$95.00**
Bracelet, Weiss, prong-set rhinestones of varied shapes & cuts on flexible rhodium, ca 1955, from $75 to ...**$95.00**
Bracelet, West Germany, German silver-tone cobra style w/prong-set Austrian crystal rhinestones, 1" W, from $125 to...**$175.00**
Brooch, Art, enameled flower w/rhinestone accents on stamen & leaves, 1960s-70s, 2½", from $45 to..........**$85.00**
Brooch, Boucher, painted enamel figural fish, 1955, from $65 to **$90.00**
Brooch, Boucher, pave-set baguette-cut rhinestones in swirling leaf shape, 1960s, from $35 to **$45.00**
Brooch, BSK, gold-tone bird on perch w/faux ruby accents, 1950s, sm, from $25 to **$35.00**

Brooch, BSK, gold-tone cat w/faux gem eyes, 1960s, from $25 to...$35.00

Brooch, Cadoro, gold-tone double bow, 1955, from $45 to $55.00

Brooch, Capri, nugget-style star w/gold-tone base, lg green glass center rhinestone (foil backed), 1960s, 3x3¾"..........$80.00

Brooch, Castlecliff, pink baroque pearl on heavy gold-plated coral branch, 1960s, from $45 to.........................$65.00

Brooch, Cini for Gumps, sterling flower form, handcrafted, 1945-'50, from $85 to.......................................$105.00

Brooch, Coro, foiled faux topaz faceted stones set in flower-like mold, 1960s...$35.00

Brooch, Coro, peacock w/multicolor enameling & rhinestones, gold electroplate, 1950s, from $55 to.......$75.00

Brooch, Danecraft, sterling repousse, 1940s, from $65 to..$80.00

Brooch, Danecraft, sterling repousse w/openwork & beading, 1950s, from $70 to..$90.00

Brooch, Danecraft, sterling shamrock, sterling hallmarked casing, 1950-60, from $35 to..................................$45.00

Brooch, gold-plated coral branches w/colored glass center stone & clear rhinestones, 1960s, 1¾x2", from $50 to...$75.00

Brooch, hallmarked Sterling, multicolor rhinestone flower, 1940s, sm & dainty, from $65 to $100.00

Brooch, HAR, gold-plated leaves among aurora borealis & dark brown rhinestones (glued in), 1950s-60s, 2¼x2¾" ..$85.00

Brooch, Hattie Carnegie, African figure w/faux coral & turquoise w/rhinestones on gold plate, 1965-70, from $150 to...$175.00

Brooch, Hobe, frog on lily pad (3-D), etched antique gold-tone, 2", from $75 to $95.00

Brooch, Hollycraft, Christmas tree w/faux gemstones of various colors, 1955-65, from $55 to $85.00

Brooch, Jomaz, cast teardrop design w/rhinestones & lg faux emerald center, ca 1955, from $95 to.................$105.00

Brooch, Joseff, oxidized brass, entended bar w/tassel, ca 1945, 4½", from $95 to..$150.00

Brooch, Judy Lee, faux pearls, aurora borealis & clear rhinestones on silver-tone metal, 1950s, 2½x4", from $60 to $80.00

Brooch, Kramer, blue aurora borealis stones on gold-tone metal, 1960s, from $45 to......................................$65.00

Brooch, Kramer, multicolor rhinestones & aurora borealis stones in filigree mounting, 1950s, from $75 to...$90.00

Brooch, Lea Stein Paris, thermoplastic boy on skateboard, 1965, from $125 to..$150.00

Brooch, Made in Austria, pewter w/oval blue cut glass cabochons, 1950s, 2x2", from $65 to $85.00

Brooch, Mimi, prong-set & faceted rhinestones on silver-tone ribbon design, 1960s, from $65 to.........................$85.00

Brooch, Miriam Haskell, gold-tone filigree & fretwork w/seed pearls & lg center pearl, ca 1955, from $85 to.....$95.00

Brooch, Sarah Coventry, abstract cushion type, rhodium plated w/clear (glued in) rhinestones, from $55 to ...$75.00

Brooch, Schreiner, flower w/prong-set blue marquise-cut rhinestones & simulated turquoise beads, gold-plated, 2¾"...$175.00

Brooch, Trifari, rhodium fleur-de-lis w/cultured pearls, 1950s, from $55 to..$75.00

Brooch, Trifari, swirling tornado-like shape w/faux pearls, baguette rhinestones, gold trifanium plated, 1¼", from $60 to...$85.00

Brooch, unmarked, amethyst rhinestones w/various cuts prong-set in chromium-plated star shape, 1950s, 2", from $35 to...$60.00

Brooch, unmarked, carved red Bakelite parrot w/hand-painted beak, 1930s, from $175 to $200.00

Brooch, unmarked, carved Lucite insect or animal, often w/painted details, ea, from $175 to $250.00

Brooch, unmarked, flower w/prong-set plastic petals & leaves, gold-plated, 1950s-60s, from $40 to..........$60.00

Brooch, unmarked, gold-tone owl w/faux tortoise-shell plastic tummy, 2½", from $40 to.................................$50.00

Brooch, unmarked, molded red Catalin lobster w/black painted eyes, 2¾", from $75 to $115.00

Brooch, unmarked, pink, blue & clear rhinestones (prong set) on oxidized silver-tone base metal filigree, 1930s, up to...$80.00

Brooch, unmarked American, red Bakelite horse w/chain reins & enameled details, glass eye, 1930s, from $195 to...$245.00

Brooch, unmarked Coro, lilac blossom of base metal w/purple & green enameling & clear rhinestones, 1940s, from $175 to...$225.00

Brooch, unmarked cushion-style flower with gray & green marquise-cut rhinestones on gold-plate, 1950s, 2¼" dia, up to...$80.00

Brooch, unsigned, clear pave-set rhinestone flower & bow, pot metal, 1930s, 4x2½", from $150 to $225.00

Brooch, unsigned, gold-plated swirl design w/lg faux pearls, 1960s, 1¾x2½", from $75 to $100.00

Brooch, unsigned, plum & clear Lucite rhinestones (glued in) form flower & bow on pot metal, 1930s, 4", from $130 to...$175.00

Brooch, Vendome, pink Austrian crystal aurora borealis beads dangle from gold-tone diamond shape, 1950s, 2½x2½"...$150.00

Brooch, Weiss, faux rubies on gold-plated heart shape, 1950s, from $25 to $35.00

Brooch, Weiss, large blue center rhinestone, gold-coated navettes, $70.00. (Photo courtesy Marcia Brown)

Buckle, unmarked, ivory celluloid bow, Patent #2108905, dated 1938, from $25 to **$45.00**

Earring, black Bakelite, egg-shaped dangles, lg, from $35 to **$50.00**

Earrings, Boucher, silver-tone pagoda shape w/dangling flowers, design #8274, from $60 to **$75.00**

Earrings, Carnegie, Austrian crystals w/red aurora borealis crystals, gold-plated, 1¼" dia, from $55 to **$75.00**

Earrings, Chanel, foiled & faceted aurora borealis stones in cluster, 1950s, from $15 to **$20.00**

Earrings, Chr Dior/Germany, faux jade & sapphires on gold-tone metal, 1967, clip style, from $55 to **$65.00**

Earrings, Coro, blue plastic flowers w/clear rhinestones forming cluster, 1950s, 2¼" dia, from $40 to...............**$75.00**

Earrings, Eisenberg, blue marquise cut rhinestones w/sm clear rhinestones, rhodium plated, 1950s, 1½", from $175 to...**$215.00**

Earrings, Eisenberg, pear shape, marquise cut & roundles of prong-set rhinestones in rhodium, clip style, 1950s.**$65.00**

Earrings, Eisenberg Ice, blue & pink imitation zircons, 1950s, from $55 to...**$65.00**

Earrings, Kim, Victorian-style dangles w/brass filigree & blue crystal beads, 3¾" L, from $75 to.......................**$110.00**

Earrings, KJL (Kenneth J Lane), faux coral & emerald w/seed pearls, 1970s, from $85 to..............................**$125.00**

Earrings, Pat Sterling, handwrought sterling w/polished agate, 1940s, from $55 to **$65.00**

Earrings, Renoir, copper, Art Moderne design, clip type, 1950-55, from $35 to.....................................**$45.00**

Earrings, Robert, seed pearls w/aurora borealis stones, 1960s, from $45 to...**$55.00**

Earrings, Sarah Coventry, prong-set clear rhinestones on gold-plate, 2¾" dangles, from $50 to....................**$70.00**

Earrings, Trifari, enamel & rhinestone flowers set in rhodium, ca 1945, from $45 to.................................**$55.00**

Earrings, unmarked, blue Bakelite & chrome, Deco styling, pierced, 1950s, from $95 to **$150.00**

Fur clip, Mazer, unfoiled Bohemian red glass & varied cut rhinestones in rhodium & gold-tone, 1950, from $75 to...**$85.00**

Necklace, Bakelite & metal w/carved celluloid beads, Egyptian profile on pendant, 1930s, from $150 to **$225.00**

Necklace, bracelet & earrings, Emmons, molded plastic flowers w/sm rhinestones on gold-plated metal w/ivory enameling...**$300.00**

Necklace, Coro, Retro-style flower & ribbon w/rhinestones on gold-plated chain, choker style, 1940s, from $125 to..**$175.00**

Necklace, Florenza, Victorian-style pendant w/black glass dangles & clear rhinestone brilliants on gold-tone chain..**$60.00**

Necklace, Germany, jade green Bakelite pendant on flat chrome chain, 1930s, from $295 to.....................**$325.00**

Necklace, Japan, 3-strand beaded bib style w/graduated molded blue plastic beads, late 1950s, from $30 to.......**$45.00**

Necklace, KJL, Egyptian thermoset faux ivory plastic pendant w/Egyptian decor on gold-plated chain, 1960s, from $55 to **$75.00**

Necklace, Monet, Art Moderne rhodium links, choker length, 1950s, from $35 to **$45.00**

Necklace, Napier, tricolor faux gemstones, flexible links, silver finish, Art Moderne design, 1960s, from $65 to......**$85.00**

Necklace, Trifari, white enameled leaves & blue enameled flowers w/silver-plated findings, collar type, from $75 to...**$125.00**

Necklace, Trifari, 4 gold-tone strands joined by bar each end, hook fastener, ca 1965, from $45 to.....................**$55.00**

Necklace, unmarked, 4-strand Austrian aurora borealis beads, hook clasp, 1960s, from $95 to **$135.00**

Necklace & earrings, Trifari, white glass beads w/golden filigree leaf accents, 1955-60, from $55 to **$75.00**

Necklace & earrings, Vendome, iridescent bugle beads, multicolor faceted crystals, aurora borealis stones, 1950s, up to **$165.00**

Pendant, Czech, antique gilded brass w/faux turquoise & garnets, w/drop, Renaissance-style design, ca 1948, from $75 to...**$85.00**

Pin, see Brooch

Ring, Cire Perdu, 14 karat yellow gold w/lg citron **$65.00**

Ring, Emmons, aurora borealis pave-set rhinestones on gold-tone metal, 1970s, from $25 to...........................**$30.00**

Ring, red Bakelite w/carved daisy pattern, ca 1935, from $175 to...**$235.00**

Ring, 12 karat yellow gold w/7.75 penny weight jade stone..**$150.00**

Ring, 14 karat rose gold w/black onyx, 10 seed pearls & gold intaglio...**$185.00**

Ring, 14 karat yellow gold, 5.5mm cabochon green jade stones...**$50.00**

Ring, 14 karat yellow gold w/emerald-cut faux ruby, modern style..**$70.00**

Ring, 14 karat yellow gold w/7.5mm cultured pearl ..**$60.00**

Ring, 18 karat yellow gold, w/1891 Indian head penny..**$75.00**

Scarf pin, Trifari, gold vermeil w/faux gemstones, 1955-65, from $95 to...**$110.00**

Necklace, Hattie Carnegie, butterfly (7x5½") with red and purple cabochons, from $650.00 to $750.00. (Photo courtesy Marcia Brown)

Johnson Bros.

There is a definite renewal of interest in dinnerware collecting right now, and just about any antique shop or mall you visit will offer a few nice examples of the wares made by this Staffordshire company. They've been in business since well before the turn of the century and have targeted the American market to such an extent that during the 1960s and '70s, as much as 70% of their dinnerware was sold to distributors in this country. They made many scenic patterns, some of which may already be familiar to you. Among them are Friendly Village, Historic America, and Old Britain Castles. They produced lovely floral patterns as well, and with the interest today's collectors have been demonstrating in Chintz, dealers tell me that Johnson Brothers' Rose Chintz and Chintz (Victorian) sell very well for them, especially the latter. In addition to their polychrome designs, they made several patterns in both blue and pink transferware.

Though some of their lines, Friendly Village, for instance, are still being produced, most are no longer as extensive as they once were, so the secondary market is being tapped to replace broken items that are not available anywhere else.

In addition to their company logo, much of their dinnerware is also stamped with the pattern name. Today they're a part of the Wedgwood group.

For more information on marks, patterns, and pricing, we recommend *Johnson Brothers Dinnerware Pattern Directory and Price Guide* by Mary J. Finegan.

Advisor: Mary J. Finegan (See Directory, Dinnerware)

Coaching Scenes, platter, 14", minimum value, $70.00.

Apple Harvest, creamer	$32.00
Apple Harvest, plate, dinner	$16.00
Apple Harvest, platter, 12"	$40.00
Autumn's Delight, cup & saucer	$17.00
Autumn's Delight, plate, bread & butter	$7.00
Autumn's Delight, plate, luncheon	$14.00
Autumn's Delight, sugar bowl, w/lid	$45.00

Barnyard King, plate, salad	$12.00
Barnyard King, platter, sm, 12"	$45.00
Barnyard King, sugar bowl, w/lid	$48.00
Century of Progress, bowl, fruit	$10.00
Century of Progress, bowl, vegetable; round	$35.00
Century of Progress, butter dish, w/lid	$60.00
Century of Progress, gravy boat	$48.00
Century of Progress, plate, salad; square or round, ea.	$14.00
Coaching Scenes, butter dish, w/lid	$55.00
Coaching Scenes, cup & saucer, jumbo	$35.00
Coaching Scenes, platter, med	$50.00
Devonshire, bowl, soup/cereal; square, round or lug, ea.	$11.00
Devonshire, plate, dinner	$16.00
Devonshire, salt & pepper shakers	$45.00
Dorchester, bowl, soup/cereal; square, round or lug, ea.	$12.00
Dorchester, creamer	$35.00
Dorchester, pitcher, minimum value	$55.00
Dorchester, plate, bread & butter	$8.00
Dorchester, sugar bowl, w/lid	$48.00
English Chippendale, creamer	$32.00
English Chippendale, plate, bread & butter	$7.00
English Chippendale, plate, dinner	$16.00
English Chippendale, platter, sm, 12"	$40.00
Fish, bowl, soup; rimmed	$15.00
Fish, coffeepot, minimum value	$85.00
Fish, plate, buffet; 10½"	$26.00
Fish, plate, salad; oval or round, ea	$12.00
Friendly Village, bowl, fruit	$8.00
Friendly Village, bowl, soup; square or round, 7", ea	$12.00
Friendly Village, bowl, vegetable; round	$25.00
Friendly Village, cake plate	$50.00
Friendly Village, cup & saucer, jumbo	$30.00
Friendly Village, egg cup	$15.00
Friendly Village, plate, chop	$50.00
Friendly Village, plate, dinner	$14.00
Friendly Village, plate, salad; square or round, ea	$10.00
Friendly Village, platter, med, 12" to 14"	$45.00
Friendly Village, sugar bowl	$30.00
Friendly Village, tureen, minimum value	$200.00
Gamebirds, creamer	$32.00
Gamebirds, egg cup	$18.00
Gamebirds, pitcher	$50.00
Gamebirds, plate, buffet size, from $24 to	$26.00
Harvest Fruit, bowl, soup; rimmed	$16.00
Harvest Fruit, plate, buffet; 10½"	$30.00
Harvest Fruit, platter, med, from 12" to 14"	$55.00
Hearts & Flowers, cup & saucer, jumbo	$35.00
Hearts & Flowers, plate, luncheon	$14.00
His Majesty, bowl, vegetable; oval	$40.00
His Majesty, gravy boat	$48.00
His Majesty, plate, buffet; minimum value	$30.00
Historic America, coaster	$8.00
Historic America, plate, luncheon	$16.00
Indian Tree, bowl, fruit	$8.00
Indian Tree, bowl, vegetable; oval	$30.00
Indian Tree, butter dish, w/lid	$50.00
Indian Tree, cake plate	$50.00

Indian Tree, gravy boat $40.00
Indian Tree, plate, bread & butter $6.00
Indian Tree, plate, dinner $14.00
Merry Christmas, plate, salad; square or round, ea.....$14.00
Merry Christmas, platter, turkey; 20½", minimum value..$200.00
Millstream, bowl, soup/cereal; square, round or lug, ea...$11.00
Millstream, bowl, vegetable; round $30.00
Millstream, plate, salad; square or round, ea $12.00
Millstream, sugar bowl, w/lid $45.00
Old Britain Castles, butter dish, w/lid $60.00
Old Britain Castles, coffee mug, minimum value $20.00
Old Britain Castles, creamer $35.00
Old Britain Castles, plate, luncheon $16.00
Old Britain Castles, platter, sm, 12" $45.00
Old Britain Castles, sugar bowl, w/lid $48.00
Olde English Countryside, coaster $7.00
Olde English Countryside, pitcher $50.00
Olde English Countryside, plate, buffet; 10½" $26.00
Olde English Countryside, salt & pepper shakers.......$45.00
Persian Tulip, bowl, fruit..$10.00
Persian Tulip, gravy boat $48.00
Persian Tulip, plate, dinner; minimum value $18.00
Rose Bouquet, bowl, soup; rimmed............................$15.00
Rose Bouquet, cup & saucer $17.00
Rose Bouquet, plate, bread & butter..........................$7.00
Rose Bouquet, plate, chop..$55.00
Rose Bouquet, platter, lg, 14", minimum value $70.00
Rose Chintz, bowl, soup/cereal; square, round or lug, ea ..$12.00
Rose Chintz, bowl, vegetable; oval $40.00
Rose Chintz, cake plate, minimum value....................$60.00
Rose Chintz, coaster..$8.00
Rose Chintz, cup & saucer, jumbo, minimum value...$40.00
Rose Chintz, plate, buffet; 10½" $30.00
Rose Chintz, plate, chop; minimum value..................$60.00
Rose Chintz, plate, luncheon $16.00
Rose Chintz, platter, lg, 14", minimum value.............$75.00
Rose Chintz, sugar bowl, w/lid $48.00
Sheraton, bowl, soup; rimmed $14.00
Sheraton, bowl, vegetable; round...............................$25.00
Sheraton, butter dish, w/lid $50.00
Sheraton, coaster..$6.00
Sheraton, coffeepot, minimum value $80.00
Sheraton, egg cup...$15.00
Sheraton, pitcher $45.00
Sheraton, plate, buffet; 10½" $24.00
Sheraton, plate, chop..$50.00
Sheraton, plate, luncheon $12.00
Sheraton, sugar bowl, w/lid..$40.00
Strawberry Fair, bowl, vegetable; round.....................$35.00
Strawberry Fair, egg cup $20.00
Strawberry Fair, plate, bread & butter $8.00
Strawberry Fair, plate, dinner, minimum value $18.00
Tally Ho, creamer $35.00
Tally Ho, plate, buffet; 10½"......................................$30.00
Tally Ho, plate, luncheon..$16.00
Tally Ho, salt & pepper shakers $48.00
Tally Ho, sugar bowl...$35.00

Twelve Days of Christmas, plate, salad; round $14.00
Wild Turkeys, bowl, fruit $10.00
Wild Turkeys, gravy boat w/fused-on base................$60.00
Wild Turkeys, plate, buffet; minimum value $30.00
Wild Turkeys, plate, salad...$14.00

Willow, platter, 14", minimum value, $60.00.

Winchester, bowl, fruit $9.00
Winchester, bowl, vegetable; oval...............................$35.00
Winchester, coaster $7.00
Winchester, coffee mug, minimum value $18.00
Winchester, pitcher $50.00
Winchester, plate, dinner $16.00

Josef Originals

Figurines of lovely ladies, charming girls, and whimsical animals marked Josef Originals were designed by Muriel Joseph George of Arcadia, California, from 1945 to 1985. Until 1960, they were produced in California. But production costs were high, and copies of her work were being made in Japan. To remain competitive, she and her partner, George Good, found a company in Japan to build a factory and produce her designs to her satisfaction. Muriel retired in 1982; however, Mr. Good continued production of her work and made new designs of his staff's creation. The company was sold in late 1985, and the name is currently owned by Applause; a limited number of figurines bear this name. Those made during the ownership of Muriel are the most collectible. They can be recognized by these characteristics: the girls have a high-gloss finish, black eyes, and most are signed. Brown-eyed figures date from 1982 through 1985; Applause uses a red-brown eye. The animals were nearly always made with a matt finish and were marked with paper labels. Later animals have a flocked coat. Our advisors, Jim and Kaye Whitaker have three books which we recommend for further study: *Josef Originals, Charming Figurines; Josef Originals, A Second Look;* and *Josef Originals, Figurines of Muriel Joseph George*. All correspondence requires a self-addressed stamped envelope.

See also Birthday Angels.

Advisors: Jim and Kaye Whitaker (See Directory, Josef Originals)

Newsletter: *Josef Original Newsletter*
Jim and Kaye Whitaker
P.O. Box 475 Dept. GS
Lynnwood, WA 98046; Subscription (4 issues): $10 per year

Africa, Little International, 4", from $28.00 to $35.00. (Photo courtesy Jim and Kaye Whitaker)

Birthday Girl, 1974 series, 12 different, Japan, 4", ea .**$40.00**
Birthday Girls, Angels, #1-#16, black eyes, Japan, ea.**$25.00**
Birthstone Dolls, 12 months, Japan, 3½", ea **$25.00**
Buggy Bugs, wire antenna, Japan, 3¼" **$20.00**

Camel, mama standing, Japan, 6¾", $55.00. (Photo courtesy Jim and Kaye Whitaker)

Caroline, pink gown & umbrella, Colonial Days, Japan, 10"..**$135.00**
Caroline from 1850 Ante-Bellum Girls, Japan, 7"......**$125.00**
Cherub on Heart Jewelry Box, Japan, 4" **$75.00**
Chihuahua from Kennel Klub series, Japan, 3½"..........**$40.00**
Chili or Dilly, pair of dogs, California, 3¼", ea..........**$40.00**
Christmas Choir Boys, Japan, 5¾", ea........................**$30.00**
Engagement Ring, girl w/ring box, Sweet Memories series, Japan, 6½" **$95.00**
English Bulldogs, 2 poses, Japan, 4½", ea..................**$20.00**

Flower Sprites, Angels, 6 poses, Japan, 3¾", ea **$35.00**
German Shepherd from Champion Dogs series, Japan, 5" **$35.00**
Gigi, pedestal girl, California, 6"................................**$75.00**
Girl in pink at piano, music box, 'Humoresque,' Japan, 5¾"..**$65.00**
Greece, California, 10¼" **$165.00**
Horoscope Angels, 12 months, Japan, 4", ea **$40.00**

Joseph II, 5½", and Marie Antoinette, 5½",$40.00 each. (Photo courtesy Jim and Kaye Whitaker)

Linda, Ballerina, California, 4¼" **$50.00**
Little Commandments, Angels, 6 poses, Japan, 3¾", ea .**$30.00**
Little International Series, various countries, Japan, 4", from $45 to **$60.00**
Little Pets, girls w/pets, 6 different, Japan, 4", ea **$35.00**
Little Pets, girls w/pets, 6 in set, Japan, 5¼", ea.........**$55.00**
Lizzy, old car, California, 2¼" **$45.00**
Mama, various poses (goes w/Mary Ann), California, 7¼"...**$95.00**
Mandy w/guitar, Musicale series, Japan, 6" **$55.00**
Mary Ann, various poses (goes w/Mama), California, 3½"...**$45.00**
Mary holding Lamb, Joy of Spring Series, Japan, 6" ...**$60.00**
Mermaid soap dish, Japan, 5"......................................**$45.00**
Nip & Tuck, pair of rabbits, California, 4", ea............**$35.00**
Persian cat family, Japan, 4-pc set, 3-4", set...............**$60.00**
Siamese cat family, 6-pc set, Japan, 2-4½", set **$65.00**
Simone, Morning Noon & Night series, California, 5½"..**$60.00**
Spring, lime green, holding umbrella, Four Seasons series, Japan, 9" **$150.00**
Spring, pink w/white bird, Four Seasons series, Japan, 5¾" **$80.00**
Spring, yellow, w/umbrella & bird on hand, Four Seasons series, Japan, 6"..**$70.00**
The Courtship, girl w/roses, Romance series, Japan, 8"..**$110.00**
Wedding party cake topper, Japan, 3½" **$55.00**
Wee Ching, Chinese boy w/dog, California, 5"..........**$35.00**
Wee Ling, Chinese girl w/cat, California, 5" **$35.00**

Keeler, Brad

California pottery is becoming quite popular among collectors, and Brad Keeler is one of the better known designers. After studying art for a time, he opened his own studio in 1939 where he created naturalistic studies of birds and animals. Sold through giftware stores, the figures were decorated by airbrushing with hand-painted details. Brad Keeler is remembered for his popular flamingo figures and his Chinese Modern Housewares. Keeler died of a heart attack in 1952, and the pottery closed soon thereafter. For more information, we recommend *The Collector's Encyclopedia of California Pottery, 2nd Edition,* by Jack Chipman.

Bowl, lettuce, #959, 4¾x11¼" **$55.00**
Bowl, tomato, w/spoon, 12" **$65.00**

Figurine, begging cocker spaniel pup, #735, 6", $45.00. (Photo courtesy Jack Chipman)

Figurine, bird of paradise, 11", from $140 to **$165.00**
Figurine, blue jay, #735, 9" **$85.00**
Figurine, crested heron, #43, 16", minimum value ...**$225.00**
Figurine, egret, blue body, #15, 9½" **$95.00**
Figurine, Siamese cat, 12", from $75 to......................**$85.00**
Figurine, Siamese cat on pillow, #928, 4½x3"............**$45.00**
Plate, lobster & leaf, 3-section, 11x9½" **$55.00**
Plate, luncheon; lobster & leaf, #891, 9x9" **$38.00**
Platter, turkey, #197, 10x12"....................................**$145.00**
Server, lobster & leaf, 3-section, #868, 8¾x9" **$35.00**
Server, lobster & leaf, 6-section, #873, 14"................**$80.00**

Kentucky Derby Glasses

Since the the late 1930s, every running of the Kentucky Derby has been commemorated with a special glass tumbler. Each year at Churchill Downs on Derby day you can buy them filled with mint juleps. In the early days this was the only place where these glasses could be purchased. Many collections were started when folks carried the glasses home from the track and then continued to add one for each successive year they attended the Derby.

The first glass appeared in 1938, but examples from then until 1945 are extremely scarce and are worth thousands — when they can be found. Because of this, many collectors begin with the 1945 glasses. There are three: the tall version, the short regular-size glass, and a jigger. Some years, for instance 1948, 1956, 1958, 1974, and 1986, have slightly different variations, so often there are more than one to collect. To date a glass, simply add one year to the last date on the winner's list found on the back.

Each year many companies put out commemorative Derby glasses. Collectors call them 'bar' glasses (as many bars sold their own versions filled with mint juleps). Because of this, collectors need to be educated as to what the official Kentucky Derby glass looks like.

Advisor: Betty L. Hornback (See Directory, Kentucky Derby and Horse Racing)

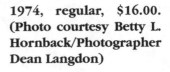

1974, regular, $16.00. (Photo courtesy Betty L. Hornback/Photographer Dean Langdon)

1940, aluminum **$800.00**
1941-1944, plastic Beetleware, ea, from $2,500 to.**$4,000.00**
1945, jigger...**$1,000.00**
1945, regular **$1,400.00**
1945, tall **$425.00**
1946 ....**$100.00**
1947 ....**$100.00**
1948, clear bottom...**$190.00**
1948, frosted bottom **$200.00**
1949 ....**$190.00**
1950 ....**$425.00**
1951 ....**$550.00**
1952 ....**$190.00**
1953 ....**$150.00**
1954 ....**$185.00**
1955 ....**$135.00**
1956, 4 variations, ea, from $150 to..........................**$250.00**
1957, gold & black on front **$110.00**
1958, Gold Bar...**$175.00**
1958, Iron Liege **$200.00**
1959 ....**$80.00**
1960 ....**$80.00**
1961 ....**$100.00**
1962 ....**$70.00**
1963 ....**$50.00**
1964 ....**$50.00**

1965	$70.00
1966	$55.00
1967	$52.00
1968	$50.00
1969	$55.00
1970	$60.00
1971	$45.00
1972	$45.00
1973	$50.00
1974, Federal, regular or mistake, ea, from $125 to	$150.00
1974, mistake (Canonero in 1971 listing on back)	$18.00
1975	$12.00
1976	$14.00
1976, plastic	$12.00
1977	$12.00
1978	$14.00
1979	$14.00
1980	$18.00
1981	$14.00
1982	$12.00
1983	$10.00

1984, $10.00.

1985	$10.00
1986	$12.00
1986 ('85 copy)	$20.00
1987	$9.00
1988	$9.00
1989	$9.00
1990	$8.00
1991	$8.00
1992	$8.00
1993	$6.00
1994	$6.00
1995	$6.00
1996	$5.00
1997	$5.00
1998	$4.00
1999	$3.00
2000	$3.00

Breeders Cup Glasses

1985	$275.00
1988	$30.00
1989	$60.00
1990	$40.00
1991	$12.00
1992	$28.00
1993	$20.00
1993, 10th Running, gold	$40.00
1994	$10.00
1995	$15.00
1996	$25.00
1997	$15.00
1998	$7.00
1999	$7.00

Festival Glasses

1968	$95.00
1984	$20.00
1985, no glass made	
1987-88, ea	$16.00
1989-90, ea	$14.00
1991-92, ea	$12.00
1993	$75.00
1994-95, ea	$10.00
1996-97, ea	$8.00
1998-99, ea	$6.00

Jim Beam Stakes Glasses

1980-81, ea	$350.00
1982	$300.00
1983	$65.00
1984	$45.00
1985	$25.00
1986	$25.00
1987-88, ea	$20.00
1988-90, ea	$15.00

1990, $15.00.

1991-93, ea $12.00
1994-95, ea $12.00
1996-97, ea $10.00
1998...$8.00
1999, the race is now sponsored by 'Gallery Furniture.com Stakes' $8.00

Shot Glasses

1987, 1½-oz, red or black, ea..................$300.00
1987, 3-oz, black.....................................$750.00
1987, 3-oz, red.....................................$1,000.00
1988, 1½-oz $40.00

1988, three-ounce, $60.00. (Photo courtesy Betty L. Hornback/Photographer Dean Langdon)

1989, 1½-oz...$35.00
1989, 3-oz $45.00
1990, 1½-oz...$35.00
1991, 1½-oz...$35.00
1991, 3-oz $40.00
1992, 1½-oz...$20.00
1992, 3-oz $25.00
1993, 1½-oz or 3-oz, ea $15.00
1994, 1½-oz or 3-oz, ea $12.00
1995, 1½-oz or 3-oz, ea $12.00
1996, 1½-oz or 3-oz, ea $12.00
1997, 1½-oz or 3-oz, ea $10.00
1998, 1½-oz or 3-oz, ea $8.00
1999, 1½-oz or 3-oz, ea $8.00

King's Crown, Thumbprint

Back in the late 1800s, this pattern was called Thumbprint. It was first made by the U.S. Glass Company and Tiffin, one of several companies who were a part of the US conglomerate, through the 1940s. U.S. Glass closed in the late '50s, but Tiffin reopened in 1963 and reissued it. Indiana Glass bought the molds, made some minor changes, and during the 1970s, they made this line as well. Confusing, to say the least! Gene Florence's *Collectible Glassware of the 40s, 50s, and 60s,* explains that originally the thumbprints were oval, but at some point Indiana changed theirs to circles. And Tiffin's tumblers were flared at the top, while Indiana's were straight. Our values are for the later issues of both companies, with the ruby flashing in excellent condition.

Bowl, bonbon; crimped, 2-handled, 8¾"................$75.00
Bowl, cone; 11¼"...$75.00
Bowl, crimped, footed....................................$85.00
Bowl, finger; 4"...$17.50
Bowl, flower floater; 12½"..............................$80.00

Bowl, ruffled, 11½", $95.00. (Photo courtesy Gene Florence)

Bowl, straight edge......................................$80.00
Bowl, wedding/candy; footed, w/lid, 10½" $155.00
Bowl, 5¾"...$20.00
Candle holder, sherbet type............................$30.00
Cheese stand $25.00
Compote, crimped, footed, 7½x12"......................$95.00
Creamer $25.00
Mayonnaise, 3-pc set $65.00
Plate, bread & butter; 5"................................$8.00
Plate, dinner; 10".......................................$37.50
Plate, party; 24".......................................$155.00
Plate, salad; 7⅜".......................................$12.00
Punch cup $15.00
Relish, 5-part, 14".......................................$95.00
Stem, cocktail; 2¼-oz $12.50
Stem, oyster cocktail; 4-oz $14.00
Stem, water goblet; 9-oz $12.00
Stem, wine; 2-oz $7.50
Tumbler, iced tea; footed, 12-oz........................$20.00
Tumbler, juice; footed, 4-oz............................$12.00
Tumbler, water; 8½-oz...................................$13.00
Vase, bud; 12¼" $90.00

Kitchen Collectibles

If you've never paid much attention to old kitchen appliances, now is the time to do just that. Check in Grandma's basement — or your mother's kitchen cabinets, for that matter. As styles in home decorating changed, so did the styles of appliances. Some have wonderful Art Deco lines, while others border on the primitive. Most of those you'll find still work, and with a thorough cleaning you'll be able to restore them to their original 'like-new' appearance. Missing parts may be impossible to replace, but if it's just a cord that's gone, you can usually find what you need at any hardware store.

Even larger appliances are collectible and are often used to add the finishing touch to a period kitchen. Please note that prices listed here are for appliances that are free of rust, pitting, or dents and in excellent working condition.

During the nineteenth century, cast-iron apple peelers, cherry pitters, and food choppers were patented by the hundreds, and because they're practically indestructible, they're still around today. Unless parts are missing, they're still usable and most are very efficient at the task they were designed to perform.

A lot of good vintage kitchen glassware is still around and can generally be bought at reasonable prices. Pieces vary widely from custard cups and refrigerator dishes to canister sets and cookie jars. There are also several books available for further information and study. If this area of collecting interests you, you'll enjoy *300 Years of Kitchen Collectibles* by Linda Campbell, and *Kitchen Antiques, 1790 – 1940*, by Kathryn McNerney. Other books include *Kitchen Glassware of the Depression Years* and *Anchor Hocking's Fire-King & More* by Gene Florence; *Collector's Encyclopedia of Fry Glassware* by H.C. Fry Glass Society; *The '50s and '60s Kitchen, A Collector's Handbook and Price Guide*, by Jan Lindenberger; and *Fire-King Fever* and *Pyrex History and Price Guide*, both by April Tvorak.

See also Aluminum; Clothes Sprinkler Bottles; Fire-King; Glass Knives; Griswold; Kitchen Prayer Ladies; Porcelier; Reamers.

Advisor: Jim Barker, Appliances (See Directory, Appliances)

Appliances

Baby bottle warmer, Sunbeam, Model B2, aluminum w/Bakelite, rocketship design, automatic, 1956 ...**$85.00**
Blender, Kenmore, Model 116-82421, 2-speed, 1951 ..**$65.00**
Can opener, Dazey, electric, ca 1960s **$28.00**
Coffee maker, Knapp-Monarch, chrome w/brown Bakelite handles, 1951 ....**$40.00**
Coffee maker, Sunbeam, Model C50, chrome w/black Bakelite handles, 1950s **$40.00**
Coffee set, coffeepot w/creamer, sugar bowl & tray, Sunbeam, Model C30C, chrome w/Bakelite handles, 1954 ....**$75.00**
Egg cooker, Sunbeam, Model E2, aluminum w/Bakelite handles & feet, 1954, 4⅝x7¾" **$30.00**

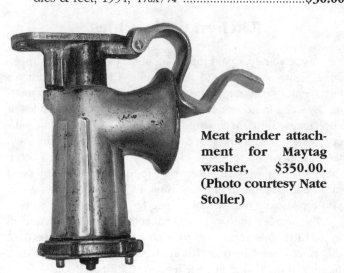

Meat grinder attachment for Maytag washer, $350.00. (Photo courtesy Nate Stoller)

Mixer, Betty Crocker, Kenmore, Model 303.82250, 1950s ..**$40.00**
Mixer, Kitchenmaid, Model 3-C, Hobart Mfg Co, w/glass bowl, 1950s **$70.00**
Percolator, General Electric, chrome w/brown Bakelite handles, 1955...**$25.00**
Toaster, Airline, chromium w/black enamel inlay, bell rings when toast is ready, ca 1939, EX, minimum value .**$25.00**
Toaster, General Electric #129T81, chrome w/brown Bakelite handles, 2-slice, 7x12", EX, minimum value **$15.00**
Toaster, Heetmaster #360-2094, chrome w/black Bakelite Art Deco handles & feet, engraved designs, EX, minimum value **$45.00**
Toaster, Kwik*Way Turnover #21-404, chrome on black base, 400 watts, 5½x7½x8", EX, minimum value **$25.00**
Toaster, Miracle #210, chrome w/Bakelite handles, 400 watts, 6½x7", EX, minimum value................................**$25.00**
Toaster, Penn-Air Pop-Down #280, aluminum w/black Bakelite handles, toast chute ea side, EX, minimum value **$100.00**
Toaster, Rosebud #25-1, chrome, black Bakelite handles & feet, rounded corners, EX, minimum value.........**$65.00**

Toaster, Son Chief, 550 watts, 115 volts, $650.00. (Photo courtesy Jim Barker)

Toaster, Sunbeam #T-9, chrome & plastic w/jewel, rounded top, ca 1942, 7¾x10", EX, minimum value...........**$45.00**
Toaster, Toastmaster #1B14, chrome w/brown Bakelite handles, 2-slice, ca 1941, EX, minimum value **$15.00**
Toaster, Universal, chrome sides lowered by turning brown Bakelite handle, 500 watts, EX, minimum value ..**$45.00**
Toaster, Westinghouse Turnover #TEC-14, chrome w/Deco linear decoration, drop-down doors, 115 volts, EX, minimum value...**$25.00**

Miscellaneous Gadgets and Glassware

Apple corer, Atceco-Std, tin, tube type, 6¾" **$20.00**
Batter jug, green, Jenkins #570..**$150.00**
Bean stringer & slicer, Bean-X, 6" **$25.00**
Bottle, water; green, flask form w/embossed panels, Hocking, 32-oz...**$27.50**
Bowl, cobalt, Hazel Atlas, 8½", w/metal holder **$38.00**
Bowl, mixing; green clambroth, 8¾" **$27.50**
Butter dish, amber, rectangular, Federal Glass, 1-lb....**$38.00**

Butter dish, green, box form, 2-lb..............................**$150.00**
Butter dish, pink, lid w/embossed B, Jeannette, 2-lb..**$185.00**
Butter dish, white, lid w/embossed BUTTER COVER, Hazel Atlas...**$30.00**
Butter tub, amber, embossed ribs, Federal.................**$33.00**
Canister, caramel, matching lid, 40-oz.......................**$80.00**
Canister, custard w/black letters, square w/metal lid.**$42.50**
Canister, Dutch boy on clear glass, red tin lid...........**$20.00**
Canister, white clambroth, square w/rounded corners, black tin lid...**$38.00**
Chopper, metal handle w/single rocker blade.............**$12.00**
Chopper, wood handle w/double steel blades...........**$25.00**
Coaster, cobalt, Hazel Atlas...**$9.00**
Colander/steamer, collaspible, tin, 10".....................**$35.00**
Corer, 3-in-1, marked Boye, Pat Nov 28, 16 Made in USA; short handle...**$15.00**

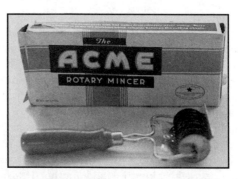

Corner shelf, plastic, Lustro-Ware, pre-zip code, $15.00.

Cruet, Caribbean Blue, Duncan....................................**$85.00**
Cruet, pink, ribbed & beaded, Imperial.......................**$45.00**
Cruet, yellow, Lancaster Glass Company.....................**$65.00**
Cup, green, slick handle...**$12.00**
Cup, measuring; green fired-on, 2-cup.......................**$12.00**
Egg basket, wireware, collapsible, wire feet, lg.........**$45.00**
Egg beater, Dover, #11, tiny beaters..........................**$70.00**
Egg lifter/whisk, spiraled springy wire w/twisted wire handle, 10"...**$18.00**
Egg slicer, Presto, heavy duty, cast aluminum frame, strong slicing wires...**$25.00**
Funnel, green, Tufglas...**$95.00**
Grater, Moran's 5 in 1 Kitchenaid, fits over bowl, grates & slices, 9½" dia..**$12.00**
Grater, nutmeg; Edgar...**$65.00**
Grater, tin, half round w/metal handle & bottom reinforcement, 7"..**$15.00**
Ice bucket, green, w/metal drainer..............................**$36.00**
Ice bucket, pink, Black Forest, Van Deman.................**$65.00**
Jar wrench, adjustable loop style, marked Berthoud Patented.**$18.00**
Jar wrench, marked The Turney Mfg Co, Detroit Mich Pat Oct 1905, pull-apart type w/teeth...............................**$18.00**

Jar wrench, marked Triumph Fruit Jar Wrench-Pat Nov 3 '03, Mfg'd by Benj P Forbes Cleveland O, 2 halves work separately...**$18.00**
Juice dispenser, pink, Mission Real Fruit Juice..........**$200.00**
Ladle, dumpling; wire, 13"..**$25.00**
Mug, green clambroth..**$35.00**

Noodle cutter/mincer, Acme, dated 1935, MIB, $20.00. (Photo courtesy Fran Carter)

Pan, measuring; Wear Ever, aluminum, 5"..................**$10.00**
Pitcher, measuring; pink, embossed ribs, Hocking, 2-cup.**$42.00**
Potato masher, circular, flat, decorative design, cast iron, 10"...**$25.00**
Potato masher, double-looped wire w/black painted handle...**$15.00**
Potato masher, 2 heavy wire concentric circles w/oak handle, restaraunt size, 14".......................................**$30.00**
Rolling pin, Silvers, doweled middle, wood handles, lg...**$60.00**

Shakers, fired-on colors, Dutch, 5", set of four, from $35.00 to $45.00. (Photo courtesy Gene Florence)

Skillet, clear, McKee Range Tec..................................**$11.00**
Soap saver, lg wire basket, wire handle, 3¾" dia.......**$35.00**
Spatula, Frank E Scott Commission Co, Sioux City Iowa, advertising on handle, heart cut-out on end of handle, 11½"...**$15.00**
Spatula, Red Moon Flour embossed on handle w/bottle opener end, heart cut-out on blade, 11¾"..........**$15.00**
Spoon, cake/mixing; slotted, handle stamped w/decorative design, 12"..**$12.00**
Spoon, cake/mixing; slotted, Rumford Cake Mix & Cream Whip, Pat Oct 6-08 stamped handle, 12".............**$18.00**
Spoon, cake/mixing; slotted, w/wooden handle w/ring at end for hanging...**$10.00**

Sundae, green, fluted..................................$18.00
Water dispenser, custard, McKee................$125.00
Water dispenser, white, McKee..................$125.00

Kitchen Prayer Ladies

The Enesco importing company of Elk Grove, Illinois, distributed a line of kitchen novelties during the 1960s that they originally called 'Mother in the Kitchen.' Today's collectors refer to them as 'Kitchen Prayer Ladies.' The line was fairly extensive — some pieces are common, others are very scarce. All are designed around the figure of 'Mother' who is wearing a long white apron inscribed with a prayer. She is more commonly found in a pink dress. Blue is harder to find and more valuable. Where we've given ranges, pink is represented by the lower end, blue by the higher. If you find her in a white dress with blue trim, add another 10% to 20%. For a complete listing and current values, you'll want to order *Prayer Lady Plus+* by April and Larry Tvorak. This line is pictured in *The Collector's Encyclopedia of Cookie Jars, Volume 1 and 2*, by Joyce and Fred Roerig (Collector Books).

Advisor: April Tvorak (See Directory, Kitchen Prayer Ladies)

Air freshener $150.00
Bank, from $145 to.....................................$175.00
Bell, from $65 to..$80.00
Candle holders, pr......................................$110.00
Canister, pink, ea..$300.00
Canister set, pk, complete, from $1,200 to.............$1,500.00
Cookie jar, blue...$495.00
Cookie jar, pink $395.00
Crumb tray or brush, from $100 to.............$150.00
Egg timer, from $100 to $135.00
Instant coffee jar, spoon-holder loop on side $125.00
Mug..$125.00
Napkin holder, pink, from $25 to..................$30.00
Picture frame, minimum value $150.00
Planter...$75.00

Plaque, 7⅜", $85.00. (Photo courtesy Pat Duncan)

Ring holder...$50.00
Salt & pepper shakers, pr, from $12 to.........$20.00

Salt and pepper shakers, rare white trimmed in blue, from $22.00 to $25.00. (Photo courtesy Pat Duncan)

Soap dish, from $35 to.................................$45.00
Spoon holder, upright, from $45 to..............$50.00
Sprinkler bottle, blue, minimum value $400.00
Sprinkler bottle, pink, minimum value $300.00
String holder, from $135 to.........................$145.00
String holder, wall mount, from $135 to......$145.00
Sugar bowl, w/spoon $60.00
Tea set, pot, sugar & creamer, from $175 to.............$275.00
Toothpick holder, 4½", from $20 to............$24.00
Vase, bud; from $80 to...............................$100.00

Kreiss & Co.

Collectors are hot on the trail of figural ceramics, and one of the newest areas of interest are those figurines, napkin dolls, planters, mugs, etc., imported from Japan during the 1950s by the Kreiss company, located in California. Though much of their early production was run of the mill, in the late 1950s, the company introduced unique new lines — all bizarre, off the wall, politically incorrect, and very irreverent — and today it's these items that are attracting so much attention. There are several lines. One is a totally zany group of caricatures called Psycho-Ceramics. There's a Beatnick series, Nudies, and Elegant Heirs (all of which are strange little creatures), as well as some that are very well done and tasteful. Several will be inset with with colored 'jewels.' Many are marked either with an ink stamp or an in-mold trademark (some are dated), so you'll need to start turning likely-looking items over to check for the Kreiss name.

There's a very helpful book now on the market, called *Kreiss Novelty Ceramics*, written by and available from our advisors, Michele and Mike King.

See also Napkin Ladies.

Advisors: Michele and Mike King (See Directory, Kreiss; Psycho Ceramics)

Beatniks

Figure, guy in green suit, slouching, hands in pockets, Dad — I'm Waiting for the World to Go Pfft!, 6", from $100 to **$125.00**

Figure, haughty blonde w/poodle on leash, Kookie, Kookie, Lend Me Your Comb, she: 6½", from $125 to....**$175.00**

Christmas Psycho Ceramics

Figure, disgruntled, leading bizarre 8-legged pet, Don't Ask Me What It Is...Found It in My Xmas Stocking, pet: 5", from $400 ....**$450.00**

Figure, pink w/outstretched arms, Christmas tree on his head, Shomebody Stole the Tree, Dear!, 6¾", from $125 to **$175.00**

Figure, Santa, furious, trapped from shoulder to hips in purple chimney, 6¾", from $125 to **$150.00**

Figure, Santa, scowling, tongue out, arms extended, Who Do I Look Like — Rin Tin Tin??, 5¾", from $75 to..**$100.00**

Figure, Santa, Yes But What Did You Get for Santa?, 6¼", from $75.00 to $100.00. (Photo courtesy Michele and Mike King)

Crazy Green-Eyed Monsters and Friends

Figure, dinosaur, 7", being lead by 2¼" caveman, 2nd caveman seated on his neck, from $100 to **$150.00**

Figure, mammoth, lg tusks, fur hair, 5¼", w/2 2½" cavemen, from $100 to..**$150.00**

Elegant Heirs

Figure, blue coat, yellow sausage curls w/green hairbow, I Never Go in for Fads, I Have My Own Ideas, 6¼", from $125 ....**$175.00**

Figure, cigarette in 1 hand, bottle in other, So I Said to the Duke of Edinburgh, 6½", from $100 to **$125.00**

Mug, man w/stringy red hair, straight black eyebrows, patched blue outfit, 4", from $125 to..................**$150.00**

Moon Beings

Figure, moon 'cat,' yellow & black with red head, white face & ruff, 'fur' hair, 4¾", from $250 to **$300.00**

Figure, pink bird-like creature w/lg pointed ears, 4¾", from $250 to..**$300.00**

The Nudies

Figure, exaggerated high forehead, bald, dazed & confused expression, 6½", from $275 to.............................**$325.00**

Mug, furrowed brow, eyes crossed, holding red valentine heart in front, 4¼", from $150 to **$200.00**

Psycho Ceramics

Ashtray, pink creature w/tongue stuck out holds blue tray overhead, 5", from $450 to **$500.00**

Bank, entreating purple creature, hands down to sides, 'fur' hair, Please!! No Slugs!!, 5¾", from $150 to........**$200.00**

Figure, blue w/black rash (Xs) & pipe cleaner antennae, blah gaze, You Say You're Sick & ...Blue, 5", from $800 to **$1,000.00**

Figure, huge open mouth, very assertive, My Mind's Made Up!, Don't Confuse Me w/Facts!, plastic hair, 5", from $400 to..**$450.00**

Figure, mouth firmly set, corks in his ears, My Mind's Made Up..., Don't Confuse Me w/Facts, 5", from $225 to............**$275.00**

Figure, pensive maroon creature, Whenever I Think, I Make Mistakes, Giant Series, 8¼", from $800 to.......**$1,000.00**

Figure, perplexed yellow creature w/red horned imp whispering in his ear, 4¾", from $600 to...................**$700.00**

Figure, pointed ears, red bubble nose, in pointed 'Dunce' hat, 6¼", from $400 to **$450.00**

Figure, purple 2-headed creature, 1 side talking & gesturing, other snarling, 5", from $275 to...........................**$325.00**

Figure, sitting w/eyes turned upward, left hand to nose as if in deep thought, spiral pipe cleaner antenna, 4¾", $350..**$400.00**

Figure, yellow creature w/cracks & fractures, Somedays I Go All to Pieces!, 4½", from $100 to.........................**$150.00**

Figure, 1 side blue, 1 side yellow, wide head-to-toe separation, Doc Said Something About a Split Personality, 5", $150 ....**$200.00**

Mug, woebegone green creature w/gun to head, Nothing Seems To Work for Me Anymore!, 5", from $125 to............**$175.00**

Miscellaneous

Cavemen (1½") and dinosaur (6½"), from $100.00 to $150.00. (Photo courtesy Michele and Mike King)

Bank, yellow 'fireman' w/removable hat, In Case of Fire Lift Up Hat, 7", from $150 to.....................................$200.00

Bell, Daffy Bell Series, 3 silly heads, sm 1 on top graduating down to very lg 1, 4½", from $25 to $75.00

Figure, Good Time Charlie on stomach on pink elephant, sm elephant on his back, A Little Fun Don't Hurt No One, 5", from $100 to.......................................$150.00

Skunk, dresser caddy and bank, 7¼", from $45.00 to $50.00. (Photo courtesy Bev and Jim Mangus)

Lamps

Aladdin Electric Lamps

Aladdin lamps have been made continually since 1908 by the Mantle Lamp Company of America, now Aladdin Mantle Lamp Company in Nashville, Tennessee. Their famous kerosene lamps are highly collectible, and some are quite valuable. Most were relegated to the storage shelf or thrown away after electric lines came through the country. Today many people keep them on hand for emergency light.

Few know that Aladdin Industries, Inc. was one of the largest manufacturers of electric lamps from 1930 to 1956. They created new designs, colorful glass, and unique paper shades. These are not only collectible but are still used in many homes today. Many Aladdin lamps, kerosene as well as electric, can be found at garage sales, antique shops, and flea markets. You can learn more about them in the books *Aladdin Electric Lamps* and *Aladdin — The Magic Name in Lamps, Revised Edition*, written by J.W. Courter, who also periodically issues updated price guides for both kerosene and electric Aladdins.

Advisor: J.W. Courter (See Directory, Lamps)

Newsletter: *Mystic Lights of the Aladdin Knights*
J.W. Courter
3935 Kelley Rd., Kevil, KY 42053. Subscription: $25 (6 issues, postpaid 1st class) per year with current buy-sell-trade information. Send SASE for information about other publications.

Bed lamp, whip-o-lite pleated shade, #653 SS, from $250 to .**$350.00**

Bedroom lamp, ceramic base, washable shade, P-64, 18", from $25 to...**$35.00**

Boudoir lamp, Allegro, Alacite, G-42, from $40 to **$50.00**

Boudoir lamp, Moonstone, G-153, from $50 to **$60.00**

Boudoir lamp, Moonstone base, G-32, from $70 to ...**$90.00**

Desk lamp, Alacite, G-202, from $200 to...................**$275.00**

Figurine lamp, classic figures, M-143, from $175 to .**$225.00**

Magic Touch lamp, ceramic base, MT-507 or MT-508, ea, from $300 to..**$350.00**

Pin-up lamp, cast white metal, plated, M-350, from $50 to .**$70.00**

Table lamp, Alacite, illuminated base, G-263A, from $50 to...**$60.00**

Table lamp, amber or ruby, G-177, from $275 to.....**$350.00**

Table lamp, black metal tripod base, original polyplastex shade, P-448, 24", from $50 to..............................**$75.00**

Table lamp, bronze metal, M-1 through M-5, ea, from $100 to **$150.00**

Table lamp, ceramic base, Volcanic brown or green, burlap shade, P-410, 35", from $40 to..............................**$60.00**

Table lamp, marble-like glass, G-2, from $300 to.....**$350.00**

Table lamp, metal & moonstone, MM-6 or MM-7, ea, from $200 to...**$250.00**

Table lamp, metal figurine, M-123, from $200 to......**$250.00**

Table lamp, Velvex, G-84, from $550 to **$600.00**

Table lamp, Vogue Pedestal, blue, E-201, from $550 to..**$600.00**

TV lamp, black iron base w/shade, M-367, from $40 to...**$50.00**

Aladdin Kerosene Mantle Lamps

Caboose lamp, Model B, galvanized steel font, B-400, from $100 to...**$150.00**

Floor lamp, Model #12, style 1251, black & gold, from $200 to...**$300.00**

Hanging lamp, brass w/glass shade, several types, Model #23, ea, from $60 to **$100.00**

Model #7, table lamp, satin brass, from $275 to.......**$350.00**

Model #12, Crystal Vase, Green Alpha art glass, #1230A, 10¼", from $150 to...**$250.00**

Model #12, Crystal Vase lamp, Variegated Verde or Tan, #1240 or #1241, 12", ea, from $200 to **$250.00**

Model B, table lamp, Corinthian, clear crystal, B-100, from $85 to...**$125.00**

Model B, table lamp, Quilt, white moonstone, B-85, from $325 to...**$400.00**

Model B, table lamp, Tall Lincoln Drape, Alacite, blue/purple w/black light, B-75, post-war (beware of new), from $125 to...**$200.00**

Model B, table lamp, Victoria, ceramic, w/oil fill, worn gold band, B-25, from $300 to **$400.00**

Model 23, table lamp, solid brass, B-2301, 1976 to present, from $50 to...**$70.00**

Table lamp, Model 23 Grand Vertiques, burmese, signed Aladdin/Fenton 1997, from $450 to **$550.00**

Table lamp, Short Lincoln Drape, ruby, signed in glass: Aladdin 1979, from $125 to **$200.00**

Wall bracket lamp, Model #6, w/font, correct burner, flame spreader & 2-part wall bracket, from $150 to **$200.00**

Table lamp, Model 12, with complete burner, EX, from $75.00 to $100.00. (Photo courtesy Bill and Treva Courter)

Young girl's torso atop large pink rose skirt, marked Germany, #14598, 5½", $175.00. (Photo courtesy Dee Boston)

Figural Lamps

Many of the figural lamps on the market today are from the 1930s, '40s, and '50s. You'll often see them modeled as matching pairs, made primarily for use in the boudoir or the nursery. They were sometimes made of glass, and *Bedroom and Bathroom Glassware of the Depression Years* by Margaret and Kenn Whitmyer (Collector Books) will prove to be an invaluable source of further information, if you're primarily interested in the glass variety. But most were ceramic, so unless another material is mentioned in our descriptions, assume that all our figural lamps are ceramic. Several examples are shown in *Collector's Guide to Made in Japan Ceramics, Books I, II,* and *III,* by Carole Bess White (Collector Books.)

See also Occupied Japan.

Advisor: Dee Boston (See Directory, Lamps)

Colonial couple (double figure), ornate attire, he standing, she seated at desk, Japan, 8" **$30.00**
Colonial couple (double figure), ornate attire w/pastels & scattered flowers, Japan, 1930s, 7½", pr, from $50 to **$80.00**
Colonial couple (double figure) standing before branching tree trunk, well dressed, white w/gold trim, Japan, 8" **$35.00**
Colonial girl in rose & yellow dress, holding blue reticule, hair piled high w/plumes, unmarked, 6" **$110.00**
Girl w/Dutch-type bonnet & lg basket bouquet, marked Germany, #32438, 6" figure on 7" base **$175.00**
Jack & Jill, Colonial-style green & lavender attire, holding water bucket or pitcher, marked Germany #13334 MHB, 8", pr...**$250.00**
Lady in pink dress w/legs exposed, marked Germany, #15567, 5½"...**$175.00**
Pierrett in short white dress w/black trim & top, detailed pedestal base, Sitzendorf/Germany, #13047, 6½" .**$225.00**
Pierrot & lady (double figure), white w/2-color polka-dots & gold trim, Japan, 7", from $25 to **$40.00**

Motion Lamps

Though some were made as early as 1920 and as late as the '70s, motion lamps were most popular during the '50s. Most are cylindrical with scenes such as waterfalls and forest fires and attain a sense of motion through the action of an inner cylinder that rotates with the heat of the bulb. Prices below are for lamps with original parts in good condition with no cracks, splits, dents, or holes. Any damage greatly decreases the value. As a rule of thumb, the oval lamps are worth a little more than their round counterparts. **Caution** — some lamps are being reproduced. Currently in production are Antique Autos, Trains, Old Mill, Ships in a Storm, Fish, and three Psychedelic lamps. The color on the scenic lamps is much bluer, and they are in a plastic stand with a plastic top. There are quite a few small motion lamps in production that are not copies of the 1950s lamps. For further information we recommend *Collector's Guide to Motion Lamps* (Collector Books), which contains full-page color photographs and useful information.

Advisors: Jim and Kaye Whitaker (See Directory, Lamps)

Antique Auto, picture frame, Econolite, 1953, 10"....**$115.00**
Antique Autos, oval, Econolite, 1957, 11"................**$125.00**
Christmas Tree, Econolite, 1950, 10½" **$75.00**
Christmas Tree, Econolite, 1950, 15" **$110.00**
Christmas Tree, Econolite, 1950, 23" **$125.00**
Colonial Fountain, Scene in Action, 1931, 13" **$145.00**
Ducks, round, pedestal base, Econolite, 1955, 14" ...**$140.00**
Forest Fire, picture frame, Econolite, 1953, 10"..........**$95.00**
Forest Fire, round, Econolite, 1955, 11"......................**$95.00**
Forest Fire, round, LA Goodman, 1956, 11" **$85.00**
Forest Fire, Scene in Action, 1931, 10" **$125.00**
Fountain of Youth, Roto-Vue Jr, 1950, 10" **$95.00**
Fountain of Youth, round, Econolite, 11" **$100.00**
Hearth, round, Econolite, 1958, 11" **$125.00**
Hopalong Cassidy, Roto-Vue Jr, 1950, 10" **$275.00**

Japanese Twilight, Scene in Action, 1931, 13" **$165.00**
Lighthouse, round, LA Goodman, 1956, 11"..............**$105.00**
Merry Go Round, Roto-Vue Jr, 1949, 10" **$130.00**
Niagara Falls, picture frame, Econolite, 1953, 10".......**$90.00**
Niagara Falls, Roto-Vue Jr, 1950, 10" **$75.00**
Niagara Falls, round, Econolite, 1955, 11" **$85.00**
Niagara Falls, round, LA Goodman, 1957, 11" **$75.00**
Niagara Falls, Scene in Action, 1931, 10"..................**$120.00**
Old Mill, round, Econolite, 1956, 11".........................**$105.00**
Psychedelic, various patterns, visual effects, 1970s, 13" ...**$65.00**

Sailboats, L.A. Goodman, 1954, 14", $110.00. (Photo courtesy Jim and Kaye Whitaker)

Seattle World's Fair, oval, Econolite, 1962, 11"..........**$150.00**
Snow Scene, round, Econolite, 1957, 11" **$120.00**
Train, picture frame, Econolite, 1953, 10"..................**$100.00**
Train, round, Econolite, 1956, 11" **$130.00**
Waterfall-Campfire, round, LA Goodman, 1956, 11" ...**$95.00**

TV Lamps

By the 1950s, TV was commonplace in just about every home in the country but still fresh enough to have our undivided attention. Families gathered around the set and for the rest of the evening delighted in being entertained by Ed Sullivan or stumped by the $64,000 Question. Pottery producers catered to this scenario by producing TV lamps by the score, and with the popularity of anything from the '50s being what it is today, suddenly these lamps are making an appearance at flea markets and co-ops everywhere.

See also Maddux of California; Morton Potteries, Royal Haeger.

Advisors: John and Peggy Scott (See Directory, Florence Ceramics)

Ballet dancer (male), painted plaster, Fiberglas shade, signed American Statuary Co, from $85 to **$95.00**
Bird, black & white, on brown log planter, 11x13" **$65.00**
Boy on dolphin, allover gold paint, signed Lane & Co, Van Nuys CA, from $95 to..**$105.00**
Coach w/horse & figures, light inside coach, painted bisque, brass base, from $100 to **$110.00**
Cockatoo w/brass base & planter, marked E21855M, from $75 to...**$90.00**

Crane, white & gold spatter, on deep planter base, 16".**$80.00**
Deer leaping over scrolling foliage (planter), green or brown, from $60 to..**$70.00**
Deer pr, Deco styling, tan w/gold trim, Kron, 15x8"..**$75.00**
Duck, flying, w/wooden base, from $82 to................**$97.00**
Duck in flight, w/planter & original plastic plants, marked Lane Co, from $75 to..**$100.00**
Gazelle (leaping) w/planter, dark green, from $70 to ..**$90.00**
Glass w/black silhouette riders, reverse-painted mountainous background, flat metal base, 8x10" **$50.00**
Horse, Deco style w/left front leg raised, w/paper shade & planter, signed Modern Art Products...1953, from $110 to **$135.00**
Horse (rearing) w/planter, black w/gold trim, 19"......**$90.00**
Horse beside stump, Deco style w/curly mane & tail, green, brown or chartreuse, from $85 to **$100.00**
Horse heads (2) between 2 planters, green or brown, unmarked, from $45 to..**$55.00**
Horse heads (3), long graceful necks, Kron, 15" **$45.00**
Horse standing on rock ledge, white, 12½x9½".........**$60.00**
Lady & swan, terra cotta or turquoise high gloss, Lane, 16", minimum value **$100.00**
Leopard, brown tones on painted plaster, 14", from $200 to **$250.00**
Madonna praying, all white, from $45 to **$55.00**
Musicians, black-painted pot metal, stand between frosted glass globe, from $120 to....................................**$135.00**
Oriental figures (2) on black sampan w/gold trim, windows light up, from $65 to **$90.00**
Owl, naturalistic, spread wings, Morton Pottery, marked Kron, lg, from $75 to...**$85.00**
Panther atop rocky ledge, Lane, 12x16" **$75.00**
Plumed feathers, painted plaster, signed FAIP, from $75 to **$90.00**
Poodle, Deco, black w/light-colored coleslaw, plaster w/Fiberglas shade, signed CMA, from $110 to...**$120.00**
Poodle & pug dog, glass eyes, Kron line, 13", from $70 to **$100.00**
Rooster, crowing, on fence, signed Lane, from $95 to...**$110.00**
Sailing ship, 2-masted, white bisque w/gilt decor, from $75 to **$95.00**
Ship, gold-colored paint on pot metal, 1 lg sail, portholes light up, from $85 to **$95.00**
Siamese cats (2), eyes light up, marked Kron, from $95 to **$110.00**
Siamese mother w/kitten, blue marble eyes, Enchanto CA **$75.00**
Siamese mother w/kitten, Kron, 1950s, 13¾x8".........**$77.50**
Siamese mother w/2 kittens, blue rhinestone eyes, Lane, 12½x3½"..**$115.00**
Siamese pr, 1 sitting, 1 recumbent, rhinestone eyes, Lane, 1956, 14" **$75.00**
Swan, green w/black details on face, light inside, holes in wings light up, from $80 to **$95.00**
Tower of Pisa, soapstone, light inside, windows light up, from $135 to..**$145.00**

Ballerina and swan, Lane, 16", minimum value, $100.00. (From the collection of John and Peggy Scott)

L.E. Smith

Originating just after the turn of the century, the L.E. Smith company continues to operate in Mt. Pleasant, Pennsylvania, at the present time. In the 1920s they introduced a line of black glass that they are famous for today. Some pieces were decorated with silver overlay or enameling. Using their own original molds, they made a line of bird and animal figures in crystal as well as in colors. The company is currently producing these figures, many in two sizes. They were one of the main producers of the popular Moon and Star pattern which has been featured in their catalogs since the 1960s in a variety of shapes and colors.

If you'd like to learn more about their bird and animal figures, *Glass Animals of the Depression Era* by Lee Garmon and Dick Spencer has a chapter devoted to those made by L.E. Smith. See also *A Collector's Guide to Modern American Slag Glass* by Ruth Grizel.

See also Eye Winker; Moon and Star.

Aquarium, King Fish, green, 7¼x15" $265.00
Basket, fireside; ruby, 13x12" $125.00
Basket, iridescent red, late $35.00
Bookend, horse, bookend, crystal, rearing, ea...........$55.00
Bowl, berry; footed, robin blue, 4" $16.00
Bowl, Dolly, red carnival $38.00
Bowl, turkey, dark blue, footed, oval, 7" $65.00
Bowl, Wigwam, flared..$30.00
Butter dish, Almond Nouveau slag, 1980 ....$45.00
Candle holder, #4041a, Almond Nouveau slag, 7½",
   ea..$25.00
Candle holder, angel, kneeling, slag, ea $25.00
Candle holders, angel, kneeling, green, pr..................$26.00
Canoe, Daisy & Button, purple carnival $25.00
Covered dish, hen on nest, #820a, Almond Nouveau slag,
   6" $50.00
Covered dish, rooster, standing, white carnival $75.00
Covered dish, turkey, milk glass $75.00

Covered dish, turkey, crystal, $35.00.

Creamer, Homestead, pink...$48.00
Figurine, bear, Almond Nouveau slag, #6654A, 4½"...$45.00
Figurine, bear, baby, head turned or straight, crystal, 3",
   ea $60.00
Figurine, bear, papa, crystal, 4x6½" $250.00
Figurine, bird, head up or down, Almond Nouveau, 5", pr..$65.00
Figurine, camel, recumbent, amber, 4½x6" $60.00
Figurine, camel, recumbent, cobalt, 4½x6" $65.00
Figurine, camel, recumbent, crystal, 4½x6" $45.00
Figurine, cock, fighting, blue, 9" $55.00
Figurine, elephant, crystal, 1¾" $12.00
Figurine, Goose Girl, amber, 5½"................................$35.00
Figurine, Goose Girl, crystal, original, 6" $25.00
Figurine, Goose Girl, ice green carnival, 5½" $60.00
Figurine, Goose Girl, red, 5½".....................................$50.00
Figurine, horse, recumbent, amberina, 9" L $150.00
Figurine, horse, recumbent, blue, 9" L.......................$115.00
Figurine, horse, recumbent, green, 9" L.....................$100.00
Figurine, praying Madonna, crystal $35.00
Figurine, rabbit, crystal, miniature..............................$10.00
Figurine, rooster, butterscotch slag, limited edition, #208...$85.00
Figurine, Scottie, black w/red trim, 6" $75.00
Figurine, Scottie, crystal, 6"...$65.00
Figurine, swan, Almond Nouveau slag, 5"...................$55.00
Figurine, swan, crystal lustre, limited edition, w/certificate,
   lg $55.00
Figurine, swan, ice pink carnival, 2"............................$15.00
Figurine, swan, milk glass w/decoration, 8½"..............$45.00
Figurine, swan, open back, #15a, Almond Nouveau slag,
   4½" $20.00
Figurine, thrush, blue frost...$20.00
Figurine, unicorn, pink, miniature................................$20.00
Lamp, fairy; turtle figural, green $25.00
Nappy, heart shape, #4630a, Almond Nouveau, 6" $25.00
Novelty, boot on pedestal, green or amber, ea...........$12.00
Novelty, coal bucket, #125a, Almond Nouveau slag, 5"..$25.00
Novelty, shoe skate, ice blue, limited edition, 4"........$25.00
Novelty, slipper, Daisy & Button, amber $8.00
Novelty, slipper, Daisy & Button, purple carnival.......$25.00
Pitcher, water; Heritage, red carnival $40.00
Pitcher, water; Hobstar, ice green, w/6 tumblers $125.00

Pitcher, water; Tiara Eclipse, green **$70.00**
Plate, Abraham Lincoln, purple carnival, #706/1195, 9" .**$40.00**
Plate, Herald, Christmas 1972, purple carnival, lg **$40.00**
Plate, Jefferson Davis, 1972, purple carnival, lg..........**$40.00**
Plate, Robert E Lee, 1972, purple carnival, lg **$40.00**
Plate, Silver Dollar Eagle, 1972, purple carnival, lg....**$40.00**
Soap dish, swan, clear, 8½" **$22.50**
Sugar bowl, Homestead, pink.................................**$8.00**
Toothpick holder, Daisy & Button, amberina..............**$12.50**
Tumbler, Bull's Eye, red carnival.............................**$22.00**
Urn, black, 2-handled, footed, 8" **$20.00**
Vase, bud; #33a, Almond Nouveau slag, 6½"............**$35.00**
Vase, corn, crystal lustre, very lg................................**$37.00**

Lefton China

China, porcelain, and ceramic items with that now familiar mark, Lefton, have been around since the early 1940s and are highly sought after by collectors in the secondary marketplace today. The company was founded by Mr. George Zoltan Lefton, an immigrant from Hungary. In the 1930s he was a designer and manufacturer of sportswear, but eventually his hobby of collecting fine china and porcelain led him to initiate his own ceramic business. When the bombing of Pearl Harbor occurred on December 7, 1941, Mr. Lefton came to the aid of a Japanese-American friend and helped him protect his property from anti-Japanese groups. Later, Mr. Lefton was introduced to a Japanese factory owned by Kowa Koki KK. He contracted with them to produce ceramic items to his specifications, and until 1980 they made thousands of pieces that were marketed by the Lefton company, marked with the initials KW preceding the item number. Figurines and animals plus many of the whimsical pieces such as Bluebirds, Dainty Miss, Miss Priss, Cabbage Cutie, Elf Head, Mr. Toodles, and Dutch Girl are eagerly collected today. As with any antique or collectible, prices vary depending on location, condition, and availability. For the history of Lefton China, information about Lefton factories, marks, and other identification methods, we highly recommend the *Collector's Encyclopedia of Lefton China, Volumes I, II, and III,* by our advisor Loretta DeLozier (Collector Books).

See also Birthday Angels; Cookie Jars.

Advisor: Loretta DeLozier (See Directory, Lefton)

Club: National Society of Lefton Collectors

Newsletter: *The Lefton Collector*
c/o Loretta DeLozier
1101 Polk St.
Bedford, IA 50833; 712-523-2289 (Mon.-Fri. 9:00-4:00), fax: 712-523-2624, or e-mail: Lefton Lady@aol.com; Dues: $25 per year (includes quarterly newsletter)

Animal, bay horse, #064, 5¼" **$50.00**
Animal, camel, Bethlehem Collection, #05381, 4".......**$10.00**

Animal, chipmunks, #4753, 11" **$95.00**
Animal, Koala bear w/cub, bisque, #4754, 10" **$130.00**
Animal, lamb w/flowers & stones, #80551, 5"............**$45.00**
Animal, Setter, #80521 ....**$52.00**
Animal, squirrel, bisque, #4749, 5" **$35.00**
Ashtray, violets & stones, #194, sm, set **$32.00**
Bank, bird nest w/stones, #90338, 5" **$65.00**
Bank, Fuzzy Dog, white, w/key, #90021, 8¼" **$65.00**
Bank, owl, bisque, #479, 6½" **$25.00**
Bank, piggy, black w/stones, #90199, 5" **$35.00**
Bell, candy cane girls, #90401, 4" **$22.00**
Bell, Forget Me Not, pink, #90460, 2¾" **$18.00**
Bird, bobolink, #1290 ....**$35.00**
Bird, butterfly, #80578, 3" & 2" w/clip **$18.00**
Bird, golden pheasant, #1060, 11¾" **$75.00**
Bird, musical, #02143, 6" **$45.00**
Bone dish, Brown Heritage Floral, #563, 8" **$15.00**

Bowl, shell shape with cherubs, #941, 9", from $400.00 to $500.00. (Photo courtesy Pat and Ann Duncan)

Box, Green Holly, $40.00.

Box, candy; Berry Harvest, #297 ....**$65.00**
Box, jewel; w/lid, #2748, 4½"...............................**$48.00**
Box, pin; Floral Bisque Bouquet, #3780, 2¾" **$18.00**
Bust, Franklin, #1146, 5½" **$25.00**
Card holder, Flower Garden, #3147 ....**$4.00**
Celery dish, Americana, #160, 12" **$55.00**
Cigarette lighter, Gold Wheat, #40111, 3" **$38.00**

Cigarette set, holder w/2 trays, #40133......................$28.00
Coffeepot, Fleur de Lis, #2910 ....$65.00
Compote, Fruit Design, #20053, 7".........................$28.00
Creamer & sugar bowl, Green Holly, #1355, from $25 to...$35.00
Creamer & sugar bowl, 50th Anniverary, #2981..........$18.00
Cup & saucer, Americana, #973.............................$35.00
Cup & saucer, Blue Rose, #1350.............................$15.00
Cup & saucer, jumbo; Grandma or Grandpa, #2594 or #2596,
    ea $12.00
Cup & saucer, tea; Dogwood Design, #2791.............$20.00
Dish, Eastern Elegance, #20567, 5".........................$32.00
Dish, Rustic Daisy, 2-compartment, w/handle, #4122...$32.00
Egg cup, Blue Paisley, #2131 ....$30.00
Egg cup, Elegant Rose, #2048................................$35.00
Egg tray, Country Squire, #1601, 12½" $28.00
Figurine, boy w/dog near tree trunk, #5051, 6"..........$56.00
Figurine, fisherman, bisque, #767, 7½".....................$70.00
Figurine, girl w/dog, pink, #4638, 4¾".....................$20.00
Figurine, Modern, all white, #1129, 5¼"....................$50.00
Figurine, Provincial boy w/duck, James, #374, 8".......$75.00

Figurine, spaniel, #80521, 5", $50.00. (Photo courtesy Loretta DeLozier)

Music box, Valentine angel, from $40.00 to $50.00. (Photo courtesy Lee Garmon)

Mug, Blue Aster, #6496, 4" $7.00
Nappy, Festival, #2632..$22.00
Pitcher & bowl, French Rose, #3383, 3¼" $25.00
Planter, black dogs, #50211, 5", pr..........................$45.00
Planter, dog w/yellow flower, #167, 6" $15.00
Planter, girl pushing cart, #50584, 4½".....................$32.00

Planter, Green Holly, boot shape, from $18 to $22.00
Planter, Ice Pink, bisque, #1183, 3¾".......................$25.00
Plaque, grapes, #455..$13.00
Plaque, oval shape w/2 angels, bisque, #1697, 6" $40.00
Plate, Brown Heritage Floral, #2222, 9" $35.00
Plate, Holly w/candy cane, red, #2617, 7½"...............$15.00
Plate, Poinsettia, #4396, 9" $22.00
Plate, To a Wild Rose, #2573, 7½" $15.00
Salt & pepper shakers, Christmas trees, #054, pr, from $12
    to..$15.00
Salt & pepper shakers, Christy, #441, 2½", pr.............$18.00
Salt & pepper shakers, Daisytime, #3362, pr..............$18.00
Salt & pepper shakers, Miss Priss, #1511, pr $35.00
Salt & pepper shakers, pink poodles, #104, pr..........$38.00
Shelf sitters, Mr & Mrs Santa Claus, #018, pr.............$55.00
Snack set, Brown Heritage Fruit, #20130 ....$38.00
Snack set, Forget Me Not, #4179 ....$12.00
Snack set, Green Holly, plate w/cup ring & teacup...$40.00
Snack set, Tree of Life Design, #20227 ....$22.00
Spice set, frying pan w/rooster design, #20601, 6-pc.$50.00
Teapot, Grape Line, #2663 ....$65.00
Teapot, Green Holly, from $55 to $70.00
Tidbit, Brown Heritage Floral, single, #20131 ....$28.00
Vase, #124, miniature, 2¾".....................................$30.00
Vase, Bird Bath, milk china, #6077...........................$30.00
Vase, Floral Bisque Bouquet, ewer form, #4209, 7"....$22.00
Vase, Luscious Lilac, #2942, 7".................................$22.00
Vase, pitcher form, blue bisque, #2184, 6" $8.00
Vase, roses, milk china, #1189, 6½" $50.00
Wall pocket, stove, Home Sweet Home, apple blossoms,
    #219, 7"...$15.00

Letter Openers

If you're cramped for space but a true-blue collector at heart, here's a chance to get into a hobby where there's more than enough diversification to be both interesting and challenging, yet one that requires very little room for display. Whether you prefer the advertising letter openers or the more imaginative models with handles sculpted as a dimensional figure or incorporating a penknife or a cigarette lighter, for instance, you should be able to locate enough for a nice assortment. Materials are varied as well, ranging from silverplate to wood. For more information, we recommend *Collector's Guide to Letter Openers* by Everett Grist (Collector Books).

Advisor: Everett Grist (See Directory, Letter Openers)

Advertising, black celluloid & French Ivory, Henry Grady
    Hotel, Atlanta GA..$30.00
Advertising, brass, Clarence A O'Brien, Patent Attorney..$35.00
Advertising, plastic, Lincoln Center NY.....................$3.00
Advertising, steel, Pittsburg Steel Co, also stamped on nail
    head $18.00
Antler & stainless steel, Nordia scene $15.00
Black onyx & sterling, Peruvian motif, design on blade..$45.00

313

Bone, cut-out totem pole $20.00

Brass, American eagle motif, plastic sheath, made in India .$12.00

Brass, George Washington bust, Souvenir of Washington DC, made by KND Co $12.00

Brass, gold-plated golf club, blade at handle $12.00

Brass, lion on wall, ornate blade, Belgium $10.00

Brass, painted dragon motif on blade, made in Taiwan .$12.00

Brass, red painted floral design on blade $6.00

Brass, Revolutionary patriot on horse, back marked England $10.00

Brass, unicorn head $12.00

Brass, upright bear on Alaskan crest $10.00

Bronze, griffin over lion head $12.00

Chrome steel, President by Peerless, Japan $5.00

Combination, bottle/letter opener, alpaca & abalone, coral eye, fish shape $20.00

Combination, paperweight/letter opener, brass, represents sword & stone $15.00

Combination, pen knife/letter opener, steel, Inck, made in France $8.00

European deer hoof handle, steel blade $15.00

Figural, copper, piano, Mammoth Cave KY $10.00

Figural, derringer, brass, Stamford CT $10.00

Figural, wood duck, hand-painted, Copyright 1987 Dakin Inc, San Francisco, made in China $8.00

Ivory, carved crocodile, tail as blade $85.00

Ivory, fancy cutouts in handle, sm $30.00

Leatherette, Duke College, gold-plated $3.00

Mother of Pearl, carved Victorian design $65.00

Pewter plate, sand dollar, Metzke $6.00

Plastic bathing beauty with flocked suit, $20.00. (Photo courtesy Everett Grist)

Plastic, beige, w/braille alphabet $10.00

Plastic, horn-like, Hawaii, w/pineapple $4.00

Plastic, pink stag, Wildlife Exhibit, Crawford Notch NH ..$6.00

Rhinestone, gold plated, jeweled handle $8.00

Silver-plated brass, sword design, American eagle w/crossed swords on shield, w/scabbard $12.00

Souvenir, silver plate & enamel, Swiss Cross, marked Meka Denmark $20.00

Souvenir, steel, Lincoln Museum, Washington DC, Lincoln bust $6.00

Souvenir, white metal, Old Faithful, Yellowstone $4.00

Steel, hand-painted camel bone plaque, scene from India w/tiger & antelope $25.00

Wood, African native head $10.00

Wood, hand-painted/carved Indian chief, The Chalet, Mt Royal Park, Montreal Cananda $20.00

Wood, Japanese-type sword used in Seppuku ceremony design, Fr Muus Falck $7.00

L.G. Wright

Until closing in mid-1999, the L.G. Wright Glass Company was located in New Martinsville, West Virginia. Mr. Wright started his business as a glass jobber and then began buying molds from defunct glass companies. He never made his own glass, instead many companies pressed his wares, among them Fenton, Imperial, Viking, and Westmoreland. Much of L.G. Wright's glass was reproductions of Colonial and Victorian glass and lamps. Many items were made from the original molds, but the designs of some were slightly changed. His company flourished in the 1960s and '70s. For more information we recommend *The L.G. Wright Glass Company* by James Measell and W.C. 'Red' Roetteis (Glass Press).

Ashtray, Daisy & Button, ruby, 5½" $20.00

Bell, Daisy & Button, ruby, 6½" $40.00

Bowl, Daisy & Button, amber, 5" $25.00

Bowl, sauce; Thistle, cobalt blue, 4½" dia $12.50

Bowl, sauce; Thistle, crystal, 4½" dia $12.00

Candy dish, Paneled Grape, amber, footed, w/lid, 6½x4" ..$40.00

Compote, Palm Beach, apple green, ca 1930, 8½" $95.00

Compote, Wild Rose, green, 13" $16.50

Covered dish, Atterbury duck, any color, unmarked, 11" ..$70.00

Covered dish, duck on flange base, amethyst w/white head $65.00

Covered dish, duck on flange base, milk glass or opaque blue w/milk glass head, ea $50.00

Covered dish, flatiron, amber, w/lid, 5x8½" $50.00

Covered dish, hen on basketweave base, amberina, red or vaseline, 7½", ea $75.00

Covered dish, hen on basketweave base, amethyst w/white head or white w/amethyst head, 7½", ea $65.00

Covered dish, hen on basketweave base, blue slag, 7½" ..$95.00

Covered dish, hen on basketweave base, chocolate, 7½" ..$95.00

Covered dish, hen on basketweave base, purple slag or caramel slag, 7½", ea, from $75 to $85.00

Covered dish, horse on basketweave base, purple slag or caramel slag, 5½", ea, from $75 to $85.00

Covered dish, owl on basketweave base, amber, 5½" .$45.00

Covered dish, owl on basketweave base, blue slag, 5½" ..$85.00

Covered dish, owl on basketweave base, custard, caramel slag or purple slag, 5½", ea, from $75 to $80.00

Covered dish, rooster on nest, red slag, 5½" **$95.00**

Covered dish, turkey on basketweave base, lilac mist, 5½"..**$55.00**

Covered dish, turtle, 'Knobby Back,' amber, lg..........**$95.00**

Covered dish, turtle, 'Knobby Back,' dark green, lg.**$135.00**

Covered dish, turtle on basketweave base, amber, 5½" .**$20.00**

Covered dish, turtle on basketweave base, purple slag, 5½", from $75 to **$85.00**

Cruet, Thumbprint, fluted **$85.00**

Cup, punch; Paneled Grape, dark green, w/cup hook, set of 12 ....**$120.00**

Goblet, Daisy & Button, ice blue, 5", set of 6............**$75.00**

Goblet, Paneled Grape, amber, 8-oz..........................**$15.00**

Goblet, wine; Paneled Grape, ruby, 2-oz...................**$20.00**

Lamp, fairy; diamond point, 3-pc, 7" **$110.00**

Lamp, fairy; Thistle, crystal, 3-pc...............................**$35.00**

Lamp, fairy; Wild Rose, green & crystal, ruffled base, 3-pc, 6"..**$40.00**

Lamp, oil; Daisy & Button, ruby, 12" **$75.00**

Lamp base, Daisy & Fern, cranberry, bulbous inverted pear form, ornate metal base **$95.00**

Lamp shade, American Beauty, embossed roses, pink overlay, 1950s-60s, 6¾x10"..**$65.00**

Mustard jar, bull's head, purple slag, no (tongue) ladle, $35.00. (Photo courtesy Everett Grist)

Pitcher, Cherries, green, 5"..**$38.00**

Plate, Log Cabin, Crystal Mist, oval, limited edition, 1971, 9", from $40 to **$50.00**

Plate, Paneled Grape, ruby, 7½", from $30 to.............**$35.00**

Salt dip, amberina, master..**$15.00**

Salt dip, Cherry, crystal, master, 1¾x3¼" **$30.00**

Salt dip, swan, crystal satin, 3¾" L.............................**$12.00**

Sleigh, Daisy and Button, large, from $150.00 to $200.00. (Photo courtesy James Measell and W. C. 'Red' Roetteis)

Sugar bowl, Paneled Grape, amber, sm......................**$15.00**

Sugar bowl, Thistle, cobalt blue, 4½" **$26.00**

Sugar shaker, Daisy & Button, cobalt opalescent, pr..**$50.00**

Tray, Daisy & Button, light blue, 3-part, 7½x4½"......**$30.00**

Tumblers, Inverted Thumbprint, cranberry, ca 1970, set of 6, from $50 to..**$60.00**

Liberty Blue

'Take home a piece of American history!,' stated an ad from the 1970s for this dinnerware made in Staffordshire, England. Blue and white depictions of George Washington at Valley Forge, Paul Revere, Independence Hall — fourteen historic scenes in all — were offered on different place-setting pieces. The ad goes on to describe this 'unique...truly unusual..museum-quality...future family heirloom.'

For every five dollars spent on groceries you could purchase a basic piece (dinner plate, bread and butter plate, cup, saucer, or dessert dish) for fifty-nine cents on alternate weeks of the promotion. During the promotion, completer pieces could also be purchased. The soup tureen was the most expensive item, originally selling for $24.99. Nineteen completer pieces in all were offered along with a five-year open stock guarantee.

Beware of 18" and 20" platters. These are recent imports and not authentic Liberty Blue. For more information we recommend Jo Cunningham's book, *The Best of Collectible Dinnerware* (Schiffer).

Advisor: Gary Beegle (See Directory, Dinnerware)

Bowl, cereal; from $12.00 to $15.00; cup and saucer, from $7.00 to $9.00.

Bowl, flat soup; 8¾", from $20 to **$22.00**

Bowl, fruit; 5", from $4.50 to **$5.50**

Bowl, vegetable; oval, from $40 to **$45.00**

Bowl, vegetable; round, from $40 to **$45.00**

Butter dish, w/lid, ¼-lb **$55.00**

Casserole, w/lid **$125.00**

Coaster..**$12.50**

Creamer, from $18 to	**$22.00**
Creamer & sugar bowl, w/lid, original box	**$80.00**
Gravy boat, from $32 to	**$38.00**
Gravy boat liner, from $22 to	**$25.00**
Mug, from $10 to	**$12.00**
Pitcher, 7½"	**$125.00**
Plate, bread & butter; 6"	**$3.00**
Plate, dinner; 10", from $6 to	**$8.00**
Plate, luncheon; scarce, 8¾"	**$24.00**
Plate, scarce, 7", from $9 to	**$12.00**
Platter, 12", from $35 to	**$45.00**
Platter, 14"	**$95.00**
Salt & pepper shakers, pr, from $38 to	**$42.00**
Soup ladle, plain white, no decal, from $30 to	**$35.00**
Soup tureen, w/lid	**$425.00**
Sugar bowl, no lid	**$10.00**
Sugar bowl, w/lid	**$28.00**
Teapot, w/lid, from $95 to	**$145.00**

License Plates

Some of the early porcelain license plates are valued at more than $500.00. First-year plates are especially desirable. Steel plates with the aluminum 'state seal' attached range in value from $150.00 (for those from 1915 to 1920) down to $20.00 (for those from the early '40s to 1950). Even some modern plates are desirable to collectors who like those with special graphics and messages.

Our values are given for examples in good or better condition, unless noted otherwise. For further information see *License Plate Values* distributed by L-W Book Sales.

Advisor: Richard Diehl (See Directory, License Plates)

Newsletter: *Automobile License Plate Collectors*
Gary Brent Kincade
P.O. Box 712, Weston, WV 26452; 304-842-3773

Magazine: *License Plate Collectors Hobby Magazine*
Drew Steitz, Editor
P.O. Box 222
East Texas, PA 18046; phone or fax: 610-791-7979; e-mail: PL8Seditor@aol.com or RVGZ60A@prodigy.com; Issued bimonthly; $18 per year (1st class, USA). Send $2 for sample copy

1919, $200.00; 1914, $300.00 (both Colorado). (Photo courtesy Richard Diehl)

1915, Indiana	**$60.00**
1918, Missouri	**$20.00**
1923, Idaho	**$35.00**
1924, Arkansas, rebuilt/repainted pr, fair	**$60.00**
1925, California	**$25.00**
1925, Louisiana, repainted	**$125.00**
1926, Connecticut	**$16.50**
1930, Maryland	**$23.00**
1931, Arizona	**$10.50**
1932, Minnesota	**$12.50**
1932, New Jersey	**$17.50**
1933, Nebraska	**$8.50**
1933, Nevada	**$30.00**
1935, Idaho	**$20.00**

1936, Rhode Island, 300th year plates, $100.00 for the pair.

1938, California	**$20.00**
1938, Pennsylvania	**$11.50**
1941, Arkansa	**$40.00**
1941, Montana	**$20.00**
1943, Kansas	**$10.50**
1944, Illinois, soybean	**$16.50**
1944, Virginia, fiberboard	**$50.00**
1946, Rhode Island, silver tab	**$40.00**
1948, Michigan	**$15.50**
1949, Iowa	**$12.50**
1949, Minnesota, Centennial	**$25.00**
1950, Ohio, waffle	**$12.50**
1951, Florida	**$40.00**
1952, Nebraska	**$6.00**
1953, Ohio	**$12.50**
1956, Utah	**$18.50**
1957, Montana	**$16.50**
1958, Texas, pr	**$18.00**
1958, Wyoming	**$8.50**
1959, British Columbia Canada	**$7.50**
1959, Indiana	**$6.50**
1960, Indiana	**$4.50**
1960, Wisconsin, tabs	**$1.00**
1961, Kansas	**$6.00**
1961, Kentucky	**$10.50**
1962, New York, pr	**$15.00**
1963, Alberta Canada	**$6.50**
1964, Alaska	**$22.00**
1965, Louisiana	**$10.50**
1966, Georgia	**$5.50**
1967, Missouri	**$7.00**

1967, Wisconsin $4.50
1969, Nevada...$8.50
1970, New Hampshire (motorcycle plate) $5.50
1970, Virginia, pr..$10.50
1971, Alabama $5.00
1971, Oklahoma $4.50
1972, Colorado, Disabled Vet............................$2.50
1972, Maine $4.50
1973, North Carolina..$4.00
1973, Washington DC, inaugural $15.50
1975, Hawaii..$10.50
1975, Oklahoma $4.50
1976, Maryland, Bicentennial $60.00
1976, Rhode Island, Ocean State $10.50
1977, Alabama (motorcycle plate) $4.50
1977, Mississippi..$3.50
1977, Yukon Canada...$12.50
1978, Washington, base undated $3.50
1979, Maine $4.50
1980, New Mexico $4.50
1980, Tennessee $4.50
1981, District of Columbia, Inaugural..................$10.50
1983, Massachusetts $6.50
1984, Alabama $3.50
1984, Delaware..$5.50
1985, North Dakota..$4.50
1987, Colorado, Association of County Clerks..............$7.50
1988, California $8.50
1988, Delaware..$6.50
1989, Indiana, POW $5.50
1989, Kentucky, horses $12.50
1991, Montana $7.50
1992, Iowa, Sesquicentennial.............................$10.50
1993, Alabama $4.50
1994, Louisianna..$9.50
1994, Montana, Veteran $9.50
1994, Texas, Lone Star......................................$3.50
1995, Arizona, cactus $3.50
1997, Arizona, desert scene...............................$6.50
1997, Southbend Indiana Taxi $5.50
1998, Indiana, Amber Waves..............................$6.50
1998, Massachusetts, Spirit $65.00

Little Red Riding Hood

This line of novelty cookie jars, canisters, mugs, teapots, and other kitchenware items was made by both Regal China and Hull. Today any piece is expensive. There are several variations of the cookie jars. The Regal jar with the open basket marked 'Little Red Riding Hood Pat. Design 135889' is worth about $350.00. The same with the closed basket goes for about $25.00 more. An unmarked Regal variation with a closed basket, full skirt, and no apron books at $600.00. The Hull jars are valued at about $350.00 unless they're heavily decorated with decals and gold trim, which can add as much as $250.00 to the basic value.

The complete line is covered in *The Collector's Encyclopedia of Cookie Jars* by Joyce and Fred Roerig (Collector Books), and again in *Little Red Riding Hood* by Mark E. Supnick.

Bank, standing $850.00
Bank, wall hanging, from $1,700 to.......................$2,000.00
Butter dish...$550.00
Canister, cereal...$1,475.00
Canister, tea...$750.00
Canisters, coffee or sugar, ea...................................$850.00

Canister, flour, $850.00.

Cookie jar, closed basket, minimum value................$360.00
Cookie jar, open basket, gold stars on apron, minumum value $675.00
Cookie jar, red spray w/gold bows, red shoes $950.00
Cookie jar, white...$200.00
Creamer, top pour, no tab handle......................$575.00
Creamer, top pour, tab handle $400.00
Lamp...$2,450.00
Match holder, wall hanging...............................$1,100.00
Mug, embossed figure, white (no color), minumum value ..$450.00
Mustard jar, w/spoon.......................................$475.00
Pitcher, batter..$500.00
Pitcher, milk; standing, 8", from $400 to...................$500.00
Planter, hanging..$575.00
Shakers, Pat Design 135889, med size, pr.............$1,100.00
Shakers, 3¼", pr..$195.00
Spice jar, square base, from $650 to $750.00
Sugar bowl, w/lid...$225.00
Teapot...$400.00
Wall pocket $450.00
Wolf jar, red base..$1,400.00
Wolf jar, yellow base $900.00

Little Tikes

For more than twenty-five years, this company (a division of Rubbermaid) has produced an extensive line of toys and playtime equipment, all made of heavy-gauge plastic, sturdily built and able to stand up to the rowdiest children and the most inclement weather. As children usually outgrow these items well before they're worn out, you'll often see them at garage sales, priced at a fraction of their original cost. We've listed a few below, along with what we feel would be a high average for an example in excellent condition. Since there is no established secondary market pricing system, though, you can expect to see a wide range of asking prices.

Barbie Canopy Bed, lavender w/white & pink polka dots & striped cloth bedding, 16x12" **$21.00**

Basketball goal, indoor/outdoor, adjusts from 4' to 6', ball included, #4803, from $12 to **$15.00**

Bench toy box, seats 2, pink & white w/lift-off lid, #7251, 34x22½x27", from $10 to **$15.00**

Bighouse Dollhouse, blue roof, pink sides & front, 5 windows & 1 doorway all w/round tops, 23x35x38"...........**$135.00**

Boy in Wheelchair w/ramp, MIB................................**$10.00**

Creative Art Studio Desk, swivel chair, built-in light table, overhead lamp, marker carousel, drawers, 40x26x30"...**$45.00**

Doll High Chair, w/baby bottle, bowl & spoon, #4429, 24¾x16½x13½", from $5 to **$7.00**

Doll stroller, built-in tray, high back, for up to 20" dolls, #4478, from $5 to..**$7.00**

Dollhouse Stable, 2 horses w/poseable riders, 1 colt, 1 orange barn cat, 4 fences, ladder, steeple for top, MIB (new)...**$50.00**

Dozer, movable parts, 22x12x10", NM **$30.00**

Dump Truck, yellow, crank handle for dumping..........**$12.00**

Easel, Super Storage, takes roll paper, features chalkboard & storage tray, #4418, from $8 to..............................**$12.00**

Fashion Vanity, shatter-resistant mirror, 4 storage compartments, seat, #4673, 32x21¾x15½", from $8 to.....**$10.00**

Grand Mansion Bedroom set, double bed, bedding & cradle, MIB..**$8.50**

Grand Mansion Bedroom set, twin beds which can make bunk beds, dresser & 2 mattresses, MIB...............**$10.00**

Grand Mansion Dining Room set, table, 4 chairs & rug, MIB..**$5.00**

Grand Mansion Kitchen set, high chair, refrigerator & sink/stove combination, MIB **$8.00**

Lawn & Garden Cart, w/watering can & 2 tools, #4451, 28x14¾x15", from $5 to **$7.00**

Little Housekeeper Laundry Center, door open, clicker knob, fully assembled, MIB **$18.00**

Little Landscaper Potting set, 3 flowerpots, spade, soil rake, watering can, basket, gloves, MIB........................**$18.00**

Mighty Voyager Pirate Ship, 2 pirates, 2 cannons, treasure chest, MIB...**$15.00**

Place Dollhouse, w/pool, desk & chair, table & chairs, easel & built-in beds, slide out patio, 17x27x20", MIB..**$45.00**

Rocking chair, #7250, 25x23x15", from $6 to.................**$8.00**

Rocking Horse, high back & low seat, #4537, 23x12x15½", from $5 to..**$7.00**

Shopping Cart, yellow, EX......................................**$23.00**

Table w/2 chairs, 21" wide, #4230, from $8 to **$12.00**

Toddler Tractor, green w/lg black & white wheels, #4032, 24x12x17", from $5 to...**$7.00**

Toy box, lift-off lid, 7 cubic feet, #7515, from $10 to.**$15.00**

Wagon, Explorer, extra lg, #4405, from $15 to...........**$20.00**

Wee Waffle Farm, complete w/box, VG **$10.00**

Longaberger Baskets

In the early 1900s in the small Ohio town of Dresden, John Wendell ('J.W.') Longaberger developed a love for hand-woven baskets. In 1973 J.W. and his fifth child, Dave, began to teach others how to weave baskets. J.W. passed away during that year, but the quality and attention to detail found in his baskets were kept alive by Dave through the Longaberger Company®.

Each basket is hand-woven, using hardwood maple splints. Since 1978 each basket has been dated and signed by the weaver upon completion. In 1982 the practice of burning the Longaberger name and logo into the bottom of each basket began, guaranteeing its authenticity as a Longaberger Basket®.

New baskets can be obtained only through sales consultants, usually at a basket home party. Collector and speciality baskets are available only for a limited time throughout the year. For example, the 1992 Christmas Collection Basket was offered only from September through December 1992. After this, the basket was no longer available from Longaberger®. Once an item is discontinued or retired, it can only be obtained on the secondary market.

This information is from *The Seventh Edition Bentley Collection Guide*, published in June 1999. See the Directory for ordering information or call 1-800-837-4394.

Advisor: Jill S. Rindfuss (See Directory, Longaberger Baskets)

Baskets

Note: values are for baskets only, unless accessories such as liners and protectors are mentioned in the description. Sizes may vary as much as one inch.

1984, darning basket, shoestring weave at base, leather handles, 4x10", minimum value, $60.00. (Photo courtesy Mary Kay Woodrow)

1979-93, Retired Mini Cradle™, no color trim or weave, no handles, wood rockers, from $85 to **$120.00**

1979-98, Retired Sm Laundry™, no color trim or weave, 2 cut-out handles, from $142 to **$185.00**

1983, JW Medium Market®, blue accent weave & trim, 1 stationary handle, brass tag: Longaberger — JW Med Market, from $1,279 to **$1,650.00**

1983-86, Retired Family Picnic™, no color trim or weave, 2 swinging handles, divided attached lid, from $326 to **$390.00**

1985, Retired Corn basket, 11½x17", from $140.00 to $275.00. (Photo courtesy Mary Kay Woodrow)

1986, Christmas Candy Cane™, red or green weave & trim, 1 stationary handle, brass tag: Longaberger Xmas Collection, from $185 to.....................................**$280.00**

1986, Medium Chore™, no color weave or trim, 2 swing handles, from $53 to.....................................**$55.00**

1986-90, Hostess Collection Lg Hamper™, no color weave or trim, attached woven lid w/knob near front, no handles, from $229 to **$305.00**

1988, All-American Cake™, red & blue weave & trim, 1 stationary handle, came w/divider shelf, from $155 to................**$225.00**

1988, Holiday Hostess Large Market™, red & green weave, red or green trim, 1 stationary handle, from $114 to...........**$150.00**

1988-97, Heartland Medium Key™, Heartland Blue shoestring weave, leather loop, metal hanging bracket, Heartland logo, from $39 to.................................**$47.00**

1990, Shades of Autumn Pie®, rust trim, green, rust & blue weave, 1 stationary handle, from $121 to **$225.00**

1990, Shamrock™, green shoestring weave, 1 swing handle, attached lid, from $120 to...................................**$175.00**

1991, Crisco® American Pie™, red & blue weave & trim, 2 swing handles, woven lid, burned-in Crisco® logo, from $355 to......................................**$500.00**

1991, Holiday Hostess Tree-Trimming™, red & green weave, red or green trim, 1 swing handle, from $163 to...**$275.00**

1992, JW Cake®, blue accent weave & trim, 2 swing handles, divider shelf, brass tag: Longaberger — JW cake, MIB, from $167 to...**$290.00**

1992-94, Booking/Promo Sweet Basil™, no color trim or weave, 2 leather ears, ⅜" weave, from $42 to **$65.00**

1992-98, Hostess Collection Wildflower™, no color weave or trim, inverted bottom, 2 double leather ears, from $94 to **$110.00**

1993, All-Star Trio™, w/liner & protector, red & blue weave & trim, 2 leather ears, from $65 to.....................**$110.00**

1993, Holiday Basket of Thanks™, natural w/red & green trim, 2 leather ears, brass tag: 1993 Longaberger Holiday Basket of Thanks, from $72 to **$115.00**

1993, Incentive Paint the Town™, green, blue & red shoestring weave, 1 stationary handle, from $100 to.**$150.00**

1993, Lg Easter™, teal shoestring weave, available stained or natural, 1 stationary handle, from $60 to.............**$80.00**

1994, Bee Basket™, rose pink & purple weave, 1 swing handle, brass tag: Celebrate Your Success, etc, from $167 to **$250.00**

1994, Boo™, orange & black weave & trim, 1 swing handle, from $93 to...**$135.00**

1994, Father's Day Tissue™, burgundy & blue trim, no handles, from $84 to...**$100.00**

1995, Horizon of Hope™, no color weave or trim, 1 stationary handle, American Cancer Society logo on bottom, from $67 ....**$95.00**

1995, Mother's Day Basket of Love™, pink weave & trim, 2 leather ears, from $74 to.....................................**$85.00**

1995, Pumpkin™, orange & black trim, 1 swing handle, from $95 to...**$150.00**

1995, Sweetheart Sweet Sentiments™, red trim & shoestring accent weave, 1 swing handle, from $67 to...........**$85.00**

1995, Traditions Family™, green trim & accent weave, 1 swing handle, brass tag, MIB, from $193 ....**$270.00**

1995-97, Woven Traditions Spring®, red, blue & green shoestring weave, 1 stationary handle, from $52 to **$65.00**

1996, Collectors Club Sm Serving Tray™, blue & green weave & trim, 2 leather braided ears, club logo on bottom, from $175 to...**$250.00**

1996, Employee Christmas Cracker™, red & green shoestring weave, no handles, from $80 to.........................**$100.00**

1996, May Series Sweet Pea™, purple weave & trim, 1 swing handle, from $78 to...**$110.00**

1997, Special Event Inaugural™, blue trim, red & blue accent weave, 1 stationary handle, pewter tag: Longaberger '97 Inaugural, from $60 to...**$75.00**

1997, 20th Century™ — 1st Edition, natural w/flag design, 1 swing handle, brass tag: 1st Edition, MIB, from $75 to..**$90.00**

1998, Collector Club 25th Anniversary™, woven flag design, 2 swing handles, pewter tag, from $170 to...............**$190.00**

1998, Grandma Bonnie's 2-Pie™, no color weave or trim, 2 swing handles, Bonnie Longaberger signature on handle, from $130 to...**$150.00**

1998, Special Event Barn Raising™, blue trim & shoestring weave, 1 swing handle, from $156 to................**$210.00**

Miscellaneous

1990, Father Christmas Cookie Mold™, inscribed on back: Longaberger Pottery, First Casting, MIB, from $92 to..**$115.00**

1990-91, Grandma Bonnie's Apple Pie Plate™, blue accents, Roseville, Ohio, embossed on bottom, MIB, from $43 to..**$60.00**

1993, Commemorative Santa Pewter Ornaments™, set of 4 in gift box, from $60 to **$105.00**

Lu Ray Pastels

This was one of Taylor, Smith, and Taylor's most popular lines of dinnerware. It was made from the late 1930s until sometime in the early '50s in five pastel colors: Windsor Blue, Persian Cream, Sharon Pink, Surf Green, and Chatham Gray.

If you'd like more information, we recommend *Collector's Guide to Lu Ray Pastels* by Kathy and Bill Meehan (Collector Books).

Baker, vegetable; gray, oval, 9½" **$30.00**
Baker, vegetable; oval, 9½" **$20.00**
Bowl, coupe soup; flat..**$15.00**
Bowl, coupe soup; gray, flat...**$25.00**
Bowl, fruit; gray, 5" **$15.00**
Bowl, fruit; 5" **$5.00**
Bowl, lug soup; tab handled **$20.00**
Bowl, mixing; 10¼", from $75 to **$85.00**
Bowl, mixing; 5½", from $75 to **$85.00**
Butter dish, gray, w/lid **$90.00**
Butter dish, w/lid **$50.00**
Casserole, w/lid **$95.00**
Chocolate creamer, AD, individual...............................**$95.00**
Chocolate cup, AD, from $70 to...................................**$80.00**
Chocolate pot, AD; from $360 to **$375.00**
Coaster/nut dish...**$65.00**
Creamer, from $8 to..**$10.00**
Cup/bowl, cream soup..**$55.00**
Egg cup, double..**$24.00**
Egg cup, double; gray..**$28.00**
Epergne, flower vase, from $110 to **$125.00**
Jug, water; footed, from $80 to **$110.00**
Nappy, vegetable; round, 8½" **$20.00**
Pitcher, fruit juice; from $130 to..................................**$150.00**
Pitcher, water; yellow, flat bottom, from $60 to..........**$75.00**
Plate, gray, 9" **$20.00**
Plate, 6"..**$3.00**
Plate, 7"..**$12.00**
Plate, 8"..**$15.00**
Plate, 9", from $10 to **$12.00**
Platter, 11½" **$16.00**
Platter, 13" **$18.00**
Sauce/gravy boat **$28.00**
Sauce/gravy boat, w/fixed stand, any color but yellow .**$35.00**
Sauce/gravy boat, w/fixed stand, yellow.....................**$22.50**
Saucer, AD; gray **$10.00**
Saucer, chocolate, from $25 to **$30.00**
Saucer, cream soup, from $22 to **$25.00**
Sugar bowl, AD; individual, w/lid...............................**$40.00**
Sugar bowl, w/lid **$15.00**

Teapot, curved spout...**$95.00**
Teapot, flat spout..**$160.00**
Tumbler, fruit juice, from $40 to **$45.00**
Tumbler, water...**$65.00**
Vase, bud...**$325.00**

Relish dish, four-part, $95.00. (Photo courtesy Kathy and Bill Meehan)

Lunch Boxes

Character lunch boxes made of metal have been very collectible for several years, but now even those made of plastic and vinyl are coming into their own.

The first lunch box of this type ever produced featured Hopalong Cassidy. Made by the Aladdin company, it was constructed of steel and decorated with decals. But the first fully lithographed steel lunch box and matching thermos bottle was made a few years later (in 1953) by American Thermos. Roy Rogers was its featured character.

Since then hundreds have been made, and just as is true in other areas of character-related collectibles, the more desirable lunch boxes are those with easily recognizable, well-known subjects — western heroes; TV, Disney, and cartoon characters; and famous entertainers like the Bee Gees and the Beatles.

Values hinge on condition. Learn to grade your lunch boxes carefully. A grade of 'excellent' for metal boxes means that you will notice only very minor defects and less than normal wear. Plastic boxes may have a few scratches and some minor wear on the sides, but the graphics must be completely undamaged. Vinyls must retain their original shape; brass parts may be tarnished, and the hinge may show signs of beginning splits. If the box you're trying to evaluate is in any worse condition than we've described, to be realistic, you must cut these prices drastically. Values are given for boxes without matching thermoses, unless one is mentioned in the line. If you'd like to learn more, we recommend *A Pictorial Price Guide to Metal Lunch Boxes and Thermoses* by Larry Aikins, and *Schroeder's Collectible Toys, Antique to Modern* (Collector Books).

Note: Watch for reproductions marked 'China.'

Metal

Adam-12, 1972, VG..**$50.00**
Addams Family, 1974, VG+...**$75.00**

Animal Friends, 1978, yellow lettering, VG+ $25.00
Auto Race, 1967, VG+ **$35.00**
Battlestar Galactica, 1978, w/thermos, EX, from $45 to..**$55.00**
Bee Gees, 1978, EX **$40.00**
Bobby Sherman, 1972, w/thermos, NM....................**$100.00**
Buck Rogers, 1979, w/thermos, EX............................**$50.00**

Bugaloos, 1971, NM, $100.00. (Photo courtesy June Moon)

Cabbage Patch Kids, 1983, VG **$10.00**
Care Bear Cousins, 1985, w/thermos, EX **$45.00**
Dark Crystal, 1982, w/thermos **$50.00**
Dr Seuss, 1970, w/thermos, M..................................**$300.00**
Duchess, 1960, w/thermos, VG+ **$135.00**
Dynomutt, 1976, EX **$50.00**
Emergency, 1977, dome top, w/thermos, EX...........**$150.00**
Flintstones & Dino, 1962, orange, VG **$140.00**
Fraggle Rock, 1984, EX **$25.00**
Frito's, 1975, VG+ **$85.00**
Gene Autry, 1954, VG+ **$200.00**
Goober & the Ghost Chasers, 1974, VG+ **$60.00**
Gremlins, 1984, w/thermos, VG+ **$20.00**
Happy Days, 1976, VG...**$30.00**
Heathcliff, 1982, w/thermos, EX.................................**$20.00**
Highway Signs, 1968, 1st design, VG+.......................**$50.00**
Holly Hobby, 1979, VG...**$10.00**
Hot Wheels, 1965, w/thermos, VG.............................**$95.00**
HR Pufnstuf, 1971, EX **$75.00**
Huckleberry Hound & Quick Draw McGraw, 1961, VG .**$70.00**
Incredible Hulk, 1978, EX..**$30.00**
Land of the Lost, 1975, w/thermos, G+ **$75.00**
Lost in Space, 1967, dome top, rare, EX...................**$425.00**
Magic of Lassie, 1978, w/thermos, EX **$85.00**
Marvel Super Heroes, 1976, w/thermos, EX...............**$45.00**

Masters of the Universe, 1983, with plastic thermos, EX, $28.00.

Monroes, 1967, EX..**$200.00**
Mork & Mindy, 1979, VG **$35.00**
Mr Merlin, 1981, w/thermos, VG...............................**$30.00**
Munsters, 1965, w/thermos, NM...............................**$250.00**
Osmonds, 1973, w/thermos, EX.................................**$75.00**
Pac Man, 1980, w/thermos, NM **$60.00**
Pathfinder, 1959, VG+ **$450.00**
Peanuts, 1976, red, w/thermos, M............................**$30.00**
Pete's Dragon, 1978, EX **$45.00**
Pigs in Space, 1977, VG **$25.00**
Pink Panther, 1984, w/thermos, M **$75.00**
Pit Stop, 1968, VG+ **$200.00**
Planet of the Apes, 1974, w/thermos, VG+ **$100.00**
Popeye, 1964, EX..**$100.00**
Popeye, 1986, w/thermos, VG **$40.00**
Raggedy Ann & Andy, 1973, VG **$35.00**
Rambo, 1985, w/thermos, M......................................**$50.00**
Rat Patrol, 1967, EX..**$145.00**
Rat Patrol, 1967, w/thermos, M **$300.00**
Rescuers Down Under, 1977, VG **$35.00**
Rifleman, 1960, VG **$400.00**
Robin Hood, 1956, G+ **$90.00**
Roy Rogers, 1957, red shirt, G...................................**$65.00**
Satellite, 1958, w/thermos, VG+ **$125.00**
School Days, 1984, features Mickey & Donald, w/thermos,
    EX **$300.00**
Secret Wars, 1984, VG **$40.00**
Six Million Dollar Man, 1978, w/thermos, EX **$95.00**
Skateboarder, 1977, w/thermos, EX **$55.00**
Snow White & the Seven Dwarfs, 1975, VG **$45.00**
Sport Goofy, 1984, VG+ **$25.00**

Star Wars, 1977, with thermos, EX, $65.00. (Photo courtesy June Moon)

Street Hawk, 1985, w/thermos, EX **$175.00**
Super Powers, 1984, w/thermos, VG **$50.00**
Superman, 1967, VG..**$135.00**
Three Little Pigs, 1982, VG, from $80 to...................**$95.00**
Thundercats, 1985, w/thermos, NM **$50.00**
Waltons, 1973, w/thermos, EX..................................**$90.00**
Zorro, 1958, VG **$145.00**
Zorro, 1966, red rim, w/thermos, EX........................**$250.00**

Plastic

Alf, 1987, red, w/thermos, NM **$18.00**

American Gladiators, 1992, red, EX............................$15.00
California Raisins, 1982, VG.....................................$15.00
Chipmunks, 1984, yellow, w/thermos, EX..................$5.00
CHiPs, 1977, NM...$30.00
Flintstones Movie, 1994, rock shape, w/thermos, NM ...$15.00
Garfield, 1978, yellow, EX..$8.00
Ghostbusters, 1986, purple, EX $20.00
Jem, 1996, purple, w/thermos, EX, from $10 to $14.00
Little Mermaid, EX $5.00
Looney Tunes, 1988, purple, w/thermos, VG $10.00
Masters of the Universe, 1983, blue, VG $10.00
Mickey Mouse Head, 1988, w/thermos, M $50.00
Miss Piggy, 1980, yellow, EX...................................$15.00
Mork & Mindy, 1978, w/thermos, EX $35.00
Mr T, 1984, orange, w/thermos, EX $30.00
Popeye & Son, 1987, yellow, 3-D, M.......................$55.00
Return of the Jedi, 1983, red, VG............................$15.00
Robot Man, 1984, EX..$20.00
Rugrats, 3-D, EX..$10.00
Simpsons, 1990, red, w/thermos, M $15.00
Superman, 1980, dome top, w/thermos, EX..............$40.00
SWAT, 1975, dome top, w/VG thermos, EX $60.00
Teenage Mutant Ninja Turtles, 1990, purple, w/thermos ..$15.00
101 Dalmatians, 1990, w/thermos, EX $10.00

Vinyl

Alvin & the Chipmunks, EX......................................$150.00
Annie, 1981, w/thermos, VG $45.00
Betsy Clark, w/thermos, M..$90.00
Crash Dummies, Tyco, w/thermos, EX......................$10.00
Dr Seuss, rare, EX..$150.00
Girl Scouts, 1960, w/thermos, EX...........................$250.00
Go-Go Dancers, 1965-66, red, EX...........................$100.00
Liddle Kiddles, King Seeley, 1968, NM....................$150.00
New Zoo Revue, 1975, w/thermos, EX......................$225.00
Peanuts, 1969, red, w/thermos, M............................$130.00

Pebbles and Bamm-Bamm, 1971, EX, $125.00.

Sesame Street, 1981, yellow, w/thermos, M $75.00
Shari Lewis & Her Friends, 1960s, EX......................$100.00
Shindig, 1960s, NM...$225.00
Soupy Sales, 1960s, blue w/red handle, EX.............$300.00
Space: 1999, 1974, G..$20.00
Swan Lake, 1960, VG+ $150.00
Wonder Woman, 1977, w/thermos, EX......................$150.00
Ziggy, 1979, orange, VG $85.00

Thermoses

Values are given for thermoses in excellent condition; all are made of metal unless noted otherwise.

Annie Oakley, 1955, metal, cork stopper, EX.............$65.00
Archies, 1969, plastic, NM......................................$40.00
Atom Ant, 1966, metal, EX.......................................$55.00
Babar, 1988, plastic, M..$3.00

Barbie, 1961, EX, $35.00.

Barbie, Midge & Skipper, 1965, metal, EX..................$50.00
Beverly Hillbillies, 1963, metal, EX $60.00
Brady Bunch, 1970, metal, VG $50.00
Crash Dummies, 1992, plastic, EX..............................$8.00
Dawn, 1970, plastic, EX $30.00
Empire Strikes Back, 1981, plastic, VG $10.00
Evel Knievel, 1974, plastic, EX $30.00
Fess Parker as Daniel Boone, 1965, metal, EX...........$75.00
Flying Nun, 1969, metal, EX.....................................$30.00
Get Smart, 1966, metal, EX......................................$75.00
Go Bots, 1984, plastic, M...$10.00
Heathcliff, 1982, plastic, EX.....................................$10.00
Hee-Haw, metal, EX $25.00
Hong Kong Phooey, 1975, plastic, EX.......................$15.00
Howdy Doody, 1977, plastic, EX................................$25.00
Mickey Mouse Club, 1976, plastic, EX.......................$10.00
Mork & Mindy, 1978, plastic, EX...............................$15.00
Muppets, 1979, plastic, EX.......................................$10.00
Road Runner, 1970, metal, EX $50.00
Robot Man & Friends, 1984, plastic, EX.....................$12.00
Scooby Doo, metal, EX...$25.00
Tom Corbett Space Cadet, 1952, metal, EX, from $75 to ..$85.00
Waltons, 1973, plastic, EX $16.00
Woody Woodpecker, 1972, plastic, G $30.00
Yogi Bear & His Friends, 1963, metal, M....................$50.00

Maddux of California

Founded in Los Angeles in 1938, Maddux not only produced ceramics but imported and distributed them as well. They supplied chain stores nationwide with well-designed figural planters, TV lamps, novelty and giftware items, and during the mid-1960s their merchandise was listed in every major stamp catalog. Because of an increasing amount of foreign imports and an economic slowdown in our own country, the company was forced to sell out in 1976. Under the new management, manufacturing was abandoned, and the company was converted solely to distribution. Collectors have only recently discovered this line, and prices right now are affordable though increasing.

#221, vase, swan, white, 12"..**$20.00**
#510, planter, swan, black, 11".................................**$18.00**
#519, TV lamp, orange rooster, 13"............................**$75.00**
#536, planter, bird in flight, 11½"............................**$20.00**
#810, TV lamp, stallion, prancing, on base, 12".........**$65.00**
#839, TV lamp, mallard, flying, natural colors, 11½"..**$45.00**
#859, TV lamp, Toro (bull), foot on mound, 11½".....**$50.00**
#892, TV lamp, Colonial ship, 10½"...........................**$40.00**

#895, TV lamp, double swan, 11½", from $50.00 to $70.00. (Photo courtesy John and Peggy Scott)

#912/#913, Chinese pheasants, airbrushed colors, 11", pr.**$30.00**
#925/#926, horses, rearing/charging, pr......................**$20.00**
#970, flamingo, flying, natural colors, 11" **$45.00**
#984, elephant, sitting, 18"..**$25.00**
#1067, shell console bowl (set), pink, 16"...................**$15.00**
#2217, Cream can, Paul Revere Co, Maddux...............**$75.00**
#3017, seashell bowl, white...**$15.00**
#3051, double leaf bowl, green, center red tomato, w/lid, 16"
    L..**$48.00**
#3304, planter, bird..**$20.00**
#7204, ashtray, pig form, natural colors, 7" L.............**$12.00**

Bank, running puppy, 5", from $75.00 to $85.00. (Photo courtesy Bev and Jim Mangus)

Cats, Deco style, black matt, 12½", facing pr..............**$50.00**
Cookie jar, Calory Hippy...**$300.00**

Cookie jar, Humpty Dumpty, c Maddux of Calif USA #2113.**$300.00**
Cookie jar, Scottie..**$75.00**
Cookie jar, Walrus...**$65.00**
Planter, rearing horse, 10x7½"....................................**$22.00**

Magazines

There are many magazines around today, but unless they're in fine condition (clean, no missing or clipped pages, and very little other damage); have interesting features (cover illustrations, good advertising, or special-interest stories); or deal with sports greats, famous entertainers, or world-renowned personalities, they're worth very little, no matter how old they are. Address labels on the fronts are acceptable, but if your magazine has one, follow these guidelines. Subtract 5% to 10% when the label is not intruding on the face of the cover. Deduct 20% if the label is on the face of an important cover and 30% to 40% if on the face of an important illustrator cover, thus ruining framing quality. If you find a magazine with no label, it will be worth about 25% more than one in about the same condition but having a label. For further information see *The Masters Price & Identification Guide to Old Magazines* (5th edition now available), *Life Magazines, 1898 to 1994,* and several other up-to-the-minute guides covering specific magazine titles, all by our advisor Denis C. Jackson.

See also TV Guides.

Advisors: Denis C. Jackson; Don Smith, Rare National Geographics (See Directory, Magazines)

Newsletter: *The Illustrator Collector's News* (Sample issue: $3.50; Subscription $18.00 per year in U.S.)
Denis C. Jackson, Editor
P.O. Box 1958
Sequim, WA 98382; 360-452-3810
www.olypen.com/ticn; e-mail: ticn@olypen.com

Better Homes and Gardens, 1933, May, VG, $6.00.

Atlantic Monthly, 1921, June, Maxfield Parrish, EX.....**$40.00**
Better Homes & Gardens, 1940, January, Walt Disney, EX..**$18.00**

Chatelaine, 1937, February, Dionne Quints, VG **$10.00**

Child Life, 1954, December, Norman Rockwell, EX....**$20.00**

Collier's, 1935, May 18, HG Wells, EX **$13.00**

Collier's, 1955, November 11, Agatha Christie, EX......**$10.00**

Cosmopolitan, 1953, May, Marilyn Monroe/Oklahoma, EX, from $50 to..**$60.00**

Cosmopolitan, 1959, February, VG.................................**$4.00**

Crawdaddy, 1970, #14, Jimi Hendrix, EX....................**$78.00**

Crawdaddy, 1978, December, Belushi/Acroyd, EX **$5.00**

Esquire, 1952, September, Esther Williams, EX **$15.00**

Family Circle, 1946, April 12, History of Broadway article/Carole Lomard photo, EX **$6.00**

Family Circle, 1946, July 26, Susan Hayward, EX.........**$6.00**

Family Circle, 1953, June, Marilyn Monroe article (part 2), EX **$20.00**

Family Circle, 1953, May, Marilyn Monroe article (part 1), EX..**$20.00**

Family Circle, 1972, July, Ted Kennedy, VG.................**$2.00**

Filmland, 1953, August, Elizabeth Taylor, EX.............**$30.00**

Forest & Stream, 1927, July, EX..................................**$8.00**

Fortune, 1940s, EX, ea, from $8 to.............................**$10.00**

Good Housekeeping, non-special edition, EX, ea, from $1 to..**$2.00**

Good Housekeeping, 1912, June, Coles Phillips cover, EX **$42.00**

Good Housekeeping, 1937, October, Pearl S Buck/Petty ads, EX **$20.00**

Good Housekeeping, 1940s-60s (issues w/articles or covers featuring famous people/events will be higher), EX, ea, $1 to...**$2.00**

Good Housekeeping, 1969, July, Marilyn Monroe, EX.**$18.00**

Gourmet, 1960s-80s, VG to VG+, ea, from $3 to **$4.00**

Harper's Bazzar, 1922, October, Erte cover, EX **$100.00**

Hollywood, 1933, September, Mae West, EX...............**$35.00**

Hollywood, 1936, April, Gloria Stewart, EX................**$30.00**

Hollywood Stars, 1958, May, Rock Hudson/Elvis, EX..**$18.00**

Hollywood Yearbook, 1953, #4, Elizabeth Taylor, EX ..**$25.00**

House & Garden, 1970s, EX, ea, from 50¢ to **$3.00**

House Beautiful, 1959, October, Frank Lloyd Wright, EX..**$12.00**

Ladies' Home Journal, 1927, April, Rose O'Neill kewpies, EX **$20.00**

Ladies' Home Journal, 1930, October, Maxfield Parrish color picture entitled 'Arizona,' VG/EX **$50.00**

Ladies' Home Journal, 1941, July, Bette Davis, EX **$14.00**

Ladies' Home Journal, 1947, May, Eleanor Roosevelt article, EX..**$4.00**

Ladies' Home Journal, 1960, January, Pat Boone, EX...**$5.00**

Ladies' World, 1913, June, Gibson girl, EX.................**$25.00**

Lady's Circle, 1968, December, Lucille Ball w/her children, EX, from $10 to..**$12.00**

Life, 1936, December 14, Archbishop Canterbury, EX.**$42.00**

Life, 1937, May 17, Dionne Quints, Rockwell ad, Babe Ruth ad, EX **$55.00**

Life, 1938, February 7, Gary Cooper, EX.....................**$38.00**

Life, 1940, January 29, Lana Turner, EX.....................**$25.00**

Life, 1942, March 30, Shirley Temple Grows Up, EX..**$27.00**

Life, 1944, December 11, Judy Garland, EX **$35.00**

Life, 1945, April 23, Harry S Truman, baseball, EX.....**$25.00**

Life, 1945, September 24, Colonel Jimmy Stewart, EX..**$18.00**

Life, 1949, August 1, Joe DiMaggio, EX......................**$65.00**

Life, 1955, January 10, Greta Garbo, EX.....................**$20.00**

Life, 1958, December 1, Ricky Nelson, EX **$20.00**

Life, 1963, December 13, John F Kennedy Memorial Edition, EX..**$25.00**

Life, 1964, August 28, Beatles, EX..............................**$40.00**

Life, 1965, July 30, Mickey Mantle, EX......................**$45.00**

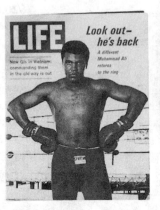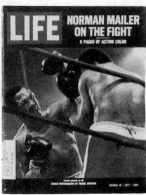

Life, 1970, October 23, Mohammed Ali, EX, $35.00; 1971, March 19, Mohammed Ali vs. Joe Frazier, EX, $30.00.

Life, 1971, July 23, Clint Eastwood, VG **$10.00**

Life, 1971, October 15, Opening of Disney World, EX...**$26.00**

Life, 1984, September, Michael Jackson, G+...............**$11.00**

Look, 1937, December 21, Shirley Temple, VG **$20.00**

Look, 1939, July 18, Vivian Leigh, EX.........................**$28.00**

Look, 1940, February 13, WWII..................................**$22.00**

Look, 1940, May 7, Judy Garland & Mickey Rooney, EX..**$25.00**

Look, 1943, January 12, Jimmy Stewart, EX................**$16.00**

Look, 1946, October 15, Ted Williams, EX **$85.00**

Look, 1956, November 13, Elvis, EX **$65.00**

Look, 1960, July 5, Marilyn Monroe, EX.....................**$20.00**

Look, 1963, December 3, Kennedys, EX......................**$12.00**

Look, 1963, January 9, Beatles article, EX **$28.00**

Look, 1968, May, Raquel Welch, EX............................**$8.00**

McCall's, 1921, August, Cummins paper dolls, EX......**$24.00**

McCall's, 1931, July, 3 NC Wyth illustrations, EX........**$18.00**

McCall's, 1940-49, EX, ea, from $2 to...........................**$5.00**

McCall's, 1951, August, Betsy McCall paper dolls, M..**$15.00**

McCall's, 1969, May, Fabulous Ford Women, VG.........**$2.00**

McCall's, 1993, November, Oprah Winfrey, VG+ **$4.00**

Modern Photography, 1954, Marilyn Monroe, EX.......**$60.00**

Modern Screen, 1935, December, Claudette Colbert, Christy art, EX..**$30.00**

Modern Screen, 1939, Deanna Durbin, EX.................**$30.00**

Modern Screen, 1944, September, Frank Sinatra, EX..**$25.00**

Modern Screen, 1953, April, Doris Day, EX **$18.00**

Modern Screen, 1968, July, Lennon Sisters, EX...........**$8.00**

Modern Teen, 1957, August, Elvis, EX.........................**$60.00**

Motion Picture, 1931, April, Marlene Dietrich, EX **$40.00**

Motion Picture, 1938, February, Katherine Hepburn, EX...**$35.00**

Movie Fan, 1949, September/October, Gregory Peck, EX..**$25.00**

Movie Life, 1943, January, Tyrone Power, EX **$25.00**
Movie Life, 1968, October, Elvis, EX **$20.00**
Movie Mirror, 1931, December, Jean Harlow, EX........**$90.00**
Movie Show, 1947, February, Linda Darnell, EX........**$18.00**
Movie Stars Parade, 1950, May, June Allyson, EX.......**$20.00**
Movie Teen Illustrated, 1962, Summer, American Bandstand, EX..**$25.00**
Movie Teen Illustrated, 1968, April, Janis Joplin/Sonny & Cher, EX..**$15.00**
Movieland, 1944, January, Ingrid Bergman, EX..........**$25.00**
Movieland, 1953, November, Janet Leigh, EX..............**$20.00**
National Geographic, 1915-16, ea **$15.00**
National Geographic, 1917-24, ea.................................**$9.00**
National Geographic, 1925-29, ea.................................**$8.00**
National Geographic, 1930-45, ea.................................**$7.00**
National Geographic, 1946-55, ea.................................**$6.00**
National Geographic, 1956-67, ea.................................**$5.50**
National Geographic, 1968-89, ea.................................**$4.50**
National Geographic, 1990-present, ea **$2.00**
Natural History, 1910-39, EX, ea, from $6 to.............**$10.00**
Newsweek, 1937, October 4, Hilter & Mussolini, EX .**$15.00**
Newsweek, 1964, February 24, Beatles, EX.................**$25.00**
Penthouse, 1985, September, Madonna, EX **$20.00**
Photoplay, 1938, July, Clark Gable, EX.......................**$30.00**
Photoplay, 1940, November, Paulette Goddard, EX....**$30.00**
PIC, 1941, September 16, Veronica Lake, EX..............**$15.00**
PIC, 1944, October 24, Lucille Ball, EX......................**$20.00**
Picture Play, 1936, July, Madge Evans, EX **$25.00**
Playboy, 1954, February, G.......................................**$850.00**
Playboy, 1955, September, G.....................................**$150.00**
Playboy, 1964, January, Marilyn Monroe tribute, EX ..**$50.00**
Playboy, 1965, February, Beatles interview, EX..........**$45.00**
Playboy, 1979, December, Raquel Welch, EX.............**$17.00**
Playboy, 1993, January, Barbi Twins, NM...................**$18.00**
Popular Mechanics, 1940-59, M, ea, from $4 to...........**$5.00**
Reader's Digest, 1940s, ea, from $3 to **$5.00**
Redbook, specialty issues range from $4 to $10 ea w/some up to **$50.00**
Redbook, 1934, December, Carole Lombard...............**$25.00**
Redbook, 1940-59, EX, ea, from $1 to **$3.00**
Redbook, 1955, July, Marilyn Monroe.......................**$50.00**
Redbook, 1956, September, Gina Lollobrigida, EX **$10.00**
Rolling Stone, 1968, #22, John Lennon, EX..............**$175.00**
Rolling Stone, 1977, September 22, Elvis, EX.............**$25.00**
Saturday Evening Post, 1945, May 26, Rockwell cover, EX..**$48.00**
Saturday Evening Post, 1956, October 13, Rockwell cover w/article featuring Eisenhower, EX **$24.00**
Saturday Evening Post, 1966, July 30, Bob Dylan, EX..**$12.00**
Saturday Evening Post, 1968, June 1, Bobby Kennedy, EX .**$8.00**
Screen Album, 1935, Jean Harlow, EX........................**$80.00**
Screen Album, 1947, Winter, June Allyson, EX **$20.00**
Screen Guide, 1936, Ginger Rogers, EX......................**$20.00**
Screen Life, 1956, September, Debbie Reynolds, EX ..**$15.00**
Screen Play, 1933, July, Mae West, EX........................**$25.00**
Screen Romances, 1937, October, Greta Garbo, EX ...**$35.00**
Screen Romances, 1944, September, Gary Cooper, EX.**$20.00**

Screen Stars, 1945, February, Errol Flynn, EX **$25.00**
Screen Stars, 1946, February, Rita Hayworth, EX........**$25.00**
Screen Stories, 1949, March, Cornel Wilde, EX...........**$22.00**
Screenland, 1934, February, Jean Harlow, EX.............**$60.00**
Screenland, 1940-57, EX, ea, from $12 to...................**$35.00**
Silver Screen, 1930s, EX, ea, from $20 to **$65.00**
Silver Screen, 1940s, EX, ea, from $20 to **$75.00**
Silver Screen, 1950s, EX, ea, from $15 to **$100.00**
Sports Illustrated, 1956, June 18, Mickey Mantle, EX..**$80.00**
Sports Illustrated, 1961, October 2, Roger Maris, EX ..**$25.00**
Sports Illustrated, 1963, March 4, Sandy Koufax, EX..**$20.00**
Sports Illustrated, 1977, Nov 28, Larry Bird/Cheerleaders, EX...**$15.00**
Sports Illustrated, 1983, January 3, Wayne Gretzky, EX..**$10.00**
Time, 1937, December 27, Disney, EX **$25.00**
Time, 1974, May 20, Richard Nixon, EX **$7.00**
True Confessions, 1936, May, Claudette Colbert, EX..**$14.00**
True Story, 1951, November, Marilyn Monroe, EX......**$35.00**
TV Digest, 1949, October, 29, Lone Ranger, EX..........**$40.00**
TV Radio Mirror, 1975, August, Michael Landon, EX.**$12.00**
TV Radio Talk, 1975, November, Ricky Nelson, EX....**$12.00**
Venture, 1964, August, Beirut/Port-Cros/etc, EX **$12.00**
Vogue, 1940, January, swimsuit cover, EX...................**$14.00**
Woman's Day, 1940, September, Jimmy Stewart, VG....**$6.00**
Woman's Day, 1957, October, 20th Anniversary issue of Queen Elizabeth & children, G+.............................**$5.00**
Woman's Home Companion, 1904, February, features Edison's home, EX...**$20.00**
Woman's Home Companion, 1925, October, Our Gang paper dolls, EX **$50.00**
Woman's Home Companion, 1933, September, Charlie Chaplin, EX **$32.00**
Woman's Home Companion, 1953, July, Marlene Dietrich, EX **$12.00**
Woman's World, 1991, December 17, Marilyn Monroe cover & art, EX..**$8.00**
Yankee, 1977, May, Parrish cover, EX.........................**$20.00**

Modern Screen, 1936, June, Christy cover, VG, $18.00 (EX, $20.00; M, $25.00).

Pulp Magazines

As early as the turn of the century, pulp magazines were beginning to appear, but by the 1930s, their popularity had literally exploded. Called pulps because of the cheap wood-pulp paper they were printed on, crime and detective stories, westerns, adventure tales, and mysteries were the order of the day. Crime pulps sold for as little as 10¢; some of the westerns were 15¢. Plots were imaginative and spicy, if not downright risque. The top three publishers were Street and Smith, Popular, and the Thrilling Group. Some of the more familiar pulp-magazine authors were Agatha Christy, Clarence E. Mulford, Erle Stanley Gardner, Ellery Queen, Edgar Rice Burroughs, Louis L'Amour, and Max Brand. Until the 1950s when slick-paper magazines signed their death warrant, they were published by the thousands. Because of the poor quality of their paper, many have not survived. Those that have are seldom rated better than very good. A near-mint to mint example will bring a premium price, since it is almost impossible to locate one so well preserved. Except for a few very rare editions, many are in the average price range suggested below — some much lower.

Advisor: J. Grant Thiessen (Pandora's Books Ltd.), Pulp Magazines (See Directory, Magazines)

Amazing Stories, 1933, April, G+ $25.00
Amazing Stories, 1934, August, G+ $12.00
Amazing Stories, 1934, June, VG $18.00
Amazing Stories, 1935, January/February, G+ $15.00
Amazing Stories, 1936, October, VG $20.00
Amazing Stories, 1939, February, VG.........................$15.00
Amazing Stories, 1945, September, VG $13.00
Amazing Stories, 1946, June, VG...............................$10.00
Amazing Stories, 1948, May, G+ $10.00
Amazing Stories, 1951, August, VG $8.00
Amazing Stories, 1955, January, VG $5.00
Amazing Stories, 1966, December, VG.........................$6.00
Amazing Stories, 1971, May, VG................................$4.00
American Boy, 1932, January, VG $15.00
American Magazine, 1942, May, VG...........................$15.00
American Rifleman, 1936, June, VG $20.00
Analog, 1960, October, VG $5.00
Analog, 1964, November, VG.....................................$6.00
Analog, 1975, August, VG $3.00
Argosy, 1932, November 5, VG $25.00
Argosy, 1934, June 30, VG $30.00
Argosy, 1939, February 11, VG..................................$50.00
Argosy, 1962, August, VG $12.00
Argosy All-Story, 1925, May 2, G+ $20.00
Astonishing, 1940, October, VG.................................$20.00
Astounding, 1937, April, G+ $20.00
Authentic, #15, VG..$15.00
Avon Fantasy Reader, #4, VG $15.00
Avon Fantasy Reader, 1947, February, VG..................$15.00
Back Brain Recluse, #6, VG $10.00
Best Detective, 1937, January, VG..............................$20.00
Bestseller Mystery, 1959, January, VG........................$10.00
Between C & D, 1983, Summer, VG............................$8.00
Beyond, 1953, July #1, VG..$8.00
Black Mask (Canadian), 1942, VG..............................$45.00

Blue Book, 1929, August, Poor $10.00
Blue Book, 1935, September, G...................................$8.00
Blue Book, 1940, April, VG.......................................$30.00
Cemetary Dance, 1991, Winter, VG............................$8.00
Charley Jones' Laugh Magazine, 1952, November, VG.$8.00
Charlie Chan, 1973, November, #1, VG $10.00
Climax, 1959, April, VG..$10.00
College Laughs, 1957, February, G+............................$5.00
Complete Adventure Novelettes, 1932, August, G+ $75.00
Confidential Detective, 1946, December, VG $10.00
Cosmic Frontiers, 1977, April, VG $5.00
Creepy, #43 or #340, VG/EX, ea.................................$6.00
Daring Crime Cases (Canadian), 1940s, Vol 5, #25, VG...$15.00
Dark Fantasy, #20, VG..$8.00
Deathrealm, 1996, Summer, #28, VG...........................$6.00
Detective Fiction Weekly, 1939, 1939, April 29, VG ...$25.00
Detective Story Magazine, 1927, March 12, VG..........$40.00
Detective Tales, 1941, VG...$30.00
Dime Western, 1951, September, VG $10.00
Doc Savage, 1938, September, VG $65.00
Doc Savage, 1940, December, VG..............................$50.00
Doc Savage, 1945, June, VG......................................$35.00
Ellery Queen, 1946, February, VG.............................$10.00
Ellery Queen, 1949, January, EX $12.00
Ellery Queen, 1955, February, VG.............................$9.00
Ellery Queen, 1956, April, EX....................................$11.00
Ellery Queen, 1956, July, VG....................................$18.00
Famous Fantastic Mysteries, 1939, November, G+ $12.00
Famous Fantastic Mysteries, 1940, March, G $8.00
Fantastic Adventures, 1948, March, G $5.00
Fantasy & Science Fiction Magazine, 1981, July, Vol 61, #1,
    Steven King, VG+ $10.00
From Unknown World, 1948, #1, G+..........................$15.00
Hitchcock Mystery Magazine, 1980, December 15, VG+ ..$5.00
Hitchcock Mystery Magazine, 1984, June, VG..............$3.00
Manhunt, 1953, February, Vol 1, #2, VG.....................$12.00
Mike Shane Mystery Magazine, 1972, November, Vol 31, #6,
    EX $5.00
Planet Stories, 1939, Winter, Vol 1, #1, VG..................$25.00
Spider Magazine, 1942, January, Vol 25, #4, VG $18.00
Startling Stories, 1939, May, Vol 1, #3, G....................$10.00
Super Science Stories, 1940, May, Vol 1, #1, G+.........$15.00
Suspense (American), 1951, Spring, Vol 1, #1, VG $8.00
Twilight Zone, 1982, October, Vol 2, #7, EX.............$10.00
Twilight Zone, 1987, April, Vol 7, #1, EX $8.00
Weird Tales, 1948, March, Vol 40, #3, VG $20.00
Weird Tales, 1950, January, Vol 42, #2, VG $22.00
Weird Tales, 1950, July, Vol 42, #5, G+.....................$15.00
Whisper, 1940, October, Vol 1, #1, G+.......................$12.00
Worlds Beyond, 1950, December, Vol 1, #1, G+.........$12.00

Marbles

There are three broad categories of collectible marbles, the antique variety, machine-made, and contemporary marbles. Under those broad divisions are many classifications.

Everett Grist delves into all three categories in his book called *Big Book of Marbles* (Collector Books).

Sulfide marbles have figures (generally animals or birds) encased in the center. The glass is nearly always clear; a common example in excellent condition may run as low as $100.00, while those with an unusual subject or made of colored glass may go for more than $1,000.00. Many machine-made marbles are very reasonable, but if the colors are especially well placed and selected, good examples sell in excess of $50.00. Peltier comic character marbles often bring prices of $100.00 and up with Betty Boop, Moon Mullins, and Kayo being the rarest and most valuable. Watch for reproductions. New comic character marbles have the design printed on a large area of plain white glass with color swirled through the back and sides.

No matter where your interests lie, remember that condition is extremely important. From the nature of their use, mint-condition marbles are very rare and may be worth as much as three to five times more than one that is near-mint. Chipped and cracked marbles may be worth half or less, and some will be worthless. Polishing detracts considerably.

Advisor: Everett Grist (See Directory, Marbles)

Akro Agate Company's box of tri-color Corkscrews, $900.00. (Collection of Gary and Sally Dolly/Photo courtesy Everett Grist)

Cat's-eye, banana; Peltier, 1" $2.00
Christmas Tree, Peltier, ⅝" $175.00
Corkscrew, clear w/opaque ribbon, ⅝" $5.00
Corkscrew, Popeye, Akro Agate, ⅝" $25.00
Corkscrew, transparent color w/opaque ribbon, ⅝"...$10.00
Goldstone, glass w/copper flakes, ¾".........................$35.00
Hurricane, Christensen Agate.........................$10.00
Ketchup & Mustard, Peltier, ⅝" $100.00
Lutz, clear swirl, ¾" $85.00
Mica, transparent blue, green or amber, w/mica flakes, ¾"...$35.00
Mica, transparent glass, clear w/mica flakes, ¾".........$25.00
Moonies, Akro Agate, ⅝" $3.00
Rebel, Peltier, ⅝" $150.00
Slag, Akro Agate, red, ⅝"....................................$10.00
Solid core swirl, ¾" $15.00
Sparkler, multicolor, Akro Agate.............................$18.00
Sulfide, chicken, 1¼"...$75.00
Superman, Peltier, ⅝"..$225.00
Transparent swirl, solid core, ¾"...........................$75.00

Sulfide, bull, 1⅞", NM, $200.00.

Match Safes

Match safes or vesta boxes, as they are known in England, evolved to keep matches dry and to protect against unintentional ignition. These containers were produced in enormous quantities over a 75-year period from various materials including silver, brass, aluminum, and gold. Their shapes and designs were limitless and resulted in a wide variety of popular and whimsical styles. They have become very sought-after collectibles and can usually be recognized by a small, rough striking surface, usually on the bottom edge. Collectors should be cautious of numerous sterling reproductions currently on the market.

Advisor: George Sparacio (See Directory, Match Safes)

Anheuser-Busch, A/eagle logo, Pat August 14 1893, nickel-plated brass, 3x1⅝", EX $125.00
Art Nouveau, nude female figure, sterling, 2⅝x1½", EX $225.00
Artillery shell, figural, sterling, English Hallmarks, 2¼x1¼", EX $495.00
Athena riding Pegasus, by Kerr, #19, sterling, 2⅝x1⅝", EX $375.00
Baby head in shirt, figural, brass, 2⅞x1½", EX.........$245.00
Baby holding rattle, figural, cylindrical, brass, 2x¾", EX $245.00
Bartholomay Beer logo, plated brass, 2½x1½", EX $85.00
Blackpool souvenir, enameled coat of arms, brass, English, 1⅞x1½", EX $100.00
Boar's head, whistle combination, figural w/bold details, brass, 3¾x1½", EX..$475.00
Cadbury litho tin for Bournville Cocoa, striker on bottom, 2½x2", EX $45.00
College motif w/football, boxing gloves & baseball, by Blackinton, sterling, 2½x1¾", EX $450.00
Devil head, figural, glass eyes, ivory horns, push nose to open, nickel-plated brass, 2x1⅜", EX $450.00
Dog motif, rectangular shape, enameled on sterling, English hallmarks, 1⅞x1⅜", EX $525.00
Dragon, figural holding sphere, 4 sharp teeth, Japanese, brass, 2¾x1⅞", EX..$375.00
Dragon motif, by Gilbert, sterling, 2⅝x1⅝", EX $225.00
Game counters w/card motif, King of Hearts, Gorham #075, silverplated, 2¾x1½", EX $275.00
Gorham, skin-like w/coins, #450, sterling, 2½x1½", EX...$310.00

Gorham sterling, embossed Indian chief, catalog #B-2507, 2⅞x1¼", $900.00. (Photo courtesy George Sparacio)

Hauck Brewing Company, nickel-plated brass, 2⅞x1⅝", EX $95.00

Heart shape, figural, sterling w/English hallmarks, 2x2", EX $285.00

Home Insurance logo on 1 side, 2 fireman on other, by Kerr, sterling, 2½x1¾", EX....................................$400.00

Indian chief, by Gorham, #B2507, sterling, 2⅞x1¼", EX .$900.00

Indian/dog motif, mica finish, insert type, nickel-plated brass ends, metal body, 2¾x1½", EX $50.00

International Tailoring logo, pillbox type, nickel-plated brass, ad inside lid, push-button release, 1⅜x2½", EX ..$60.00

Jack knife, figural w/simulated blades & corkscrew, plated brass, 2½x1", EX...$275.00

Kate Greenaway, Springtime motif, copper, 3x1½", EX..$70.00

Knight on horseback, castle background, sterling, 2¾x1⅜", EX $160.00

Mother w/baby, Love's Dream motif, slant top, by Unger, sterling, 2⅝x2", EX $325.00

Mussel shell, fluted design, figural, brass, 2x1⅛", EX...$165.00

Nymphs & Satyr motif, by Kerr, #17, sterling, 2⅝x1⅝", EX $325.00

Privy, figural, w/brass man in top hat, nickel-plated brass, 2x¾x½", EX $295.00

Sailor/ship motif, book shape, vulcanite, 2x1½", EX..$150.00

Seal/safe combination, Rd#603, brass, English, 2½x¾", EX..$125.00

Shoe, figural, inlaid w/mother-of-pearl, papier-mache, sand striker on sole, 3x¾", EX $125.00

Shoe, figural, lid on top, pewter, 3¼x1½", EX.........$150.00

Sorrento ware, inlaid top w/lady motif, sandpaper striker, 2¾x1½", EX $125.00

Stamp/safe combination, Pat October 11, 1892, double lid, aluminum, 2⅝x1⅜", NM $100.00

Trousers/overalls, figural, advertising on lid, pewter, 2⅞x1¼", EX $135.00

US Cartridge Company, embossed US & bullet plus prone man w/rifle, silverplated, 2⅝x1½", EX $195.00

Velocity Oil/auto motif, insert type, plated brass, 2¾x1½", EX $200.00

Max, Peter

Born in Germany in 1937, Peter Max came to the United States in 1953 where he later studied art in New York City.

His work is colorful and his genre psychedelic. He is a prolific artist, best known for his designs from the '60s and '70s that typified the 'hippie' movement. In addition to his artwork, he has also designed housewares, clothing, toys, linens, etc. In the 1970s, commissioned by Iroquois China, he developed several lines of dinnerware in his own distinctive style. Today, many of those who were the youth of the hippie generation are active collectors of his work.

Advisor: Richard Synchef (See Directory, Beatnik and Hippie Collectibles)

Ashtray, stylized dove flies below the word Dove, Iroquois China, logo on front, 6¼" dia $80.00

Binder, 3-ring; multicolored butterfly w/man's face in center, design on sides & on spines, 1970s $45.00

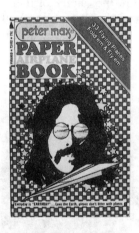

Book, paper airplanes, Fold 'em & Fly 'em, 1971, complete, EX, $50.00. (Photo courtesy Richard Synchef)

Jeans, bell-bottom; white, 2 front pockets w/pink sailboats w/face in sail design, Peter Max patch & Wrangler label, EX...$43.00

Magazine, Peter Max #2, articles & artwork, w/24x36" poster still in spine, 1970, EX..$48.00

Inflatable pillow, one of eight designs, each, $100.00. (Photo courtesy Richard Synchef)

Plate, Checkerboard (Opticon), purple checked center circled by yellow, blue & red, white edge, 10" dia .$55.00

Poster, Life Is Beautiful Stay Alive Don't Smoke Cigarettes, American Lung Society, 24x36", EX....................$150.00

Poster, Make Every Day Earth Day, multicolored, 27½x24" $75.00

Poster, of his painting Blue Flowers, exhibited at Monte Carlo 1992, signed Love & Peace — Max 92, NM **$110.00**

Poster, Peace by the Year 2000 — I Love the World, for United Nations Bookstore, 1989, 24x28" **$60.00**

Poster, picture of 1938 Liberty coin, for March of Dimes 50th Anniversary, 1988, 20x26" **$38.00**

Poster/sticker, Arizona Tea, Liberty head logo, for vendors only, 11x13", NM **$20.00**

Puzzle, Carousel Mindflowers, Springbok Editions, 1967, 450+pcs, 20½" square..**$75.00**

Sheet set, twin flat sheet & 2 pillowcases, Cosmic Flower Watchers, Tastemaster by Mohawk, EX **$100.00**

Sleeping bag, colorful flower power design on white background, w/drawstring tote bag, 67x76"................**$90.00**

Stamp sheet, commemorating Bobby Jones, Expo '74, Scott #1527, 1974, NM+ **$22.00**

Sunglasses, rose-colored lenses, multicolored frames, logo on side, EX...**$80.00**

Tie, black w/colorful shapes, Neomax, 100% silk, 1990 ..**$30.00**

Tote bag, lady running on blue background w/white stars in purple sky, vinyl, 1968, 12x15"............................**$65.00**

Tray, 2 profiles on striped background, lithographed, original back label, EX..**$35.00**

Tumbler, man stands among red & black planets & stars on yellow background, plastic, marked, 1972, 7½", from $10 to...**$45.00**

Yo-yo, purple, black & blue butterfly in white ring w/yellow border, Duncan, 2¼" dia, EX (in cello w/cut card) .**$25.00**

McCoy Pottery

This is probably the best known of all American potteries, due to the wide variety of goods they produced from 1910 until the pottery finally closed only a few years ago.

They were located in Roseville, Ohio, the pottery center of the United States. They're most famous for their cookie jars, of which were made several hundred styles and variations. (For a listing of these, see the section entitled Cookie Jars.) McCoy is also well known for their figural planters, novelty kitchenware, and dinnerware.

They used a variety of marks over the years, but with little consistency, since it was a common practice to discontinue an item for awhile and then bring it out again decorated in a manner that would be in sync with current tastes. All of McCoy's marks were 'in the mold.' None were ink stamped, so very often the in-mold mark remained as it was when the mold was originally created. Most marks contain the McCoy name, though some of the early pieces were simply signed 'NM' for Nelson McCoy (Sanitary and Stoneware Company, the company's original title). Early stoneware pieces were sometimes impressed with a shield containing a number. If you have a piece with the Lancaster Colony Company mark (three curved lines — the left one beginning as a vertical and terminating as a horizontal, the other two formed as 'C's contained in the curve of the first), you'll know that your piece was made after the mid-'70s when McCoy was owned by that group. Today even these later pieces are becoming collectible.

If you'd like to learn more about this company, we recommend *The Collector's Encyclopedia of McCoy Pottery* and *The Collector's Encyclopedia of Brush-McCoy Pottery*, both by Sharon and Bob Huxford; and *McCoy Pottery, Collector's Reference & Value Guide, Vols 1 & 2,* by Bob and Margaret Hanson and Craig Nissen. All are published by Collector Books.

A note regarding cookie jars: beware of *new* cookie jars marked McCoy. It seems that the original McCoy pottery never registered their trademark, and for several years it was legally used by a small company in Rockwood, Tennessee. Not only did they use the original mark, but they reproduced some of the original jars as well. If you're not an experienced collector, you may have trouble distinguishing the new from the old. Some (but not all) are dated #93, the '#' one last attempt to fool the novice, but there are differences to watch for. The new ones are slightly smaller in size, and the finish is often flawed. They have also used the McCoy mark on jars never produced by the original company, such as Little Red Riding Hood and the Luzianne mammy. Only lately did it become known that the last owners of the McCoy pottery actually did register the trademark; so, having to drop McCoy, they have since worked their way through two other marks: Brush-McCoy and (currently) BJ Hull.

See Also Cookie Jars.

Newsletter: *NM Xpress*
Carol Seman, Editor
8934 Brecksville Rd., Suite 406, Brecksville, OH 44141

Bookend planters, ca 1955, from $150.00 to $200.00 for the pair. (Photo courtesy Margaret and Bob Hansen and Craig Nissen)

Ashtray, flower form w/bird perched on edge of petal, green, pink, blue, or yellow, no mark, 1951, 5¼", from $20 to **$25.00**

Ashtray, round stylized fish shape, gold or brown gloss glaze, marked McCoy USA, 1973-76, from $10 to..........**$15.00**

Ashtray, swirled oval shape w/row of comma-shaped rests in center, marked McCoy, 8", from $25 to **$35.00**

Bank, cats w/barrel, various matt finishes, marked MCP, from $65 to..**$80.00**

Bank, covered bridge, matt finish, marked MCP, from $75 to..**$95.00**

Bank, Lucky Penny Puppy, brown gloss glaze, from $50 to..**$60.00**

Bank, safe, black gloss glaze, marked McCoy, from $55 to.**$65.00**

Basket planter, basketweave w/double handle, gold trim, marked McCoy, 1957, 5¼x9", from $65 to **$80.00**

Basket vase, ruby tulip petals w/green leaves & handle on ivory, marked McCoy, 1954, 9x5½", from $90 to...**$110.00**

Bird feeder, tall hut form w/oval opening, chain hanger, no mark, from $40 to.................................**$60.00**

Biscuit jar, marked Esmond USA, 1950s-60s, from $35 to..**$40.00**

Bookends, bird pr & blossom branch, solid pastel color, marked NM, 1940s, 6", pr, from $175 to............**$225.00**

Bookends, tulip candle holders, solid pastel color or mustard rust, marked NM, 1940s, 6", pr, from $125 to **$150.00**

Butter crock, hammered design, 1970s, from $15 to ..**$20.00**

Candy dish, gondola shape, marked McCoy, 1955, from $60 to...**$75.00**

Centerpiece, footed shell dish w/turned-up end, yellow, salmon, or chartreuse, 1955, 9½x10¾", from $60 to **$75.00**

Centerpiece, long oval boat shape w/candle holders at either end & round well in center, matt green, 15", from $35 to **$40.00**

Coffee serving set, repeated steaming mug & medallion design, #712, 1965, pot+4 mugs, from $100 to ..**$120.00**

Creamer & sugar bowl, ivy motif w/twig handles on ivory, marked McCoy, 1950s, 8-oz, ea, from $15 to.......**$20.00**

Cruets, oil & vinegar; w/cork stoppers, green drip glaze, 1970s, set, from $15 to **$25.00**

Decanter set, Jupiter 60 Iron Horse McCormick Train, w/locomotive, tender, mail car & passenger car, 1969, from $250 to..**$350.00**

Drawer pulls, heart, pig, duck, dog or bear, 1970s, from $50 to...**$75.00**

Flower bowl ornament, peacock, white, no mark, from $100 to...**$125.00**

Flower holder, bulbous, vertical ribs, embossed flowers, any except yellow or rose, NM, 1930s-40s, 3½", from $20 to..**$30.00**

Flower holder, bulbous, vertical ribs, embossed flowers, yellow or rose, marked NM, 1930s-40s, 3½", from $40 to...**$50.00**

Flower holder, fish, bead design, any except yellow & rose, marked NM, 1930s-40s, 4¼", from $35 to.............**$50.00**

Flower holder, fish, bead design, yellow or rose, marked NM, 1930s-40s, 4¼", from $60 to.....................**$80.00**

Flower holder, pigeon, stylized form, any except yellow or rose, marked NM, 1930s-40s, 4", from $30 to.......**$40.00**

Flower holder, pigeon, stylized form, yellow or rose, marked NM, 1930s-40s, 4", from $60 to..............**$80.00**

Flower holder, pitcher, flat-sided w/embossed flowers, any except yellow, rose & non-production, NM, 4", from $20 to...**$30.00**

Flower holder, pitcher, flat-sided w/embossed flowers, yellow, rose or non-production colors, marked NM, 4", from $40 to...**$50.00**

Frame for mirror, vertical oval, blue & white speckle, no mark, early 1980s, 13x7½", from $40 to **$50.00**

Jardiniere, terra-cotta clay-pot shape, white, yellow, or green, marked McCoy, 1960s, 12½", from $50 to...........**$75.00**

Jardiniere, vertical ribs w/berries & leaves on rim, pink, ivory, or chartreuse, 1955, marked McCoy, 7½", from $100 ....**$125.00**

Jardiniere, Wild Rose, flat-sided w/flared petal rim, pastel colors, marked McCoy, 1952, sm, from $75 to.....**$90.00**

Jardiniere & pedestal, Berries & Leaves, no mark, 1930s-40s, 7" jardiniere & 6½" pedestal **$250.00**

Jardiniere & pedestal, onyx & matt glazes, 8½" jardiniere & 12½" pedestal, from $250 to................................**$350.00**

Lamp, mermaid seated on rock w/lg seashell, red & gray, no mark, 9¾x6", from $200 to **$300.00**

Lamp, rearing horse form, various glazes, unmarked, 1950s, 8½", from $65 to..**$95.00**

Lamp, white urn w/ornate handles & embossed cold-painted floral design, 1940s, from $100 to **$150.00**

Mug, hammered design, 1970s, from $10 to **$15.00**

Mug, various sports balls w/feet, no mark, 1988, from $20 to..**$30.00**

Napkin holder, rusty orange w/vertical striations, Esmond line, 1950s-60s, 5¼", from $35 to **$45.00**

Oil jar, no handles, various glazes, marked NM, 1930s, 12", from $125 to..**$200.00**

Oil jar, w/handles at rim to top of shoulder, matt glaze, 18", from $250 to..**$300.00**

Paperweight, baseball glove, brown gloss glaze, 5", from $75 to..**$100.00**

Pitcher, butterfly design w/long curved handle, marked NM, 10", from $150 to..**$225.00**

Pitcher & bowl set, sailing ship motif, marked McCoy, 1973, 8" pitcher & 9½x1½" oval bowl, from $60 to **$80.00**

Pitcher vase, parrot form, green or brown, marked McCoy, 1952, 7", from $150 to...**$200.00**

Pitcher vase, Sunburst Gold w/ivory interior, marked McCoy w/24k stamp, 1957, 6", from $40 to......................**$50.00**

Planter, baby carriage, What About Me? lettered on base, gold trim, marked McCoy, 1955, 6x7¾", from $100 to..**$120.00**

Planter, baby grand piano, black w/white & yellow trim, marked McCoy, 1959, 5x6", from $100 to...........**$150.00**

Planter, ball form (footed) w/scalloped rim, marked NM, 1940s, 3½", from $60 to **$75.00**

Planter, ball form w/slanted opening, Garden Club line, marked McCoy, 1958, 5¾", from $25 to **$35.00**

Planter, bird w/head turned back, yellow or turquoise, marked NM, sm..**$60.00**

Planter, carriage w/removable parasol, green or black w/yellow trim, marked McCoy, 1955, 8x9", from $150 to **$200.00**

Planter, cat resting w/lg bow under chin, gold trim, marked McCoy, 1953, 4x7", from $75 to **$100.00**

Planter, caterpiller form, marked Floraline USA, 13½", from $30 to..**$40.00**

Planter, cowboy hat w/feathers, gold trim, marked McCoy, 1956, 8x3", from $65 to **$90.00**

Planter, crown shape w/jeweled butterfly, marked McCoy, from $85 to..**$125.00**

Planter, dog dragging jacket in mouth beside holder, solid pastels, marked NM, 1940s, 5x7", from $60 to **$75.00**

Planter, duck w/parasol & leaves on back, yellow or white w/orange & green, marked McCoy, 1954, 7½", from $100 to...**$150.00**

Planter, Dutch shoe w/bird-on-branch & flower motif, 8", from $30 to...**$40.00**

Planter, hobby horse, gold trim, marked McCoy, 1955, 6½x8", from $100 to...**$125.00**

Planter, horse (saddled) w/holder, solid pastels, marked NM, 1940s, 5x7", from $75 to.................................**$90.00**

Planter, orange-shaped bowl on leaf base, from $40 to ..**$60.00**

Planter, plow boy on horse at trough, marked McCoy, 1955, 7x8", from $100 to...**$125.00**

Planter, rodeo cowboy, bucking bronco, or calf roping motif, marked McCoy, 1956, 7¾", from $150 to **$200.00**

Planter, stretch dachshund, 1940s, light blue, from $175 to...**$225.00**

Planter, triple flower form, brown, marked McCoy, 1956, 4½x12½", from $95 to...**$125.00**

Planter, turtle, green or chartreuse drip, marked McCoy, 1955, from $150 to...**$200.00**

Planter, wheelbarrow w/rooster on front wheel, marked McCoy, 1955, from $100 to...**$125.00**

Planter, wishing well, gold trim, marked McCoy, 1950, 6¾", from $30 to...**$40.00**

Planter, zebra, rare, minimum value, $550.00.

Planter (porch jar), flowerpot w/leaves-&-rings & ribbed design, white or green, marked NM, 1940s, 11", from $150 to...**$200.00**

Platter, leaf shape w/butterfly, marked NM, 14", depending on color from $250 to...**$400.00**

Platter, oval w/turkey motif w/airbrushed colors, 1960s, 19", from $80 to...**$100.00**

Reamer, yellow or white, 1949, 8", from $45 to..........**$60.00**

Spoon rest, butterfly design, glossy green or yellow, marked McCoy, 1953, 4x7½", from $100 to.....................**$150.00**

Teapot, ivy motif w/twig handle, marked McCoy, 1950s, 6-cup, from $40 to...**$50.00**

Umbrella stand, cylinder w/vertical leaf design, matt or gloss, no mark, 19", from $250 to.................................**$350.00**

Vase, Antique Curio Line, 5-finger fan shape w/grapes & leaves, marked McCoy, 1962, 10", from $60 to **$75.00**

Vase, Butterfly, castle gate shape, marked USA, 6x7", from $150 to...**$200.00**

Vase, butterfly design w/long curved handles, marked USA, 10", from $150 to...**$225.00**

Vase, castle gate shape, solid pastel colors, no mark, 6x7", from $150 to...**$200.00**

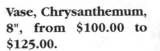

Vase, Chrysanthemum, 8", from $100.00 to $125.00.

Vase, Corinthian Garden, marked McCoy, 1969, 11", from $30 to...**$40.00**

Vase, cylinder w/low pedestal, plain green, white or black, marked Floraline USA, 9¼", from $15 to.............**$20.00**

Vase, goblet, vertical ribs, marked Floraline, 6½", from $15 to...**$25.00**

Vase, grapes & leaves (double cluster form), gold grape w/green & brown leaves, marked McCoy, 1951, 9", from $100 to...**$150.00**

Vase, Grecian, marked McCoy, 1956, 9½", from $100 to...**$150.00**

Vase, integral handles, embossed leaf design at neck, matt colors, 1930s, 12", from $200 to **$300.00**

Vase, ivy design on white w/brown-trimmed rim, base & twig handles, marked McCoy, 1953, 9", from $100 to ..**$150.00**

Vase, melon ribs & sm handles at shoulder, various matt colors, 1940s, 12", from $100 to **$150.00**

Vase, mug w/pedestal foot & ear-shaped handle, matt finish, marked Floraline USA, 6", from $15 to **$25.00**

Vase, ram's head, 1950s, 9½", from $125 to..............**$175.00**

Vase, swan (stylized), gold trim, marked McCoy, 1956, 9", from $75 to...**$100.00**

Vase, triple lilies w/leaves on rectangular base, white or yellow w/gold trim, marked McCoy, 1955, 8½", from $100 to...**$125.00**

Vase, upright cat form (stylized), matt gray, black, or white, marked McCoy, 1960, 14", from $200 to............**$250.00**

Vase, Wild Rose, flared, pastel colors, marked McCoy, 1952, 8", from $75 to...**$90.00**

Wall candle holder, fluted tear-drop shape w/cup holder on shelf, white w/floral decal, no mark, 1970s, 11", from $25 to...**$35.00**

Wall pocket, apple w/leaf branch, 1950s, from $50 to.**$60.00**

Wall pocket, bananas w/leaf branch, 1950s, from $125 to **$150.00**

Wall pocket, Blossomtime, fan shape w/pink blossom branch, marked McCoy, 1946, 8", from $95 to...**$130.00**

Wall pocket, clown w/full ruffled collar & pointed hat, white w/red trim, marked McCoy, 1940s, 8", from $100 to.**$150.00**

Wall pocket, cone shape w/scalloped rim, blue & white speckled effect, no mark, early 1980s, 9½", from $35 to..**$50.00**

Wall pocket, lily bud design, embossed, white, marked McCoy, from $250 to **$300.00**

Wall pocket, umbrella form, gold trim, no mark, 1955, 8¾", from $150 to **$200.00**

Wall pocket, violin, marked McCoy, mid-1950s, 10½", from $100 to **$150.00**

Wall pocket, birdbath, decorated blue, yellow, or green glaze, marked, 1940s, 6½x5", from $85.00 to $100.00. (Photo courtesy Margaret and Bob Hanson and Craig Nissen)

Brown Drip Dinnerware

One of McCoy's dinnerware lines that was introduced in the 1960s is beginning to attract a following. It's a glossy brown stoneware-type pattern with frothy white decoration around the rims. Similar lines of brown stoneware were made by many other companies, Hull and Pfaltzgraff among them. McCoy simply called their line 'Brown Drip.'

Baker, oval, 09"..**$10.00**
Baker, oval, 10½"..**$10.00**
Baker, oval, 12½", from $18 to...................................**$22.00**
Bean pot, individual, 12-oz..................................**$4.00**
Bean pot, 1½-qt, from $15 to.....................................**$20.00**
Bean pot, 3-qt, from $25 to **$30.00**
Bowl, cereal; 6"...**$6.00**
Bowl, lug soup; 12-oz **$8.00**
Bowl, lug soup; 18-oz **$10.00**
Bowl, spaghetti or salad; 12½"..............................**$20.00**
Bowl, vegetable; divided.....................................**$12.00**
Bowl, vegetable; 9"..**$12.00**
Butter dish, ¼-lb..**$15.00**
Candle holders, pr, from $18 to.............................**$22.00**
Canister, Coffee...**$45.00**
Casserole, 2-qt..**$15.00**
Casserole, 3½-qt..**$20.00**
Casserole, 3-qt, w/hen-on-nest lid, from $45 to..........**$50.00**
Corn tray, individual, from $15 to..........................**$20.00**
Creamer **$5.00**
Cruet, oil & vinegar, ea, from $12 to **$15.00**
Cup, 8-oz...**$5.00**

Custard cup, 6-oz..**$4.00**
Gravy boat, from $12 to..**$15.00**
Mug, pedestal base, 12-oz......................................**$7.50**
Mug, 12-oz, from $6 to..**$8.00**
Mug, 8-oz..**$5.00**
Pie plate, 9", from $15 to **$18.00**
Pitcher, jug style, 32-oz **$20.00**
Plate, dinner; 10"...**$10.00**
Plate, salad; 7"..**$6.50**
Plate, soup & sandwich; w/lg cup ring **$10.00**
Platter, fish form, 18"...**$32.00**
Platter, oval, 14", from $12 to **$18.00**
Salt & pepper shakers, pr, from $6 to......................**$9.00**
Saucer **$3.00**
Souffle dish, 2-qt...**$9.50**
Teapot, 6-cup, from $18 to **$22.00**
Trivet, concentric circles, round **$12.00**

Melmac Dinnerware

The postwar era gave way to many new technologies in manufacturing. With the discovery that thermoplastics could be formed by the interaction of melamine and formaldehyde, Melmac was born. This colorful and decorative product found an eager market due to its style and affordability. Another attractive feature was its resistance to breakage. Who doesn't recall the sound it made as it bounced off the floor when you'd accidentally drop a piece.

Popularity began to wane: the dinnerware was found to fade with repeated washings, the edges could chip, and the surfaces could be scratched, stained, or burned. Melmac fell from favor in the late '60s and early '70s. At that time, it was restyled to imitate china that had become popular due to increased imports.

As always, demand and availability determine price. Our values are for items in mint condition only; pieces with scratches, chips, or stains have no value. Lines of similar value are grouped together. As there are many more manufacturers other than those listed, for a more thorough study of the subject we recommend *Melmac Dinnerware* by Gregory R. Zimmer and Alvin Daigle Jr.

See also Russel Wright.

Advisors: Gregory R. Zimmer and Alvin Daigle Jr. (See Directory, Melmac)

Aztec, Debonaire, Flite-Lane, Mar-Crest, Restraware, Rivieraware, Stetson, Westinghouse

Bowl, cereal; from $2 to..**$3.00**
Bowl, serving; from $4 to.......................................**$5.00**
Bowl, soup; from $3 to..**$4.00**
Butter dish, from $5 to..**$7.00**
Cup & saucer, from $2 to.......................................**$3.00**
Gravy boat, from $5 to..**$6.00**
Plate, bread; from $1 to...**$2.00**

Plate, dinner; from $2 to	**$3.00**
Plate, salad; from $2 to	**$3.00**
Salt & pepper shakers, from $4 to	**$5.00**
Sugar bowl, w/lid, from $3 to	**$4.00**
Tumbler, 10-oz, from $7 to	**$8.00**
Tumbler, 6-oz, from $6 to	**$7.00**

Boontoon, Branchell, Brookpark, Harmony House, Prolon, Watertown Lifetime Ware

Branchell, divided vegetable, from $8.00 to $10.00; butter dish, from $10.00 to $12.00; salt and pepper shakers, from $6.00 to $8.00 for the pair. (Photo courtesy Gregory R. Zimmer and Alvin Daigle Jr.)

Bowl, cereal; from $4 to	**$5.00**
Bowl, divided vegetable; from $8 to	**$10.00**
Bowl, fruit; from $3 to	**$4.00**
Bowl, serving; from $8 to	**$10.00**
Bowl, soup; w/lid, from $5 to	**$6.00**
Bread tray, from $8 to	**$10.00**
Casserole, w/lid, from $20 to	**$25.00**
Creamer, from $5 to	**$6.00**
Cup & saucer, from $3 to	**$4.00**
Gravy boat, from $6 to	**$8.00**
Jug, w/lid, from $20 to	**$25.00**
Plate, bread; from $2 to	**$3.00**
Plate, compartment; from $10 to	**$12.00**
Plate, dinner; from $4 to	**$5.00**
Plate, salad; from $4 to	**$5.00**
Platter, from $8 to	**$10.00**
Salad tongs, from $12 to	**$15.00**
Sugar bowl, from $6 to	**$8.00**
Tidbit tray, 2-tier, from $12 to	**$15.00**
Tidbit tray, 3-tier, from $15 to	**$18.00**
Tumbler, 10-oz, from $12 to	**$15.00**
Tumbler, 6-oz, from $10 to	**$12.00**

Fostoria, Lucent

Bowl, cereal; from $7 to	**$9.00**
Bowl, serving; from $15 to	**$18.00**
Butter dish, from $15 to	**$18.00**
Creamer, from $8 to	**$10.00**

Cup & saucer, from $8 to	**$12.00**
Plate, bread; from $3 to	**$4.00**
Plate, dinner; from $6 to	**$8.00**
Platter, from $12 to	**$15.00**
Relish tray, from $15 to	**$18.00**
Sugar bowl, w/lid, from $12 to	**$15.00**

Metlox Pottery

Founded in the late 1920s in Manhattan Beach, California, this company initially produced tile and commercial advertising signs. By the early '30s, their business in these areas had dwindled, and they began to concentrate their efforts on the manufacture of dinnerware, figurines, and kitchenware. Carl Gibbs has authored *Collector's Encyclopedia of Metlox Potteries*, published by Collector Books, which we recommend for more information.

Carl Romanelli was the designer responsible for modeling many of the figural pieces they made during the late '30s and early '40s. These items are usually imprinted with his signature and are very collectible today. Coming on strong is their line of 'Poppets,' made from the mid-'60s through the mid-'70s. There were eighty-eight in all, whimsical, comical, sometimes grotesque. They represented characters ranging from the seven-piece Salvation Army Group to royalty, religious figures, policemen, and professionals. They came with a name tag, some had paper labels, others backstamps. If you question a piece whose label is missing, a good clue to look for is pierced facial features.

Poppytrail was the trade name for their kitchen and dinnerware lines. Among their more popular patterns were California Ivy, California Provincial, Red Rooster, Homestead Provincial, and the later embossed patterns, Sculptured Grape, Sculptured Zinnia, and Sculptured Daisy.

Some of their lines can be confusing. There are two 'rooster' lines, Red Rooster (red, orange, and brown) and California Provincial (this one is in dark green and burgundy), and two 'homestead' lines, Colonial Homestead (red, orange, and brown like the Red Rooster line) and Homestead Provincial. Just remember the Provincial patterns are done in dark green and burgundy. See also Cookie Jars.

Advisor: Carl Gibbs, Jr. (See Directory, Metlox)

Dinnerware

#200 series, butter dish, w/lid	**$55.00**
#200 series, cup, Tom & Jerry	**$18.00**
#200 series, plate, chop; 12"	**$30.00**
#200 series, salt & pepper shakers, S&P shape, pr	**$24.00**
Antique Grape, pitcher, 1¼-qt	**$55.00**
Blueberry Provincial, bowl, salad; 11⅛"	**$70.00**
Blueberry Provincial, creamer, 6-oz	**$22.00**
California Aztec, bowl, soup	**$28.00**
California Aztec, jam & jelly	**$75.00**
California Aztec, plate, salad	**$18.00**

California Golden Blossom, bowl, vegetable; w/lid ...**$95.00**
California Ivy, bowl, cereal; 6¾" **$16.00**
California Ivy, creamer **$28.00**
California Ivy, egg cup **$35.00**
California Ivy, gravy boat **$35.00**
California Ivy, mug, 7-oz. **$24.00**
California Ivy, plate, dinner; 10¼" **$15.00**

California Ivy, salt and pepper shakers, $28.00 for the pair.

California Ivy, tumbler, 13-oz **$35.00**
California Peach Blossom, plate, chop.....................**$75.00**
California Peach Blossom, plate, salad **$12.00**
California Provincial, coaster, 3¾" **$30.00**
California Provincial, egg cup......................**$45.00**
California Provincial, plate, dinner; 10"......................**$20.00**
California Provincial, sprinkling can **$115.00**
Chantilly Blue, cup **$10.00**

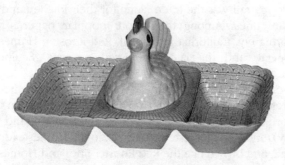

Cock-a-Doodle-Do Artware, three-section basket with lift-off rooster, from $45.00 to $50.00. (Photo courtesy Lee Garmon)

Colonial Heritage, butter dish, w/lid..........................**$65.00**
Colonial Heritage, platter, oval, med.......................**$40.00**
Della Robbia, platter, sm, 9⅝" **$40.00**
Homestead Provincial, creamer, 6-oz......................**$32.00**
Homestead Provincial, oil cruet, w/lid, 7-oz **$45.00**
Homestead Provincial, plate, dinner; 10".................**$20.00**
Homestead Provincial, salt & pepper shakers, pr.......**$32.00**
Jamestown, plate, dinner; 10"......................**$12.00**
La Mancha, gravy boat, 12-oz......................**$30.00**
La Mancha, sugar bowl, w/lid, 12-oz......................**$28.00**
La Mancha, teapot, 6-cup......................**$95.00**
Lotus, cup, 7-oz **$12.00**

Lotus, plate, crescent salad; 8"......................**$38.00**
Navajo, bowl, fruit......................**$14.00**
Navajo, mug, expresso......................**$20.00**
Navajo, sauce boat......................**$35.00**
Provincial Blue, bowl, vegetable; 7⅛" **$55.00**
Provincial Blue, cup, 6-oz......................**$15.00**
Provincial Blue, egg cup **$45.00**
Provincial Blue, tumbler, 11-oz......................**$45.00**
Provincial Rose, mug, 8-oz......................**$24.00**
Red Rooster Provincial, buffet server, 12¼" dia **$75.00**
Red Rooster Provincial, canister, flour **$90.00**
Red Rooster Provincial, salt & pepper mill, pr..........**$120.00**
Sculptured Daisy, creamer, 6-oz......................**$25.00**
Sculptured Daisy, plate, dinner; 10½" **$13.00**
Sculptured Grape, bowl, vegetable; 9½" **$50.00**
Sculptured Grape, salad fork & spoon........................**$70.00**
Sculptured Grape, saucer, 6⅛"......................**$4.00**

Sculptured Grape, sugar canister with lid, large, from $65.00 to $70.00. (Photo courtesy Carl Gibbs Jr.)

Sculptured Zinnia, plate, dinner; 10½" **$13.00**
Sculptured Zinnia, plate, salad; 7½".........................**$10.00**
Vineyard, jam & jelly, 8¼" **$45.00**
Woodland Gold, bowl, cereal; 5⅝" **$14.00**
Woodland Gold, tumbler, 12-oz......................**$25.00**
Yorkshire, candle holder **$30.00**
Yorkshire, celery dish **$30.00**
Yorkshire, relish, handled, 5-part **$65.00**
Yorkshire, sherbet......................**$24.00**

Poppets

Angelica, angel, 7⅝" **$55.00**
Chimney sweep, 7¾" **$55.00**
Colleen, girl w/coiled hair, 7¼" **$45.00**
Doc, w/4" bowl......................**$45.00**
Eliza, flower vendor, 5⅝" **$55.00**
Grace, Princess......................**$45.00**
Hawaiian Girl, 4¾" **$35.00**
Mary Lou, seated lady, 9" **$45.00**
Myra & Mattie, mother & daughter, 8¼"......................**$60.00**
Nellie, girl w/bird, 8⅝" **$55.00**
Raymond, barrister, w/4" bowl **$55.00**
Sam, little boy, 5¾" **$35.00**
Schultz, tradesman/grocer, 8½" **$55.00**

Miscellaneous

Aardvark, miniature	$125.00
American Royal Horse, Arabian, Nostalgia Line, 7¾x8¾"	$115.00
American Royal Horse, Clydesdale, Nostalgia Line, 9x9"	$200.00
Bambi, tail up, Disney, sm	$225.00
Bambi, w/butterfly, Disney	$250.00
Barrel wagon, Nostalgia Line, 11x8"	$100.00
Bathtub, Nostalgia Line, 7½" L	$60.00
Caterpiller, miniature	$30.00
Dinosaur, miniature, 4½"	$195.00
Donald Duck (Three Caballeros), Disney	$350.00
Drum table, Nostalgia Line	$45.00
Dwarf, any, Disney	$250.00
Flower (Bambi), Disney, med	$100.00
Giraffe, miniature, 5¾"	$145.00
Hansom cab, Nostalgia Line, 13x7x5¼"	$80.00
Heron, miniature, 6½"	$45.00
Lady (Lady & the Tramp), sitting, Disney, 1¾"	$125.00
Mamma or Papa, Nostalgia Line, ea	$65.00
Michael (Peter Pan), Disney	$180.00
Mickey Mouse, Disney	$400.00
Pluto, sniffing, Disney	$250.00
Santa, Nostalgia Line	$95.00
Shark, miniature, 6"	$90.00
Squirrel, miniature, 2"	$35.00
Thumper (Bambi), Disney, lg	$95.00
Timothy Mouse (aka Dumbo Mouse), miniature, 1¼"	$250.00
Tweedle Dee or Tweedle Dum, Disney, ea	$250.00
Victorian carriage, Nostalgia Line, 10½"	$100.00
Watering trough, Nostalgia Line, 15" L	$100.00
White Rabbit (Alice in Wonderland), Disney	$275.00

Milk Bottles

Between the turn of the century and the 1950s, milk was bought and sold in glass bottles. Until the '20s, the name and location of the dairy was embossed in the glass. After that it became commonplace to pyro-glaze (paint and fire) the lettering onto the surface. Farmers sometimes added a cow or some other graphic that represented the product or related to the name of the dairy.

Because so many of these glass bottles were destroyed when paper and plastic cartons became popular, they've become a scarce commodity, and today's collectors have begun to take notice of them. It's fun to see just how many you can find from your home state — or try getting one from every state in the union!

What makes for a good milk bottle? Collectors normally find the pyro-glaze decorations more desirable, since they're more visual. Bottles from dairies in their home state hold more interest for them, so naturally New Jersey bottles sell better there than they would in California, for instance. Green glass examples are unusual and often go for a premium; so do those with the embossed baby faces. (Watch for reproductions here!) Those with a 'Buy War Bonds' slogan or a patriot message are always popular, and cream-tops are good as well.

Some collectors enjoy adding 'go-alongs' to enhance their collections, so the paper pull tops, advertising items that feature dairy bottles, and those old cream-top spoons will also interest them. The spoons usually sell for about $6.00 to $10.00 each.

For more information, we recommend *Udderly Delightful* and *Udderly Beautiful* by John Tutton, whose address may be found in the Directory under Bottles.

Newsletter: *The Milk Route*
National Association of Milk Bottle Collectors, Inc.
Thomas Gallagher
4 Ox Bow Rd., Westport, CT 06880-2602; 203-454-1475

Newsletter: *Creamers*
Lloyd Bindscheattle
P.O. Box 11, Lake Villa, IL 60046-0011; Subscription: $5 for 4 issues

Arden, milkman in red pyro, very long straight neck, round, ½-pt	$45.00
Ayrhill Farms Inc, Adams Mass, red pyro, round, qt	$4.50
Bellows Falls Co-Operative Creamery Inc Bellows Falls VT... embossed on clear, round, ½-pt, EX	$9.00
Blueridge Creamery, Luray V embossed in clear, round, qt	$14.00
Brook Field Dairy, back: farm scene, orange pyro, double baby face top, square, qt	$50.00
Canadian Pacific embossed in clear, round, ½-pt	$45.00
Central Dairy Milk Co, Rockford Ill embossed in clear, round, qt	$5.00
Cloverleaf Dairy Inc Milk Havervill, 4-leaf clover embossed in clear, round, qt, EX	$18.00
Dale Bish's Dairy, 1923-1953, New Bethelhem PA, red pyro, square, cream	$45.00
Dighton Rock Farm Elliot F Walker...Farm Producer of Grade A Milk, orange pyro, round, pt, EX	$9.00
Eddy Dairy Newington Conn, For Breakfast Brunch Lunch..., orange & brown pyro, qt	$9.00
Edgar Road Dairy, Linden NJ, Deposit embossed in clear, round, qt	$8.00
EM Dwyer Dairy, Weymouth (MA), There Is No Substitute.... embossed in clear, round, qt	$7.00
Escanaba Dairy, boy & girl kissing, back: Drink More... & cow, red pyro, round, ½-pt	$15.00
Excelsior Sanitary...Chas F Rothenhoefer, reverse: Bottle Is Not Sold Property of..., embossed in clear, round, ½-pt	$9.00
Farmer's Co-Operative Milk Exchange of Westfield embossed in clear, round, ½-pt	$7.50
Gnagy's Dairy, Meyersdale PA, Buttercup & cow's head on back, red pyro, creamer, ¾-oz	$30.00
Guarding Your Health w/Toy Soldier-Jones Dairy Products, red pyro, round, ½-pt	$18.00
Gulf Hill Dairy, cow & bull's head, Country Fresh Milk, orange pyro, square, pt	$8.50

Hampden (cow's head) Creamery Co embossed in clear, tin top, ½-pt...$75.00

Hershey Farms Inc, 527 W 36th St NY City embossed in clear, round, ½-pt $12.00

Highlawn Farm Lenox Mass embossed in clear, round, ½-pt...$6.00

Hillside Farms Oaklawn RI, orange pyro, square, qt....$6.50

Honicker's Dairy, St Clair PA, baby face top, round, qt...$45.00

Hood on 4 sides on shoulder, row of dots completely surround neck, square, ½-pt, EX................................$5.00

JA McKinney Dairy Milk Bottle, Paducah KY embossed in glass, round, pt $20.00

John Joaquin Fall River, Mass, lg J monogram embossed in clear, ribbed neck, round, qt $10.00

Johnson's Pasturized Dairy Products embossed in glass, round, qt...$9.00

Kendall Belmont Cream, back: This Bottle To Be Washed... embossed on clear, round, ½-pt $5.00

Maple Farms Milk Co Boston Mass, lg monogram on shoulder embossed in clear, round, qt, EX.....................$7.00

Martin & Oliveira Fall River, cow's head, back: Store Bottle embossed in clear, round, pt $18.00

McCellain's All Star Milk & Hopalong Cassidy, red & black pyro, square, qt...$50.00

Missouri Pacific Lines, Sunnymead Farm, Bismark Missouri, red pyro, round, wide mouth, ½-pt $35.00

Modern Dairy, Fallon Nev, barn scene, bk: crossing guard & 2 kids, Be Careful..., green pyro, round, qt........$100.00

Modern Dairy Company, cow's head, Drink Fresh Buttermilk, boy & girl, brown pyro, round, qt, EX...................$25.00

Morningside Farm, Stockton CA, farm building, sun, trees, cow etc in orange pyro, round, qt $15.00

Muller's Dairy, Whiteboro NY embossed on clear, square, gill $22.00

Pegues & Holloway, Jackson Tenn Phone 943J, boy on back, blue pyro, round, 5", EX $17.50

Price's & cow, red pyro, square, qt............................$12.00

Reads Dairy Grade A Milk Seekonk MA, circle w/sunburst, orange pyro, Old English lettering, round, pt, EX .$12.00

Sanitary's Best by Test Milk, blue and red, cream top, ½-pint, $20.00.

Santa Fe on cross in circle, orange pyro, square, ½-pt...$10.00

Speedwell Farms, cow's head, back: Wash & Return embossed in clear, tin top, ½-pt.........................$70.00

Turner Center System, back: This Bottle Not Sold But Lent On embossed in clear, 1-pt...........................$15.00

Universal Store Bottle, Store Bottle 5¢ embossed in clear, round, qt...$5.00

White's Farm Dairy, Fresh From..., cow's head, orange & red pyro, square, qt, EX...$7.00

Model Kits

By far the majority of model kits were vehicular, and though worth collecting, especially when you can find them still mint in the box, the really big news is the figure kits. Most were made by Aurora during the 1960s. Especially hot are the movie monsters, though TV and comic strip character kits are popular with collectors too. As a rule of thumb, assembled kits are valued at about half as much as conservatively priced mint-in-box kits. The condition of the box is just as important as the contents, and top collectors will usually pay an additional 15% (sometimes even more) for a box that retains the factory plastic wrap still intact. For more information, we recommend *Aurora History and Price Guide* by Bill Bruegman (Cap'n Penny Productions) and *Classic Plastic Model Kits* by Rick Polizzi. *Schroeder's Toys, Antique to Modern,* contains prices and descriptions of hundreds of models by a variety of manufacturers. (The latter two books are published by Collector Books.)

Club: *International Figure Kit Club*

Magazine: *Kit Builders* Magazine
Gordy's
P.O. Box 201
Sharon Center, OH 44274-0201
216-239-1657 or fax: 216-239-2991

Magazine: *Model and Toy Collector Magazine*
137 Casterton Ave., Akron, OH 44303
216-836-0668 or fax: 216-869-8668

Academy, ZZ Gundum, Desert-Zaku Mobile Suit, #31, 1974, MIB $15.00

Addar, Jaws Diorama, #3231, 1975, MIB (sealed) $50.00

AEF, Aliens, Ferro, #AM-11, 1980s, MIB.....................$26.00

AEF, Aliens, Sgt Apone, #AM-5, 1980s, MIB $26.00

Airfix, Ankylosaurus, #3802, 1981, MIB $30.00

Airfix, Skeleton, #301, 1970, MIB $20.00

AMT, BJ & the Bear, KW Aerodyne & Trailer, #7705, MIB (sealed) $35.00

AMT, Farrah's Foxy Vette, #3101, 1970s, MIB (sealed)..$35.00

AMT, Klingon Cruiser, #952, 1970s, MIB (sealed) $30.00

AMT, Man From UNCLE, Car, #912, MIB $220.00

AMT, Star Trek, USS Enterprise, #921, 1967, MIB (sealed) .$190.00

AMT, Star Trek: The Motion Picture, USS Enterprise, #970, 1979, MIB $70.00

AMT/Ertl, Back to the Future, Delorian, #6122, 1991, MIB (sealed) **$35.00**

AMT/Ertl, Batman (movie), Batmobile, #6877, 1989, MIB (sealed) **$15.00**

AMT/Ertl, Gigantics, Colossal Mantis, #8389, 1996, MIB (sealed) **$15.00**

Anubus, Jonny Quest, Robot Spy, #9206, 1992, MIB..**$60.00**

Arii, Orguss Flier, #503, MIB.................................**$15.00**

Aurora, Batmobile, #486, 1966, MIB **$500.00**

Aurora, Captain Action, #480, 1966, MIB (sealed), from $250 to **$290.00**

Aurora, Comic Scenes, Batman, #187, 1974, MIB (sealed)..**$90.00**

Aurora, Comic Scenes, Tarzan, #181, 1974, MIB (sealed), from $50 to...**$70.00**

Aurora, Creature, 1963, MIB, $275.00. (Photo courtesy June Moon)

Aurora, Dr Jekyll as Mr Hyde, #482, 1972, MIB........**$250.00**

Aurora, Frankenstein, #423, 1961, MIB.....................**$400.00**

Aurora, Green Beret, #413, 1966, assembled...............**$60.00**

Aurora, Invaders, Flying Saucer, #256, 1975, MIB (sealed)...**$120.00**

Aurora, Monster Scenes, Pendulum, #63, 1971, MIB ..**$140.00**

Aurora, Mummy, #427, 1963, MIB.............................**$250.00**

Aurora, Prehistoric Scenes, Cro-Magnon Man, #730, 1971, MIB **$100.00**

Aurora, Prehistoric Scenes, Cro-Magnon Woman, 1971, MIB **$100.00**

Aurora, Robin the Boy Wonder, #488, 1966, M (NM sealed box) **$100.00**

Aurora, Spider-Man, #182, 1974, MIB (sealed).........**$160.00**

Aurora, Superboy, #478, 1974, M (VG sealed box) **$65.00**

Aurora, White-Tail Deer, #403, 1962, MIB **$75.00**

Aurora, Whoozis (Denty), #203, 1966, MIB................**$90.00**

Aurora, Wolfman, #450, 1972, MIB **$120.00**

Aurora, 2001: A Space Odyssey, Space Shuttle Orion, #252, 1975, MIB (sealed).....................................**$170.00**

Bachmann, Animals of the World, Cow & Calf, #7201, 1959, MIB **$60.00**

Bachmann, Birds of the World, Blue Bird, 1960s, M (EX sealed box)...**$35.00**

Bachmann, Dogs of the World, Pointer, #8006, 1959, MIB...**$40.00**

Bandai, Godzilla, #502526, 1984, MIB......................**$50.00**

Bandai, Kinggidrah, #3533, 1990, MIB.....................**$40.00**

Bandai, Silly Dracula, #503867, 1985, MIB **$20.00**

Billiken, Laser Blast Alien, 1988, vinyl, MIB............**$100.00**

Billiken, Mole People, 1984, vinyl, NM (EX+ box) **$65.00**

Dark Horse, Frankenstein, #22, 1991, MIB...............**$130.00**

Dark Horse, Predator II, #240131, 1994, MIB...........**$175.00**

Dimensional Designs, Outer Limits, The Mice (Chromite), MIB...**$100.00**

Eldon, Matador Missile & Launcher, 1960, MIB...........**$75.00**

Entex, 1st Dune Buggy, M (EX box).........................**$35.00**

Fujimi Mokei, Mad Police, Interceptor Car, #2, 1980s, MIB **$50.00**

Fundimensions, Six Million Dollar Man Bionic Bustout, MIB **$40.00**

Geometric Designs, Clash of the Titans, Medusa, vinyl or resin, 1994, MIB...**$60.00**

Hasegawa, Boeing F4B-4 Biplane, 1970s, MIB (sealed) .**$30.00**

Hawk, Explorer 18 Satellite, #553, 1968, MIB **$70.00**

Hawk, Weird-Ohs, Digger Way-Out Dragster, #530, 1963, MIB **$100.00**

Hawk, Weird-Ohs, Freddy Flameout, #533, 1963, MIB...**$75.00**

Horizon, Batman, #12, 1989, MIB..............................**$80.00**

Horizon, Bram Stoker's Dracula (Bat-Type), #42, 1992, MIB **$50.00**

Horizon, Jurassic Park, Spitter Dilophosaur, #62, 1993, MIB **$90.00**

Horizon, Marvel Universe, Dr Doom, #17, 1991, MIB ..**$40.00**

Horizon, Marvel Universe, Incredible Hulk, #13, 1990, MIB **$40.00**

Horizon, Marvel Universe, Thor, #25, 1993, MIB **$50.00**

Horizon, Robocop, #10, 1989, MIB **$60.00**

Horizon, Terminator 2 Judgement Day, 1991, M (EX+ box)..**$35.00**

Ideal, Jaguar XK-120 Fix-It Car, complete, NM (NM box)..**$115.00**

Imai, Captain Blue, #1209, 1982, MIB......................**$10.00**

Imai, Captain Scarlet, Spectrum Helicopter, #2015, 1992, MIB **$80.00**

Imai, Orguss, Dark Phoenix, #16, 1991, MIB **$40.00**

Imai, Orguss, Thing, #25, 1993, MIB........................**$50.00**

ITC, Collie, #3815, 1959, MIB **$35.00**

ITC, Midget Models, Covered Wagon & Stagecoach, #3749, 1962, MIB **$30.00**

KGB, Batman (1960s TV), Batgirl on Cycle, MIB........**$50.00**

Lindberg, Monsters, Krimson Terror, #272, 1965, MIB..**$130.00**

Lindberg, Northrop Snark Missile, #687, 1988, MIB (sealed)..**$40.00**

Lunar Models, Lost in Space, Space Pod, #SF016, MIB...**$110.00**

Monogram, Backdraft (movie), Fire Chief Car, #6250, 1991, MIB **$20.00**

Monogram, Battle Star Galactica, Space Fighter Raider, #6026, 1978, MIB (sealed)...**$100.00**

Monogram, Blue Thunder Helicopter, #6036, 1984, MIB..**$30.00**

Monogram, Dracula, #6008, 1983, MIB.....................**$70.00**

Monogram, Frankenstein, #6007, 1983, MIB...............**$70.00**
Monogram, Miami Vice, Ferrari Testarossa, #2756, 1987, MIB (sealed)..**$20.00**
Monogram, Rambo, Chopper & Riverboat, #6039, 1985, MIB (sealed)..**$30.00**
Monogram, Space Buggy, #194, 1969, MIB...............**$100.00**
Monogram, Young Astronauts, Mercury & Atlas Booster, #5910, 1987, MIB (sealed).....................................**$50.00**
MPC, Advanced Dungeons & Dragons, Dungeon Invaders, #2102, 1982, MIB...**$28.00**
MPC, Batman, #1702, 1984, MIB (sealed)....................**$50.00**
MPC, Black Hole, Maximillian Robot, #1982, 1979, MIB (sealed)..**$45.00**
MPC, Disney's Pirates of the Caribbean, Fate of the Mutineers, #5004, 1972, MIB...............................**$120.00**
MPC, Dukes of Hazzard, General Lee, #3058, 1981, MIB (sealed)..**$120.00**
MPC, Knight Rider, KITT, #675, 1983, MIB.................**$50.00**
MPC, Pilgrim Space Station, #9001, 1970, MIB............**$50.00**
MPC, Star Wars, R2-D2, #1912, 1978, MIB.................**$50.00**
MPC, Superman, #1701, 1984, MIB (sealed)................**$60.00**
Nitto, Crusher Joe, BMW-A795 Car, #23016, MIB........**$15.00**
Palmer, Animals of the World, Kodiak Bear, #22, 1950s, MIB...**$30.00**
Pyro, Deluxe Classics, VW Sun Roof Sedan, MIB.......**$60.00**
Pyro, US Marshall Wyatt Earp, #278, 1958, MIB........**$120.00**
Revell, Apollo Lunar Spacecraft, #1838, 1969, MIB (sealed) **$175.00**
Revell, CHiPs, Kawasaki, #7800, 1980, MIB (sealed)..**$30.00**
Revell, Dune, Sand Worm, #1778, 1985, MIB............**$70.00**
Revell, Flash Gordon & the Martian, #1450, 1965, MIB..**$170.00**
Revell, Hardy Boys Van, #1398, 1977, MIB (sealed)...**$40.00**
Revell, James Bond 007, Moonraker Space Shuttle, #4306, 1979, M (VG+ sealed box) **$25.00**
Revell, Laser Battle Stations, #4534, 1984, MIB **$30.00**
Revell, Magnum PI, 308 GTS Ferrari, #7378, 1982, MIB...**$20.00**
Revell, Robotech, Commando, #1199, lg, 1984, MIB..**$50.00**
Revell, Space Transport Sanger, #4804, 1991, MIB......**$35.00**
Revell, USN Bendix Talos Missile, #1808, 1957, MIB..**$80.00**
Screamin', Mary Shelly's Frankenstein, #1400, 1994, assembled...**$30.00**
Screamin', Star Wars, C-3PO, #3500, 1993, MIB **$45.00**
Testors, Grodies! (Weird-Ohs), Steel Pluckers, #547, 1983, MIB...**$50.00**
Toy Biz, Incredible Hulk, #48656, 1996, MIB (sealed) .**$25.00**
Tsukuda, Ghost Busters, Terror Dog, #16, 1984, MIB..**$120.00**
Union, Shuttle Challenger, #16, 1980s, MIB (sealed) ..**$10.00**

Modern Mechanical Banks

The most popular (and expensive) type of bank with today's collectors are the mechanicals, so called because of the antics they perform when a coin is deposited. Over three hundred models were produced between the Civil War period and the first World War. On some, arms wave, legs kick, or mouths open to swallow up the coin — amusing nonsense

intended by the inventor to encourage and reward thriftiness. Some of these original banks have been known to sell for as much as $20,000.00 — well out of the price range most of us can afford! So many opt for some of the modern mechanicals that are available on the collectibles market, including Book of Knowledge and James D. Capron, which are reproductions marked to indicate that they are indeed replicas. But beware — unmarked modern reproductions are common.

Advisor: Dan Iannotti (See Directory, Banks)

Auto Bank, John Wright, edition of 250, 1974, M.....**$725.00**
Bad Accident, James D Capron, M............................**$995.00**
Betsy Ross, Davidson/Imswiller, blue dress, edition of 300, 1976, M...**$975.00**
Butting Buffalo, Book of Knowledge, M **$340.00**
Cabin Bank, Book of Knowledge, NM **$350.00**
Decoy Hen Bank, Reynolds, 1974, edition of 10......**$600.00**
John Paul Jones, Franklin Mint, I Have Not Yet Begun To Fight, 1986, NM...**$550.00**
Leap Frog, Book of Knowledge, MIB **$450.00**
Magic Bank, James D Capron, M **$975.00**
North Pole, John Wright, simulates an old ice cream maker, scarce, M...**$125.00**
Penny Pineapple, Richards & Wilton, commemorating Hawaii becoming the 50th state, NM.................**$545.00**
Punch & Judy, Book of Knowledge, M.....................**$375.00**
Reagan O'Neill Feud, Miley's, political, bronze finish, 1983, NM **$550.00**
St Nickolas Bank, Reynolds, 1975, edition of 50.......**$775.00**
Teddy & the Bear, Book of Knowledge, NM **$375.00**
Toy Collector Bank, Reynolds, 1972, unlimited edition.**$650.00**
Train Man Bank, Reynolds, 1971, edition of 30 ....**$350.00**
Trick Dog, James D Capron, NM...............................**$625.00**

Uncle Louis, Reynolds #58M, 1997, edition of 50, $295.00. (Photo courtesy Charlie Reynolds)

Uncle Remus, Book of Knowledge, M.......................**$475.00**
Uncle Sam, Richards & Wilton, scarce rear-trap version, NM **$495.00**

Moon and Star

Moon and Star (originally called Palace) was first produced in the 1880s by John Adams & Company of Pittsburgh. But because the glassware was so heavy to transport, it was made for only a few years. In the 1960s, Joseph Weishar of Wheeling, West Virginia, owner of Island Mould & Machine Company, reproduced some of the original molds and incorporated the pattern into approximately forty new and different items. Two of the largest distributors of this line were L.E. Smith of Mt. Pleasant, Pennsylvania, who pressed their own glass, and L.G. Wright of New Martinsville, West Virginia, who had theirs pressed by Fostoria and Fenton. Both companies carried a large and varied assortment of shapes and colors. Several other companies were involved in its manufacture as well, especially of the smaller items. All in all, there may be as many as one hundred different pieces, plenty to keep you involved and excited as you do your searching.

The glassware is already very collectible, even though it is still being made on a limited basis. Colors you'll see most often are amberina (yellow shading to orange-red), green, amber, crystal, light blue, and ruby. Pieces in ruby and light blue are most collectible and harder to find than the other colors, which seem to be abundant. Purple, pink, cobalt, amethyst, tan slag, and light green and blue opalescent were made, too, but on a lesser scale.

Current L.E. Smith catalogs contain a dozen or so pieces that are still available in crystal, pink, cobalt (lighter than the old shade), and these colors with an iridized finish. A new color was introduced in 1992, teal green, and the water set in sapphire blue opalescent was pressed in 1993 by Weishar Enterprises. They are now producing limited editions in various colors and shapes, but they are marking their glassware 'Weishar,' to distinguish it from the old line. Cranberry Ice (light transparent pink) was introduced in 1994.

Our values are given for ruby and light blue. For amberina, green, and amber, deduct at least 30%. These colors are less in demand, and unless your prices are reasonable, you may find them harder to sell. Read *Mysteries of the Moon and Star* by George and Linda Breeze for more information.

Cruet, 6¾", from $65.00 to $75.00.

Ashtray, allover pattern, moons form scallops along rim, 4 rests, 8" dia..**$25.00**
Ashtray, moons at rim, star in base, 6-sided, 5½".......**$18.00**
Ashtray, moons at rim, star in base, 6-sided, 8½".......**$25.00**
Banana boat, allover pattern, moons form scallops along rim, 9", from $28 to...**$32.00**
Banana boat, allover pattern, moons form scallops along rim, 12"..**$45.00**
Basket, allover pattern, moons form scallops along rim, footed, incurvate upright handles, 4", from $15 to.....**$22.00**
Basket, allover pattern, moons form scallops along rim, solid handle, 9", from $50 to...**$65.00**
Bell, pattern along sides, plain rim & handle, from $35 to..**$45.00**
Bowl, allover pattern, footed, crimped rim, 7½", from $25 to..**$35.00**
Butter dish, allover pattern, scalloped foot, patterned lid & finial, 6x5½" dia..**$45.00**
Butter dish, allover pattern, stars form scallops along rim of base, star finial, oval, ¼-lb, 8½"...........................**$50.00**
Butter/cheese dish, patterned lid, plain base, 7" dia, from $50 to..**$65.00**
Cake plate, allover pattern, low collared base, 13" dia, from $50 to...**$60.00**
Cake salver, allover pattern w/scalloped rim, raised foot w/scalloped edge, 5x12" dia, from $50 to............**$60.00**
Cake stand, allover pattern, plate removes from standard, 2-pc, 11" dia...**$75.00**
Candle bowl, allover pattern, footed, 8", from $25 to.**$30.00**
Candle holder, allover pattern, bowl style w/ring handle, 2x5½", ea...**$18.00**
Candle holders, allover pattern, flared & scalloped foot, 6", pr, from $40 to...**$50.00**
Candle holders, allover pattern, flared base, 4½", pr, from $20 to..**$25.00**
Candle lamp, patterned shade, clear base, 2-pc, 7½", from $20 to..**$25.00**
Candy dish, allover pattern on base & lid, footed ball shape, 6"..**$25.00**
Canister, allover pattern, 1-lb or 2-lb, from $12 to......**$15.00**
Canister, allover pattern, 3½-lb or 5-lb, from $18 to ..**$22.00**
Chandelier, dome shape, 14" dia, w/font, amber, from $300 to..**$365.00**
Chandelier, ruffled dome shape w/allover pattern, amber, 10"..**$100.00**
Cheese dish, patterned base, clear plain lid, 9½", from $65 to **$70.00**
Compote, allover pattern, footed, flared crimped rim, 5", from $15 to...**$22.00**
Compote, allover pattern, raised foot, patterned lid & finial, 7½x6", from $30 to...**$40.00**
Compote, allover pattern, raised foot on stem, patterned lid & finial, 10x8", from $50 to...............................**$65.00**
Compote, allover pattern, raised foot on stem, patterned lid & finial, 12x8", from $60 to...............................**$75.00**
Compote, allover pattern, scalloped foot on stem, patterned lid & finial, 8x4", from $35 to **$40.00**

Compote, allover pattern, scalloped rim, footed, 5½x8", from $28 to **$35.00**

Compote, allover pattern, scalloped rim, footed, 5x6½", from $15 to...**$20.00**

Compote, allover pattern, scalloped rim, footed, 7x10", from $35 to...**$45.00**

Console bowl, allover pattern, scalloped rim, flared foot w/flat edge, 8"..**$25.00**

Creamer, allover pattern, raised foot w/scalloped edge, 5¾x3"..**$35.00**

Creamer & sugar bowl (open), disk foot, sm, from $25 to **$35.00**

Decanter, bulbous w/allover pattern, plain neck, foot ring, original patterned stopper, 32-oz, 12", from $75 to........**$90.00**

Epergne, allover pattern, 1-lily, flared bowl, scalloped foot, minimum value **$95.00**

Epergne, allover pattern, 2-pc, 9", minimum value **$65.00**

Fairy lamp, cylindrical dome-top shade, 6", from $25 to.**$35.00**

Jardiniere, allover pattern, patterned lid & finial, 9¾", minimum value...**$85.00**

Jardiniere/cracker jar, allover pattern, patterned lid & finial, 7¼", minimum value **$65.00**

Jardiniere/tobacco jar, allover pattern, patterned lid & finial, 6", minimum value..**$45.00**

Jelly dish, allover pattern, patterned lid & finial, stemmed foot, 10½", from $55 to **$65.00**

Jelly dish, patterned body w/plain flat rim & disk foot, patterned lid & finial, 6¾x3½"......................................**$35.00**

Lamp, miniature; amber **$145.00**

Lamp, miniature; blue, from $185 to.........................**$225.00**

Lamp, miniature; green **$185.00**

Lamp, miniature; milk glass **$245.00**

Lamp, miniature; red **$235.00**

Lamp, oil or electric; allover pattern, all original, amber, from $175 to...**$200.00**

Lamp, oil or electric; allover pattern, all original, red or light blue, 24", minimum value...................................**$350.00**

Lamp, oil; allover pattern, all original, common, 12", from $75 to...**$100.00**

Lighter, allover patterned body, metal fittings, from $40 to..**$50.00**

Nappy, allover pattern, crimped rim, 2¾x6", from $12 to....**$18.00**

Plate, patterned body & center, smooth rim, 8"..........**$35.00**

Relish bowl, 6 lg scallops form allover pattern, 1½x8"...**$35.00**

Relish dish, allover pattern, 1 plain handle, 2x8" dia, from $35 to...**$40.00**

Relish tray, patterned moons form scalloped rim, star in base, rectangular, 8" **$35.00**

Salt & pepper shakers, allover pattern, metal tops, 4x2", pr, from $25 to...**$35.00**

Salt cellar, allover pattern, scalloped rim, sm flat foot..**$8.00**

Soap dish, allover pattern, oval, 2x6" **$12.00**

Spooner, allover pattern, straight sides, scalloped rim, raised foot, 5¼x4", from $45 to.....................................**$50.00**

Sugar bowl, allover pattern, patterned lid & finial, sm flat foot, 5¼x4", from $35 to.......................................**$40.00**

Sugar bowl, allover pattern, straight sides, patterned lid & finial, scalloped foot, 8x4½", from $35 to.............**$40.00**

Sugar shaker, allover pattern, metal top, 4½x3½" **$50.00**

Syrup pitcher, allover pattern, metal lid, 4½x3½", from $65 to...**$75.00**

Toothpick holder, allover pattern, scalloped rim, sm flat foot...**$10.00**

Tumbler, juice; no pattern at rim or on disk foot, 5-oz, 3½", from $12 to...**$15.00**

Tumbler, no pattern at rim or on disk foot, 7-oz, 4¼", from $12 to...**$15.00**

Tumbler, juice; 4¼", from $18.00 to $22.00; Goblet, water; 5¾", from $15.00 to $22.00; Tumbler, iced tea; 5", from $18.00 to $22.00; Sherbet, 4½", from $25.00 to $28.00; Goblet, wine; 4½", from $12.00 to $15.00; Tumbler, juice, short pedestal foot, from $18.00 to $20.00.

Pitcher, water; 7½", from $65.00 to $80.00.

Mortens Studios

During the 1940s, a Swedish sculptor by the name of Oscar Mortens left his native country and moved to the United States, settling in Arizona. Along with his partner, Gunnar Thelin, they founded the Mortens Studios, a firm that specialized in the manufacture of animal figurines. Though he preferred dogs of all breeds, horses, cats, and wild animals were made, too, but on a much smaller scale.

The material he used was a plaster-like composition molded over a wire framework for support and reinforcement. Crazing is common, and our values reflect pieces with a moderate amount, but be sure to check for more serious damage before you buy. Most pieces are marked with either an ink stamp or a paper label.

Bloodhound, #877, 7" L $150.00
Boston Terrier, sitting, #793, 5½"................................$70.00
Boxer, #551, mini...$65.00
Boxer, fawn, standing, #755, 5½"...............................$75.00
Chow pup, brown, #816, 3"..$50.00
Cocker Spaniel, lying down, #516, 4½" L....................$50.00

Collie, 6", $100.00.

Collie pup, #818, mini..$55.00
Colt, standing, #714, 5x4½" $65.00
Dachshund, standing, #866, 6" L..................................$65.00
Dalmatian, #854, 7½" L...$95.00
Doberman, #785, black & rust, 6½"..............................$95.00
German Shepherd, #556, mini.....................................$65.00
Greyhound, gray, #747, 6¾".......................................$100.00
Horse, filly, chestnut brown, #716, 8½".......................$95.00
Horse, golden-brown, running, #724, 7" L $100.00

Horse, rearing, 9", $110.00.

Horse, stallion, rearing, #662, 4¾" $95.00
Irish Setter, #856, standing, mahogany, 5½x7¼".........$95.00
Norwegian Elkhound, gray, #764, 5⅛" $110.00
Pekinese, #553, mini..$65.00
Pointer pup, recumbent, #503, 5" L.............................$75.00
Pug, #738, buff, 4x5"..$125.00
Springer Spaniel, #745C, black spotted, 5¾x4¾".........$95.00

Morton Pottery

Six different potteries operated in Morton, Illinois, during a period of ninety-nine years. The first pottery, established by six Rapp brothers who had immigrated from Germany in the mid-1870s, was named Morton Pottery Works. It was in operation from 1877 to 1915 when it was reorganized and renamed Morton Earthenware Company. Its operation, 1915 – 1917, was curtailed by World War I. Cliftwood Art Potteries, Inc. was the second pottery to be established. It operated from 1920 until 1940 when it was sold and renamed Midwest Potteries, Inc. In March 1944 the pottery burned and was never rebuilt. Morton Pottery Company was the longest running of Morton's potteries. It was in operation from 1922 until 1976. The last pottery to open was the American Art Potteries. It was in production from 1947 until 1961.

All of Morton's potteries were spin-offs from the original Rapp brothers. Second, third, and fourth generation Rapps followed the tradition of their ancestors to produce a wide variety of pottery. Rockingham and yellow ware to Art Deco, giftwares, and novelties were produced by Morton's potteries.

To learn more about these companies, we recommend *Morton's Potteries: 99 Years, Vol. II,* by Doris and Burdell Hall.

Advisors: Doris and Burdell Hall (See Directory, Morton Pottery)

Planters, male or female rabbit, Morton Pottery Works, $18.00 each. (Photo courtesy Doris and Burdell Hall)

Morton Pottery Works — Morton Earthenware Company, 1877 – 1917

Acorn, bank, brown $50.00
Crock, sauerkraut; Rockingham, w/press, 4-gal........$150.00
Cuspidor, Rockingham, 7"...$50.00
Jardiniere, cobalt, 7"...$60.00
Jug, Rockingham, 8-pt..$125.00
Mug, yellow ware, banded, 1-pt..................................$85.00
Paperweight, buffalo, brown, w/advertising, 2½".......$55.00
Pie plate, brown Rockingham, 9"................................$25.00
Pitcher, green, brown & yellow multicolor, #245, 6" ..$125.00

341

Cliftwood Art Potteries, Inc., 1920 – 1940

Ashtray, brown chocolate drip, w/holders for cigarettes & matches **$40.00**

Bowl, Viking ship, 14" L, w/dragon candle holder, ivory/turquoise, 6" **$200.00**

Creamer, cow figural, brown drip chocolate, 6½x3½x1½" .**$75.00**

Dinnerware in apple green: plate, 10", $25.00; sugar bowl with lid, $25.00; creamer, $20.00. (Photo courtesy Doris and Burdell Hall)

Dinnerware, compote, mint matt ivory, 4x6½" **$24.00**

Dinnerware, sweetmeat bowl, green & yellow drip, w/lid **$50.00**

Figurine, elephant, trumpeting, extended tusks, mulberry, 9½" L **$55.00**

Jardiniere, brown chocolate drip, 5½" **$35.00**

Miniature, lion, yellow/brown, 6x3¼x1" **$70.00**

Radio speaker, 3 animal paw feet, brown drip, 16¾" ..**$100.00**

Stein, barrel shape, German motto on white, 4½" **$30.00**

Wine jug, musical, plays polka, brown drip, 9" **$125.00**

Midwest Potteries, Inc., 1940 – 1944

TV lamp, poodle and pug, air-brushed natural colors, Kron line, 11", $75.00. (Photo courtesy Doris and Burdell Hall)

Ashtray, hand on tray, 14k gold, 4½" **$25.00**

Figurine, canary pr on stump, yellow & gold decoration, 4½" **$30.00**

Figurine, duck, stylized, brown & green, 12" **$25.00**

Figurine, horse, rearing, brown drip, 10¾" **$35.00**

Figurine, stallion (wild horse), rearing, 14k gold, 10¾".**$40.00**

Miniature, camel, brown, 2" **$10.00**

Miniature, polar bear, white, 2" **$10.00**

Planter, cat, hole for cactus 'tail,' white, 4" **$12.00**

Shadow lamp base for lg figurals, yellow & green drip, 17½x7½x5½" **$60.00**

Shelf sitters, Oriental boy & girl, black & white w/gold, 3½", pr **$30.00**

Wall pocket, corner style, underglaze decor **$20.00**

Morton Pottery Company, 1922 – 1976

Christmas item, lollipop tree, holes for sticks, green, 9¼".**$30.00**

Christmas item, Santa Claus, cranberry/nut/ashtray **$15.00**

Christmas item, Santa Claus, planter/vase, 9½" **$35.00**

Christmas item, sleigh, red, #772...............................**$30.00**

Easter item, bunny (boy) in top hat/vest, figurine, brown & blue, 9½" **$18.00**

Easter item, bunny w/carrot, basket/planter, white & pink, #435, 5¼" **$20.00**

Figurine, bison, brown, 7" **$75.00**

Figurine, elephant, trumpeting, gray, 10"..................**$40.00**

Figurine, seeing-eye dog, black, 5¾" **$20.00**

Lamp, Easter bunny w/carrot, male **$40.00**

Lamp, old woman shoe house **$35.00**

Lamp, teddy bear..**$35.00**

Political giveaway, ashtray, Nixon, red **$25.00**

Political giveaway, figurine, donkey, Kennedy, brown, 2"..**$40.00**

Political giveaway, figurine, elephant, miscellaneous names, blue or gray, 2" **$20.00**

Political giveaway, ring holder, elephant, Nixon, 4"...**$40.00**

Thanksgiving item, turkey, cookie jar, chick finial, yellow & brown spatter..**$90.00**

Thanksgiving item, turkey, planter, natural colors, #3335, lg **$35.00**

Valentine item, heart vase, red, #428, 5¾"..................**$12.00**

Valentine item, heart vase, red, #953, 3½"..................**$8.00**

American Art Potteries, 1947 – 1963

Bowl, water lily blossom, blue & pink spray, 3¼x5" .**$15.00**

Candlestick, black, 3 cups, #140, 6x7½" **$30.00**

Creamer, bird figural, tail handle, black & gray spray ..**$15.00**

Doll parts, 3" head & appendages, hand-painted natural colors **$60.00**

Figurine, hog, Hampshire, natural colors, 5½"............**$35.00**

Flower frog, bird on stump, #98, 8½"..........................**$15.00**

Flower frog, turtle, #411, 2" **$12.00**

Mint dish, flat flower blossom, green, brown & mauve spray, 5½" dia...**$7.00**

Planter, hog, Hampshire, black w/white band, 5½" ...**$20.00**

Planter, rabbit beside stump, brown, white, pink & green spray, 4¾" **$15.00**

TV lamp, rearing horse, green & black, #327, 9x8x6" ..**$36.00**

Vase/flower frog, inverted mushroom form, green & yellow spray, 4¾" **$15.00**

Wall pocket, apple & leaf, #127, 6½".............$18.00
Wall pocket, teapot, decorated, #79, 4" $22.00

Ewers, Norwood label, from $18.00 to $25.00. (Photo courtesy Doris and Burdell Hall)

Moss Rose

Though the Moss Rose pattern has been produced by Staffordshire and American pottery companies alike since the mid-1800s, the line we're dealing with here was primarily made between the late 1950s into the 1970s by Japanese manufacturers. Even today you'll occasionally see a tea set or a small candy dish for sale in some of the chain stores. (The collectors who're already picking this line up refer to it as Moss Rose, but we've seen it advertised under the name 'Victorian Rose.') The pattern consists of a briar rose with dark green mossy leaves on stark white glaze. Occasionally an item is trimmed in gold. In addition to dinnerware, many accessories and novelties were also made.

Refer to *Schroeder's Antiques Price Guide* (Collector Books) for information on the early Moss Rose pattern.

Advisor: Geneva Addy (See Directory, Imperial Porcelain)

Bell $10.00
Bowl, sauce...$4.00
Bowl, soup..$8.00
Bud vase...$15.00
Butter dish..$25.00
Candy dish, fluted, w/lid...................................$20.00
Child's set, complete in box $165.00
Chocolate pot...$23.00
Cigarette box w/2 attached ashtrays (self-contained set) ..$25.00
Cottage cheese dish..$15.00
Creamer & sugar bowl, w/lid $15.00
Cup & saucer..$6.00
Cup & saucer, demitasse $8.00
Egg cup..$9.00
Fairy lamp $18.00
Incense burner, gold trim, 3-footed, w/domed lid, 3¼" .$15.00
Lamp, vanity or dresser; oil burning, 10", pr.............$75.00
Mirror, on stand $15.00
Mirror, sm, standing, w/pin-dish base......................$10.00

Nut dish w/4 nut cups $35.00
Perfume bottle, w/stopper $15.00
Pin tray, butterfly shape....................................$15.00
Plate, dinner $7.00
Plate, salad..$5.00
Platter..$15.00
Port wine stopper $10.00
Salt & pepper shakers, pr $10.00
Smoke set, flat tray w/4 ashtrays & lighter................$30.00
Soap dish..$10.00
Tea set, stacking, creamer & sugar bowl set atop teapot..$25.00
Teapot, demitasse $30.00
Teapot, electric...$22.00
Teapot, regular...$30.00
Tidbit tray, 2-tiered...$15.00
Trays, butterfly shaped, stacking set of 4 ....$15.00

Motion Clocks (Electric)

Novelty clocks with some type of motion or animation were popular in spring-powered or wind-up form for hundreds of years. Today they bring thousands of dollars when sold. Electric-powered or motor-driven clocks first appeared in the late 1930s and were produced until quartz clocks became the standard, with the 1950s being the era during which they reached the height of their production.

Four companies led their field. They were Mastercrafters, United, Haddon, and Spartus in order of productivity. Mastercrafters was the earliest and longest-lived, making clocks from the late '40s until the late '80s. (They did, however, drop out of business several times during this long period.) United began making clocks in the early '50s and continued until the early '60s. Haddon followed in the same time frame, and Spartus was in production from the late '50s until the mid-'60s.

These clocks are well represented in the listings that follow; prices are for examples in excellent condition and working. With an average age of forty years, many now need repair. Dried-out grease and dirt easily cause movements and motions not to function. The other nemesis of many motion clocks is deterioration of the fiber gears. Originally intended to keep the clocks quiet, fiber gears have not held up like their metal counterparts. For fully restored clocks, add $50.00 to $75.00 to our values. (Full restoration includes complete cleaning of motor and movement, repair of same; cleaning and polishing face and bezel; cleaning and polishing case and repairing if necessary; and installing new line cord, plug, and light bulb if needed.) Brown is the most common case color for plastic clocks. Add 10% to 20% or more for cases in onyx (mint green) or any light shade. If any parts noted below are missing, value can drop one-third to one-half. We must stress that 'as is' clocks will not bring these prices. Deteriorated, nonworking clocks may be worth less that half of these values.

Note: When original names are not known, names have been assigned.

Advisors: Sam and Anna Samuelian (See Directory, Motion Clocks)

Haddon

Based in Chicago, Illinois, Haddon produced an attractive line of clocks. They used composition cases that were hand painted, and sturdy Hansen movements and motions. This is the only clock line for which new replacement motors are still available.

Granny rocking (Home Sweet Home) **$125.00**
Rocking Horse (Rancho), composition, from $150 to ..**$200.00**
Tetter Totter, children on seesaw, from $125 to **$175.00**

Mastercrafters

Based in Chicago, Illinois, this company produced many of the most appealing and popular collectible motion clocks on today's market. Cases were made of plastic, with earlier examples being a sturdy urea plastic that imparted quality, depth, and shine to their finishes. Clock movements were relatively simple and often supplied by Sessions Clock Company, who also made many of their own clocks.

Airplane, Bakelite & chrome, from $175 to **$225.00**
Blacksmith, plastic, from $75 to **$100.00**
Carousel, plastic, carousel front, from $175 to **$225.00**
Church, w/bell ringer, plastic **$100.00**
Fireplace, plastic, from $60 to **$90.00**
Swinging Bird, plastic, w/cage front, from $125 to ..**$150.00**
Swinging Girl, plastic, from $100 to..........................**$125.00**
Swinging Playmates, plastic, w/fence, from $100 to.**$125.00**
Waterfall, plastic...**$100.00**

Spartus

This company made clocks well into the '80s, but most later clocks were not animated. Cases were usually plastic, and most clocks featured animals.

Cat, w/flirty eyes, plastic, from $25 to **$40.00**
Panda Bear, plastic, eyes moves, from $25 to.............**$40.00**
Water Wheel (L style), plastic, from $20 to **$30.00**
Waterfall & Wheel, plastic, from $50 to.......................**$75.00**

United

Based in Brooklyn, New York, United made mostly cast-metal cases finished in gold or bronze. Their movements were somewhat more complex than Mastercrafters'. Some of their clocks contained musical movements, which while pleasing can be annoying when continuously run.

Ballerina, wooden, from $75 to....................................**$125.00**
Bobbing Chicks, metal case, various colors, from $35 to .**$50.00**
Bobbing Chicks, wooden house, green & red, from $40 to .**$60.00**

Cowboy w/Rope, metal, wooden base, from $100 to..**$150.00**
Dancers, metal w/square glass dome, from $100 to.**$150.00**

Davy Crockett, metal, 10", rare, $650.00. (Photo courtesy Phil Helley)

Fireplace, metal, gold, from $50 to **$75.00**
Fireplace, w/man & woman, spinning wheel & moving fire,
  from $125 to...**$150.00**
Fishing Boy, metal, fishing pole & fish move, from $125
  to...**$150.00**
Huck Finn, fishing pole & fish move, from $150 to.**$175.00**
Hula Girl & Drummer, wooden, from $200 to..........**$250.00**
Majorette w/Rotating Baton, from $75 to **$125.00**
Owl, metal on wooden base, eyes move, from $75 to..**$100.00**
Windmill, pink plastic case, minor cracks in plastic, from $75
  to...**$125.00**

Miscellaneous

God Bless America, flag waves, from $75 to **$100.00**
Klocker Spaniel, from $50 to **$75.00**
Poodle, various colors, from $75 to.........................**$100.00**

Motorcycle Collectibles

At some point in nearly everyone's life, they've experienced at least a brief love affair with a motorcycle. What could be more exhilarating than the open road — the wind in your hair, the sun on your back, and no thought for the cares of today or what tomorrow might bring. For some, the passion never diminished. For most of us, it's a fond memory. Regardless of which description best fits you personally, you will probably enjoy the old advertising and sales literature, books and magazines, posters, photographs, banners, etc., showing the old Harleys and Indians, and the club pins, dealership jewelry and clothing, and scores of other items of memorabilia in which collectors are now beginning to show considerable interest. For more information and a lot of color photographs, we recommend *Motorcycle Collectibles With Values* by Leila Dunbar (Schiffer). See also License Plates.

Advisor: Bob 'Sprocket' Eckardt (See Directory, Motorcycles)

Ad, Harley-Davidson, paper on cardboard, Step In & See The 1924...Then Let's Go For A Ride!, cycle w/sidecar, 34x26", G+..**$250.00**

Ad, Indian Motorcycles, paper, Announcing The New 1935..., sleek Indian head in full headdress, red on white, 14x45", EX..**$425.00**

Badge, Indian Motorcycles, round w/profile of Indian in full headdress & Indian in script below, silver-tone on red, EX **$135.00**

Banner, Harley-Davidson Drop-Forged Forks, paper, image of 1930 cycle, EX **$525.00**

Brochure, 1940 Indian Spring Frame Motorcycles, 2-color, EX **$90.00**

Brochure, 1966 Triumph, covers different bikes, 16 pages, EX **$55.00**

Catalog, Guaranteed Motorcycle Supplies 13th Annual Catalogue, 1916, Motorcycle Equipment Co, 70 pages, VG+ **$150.00**

Catalog, Harley-Davidson, 1975, EX.........**$45.00**

Catalog, Indians 1928 Series, 6x9½", VG...............**$200.00**

Clock, Harley-Davidson, octagonal light-up w/glass front, decorative border around numbers & logo, 18x18", M **$1,400.00**

Clock, Indian Motorcycles, round metal frame w/glass lens, black numbers & red lettering on white, 18½" dia, NM+......................................**$1,700.00**

Decal, Oilzum Motorcycle Oil, triangle shape w/extended lettered band & silhouette motorcyclist, 1950s, 4", M **$50.00**

Envelope, Indian Motorcycle logo in corner, 8x9", EX ..**$15.00**

Flyer, Hells Angels Poker Run, w/special guest Canned Heat, September 15, 1996, 8½x11" (framed)..................**$80.00**

Flyer, Indian Motorcycle Sidecar, features detailed text & graphics of sidecar, red accents, framed, image: 16x12", EX **$135.00**

Folder, Indian Scout The Universal Motorcycle, photos of Indian scaling Multnomah Falls, 6x8½", EX **$125.00**

Handbill, Harley-Davidson for 1940, EX....................**$65.00**

Hat, Harley-Davidson, black w/white bill & silver-tone band, winged patch, EX **$250.00**

Helmet & goggles, fitted leather hat w/metal goggles #AN6530, EX **$200.00**

Horn, Cushman Eagle, Balkamp, MIB (EX box).........**$25.00**

Kidney belt, dice & club name incised on leather, 40", EX..**$50.00**

Magazine, Enthusiast, May 1956, cover pictures 21-year-old Elvis on his 3rd Harley, NM...............................**$450.00**

Manual, owner's; 1974 Triumph Trident, 4 pages, VG .**$20.00**

Match holder, Indian Motorcycles, brass box w/embossed image of Indian framed by lettering, 2x1½", EX..**$550.00**

Money clip, AMA Award, dated 1961, MOC...............**$70.00**

Oil can, Harley-Davidson Genuine Refinery Sealed Oil, 1-qt, black logo on orange, NM+..................................**$400.00**

Oil can, Harley-Davidson's Premium II, 1-qt, cardboard w/metal top & bottom, 1980, VG..........................**$25.00**

Oil can, Indian Premium Motorcycle Oil, 1-qt, round Indian logo above lettering, red, white & black, NM+..**$250.00**

Patch, 1988 Harley Owners, spread-wing eagle logo & HOG over light blue background, 6", EX......................**$10.00**

Pin, Harley-Davidson, Jerome Implements, 1978, gold wash w/red, white & blue enameled inlay, 1" dia, EX .**$17.00**

Pin, Outlaw Motorcycle Club, EX..............................**$50.00**

Pin-back button, Indian Motorcycles, Indian head in profile encircled by bands w/lettering, ¾" dia, EX..........**$80.00**

Plate holder, Harley-Davidson logo on brass, marked Made in USA on bottom, EX....................................**$20.00**

Pocket watch, Harley-Davidson, silver-tone w/logo on face, 1920s, EX..**$725.00**

Postcard, Indian Motorcycles, photo image of man on early motorcycle, 4x6", EX+...................................**$60.00**

Poster, Harley-Davidson Wins All 1940 Class A & Class B Hillclimb Championships, multicolored, 24x37", NM **$500.00**

Poster, It's New! The Indian Brave Only $345.00..., motorcycle picture on red dot w/white background, 29x22", NM..**$300.00**

Program, 1959 National Motorcycle Championship, Sacramento CA, VG **$28.00**

Program, 1962 AMA 25th Annual Winter Motorcycle Classics, Daytona International Speedway, EX...................**$65.00**

Screwdriver, Harley-Davidson, nickel-plated handle w/engraved lettering, 5", EX............................**$115.00**

Shot glass, Harley-Davidson 95th Anniversary, 95 Years of Great Motorcycles, 1903-1998, bar & shield logo, pewter, M..**$27.00**

Sign, Harley-Davidson Motor Cycles, diecut eagle & emblem outlined w/neon, multicolored, 1980s, 25x36", NM......**$700.00**

Sign, Indian Motorcycles/Authorized Dealer, enamel flange, red, black & white on yellow, w/logo, 1940s, 26" dia, EX...**$550.00**

Stick pin, Indian Motorcycles, round metal Indian head emblem on end, gold-tone, ½" dia, EX.............**$180.00**

Tie bar, AMA Gypsy Tour Award, brass w/AMA logo, EX.**$20.00**

Trophy ashtray, marked Geuirie, 1930s, 9", rare, from $200.00 to $300.00. (Photo courtesy Bob 'Sprocket' Eckardt)

Watch fob, AMA Gypsy Tours 1925, triangular w/green, yellow & red cloisonne detail, leather strap, VG **$55.00**

Windbreaker, Harley-Davidson, 1970s, EX **$50.00**

Wristwatch, Harley-Davidson, rectangular face w/bowed sides, black leather band, Elgin, VG **$600.00**

Movie Posters and Lobby Cards

Although many sizes of movie posters were made and all are collectible, the preferred size today is still the one-sheet, 27" wide and 41" long. Movie-memorabilia collecting is as diverse as films themselves. Popular areas include specific films such as *Gone With the Wind, Wizard of Oz,* and others; specific stars — from the greats to character actors; directors such as Hitchcock, Ford, Speilberg, and others; specific film types such as B-Westerns, all-Black casts, sports related, noir, '50s teen, '60s beach, musicals, crime, silent, radio characters, cartoons, and serials; specific characters such as Tarzan, Superman, Ellery Queen, Blondie, Ma and Pa Kettle, Whistler, and Nancy Drew; specific artists like Rockwell, Davis, Frazetta, Flagg, and others; specific art themes, for instance, policeman, firemen, horses, attorneys, doctors, or nurses (this list is endless). And some collectors just collect posters they like. In the past twenty years, movie memorabilia has steadily increased in value, and in the last few years the top price paid for a movie poster has reached $453,500.00. Movie memorabilia is a new field for collectors. In the past, only a few people knew where to find posters. Recently, auctions on the east and west coasts have created much publicity, attracting scores of new collectors. Many posters are still moderately priced, and the market is expanding, allowing even new collectors to see the value of their collections increase.

Advisors: Cleophas and Lou Ann Wooley, Movie Poster Service (See Directory, Movie Posters)

Gentlemen Prefer Blondes, 20th Century Fox, 1953, one-sheet, linen backed, 41x27", NM, $850.00.

Abbott & Costello in Dr Jekyll & Mr Hyde, lobby card #6, w/Boris Karloff, 1953, 11x14", EX **$65.00**

All American Boy, Jack Armstrong, 1947, 6-sheet, 81x81", EX..**$500.00**

Animal House, John Belushi, 1978, 41x27", EX **$50.00**

Aristocats, Disney animation, 1971, 41x27", EX **$60.00**

Attack of the Jungle Woman, 1959, 22x14", EX...........**$50.00**

Back Street, window card, Susan Hayward, 1961, EX ..**$25.00**

Bambi, Disney animation, 1966 reissue, 6-sheet, EX ..**$65.00**

Beast From Haunted Cave, monster graphics, 1959, 41x27", EX **$100.00**

Bedtime Story, Fredric March & Loretta Young, 1941, styles A or B, 41x27", EX, ea **$65.00**

Betrayed, Clark Gable, Lana Turner & Victor Mature, 1954, 3-sheet, EX...**$75.00**

Big Jake, John Wayne & Richard Boone, 1971, 41x27", EX...**$50.00**

Black Sunday, Barbara Steele, 1961, 40x30", EX.........**$85.00**

Blade Runner, Harrison Ford & Sean Young, 41x27", EX .**$65.00**

Boom Town, lobby cards, Clark Gable & Spencer Tracy, 3 different, 1946, ea **$15.00**

Bridge of San Luis Rey, Lynn Bari, 1944, 41x27", EX .**$50.00**

Cahill: US Marshall, John Wayne, 1973, 41x27", EX...**$40.00**

Casablanca, Humphrey Bogart & Ingrid Bergman, 1992 commemorative reissue, 41x27", NM **$25.00**

Charlie Chan in the Golden Eye, lobby card, Roland Winters, 5 different ea w/Chan, 1948, EX, ea **$18.00**

Charlie Chan in the Golden Eye, Roland Winters, 1948, 3-sheet, EX **$175.00**

China Sky, window card, Randolph Scott, 1945 ....**$40.00**

Christmas in Connecticut, Barbara Stanwyck, Dennis Morgan & Sydney Greenstreet, 1945, 3-sheet, EX...........**$250.00**

Cleopatra, Cecil B DeMille w/Claudette Colbert, 1952 reissue, 41x27", EX **$85.00**

Corridors of Blood, Boris Karloff, 1963, 41x27", EX ...**$50.00**

Country Girl, insert, Grace Kelly, Bing Crosby & William Holden, 1954, EX **$50.00**

Crazy for Love, Brigitte Bardot, 1960, 41x27", EX......**$60.00**

Cult of the Cobra, Can a Woman's Beauty Be Changed...?, Faith Domergue & Richard Long, 1955, 41x27", EX........**$100.00**

Cyclops, Lon Chaney, 1956, 1956, 41x27", EX **$225.00**

Dark Mountain, Robert Lowery & Ellen Drew, 1944, 41x27", EX...**$40.00**

Day of the Triffids, Beware of Triffids..., graphics of killer plant, 1962, 41x27", EX **$150.00**

Day's Journey Into Night, lobby cards, Katharine Hepburn, set of 4, EX..**$35.00**

Death of a Salesman, insert, Arthur Miller classic w/Fredric March, 1952, EX..**$65.00**

Desire Under the Elms, insert, Sophia Loren, 1958, EX ..**$35.00**

Diamonds Are Forever, Sean Connery as Bond, 1971, 41x27", EX...**$50.00**

Dick Tracy's Dilemma, lobby card, 1947, 14x11", EX+ ..**$65.00**

Earth Vs the Flying Saucers, lobby card, full-color scene w/robot in the park, 1956, 11x14", EX...................**$75.00**

Electronic Monster, Rod Cameron, 1960, 22x14", EX..**$50.00**

Elmer Gantry, Burt Lancaster & Jean Simmons, 1960, 6-sheet, M...**$125.00**

Exile, Douglas Fairbanks Jr, 1947, 41x27", EX............**$50.00**

Family Plot, last Hitchcock film, Bruce Dern, 1976, 44x27", EX...**$35.00**

First Men in the Moon, HG Wells Astounding Adventure in Dynamation!, Ray Harryhausen effects, 1964, 41x27", EX..**$65.00**

Four Feathers, window card, William Powell, Richard Arlen & Fay Wray, close-up of Powell & co-star, 1929, 22x14", EX $150.00

Frenzy, Hitchcock classic, 1972, w/insert, 1972, 44x27", EX $40.00

Friday the 13th, They Were Warned..., moonlit night in the woods w/knife dripping blood, 1980, 41x27", EX .$45.00

Friendly Persuasion, Gary Cooper & Anthony Perkins, 1956, rare B style, 22x14", EX..................................$50.00

From Russian w/Love, Sean Connery as Bond, 1964, 41x27", EX $175.00

Georgy Girl, Lynn Redgrave & James Mason, 1966, 41x27", EX $25.00

Godfather, Marlon Brando, 1972, 22x14", EX.............$50.00

Godfather II, Robert DeNiro, 1974, 40x30", EX...........$45.00

Going My Way, Bing Crosby, 1944, 41x27", EX........$200.00

Gold Rush, Charlie Chaplin, 1942 reissue, 28x22", EX..$225.00

Goldfinger, Sean Connery as Bond, 1964, 41x27", EX..$300.00

Gone w/the Wind, Clark Gable & Vivien Leigh, 1961 reissue, 41x27", EX $200.00

Green Hornet, Van Williams & Bruce Lee, 1977, 41x27", NM $100.00

Hang 'Em High, Clint Eastwood, 1968, 40x30", EX.....$50.00

Hell's Angels, Jean Harlow & Ben Lyon, 1940s reissue, 28x22", EX+...$425.00

High Noon, window card, Gary Cooper w/smoking gun in hand, black & white w/yellow border, 1952, 22x14", VG+..$225.00

Horrors of the Black Museum, 1958, 41x27", EX........$65.00

Indiscreet, Cary Grant & Ingrid Bergman, 1958, 41x27", EX $125.00

It's a Wonderful Life, James Stewart & Donna Reed, 1990 reissue, 41x27", NM $25.00

Jason & the Argonauts, 1963, 41x27", EX $65.00

Judgment at Nuremberg, Spencer Tracy, Marlene Dietrich, Judy Garland & Montgomery Clift, 1961, 40x30", EX $150.00

Kiss Me Kate, Kathryn Grayson, Howard Keel & Ann Miller, 1953, 41x27", EX...$100.00

Kiss of the Vampire, Clifford Evans, 1963, 41x27", EX .$65.00

Lady & the Tramp, Disney animation, 1962, 41x27", EX .$50.00

Lion in Winter, Peter O'Toole & Katharine Hepburn, 1968, 22x14", EX $35.00

Lost World, Michael Rennie, Jill St John, Claude Reins, 1960, 41x27", EX $65.00

Love Slaves of the Amazon, Curt Siodmak classic, 1957, 6-sheet, EX $125.00

Machine Gun Kelly, insert, Charles Bronson, 1958, EX ..$50.00

Man in the Iron Mask, Joan Bennett & Louis Hayward, 1947 reissue, 41x27", EX $40.00

Manchurian Candidate, Frank Sinatra & Laurence Harvey, 1962, 6-sheet, EX $85.00

Miller's Beautiful Wife, Sophia Loren, 1957, 41x27", EX ..$50.00

Muscle Beach Party, Frankie Avalon & Annette Funicello, 1964, 40x30", EX $65.00

New Adventures of Batman & Robin, lobby cards, Columbia, 1949, sepia tones, set of 8 from serial, 11x14", EX...$60.00

Night of the Iguana, Tennessee Williams classic w/Richard Burton, Deborah Kerr & Ava Gardner, 1964, 41x27", EX $50.00

North by Northwest, classic Hitchcock w/Cary Grant, Eva Marie Saint & James Mason, 1959, 22x14", EX $85.00

Nyoka & the Tiger Men, reissue of Perils of Nyoka, Kay Aldridge & Clayton Moore, 1955, 41x27", EX.....$100.00

One Spy Too Many (feature version of Man From UNCLE), 1966, 41x27", EX $50.00

Platinum Blonde, window card, Jean Harlow, 1950, EX .$50.00

Quiet Man, John Wayne & Maureen O'Hara, double-sided, 1951, 3-sheet, EX $400.00

Rear Window, window card, James Stewart & Grace Kelly, 1954, EX $125.00

Ring of Fire, insert, Mickey Spillane, 1954, EX...........$35.00

Rio Lobo, John Wayne, Give 'Em Hell John above image, 1971, 41x27", EX $50.00

Road to Bali, Bing Crosby, Bob Hope & Dorothy Lamour, 1952, 41x27", EX $175.00

Rooster Cogburn, John Wayne & Katharine Hepburn, 1975, 41x27", VG+ $40.00

Sabrina, lobby card, Audrey Hepburn & William Holden, 1954, EX $35.00

Shane, Allan Ladd, Jean Arthur, Van Heflin & Brandon DeWilde, 1959 reissue, 41x27", EX.........................$50.00

Suddenly, Frank Sinatra, 1954, 3-sheet, EX $85.00

The Defector, Montgomery Clift (his last film), 1966, 22x14", EX..$25.00

The Good, The Bad & The Ugly, window card, Clint Eastwood, 1968, M..$75.00

The Racket, Robert Mitchum, Liz Scott & Robert Ryan, RKO graphics, 3-sheet, EX $125.00

The Shootist, John Wayne (last film), Amsel artwork, 1976, 41x27", VG $60.00

The Sun Also Rises, window card, Errol Flynn & Tyrone Power, 1957, 1857, EX...$35.00

The Terror, Jack Nicholson (not pictured), image of Boris Karloff looking at spider web w/trapped woman, 1963, 41x27", EX $65.00

This Island Earth, lobby card, full-color scene showing flying saucer approaching Earth, 1955, 11x14", EX $125.00

Three Little Words, Fred Astaire & Red Skelton, black & white w/red, yellow & blue highlights, 1950, 41x27", EX..$100.00

Three Worlds of Gulliver, shows bottom half of Gulliver as a giant, 1960, 41x27", EX...$65.00

Tobacco Road, Gene Tiereny & Dana Andrews, 1956 reissue, 22x14", EX $45.00

Two for the Road, Audrey Hepburn & Albert Finney, 1967, 44x27", EX $50.00

Two Mules for Sister Sara, Clint Eastwood & Shirley McLaine, 1970, 22x14", EX...$35.00

War & Peace, Hepburn & Fonda, w/insert, 22x14", EX..$65.00

Weird Woman, Soft Arms Killing w/a Voodoo Curse!, Lon Chaney 1952 reissue, 28x22", EX $200.00

Wild One, insert, Marlon Brando, 1954, EX $650.00

Zorro Rides Again, Duncan Renaldo & John Carrol, 1959, 41x27", EX $65.00

Zulu, Michael Caine & Stanley Baker, 1963, 41x27", EX..$65.00

Napkin Dolls

Cocktail, luncheon, or dinner..., paper, cotton, or damask..., solid, patterned, or plaid — regardless of size, color, or material, there's always been a place for napkins. In the late 1940s and early 1950s, buffet-style meals were gaining popularity. One accessory common to many of these buffets is now one of today's hot collectibles — the napkin doll. While most of the ceramic and wooden examples found today date from this period, many homemade napkin dolls were produced in ceramic classes of the 1970s and '80s.

For information on napkin dolls as well as egg timers, string holders, children's whistle cups, baby feeder dishes, razor blade banks, pie birds, laundry sprinkler bottles, and other unique collectibles from the same era, we recommend *Collectibles for the Kitchen, Bath and Beyond*; for ordering information see our advisor's listing in the Directory.

Advisor: Bobbie Zucker Bryson (See Directory, Napkin Dolls)

Betson's yellow Colonial lady, bell clapper, marked Hand Painted Japan, 8½", from $75 to..............................**$90.00**
California Originals, toothpick holder basket over head, foil label, 13¾", from $75 to...**$85.00**
California Originals, white Spanish dancer w/gold trim, splits in rear only, foil label, 13", from $110 to **$125.00**
Enesco, Genie at Your Service, holding lantern, paper label, 8", from $120 to **$130.00**
Goebel, half doll on wire frame, marked Goebel, W Germany, ca 1957, 9", from $175 to **$195.00**
Holland Mold, Daisy, No 514, 7¼", from $75 to.........**$90.00**
Holland Mold, Rebecca No H-265, 10½", from $130 to.**$155.00**
Holland Mold, Rosie, No H-132, 10¼", from $55 to...**$65.00**
Holt Howard, pink Sunbonnet Miss, marked Holt Howard 1958, 5", from $85 to...**$115.00**
Japan, angel, pink, holding flowers, 5⅜", from $95 to.**$125.00**
Japan, lady in green w/pink umbrella, bell clapper, unmarked, 9"..**$80.00**
Japan, lady in pink dress w/blue shawl & yellow hat, 8½", from $60 to..**$75.00**
Japan, Santa, marked Chess, 1957, 6¾", from $95 to.**$115.00**
Kreiss & Co, blue lady w/candle holder behind hat, from $60 to **$75.00**
Kreiss & Co, green lady holding fan, candle holder behind fan, marked, 8¾", from $70 to...............................**$90.00**
Kreiss & Co, yellow doll w/gold trim holding muff, jeweled eyes, candle holder in top of hat, marked, 10", from $95 to..**$110.00**
Kreiss & Co, yellow doll w/poodle, jeweled eyes, necklace & ring, candle holder behind hat, marked, 10¾", from $95 to..**$115.00**
Man (bartender), holding tray w/candle holder, 8¾", from $95 to **$110.00**
Metal, silhouette of Deco woman, black & gold w/wire bottom, 8⅞", from $100 to **$125.00**
Miss Versatility Cocktail Girl, 13", from $65 to **$85.00**

Pink and white dress with holes, tray over head for toothpicks, 9¼", from $65.00 to $75.00. (Photo courtesy Bobbie Zucker Bryson)

Rooster, white w/red & black trim, slits in tail for napkins, w/egg salt & pepper shakers, from $35 to..........**$45.00**
Sevy Etta, wood w/marble base, marked USD Patent No 159,005, 11½", from $35 to **$45.00**
Swedish doll, wooden, marked Patent No 113861, 12", from $25 to...**$35.00**
Wooden Jamaican lady, movable arms, papel label: Ave 13 Nov 743, A Sinfonia, Tel 2350 Petropolis, 6", from $65 to **$85.00**
Wooden pink & blue doll w/strawberry toothpick holder on head, 8", from $60 to..**$75.00**
Yamihaya Bros, lady holding yoke w/bucket salt & pepper shakers, hat conceals candle holder, from $100 to........**$135.00**

New Martinsville

Located in a West Virginia town by the same name, the New Martinsville Glass Company was founded in 1901 and until it was purchased by Viking in 1944 produced quality tableware in various patterns and colors that collectors admire today. They also made a line of glass animals which Viking continued to produce until they closed in 1986. In 1987 the factory was bought by Mr. Kenneth Dalzell who reopened the company under the title Dalzell-Viking. He used the old molds to reissue his own line of animals, which he marked 'Dalzell' with an acid stamp. These are usually priced in the $50.00 to $60.00 range. Examples marked 'V' were made by Viking for another company, Mirror Images. They're valued at $15.00 to $35.00, with colors sometimes higher.

Advisor: Roselle Schleifman (See Directory, Elegant Glass)

Basket, Janice, crystal, oval, 10x12" **$85.00**
Bowl, fruit; Janice, crystal, ruffled top, 12".................**$55.00**
Bowl, Prelude, crystal, 12" **$50.00**
Bowl, Radiance, ruby w/Prelude etch, 12"....................**$60.00**
Candlestick, Janice, light blue, #4554, 5" **$45.00**
Candy box, Prelude, crystal, 3-footed, w/lid, 7" **$65.00**
Champagne, Prelude **$22.00**
Condiment set: tray & 2 covered jars, Janice, crystal..**$60.00**

Cordial, Radiance, red $35.00
Cup, punch; Mildred, Hostmaster, amber $17.00
Figurine, bear, baby, crystal, head turned or straight, 3",
    ea $60.00
Figurine, bear, papa, crystal, 4x6½" $250.00
Figurine, chick, crystal frost, 1" $25.00
Figurine, eagle, crystal, 8" $85.00
Figurine, German shepherd, crystal, 5" $75.00
Figurine, horse, crystal, head up, 8" $95.00
Figurine, piglet, crystal, standing $95.00
Figurine, rabbit, mama, crystal $350.00
Figurine, seal, baby w/ball, crystal $60.00
Figurine, seal, candlesticks, crystal, lg, pr $150.00
Figurine, seal w/ball, candle holder, black, rare, ea.$650.00
Figurine, ship, bookend, crystal, ea $55.00
Figurine, swan, candle holders, ruby, pr $70.00
Figurine, tiger, crystal, head up, 6½" $225.00
Figurine, woodsman, crystal, square base, 7⅜" $135.00
Goblet, water; Hilton, clear w/blue band $9.00
Jug, ruby..$90.00
Mint dish, Radiance, light blue, handles, #4237, 5" $45.00
Pitcher, Oscar, red..$95.00
Plate, torte; Prelude, 14"...$55.00

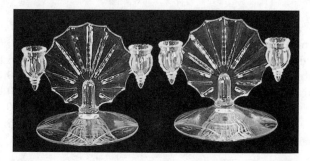

Radiance, candle holders, crystal, wheel cut, pair, $130.00.

Relish, Janice, light blue, handled, 6" $35.00
Relish, Radiance, light blue, #4228, 8½" $55.00
Tumbler, Amy, footed, #34 ....$20.00
Vase, Prelude, crystal, footed, 11" $75.00
Wine, Hostmaster, Mildred, ruby, 4x2¼" $8.00

Niloak Pottery

The Niloak Pottery company was the continuation of a quarter-century-old family business in Benton, Arkansas. Known as the Eagle Pottery in the early twentieth century, its owner was Charles Dean Hyten who continued in his father's footsteps making utilitarian wares for local and state markets. In 1909 Arthur Dovey, an experienced potter formerly from the Rookwood Pottery of Ohio and the Arkansas-Missouri based Ouachita Pottery companies, came to Benton and created America's most unusual art pottery. Introduced in 1910 as Niloak (kaolin spelled backwards), Dovey and Hyten produced art pottery pieces from swirling clays with a wide range of artificially created colors including red, blue, cream, brown, gray, and later green. Connected to the Arts & Crafts Movement by 1913, the pottery was labeled as Missionware (probably due to its seeming simplicity in the making). Missionware (or swirl) production continued alongside utilitarian ware manufacturing until the 1930s when economic factors led to the making of another type of art pottery and later to (molded) industrial castware. In 1931 Niloak Pottery introduced Hywood Art Pottery (marked as such), consisting of regular glaze techniques including overspray, mottling, and drips of two colors on vases and bowls that were primarily hand thrown. It was short-lived and soon replaced with the Hywood by Niloak (or Hywood) line to increase marketing potential through the use of the well-recognized Niloak name. Experienced potters, designers, and ceramists were involved at Niloak; among them were Frank Long, Paul Cox, Stoin M. Stoin, Howard Lewis, and Rudy Ganz. Many local families with long ties to the pottery included the McNeills, Rowlands, and Alleys. Experiencing tremendous financial woes by the mid-1930s, Niloak came under new management which was led by Hardy L. Winburn of Little Rock. To maximize efficiency and stay competetive, they focused primarily on industrial castware such as vases, bowls, figurines, animals, and planters. Niloak survived into the late 1940s when it became known as the Winburn Tile Company of North Little Rock; it still exists today.

Virtually all of Niloak Missionware/swirl pottery is marked with die stamps. The exceptions are generally fan vases, wall pockets, lamp bases, and whiskey jugs. Be careful when you buy unmarked swirl pottery — it is usually Evans pottery (made in Missouri) which generally has either no interior glaze or is chocolate brown inside. Moreover, Evans made swirl wall pockets, lamp bases, and even hanging baskets that find their way on to today's market and are sold as Niloak. Niloak stickers are often placed on these unmarked Evans pieces — closely examine the condition of the sticker to determine if it is damaged or mutilated from the transfer process.

For more information, we recommend *The Collector's Encyclopedia of Niloak Pottery* (Collector Books) by our advisor David Edwin Gifford, a historian of Arkansas pottery.

Advisor: David Edwin Gifford (See Directory, Niloak)

Mission Ware

Humidor, predominately red, first art mark, $350.00. (Photo courtesy David Edwin Gifford)

Ashtray/match holder, 2 rests, 4½" dia $225.00
Bean pot, w/handles & lid, early mark, 7¼"............ $325.00
Box, w/lid, 2x2½x2½" $135.00
Clock, replaced quartz movement within round 4½"
    frame $425.00
Flower frog, unmarked, 1x2½" $82.00
Matchstick holder, slightly flared base, 1½" dia $85.00
Stein/mug, marked Patent Pend'g, 4¼" $300.00
Tumbler, 4½" $110.00
Vase, bulbous, 2nd art mark, 5½" $100.00
Vase, classic form, flared rim, marked Patent Pend'g,
    10¼".. $325.00
Vase, cylindrical, bottle neck w/flared rim, 1st art mark,
    10" $275.00
Water bottle, w/cork-wrapped stopper, 8½" $410.00

Miscellaneous

Ashtray, swan figure w/2 rests, gloss, N mark, 5½" ... $35.00
Bowl, Peter Pan resting on top, gloss, 8" $55.00
Box, woven design, gloss, marked Niloak in block letters,
    3½x5 .... $50.00
Candle holder, leaf design, gloss, marked Niloak in let-
    ters, 3½" $45.00

**Clown, 7½", $45.00; elephant, 6", $38.00. (Photo
courtesy David Edwin Gifford)**

Creamer, cow w/tail handle, unmarked (sticker only), gloss,
    4½" L.. $85.00
Ewer, exaggerated handle & spout, gloss, mini, 2¾" . $28.00
Figurine, deer, alert pose w/extended ears, matt, 10" . $98.00
Figurine, dog, I'm Lost on tag, 2½"...................... $28.00
Figurine, elephant w/trunk extended, matt, 7½" L..... $75.00
Figurine, razorback hog, w/or w/o U of A, matt, 4" . $100.00
Figurines, birds, various, matt, N mark, 2x2¾", ea $12.00
Figurines, various, 1½x3", ea, from $10 to $25.00
Pitcher, ball form w/ice lip, gloss, marked Niloak in block
    letters, 7½" $36.00
Planter, Aladdin lamp style, gloss, 4x5½" $20.00
Planter, duck, standing, well detailed, gloss, impressed mark,
    4¼" $21.50
Planter, elephant balanced on drum, matt, marked Niloak in
    block letters, 6½" $38.00

Planter, fox w/lg bushy tail resting, gloss, 5½" L........ $45.00
Planter, wooden shoe, matt, w/sticker, 4½" L............ $11.00
Shakers, various shapes, 1¾x3", pr, from $15 to $35.00
Strawberry jar, 6 bud-shaped openings, matt, marked Niloak
    in block letters, 9½"...................................... $65.00
Vase, bud; stacked pedestal base, matt, marked Hywood by
    Niloak, 8½".. $35.00
Vase, ribbed fan shape w/flared base, matt, marked Hywood
    by Niloak, 7¼" $37.00
Vase, Winged Victory, 7" $16.00

Novelty Radios

Novelty radios come in an unimaginable variety of
shapes and sizes from advertising and product shapes to
character forms, vehicles, and anything else the manufacturer might dream up. For information on these new, fun collectibles read *Collector's Guide to Novelty Radios* by Marty
Bunis and Robert Breed, and *Schroeder's Collectible Toys,
Antique to Modern* (Collector Books).

Advisor: Marty and Sue Bunis (See Directory, Novelty
Radios)

Agway Super Latex paint can, EX $30.00
Animal Crackers, Keebler, braided handle, EX........... $70.00
Austin Quality Crackers, 4⅜x3", EX $65.00
Automash Potato Mix, French's, EX $30.00
Budweiser, Isis model #39, EX $30.00
Cheez-It Snack Crackers, Sunshine, Isis model #39, EX . $30.00
Coca-Cola Classic, Isis Billboard, EX.......................... $85.00

**Coca-Cola Vending
Machine, China,
1989, MIB, $65.00.
(Photo courtesy
June Moon)**

Duracell Alkaline Battery, D cell, 5½" $50.00
Exide Ultra Start Battery, USA, EX........................... $75.00
Fujicolor Super HR, Isis model #39, EX.................... $30.00
Gain Baby Formula, EX....................................... $85.00
Heileman's Old Style Beer, EX $60.00
Heineken Lager Beer, EX...................................... $45.00
Hippo, dancing, 3-D, Hong Kong, EX $30.00
Hydrox Cookies, Sunshine, Isis model #39, EX $30.00

Kangaroo, boxing gloves, Official Product of America Cup Defense, 1987, Korea, 11" **$85.00**
King Cobra, Premium Malt Liquor, Isis model #103, EX.**$30.00**
Kitchen Tunes, combination radio/can opener, Hamilton Beach, EX..................**$25.00**
Light 'N Lively Lowfat Cottage Cheese, Isis model #103, EX **$45.00**
Little Debbie Swiss Cake Rolls, Isis model #103, EX ..**$30.00**
Marlboro, pack form, Hong Kong, 2½x3½", EX.........**$85.00**

Mickey Mouse, ears are controls, marked Walt Disney Productions, 3x3x1¼", $15.00. (Photo courtesy Lee Garmon)

Midland Enterprises, First on the River, 3x5", EX........**$30.00**
Moosehead Beer, FM only, 1½x3¾", EX **$30.00**
Nesquik Milk Shake Mix, Nestle's, strawberry flavor, EX..**$45.00**
Old Spice, Isis aerosol can radio, model #105, FM only, 7", EX..................**$85.00**
Olympia Pale Export Beer, EX..................**$45.00**
Power 99FM, Energizer Bunny on front, Isis model #39, EX **$45.00**
RADIO CKST 1070, red letters spelling radio, Isis model #20-1, EX..................**$45.00**
Royal Caribbean Cruise Lines, can shape, white w/red & blue logo, EX..................**$45.00**
Seashell, pendant w/24" chain, Hong Kong, 3¼x3¼", EX..................**$85.00**
The Club, Trump PLaza, Isis model #39, EX..............**$30.00**
Wix Oil Filter #51068, white w/red lettering, EX........**$60.00**

Novelty Telephones

Novelty telephones modeled after products or advertising items are popular with collectors — so are those that are character related. For further information we recommend *Schroeder's Collectible Toys, Antique to Modern* (Collector Books).

AC Sparkplug, EX **$35.00**
Alvin, 1984, 15", M..**$60.00**
Bart Simpson, Columbia Tel-Com, 1990s, MIB...........**$35.00**
Batmobile (Batman Forever), MIB, from $35 to.........**$50.00**
Crest Sparkle, NMIB **$50.00**
Ghostbusters, M **$100.00**
Gumball Machine, MIB **$135.00**
Keebler Elf, NM **$100.00**
Kermit the Frog, candlestick-type, MIB..................**$80.00**

Mario Brothers, 1980s, MIB..................**$50.00**
Mickey Mouse, 1988, MIB..................**$50.00**
Oscar Meyer Weiner, EX **$65.00**

Raggedy Ann Talking Telephone, Copyright Bobbs-Merrill, 1980, 9", from $20.00 to $25.00. (Photo courtesy Kim Avery)

Snoopy, as Joe Cool, 1980s, MIB **$55.00**
Snoopy & Woodstock, American Telephone Corporation, 1976, touch-tone, EX..................**$100.00**
Spider-Man Climbing Down Chimney, NM, from $165 to .**$200.00**
Super Bowl XIX, full-size helmet, w/handset, NM.....**$70.00**
Winnie the Pooh, square base, M, from $225 to **$250.00**
Ziggy, 1989, MIB..................**$75.00**

Occupied Japan Collectibles

Some items produced in Japan during the period from the end of WWII until the occupation ended in 1952 were marked Occupied Japan. No doubt much of the ware from this era was marked simply Japan, since obviously the 'Occupied' term caused considerable resentment among the Japanese people, and they were understandably reluctant to use the mark. So even though you may find identical items marked simply Japan or Made in Japan, only those with the more limited Occupied Japan mark are evaluated here.

Assume that the items described below are ceramic unless another material is mentioned. For more information, we recommend *The Collector's Encyclopedia of Occupied Japan* (there are five in the series) by Gene Florence. (All are published by Collector Books.)

Newsletter: *The Upside Down World of an O.J. Collector*
The Occupied Japan Club, c/o Florence Archambault
29 Freeborn St., Newport, RI 02840-1821
Published bimonthly. Information requires SASE.

Ashtray, Indian head in profile, embossed detail, tan lustre, 3½" **$12.50**
Ashtray, copper w/embossed image of sailboat in center & decorative rim, embossed SNK in diamond..........**$5.00**

Biscuit/cookie jar, red tomato form w/rattan handle, Maruhonware w/K in circle, from $85 to **$100.00**

Cigarette box, Chinese man carrying box w/dragon on lid, gold trim, 6½" **$30.00**

Coaster, papier-mache, rose design, marked Isco alcohol proof, from $2.50 to................................**$4.00**

Coasters in box, papier-mache, set of 8, from $30 to.**$35.00**

Cornucopia, white bisque w/pink embossed & applied roses & green leaves, gold trim on rim & footed base, Lamore/GZL USA.......................................**$40.00**

Creamer & sugar bowl, silver-tone metal w/embossed decoration, footed, embossed w/rising sun mark........**$17.50**

Crumb pan, metal w/embossed images of New York sights w/decorative rim..............................**$12.50**

Cup & saucer, demitasse; black w/white lacy flower design around middle, gold-trimmed handle, green HB in diamond..**$15.00**

Cup & saucer, demitasse; black w/2 flowers, slightly scalloped rim, gold trim, Ardalt HP Lenwile China 6195.......**$22.50**

Cup & saucer, demitasse; gold decoration on rust swirled form w/scalloped rim, ornate gold handle...........**$12.50**

Cup & saucer, white w/black decoration over red hearts around rim on cup & saucer, gold trim, red mark..**$10.00**

Dish, fish form, tan lustre w/blue tint, circle K mark.**$12.50**

Dish, leaf form, brown w/white sunflower & blue leaves, handled, embossed Made In Occupied Japan......**$10.00**

Dish, metal leaf form w/bunch of grapes embossed at 1 side **$4.00**

Dish, shell form, white w/scene of couple on path, gold trim, blue elephant A symbol, sm **$8.00**

Dish, square & flat w/Oriental scene on white, black rim, 6x6"...**$20.00**

Fan, paper w/wooden stick handle, unfolds to form circle w/rainbow of colors **$3.00**

Fans, paper folding type w/wooden sticks, various decorative scenes & images, ea **$10.00**

Figurine, boy playing concertina, 2½" **$3.00**

Figurine, cherub on handle of leaf-formed basket, bisque w/pink & gold trim, 5"..................................**$60.00**

Figurine, cherub sitting on upright cornucopia playing concertina, bisque w/pink & gold trim, marked HP Andrea, 5¼"..**$70.00**

Figurine, colonial couple in working-class clothing playing musical instruments, bisque, 7½", pr **$65.00**

Figurine, colonial couple w/man seated serenading lady w/flute, embossed gold-trimmed base, 7", from $75 to **$85.00**

Figurine, colonial couple w/sled & dog, embossed gold trim on base, 5¾", from $200 to **$250.00**

Figurine, dancing boy & girl on ovoid base, heads tilted back as if ready to twirl, bisque **$25.00**

Figurine, dancing lady holding up skirt w/both hands, Hadson w/anchor mark, 3½"........................**$15.00**

Figurine, dancing lady w/hands behind head w/hat & swirling skirt, white w/painted face, gold trim, 5½" **$17.50**

Figurine, Dutch girl w/head tilted & hand to face standing on round base w/milk can, from $15 to **$20.00**

Figurine, Dutch peasant couple, strong colors, gold-trimmed bases, red mark, 8¼", pr, from $65 to **$75.00**

Figurine, elf on caterpillar, pastel colors w/brown dots on caterpillar, 3½" **$15.00**

Figurine, girl in long mid-19th century dress w/song book, Ucago, 5¾"....................................**$40.00**

Figurine, girl musicians in robes playing concertina, mandolin & bass, 5¾", ea **$22.00**

Figurine, girl shelf sitter, in dress w/bow in hair, legs crossed at ankles **$17.50**

Figurine, horses (2) jumping on elongated base, glossy brown w/black manes & tails, blue circle T mark, 5" **$50.00**

Figurine, lady with net dress, 9", from $50.00 to $60.00. (Photo courtesy Gene Florence)

Figurine, ladybug baseball player w/bat, 2¼" **$8.00**

Figurine, ladybug w/broom, brown, #92796, 4".........**$12.00**

Figurine, Mexican lady w/lg hat & long pigtails holding basket at waist w/1 hand, striped sarape on shoulder, Ucagco, 7" **$40.00**

Figurine, Mexican on donkey, multicolored whimsical depiction on white base w/gold trim, red mark, 8¼" ..**$30.00**

Figurine, Mexican standing next to sm donkey, bisque, realistic depiction, ornate base w/gold trim, 8".........**$30.00**

Figurine, musketeer bust on pedestal, bisque, lg **$30.00**

Figurine, organ grinder w/monkey, colorful whimsical figure on round white base w/gold trim, red mark, 6" ..**$25.00**

Figurine, Oriental girl seated between 2 baskets w/parasol behind head, white base w/gold trim, red mark, 5" **$17.50**

Figurine, Oriental lady standing w/hands crossed at chest holding fan, gray & black w/round black base, 8".........**$20.00**

Figurine, pastoral couple standing by fences, bisque, 8", pr, from $100 to................................**$125.00**

Figurine, peacock w/head up & tail curled around feet, multicolored w/gold trim, 5"........................**$20.00**

Figurine, peasant lady w/basket of fruit on head & man w/bouquet of flowers, bisque, 6½", pr.................**$60.00**

Ice bucket w/tongs, red lacquered metal w/colorful florals, sm, from $35 to................................**$50.00**

Lamp, Chinese boy seated Indian style on platform reading, bright colors, metal 4-footed base, 6" **$40.00**

Lamp, cowboy figure on square base, bisque, red mark, 7½"..**$40.00**

Lamp base, double-sided wooden square form on base w/Oriental-type painted tree & leaf design w/lacquered finish...**$75.00**

Marmalade, white beehive house w/chimney on green lid, marked w/T in circle..**$20.00**

Match holder, coal hod, white or black w/scenes & gold trim, red or green mark, ea **$12.50**

Miniature baskets, various florals, 1¼" to 2", ea, from $3 to..**$6.00**

Mug, toby style w/mustache, about 4"....................**$35.00**

Needle packets, various..**$5.00**

Novelty, celluloid dog, setter-type w/collar.............**$12.50**

Novelty, celluloid doll, jointed, molded hooded outfit in yellow w/red neck bow & shoes, sm.....................**$25.00**

Novelty, celluloid doll, nude standing w/legs molded together, jointed arms, about 3"..................................**$17.50**

Novelty, celluloid donkey w/nodding head, from $30 to.**$35.00**

Novelty, cowboy boot, tan on cream w/blue floral accents, 6½"...**$8.00**

Novelty, hanger, papier-mache bird w/feathers, from $15 to **$20.00**

Novelty, miniature coffeepot w/lid, blue w/embossed pink rose & green leaves, from $8 to **$10.00**

Novelty, miniature pitcher, Wedgwood urn style w/lady playing mandolin, 2½", from $8 to **$10.00**

Novelty, miniature satchels, various decorations, red mark, 2", ea, from $4 to **$5.00**

Novelty, miniature teapots, various glazes & decorations, ea, from $8 to...**$10.00**

Novelty, miniature wheelbarrow, applied roses, spoked wheel, 1½x5", from $8 to...**$10.00**

Novelty, miniature wheelbarrow, blue w/embossed pink rose, green mark, from $4 to **$5.00**

Novelty, pipe-cleaner rooster w/felt comb & waddle, sm .**$12.50**

Novelty, Rag Time Band, boxed set of 6 figures atop wooden barrels, ea $4 or set from $25 to.....................**$30.00**

Novelty, wooden sampan boat on base w/Chinese symbols, sm **$15.00**

Planter, cucumber form in green glossy glaze w/yellow & black accents **$10.00**

Planter, dog w/whimsical chubby face & neck bow sitting upright, cream w/light pastel airbrushing, Arch emblem, 4"...**$6.00**

Planter, elf in red w/white collar leaning against light brown tree trunk, vegetation at bottom, high gloss, 5" ...**$18.00**

Planter, horse-drawn covered wagon, airbrushed pastel colors w/black wheels..**$7.00**

Planter, kitten sitting upright next to basket, black & white high gloss, horseshoe emblem, 3⅝"..................**$9.00**

Planter, seashell nestled on base of seaweed, browns, tans & muted greens in semigloss, blue mark **$15.00**

Planter, shoe w/treaded sole & bouquet of applied flowers on laces, blue airbrushing w/multicolored flowers, 3½"...**$8.00**

Planter, speedboat w/driver on waves, brushed colors.**$20.00**

Planter, zebra, whimsical...**$12.00**

Relish dish, 2-part w/bees on honeycomb design & bee in center, marked w/T in circle............................**$20.00**

Ring box, round Wedgwood style w/beveled lid **$20.00**

Sewing kit, sm round tin w/pincushion top, holds spools of thread & thimble..**$20.00**

Snack set, cup & plate, marked w/red G in ivy, from $12 to...**$15.00**

Souvenir ashtray, Florida, shaped like state w/name & theme images on white, gold-trimmed edge, Burger of Miami..**$15.00**

Souvenir ashtray, New York, metal oval w/embossed image of Statue of Liberty & skyline, decorative rim, Enco 2T388 ....**$12.50**

Souvenir plate, Niagara Falls, painted scene, plain rim w/gold trim **$10.00**

Stein, 3 Musketeers w/musical instruments in tavern scene, white or brown rim, 6½", ea **$25.00**

Tea set, teapot w/4 cups & saucers, white w/allover pink floral design & green leaves, from $60 to................**$75.00**

Teapot, beehive form w/white honeycomb design & bee finial, green handle & spout, marked w/T in circle **$45.00**

Teapot, stoneware, ridged ball shape w/bamboo handle, marked w/K in circle, from $30 to.......................**$35.00**

Tray, papier-mache, rectangular, lg, from $15 to **$17.50**

Tray, papier-mache, rectangular, sm, from $8 to **$10.00**

Umbrella, paper w/colorful design, 36" dia, from $25 to..**$30.00**

Vase, lg applied pink rose w/3 leaves & embossed tan vines on green airbrushed bulbous body w/cylindrical neck, 4¼"...**$20.00**

Vase, urn style w/embossed pale blue floral design on pale pink, scrolled handles at neck, 6¼" **$25.00**

Wall plaques, bisque, Chinese man or woman & garden scene w/stream embossed on ovals w/decorative borders, ea **$25.00**

Wall plaques, chalkware, Japanese couple in motion w/baskets, bright colors, ea **$25.00**

Wall shelf unit, lacquerware, colorful Oriental scene painted on back w/top painted white to resemble Mt Fugi.......**$60.00**

Old MacDonald's Farm

This is a wonderful line of novelty kitchenware items fashioned as the family and the animals that live on Old MacDonald's Farm. It's been popular with collectors for quite some time, and prices are astronomical, though they seem to have stabilized, at least for now.

These things were made by the Regal China Company, who also made some of the Little Red Riding Hood items that are so collectible, as well as figural cookie jars, 'hugger' salt and pepper shakers, and decanters. The Roerigs devote a chapter to Regal in their book *The Collector's Encyclopedia of Cookie Jars* and, in fact, show the entire Old MacDonald's Farm line.

Advisor: Rick Spencer (See Directory, Regal China)

Butter dish, cow's head...$220.00
Canister, flour, cereal or coffee, med, ea...................$220.00
Canister, pretzels, peanuts, popcorn, chips or tidbits, lg,
    ea...$300.00
Canister, salt, sugar or tea, med, ea $220.00
Canister, cookies, lg..$300.00

Canister, soap, large, $300.00. (Photo courtesy Pat and Ann Duncan)

Cookie jar, barn...$275.00
Creamer, rooster $110.00
Grease jar, pig..$175.00
Pitcher, milk $400.00
Salt & pepper shakers, boy & girl, pr $75.00
Salt & pepper shakers, churn, gold trim, pr...............$90.00
Salt & pepper shakers, feed sacks w/sheep, pr........$195.00
Spice jar, assorted lids, sm, ea..................................$100.00
Sugar bowl, hen..$125.00
Teapot, duck's head $250.00

Paper Dolls

One of the earliest producers of paper dolls was Raphael Tuck of England, who distributed many of their dolls in the United States in the late 1800s. Advertising companies used them to promote their products, and some were often included in the pages of leading ladies' magazines.

But over the years, the most common paper dolls have been those printed on the covers of a book containing their clothes on the inside pages. These were initiated during the 1920s and because they were inexpensive retained their popularity even during the Depression years. They peaked in the 1940s, but with the advent of television in the '50s, children began to loose interest. Be sure to check old boxes and trunks in your attic; you just may find some!

But what's really exciting right now are those from more recent years — celebrity dolls from television shows like 'The Brady Bunch' or 'The Waltons,' the skinny English model Twiggy, and movie stars like Rock Hudson and Debbie Reynolds. Our values are for paper dolls in mint, uncut, original condition. Just remember that cut sets (even if all origi-

nal components are still there) are worth only about half as much. Damaged sets or those with missing pieces should be priced accordingly. Prices below are for uncut and original paper dolls in mint condition.

If you'd like to learn more about them, we recommend *Collector's Guide to Paper Dolls* (there are two in the series) and *Collector's Guide to Magazine Paper Dolls,* all by Mary Young. Other references: *Schroeder's Collectible Toys, Antique to Modern;* and *Toys, Antique and Collectible,* by David Longest. (All of these books are published by Collector Books.)

Advisor: Mary Young (See Directory, Paper Dolls)

Newsletter: *Paper Dolls News*
Ema Terry
P.O. Box 807
Vivian, LA 71082; Subscription: $12 per year for 4 issues; want lists, sale items and trades listed

Annie Oakley, Whitman #1960, 1956...........................$75.00
Archie, Whitman #4743, 1969 ....$28.00
Baby Show, Lowe #1021, 1940....................................$75.00
Badgett Quadruplets, Saalfield #2348, 1941...............$125.00

Brownie Scout Paper Doll, one doll with mohair, deJournett Mfg., uncut, MIB, from $30.00 to $40.00.

Carmen Miranda, Whitman #995, 1942......................$160.00
Cradle Tots, 8-page book, Merrill #3455, 1945............$90.00
Donna Reed, Saalfield #4412, 1959 ....$65.00
Dotty Double, Saalfield #977, 1933 ....$50.00
Dr Kildare, Lowe #955 ....$25.00
Eve Arden, Saalfield #4310, 1953 ....$125.00
Gene Autry's Melody Ranch, Whitman #990, 1950...$100.00
Girls in the War (Turnabout), Lowe #1028, 1943......$125.00
Golden Girl, Merrill #1543, 1953 ....$75.00
Hayley Mills 'The Moonspinners,' Whitman #1960, 1964..$50.00
Here's Sally/Here's Sunny, Whitman #915, 1939.........$75.00
High School Dolls, Merrill #1551, 1948........................$75.00
Hollywood Personalities, Lowe #1049, 1941, minimum
    value $200.00
Honeymooners, Lowe #2560, 1956 ....$250.00
Jeanette MacDonald, Merrill #3460, 1941, minimum value..$175.00
Judy Garland, Whitman #980, 1941............................$200.00
Kim Novak, Saalfield #4409, 1957 ....$125.00

Laugh-In Party, Saalfield #6045, 1969............................$50.00
Little Family & Their Little House, Merrill #1561, 1949.$85.00
Little Women, Lowe #1030, 1941..................................$65.00
Little Women, Saalfield #1345, 1963 ....$35.00
Margaret O'Brien, Whitman #964, 1946.......................$100.00
Mary Poppins, Whitman #1982, 1964.............................$35.00
Mod Fashions Featuring Jane Fonda, Saalfield #4469,
    1966...$45.00
Mommy & Me, Whitman #977, 1954...............................$30.00
Mother & Daughter, Saalfield, #1330, 1962..................$25.00
My Fair Lady, Columbia Broadcasting #2960-2, 1965 .$50.00
Nanny & the Professor, Artcraft #4213, 1970 ....$40.00
Oklahoma! A Golden Paper Doll Story Book, Simon &
    Schuster, 1956...$95.00
Ozzie & Harriet, Saalfield #4319, 1954.......................$125.00
Partridge Family, Artcraft #5137, 1971.........................$50.00

Partridge Family, Saalfield #6050, 1971, uncut, M, from $45.00 to $55.00.

Patti Page, Lowe #2406, 1957 ....$75.00
Pink Wedding, 8-page book, Merrill #1559, 1952 ....$65.00
Quiz Kids, Saalfield #2430, 1942 ....$150.00
Raggedy Ann & Andy, Whitman #1977-23, 1980 ....$18.00
Rhonda Fleming, Saalfield #4320, 1954......................$100.00
Riders of the West, Saalfield #2716, 1950....................$35.00
Robin Hood & Maid Marian, Saalfield #2748, 1956.....$75.00
Rock Hudson, Whitman #2087, 1957 ....$65.00
Roy Rogers, Whitman #995, 1948.................................$125.00
Roy Rogers & Dale Evans, Whitman #2197, 1952.......$85.00
Shari Lewis & Her Puppets, Saalfield #6060, 1960......$60.00
Shirley Temple, Saalfield #1715, 1935, minimum value ..$175.00
Snow White & the Prince, Whitman #4732, 1967 ....$35.00
Sunshine Family, Whitman #1976, 1974.......................$15.00
Sweet-Treat Kiddles, Whitman #1993-59, 1969............$55.00
Toni Hair-Do Cut-Out Dolls, Lowe #1284, 1950..........$65.00
Trica, Saalfield #4248, 1970...$40.00
Tyrone Power & Linda Darnell, Merrill #3438, 1941..$275.00
Walking Paper Doll Family, Saalfield #1074, 1934......$85.00
Walt Disney's Mouseketeer Cut-Outs, Whitman #1959,
    1957 ....$60.00
Walt Disney's Mouseketeer Annette, Whitman #1958, 1956..$50.00
White House, Saalfield #4475, 1969 ....$40.00

Pencil Sharpeners

The whittling process of sharpening pencils with pocketknives was replaced by mechanical means in the 1880s. By the turn of the century, many ingenious desk-type sharpeners had been developed. Small pencil sharpeners designed for the purse or pocket were produced in the 1890s. The typical design consisted of a small steel tube containing a cutting blade which could be adjusted by screws. Mass-produced novelty pencil sharpeners became popular in the late 1920s. The most detailed figurals were made in Germany. These German sharpeners that originally sold for less than a dollar are now considered highly collectible!

Disney and other character pencil sharpeners have been produced in Catalin, plastic, ceramic, and rubber. Novelty battery-operated pencil sharpeners can also be found. For over fifty years pencil sharpeners have been used as advertising giveaways — from Baker's Chocolates and Coca-Cola's metal figurals to the plastic 'Marshmallow Man' distributed by McDonald's. As long as we have pencils, new pencil sharpeners will be produced, much to the delight of collectors.

Advisors: Phil Helley; Martha Hughes (See Directory, Pencil Sharpeners)

Bakelite, Baby Hep, WDP, round.................................$30.00
Bakelite, Bambi, WDP, round, 1"..................................$55.00
Bakelite, Br'er Fox, round & fluted, 1⅜" $45.00
Bakelite, Cinderella, decal, round, EX $85.00
Bakelite, Donald Duck, decal, round, 1", EX $35.00
Bakelite, Dopey, figural, 1¾", EX...............................$125.00
Bakelite, elephant, 1⅝", from $50 to $65.00
Bakelite, Goofy, round & fluted, 1½" $50.00
Bakelite, Hep Cats, round & fluted, 1⅜" $40.00
Bakelite, Jiminy Cricket, decal, rectangular, EX..........$40.00
Bakelite, Joe Carioca, decal, rectangular, EX..............$40.00
Bakelite, Lampwick, WDP, figural, 1¾" $65.00
Bakelite, mantel clock, Germany, 2".............................$50.00
Bakelite, Pablo, round & fluted, 1" $45.00
Bakelite, Panchito, WDP, round, 1"..............................$40.00
Bakelite, paneled cylinder, 2½".....................................$12.00
Bakelite, pig, 1⅜" $75.00
Bakelite, Popeye, decal, round, EX..............................$80.00

Bakelite, red airplane, 2½" wide, from $35.00 to $45.00. (Photo courtesy Timothy Northup)

Bakelite, scottie dog, 1⅝", from $25 to......................$40.00
Bakelite, Snow White, WDE, figural, 1¾"....................$78.00
Bakelite, Thumper, WDP, round, 1"............................$50.00
Bakelite, US Army tank, 2"..$60.00
Bakelite, USA Army plane...$80.00
Bakelite, Walt Disney's train, figural, 1¾"..................$85.00
Bakelite, 1" sharpener on key chain w/Humble/Esso
    tag $25.00
Bakelite, 1939 NY World's Fair..................................$80.00
Celluloid, Japan, pelican, 3".....................................$130.00
Metal, alarm clock, Japan...$40.00
Metal, banjo, w/glass back, Germany, 2¾"...............$60.00
Metal, British guard in guard house, Germany, 1½"..$75.00
Metal, Charlie Chaplin, Germany, 2¼"....................$125.00
Metal, Coke bottle, Bavaria, 1¾"..............................$40.00
Metal, cuckoo clock, Germany, 2¼".........................$130.00
Metal, Eiffel Tower, Germany, 2¼"............................$90.00
Metal, Felix the Cat, 1½"...$175.00
Metal, frog w/crown, Germany, 1".............................$75.00
Metal, Great Dane, Germany, 2"................................$85.00
Metal, piano player, Germany, 2"...............................$90.00
Metal, rifle, Japan, 3½"..$75.00
Metal, soccer player, Germany, 1¾".........................$100.00
Metal, stop-&-go light, 2¼".......................................$70.00
Metal, Uncle Sam walking, 2"....................................$65.00
Occupied Japan, Black Uncle Sam w/bow tie..........$150.00
Occupied Japan, bulldog head, 1½"...........................$95.00
Occupied Japan, clown w/bow tie $75.00
Occupied Japan, Indian chief head............................$80.00
Occupied Japan, smiling pig w/hat.............................$80.00
Plastic, Batman figure holding a red bat, 1973, 3", EX .$15.00
Plastic, Bireley's soda bottle, 3"................................$25.00
Plastic, giraffe, press tail, head bobs, 4"....................$18.00
Plastic, Mummy (Universal Monsters), Universal Pictures,
    1960s, 3", EX $40.00
Plastic, Ronald McDonald, 2"....................................$15.00
Plastic, Sunbeam Bread, 1" $15.00

Plastic, Snoopy Fire Truck, United Features, 1958, $12.00.

Pennsbury Pottery

From the 1950s throughout the '60s, this pottery was sold in gift stores and souvenir shops along the Pennsylvania Turnpike. It was produced in Morrisville, Pennsylvania, by Henry and Lee Below. Much of the ware was hand painted in multicolor on caramel backgrounds, though some pieces were made in blue and white. Most of the time, themes centered around Amish people, barber shop singers, roosters, hex signs, and folksy mottos.

Much of the ware is marked, and if you're in the Pennsylvania/New Jersey area, you'll find a lot of it. It's fairly prevalent in the Midwest as well and can still sometimes be found at bargain prices. If you'd like to learn more about this pottery, we recommend *Pennsbury Pottery Video Book* by Shirley Graff and BA Wellman.

Advisor: Shirley Graff (See Directory, Pennsbury)

Plaque, Banking, 8" long, from $40.00 to $50.00.

Ashtray, cereal; Rooster, 5½" $15.00
Ashtray, It's Making Down...$18.00
Ashtray, Wonders Me, 4" $18.00
Bowl, Rooster, heart shape, 6"....................................$40.00
Bowl, Rooster, plain edge, 6¼"...................................$20.00
Bowl, salad; Folkart, 13" $30.00
Box, cigarette; Eagle, 2½x4¼"....................................$50.00
Butter dish, Bird Over Heart.......................................$30.00
Butter dish, 3 Tulips $85.00
Cake stand, Amish children, 11"..................................$95.00
Candlesticks, Bird Over Heart, 2x5", pr......................$90.00
Candlesticks, Rooster, 2x5", pr...................................$60.00
Canister, Folkart, Tea, 6½"..$100.00
Canister, Rooster, Coffee, wooden lid, 6½"..............$100.00
Casserole, Folkart, w/lid, 7" dia.................................$40.00
Casserole, Rooster, w/lid, 5" dia................................$40.00
Chip 'n dip, Rooster, 11" $85.00
Coaster, Luigi..$20.00
Coffeepot, Hex, 6-cup, 8½"...$40.00
Compote, Rooster, footed, 5"......................................$25.00
Creamer, Rooster, 2½"..$30.00
Cruet, Rooster..$40.00
Cup & saucer, Rooster..$35.00
Egg cup, Rooster..$20.00
Hot plate, Rooster, in electric metal frame $80.00
Mug, beer; Swallow the Insult....................................$40.00
Mug, coffee; Amish Couple, 3¼"...............................$27.50
Pie pan, Hex Star...$60.00
Pitcher, Amish man & heart, 4" $35.00

Pitcher, Rooster, 2½".................................$25.00
Plaque, Amish family, 8" **$55.00**
Plaque, Eagle, 13" **$60.00**
Plaque, Hear Ye..., Swallow the Insult, 6" dia **$50.00**
Plaque, Making Pie, 6" dia............................**$55.00**
Plaque, Ship, Barkentine 1880, 7½x5½" **$75.00**
Plate, Family, 11" in factory frame **$60.00**
Plate, Folkart, 10".....................................**$20.00**
Plate, Rooster, 11".....................................**$45.00**
Platter, Folkart, 14x11"...............................**$30.00**
Platter, Rooster, 14"..................................**$70.00**

Snack set, Rooster, from $20.00 to $25.00.

Sugar bowl, Rooster, w/lid.............................**$30.00**
Teapot, Rooster, 4-cup.................................**$65.00**
Tile, Harvest, 6" square **$12.00**
Tray, Laurel Ridge, tan, 8½x5¼" **$40.00**
Vinegar & oil set, Amish, pr **$125.00**
Wall pocket, Rooster...................................**$55.00**

Pepsi-Cola

People have been enjoying Pepsi-Cola since before the turn of the century. Various logos have been registered over the years; the familiar oval was first used in the early 1940s. At about the same time, the two 'dots' between the words Pepsi and Cola became one, though more recent items may carry the double-dot logo as well, especially when they're designed to be reminiscent of the old ones. The bottle cap logo came along in 1943 and with variations was used through the early '60s.

Though there are expensive rarities, most items are still reasonable, since collectors are just now beginning to discover how fascinating this line of advertising memorabilia can be. There are three books in the series called *Pepsi-Cola Collectibles*, written by Bill Vehling and Michael Hunt, which we highly recommend. Another good reference is *Introduction to Pepsi Collecting* by Bob Stoddard. Two general advertising guides that include Pepsi-Cola information are *Huxford's Collectible Advertising* by Sharon and Bob Huxford, and *Value Guide to Advertising Memorabilia* by B.J. Summers (both are published by Collector Books).

Note: In the descriptions that follow, the double-dot logo is represented by the equal sign.

Advisor: Craig and Donna Stifter (See Directory, Pepsi-Cola)

Newsletter: *Pepsi-Cola Collectors Club Express*
Bob Stoddard, Editor
P.O. Box 817
Claremont, CA 91711; Send SASE for information.

Sign, cardboard, self framed, 1940, 24x34", $650.00. (Photo courtesy Craig and Donna Stifter)

Ashtray, chrome bowl w/enameled bottle cap opposite chrome cigarette rest, 1950s, 3½" dia, NM **$75.00**
Ballpark vendor carrier, white oval logo & stripes on blue, Drink Pepsi-Cola in red, w/strap, 1950s, 6x19", VG............**$175.00**
Blotter, Pepsi & Pete The Pepsi-Cola Cops, 1939, EX+...**$80.00**
Calendar, 1941, Pepsi=Cola Hits The Spot, complete, EX+...**$325.00**
Calendar, 1943, American Art Series, complete, EX+..**$85.00**
Clock, List-O-Matic, square w/numbers & bottle cap embossed on front, Drink Pepsi=Cola Now!, 14x14", EX **$275.00**
Clock, round light-up w/Drink Pepsi-Cola bottle cap on yellow background, Swihart, 1950s, 15" dia, EX.....**$375.00**
Dispenser, plastic box w/stainless steel parts, red, white & blue w/Pepsi & bottle-cap logos, 1960s, VG+....**$250.00**
Door plate, Enjoy A Pepsi/Pepsi-Cola bottle caps on yellow & white, 1954, 14x4", EX+ **$230.00**
Fan, cardboard w/wooden handle, Drink Pepsi=Cola/12-Ounce Bottles 5¢ w/Pepsi cops on reverse, 1940, 12", NM+ **$120.00**
Fountain pen, red Pepsi=Cola logo w/blue & white stripes, VG **$35.00**
Lighter, can shape, 3-quarter bottle cap logo on silver-blue w/white diagonal stripes, 1960s, EX+ **$50.00**
Mechanical pencil, bottle cap logo, NM **$30.00**
Menu board, plastic, Sugar Free Diet Pepsi logo on yellow at left of white menu slots, yellow border, 13x35", NM+ **$40.00**
Menu board, tin, Drink Pepsi=Cola/Bigger-Better, blackboard w/wood-look frame & red rope border, 1940s, 30x20", NM+ **$250.00**
Money clip, brass & chrome dollar sign, 1950s, 2", NM+ ..**$65.00**
Paperweight, glass, rectangular w/rounded corners, Pepsi=Cola logo, VG **$50.00**
Pin-back button, Have A Pepsi/Refresh Without Filling, bottle cap logo, blue/yellow/blue, square w/rounded corners, EX **$35.00**
Salt & pepper shakers, early bottles w/Pepsi=Cola oval labels, EXIB, pr **$165.00**

Sign, cardboard, Ice Cold, bottle caps flank lettering on icicle background, 13x35", EX+ $40.00

Sign, cardboard, The Light Refreshment, girl leaning on birdcage w/parakeet perched on finger, 1957, 11x25", EX+ ...$100.00

Sign, cardboard, The Light Refreshment/Refreshes Without Filling, 2-sided, party girl/pinup girl, 25x37", EX ..$150.00

Sign, celluloid hanger, Ice Cold Pepsi=Cola Sold Here, red, white & blue button, 1930s-40s, 9" dia, EX+ $425.00

Sign, plastic light-up, Have A Pepsi For Light Refreshment, girl w/bottle & cap logo at ends, 1950s, horizontal, EX $500.00

Sign, porcelain bottle cap, Pepsi-Cola logo, 19", EX ..$325.00

Sign, tin, More Bounce To The Ounce!, bottle bursting through paper next to bottle cap on blue, 1940s, horizontal, NM...$1,000.00

Sign, tin, Tops..., shows row of bottle caps receding over the horizon, 1950s, 16x37", EX $500.00

Syrup can, white w/red drum graphics, EX+ $100.00

Thermometer, tin, Have A Pepsi/The Light Refreshment, 3-quarter bottle cap logo below, yellow & white, 1956, 27", EX $150.00

Toy truck, plastic '60s Ford delivery w/Tome Pepsi (Spanish) on center divider, 5 cases, red, white & blue, 7½", EX+ $250.00

Tray, Pepsi-Cola/Bigger & Better, w/stylized flowers, 1940, 11x14", EX $50.00

Tray, shows top view of bottles in ice, 1940s, 12x12", NM...$20.00

Perfume Bottles

Here's an area of bottle collecting that has come into its own. Commercial bottles, as you can see from our listings, are very popular. Their values are based on several factors. For instance, when you assess a bottle, you'll need to note: is it sealed or full, does it have its original label, and is the original package or box present.

Figural bottles are interesting as well, especially the ceramic ones with tiny regal crowns as their stoppers.

Advisor: Monsen & Baer (See Directory, Perfume Bottles)

Club: International Perfume Bottle Association (IPBA)
Coleen Abbot, Membership Secretary
396 Croton Rd.
Wayne, PA 19087; Membership: $45 USA or $50 Canada

Annich Geutal of Paris, frosted glass oval w/metal butterfly stopper, 4" $20.00

Armani, rectangular w/shaped sides, full, 1¾" $5.00

Balenciaga, Cialenga, horizontal rectangle, conforming stopper, full, 1¼" $5.00

Bob Mackie, black, spherical, full, 2", in sealed box ..$60.00

Bourjois, Evening in Paris, set of 5 gold-enameled bottles w/gold caps & labels, in gold & blue lace foil box, EX $165.00

Chanel, #22, squared, full, 2½".................................$10.00

Christian Dior, Miss Dior, slender urn shape w/some contents, 3¾", in gray box w/ribbon $65.00

Ciro, Danger, irregular stepped sides, corresponding black stopper, full, 4"...$80.00

Ciro, Danger, squared, miniature, 1¼", original box ..$30.00

Ciro, New Horizons, rectangle widens toward bottom, Deco stopper, bottom label, 1¼" $25.00

Ciro, Originals, set of 5 replica minis in individual boxes, unused, in presentation box $145.00

Corday, Fame, perfume solid golden birdcage w/lovebirds, (wax perfume still present), 2¼", in foil box w/foliage $120.00

Corday, Tourjours Moi, gold molded-in 'wings,' metal top, 2¼" $25.00

Coty, Paris, set w/Eau de Toilette & perfume, both clear w/gold caps, sm bottle in gold swan, both full, in foil box $120.00

D'Orsay, Divine, slender w/twisting panels, disk-shaped stopper, 5¾" $40.00

Elizabeth Arden, Mèmoire Chèrie, frosted, shaped as a woman w/her arms folded, 3" $265.00

Elizabeth Arden, On Dit, miniature, multi-faceted clear bottle & stopper, 2 women on gold label, 2" $200.00

Evening in Paris, five bottles, in original box, $125.00. (Photo courtesy Monsen & Baer Auctions)

Fabergè, Flambeau, whistle bottle, full, w/hang tag, 3", in box...$25.00

Givenchy, L'Interdit, 1½"...$5.00

Guerlain, Nahèma, shouldered/flattened, 1½"..............$7.00

Jean d' Albret, Ecusson, 1½"......................................$5.00

Jean Patou, Moment Supreme, flattened triangle shape, quality crystal, full/sealed, 4¼" $55.00

Jovan, Sculptura, gold nude figure on black base, 2¾".$35.00

Lenthèric, Confetti, bowling-pin shape w/diagonal ruffles, butterfly stopper, ½ full, all labels, 7½" $65.00

Lenthèric, Dark Brilliance, frosted, angular shoulders, knot of yarn as stopper, empty, 3", in black box w/wear ..$95.00

Lenthèric, Tweed, square w/wooden overcap, 2¼", in book presentation (& outer box) titled Christmas Carol, full .$145.00

Lucretia Vanderbilt, Concentrated Perfume, 2½" hexagonal bottle, w/Face Powder #21 (unopened), w/pamphlet, in box...$100.00

Luxor, La Richesse, flattened disk shape, partially full, 1¼"...**$20.00**

Marquay, Prince Douka, frosted stopper molded as prince's head, w/cloth cape, empty, 3"...........................**$140.00**

Matchabelli, Golden Autumn, crown shape w/gold enamel, sealed, 1¾", in Lucite box......................**$120.00**

Matchabelli, Infanta, crown shape w/brass cap, full, label on bottom, 1¾"...**$85.00**

Max Factor, Primitif, 2" bottle held by black cat, under plastic dome...**$25.00**

Richard Hudnut, Sweet Orchid, frosted rectangle w/embossed leaves, colorful label, full, 3", in box.....................**$175.00**

Schiaperelli, Shocking, miniature, clear dressmaker's dummy shape, full, 2", in book-form presentation & outer box..**$165.00**

Vigney, Le Golliwogg, frosted flattened oval w/black glass stopper molded as golliwogg, paper label face, 2½", EX...**$450.00**

Vigny, Echo Troublant, green opaque w/clear green stopper, stepped 'flatiron'-shaped sides, France on botton, 2½"...**$200.00**

Vivaudou, Narcisse de Chine, clear tester w/long dauber & brass overcap, full, 3", in floral box......................**$75.00**

Worth, Imprudence, flattened/shouldered, molded w/chevrons, blue label, full, 2", in cream-colored box.............**$130.00**

Pez Candy Dispensers

Though Pez candy has been around since the late 1920s, the dispensers that we all remember as children weren't introduced until the 1950s. Each had the head of a certain character — a Mexican, a doctor, Santa Claus, an animal, or perhaps a comic book hero. It's hard to determine the age of some of these, but if yours have tabs or 'feet' on the bottom so they can stand up, they were made in the last ten years. Though early on, collectors focused on this feature to evaluate their finds, now it's simply the character's head that's important to them. Some have variations in color and design, both of which can greatly affect value.

Condition is important; watch out for broken or missing parts. If a Pez is not in mint condition, most are worthless. Original packaging can add to the value, particularly if it is one that came out on a blister card. If the card has special graphics or information, this is especially true. Early figures were sometimes sold in boxes, but these are hard to find. Nowadays you'll see them offered 'mint in package,' sometimes at premium prices. But most intense Pez collectors say that those cellophane bags add very little if any to the value.

For more information, refer to *A Pictorial Guide to Plastic Candy Dispensers Featuring Pez* by David Welch; *Schroeder's Collectible Toys, Antique to Modern* (Collector Books); and *Collecting Toys #6* by Richard O'Brien.

Advisor: Richard Belyski (See Directory, Pez)

Newsletter: *Pez Collector's News*

Richard and Marianne Belyski, Editors
P.O. Box 124
Sea Cliff, NY 11579; 516-676-1183; www.peznews.com;
Subscription: $19 for 6 issues

Arlene, w/feet, from $3 to...**$5.00**
Bambi, no feet **$65.00**
Bouncer Beagle, w/feet **$6.00**
Captain Hook, no feet..**$85.00**
Clown w/Collar, no feet..**$65.00**
Cool Cat, w/feet...**$75.00**
Donald Duck's Nephew, no feet.....................................**$30.00**
Donkey, w/feet, whistle head...**$10.00**
Droopy Dog (A), no feet, plastic swivel ears, MIP **$25.00**
Fat-Ears Rabbit, no feet, pink head..............................**$20.00**

Fireman, no feet, $95.00; Policeman, no feet, $65.00. (Photo courtesy June Moon)

Frog, w/feet, whistle head **$40.00**
Gargamel, w/feet **$5.00**
Henry Hawk, no feet..**$65.00**
Indian, w/feet, whistle head **$20.00**
Inspector Clouseau, w/feet **$5.00**
Jerry Mouse, w/feet, painted face **$60.00**
Jerry Mouse, w/feet, plastic face **$15.00**
Koala Bear, w/feet, whistle head..............................**$40.00**
Lamb, w/feet, whistle head..**$20.00**
Lucy, w feet, from $1 to..**$3.00**
Merlin Mouse, w/feet **$20.00**
Mickey Mouse, w/feet, from $1 to **$3.00**
Miss Piggy, w/feet, eyelashes **$15.00**
Odie, w/feet..**$5.00**
Olive Oyl, no feet..**$200.00**
Panda, no feet diecut eyes...**$30.00**
Parrot, w/feet, whistle head..**$10.00**
Pink Panther, w/feet...**$5.00**
Pirate, no feet..**$45.00**
Pluto, no feet, red...**$10.00**
Practical Pig (B), no feet **$30.00**
Psychedelic Hand, remake, black or pink, MOC, ea ..**$20.00**
Raven, no feet, yellow beak **$60.00**
Rhino, w/feet, whistle head **$10.00**
Road Runner, w/feet...**$15.00**

Rooster, w/feet, white or yellow head, ea..................$30.00
Santa Claus (C), no feet, from $5 to..........................$15.00
Sheik, no feet..$30.00
Skull (A), no feet, from $5 to $10.00
Snow White, no feet..$200.00

Space Gun, MIP, minimum value, $150.00.

Speedy Gonzales (A), w/feet.......................................$15.00
Speedy Gonzales (B), no feet, from $1 to.....................$3.00
Spider-Man, w/feet, from $1 to....................................$3.00
Spike, w/feet..$6.00
Thor, no feet $300.00
Thumper, w/feet, no copyright....................................$45.00
Tiger, w/feet, whistle head $10.00
Tom, w/feet, painted face $6.00
Tom, w/feet, plastic face...$15.00
Tweety Bird, no feet..$10.00
Tweety Bird, w/feet, from $1 to....................................$3.00
Valentine Heart, from $1 to...$3.00
Wile E Coyote, w/feet..$45.00
Wolfman, no feet $300.00

Pfaltzgraff Pottery

Pfaltzgraff has operated in Pennsylvania since the early 1800s making redware at first, then stoneware crocks and jugs, yellow ware and spongeware in the '20s, artware and kitchenware in the '30s, and stoneware kitchen items through the hard years of the '40s. In 1950 they developed their first line of dinnerware, called Gourmet Royale (known in later years as simply Gourmet). It was a high-gloss line of solid color accented at the rims with a band of frothy white, similar to lines made later by McCoy, Hull, Harker, and many other companies. Although it also came in pink, it was the dark brown that became so popular. Today these brown stoneware lines have captured the interest of young collectors as well as the more seasoned, and they all contain more than enough unusual items to make the hunt a bit of a challenge and loads of fun.

The success of Gourmet was just the inspiration that was needed to initiate the production of the many dinner-ware lines that have become the backbone of the Pfaltzgraff company.

A giftware line called Muggsy was designed in the late 1940s. It consisted of items such as comic character mugs, ashtrays, bottle stoppers, children's dishes, a pretzel jar, a cookie jar, etc. All of the characters were given names. It was very successful and continued in production until 1960. The older versions have protruding features, while the later ones were simply painted on.

Village, an almond-glazed line with a folksy, brown stenciled tulip decoration, is now discontinued. It's a varied line with many wonderful, useful pieces, and besides the dinnerware itself, the company catalogs carried illustrations of matching glassware, metal items, copper accessories, and linens. Of course, all Pfaltzgraff is of the highest quality, and all these factors add up to a new area of collecting in the making. Several dinnerware lines are featured in our listings. To calculate the values of Yorktowne, Heritage, and Folk Art items not listed below, use Village prices.

For further information, we recommend *Pfaltzgraff, America's Potter,* by David A. Walsh and Polly Stetler, published in conjunction with the Historical Society of York County, York, Pennsylvania.

Christmas Heritage, bowl, soup/cereal; #009, 5½", from $2 to $3.50
Christmas Heritage, cheese tray, #533, 10½x7½", from $5 to..$7.00
Christmas Heritage, pedestal mug, #290, 10-oz.............$4.50
Christmas Heritage, plate, dinner; #004, 10", from $4 to .$5.50
Gourment Royale, ashtray, #AT32, skillet shape, 9", from $10 to..$15.00
Gourmet Royale, ashtray, #321, 7¾", from $12 to $15.00
Gourmet Royale, ashtray, 12", from $15 to..................$18.00
Gourmet Royale, baker, #321, oval, 7½", from $18 to..$20.00
Gourmet Royale, baker, #323, 9½", from $20 to........$24.00
Gourmet Royale, bean pot, #11-1, 1-qt, from $20 to..$22.00
Gourmet Royale, bean pot, #11-2, 2-qt, from $28 to..$30.00
Gourmet Royale, bean pot, #11-3, 3-qt....................$35.00
Gourmet Royale, bean pot, #11-4, 4-qt....................$45.00
Gourmet Royale, bean pot, #30, w/lip, lg, from $45 to..$50.00
Gourmet Royale, bean pot warming stand.................$12.00
Gourmet Royale, bowl, #241, oval, 7x10", from $15 to.$20.00
Gourmet Royale, bowl, cereal; #934SR, 5½" $6.00
Gourmet Royale, bowl, mixing; 6", from $8 to...........$10.00
Gourmet Royale, bowl, mixing; 8", from $12 to........$14.00
Gourmet Royale, bowl, salad; tapered sides, 10", from $18 to...$25.00
Gourmet Royale, bowl, soup; 2¼x7¼", from $6 to $8.00
Gourmet Royale, bowl, spaghetti; #319, shallow, 14", from $15 to...$20.00
Gourmet Royale, bowl, vegetable; #341, divided, from $15 to $20.00
Gourmet Royale, butter dish, #394, ¼-lb stick type ...$12.00
Gourmet Royale, butter warmer, #301, stick handle, double spout, 9-oz, w/stand, from $18 to $22.00
Gourmet Royale, candle holders, tall, w/finger ring, 6", pr, from $25 to..$35.00

Gourmet Royale, canister set, 4-pc, from $60 to.........**$75.00**

Gourmet Royale, casserole, hen on nest, 2-qt, from $75 to.**$95.00**

Gourmet Royale, casserole, individual; #399, stick handle, 12-oz, from $10 to **$12.00**

Gourmet Royale, casserole, stick handle, 1-qt, from $15 to **$18.00**

Gourmet Royale, casserole, stick handle, 3-qt, from $25 to **$30.00**

Gourmet Royale, casserole, stick handle, 4-qt, from $32 to **$40.00**

Gourmet Royale, casserole-warming stand..................**$10.00**

Gourmet Royale, chafing dish, w/handles, lid & stand, 8x9", from $30 to...**$35.00**

Gourmet Royale, cheese shaker, bulbous, 5¾", from $18 to..**$22.00**

Gourmet Royale, chip 'n dip, #306, 2-pc set, w/stand, from $28 to...**$30.00**

Gourmet Royale, chip 'n dip, #311, molded in 1 pc, 12", from $18 to...**$22.00**

Gourmet Royale, coffee server, on metal & wood stand, 10¾", from $100 to..**$125.00**

Gourmet Royale, coffeepot, #303, 10-cup, from $35 to..**$45.00**

Gourmet Royale, creamer, #382, from $5 to.................**$7.00**

Gourmet Royale, cruet, coffeepot shape, fill through spout, 5", from $20 to...**$22.00**

Gourmet Royale, cup, from $2 to.................................**$3.00**

Gourmet Royale, cup & saucer, demitasse **$18.00**

Gourmet Royale, egg/relish tray, 15" L, from $22 to ..**$28.00**

Gourmet Royale, gravy boat, #426, 2-spout, lg, +underplate, from $14 to.....................................**$16.00**

Gourmet Royale, gravy boat, w/stick handle, 2-spout, from $15 to...**$20.00**

Gourmet Royale, jug, #384, 32-oz, from $32 to **$36.00**

Gourmet Royale, jug, #386, ice lip, from $40 to.........**$48.00**

Gourmet Royale, ladle, sm, from $12 to.....................**$15.00**

Gourmet Royale, ladle, 3½" dia bowl w/11" handle, from $18 to...**$20.00**

Gourmet Royale, Lazy Susan, #220, 5-part, molded in 1 pc, 11", from $22 to...**$28.00**

Gourmet Royale, Lazy Susan, #308, 3 sections w/center bowl, 14", from $32 to...**$36.00**

Gourmet Royale, mug, #391, 12-oz, from $6 to.........**$8.00**

Gourmet Royale, mug, #392, 16-oz, from $12 to........**$14.00**

Gourmet Royale, pie plate, #7016, 9½", from $14 to.**$18.00**

Gourmet Royale, plate, dinner; #88R, from $3.50 to.....**$4.50**

Gourmet Royale, plate, egg; holds 12 halves, 7¾x12½", from $20 to...**$22.00**

Gourmet Royale, plate, grill; #87, 3-section, 11", from $18 to..**$20.00**

Gourmet Royale, plate, salad; 6¾", from $3 to.............**$4.00**

Gourmet Royale, plate, steak; 12", from $15 to **$20.00**

Gourmet Royale, platter, #320, 14", from $20 to........**$25.00**

Gourmet Royale, platter, #337, 16", from $25 to........**$30.00**

Gourmet Royale, rarebit, #330, w/lug handles, oval, 11", from $15 to...**$18.00**

Gourmet Royale, rarebit, w/lug handles, oval, 8½", from $10 to..**$12.00**

Gourmet Royale, relish dish, #265, 5x10", from $15 to..**$17.00**

Gourmet Royale, roaster, #325, oval, 14", from $30 to.**$35.00**

Gourmet Royale, roaster, #326, oval, 16", from $50 to.**$60.00**

Gourmet Royale, salt & pepper shakers, #317/318, 4½", pr, from $12 to...**$14.00**

Gourmet Royale, salt & pepper shakers, bell shape, pr, from $25 to...**$35.00**

Gourmet Royale, scoop, any size, from $15 to..........**$18.00**

Gourmet Royale, serving tray, round, 4-section, upright handle in center **$22.00**

Gourmet Royale, shirred egg dish, #360, 6", from $10 to.**$12.00**

Gourmet Royale, souffle dish, #393, 5-qt, +underplate, from $65 to...**$70.00**

Gourmet Royale, sugar bowl, from $5 to **$7.00**

Gourmet Royale, teapot, #381, 6-cup, from $18 to.....**$22.00**

Gourmet Royale, three-part tray, 15½" long, minimum value, $35.00.

Gourmet Royale, tray, tidbit; 2-tier, from $15 to **$18.00**

Heritage, butter dish, #002-028, from $6 to **$8.00**

Heritage, cake/serving plate, #002-529, 11¼" dia, from $9 to..**$12.00**

Heritage, cup & saucer, #002-002, 9-oz.......................**$3.00**

Heritage, soup tureen, #002-160, 3½-qt, from $25 to.**$35.00**

Muggsy, ashtray **$125.00**

Muggsy, bottle stopper, head, ball shape **$85.00**

Muggsy, canape holder, Carrie, lift-off hat pierced for toothpicks, from $125 to..................................**$150.00**

Muggsy, cigarette server...**$125.00**

Muggsy, clothes sprinkler bottle, Myrtle, Black, from $225 to...**$260.00**

Muggsy, clothes sprinkler bottle, Myrtle, white, from $195 to...**$225.00**

Muggsy, cookie jar, character face, minimum value.**$250.00**

Muggsy, mug, action figure (golfer, fisherman, etc), any, from $65 to...**$85.00**

Muggsy, mug, Black action figure...............................**$125.00**

Muggsy, mug, character face, ea, from $35 to **$38.00**

Muggsy, shot mug, character face, from $45 to **$50.00**

Muggsy, tumbler **$60.00**

Muggsy, utility jar, Handy Harry, hat w/short bill as flat lid, from $175 to.....................................**$200.00**

Planter, donkey, brown drip glaze, common, 10", from $15 to..**$20.00**

Planter, elephant, brown drip glaze, scarce, from $90 to..**$110.00**

Village, baker, #236, rectangular, tab handles, 2-qt, from $12 to..**$15.00**

Village, baker, #237, square, tab handles, 9", from $9 to..**$12.00**

Village, baker, #24, oval, 10¼", from $8 to **$10.00**
Village, baker, #240, oval, 7¾", from $6 to...................**$8.00**

Village, bean pot, 2½-quart, $35.00.

Village, beverage server, #490, from $24 to................**$28.00**
Village, bowl, batter; w/spout & handle, 8", from $30 to...**$35.00**
Village, bowl, fruit; #008, 5"..**$4.00**
Village, bowl, mixing; #453, 1-qt, 2-qt, & 3-qt, 3-pc set, from $40 to **$50.00**
Village, bowl, rim soup; #012, 8½"..............................**$6.00**
Village, bowl, serving; #010, 7", from $8 o.................**$10.00**
Village, bowl, soup/cereal; #009, 6" **$4.50**
Village, bowl, vegetable; #011, 8¾", from $12 to **$15.00**
Village, bread tray, 12", from $15 to **$18.00**
Village, butter dish, #028...**$8.00**
Village, canisters, #520, 4-pc set, from $50 to.............**$60.00**
Village, casserole, w/lid, #315, 2-qt, from $18 to........**$25.00**
Village, coffee mug, #89F, 10-oz, from $4 to................**$5.50**
Village, coffeepot, lighthouse shape, 48-oz, from $30 to**$35.00**
Village, cookie jar, #540, 3-qt, from $15 to..................**$20.00**
Village, creamer & sugar bowl, #020, from $9 to **$12.00**
Village, cup & saucer, #001 & #002.............................**$3.50**
Village, flowerpot, 4½"..**$15.00**
Village, gravy boat, #443, w/saucer, 16-oz, from $12 to ..**$15.00**
Village, ice bucket, canister w/lid **$175.00**
Village, onion soup crock, #295, stick handle, sm, from $4 to **$5.50**
Village, pedestal mug, #90F, 10-oz **$4.50**
Village, pitcher, #416, 2-qt, from $20 to......................**$25.00**
Village, plate, dinner; #004, 10¼", from $3 to..............**$4.50**
Village, platter, #016, 14", from $15 to **$18.00**
Village, soup tureen, #160, w/lid & ladle, 3½-qt, from $40 to **$45.00**
Village, spoon rest, #515, 9" L, from $6 to....................**$7.50**
Village, table light, #620, clear glass chimney on candle holder base, from $12 to **$14.00**

Pie Birds

Pie birds are hollow, china, or ceramic kitchen utensils. They date to the 1800s in England, where they were known as pie vents or pie funnels. They are designed to support the upper crust and keep it flaky. They also serve as a steam vent to prevent spill over.

Most have arches on the base and they have one, and *only* one, vent hole on or near the top. There are many new pie birds on both the US and British markets. These are hand painted rather than airbrushed like the older ones.

The Pearl China Co. of East Liverpool, Ohio, first gave pie birds their 'wings.' Prior to the introduction in the late 1920s of an S-neck rooster shape, pie vents were non-figural. They resembled inverted funnels. Funnels which contain certain advertising are the most sought after.

The first bird-shaped pie vent produced in England was designed in 1933 by Clarice Cliff, a blackbird with an orange beak on a white base. The front of the base is imprinted with registry numbers. The bird later carried the name Newport Pottery; more recently it has been marked Midwinter Pottery.

Advisor: Linda Fields (See Directory, Pie Birds)

Aluminum pie funnels, England, ea **$25.00**

Benny the Baker, Cardinal China Co., Carteret, NJ, holds pie crimper and cake tester, 1946 – 60, from $125.00 to $135.00. (Photo courtesy Linda Fields)

Bird on Nest, Artesian Galleries, copyright mark, 1950s, from $200 to...**$250.00**
Blackbird, thin necked, marked Scotland, from $60 to **$75.00**
Blackbird, white head, teardrop eyes, Australia, from $40 to **$60.00**
Blackbird on white base, orange beak, Clarice Cliff, from $45 to **$50.00**
Blue & White bird on white base, Royal Worcester, 2-pc (ea marked), from $95 to **$100.00**
Chef, marked The Servex Chef, from $125 to...........**$140.00**
Chick, Josef Original, 1950s-70s, from $45 to..............**$50.00**
Cutie Pie, Josef Original (or A Lorrie Design), hen wearing bonnet, from $75 to..**$100.00**
Duck (or Swan) head, brown w/yellow beak, from $150 to **$175.00**
Dutch girl, multipurpose kitchen tool, from $150 to ..**$195.00**
Eagle, marked Sunglow, golden color, from $75 to....**$85.00**
Elephant, marked Nutbrown, white, tan or gray, respectively, from $75 to **$175.00**

Elephant on drum, marked CCC (Cardinal China Co), solid pink base, swirl base or XXX base, respectively, from $120 to...**$200.00**

Fred the Flour Grater, original has dots for eyes, from $65 to..**$75.00**

Fruits: apple, peach or cherries, import, ea, from $350 to .**$400.00**

Funnel, marked Grimwade Perfection.......................**$110.00**

Funnel, marked Squab vit porcelain...........................**$75.00**

Funnel, pagoda, marked Gourmet Pie Cup, Reg No 369793..**$75.00**

Funnel, pagoda, marked Nutbrown...........................**$95.00**

Funnel, plain aluminum, from $10 to.........................**$15.00**

Funnel, plain white w/rosebud on top, from $150 to .**$175.00**

Funnel, yellow ware, marked Mason Cash (paper label), new, from $15 to...**$18.00**

Half Bird, black, w/scalloped or triangle bottom, from $65 to..**$70.00**

Long-neck Pie Duckling, American Pottery Co, blue, yellow or pink, 1940s, from $50 to.................................**$75.00**

Mammy and Dutch Girls with outstretched arms, maker unknown, multipurpose kitchen utensils, each holds measuring spoons in her arms, bases rested atop inverted measuring cups, from $125.00 to $150.00 each. (Photo courtesy Linda Fields)

Pie Boy, green sombreros on outfit, from $350 to ...**$400.00**

Rooster, Cleminson Pottery, marked 'C' encircling a 'b', from $45 to...**$50.00**

S-neck rooster, Pearl China Co, colors other than pink trimmed w/blue base, from $150 to....................**$175.00**

S-neck rooster, pink trimmed w/blue base, Pearl China Co, from $110 to..**$115.00**

Songbird, LaPere, cream or black w/gold trim, ea, from $125 to..**$150.00**

Welsh Lady, marked Cymru, from $75 to....................**$95.00**

Pierce, Howard

Even though Howard Pierce began his career creating vases, nut bowls, and dishware such as creamers, cups, and saucers, he will no doubt be remembered more for his porcelain wildlife pieces. Howard and his wife, Ellen Van Voorhis, whom he had met in National City, California, created a vast array of pieces for more than five decades.

His formal education included training at the Chicago Art Institute, California's Pomona College, and the University of Illinois. For a brief time Howard worked alongside William Manker, and some of Howard's pieces have been mistaken as Manker's work. This influence was particularly strong in the early two-tone pieces such as the nut dishes and some vases. Various colors were utilized: the outer glaze might be a deep green with the inner glaze a light apple green; maroon was paired with yellow, and there were several other combinations as well.

Not only was Pierce creative with his designs, he also used imagination in selecting his materials. Pewter was perhaps the first material that he worked in, having become familiar with its properties after designing lapel pins of both pewter and copper. He dabbled in polyurethane for only a short time (he soon found he was allergic to it), so today polyurethane pieces are rare and costly. He used aluminum and bronze to make a few items, also Hydrocal, bisque, cement, and porcelain (some with Mount St. Helen's ash). Howard was a talented painter and created some of their paper Christmas cards. But his favorite material was porcelain, and by far, his love for wildlife was predominate in the pieces he designed.

Howard's earliest mark was probably 'Howard Pierce' (in block letters) on his metalware, mostly on the lapel pins. When he and Ellen moved to Claremont, California, the mark became 'Claremont Calif. Howard Pierce,' usually with a stock number. A rubber stamp was used later to stamp 'Howard Pierce Porcelains.' Eventually 'Porcelains' was omitted. Not all pieces are marked, especially when they belong to a two- or three-piece set. Generally only the larger is marked.

In 1992, due to Howard's poor health, they destroyed all the molds they had ever created. Later his health improved, and he was able to work a few hours a week, creating miniatures of some of his original models and designing new ones as well. These miniatures are marked simply 'Pierce,' with what appears to be a stamp. Howard Pierce passed away in February 1994. For further information see *Collector's Encyclopedia of Howard Pierce Porcelain* by Darlene Hurst Dommel (Collector Books).

Advisor: Susan Cox (See Directory, California Pottery)

Figurines, fish pair, purple with black stripes, 4¾" and 3¼", $155.00. (Photo courtesy Susan Cox)

Ashtray, light lava gray outside, cobalt blue inside, tri-point high-style **$75.00**

Bowl, gondola shape, 5x9½" **$65.00**

Candle holder, angel, gold leaf, 8" **$65.00**

Figurine, cat & kitten, brown on white, 9", 4", pr **$150.00**

Figurine, chickens, brown on white, 6", 9", pr **$175.00**

Figurine, coyote, howling, granite-like glaze, 5¾" **$80.00**

Figurine, decoy-like duck, matt glaze, 6" L **$75.00**

Figurine, giraffes, brown agate, 1950s, 10½", pr **$350.00**

Figurine, goose, late 1940s-50s, 11" **$100.00**

Figurine, goose taking flight, gold leaf, 6" **$40.00**

Figurine, horse, windblown, matt black w/speckled mane & tail, 8x7" **$195.00**

Figurine, native couple, brown on white, 7, 7½", pr .**$165.00**

Figurine, parakeet on base, yellow & black, 5" **$60.00**

Figurine, penguin, matt black & white, 4¾", 3½", pr ..**$125.00**

Figurine, polar bear, brown on white, 6½" **$150.00**

Figurine, rabbit, long eared, brown, #102-P, ca 1953, 10½" **$100.00**

Figurine, roadrunner, running, 8" L **$90.00**

Floral container, pr of squirrels on tree stump, 11½x7" ..**$285.00**

Vase, mottled green high glaze, 7¼" **$85.00**

Vase, ovoid w/giraffe at base, cream, #250-P, 7" **$125.00**

Vase, speckled green, silken white giraffe & palm tree in open center, 9" **$130.00**

Vases, white bisque figural inserts, from $130.00 to $165.00 each. (Photo courtesy Pat and Kris Secor)

Pin-Back Buttons

Literally hundreds of thousands of pin-back buttons are available; pick a category and have fun! Most fall into one of three fields — advertising, political, and personality related, but within these three broad areas are many more specialized groups. Just make sure you buy only those that are undamaged, are still bright and unfaded, and have well-centered designs and properly aligned printing. The older buttons (those from before the 1920s) may be made of celluloid with the cardboard backing printed with the name of a company or a product.

See also Political.

Advisor: Michael McQuillen (See Directory, Pin-Back Buttons)

Aladdin, all characters shown **$4.00**

Always Shoot Winchester, bull's-eye target w/W on inner circle, 1", NM...**$32.00**

America's First Orbital Spaceman, Astronaut John Glenn, image in space helmet, 1962, 3½", NM.................**$30.00**

America's Getting Into Training, Amtrak logo, black & gold, 2¼" **$3.00**

Archie's Official Fan Club, 1968, 1½"..............................**$6.00**

Ask Your Grocer for Ferguson's White Seal Bread, blue & white, 1¼", EX...**$4.50**

Babe Ruth Baseball Club, 1970s, 1½" **$6.00**

Beverly Hills 90210, color cast portrait, 4"...................**$2.00**

Buck Jones for US Marshall, red & black, EX **$5.00**

Buster Brown Walking Club, 1920s, oval, EX.............**$25.00**

Captain Kirk & Mr Spock, black & white photo images, 1976, 2¼", M..**$8.00**

Casper the Friendly Ghost, 1950s **$20.00**

Charge, Bring Back the Bullmoose Party!..., image of Bullwinkle yelling, 1964, 2¼", EX **$20.00**

Chip 'N Dale Rescue Rangers, 1990, 3" **$5.00**

Dale Evans, black & white photo on green, 1950s, 1½"...**$25.00**

Davy Crockett King of the Frontier, black & white photo on yellow, 1950s, 1¼"..**$35.00**

Donald Duck's 50th Birthday, multicolor.....................**$7.50**

Elsie the Cow for President, red, white & blue, 1960s, 3"..**$25.00**

ET & Elliot, color photo, Universal Studios, 1982, 6", NM....**$5.00**

Evel Knievel Snake River Canyon, September 3, 1974, M....**$8.00**

Fabian, name in script, no image, early 1960s, 1", EX..**$15.00**

Ford Mustang's 20th Anniversary, 1984, 3", EX.............**$5.00**

Frankenstein, name under bust image, 1960s, EX **$10.00**

GE Safety Committee, red, gold & green, ⅞", EX.........**$8.00**

Green Hornet Agent, 1960s, 4", EX..............................**$15.00**

Harlem Globetrotters, 1970s, 3", $15.00.

H-eeey!, Fonzie of Happy Days, 1975, Paramount Pictures Corp **$8.00**

Howdy Doody Time, Howdy's face, orange & black, 1980s, EX...**$3.00**

I Go Pogo, 1956, ⅞", NM...**$22.00**

I'm Gonna Be King, image of Simba from Lion King, 1993, 2¼", NM..**$5.00**

Indian Apple-Us (Indianapolis) Gloves, apple logo in center, banded edge, 1930s, ⅞", EX............................**$10.00**

Jackie Gleason Fan Club/And Awa-a-ay We Go!!!, w/Jackie in checked suit, blue on white, tin litho, 1950s, 1½", EX..**$35.00**

James Dean, black & yellow portrait, 1980s, EX..........**$2.00**

Jetson, Kool-Aid giveaway at movie theaters, oval, EX ..**$5.00**

Joe DiMaggio, New York Yankees, black & white photo, 1¾", EX...**$20.00**

John Wayne Western Saddle Kings Series, black & green, 1¾", M **$12.00**

Johnston Fudge Sundae, red, white & blue, 1940s, 2¼", EX **$20.00**

Jurassic Park, multicolor, 1¾", NM **$3.00**

Knott's Berry Farm, Friendliest Place in the West, white & gold litho tin, 2", M...................................**$12.00**

Latest Greatest Plymouth/Four Years Better, EX **$25.00**

Leave It to Beaver, black & white shot of Beaver & Wally, 1980s **$2.00**

Majestic Ranges, stove on ship's flag, multicolored, ⅞", EX **$10.00**

Mickey Mantle, Lee Jeans, 1960s, 3", NM **$15.00**

Mickey Mouse Club, 1970s, 3" **$8.00**

Mummy, name under bust image, EX..........................**$10.00**

Nixon's the One, red & white, 1⅜", EX......................**$3.00**

Party Animal, image of Woodstock, 1990, MOC...........**$4.00**

Pebbles Flintstone, 1972, 2", EX **$15.00**

Philadelphia Phillies 1950 Champs, 1¾" **$15.00**

Pocahontas, I Was There, Wang Center, Boston, 1995, rectangular, NM **$8.00**

Red Goose Club Member, red on white, 1940s, 1¼", EX..**$15.00**

Remember Pearl Harbor, shows American flag, red, white & blue, 1¼", EX **$20.00**

Remington-UMC, white on red, VG **$15.00**

Rescuers Down Under, w/map background, 1980s, NM ..**$5.00**

Rin-Tin-Tin, Screen Gems, 1956, head shot, NM **$20.00**

San Diego Chargers, 1960s logo, ¾", EX **$5.00**

Snoopy Fan Club, litho tin, 2¼", EX **$6.00**

Snow White Jingle Club, red, white & blue, 1938, 3", EX..**$150.00**

Stephen King's Sleepwalkers, paw silhouette on red, Columbia Pictures, 1992, EX..............................**$4.50**

Tea Keeps You Cool, blue & white, 1940s, 1⅜", EX **$3.00**

Teenage Mutant Ninja Turtles, white ground, NM **$5.00**

Tom & Jerry, Sunbeam Bread premium, 1960s, 1¼" **$6.00**

Under Achiever & Proud of It Man, Bart Simpson, green ground, 6", MIP **$4.00**

Wolf Man, name under bust image, 1960s, EX............**$10.00**

1950 Ducks Unlimited, Bluebill on light blue ground, EX, $60.00.

Kellogg's Pep Pins

Chances are if you're over fifty, you remember them — one in each box of PEP (Kellogg's wheat-flake cereal that was among the first to be vitamin fortified). There were eighty-six in all, each carrying the full-color image of a character from one of the popular cartoon strips of the day — Maggie and Jiggs, the Winkles, Dagwood and Blondie, Superman, Dick Tracy, and many others. Very few of these cartoons are still in print.

The pins were issued in five sets, the first in 1945, three in 1946, and the last in 1947. They were made in Connecticut by the Crown Bottle Cap Company, and they're marked PEP on the back. You could wear them on your cap, shirt, coat, or the official PEP pin beanie, an orange and white cloth cap made for just that purpose. The Superman pin — he was the only D.C. Comics Inc. character in the group — was included in each set.

Values are given for pins in near mint condition; prices should be sharply reduced when foxing or fading is present. Any unlisted pins are worth from $10.00 to $15.00.

Advisor: Doug Dezso (See Directory, Candy Containers)

Bo Plenty, NM...**$30.00**

Corky, NM...**$16.00**

Dagwood, NM..**$30.00**

Dick Tracy, NM..**$30.00**

Early Bird, NM...**$6.00**

Fat Stuff, NM...**$15.00**

Felix the Cat, NM..**$85.00**

Flash Gordon, NM...**$30.00**

Flat Top, NM..**$30.00**

Goofy, NM...**$10.00**

Gravel Girtie, NM...**$15.00**

Harold Teen, NM..**$15.00**

Inspector, NM..**$12.50**

Jiggs, NM...**$25.00**

Judy, NM..**$10.00**

Kayo, NM...**$20.00**

Little King, NM...**$15.00**

Little Moose, NM...**$15.00**

Maggie, NM...**$25.00**

Mama De Stross, NM...**$30.00**

Mama Katzenjammer..**$25.00**

Mamie, NM..**$15.00**

Moon Mullins, NM...**$10.00**

Navy Patrol, NM...**$6.00**

Olive Oyl, NM..**$30.00**

Orphan Annie, NM...**$25.00**

Pat Patton, NM..**$10.00**

Perry Winkle, NM...**$15.00**

Phantom, NM...**$80.00**

Pop Jenks, NM...**$15.00**

Popeye, NM...**$30.00**

Rip Winkle, NM..**$20.00**

Skeezix, NM...**$15.00**

Superman, NM...**$45.00**

Toots, NM..**$15.00**

Uncle Walt, NM..**$20.00**

Uncle Willie, NM..**$12.50**

Winkles Twins, NM $90.00
Winnie Winkle, NM $15.00

Pinup Art

Some of the more well-known artists in this field are Vargas, Petty, DeVorss, Elvgren, Moran, Ballantyne, Armstrong, and Phillips, and some enthusiasts pick a favorite and concentrate their collections on only his work. From the mid-thirties until well into the fifties, pinup art was extremely popular. As the adage goes, 'Sex sells.' And well it did. You'll find calendars, playing cards, magazines, advertising, and merchandise of all types that depict these unrealistically perfect ladies. Though not all items will be signed, most of these artists have a distinctive, easily identifiable style that you'll soon be able to recognize.

Unless noted otherwise, values listed below are for items in at least near-mint condition.

Advisor: Denis Jackson (See Directory, Pinup Art)

Newsletter: *The Illustrator Collector's News*
Denis Jackson, Editor
P.O. Box 1958
Sequim, WA 98382; 360-452-3810
http://www.olypen.com/ticn, e-mail: ticn@olypen.com

Calendar, 1947, illustrated by Elvgren, 12x8", M (with original mailer), $135.00. (Photo courtesy Denis Jackson)

Album, Follies Bergere, 1930, EX $45.00
Arcade card, Elvgren, What a Break, color, EX............$5.00
Ashtray, metal w/painted image of nude blond by coffee table, late 1950s, M $15.00
Blotter, DeVorss, redhead on divan wearing yellow dress & white fur jacket, saleman's sample, 3¾x8¼", NM...$10.00
Blotter, Elvgren, Drawing Attention, saleman's sample, girl w/easel & brush, 1950s, 4x9", NM, from $12 to...$15.00
Blotter, Moran, No Kisses & a Girl & Her Honey...Soon Parted, girl in sunsuit, w/1953 calendar, 3x4", NM, from $12 to...$15.00

Book, Pinup, A Modest History, Mark Garbor, 1972, hardbound, EX $35.00
Calendar, Armstrong, 1956, brunette in black & white gown w/black gloves seated in seductive pose, 33½x16", VG+ $100.00
Calendar, Armstrong, 1957, brunette in black gown seated in seductive pose, 33½x16", EX...........................$110.00
Calendar, Ben-Hur Baz, 1955, girl in blue shorts & yellow T-shirt kneeling w/a come-on gesture, 33½x16", EX+........$100.00
Calendar, Esquire, 1947, in original sleeve, NM $80.00
Calendar, Moran, 1949, blond in yellow 2-pc swimsuit & spike heels stands w/hands on hips, 33½x16", EX, from $60 to...$70.00
Calendar, Randall, 1961, complete, EX $55.00
Calendar top, Medcalf, Victor Gaskets & Oil Seals, windblown girl in yellow sweater & blue skirt w/umbrella, 24x19", EX $100.00
Calendar top, Pepsi-Cola, redheaded beach beauty in white suit kneeling seductively w/hands behind head, 21x17", EX $150.00
Cartoon, Petty, I Suppose This Bum Check Is Your Idea of a Joke!, Esquire, April 1937, EX...............................$20.00
Cartoon, Petty, This Is His Secretary Speaking, blond girl on sofa w/phone, Esquire, September 1935, M.........$22.00
Fan, Armstrong, Queen of the Ball, redhead in green hat looks over shoulder, stapled wood handle, 1980s repro, 9x8", EX $15.00
Gatefold, Petty, redheaded Irish girl in green pants, jacket & top, True Magazine, EX...$30.00
Gatefold, Vargas, Torch Singer, Esquire, February 1945, EX $30.00
Gatefold, Vargas, V Mail for a Soldier, pretty blond in blue & white ruffles, Esquire, 1943, EX+..........................$30.00
Letter opener, Elvgren, plastic diecut nude in slotted folder w/painted dress, 1950s, 8½", NM.........................$35.00
Magazine, Beau #3, Aug 1966, Jayne Mansfield cover w/nude models inside, NM...$35.00
Magazine, Cabaret Quarterly #5, 1956, Jayne Mansfield cover, nude models inside, spiral-bound, M....................$35.00
Magazine, Humorama #4, January 1958, w/Ward cartoons & posing models, 1st inside page features Betty Page, EX+...$30.00
Magazine, Modern Man, June 1956, Marilyn Monroe cover (black & white) w/model & star photos inside, EX..$65.00
Memo pad, Elvgren, Perfect Form, ballerina at bar in snug leotard, 1945-55, NM $10.00
Mutoscope card, Elvgren, What's Cooking, EX $9.00
Mutoscope card, Mozert, A Run on Sugar, EX $9.00
Paint-by-number canvas, blue line art of nude dipping feet in pool on white, 1950s, 18x24", unused, EX..........$35.00
Paint-by-number canvas, blue line art of nude model seated at edge of waterfall on white, 1950s, 18x24", unused, EX...$35.00
Playing cards, Art Studies, ea card pictures different nude model & has trademark Wolf, 1950s, complete, NMIB........$45.00
Playing cards, Elvgren Top Hat designs, Creative Playing Cards, 1950s, complete, NMIB.........................$100.00

Print, D'Armaro, Danger!, cowgirl by split-rail fence, early 1950s, 17x12", NM $35.00

Print, Elvgren, Hitch in Time, girl adjusting garter belt, sm, NM $18.00

Print, Erbit, girl in pink evening gown on stairway, ca 1942, 18x12", EX $60.00

Print, Petty, advertising Acme Brewing Co, girl lying on stomach in long gown talking on phone, framed, 12x25", EX $150.00

Puzzles, #AP 118 (Avis Miller) or #AP 131 (Carol O'Neal), sm can, ea $15.00

Shot glass, Playboy Playmate w/key painted on glass, 1960s, M $40.00

Sign, diecut cardboard, Bireley's, brunette in tight-fitting gold sweater & white shorts jumping rope, 40x24", NM+..$475.00

Sign, diecut cardboard, Tartan Lotion & Cream, blond beach beauty in white 1-pc suit kneeling by Dalmatian, 37x29", EX+ $60.00

Sign, diecut tin, Fram, blond in bikini holding Fram oil filter, ad panel below, Tribisort art, 16x5½", VG+ $250.00

Sign, diecut tin, Veedol, blond ice skater in skimpy yellow suit w/advertising chest banner, 17x9½", EX+ $1,400.00

Sign, diecut tin, Veedol, blond ice skater in white skort w/ad banner between feet, 18x6", EX+ $110.00

Sign, diecut tin, Veedol, figure of blond ice skater in white & orange swimsuit w/product sign below, 14½x5½", EX $1,200.00

Tumbler, Petty, w/full-color illusion decal, 1940s, 4½", EX.$15.00

Playing Cards

Here is another collectible that is inexpensive, easy to display (especially single cards), and very diversified. Among the endless variations are backs that are printed with reproductions of famous paintings and pinup art, carry advertising of all types, and picture tourist attractions and world's fair scenes. Early decks are scarce, but those from the '40s on are usually more attractive anyway, so pick an area that interests you most and have fun! Though they're usually not dated, you may find some clues that will help you to determine an approximate date. Telephone numbers, zip codes, advertising slogans, and patriotic messages are always helpful.

Everett Grist has written an informative book, *Advertising Playing Cards* (published by Collector Books), which we highly recommend to anyone interested in playing cards with any type of advertising.

Club/Newsletter: American Antique Deck Collectors;
52 Plus Joker Club
Clear the Decks, quarterly publication
Ray Hartz, Past President
P.O. Box 1002
Westerville, OH 43081; 614-891-6296

Aces of the Turf, Brown & Bigelow, horse paintings by Palenske, double deck, EXIB..............................$10.00

Air Indian, 1st Class in red on white, 52+Joker, MIB .$12.50

Alice in Wonderland, Western Publishing, double deck, 1950s, 52 no Joker, VGIB..............................$20.00

Amalgamated Meat Cutters & Butcher Workmen of N America, different leader ea card, 52+2 different Jokers, NMIB..............................$20.00

Army & Navy Playing Cards, Russell & Morgan 1981 reproductions of 1881 cards, MIB (presentation) w/booklet $75.00

Bannister Babies, black & white baby pictures, narrow double deck, 52+2 Jokers+booklet, VG in paper box........$10.00

Bay City Rollers, color photos of 1980s rock singing group, 52+2 Jokers, NM, no box..............................$10.00

Bicentennial Presentation Set, US Playing Cards, American Revolution flags, 1976, 6 M (sealed) decks in special case $25.00

Black Velvet, narrow nonstandard, 1974, double deck, MIB/NMIB $20.00

Bulldog Squeezers, US Playing Cards, Squeezer & TGrip backs, 52 w/no Joker, VGIB $50.00

Card Tricks, Hit the Deck, San Francisco, gay theme, Queens are cross-dressers, NMIB..............................$25.00

Colonial Art, Morgan Press, Hastings-on-Hudson, NY, 52 scenes of early America, DL Bloch, 1980s, 52+Joker, NMIB...$20.00

Coolidge Dogs, Monsey Products, dogs playing cards, 1950s, M, sealed $10.00

Dallas Cowboy Cheerleaders, color photos of different cheerleaders, 52+2 Jokers+extra card, NMIB.................$10.00

Death Filter, Occabot Group, 52 ways to stop smoking, 1985, 52+2 skeleton Jokers, EXIB..............................$10.00

Don Celender's Artball, heads of modern artists on NFL players' bodies, 1972, NM, no box..............................$37.00

Early Americana, Shackman, NY, 54 paintings on cards, 1990s, NM, no box..............................$10.00

Egypt, Tutankhamen, wide, golden mask on backs, M in broken box $32.00

Emanuelle, erotic transformation cards, Patric Cuenol for Intercol, 1986, M, sealed $10.00

Gerber Baby, Left: face on white, single deck, $7.00; Right: face on Modilac can, blue and white, double deck, MIB, $12.00. (Photo courtesy Joan Stryker Grubaugh)

Goldwater For President, AU H20 on backs, face on courts, 1966, MIB, sealed..............................$50.00

Green Cross for Safety, National Safety Council, 54 safety suggestions, 1954, 52+2 different Jokers, EXIB **$10.00**

Happy Cards, Germany, 1966, 52+2 Jokers+extra card, M, sealed...**$15.00**

Iron Fireman, blue disk backs, ca 1960, M, no box ...**$16.00**

James Bond, paintings from various Bond films on courts, 1987, 52+Joker+extra card, NM, no box **$10.00**

Kennedy Kards, Humor House, Kennedy family caricatures, red backs, 1963, MIB, sealed **$20.00**

Kissproof, Kissproof Girl backs, narrow, 52+Joker+ad card, VG in torn box..**$40.00**

Liquid Blue, Druggy art w/roses for hearts, moons for spades, etc, 1992, 52+2 Jokers+extra card, M in draw-string bag..**$10.00**

Man From UNCLE, Ed-U Cards, scenes on pip cards, actors photos on courts, 1965, 52+2 Jokers, NMIB **$10.00**

Politicards, drawings by Donald Gates, 1984, MIB, sealed .**$15.00**

Ripley's Believe It or Not, Stancraft, 53 cartoons, 1963, 52+2 Jokers, EXIB **$15.00**

Rockwell International Space Deck, astronaut kings & queens, 52+2 robot Jokers, NMIB **$35.00**

Samuel Hart Pharo, repro, no indices, 1-way courts, printed on cheap paper, 52 complete, M, no box **$35.00**

Snoopy Playing Cards, Hallmark, Snoopy as sports fan backs, 52+2 Jokers, NMIB...**$10.00**

Tee Up, Creative Playing Cards, golf humor, 1962, M in book-style case **$20.00**

Texas White House, historical facts about LBJ on ea card, 1966, MIB, sealed...**$15.00**

Tiffany, US Playing Cards, repro transformation courts, double deck, ea MIB...**$22.00**

Union & Confederate Generals, US Games, repro of Nelson 1863 originals, double deck w/identification cards, M, sealed **$15.00**

US Lines, red & blue backs, double deck, ea 52+Joker, ea VGIB **$20.00**

Vanity Fair, US magazine covers on 10s through aces, 52+2 special Jokers, NMIB **$25.00**

WC Fields, JL Brown, black & white scenes & memorable quotes, 1971, NMIB **$15.00**

Winstanley Geographical Cards, repro of 1676 Worshipful Co collection, edition of 275 w/leaflet, MIB, sealed..**$12.00**

Woman's World, lady in lg hat, wide, 52+Joker, G in torn box...**$32.00**

Political Memorabilia

Political collecting is one of today's fastest-growing hobbies. Between campaign buttons, glassware, paper, and other items, collectors are scrambling to acquire these little pieces of history. Before the turn of the century and the advent of the modern political button, candidates produced ribbons, ferrotypes, stickpins, banners, and many household items to promote their cause. In 1896 the first celluloid (or cello) buttons were used. Cello refers to a process where a paper disc carrying a design is crimped under a piece of celluloid (now acetate) and fastened to a metal button back. In the 1920s the use of lithographed (or litho) buttons was introduced.

Campaigns of the 1930s through the '90s have used both types of buttons. In today's media-hyped world, it is amazing that in addition to TV and radio commercials, candidates still use some of their funding to produce buttons. Bumper stickers, flyers, and novelty items also still abound. Reproductions are sometimes encountered by collectors. Practice and experience are the best tools in order to be aware.

One important factor to remember when pricing buttons is that condition is everything. Buttons with any cracks, stains, or other damage will only sell for a fraction of our suggested values. Listed below are some of the items one is likely to find when scrutinizing today's sales.

For more information about this hobby, we recommend you read Michael McQuillen's monthly column 'Political Parade' in *Antique Week* newspaper.

Advisor: Michael McQuillen (See Directory, Political)

Club: A.P.I.C. (American Political Items Collectors) of Indiana
Michael McQuillen
P.O. Box 50022
Indianapolis, IN 46250-0022; e-mail: buttons@oaktree.net; National organization serving needs of political enthusiasts; send SASE for more information

Ashtray, I Like Ike, ceramic, red, white & blue, square..**$25.00**

Badge, Connecticut Constitutional Convention of 1956, staff member, EX...**$35.00**

Badge, GOP Republican National Convention, Kansas City, MO, Honored Guest, red, white & blue ribbon, 1976, EX..**$35.00**

Ballpoint pen, Spiro T Agnew, facsimile signature w/Vice President's seal..**$30.00**

Bandanna, Ike For President, red, white & blue w/stars & stripes on shield & stars on background, EX **$65.00**

Bank, Abraham Lincoln, bust w/name on base, Banthrico Inc USA, 5½x3½x2", EX **$20.00**

Bank, FDR/Happy Days, barrel shape, 5", EX **$15.00**

Bookends, John & Jacqueline Kennedy, gold-painted plaster, 5", pr, EX...**$40.00**

Brochure, Ronald Reagan as host of GE Theatre, promotion for GE's role in US defense, 1954, 14x10½", EX ..**$20.00**

Bumper Sticker, Democrats for Nixon...........................**$2.00**

Bumper sticker, Kennedy-Johnson, orange & black, unused **$7.00**

Button, All the Way w/Adlai, Stevenson portrait, 1956, 1", EX **$15.00**

Button, America's First Lady, Jacqueline Kennedy surrounds black & white photo, blue & red border, EX **$85.00**

Button, Eisenhower Inauguration picturing the Eisnehowers & Nixons, 1957, 4", EX+......................................**$45.00**

Button, Goldwater in '64 surrounds black & white photo on gold background, EX...**$4.00**

Button, I'm With Magic!, Clinton/Gore, $100.00.

Button, In Memory of LBJ, 1908-1973, 4" $10.00
Button, Jimmy Carter For President, photo, 3" $6.00
Button, McGovern-Eagleton, blue & white, 7⁄8" $3.00
Button, Nixon-Agnew flasher, 2½", EX.....................$15.00
Button, Perot For President in '92 surrounds photo & flag, EX..$5.00
Button, Richard Nixon & Spiro Agnew Inauguration, dated, January 20, 1969, w/ribbon, 3", EX.....................$15.00
Button, Roosevelt/Truman jugate, brown & white, 1944, 1", EX...$85.00
Button, Thomas E Dewey For President, 3", EX+ $25.00
Button, Vote Gore, shows Senator Gore Sr of Tennessee, blue & white flasher........................$15.00
Button, We Want Mamie, portrait, red, white & blue, EX..$18.00
Cane, Gerald Ford, wood w/elephant handle............$30.00
Clicker, Click w/Dick, w/image NM.....................$10.00
Coaster, I Like Ike in bold red letters in center, cork.$15.00
Coloring book, JFK, caricature cartoons inside, unused ..$35.00
Coloring book, Reagan biography, Miller Publications, Hanover Ill, 1981, unused, M...............$12.50
Dart board, Stick Dick (Nixon), 11½" square, NM......$25.00
Doll, Santa w/George Bush's face, squeeze rubber, EX...$20.00
Doll, Ted Kennedy, cloth w/caricature features, 1980, 5½", EX.......................................$15.00
Doll, Tricky Dicky, rubber, 5", NMOC $25.00
Figure, Barry Goldwater, Remco, 1964, NMIB............$35.00
Figure, Lyndon Johnson, plastic, Remco, 5", MIB.......$35.00
Game, Barrel of Clintons, NM...........................$12.00
Game, Barry Goldwater's 1964 Presidential Election, MOC $30.00
Game, The Kennedys, NMIB (Mt Rushmore caricatures on box) $55.00
Invitation, Ronald Reagan inaugural, 1981 ....$15.00
Jigsaw puzzle, Spiro Agnew as Superman, MIB..........$20.00
Key, Democratic Convention, brass, lg, 1968.............$20.00
License plate, Coolidge For President, red on white w/red border, EX $120.00
License plate, LBJ For the USA, red, white & blue $25.00
Mask, Jackie Kennedy, thin plastic, 1960, EX............$40.00
Mask, John Kennedy, thin plastic, 1960, EX...............$40.00
Matchbook cover, Let Us Now Close Ranks, Reagan & Ford portraits, blue & red on white, NM $6.00
Mechanical pencil, MacArthur portrait in blue, 2 flags on white band, unusual, EX...................$65.00
Medal, Eisenhower & Lincoln Republican Centennial, 1954, 2½", EX.....................................$15.00

Membership card, Truman & Barkley, 1948, EX.........$45.00
Money clip, John F Kennedy, 1917-1963, MIB...........$10.00
Mug, Jimmy Carter caricature, brown cermaic...........$20.00
Music box, Richard Nixon, w/wind-up dancer, plays 'Ta Ra Ra Boom De Yea,' 1972, NM $175.00
Nodders, John & Jackie Kennedy, pr........................$275.00
Paperweight, FDR bust, A New Deal, heavy metal, EX..$55.00
Pencil, Nixon portrait, King Richard XXXVII, Watergate Hotel...Coronation January 1975, M........$8.00
Pocket mirror, RFK Destined To Become President surrounds photo, red, white & blue, EX...............$35.00
Pocket mirror, William McKinley Memorial, multicolored, 1920s, EX..........................$25.00
Postcard, Nixon family portrait, black & white, postmarked Inaugural Day, 1969 ....$15.00
Poster, Hello!, My Name Is Jimmy Carter, I'm Running For President, black & green on white cardboard, EX.$16.00
Poster stamp, GOP elephant, 1956, M $4.00
Radio, Jimmy Carter w/peanut body, vinyl strap, MIB.$30.00
Snowdome, Douglas MacArthur, 1940s, NM...............$38.00
Ticket, John F Kennedy campaign appearance, Time of Greatness, blue, NM $40.00
Tie tac, Vote Adlai, flasher, EX $15.00

Ticket, Inaugural Gala, January 19th, 1949, $40.00.

Toy, Watergate Bug, plastic, mechanical, MIB............$40.00
Tray, FD Roosevelt image w/White House, 10x13", EX.$50.00
Wristwatch, Ross Perot, 1991, MIB $25.00
Wristwatch, Spiro T Agnew, All American Time Co, caricature face, nonworking.....................$30.00

Porcelier China

The Porcelier Manufacturing Company was founded in East Liverpool, Ohio, in 1926. They moved to Greensburg, Pennsylvania, in 1930, where they continued to operate until closing in 1954. They're best known for their extensive line of vitrified china kitchenware, but it should also be noted that they made innumerable lighting fixtures.

The company used many different methods of marking their ware. Each mark included the name Porcelier, usually written in script. The mark can be an ink stamp in black, blue, brown, or green; engraved into the metal bottom plate (as on electrical pieces); on a paper label (as found on lighting fixtures); incised block letters; or raised block letters.

With the exception of sugar bowls and creamers, most pieces are marked.

The values below are suggested for pieces in excellent condition. Our advisor for this category, Susan Grindberg, has written the *Collector's Guide to Porcelier China, Identification and Values* (Collector Books).

Advisor: Susan Grindberg (See Directory, Porcelier)

Club/Newsletter: Porcelier Collectors Club
21 Tamarac Swamp Rd.
Wellingford, CT 06492
Porcelier Paper Newsletter, $2.50 for sample copy

Miniature Rose percolator, sugar bowl with lid and creamer set, $175.00. (Photo courtesy Susan Grindberg)

Ball jug, Beehive Crisscross	**$70.00**
Bean pot, Basketweave Cameo, individual	**$10.00**
Boiler, Rope Bow, 6-cup	**$35.00**
Casserole, Country Life Series, w/lid, 9½"	**$85.00**
Creamer, Basketweave Wild Flowers	**$12.00**
Creamer, Beehive Floral Spray	**$10.00**
Creamer, Black-Eyed Susan Hostess set	**$12.00**
Creamer, Geometric Wheat	**$12.00**
Creamer, Goldfinches	**$12.00**
Creamer, Medallion	**$10.00**
Creamer, Orange Poppy Hostess set	**$12.00**
Decanter, Oriental Deco	**$60.00**
Electric percolator, Pink Flower Hostess set	**$75.00**
Electric percolator, Scalloped Wild Flowers	**$110.00**
Electric urn, White Flower Platinum set	**$95.00**
Lamp, table; Antique Rose decal	**$45.00**
Mugs, Wildlife series, w/gold trim, ea	**$35.00**
Pitcher, Chevron, 2-cup	**$25.00**
Pitcher, disc; 1939 New York World's Fair, 5"	**$150.00**
Pot, Colonial, Black-Eyed Susan, 6-cup	**$45.00**
Pretzel jar, Serv-All Line, platinum	**$75.00**
Refrigerator beverage coolers, rectangular	**$75.00**
Sugar bowl, Black-Eyed Susan Percolator set, #710	**$12.00**
Sugar bowl, Dutch Boy & Girl	**$8.00**
Sugar bowl, Paneled Rose	**$12.00**
Sugar bowl, Pink Flower Platinum set	**$8.00**

Sugar bowl, Silhouette Hostess set	**$12.00**
Syrup jar, Barock-Colonial, ivory, red or blue, #2012	**$45.00**
Teapot, American Beauty Rose, 6-cup	**$35.00**
Teapot, Basketweave Floral, w/decorated dripper, 6-cup	**$55.00**
Teapot, Cobblestone I & II, 6-cup	**$30.00**
Teapot, Flamingo, 6-cup	**$40.00**
Teapot, Floral Trio, 4-cup	**$30.00**
Teapot, Hearth, w/gold trim, 8-cup	**$40.00**
Teapot, Mexican, 6-cup	**$40.00**
Teapot, Nautical, 2-cup	**$40.00**
Teapot, Pears, 4-cup	**$25.00**
Teapot, Rose & Wheat, 2-cup	**$30.00**
Teapot, Tree Trunk, 6-cup	**$35.00**

Postcards

Postcards are not just to mail home when you're on vacation; for more than one hundred years, they've also served to document changes in social history. Deltiology, the study of postcards, is a major hobby for people of all ages, backgrounds and financial strata. There are still penny postcards, and there are others that can run into the thousands of dollars; but the average card is valued at $2.00 to $8.00 on today's market. Art Nouveau, Poster Art, Real Photo, and Signed Artist cards are most collectible. Note that cards with tiny images and florals may be old but have almost no value. Condition is all important.

Advisor: Pamela E. Apkarian-Russell (See Directory, Postcards)

Advertising

Butterfly Pipes, Art Deco, w/butterfly	**$45.00**
Conserves 'le Soleil,' fat cook w/products in his arms	**$50.00**
Dennison Mfg Co, Framingham MA, white border	**$4.00**
Fire-Chief Gasoline, w/chrome of Ed Wynn	**$15.00**
Government postal, Man & Wife Wanted, shows car to be given as bonus, ad for Coffee Co OH	**$14.00**
Rice Krispies, showing Snap, Crackle & Pop	**$8.00**
Snowdrift Lard, can w/rabbit in cotton field	**$25.00**

Artist Signed

Bainsfather, Bruce; war humor	**$10.00**
Brundage, boy w/candle kneels by jack-o'-lantern, cat peers around from other side, German, #121	**$20.00**
Brundage, boy w/untied shoelace, top hat & yellow coat walks away while girl w/big blue bows reads Valentine	**$10.00**
Brundage, Tuck series #120, boy holds jack-o'-lantern up as cat on his shoulder stands between them	**$25.00**
Brundage, Tuck series #174, boy w/jack-o'-lantern in hand, green jacket, red hat	**$15.00**
Buss, Deco garden, couple in French period costume dance under moon	**$15.00**
Clappsaddle, angel carrying lilies, lavender background	**$10.00**

Clappsaddle, Christmas, kneeling angel w/toys **$10.00**
Clappsaddle, Easter, angel in lavender robe, silver border .**$8.00**
Ebner, Pauli; 3 children under flowering tree look at Easter eggs **$12.50**
Elliot, Katherine; woman w/muff in circle, snow falling ..**$8.00**
Fisher, Harrison; bride **$14.00**
Heinmulier, Thanksgiving, man & woman hold stick w/hanging pumpkin turkey below **$6.00**
Helle, music & children in uniform, 'God Save the King' ..**$10.00**
Koehler, Mela; girl in skirt on skis **$125.00**
Mucha, Slavia Vzajemne Pojistovaci Banka, Art Nouveau .**$150.00**
Nash, Christmas, 2 children carrying holly & gifts **$5.00**
Nash, Halloween, 2 Deco nude witches silhouette on gray **$25.00**
O'Neil, Rose; Kewpies w/Santa **$45.00**
Parrish, Maxfield; Broadview **$45.00**
Parrish, Maxfield; tea house **$75.00**
Phillips, Cole; fade out: woman's arms & back side of man's head fade out **$15.00**
Roulan, Edward; 10 cards from 'Chantecler' in original envelope, French **$55.00**
Solomko, woman (semi-clad in veils) w/cougar **$20.00**
Sowerby, Millicent; Phyllis (pretty little girl)...............**$20.00**
Wall, Bernhardt; woman in lg hat holds jack-o'-lantern, 2 cats gaze at her hat, sepia **$15.00**
Whitney, child dressed in green period clothing carrying Christmas packages...**$5.00**
Winch, girl in white holds hands w/owl & jack-o'-lantern man, 1913...**$145.00**
Winch, witch on owl, 3 dwarfs on bats fly through sky, 'A Halloween' **$125.00**

Holidays (not artist signed)

Christmas, angel w/cherubs about her reads card, gold embellishments **$8.00**
Christmas, Greetings From Florida, train going through orchard...**$3.00**
Christmas, Santa in silk suit **$40.00**
Christmas, Tuck series #512, girl in red coat w/basket knocks on door **$6.00**
Easter, silk clothes on 2 children in yard, girl in blue dress & boy in red hat & white silk sash **$10.00**

Halloween, Guid luck tae yea this Hallowe'en, pre-1920, $10.00. (Photo courtesy Pamela Apkarian-Russell)

Valentine, little girl on rocking horse being stopped by little boy policeman, Whitney **$6.00**
Valentine, 2 cherubs trying to pick 4-leaf clover on a cliff, PFB..**$7.00**

Locations, Landmarks, and Attractions

Akron OH, Rubber Manufacturer of the World, linen...**$6.00**
American Steel Foundries, Alliance OH, #11002 ....**$10.00**
Austria-Hungary, woman in national dress w/banner, Alps behind her, sm size **$12.00**
Boston view, w/baked beans pot....................................**$4.00**
Busy street scene, Harrison NY, 1910 ....**$6.00**
Canton OH, Main St, linen...**$3.00**
Chefoo, China, street scene, 1913..................................**$5.00**
Chemins De Fer De L'etat Excursions en Bretagne, art poster **$15.00**
DeKalb St Looking West, Camden SC, 1923 ....**$5.00**
Fenway Park, game in progress, linen.........................**$12.00**
Fisherman's Wharf, San Francisco, linen......................**$2.50**
Foating dry dock, Jacksonville FL.................................**$5.00**
Gem Theatre, Peakes Isle ME, #2199 ....**$6.00**
Granite State Hotel in Ocean Park ME, tennis courts ...**$5.00**
Hamilton Hotel (front view), Bermuda **$4.00**
Hood College, Frederick MD, linen................................**$2.00**
Hotel Metropole in London, litho................................**$10.00**
Ice Blockade in St Mary's River **$5.00**
Lawrence MA, buildings, copper window card.............**$5.00**
Lobster King Harry Hachney & His Lobster Waitress, Atlantic City..**$10.00**
Mexican soldiers on duty, Matamoros, Mexico **$6.00**
Montreal, St Catherine's St, looking east of the busy main street **$5.00**
Montreal harborfront & St Helen's Island, busy area....**$6.00**
Napoli, early litho view..**$10.00**
Neely's Ginnery & Cotton Warehouse, Waynesboro GA, busy scene **$7.00**
Oxford MI Baptist Church, advertising for postcard publishing on back from Newfield & Newfield...............**$10.00**
Restwell Motel H'way 41, Vincennes IN, linen.............**$6.00**
Richmond Hotel No Adams MA, 1907, copper enhancement **$6.00**
Salute From Camp Croft S Carolina, McArthur...........**$12.00**
Shangri-La Restaurant, Lake Winnipesaukee (interior), chrome..**$4.00**
State House, Dover DE, heavy gold embellishment **$6.00**
Tea House, 1914, North Salem NY................................**$4.00**

Real Photo

African maiden w/tribal scarring **$14.00**
Beautiful woman, tinted..**$15.00**
Boy in pedal car, tinted...**$15.00**
Brigitte Helm, in Russian-style winter outfit **$20.00**
Fay Wray in King Kong's hand....................................**$14.00**
Gina Lollobrigida in strapless gown & coat over 1 shoulder..**$12.00**

Greta Garbo in the arms of Nils Asther **$15.00**
Greta Garbo w/Conrad Nagel who is in military uniform .**$14.00**
House (unidentified)..**$1.00**
Little girl w/doll, tinted...**$14.00**
Little girl w/muff, tinted **$9.00**
Lowell MA, man in 1913 car waves to people on main street, readable license plate..................................**$35.00**
Mary Pickford, French **$12.00**
Near Eastern Orphans From Armenian Genocide, in front of pyramid..**$15.00**
Nude lady w/vase, tinted...**$35.00**
Nude lady w/veil **$22.00**
Pola Negri, French..**$12.00**
Shirley Temple in blue-tinted full-length dress............**$25.00**
St Stanislav's Church, Winchester NH, ca 1914 ....**$20.00**
Stately home in Katonah NY, 1906.............................**$10.00**
Teddy Roosevelt in VT..**$40.00**

Steamships and Boats

Block Island RI, member of Spartan's crew being rescued from ship **$7.00**
Boat loading cotton at wharf, Memphis TN **$4.00**
Ferry boat, Vischer's Ferry, NY..................................**$4.00**
SS Pocahontas Near Norfolk, linen, 1944...................**$4.00**
Steam boat loading, Louisville KY, white border **$4.00**
Steamer, Mt Washington Lake, Winnipesaukee NH, Tuck .**$4.50**
Steamer City of Detroit, white border, 1915 ....**$4.50**
Steamer Marguerite, Moosehead Lake, ME **$4.00**
Steamer Put-In-Bay, 1911 ....**$5.00**
Steamer Theodore Roosevelt, at night, Chicago, 1912..**$5.00**
Steamer White Star, Tashmoo MI, 1909......................**$5.00**

Trains and Depots

Grand Trunk Railway Station, Brantford, Ontario Canada .**$8.00**
Ill Central Depot, Champaign IL, train arriving.............**$6.00**
Little girl in purple w/muff waits for coming train **$8.00**
Railroad station, Garrison NY, 1914, sepia...................**$7.00**
Southern Railway Station, Black Mountain NC, linen.**$10.00**
Train, #7044, June 18, 1909, en route to Mt McClellan CO, passengers pose by train, snow walls on ea side of tracks **$8.00**
Train at Midlake Station, Salt Lake UT **$8.00**
Train in station, Mount Vernon NY, A8516, black & white...**$7.00**
Train station, Woodlawn PA, white border...................**$10.00**
Train station at Castle Rock CO **$8.00**
Union Pacific Depot, Las Vegas NV, linen **$7.00**

Miscellaneous

Adolf Hitler, portrait..**$15.00**
Airbrushed embossed baseball player...........................**$18.00**
Airbrushed embossed heart of flowers in purple, 'To My Sweetheart' in gold **$2.00**
Birthday, w/violets...**$.50**

Bonzo w/glass eyes, 'My Love Is Like a Red Red Rose' (not by Studdy-Alpha publishing) **$20.00**
British fighter bomber, 'Keep 'em Flying' **$7.00**
Cameo embossed 'Vive La RF France' **$12.00**
Child angel w/cornucopia of flowers walks through stars..**$6.00**
Children playing w/snowman, artist MEP, 1921 ....**$4.00**
Fisherman being photographed w/fish 5 times his size, comic, linen..**$4.00**
Flags & shields, US & Italy w/eagle in between **$8.00**
Greatest Mother in the World, Red Cross poster, UK .**$15.00**
Lady applying mascara, signed artist...........................**$16.00**
Leather, w/dog **$5.00**
Linen, comic, man & sexy woman at bar w/bartender ..**$4.00**
Penny Dreadful, The Boarding House Lady, Myer **$8.00**
Prince Arisugawa portrait, Japanese art **$25.00**
Princess Grace & Prince Rainier of Monaco, cameos above view of Monte Carlo, black & white...................**$10.00**
Puppies (3) in black top hats **$10.00**

Powder Jars

Ceramics

With figural ceramics becoming increasingly popular, powder jars are desired collectibles. Found in various subjects and having great eye appeal, they make interesting collections. For more information we recommend *Collector's Guide to Made in Japan Ceramics* (there are three in series) by Carole Bess White (Collector Books).

Advisor: Carole Bess White (See Directory, Japan Ceramics)

Bamboo w/flower motif, black & white on orange, Japan, 3½" dia, from $15 to.............................**$20.00**
Colonial lady, blue hoop skirt, ¾-figure lid, Japan, 7", from $30 to..**$45.00**
Colonial lady, rose in right hand, bouquet held in front, lid extends to hip line, Japan, 7", from $125 to **$165.00**
Dog pr, white w/black ears etc, atop basketweave lid (w/fruit decal) & bowl, Japan, 4", from $25 to **$45.00**
Flapper, orange coat w/white trim, yellow & blue hat, head & shoulders as lid, bowl as mid section, Japan, 4", from $70 to.**$85.00**
Flowers in relief (red, blue & green) over entire dome lid, yellow bowl, Japan, 3¾" dia................................**$20.00**
Garden scene, on white background w/blue border, solid blue jar w/gold trim, Noritake, 4¾" dia...............**$65.00**
Heart shape, Oriental lady w/fan on heart shape in center of lid, Noritake, 3", from $300 to **$400.00**
Lady, half-figure in pink dress w/hands folded, floral decor on pink jar, Noritake, 5", from $295 to..............**$355.00**
Lady, hoop skirt as lid & bowl, gold & multicolored lustre glazes, Goldcastle, 4", from $65 to......................**$85.00**
Landscape, fall scene, earth tones, Noritake, green mark #27, 3½" dia **$75.00**
Oriental lady w/parasol in orange dress atop purple lustre scalloped lid & jar, Noritake, from $295 to **$355.00**

Owl, multicolor lustre glaze, Japan, 4½", from $60.00 to $85.00. (Photo courtesy Carole Bess White)

Pierrot, yellow costume w/multicolored trim, Goldcastle, 4¼", from $75 to...**$100.00**

Rabbit, ear cocked, on hexagonal lid & bowl, yellow w/multicolored trim, Japan, 5¼", from $45 to **$65.00**

Glassware

Glassware items such as powder jars, trays, lamps, vanity sets, towel bars, and soap dishes were produced in large quantities during the Depression era by many glasshouses who were simply trying to stay afloat. They used many of the same colors as they had in the making of their colored Depression glass dinnerware that has been so popular with collectors for more than thirty years.

Some of their most imaginative work went into designing powder jars. Subjects ranging from birds and animals to Deco nudes and Cinderella's coach can be found today, and this diversity coupled with the fact that many were made in several colors provides collectors with more than enough variations to keep them interested and challenged.

Advisor: Sharon Thoerner, Glass Powder Jars (See Directory, Powder Jars)

Annabella, pink transparent.......................................**$175.00**
Annette w/2 dogs, crystal **$85.00**
Babs II, pink frost, 3-footed, sm version **$155.00**
Ballerina, pink frost...**$255.00**
Bassett hound, green frost **$195.00**
Bassett hound, pink frost, from $145 to **$165.00**
Cameo, green frost **$275.00**
Carrie, black, draped nude figural stem **$195.00**
Cinderella's Coach, pink frost w/black lid, rectangular body, sm footrest for coachman, lg.............................**$195.00**
Cleopatra II, crystal, shallow base, deep lid, 4¾".......**$95.00**
Crinoline Girl, crystal, off-the-shoulder gown, flowers in right hand, embossed bows on skirt.............................**$40.00**
Crinoline Girl, pink frost, off-the-shoulder gown, flowers in right hand, embossed bows on skirt..................**$120.00**
Dancing Girl, blue transparent, feminine features, rope trim at top of base...**$480.00**
Dancing Girl, green frost, feminine features, rope trim at top of base...**$120.00**

Delilah II, green frost..**$95.00**
Dolly Sisters, green frost **$225.00**
Elephant w/carousel base, green frost......................**$255.00**
Elephants battling, pink frost....................................**$135.00**
Godiva, satin, nude seated on diamond-shaped base.**$185.00**
Gretchen, green transparent **$195.00**
Horse & coach, pink frost, round **$350.00**
Jackie, Jade-ite...**$275.00**
Joker, green transparent **$85.00**
Lillian III, crystal, stippled lid, w/hexagonal band......**$50.00**
Lillian VII, pink frost, cone-shaped base **$250.00**
Lovebirds, green frost...**$100.00**
Martha Washington, crystal, Colonial lady between boy & girl...**$60.00**
Martha Washington, green frost, Colonial lady between boy & girl...**$150.00**
Martha Washington, pink frost, Colonial lady between boy & girl...**$130.00**
Minstrel, crystal..**$50.00**
Minstrel, crystal w/green paint **$85.00**
My Pet, 3 Scotties on lid, crystal..............................**$75.00**
My Pet, 3 Scotties on lid, pink transparent..............**$225.00**
Penguins, pink frost, dome top.................................**$300.00**
Rapunzel, pink or green frost, ea.............................**$250.00**
Rin-Tin-Tin, green transparent.................................**$225.00**
Scottie, puff box, Akro Agate, blue..........................**$140.00**
Scottie, puff box, Akro Agate, milk glass **$115.00**
Southern Belle, green frost **$250.00**
Sphinx, yellow frost..**$275.00**

Spike Bulldog, green frost, $155.00. (Photo courtesy Sharon Thoerner)

Spike Bulldog, pink frost **$125.00**
Terrier, pink frost, sm base **$135.00**
Terrier on lg base, pink transparent, rare.................**$300.00**
Twins, green frost..**$150.00**
Vamp, pink frost, flapper's head forms finial **$155.00**
Victorian Lady, green frost **$250.00**
Wendy, satin, flapper girl w/arms outstretched, beaded necklace..**$65.00**

Purinton Pottery

The Purinton Pottery Company moved from Ohio to Shippenville, Pennsylvania, in 1941 and began producing several lines of dinnerware and kitchen items hand painted with fruits, ivy vines, and floral designs in bold brush strokes of color on a creamy white background. The company closed in 1959 due to economic reasons.

Purinton has a style that's popular today with collectors who like the country look. It isn't always marked, but you'll soon recognize its distinct appearance. Some of the rarer designs are Palm Tree, Peasant Garden, and Pennsylvania Dutch, and examples of these lines are considerably higher than the more common ones. You'll see more Apple and Fruit pieces than any, and in more diversified shapes.

For more information we recommend *Purinton Pottery, An Identification and Value Guide,* by Susan Morris.

Advisor: Susan Morris (See Directory, Purinton Pottery)

Apple, ashtray, 5½" L $40.00
Apple, baker, 7" $30.00
Apple, bean pot, 3¾" $50.00
Apple, bottle, oil & vinegar; tall, 1-pt, 9½", pr...........$95.00
Apple, bowl, fruit; plain border, 12" $35.00
Apple, canister, sugar or tea; square, 5½" $50.00
Apple, dish, jam & jelly; 5½" $45.00
Apple, dish, pickle; 6" $30.00
Apple, jar, marmalade; 4½" $50.00
Apple, jug, honey; 6¼" $55.00
Apple, jug, 5-pt, 8" $85.00
Apple, mug, beer; 16-oz, 4¾" $55.00

Apple, pitcher, beverage; two-pint, 6½", $65.00.

Apple, plate, breakfast; 8½"..$12.00
Apple, plate, chop; scalloped border, 12"...................$40.00
Apple, plate, lap; 8½" $15.00
Apple, platter, grill; indentations, 12"........................$45.00
Apple, salt & pepper shakers, jug style, miniature, 2½",
    pr...$20.00
Apple, saucer, 5½"..$3.00
Apple, teapot, 6-cup, 6½" $70.00
Apple, tray, roll; 11" $35.00
Apple, tumbler, 12-oz, 5" $20.00
Apple, wall pocket, 3½"...$40.00
Chartreuse, bowl, vegetable; open, 8½" $25.00
Chartreuse, mug, juice; 6-oz, 2½".................................$15.00
Chartreuse, plate, chop; 12"...$25.00
Chartreuse, salt & pepper shakers, jug style, miniature, 2½",
    pr...$30.00

Chartreuse, saucer, 5½"..$3.00
Crescent Flower, coaster, 3½".....................................$40.00
Crescent Flower, plate, breakfast; 8½".........................$35.00
Crescent Flower, vase, handled, 7½".........................$125.00
Fruit, bottle, vinegar; cobalt trim, 1-pt, 9½" $35.00
Fruit, bowl, range; w/lid, cobalt trim, labeled Fats, 5½" ...$45.00
Fruit, canister, cobalt trim, oval, 9"...........................$65.00
Fruit, coffeepot, w/drip filter, 8-cup, 11" $85.00
Fruit, cup & saucer, complementary, no fruit design, 2½",
    5½"..$13.00
Fruit, dish, cocktail; sea horse center handle, 11¾" ...$55.00
Fruit, jar, grease; 5½"..$45.00
Fruit, jug, 5-pt, 8"...$75.00
Fruit, plate, lap; 8½"...$30.00
Fruit, relish, wood or metal handle, 3-part, 10" $45.00
Fruit, salt & pepper shakers, jug style, miniature, 2½", pr ..$20.00
Fruit, salt & pepper shakers, range style, 4", pr.........$40.00
Fruit, sugar bowl & creamer, miniature, 2"..................$30.00
Fruit, teapot, individual, 2-cup, 4".............................$45.00
Fruit, teapot, 6-cup, 6"..$55.00
Heather Plaid, creamer, 3"..$20.00
Heather Plaid, jar, grease; w/lid, 5½"..........................$60.00
Heather Plaid, jug, 5-pt, 8"..$75.00
Heather Plaid, mug, handled, 8-oz, 4".........................$25.00
Heather Plaid, plate, salad; 6¾"..................................$10.00
Heather Plaid, platter, meat; 12".................................$30.00
Heather Plaid, saucer, 5½"..$3.00
Heather Plaid, tray, roll; w/stand................................$35.00
Heather Plaid, wall pocket, 3½"...................................$35.00
Intaglio, baker, 7"...$20.00
Intaglio, cookie jar, oval, 9½"....................................$75.00
Intaglio, decanter, miniature, 5".................................$35.00
Intaglio, dish, jam & jelly; 5½" $40.00
Intaglio, mug, beer; 16-oz, 4¾"...................................$40.00
Intaglio, pitcher, beverage; 2-pt, 6¼"..........................$55.00
Intaglio, pitcher, gravy; TS & T mold, 3¾" $65.00
Intaglio, plate, breakfast; 8½".....................................$10.00
Intaglio, plate, chop; 12"..$25.00
Intaglio, relish, metal handle, 3-part, 10"....................$45.00
Intaglio, saucer, 5½"..$3.00
Intaglio, sugar bowl, w/lid, 5".....................................$30.00
Intaglio, tidbit, 2-tiered, 10" $55.00
Intaglio, tray, roll; 11"...$35.00
Ivy-Red Blossom, creamer, 3½"...................................$15.00
Ivy-Red Blossom, mug, juice; 6-oz, 2½".......................$15.00
Ivy-Yellow Blossom, creamer, 3½"...............................$15.00
Ivy-Yellow Blossom, Kent jug, 1-pt, 4½".....................$30.00
Maywood, bowl, cereal; 5¼"...$8.00
Maywood, bowl, salad; 11"..$25.00
Maywood, cup, 2½"..$8.00
Maywood, dish, pickle; 6"...$15.00
Maywood, plate, lap; 8½"...$10.00
Maywood, relish, 3-part, 10".......................................$35.00
Maywood, teapot, 6-cup, 6½".......................................$45.00
Ming Tree, cup, 2½"...$20.00
Ming Tree, plate, chop; 12"...$55.00
Ming Tree, saucer, 5½"..$10.00

Mountain Rose, bean pot, 3¾" $65.00
Mountain Rose, decanter, 5" $45.00
Mountain Rose, plate, dinner; 9¾" $25.00
Mountain Rose, relish, 3-part, 10" $75.00
Mountain Rose, tumbler, 12-oz, 5" $35.00
Normandy Plaid, bowl, dessert; 4" $8.00
Normandy Plaid, bowl, fruit; 12" $35.00
Normandy Plaid, bowl, vegetable; divided, 10½"......$30.00
Normandy Plaid, candy dish, 6¼" $35.00

Normandy Plaid, cookie jar, $70.00. (Photo courtesy Susan Morris)

Normandy Plaid, creamer & sugar bowl, miniature, 2",
    pr...$30.00
Normandy Plaid, dish, w/lid, 9" $55.00
Normandy Plaid, jug, mug; 8-oz, 4¾" $40.00
Normandy Plaid, jug, 5-oz, 8" $75.00
Normandy Plaid, mug, beer; 16-oz, 4¾"...............$40.00
Normandy Plaid, shaker, Pour-N-Shake; 4¼" $30.00
Peasant Garden, pitcher, Rubel mold, 5"..................$150.00
Peasant Garden, plate, chop; 12" $200.00
Peasant Garden, plate, lap; 8½" $110.00
Peasant Garden, salt & pepper shakers, jug style, miniature,
    2½", pr...$75.00
Pennsylvania Dutch, baker, 7" $45.00
Pennsylvania Dutch, bowl, dessert; 4" $15.00
Pennsylvania Dutch, cookie jar, w/wooden lid, square,
    9½" $110.00
Pennsylvania Dutch, creamer, 3½"........................$40.00
Pennsylvania Dutch, planter, basket; 6¼"...............$85.00
Pennsylvania Dutch, plate, salad; 6¾" $20.00
Pennsylvania Dutch, relish, pottery handle, 3-part, 10" ..$75.00
Pennsylvania Dutch, salt & pepper shakers, Pour-N-Shake;
    4¼", pr..$100.00
Pennsylvania Dutch, soup & sandwich (cup & plate), 2¼x4",
    11" dia, set..$75.00
Pennsylvania Dutch, wall pocket, 3½".....................$65.00
Petals, baker, 7"...$35.00
Petals, jug, honey; 6¼" $45.00
Petals, mug, juice; 6-oz, 2½" $15.00
Petals, plate, breakfast; 8½" $15.00
Provincial Fruit, bowl, cereal; 5¼" $20.00
Provincial Fruit, cup, 2½"..$15.00

Provincial Fruit, plate, salad; 6¾"...........................$15.00
Provincial Fruit, platter, meat; 11" $50.00
Provincial Fruit, tumbler, 12-oz, 5".........................$25.00
Saraband, bowl, vegetable; open, 8½".....................$15.00
Saraband, canister, flour or coffee; 7½" $35.00
Saraband, mug, beer; 16-oz, 4¾" $20.00
Saraband, plate, chop; 12" $25.00
Saraband, plate, lap; 8½" $15.00
Saraband, salt & pepper shakers, stacking, 2¼", pr....$25.00
Saraband, saucer, 5½"..$5.00
Seaform, plate, dinner; 10"......................................$25.00
Seaform, platter, meat; 12" $50.00
Seaform, salt & pepper shakers, 3", pr $55.00
Seaform, saucer, 5½"...$8.00
Tea Rose, creamer & sugar bowl, w/lid, 3½", set.....$85.00
Tea Rose, planter, 5" $65.00
Tea Rose, plate, salad; 6¾" $20.00
Tea Rose, salt & pepper shakers, jug style, miniature, 2½",
    pr $50.00
Tea Rose, saucer, 5½"...$8.00
Turquoise, bowl, vegetable; divided, 10½" $35.00
Turquoise, butter dish, 6½" $75.00
Turquoise, cup, 2½" $10.00
Turquoise, plate, dinner; 9¾" $15.00
Turquoise, salt & pepper shakers, stacking, 2¼", pr..$30.00

Puzzles

The first children's puzzle was actually developed as a learning aid by an English map maker, trying to encourage the study of geography. Most nineteenth-century puzzles were made of wood, rather boring, and very expensive. But by the Victorian era, nursery rhymes and other light-hearted themes became popular. The industrial revolution and the inception of color lithography combined to produce a stunning variety of themes ranging from technical advancements, historical scenarios, and fairy tales. Power saws made production more cost effective, and wood was replaced with less expensive cardboard.

As early as the '20s and '30s, American manufacturers began to favor character-related puzzles, the market already influenced by radio and the movies. Some of these were advertising premiums. Die-cutters had replaced jigsaws, cardboard became thinner, and now everyone could afford puzzles. During the Depression they were a cheap form of entertainment, and no family get-together was complete without a puzzle spread out on the card table for all to enjoy.

Television and movies caused a lull in puzzle making during the '50s, but advancements in printing and improvements in quality brought them back strongly in the '60s. Unusual shapes, the use of fine art prints, and more challenging designs caused sales to increase.

If you're going to collect puzzles, you'll need to remember that unless all the pieces are there, they're not of much value, especially those from the twentieth century. The condition of the box is important as well. Right now there's a lot of interest in puzzles from the '50s through the '70s that feature popular TV shows and characters from that era. Remember, though a frame-tray puzzle still sealed in its original wrapping may be worth $10.00 or more, depending on the subject matter and its age, a well used example may well be worthless as a collectible.

To learn more about the subject, we recommend *Character Toys and Collectibles* and *Toys, Antique and Collectible*, both by David Longest; and *Schroeder's Toys, Antique to Modern*. (All are published by Collector Books.) *Toys of the Sixties, A Pictorial Guide*, by Bill Bruegman (Cap'n Penny Productions) is another good source of information.

Newsletter: *Piece by Piece*
P.O. Box 12823
Kansas City, KS 66112-9998; Subscription: $8 per year

Alf, jigsaw, 100 pcs, EXIB **$5.00**
Alice in Wonderland, jigsaw, Jaymar, complete, EXIB..**$30.00**
Aquaman, jigsaw, Whitman, 1968, 100 pcs, MIB **$40.00**
Archie, jigsaw, Jaymar, 1969, complete, MIB..............**$40.00**
Batman, jigsaw, Control Room Chaos, 1966, 260 pcs, EXIB **$65.00**
Batman & Robin, frame-tray, Whitman #4518, 1966, EX...**$12.00**
Battlestar Galactica, jigsaw, Parker Bros, 1978, 140 pcs, MIB (sealed) **$15.00**
Beatles, jigsaw, Yellow Submarine, Jaymar, 650 pcs, NMIB **$150.00**
Beverly Hillbillies, frame-tray, Jaymar, 1963, complete, NM **$20.00**
Beverly Hillbillies, jigsaw, Jaymar, 1963, complete, MIB..**$20.00**
Brady Bunch, frame-tray, Whitman, 1972, complete, M ..**$45.00**
Buzz Lightyear & Woody, jigsaw, 60 pcs, MIB..............**$8.00**
Captain America, frame-tray, Whitman, 1966, complete, 14x11", M.............................**$50.00**
Captain Kangaroo, jigsaw, Fairchild, 1950s, complete, EXIB **$25.00**
Captain Kool & the Kongs, frame-tray, Whitman, 1978, complete, EX **$12.00**
Charlie's Angels, jigsaw, HG Toys, 1976, 250 pcs, MIB ..**$30.00**
Dallas, jigsaw, features, JR, Warren, 1980, EXIB **$20.00**
Daniel Boone, frame-tray, Wilderness Scout, Jaymar #2722, EX.............................**$20.00**
Dark Shadows, jigsaw, Milton Bradley, 1969, NM (EX box).............................**$65.00**
Dick Tracy, jigsaw, Jaymar, 1961, 60 pcs, MIB............**$50.00**
Dilly Dally the Human Bullet, frame-tray, Whitman, 1950s, complete, EX.............................**$40.00**
Donnie & Marie Osmond, frame-tray, Whitman, 1977, complete, M.............................**$20.00**
Dr Kildare, jigsaw, Milton Bradley, 1962, complete, NMIB.............................**$35.00**
Dudley Do-Right, jigsaw, Whitman, 100 pcs, NM (EX box).**$30.00**
Eight Is Enough, jigsaw, American Publishing, 1978, complete, MIB.............................**$15.00**
Emergency, jigsaw, American Publishing, 1975, complete, NM (NM canister).............................**$50.00**

Farrah Fawcett, jigsaw, American Publishing, 1977, 200 pcs, EXIB.............................**$30.00**

Flipper, jigsaw, Whitman, 1967, NMIB, $15.00. (Photo courtesy Greg Davis and Bill Morgan)

Fonzie, jigsaw, HG Toys, 1976, complete, EX (EX canister).............................**$15.00**
Fox & the Hound, frame-tray, Jaymar, 2 different, EX, ea.............................**$6.00**
Frankenstein, frame-tray, Universal, 1991, M (sealed)..**$5.00**
Goldfinger, jigsaw, Milton Bradley, 1965, complete, VG (VG box).............................**$35.00**
Goofy, frame-tray, set of 2 w/Goofy on pogo stick & Goofy in garden, Whitman, 1940s, NMIB.............................**$85.00**
Green Hornet, frame-tray, Whitman, 1966, set of 4, MIB.**$75.00**
Gunsmoke, frame-tray, Whitman, 1958, complete, EX.**$30.00**
Gunsmoke, jigsaw, Whitman, 1969, 100 pcs, NM (EX box).............................**$45.00**

Hair Bear Bunch, jigsaw, Western Publishing/ Whitman, 1974, 14x18", EX, $5.00. (Photo courtesy Bob Armstrong)

Happy Days, jigsaw, HG Toys, 1976, complete, NMIB...**$35.00**
Hot Wheels, frame-tray, 1986, EX.............................**$5.00**
Howdy Doody, frame-tray, Howdy Goes West, Whitman, 1954, complete, EX.............................**$40.00**
Incredible Hulk, jigsaw, Whitman, 1979, 100 pcs, MIB ..**$25.00**
Janet Jackson, jigsaw, Milton Bradley, 1991, complete, MIB.............................**$10.00**
Josie & the Pussycats, jigsaw, Hope, 1972, complete, EX (EX tin canister).............................**$30.00**
Kermit the Frog, frame-tray, Fisher-Price, 1981-82, complete, M.............................**$5.00**

Lady & the Tramp, frame-tray, Whitman #4452, 1964, EX ..**$10.00**
Land of the Giants, jigsaw, Whitman Jr, 1960s, round, complete, EXIB **$35.00**
Lassie, frame-tray, Whitman, 1966, complete, 14x9", NM..**$35.00**
Lassie, jigsaw, Whitman Big Little Book series, 1960s, complete, NMIB **$50.00**

Little House on the Prairie, jigsaw, HG Toys, #490-5, 1978, MIB, $15.00. (Photo courtesy Greg Davis and Bill Morgan)

Lone Ranger, jigsaw, Milton Bradley, 1980, 250 pcs, MIB......................**$65.00**
Love Boat, jigsaw, HG Toys, 1978, 150 pcs, MIB **$15.00**
Madonna, jigsaw, Milton Bradley, 1990, 500 pcs, MIB .**$10.00**
Man From UNCLE, jigsaw, Illya, Milton Bradley, 1966, VG+ **$35.00**
Marvel Super Heroes, jigsaw, Milton Bradley, 1967, 100 pcs, MIB **$100.00**
MC Hammer, jigsaw, Milton Bradley, 1990, 500 pcs, MIB **$8.00**
Mighty Mouse, frame-tray, Jaymar, 1950s, complete, NM......................**$15.00**
Mighty Mouse Playhouse, jigsaw, Fairchild, 1956, complete, MIB **$20.00**
Muppets, frame-tray, Fisher-Price, 1981-82, complete, M..**$15.00**
New Kids on the Block, jigsaw, Milton Bradley, 1990, 500 pcs, MIB.....................**$8.00**
Patty Duke, jigsaw, Whitman Jr, 1963, 100 pcs, EXIB...**$45.00**
Paula Abdul, jigsaw, Milton Bradley, 1990, 500 pcs, MIB ..**$8.00**
Penelope Pitstop, frame-tray, Whitman, complete, NM ...**$25.00**
Planet of the Apes — On Patrol, jigsaw, HG Toys, 1967, complete, EX (EX canister) **$40.00**
Quick Draw McGraw, frame-tray, Whitman, 1960, complete, EX........................**$25.00**
Raggedy Ann & Andy, frame-tray, Home Sweet Home, Playskool, 1987, complete, M **$15.00**
Road Runner, jigsaw, Whitman, 1980, EXIB **$20.00**
Rod Stewart, jigsaw, 1873, complete, MIB...................**$40.00**
Simpsons, jigsaw, Milton Bradley, several different, 250 pcs, MIB, ea **$15.00**
Snow White & the Seven Dwarfs, jigsaw, Jaymar, complete, EXIB........................**$25.00**
Space Ghost, jigsaw, Whitman, 1967, 100 pcs, MIB ...**$25.00**
Spider-Man w/Thor, jigsaw, 4-G Toys, 1974, 75 pcs, MIB..**$40.00**
Star Trek, frame-tray, Whitman, 1978, complete, M....**$15.00**

Superboy, frame-tray, Whitman, 1968, complete, 14x11", NM.................................**$50.00**
Superman, frame-tray, Whitman, 1966, complete, 11x8", NM.................................**$25.00**
Superman, jigsaw, Whitman, 1966, 100 pcs, MIB **$25.00**
Sword in the Stone, frame-tray, Whitman, 1963, complete, EX **$20.00**
Thunderball, jigsaw, Milton Bradley, 1965, complete, EXIB **$40.00**
Tom & Jerry, frame-tray, Whitman, 1959, complete, NM..**$25.00**
Top Cat, frame-tray, Whitman, 1960s, complete, MIP.**$25.00**
Underdog, jigsaw, APC, 1978, 100 pcs, MIB **$25.00**
Village People, jigsaw, American Publishing, 1978, complete, MIB **$20.00**
Voyage to the Bottom of the Sea, jigsaw, Milton Bradley, 1966, NMIB...........................**$85.00**
Welcome Back Kotter, jigsaw, HG toys, 1976, 250 pcs, MIB..................................**$20.00**
Wild Bill Hickok, jigsaw, Built Rite, 1956, 100 pcs, EXIB...**$25.00**
Wyatt Earp, jigsaw, Whitman, 1960s, complete, NMIB.......**$25.00**

Yosemite Valley, plywood, Joseph Straus, ca 1930s, 12x9", EX (original box), $20.00. (Photo courtesy Bob Armstrong)

Zorro, frame-tray, 1957, complete, EX **$35.00**
ZZ Top, jigsaw, 1980s, complete, NM (NM canister)..**$35.00**
101 Dalmatians, frame-tray, Jaymar #2720-29, EX.......**$10.00**

Railroadiana

It is estimated that almost two hundred different railway companies once operated in this country, so to try to collect just one item representative of each would be a challenge. Supply and demand is the rule governing all pricing, so naturally an item with a marking from a long-defunct, less prominent railroad generally carries the higher price tag.

Railroadiana is basically divided into two main categories, paper and hardware, with both having many subdivisions. Some collectors tend to specialize in only one area — locks, lanterns, ticket punches, dinnerware, or timetables, for example. Many times estate sales and garage sales are good sources for finding these items, since retired railroad employees often kept such memorabilia as keepsakes. Because many of these items are very unique, you need to get to know as much as possible about railroad artifacts in order to be able to recognize and evaluate a good piece. For more information we recommend *Railroad Collectibles, Revised 4th Edition,* by Stanley L. Baker (Collector Books).

Advisors: Fred and Lila Shrader; John White, Grandpa's Depot (See Directory Railroadiana)

Dinnerware

Ashtray, C&O, Chessie, no back stamp, 4" **$125.00**
Ashtray, CB&Q, Violets & Daisies, no back stamp, 4½" square **$68.00**
Bowl, berry; C&O, Staffordshire, bottom stamp, 5½". **$150.00**
Bowl, berry; T&P, Eagle, bottom stamp, 5¼" **$125.00**
Bowl, bouillon; GN, Mountains & Flowers, w/out handles, bottom stamp **$125.00**
Bowl, cereal; CMStP&P, Traveler, bottom stamp, 6¼".. **$128.00**
Bowl, cereal; SP, Prairie Mountain Wildflowers, bottom stamp, 6" **$110.00**
Bowl, rim soup; CB&Q, Voilets & Daisies, bottom stamp, 9" **$225.00**
Bowl, rim soup; UNC, Shield, top logo, no back stamp, 9" **$95.00**
Butter pat, B&O, Capitol, top logo, 3¼" **$135.00**
Butter pat, CB&Q, Galatea, no back stamp, 3¼" **$135.00**
Butter pat, CRI&P, LaSalle, no back stamp, 3½" **$195.00**
Butter pat, N&W, Cavalier, no back stamp, 4" **$85.00**
Butter pat, SP, Prairie Mountain Wildflowers, bottom stamp, 3" **$210.00**
Chocolate pot, B&O, Centenary, bottom stamp, w/lid ... **$295.00**
Compote, CMStLP&P, Galatea, footed, no back stamp, 6½" **$275.00**
Creamer, ATSF, California Poppy, w/handle, no back stamp, individual, 3" **$185.00**
Creamer, NYC, Dewitt Clinton, side logo, bottom stamp, 4½" **$65.00**
Creamer, PRR, Purple Laurel, w/out, bottom stamp, individual, 2" **$85.00**
Creamer, Pullman, Calumet, w/handle, side mark, individual, 2½" **$250.00**
Cup & saucer, ATSF, California Poppy, no back stamp .. **$175.00**
Cup & saucer, B&O, Capitol, side logo, no back stamp, demitasse **$195.00**
Cup & saucer, B&O, Centenary, bottom stamp, demitasse **$110.00**
Cup & saucer, CM&PS, Olympian, top logo **$12.00**
Cup & saucer, FEC, Mistic, no back stamp, demitasse .**$26.00**
Cup & saucer, PRR, Broadway, no back stamp, demitasse **$265.00**
Cup & saucer, SRR, Piedmont, bottom stamp, demitasse... **$63.00**
Egg cup, CN, Prince Edward, bottom stamp, 3¼" **$35.00**
Egg cup, UP, Desert Flower, sm pedestal, bottom stamp, 2½" **$95.00**
Egg cup, WP, Feather River, side logo, 3¼" **$325.00**

Gravy boat, B&O, Capitol, side logo **$225.00**
Gravy boat, StL&SF, Denmark, no back stamp............ **$65.00**
Hot food cover, CMStP&P, Traveler, no back stamp, 5¾" dia **$95.00**
Ice cream dish, CN, Bonaventure, w/tab handle, top logo, 5" **$85.00**
Ice cream dish, NYC, Dewitt Clinton, w/tab handle, bottom stamp, 5½".. **$90.00**
Mustard pot, UP, Harriman Blue, bottom stamp, w/lid, 2¾" **$145.00**
Plate, ACL, Flora of the South, bottom stamp, 9¼" ..**$225.00**
Plate, ATSF, Bleeding Blue, top mark, 5½" **$150.00**
Plate, ATSF, California Poppy, no back stamp, 10"...**$165.00**
Plate, B&O, Capitol, top logo, 6" **$65.00**

Plate, CB&CQ RR, Chessie logo, 9¾", $285.00.

Plate, D&RGW, Prospector, no back stamp, 9" **$145.00**
Plate, GN, Oriental, no back stamp, 6½" **$90.00**
Plate, NP, Monad, no back stamp, 5½" **$75.00**
Plate, NYNH&H, Merchants, bottom stamp, 8½" **$175.00**
Plate, PRR, Keystone, bottom stamp, 9" **$125.00**
Plate, Pullman, Indian Tree, no back stamp, 6½" **$49.00**
Plate, service; MKT, Alamo w/cobalt border, no back stamp, 10½".. **$425.00**
Plate, service; MP, State Flowers, top logo, no back stamp, 10½" **$250.00**
Plate, service; PRR, Gotham, bottom stamp, 10½"....**$175.00**
Plate, SP, Prairie Mountain Wildflowers, no back stamp, 9½" **$75.00**
Plate, WP, Feather River, no back stamp, 5½"............ **$65.00**
Platter, B&O, Derby, bottom stamp, 9x5" **$90.00**
Platter, C&O, George Washington, bottom stamp, 9½x6½"..**$265.00**
Platter, NYC, Dewitt Clinton, bottom stamp, 12½x8½"......**$125.00**
Platter, NYC, Vanderbilt, bow style, back stamp, 8½x5½" ..**$95.00**
Platter, SP, Sunset, top logo, no back stamp, 14½x10"..**$250.00**
Platter, UP, Challenger, bottom stamp, 9½x8" **$65.00**
Ramekin, L&N, Regent, no back stamp, 3½"............... **$95.00**
Relish, CB&Q, Violets & Daisies, no back stamp, 10x4¾".**$110.00**
Relish, CNJ, Sea Gull, no back stamp, 10½x5" **$210.00**
Sauce boat, WP, Feather River, side logo, no back stamp..**$265.00**
Sherbet, PRR, Keystone, pedestal foot, side logo **$165.00**
Sugar bowl, KCS, Roxbury, no back stamp, open......**$42.00**
Teapot, D&RGW, Blue Adam, no back stamp, w/lid .**$165.00**

Teapot, NP, Verde Green w/YPL side logo, w/lid **$285.00**
Teapot, UP, Winged Streamliner, no back stamp, 24-oz...**$165.00**

Glassware

Ashtray, B&O, 5", from $20.00 to $25.00.

Ashtray, McCloud RR, red logo, 3½" dia **$18.00**
Ashtray, Rock Island, clear w/black & red bearskin logo ..**$10.00**
Bottle, milk; Missouri Pacific embossed on clear, 1-qt..**$75.00**
Bottle, milk; MOPAC, buzz saw logo, ½-pt **$20.00**
Bottle, milk; MP, buzz saw logo, side mark, red enamel, ½-pt...**$25.00**
Champagne, NYC, NYC side mark, 4½" **$25.00**
Cocktail set, UP, mixer+2 roly poly 2½" tumblers, logo .**$45.00**
Cordial, NYC, NYC System gold logo, 4".................**$50.00**
Double shot, Sante Fe, straight sides, weighted base, 2-oz, 2½"...**$50.00**
Goblet, UP w/enamel shield logo, side mark, footed, 5½" **$15.00**
Pitcher, water; M&StL, silverplated frame, Albert Pick & Co, 1928 ....**$365.00**
Roly poly, CRI&P, Route of the Rockets side logo, 2¼"...**$24.00**
Roly poly, Wabash, flag & train, red & blue, 3¼".......**$15.00**
Shot glass, UP, white enamel lettering, 2½" **$26.00**
Tumbler, ATSF, Sante Fe (script letters) in white enamel, 5½" **$18.00**
Tumbler, Erie, amethyst, slant sides, 3¼x3" **$38.00**
Tumbler, juice; ATSF, Sante Fe in white enamel (cursive), 4"...**$14.00**
Tumbler, juice; CMStP&P, etched box logo, side mark, 3¼"...**$32.00**
Tumbler, NYC, side logo, 4" **$14.00**
Tumbler, NYC, 1964 World's Fair w/trains in black & gold, 6¾"...**$10.00**
Wine, CN, etched w/3 pinstripes, stem, 3½"..............**$65.00**
Wine, Sante Fe, tulip style, 6", 4 for **$150.00**

Lanterns

B&M Signal Co, bell bottom, clear unmarked globe, repaired, VG...**$150.00**
BMStP&P, Adlake Kero, clear unmarked globe, short, EX .**$70.00**
C&NW, Adams & Westlake, clear marked globe, short **$100.00**
CB&Q, Adams & Westlake, red etched globe, short, EX .**$125.00**

CPR, ET Wright, western lettering, wire bottom, tall globe, EX **$150.00**
D&SL, Adams & Westlake, top mark, tall unmarked melon globe, Pat 1909 ....**$350.00**
FW&DC, Adams & Westlake, clear unmarked globe ..**$100.00**
L&A, Handlan, tall flat dome, 4½" amber globe, EX ..**$125.00**
ME Central, Dietz Vesta, blue unmarked globe, tall .**$200.00**
N&W, Adlake Reliable, clear globe, tall, G................**$175.00**
NY Central, Dietz Vesta, later #6 version, 9½" **$90.00**
NYNH&H, Vulcan #39 Dietz, clear marked globe, tall .**$150.00**
PCC&StL, Adlake Reliable, bell bottom, clear marked globe, tall **$200.00**
Pennsylvania Lines, Adlake Reliable, clear marked globe, tall **$200.00**
PRR, Dressel, flat vertical ribs, clear unmarked globe, short **$75.00**
Unmarked, Handlan Buck, bell bottom, cobalt globe ..**$250.00**
WC, Adams & Westlake, Soo Line, 5⅜" red etched globe, EX **$200.00**

Linens

Blanket, CA Zephyr logo in brown, wool, 58x84"....**$245.00**
Blanket, GN, woven goat logo, brown & rose, wool, 67x84" **$295.00**
Hand towel, ATSF woven in blue center stripe, 24x16" **$12.00**
Hand towel, Pullman, blue stripe, no date, 24x16", up to...**$12.00**
Hand towel, Soo Line 1925 woven on blue stripe, 24x16" **$28.00**
Headrest cover, Denver Zephyr, brown on tan, 15x18" **$35.00**
Headrest cover, N&W, red & tan, w/ticket pocket, 15x18" **$18.00**
Headrest cover, SCL, yellow & green beach scene, 15x26" **$21.00**
Jacket, CPR trainman's, old style, gray.........................**$40.00**
Napkin, Sante Fe, old script, white on white, 19½" square **$15.00**
Napkin, SP, Sunset logo w/poppies, white on white, 24" square **$31.00**
Napkin, UP, sewn Union Pacific in blue on white, 18" square **$11.00**
Sheet, CA Zephyr printed over Pullman, berth size....**$19.00**
Shop cloth, C&NW logo w/safety slogans, unused, 15x17"...**$13.00**
Tablecloth, C&NW, 400 logo in center, cotton, 54x40".**$4.00**
Tablecloth, PRR, woven Keystone logo on tan & light brown, 32x48" **$42.00**
Trousers & jacket, GN, goat logo & GN buttons **$115.00**
Uniform, VIA Rail trainman's, 2-pc, red pants stripe, M..**$135.00**

Locks

Shanty, ATSF, steel...**$35.00**
Switch, CC&O, steel...**$25.00**

Switch, D&RG, brass, sm $295.00
Switch, MR&BT Lead Belt Short Line, cast brass, NM...$375.00
Switch, NRR (on back), brass $175.00
Switch, SR, brass, SR w/arrow on back $75.00
Switch, VGN, steel, w/brass marked key....................$85.00

Silverplate

Ashtray & matchbook holder, FEC, side logo & bottom
   stamp, 5½x4½" $125.00
Butter icer, SP, w/lid, SP & Sunset side logo, Reed & Barton,
   4x3" $165.00
Butter pat, California Zephyr, bottom stamp, International,
   3½" $55.00
Carafe frame w/glass insert, NYC, bottom stamp, Reed &
   Barton, 10"...$245.00
Coffeepot, ATSF, hinged lid, bottom stamp, Reed & Barton,
   14-oz $110.00
Coffeepot, T&P, Reed & Barton, bottom stamp, 10-oz .$150.00
Creamer, DL&W, back stamp, Reed & Barton, individual, 2-
   oz $110.00
Creamer, GN, w/hinged lid, side logo, bottom stamp,
   International, 4-oz...$75.00
Fork, dinner; ACL logo, Cromwell, top mark,
   International...$22.00
Fork, pickle; Fred Harvey, Albany $19.00
Gravy boat, UP, 4-oz, G $75.00
Hot food cover, NP, NP YPL side logo, oval, International .$175.00
Ice tongs, UP, Sierra, UPRR cursive side mark, Reed &
   Burton, 7" $165.00
Knife, butter; GN, Hutton, hollow handle, top mark,
   International...$22.00
Knife, luncheon; PA RR, Broadway, top mark $15.00
Knife, place; BR, Modern.......................................$12.00
Ladle, sauce; T&P, Sierra, top mark in cursive, Reed &
   Barton $135.00
Menu holder, CR&P w/side marked Golden Rocket logo &
   bottom stamp $175.00
Menu holder, UP, half-moon shape, bottom stamp, 1954 ..$125.00
Mustard, UP, Winged Streamliner, glass insert............$85.00
Sherbet, GN, pedestal foot, 1946............................$100.00
Spoon, bouillon; ATSF, Cromwell, top mark, International ..$19.00
Spoon, iced tea; NYC, Century................................$12.00
Spoon, mustard; PRR, Kings, top mark in cursive,
   International $59.00
Spoon, soup; SP, w/Winged Ball logo, Broadway, top mark,
   International $15.00
Spoon, sugar; B&O, Clovelly, top mark, Reed Barton..$45.00
Sugar bowl, CB&Q, Rubington Route side logo, w/lid & han-
   dles, 8-oz..$165.00
Sugar bowl, Pullman, back stamp, w/lid & handles,
   International, 7-oz..$100.00
Sugar tongs, PRR, Kings, raised side logo, International ..$110.00
Sugar tongs, Wabash, Paisley, side logo, Rogers $135.00
Syrup, ATSF, attached tray, bottom stamp, Reed & Barton, 8-
   oz $118.00
Syrup, UP, attached tray, 1947, 4-oz........................$95.00

Tea strainer, CP, top mark, Mappin & Webb $75.00
Tray, Pullman, deep-dish, International, 9x5"............$85.00
Tray, serving; Pullman, dated 1929, 14x11".............$125.00
Tray, tip; WP, Feather River Route top mark, International,
   6½"...$75.00
Tureen, soup; RI, peaked finial, Wallace, bottom stamp, 1927,
   +tray..$175.00

Miscellaneous

Badge, Amtrak conductor's, gold-tone metal w/black,
   1½x2¾"..$28.00
Badge, breast; LA Union Passenger Terminal Police, w/eagle,
   1920s $77.00
Badge, C&S brakeman's, rectangular, black paint, scarce,
   EX..$150.00
Badge, cap; ATSF Brakeman, blue enamel on German sil-
   ver $79.00
Badge, CB&Q brakeman's, black paint, 2¾" L..........$100.00
Badge, CPR police officer's, gray cloth w/gold bullion ..$25.00
Badge, hat; CN Police, Queen's crown over new logo,
   NM...$65.00
Badge, hat; M&StL brakeman's...............................$110.00
Badge, NP brakeman's, black paint, 4" L $100.00
Bandana, ATSF logo, cowboy theme, cotton & polyester, 32"
   square $13.00
Billfold, C&O, Chessie imprint on black leather, plastic win-
   dows $77.00
Blotter, MP, Missourian, 4-digit phone number, 4x9" ..$12.00
Book, Nothing Could Be Finer, Sandknop, softcover,
   1977 ....$35.00
Booklet, History of RR Handcar, 1972 reprint, 40
   pages $38.00
Booklet, MP, Eastern Colorado (real-estate promo), pre-
   1900 ....$80.00
Booklet, Pullman Accommodations, 29 pages, 5½x7¾" ..$18.00
Bridge score pad, L&N, 8½x3½" $13.00
Bucket, Erie, canvas w/rope bale, 1-gal+ capacity $49.00
Button, B&O, brass, Waterbury, ⅞"...........................$10.00
Button, Long Island RR, brass, Waterbury, ⅞"............$11.00

Calendar, 1929 Pennsylvania Railroad, 30x29", VG, $210.00.

Calendar, ATSF, Couse Indian scene, complete, 1962,
   14x24"..$28.00
Calendar, MP, plastic, 1955, pocket size........................$8.00

Calendar, PA RR, tri-month, 1954, complete..............**$120.00**

Catalog, Adlake Hardware & Fixtures, ca 1950, 90 pages, 8½x11"...**$55.00**

Fan, hand; MKT logo & blue bonnets on cardboard w/vase-shaped handle..**$38.00**

Handkerchief, Chessie, Peake & kittens, C&O logo, 15" square **$52.00**

Hat, VIA Rail Conductor's, MIB **$50.00**

Letterhead, T&P logo, unused, 8½x11".........................**$6.00**

Lighter, cigarette; MOPAC logo, Zippo, 1973..............**$48.00**

Lighter, M&StL, Peoria Gateway, Safety First **$45.00**

Match book, MKT, w/logo, 1940s-50s, unused..............**$5.00**

Menu, CP, child's, diecut, whimsical animal illustrations, 1940s...**$54.00**

Menu, Fred Harvey, Portland Rose, 1943, 7x10", EX..**$65.00**

Money bag; CStPM&O, black stamp on cotton, 5x10"....**$22.00**

Paperweight, CM&StP Ry, Walking Bear, Puget Sound Electrified...**$80.00**

Pencil, mechanical; Rock Island, Travel & Ship, Route of Rockets **$60.00**

Pencil, mechanical; UP, Road of Streamliners & Challengers **$25.00**

Pin-back, Milwaukee Road Hiawatha Club, celluloid.**$15.00**

Pocketknife, MOPAC buzz saw logo, 2½" L................**$25.00**

Ruler, M&StL Ry, metal...**$15.00**

Sign, Seaboard Coast Line RR, painted metal, black on yellow, 22" dia, EX..**$70.00**

Tag, luggage; T&P logo on leather, window for passenger's name **$55.00**

Razor Blade Banks

Razor blade banks are receptacles designed to safely store used razor blades. While the double-edged disposable razor blades date back to as early as 1904, ceramic and figural razor blade safes most likely were not produced until the early 1940s. The development of the electric razor and the later disposable razors did away with the need for these items, and their production ended in the 1960s.

Shapes include barber chairs, barbers, animals, and barber poles, which were very popular. Listerine produced a white donkey and elephant in 1936 with political overtones. They also made a white ceramic frog. These were used as promotional items for shaving cream. Suggested values are based on availability and apply to items in near-mint to excellent condition. Note that regional pricing could vary.

Advisor: Debbie Gillham (See Directory, Razor Blade Banks)

Barber, wood w/Gay Blade bottom, unscrews, Woodcraft, 1950, 6", from $65 to **$75.00**

Barber, wood w/key & metal holders for razor & brush, 9", from $85 to...**$95.00**

Barber bust w/handlebar mustache, coat & tie, from $55 to..**$65.00**

Barber chair, lg or sm, from $100 to..........................**$125.00**

Barber head, different colors on collar, Cleminson, from $30 to..**$40.00**

Barber holding pole, Occupied Japan, 4", from $50 to ..**$60.00**

Barber pole, red & white, w/ or w/out attachments & various titles, from $20 to..**$25.00**

Barber pole w/barber head & derby hat, white, from $35 to..**$40.00**

Barber pole w/face, red & white, from $30 to...........**$35.00**

Barber standing in blue coat & stroking chin, from $75 to **$80.00**

Barber w/buggy eyes, pudgy full body, Gleason look-alike, from $65 to...**$75.00**

Barber with handlebar mustache (no tie), Lipper & Mann, from $75.00 to $95.00. (Photo courtesy Debbie Gillham)

Barbershop quartet, 4 singing barber heads, from $95 to ...**$125.00**

Box w/policeman holding up hand, metal, marked Used Blades, from $90 to **$125.00**

Dandy Dans, plastic w/brush holders, from $30 to....**$40.00**

Frog, green, marked For Used Blades, from $65 to....**$75.00**

Half barber pole, hangs on wall, may be personalized w/name, from $60 to...**$70.00**

Half shaving cup, hangs on wall, marked Gay Blades w/floral design, from $65 to...**$75.00**

Half shaving cup, hangs on wall, marked Gay Old Blade w/quartet, from $65 to **$75.00**

Listerine donkey, from $20 to.....................................**$30.00**

Listerine elephant, from $25 to...................................**$35.00**

Listerine frog, from $15 to...**$20.00**

Looie, right- or left-hand version, from $85 to.........**$100.00**

Man shaving, mushroom shape, Cleminson, from $25 to..**$30.00**

Razor Bum, from $95 to...**$125.00**

Safe, green, marked Razor on front, from $55 to **$65.00**

Shaving brush, ceramic, wide style w/decal, from $50 to...**$60.00**

Tony the Barber, Ceramic Arts Studio, from $85 to....**$95.00**

Reamers

Reamers were a European invention of the late 1700s, devised as a tool for extracting liquid from citrus fruits, which was often used as a medicinal remedy. Eventually the concept of freshly squeezed juice worked its way across the oceans. Many early U.S. patents (mostly for wood reamers) were filed in the mid-1880s, and thanks to the 1916 Sunkist

'Drink An Orange' advertising campaign, the reamer soon became a permanent fixture in the well-equipped American kitchen. Most of the major U.S. glass companies and pottery manufacturers included juicers as part of their kitchenware lines. However, some of the most beautiful and unique reamers are ceramic figures and hand-painted, elegant china and porcelain examples. The invention of frozen and bottled citrus juice relegated many a reamer to the kitchen shelf. However, the current trend for a healthier diet has garnered renewed interest for the manual juice squeezer.

Most of the German and English reamers listed here can be attributed to the 1920s and '30s. Most of the Japanese imports are from the 1940s.

Advisor: Bobbie Zucker Bryson (See Directory, Reamers)

Newsletter: *National Reamer Collectors Association*
Debbie Gillham
47 Midline Ct., Gaithersburg, MD 20878, 301-977-5727
e-mail: reamers@erols.com or http://www.reamers.org

Ceramics

Baby's, 2-pc, pink w/white kitten in blue pajamas, pink, blue, green & white top, Japan, 4", from $75 to ..**$85.00**

Baby's Orange, 2-pc, red & white, Japan, 4½" **$55.00**

Black face & hands, red coat & blue pants, 4¾", from $500 to...**$600.00**

Child's, 2-pc, orange lustre w/red, blue & yellow flowers, 2", from $100 to..**$125.00**

Clown, brown body & hat, blue button & collar, 6", from $95 to...**$125.00**

Clown, lime green & white, 4¾", from $95 to..........**$125.00**

Clown, polka dots, lustre hat, Japan, 4½", from $125 to .**$135.00**

Clown, Sourpuss, w/saucer, 4¾", from $115 to **$135.00**

Clown, 2-pc, tan & light blue w/pig head, 5", from $185 to...**$225.00**

Clown, 2-pc, wearing tuxedo, 5½", from $125 to.....**$150.00**

Cottage, Carlton Ware (England), yellow w/orange & green trim, 4", from $95 to...**$125.00**

Floral w/gold, Nippon, 2-pc.......................................**$195.00**

Floral w/gold, Royal Rudolstadt, 2-pc......................**$250.00**

Germany, Goebel, Winnie-the-Pooh, yellow w/white top, 4½"...**$300.00**

House, 2-pc, beige w/green trees & tan branches, blue door & windmill, Japan, 4½"..**$185.00**

Lemon, 2-pc, yellow w/green leaves, gold trim, Japan, 4", from $65 to...**$85.00**

Orange, 2-pc, Orange for Baby, yellow w/blue flowers, Goebel, 3½"..**$135.00**

Pear, 3-pc, white w/black flowers & leaves, gold trim, Japan, 4¾", from $55 to.......................................**$65.00**

Pitcher, 2-pc, beige w/multicolor flowers & black trim, Japan, 8¾"...**$50.00**

Pitcher, 2-pc, beige w/red & yellow flowers, black trim, Japan, 8½", w/6 cups, from $50 to **$65.00**

Pitcher, 2-pc, black w/gold wheat, 8" **$45.00**

Pitcher, 2-pc, cream w/lavender lillies & green leaves, Universal Cambridge, 9".....................................**$185.00**

Pitcher, 2-pc, rose w/yellow & lavender flowers, green leaves, Japan, 7", +6 cups **$65.00**

Pitcher, 2-pc, rust leaves, dark blue trim, 3½" **$45.00**

Pitcher, green with blue and brown flowers, green leaves, tan trim, Japan, 8½", with six cups (only one shown), from $55.00 to $65.00. (Photo courtesy Bobbie Zucker Bryson)

Red Wing USA, cream, 6¾" **$125.00**

Rose, pink w/green leaves, Germany, 1¾" **$225.00**

Sailboat, yellow or red, 3", ea **$125.00**

Saucer, cream, tan & maroon w/blue trim, England, 3¼" dia, from $90 to..**$100.00**

Saucer, white w/pink flowers & green leaves, Germany, 4½" dia, from $85 to **$100.00**

Saucer, 2-pc, France, Ivoire Corbelle, Henriot Quimper #1166, 4¼", from $350 to....................................**$400.00**

Sleeping Mexican, 2-pc, green shirt, red pants, gold top, Japan, 4¾", from $150 to....................................**$185.00**

Sourpuss, 4¾", from $100 to **$125.00**

Teapot, 2-pc, white w/red flowers & trim, Prussia/Germany/Royal Rudolstadt, 3¼" **$150.00**

Teapot, 2-pc, white w/yellow & maroon flowers, Nippon, 3¼"...**$90.00**

Teapot, 2-pc, yellow, tan & white, England/Shelley, 3½", from $90 to...**$100.00**

USA, Ade-O-Matic Genuine Coorsite Porcelain, green, 9"..**$150.00**

USA, Jiffy Juicer, US Pat 2,130,755, Sept 2, 1928, yellow, 5¼"...**$85.00**

Glassware

Amber, Cambridge...**$600.00**

Black, loop handle, embossed Sunkist, from $650 to...**$800.00**

Chalaine blue, embossed Sunkist, from $200 to **$225.00**

Clambroth, boat shape, from $150 to **$185.00**

Cobalt, crisscross cone, loop handle, Hazel Atlas, from $275 to...**$300.00**

Crystal, crisscross cone, tab handle, Hazel Atlas, from $18 to...**$22.00**

Crystal, Glasbake, McKee on handle, from $70 to......**$75.00**

Crystal, spout opposite handle, Indiana Glass, from $25 to..**$28.00**

Crystal, tab handle, Cambridge, from $25 to..............**$28.00**

Crystal w/painted-on flowers & oranges, loop handle, Westmoreland, from $60 to....................................**$65.00**

Custard, loop handle, embossed Sunkist, from $35 to .**$40.00**

Custard w/red trim, loop handle, embossed Sunkist, from $30 to...**$35.00**

Emerald green, Fry, tab handle, from $35 to **$40.00**

Green, baby's, 2-pc, Westmoreland.............................**$185.00**

Green, embossed Lindsay, from $450 to **$500.00**

Green, loop handle, footed, Cambridge, from $500 to...**$600.00**

Green, loop handle, Westmoreland, from $95 to......**$110.00**

Green, pointed cone, tab handle, Federal Glass, from $25 to..**$28.00**

Green, ribbed, loop handle, Federal Glass, from $30 to...**$35.00**

Green, ribbed, w/seed dam, tab handle, Federal Glass, from $25 to...**$28.00**

Green, spout opposite handle, Indiana Glass, from $35 to..**$40.00**

Green, tab handle, Hazel Atlas, from $25 to **$28.00**

Green, tab handle, Jeannette, from $25 to **$28.00**

Green, 4-cup pitcher w/reamer top, footed, Anchor Hocking, from $35 to..**$40.00**

Green, 4-cup pitcher w/reamer top, marked A&J, Hazel Atlas, from $40 to...**$45.00**

Jade-ite, embossed Sunkist, from $35 to.....................**$45.00**

Jade-ite, 2-cup measure w/reamer top, angled handle, Jeannette, from $35 to..**$40.00**

Pink, Hex Optic, bucket container w/reamer top, Jeannette, from $40 to...**$45.00**

Pink, loop handle, Cambridge, from $200 to...........**$225.00**

Pink, loop handle, Westmoreland, from $90 to **$100.00**

Pink, ribbed, loop handle, Federal Glass, from $35 to..**$40.00**

Red, 2-cup measure w/reamer top, Hazel Atlas, from $40 to..**$45.00**

Skokie green, pointed cone, loop handle, embossed Sunkist, from $60 to..**$65.00**

Transparent green, embossed Sunkist, from $50 to....**$55.00**

White, embossed Valencia, square handle, from $100 to..**$120.00**

White, 4-cup stippled pitcher w/reamer top, Hazel Atlas, from $30 to...**$35.00**

White opalescent, embossed Sunkist, McKee, 6", from $85.00 to $140.00 (value determined by amount of opalescence).

Metal

Aluminum tilt-model, Seald Sweet Juice Extractor, attaches to counter, 13" **$60.00**

Green metal base, white porcelain bowl & cone, 3-pc, Presto Juice National Electric Appliance Corp, 7⅝", from $110 to...**$125.00**

Metal, Quam-Nicholas Co, Chicago IL, Kwicky Juicer, 5½", from $8 to...**$10.00**

Silverplate, Meriden SP Co International, S Co, 2-pc, 4⅝" dia **$95.00**

Silverplate, 2-pc, cocktail shaker, Germany, 7", from $85 to...**$100.00**

Sterling silver, Black & Starr, 3¾" dia, from $300 to.**$350.00**

Records

Records are still plentiful at flea markets and some antique malls, but albums (rock, jazz, and country) from the '50s and '60s are harder to find in collectible condition (very good or better). Garage sales are sometimes a great place to buy old records, since most of what you'll find there have been stored more carefully by their original owners.

There are two schools of thought concerning what is a collectible record. While some collectors prefer the rarities — those made in limited quantities by an unknown who later became famous, or those aimed at a specific segment of music lovers — others like the vintage Top-10 recordings. Now that they're so often being replaced with CDs, we realize that even though we take them for granted, the possibility of their becoming a thing of the past may be reality tomorrow.

Whatever the slant your collection takes, learn to visually inspect records before you buy them. Condition is one of the most important factors to consider when assessing value. To be judged as mint, a record may have been played but must have no visual or audible deterioration — no loss of gloss to the finish, no stickers or writing on the label, no holes, no skips when it is played. If any of these are apparent, at best it is considered to be excellent, and its value is at least 50% lower than a mint example. Many of the records you'll find that seem to you to be in wonderful shape would be judged only very good, excellent at the most, by a knowledgeable dealer. Sleeves with no tape, stickers, tears, or obvious damage at best would be excellent; mint condition sleeves are impossible to find unless you've found old store stock.

Be on the lookout for colored vinyl or picture discs, as some of these command higher prices; in fact, older Vogue picture disks commonly sell in the $50.00 to $75.00 range, some even more. It's not too uncommon to find old radio station discards. These records will say either 'Not for Sale' or 'Audition Copy' and may be worth more than their commercial counterparts. Our values are based on original issue — remember to cut these prices drastically when condition is less than described.

If you'd like more information, we recommend *American Premium Record Guide* by L.R. Docks.

Advisor: L.R. Docks (See Directory, Records)

45 rpm

Values for 45 rpms are 'with dust jacket'; if no jacket is present, reduce these prices by at least 50%.

Avalon, Frankie, Venus, Chancellor 1031, 1960, NM...**$50.00**
Banana Splits, The Tra La La Song, 1970, NM.............**$25.00**
Beach Boys, Fun Fun Fun, Capitol 5118, 1964, NM ...**$30.00**
Benton, Brook; The Ties That Bind, Mercury 71566, 1960, NM **$20.00**
Berry, Chuck; No Particular Place To Go, Chess 1898, 1964, NM **$50.00**
Blondie, Private Stock 45141, 1977, NM **$10.00**
Booker T & the MG's, Green Onions, Volt 102, 1962, NM...**$30.00**
Bowie, David; Can't Help Thinking About Me, Warner Bros 5815, 1966, VG..**$50.00**
Cannon, Freddy; Tallahassee Lassie, Swan 4031, 1959, NM...**$35.00**
Cascades, A Little Like Lovin', RCA Victor, 47-8206, 1963, NM **$30.00**
Champs, Tequilla, Challenge 1016, 1958, NM **$40.00**
Checker, Chubby; Let's Twist Again, Parkway 824, 1961, NM...**$35.00**
Clanton, Jimmy; Go Jimmy Go, Ace 575, 1959, NM...**$30.00**
Clark, Dee; Hey Little Girl, Abner 1029, 1959, NM.....**$50.00**
Cooke, Sam; Cupid, RCA Victor 47-7883, 1961, NM..**$25.00**
Crawford, Johnny; Daydreams, Del-Fi 4165, 1961, NM .**$25.00**
Dave Clark Five, Bits & Pieces, Epic 9671, M **$10.00**
Deep Purple, Hush, Tetregrammaton 1503, 1968, NM .**$30.00**
Diamonds, High Sign, Mercury 71291, 1958, NM........**$75.00**
Donovan, Mellow Yellow, Epic 10098, 1966, NM **$15.00**
Earls, The; Remember Me, Old Town 1181, 1965, NM..**$50.00**
Eddy, Duane; Peter Gunn, Jamie 1168, 1960, NM **$35.00**

Eddy, Duane; Ring of Fire/Bobbie, Jamie 1187, VG, from $15.00 to $20.00.

Four Seasons, Sherry, Vee Jay 456, 1962, NM **$35.00**
Francis, Connie; Second Hand Love, MGM 13074, 1967, NM .**$10.00**
Haley, Bill & the Comets; Rock Around the Clock, Decca 29124, VG...**$20.00**

Hodges, Eddie; I'm Gonna Knock on Your Door, Cadence 1397, 1961, NM **$25.00**
Isley Brothers, The Drag, Gone 5048, 1958, NM **$100.00**
Jan & Dean, Dead Man's Curve, Liberty 55672, 1964, NM..**$30.00**
King, Ben E; Stand By Me, Atco 6194, 1961, NM **$25.00**
Lennon, John; Mind Games, Apple P-1868, 1973, NM..**$40.00**
Lewis, Jerry Lee; Great Balls of Fire, Sun 281, 1957, NM ..**$50.00**
Lyman, Frankie & the Teenagers; Why Do Fools Fall in Love?, Gee 1002, gold & red label, 1956, NM **$100.00**
Marvelettes, The; Please Mr Postman, Tamla, 54046, 1961, EX..**$50.00**
Nelson, Ricky; Travelin' Man/Hello Mary Lou, Imperial 5741, 1961, NM..**$30.00**
Orbison, Roy; Crying/Candy Man, Monument 447, 1961, NM..**$30.00**
Perkins, Carl; Pink Pedal Pushers, Columbia 41131, 1958, NM..**$75.00**
Pitney, Gene; Town Without Pity, Musicor 1009, 1961, NM..**$25.00**

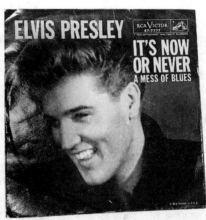

Presley, Elvis; It's Now or Never/A Mess of Blues, RCA Victor #47-7777, EP, VG, $35.00 to $40.00.

Queen, We Are the Champions, Elektra 45441, 1977, NM...**$6.00**
Rip Cords, Hey Little Cobra, Columbia 42921, yellow vinyl, 1963, NM **$50.00**
Royal, Billy Joe; Down in the Boondocks, Columbia 43305, red vinyl, 1965, NM **$40.00**
Shannon, Del; Runaway, Big Top 3067, 1961, NM **$35.00**
Taylor, James; Carolina on My Mind, Apple 1805, 1969, NM..**$30.00**
Turner, Ike & Tina; I Wanna Jump, Minit 32077, 1969, NM..**$25.00**
Untouchables, Poor Boy Needs a Preacher, Madison 128, 1960, NM **$35.00**
Ventures, Walk Don't Run/The McCoy, Dolton 25X, 1960, NM **$35.00**
Yardbirds, For Your Love, Epic 9709, 1965, NM **$40.00**

78 rpm

Autry, Gene; Wild Cat Mama, Victor 23642, EX..........**$75.00**
Baker, Buddy; Box Car Blues, Victor 21549, VG **$15.00**

Big Richard, Pig Meat Mama, Varsity 6063, EX............**$15.00**

Carter Family, Keep on the Sunny Side, Bluebird 5006, NM...**$10.00**

Cotton Club Orchestra, Down & Out Blues, Columbia 287-D, EX...**$40.00**

Dells, Time Makes You Change, Vee-Jay 258, EX.......**$30.00**

Domino, Fats; Boogie Woogie Baby, Imperial 5065, EX...**$15.00**

Four Tunes, I Understand Just How You Feel, Jubilee 5132, EX...**$25.00**

Garland, Judy; Stompin' at the Savoy, Decca 848, EX..**$8.00**

Ink Spots, The Gypsy, Decca 18817, VG.....................**$15.00**

Mills Brothers, Diga Diga Doo, Brunswick 6519, EX..**$14.00**

Page, Patti; I Went to Your Wedding, Mercury 5899, EX .**$20.00**

Prairie Ramblers, Blue River, Bluebird 5302................**$25.00**

Ray Brothers, Jake Legg Wobble V-40281, EX............**$50.00**

Ritter, Tex; Nobody's Darling But Mine, Champion 45153, NM..**$10.00**

LP Albums

Atkins, Chet; Picks on the Beatles, RCA 3531, NM.....**$20.00**

Beatles, Rock 'N Roll Music, Capitol SKBO-1137, set of 2, EX...**$35.00**

Brown, James; Please Please Please, King 610, EX.....**$50.00**

Cannibal & the Head Hunters, Land of a 1,000 Dances, NM..**$50.00**

Checker, Chubby; Twist With..., Parkway 7001, EX....**$25.00**

Cristie, Lou; Lightnin' Strikes, MCA 4360, NM..........**$25.00**

Domino, Fats; Fats Domino Swings, Liberty, NM........**$35.00**

Eddy, Duane; $1,000,000.00 Worth of Twang, Jamie 3014, EX..**$30.00**

Ellington Jazz Party in Stereo, Columbia CS8127, EX .**$20.00**

Francis, Connie; More Greatest Hits, MGM E-3893, VG...**$15.00**

Guess Who, Canned Heat, RCA 4157, NM **$20.00**

Hey There It's Yogi Bear, Columbia Pictures/1964, EX+ (EX+ sleeve)...**$25.00**

Jones, Jack; Call Me Irresponsible, Kapp 3328, EX.....**$35.00**

Little Richard, Here's Little Richard, Specialty, EX **$100.00**

Martin, Dean; Gentle on My Mind, Reprise RS 6330, EX..**$15.00**

Monkees, Meet the Monkees, Colgems 101, EX..........**$20.00**

Monkees, Then & Now...The Best of the Monkees, Arista AL9-8432, 1986 reissue, set of two, EX, from $10.00 to $15.00.

Paul & Paula, Sing for Young Lovers, Philips 200-078, NM **$50.00**

Righteous Brothers, Just Once in My Life, Phillies Records PHLP 4008, NM..**$25.00**

Snow, Hank; Big Country Hits — Songs I Hadn't Recorded Till Now, LSP-2458, EX...**$10.00**

Van Dyke, Dick; Songs I Like, Command Records RS-86OSD, M **$40.00**

Vee, Bobby; Just Today, Liberty LST-7554, EX **$20.00**

Young, Neil; Harvest, Reprise 2032, NM.....................**$20.00**

Red Wing

For almost a century, Red Wing, Minnesota, was the center of a great pottery industry. In the early 1900s several local companies merged to form the Red Wing Stoneware Company. Until they introduced their dinnerware lines in 1935, most of their production centered around stoneware jugs, crocks, flowerpots, and other utilitarian items. To reflect the changes made in 1935, the name was changed to Red Wing Potteries Inc. In addition to scores of lovely dinnerware lines, they also made vases, planters, flowerpots, etc., some with exceptional shapes and decoration.

Some of their more recognizable lines of dinnerware and those you'll most often find are Bob White (decorated in blue and brown brush strokes with quail), Tampico (featuring a collage of fruit including watermelon), Random Harvest (simple pink and brown leaves and flowers), and Village Green (or Brown, solid-color pieces introduced in the '50s). Often you'll find complete or nearly complete sets, and when you do, the lot price is usually a real bargain.

If you'd like to learn more about the subject, we recommend *Red Wing Stoneware, An Identification and Value Guide,* and *Red Wing Collectibles*, both by Dan and Gail DePasquale and Larry Peterson. B.L. Dollen has written a book called *Red Wing Art Pottery*. All are published by Collector Books.

Advisors: Wendy and Leo Frese, Artware (See Directory, Red Wing); and B.L. and R.L. Dollen, Dinnerware (See Directory, Red Wing)

Club/Newsletter: *Red Wing Collectors Newsletter*
Red Wing Collectors Society, Inc.
Doug Podpeskar, membership information
624 Jones St., Eveleth, MN 55734-1631; 218-744-4854.
Please include SASE when requesting information.

Artware

Bowl, boat type, gloss gray exterior w/coral interior, #1382, 1950s, 12" L...**$42.00**

Bowl, console; scalloped edge, semi-matt salmon, #1620, 1950s, 10" **$25.00**

Bowl, console; Tropicana, chartreuse, #B-2014, 14" ...**$25.00**

Bowl, console; Tropicana, maroon, #B-2014, 14" **$60.00**

Bowl, flat, gloss brown exterior w/orange interior, #414, 1950s, 7" **$20.00**

Bowl, gloss gray exterior w/coral interior, teardrop shape, Textura Line, #B-2108, 1960s, 11¼".......$30.00

Bowl, leaf shape, gloss luster blue exterior w/coral interior, detailed vein inside & bottom, #1251, 1950s, 12" ..$25.00

Bowl, matt snow white exterior w/orange interior, silver wing label, Belle Line, #881, 1960s, 8"..................$40.00

Bowl, sgrafitto, #M-4001, 7"................................$50.00

Candle holders, ivy, gloss dark green, #B-2505, 1960s, 4½", pr...$25.00

Candle holders, petal shape, gloss gray exterior w/coral interior, #B-1411, 1950s, 4", pr.....................$25.00

Candle holders, teardrop shape, gloss cinnamon, #1409, bottom marked, 1960s, 5", pr.............................$25.00

Compote, flecked Nile Blue exterior w/Colonial Buff interior, gold wing label, #5022, 1950s, 7".........$30.00

Compote, semi-matt coral exterior w/yellow interior, cherubs around foot, #761, 1960s, 6" $60.00

Cornucopia, flecked Nile Blue exterior w/Colonial Buff interior, footed to lay on side, #443, 1950s, 10" $30.00

Ewer, Magnolia, #1012, 7"..................................$35.00

Figurine, girl, #1121, 8¾"...................................$500.00

Jardiniere, semi-matt Cypress Green exterior w/yellow interior, pedestal, #110, 1960s, 10" dia $25.00

Pelican ash receiver, green, $175.00. (Photo courtesy Leo and Wendy Frese)

Pitcher, ball form, Dutch Blue, #547, 7½" $60.00

Pitcher, ball form, orange, #547, 7½".....................$35.00

Pitcher, ball form, yellow, #547, 7½" $35.00

Pitcher/vase, gloss cinnamon, vertically grooved, #819, 1960s, 12" $30.00

Planter, gloss yellow basketweave design exterior w/semi-matt brown interior, #432, 1950s, 13" L $20.00

Planter, lady's boot, semi-matt white exterior w/green interior, silver wing label, #651, 1960s, 6" $80.00

Planter, shelf; fleck yellow exterior w/light green interior, #1552, 1950s, 6"......................................$20.00

Vase, bird, yellow, #1296, 10".............................$75.00

Vase, bud; cherub, #821, 8".................................$350.00

Vase, bud; handled, #1510, 8".............................$12.00

Vase, cloverleaf design, gloss fleck Zephyr Pink, #1556, 1950s, 6"...$30.00

Vase, contoured, gloss blue exterior w/coral interior, #1202, 1950s, 5½"..$20.00

Vase, Dutch Blue, #505, 7½"................................$60.00

Vase, fan form, maroon, #892, 7½"........................$60.00

Vase, fan form, white, #892, 7½"...........................$30.00

Vase, fan shape, gloss maroon exterior w/blue interior, #892, 1960s, 7½"..$50.00

Vase, Georgia Rose, white/brown flower, #200F, 10" .$350.00

Vase, gloss celadon exterior w/Mandarin Orange interior, Prismatique Line, #798, 1960s, 8" $75.00

Vase, gloss dark green exterior w/yellow interior, Tropicana Line, embossed Desert Flower, #B-2004, 1960s, 10".$30.00

Vase, gloss tan fleck exterior w/dark green interior, Textura Line, #B-2105, 1960s, 10" $30.00

Vase, Magnolia, #1216, 8"..................................$60.00

Vase, Magnolia, #976, 10"..................................$150.00

Vase, maroon, #505, 7½".....................................$45.00

Vase, prism type, semi-matt Cypress Green, #1633, 1960s, 7"..$30.00

Vase, rooster, chartreuse, #M-1438, 10".................$75.00

Vase, semi-matt white bamboo motif w/green interior, #1400, 1960s, 8" $25.00

Vase, shell type, semi-matt orange exterior w/white interior, #1295, 1950s, 7" $25.00

Vase, swirl, gloss yellow, #1590, 1950s, 10" $30.00

Vase, trophy style, gloss maroon exterior w/gray interior, #871, 1950s, 7½"...$50.00

Vase, white, double-handled, #734, 9" $60.00

Vase, yellow, #505, 7½" $25.00

Wall pocket, guitar, blue, #M-1484, 13½" $50.00

Dinnerware

Bob White, cup and saucer, $20.00; dinner plate, 10½", $20.00. (Courtesy B.L. and R.L. Dollen)

Blossom Time, cup, from $4 to $8.00

Bob White, bowl, cereal $22.00

Bob White, bowl, divided vegetable.........................$32.00

Bob White, casserole, 2-qt......................................$45.00

Bob White, cocktail tray..$75.00

Bob White, creamer...$30.00

Bob White, hors d'oeuvres bird................................$50.00

Bob White, pitcher, sm...$45.00

Bob White, pitcher, water; sm $45.00

Bob White, plate, 6"...$7.00

Bob White, plate, 8"...$8.00

Bob White, platter, 13" $45.00
Bob White, platter, 20" $67.50
Bob White, relish, 3-part $50.00
Bob White, salt & pepper shakers, tall, pr $40.00
Bob White, sugar bowl, w/lid $25.00
Bob White, trivet, ceramic $100.00
Capistrano, bowl, berry; 5½" $8.00
Capistrano, bowl, lug vegetable; 8" $12.00
Capistrano, platter, 13" $35.00
Capistrano, saucer $4.00
Chevron, drip jar $37.50
Chevron, plate, salad; 8" $7.50
Chevron, teapot, 6-cup $55.00
Lotus, beverage pot $32.50
Lotus, bowl, dessert; 5" $6.00
Lotus, butter dish $28.00

Lotus, cup and saucer, $15.00; dinner plate, 10½", $20.00; salad plate, 7", $7.00. (Photo courtesy B.L. and R.L. Dollen)

Lotus, gravy boat $30.00
Lotus, salt & pepper shakers, pr $20.00
Lotus, spoon rest $30.00
Magnolia, bowl, salad; lg $15.00
Magnolia, saucer $4.00
Morning Glory, bowl, rim soup $14.00
Morning Glory, creamer $15.00
Morning Glory, plate, 10½" $22.00
Pepe, bean pot, w/lid $36.00
Pepe, creamer $10.00
Pepe, platter, 15" $30.00
Pepe, salt & pepper shakers, pr $17.50
Plum Blossom, bowl, sauce $10.00
Plum Blossom, saucer $5.00
Provincial, bean pot, tan w/red lid, 5-qt, from $16 to..$30.00
Random Harvest, bowl, salad; 12" $45.00
Random Harvest, cup & saucer $17.50
Random Harvest, gravy boat $35.00
Random Harvest, pitcher, water; 2-qt $44.00
Random Harvest, plate, 8½" $15.00
Random Harvest, sugar bowl, w/lid $27.50
Reed, bowl, vegetable; tab handles, 9" $22.50
Reed, egg cup $25.00

Reed, jug, ball form, 32-oz $38.00
Reed, plate, 8½" $7.50
Reed, salt & pepper shakers, pr $15.00
Reed, teapot, 6-cup $48.00
Round-Up, bowl, divided vegetable $95.00
Round-Up, bowl, salad; 10½", from $85 to $95.00
Round-Up, butter dish $200.00
Round-Up, casserole, 2-qt $95.00
Round-Up, creamer $50.00
Round-Up, cup & saucer $55.00
Round-Up, jug, 60-oz $130.00
Round-Up, plate, 6½" $18.50
Round-Up, platter, 13" $90.00
Smart Set, bowl, salad; 10½", from $45 to $75.00
Smart Set, bowl, salad; 5½" $15.00
Smart Set, bowl, soup $17.50
Smart Set, creamer $25.00
Smart Set, cruets, w/stopper & stand, pr, from $165 to ..$185.00
Smart Set, cup & saucer $38.00
Smart Set, plate, dinner; 10½" $35.00
Smart Set, plate, 6½" $12.00
Smart Set, relish, 3-part $45.00
Tampico, beverage server, w/lid $90.00
Tampico, bowl, cereal $16.00
Tampico, bowl, salad; 12" $85.00
Tampico, butter dish, ¼-lb $50.00
Tampico, creamer $30.00
Tampico, cup & saucer $30.00
Tampico, gravy boat w/stand $70.00
Tampico, nut bowl, 5-section $80.00
Tampico, plate, luncheon; 8½" $20.00
Tampico, plate, 6" $9.00
Tampico, plate, 8½" $20.00
Tampico, salt & pepper shakers, pr $32.00
Tampico, trivet, 6½" $75.00
Town & Country, bowl, vegetable; sand, 8" $35.00
Town & Country, bowl, 5" $15.00
Town & Country, casserole, marmite, chartreuse, individual ..$35.00
Town & Country, casserole, stick handle, w/lid, lg ..$125.00
Town & Country, coffee mug $48.00
Town & Country, cup & saucer, forest green w/white interior ..$35.00
Town & Country, plate, bronze, 10½" $45.00
Town & Country, plate, gray, 8" $20.00
Town & Country, plate, 10½" $30.00
Town & Country, relish, 9" $24.00
Town & Country, salt & pepper shakers, Shmoo shape, mixed colors, pr ..$75.00
Town & Country, sugar bowl, bronze, w/lid $65.00
Town & Country, teapot, sand $275.00

Regal China

Perhaps best known for their Beam whiskey decanters, the Regal China company (of Antioch, Illinois) also produced some exceptionally well-modeled ceramic novelties, among them their 'hugger' salt and pepper shakers, designed by artist Ruth Van Telligen Bendel. Facing pairs made to 'lock' together arm-in-arm, some huggies are signed Bendel while others bear the Van Telligen mark. Another popular design is her Peek-a-Boo Bunny line, depicting the coy little bunny in the red and white 'jammies' who's just about to pop his buttons. (The cookie jar has been reproduced.)

See also Cookie Jars; Old MacDonald's Farm.

Advisor: Rick Spencer (See Directory, Regal)

Bendel Shakers

Bears, white w/pink & brown trim, pr.....................$100.00
Bunnies, white w/black & pink trim, pr....................$135.00
Kissing pigs, gray w/pink trim, pr............................$375.00

Love Bugs, burgundy, large, $165.00 for the pair.

Love bugs, green, sm, pr..$65.00

Van Telligen Shakers

Bears, brown, pr..$24.00
Boy & dog, black, pr...$125.00
Boy & dog, white, pr...$62.00
Bunnies, solid colors, pr..$26.00
Ducks, pr...$32.00
Dutch boy & girl, pr...$42.00
Mary & lamb, pr..$58.00

Peek-a-Boo cookie jar, $1,500.00; Salt and pepper shakers, large, $500.00 for pair (original only, beware of reproductions). (Photo courtesy Fred and Joyce Roerig)

Peek-a-Boo, peach trim, rare, lg, pr.....................**$585.00**
Peek-a-Boo, red dots, sm, pr.................................**$240.00**
Peek-a-Boo, solid white, lg, pr..............................**$400.00**
Peek-a-Boo, solid white, sm, pr............................**$200.00**
Peek-a-Boo, white w/gold trim, lg, pr...................**$450.00**

Miscellaneous

Banks, kissing pigs, Bendel, lg, pr..........................**$425.00**
Creamer, cat...**$175.00**
Salt & pepper shakers, A Nod to Abe, 3-pc set........**$250.00**
Salt & pepper shakers, cat, pr................................**$225.00**
Salt & pepper shakers, clown, pr............................**$450.00**
Salt & pepper shakers, FiFi, pr...............................**$450.00**
Salt & pepper shakers, Fish C Miller, pr...................**$65.00**
Salt & pepper shakers, pig, pink, marked C Miller, 1-pc ..**$95.00**
Salt & pepper shakers, tulip, pr...............................**$50.00**
Salt & pepper shakers, Vermont Leaf People, 3-pc ..**$150.00**
Sugar bowl, cat...**$175.00**
Sugar bowl, tulip, tall...**$100.00**
Teapot, tulip, tall..**$125.00**

Restaurant China

Restaurant china, also commonly called cafe ware, diner china, institutional china, hotelware, or commercial china, is specifically designed for use in commercial food service. In addition to restaurants, it is used on board airplanes, ships, and trains, as well as in the dining areas of hotels, railroad stations, airports, government offices, military facilities, corporations, schools, hospitals, department and drug stores, amusement and sports parks, churches, clubs, and the like. Though most hotelware produced in America before and at the turn of the century has a heavy gauge nonvitrified body, vitrified commercial china made post-1910 includes some of the finest quality ware ever produced, far surpassing that of nonvitrified household products. A break- and chip-resistant rolled or welted edge is still frequently used, though no longer a concern on the very durable high alumina content bodies introduced in the 1960s. In addition, commercial tableware is also made of porcelain, glass-ceramic, glass laminate, glass, melamine, pewter-like metal, and silverplate. Airlines use fine gauge china in first class, due to space and weight factors. And beginning in the late 1970s, fine gauge porcelain and bone china became a popular choice of upscale American restaurants, hotels, and country clubs. To reduce loss from wear, most decoration is applied to bisque, then glazed and glaze fired (i.e. underglaze) or to glaze-fired ware, then fired into the glaze (i.e. in-glaze). Until the 1970s many restaurants regularly ordered custom-decorated white-, deep tan-, blue-, or pink-bodied patterns. However, it is estimated that more than 80% of today's commercial ware is plain or embossed white. For decades collectors have searched for railroad and ship china. Interest in airline china is on the rise. Attractive standard (stock) patterns are now also sought by many. Western motifs and stencil airbrushed designs are especially treasured. The popularity of high quality American-made Oriental designs has increased. Most prefer traditional medium-heavy gauge American vitrified china, though fine china collectors no doubt favor the commercial china products of Pickard or Royal Doulton. While some find it difficult to pass up any dining concern or transportation system top-marked piece, others seek ware that is decorated with a military logo or department store, casino, or amusement park name. Some collect only creamers, other butters or teapots. Some look for ware made by a particular manufacturer (e.g. Tepco), others specific patterns such as Willow or Indian Tree, or pink, blue, or tan body colors. It is currently considered fashionable to serve home-cooked meals on mismatched top-marked hotelware. Reminiscent of days gone by, pre-1960s restaurant or railroad china brings to mind pre-freeway cross-country vacations by car or rail when dining out was an event, unlike the quick stops at today's fast-food and family-style restaurants. For a more through study of the subject, we recommend *Restaurant China, Identification & Value Guide for Restaurant, Airline, Ship & Railroad Dinnerware, Volume 1* and *Volume 2,* by Barbara Conroy (Collector Books); her website with a list of contents and details of her book is listed in the Directory.

In the lines below, TM indicates top marked or side marked.

Advisor: Barbara Conroy (See Directory, Dinnerware)

Restaurant, Hotel, Department and Drug Store, and Company Cafeteria

A Sabella's TM (San Francisco) cup & saucer, Jackson, 1980s $30.00

Alsonette Hotel palm tree pattern 7" plate, Mayer & Alsonette Hotels backstamp, 1960 date code.......................$14.00

Amelio's (San Francisco) TM ashtray, Syracuse Econo-Rim, 1955 date code..$12.00

Andersen Pea Soup TM footed mug, Hall, 1960s.......$28.00

Andy's Drive-in 6½" plate, car hop above Andy's TM, Tepco, 1940s-50s $95.00

Antoine's Restaurant (New Orleans) TM cream pitcher, Syracuse, 1964 date code $35.00

Astor Hotel TM butter pat, Haviland, 1930s $25.00

Aunt Jemima's Kitchens TM fruit, Walker, 1950s, minimum value $90.00

Blackhawk Hotel 11" platter, name & Indian TM, Syracuse, 1930s, minimum value..$40.00

Branding Iron brown on tan body 6" plate, Tepco $30.00

Cal-Neva Biltmore TM ashtray, Wallace, 1951, minimum value $45.00

Chicken in the Rough TM 10" platter, Syracuse, 1950s..$60.00

Copper Penny TM 9¾" plate, Shenango, 1960s $22.00

Denny's mug, straight line text TM, Diversified Ceramics (DCC backstamp)..$9.00

Disneyland 6½" plate, D TM, Homer Laughlin, 1980s.$22.00

Dunkin' Donuts mug, capital letters TM, Bell Terr or Rego China..$14.00

Early California 13" compartment plate, red on white body, Tepco..$110.00

El Rancho creamer, brown on tan body, Wallace, 1950s..$35.00

Fairmont Hotel (San Francisco) AD cup & saucer, black script TM, Shenango, 1964 date code............................$20.00

Ford soup plate, green transfer-printed Ford Rotunda, Shenango 1954 date code $80.00

Foster's grapefruit, chef's head w/name on hat TM, Scammell, early 1950s...$20.00

Franciscan Restaurant (San Francisco) 6½" plate, full-color monk w/halo TM, Syracuse, 1981 date code $18.00

General Motors Training Center TM 9" plate, Jackson, 1964 date code..$45.00

Hilton Hotels 9" plate, embossed H rim, Corning Pyroceram $20.00

Hobo Joe TM 6½" plate, HF Coors $22.00

Howard Johnson's cream pitcher, maroon 'Simon & Pieman' TM, Shenango, 1960s, minimum value $38.00

Howard Johnson's 9" plate, maroon scenic rim, Mayer, 1951 date code..$40.00

Inter-Continental Hotels TM ivory-glazed porcelain ashtray $6.00

International House of Pancakes TM 7¼" plate, coral & navy-banded rim, Homer Laughlin, 1990s $12.00

Iroquois China 9" sample plate, multi-TM, pre-1920 ..$140.00

Jade-ite heavy-gauge restaurant ware mug, Fire-King G612 ....$24.00

Liggett's Drugstore TM 7" plate, Warwick, 1920s-40s..$28.00

Little America footed mug, penguin TM $9.00

Little Tavern Shops TM mug, Shenango, 1953 date code.$40.00

Marriott Hotels footed mug, stylized M TM, Homer Laughlin, 1970s..$14.00

Mel's Drive-In cup, Ultima, 1985+ $15.00

Mets Stadium TM 10½" plate, scalloped edge & brown rim, Syracuse..$70.00

Milk Farm mug, cow over moon TM, Syracuse, 1964 date code, minimum value..$65.00

Mister Donut TM cup & saucer, Buffalo, 1970s, minimum value $15.00

Olympic Club (San Francisco) TM 6" plate, Syracuse, 1961 date code..$20.00

Ox Head cereal, burgundy on white body, Tepco $28.00

Palace Hotel (San Francisco) candlestick, PH TM, ca 1910s, Bauscher..$32.00

Pere Marquette Hotel (Peoria, Illinois) TM bouillon, Buffalo, ca 1930s..$14.00

Riveria Hotel & Casino (Las Vegas) cream pitcher, crown over R TM, Wallace, late 1950s, minimum value $35.00

Rodeo 8" plate, multicolor on tan body, Wallace, 1950s...$40.00

Rusty Pelican (chain restaurant located in 6 states) TM mug, Burden China $10.00

Sam's Hof Brau TM mug, Tepco, 1950s-60s $30.00

Sambo's cup, clown TM, Wallace, late 1950s, minimum value $75.00

Sarah Siddons TM (Ambassador Hotel East's Pump Room, Chicago) cream pitcher, Duraline Grindley Hotelware, 1966 date code..$30.00

Steak 'n Shake TM 6" plate, Shenango, 1970 date code....**$18.00**

Tepco TM sample ashtray w/spattered rim, ca 1940s, minimum value......................**$45.00**

Tim Horton's Donuts TM mug, Dunn Bennett, 1970s......**$18.00**

Toddle House TM covered mustard, Iroquois, ca 1930s..**$50.00**

Trocadero Hotel (Miami Beach, Florida) TM fruit, Buffalo Colorido Lamelle, 1930s **$22.50**

Walgreens TM footed mug, Shenango, 1975 date code...**$19.00**

Western Traveler 10" plate, brown on tan body, Tepco, 1940s-50s **$55.00**

White Castle mug, black TM, Mayer, 1951 date code.**$38.00**

White Tower TM 7" plate, Sterling, 1930s...................**$40.00**

Woolworth's TM 7½" plate, Syracuse, 1930 date code .**$42.00**

Transportation and Military China

Air France butter pat, stylized blue & gold dragon TM, Bernardaud & Co, 1970-90s **$18.00**

Alaska Airline 'Gold Coast' TM cup & saucer, Rackett, 1980s **$22.00**

American Airlines plastic molded cup, embossed AA topmark.........................**$2.00**

American Embassy (Paris, France) 4½" long fine-gauge TM tray, Haviland, 1920s **$25.00**

American Orient Express TM AD cup & saucer, China Concepts, 1997.........................**$50.00**

American President Lines room service sugar, eagle TM, Syracuse.........................**$24.00**

BWIA 6½" casserole, gold TM, Pfaltzgraff, 1980s..........**$9.00**

Chesapeake & Ohio ashtray, Chessie cat TM, Syracuse, 1955-62, minimum value.........................**$85.00**

Delta Air Lines 8" plate, 'Widget' TM, Mayer or ABCO .**$9.00**

Department of the Navy TM handled bouillon, 1950s-present **$12.50**

Elders & Ffyes Ltd TM AD cup & saucer, Dunn Bennett, 1950s.........................**$75.00**

French Line 9" soup, squared CGT TM, GDA, 1950s .**$65.00**

Greyhound Post House topmarked plate, Syracuse, 6¼", $22.00. (Photo courtesy Barbara Conroy)

London & North East Railway (LNER TM) 13" platter, Minton, ca 1920s **$70.00**

Manitou Steamship Co TM sauce boat, Union Porcelain Works, ca 1890s, minimum value **$75.00**

McClain Airlines cup & saucer (cup only TM), Rego, 1986-88 ....**$28.00**

Northwest Airlines 'Regal Imperial' TM bowl, Royal Doulton, mid-1980s **$18.00**

Norwegian American Cruises ashtray, NAC top mark, Pillvuyt, 1981 date code **$11.00**

Prudential Lines 8" platter, P in compass TM, Jackson, Paul, McCobb **$28.00**

Royal Cruise Line TM mug, Porsgrund, 1982 date code ...**$12.00**

Singapore Airline gold TM & maroon border design 6½" plate, 1990s.........................**$16.00**

Southern Pacific Daylight cup & saucer, peach matt, Franciscan/So Pacific Lines or SPC Co backstamp, 1939-early '40s, minimum **$500.00**

Southern Pacific Prairie Mountain Wild Flowers cup & saucer, Syracuse, 1930s-50s, minimum value **$95.00**

Sun Line TM 6" plate, Richard-Ginori, 1980s...............**$28.00**

TWA Royal Ambassador cup & saucer, red & gold RA TM, Rosenthal, 1960s-75 ....**$30.00**

TWA 6" plate, red & gold TWA TM, Michaud, Rego or ABCO **$8.00**

Union Pacific Winged Streamliner cup & saucer **$75.00**

United Air Lines cup & saucer, 'U' UNITED TM, Wessco, 1980s **$20.00**

United Air Lines 6" casserole, blue exterior, no TM, Coors Porcelain, dated 1951 ....**$16.00**

United Air Lines 6½" plate, Syracuse Silhouette backstamp, 1960s **$30.00**

United States Army Corps of Engineers, logo in flag TM 8" plate, Scammell, 1930s **$28.00**

United States Army Medical Department, cream pitcher, 1940s **$14.00**

US Army Transport sauce boat, USAT clover TM, Syracuse, 1942 date code.........................**$24.00**

US Navy Wardroom Officer's Mess cup & saucer, anchor TM.........................**$20.00**

Rock 'n Roll Memorabilia

Ticket stubs and souvenirs issued at rock concerts, posters of artists that have reached celebrity status, and merchandise such as dolls, games, clothing, etc., that was sold through retail stores during the heights of their careers are just the things that interest collectors of rock 'n roll memorabilia. Some original, one-of-a-kind examples — for instance, their instruments, concert costumes, and personal items — often sell at the large auction galleries in the East where they've realized very high-dollar prices. For more information we recommend *Rock-N-Roll Treasures* by Joe Hilton and Greg Moore (Collector Books). Greg has also written *A Price Guide to Rock and Roll Collectibles* which is distributed by L-W Book Sales. *Collector's Guide to TV Toys and Memorabilia* by Greg Davis and Bill Morgan contains additional information and photos. (It is also published by Collector Books.)

See also Beatles Collectibles; Elvis Presley Memorabilia; Magazines; Movie Posters; Pin-Back Buttons; Records.

Advisor: Bojo/Bob Gottuso (See Directory, Character and Personality Collectibles)

AC/DC, scarf, Back in Black/European Tour 1980-81, 48" L, EX (unused) $22.00

Alice Cooper, concert ticket, Jackson MS, June 6, 1975, NM (unused) $25.00

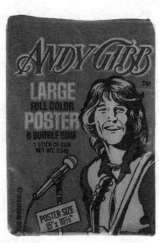

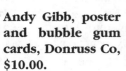

Andy Gibb, poster and bubble gum cards, Donruss Co, $10.00.

Bee Gees, transistor radio, Vanity Fair, 1979, 5½" $15.00

Blondie, International Fan Club Book, #2, 1981, NM.$10.00

Blondie, promotional soap, color photo in center, 3½" oval, MIP..........$20.00

Bob Dylan, poster, House of Blues, Atlanta, Aug 3-4, 1996, 17x11", NM..........$50.00

Bob Seger & the Silver Bullet Band, foam rock, Like a Rock Album, 1980, 4x5", M $18.00

Bobby Sherman, book, Secret of Bobby Sherman, 1971, NM..........$25.00

Bobby Sherman, Love Beads, 1971, M, from $40 to...$50.00

Bobby Sherman, necklace, black suede choker w/gold trim, 1971, M..........$60.00

Bobby Sherman, ring, Love & Peace, 1971, M..........$25.00

Bonnie Raitt, concert poster, Smith Center, April 9, 1978, 17½x11½", NM..........$75.00

Boy George, doll, cloth, 1984, NM..........$100.00

Boy George & the Culture Club, book, 1984, NM $18.00

Boy George & the Culture Club, puffy stickers, 1984, set of 6, M..........$12.00

Cars, matchbook, Candy-O, Elektra, M (unused)........$15.00

Cheap Trick, security sticker, Dream Police album, 1979, 3x3", M (unused) $10.00

Chubby Checker, limbo bar w/record, Whamo, 1962, EX..........$125.00

Crosby, Stills & Nash, whistle, Whistle Down the Wire, ABC Records, EX..........$15.00

Dave Clark 5, tour book, 1964, lg format, EX..........$35.00

David Bowie, sweatshirt, navy blue w/embroidered logo of Serious Moonlight tour, 1983, M (unused)..........$22.00

David Cassidy, guitar, Carnival Toys, 1970s, MIB $100.00

David Cassidy, slide-tile puzzle, 1970s, M..........$30.00

Dick Clark/American Bandstand, cuff links & tie clasp, brass figures of dancing couple & lettering, 3-pc set, MIB $50.00

Dick Clark/American Bandstand, diary, vinyl, 1958, 4x4", EX..........$125.00

Dick Clark/American Bandstand, record case, 1958, EX..........$75.00

Donny & Marie Osmond, diary, Continental Plastics, 1977, EX, unused $18.00

Donny & Marie Osmond, microphone, LJN, 1977, MIB ..$35.00

Doors, bumper sticker, orange & white on blue, promo from WPU NY rock station, 1970s, 12" L, M..........$8.00

Doors, concert ticket, KNRT Theater, Sept 27, 1967, NM (unused) $300.00

Doors, stationery, 1960s, NM..........$100.00

Eric Clapton, comic, color cover, info on Eric, Rock & Roll Comics, 1st printing, 1993, M..........$8.00

Fleetwood Mac, pin, radio promo for June 1977 concert at Madison Square Gardens, black & white tin litho, 2¼" dia, M..........$12.00

Go Gos, button, We Got the Beat, girls on pink image, 1" dia, M..........$17.50

Grateful Dead, postcard, BG-263, Dec 31, 1970, NM .$30.00

Hard Rock Cafe, pin, Bangkok Earth Day, multicolored enamel, M..........$20.00

Herman's Hermits, pin-back button, I Love Herman's Hermits, pictures group, red & white, 1960s, 3½", EX $15.00

Jackson 5, banner, I Love the Jackson 5, white lettering on black felt w/red trim, 1960s-70s, 29", NM..........$25.00

Jerry Garcia Band, baseball shirt, 1978 concert tour, off white w/blue sleeves, by ABCO, M (unused)..........$22.00

Joe Cocker, concert button, Central Park Music Festival, New York City, tin w/litho photo, 1980, 2½" dia, EX ..$10.00

John Denver, belt buckle, brass w/color image of Denver performing, Rock Visuals Inc, 1976, EX..........$25.00

Kinks, concert ticket, Universal Amphitheater, June 23, 1978, unused, NM..........$20.00

KISS, belt buckle, brass w/logo, 1976, NM..........$35.00

KISS, bracelet, stylized logo, gold colored w/chain, ca 1970s, M..........$8.00

KISS, fan club kit, Kiss Army, complete, M..........$75.00

KISS, iron-on transfers, M (unused) $10.00

KISS, necklace, gold-tone in shape of logo, fan club premium, 1970s, M..........$35.00

KISS, poster, Honda Kissmobile & group photo, 1979, M..........$250.00

KISS, sweatshirt, 1992 Convention at New Jersey Meadowlands, heavy cotton w/puffed silk screening, Jerzees, M (unused)..........$22.00

KISS, wastebasket, metal pail w/graphics of group posing & performing, P&K Products, 1970s, 19", EX........$230.00

Led Zeppelin, program, Knebworth Park, Aug 11, 1979, VG+..........$200.00

MC Hammer, backpack, vinyl, 2 different styles, Bustin Products, 15", M..........$20.00

MC Hammer, hand-held video game, Tiger Electronics LCD, 1991, MIP......................**$25.00**

Michael Jackson, bumper sticker, full-color image, 1984, EX......................**$5.00**

Michael Jackson, cassette & glove set, Motown, 1984, MIP......................**$25.00**

Michael Jackson, key chain, 1988 concert promo, brass, M......................**$12.00**

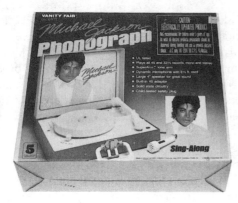

Michael Jackson, Sing-Along Phonograph, MIB, $50.00.

Michael Jackson, wallet, nylon, various colors, 1984, M...**$12.00**

Monkees, book, Who's Got the Button, Whitman, 1967, NM......................**$20.00**

Monkees, fan club kit, complete, 1967, EX (EX mailer)...**$150.00**

Monkees, pillow, red w/guitar logo in white & white daisies w/reverse in red, inflatable, recent, 16x16", MIP .**$10.00**

Monkees, playing cards, complete, Raybert, 1967, MIB...**$65.00**

Monkees, record case, Mattel, 1966, NM **$150.00**

Monkees, sunglasses, w/gold chain, 1960s, EX...........**$60.00**

Monkees, tour book, 1960s, 12x12", VG......................**$35.00**

Neil Young, program, Crazy Horse, 1987 North American Tour, EX......................**$35.00**

New Kids on the Block, balloons, Unique, 1990, MIP .**$5.00**

New Kids on the Block, microphone, Big Step Products, 1990, MIB **$20.00**

Olivia Newton John, T-shirt iron-on, photo of young Olivia, 1976 ....**$10.00**

Ozzy Ozbourne, scarf, Blizzard of Ozz album tour, skull w/horns logo on ea end, 48" L, M (unused)........**$18.00**

Paul McCartney, shirt, band photo w/Linda on front, tour dates on back, 1989-90, NM......................**$18.00**

Peter, Paul & Mary, concert ticket, April, 8, 1966, unused, NM......................**$75.00**

Phil Collins, handkerchief, No Jacket Required tour, 24x24", M (unused)......................**$18.00**

Pink Floyd, postcard, Cheetah Club, colored graphics, ca 1980s, M......................**$8.00**

Pink Floyd, T-shirt, logo on front, dates & venues on back, 1994 tour, heavy cotton, by Brockum, M (unused)...........**$18.00**

Police, cap, 1983 Syncronicity Tour, black w/group name, tour name & logo, M......................**$15.00**

Rolling Stones, handbill, for movie at Sony Imax theatre, tongue logo, 10x4", M **$7.00**

Rolling Stones, key chain, Musidor, 1983, MOC...........**$8.00**

Rolling Stones, pennant, felt, 1960s, M......................**$75.00**

Rolling Stones, program, 1966 US tour, EX..............**$150.00**

Rolling Stones, puffy stickers, set of 6 on photo display card, M......................**$6.00**

Rolling Stones, ring, tongue logo, silver or bronze metal, adjustable, M......................**$15.00**

Rolling Stones, sticker album, Stanley, 1983, NM **$15.00**

Sonny & Cher, tour program, 1972-73, 10x13", EX.....**$35.00**

Sun Records, invoice for 45s, 1959, NM......................**$25.00**

Supremes, flyer, Lincoln Center Philharmonic Hall, Oct 15, 1925, 9x6", NM......................**$100.00**

Three Dog Night, banner, I Love Three Dog Night, white lettering on blue felt w/yellow trim, 1960s-70s, 29", NM......................**$25.00**

U2, security T-shirt, Unforgetable Fire tour, 1984, M (never worn) **$18.00**

Van Halen, puffy stickers, 1980s, MIP......................**$10.00**

Vanilla Ice, Rap Microphone, THQ, 1991, MIB **$25.00**

Who, sticker sheet, features Who & WPU (NY rock station), 2 lg & 5 sm, ca 1970s, 8½x7", M (unused)............**$8.00**

Yes, headband, 90210 tour, black w/tour/album logo on front, 1984, 36" L, M......................**$15.00**

ZZ Top, mirror, 1980s, 6x6", M..................**$10.00**

Rookwood

Although this company was established in 1879, it continued to produce commercial artware until it closed in 1967. Located in Cincinnati, Ohio, Rookwood is recognized today as the largest producer of high-quality art pottery ever to operate in the United States.

Most of the pieces listed here are from the later years of production, but we've included some early pieces as well. With few exceptions, all early Ohio art pottery companies produced an artist-decorated brown-glaze line — Rookwood's was called Standard. Among their other early lines were Sea Green, Iris, Jewel Porcelain, Wax Matt, and Vellum.

Virtually all of Rookwood's pieces are marked. The most familiar mark is the 'reverse R'-P monogram. It was first used in 1886, and until 1900 a flame point was added above it to represent each passing year. After the turn of the century, a Roman numeral below the monogram was used to indicate the current year. In addition to the dating mark, a die-stamped number was used to identify the shape.

The Cincinnati Art Galleries held two large and important cataloged auctions in 1991. The full-color catalogs contain a comprehensive history of the company, list known artists and designers with their monograms (as well as company codes and trademarks), and describe each lot thoroughly. Collectors now regard them as an excellent source for information and study.

Ashtray, #1084, 1946, owl form, dark green, 7x6"....**$250.00**

Ashtray, #1139, 1945, rook form, light green, 7½" ...**$275.00**

Bookends, #2274, 1946, rook form, wine madder, lg, pr...**$650.00**

Bookends, #2655, 1946, owl form, chartreuse, 6", pr.......**$275.00**

Bookends, #2836, 1956, cactus flower, brown, 3½".$250.00
Bowl, #6180, 1945, turquoise, fluted, 7¾"................$150.00
Bowl, console; #6825, 1949, light green, 13x5".........$160.00
Candle holders, #1773, 1926, sea horse figural, ivory, 4",
    EX...$305.00
Cigarette box, #6451, 1950, brown, 3½"....................$195.00
Face, #2457, 1949, Italian model, beige, 5½"...........$195.00
Figurine, #2832, 1946, pheasant, chartreuse, crazed, 13"
    L $450.00
Flower frog, #2336, 1921, satyr, raspberry, 6½".......$525.00
Font, #6975, 1947, St Francis Holy Water, wine madder,
    10"...$250.00
Lamp base, unknown number, 1949, cream, undrilled,
    7½" $225.00
Smoke set, #7081A, 1951, maroon, 2-pc, 7" L..........$160.00
Stein, Weideman; 1948, high glaze, 5½".....................$595.00
Sugar bowl, #2800, 1930, Blue Ship, high glaze......$170.00
Trivet, #2351, 1951, w/gull design, yellow, 5⅝".......$275.00
Trivet, #7131, 1957, w/pointsettia design, light brown, 7"
    dia $225.00
Vase, #63, 1938, mottled blue matt, 2-handled, 4¼".$195.00
Vase, #778, 1946, tan, narrow neck, 9¾"...................$140.00
Vase, #2236, 1916, ivory & pink, flared, 5¼" $375.00
Vase, #2592, 1950, w/embossed cattails, wine madder,
    5"..$150.00
Vase, #2840, 1926, gray matt, rectangular, 5¾" $170.00
Vase, #2854, 1940, white matt, molded, 4½".............$225.00
Vase, #6214, 1934, embossed deer design, gray/blue matt,
    4¼"...$245.00
Vase, #6214, 1942, molded w/deer design, blue green,
    4½" $225.00
Vase, #6218, 1937, white matt, molded, 6¼".............$245.00
Vase, #6363, 1946, light blue, molded, 6".................$160.00
Vase, #6449E, 1937, khaki matt, 2-handled, 8".........$175.00
Vase, #6509, 1943, molded w/butterfly design, white matt,
    4½"...$175.00
Vase, #6534, 1935, white exterior, green interior, pedestal,
    6¾"...$325.00
Vase, #6957, 1958, w/molded lamb design, pink, 4½" ..$140.00
Vase, #7088, 1951, wine madder, molded S shape, 6"...$175.00
Vase, #7133, 1957, gunmetal & pink, pedestal, sm, 3"...$165.00
Vase, bud; #2546-C, 1921, black matt, 10½"..............$395.00

Vases, blue matt glaze with molded floral bouquets, style #6376, signed and dated 1934, 7½", $660.00 for the pair.

Rooster and Roses

Back in the 1940s, newlyweds might conceivably have received some of this imported Japanese-made kitchenware as a housewarming gift. They'd no doubt be stunned to see the prices it's now bringing! Rooster and Roses (Ucagco called it Early Provincial) is one of those lines of novelty ceramics from the '40s and '50s that are among today's hottest collectibles. Ucagco was only one of several importers whose label you'll find on this pattern; among other are Py, ACSON, Norcrest, and Lefton. The design is easy to spot — there's the rooster, yellow breast with black crosshatching, brown head and, of course, the red crest and waddle, large full-blown roses with green leaves and vines, and a trimming of yellow borders punctuated by groups of brown lines. (You'll find another line having blue flowers among the roses, and one with a rooster with a green head and a green borders. These are not considered Rooster and Roses by purist collectors, though there is a market for them as well.) The line is fun to collect, since shapes are so diversified. Even though there has been relatively little networking among collectors, more than eighty items have been reported and no doubt more will surface.

Advisor: Jacki Elliott (See Directory, Rooster and Roses)

Ashtray, rectangular, 3x2"..$9.50
Ashtray, round or square, sm, from $15 to.................$25.00
Ashtray, square, lg, from $25 to $35.00
Basket, flared sides, 6", from $45 to $65.00
Bell, from $35 to...$55.00
Bell, rooster & chicken on opposing sides, from $35 to...$55.00
Biscuit jar, w/wicker handle, from $65 to...................$95.00
Bonbon dish, pedestal base, minimum value $55.00
Bowl, cereal; from $14 to..$25.00
Bowl, rice; on saucer, from $25 to...............................$35.00
Bowl, 8"...$25.00
Box, 4½x3½", from $25 to...$35.00
Bread plate, from $15 to $25.00
Butter dish, ¼-lb, from $20 to......................................$25.00
Candle warmer (for tea & coffeepots), from $15 to ...$25.00
Candy dish, flat chicken-shaped tray w/3-dimensional chick-
    en head, made in 3 sizes, from $40 to $65.00
Candy dish, w/3-dimensional leaf handle, from $25 to ..$45.00
Canister set, round, 4-pc, from $150 to $175.00
Canister set, square, 4-pc, from $100 to $150.00
Canister set, stacking, minimum value......................$150.00
Carafe, no handle, w/stopper lid, 8", from $65 to......$85.00
Carafe, w/handle & stopper lid, 8".............................$85.00
Casserole dish, w/lid $65.00
Castor set in revolving wire rack, 2 cruets, mustard jar & salt
    & pepper shakers, rare, from $75 to..................$125.00
Chamberstick, saucer base, ring handle, from $20 to.$25.00
Cheese dish, slant lid, from $40 to.............................$55.00
Cigarette box w/2 trays, hard to find, from $40 to.....$65.00
Coaster, ceramic disk embedded in round wood tray, mini-
    mum value..$35.00
Coffee grinder, rare, from $85 to................................$150.00

Condiment set and four spice containers in wood and wire rack, from $100.00 to $125.00. (Photo courtesy Jacki Elliott)

Cookie jar, ceramic handles, from $85 to **$100.00**
Creamer & sugar bowl, w/lid, lg **$25.00**
Creamer & sugar bowl on rectangular tray, from $35 to ..**$40.00**
Cruets, cojoined w/twisted necks, sm **$20.00**
Cruets, oil & vinegar, flared bases, pr, from $25 to **$30.00**
Cruets, oil & vinegar, square, lg, pr, from $30 to.......**$35.00**
Cruets, oil & vinegar, w/salt & pepper shakers in shadow box, from $55 to **$75.00**
Cup & saucer, from $15 to...**$25.00**
Demitasse pot, w/4 cups & saucer, from $100 to.....**$150.00**
Demitasse pot, w/6 cups & saucers, from $125 to ...**$175.00**
Egg cup, from $20 to...**$25.00**
Egg cup on tray, from $35 to **$45.00**
Egg plate, from $45 to..**$55.00**
Flowerpot, buttress handles, 5", from $35 to..............**$45.00**
Hamburger press, wood w/embedded ceramic tray, round, minimum value **$24.00**
Instant coffee jar, no attached spoon holder on side, minimum value...**$35.00**
Instant coffee jar, spoon-holder tube on side, from $20 to ..**$30.00**
Jam & jelly containers, cojoined, w/lids & spoons, from $35 to..**$45.00**
Jam jar, attached underplate, from $35 to....................**$45.00**
Ketchup or mustard jar, flared cylinder w/lettered label, ea, from $25 to...**$30.00**
Lamp, pinup, made from either a match holder or a salt box, ea, from $75 to **$100.00**
Lazy Susan on wood pedestal, round covered box at center, 4 sections around outside (2 w/lids), from $150 to ..**$250.00**
Marmalade, round base w/tab handles, w/lid & spoon, minimum value, from $35 to..**$55.00**
Match holder, wall mount, from $45 to **$65.00**
Measuring cup set, 4-pc w/matching ceramic rack, from $45 to..**$65.00**
Measuring spoons on 8" ceramic spoon-shaped rack, from $40 to...**$55.00**
Mug, rounded bottom, med, from $15 to....................**$25.00**

Mug, straight upright bar handle, lg, from $15 to.......**$25.00**
Napkin holder, from $30 to **$40.00**
Pipe holder/ashtray, from $30 to.................................**$40.00**
Pitcher, bulbous, 5", from $25 to.................................**$30.00**
Pitcher, lettered Milk on neck band, from $22.50 to ..**$35.00**
Pitcher, 3½", from $15 to **$20.00**
Planter, rolling pin shape, minimum value.................**$50.00**
Plate, dinner; from $25 to **$35.00**
Plate, luncheon; from $15 to **$25.00**
Plate, side salad; crescent shape, hard to find, from $50 to **$60.00**
Platter, 12", from $35 to..**$55.00**
Recipe box, from $25 to...**$35.00**
Relish tray, 2 round wells w/center handle, 12", from $22 to **$28.00**
Relish tray, 3 wells w/center handle, from $45 to **$55.00**
Rolling pin, minimum value **$50.00**
Salad fork, spoon & salt & pepper shakers w/wooden handles, on ceramic wall-mount rack, minimum value **$55.00**
Salad fork & spoon w/wooden handles on ceramic wall-mount rack, from $45 to **$65.00**
Salt box, wooden lid, from $45 to **$55.00**
Slipper, 3-dimensional rose on toe, rare, minimum value **$85.00**
Snack tray w/cup, oval, 2-pc, minimum value...........**$45.00**
Snack tray w/cup, rectangular, 2-pc, from $50 to.......**$60.00**

Spice canisters, small, set of four, from $85.00 to $125.00.

Syrup pitcher, w/2 sm graduated pitchers on tray, minimum value **$45.00**
Toast holder, minimum value **$75.00**
Wall pocket, lavabo, 2-pc, mounted on board, from $85 to **$125.00**
Wall pocket, scalloped top, bulbous bottom, from $75 to.**$80.00**
Wall pocket, teapots, facing ea other, pr, minimum value **$110.00**

Roselane Sparklers

Beginning as a husband and wife operation in the late 1930s, the Roselane Pottery Company of Pasadena, California, expanded their inventory from the figurines they originally sold to local florists to include a complete line of decorative items that eventually were shipped to Alaska,

South America, and all parts of the United States.

One of their lines was the Roselane Sparklers. Popular in the '50s, these small animal and bird figures were airbrush decorated and had rhinestone eyes. They're fun to look for, and though prices are rising steadily, they're still not terribly expensive.

If you'd like to learn more, there's a chapter on Roselane in *The Collector's Encyclopedia of California Pottery, Second Edition,* by Jack Chipman.

Advisor: Lee Garmon (See Directory, Advertising, Reddy Kilowatt)

Angelfish, 4½", from $20 to **$25.00**
Basset hound, sitting, 4", from $15 to **$18.00**
Basset hound pup, 2", from $12 to **$15.00**
Bulldog, fierce expression, looking right, 2", from $12 to..**$15.00**
Bulldog, fierce expression, looking up & right, jeweled collar, lg, from $22 to **$25.00**
Bulldog, sitting, slender body, looking right, 6"..........**$25.00**
Cat, recumbent, head turned right, tail & paws tucked under body, from $20 to **$25.00**
Cat, Siamese, sitting, looking straight ahead, jeweled collar, 7", from $25 to **$28.00**
Cat, sitting, head turned right, tail out behind, from $25 to **$28.00**
Cat, standing, head turned left, tail arched over back, jeweled collar, 5½", from $20 to...**$25.00**
Cat mother, looking straight ahead, 4½", w/kitten (same pose), 2-pc set, from $25 to...................................**$30.00**
Chihuahua, sitting, left paw raised, looking straight ahead, 6½" **$25.00**
Cocker spaniel, 4½"..**$20.00**
Deer, standing, head turned right, looking downward, 5½" **$25.00**
Deer w/antlers, standing jeweled collar, 4½", from $22 to **$28.00**
Elephant, sitting on hind quarters, 6".........................**$25.00**
Elephant, trunk raised, striding, jeweled headpiece, 6" ..**$25.00**
Fawn, legs folded under body, 4x3½" **$25.00**
Fawn, upturned head, 4x3½" **$20.00**
Fawn, 4½x1½" **$20.00**
Frog, 2½", from $25 to..**$30.00**

Kangaroo mama with babies, rare, from $40.00 to $45.00. (Photo courtesy Lee Garmon)

Kitten, sitting, 1¾" **$12.00**
Owl, very stylized, lg round eyes, teardrop-shaped body, lg..**$25.00**
Owl, 3½" **$15.00**
Owl, 5¼" **$25.00**
Owl, 7" **$30.00**
Owl baby, 2¼", from $12 to **$15.00**
Pig, lg...**$25.00**
Pouter pigeon, 3½"...**$20.00**
Raccoon, standing, 4½", from $20 to **$25.00**
Whippet, sitting, 7½", from $25 to **$28.00**

Rosemeade

The Wahpeton Pottery Company of Wahpeton, North Dakota, chose the trade name Rosemeade for a line of bird and animal figurines, novelty salt and pepper shakers, bells, and many other items which were sold from the 1940s to the '60s through gift stores and souvenir shops in that part of the country. They were marked with either a paper label or an ink stamp; the name Prairie Rose was also used. See *Collector's Encyclopedia of the Dakota Potteries* by Darlene Hurst Dommel (Collector Books) for more information.

Advisor: Bryce Farnsworth (See Directory, Rosemeade)

Club: North Dakota Pottery Collectors Society
Sandy Short
Box 14, Beach, ND 58621; 701-872-3236. Annual dues: $15; sponsors annual convention and includes four newsletters

Ashtray, Dakota Territory Centennial, white, 7" square .**$75.00**
Ashtray, wheat design, blue, 2 rests, 4¼" dia..............**$45.00**
Basket, pink, 4¼x5"..**$55.00**
Bells, tea; tulip shape, Art Nouveau, maroon, blue, yellow or pink, 3¾", ea, from $125 to...............................**$150.00**
Figurine, buffalo, bronze, 6½x8½", from $400 to.....**$500.00**
Figurine, Chinese ring-necked pheasant (cock), 7x11½" ..**$300.00**

Figurine, cock pheasant, 14", $525.00. (Photo courtesy Bryce Farnsworth)

Figurine, dog, sits begging, solid, 2¾".....................**$100.00**

Figurine, skunks (2), black & white, 1½", ¾", pr **$25.00**
Mug, Minnesota Centennial, brown, 3"......................**$65.00**
Pin, meadowlark, 2x2", from $375 to.........................**$450.00**
Planter, deer, 8"..**$75.00**
Planter, peacock, 7½"...**$200.00**
Planter w/bird flower frog, 3½x7½" **$75.00**
Salt & pepper shakers, chicken, lg, 3¼", pr **$95.00**
Salt & pepper shakers, fish, pink, 2¾", pr...................**$70.00**
Salt & pepper shakers, flamingos, pink on brown post stump,
 3¾", pr..**$85.00**
Salt & pepper shakers, Paul Bunyon (bust) & Babe the Blue
 Ox (bust), 2¼", pr **$150.00**
Salt & pepper shakers, swans, 2", pr **$95.00**
Salt & pepper shakers, tulips, pink, 2¼", pr **$60.00**
Spoon rest, flying pheasant, 3¼x5½"...........................**$75.00**
Spoon rest, tulip, 5½", from $50 to.............................**$75.00**
Sugar & creamer, corn design, from $35 to.................**$55.00**
TV lamp, Palomino horse, 9½", from $475 to...........**$525.00**
Vase, early glaze, aqua interior, 4", from $50 to.........**$75.00**
Vase, embossed wheat design, 7"..................................**$75.00**
Vase, ruffled rim, made to look hand thrown, 4" **$55.00**
Wall hanging, mallard, 6" dia......................................**$75.00**

Roseville Pottery

This company took its name from the city in Ohio where they operated for a few years before moving to Zanesville in the late 1890s. They're recognized as one of the giants in the industry, having produced many lines of the finest in art pottery from the beginning to the end of their operations. Even when machinery took over many of the procedures once carefully done by hand, the pottery they produced continued to reflect the artistic merit and high standards of quality the company had always insisted upon.

Several marks were used over the years as well as some paper labels. The very early art lines often carried an applied ceramic seal with the name of the line (Royal, Egypto, Mongol, Mara, or Woodland) under a circle containing the words Rozane Ware. From 1910 until 1928 an Rv mark was used, the 'v' being contained in the upper loop of the 'R.' Paper labels were common from 1914 until 1937. From 1932 until they closed in 1952, the mark was Roseville in script, or R USA. Pieces marked RRP Co Roseville, Ohio, were not made by the Roseville Pottery but by Robinson Ransbottom of Roseville, Ohio. Don't be confused. There are many jardinieres and pedestals in a brown and green blended glaze that are being sold at flea markets and antique malls as Roseville that were actually made by Robinson Ransbottom as late as the 1970s and '80s. That isn't to say they don't have some worth of their own, but don't buy them for old Roseville.

Most of the listings here are for items produced from the 1930s on — things you'll be more likely to encounter today. If you'd like to learn more about the subject, we recommend *The Collector's Encyclopedia of Roseville Pottery, Vols. 1 and 2,* by Sharon and Bob Huxford (Collector Books); *A Price Guide to Roseville Pottery by the Numbers* by John Humphries

(L&W Book Sales); *Roseville in All Its Splendor* by Jack and Nancy Bomm (L&W Book Sales); and *Collector's Compendium of Roseville Pottery, Vols. 1 and 2,* by R.B. Monsen (Monsen & Baer). The Monsen book is the source of the Futura reference names used in our descriptions. Note: use the low side of the Pine Cone range of values for green, the high side for blue, and mid-range for brown.

Newsletter: *Rosevilles of the Past*
Nancy Bomm, Editor
P.O. Box 656
Clarcona, FL 32710-0656
Subscription: $19.95 per year for 6 to 12 newsletters

Apple Blossom, bowl, #326-6, 2½x6½" **$95.00**
Apple Blossom, vase, #388-10, 10"............................**$175.00**
Apple Blossom, window box, #368-8, 2½" **$95.00**
Artwood, planter, #1055-9, 7x9½"...............................**$95.00**
Baneda, bowl, no mark, 3½x10".................................**$400.00**
Baneda, vase, no mark, 8" **$600.00**
Baneda, vase, silver paper label, 4½" **$325.00**
Bittersweet, cornucopia, #857-4, 4½"..........................**$95.00**
Bittersweet, planter, #827-8, 11½"............................**$120.00**
Bittersweet, vase, #874-7, 7"......................................**$125.00**
Blackberry, candle holders, black paper label, 4½", pr ..**$400.00**
Blackberry, jardiniere, no mark, 7" **$375.00**
Blackberry, vase, sm silver label, 6"..........................**$350.00**
Blackberry, wall pocket, black paper label..............**$850.00**
Bleeding Heart, bowl vase, #377-4, 4"......................**$110.00**
Bleeding Heart, console bowl & frog, #384-14 & #40,
 17" **$250.00**
Bleeding Heart, plate, #381-10 ....**$175.00**

Bushberry, basket, #372-12, $350.00.

Bushberry, hanging basket, marked USA, 7"............**$375.00**
Bushberry, mug, #1-3½, 3½" **$125.00**
Bushberry, vase, #156-6, 6".......................................**$150.00**
Bushberry, vase, #32-7, 7"..**$125.00**
Capri, ashtray, #598-9, 9"..**$45.00**
Capri, leaf dish, #532-16, 16" **$35.00**
Capri, shell dish, #C-1120, 13½"................................**$60.00**
Capri, window box, #569-10, 3x10" **$45.00**

Cherry Blossom, bowl, 5" $300.00
Cherry Blossom, jardiniere, 10" $800.00
Cherry Blossom, jug vase, paper label, 7"....$400.00

Cherry Blossom, vase, 8", from $600.00 to $650.00.

Clemana, bowl, #281-5, 4½x6½" $225.00
Clemana, flower frog, #23, 4" $175.00
Clemana, vase, #754-8, 8½" $350.00
Clematis, candle holder, #1155-2, 2½" $60.00
Clematis, flower arranger, #102-5, 5½" $75.00
Clematis, flower frog, #50, 4½" $75.00
Clematis, vase, #108, 8" $125.00
Columbine, candle holders, #1146-4½, 5", pr...$150.00
Columbine, vase, #151-8, 8" $200.00
Cosmos, console bowl, #374-14, 15½" $250.00
Cosmos, vase, #134-4, 4" $110.00
Cosmos, vase, #905-8, 8" $150.00
Cremona, bowl, 9" $125.00
Cremona, candle holder, black paper label, 4"....$85.00
Cremona, flower frog $75.00
Dahlrose, triple bud vase, black paper label, 6"....$150.00
Dahlrose, vase, black paper label, 6"..........$150.00
Dawn, ewer, #834-16, 16" $550.00
Dawn, vase, #827, 6" $200.00
Dawn, vase, #828, 8" $200.00
Dogwood II, basket, no mark, 6" $150.00
Dogwood II, boat planter, no mark, 6" $175.00
Earlam, candlestick, black paper label, 4"....$275.00
Earlam, planter, no mark, 5½x10½"............$150.00
Falline, bowl, no mark, 11" $250.00
Falline, vase, no mark, 9" $600.00
Falline, vase, sm silver label, 6" $425.00
Ferella, candlesticks, no mark, 4½", pr......$500.00
Florane, bowl, 10"............................$30.00
Florane, bowl, 12"............................$75.00
Florane, bud vase, 7".........................$35.00
Florentine, double bud vase, Rv ink stamp, 6"....$110.00
Florentine, vase, Rv ink stamp, 6½"..........$100.00
Florentine, wall pocket, Rv ink stamp, 9½" $225.00
Foxglove, flower frog, #46, 4" $135.00
Foxglove, tray, 8½"..........................$110.00
Foxglove, vase, #51-10, 10" $225.00
Freesia, basket, #390-7, 7"...................$150.00

Freesia, bowl, #669-4, 4" $95.00
Freesia, flowerpot w/saucer, #670-5, 5½".....$150.00
Freesia, vase, #121-8, 8" $130.00
Fuchsia, console bowl & frog, #353-14 & #37 ....$325.00
Fuchsia, vase, #893-6, 6" $150.00
Fuchsia, vase, #898-8, 8" $275.00
Futura, vase, Beehive, #406-8, from $600 to $700.00
Futura, vase, Cone, #401-8, from $450 to......$600.00
Futura, vase, Little Blue Triangle, #383-8, from $300 to..$375.00
Futura, vase, Sand Toy, 4", from $400 to......$500.00
Futura, vase, Telescope, #382-7, from $250 to....$325.00
Futura, wall pocket, 8", from $475 to $550.00
Gardenia, basket, #610-12, 12" $225.00
Gardenia, bowl, #64105, 5" $100.00
Gardenia, vase, #658-10, 10" $150.00
Iris, bowl vase, #647-3, 3½" $85.00
Iris, pillow vase, #922-8, 8½" $200.00
Iris, vase, #923-8, 8" $175.00
Ivory II, cornucopia, #2, 5½x12" $60.00
Ivory II, ewer, #941-10, 10½" $75.00
Ivory II, hanging basket, no mark, 7" $100.00
Ixia, console bowl, #330-7, 3½x10½" $125.00
Ixia, vase, #856-8, 8½" $150.00
Jonquil, bowl, no mark, 3" $150.00
Jonquil, candlestick, no mark, 4" $125.00
Jonquil, vase, sm black paper label, 8".......$300.00

Jonquil, vase, paper label, 12", from $800.00 to $900.00.

La Rose, bowl, Rv ink stamp, 6"...............$75.00
La Rose, double bud vase, Rv ink stamp $125.00
Laurel, bowl, silver paper label, 7" $200.00
Laurel, vase, silver paper label, 8" $325.00
Luffa, candlestick, no mark, 5" $175.00
Luffa, jardiniere, silver paper label, 5¼" base dia.....$350.00
Luffa, lamp, no mark, blue & green, 9½"......$600.00
Magnolia, ashtray, #28, 7" $125.00
Magnolia, basket, #386-12, 12" $225.00
Magnolia, conch shell, #453-6, 6½".........$110.00
Magnolia, vase, #180-6, 6" $110.00
Mayfair, bowl, #1119-9, 10" $60.00
Mayfair, flowerpot, #71-4, 4½"...............$45.00

Mayfair, planter, #1113-8, 3½x8½" **$60.00**
Mayfair, vase, #1106-12, 12½" **$75.00**
Ming Tree, basket, #509-12, 13" **$300.00**
Ming Tree, bowl, #526-9, 4x11½" **$110.00**
Ming Tree, planter, 4x8½" **$110.00**
Mock Orange, pillow vase, #930-8, 7" **$115.00**
Mock Orange, planter, #931-8, 3½x9" **$125.00**
Mock Orange, window box, #956-8, 8½" **$95.00**
Moderne, comport, #297-6, 6" **$150.00**
Moderne, vase, #299, 6½" **$175.00**
Montacello, basket, no mark, brown, 6½" **$500.00**
Montacello, vase, no mark, 5" **$300.00**
Morning Glory, basket, white, sm silver paper label,
　10½" **$500.00**
Morning Glory, console bowl, green, 11½" L **$350.00**
Morning Glory, flowerpot, green, 5" **$250.00**
Morning Glory, vase, white, no mark, 15" **$950.00**
Moss, console bowl, 13" **$250.00**
Moss, pillow vase, #781-8, 8" **$225.00**
Moss, triple bud vase, #1108, 7" **$400.00**
Orian, candle holder, no mark, 4½" **$95.00**
Orian, console bowl, no mark, 5" **$200.00**
Orian, vase, #733-6, 6" **$125.00**
Peony, basket, #379-12, 11" **$275.00**
Peony, bookend, #11, 5½", ea **$110.00**
Peony, planter, #387-8, 10" **$95.00**
Peony, tray, no mark, 8" **$100.00**
Pine Cone, double tray, no mark, 13", from $275 to..**$325.00**
Pine Cone, pillow vase, #845-8, 8", from $350 to.....**$500.00**
Pine Cone, pitcher, #708-9, 9½", from $800 to **$1,000.00**
Pine Cone, planter, #124, 5", from $225 to..............**$300.00**
Pine Cone, vase, #747-10, 10½", from $400 to.........**$550.00**
Poppy, basket, #348-12, 12½" **$400.00**
Poppy, bowl, #642-3, 3½" **$85.00**
Poppy, vase, #346-6, 6" **$150.00**
Primrose, vase, #761-6, 6½" **$150.00**
Raymor, ashtray, #203, from $65 to.........................**$80.00**
Raymor, bean pot, individual; #195, from $40 to........**$50.00**
Raymor, bowl, divided vegetable; #165, 13", minimum
　value **$75.00**
Raymor, bowl, salad; #161, 11½", from $50 to..........**$75.00**
Raymor, bowl, vegetable; divided, #165, 13", minimum
　value **$65.00**
Raymor, butter dish, #181, 7½" **$75.00**
Raymor, casserole, #183, 11" **$60.00**
Raymor, casserole, individual; #199, 7½", from $50 to.**$65.00**
Raymor, corn server, individual, #162, 12½" **$50.00**
Raymor, gravy boat, #190, 9½", from $30 to.............**$50.00**
Raymor, pitcher, #189, 10", from $150 to..................**$175.00**
Raymor, plate, dinner; #152, 10½", from $20 to.........**$25.00**
Raymor, platter, #163, from $50 to **$75.00**
Raymor, shirred egg, #200, 10" **$60.00**
Raymor, teapot, #174..**$200.00**
Raymor, trivet, for casserole, #186...........................**$50.00**
Rosecraft Vintage, bowl, lg Rv ink stamp, 6" **$100.00**
Rosecraft Vintage, candlestick, lg Rv ink stamp, 8" ..**$250.00**
Rosecraft Vintage, vase, lg Rv ink stamp, 5" **$125.00**

Rozane, bowl, #5-8, 8½" **$95.00**
Rozane, bud vase, #2, 6" **$85.00**
Rozane, vase, #10-12, 12" **$125.00**
Russco, double bud vase, no mark, 8½" **$125.00**
Russco, vase, gold paper label, 14½" **$250.00**
Silhouette, box, #740, 4½" **$125.00**
Silhouette, vase, #780-6, 6" **$85.00**
Snowberry, console bowl, #1BL-8, 11" **$110.00**
Snowberry, tray, #1V2-7, 7½" **$110.00**
Snowberry, vase, #V-6, 6" **$95.00**
Sunflower, vase, no mark, 7" **$495.00**

**Sunflower, vase, 10",
from $1,500.00 to
$1,800.00.**

Teasel, vase, #881-6, 6" **$110.00**
Teasel, vase, #888-12, 12" **$275.00**
Thorn Apple, hanging basket, 7" **$400.00**
Thorn Apple, triple bud vase, #1120, 6" **$200.00**
Thorn Apple, vase, #820-9, 9½" **$225.00**
Topeo, no mark, 3x11½" **$140.00**
Topeo, vase, no mark, 14" **$550.00**
Topeo, vase, silver paper label, 6" **$200.00**
Tourmaline, pillow vase, no mark, 6" **$125.00**
Tourmaline, vase, silver paper label, 8" **$125.00**
Tuscany, candle holders, no mark, 4", pr...................**$125.00**
Tuscany, console bowl, no mark, 11" **$150.00**
Velmoss, bowl, no mark, 3x11" **$200.00**
Velmoss, vase, no mark, 12½" **$400.00**
Velmoss II, double bud vase, gold paper label, 8" ...**$175.00**
Velmoss II, double cornucopia, gold paper label, 8½" ...**$225.00**
Water Lily, bowl, #663, 3" **$85.00**
Water Lily, flower frog, #48, 4½" **$95.00**
Water Lily, vase, #78-9, 9" **$225.00**
White Rose, double candle holder, #1143, 4".........**$150.00**
White Rose, vase, #978-4, 4" **$90.00**
White Rose, vase, #980-6, 5" **$110.00**
Wincraft, basket, #210-12, 12" **$300.00**
Wincraft, bookends, #259, 6½", pr..........................**$175.00**
Wincraft, cornucopia, #221-8, 9x5".........................**$95.00**
Windsor, basket, sm black paper label, 4½" **$350.00**
Windsor, bowl, no mark, 3½x10½" **$175.00**
Windsor, lamp base, no mark, 7"..............................**$600.00**
Wisteria, bowl vase, no mark, 5" **$350.00**
Wisteria, hanging basket, no mark, 7½" **$550.00**

Zephyr Lily, bud vase, #201-7, 7½" **$85.00**
Zephyr Lily, cornucopia, #204-8, 8½" **$95.00**
Zephyr Lily, hanging basket, no mark, 7½" **$175.00**

Zephyr Lily, tray, 14½" long, from $150.00 to $200.00.

Royal China

The dinnerware made by Royal China of Sebring, Ohio, has become very collectible, the lines mentioned here in particular. All are found on the same standard company shapes. The most popular are their Currier and Ives and Blue Willow patterns, both decorated with blue machine-stamped designs on white backgrounds, but interest in the other patterns is growing all the time. Memory Lane is decorated with red stampings of rural life, Colonial Homestead and Old Curiosity Shop both have green designs, and Fair Oaks has a brown motif with multicolor accents. Buck's County is decorated with gold stamping on a yellow background. Each line has a distinctive border design that will help you identify the pattern on the many unmarked pieces. Of the two green lines, Old Curiosity Shop's border depicts hinges and pulls, while Colonial Homestead's represents wooden frames with nailed joints. The Willow pattern was made in both blue and pink, but pink is hard to find and not as collectible. Tradition is an allover Jacobean-type floral, and though it's often found in pink, it comes in other colors as well.

Most of these lines had matching glassware. With the exception of Currier and Ives, expect to pay about $8.00 for the old-fashioned (3¼"); $8.00 for the six-ounce juice (3½"); $12.00 for the nine-ounce water (4¾"); and $16.00 for the 14-ounce iced tea, which is rare. Any size or style in Currier and Ives goes for around $7.00 to $18.00 each.

Advisors: BA Wellman and John Canfield (See Directory, Dinnerware)

Newsletter: *Currier and Ives China by Royal*
c/o Jack and Treva Hamlin
R.R. 4, Box 150, Kaiser St., Proctorville, OH 45669; 614-886-7644

Newsletter: *Currier and Ives Quarterly Newsletter*
c/o Patty Street
P.O. Box 504, Riverton, KS 66770; 316-848-3529

Club: C&I Dinnerware Collectors
E.R. Aupperle, Treasurer
29470 Saxon Road
Toulon, IL 61483; 309-896-3331, fax: 309-856-6005

Blue Willow, ashtray, 5½" **$12.00**
Blue Willow, bowl, cereal; 6¼" **$12.00**
Blue Willow, bowl, fruit nappy; 5½" **$6.50**
Blue Willow, bowl, soup; 8¼" **$10.00**

Blue Willow, vegetable bowl, 10", $22.00.

Blue Willow, butter dish, ¼-lb **$35.00**
Blue Willow, cake plate, w/handles, 10½" **$20.00**
Blue Willow, casserole **$95.00**
Blue Willow, creamer **$6.00**
Blue Willow, cup & saucer **$6.00**
Blue Willow, gravy boat **$18.00**
Blue Willow, pie plate, 10" **$30.00**
Blue Willow, plate, bread & butter; 6¼" **$3.00**
Blue Willow, plate, dinner; 10" **$6.00**
Blue Willow, plate, salad; 7¼" **$7.00**
Blue Willow, platter, 13" **$28.00**
Blue Willow, salt & pepper shakers, pr **$18.00**
Blue Willow, sugar bowl, w/lid **$12.00**
Blue Willow, teapot **$125.00**
Blue Willow, tray, tidbit; 2-tier **$65.00**
Buck's County, ashtray, 5½" **$7.00**
Buck's County, bowl, soup; 8½" **$9.00**
Buck's County, bowl, vegetable; 10" **$22.00**
Buck's County, cake plate, w/handles, 10½" **$18.00**
Buck's County, casserole, w/lid **$125.00**
Buck's County, creamer **$5.00**
Buck's County, cup & saucer **$5.00**
Buck's County, gravy boat **$22.00**
Buck's County, plate, bread & butter; 6¼" **$2.00**
Buck's County, plate, dinner; 10" **$4.00**
Buck's County, platter, oval **$25.00**
Buck's County, salt & pepper shakers, pr **$18.00**
Buck's County, sugar bowl, w/lid **$12.00**
Buck's County, teapot **$95.00**
Colonial Homestead, bowl, cereal; 6¼" **$10.00**
Colonial Homestead, bowl, fruit nappy; 5½" **$4.00**
Colonial Homestead, bowl, soup; 8¼" **$9.00**
Colonial Homestead, bowl, vegetable; 10" **$20.00**

Colonial Homestead, cake plate, tab handles, 10½"...**$15.00**
Colonial Homestead, casserole, angle handles, w/lid.**$75.00**
Colonial Homestead, chop plate, 12".........................**$18.00**
Colonial Homestead, creamer.....................................**$5.00**
Colonial Homestead, cup & saucer **$5.00**
Colonial Homestead, gravy boat **$15.00**
Colonial Homestead, pie plate **$25.00**
Colonial Homestead, plate, bread & butter; 6"............**$2.00**
Colonial Homestead, plate, dinner; 10".......................**$4.00**
Colonial Homestead, plate, salad; rare, 7¼".................**$6.00**
Colonial Homestead, platter, oval, 13".......................**$24.00**
Colonial Homestead, salt & pepper shakers, pr..........**$15.00**
Colonial Homestead, sugar bowl, w/lid......................**$12.00**
Colonial Homestead, teapot.......................................**$85.00**
Currier & Ives, ashtray, 5½"......................................**$15.00**
Currier & Ives, bowl, cereal; round (various sizes made) ...**$15.00**
Currier & Ives, bowl, fruit nappy; 5½".........................**$5.00**
Currier & Ives, bowl, salad/cereal; tab handle, 6¾" ...**$25.00**
Currier & Ives, bowl, soup; 8½"................................**$14.00**
Currier & Ives, bowl, vegetable; 10" **$28.00**
Currier & Ives, bowl, vegetable; 9" **$22.00**
Currier & Ives, butter dish, Fashionable, ¼-lb **$50.00**
Currier & Ives, butter dish, Road Winter, ¼-lb...........**$40.00**

Currier and Ives, casserole, angle handles, $115.00.

Currier & Ives, casserole, tab handles, w/lid............**$165.00**
Currier & Ives, clock plate, factory, electric **$190.00**
Currier & Ives, clock plate, non-factory.....................**$50.00**
Currier & Ives, creamer, angle handle........................**$8.00**
Currier & Ives, creamer, round handle, tall **$48.00**
Currier & Ives, cup & saucer **$6.00**
Currier & Ives, gravy boat, pour spout **$25.00**
Currier & Ives, gravy boat, tab handles, w/liner (like 7"
    plate), from $100 to..**$135.00**
Currier & Ives, gravy ladle, 3 styles, ea **$35.00**
Currier & Ives, lamp, candle; w/globe.......................**$250.00**
Currier & Ives, mug, coffee; very rare, from $45 to....**$65.00**
Currier & Ives, pie baker, 10", (depending on picture) from
    $30 to...**$90.00**
Currier & Ives, plate, bread & butter; 6⅜".................**$2.00**
Currier & Ives, plate, calendar; ca 1969-86, ea, from $25
    to...**$100.00**
Currier & Ives, plate, chop; Getting Ice, 11½" **$35.00**
Currier & Ives, plate, chop; Getting Ice, 12¼" **$38.00**
Currier & Ives, plate, chop; Rocky Mountains, 11½"..**$65.00**
Currier & Ives, plate, dinner; 10".............................**$7.00**
Currier & Ives, plate, luncheon; very rare, 9"............**$25.00**

Currier & Ives, plate, salad; 7", rare **$15.00**
Currier & Ives, plate, snack; w/cup & well, 9", from $60
    to..**$90.00**
Currier & Ives, platter, oval, 13" **$35.00**
Currier & Ives, platter, tab handles, 10½" dia **$18.00**
Currier & Ives, salt & pepper shakers, pr...................**$30.00**
Currier & Ives, sugar bowl, angle handle...................**$15.00**
Currier & Ives, sugar bowl, no handles, flared top **$48.00**
Currier & Ives, sugar bowl, no handles, w/lid...........**$35.00**
Currier & Ives, teapot, many different styles & stampings,
    from $110 to...**$150.00**
Currier & Ives, tidbit tray, 2- or 3-tier, abundant in numbers,
    from $50 to...**$100.00**
Currier & Ives, tumbler, iced tea; glass, 12-oz, 5½"....**$18.00**
Currier & Ives, tumbler, juice; glass, 6-oz, 3½" **$7.00**
Currier & Ives, tumbler, old-fashioned; glass, 3¼".......**$7.00**
Currier & Ives, tumbler, water; glass, 4¾" **$15.00**
Fair Oaks, bowl, divided vegetable.............................**$45.00**
Fair Oaks, bowl, soup **$15.00**
Fair Oaks, bowl, vegetable; 9" **$30.00**
Fair Oaks, butter dish **$45.00**
Fair Oaks, casserole **$135.00**
Fair Oaks, creamer..**$12.00**
Fair Oaks, cup & saucer **$8.00**
Fair Oaks, plate, bread & butter **$3.00**
Fair Oaks, plate, dinner; 10" **$10.00**
Fair Oaks, platter, tab handles, 10½" **$22.00**
Fair Oaks, salt & pepper shakers, pr **$22.00**
Fair Oaks, sugar bowl, w/lid **$18.00**
Fair Oaks, teapot **$125.00**
Memory Lane, bowl, cereal; 6¼" **$9.00**
Memory Lane, bowl, fruit nappy; 5½" **$3.00**
Memory Lane, bowl, soup; 8½"....................................**$7.50**
Memory Lane, bowl, vegetable; 10" **$25.00**
Memory Lane, butter dish, ¼-lb **$30.00**
Memory Lane, creamer..**$6.00**
Memory Lane, gravy boat **$18.00**
Memory Lane, gravy boat liner, from $12 to **$15.00**
Memory Lane, plate, bread & butter; 6⅜".....................**$2.00**
Memory Lane, plate, chop; 12" **$25.00**
Memory Lane, plate, luncheon; rare, 9¼"....................**$25.00**

**Memory Lane, plate, 10", $6.00; ashtray, from
$10.00 to $12.00; cup and saucer, $5.00.**

Memory Lane, plate, salad; rare, 7" **$10.00**
Memory Lane, platter, tab handles, 10½" **$15.00**
Memory Lane, platter, 13" **$25.00**
Memory Lane, salt & pepper shakers, pr **$15.00**
Memory Lane, sugar bowl, w/lid..................................**$9.00**
Memory Lane, tumbler, iced tea; glass **$15.00**
Memory Lane, tumbler, juice; glass **$8.00**
Old Curiosity Shop, bowl, fruit nappy; 5½" **$4.00**
Old Curiosity Shop, bowl, soup/cereal; 6½" **$10.00**
Old Curiosity Shop, bowl, vegetable; 10" **$25.00**
Old Curiosity Shop, bowl, vegetable; 9" **$22.00**
Old Curiosity Shop, casserole......................................**$90.00**
Old Curiosity Shop, creamer..**$6.00**
Old Curiosity Shop, cup & saucer **$5.00**
Old Curiosity Shop, plate, bread & butter; 6⅜" **$3.00**
Old Curiosity Shop, plate, dinner; 10" **$5.00**
Old Curiosity Shop, platter, tab handles, 10½" **$15.00**
Old Curiosity Shop, salt & pepper shakers, pr...........**$15.00**
Old Curiosity Shop, sugar bowl, w/lid..........................**$9.00**
Old Curiosity Shop, teapot **$115.00**
Tradition, bowl, fruit nappy; 5½" **$3.00**
Tradition, bowl, vegetable; 10" **$20.00**
Tradition, creamer..**$5.00**
Tradition, cup & saucer **$5.00**
Tradition, gravy boat **$15.00**
Tradition, plate, dinner; 10" **$6.00**
Tradition, platter, tab handles, 10½" **$20.00**
Tradition, sugar bowl...**$8.00**

Royal Copley

This is a line of planters, wall pockets, vases, and other novelty items, most of which are modeled as appealing animals, birds, or human figures. They were made by the Spaulding China Company of Sebring, Ohio, from 1942 until 1957. The decoration is underglazed and airbrushed, and some pieces are trimmed in gold (which can add 25% to 50% to their values). Not every piece is marked, but they all have a style that is distinctive. Some items are ink stamped; others have (or have had) labels.

Royal Copley is really not hard to find, and unmarked items may sometimes be had at bargain prices. The more common pieces seem to have stabilized, but the rare and hard-to-find examples are showing a steady increase. Your collection can go in several directions; for instance, some people choose a particular animal to collect. If you're a cat lover, they were made in an extensive assortment of styles and sizes. Teddy bears are also popular; you'll find them licking a lollipop, playing a mandolin, or modeled as a bank, and they come in various colors as well. Wildlife lovers can collect deer, pheasants, fish, and gazelles, and there's also a wide array of songbirds.

If you'd like more information, we recommend *Collector's Guide to Royal Copley plus Royal Windsor & Spaulding, Books I and II,* by Joe Devine.

Advisor: Joe Devine (See Directory, Royal Copley)

Bank, pig in striped shirt, paper label, 4½", from $50 to ...**$55.00**
Bank, teddy bear, paper label, 7½", rare, from $125 to ...**$150.00**
Figurine, cockatoo, full body, raised letters, 8", from $40
to..**$45.00**
Figurine, cocker spaniel, paper label, 6¼", from $20 to....**$25.00**
Figurine, dancing lady, several color variations, 8", ea, from
$100 to...**$150.00**
Figurine, deer & fawn, raised letters, 8½", from $40 to ...**$45.00**
Figurine, flycatcher, several color variations, paper label, 8",
ea, from $40 to...**$45.00**
Figurine, hen standing in straw, No 1, paper label, 5½", from
$30 to...**$35.00**
Figurine, kitten w/ball of yarn, paper label, 6½", from $40
to..**$45.00**
Figurine, lark, full body, several color variations, 6½", ea,
from $20 to..**$24.00**

Figurines, mallard pair, Royal Windsor, 6¼", 8½", from $175.00 to $200.00 for the pair. (Photo courtesy Joe Devine)

Figurine, Oriental boy or girl, several color variations, paper
label, 7½", ea, from $20 to **$24.00**
Figurine, rooster, Banty, paper label, 6½", from $50 to..**$60.00**
Figurine, rooster standing in straw, No 1, paper label, 5½",
from $30 to..**$35.00**
Figurine, sparrow, several color variations, paper label, 5",
ea, from $12 to...**$16.00**
Figurine, swallow, full body, several color variations, paper
label, ea, from $25 to **$30.00**
Pitcher, Floral Beauty, green stamp or raised letters, any color
except cobalt, ea, from $45 to **$50.00**
Pitcher, floral decal on ivory, gold stamp, 6", from $12 to..**$14.00**
Pitcher, Pome Fruit, tan, green stamp, 8", from $45 to...**$50.00**
Planter, angel, blue or pink, paper label, 8", ea, from $40
to..**$45.00**
Planter, birdhouse w/bird atop, paper label, 8", from $100
to..**$110.00**
Planter, cocker spaniel w/basket, paper label, 5½", ea, from
$20 to...**$25.00**
Planter, deer & doe in relief, ivory, paper label, 7½", from
$15 to...**$20.00**
Planter, deer & fawn in relief, gold trim, footed, rectangular,
6", from $40 to...**$45.00**
Planter, deer on stump, full body, paper label, 8", from $40
to..**$45.00**

Planter, dog & mailbox, paper label, 7¾", from $30 to ..**$35.00**

Planter, Dogwood, paper label, oval, 4½", from $12 to .**$15.00**

Planter, Dutch boy or girl w/bucket, several color variations, paper label, 6", ea, from $25 to............................**$30.00**

Planter, elf & stump, paper label, 6", from $35 to **$40.00**

Planter, farm boy or girl, boy w/fishing pole, several colorations, raised letters, 6½", ea, from $30 to........**$35.00**

Planter, fighting cock, paper label, 6½", from $45 to .**$50.00**

Planter, gazelles in relief, ivory, 6", from $15 to **$20.00**

Planter, girl in pigtails, cobalt & yellow, raised letters, 7", from $70 to..**$75.00**

Planter, grazing horse, full body, paper label, 4¾", from $28 to..**$32.00**

Planter, horse in relief, black on ivory, paper label, 6", from $15 to..**$20.00**

Planter, kitten & boot, paper label, 7½", from $50 to..**$55.00**

Planter, kitten on stump, paper label, 6½", from $30 to ..**$35.00**

Planter, Oriental boy or girl w/basket on back, paper label, 8", ea, from $40 to **$45.00**

Planter, teddy bear on tree stump, paper label, 5½", from $20 to **$25.00**

Planter, teddy bear, 6½", from $55.00 to $60.00.

Planter, wood duck, paper label, 5½", from $20 to....**$25.00**

Planter, woodpecker, several color variations, green stamp or raised letters, 6", ea, from $20 to.........................**$25.00**

Planter/wall pocket, boy or girl in wide-brimmed hat, hand under cheek, raised letters, 7½", ea, from $40 to ..**$45.00**

Planter/wall pocket, Chinese boy or girl in wide-brimmed hats, raised letters, 7½", ea, from $24 to **$28.00**

Vase, Bow & Ribbon, several color variations, paper label, footed, 6½", from $14 to **$18.00**

Vase, Ivy, dark green on ivory, paper label, footed, 7", from $10 to..**$12.00**

Vase, mare & foal, raised letters, 8½", from $30 to.....**$35.00**

Vase, Oriental style w/dragon motif, paper label, footed, 5½", from $12 to...**$15.00**

Vase, rooster, paper label, 7", from $40 to **$45.00**

Vase, stylized leaf, paper label, 8¼", from $12 to.......**$15.00**

Royal Haeger

Many generations of the Haeger family have been associated with the ceramic industry. Starting out as a brickyard in 1871, the Haeger Company (Dundee, Illinois) progressed to include artware in their production as early as 1914. That was only the beginning. In the '30s they began to make a line of commercial artware so successful that as a result a plant was built in Macomb, Illinois, devoted exclusively to its production.

Royal Haeger was their premium line. Its chief designer in the 1940s was Royal Arden Hickman, a talented artist and sculptor who also worked in mediums other than pottery. For Haeger he designed a line of wonderfully stylized animals and birds, high-style vases, and human figures and masks with extremely fine details.

Paper labels were used extensively before the mid-'30s. Royal Haeger ware has an in-mold script mark, and their Flower Ware line (1954 – 1963) is marked 'RG' (Royal Garden).

Collectors need to be aware that certain glazes can bring two to three times more than others. For those wanting to learn more about this pottery, we recommend *Haeger Potteries Through the Years* by David D. Dilley (L-W Book Sales).

Advisor: David D. Dilley (See Directory, Royal Haeger)

Club: Haeger Pottery Collectors of America
Lanette Clarke
5021 Toyon Way
Antioch, CA 94509, 510-776-7784; Monthly newsletter available

Ashtray, A Century of Progress, 1933-34, green, 3" **$40.00**

Ashtray, Brown Earth Graphic Wrap, #2124, 7x7x2"...**$15.00**

Bank, dog, white transparent ('bone ash' glaze), #8034, 7½x8½"..**$60.00**

Bookends, Water Lily, green w/white flowers, #R-1144, ca 1952, 5x5x7½", pr...**$75.00**

Bowl, dark purple w/light blue & white, scalloped edge, #R-759, 3x6½" dia **$60.00**

Bowl, Mauve Agate w/daisy relief, #R-442, not marked, 18¼x6¼x4¾"..**$45.00**

Bowl, scalloped & wavy, white, #334, 15x7½x2" **$20.00**

Bowl, shell shape, chartreuse & silver spray, #R-297, 14x7½x2¾"...**$25.00**

Candle holder, bow, blue, #3277, ca 1947, 7½x3¼" dia ..**$75.00**

Candle holders, Rosebud, Cloudy Blue, #R-438, not marked, 4¼x1⅛", pr...**$15.00**

Candle holders, starfish, Pearl Gray Drip, #R-968, pr.**$35.00**

Covered dish, rooster on lid (Sascha Brastoff), Roman Bronze, #8170, 9x5x3" **$150.00**

Creamer & sugar bowl, white, solid handles, #575, ca 1936 ..**$35.00**

Figural, pigeon, wings spread, #650, 9½"...................**$30.00**

Figurine, Bucking Bronco, amber, #R-424, ca 1940s, 13" ..**$200.00**

Figurine, bull, Mallow, #R-379, 12x3½x6½" **$600.00**

Figurine, cockatoo, pink, #7, not marked, 1933, 4x3" ..**$15.00**

Figurine, cocker spaniel, brown w/black tail, #R-777, not marked, ca 1950, 5½x2¼x3" **$75.00**

Figurine, donkey w/cart, blue, #3296, ca 1943, 5x3x3" ..**$20.00**

Figurine, Egyptian cat, Mandarin Orange, 1 glass eye, #616, ca 1950s, 15½" **$75.00**

Figurine, elephant, chartreuse & honey, #R-784, crown foil label, 8¼x3¾x6" **$40.00**

Figurine, fawn, sitting, dark brown base w/muddy brown overglaze, #R-413, not marked, ca 1949, 6½x3x6½" **$35.00**

Figurine, flying fish (3), teal & yellow, paper tag, #R-138, 8x4x9" **$200.00**

Figurine, horse head, Desert Red on ebony base, not marked, ca mid-1930s, 4¾x4¾x9" **$175.00**

Figurine, Indian on horse, Desert Red, #R-721, minimum value, $750.00. (Photo courtesy David Dilley)

Figurine, panther, lying, Oxblood, #R-649, 7¼x2½x2⅝" .. **$35.00**

Figurine, peasant woman, Green Agate, w/out potatoes in basket, R-383 .... **$75.00**

Figurine, peasant woman, #R-383, w/potatoes in basket (earliest version) **$150.00**

Figurine, pheasant, Mauve Agate, #R-165, 11x6x10¼" .. **$75.00**

Figurine, pheasant hen, Mauve Agate, #R-434, not marked, 15x4½x5¼" **$40.00**

Figurine, polar bear, sitting, gray-white ('bone ash' glaze), #R-375b, not marked, ca 1942, 6½x5x6⅞" **$75.00**

Figurine, prospector, amber, #R-479, 11¼x7" **$175.00**

Figurine, rooster, Burnt Sienna, #612, ca 1973, 8½x4x11" . **$40.00**

Figurine, tigress on base, amber, #R-314, 10¼x4¼x11" ... **$100.00**

Flower frog, frog, chartreuse, crown foil label, #R-838, 4½x3¼x3¾" **$75.00**

Flower frog, nude sitting, Peach Agate, #R-189 .... **$150.00**

Flower frog, nude w/seal block, Green Briar, #R-364, not marked, ca 1946, 13¼" **$125.00**

Hanging basket, owl, Bennington Brown Foam, #5015-H, 8½x7" **$50.00**

Lamp, Parrot on Tree, Green Agate & yellow decorated, #5202, not marked, ca 1947, 17" **$250.00**

Lamp, wall; horse head, ebony, #5240, crown foil label, ca 1947, 9¼" **$125.00**

Lighter, blue w/black streams, #8167, not marked, round, 3½" H, 3" dia **$25.00**

Lighter, boot, #8054, ca 1967, 4¼x2x9¼" **$20.00**

Pitcher, Mexican head, Green Briar, #R-698, 7½x4¼x7⅜" .. **$45.00**

Planter, baby buggy, pink, #3280-B, not marked, ca 1942, 6x2½x5½" **$15.00**

Planter, barnyard riders, silver spray w/yellow figures & chartreuse base, #R-596, 13", minimum value **$500.00**

Planter, Brown Earth Graphic Wrap, #4185X, 9½x5½" .. **$60.00**

Planter, Colonial Girl w/basket, chartreuse, #3318, not marked, 6½x4¾x9" **$25.00**

Planter, duck, Jade Crackle, #R-1844, 8x7x6½" **$25.00**

Planter, fish, yellow, #14, not marked, ca 1936, 3½x1½x3½" **$15.00**

Planter, goat w/basket on back, Sable, #R-1734, foil crown label, 13x4¼x9½" **$100.00**

Planter, lemon peel glaze (rarest of 'peel' glazes), upside-down hat shape, #3178, 6½" **$175.00**

Planter, peacock, Mauve Agate, #R-453, 9¾x3⅛x10" . **$50.00**

Planter, raccoon w/bucket, Bennington Brown Foam, #5073, 9x5½" **$35.00**

Planter, rooster, #R-1741, $250.00.

Planter, teddy bear, chartreuse, #616, not marked, ca 1938, 7x3¼x4¾" **$15.00**

Planter, triple ball, Oxblood, #R-852, foil label, 11¼x4¾x3⅝" **$20.00**

Planter, turkey, red & black, #R-1761, 14x10x12" **$150.00**

Planter, wheelbarrow, Briar Agate, #R-1462, ca 1964, 9½x6x5½" **$15.00**

Sign, Haeger in brown letters, 8¾" **$35.00**

Toe Tapper, musician, 4½"-11½", ea **$75.00**

Vase, basket w/fruit, Peach Agate, #R131, not marked, 10¼x3x9" **$65.00**

Vase, Bird of Paradise, Cloudy Blue, #R-186, 9x4¼x13⅛" **$75.00**

Vase, butterfly, Mauve Agate, #R-422, ca 1940, 9x3¾x5½" **$40.00**

Vase, Dancing Girl, green, #3105, not marked, 5¼x8" .. **$20.00**

Vase, Elm Leaf, Green Briar, #R-320, ca 1947, 6x12½" ... **$25.00**

Vase, Laurel Wreath Bow, Mauve Agate, #R-303, 7¾x4x12" **$75.00**

Vase, lemon peel (rarest of the 'peel' glazes), cylinder, #4162X, 7" **$95.00**

Vase, lemon peel (rarest of the 'peel' glazes), lg handles, #4208X, 15" **$275.00**

Vase, Seminole Orange (squiggles), #4171X, 15" (other glazes will be 75% less) **$225.00**

Vase, Seminole Orange Glaze (squiggles), #4160X, cylinder, 12" (other glazes are 75% less) **$150.00**

Vase, swan, matt white, #3276, not marked, ca 1946, 5½x3½x9½" **$20.00**

Wall pocket, fish, Antique, #R-16275, crown label, 13¼x6½x3¼" **$125.00**

Rozart

George and Rose Rydings (Kansas City, Missouri) were aspiring potters, who in 1969 set about to produce a line of fine underglaze art pottery. They inherited some vintage American-made artware which they very much admired and set about trying to unravel the enigma of ceramic chemistry used by the old masters. Early in the 1970s, Fred Radford, grandson of Albert Radford, a well-known, remarkably talented artist who had made his presence felt in the Ohio pottery circles (ca 1890s – 1904), offered them ideas about glazing techniques, chemistry, etc., and allowed them to experiment with his grandfather's formula for Jasperware (which he had produced in his own pottery). It was then that the Ryding's pottery acquired a different look — one very reminiscent of the wares made by the turn-of-the century American art pottery masters.

Rozart (as they named their pottery) has created may lines since its beginning: Twainware, Sylvan, Cameoware, Rozart Royal, Rusticware, Deko, Krakatoa, and Sateen to mention a few. All of their pottery is marked in some fashion. Though some items have been found with paper labels, they did not come from the Rydings. You will almost always find the initials of the artist responsible for the decorating and a date code, created in one of two ways: two digits, for example '88' denoting 1988, or a month (represented by a number) separated by a slash followed by the two-digit year. The earliest mark known is 'Rozart' at the top of a circle, 'Handmade' in the center, and 'K.C.M.O.' (Kansas City, Missouri) at the bottom. In the early years, a stylized paint brush was sometimes added to the mark as well. Other marks followed over the years, including a seal which was used extensively.

The Rydings' venture quickly involved several family members, some of which developed their own lines, themes, and designs. George signs his pieces in one of three ways: 'GMR,' 'GR,' or 'RG' (with a backwards R). In the early years George worked on Twainware, Jasperware, and Cameoware. He has many wheel-thrown pieces to his credit.

Rose, who is very knowledgable about Native Americans, does scenics and portraits, using painstaking care to authenticate the exact history of a particular tribe and their culture. Her mark is either 'RR' or 'RRydings,' both written on an angle.

Four of the seven Rydings children have worked in the pottery as well, becoming decorators in their own right. Anne Rydings White designed and executed many original pieces in addition to her work on the original Twainware line, which she signed 'AR.' (Before her marriage, she used this mark or simply 'Anne.') She is still actively involved; her later creations are signed 'ARW.' Susan Rydings Ubert has specialized in design pieces (mostly Sylvan) and is an accomplished sculptor and mold maker. She signs her pieces with an 'S' over the letter R. Susan's daughter, Maureen, does female figures in the Art Deco style. Rebecca 'Becky' Rydings White, now a commercial artist, early on designed such lines as Fleamarket (depicting typical flea market scenes and mer-

chandise), Nature's Jewels, and Animal, which she marked with the name of the line as well as her initials (B over the letter R). (When collecting Rozart, use caution if you want a particular artist's work; with two Rydings children married to two unrelated White families, it would be easy to confuse the artists and their place in history.)

Of all the children, Cynthia Rydings Cushing has always been the most prolific. Her Kittypots line depicts animated cats and kittens involved in a variety of activities on vases, jars, etc., utilizing their Rusticware glazes and shapes (usually 3" to 4" high). Her earlier work is signed with a 'C' over the 'R'; today she uses the initials 'CRC.'

The Rozart Pottery is still active today, and while prices for the older pieces have been climbing steadily for several years, they are still affordable.

Watch for the release of a book on this subject, written by our advisor Susan Cox. (She will welcome photos or additional information.)

Advisor: Susan Cox (See Directory, California Pottery)

Figurine, poodle, reclining, Krakatoa line, 1970, 6" L...**$125.00**
Ginger jar, flower motif, w/lid, ca 1975, 3¾" **$75.00**
Jardiniere, Cameoware, 3 sculptured frogs, mid-1980s, 11" **$95.00**
Jardiniere, Westerm theme, Cindy Cushing, w/base, 1981, 16" **$150.00**
Jug, Rusticware, Cleopatra, mid-1980s, 22"................**$350.00**
Sign, Rozart Pottery in script, base across front, 1998, 5½" **$20.00**
Sign, Rozart Pottery in script, sm vertical base, 1985, 5½" **$35.00**

Tankard, part of the Twainware series, very scarce with lid, artist Anne Rydings, 1974, 9½", $325.00. (Photo courtesy Susan Cox)

Tile, Danielle nude, Deko line, Susan Ubert, 1998, 10" **$68.00**
Tile, Two Moons Chief Joseph, Rose Rydings, 1974, 6" square **$55.00**
Vase, Animal by Becky Rydings, 2 handles, 1988, 9¾" .**$95.00**
Vase, Deko line w/dancing nude, narrow base, mid-1980s, 12" **$210.00**

Vase, Kittypots, animal motif, Cindy Cushing, 1998, 3"...**$25.00**
Vase, Nature's Jewels by Becky Rydings, butterfly motif, 4" **$24.00**

Vases, Rusticware: Indian Chief (1981 – 1982), artist Rose Rydings, 8", $175.00; Pillow shape, artist Anne Rydings, 6", $135.00. (Photo courtesy Susan Cox)

Vase, stonewall w/flowers, wheel-thrown, GR, 7½" ...**$95.00**
Vase, Twainware, Tom the Retired Painter, limited edition of 2,500, 6" **$155.00**
Vase, winter scene, Dove Gray glaze, GR, 1999, 9"..**$100.00**
Water set, pitcher & 4 mugs, horse motif, marked CRC..**$235.00**

RumRill

RumRill-marked pottery was actually made by other companies who simply provided the merchandise that George Rumrill marketed from 1933 until his death in 1942. Rumrill designed his own lines, and the potteries who filled the orders were the Red Wing Stoneware Company, Red Wing Potteries, Shawnee (but they were involved for only a few months), Florence, and Gonder. Many of the designs were produced by more than one company. Examples may be marked RumRill or with the name of the specific pottery.

For more information we recommend *Red Wing Art Pottery* by B.L. Dollen (Collector Books).

Advisors: Wendy and Leo Frese, Three Rivers Collectibles (See Directory, Rum Rill)

Basket, #348, Lilac **$75.00**
Bookends, #396, polar bear, black, pr.....................**$450.00**
Bowl, #314, Mandarin, Dutch Blue, original sticker ...**$75.00**
Bowl, #314, Mandarin, white w/green interior...........**$40.00**
Bowl, #567, Athena Series, nude holding bowl, white w/green interior..**$350.00**
Bowl, #646, Snowdrop, 3-ftd, 3½x9" **$125.00**
Bowl, console; #625, Vintage, green, 10" **$75.00**
Candle holder, #240, Continental, white, 2-light, 9" .**$125.00**
Ewer, #220, Neptune w/sea dragons design, sea dragon handles, ivory w/turquoise interior, 10½"...............**$50.00**
Ewer, #295, Classic Group, Riviera White w/blue interior, 10" **$50.00**

Ivy ball, #601, Suntan, 8" **$125.00**
Jardiniere, #304, jade green **$35.00**
Planter, #H-36, hat shape, peach (cameo)................**$25.00**
Planter, #H-36, hat shape, white............................**$25.00**
Vase, #G-2, mint green, handles............................**$40.00**
Vase, #H-32, pearly pink/maroon (rare color) **$50.00**
Vase, #L-10, embossed floral, 11½", NM..................**$125.00**
Vase, #L-3, mint green, 2-handled **$30.00**
Vase, #256, Fluted, Dutch Blue w/white stippling, 6"...**$50.00**
Vase, #302, green...**$45.00**
Vase, #318, light green matt...................................**$45.00**
Vase, #447, white...**$25.00**
Vase, #504, turquoise w/mottling **$30.00**
Vase, #536, Manhattan, Dutch Blue, 9", NM..............**$75.00**
Vase, #537, fan form..**$48.00**
Vase, #635, green...**$35.00**
Vase, #636, Dutch Blue, 6"....................................**$75.00**
Vase, #668, Neoclassic, 7" **$125.00**
Vase, bud; #329, mottled blue **$45.00**

Bud vase, Goldenrod glaze, #270, $50.00. (Photo courtesy Wendy and Leo Frese)

Russel Wright Designs

One of the country's foremost industrial designers, Russel Wright, was also responsible for several lines of dinnerware, glassware, and spun aluminum that have become very collectible. American Modern, produced by the Steubenville Pottery Company (1939 – 1959) is his best known dinnerware and the most popular today. It had simple, sweeping lines that appealed to tastes of that period, and it was made in a variety of solid colors. Iroquois China made his Casual line, and because it was so serviceable, it's relatively easy to find today. It will be marked with both Wright's signature and 'China by Iroquois.' His spun aluminum is highly valued as well, even though it wasn't so eagerly accepted in its day, due to the fact that it was so easily damaged.

If you'd like to learn more about the subject, we recommend *The Collector's Encyclopedia of Russel Wright, Second Edition,* by Ann Kerr (Collector Books).

Note: Values are given for solid color dinnerware unless a pattern is specifically mentioned.

American Modern

The most desirable colors are Canteloupe, Glacier Blue, Bean Brown, and White; add 50% to our values for these colors. Chartreuse is represented by the low end of our range; Cedar, Black Chutney, and Seafoam by the high end; and Coral and Gray near the middle. To evaluate patterned items, deduct 25%.

Bowl, fruit; lug handle, from $15 to	**$20.00**
Coffeepot, AD, from $100 to	**$150.00**
Creamer, from $12 to	**$15.00**
Cup & saucer, AD, from $25 to	**$30.00**

Divided vegetable dish, from $85.00 to $120.00; sauce boat, 13", from $35.00 to $40.00.

Gravy boat, 10½", from $20 to	**$25.00**
Pickle dish, from $15 to	**$18.00**
Pitcher, water; from $100 to	**$150.00**
Plate, chop; from $30 to	**$45.00**
Plate, dinner; 10", from $10 to	**$12.00**
Sugar bowl, from $15 to	**$20.00**

Iroquois Casual

To price Brick Red, Aqua, and Cantaloupe Casual, double our values; for Avocado, use the low end of the range. Oyster, White, and Charcoal are at the high end.

Bowl, cereal; redesigned, 5", from $12 to	**$15.00**
Bowl, fruit; 9½-oz, 5½", from $10 to	**$12.00**
Bowl, soup; redesigned, 18-oz, from $20 to	**$22.00**
Butter dish, ½-lb, from $65 to	**$100.00**
Casserole, 2-qt, 8", from $40 to	**$60.00**
Creamer, redesigned, from $15 to	**$25.00**
Cup & saucer, coffee; from $15 to	**$20.00**
Gravy boat, 12-oz, 5¼", from $12 to	**$18.00**
Gumbo, flat soup; 21-oz, from $30 to	**$35.00**
Mug, 13-oz, from $95 to	**$165.00**
Pepper mill, from $200 to	**$225.00**
Plate, chop; 13⅞", from $30 to	**$50.00**
Plate, salad; 7½", from $9 to	**$12.00**

Knowles

The high end of the range should be used to evaluate solid-color examples.

Bowl, soup/cereal; 6¼", from $14 to	**$16.00**
Pitcher, 2-qt, from $150 to	**$175.00**
Plate, dinner; 10¾", from $12 to	**$15.00**
Platter, oval, 13", from $25 to	**$45.00**
Sauce boat, from $25 to	**$35.00**
Teapot, from $175 to	**$250.00**

Plastic

These values apply to Home Decorator, Residential, and Flair (which is at the high end of the range). Copper Penny and Black Velvet items command 50% more. Meladur items are all hard to find in good condition, and values can be basically computed using the following guidelines (except for the fruit bowl, which in Meladur is valued at $7.00 to $8.00).

Meladur: Dinner plate, 9", from $8.00 to $10.00; Salad plate, 7", from $8.00 to $10.00; Soup bowl, 12-ounce, from $10.00 to $12.00; Cup and saucer, from 10.00 to $15.00. (Photo courtesy Ann Kerr)

Bowl, fruit; #707, from $13 to	**$15.00**
Bowl, vegetable; oval, deep, from $15 to	**$20.00**
Bowl, vegetable; oval, shallow, #708, from $15 to	**$20.00**
Creamer, #711, from $10 to	**$12.00**
Plate, bread & butter; #705, from $3 to	**$6.00**
Plate, dessert; 6¼", from $5 to	**$6.00**
Platter, #710, from $20 to	**$25.00**
Sugar bowl, w/lid, #712, from $12 to	**$15.00**
Tumbler, #715, from $15 to	**$18.00**

Spun Aluminum

Bun warmer, from $65 to	**$75.00**
Cheese knife, from $75 to	**$100.00**
Ice bucket, from $75 to	**$100.00**
Muddler, from $75 to	**$100.00**
Pitcher, sherry; from $250 to	**$275.00**
Vase, 12", from $150 to	**$175.00**

Sterling

Values are given for undecorated examples.

Bowl, onion soup; 10-oz, from $20 to **$25.00**
Celery dish, 11¼", from $20 to **$30.00**
Cup, 7-oz, from $10 to **$15.00**
Pitcher, cream; 9-oz, from $14 to **$16.00**
Plate, salad; 7½", from $8 to...............................**$10.00**
Platter, oval, 13⅝", from $20 to **$30.00**

White Clover (for Harker)

Creamer, clover decorated, from $18 to....................**$20.00**
Cup, from $12 to..**$15.00**
Dish, vegetable; w/lid, 8¼", from $40 to....................**$45.00**
Gravy boat, clover decorated, from $25 to.................**$35.00**
Plate, barbecue; color only, 11", from $20 to.............**$25.00**
Plate, jumbo; clover decorated, 10", from $16 to........**$18.00**

Salt Shakers

Probably the most common type of souvenir shop merchandise from the '20 through the '60s, salt and pepper shakers can be spotted at any antique mall or flea market today by the dozens. Most were made in Japan and imported by various companies, though American manufacturers made their fair share as well. When even new shakers retail for $10.00 and up, don't be surprised to see dealers tagging the better vintage varieties with some hefty prices.

'Miniature shakers' are hard to find, and their prices have risen faster than any others'. They were all made by Arcadia Ceramics (probably an American company). They're under 1½" tall, some so small they had no space to accommodate a cork. Instead they came with instructions to 'use Scotch tape to cover the hole.'

Advertising sets and premiums are always good, since they appeal to a cross section of collectors. If you have a chance to buy them on the primary market, do so. Many of these are listed in the Advertising Character Collectibles section of this guide.

Right now, the market has softened on low-end shakers (they're as much as 10% to 15% down), but the more desirable shakers have seen a dramatic increase in values. There are several good books which we highly recommend to help you stay informed: *Salt and Pepper Shakers, Identification and Values, Vols I, II, III,* and *IV,* by Helene Guarnaccia; and *The Collector's Encyclopedia of Salt and Pepper Shakers, Figural and Novelty, First* and *Second Series,* by Melva Davern. All are published by Collector Books.

See also Advertising Character Collectibles; Breweriana; Condiment Sets; Holt Howard; Occupied Japan; Regal China; Rosemeade; Shawnee; Vandor, and other specific companies.

Advisor: Judy Posner (See Directory, Salt and Pepper Shakers)

Club: Novelty Salt and Pepper Club
c/o Irene Thornburg, Membership Coordinator
581 Joy Rd.
Battle Creek, MI 49017
Publishes quarterly newsletter and annual roster. Annual dues: $20 in USA, Canada, and Mexico; $25 for all other countries

Advertising

Blue Nun Wine, from $125.00 to $150.00 for the pair. (Photo courtesy Helene Guarnaccia)

Borden's Elsie & Elmer, ceramic, half-figures in chef hats, 1940s, scarce, pr **$150.00**
Burger Chef, plastic, white containers w/red & white logos & marked Nowhere Else, pr **$15.00**
Coppertone Sun Tan Lotion, ceramic figure of little girl & dog tugging at her bottom, pr, from $75 to..............**$150.00**
Greyhound buses, painted metal w/white tops & blue trim, Japan, pr, from $45 to **$55.00**
Hershey's Milk Chocolate mugs, ceramic, white w/brown & silver candy wrapper middle, pr **$20.00**
Luzianne Mammys, plastic, reproductions w/red skirts (originals had green skirts), pr, from $150 to.............**$200.00**
Magic Chef, plastic chef figures w/jug-type bodies, white w/red hats & trim, black-painted features & bow tie, pr **$55.00**
Mason jars, glass w/metal caps, pr.............................**$10.00**
Mobiloil Special cans, red winged horse w/red & blue lettering on silver & white label, pr.............................**$25.00**
Sandman Port Wine, ceramic miniature replicas of figural wine decanter made by Wedgwood, black w/gold lettering, pr **$95.00**
Schlitz beer cans in cardboard holder, new, pr **$15.00**
Seven-Up bottles, glass w/metal caps, red, white & green bubble girl label, older, pr **$20.00**
Tappan Ranges, Harvest Gold, dated 1976, 1-pc **$28.00**
TWA, plastic, red w/white logos, pr...........................**$45.00**
Virginia Dare Beverages, glass bottles w/blue-on-white painted labels, metal caps, pr **$10.00**

Animals, Birds, and Fish

Bear in car, ceramic, yellow & pink bear in green car w/yellow nose & orange wheels, 2-pc....................**$35.00**

Beetle musicians, ceramic, 1 playing violin in black top hat & 1 holding music in white hat, both in brown shoes, pr.................**$15.00**

Birds in swing, ceramic, 2 birds looking up w/mouths open in branch swing resting on tree trunk posts w/blossoms, 2-pc....................**$35.00**

Birds pecking, ceramic, blue lustre w/gold trim, yellow bases, pr.................**$10.00**

Brahma bulls, bisque, in walking stance, gray airbrushing w/black bridle bits, pinkish ears & mouth, pr.....**$22.00**

Bull dogs w/ears up, bone china, sitting upright, white w/brown airbrushing, pr.................**$25.00**

Cardinals on tree stumps, bisque, red w/black accents, white stumps w/light brown accents, pr.................**$10.00**

Cat couple dressed, ceramic, she w/hand on hip appearing to scold, he standing w/fish & winking, multicolors, 1940s, pr.................**$30.00**

Cat in curled postion, ceramic, head nestled in body, white w/pink airbrushed body, black features & tail, 2-pc .**$20.00**

Cat on piano, ceramic, white kitten playing atop black baby grand piano, 2-pc **$20.00**

Cat pr on rotary phones, ceramic, he w/eyes open, she w/eyes shut, tan speckle w/red ears, black & white dials, pr.................**$10.00**

Cats in Deco style, ceramic, sitting upright, white w/yellow dots outlined in blue, blue & yellow striped tails, pr **$18.00**

Cats stretching, ceramic, stylized form, black airbrushing, Dan Brechner & Co, from $15 to **$35.00**

Cats w/necks crossed, ceramic, sleek pose, glossy black w/gold collars & paws, red ears & collar trim, 1-pc.................**$24.00**

Chicken holding 2 egg shakers, ceramic, white w/light brown airbrushing, red comb & wattle, brown eggs, semigloss, 3-pc.................**$15.00**

Chickens in stylized form, ceramic, ball heads on rounded bodies & bases, white w/red & green painted floral design, pr.................**$10.00**

Chickens w/black & white speckles, ceramic, red combs, yellow beaks & feet, green grass, lg & sm, pr.........**$10.00**

Chicks in a basket, ceramic, chicks breaking out of eggs in woven basket w/twisted handle & flowers, multicolored, 3-pc.................**$18.00**

Circus elephant on ball, ceramic, w/trunk up, gray airbrushing w/red & blue hat, pink & white ball, 2-pc, from $15 to.................**$35.00**

Circus horses, ceramic, standing w/front hooves on star drum & facing ea other, tan & brown w/blue trim, pr.................**$22.00**

Circus lion on tub, ceramic, brown & tan detailed lion rearing on white tub w/red & blue spots, 2-pc, from $15 to **$20.00**

Circus monkey on tub, ceramic, brown detailed monkey tipping red hat on white drum w/blue & red dots, 2-pc, from $15 to.................**$35.00**

Circus monkeys, ceramic, sitting w/hands around knees & heads cocked, light blue w/gold hats & trim, pr .**$15.00**

Cow couple w/halos, bone china, white w/flowers & rhinestones, gold halos, horns, hooves & tails, pr **$24.00**

Cow w/2 saddle milk pails, ceramic, white w/black spots, 3-pc **$15.00**

Cows w/cartoon features, ceramic, sitting upright w/bow ties, eyes open/closed, glossy pink & yellow airbrushing, pr.................**$8.00**

Dachshund split in half, ceramic, white w/brown spots, 2-pc.................**$12.00**

Dachshunds, ceramic, 1 lg & 1 sm, brown w/red & white back blankets, gold trim, pr.................**$20.00**

Deer in playful poses on grassy bases, ceramic, natural airbrushed colors, pr.................**$8.00**

Dog & bear rocking on post, ceramic, 1-pc dog & bear facing ea other on 2 T posts on base, 2-pc.................**$22.00**

Dog & cat in gingham & calico, ceramic, white w/multicolored decoration, pr.................**$25.00**

Dog in curled postion, ceramic, head nestled in body, tan w/black airbrushed spots, 2-pc **$20.00**

Dog in doghouse, ceramic, sign above reads Sad Sack & 1 at side reads Beware of Dog, white w/black spots, pr.........**$35.00**

Dog w/2 saddle flower baskets, ceramic, standing w/nose up, multicolored, 3-pc.................**$8.00**

Dogs w/cartoon features, ceramic, 1 sitting upright & 1 begging w/1 ear up, white w/black ears, red & blue collars, pr.................**$15.00**

Donkey cart w/chickens on baskets, ceramic, multicolored, 3-pc.................**$20.00**

Donkey w/Mexican rider & 2 saddle baskets, glossy dark brown w/multicolored & gold trim, 3-pc.................**$15.00**

Ducks in stylized form, clay, heads turned, tan w/gray, yellow, & green accents, black line detail, Mexico, pr.........**$7.00**

Ducks w/cartoon features wearing bonnets, ceramic, glossy black w/white eyes, red neck bows & trim, pr......**$8.00**

Elephant cart w/fire wood shakers, ceramic, white & pastel elephant in black hat, yellow & brown cart & shakers, 3-pc.................**$28.00**

Elephants w/stuffed look, ceramic, standing w/trunks reaching out & up, white w/stitching & floral trim, pink bows, pr.................**$10.00**

Fish in top hats, ceramic, upright, white w/black hats & details, pr.................**$25.00**

Fish nodders, porcelain, green fish atop fancy white base marked Salt & Pepper in gold script & pink roses, 3-pc.................**$35.00**

Fish w/puffy cheeks, ceramic, white w/very light airbrushing & heavy black details, pr **$12.00**

Frog musicians, ceramic, playing tuba & accordion, multicolored w/both wearing black hats, pr.................**$25.00**

Frogs on ovoid base, ceramic, angular forms in leap-frog positions, airbrushed colors, green base, 3-pc **$15.00**

Frogs w/cartoon features on wire umbrella holder, ceramic, green, 3-pc **$22.00**

Giraffes, ceramic, white w/black spots & speckles, gold ears, manes & tails, pr, from $10 to **$15.00**

Grasshoppers on watermelon slices, ceramic, realistic, glossy, pr.................**$15.00**

Greyhound dogs, bone china, in sleek racing form, light gray & white, pr, from $20 to **$25.00**

Hen w/chick in egg, bisque, hen w/head turned back & chick bursting through egg, multicolored, pr.......**$18.00**

Hippos w/heads down on grassy bases, ceramic, dark gray airbrushing in semigloss finish, pr.........................**$12.00**

Horse heads, ceramic, 1 w/nose down & 1 w/nose up, wavy manes, yellowish brown speckle, pr.....................**$25.00**

Horses in stylized form, ceramic, white w/brown manes & tails, pr..**$10.00**

Horses rearing, bone china, 1 black w/white accents & 1 tan w/white accents, pr...**$15.00**

Kangaroos dressed in top hats & tails, ceramic, nesting set w/baby kangaroo w/bouquet nestled in lap of father, pr **$125.00**

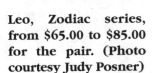 

Leo, Zodiac series, from $65.00 to $85.00 for the pair. (Photo courtesy Judy Posner)

Lions w/cartoon features, ceramic, sitting upright w/lg scraggly manes, beady close-set eyes, deep yellow, pr.**$25.00**

Lions w/realistic features, bone china, wide stance, white w/brown airbrushing & black details, pr..............**$15.00**

Monkey couple dressed up, ceramic, standing, he tipping his hat, glossy multicolored glazes, pr **$20.00**

Monkey w/baby, ceramic, detailed w/baby standing on mother's arm, glossy light brown w/dark brown & black trim, pr..**$30.00**

Mouse holding 2 cheese shakers, ceramic, white w/gray airbrushing, pinkish ears, yellow & orange cheese wedges, 3-pc **$15.00**

Mouse on wedge of cheese, ceramic, sitting upright, white w/pink ears, green hat w/red feather, yellow cheese, 2-pc **$15.00**

Ostriches w/cartoon features, ceramic, walking on grassy bases, 1 looking back at the other, purple, pr **$22.00**

Owl couple w/cartoon features, ceramic, brown w/white & red rings around eyes (open/closed), yellow daisy trim, pr...........**$15.00**

Penguin chefs, ceramic, round heads w/lg round eyes, white chef hats, 1 w/arms wide spread & 1 w/arms half spread, pr.**$15.00**

Penguin in car pulling trailer w/girl penguin, ceramic, pastel colors, glossy, 2-pc **$45.00**

Penguins, white swirled glass bodies w/black plastic heads & flippers, w/box marked Penguin Pals, pr **$15.00**

Pig nursing baby pig, ceramic, white w/black spots, pr...**$25.00**

Pigs w/floral decoration, bone china, standing w/heads cocked & ears flared, white w/pink & yellow applied flowers, pr **$8.00**

Pigs w/satisfied expressions, ceramic, 1 lying on stomach & 1 sitting upright, pink w/dark blue spots, black feet, pr **$10.00**

Pigs w/stylized cartoon features, ceramic, standing w/happy expressions, white w/pink & green floral design, sm, pr..**$15.00**

Rabbit in hat, ceramic, coming out w/rump in hat & legs & feet up, white w/brown eyes & toes, pink accents, 2-pc.**$12.00**

Rainbow Trout (marked on base), ceramic, jumping upright out of water, multicolored, glossy, pr **$25.00**

Scottie dogs, bisque, sitting upright, pr **$15.00**

Seals, ceramic, 1 w/head up & 1 w/head down & flippers out, glossy black, pr **$8.00**

Siamese cats, ceramic, sitting upright, white w/brown airbrushing, rhinestone eyes, pr **$18.00**

Snakes in coiled postion, ceramic, heads up ready to strike, light green w/black spots & accents, red eyes & mouths, pr..**$10.00**

Whales w/toothy smiles & tails up, ceramic, brown airbrushing, pinkish teeth, pr **$12.00**

Black Americana

Boy & girl busts, ceramic, dark brown skin, pink lips, she in yellow straw hat & blue & white bodice, glossy, pr ...**$165.00**

Boy & girl eating watermelon, ceramic, dark brown skin, seated on chairs, glossy, pr..................................**$125.00**

Boy & girl eating watermelon, ceramic, dark brown skin, w/side-glance goggly eyes, white toothy smiles, 1940s, pr ...**$100.00**

Boy on cotton bale, ceramic, black skin, white smile, white shirt & blue overalls, glossy, Iowa State Fair, 1955, 2-pc **$150.00**

Boy sitting w/watermelon in lap, ceramic, mouth open, black skin w/brown hair, white eyes w/lg black dots, glossy, 2-pc **$110.00**

Boy w/2 watermelon slices resting on knees, brown skin, brown pants, white shirt, blue hat, glossy, 3-pc ..**$110.00**

Boys in turbans marked Mammy's Salt & Mammy's Pepper, ceramic, multicolored, glossy, pr..........................**$75.00**

Boys shooting dice on tray, bisque, multicolored, 3-pc...**$95.00**

Butler & Mammy, ceramic, dark brown skin, he in black jacket, white pants w/blue stripe, she in orange & green plaid, pr...**$110.00**

Chef & Mammy heads, ceramic, dark brown skin, she scolding & he winking, glossy, marked Made in Japan, 1930s, pr **$110.00**

Chef & Mammy marked New Orleans, ceramic, black skin, white aprons w/red spoons, she in red bandanna, pr **$35.00**

Chef & Mammy marked Peppy & Salty, ceramic, black skin, she w/hands on hips & he holding red spoon, Pearl China, pr..**$150.00**

Chef carrying milk can shakers, ceramic, black skin, side glance, white ring around mouth, lg feet, 3-pc..**$150.00**

Chef carrying 2 watermelon slices on trays, brown skin w/white hat & apron, embossed flowers on heart-shaped base, 3-pc **$110.00**

Chef heads, walnut heads w/white cork hats, applied eyes w/painted mouths, pr.............................**$28.00**

Gardening kids, ceramic, sepia skin, w/rake & pitch fork, he in blue overalls, she in pink dress, gold trim, glossy, pr **$225.00**

Head & watermelon slice, ceramic, brown head w/red-orange tam & lg lips, white eyes w/sm black dots, semi-gloss, 2-pc **$65.00**

Jonah (Native boy) on whale, ceramic, brown skin, black whale w/toothy grin, glossy, 2-pc **$95.00**

Mammies w/hands clasped at waist, ceramic, brown skin, exaggerated features, white w/red & blue dots & plaids aprons, pr.............................**$135.00**

Mammies w/hands on hips, ceramic, black skin, 1 in yellow dress w/red bandanna & trim, other in blue, marked S&P, pr **$45.00**

Mammy carrying basket shakers w/shoulder brace, ceramic, brown skin, yellow apron w/green stripes, 1950s, 3-pc **$175.00**

NASSAU police, ceramic, light brown skin, standing w/hands behind backs, white & black, helmets marked S&P, glossy, pr **$45.00**

Native & drum, ceramic, brown skin, standing w/1 hand on hip & other to head, white & brown drum, pr **$75.00**

Native boys on eggplants, ceramic, brown skin, color on bottom (repros have no color there, their value: $10 to $15), pr **$65.00**

Native boys on heads of lettuce, ceramic, brown skin, color on bottom (repro: no color on bottom w/value up to $15), pr **$65.00**

Native busts, ceramic, brown skin, 1 w/bone in hair & toothy smile, other w/white nose ring & bone necklace, glossy, pr.............................**$65.00**

Native couple in grass skirts, ceramic, brown skin, she w/pink bow in hair, he bent forward w/hands behind back, pr **$35.00**

Native couple w/shields, ceramic, airbrushed brown skin w/black hair, blue & pink shields w/facial features, pr **$35.00**

Natives on elephant toothpick holder, wood, black bead figures w/painted skirts on natural wood elephant, 3-pc **$50.00**

Porter carrying bags marked S&P, painted wood bead body w/angled bags, multicolored, 3-pc **$75.00**

Rastus & Liza, wood painted yellow w/black accents & red lips, pr.............................**$35.00**

Tropical ladies w/baskets on heads marked S&P, ceramic, brown-skinned half figures in red dresses w/white collars, pr **$65.00**

Character

Aladdin playing instrument & magic lamp, ceramic, white figure w/flesh face & gold accents, gold lamp, pr...**$30.00**

Captain Midnight & Joyce, chalkware, multicolored, pr, from $25 to.............................**$55.00**

Cat & the fiddle, ceramic, green cat & brown fiddle, black trim, 2-pc **$40.00**

Dick Tracy & Junior, chalkware, red & yellow, pr......**$45.00**

Garfield the Cat as chef w/spoon & fork in ea hand, ceramic, pr, from $35 to.............................**$65.00**

Goldilocks, ceramic, holding book titled The Three Bears, green dresses w/white aprons, red hair bows, name in gold, pr.............................**$35.00**

Goose w/golden egg shakers, plastic, white goose opens to expose 2 golden egg shakers, 4-pc.............................**$18.00**

Hare & the Tortoise, ceramic, both upright w/arms outstretched & wearing shoes, white w/pastel accents, pr.............**$15.00**

Humpty Dumpty couple, ceramic, legs spread in sitting position looking sideways, red, white, blue, black, pr.**$25.00**

Humpty Dumpty sitting on wall, plastic, all red, pr ...**$20.00**

Jack & Jill, chalkware, she w/bucket, he on head w/feet up, pr.............................**$45.00**

Little Orphan Annie & Sandy, chalkware, pr.............**$45.00**

Mary Had a Little Lamb, ceramic, standing w/lamb on base, gray & white w/black accents, gold trim & writing on base, pr.............................**$28.00**

Mickey Mouse, plastic, blue, red, and yellow clothes, made for Wilton, marked Walt Disney Production in Hong Kong, 1972, from $25.00 to $35.00 for the pair. (Photo courtesy Helene Guarnaccia)

Moon Mullins & Kayo, chalkware, mostly yellow w/multicolored accents, pr, from $25 to.............................**$35.00**

Mouse atop clock (Hickery, Dickery, Dock...), ceramic, gray mouse w/honey-colored clock, black trim, 2-pc, pr.**$25.00**

Noah w/list of animals & ark, ceramic, white figure w/green & gold trim, glossy brown ark, pr, from $18 to ...**$25.00**

Old Woman & shoe, ceramic, white lady w/gray hair & blue trim, white shoe w/brown wash & blue roof, glossy, pr **$40.00**

Pinocchio, ceramic, sitting, multicolored, glossy, pr.**$125.00**

Queen of Hearts, ceramic, red & white w/gold crown, trim & writing on base, pr **$45.00**

Red Riding Hood, ceramic, red & white w/black baskets, gold trim & writing on base, pr.............................**$45.00**

Shmoo, chalkware, white w/red, green & black details, pr, minimum value **$150.00**

Snoopy as chef & Woodstock on stock pot, white w/black & yellow accents, pr.............................**$65.00**

Snoopy as Red Baron, chalkware, white w/black goggles & accents, pink bow tie, pr **$50.00**

Tom Sawyer & Huck Finn, ceramic, 1 standing holding cat by tail & 1 standing w/schoolbooks, pr **$55.00**

Fruit, Vegetables, and Other Food

Apples, ceramic, realistic w/red, yellow & white shading, glossy, pr **$8.00**

Apples, ceramic, realistic Delicious type w/red shading to yellow at bottom, pr **$7.00**

Asparagus spears, ceramic, realistic, pr **$5.00**

Baked potato, from $8.00 to $10.00 for the pair. (Photo courtesy Helene Guarnaccia)

Banana & pineapple boxers, ceramic, standing, fruit heads w/human bodies, pr **$45.00**

Banana island couple, ceramic, he playing drum & wearing hat, she w/lei around neck & dancing, pr **$45.00**

Bananas, ceramic, realistic, pr **$7.00**

Cabbage girls, ceramic, realistic girl heads in green cabbage bonnets & coats, pr **$35.00**

Carrots, ceramic, bunched, standing upright, orange w/green tops, pr **$12.00**

Celery people, ceramic, cartoon features, sitting, yellow & purple clothing w/black shoes, glossy, pr **$30.00**

Cookies, ceramic, Oreo type marked Cookies, glossy, pr ... **$22.00**

Corn, ceramic, 2 ears lying side by side, 1-pc **$12.00**

Corn on corn tray, ceramic, 2 realistic ears standing upright on tray, 3-pc **$12.00**

Corn people, ceramic, ears of corn w/painted features, black shoes, glossy, pr **$25.00**

Cucumbers, ceramic, green & yellow, 1-pc **$12.00**

Cupcakes, brown w/multicolored speckles & red cherries on white tops, glossy, pr **$8.00**

Eggplant & cabbage referees, ceramic, glossy, pr **$65.00**

Fried eggs, plastic, yoke shakers, 3-pc **$12.00**

Gourds, ceramic, standing upright, 2 different in yellow & green, glossy, pr **$5.00**

Ice-cream cones, ceramic, yellow, glossy, pr **$15.00**

Oranges, ceramic, orange w/green leaf & stem tops, glossy, pr **$12.00**

Pea pods w/tray, ceramic, realistic w/shades of green, white & yellow, 3-pc **$15.00**

Peaches, ceramic coated w/fuzz, pr **$12.00**

Peanut girls, ceramic, peanut heads w/girl features, green bodies w/gold trim, glossy, pr **$38.00**

Pears, ceramic, upright, yellow w/brown specks & short brown stems, pr **$7.00**

Potatoes, ceramic, realistic brown w/defined eyes, pr . **$5.00**

Pretzel twists, ceramic, realistic, J Rayton, California, pr ... **$10.00**

Strawberries, ceramic, red w/green screwed-on bases, pr .. **$10.00**

Watermelon slices, ceramic, realistic, glossy, pr **$8.00**

Holidays and Special Occasions

Anniversary hearts, bone china, footed, white w/dove motif, Happy Anniversary in gold w/gold trim, pr **$10.00**

Birthday cake & slice on plate, ceramic, yellow cake w/white & pink icing on white plates w/gold server & fork, pr **$16.00**

Christmas mice atop wedges of cheese marked S&P, ceramic, gray mice in red & white Santa hats, yellow cheese, pr **$15.00**

Christmas mouse sleeping on wedge of cheese, ceramic, in stocking hat & 2 stockings hung on side of cheese, 2-pc **$15.00**

Christmas piano, plastic, red, white & green upright w/Christmas sheet music, 3-pc **$18.00**

Christmas pigs w/cartoon features, ceramic, sitting upright & grinning, white w/red, green & black accents, pr . **$20.00**

Devils, chalkware, half figures, painted red w/yellow & green accents, pr **$25.00**

Easter egg & bunny, ceramic, white bunny w/pastel-decorated egg, pr **$12.00**

Father Time & grandfather clock, ceramic, white figure & honey brown clock w/gold trim, Pointsetta Studio, pr **$65.00**

Jack-o'-lanterns wearing witches' hats, ceramic, bright orange w/black features, black hats w/yellow & green, glossy, pr **$28.00**

Pilgrim couple, ceramic, he holding ears of corn, she holding flowers, black & white, Hallmark, pr **$12.00**

Santa & Mrs Claus dancing, ceramic, glossy, 1986, pr .. **$20.00**

Santa & Mrs Claus kissing, ceramic, bent at waist & facing ea other, glossy, 1986, pr **$12.00**

Santa & tree, ceramic, Santa seated in green chair, green coiled-built tree w/red dots, pr **$12.00**

Santa & tree, ceramic, Santa standing, green coil-built tree, pr **$15.00**

Snowman couple holding letters S&P, bisque bodies w/glazed hats & letters in red & green, pr **$10.00**

Snowman couple w/gifts, bone china, white w/black & red hats, gifts & mittens, gold trim, pr **$10.00**

Valentine hearts on floral tray w/arrow, ceramic, red heart shakers, gold-trimmed white tray w/blue & green, 3-pc **$16.00**

Wedding couple on wire altar, porcelain, he holding top hat in crook of arm, she in real net dress, Dan Brechner, 3-pc **$45.00**

Household Items

Bed & pillow, ceramic, white w/pink & blue accents, glossy, 2-pc **$25.00**

Candlesticks, ceramic, red & white candles w/yellow flames, green holders w/handles, glossy, pr **$10.00**

Chair & ottoman, ceramic, brown w/white & green accents, glossy, pr **$15.00**

Coffeepot, plastic, chrome-look double pots w/black trim, in box marked Salt & Pepper Set, 2-pc **$18.00**

Faucets, white china w/red & blue taps, pr **$15.00**

Fireplace w/andirons, plastic, white w/brown stone-look, gold andiron shakers, 3-pc **$10.00**

Ice boxes, plastic, realistic wood-look, pr **$7.00**

Iron on stand, ceramic, glossy black iron on brown footed stand, Sarsaparilla, pr **$8.00**

Mixer & bowl, plastic, chrome-look & black w/clear bowl & beaters, beaters are shakers & bowl holds sugar, 4-pc **$25.00**

Piano, plastic, black & gold upright, 3-pc **$12.00**

Potbellied coal stove & bucket, ceramic, brown & black, glossy, pr **$10.00**

Rolling pin & scoop, ceramic, white w/maroon floral design, glossy, pr **$15.00**

Rotisserie w/roasting chickens, plastic, realistic w/clear front marked Rotisserie in script, chrome-look & black, 3-pc **$125.00**

Sewing machine, plastic, treadle machine w/drawers as shakers, realistic, 3-pc **$22.00**

Shaving mug & brush, ceramic, yellow mug, black brush w/white bristles, glossy, pr **$15.00**

Sofa & chair, ceramic, tufted backs, blue & yellow, pr..**$25.00**

Stove & refrigerator, ceramic, 1940s vintage, white w/red trim, glossy, pr **$20.00**

Telephone, ceramic, black rotary dial type, glossy, 2-pc.**$35.00**

Television, ceramic, black & white w/black image of Beatles performing on screen, 2-pc **$20.00**

Thimble & spool of thread, ceramic, black & white, glossy, pr **$12.00**

Toaster & toast, ceramic, white toaster w/brown & yellow toast, glossy, pr **$12.00**

Toaster w/2 slices of toast, plastic, black & white, 3-pc.**$15.00**

Toothbrush & tube of toothpaste, ceramic, green brush w/yellow tube, glossy, pr **$15.00**

Miniatures

Barn & hay wagon, ceramic, dark red barn w/black roof & 2 sm gold domes, yellow hay wagon w/gold hubs, pr **$45.00**

Bathtub & kettle, ceramic, white tub w/pink & gold trim, speckled kettle w/gold-trimmed handle, pr **$50.00**

Book & hurricane lamp, ceramic, gold-trimmed black book w/white & maroon lamp, glossy, pr **$22.00**

Box of chocolates & bouquet of flowers, ceramic, pink & white box w/gold chocolates, white flowers w/pink & green, pr **$45.00**

Camera & photo album, ceramic, beige camera & black & white open album w/gold trim, pr........................**$65.00**

Change purse & pocket watch, ceramic, gold-trimmed maroon purse & white watch w/numbers & hands, glossy, pr **$22.00**

Chocolate candies in paper wrap, ceramic, gold pc & brown pc in real brown paper, pr..............................**$30.00**

Coffeepot w/full cup on saucer, ceramic, ball-shaped pot w/gold handle appearing to be full, white cup & saucer, pr **$25.00**

Comb & brush w/mirror, ceramic, oval mirror w/blue bow on pink ruffled footed frame, pr **$45.00**

Cowboy boots, ceramic, brown w/gold trim, glossy, pr.**$40.00**

Diary & stack of love letters, ceramic, pink diary, white letters w/pink bow, glossy, pr **$65.00**

Dog & bowl of dog food, ceramic, pale yellow dog w/front paws & head down w/rump up looking at bowl of food, glossy, pr **$45.00**

Dustpan & whisk broom, ceramic, green & yellow w/gold trim, pr **$22.00**

Fish on boat & fisherman in water, ceramic, pr.........**$65.00**

Garden gate w/lady's hat, ceramic, open gate arched w/pink roses & green foliage, pale pink hat w/blue & gold trim, pr **$65.00**

Ice skates & sled, ceramic, white & brown w/gold trim, glossy, pr **$45.00**

Ice-cream churn & dish of ice cream w/spoon, ceramic, wood-look bucket, gold trim, pr **$26.00**

Lobster & oyster, ceramic, red lobster w/black eyes, black & white open oyster shell, glossy, pr....................**$45.00**

Lock & keyhole, ceramic, gray key & honey gold keyhole, pr **$45.00**

Mouse & mouse trap, ceramic, gray mouse w/pink ears, white trap w/yellow cheese, gold trim, glossy, pr **$40.00**

Pancakes on plate & syrup jar, ceramic, w/gold knife & fork on sides on plate, glossy, pr................................**$40.00**

Picnic table & stone barbecue, ceramic, silver trim, pr..**$55.00**

Pipe & slippers, ceramic, deep pink slippers, cream & black pipe w/gold trim, glossy, pr **$20.00**

Roller skates, ceramic, white w/gold trim, glossy, pr.**$35.00**

Rolling pin & pan of biscuits, ceramic, white w/red handles, browned biscuits in gray pan, pr **$30.00**

Saloon doors & spittoon, ceramic, honey gold, pr **$55.00**

Sausage & eggs, ceramic, 2 sausage links on plate w/2 eggs, glossy, 2-pc.. **$45.00**

Scarecrow & gathered cornstalks w/pumpkin, ceramic, glossy, pr **$75.00**

Stop sign & car, ceramic, red round sign on white pedestal, purple touring car, glossy, pr **$75.00**

Turkey on platter & covered roasting pan, ceramic, gray-speckled pan, golden turkey, pr............................**$45.00**

Violin & accordion, ceramic, maroon-colored violin, brown accordion, pr **$40.00**

People

Angels, ceramic, standing w/praying hands, eyes closed, blue hair & robes w/white faces & wings, pr **$12.00**

Bellhops holding flowers, ceramic, white w/brown, blue & black accents, pr...**$15.00**

Bikini girls sunbathing w/hats over faces, ceramic, red & blue, pr **$35.00**

Bride & groom, porcelain, standing, she w/bouquet, he holding hat at side, white w/blond hair, gold & black trim, pr........**$18.00**

Butler & maid, ceramic, butler w/eyes closed & towel over arm, maid w/hands on hips, black & white w/gold trim, pr...$35.00

Chef heads marked S&P, ceramic, white w/black hair & mustaches, red noses, pr.................................$15.00

Clown w/ball, ceramic, green clown, yellow ball, glossy, 2-pc $20.00

Colonial couple, ceramic, standing in elegant dress, white w/pink flowers, gold trim, she w/yellow hair, pr..$12.00

Couple in metal car holder, ceramic, he in black hat w/brown hair, she in yellow hat w/yellow hair, 3-pc.............$25.00

Couple w/weird cartoon features on park bench, ceramic figures w/green wood bench, multicolored, glossy, 3-pc......$25.00

Deep sea diver w/treasure chest, ceramic, white, black & brown, glossy, pr.................................$22.00

Doctor & nurse w/boy & girl look, painted porcelain heads w/white glossy uniforms, black & gold trim, pr..$20.00

Dutch boy carring water buckets over shoulders, red & black w/gold shoes, 3-pc.................................$15.00

Dutch couple kissing, ceramic, red, brown, white, black & yellow, pr.......................................$12.00

Eskimo couple on wood bench kissing, ceramic, olive green coats w/white trim, yellow mittens, black hair & boots, 3-pc...$10.00

Geisha girls, ceramic, half-figures holding fans, green kimonos w/multicolored accents, glossy, pr $18.00

Girl heads, ceramic, full-face girls w/yellow hair, white hats w/plaid design & blue daisies, blue bow tires, pr..$18.00

Glee & Glum clowns, ceramic, white & black w/gold trim, pr $45.00

Graduate boy & girl, porcelain, she in yellow banana curls, gray, black & white, pr $10.00

Graduates, ceramic, standing looking up w/books under arms & holding diplomas, black robes & hats w/white tassels, pr...$10.00

Grandma & grandpa in rocking chairs reading, ceramic, multicolored, glossy, pr.....................................$10.00

Hummel-type boy & girl gathering wood, ceramic, multicolored, matt, pr....................................$15.00

Indian couple in drum base, ceramic, multicolored heads, white base w/embossed Indian decor & gold trim, nodders, 3-pc..$55.00

Laughing couple heads, ceramic, pr..........................$8.00

Mermaids, bisque, girls in ponytails, 1 winking & 1 w/hands under chin, white hair, green bottoms w/gold accents, pr $45.00

Mexican cowboys saluting on performing horses on grassy bases, ceramic, multicolored, glossy, pr $10.00

Nuns, ceramic, round heads w/round noses, holes for eyes & mouth, black & white w/flesh faces, pr...........$25.00

Old couple in rocking chairs, ceramic, he smoking pipe & she knitting, glossy, pr......................................$15.00

Organ grinder w/monkey, ceramic, stout figure w/gray hair & dark brown mustache, monkey atop grinder, multicolored, 2-pc...$25.00

Peppy Pa & Salty Ma, ceramic, standing w/noses in air, white w/multicolored pastel accents, pr $10.00

Pirate boy & treasure chest, ceramic, multicolored, pr.$22.00

Scottish boy & girl kissing, ceramic, white w/brown & black costumes, black hats, pr.............................$15.00

Sea captains looking up, ceramic, black & white w/gray beards, gold decoration on hats, pr.....................$12.00

Seaman heads w/pipes, ceramic, white w/yellow beards, black pipes & bills on hats, white neck bases w/painted rings, pr...$22.00

Shopping lady and gent, 6", from $85.00 to $95.00 for the pair. (Photo courtesy Judy Posner)

US Mail boy & girl, ceramic, w/marked bags over shoulders, she w/mail in hand, he waving, blue w/red & black shoes, pr...$15.00

Souvenir

British bobbie & palace guard, ceramic, red & black, pr..$15.00

Cape Cod fisherman, ceramic, standing on marked bases in yellow slickers & hats, pr.....................................$12.00

Disneyland castle on tray, metal, split in half, 3-pc..$125.00

Eisenhower Lock/St Lawrence Seaway, ceramic, sculptural w/boat going through lock, pr.............................$40.00

Eskimo couple marked Canada, chalkware, cartoon features, he w/eyes open & toothy grin, she w/eyes & mouth closed, pr...$15.00

Feet w/painted toenails, ceramic, marked I Walked My Feet Off In Maine, pr.......................................$22.00

Grand Ole Opry Since 1925, ceramic, brown wood-look kegs w/white & brown end labels, pr.........................$12.00

Mouse popping out of loaf of bread, ceramic, gold label reading Souvenir of St Augustine FL, 2-pc...........$15.00

Niagara Falls, ceramic, 1 marked Niagara & 1 marked Falls w/boat, pr...$25.00

Riverboat w/smokestack shakers, cermaic, label marked Souvenir of Norfolk VA, multicolored, 3-pc..........$15.00

Strasburg (PA) Railroad workers, ceramic, 1 looking at watch & 1 w/lantern & hand on hip, glossy, marked bases, pr $35.00

Streetcars marked Desire & New Orleans, ceramic, golden yellow, glossy, pr.....................................$12.00

Washington DC, metal, Capitol Building & Washington Monument on tray w/embossed image of Capitol, gold-tone, 3-pc $25.00

Miscellaneous

ABC blocks & ball, ceramic, 3 stacked blocks in white w/red & blue trim & white ball w/red & blue swirl, pr .**$22.00**

Aircraft carrier & plane, ceramic, gray boat w/yellow plane, black trim, glossy, 2-pc **$35.00**

Automobiles, metal, 1918 Ford touring cars w/tops down, green, pr **$35.00**

Binoculars, ceramic, white lustre finish w/gold trim, pr ..**$15.00**

Binoculars marked S&P, ceramic, white w/gold decoration & trim, 3-pc..**$10.00**

Bow tie & collar, ceramic, white collar, blue bow tie w/black dots, 2-pc...**$10.00**

Boxing gloves & bag, ceramic, glossy magenta, pr **$12.00**

Bus & fire engine w/cartoon facial features, ceramic, crudely painted in multicolors, semigloss, pr **$30.00**

Confederate infantry & officers' hats, ceramic, light blue & black w/flag symbols, glossy, pr **$10.00**

Fire helmets marked S&P, pottery, white w/red lettering & red top button, lg, pr..**$10.00**

Houses (brick) marked God Bless Our Mortgaged Home on roofs, ceramic, pastel pink & blue, pr **$12.00**

Houses on tray, porcelain, steep-pitched roofs, white w/tan & blue lustre, black trim, sm, 3-pc........................**$15.00**

Jack-in-the boxes, chalkware, red & white w/blue & black trim, pr...**$22.00**

King & Queen of Diamonds, ceramic, diamond shapes, white w/gold trim, pr..**$15.00**

Lighthouse & sailboat on base, ceramic, multicolored, semigloss, 3-pc **$18.00**

Race cars marked Salt & Peppy, ceramic, 1 pink & 1 blue, glossy, pr **$25.00**

Rocket & moon, ceramic, gray rocket, yellow crescent moon w/human features, pr..**$45.00**

Sailboats on wavy base w/sailboat handle, ceramic, multicolored, 3-pc **$15.00**

Semi truck marked S&P Co, ceramic, green, 2-pc **$35.00**

Stop & Caution street signs, ceramic, octagonal, pr ...**$15.00**

Tire & nail, ceramic, light gray tire & light blue nail, glossy, pr.**$12.00**

Trolley cars, ceramic, pink w/embossed passengers in blue, pr..**$8.00**

Tugboats w/cartoon features, ceramic, red, white & blue w/black details, pr..**$15.00**

Typewriter & ink bottle, ceramic, black, glossy, pr **$24.00**

Violin & case, ceramic, glossy honey gold violin w/brown-speckled honey gold case, pr...............................**$15.00**

Violin & mandolin, ceramic, brown sides w/green & yellow fronts, pr **$10.00**

Windmills, ceramic, white w/embossed brown blades, black roofs, greenery on sides, brown railing above door, matt, pr.**$12.00**

Yarn doll boy & girl, ceramic, gray w/cold-painted red trim, pr.**$25.00**

Schoop, Hedi

One of the most successful California ceramic studios was founded in Hollywood by Hedi Schoop, who had been educated in the arts in Berlin, Germany. She had studied not only painting but sculpture, architecture, and fashion design as well. Fleeing Nazi Germany with her husband, the famous composer Frederick Holander, Hedi settled in California in 1933 and only a few years later became involved in producing novelty giftware items so popular that they were soon widely copied by other California companies. She designed many animated human figures, some in matched pairs, some that doubled as flower containers. (Many of the 'figurines' listed are in fact flower containers.) All were hand painted and many were decorated with applied ribbons, sgraffito work, and gold trim. To a lesser extent, she modeled animal figures as well. Until fire leveled the plant in 1958, the business was very productive. Nearly everything she made was marked.

If you'd like to learn more about her work, we recommend *The Collector's Encyclopedia of California Pottery, Second Edition,* by Jack Chipman (Collector Books).

Advisors: Susan Cox (See Directory California Pottery)

Bowl formed by swirl of gown, pink with black overspray, applied roses, $110.00.

Candle holder, mermaid holding shells in each hand, 13½" .**$450.00**

Cookie jar, King or Queen, 12", 12½", ea **$600.00**

Figurine, boy angel, waist up, 8"................................**$85.00**

Figurine, Chinese girl crouched down w/separate hanging lantern, 7"..**$85.00**

Figurine, Chinese musicians, 11", pr......................**$275.00**

Figurine, clown playing cello, overglaze platinum, 12½" **$275.00**

Figurine, Conchita, w/2 baskets, 12½" **$165.00**

Figurine, Debutante, handmade flowers, 12½".........**$165.00**

Figurine, hula dancer, 11", from $225 to **$250.00**

Figurine, Hungarian man & woman, #57, #58, 10½", 10", pr..**$250.00**

Figurine, Josephine, holding sm black bowl, 13" **$250.00**

Figurine, Love Boat, 1939, 6x10½"...........................**$280.00**

Figurine, My Sister & I, Dutch boy & girl, boy w/sm hanging baskets, pr..**$250.00**

Figurine, Repose, female holding bowl, tinted bisque w/high glaze **$165.00**

Figurine, Strongman, circus clown lifting barbell, 12x12", minimum value..**$275.00**

Figurine, Vienna, w/baskets, 13½"..........................**$175.00**

Flower frog, dancing girls, 8" **$250.00**

Flower holder, gardening girl, w/bucket & watering can, 7x6"...**$85.00**

Flower holder, lady of hearts, light blue dress w/pink trim, 7" **$85.00**

Flower holder, Marguerita, 12½", from $125 to **$145.00**

Flower holder, Tyrolean girl, holding skirt in both hands, 11½"...**$110.00**

Flower holder/lamp base, Colbert (Claudette), white dress, blue baskets, 11½"..**$150.00**

Jardiniere, Chinese style, blue w/gold trim, 7½" **$100.00**

Scouting Collectibles

Collecting scouting memorabilia has long been a popular pastime for many. Through the years, millions of boys and girls have been a part of this worthy organization founded in England in 1907 by retired Major-General Lord Robert Baden-Powell. Scouting has served to establish goals in young people and help them to develop leadership skills, physical strength, and mental alertness. Through scouting, they learn basic fundamentals of survival. The scouting movement came to the United States in 1910, and the first World Scout Jamboree was held in 1911 in England. If you would like to learn more, we recommend *A Guide to Scouting Collectibles With Values* by R.J. Sayers (ordering information is given in the Directory).

Advisor: R.J. Sayers (See Directory, Scouting Collectibles)

Boy Scouts

Ashtray, National Jamboree, souvenir w/logo, 1973 .....**$3.00**

Bank, Cub Scout, composition bust of Cub **$20.00**

Belt buckle, #d for staff, limited edition, 1989 ....**$45.00**

Belt buckle, National Jamboree, special Max Silber issue, limited edition of 1,000, 1969 ....**$50.00**

Belt buckle, 1985 World Jamboree, Max Silber issue of 125 ....**$50.00**

Blotter, Onward for God & Country, BSA, 1950s, w/scouts..**$5.00**

Book, Lost Patrol, 1913, EX **$12.00**

Bookends, Official BSA, Cub Scout issue, pressed wood, 1940s, pr **$15.00**

Camera, Official Box Camera, Senica type, 1930s, complete in litho box...**$75.00**

Cap, Official, red beret w/patch **$3.00**

Card, membership; plastic, ring at top, 4-page, 1919 .**$15.00**

Cards, Christmas; w/envelopes, 25 in red box, set.....**$10.00**

Compass, black plastic, 8-point side, 1935 ....**$20.00**

Compass, red plastic, 1930, 8-point side....................**$20.00**

Cup, loving; sterling, 1920s, 12" **$50.00**

Decal, Full 1st Class, silver, 1930s **$3.00**

Decal, Historical Trails Award, red border...................**$2.00**

Figure, Boy Scout stalking, hollow, painted................**$25.00**

First Aid kit, Bauer & Black, rectangular, in kakai case ...**$15.00**

First Aid kit, Johnson & Johnson, tin, square, flip lid type..**$8.00**

Flashlight, Ever Ready, red head, 3-battery type...........**$3.00**

Game, Target Ball, marble shooting game, 1920 ......**$125.00**

Handkerchief, Cub Scout, blue w/Cub promise............**$4.00**

Hikemeter (pedometer), w/compass in back, belt hanger, 1930s...**$22.50**

Kit, woodburning; w/wood & cord..............................**$20.00**

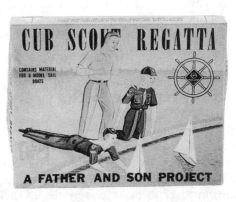

Model Sail Boats, #1698, wood and white plastic, complete, $30.00.

Mug, Regional; ceramic, old regions, set of 12 in box .**$25.00**

Pamphlet, Fun Around the Campfire, Boy Scouts of America **$4.00**

Pamphlet, Guide for Good Camping, BSA, 1954 ....**$2.00**

Pen, ink; 1940s scout emblem, Parker Bros **$7.50**

Pennant, World Jamboree, blue, woven w/logo, 1963 .**$15.00**

Pin, Strengthen the Arms of Liberty, stick-back **$3.00**

Pitcher, water; ceramic, scout & Baden-Powell (bust), English, 1920s **$100.00**

Plate, ceramic, Rockwell-Gorham, Campfire Story......**$30.00**

Postcard, Blazing a Trail, 1914, color, #4 in series.....**$10.00**

Postcard, Hero of the Day, scout w/flag, 1920.............**$7.00**

Postcard, Official World Jamboree, w/logo, 1947 ....**$10.00**

Postcard, 1957 World Jamboree, w/official stamp.........**$4.00**

Poster, John Glenn-Space Scout, 1960s......................**$10.00**

Record, Boy Scouts in Switzerland, 1920, 78 rpm.......**$15.00**

Record, Morse Code Made Easy, 1950, 78 rpm...........**$15.00**

Ring, full 1st Class, sterling......................................**$10.00**

Sheet music, A Good Turn, for piano, color cover, Murphy, 1912 ....**$10.00**

Signal set, Official Triple; metal #1092.....................**$35.00**

Tie bar, Eagle Scout, sterling, clip-on, logo **$5.00**

Wallet, Cub Scout, National issue, vinyl.......................**$4.00**

Watch, Official BSA, Midget Radiolite Army Strap, #1364, 1919 ....**$75.00**

Watch, pocket; Official Boy Scout, Seven-Seas, #1270, 1941 ....**$35.00**

Watch fob, Official Troop Committee, white enamel, #312 ....**$200.00**

Woodcarving kit, complete, #1241 ....**$25.00**

Girl Scouts

Armband, Senior Service Scout..................................**$20.00**

Camera, box type, Official GSA, Falcon, 1940 ....**$30.00**

Cup, collapsible; Girl Scout, aluminum, 1950..............**$5.00**

Doll, Girl Scout, Effanbee, 1965, MIB **$30.00**

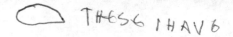 THESE I HAVE

Dress, Brownie, w/orange necktie, membership card, 1950s, M **$20.00**

Flags, signal; Official GSA, wooden handles, 1920 .....**$15.00**

Medal, Life Saving, bronze, 1916, Maltese cross **$200.00**

Pin, Mariner, 1940 ....**$15.00**

Pin, Wing Scouting, 1941 ....**$35.00**

Uniform, Official GSA, top & skirt, khaki, 1917-23, no badges **$75.00**

Shawnee Pottery

In 1937 a company was formed in Zanesville, Ohio, on the suspected site of a Shawnee Indian village. They took the tribe's name to represent their company, recognizing the Indians to be the first to use the rich clay from the banks of the Muskingum River to make pottery there. Their venture was very successful, and until they closed in 1961, they produced many lines of kitchenware, planters, vases, lamps, and cookie jars that are very collectible today.

They specialized in figural items. There were 'Winnie' and 'Smiley' pig cookie jars and salt and pepper shakers; 'Bo Peep,' 'Puss 'n Boots,' 'Boy Blue,' and 'Charlie Chicken' pitchers; Dutch children; lobsters; and two lines of dinnerware modeled as ears of corn.

Values sometimes hinge on the extent of an item's decoration. Most items will increase by 50% to 200% when heavily decorated and gold trimmed.

Not all of their ware was marked Shawnee; many pieces were simply marked USA with a three- or four-digit mold number. If you'd like to learn more about this subject, we recommend *Shawnee Pottery, The Full Encyclopedia,* by Pam Curran; *The Collector's Guide to Shawnee Pottery* by Duane and Janice Vanderbilt; and *Shawnee Pottery, Identification & Value Guide,* by Jim and Bev Mangus.

See Also Cookie Jars.

Advisor: Rick Spencer (See Directory, Shawnee)

Club: Shawnee Pottery Collectors' Club
P.O. Box 713
New Smyrna Beach, FL 32170-0713. Monthly nationwide newsletter. SASE (c/o Pamela Curran) required when requesting information. Optional: $3 for sample of current newsletter

Creamer, elephant, white w/gold trim, marked Pat USA **$210.00**

Creamer, Pennsylvania Dutch, marked USA 12 ....**$95.00**

Creamer, Puss 'n Boots, all gold, marked Pat Puss 'n Boots ..**$480.00**

Creamer, Puss 'n Boots, cream, marked Pat Puss 'n Boots ...**$55.00**

Creamer, quill, ball jug shape, marked USA 12 ....**$135.00**

Creamer, Smiley the Pig, clover bud, marked Pat Smiley .**$100.00**

Creamer, Smiley the Pig, yellow & blue w/gold, marked Shawnee 86 ....**$195.00**

Creamer, Snowflake, marked USA **$20.00**

Creamer, tilt; Pennsylvania Dutch, mk USA 10 ....**$135.00**

Creamer, tilt; yellow, marked USA 10 ....**$50.00**

Pitcher, Bo Peep, blue bonnet, marked Pat Bo Peep .**$110.00**

Pitcher, Boy Blue, gold trim, marked Shawnee 46 ...**$240.00**

Pitcher, Charlie Chicken, gold & decals, marked Chanticleer **$360.00**

Pitcher, jug; Flower & Fern **$60.00**

Pitcher, Sunflower, marked USA **$95.00**

Planter, baby shoe on base, marked USA **$12.00**

Planter, birds on driftwood, marked Shawnee #502 ...**$50.00**

Planter, blow fish, marked USA **$8.00**

Planter, boy & wheelbarrow, marked USA #750 ....**$18.00**

Planter, cat, marked USA **$15.00**

Planter, centerpiece; Cameo, marked Shawnee USA #2503, 10" **$15.00**

Planter, chick & egg, marked Shawnee USA #730 ......**$40.00**

Planter, dancing lamb, marked USA **$25.00**

Planter, dog in a boat, marked Shawnee #736 ....**$22.00**

Planter, Elegance, cone form, w/brass-plated stand, no mark, 7" **$45.00**

Planter, Fairy Wood, marked Shawnee USA #1201, 4½" ...**$8.00**

Planter, Madonna, marked USA **$30.00**

Planter, pixie & wheelbarrow, no mark **$15.00**

Planter, rocking horse, marked USA 526, from $22.00 to $24.00. (Photo courtesy Jim and Bev Mangus)

Planter, squirrel & stump, gold, marked Shawnee #664 ..**$20.00**

Planter, wing form, Touchè, marked Shawnee #1015, 11" .**$10.00**

Planter, zebra & stump, no mark **$22.00**

Shakers, Bo Peep & Sailor Boy, gold trim, sm, pr **$95.00**

Shakers, Charlie Chicken, gold trim, lg, pr **$95.00**

Shakers, cottage, marked USA 9, sm, pr **$210.00**

Shakers, Dutch boy & girl, Great Northern, lg, pr **$330.00**

Shakers, Dutch boy & girl, lg, pr **$75.00**

Shakers, Flower & Fern, square, lg, pr **$30.00**

Shakers, Muggsy, blue bow w/gold, lg, pr **$250.00**

Shakers, owl, green eyed, sm, pr **$35.00**

Shakers, Smiley the Pig, peach bib w/gold & decals, lg, pr **$300.00**

Shakers, Smiley the Pig, red bib, lg, pr **$155.00**

Shakers, Sunflower, lg, pr **$60.00**

Shakers, Swiss boy & girl, gold trim, lg, pr **$60.00**

Shakers, Winnie & Smiley, clover bud, sm, pr **$75.00**

Shakers, Winnie & Smiley, gold trim, sm, pr **$120.00**

Shakers, Winnie & Smiley, hearts, lg, pr **$180.00**

Teapot, blue & red flower w/gold, marked USA **$75.00**

Teapot, clover bud, marked USA **$115.00**

Teapot, cottage, marked USA 7 ....**$360.00**

Teapot, elephant, blue, green or yellow, marked USA..**$180.00**

Teapot, embossed rose, solid gold, marked USA **$240.00**

Teapot, Granny Ann, green apron, marked Pat Granny Ann **$130.00**

Teapot, Pennsylvania Dutch, marked USA #14, 14-oz..**$85.00**

Teapot, Pennsylvania Dutch, w/gold, 18-oz, marked USA 18..**$130.00**

Teapot, red flower w/gold, marked USA...................**$70.00**

Teapot, Snowflake, green, sm, marked USA **$30.00**

Teapot, Tom Tom, marked Tom the Piper's Son Pat USA ..**$120.00**

Corn Ware

Bowl, fruit; King or Queen, #92, 6" **$48.00**

Bowl, mixing; Corn King, #6, 6½" **$35.00**

Bowl, mixing; King or Queen, #5, 5".......................**$30.00**

Bowl, soup/cereal; King or Queen, #94 ....**$55.00**

Butter dish, King or Queen, w/lid, #72 ....**$60.00**

Casserole, individual, King or Queen, #73 ....**$60.00**

Cookie jar, King or Queen, #66............................**$240.00**

Corn roast set, Corn Queen, #108...........................**$165.00**

Creamer, King or Queen, #70 ....**$30.00**

Dish, vegetable; King or Queen, #95, 9" **$45.00**

Jug, King or Queen, #71, 40-oz................................**$80.00**

Mug, King or Queen, #69, 8-oz................................**$55.00**

Plate, King or Queen, #68, 10"...............................**$35.00**

Platter, King or Queen, #96, 12"..............................**$55.00**

Popcorn set, King or Queen..................................**$275.00**

Salt & pepper shakers, King or Queen, no mark, 3¼", pr.**$20.00**

Salt & pepper shakers, King or Queen, 5¼", pr **$30.00**

Table set, Corn Queen, #102..................................**$55.00**

Teapot, King or Queen, #75, 30-oz..........................**$85.00**

Town & Country snack set, Corn King, #101...........**$275.00**

Lobster Ware

Bowl, batter; handled, #928.................................**$100.00**

Bowl, mixing/open baker; #915, 5"..........................**$44.00**

Bowl, mixing/open baker; #919, 9"..........................**$62.00**

Bowl, salad/spaghetti; #922 ....**$80.00**

Casserole, French; #900, 10-oz **$19.00**

Casserole, French; #902, 16-oz **$31.00**

Casserole, French; white w/red lobster finial, stick handle, #904, 2-qt..**$46.00**

Creamer & sugar bowl, w/lid, #910 ....**$138.00**

Creamer jug, #921...**$100.00**

Hors d'oeuvre holder, #932, 7¼"..........................**$280.00**

Range set, #906, 4-pc, in box **$88.00**

Relish, lobster finial, #926, 5½" **$100.00**

Salad set, #924, 9-pc...**$345.00**

Snack jar/bean pot, lobster finial, #925 ....**$310.00**

Spoon holder, double; lobster finial, #935, 8½"........**$280.00**

Valencia

Ashtray...**$24.00**

Casserole, 7½"..**$75.00**

Chop plate, 15"...**$52.00**

Comport, 12" **$45.00**

Covered dish, ftd, 8" **$75.00**

Covered mustard...**$24.00**

Covered onion soup **$30.00**

Cup & saucer, coffee; after-dinner, no mark **$65.00**

Dessert, 6" **$17.00**

Flower vase, 10"...**$28.00**

Ice pitcher, marked USA **$40.00**

Pie server, 9" **$85.00**

Plate, deep, 8" **$24.00**

Plate, 9¾" **$21.00**

Relish tray, no mark **$115.00**

Sugar bowl, w/lid, no mark **$17.00**

Waffle set, 5-pc **$205.00**

Candle holders, bulb type, from $12.00 to $14.00 each. (Photo courtesy Jim and Bev Mangus)

Sheet Music

Flea markets are a good source for buying old sheet music, and prices are usually very reasonable. Most examples can be bought for less than $5.00. More often than not, it is collected for reasons other than content. Some of the cover art was done by well-known illustrators like Rockwell, Christy, Barbelle, and Starmer, and some collectors like to zero in on their particular favorite, often framing some of the more attractive examples. Black Americana collectors can find many good examples with Black entertainers featured on the covers and the music reflecting an ethnic theme.

You may want to concentrate on music by a particularly renowned composer, for instance George M. Cohan or Irving Berlin. Or you may find you enjoy covers featuring famous entertainers and movie stars from the '40s through the '60s, for instance. At any rate, be critical of condition when you buy or sell sheet music. As is true with any item of paper, tears, dog ears, or soil will greatly reduce its value.

If you'd like a more thorough listing of sheet music and prices, we recommend *The Sheet Music Reference and Price Guide* by Anna Marie Guiheen and Marie-Reine A. Pafik (Collector Books), and *The Collector's Guide to Sheet Music* by Debbie Dillon.

A Lot of Livin' To Do, Lee Adams & Charles Strouse, Movie: Bye Bye Birdie, 1960 ....**$5.00**

Ace in the Hole, Cole Porter, Movie: Let's Face It, 1943...**$5.00**

After Twelve O'Clock, Hoagy Carmichael & Johnny Mercer, 1932..**$5.00**

All Aboard, Oliver Wallace, Frank Churchill & Ned Washington, Movie: Dumbo, 1941.........................**$15.00**

All Alone, Irving Berlin, 1924 ....**$10.00**

All or Nothin', Rodgers & Hammerstein II, Musical: Oklahoma, 1943..**$8.00**

America, Stephen Sondheim & Leonard Bernstein, Movie: West Side Story, 1957...**$5.00**

American Born, Eugene Kenney, Pfeiffer cover artist, 1914...**$15.00**

Angel May Care, Ary Barroso & Erin Drake, Movie: The Three Cabaleros (Disney), 1945............................**$15.00**

Arms for the Love of America, Irving Berlin, 1941 .....**$10.00**

Around the World in 80 Days, Harold Adamson & Victor Young, Movie: same title, 1956.............................**$5.00**

As Time Goes By, Movie: Casablanca, Humphrey Bogart & Ingrid Bergman photo cover..............................**$15.00**

Atlantic City Pageant, John Philip Sousa, 1927............**$15.00**

Babes on Broadway, Ralph Freed & Burton Lane, Judy Garland photo cover, 1942..................................**$10.00**

Ballin' the Jack, Jim Burris & Chris Smith, Movie: That's My Boy, Martin & Lewis photo cover, 1951..................**$5.00**

Barnum Had the Right Idea, George M Cohan...........**$15.00**

Beautiful Blue Danube, Johann Strauss, 1933 ....**$2.00**

Best Man, Roy Alfred & Fred Wise, Nat King Cole Trio photo cover, 1946 ....**$5.00**

Bianca, Cole Porter, Musical: Kiss Me Kate, 1948 ....**$5.00**

Bird Song, CS Courtenay, dedicated to the Audubon Society of America, 1912...**$10.00**

Blue September, Mitchell Parish & Peter DeRose, 1940..**$5.00**

Boin-N-N-NG, Sam Stept, Kay Kyser photo cover, 1947..**$5.00**

Bouquet of Roses, Steve Nelson & Bob Hilliard, Eddy Arnold photo cover, 1948 ....**$3.00**

Broken Promise, James Goldsborough, Movie: Jamboree, The Four Coins photo cover, 1957...........................**$5.00**

Bus Stop Song, Darby, Movie: Bus Stop, Marilyn Monroe & Don Murray photo cover, 1956.............................**$10.00**

Cabarabia, Mitchell, Flatow & Gumble, Musical: Cabaret, 1966..**$3.00**

Casey, The Pride of Them All, Ray Gilbert, Ken Darby & Eliot Daniel, Movie: Make Mine Music, Disney, 1946 ..**$10.00**

Chicka Boom, Bob Merrill, 1953...................................**$5.00**

Chitty-Chitty Bang-Bang, Sherman & Sherman, Movie: same title, Dick Van Dyke & Sally Ann Howes photo cover, 1968...**$5.00**

Coax Me a Little Bit, Charles Tobias & Mat Simon, Andrews Sisters photo cover, 1946....................................**$5.00**

Comin' Thro' the Rye, Robert Burns, Bob Crosby photo cover, 1938 ....**$3.00**

Cool, Stephen Sondheim & Leonard Bernstein, Movie: West Side Story, 1957...**$5.00**

Cover Girl, Ira Gershwin & Jerome Kern, Movie: same title, 1944...**$5.00**

Cuban Pete, Jose Norman, Desi Arnaz & King Sisters, 1946...**$5.00**

Daughter of Jole Blon, Bart Dawson, 1948 ....**$5.00**

David & Bathsheba, Jenkins, Allen & Roberts, Movie: same title, 1951 ....**$3.00**

Day-Dreaming, Gus Kahn & Jerome Kern, Bing Crosby photo cover, 1941 ....**$5.00**

Dime a Dozen, Cindy Walker, Sammy Kaye photo cover, 1949...**$3.00**

Doctor Doolittle, Bricusse, Movie: same title, Rex Harrison photo cover, 1967 ....**$3.00**

Don't Let Me Down, John Lennon & Paul McCartney, Lennon & McCartney photo cover, 1969 ....**$30.00**

Don't Let the Stars Get in Your Eyes, Slim Willet, Perry Como photo cover, 1952 ....**$5.00**

Down T'Uncle Bill's, Hoagy Carmichael & Johnny Mercer, 1934...**$5.00**

Dreamer's Holiday, Kim Gannon & Mabel Wayne, Vic Damone photo cover, 1949...**$5.00**

Drum Beat, Washington & Young, Movie: same title, Allan Ladd & Audrey Dalton photo cover, 1954 ....**$5.00**

Encore, J Fred Coots, Eddy Howard photo cover, 1947 ...**$5.00**

Ev'rything I've Got, Lorenz Hart & Richard Rodgers, Movie: All's Fair, 1942 ....**$5.00**

Extra, Extra, Irving Berlin, Musical: Miss Liberty, 1949 .**$5.00**

Fanny, Rome, Movie: same title, Leslie Caron, Maurice Chevalier & Charles Boyer photo cover, 1954......**$10.00**

Fiddle Dee Dee, Sam Cahn and Jule Styne, from movie 'Its a Great Feeling,' Dennis Morgan, Doris Day, and Jack Carson photo cover, 1949, $10.00. (Photo courtesy Guiheen & Pafik)

Fire & Rain, James Taylor, James Taylor photo cover, 1969...**$5.00**

Fly Me to the Moon, Bart Howard, Bart Howard photo cover, 1954...**$5.00**

For Once In My Life, Ronald Miller & Orlando Murden, Tony Bennett photo cover, 1967 ....**$5.00**

Galveston, Webb, Glen Campbell photo cover, 1968 ...**$5.00**

Gangster's Warning, Gene Autry, Curt Poulton photo cover, 1932...**$5.00**

Ghost Riders in the Sky, Vaughn Monroe signed photo cover, 1947 ....**$20.00**

Gigi, Alan J Lerner & Frederick Loewe, Movie: same title, 1958...**$5.00**

Give Me a Hundred Reasons, Ann Jones, 1949............**$5.00**

Go Away Little Girl, Carole King, Donny Osmond photo cover, 1962 ....**$5.00**

Goodbye Sue, Rule, Ricca & Loman, Morton Downey photo cover, 1943 ....**$3.00**

Goodnight Irene, Huddie Ledbetter & John Lomax, The Weavers & Gordon Jenkins photo cover, 1950.......**$3.00**

Guitar Boogie, Arthur Smith, Arthur Smith photo cover, 1946..**$5.00**

Gypsy, Billy Reid, Sammy Kaye photo cover, 1947 ......**$5.00**

Half As Much, Curley Williams, Rosemary Clooney photo cover, 1951 ....**$5.00**

Halls of Ivy, Henry Russell & Vicki Knight, 1950..........**$5.00**

Haven't the Time for the Pain, Jacob Brackman, Carly Simon photo cover, 1974 ....**$5.00**

He's a Right Guy, Cole Porter, Movie: Something for the Boys, 1942 ....**$5.00**

Headless Horseman, Don Raye & Gene DePaul, Movie: Adventures of Ichabod Crane & Mr Toad, Disney, 1949..**$10.00**

Heart, Richard Adler & Jerry Ross, Musical: Damn Yankees, 1955...**$5.00**

Hello Dolly, Jerry Herman, Musical: same title, 1963 ...**$5.00**

Hey Jude, John Lennon & Paul McCartney, Beatles photo cover, 1968 ....**$25.00**

Hey There, Richard Adler & Jerry Ross, Musical: The Pajama Game, 1954...**$5.00**

Ho Ho Song, Red Buttons & Joe Darion, Red Buttons photo cover, 1953 ....**$5.00**

Honey, Bobby Russell, Bobby Goldsboro photo cover, 1968...**$3.00**

Hooray, Leo Robin & Harold Arlen, Movie: Casbah, 1948..**$5.00**

How Great Thou Art, Hine, 1955 ....**$5.00**

How Lucky You Are, O'Conner & Maurice, 1946 ....**$5.00**

I Bring You a Song, Frank Churchill & Larry Morey, Movie: Bambi, Disney, 1942..**$10.00**

I Don't Want To Be Hurt Anymore, McCarthy, Nat King Cole photo cover, 1962 ....**$3.00**

I Enjoy Being a Girl, Rodgers & Hammerstein II, Movie: Flower Drum Song, 1961..**$5.00**

I Hear the Music Now, Seelen & Fain, Movie: The Jazz Singer, Danny Thomas & Peggy Lee photo cover, 1953 ....**$5.00**

I Love Paris, Cole Porter, Musical: Can Can, 1953 ....**$3.00**

I Remember When, Ed Sarche & Percy Haid, The Song Smiths photo cover, 1951 ....**$3.00**

I Walk Alone, Herbert W Wilson, 1943 ....**$5.00**

I Want To Be Loved Like a Baby, Randy Ryan & Sam Wall, 1945 ....**$5.00**

I Will Wait for Love, Williams & Shaper, Movie: A Nice Girl Like Me, 1969 ....**$3.00**

I Wish, Roberts & Fisher, 1945...................................**$3.00**

I Wish I Had a Daddy in the White House, Bud Burtson, Kitty Kallen photo cover, 1951 ....**$5.00**

I'll Be Around, Alec Wilder, Mills Brothers photo cover, 1942...**$3.00**

I'll Dance at Your Wedding, Frank Loesser & Hoagy Carmichael, Movie: Mr Bug Goes to Town, 1941...**$5.00**

I'll Share It All With You, Irving Berlin, Movie: Annie Get Your Gun, 1946 ....**$5.00**

I'm Alright, Loggins, Movie: Caddyshack, Bill Murray, Rodney Dangerfield & Chevy Chase photo cover, 1980......**$3.00**

I'm Gonna Live Till I Die, Al Hoffman, Walter Kent & Mann Curtis, Danny Scholl photo cover, 1950 ....**$3.00**

I'm Henry the Eighth, Fred Murray & RP Weston, Herman's Hermits photo cover, 1965 ....**$3.00**

I'm On a See-Saw, Desmond Carter & Vivian Ellis, Musical: Jack & Jill, 1934...**$3.00**

I'm the Greatest Father of Them All, Jerome, Lilley & Foy, Movie: The Seven Little Foys, Bob Hope photo cover, 1955...**$5.00**

I've Got My Love To Keep Me Warm, Irving Berlin, Les Brown photo cover, 1937...**$5.00**

If I Had a Wishing Ring, Marla Skelton & Louis Alter, Movie: Breakfast in Hollywood, 1945....................................**$5.00**

If I Were a Bell, Jo Swerling, Abe Burrows & Frank Loesser, Musical: Guys & Dolls, 1950 ....**$5.00**

If I Were a Carpenter, Tim Hardin, June & Johnny Cash photo cover, 1966 ....**$3.00**

In a World of My Own, Bob Hilliard & Sammy Fain, Movie: Alice in Wonderland, Disney, 1951 ....**$10.00**

In the Arms of Love, Henry Mancini, Jay Livingston & Roy Evans, Movie: What Did You Do in the War Daddy?, 1966..**$2.00**

In the Good Old Summertime, Ren Shields & George Evans, 1958..**$3.00**

In the Land of Beginning Again, G Clarke & GW Meyer, Movie: The Bells of St Mary's, Bing Crosby photo cover, 1946..**$5.00**

In the Moon Mist, Jack Lawrence, Jerry Wald photo cover, 1946..**$3.00**

Inka Dinka Doo, Durante & Ryan, Movie: Palooka, Jimmy Durante photo cover, 1933 ....**$10.00**

It Looks Like Rain in Cherry Blossom Lane, Edgar Leslie & Joe Burke, Guy Lombardo photo cover, 1937......**$10.00**

It Was Written in the Stars, Leo Robin & Harold Arlen, Movie: Casbah, 1948 ....**$5.00**

It's Impossible, A Manzanero & Sid Wayne, Perry Como photo cover, 1968 ....**$5.00**

It's So Nice To Have a Man Around the House, Jack Elliot & Harold Spina, Dinah Shore photo cover, 1950.....**$10.00**

Jambalaya, Hank Williams, Hank Williams photo cover, 1952..**$3.00**

Joobalai, Leo Robin & Ralph Rainger, Movie: Paris Honeymoon, Bing Crosby & Shirley Ross photo cover, 1938..**$5.00**

Just an Old Love of Mine, Peggy Lee & Dave Barbour, Peggy Lee & Dave Barbour photo cover, 1947.................**$5.00**

Just for Fun, Livingston & Evans, Movie: My Friend Irma, Marie Wilson, John Lund & Martin & Lewis photo cover, 1949..**$5.00**

Katrina, Don Raye & Gene DePaul, Movie: Adventures of Ichabod Crane & Mr Toad, Disney, 1949.............**$10.00**

Kickin' a Hole in the Sky, Rose, MacDonald & Greer, Movie: Be Yourself, Fannie Brice photo cover, 1930 ....**$10.00**

La Cucaracha, Carl Field, Don Pedro photo cover, 1935 ..**$5.00**

Last Waltz, Less Reed & Barry Mason, Englebert Humperdinck photo cover, 1967 ....**$3.00**

Lawrence of Arabia, Maurice Jarre, Movie: same title, 1962..**$5.00**

Let Freedom Ring, Sheeley & Mossman, Starmer cover artist, 1940 ....**$10.00**

Let's Not Talk About Love, Cole Porter, Movie: Let's Face It, 1943...**$5.00**

Let's Sing a Gay Little Spring Song, Frank Churchill & Larry Morey, Movie: Bambi, Disney, 1942.....................**$10.00**

Life Goes On, Theodorakis, Movie: Zorba the Greek, Anthony Quinn photo cover, 1966..........................**$5.00**

Little Bit Independent, Edgar Leslie & Joe Burke, Ozzie & Harriet photo cover, HBK cover artist, 1935...........**$5.00**

Little Did I Know, Nick & Charles Kenny & Abner Silver, Kate Smith photo cover, 1943................................**$10.00**

Little Toot, Allie Wrubel, Movie: Melody Time, Disney, 1948...**$10.00**

Living the Life I Love, Seelen & Fain, Movie: The Jazz Singer, Danny Thomas & Peggy Lee photo cover, 1953....**$5.00**

Love & Marriage, Sammy Cahn & James Van Heusen, Movie: Our Town, Frank Sinatra photo cover, 1955...........**$5.00**

Magic of Your Love, Kahn, Grey & Lehar, Movie: Balalaika, Nelson Eddy & Ilone Massey photo cover, 1939....**$8.00**

Make Way for Tomorrow, Jerome Kern, Ira Gershwin & EY Harburg, Movie: Cover Girl, Rita Hayworth photo cover, 1944...**$8.00**

Man That Got Away, Arlen & Gershwin, Movie: A Star Is Born, Judy Garland photo cover, 1954 ....**$10.00**

Maria, Rodgers & Hammerstein II, Movie: The Sound of Music, Julie Andrews & Christopher Plummer photo cover, 1959 ....**$8.00**

May You Always, Larry Markes & Dick Charles, McGuire Sisters photo cover, 1958.....................................**$5.00**

Me & My Melinda, Irving Berlin, 1942.........................**$10.00**

Memories of You, Andy Razaf & Eubie Blake, Steve Allen & Donna Reed photo cover, 1944.............................**$10.00**

Milkman, Keep Those Bottles Quiet, Don Raye & Gene DePaul, Movie: Broadway Rhythm, Ginny Simms & Tommy Dorsey, 1944......................................**$5.00**

Mister Five By Five, Don Raye & Gene DePaul, Movie: Behind the 8 Ball, Holley cover artist, 1942...........**$5.00**

Money Isn't Everything, Rodgers & Hammerstein II, Musical: Alegro, 1951 ....**$5.00**

Moonlight in Vermont, John Blackburn & Karl Suessdorf, 1945..**$5.00**

Music Stopped, Harold Adamson & Jimmy McHugh, Movie: Higher & Higher, Frank Sinatra photo cover, 1943 .**$5.00**

Mutual Admiration Society, Matt Dubey & Harold Karr, Musical: Happy Hunting, Ethel Merman photo cover, 1956...**$5.00**

My Cup Runneth Over, Tom Jones & Harvey Schmidt, Musical: I Do! I Do!, 1966 ....**$5.00**

My Heart Cries for You, Carl Sigman & Percy Faith, Guy Mitchell photo cover, 1950...................................**$5.00**

My Mother Would Love You, Cole Porter, Movie: Panama Hattie, 1942...**$5.00**

My Mother's Waltz, Dave Franklin, Bing Crosby photo cover, 1945 ....**$5.00**

My Sister & I, Hy Zaret, Joan Whitney & Alex Kramer, Im-Ho cover artist, 1941 ....**$5.00**

Naughty But Nice, Mercer & Warren, Movie; The Belle of New York, Fred Astaire & Vera Ellen photo cover, 1952 ....**$5.00**

Never So Beautiful, Jay Livingston & Ray Evans, Movie: Here Comes the Girls, 1953...**$5.00**

Night of My Nights, Robert Wright & Chet Forest, Musical: Kismet, 1953 ....**$5.00**

No Other Love, Rogers & Hammerstein, Movie: Me & Juliet, 1953...**$5.00**

No Two People, Frank Loesser, Movie: Hans Christian Anderson, Danny Kaye photo cover, 1951 ....**$10.00**

Now & Then, There Is a Fool Such As I; Trader, Harry Snow photo cover, 1952 ....**$5.00**

Now That I Need You, Frank Loesser, Movie; Red, Hot & Blue, Bette Hutton & Victor Mature photo cover, 1949......**$5.00**

Oklahoma, Rodgers & Hammerstein II, Musical: same title, Holley cover artist, 1943.....................................**$5.00**

Old Home Guard, Sherman & Sherman, Movie: Bedknobs & Broomsticks, Angela Lansbury & David Tomlinson, 1971..**$3.00**

Old Music Master, Johnny Mercer & Hoagy Carmichael, Movie: True to Life, 1943 ....**$5.00**

On the Atchison, Topeka, and the Santa Fe, Mercer and Warren, from movie 'Harvey Girls,' Garland photo cover, 1934, $15.00. (Photo courtesy Guiheen & Pafik)

On the Street Where You Live, Lerner & Lowe, Movie: My Fair Lady, 1956 ....**$5.00**

On Top of Old Smokey, Peter Seeger, 1951.................**$3.00**

Once in Love With Amy, Frank Loesser, Musical: Where's Charley, Ray Bolger caricature, 1948.....................**$10.00**

Oops!, Mercer & Warren, Movie: Belle of New York, Fred Astaire & Vera Ellen, 1952..**$8.00**

Over the Rainbow, EY Harburg & Harold Arlen, Movie: Wizard of Oz, Judy Garland photo cover, 1939 ...**$35.00**

Pennies From Heaven, John Burke & Arthur Johnston, Movie: same title, Bing Crosby photo cover, 1936.**$5.00**

Poor Jud, Rodgers & Hammerstein II, Musical: Oklahoma, 1943...**$5.00**

Pretending, Marty Symes & Al Sherman, Bing Crosby photo cover, 1946 ....**$5.00**

Put On a Happy Face, Lee Adams & Charles Strause, Movie; Bye Bye Birdie, 1960 ....**$5.00**

Rainbow, Russ Hamilton, 1957 ....$5.00

Ready To Take a Chance Again, Gimbel & Fox, Movie: Foul Play, Chevy Chase & Goldie Hawn, 1978...............$5.00

Reciprocity, Sally Benson, Walter Kent & Kim Gannon, Movie: Seventeen, 1951 ....$5.00

Rock-A-Bye Your Baby With a Dixie Melody, Joe Young, Sam E Lewis & Jean Schwartz, Jerry Lewis photo cover, 1946 ....$5.00

Rose in Her Hair, Harry Warren & Al Dubin, Movie: Broadway Gondolier, Dick Powell photo cover, 1935 ....$8.00

Rudolph the Red-Nosed Reindeer, Johnny Marks, 1949 .$5.00

School Days, Will D Cobb & Gus Edwards, Movie: The Star Maker, Bing Crosby photo cover, Im-Ho cover artist, 1936 ....$10.00

Secret Love, Paul Francis & Sammy Fain, Movie; Calamity Jane, Doris Day & Howard Keel photo cover, 1953..........$5.00

Sewing Machine, Frank Loesser, Movie: The Perils of Pauline, Betty Hutton & John Lund photo cover, 1947.......$5.00

Shenanigans, Carl Sigman & William Whitlock, Irish, 1949.......................$5.00

Shoo-Shoo, Phil Moore, Movie: Beautiful But Broke, Andrews Sisters, 1943 ....$5.00

Since I Kissed My Baby Goodbye, Cole Porter, Movie: You'll Never Get Rich, 1941 ....$5.00

Sit Down You're Rocking the Boat, Jo Swerling, Abe Burrows & Frank Loesser, Musical: Guys & Dolls, 1950.......$5.00

Small Town Girl, Kahn, Stothart & Ward, Movie: same title, Robert Taylor & Janet Gayner photo cover, 1936 ..$10.00

So Long, It's Been Good To Know Yuh, Woody Guthrie, Don Cherry photo cover, 1950 ....$5.00

Some of These Days, Shelton Brooks, Sophie Tucker photo cover, Starmer cover artist, 1937.......................$15.00

Sometime Remind Me To Tell You, Leigh Harline, Movie: Station West, Dick Powell & Jane Greer photo cover, 1958.......................$5.00

Song of the South, Sam Coslow & Arthur Johnston, Movie: same title, Disney, 1946 ....$10.00

Sound of Music, Rodgers & Hammerstein II, Movie: same title, George Martin cover artist, 1959 ....$5.00

Stars & Stripes on Iwa Jima, Bob Wills & Cliff Johnson, Bob Wills photo cover, WWII, 1945.......................$10.00

String of Pearls, Jerry Gray, Movie: The Glenn Miller Story, James Stewart & June Allyson, 1954.......................$5.00

Stupid Girl, Mick Jagger & Keith Richards, Rolling Stones photo cover, 1966 ....$5.00

Sunday, Rodgers & Hammerstein II, Movie: Flower Drum Song, Nancy Kwan photo cover, 1961 ....$5.00

Sunflower, Mack David, 1948 ....$5.00

Sweet Violets, Cy Coben & Charles Grean, Dinah Shore photo cover, 1951 ....$5.00

Take It From There, Leo Robin & Ralph Rainger, Movie: Coney Island, Betty Grable photo cover, 1943.......$5.00

Tea For Two, Irving Ceasar & Otto Harbach, Movie: No No Nanette, Anna Neagle photo cover, 1940.................$5.00

Ten Pins in the Sky, Joseph McCarthy & Milton Ager, Movie: Listen Darling, 1938 ....$5.00

Tennessee Waltz, Redd Stewart & Pee Wee King, Wayne King photo cover, 1948 ....$5.00

Thanks a Million, Arthur Johnson & Gus Kahn, Movie: same title, Dick Powell photo cover, 1948 ....$5.00

That's All Brother, Mack David & Jerry Livingston, Kay Kyser photo cover, 1939 ....$5.00

There Is a Tavern in Town, Harry Henneman, 1942 ....$5.00

There Once Was a Man, Richard Alder & Jerry Ross, Musical: The Pajama Game, 1954.......................$5.00

There'll Always Be an England!, Ross Parker & Hughie Charles, 1939.......................$10.00

Thing, Charles R Grean, Phil Harris photo cover, 1950 ..$5.00

This Heart Is Mine, Freed & Warren, Movie: Ziegfeld Follies, Fred Astaire & Lucille Bremer photo cover, 1944 ..$8.00

This Is the Moment, Leo Robin & Fredrick Hollander, Movie: That Lady in Ermine, Betty Grable photo cover, 1948 ....$10.00

Till There Was You, Meredith Wilson, Movie: The Music Man, 1950.......................$5.00

Tomorrow Is Forever, Max Steiner & Charlie Tobias, Movie: same title, Claudette Colbert, 1945 ....$5.00

Tonight, Stephen Sondheim & Leonard Bernstein, Movie: West Side Story, 1957.......................$5.00

Too Good To Be True, Eliot Daniel & Buddy Kaye, Movie: Fun & Fancy Free, Disney, 1947 ....$10.00

Turntable Song, Robin & Green, Movie: Something in the Mind, Deanna Durbin photo cover, 1947 ....$5.00

Twist, Hank Ballard, 1959 ....$3.00

Very Good Advice, Bob Hilliard & Sammy Fain, Movie: Alice in Wonderland, Disney, 1951.......................$10.00

Volare, Mitchell Parish & Domenico Modungo, McGuire Sisters photo cover, 1958.......................$3.00

Waco, Blair & Haskell, Movie: same title, Jane Russell & Howard Keel photo cover, 1966.......................$5.00

Wait Until Dark, Livingston, Evans & Mancini, Movie: same title, Audrey Hepburn photo cover, 1967 ....$8.00

Watermelon Weather, Paul Francis & Hoagy Carmichael, Perry Como & Eddie Fisher photo cover, 1952......$5.00

We Open in Venice, Cole Porter, Musical: Kiss Me Kate, 1948.......................$5.00

What Did You Do in the Infantry, Frank Loesser, WWII, 1943.......................$5.00

What Is a Husband?, Gene Piller & Ruth Roberts, Steve Allen & Garry Moore photo cover, 1955.......................$5.00

When I Close My Eyes & Dream, Earl Abel, Rudy Vallee photo cover, Leff cover artist, 1930 ....$10.00

When I See an Elephant Fly, Oliver Wallace, Frank Churchill & Ned Washington, Movie: Dumbo, Disney, 1941.$10.00

When I Write My Song, Ted Mossman & Bill Anson, 1947..$5.00

When the Sun Comes Out, Ted Koeler & Harold Arlen, 1941.......................$3.00

When You Wish Upon a Star, Leigh Harline & Ned Washington, Movie: Pinocchio, Disney, 1940.......$10.00

Where the Mountains Meet the Moon, Remus Harris & Irving Melsher, 1940.......................$3.00

Who Can I Turn To?, Leslie Bricusse & Anthony Newley, 1964.......................$3.00

Who's Afraid of the Big Bad Wolf?, Ann Ronell & Frank Churchill, Mickey Mouse photo cover, 1934.........**$10.00**

Why Fight the Feeling, Frank Loesser, Movie: Let's Dance, Fred Astaire & Betty Hutton photo cover, 1950 ...**$10.00**

Why?, Bob Marcucci & Peter DeAngelis, Frankie Avalon signed photo cover, 1969 ....**$5.00**

Wish You Were Here, Harold Rome, Musical: same title, Slim Aarons cover artist, 1952 ....**$5.00**

Without You, Ray Gilbert, Osvaldo Farres, Movie: Make Mine Music, Disney, 1942......................................**$10.00**

Woody Woodpecker, George Tibbles & Ramey Idriss, 1947 ....**$5.00**

Yesterday, John Lennon & Paul McCartney, 1965.........**$5.00**

You Can't Win, Smalls, Movie: The Wiz, Diana Ross, Nipsey Russell, Ted Ross & Michael Jackson photo cover, 1975..**$10.00**

You Do, Mack Gordon & Joseph Myrow, Movie: Mother Wore Tights, Betty Grable & Dan Dailey photo cover, 1947..**$5.00**

You Gotta Be a Football Hero, Al Sherman, Buddy Fields & Al Lewis, Don Bestor photo cover, Sports, 1933..**$15.00**

You Know How Talk Gets Around, Fred Rose, Eddy Arnold photo cover, 1949 ....**$5.00**

You Won't Be Satisfied, Freddy James & Larry Stork, Perry Como photo cover, 1945 ....**$5.00**

You'll Always Be the One I Love, Sunny Skylar & Ticker Freeman, Movie: Song of the South, Disney, 1946 .**$10.00**

You're a Natural, Frank Loesser & Manning Sherwin, Movie: College Swing, 1938..**$5.00**

You've Got Something, Cole Porter, Movie: Red, Hot & Blue, 1936 ....**$10.00**

Yours, Mine & Ours, Sheldonn & Karlin, Movie: same title, Henry Fonda & Lucille Ball photo cover, 1968 ......**$8.00**

Shell Pink Glassware

Here's something relatively new to look for this year — lovely soft pink opaque glassware made by the Jeannette Glass Company for a short time during the late 1950s. Prices, says expert Gene Florence, have been increasing by leaps and bounds! You'll find a wide variance in style from piece to piece, since the company chose shapes from several of their most popular lines to press in the satiny shell pink. Refer to *Collectible Glassware from the 40s, 50s, and 60s,* by Mr. Florence for photos and more information.

Ashtray, butterfly shape...**$25.00**
Base, for Lazy Susan, w/ball bearings **$150.00**
Bowl, Florentine, footed, 10" **$30.00**
Bowl, Gondola, 17½" **$40.00**
Bowl, Holiday, footed, 10½"..**$45.00**
Bowl, Lombardi, design in center, 4-footed, 11" **$42.00**
Bowl, Napco #2250, w/berry design, footed...............**$15.00**
Bowl, Pheasant, footed, 8" **$37.50**
Bowl, Wedding, w/lid, 6½"..**$22.50**
Cake plate, Anniversary **$195.00**
Cake stand, Harp, 10"..**$45.00**

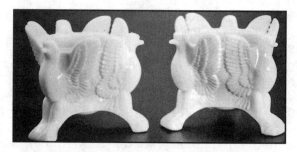

Candle holders, Eagle, $85.00 for the pair.

Candle holders, 2-light, pr **$45.00**
Candy dish, Floragold, 4-footed, 5¼".........................**$20.00**
Candy dish, square, w/lid, 6½" **$30.00**
Candy jar, Grapes, 4-footed, w/lid, 5½" **$20.00**
Candy jar bottom, National **$10.00**
Celery/relish, 3-part, 12½" **$45.00**
Cigarette box, butterfly finial **$225.00**
Comport, Napco #2256, square **$12.50**
Compote, Windsor, 6" **$20.00**
Cookie jar, w/lid, 6½" **$95.00**
Creamer, Baltimore Pear..**$15.00**
Cup, punch; 5-oz **$6.00**
Honey jar, beehive shape, notched lid **$40.00**
Pitcher, Thumbprint, footed, 24-oz **$2,750.00**
Pot, Napco #2249, crosshatch design..........................**$15.00**
Powder jar, w/lid, 4¾"...**$45.00**
Punch base, 3½"..**$45.00**
Punch bowl, 7½-qt..**$85.00**
Punch ladle, pink plastic..**$20.00**
Relish, Vineyard, octagonal, 4-part, 12" **$40.00**
Stem, sherbet; Thumbprint, 5-oz **$10.00**
Stem, water goblet; Thumbprint, 8-oz..........................**$12.50**
Sugar bowl, Baltimore Pear, footed, w/lid..................**$20.00**
Tray, Harp, 2-handled, 12½x9¾"..................................**$60.00**
Tray, Lazy Susan, 5-part, 13½".....................................**$75.00**
Tray, snack; w/cup indent, 7¾x10"................................**$9.00**
Tray, Venetian, 6-part, 16½"..**$40.00**
Tray, 5-part, 2 handles, 15¾"...**$75.00**
Tumbler, juice; Thumbprint, footed, 5-oz **$8.00**
Vase, cornucopia, 5" **$15.00**
Vase, heavy bottom, 9"..**$125.00**
Vase, 7" **$35.00**

Shirley Temple

Born April 23, 1928, Shirley Jane Temple danced and smiled her way into the hearts of America in the movie *Stand Up and Cheer*. Many successful roles followed and by the time Shirley was eight years old, she was #1 at box offices around the country. Her picture appeared in publications almost daily, and any news about her was news indeed. Mothers dressed their little daughters in clothing copied after hers and coiffed them with Shirley hairdos.

The extent of her success was mirrored in the unbeliev-able assortment of merchandise that saturated the retail market. Dolls, coloring books, children's clothing and jewelry, fountain pens, paper dolls, stationery, and playing cards are just a few examples of the hundreds of items that were available. Shirley's face was a common sight on the covers of magazines as well as in the advertisements they contained, and she was the focus of scores of magazine articles.

Though she had been retired from the movies for nearly a decade, she had two successful TV series in the late '50s, *The Shirley Temple Story-Book* and *The Shirley Temple Show.* Her reappearance caused new interest in some of the items that had been so popular during her childhood, and many were reissued.

Always interested in charity and community service, Shirley became actively involved in a political career in the late '60s, serving at both the state and national levels.

If you're interested in learning more about her, we recommend *Shirley Temple Dolls and Collectibles* by Patricia R. Smith; *Toys, Antique and Collectible,* by David Longest; and *Shirley in the Magazines* by Gen Jones.

Note: The pin-back button we describe below has been reproduced, so has the cobalt glassware with Shirley's likeness. Beware!

Advisor: Gen Jones (See Directory, Character and Personality Collectibles)

Newsletter: *Lollipop News*
P.O. Box 6203, Oxnard, CA 93031; Dues: $14 per year

Newsletter: *The Shirley Temple Collectors News*
8811 Colonial Rd., Brooklyn, NY 11209; Dues: $20 per year; checks payable to Rita Dubas

Ad sheet from Sears catalog, 1936, NM **$10.00**
Autograph, as adult, common **$10.00**
Barette, pink, NM...**$20.00**
Bath Drum, Kerk Guild, originally held Castille soap, cardboard w/Shirley in drum major hat, 4" dia, EX....**$75.00**
Book, Heidi, Random House, Shirley Temple edition, 1st printing, EX **$30.00**
Book, How I Raised Shirley Temple, 1935, EX..........**$25.00**
Book, Now I Am Eight, M **$32.00**
Book, Shirley Temple in The Little Colonel, Saalfield #1895, 1935, EX...**$30.00**
Book, Shirley Temple's Favorite Poems, hardcover, EX .**$45.00**
Book, Susannah of the Mounties, 1st Shirley Temple edition, 1936, EX...**$15.00**
Christmas card, Hallmark, 1935, M...........................**$30.00**
Coloring book, Little Princess, 1939, EX...................**$110.00**
Coloring book, Shirley Temple Crossing the Country, M, minimum value..**$35.00**
Doll, celluloid, Japan, 5", M.......................................**$185.00**
Doll, celluloid, Japan, 8", M.......................................**$245.00**
Doll, composition, 11", 1934 to late 1940s, M..........**$950.00**
Doll, composition, 13", M **$700.00**
Doll, composition, 16", open-close eyes, open-mouth smile, Germany, 1936, M, minimum value....................**$600.00**

Doll, composition, 17" to 18", Ideal, M, from $875 to ..**$950.00**
Doll, composition, 25", cowgirl, M **$1,500.00**
Doll, composition, 7" to 8", Japan, M **$245.00**
Doll, painted bisque w/molded hair, Japan, 6", M ...**$250.00**
Doll, plastic & vinyl, 1982-83, 8", M..........................**$30.00**
Doll, plastic & vinyl, 1982-83, 12", M........................**$40.00**
Doll, vinyl, 1950s, 12", M..**$225.00**
Doll, vinyl, 1950s, 15", M..**$265.00**
Doll, vinyl, 1950s, 17", M..**$325.00**
Doll, vinyl, 1950s, 19", M..**$400.00**
Doll, vinyl, 1950s, 36", M..**$1,600.00**
Doll, vinyl, 1972, Montgomery Ward, 17", M **$165.00**
Doll, vinyl, 1973, 6", M...**$125.00**
Fan, paper w/stick handle, shows teen photo & Royal Crown Cola advertising, 7", EX.......................................**$35.00**
Figurine, chalkware, 6", EX..**$185.00**
Figurine, chalkware, 12½", EX **$275.00**
Handkerchief, Little Colonel in corners, 1930s, M **$30.00**
Magic slate, Saalfield #8806, 1959, EX......................**$25.00**
Mug, portrait on cobalt glass, M.................................**$40.00**

Paper doll, Shirley Temple Standing Doll, Saalfield #1727, 1935, boxed set, minimum value, $60.00.

Paper dolls, Saalfield #1759, 1959, uncut, minimum value...**$25.00**
Pin-back button, My Friend Shirley Temple, face on red, 1930s **$35.00**
Plate, Baby Take a Bow...**$65.00**
Plate, Poor Little Rich Girl, MIB.................................**$40.00**
Pocket mirror, Shirley Temple as Heidi, 1937, NM **$35.00**
Poster, Susannah of the Mounties, 41x27", G............**$150.00**
Program, The Bachelor & the Bobby Soxer, 8 pages, NM...**$15.00**
Program, Tournament of Roses, 1939, 38 pages, EX ..**$20.00**
Ring, Club; face, sterling, 1930s, rare........................**$300.00**
Sheet music, The Good Ship Lollipop, NM **$15.00**
Tea set, pink & white w/floral design, serves 2, 1959, MIB, minimum value **$50.00**
Teddy bear, Bearly Temple, NM.................................**$50.00**
Writing tablet, Western, 1935, M................................**$40.00**

Shot Glasses

Shot glasses come in a wide variety of colors and designs. They're readily available, inexpensive, and they don't take a lot of room to display. Most sell for $5.00 and under, except cut glass, carnival glass, Depression glass, or pressed glass. Colored glass, those with etching or gold trim, or one that has an unusual shape — squared or barrel form, for instance — fall into a slightly higher range. Several advertising shot glasses, probably the most common type of all, are described in our listings. Soda advertising is unusual and may drive the value up to about $12.00 to $15.00.

Both new and older glasses alike sell for a little more in the Western part of the country. One-of-a-kind items or oddities are a bit harder to classify, especially sample glasses. Many depend on the elaborateness of their designs as opposed to basic lettering. These values are only estimates and should be used as a general guide. The club welcomes your suggestions and comments. For more information, we recommend *Shot Glasses: An American Tradition,* and *The Shot Glass Encyclopedia*, both by Mark Pickvet.

Note: Values for shot glasses in good condition are represented by the low end of our ranges, while the high end reflects estimated values for examples in mint condition.

Advisor: Mark Pickvet (See Directory, Shot Glasses)

Barrel shaped, from $5 to **$7.50**
Black porcelain replica, from $3.50 to **$5.00**
Carnival colors, plain or fluted, from $100 to **$150.00**
Carnival colors, w/patterns, from $125 to **$175.00**
Colored glass tourist, from $4 to **$6.00**
Culver 22k gold, from $6 to...**$8.00**
Depression, colors, from $10 to **$12.50**
Depression, colors w/patterns or etching, from $17.50 to ..**$25.00**
Depression, tall, general designs, from $10 to **$12.50**
Depression, tall, tourist, from $5 to..............................**$7.50**
Frosted w/gold designs, from $6 to **$8.00**
General, advertising, from $4 to **$6.00**
General, etched designs, from $5 to **$7.50**
General, porcelain, from $4 to..**$6.00**
General, w/enameled design, from $3 to **$4.00**
General, w/frosted designs, from $3.50 to....................**$5.00**
General, w/gold designs, from $6 to **$8.00**
General tourist, from $3 to..**$4.00**
Inside eyes, from $5 to...**$7.50**
Iridized silver, from $5 to..**$7.50**
Mary Gregory or Anchor Hocking Ships, from $150 to ..**$200.00**
Nudes, from $25 to...**$35.00**
Plain, w/or w/out flutes, from 75¢ to **$1.00**
Pop or soda advertising, from $12.50 to.....................**$15.00**
Porcelain tourist, from $3.50 to......................................**$5.00**
Rounded European designs w/gold rims, from $4 to...**$6.00**
Ruby flashed, from $35 to...**$50.00**
Sayings & toasts, 1940s-50s, from $5 to **$7.50**
Sports, professional teams, from $5 to.........................**$7.50**
Square, general, from $6 to...**$8.00**
Square, w/etching, from $10 to **$12.50**
Square, w/pewter, from $12.50 to **$15.00**
Square, w/2-tone bronze & pewter, from $15 to **$17.50**
Standard glass w/pewter, from $7.50 to.......................**$10.00**
Steuben crystal, from $150 to **$200.00**

Taiwan tourist, from $2 to...**$3.00**

Take a Shot, chrome finish, four shots contained in each bullet, marked variously Japan or USA, from $25.00 to $30.00 for each set. (Photo courtesy Steven Visakay)

Tiffany, Galle or fancy art, from $600 to **$800.00**
Turquoise & gold tourist, from $6 to **$8.00**
Whiskey or beer advertising, modern, from $5 to........**$7.50**
Whiskey sample glasses, from $30 to **$250.00**
19th-century cut patterns, from $35 to........................**$50.00**

Silhouette Pictures

These novelty pictures are familiar to everyone. Even today a good number of them are still around, and you'll often see them at flea markets and co-ops. They were very popular in their day and never expensive, and because they were made for so many years (the '20s through the '50s), many variations are available. Though the glass in some is flat, in others it is curved. Backgrounds may be foil, a scenic print, hand tinted, or plain. Sometimes dried flowers were added as accents. But the characteristic common to them all is that the subject matter is reverse painted on the glass. People (even complicated groups), scenes, ships, and animals were popular themes. Though quite often the silhouette was done in solid black to create a look similar to the nineteenth-century cut silhouettes, colors were sometimes used as well.

In the '20s, making tinsel art pictures became a popular pastime. Ladies would paint the outline of their subjects on the back of the glass and use crumpled tinfoil as a background. Sometimes they would tint certain areas of the glass, making the foil appear to be colored. This type is popular with with collectors of folk art.

If you'd like to learn more about this subject, we recommend *The Encyclopedia of Silhouette Collectibles on Glass* and *1996 – 97 Price Guide for Encyclopedia of Silhouette Collectibles on Glass* by Shirley Mace. These books show examples of Benton Glass pictures with frames made of metal, wood, plaster, and plastic. The metal frames with the stripes are most favored by collectors as long as they are in good condition. Wood frames were actually considered deluxe when silhouettes were originally sold. Recently some convex glass silhouettes from Canada have been found, nearly identical to the ones made by Benton Glass except for their brown tape frames. Backgrounds seem to be slightly different as well. Among the flat glass silhouettes, the ones signed by Diefenbach are the most expensive. The wildflower pictures, especially ones with fine lines and good detail, are becoming popular with collectors.

Advisor: Shirley Mace (See Directory, Silhouette Pictures)

Convex Glass

Child plays w/cat while mother watches, BG 68-7B, Benton Glass Company **$60.00**
Couple putting final touches on snowman, BG 45-159, Benton Glass Company....................................**$45.00**
Couple sit while having drinks, BG 68-29, Benton Glass Company **$40.00**
Horse & rider jumping fence, BG 68-198, Benton Glass Company **$40.00**
Indian chief stands w/horse overlooking wagon train in valley, BG 45-203, Benton Glass Company..............**$35.00**
Kittens (2) watch baby ducks enter water, BG 45-191, Benton Glass Company **$30.00**
Lady looks upon well on hill, BG 45-182, Benton Glass Company **$30.00**
Lady playing piano, BG 45-172, Benton Glass Company .**$30.00**
Lady w/parasol, plate, BI 9D-1, Bilderback's Inc, 9" dia...**$35.00**
Man & boy in sailor suits look at sunset over ocean, BG 45-122, Benton Glass Company....................................**$35.00**
Man sits blowing bubbles from long pipe w/boy watches, BG 45-118, Benton Glass Company **$35.00**
Man smoking pipe & reading newspaper, BG 45-15, Benton Glass Company **$25.00**
Man standing in fishing boat w/boy & dog, BG 45-212, Benton Glass Company....................................**$28.00**
Mother & son w/Dearest Mother poem in upper corner, BG 68-129, Benton Glass Company....................**$35.00**
Scottie dog barks at bird on fence, BG 45-185, Benton Glass Company **$30.00**
Scottie dog chases butterfly, BG 45-186, Benton Glass Company **$30.00**
Scout on hill overlooks passing wagon train, BG 45-204, Benton Glass Company....................................**$30.00**
Snowland Splender, BA 45-2, advertising, Baco Glass Plaque....................................**$30.00**
This Little Piggy, baby plays w/toes, BG 68-100, Benton Glass Company **$38.00**
Woman shoots bow & arrow while man looks on, BG 45-77, Benton Glass Company....................................**$30.00**

Flat Glass

Boy fishing while flock of geese fly overhead, NE 5½ 7½-1, Newton Manufacturing..**$30.00**
Child says prayers at bedside w/dog, MF 34-37, unknown manufacturer....................................**$20.00**

Colonial Lady, plate, Harker, ca 1930s........................**$45.00**
Couple embrace, FL 3½ 3½-3, Flowercraft.................**$40.00**
Courtship, RE 44-83, Reliance Products **$22.00**
Cowboy on horse looks out over canyon, 'Souvenir-Yellowstone Park, Wyoming-Hayes, Inc,' NE 45-19, Newton Manufacturing **$25.00**
Elfin Music, RI 57-760, C&A Richards **$140.00**
Gallant, man bows for lady as they cross paths, DE 45-25, Deltex Products Company............................**$38.00**
Girl w/3 ducks under tree on a windy day, DE 921-11, Deltex Products Company............................**$30.00**
Good Night, couple at gate kissing, BB 46-2, Buckbee-Brehm Company **$24.00**
Hidden Pond, plaster, 2 nude ladies take a swim, BB 68-10, Buckbee-Brehm Company **$20.00**
Homeward Bound, sailing ship, RE 45-112 ....**$15.00**
Kittens (2) watch butterfly, BH 48-1, unknown manufacturer....................................**$8.00**
Lady dancing w/musicians & other dancers in background, BB 710-26, Buckbee-Brehm Company.................**$30.00**
Lady standing on stool lighting candles on fireplace mantel, AP 810-20, Art Publishing Company **$25.00**
Little girl watching bird w/Mother poem underneath, VO 711-1, PF Volland....................................**$50.00**
Love Letter, plaster, lady at desk kissing letter, BB46-3, Buckbree-Brehm Company **$23.00**
Out Where the West Begins, 2 cowboys having coffee at campfire w/horses in background, NE 810-4, Newton Manufacturing **$28.00**
Robin, RE 710-22, Reliance Products, NRA stamp 12-33..**$22.00**
Swan pond, RE 711-2, Reliance Products **$30.00**

Untitled, RF 5D-7, with wood frame, 5" diameter, $20.00. (Photo courtesy Shirley and Ray Mace)

Silverplated and Sterling Flatware

The secondary market is being tapped more and more as the only source for those replacement pieces needed to augment family heirloom sets, and there are many collectors who admire the vintage flatware simply because they appreciate its beauty, quality, and affordability. Several factors influence pricing. For instance, a popular pattern though plentiful may be more expensive than a scarce one that might be passed over because it very likely would be difficult to collect. When you buy silverplate, condition is very important, since replating can be expensive.

Pieces with no monograms are preferred. To evaluate monogrammed items, deduct 20% from fancy or rare examples; 30% from common, plain items; and 50% to 70% if they are worn.

Dinner knives range in size from 9⅜" to 10"; dinner forks from 7⅜" to 7¾". Luncheon knives are approximately 8½" to 8¾", while luncheon forks are about 6¾" to 7". Place knives measure 8⅞" to 9¼", and place forks 7⅛" to 7¼".

Our values are given for flatware in excellent condition. Matching services often advertise in various trade papers and can be very helpful in locating items. One of the best sources we are aware of is *The Antique Trader*, they're listed with the trade papers in the back of this book.

If you'd like to learn more about the subject, we recommend *The Standard Encyclopedia of American Silverplate,* by Frances M. Bones and Lee Roy Fisher, and *Silverplated Flatware, Revised Fourth Edition,* by Tere Hagan (both published by Collector Books).

Advisor: Rick Spencer (See Directory, Regal)

Silverplate

Adoration, 1939, place set, International, 40-pc........**$145.00**
Adoration, 1939, wood box, 2-drawer, International, from $20 to..**$40.00**
Adoration, 1939, wooden box, single lid, International, from $15 to..**$25.00**
Affection, baby spoon/fork, Community Plate............**$15.00**
Affection, feeding spoon, Community Plate.................**$8.00**
Affection, fruit spoon, Community Plate......................**$8.00**
Assyrian Head, cheese scoop, hollow handle...........**$195.00**
Assyrian Head, 1886, crumber, engraved, 1847 Rogers .**$150.00**
Assyrian Head, 1886, demitasse spoon, 1847 Rogers .**$18.00**
Assyrian Head, 1886, dinner fork, 1847 Rogers **$20.00**
Assyrian Head, 1886, gravy tureen, oval, covered, 1847 Rogers..**$395.00**
Assyrian Head, 1886, soup ladle, 1847 Rogers, med ..**$150.00**
Baroque Rose, 1967, steak knife, Oneida...................**$12.00**
Baroque Rose, 1967, youth set, Oneida, 3-pc.............**$22.00**
Bridal Wreath, 1950, dinner setting, Oneida, 4-pc......**$15.00**
Bridal Wreath, 1950, oval soup, Oneida......................**$5.00**
Bridal Wreath, 1950, tomato server, Oneida..............**$22.00**
Classic Filigree, 1937, gravy ladle, Wallace..............**$14.00**
Classic Filigree, 1937, teaspoon, Wallace...................**$4.00**
Diana, 1910, berry spoon, Alvin................................**$28.00**
Diana, 1910, bouillon spoon, Alvin.............................**$6.00**
Diana, 1910, teaspoon, Alvin......................................**$6.00**
Esperanto, 1967, oval soup, 1847 Rogers....................**$5.00**
Esperanto, 1967, pierced pie server, 1847 Rogers.......**$12.00**
Esperanto, 1967, viande knife, 1847 Rogers................**$5.00**
Flair, 1956, bonbon dish, International......................**$15.00**
Flair, 1956, dinner setting, International, 4-pc............**$27.00**
Flair, 1956, serving dish, International, 9x13"............**$80.00**
Flair, 1956, tray, oval, International............................**$55.00**

Flair, 1956, water pitcher, International....................**$125.00**
Garland, 1965, dinner set, 1847 Rogers, 60-pc, serves 12...**$250.00**
Garland, 1965, master butter, 1847 Rogers..................**$6.00**
Garland, 1965, sugar spoon, 1847 Rogers....................**$6.00**
Garland, 1965, tablespoon, 1847 Rogers......................**$8.00**
Heraldic, 1916, cheese knife, hollow handle, 1847 Rogers..**$25.00**
Heraldic, 1916, ice cream fork, 1847 Rogers..............**$16.00**
Heraldic, 1916, ice cream spoon, 1847 Rogers...........**$12.00**
Heraldic, 1916, pickle fork, long handle, 1847 Rogers .**$16.00**
Interlude, 1971, fruit spoon, International....................**$8.00**
Interlude, 1971, tablespoon, pierced, International.....**$12.00**
Interlude, 1971, trowel/pastry server, International, lg .**$25.00**
Joan, 1898, beef fork, Wallace..................................**$24.00**
Joan, 1898, ice cream fork, Wallace..........................**$24.00**
Joan, 1898, salad fork, Wallace.................................**$15.00**
Joan, 1898, soup ladle, Wallace................................**$80.00**
Joan, 1898, sugar tongs, Wallace..............................**$22.00**
King, 1890s to present, crumb knife (many manufacturers)..**$75.00**
King, 1890s to present, dinner fork (many manufacturers) ...**$10.00**
King, 1890s to present, teaspoon (many manufacturers) **$8.00**
Legacy, 1928, iced teaspoon, International..................**$6.00**
Legacy, 1928, salad set, olive wood, International......**$65.00**
Legacy, 1928, viande fork, International.......................**$6.00**
Legacy, 1928, viande knife, International.....................**$6.00**
Modern Baroque, 1969, baby fork, Oneida.................**$12.00**
Modern Baroque, 1969, fish knife, Oneida.................**$10.00**
Modern Baroque, 1969, youth set, Oneida, 3-pc........**$22.00**
Morning Glory, 1954, gravy ladle, Wallace................**$14.00**
Morning Glory, 1954, sugar spoon, Wallace................**$4.00**
Narcissus, 1935, cocktail fork, National......................**$5.00**
Narcissus, 1935, dinner set, National, 40-pc.............**$140.00**
New Century, 1898, cake serving fork, International..**$20.00**
New Century, 1898, gumbo soup, International..........**$10.00**
Olive, 1850s on, nut pick, 1847 Rogers.......................**$4.00**
Orange Blossom, 1910, fruit spoon..............................**$4.00**
Orange Blossom, 1910, youth fork.............................**$16.00**
Orange Blossom, 1910, youth knife............................**$14.00**
Pickwick, 1938, dinner fork, International....................**$6.00**
Pickwick, 1938, dinner knife, International...................**$6.00**
Queen Bess, 1946, candlestick, 2-light, pr................**$165.00**
Queen Bess, 1946, luncheon setting, 4-pc.................**$14.00**
Reverie, 1937, cream soup spoon, Nobility Plate.........**$5.00**
Reverie, 1937, roast carving set, Nobility Plate, 3-pc ..**$50.00**
Romance II, 1952, pie server, hollow handle, Holmes & Edwards..**$18.00**
Romance II, 1952, sugar tongs, Holmes & Edwards...**$20.00**
Romance II, 1952, tomato server, Holmes & Edwards..**$28.00**
Romance II, 1952, viande setting, Holmes & Edwards, 4-pc..**$15.00**
Rosemont, 1930, bouillon spoon, Gorham.................**$10.00**
Rosemont, 1930, fruit knife, hollow handle, Gorham.**$16.00**
Rosemont, 1930, luncheon knife, Gorham....................**$8.00**
Sierra, 1914, demitasse spoon, Reed & Barton............**$5.00**
Sierra, 1914, sauce ladle, Reed & Barton...................**$13.00**
Sierra, 1914, tablespoon, Reed & Barton.....................**$9.00**
Silver Arbor, individual butter spreader, Oneida..........**$4.00**

Silver Arbor, place fork, Oneida $6.00
Silver Arbor, teaspoon, Oneida.................................$3.00
Spring Charm, 1950, berry spoon, Wm Rogers $12.00
Spring Charm, 1950, desert server, pierced, Wm Rogers ..$10.00
Spring Charm, 1950, dinner setting, Wm Rogers, 4-pc.$16.00
Twilight, 1956, cocktail fork, Oneida $5.00
Twilight, 1956, dinner setting, Oneida, 4-pc $16.00
Twilight, 1956, sugar spoon, Oneida $6.00
Vanessa, 1968, demitasse spoon, Wm A Rogers...........$4.00
Vanessa, 1968, dinner setting, Wm A Rogers, 5-pc.....$25.00
Vanessa, 1968, iced teaspoon, Wm A Rogers $8.00
Vanessa, 1968, soup spoon, oval, Wm A Rogers..........$5.00
Violet, 1905, dinner fork, SL & GH Rogers................$12.00
Violet, 1905, dinner knife, hollow handle, SL & GH
    Rogers $24.00
Wisteria, 1966, jelly server, Reed & Barton................$12.00
Wisteria, 1966, master butter spreader, Reed & Barton...$8.00
Wood Song, 1958, cold meat fork, Holmes & Edwards..$12.00
Wood Song, 1958, pastry fork, Holmes & Edwards $6.00

Sterling

American Classic, jelly server, Easterling.....................$25.00
American Classic, luncheon setting, Easterling, 4-pc ..$65.00
American Classic, tablespoon, Easterling.....................$45.00
Aspen, place fork, Gorham...$22.00
Aspen, place knife, Gorham $20.00
Aspen, sugar spoon, Gorham $18.00
Bell Rose, bonbon server, Oneida...............................$20.00
Belle Rose, place setting, Oneida, 4-pc $60.00
Cascade, iced teaspoon, Towle $22.00
Cascade, luncheon setting, Towle, 4-pc......................$60.00
Cascade, relish scoop, Towle.....................................$25.00
Chapel Bells, cream soup spoon, Alvin $16.00
Chapel Bells, individual butter spreader, hollow handle,
    Alvin..$18.00
Chapel Bells, luncheon set, Alvin, 48-pc $725.00
Chapel Bells, olive spoon, Alvin $35.00
Chapel Bells, tablespoon, pierced, Alvin $42.00
Colonial Theme, individual butter spreader, hollow handle,
    Lunt..$18.00
Colonial Theme, sugar spoon, Lunt $22.00
Courtship, butter pick, International $26.00
Courtship, candlesticks, 3-light, International, pr......$175.00
Courtship, cheese scoop, International........................$26.00
Decor, ice cream fork, Gorham $30.00
Decor, place setting, Gorham, 4-pc.............................$125.00
Enchanting Orchid, black plastic salad set, Westmoreland $50.00
Enchanting Orchid, demitasse spoon, Westmoreland.$14.00
Enchanting Orchid, gravy ladle, Westmoreland $42.00
Enchanting Orchid, place setting, Westmoreland, 4-pc...$62.00
French Provincial, cream soup spoon, Towle $28.00
French Provincial, dinner setting, Towle, 4-pc.........$110.00
French Provincial, individual butter spreader, flat handle,
    Towle $24.00
French Provincial, mustard ladle, Towle....................$29.00
French Provincial, ramekin fork, Towle......................$26.00

French Provincial, strawberry fork, Towle.................$24.00
Golden Scroll, 1977, cocktail fork, Gorham $30.00
Golden Scroll, 1977, place setting, Gorham, 4-pc.....$170.00
Golden Scroll, 1977, place spoon, Gorham.................$45.00
Inaugural, gravy ladle, State House............................$42.00
Inaugural, grill set, State House, 4-pc.........................$49.00
Inaugural, ice cream fork, State House.......................$20.00
Inaugural, soup spoon, oval, State House $24.00
Inaugural, sugar spoon, State House...........................$20.00
Inaugural, tablespoon, State House.............................$39.00
Joan of Arc, gumbo soup, International $36.00
Joan of Arc, luncheon set, International, 4-pc............$92.00
Lyric, cream soup, Gorham...$19.00
Lyric, fruit spoon, Gorham...$21.00
Lyric, luncheon set, Gorham, 4-pc..............................$66.00
Margaret Rose, berry spoon, National $50.00
Margaret Rose, luncheon set, National, 4-pc $50.00
Margaret Rose, youth set, National.............................$50.00
Monte Cristo, place setting, Towle, 4-pc.....................$80.00
Monte Cristo, place spoon, Towle...............................$28.00
Monte Cristo, tablespoon, Towle.................................$45.00
Nocturne, lemon fork, Gorham $20.00
Nocturne, luncheon fork, Gorham $18.00
Nocturne, master butter spreader, flat handle, Gorham..$20.00
Nocturne, steak carving set, Gorham, 2-pc $55.00
Nocturne, teaspoon, Gorham......................................$12.00
Prelude, hooded asparagus server, International $240.00
Prelude, lobster pick, International $28.00
Prelude, place set, International, 60-pc $1,050.00
Prelude, sauce ladle, International $24.00
Rose Elegance, soup spoon, oval, Lunt.......................$28.00
Rose Solitaire, bonbon server, Towle.........................$30.00
Savannah, cold meat fork, Reed & Barton..................$65.00
Tranquility, berry spoon, Fine Arts.............................$60.00
Tranquility, pie/cake server, Fine Arts $30.00
Tranquility, salad fork, Fine Arts $19.00
Victoria, cheese scoop, Frank Whiting........................$24.00
Victoria, luncheon set, Frank Whiting, 4-pc $60.00
Waltz of Spring, cold meat fork, Wallace....................$70.00
Waltz of Spring, demitasse spoon, Wallace.................$20.00
Waltz of Spring, place setting, Wallace, 4-pc.............$105.00
Winslow, lemon fork, Kirk...$28.00
Winslow, luncheon setting, Kirk, 4-pc $90.00
Young Love, olive fork, Oneida $19.00
Young Love, place setting, Oneida, 4-pc.....................$59.00
Young Love, sauce ladle, Oneida................................$24.00

Skookum Indian Dolls

The Skookums Apple Packers Association of Wenatchee, Washington, had a doll made from their trademark. Skookum figures were designed and registered by a Montana woman, Mary McAboy, in 1917. Although she always made note of the Skookum's name, she also used the 'Bully Good' trademark along with other information to inform the buyer that 'Bully Good' translated is 'Skookums.' McAboy had an article published in the March 1920 issue of *Playthings* magazine explaining the history of Skookum dolls. Anyone interested can obtain this information on microfilm from any large library.

In 1920 the Arrow Novelty Company held the contract to make the dolls, but by 1929 the H.H. Tammen Company had taken over their production. Skookums were designed with life-like facial characteristics. The dried apple heads of the earliest dolls did not last, and they were soon replaced with heads made of a composition material. Wool blankets formed the bodies that were then stuffed with dried twigs, leaves, and grass. The remainder of the body was cloth and felt.

Skookum dolls with wooden legs and felt-covered wooden feet were made between 1917 and 1949. After 1949 the legs and feet were made of plastic. The newest dolls have plastic heads. A 'Skookums Bully Good Indians' paper label was placed on one foot of each early doll. Exact dating of a Skookum is very difficult. McAboy designed many different tribes of dolls simply by using different blanket styles, beading, and backboards (for carrying the papoose).

Advisor: Jo Ann Palmieri (See Directory, Skookum Dolls)

Child, plastic legs, 6" to 8", from $35 to **$50.00**
Child, plastic legs, 8" to 10", from $50 to **$75.00**
Female w/papoose, wooden legs, 14" to 16", from $250 to.**$300.00**
Female w/papoose, wooden legs, 10" to 12", from $150 to.**$200.00**
Female w/papoose, wooden legs, 8" to 10", from $75 to.....**$150.00**
Male, wooden legs, 10 to 12", from $175 to **$250.00**
Male, wooden legs, 14" to 16", from $300 to **$4.00**
Male, wooden legs, 8" to 10", from $100 to............**$175.00**

Soda-Pop Memorabilia

A specialty area of the advertising field, soft-drink memorabilia is a favorite of many collectors. Now that vintage Coca-Cola items have become rather expensive, interest is expanding to include some of the less widely known sodas — Grapette, Hires Root Beer, and Dr. Pepper, for instance.

If you want more pricing information, we recommend *Huxford's Collectible Advertising* by Sharon and Bob Huxford (Collector Books).

See also Coca-Cola; Pepsi-Cola.

Advisors: Craig and Donna Stifter (See Directory, Soda-Pop Memorabilia)

Newsletter: National Pop Can Collectors
5417 Midvale Dr. #4
Rockford, IL 61108-2325; Send for free information

Ashtray, Seven-Up, glass, square w/rounded corners, decorative border around logo in center, G.................**$15.00**
Bill hook, Seven-Up, celluloid button, I'd Hang For A Chilled 7-Up, EX+...**$35.00**
Bottle topper, Dr Pepper, diecut cardboard, pictures Edith Luce, NM...**$32500**

Bottle topper, Royal Crown Cola, cardboard, Santa in wreath w/bottle, EX **$20.00**
Calendar, A-Treat Beverages, 1959, complete, EX......**$85.00**
Calendar, Dr Pepper, 1951, complete, EX+ **$200.00**
Calendar, Kist Beverages, 1946, complete, NM+.......**$185.00**
Calendar, Mission Beverages, 1953, complete, 25x14", NM **$125.00**
Calendar, Seven-Up, 1953, complete, EX+...................**$75.00**
Clock, Nehi, round w/glass front, metal frame, Drink Nehi Orange & Other Flavors on yellow dot, 15" dia, NM................**$325.00**
Dislay, Seven-Up, bottle embedded in glass iceberg, 1940s-50s, 9x7x8", NM.......................................**$375.00**
Dispenser, Orange-Crush, ribbed glass bowl on round aluminum base, diamond logo, porcelain top w/aluminum pump, EX+..**$425.00**
Distance chart, Nesbitt's, cardboard w/steel frame, shows distance from central point to US cities, 1955, 31x7", EX+..**$50.00**
Door pull, Kist Beverages, advertising on backplate w/black handle, EX+.......................................**$115.00**
Fan pull, Dr Pepper, cardboard, beach girl w/umbrella, G..**$100.00**
Menu board, Mission Beverages, cardboard, Mission of California, menu slots flanking bottle & fruit, 13x32", NM...**$100.00**
Mug, Hires, ceramic barrel shape, Drink Hires Root Beer lettered above pointing Hires Boy, Mettlach, 4", EX+ **$250.00**
Picnic cooler, Royal Crown Cola, metal box w/locking handle, red embossed lettering on yellow, 20x18x12", EX...**$165.00**
Recipe book, Hires, EX **$65.00**
Sign, Donald Duck Cola, diecut cardboard standup, Tops For Flavour, bottle cap & hand-held bottle in ice, 1950s, 26", NM..**$150.00**
Sign, Dr Pepper, porcelain, round w/Drink Dr Pepper & 10-2-5 on red, white & red background, 10" dia, NM.**$700.00**
Sign, Grapette, porcelain, oval, Grapette Soda/Imitation Grape Flavor, red, white & blue, 10x17", EX **$300.00**
Sign, Kist Beverages, tin bottle cap shape, Kist/The Drinks w/Real Flavor, red, white & blue, dated 6-59, 15" dia, EX+..**$180.00**
Sign, Nehi, embossed tin, Nehi Quality Beverages lettered below on white, 1940s, 20x6", EX...................**$125.00**
Sign, Nesbitt's, cardboard, Drink Nesbitt's California Orange on disk upper right of family barbecue, 1940s, 24x36", EX+..**$250.00**
Sign, Royal Crown Cola, tin bottle shape, 1952, 60", NM...**$375.00**
Sign, Seven-Up, tin, You Like 7-Up/It Likes You on red oval w/bubbles, white raised rolled rim, 1947, 40x30", VG+...**$150.00**
Stamp holder, Orange-Crush, celluloid book shape, ...Pure Sugar Beverages, Whitehead & Hoag, 1x1", EX.**$90.00**
Thermometer, Grapette, tin, Remember To Buy..., bottle next to gauge, 15", EX..**$125.00**
Thermometer, Royal Crown Cola, tin, red w/yellow arrow pointing up, 1960s, 26", NM...............................**$275.00**
Tie clip, Seven-Up, enameled logo on bar, EX..........**$15.00**

Tray, NuGrape, A Flavor You Can't Forget, oval image of hand-held bottle, rectangular, 13x11", VG **$75.00**
Wall lamps, Bireley's, bottle-shaped glass lamps painted orange w/embossed name, silver spiral brackets, 12", EX, pr **$800.00**

Sign, Orange-Crush, masonite, 1940s, 18x48, $400.00. (Photo courtesy Craig and Donna Stifter)

Soda Bottles With Painted Labels

The earliest type of soda bottles were made by soda producers and sold in the immediate vicinity of the bottling company. Many had pontil scars, left by a rod that was used to manipulate the bottle as it was blown. They had a flat bottom rather than a 'kick-up,' so for transport, they were laid on their side and arranged in layers. This served to keep the cork moist, which kept it expanded, tight, and in place. Upright the cork would dry out, shrink, and expel itself with a 'pop,' hence the name 'soda pop.'

Until the '30s, the name of the product or the bottler was embossed in the glass or printed on a paper label (sometimes pasted over reused returnable bottles). Though a few paper labels were used as late as the '60s, nearly all bottles produced from the mid-'30s on had painted-on (pyro-glazed) lettering, and logos and pictures were often added. Imaginations ran rampant. Bottlers waged a fierce competition to make their soda logos eye catching and sales inspiring. Anything went! Girls, airplanes, patriotic designs, slogans proclaiming amazing health benefits, even cowboys and Indians became popular advertising ploys. This is the type you'll encounter most often today, and collector interest is on the increase. Look for interesting, multicolored labels, rare examples from small-town bottlers, and those made from glass in colors other than clear or green. If you'd like to learn more about them, we recommend *The Official Guide to Collecting Applied Color Label Soda Bottles* by Thomas E. Marsh.

Advisor: Thomas Marsh, Painted-Label Soda Bottles (See Directory, Soda-Pop Collectibles)

American Beverages, clear glass, 12-oz **$10.00**
Big Chief, clear glass, any size **$20.00**

Big Red, clear glass, 10-oz...**$10.00**
Big Ten, clear glass, 10-oz...**$10.00**
Brown Cow, clear glass, Dyersburg TN, 8-oz **$15.00**
Chex, green glass, 7-oz..**$10.00**
Cleo Cola, green glass w/out belly button, 12-oz.....**$150.00**
Cott Nectar Beverages, clear glass, 12-oz **$15.00**
Diamond Beverage, clear glass, 7-oz **$10.00**
Dr Pepper, clear glass, 10-oz......................................**$45.00**
Five Points, green glass, 1-qt......................................**$15.00**
Frost King, clear glass, 7-oz..**$45.00**
Harris, green glass, 12-oz..**$20.00**
Icy, clear glass, 10-oz..**$15.00**
Kik, clear glass, 12-oz...**$25.00**
Life, green glass, 10-oz..**$10.00**
Mission Beverage, clear glass, 1-qt.............................**$15.00**
Mosso's, green glass, 1-qt..**$15.00**
Nugget, clear glass, 12-oz **$15.00**
Pepsi-Cola, clear glass, 1-qt **$25.00**
Plantation, green glass, 7-oz..**$10.00**
Quench, green glass, 8-oz..**$15.00**
Royal Palm, clear glass, 6-oz......................................**$15.00**
Sandy's, clear glass, 10-oz...**$10.00**
Seven-Up, green glass, 7-oz...**$15.00**
Ski-Club, clear glass, 7-oz...**$15.00**
Solo, clear glass, 12-oz..**$25.00**
Sterling, clear glass, 7-oz...**$10.00**
Tea-Cola, clear glass, 6½-oz..**$15.00**
Up Town, green glass, 1-qt..**$15.00**
Virginia Bell, clear glass, 10-oz...................................**$20.00**
Walker's Root Beer, amber glass, Melrose MA, 1953, 1-qt..**$125.00**
Zeps Sparkling Pale Dry Ginger Ale, green glass, 1-qt.........**$20.00**

Sporting Goods

Catalogs and various ephemera distributed by sporting good manufacturers, ammunition boxes, and just about any other item used for hunting and fishing purposes are collectible. In fact, there are auctions devoted entirely to collectors with these interests.

One of the most best-known companies specializing in merchandise of this kind was the gun manufacturer, The Winchester Repeating Arms Company. After 1931, their mark was changed from Winchester Trademark USA to Winchester-Western. Remington, Ithaca, Peters, and Dupont are other manufacturers whose goods are especially sought after.

Advisor: Kevin R. Bowman (See Directory, Sports Collectibles)

Ad sheet, Iver Johnson's 410 double, 6x3" (double sided), EX..**$20.00**
Ashtray, Winchester Western, black glass, 3½", M......**$25.00**
Badge, employee's; Remington, Denver ordnance plant, picture of lady, EX..**$40.00**
Book, Gunsmith Kinks, by Frank Brownell, hardback w/dust jacket, 1981, 496 pages, EX...................................**$15.00**
Book, Main Street Pocket Guide to American Longarms, by Michael Madaus, paperback, 1981, 255 pages, M.**$10.00**

Book, Modern Fishing Tackle, by Vlad Evanoff, 1961, 211 pages, hardback w/dust jacket, EX **$15.00**

Book, Nosler Reloading Manual, #1, hardback, 1976, 222 pages, EX **$20.00**

Book, Olt's Hunting Handbook, by Bert Popowski, hardback w/no dust jacket, 1st edition, 1948, 167 pages, EX .. **$25.00**

Book, Sport Fishing Boats, by Kip Farrington Jr, 1949, 154 pages, hardback w/poor dust jacket **$15.00**

Book, Trapshooting & Skeet, by Jimmy Robinson, hardback w/faded cover, 1942, 224 pages, EX **$20.00**

Booklet, Al Foss's pork rind minnows, 14 pages, 3x4", EX **$45.00**

Booklet, Browning models, 1939, fold-out, opens to 24x12", EX **$30.00**

Booklet, Du Pont, Brush Stubble & Marsh, early, G, $75.00. (Photo courtesy Kevin Bowman)

Booklet, history of deer in Nebraska in 1957, 37 pages, 6x9", VG **$10.00**

Booklet, Peters Cartridges, What Happens After the Shot Is Fired?, 1928, rare, 5x8", EX **$35.00**

Box, Browning shotshells, 20 gauge, #2 shot, 3", 45 power shells, G **$25.00**

Box, shell; Winchester Bicentennial, 30-30 cal, M **$25.00**

Box, shotshell; Western Xpert, miniature, EX **$8.00**

Call, coon preditor; Thomas, MIB **$15.00**

Call, deer; Faulk's D-50, MIB (w/display box) **$20.00**

Call, goose; Sure Shot #950, MIB **$30.00**

Call, quail; Herter's, MIB **$30.00**

Call, turkey; Winchester, XX magnum by Ray Eye, limited edition, M (plastic box) **$30.00**

Call, turkey; Olt #F-6, MIB **$25.00**

Catalog, Remington Small Cartridges, game boxes on inside front cover, 1922, 56 pages, 6x3½", EX **$70.00**

Catalog, South Bend, Fish & Feel It, 1942, 136 pages (50+ color pages), 5x6", EX **$60.00**

Clay target thrower, Allison-Faulkner Corp, sm **$35.00**

Ear plugs, Savage Arms Inc, soft foam, MIP **$5.00**

Golf ball, Winchester, w/horse & rider, M **$25.00**

Gun grease, Gunslick, MIB **$15.00**

Ink blotter, Dupont, 3 panels w/a dog, load data & logo, 9x4", M **$50.00**

Lawn sprinkler, Western Cartridge, sm brass w/Western logo & address, EX **$125.00**

Letter opener, marked Kynoch Ltd on handle, white plastic, 9x1", EX **$35.00**

Mug, drinking; Winchester Super-X, red w/picture of Nilo the Winchester lab, M **$25.00**

Patch, Federal, for shooting 25 straight in trap, shotshell shape, M **$5.00**

Pin-back, Ducks Unlimited, pictures Cinnamon Teal, by Gilder, 1988, round, M **$10.00**

Pin-back, Winchester, Winchester Is Returning, 2 eyes & a mouth, M **$20.00**

Playing cards, Winchester, pictures ducks & a lab in a marsh, M (sealed) **$25.00**

Postcard, Iver Johnson's Arms & Cycle Works, color picture of plant in Fitchburg MA, postmarked 1920, EX .. **$25.00**

Postcard, New York Knife Works, Walden NY, black & white of factory, postmarked 1905, EX **$25.00**

Poster, Winchester Bird Buster II, 17x29", M **$30.00**

Powder flask, Dixon & Sons, plain brass, EX **$95.00**

Powder flask, Sykes, plain brass w/few dents, rare **$95.00**

Price list, Western Super-X & Xpert, January 3, 1950, 13 pages, w/letter from Western to retailers, 8½x11", NM **$20.00**

Print, Dupont, of Wilson Snipe, by Lynn Bogue Hunt, 1917, VG **$25.00**

Reel, Pfleuger Fas-Kast, w/box & papers, VG **$25.00**

Shot tube, Federal XL, plated copper, shotshell shape, full, 3", M **$15.00**

Shot tube, Peters air rifle, Kings Mill, OH address, 2¾", EX **$30.00**

Ticket stub, Ducks Unlimited, Woodbury NJ, 1962, VG . **$8.00**

Tin, Browning gun oil, gold & black w/plastic top, G . **$20.00**

Tin, Remington gun oil, yellow & black, w/cartoon characters, VG **$60.00**

Tin, Schultze gunpowder, label w/London address, slide top, EX **$85.00**

Sports Collectibles

When the baseball card craze began sweeping the country a decade ago, memorabilia relating to many types of sports began to interest sports fans. Today ticket stubs, autographed baseballs, sports magazines, and game-used bats and uniforms are prized by baseball fans, and some items, depending on their age or the notoriety of the player or team they represent, may be very valuable. Baseball and golfing seem to be the two sports most collectors prefer, but hockey and auto racing are gaining ground. Game-used equipment is sought out by collectors, and where once they preferred only items used by professionals, now the sports market has expanded, and collectors have taken great interest in the youth equipment endorsed by many star players now enshrined in their respective Halls of Fame. Some youth equipment was given away as advertising premiums and bear that company's name or logo. Such items are now very desirable.

See also Autographs; Indianapolis 500 Memorabilia; Magazines; Motorcycle Memorabilia; Pin-Back Buttons; Puzzles.

Advisors: Don and Anne Kier (See Directory, Sports Collectibles)

Alarm clock, w/various baseball teams, Westclox/Team Mate, 1970s, MIB, ea **$45.00**

Badge, Masters, 1978, green & white, EX.....................$40.00

Banner, Indiana University NCAA Champions, 1940/1953/ 1976/1981/1987, 5 sm balls for ea year, black & white on red, M $35.00

Baseball, American League All Stars autographed, 15 signatures, Official American League ball, NM $265.00

Baseball, Joe DiMaggio autographed, Official American League ball, M...$175.00

Baseball, Leo Durocher autographed, Official National League ball, VG+ $40.00

Baseball, Mickey Mantle autographed, Official American League ball, M...$95.00

Baseball, 1946 Boston Braves team, 27 signatures, Official National League ball, EX....................................$195.00

Baseball, 1975 LA Dodgers team, 18 signatures, Official National League ball, EX....................................$135.00

Basketball, Harlem Globetrotters, red, white & blue w/red on white Harlem & yellow on blue Globetrotters, MacGregor, EX...$30.00

Book, 5th Anniversary of the Super Bowl, by Don Smith & Art Poretz, 1971, soft cover, 61 pages, 4¾x6", VG.$8.00

Book cover, Yankees team photo w/Mickey Mantle sitting in center, 1968, NM $25.00

Button, 1984 World Series National Champions, San Diego Padres, Padres color & World Series logo, 3½" dia .$12.00

Card, basketball, Scottie Pippen, Fleer, 1988-89, NM+..$12.00

Card, hockey, Wayne Gretzky, Topps, 1979, EX.........$35.00

Card set, basketball, Topps, 1969-70, complete set of 99, EX+ .$425.00

Card set, football, Topps, 1957, complete set of 155, EX..$925.00

Comic book, Yankees, Story of the 1951 World Champions & Great Yankee Teams of the Past, Fawcett, 1952, EX............$125.00

Cup, Chicago Bulls, Repeat the 3-Peat, 1998, NM $10.00

Cup, Yogi Berra/Yoo-Hoo, white plastic w/blue image & Yoo-Hoo logo on back, 1960s, 5", EX...................$38.00

Figurine, Nebraska Cornhuskers, Graduate series, BPI Collectibles, late 1980s, MIB $26.50

Games, 6 board games featuring Mickey Mantle's Big League Baseball, Football, Basketball, etc, Gardner Toys, 1950s, EXIB..$200.00

Jersey, baseball; St Louis Cardinals, red (away color), Russell Athletics, souvenir, not game-used, M $35.00

Lapel pin, 1964 Olympic Games in Tokyo, for swimming, gold-colored, EX $25.00

Magazine, Sport, Jerry West on cover, March 1965, EX .$20.00

Magazine, Sports Illustrated, NCAA Tournament, Duke's the Team To Beat, March, 1986 ....$10.00

Magazine, Sports Illustrated, Pete Maravich cover, November 12, 1973, NM $35.00

Nodder, Giants, 1960s, 4", NM (VG box marked My Favorite baseball Team)...$125.00

Nodder, Los Angeles Dodgers, 1960s, 4", NM (EX box marked My Favorite Baseball Team)...................$145.00

Pennant, LA Dodgers, blue & white, early 1960s, 14x5", EX $20.00

Pennant, San Fransisco Giants, red letters on blue background, w/white baseball w/Golden Gate Bridge & batter, 1962, NM $85.00

Pillowcase, LA Dodgers, logo, standard size, 20x26", MIB (sealed) $10.00

Plates, Meadowlands Race Track, 5 different w/caricature drawings & names of jockeys, Belcrest China, 1983, 8", NM, ea $35.00

Postcard, Briggs Stadium, Home of Detroit Tigers, linen type, 1946, EX..$25.00

Postcard, copy of serigraph of Jordan, Leroy Neiman, 1991, 8x6", M..$10.00

Poster, 1986-87 Boston Celtics, pictures of all 5 starters, Boston Globe insert, 17x13", M............................$15.00

Poster/program/schedule, WNBA, Tennessee vs Portland, Chamique Holdsclaw on cover, November 13, 1998, 11x17", EX...$22.00

Program, Baltimore Orioles, All-Star edition, Cal Ripken & Kirby Puckett on cover, 1993, M $25.00

Program, Harlem Globetrotters, 31st season, 1957, EX..$25.00

Program, Toronto Raptors vs Chicago Bulls, Jordan's last game, March 9, 1998, EX $18.00

Program, Yankees/Pirates World Series, 1960, EX.......$75.00

Programs: 1940 All-Star Game, played at Sportsman's Park, St. Louis, MO, EX, $275.00; Bob Feller's All-Stars Vs. Satchel Paige's All-Stars, 1946, EX, $385.00.

Program, 1980 NBA All-Star Game, EX......................$30.00

Program, 1987 NCAA Final Four, played at Super Dome, EX..$20.00

Program, 1989 NCAA Final Four, Michigan vs Seton Hall at Seattle, EX...$15.00

Salt & pepper shakers, Florida Gators, mascots in cheerleading outfits, BPI Collectibles, late 1980s, MIB, pr ..$20.00

Salt & pepper shakers, Georgia Bulldogs, mascots in cheerleading outfits, late 1980s, BPI Collectibles, MIB, pr........$20.00

Salt & pepper shakers, Tennessee Volunteers mascots in cheerleading outfits, BPI Collectibles, late 1980s, MIB, pr...$15.00

Schedule, 1950 Cleveland Indians, complete, M.........$30.00

Schedule, 1974-75 Boston Celtics, triple fold, issued by Carling Black Label Beer, M..................................$10.00

Stand-up, Ken Griffey Jr, Upper Deck, logo & facsimile signature, MIB..$35.00

Statue, Nolan Ryan, Texas Rangers away uniform, Hartland, limited edition, 1993, MIB.....................................$50.00

Stein, Denver Broncos, Super Bowl XXXIII Champions, embossed player images, white w/color decal, 6", NM.............$32.00

Ticket, 1980 Olympics at Lake Placid, for ice hockey, w/stub, EX...............**$25.00**
Ticket stub, 1993 NBA Finals in Phoenix vs Chicago, Jordan & Barkley pictured, EX...............**$12.00**
Tickets, 1967 LA Lakers playoff, strips (2) for games 3-9, EX...............**$10.00**
Yearbook, Detroit Tigers, 1955, EX...............**$75.00**
Yearbook, New York Yankees, 1959, EX...............**$95.00**
Yearbook, Washington Nationals, 1955, EX...............**$80.00**

St. Clair Glass

Since 1941, the St. Clair family has operated a small glasshouse in Elwood, Indiana. They're most famous for their lamps, though they've also produced many styles of toothpick holders, paperweights, and various miniatures as well. Though the paperweights are usually stamped and dated, smaller items may not be marked at all. In addition to various colors of iridescent glass, they've also made many articles in slag glass (both caramel and pink) and custard. For more information, we recommend *St. Clair Glass Collector's Book* by Bonnie Pruitt (see Directory, St. Clair).

Bell, Fruit Pattern, blue carnival...............**$40.00**
Bell, pansy; ice blue...............**$100.00**
Bell, sulfide, carnival glass...............**$100.00**
Bowl, pedestal; pink slag, from $150 to...............**$175.00**
Candle holder, sulfide, any color, from $75 to...............**$85.00**
Creamer & sugar bowl, Paneled Grape, cobalt carnival...**$75.00**
Figurine, bird, yellow, sm...............**$40.00**
Figurine, Dolphin, green carnival...............**$100.00**
Goblet, Wild Flower, ice blue carnival...............**$35.00**
Insulator, marigold carnival...............**$110.00**
Paperweight, sulfide, apple...............**$75.00**
Paperweight, sulfide, Betsy Ross...............**$275.00**
Paperweight, sulfide, cameo, windowed...............**$300.00**
Paperweight, sulfide, kitten, from $140 to...............**$165.00**
Paperweight, sulfide, rose, windowed & etched...**$1,350.00**
Pen holder, Indian...............**$65.00**
Perfume bottle, Paul St Clair...............**$95.00**
Perfume bottle, sulfide, carnival...............**$100.00**
Plate, Elwood Glass Festival, all colors...............**$30.00**
Plate, JF Kennedy...............**$100.00**
Plate, Kewpie, cobalt...............**$225.00**
Plate, Reagan/Bush, all colors, ea...............**$35.00**
Ring holder, sulfide, any color, from $75 to...............**$85.00**
Toothpick holder, Kingfisher...............**$50.00**
Toothpick holder, Sheaf of Wheat, any color...............**$45.00**
Toothpick holder, Shriner's Hat (Fez), red or red carnival, ea...............**$150.00**
Toothpick holder, sulfide, flowers, blue...............**$75.00**
Toothpick holder, swans, blue carnival...............**$45.00**
Toothpick holder, Wreath of Cherry, cobalt...............**$30.00**
Tumbler, Grape & Cable, amethyst...............**$35.00**
Tumbler, lemonade; Paneled Grape, ice blue...............**$125.00**
Vase, sulfide, pink slag...............**$125.00**

Stanford Corn

Teapots, cookie jars, salt and pepper shakers, and other kitchen and dinnerware items modeled as ears of yellow corn with green shucks were made by the Stanford company, who marked most of their ware. The Shawnee company made two very similar corn lines; just check the marks to verify the manufacturer.

Butter dish...............**$50.00**
Casserole, 8" L...............**$40.00**
Cookie jar...............**$85.00**

Creamer and sugar bowl, $50.00.

Cup...............**$15.00**
Pitcher, 7½"...............**$60.00**
Plate, 9" L...............**$32.00**
Relish tray...............**$40.00**
Salt & pepper shakers, sm, pr...............**$28.00**
Salt & pepper shakers, 4", pr...............**$28.00**
Spoon rest...............**$25.00**
Teapot...............**$70.00**
Tumbler...............**$30.00**

Stangl Birds

The Stangl Pottery Company of Flemington and Trenton, New Jersey, made a line of ceramic birds which they introduced in 1940 to fulfill the needs of a market no longer able to access foreign imports, due to the onset of WWII. These bird figures immediately attracted a great deal of attention. At the height of their productivity, sixty decorators were employed to hand paint the birds at the plant, and the overflow was contracted out and decorated in private homes. After WWII, inexpensive imported figurines once again saturated the market, and for the most part, Stangl curtailed their own production, though the birds were made on a very limited basis until as late as 1978.

Nearly all the birds were marked. A four-digit number was used to identify the species, and some pieces were signed by the decorator. An 'F' indicates a bird that was decorated at the Flemington plant.

Advisors: Popkorn Antiques (See Directory, Stangl)

Club: Stangl/Fulper Collectors Club
P.O. Box 538
Flemington, NJ 08822
Yearly membership: $25 (includes quarterly newsletter)

Allen Hummingbird, #3634, 4"....................................$85.00
Audubon Warbler, #3755, 4¼".............................$400.00
Bird of Paradise, #3408, 5"...................................$125.00
Black Poll Warbler, #3819 ....$200.00
Blue Jay w/leaf, #3716 ....$675.00
Brewers Blackbird, #3591 ....$150.00
Broadtail Hummingbird, #3626, blue flowers, 6½" ...$175.00
Cardinal, #3444, pink, revised $100.00
Carolina Wren, #3590 ....$165.00
Chestnut-Backed Chickadee, #3811 ....$165.00
Chickadees, #3581, black & white $300.00
Chickadees, #3581, brown & white........................$200.00
Cliff Swallow, #3852, 3½" $150.00
European Finch, #3922 ....$1,000.00
Feeding Duck, #3250C, Antique Gold....................$40.00
Goldfinch, #3849..$150.00
Goldfinches, #3635, group......................................$220.00

Indigo Bunting, #3589, $85.00.

Kentucky Warbler, #3598................................$60.00
Magpie-Jay, #3758, 10½"...........................$1,200.00
Nuthatch, #3593 ....$65.00
Oriole, #3402, revised version, 3½" $65.00
Owl, #3407...$350.00
Parakeets, #3582D, blue................................$275.00
Parakeets, #3582D, green..............................$200.00
Parrot, #3449 ....$150.00
Penguin, #3274 ....$500.00
Prothonotary Warbler, #3447.........................$75.00
Red-Breasted Nuthatch, #3851 ....$85.00
Redstarts, #3490D, pr.....................................$225.00
Rufous Hummingbird, #3585, 3".....................$75.00
Scarlet Tanager, #3750D, pink, 8", pr...........$450.00
Titmouse, #3592...$65.00
Turkey, #3275 ....$500.00
Western Bluebird, #3815 ....$450.00
Yellow-Headed Verdin, #3921, minimum value.....$1,250.00

Stangl Dinnerware

The Stangl Company of Trenton, New Jersey, grew out of the Fulper company that had been established in Flemington early in the 1800s. Martin Stangl, president of the company, introduced a line of dinnerware in the 1920s. By 1954, 90% of their production centered around their dinnerware lines. Until 1942 the clay they used was white firing, and decoration was minimal — usually simple one-color glazes. In 1942, however, the first of the red-clay lines that have become synonymous with the Stangl name was created. Designs were hand carved into the greenware, then hand painted. More than one hundred different patterns have been cataloged. From 1974 until 1978, a few lines previously discontinued on the red clay were reintroduced with a white clay body. Soon after '78, the factory closed.

If you'd like more information on the subject, read *Stangl Pottery* by Harvey Duke.

Advisors: Popkorn Antiques (See Directory, Stangl)

Amber Glo, bowl, 8"...$20.00
Amber Glo, coffee server....................................$75.00
Amber Glo, gravy boat, w/underplate $20.00
Antique Gold, compote, lace edge, footed, 4x9½" ...$20.00
Antique Gold, cornucopia, #5066, 11" $35.00
Apple Delight, mug...$30.00
Apple Delight, plate, luncheon...........................$10.00
Bachelor's Button, plate, 12"..............................$30.00
Black Gold, apple tray, #3546, 13"......................$40.00
Black Gold, heart dish, #3788, 8".......................$20.00
Blueberry, bowl, fruit; 5½"..................................$15.00
Blueberry, butter dish...$55.00
Blueberry, sandwich tray, center handle, 10"......$15.00
Carnival, plate, 8"...$10.00
Carnival, salt & pepper shakers, pr....................$16.00
Country Garden, bowl, flat soup..........................$20.00
Country Garden, bowl, 8"....................................$35.00
Country Garden, cup & saucer............................$16.00
Country Garden, pitcher, 1-pt.............................$40.00
Country Life, bread tray, w/hen & chicks $275.00
Country Life, chop plate, barn............................$350.00
Country Life, cup & saucer.................................$65.00
Festival, bowl, divided vegetable $30.00
Festival, bowl, fruit...$12.00
Festival, casserole, w/serving lid, 8"...................$60.00
Festival, goblet, Terra Rose, 5¾"........................$25.00
Festival, plate, Terra Rose, 10"...........................$18.00
First Love, bowl, salad; 10".................................$35.00
First Love, casserole, stick handle, 6"..................$15.00
First Love, plate, 8"..$10.00
Florette, gravy boat...$15.00
Florette, plate, 11"...$20.00
Florette, plate, 6"...$7.00
Fruit, bowl, salad; Terra Rose, 12".......................$65.00
Fruit, cruet, w/stopper...$60.00
Fruit, cup & saucer...$17.00
Fruit, relish tray...$40.00
Garden Flower, casserole, 8" $60.00
Garland, plate, 8"...$16.00
Golden Blossom, egg cup....................................$15.00

Golden Blossom, mug..**$25.00**
Golden Blossom, platter, 12" dia...........................**$25.00**
Golden Harvest, ashtray, rectangular.......................**$22.50**
Golden Harvest, bowl, fruit; 5½".............................**$12.00**
Golden Harvest, bread tray.....................................**$28.00**
Golden Harvest, plate, 10".......................................**$12.00**
Golden Harvest, relish tray.....................................**$18.00**
Golden Harvest, sugar bowl....................................**$15.00**
Golden Harvest, teapot..**$50.00**
Granada Gold, cornucopia, #5066..........................**$40.00**
Granada Gold, double pear dish, center basket handle, #3782.**$20.00**
Holly, creamer..**$30.00**
Holly, plate, dinner..**$50.00**
Kiddieware, cup, Ranger Boy, from $100 to............**$125.00**
Kiddieware, dish, Ducky Dinner, 3-part, w/cup.......**$195.00**
Kiddieware, dish, Five Little Pigs...........................**$300.00**
Kiddieware, dish & cup, Barnyard Friends..............**$175.00**
Laurel, carafe...**$75.00**
Magnolia, bowl, centerpiece; 12"............................**$75.00**
Magnolia, bowl, fruit; 5½".......................................**$12.00**
Magnolia, plate, 10"..**$16.00**
Magnolia, plate, 6"..**$5.00**
Mediterranean, platter, Casual................................**$60.00**
Orchard Song, bread tray..**$35.00**
Orchard Song, coaster...**$5.00**
Orchard Song, gravy boat.......................................**$15.00**

Orchard Song, pitcher, pint, from $20.00 to $25.00.

Orchard Song, salt & pepper shaker, pr.................**$16.00**
Provincial, bowl, fruit, 5½"......................................**$12.00**
Provincial, bowl, lug soup.......................................**$12.00**
Provincial, plate, dinner...**$15.00**
Provincial, plate, 6"...**$5.00**
Provincial, plate, 8"..**$10.00**
Scupltured Fruit, plate, 10".....................................**$14.00**
Sportsmen, plate, Canvas Back, 11".........................**$60.00**
Starflower, cup & saucer..**$15.00**
Starflower, plate, 8"..**$12.00**
Thistle, bowl, fruit..**$12.00**
Thistle, coaster..**$25.00**
Thistle, gravy, w/stand..**$38.00**
Thistle, relish..**$25.00**
Thistle, salt & pepper shakers, pr...........................**$20.00**
Thistle, teapot...**$100.00**
Town & Country, chop plate, blue..........................**$75.00**

Town & Country, coffeepot, blue...........................**$100.00**
Town & Country, mold, blue, fluted, 6"....................**$50.00**
Town & Country, teapot, blue.................................**$125.00**
Tulip, bean pot, blue or yellow, w/lid.....................**$55.00**

Star Trek Memorabilia

Trekkies, as fans are often referred to, number nearly 40,000 today, hold national conventions, and compete with each other for choice items of Star Trek memorabilia, some of which may go for hundreds of dollars.

The Star Trek concept was introduced to the public in the mid-1960s through a TV series which continued for many years in syndication. An animated cartoon series (1977), the release of six major motion pictures (1979 through 1989), and the success of 'Star Trek: The Next Generation' (Fox network, 1987) all served as a bridge to join two generations of loyal fans.

Its success has resulted in the sale of vast amounts of merchandise, both licensed and unlicensed, such as clothing, promotional items of many sorts, books and comics, toys and games, records and tapes, school supplies, and party goods. Many of these are still available at flea markets around the country. An item that is 'mint in box' is worth at least twice as much as one in excellent condition but without its original packaging. For more information, refer to *Modern Toys, American Toys, 1930 – 1980,* by Linda Baker, and *Schroeder's Collectible Toys, Antique to Modern.* (Both are published by Collector Books.)

Bop bag, Spock, 1975, M...**$50.00**
Calendar, 1975, Star Trek Animated Calendar, Lincoln
   Enterprises, #0104, NM.......................................**$10.00**
Figure, Applause, Deep Space 9, Kira Nerys, Odo, Quark or
   Sisko, 10", MIP, ea...**$10.00**
Figure, Applause, Next Generation, Kirk, La Forge, Picard,
   Riker or Worf, 10", MIP, ea................................**$10.00**
Figure, Ertl, Star Trek III, Klingon Leader or Spock, 3¾",
   MOC, ea...**$30.00**
Figure, Galoob, Next Generation, Data, 1st series, blue or
   spotted face, 3¾", MOC......................................**$125.00**
Figure, Galoob, Next Generation, Data, 3rd series, 3¾", MOC.**$20.00**
Figure, Galoob, Next Generation, Data, 4th series, 3¾", MOC.**$8.00**
Figure, Galoob, Next Generation, Tasha Yar, 3¾", MOC..**$20.00**
Figure, Mego, 1974-76, Cheron or the Keeper, 2nd series, 8",
   MOC, ea from $250 to...**$300.00**
Figure, Mego, 1974-76, Kirk, Klingon or Spock, 1st series, 8",
   MOC, ea...**$55.00**
Figure, Mego, 1974-76, McCoy or Uhura, 1st series, 8", MOC,
   ea from $150 to...**$175.00**
Figure, Mego, 1979, Motion Picture, Cheron, 12", NM..**$85.00**
Figure, Mego, 1979, Motion Picture, Decker, 3¾", MOC, from
   $20 to..**$30.00**
Figure, Mego, 1979, Motion Picture, Ilia, 12", MIB, from $75 to.**$100.00**
Figure, Mego, 1979, Motion Picture, Ilia, 3¾", MOC..**$20.00**
Figure, Mego, 1979, Motion Picture, Kirk, McCoy or Spock,
   3¾", MOC, from $40 to.......................................**$50.00**

Figure, Mego, 1979, Motion Picture, Klingon, 12", MIB, from $200 to **$250.00**

Figure, Playmates, Deep Space 9, Dukat, Gil, Kira, O'Brien or Quark, MOC, ea................................**$15.00**

Figure, Playmates, Next Generation, Admiral Kirk, MOC....**$25.00**

Figure, Playmates, Next Generation, Borg, Data, La Forge, Picard or Troi, 1st series, MOC, ea.....................**$20.00**

Iron-on transfers, 4 different, General Mills, 1979, M, ea ...**$5.00**

Kite, Star Trek III, M **$25.00**

Patch, USS Enterprise, starboard profile on black background, 3x4", M **$3.00**

Patch, Welcome Committee, 1976, 3x4" oval, M **$5.00**

Pin-back button, crew photo, Paramount Pictures, 1974, 3½x2¼", NM...**$4.00**

Plate, Spock, Ernst/Paramount Pictures, 8½", M **$40.00**

Playset, Command Communications Console, Mego, 1976, MIB **$150.00**

Playsuit, Mr Spock, cloth suit w/plastic mask, Ben Cooper, 1975, EXIB..**$35.00**

Postcard set, Motion Picture, 1979, complete, M **$40.00**

Program, International Convention, 1976, 24 pages, EX ...**$25.00**

Puzzle Cube, Next Generation, turn cube to reveal 9 photos, Applause, M..**$5.00**

Stickpin, I Am a Trekki, Lincoln Enterprises, 1976, EX.**$5.00**

Tablet, features Captain Kirk w/phaser rifle, 1967, unused, NM **$20.00**

Vehicle, Ferengi Fighter, Next Generation, Galoob, 1989, NRFB..**$55.00**

Vehicle, USS Enterprise, diecast metal, Dinky, 1970s, 4", MOC..**$15.00**

Vehicle, USS Enterprise, Star Trek II, Corgi, 1982, MOC, from $18 to...**$25.00**

Writing tablet, Spock, 1970, EX................................**$5.00**

Star Wars

In the late '70s, the movie 'Star Wars' became a box office hit, most notably for its fantastic special effects and its ever-popular theme of space adventure. Two more movies followed, 'The Empire Strikes Back' in 1980 and 'Return of the Jedi' in 1983. After the first movie, an enormous amount of related merchandise was released. A large percentage of these items was action figures, made by the Kenner company who used the logo of the 20th Century Fox studios (under whom they were licensed) on everything they made until 1980. Just before the second movie, Star Wars creator, George Lucas, regained control of the merchandising rights, and items inspired by the last two films can be identified by his own Lucasfilm logo. Since 1987, Lucasfilm Ltd. has operated shops in conjunction with the Star Tours at Disneyland theme parks.

What to collect? First and foremost, buy what you yourself enjoy. But remember that condition is all-important. Look for items still mint in the box. Using that as a basis, if the box is missing, deduct at least half from its mint-in-box value. If a major accessory or part is gone, the item is basically worthless. Learn to recognize the most desirable, most valuable items. There are lots of Star Wars bargains yet to be had!

Original packaging helps date a toy, since the package or card design was updated as each new movie was released. Naturally, items representing the older movies are more valuable than later issues. For more coverage of this subject, refer to *Schroeder's Collectible Toys, Antique to Modern* (Collector Books).

Belt, Return of the Jedi, Lee, 1983, EX.........................**$8.00**

Card game, Return of the Jedi, Parker Bros, 1983, MIB (sealed) **$10.00**

Case, Darth Vader, complete w/header card, NM.......**$35.00**

Case, Star Wars, vinyl w/cardboard insert, EX **$16.00**

Chewbacca Bandolier Strap, holds small action figures and weapons, Kenner, 1983, MIB, from $18.00 to $24.00. (Photo courtesy June Moon)

Comb & Keeper, Return of the Jedi, MOC **$18.00**

Darth Vader's Star Destroyer, Star Wars, complete, VG...**$60.00**

Doll, Chewbacca, Kenner, 1977, 21", MIP **$125.00**

Erasers, Return of the Jedi, set of 3, Stuart Hall, 1983, MOC...**$5.00**

Figure, Admiral Ackbar, Return of the Jedi, 3¾", MOC .**$25.00**

Figure, Anakin Skywalker, Star Wars, w/accessories, 3¾", NM **$30.00**

Figure, AT-AT Commander, Empire Strikes Back, 3¾", NM (G card)..**$24.00**

Figure, AT-AT Driver, Return of the Jedi, 3¾", MOC..**$26.00**

Figure, B-Wing Pilot, Return of the Jedi, 3¾", MOC...**$12.00**

Figure, Barada, Power of the Force, 3¾", MOC..........**$60.00**

Figure, Ben Obi-Wan Kenobi, Power of the Force, 3¾", MOC...**$130.00**

Figure, Ben Obi-Wan Kenobi, Star Wars, w/accessories, 3¾", NM **$20.00**

Figure, Ben Obi-Wan Kenobi, 12", MIB, fom $350 to..**$375.00**

Figure, Bespin Security Guard, Empire Strikes Back, Black or Caucasian, w/accessories, 3¾", NM, ea...................**$8.00**

Figure, Bib Fortuna, Return of the Jedi, 3¾", MOC....**$20.00**

Figure, Biker Scout, Return of the Jedi, 3¾", MOC.....**$28.00**

Figure, Boba Fett, 12", M (EX box) **$95.00**

Figure, C-3PO, Star Wars, w/accessories, 3¾", NM.....**$10.00**

Figure, C-3PO, 12", EX (VG box)..............................**$130.00**

Figure, Chewbacca, Empire Strikes Back, 3¾", MOC .**$35.00**

Figure, Chewbacca, 14", EX.....................................**$35.00**

Figure, Chief Chirpa, Return of the Jedi, w/accessories, 3¾", NM...**$8.00**

Figure, Chief Chirpa, Return of the Jedi, 3¾", MOC...**$27.00**

Figure, Darth Vader, Return of the Jedi, 3¾", MOC....**$40.00**

Figure, Darth Vader, 14", EX.............................**$35.00**

Figure, Death Squad Commander, Empire Strikes Back, 3¾", MOC...**$75.00**

Figure, Dulok Scout, Ewoks, 3¾", MOC..................**$15.00**

Figure, Emperor, Return of the Jedi, 3¾", MOC.........**$35.00**

Figure, Gammorean Guard, Return of the Jedi, 3¾", MOC...**$18.00**

Figure, Greedo, Empire Strikes Back, 3¾", MOC, from $85 to...**$100.00**

Figure, Greedo, Star Wars, w/accessories, 3¾", NM ...**$10.00**

Figure, Han Solo, Return of the Jedi, lg head, 3¾", MOC..**$75.00**

Figure, Han Solo, Return of the Jedi, sm head, Bespin outfit, 3¾", MOC..**$55.00**

Figure, Han Solo, 12", NM (VG box) **$375.00**

Figure, Imperial Commander, Return of the Jedi, 3¾", MOC...**$25.00**

Figure, Imperial Gunner, Power of the Force, 3¾", MOC..**$100.00**

Figure, Imperial TIE Fighter Pilot, Return of the Jedi, 3¾", MOC...**$45.00**

Figure, Jawa, Return of the Jedi, 3¾", MOC.............**$65.00**

Figure, Jawa, Star Wars, 3¾", w/accessories, NM........**$18.00**

Figure, Jawa, 12", MIB..................................**$225.00**

Figure, King Gorneesh, Ewoks, 3¾", MOC **$19.00**

Figure, Lando Calrissian, Empire Strikes Back, w/accessories, 3¾", NM...**$12.00**

Figure, Lobot, Empires Strikes Back, 3¾", MOC.........**$30.00**

Figure, Logray (Ewok Medicine Man), Return of the Jedi, 3¾", MOC..**$35.00**

Figure, Luke Skywalker, Empire Strikes Back, Bespin outfit, MOC...**$90.00**

Figure, Luke Skywalker, Power of the Force, Battle Poncho, 3¾", MOC..**$80.00**

Figure, Luke Skywalker, 12", EX (VG box) **$285.00**

Figure, Paploo, Power of the Force, 3¾", MOC..........**$45.00**

Figure, Power Droid, Return of the Jedi, 3¾", MOC ..**$35.00**

Figure, Princess Leia Organa, Empire Strikes Back, Bespin outfit, w/accessories, NM **$25.00**

Figure, Princess Leia Organa, Return of the Jedi, Boushh disguise, 3¾", M (NM card) **$35.00**

Figure, Princess Leia Organa, Star Wars, Boushh disguise, w/accessories, 3¾", NM **$18.00**

Figure, Princess Leia Organa, 12", NM...................**$100.00**

Figure, Prune Face, Return of the Jedi, 3¾", MOC.....**$17.00**

Figure, Rancor Keeper, Return of the Jedi, 3¾", MOC .**$12.00**

Figure, Rebel Commando, Return of the Jedi, 3¾", MOC..**$18.00**

Figure, Rebel Soldier, Empire Strikes Back, 3¾", MOC.......**$35.00**

Figure, Rebel Soldier, Return of the Jedi, Hoth battle gear, 3¾", M (EX+ card) **$25.00**

Figure, Ree-Yees, Return of the Jedi, 3¾", MOC.........**$15.00**

Figure, R2-D2, Empire Strikes Back, 3¾", MOC..........**$45.00**

Figure, R2-D2, remote control, 12", MIB..................**$125.00**

Figure, R5-D4, Star Wars, w/accessories, 3¾", NM.......**$8.00**

Figure, Snaggletooth, Empire Strikes Back, 3¾", MOC..**$60.00**

Figure, Star Destroyer Commander, Empire Strikes Back, 3¾", MOC..**$35.00**

Figure, Stormtrooper, Return of the Jedi, 3¾", MOC.**$35.00**

Figure, Ugnaught, Empire Strikes Back, 3¾", MOC....**$40.00**

Figure, Ugnaught, Return of the Jedi, 3¾", MOC.......**$28.00**

Figure, Urgah, Ewoks, 3¾", MOC........................**$19.00**

Figure, Weequay, Return of the Jedi, 3¾", MOC.......**$18.00**

Figure, Yoda, Empire Strikes Back, orange snake, 3¾", MOC...**$50.00**

Figure, 2-1B, Return of the Jedi, 3¾", MOC **$35.00**

Figure, 4-Lom, Return of the Jedi, 3¾", MOC **$50.00**

Figure, 8D8, Return of the Jedi, 3¾", MOC................**$25.00**

Magnets, Return of the Jedi, set of 4, MOC...............**$25.00**

Mask, Admiral Ackbar, hard plastic, Don Post, EX **$50.00**

Mask, C-3PO, hard plastic, Don Post, EX **$50.00**

Mask, Darth Vader, hard plastic, Don Post, EX...........**$65.00**

Mask, Yoda, hard plastic, Don Post, EX **$45.00**

Mug, Ben Obi-Wan Kenobi, California Originals, M.**$175.00**

Night light, Return of the Jedi, 6 different, MIP.........**$10.00**

Pencil pouch, Return of the Jedi, Stuart Hall, vinyl w/zipper, 1983, MIP...**$12.00**

Pin, C-3PO figure, metal, EX.............................**$4.00**

Playset, Bespin Control Room, Star Wars, Micro Collection, MIB **$50.00**

Playset, Bespin Gantry, Star Wars, Micro Collection, EX...**$25.00**

Playset, Cloud City, EX (EX box) **$300.00**

Playset, Death Star Compactor, Star Wars, Micro Collection, MIB **$85.00**

Playset, Ewok Village, Return of the Jedi, MIB........**$100.00**

Playset, Imperial Attack Base, EX (EX box) **$65.00**

Playset, Radar Laser Cannon, Return of the Jedi, NMIB ..**$20.00**

Presto Magix Transfer Set, Return of the Jedi, NRFB.**$10.00**

Record tote, Star Wars, w/6 records, VG **$30.00**

Vehicle, Boba Fett's Slave I, Empire Strikes Back, EX (VG box)...**$75.00**

Vehicle, Darth Vader TIE Fighter, Star Wars, NMIB.....**$75.00**

Vehicle, Endor Forest Ranger, NRFB **$25.00**

Vehicle, Ewok Assault Catapult, NRFB.......................**$25.00**

Vehicle, Imperial Troop Transport, EX (EX box) **$65.00**

Vehicle, Jawa Sand Crawler, with remote control and all accessories, NM, from $300.00 to $350.00. (Photo courtesy June Moon)

Vehicle, Landspeeder, Star Wars, EX (VG box) **$40.00**

Vehicle, Scout Walker, Return of the Jedi, complete, NM (VG box) **$50.00**

Vehicle, X-Wing Fighter, Return of the Jedi, NMIB.....**$75.00**

Vehicle, Y-Wing Fighter, Star Wars, EX **$55.00**

Steiff Animals

These stuffed animals originated in Germany around the turn of the century. They were created by Margaret Steiff, whose company continues to operate to the present day. They are identified by the button inside the ear and the identification tag (which often carries the name of the animal) on their chest. Over the years, variations in tags and buttons help collectors determine approximate dates of manufacture.

Teddy bear collectors regard Steiff bears as some of the most valuable on the market. When assessing the worth of a bear, they use some general guidelines as a starting basis, though other features can come into play as well. For instance, bears made prior to 1912 that have long gold mohair fur start at a minimum of $75.00 per inch. If the bear has dark brown or curly white mohair fur instead, that figure may go as high as $135.00. From the 1920 to 1930 era, the rule of thumb would be about $50.00 minimum per inch. A bear (or any other animal) on cast-iron or wooden wheels starts at $75.00 per inch; but if the tires are hard rubber, the value is much lower, more like $27.00 per inch.

It's a fascinating study which is well covered in *Teddy Bears and Steiff Animals, First, Second,* and *Third Series,* by Margaret Fox Mandel. Also see Cynthia Powell's *Collector's Guide to Miniature Teddy Bears.*

Newsletter/Club: *Collector's Life*
The World's Foremost Publication for Steiff Enthusiasts
Beth Savino
P.O. Box 798
Holland, OH 43528; 1-800-862-TOYS; fax: 419-473-3947

Foxy Dog, original ribbon and chest tag, 1950, 3¼", EX, $85.00. (Photo courtesy Margaret Fox Mandel)

Baby Chick, spotted Dralon w/felt comb, plastic feet & beak, all ID, 1971, 4", NM.................$85.00
Bazi Dog, mohair, plastic eyes, original blue collar, chest tag, 1960s, 4", NM.................**$110.00**
Bear, Margaret Strong, cinnamon mohair, brass button & cloth stock tag, 1982-90, 9", NM.................**$125.00**
Bendy Panda, mohair, all ID, 1960s, 3", NM.................**$325.00**
Biggie Beagle, mohair, glass eyes, original red collar, all ID, 1950s, 4", EX.................**$100.00**
Bird, mohair & felt w/plastic legs & beak, all ID, 1969, 4", M.................**$150.00**
Boxer Dog, mohair w/velvet chin, glass eyes, original blue leather collar, all ID, 1954, 4", NM.................**$165.00**

Clownie Clown, original outfit, chest tag, 5", M.......**$100.00**
Cockie Dog, mohair, glass eyes, original red leather collar, chest tag, 4", EX.................**$100.00**
Crabby Lobster, glass eyes, all ID, 4½", M.............**$350.00**
Fawn, mohair, glass eyes, no ID, 9", VG.................**$50.00**
Floppy Beagle, sleeping, mohair, original ribbon, chest tag, 8", NM.................**$125.00**
Floppy Ele Elephant, gray mohair w/red felt bib, all ID, NM.................**$150.00**
Gago Chinchilla, Dralon & felt, all ID, 5½", M.........**$200.00**
Gaty Alligator, all ID, 1968, 14", NM.................**$150.00**
Goldy Hamster, mohair, glass eyes, all ID, 4", NM...**$100.00**
Halloween Cat, black mohair, plastic eyes, original ribbon, raised script button, 9½", NM.................**$175.00**
Hoppy Rabbit, mohair, glass eyes, original ribbon & bell, all ID, 1968, 9", NM.................**$265.00**
Horse, mohair, plastic eyes, red bridle, all ID, 1968-76, 6½", M.................**$125.00**
Kangoo Kangaroo, w/original joey, all ID, 1959, 5", NM...**$125.00**
Kitty, tiger-striped mohair, glass eyes, fully jointed, original ribbon & chest tag, 4", EX.................**$150.00**
Lama Llama, mohair & velvet w/airbrushing, all ID, 1957-58, 6", M.................**$200.00**
Manni Rabbit, mohair, glass eyes, original ribbon, all ID, 1961-64, 6½", NM.................**$265.00**
Manni Rabbit, mohair, plastic eyes, original ribbon & bell, chest tag, 1960s, 3½", NM.................**$135.00**
Maxi Mole, mohair, all ID, 1964, 4", M.................**$135.00**
Molly Dog, puppet, mohair, glass eyes, no ID, 1950s, 9", EX.................**$65.00**
Molly Dog, white mohair w/red-brown tipping, glass eyes, raised script button & remnant stock tag, 1950s, 7", NM....**$200.00**
Nagy Beaver, mohair, plastic eyes, chest tag, 1960s, 7", NM.................**$125.00**
Nagy Beaver, mohair w/felt hands & feet, glass eyes, all ID, 1958, 3¾", M.................**$100.00**
Neander Caveman, felt w/rubber face, mohair suit, all ID, 1968, 8", M.................**$485.00**
Niki Rabbit, mohair, glass eyes, fully jointed, original ribbon, raised script button & stock tag, 7", M.................**$400.00**
Original Teddy, caramel mohair, glass eyes, fully jointed, raised script button, 1950s, 5½", VG.................**$200.00**
Original Teddy, gold mohair, black bead eyes, fully jointed, chest tag, 1950s, 3½", EX.................**$265.00**
Original Teddy, tan mohair, all ID, 1968, 9", M.......**$175.00**
Ossi Rabbit, mohair & Dralon, incised button, 6", NM...**$60.00**
Peggy Penguin, mohair, glass eyes, chest tag, 3", NM..**$110.00**
Peky Dog, mohair, all ID, 6", M.................**$100.00**
Pieps Mouse, gray over white mohair, all ID, M.........**$75.00**
Pieps Mouse, white mohair, all ID, M.................**$100.00**
Pony, mohair, glass eyes, original red leather saddle & plastic reins, chest tag, 1950s, 5", NM.................**$125.00**
Rabbit, Dralon, glass eyes, chest tag, 1956-67, 6", NM..**$100.00**
Rabbit, puppet, mohair, plastic eyes, no ID, 9", EX....**$50.00**
Raccy Raccoon, mohair, glass eyes, stock tag, 6", EX...**$100.00**
Schwarzbar Bear, black mohair w/red stitched claws, fully jointed, brass button & stock tag, 6", NM.................**$125.00**

Snucki Goat, all ID, 1960s, 4", M...............**$85.00**

Squirrel, puppet, mohair w/felt hands & feet, glass eyes, 8½", NM **$75.00**

Tabby Cat, mohair, glass eyes, original ribbon & bell, no ID, 1950s, 5½", NM...............**$85.00**

Tessie Schnauzer, gray mohair, glass eyes, original red collar, chest tag, 4½", NM **$150.00**

Vario Rabbit, mohair, glass eyes, raised script button & stock tag, 5", EX...............**$100.00**

Woolie Bird, raised script button & stock tag, 1949, 2", NM **$50.00**

Woolie Cat, black & white, green plastic eyes, original red ribbon, raised script button & stock tag, 3", M **$85.00**

Woolie Fish, green & yellow, raised script button & stock tag, 1968, 1½", NM...............**$35.00**

Woolie Mouse, no ID, NM **$25.00**

Woolie Owl, incised button & stock tag, 1971, 2", NM..**$35.00**

Woolie Parrot, plastic feet, incised button & stock tag, 1971, 2½", M **$65.00**

Zicky Goat, mohair, glass eyes & wood horns, original ribbon & bell, chest tag, 6", EX **$100.00**

Zotty Bear, mohair, glass eyes, original ribbon & chest tag, 7", NM **$300.00**

String Holders

Today we admire string holders for their decorative nature. They are much sought after by collectors. However, in the 1800s, they were strictly utilitarian, serving as dispensers of string used to wrap food and packages. The earliest were made of cast iron. Later, advertising string holders appeared in general stores. They were made of tin or cast iron and were provided by companies pedaling such products as shoes, laundry supplies, and food. These advertising string holders command the highest prices.

These days we take cellophane tape for granted. Before it was invented, string was used to tie up packages. String holders became a staple item in the home kitchen. To add a whimsical touch, in the late 1920s and 1930s, many string holders were presented as human shapes, faces, animals, and fruits. Most of these novelty string holders were made of chalkware (plaster of Paris), ceramics, or wood fiber. If you were lucky, you might have won a plaster of Paris 'Super Hero' or comic character string holder at your local carnival. These prizes were known as 'carnival chalkware.' The Indian string holder was a popular giveaway, so was Betty Boop and Superman.

Our values reflect string holders in excellent condition.

Advisor: Ellen Bercovici (See Directory, String Holders)

Apple, many variations, chalkware, from $25 to **$50.00**

Apple w/face, ceramic, Py, from $100 to.................**$150.00**

Babies, 1 happy, 1 crying, ceramic, Lefton, pr, from $250 to...............**$300.00**

Bananas, chalkware, from $85 to **$95.00**

Bird, 'String Nest Pull,' ceramic, from $40 to..............**$60.00**

Bird on branch, scissors in head, ceramic, from $85 to.**$100.00**

Birdcage, red & white w/green leaves & yellow bird, chalkware, from $100 to **$150.00**

'Blue' Riding Hood, chalk, minimum value, $250.00. (Photo courtesy Ellen Bercovici)

Bonzo (dog) w/bee on chest, ceramic, from $150 to...**$200.00**

Boy, top hat & pipe, eyes to side, chalkware, from $50 to .**$60.00**

Bride, ceramic, from $100 to **$125.00**

Bride & bridesmaids, ceramic, from $100 to **$125.00**

Butler, Black man w/white lips & eyebrows, ceramic, minimum value **$300.00**

Chef, chalkware, from $50 to **$75.00**

Chef, Rice Crispy, chalkware, from $125 to **$150.00**

Chef w/rolling pin, full figure, chalkware, from $75 to ..**$100.00**

Cherries, chalkware, from $125 to **$200.00**

Clown w/string around tooth, chalkware, from $150 to..**$200.00**

Dog, Scottie, ceramic, from $125 to...............**$200.00**

Dutch girl's head, chalkware **$50.00**

Elephant, yellow, England, ceramic, from $50 to **$60.00**

Girl in bonnet, eyes to side, chalkware, from $50 to .**$60.00**

Granny in rocking chair, Py, ceramic, from $100 to.**$150.00**

Groom & bridesmaids, ceramic, from $100 to **$125.00**

Heart, puffed, Cleminson, ceramic, from $75 to.......**$100.00**

House, Cleminson, ceramic, from $125 to.................**$175.00**

Iron w/flowers, ceramic, from $100 to **$150.00**

Jester, chalkware, from $125 to **$175.00**

Kitten w/ball of yarn, ceramic...............**$65.00**

Kitten w/ball of yarn, ceramic, homemade **$65.00**

Little Red Riding Hood, chalkware, minimum value ..**$250.00**

Maid, Sarsaparilla, ceramic, 1984, from $95 to..........**$125.00**

Mammy, full figured, plaid & polka-dot dress, ceramic, from $125 to...............**$200.00**

Mammy face, many variations, chalkware, from $250 to ...**$300.00**

Man in top hat w/pipe, from $65 to **$85.00**

Mouse, Josef Originals, ceramic, from $80 to.............**$90.00**

Penguin, ceramic, from $65 to...............**$85.00**

Pig w/flowers, ceramic, from $100 to **$150.00**

Pirate & gypsy, wood fiber, pr, from $100 to............**$125.00**

Rooster, Royal Bayreuth, ceramic, from $400 to **$600.00**

Rose, chalkware, from $125 to **$175.00**

Rosie the Riveter, chalkware, from $125 to **$175.00**

Sailor boy, chalkware, from $125 to **$175.00**

Senor, chalkware, from $50 to...............**$75.00**

Senora, chalkware, from $125 to..............................$200.00
Soldier, head w/cap, chalkware, from $50 to.............$75.00
Witch in pumpkin, winking, ceramic, from $125 to.$175.00
Woman w/turban, chalkware, from $125 to.............$150.00

Swanky Swigs

These glass tumblers, ranging in size from 3⅛" to 5⅝", were originally distributed by the Kraft company who filled them with their cheese spread. They were introduced in the 1930s and used until sometime during the war, but they were brought back soon after and used to some extent until the late 1970s. There are approximately 223 different variations of colors and patterns ranging from sailboats, bands, animals, dots, stars, checkers, etc.

Here is a listing of some of the harder-to-find examples: In the small (Canadian) size (about 3¹⁄₁₆" to 3¼") look for Band No. 5 (two red and two black bands); Galleon (2 ships on each example, made in five colors — black, blue, green, red, and yellow); Checkers (made in four color combinations — black and red, black and yellow, black and orange, and black and white, all having a top row of black checks); and Fleur-De-Lis (black fleur-de-lis with a bright red filigree motif).

In the regular size (about 3⅜" to 3⅞") look for Dots Forming Diamonds (diamonds made up of small red dots); Lattice and Vine (white lattice with flowers in these combinations — white and blue, white and green, and white and red); Texas Centennial (a cowboy and horse in these colors — black, blue, green, and red); three special issues with dates of 1936, 1938, and 1942; and Tulip No. 2 (available in black, blue, green, and red).

In the large (Canadian) size (about 4³⁄₁₆" to 5⅝" you'll find Circles and Dot (circles with a small dot in the middle, in black, blue, green, and red); Star No. 1 (small scattered stars, made in black, blue, green, and red); Cornflower No. 2 (in dark blue, light blue, red, and yellow); Provincial Cress (made only in red/burgundy with maple leaves); and Antique No. 2 (assorted antiques on each, made in lime green, deep red, orange, blue, and black).

Even the lids are collectible and are valued at a minimum of $3.00, depending on condition and the advertising message they convey.

For more information we recommend *Collectible Glassware of the 40s, 50s, and 60s,* and *The Collector's Encyclopedia of Depression Glass,* both by Gene Florence; and *Collectible Drinking Glasses* by Mark Chase and Michael Kelly.

Note: All are USA issue unless noted Canadian.

Advisor: Joyce Jackson (See Directory, Swanky Swigs)

Antique #1, black, blue, brown, green, orange or red, Canadian, 3¼", ea $8.00
Antique #1, black, blue, brown, green, orange or red, Canadian, 1954, 4¾", ea.............................$20.00
Antique #1, black, blue, brown, green, orange or red, 1954, 3¾", ea...$3.00

Antique #2, lime green, deep red, orange, blue or black, Canadian, 1974, 4⅝", ea.........................$25.00
Bachelor Button, red, green & white, 1955, 3¾" $3.00
Bachelor Button, red, white & green, Canadian, 1955, 3¼" $6.00
Bachelor Button, red, white & green, Canadian, 1955, 4¾" $15.00
Band #1, red & black, 1933, 3⅜"....................................$3.00
Band #2, black & red, Canadian, 1933, 4¾"...............$20.00
Band #2, black & red, 1933, 3⅜".....................................$3.00
Band #3, white & blue, 1933, 3⅜" $3.00
Band #4, blue, 1933, 3⅜" $3.00
Bicentennial Tulip, green, red or yellow, 1975, 3¾", ea ...$15.00
Blue Tulips, 1937, 4¼", from $3 to $6.00
Bustlin' Betty, blue, brown, green, orange, red or yellow, Canadian, 1953, 3¼", ea......................$8.00
Bustlin' Betty, blue, brown, green, orange, red or yellow, Canadian, 1953, 4¾", ea......................$20.00
Bustlin' Betty, blue, brown, green, orange, red or yellow, 1953, 3¾", ea..$3.00
Carnival, blue, green, red or yellow, 1939, 3½", ea......$6.00
Checkerboard, white w/blue, green or red, Canadian, 1936, 4¾", ea...$20.00
Checkerboard, white w/blue, green or red, 1936, 3½", ea...$20.00
Circles & Dot, any color, 1934, 3½", ea $4.00
Circles & Dot, black, blue, green or red, Canadian, 1934, 4¾", ea...$20.00
Coin, clear & plain w/indented coin decor around base, Canadian, 1968, 3⅛" or 3¼", ea $2.00
Coin, clear & plain w/indented coin decor around base, 1968, 3¾"...$1.00
Colonial, clear w/indented waffle design around middle & base, 1976, 3¾", ea.....................................$.50
Colonial, clear w/indented waffle design around middle & base, 1976, 4⅜", ea.....................................$1.00
Cornflower #1, light blue & green, Canadian, 1941, 4⅝", ea $20.00
Cornflower #1, light blue & green, Canadian, 3¼", ea.$8.00
Cornflower #1, light blue & green, 1941, 3½", ea.........$3.00
Cornflower #2, dark blue, light blue, red or yellow, Canadian, 1947, 3¼", ea................................$8.00
Cornflower #2, dark blue, light blue, red or yellow, Canadian, 1947, 4¼", ea................................$20.00
Cornflower #2, dark blue, light blue, red or yellow, 1947, 3¼", ea..$3.00
Crystal Petal, clear & plain w/fluted base, 1951, 3½", ea .$2.00
Dots Forming Diamonds, red, 1935, 3½", ea $25.00
Ethnic Series, lime green, royal blue, burgundy, poppy red or yellow, Canadian, 1974, 4⅝", ea $20.00
Forget-Me-Not, dark blue, light blue, red or yellow, Canadian, 3¼", ea..$8.00
Forget-Me-Not, dark blue, light blue, red or yellow, 1948, 3½", ea...$3.00
Galleon, black, blue, green, red or yellow, Canadian, 1936, 3⅛", ea..$30.00
Hostess, clear & plain w/indented groove base, Canadian, 1960, 3⅛" or 3¼", ea $2.00

Hostess, clear & plain w/indented groove base, Canadian, 1960, 5⅝", ea..**$5.00**

Hostess, clear & plain w/indented groove base, 1960, 3¾", ea.**$1.00**

Jonquil (Posy Pattern), yellow & green, Canadian, 1941, 3¼"..**$8.00**

Jonquil (Posy Pattern), yellow & green, Canadian, 1941, 4⅝", ea **$20.00**

Jonquil (Posy Pattern), yellow & green, 1941, 3½", ea.**$3.00**

Kiddie Kup, black, blue, brown, green, orange or red, Canadian, 1956, 3¼", ea..**$6.00**

Kiddie Kup, black, blue, brown, green, orange or red, Canadian, 1956, 4¾", ea..**$20.00**

Kiddie Kup, black, blue, brown, green, orange or red, 1956, 3¾", ea..**$3.00**

Lattice & Vine, white w/blue, green or red, 1936, 3½", ea...**$25.00**

Petal Star, clear, 50th Anniversary of Kraft Cheese Spreads, 1933-1983, ca 1983, 3¾", ea..**$1.00**

Petal Star, clear w/indented star base, Canadian, 1978, 3¼", ea..**$2.00**

Petal Star, clear w/indented star base, 1978, 3¾", ea......**$.50**

Plain, clear, like Tulip #1 w/out design, 1940, 3½", ea...**$4.00**

Plain, clear, like Tulip #3 w/out design, 1951, 3⅞", ea...**$5.00**

Provincial Crest, red & burgundy, Canadian, 1974, 4⅝", ea...**$25.00**

Sailboat #1, blue, 1936, 3½", ea **$12.00**

Sailboat #2, blue, green, light green, or red, 1936, 3½", ea **$12.00**

Sailboats, #2, any color, 1936, from $8 to....................**$10.00**

Special Issue, Del Monte Violet, Greetings From Kraft, 1942, 3½", ea...**$50.00**

Special Issue, Greetings From Kraft, California Retail Grocers Merchants Assn, Del Monte CA 1938, red, 1938, 3½"...**$50.00**

Special Issue, Lewis-Pacific Dairymen's Assn, Kraft Foods Co, Sept 13, 1947, Chehalis WA, 1947, 3½", ea...........**$50.00**

Special Issue, Pasadena blue sailboat, Greetings From Kraft, blue, 1936, 3½" **$50.00**

Sportsmen Series, red hockey, blue skiing, red football, red baseball, or green soccer, Canadian, 1976, 4⅝", ea.**$25.00**

Stars #1, black, blue, green, red or yellow, Canadian, 1934, 4¾", ea...**$20.00**

Stars #1, black, blue, green or red, 1935, 3½", ea **$4.00**

Stars #1, yellow, 1935, 3½", ea **$25.00**

Stars #2, clear w/orange stars, Canadian, 1971, 4⅝", ea **$12.00**

Texas Centennial, black, blue, green or red, 1936, 3½", ea.**$30.00**

Tulip (Posy Pattern), red & green, Canadian, 1941, 3¼", ea ..**$8.00**

Tulip (Posy Pattern), red & green, Canadian, 1941, 4⅝", ea.**$20.00**

Tulip (Posy Pattern), red & green, 1941, 3½", ea **$4.00**

Tulip #1, black, blue, green, red or yellow, Canadian, 3¼", ea.**$8.00**

Tulip #1, black, blue, green, red or yellow, 1937, 3½", ea.**$4.00**

Tulip #1, black, blue, green or red, Canadian, 1937, 4⅝", ea **$20.00**

Tulip #2, black, blue, green or red, 1938, 3½", ea **$20.00**

Tulip #3, dark blue, light blue, red or yellow, Canadian, 1950, 4¾", ea...**$20.00**

Tulip #3, dark blue, light blue, red or yellow, Canadian, 3¼", ea..**$8.00**

Tulip #3, dark blue, light blue, red or yellow, 1950, 3⅞", ea.**$3.00**

Violet (Posy Pattern), blue & green, Canadian, 1941, 3¼", ea.**$8.00**

Violet (Posy Pattern), blue & green, Canadian, 1941, 4⅝", ea.**$20.00**

Violet (Posy Pattern), blue & green, 1941, 3½", ea.......**$4.00**

Wildlife Series, black bear, Canadian goose, moose, or red fox, Canadian, 1975, 4⅝", ea **$20.00**

Syroco

Syroco Inc. originated in New York in 1890 when a group of European wood carvers banded together to produce original hand carvings for fashionable homes of the area. Their products were also used in public buildings throughout upstate New York, including the state capitol. Demand for those products led to the development of the original Syroco reproduction process that allowed them to copy original carvings with no loss of detail. They later developed exclusive hand-applied color finishes to further enhance the product, which they continued to improve and refine over ninety years.

Syroco's master carvers use tools and skills handed down from father to son through many generations. Woods used, depending on the effect called for, include Swiss pear wood, oak, mahogany, and wormy chestnut. When a design is completed, it is transformed into a metal cast through their molding and tooling process. A compression mold system using wood fiber was employed from the early 1940s to the 1960s. Since 1962 a process has been in use in which pellets of resin are injected into a press, heated to the melting point, and then injected into the mold. Because the resin is liquid, it fills every crevice, thus producing an exact copy of the carver's art. It is then cooled, cleaned, and finished.

Other companies have produced similar items, among them are Multi Products, now of Erie, Pennsylvania. It was incorporated in Chicago in 1941 but in 1976 was purchased by John Hronas. Multi Products hired a staff of artists, made some wood originals and developed a tooling process for forms. They used a styrene-based material, heavily loaded with talc or calcium carbonate. A hydraulic press was used to remove excess material from the forms. Shapes were dried in kilns for seventy-two hours, then finished and, if the design required it, trimmed in gold. Their products included bears, memo pads, thermometers, brush holders, trays, plaques, nut bowls, napkin holders, etc., which were sold mainly as souvenirs. The large clocks and mirrors were made before the 1940s and may sell for as much as $100.00 and more, depending on condition. Syroco used gold trim, but any other painted decoration you might encounter was very likely done by an outside firm. Some collectors prefer the painted examples and tend to pay a little more to get them. You may also find similar products stamped 'Ornawood,' 'Decor-A-Wood,' and 'Swank.'

See also Motion Clocks.

Advisor: Doris J. Gibbs (See Directory, Syroco)

Ashtray, double, glass bowls, cigarette compartment in center, from $10 to **$20.00**

Ashtray, floral at sides, rectangular receptacle, from 2 to 4 rests, Syroco, 4x6", from $6 to **$10.00**

Ashtray, florals at square sides, round receptacle, from 2 to 4 rests, Syroco, 5½x5½", from $7 to **$10.00**

Ashtray, steer & building on sides, marked Alamo TX, from $3 to **$10.00**

Barometer, ship's captain at wheel, round mechanism at wheel's center, from $10 to....................................**$15.00**

Bookends, Diana the Huntress w/hound, pr, from $10 to **$15.00**

Bookends, End of the Trail, pr, from $10 to **$15.00**

Bookends, lg wild rose, pr, from $10 to......................**$15.00**

Bookends, Mount Rushmore, pr, from $10 to **$15.00**

Box, bear, waterfall & trees on lid, marked Yellowstone National Park, 3½x4½", from $5 to **$7.00**

Box, cowboy boots & saddle on lid, w/paper label...**$12.50**

Box, deer & trees, 4½x6", from $4 to **$6.00**

Box, floral design at sides & on lid, Syroco, 5½x5½", from $5 to **$10.00**

Box, rope design on lid, velvet lining, Syroco, 6x6", from $10 to **$15.00**

Box, standing dog on lid, 4x6", from $5 to **$10.00**

Box, swirl design, 5½x7", from $8 to..........................**$10.00**

Brush holder, ship w/white triple mainsails, 4½", from $7 to **$12.00**

Brush holder, 2 drunks w/keg, 5", from $5 to **$10.00**

Brush holder, 4 puppies in basket, from $8 to **$10.00**

Figure, Cape Cod fisherman & woman, painted, pr, from $6 to **$15.00**

Figure, musician, painted, from $10 to **$15.00**

Figure, seated Indian, from $6 to **$10.00**

Picture frame, 3x2½" **$6.00**

Picture frame, 8x5½", from $6 to **$12.00**

Pipe holder, 2 horses at gate, 3 rests, from $12 to **$15.00**

Plate, barn & silo pastoral scene at center, fruits & vegetables at rim, 8", from $2 to **$5.00**

Plate, pine cones & leaves, 4", from $2 to...................**$5.00**

Thermometer, captain at ship's wheel, painted, marked Copyright Thad Co, 4"..**$15.00**

Thermometer, Scottie dogs at sides, magnet at bottom, 4", from $5 to **$10.00**

Tie rack, bartender behind bar w/bottles, painted, 6x9½", from $10 to..**$20.00**

Tie rack, Indian chief, 5", from $10.00 to $20.00. (Photo courtesy Doris Gibbs)

Tie rack, pointer dog at top, metal hangers, 7x12", from $10 to **$20.00**

Tray, flowers, marked Multi Products, 11" L, from $8 to...**$14.00**

Wall plaque, crucifix, white, 8", from $5 to................**$10.00**

Wall plaque, Our Mother of Perpetual Help, 4x5", from $5 to **$10.00**

Wall plaque, Scottie dog, repainted, 6", from $2 to......**$8.00**

Wall shelf, floral w/acanthus leaf, bead trim at top edge, Multi Products, 9x7", pr, from $7 to.....................**$12.00**

Taylor, Smith and Taylor

Though this company is most famous for their pastel dinnerware line, LuRay, they made many other patterns, and some of them are very collectible in their own right. They were located in the East Liverpool area of West Virginia, the 'dinnerware capitol' of the world. Their answer to HLC's very successful Fiesta line was Vistosa. It was made in four primary colors, and though quite attractive, the line was never developed to include any more than twenty items. Other lines/shapes that collectors especially look for are Taverne (also called Silhouette — similar to a line made by Hall), Conversation (a shape designed by Walter Dorwin Teague, 1950 to 1954), and Pebbleford (a textured, pastel line on the Versatile shape, made from 1952 to 1960).

For more information we recommend *Collector's Guide to LuRay Pastels* by Bill and Kathy Meehan (Collector Books), which covers several dinnerware lines in addition to LuRay.

Note: To evaluate King O'Dell, add 15% to the values we list for Conversation. For Boutonniere, add 15% to our Ever Yours values; and for Dwarf Pine, add the same amount to the values suggested for Versatile.

See also LuRay Pastels.

Castle, platter, sm...**$20.00**

Castle, teacup **$5.00**

Center Bouquet, platter, lg..**$30.00**

Conversation, coffee server...**$20.00**

Conversation, jug, water...**$25.00**

Conversation, plate, salad **$2.00**

Conversation, sugar bowl, w/lid....................................**$5.00**

Delphian Rose, plate, 9"..**$9.00**

Dogwood, sauce boat **$18.00**

Empire, cake plate..**$10.00**

Empire, teapot, curved spout.......................................**$20.00**

English Abbey, casserole..**$35.00**

Ever Yours, bowl, vegetable; round **$3.00**

Ever Yours, cake server..**$15.00**

Ever Yours, dessert dish **$1.75**

Ever Yours, saucer **$1.00**

Ever Yours, tray, utility..**$8.00**

Laurel, plate, 6"...**$1.75**

Laurel, platter, 13"...**$6.00**

Paramount, creamer...**$5.00**

Paramount, jug, batter; w/lid **$40.00**

Paramount, pickle...**$7.00**

Pebbleford, bowl, vegetable; round, sm $6.00
Pebbleford, egg cup, double $10.00
Pebbleford, plate, bread & butter.................................$2.50
Pebbleford, plate, chop..$15.00
Pebbleford, platter, 11" $6.00

Pebbleford, syrup pitcher, $20.00. (Photo courtesy Bill and Kathy Meehan)

Taverne (Silhouette), bowl, fruit....................................$7.00
Taverne (Silhouette), bowl, lug soup; tab handled.....$15.00
Taverne (Silhouette), saucer, St Denis.........................$7.00
Taverne (Silhouette), teacup.......................................$10.00
Taylorton, casserole, w/lid..$23.00
Taylorton, creamer...$2.75
Taylorton, platter, round, 11" $6.00
Versatile, butter dish, w/lid $5.50
Versatile, creamer...$2.75
Versatile, plate, dinner $2.00
Versatile, sauce boat $4.00
Versatile, teapot..$20.00
Vistosa, bowl, fruit..$15.00
Vistosa, bowl, salad; footed, 12" $200.00
Vistosa, creamer...$20.00
Vistosa, egg cup, footed...$35.00
Vistosa, jug, water, 2-qt $85.00
Vistosa, nappy..$50.00
Vistosa, plate, chop; 12" $40.00
Vistosa, plate, chop; 15" $50.00
Vistosa, plate, 7"..$18.00
Vistosa, plate, 9"..$20.00
Vistosa, saucer, coffee; AD..$20.00
Vistosa, saucer, tea..$7.00
Vogue, bowl, soup..$2.50
Vogue, cake plate $10.00
Vogue, creamer..$3.50
Vogue, teacup...$2.50

Tiara Exclusives

Collectors are just beginning to take notice of the glassware sold through Tiara in-home parties, their Sandwich line in particular. A branch of the Lancaster Colony Corp., the Tiara Division closed in 1998. Several companies were involved in producing the lovely colored glassware they marketed over the years, among them Indiana Glass, Fenton, Dalzell Viking, and L.E. Smith.

Note: Home Interiors has just introduced Tiara Sandwich glass and the square honey box in a lovely transparent amethyst color (Plum). They are using the Tiara brand name, and pieces appear to be from Tiara molds.

Advisor: Mandi Birkinbine (See Directory, Tiara)

Crown Dinnerware

In the mid-1980s Tiara made Crown Dinnerware in Imperial Blue. This is the pattern most collectors know as King's Crown Thumbprint. The color is a rich medium blue and brighter than cobalt.

Cup $3.00
Goblet, stemmed, 8-oz $5.00
Plate, bread; 8" $5.00
Plate, dinner; 10"...$7.00
Saucer $2.00

Honey Boxes

One of Tiara's more popular items was the honey box or honey dish. It is square with tiny tab feet and an embossed allover pattern of bees and hives. The dish measures 6" tall with the lid and was made in many different colors, ranging in value from $15.00 up to $50.00, depending on the color.

Amber $15.00
Black...$29.00
Chantilly (pale) Green $50.00
Clear..$40.00
Light blue $25.00

Sandwich Pattern

In the late 1960s, Tiara contracted with Indiana to produce their famous line of Sandwich dinnerware (a staple at Indiana Glass since the late 1920s). Over the years, it has been offered in many colors: ruby, teal, crystal, amber, green, pink (officially named Peach), blue, and others in limited amounts. We've listed a few pieces of Tiara's Sandwich below, and though the market is unstable and tends to vary from region to region, our estimates will serve to offer an indication of current asking prices. Because this glass is not rare and is relatively new, collectors tend to purchase only items in perfect condition. Chips or scratches will decrease value drastically.

Unless you're sure of what you're buying, though, don't make the mistake of paying 'old' Sandwich prices for Tiara. With most items, the quickest way to tell Anchor Hocking's Sandwich from Tiara and Indiana Sandwich is by looking at the flower in the pattern. The Tiara/Indiana flower is outlined with a single line and has convex petals. Anchor Hocking's flower is made with double lines, so it has a more complex appearance, and the convex area in each petal is tiny. To learn more about the two lines, we recommend

Collectible Glassware from the 40s, 50s, and 60s, by Gene Florence (Collector Books).

Basket, amber, 10"	$35.00
Bowl, berry; amber, 4"	$3.50
Bowl, vegetable; amber, 8"	$12.00
Bowl, vegetable; Chantilly Green, 8"	$17.00
Butter dish, amber, domed lid, 6"	$25.00

Butter dish, Chantilly green, domed lid, 6", $35.00.

Canister, amber, 26-oz, 5⅝"	$8.00
Canister, amber, 38-oz, 7½"	$10.00
Canister, amber, 52-oz, 8⅞"	$15.00
Celery tray/oblong relish, amber, 10⅜x4⅜"	$15.00
Celery tray/oblong relish, midnight blue, 10⅜x4⅜"	$18.50
Coaster, amber	$3.00
Compote, amber, 8"	$17.50
Creamer & sugar bowl, midnight blue, round, flat, pr	$15.00
Cup, coffee; amber, 9-oz	$3.00
Cup, snack/punch; crystal, 6-oz	$2.00
Egg tray, amber, 12"	$15.00
Egg tray, Chantilly Green, 12"	$20.00
Egg tray, Spruce Green, 12"	$15.00
Goblet, Spruce Green, 8-oz	$5.50
Napkin holder, amber, footed fan shape	$22.00
Plate, dinner; amber, 10"	$9.50
Plate, salad; amber, 8"	$7.00
Salt & pepper shakers, amber, pr	$13.00
Saucer, amber	$2.00
Tray, oval snack; crystal (goes w/punch cup), 8⅜x6¾"	$3.00

Tire Ashtrays

Manufacturers of tires issued miniature versions containing ashtray inserts that they usually embossed with advertising messages. Others were used as souvenirs from World's Fairs. The earlier styles were made of glass or glass and metal, but by the early 1920s, they were replaced by the more familiar rubber-tired variety. The inserts were often made of clear glass, but colors were also used, and once in awhile you'll find a tin one. The tires themselves were usually black; other colors are rarely found. Hundreds have been produced over the years; in fact, the larger tire companies still issue them occasionally, but you no longer see the details or colors that are evident in the pre-WWII ashtrays. Although the common ones bring modest prices, rare examples sometimes sell for up to several hundred dollars. For ladies or non-smokers, some miniature tires contained a pin tray.

For more information we recommend *Tire Ashtray Collector's Guide* by Jeff McVey.

Advisor: Jeff McVey (See Directory, Tire Ashtrays)

Allray Duster Tires, plastic insert, plastic 6" tire	$35.00
BF Goodrich Comp T/A, imprinted insert, 6" high performance tire	$30.00
Bridgestone Radial RD-201 165SR13, clear imprinted insert, Japan, 5⅞" tire	$35.00
Cooper Cobra Radial GT 75th Anniversary, clear insert imprinted 1989, 5⅞" tire	$30.00
Dominion Royal Heavy Duty 7.00-19, amber embossed insert, Canada, 6½" tire	$100.00
Falls Evergreen Tube, green rubber innertube ashtray, Weller Pottery insert	$175.00
Firestone, red & black mottled plastic insert w/3 rests, plastic 6" tire	$20.00
Firestone Balloon 9.75-24, bluish-green insert embossed 'F the Mark of Quality'	$200.00
Firestone Steel Radial 500, clear imprinted insert, 6" tire	$25.00
General Streamline Jumbo, green embossed insert, 5" tire	$65.00
Gislaved 8.25-20 10 Lager Rayon, clear embossed insert, Sweden, 6¼" truck tire	$50.00
Goodrich Silvertown - The Safest Tire Ever Built, embossed, marbleized insert	$50.00
Goodyear Eagle, clear imprinted insert, motorcycle knobby tire	$100.00

Goodyear Vector, clear insert with manufacturer's imprint, 6" tire, $25.00. (Photo courtesy Jeff McVey)

Goodyear Wrangler Radial, clear imprinted insert, wide 6½" SUV tire	$40.00
Goodyear 3-T Custom Super Cushion, clear imprinted insert, 5¾" tire	$35.00
Hood Deep Cleat HB, clear imprinted insert, 6⅛" tractor tire	$50.00
Kelly Springfield Commercial Heavy Duty Tread 10.00-20, clear insert, 6⅛" truck tire	$45.00
Mohawk Cord Balloon 33x6.00 for 21x5" rim, amber or green wheel insert, ea	$100.00

Ohtsu Radialace Ultra 70 185/70HR13, clear imprinted insert, Japan, 5¾" tire $35.00

Pennsylvania Pennsylvania, clear insert, 5½" tire $35.00

Republic Staghound, green embossed insert, solid truck tire..$150.00

Seiberling RT/78 Steel Radial, clear imprinted insert, 6⅛" tire .$50.00

Tyer Rubber Co, unusual 'Tyer' ashtray, various rubber goods depicted on sidewall..................$100.00

Uniroyal Master, clear imprinted insert, 6" tire w/both red & white stripes.........................$45.00

Western Auto, red & black plastic insert w/3 rests, plastic 6" tire..$40.00

Tobacco Collectibles

Until lately, the tobacco industry spent staggering sums advertising their products, and scores of retail companies turned out many types of smoking accessories such as pipes, humidors, lighters, and ashtrays. Even though the smoking habit isn't particularly popular nowadays, collecting tobacco-related memorabilia is! See *Huxford's Collectible Advertising* (Collector Books) by Sharon and Bob Huxford for more information.

See also Advertising Character Collectibles, Joe Camel; Cigarette Lighters.

Club: Tobacciana
Chuck Thompson and Associates
P.O. Box 11652
Houston, TX 77293; Send SASE for free list of publications

Club/Newsletter: *Tobacco Jar*
Society of Tobacco Jar Collectors
Charlotte Tarses, Treasurer
3011 Falstaff Road #307
Baltimore, MD 21209; Dues: $30 per year ($35 outside of U.S.)

Sign, flange; Chesterfield Cigarettes, porcelain, 1950, 17x11", EX, $110.00.

Ashtray/cigarette holder, Fatima Turkish Cigarettes, porcelain, octagonal w/square cup, white w/gold trim, 5x6", EX $140.00

Box, wood, Boot Jack Plug Tobacco, oval label, 13x4", EX+..................................$25.00

Canister, tin, City Club, red w/graphics, dome top, 5½x4", EX+..................................$335.00

Canister, tin, Hand Made Flake Cut, shouldered w/smaller round slip lid, EX+ $275.00

Canister, tin, US Marine Cut Plug, shouldered w/smaller round slip lid, red, EX+..................$600.00

Chair, Piedmont Cigarettes, wood folding type w/blue & white porcelain sign back, EX...........$190.00

Charger, tin, Prince Albert Tobacco, The National Smoke, man smoking pipe & pocket tin on back, gold trim, 24" dia, G..................................$450.00

Cigar box, Citizen's Club, images of chess & pool games, VG+..................................$350.00

Cigar box label, inner lid, Dante, images from poem Divine Comedy, 6x9", M $125.00

Cigar box label, outer, Fine Domestic, partially nude Indian maiden, 4½x4½", EX....................$100.00

Cigar box label, sample, Duc De Montensier, George L Schlegel litho #1782, EX..................$100.00

Cigar cutter, Charles Denby Cigars, reverse-glass top mounted on fancy footed nickel-plated base, G $150.00

Cigarette paper dispenser, Top, metal w/black lettering & cigarette graphic on white, vertical, EX $35.00

Cigarette papers, Great Puff Tobacco, image of pouch w/man in mustache & goatee & hat, EX $70.00

Door plate, metal, Copenhagen, white on black, vertical w/square corners, EX....................$45.00

Door plate, porcelain, Chesterfield Cigarettes, ...They Satisfy/And The Blend Can't Be Copied, white on blue, 9x4", NM+..................................$325.00

Flyer, Edgeworth Smoking Tobacco, Christmas/A Gift That Warms A Man's Heart Only $1.00, w/envelope, 12x9", VG+..................................$45.00

Humidor, glass, Tuxedo Tobacco, octagonal w/knob lid, paper label, NM $85.00

Humidor, tin, Hi-Plane Smooth Cut Tobacco, red, EX+..$200.00

License plate attachment, Lucky Strike Cigarettes, tin & plastic, round red & white symbol w/pouch, saleman's sample, EX..................................$190.00

Pocket tin, Bond Street, sample, short, NM..............$125.00

Pocket tin, Briggs Pipe Mixture, Complimentary, full size, EX+..................................$115.00

Pocket tin, Charm of the West, yellow, flat, EX........$300.00

Pocket tin, Eden Cube Cut, red, EX....................$300.00

Pocket tin, Edgeworth Ready-Rubbed, sample, blue, 2", EX+ $75.00

Pocket tin, Tuxedo Tobacco, man in hat, green, NM+ (sealed)...$45.00

Pocket tin, Whip Ready Rolled, green, tall, NM+ $675.00

Postcard, Chesterfield Cigarettes, It's A Chesterfield, head image of doughboy w/cigarette, Lyendecker, EX ..$35.00

Product display box, Our Advertiser Smoking Tobacco 5¢, diecut cardboard, complete w/24 full pouches & papers, EX+ $340.00

Sign, cardboard, Chesterfield Cigarettes, I'll Light Your..., actress Maureen O'Hara & fighter pilot, 23x22", NM $170.00

Sign, cardboard, Kool Cigarettes/Mildly Mentholated, girl in swimsuit riding the waves on cigarette pack, 18x12", NM...$40.00

Sign, cardboard, Raleigh, lady's head w/patriotic red, white & blue head bow, cigarette pack & banner below, 18x12", NM **$25.00**

Sign, cardboard display, Forty-Four (44)/Old Time Quality 5¢..., diecut Indian scout in headdress w/open box, 32x21", VG **$260.00**

Sign, cardboard hanger, Kool, Buy Your Cigarettes Here..., 2-sided diecut penguin descending w/parachute, 7x6", NM **$50.00**

Sign, paper on glass, Boot Jack Chewing Tobacco, Above All.../Costliest Because Best, gold on browns & black, 12x8", VG **$85.00**

Sign, paper over cardboard, Edgeworth, image of man w/4 dogs & 3 product packs, self-framed, 17x26", EX..**$180.00**

Sign, porcelain, Helmar Turkish Cigarettes, white lettering on black, white line border, 12x36", EX+.................**$135.00**

Sign, porcelain, Mail Pouch, Chew/Smoke...Treat Yourself To The Best, white & yellow lettering on blue, 11x36", EX+.**$300.00**

Sign, porcelain, RC Sullivan's 7-20-4 Cigar/Famous For Quality/Factory Manchester NH, white & yellow on red, 12x30", EX+ **$400.00**

Sign, reverse-painted glass, Honeymoon Cigars 5¢, silver leaf on black, w/crescent moon & 3 stars, framed, 12x19", NM+ **$425.00**

Sign, tin, Clown Cigarettes, Smoke.../A Balanced Blend, white & yellow on blue w/yellow frame, embossed, 14x10", VG...**$85.00**

Sign, tin, Devilish Good Cigar 5 Cents/None Better, shows open cigar box w/3 boys on lid, embossed, 10x14", EX.**$375.00**

Sign, tin, Harvester Cigar 5¢/Heart of Havana..., oval w/rolled rim, image of lady's head above lettering, 13x9", EX **$130.00**

Sign, tin, Philip Morris, Call For..., black & red lettering w/bellhop & cigarette on yellow, red trim, 10x25", EX+...**$50.00**

Store bin, tin, Mail Pouch Tobacco, white & yellow on dark blue, 10x14", EX **$325.00**

Store bin, tin, Sweet Cuba Fine Cut 5¢, slant top, yellow, EX+ **$340.00**

Store tin, Forest Giant Tobacco, round w/square lid, VG.**$300.00**

Store tin, Nic Nac Chewing Tobacco/5¢ Packets, round w/smaller round slip lid, yellow, G **$350.00**

String holder, tin, Mail Pouch Chew & Smoke Tobacco, pouch rises along side as string is pulled, HD Beach litho, 20", G...**$2,350.00**

Thermometer, porcelain, Mail Pouch Tobacco, Treat Yourself To The Best..., white & yellow on dark blue, 39", EX+ **$180.00**

Thermometer, tin, Grads Cigarettes, white on red, curved top & bottom, Canada, 39", NM **$100.00**

Thermometer, tin, La Fendrich Cigar/Always A Cool Smoke, red & yellow, 25½"x10½", EX+ **$190.00**

Tin, Bohemian Mixture No 1, horizontal box, gold on green, holds 100, 2x3x6", EX+ **$60.00**

Tin, Bond of Union Smoking Mixture, horizontal box w/rounded corners, EX+...**$80.00**

Tin, Charles Denby Cigars, vertical square w/slip lid, paper label w/oval portrait, EX+ **$35.00**

Tin, Charles Thomson 5¢ Cigar, vertical square w/portrait image on yellow, 5", EX+ **$110.00**

Tin, Club Chewing Tobacco, round w/key-wind lid, yellow & blue, NM...**$30.00**

Tin, Fiona Cigars, round w/slip lid, shows exotic lady, Liberty Can Co, EX+...**$440.00**

Tobacco pouch, Huntington Smoking Tobacco, cloth w/paper label, red & yellow, 2-oz, EX...............**$285.00**

Tobacco sample packet, Mail Pouch Sweet Chewing Tobacco, red & blue on gold, NM **$18.00**

Tobacco tag, BF Hanes Hot Stuff, rectangular w/red pepper on yellow background, EX **$30.00**

Tobacco tag, Catcher, yellow oval w/graphics & red lettering, EX...**$20.00**

Tobacco tag, Flirt, round w/scalloped edge, embossed w/lady's head & fan, yellow, EX...........................**$25.00**

Tobacco tag, Old Joe, round w/name & image of Black man on yellow background, EX **$55.00**

Toothbrush Holders

Novelty toothbrush holders have been modeled as animals of all types, in human forms, and in the likenesses of many storybook personalities. Today all are very collectible, especially those representing popular Disney characters. Most of these are made of bisque and are decorated over the glaze. Condition of the paint is an important consideration when trying to arrive at an evaluation.

For more information, refer to *Pictorial Guide to Toothbrush Holders* by Marilyn Cooper.

Advisor: Marilyn Cooper (See Directory, Toothbrush Holders)

Bear w/Scarf & Hat, Japan, 5½", from $80 to **$95.00**

Betty Boop w/Toothbrush & Cup, KFS, 5", from $85 to..**$100.00**

Big Bird, Taiwan (RCC), 4½", from $80 to **$90.00**

Bonzo, Japan, 6", from $80 to **$95.00**

Candlestick Maker, Japan (Goldcastle), 5", from $70 to..**$85.00**

Cat, Japan (Goldcastle), 6", from $70 to **$90.00**

Cat on Pedestal, Japan (Diamond T), 6", from $150 to.**$175.00**

Cat w/Bass Fiddle, Japan, 6", from $115 to..............**$135.00**

Circus Elephant, Japan, 5", from $85 to...................**$100.00**

Clown Head w/Bug on Nose, Japan, 5", from $150 to...**$180.00**

Dalmatian, Germany, 4", from $170 to **$190.00**

Donald Duck, WDE, bisque, 5", from $250 to **$300.00**

Ducky Dandy, Japan, 4", from $150 to.....................**$175.00**

Dutch Boy & Girl Kissing, Japan, 6", from $55 to **$65.00**

Dwarfs in Front of Fence (Sleepy & Dopey), Japan/WDE, bisque, 3½" **$1,275.00**

Humpty Dumpty, Pat Pending, bisque, 5½", from $200 to.**$225.00**

Little Red Riding Hood, Germany (DRGM), 5½", from $200 to...**$225.00**

Mary Poppins, Japan, 6"...**$150.00**

Mickey Mouse, Donald Duck & Minnie, Japan/WDE, 4½", from $300 to...**$375.00**

Mickey Mouse & Pluto, WDE, 4½", from $250 to.....**$300.00**

Musician, Japan, 4½", from $55.00 to $65.00 each. (Photo courtesy Carole Bess White)

Old Mother Hubbard, Germany, 6", from $350 to **$410.00**
Penguin, Japan, 5½", from $85 to **$100.00**
Pinocchio & Figaro, Shafford, 5", from $500 to **$525.00**
Popeye, Japan, bisque, 5" **$500.00**
Three Bears w/Bowls, Japan (KIM USUI), 4", from $90 to .**$125.00**
Three Little Pigs w/Piano, WDE, bisque, 5", from $150 to.**$175.00**
Traffic Cop, Germany, Don't Forget the Teeth, 5", from $350
    to...**$375.00**
Uncle Willie, Japan/FAS, 5", from $85 to **$100.00**

Toys

Toy collecting has long been an area of very strong activity, but over the past decade it has literally exploded. Many of the larger auction galleries have cataloged toy auctions, and it isn't uncommon for scarce nineteenth-century toys in good condition go for $5,000.00 to $10,000.00 and up. Toy shows are popular, and there are clubs, newsletters, and magazines that cater only to the needs and wants of toy collectors. Though once buyers ignored toys less than thirty years old, in more recent years, even some toys from the '80s are sought after.

Condition has more bearing on the value of a toy than any other factor. A used toy in good condition with no major flaws will still be worth only about half (in some cases much less) as much as one in mint (like new) condition. Those mint and in their original boxes will be worth considerably more than the same toy without its box.

There are many good toy guides on the market today including *Modern Toys, American Toys, 1930 to 1980,* by Linda Baker; *Collecting Toys* and *Collecting Toy Trains* by Richard O'Brien; *Schroeder's Collectible Toys, Antique to Modern; Elmer's Price Guide to Toys* by Elmer Duellman; *Toys of the Sixties, A Pictorial Guide,* by Bill Bruegman; *Occupied Japan Toys With Prices* by David C. Gould and Donna Crevar-Donaldson; *Toys, Antique and Collectible, Antique and Collectible Toys, 1870 – 1950, Cartoon Toys and Collectibles,* and *Character Toys and Collectibles*, all by David Longest; and *Collector's Guide to Tinker Toys* by Craig Strange. More books are listed in the subcategory narratives that follow. With the exception of O'Brien's (Books Americana) and Bruegman's (Cap't Penny Productions), all the books we've referred to are published by Collector Books.

See also Advertising Character Collectibles; Breyer Horses; Bubble Bath Containers; Character Collectibles; Disney Collectibles; Dolls; Fast-Food Collectibles; Fisher-Price; Halloween; Hartland Plastics Inc.; Model Kits; Paper Dolls; Games; Puzzles; Star Trek; Star Wars; Steiff Animals; Trolls.

Action Figures and Accessories

Back in 1964, Barbie dolls were sweeping the feminine side of the toy market by storm. Hasbro took a risky step in an attempt to capture the interest of the male segment of the population. Their answer to the Barbie doll craze was GI Joe. Since no self-respecting boy would admit to playing with dolls, Hasbro called their boy dolls 'action figures,' and to the surprise of many, they were phenomenally successful. Today action figures generate just as much enthusiasm among toy collectors as they ever did among little boys.

Action figures are simply dolls with poseable bodies. Some — the original GI Joes, for instance, were 12" tall, while others were 6" to 9" in height. In recent years, the 3¾" figure has been favored. GI Joe was introduced in the 3¾" size in the '80s and proved to be unprecedented in action figure sales. (See also GI Joe.)

In addition to the figures themselves, each company added a full line of accessories such as clothing, vehicles, play sets, weapons, etc. — all are avidly collected. Be aware of condition! Original packaging is extremely important. In fact, when it comes to the recent issues, loose, played-with examples are seldom worth more than a few dollars.

For more information, refer to *Collectible Action Figures* by Paris and Susan Manos, *Mego Toys* by Wallace M. Crouch, and *Collector's Guide to Dolls in Uniform* by Joseph Bourgeois. (All are published by Collector Books.)

Club: The Mego Adventurers Club
Old Forest Press, Inc.
PMB 195, 223 Wall St.
Huntington, NY 11743; Membership: $18.95 per year ($30 foreign); Includes 6 issues of *Mego Head,* the official club newsletter

A-Team, figures, Cobra, Python, Rattler or Viper, Galoob,
    6½", MOC, ea...**$22.00**
Action Jackson, accessory, Aussie Marine outfit, Mego,
    MIB **$15.00**
Action Jackson, accessory, Surf & Scuba outfit, Mego,
    MIB **$12.00**
Action Jackson, figure, Action Jackson, Army fatigues, red
    hair, Mego, 8", EX..**$20.00**
Adventures of Indiana Jones, figure, Indiana Jones, Kenner,
    4", NM..**$50.00**
Adventures of Indiana Jones, figure, Marion Ravenwood,
    Raiders of the Lost Ark, Kenner, 3¾", MOC.......**$200.00**
Adventures of Indiana Jones, playset, Wells of the Soul,
    MIB **$100.00**
Aliens, accessories, Evac Fighter or Power Loader, Kenner,
    MIB, ea **$30.00**
Aliens, figures, Arachnid, King, Queen or Swarm, Kenner,
    MOC, ea..**$25.00**
Aliens, playset, Queen Hive, Kenner, MIB **$50.00**

Batman (Animated Series), accessory, Joker Mobile, Kenner, MOC..**$30.00**

Batman (Animated Series), accessory, Triple Attack Jet, Kenner, MOC...**$20.00**

Batman (Animated Series), figure, Manhunt, Kenner, MOC.**$25.00**

Batman (Animated Series), figures, Bane, Bruce Wayne or Ras A Gual, Kenner, MOC.................................**$20.00**

Batman (Animated Series), figures, Clayface, Killer Kroc, Poison Ivy or Scarecrow, Kenner, MOC, ea **$30.00**

Batman Returns, accessory, Robin's Jet Foil Cycle, Kenner, MIB **$30.00**

Batman Returns, carring case, triangular, holds 12 figures, Tara Toy, EX...**$30.00**

Battlestar Galactica, accessory, Colonial Scarab, Mattel, M (NM Canadian box) **$60.00**

Battlestar Galactica, figure, Colonial Warrior, Mattel, 12", VG.**$30.00**

Beetlejuice, accessory, Vanishing Vault, Kenner, 1990, MIB.**$15.00**

Beetlejuice, figures, Showtime Beetlejuice, Spinhead Beetlejuice or Shishkebab Beetlejuice, Kenner, 1989, MOC, ea.**$15.00**

Best of the West, figure, Geronimo, complete, Marx, NM (EX box) **$140.00**

Best of the West, figure, Johnny West, complete, Marx, VG .**$40.00**

Best of the West, horse, Comanche, complete, Marx, EX (EX Fort Apache Fighters box) **$125.00**

Best of the West, playset, Circle X Ranch, Marx, MIB.....**$175.00**

Big Jim, accessory, Sports Camper w/Boat, Mattel, MIB...**$50.00**

Big Jim, figures, Dr Steel, Torpedo Fist, Warpath or Whip, complete, Mattel, EX, ea from $25 to....................**$30.00**

Big Jim, outfit, Jungle Vet, Mattel, MIP **$15.00**

Big Jim, playset, Kung Fu Studio, Mattel, MIB **$85.00**

Buck O'Hare, figures, Commander Dogstar, Dead-Eye Duck, Stormtoad Trooper or Toadborg, Hasbro, MOC, ea...**$10.00**

Buck Rogers in the 25th Century, figures, Draco, Killer Kane or Walking Twiki, Mego, 3¾", M, ea.....................**$25.00**

Captain Action, accessory, Silver Streak Amphibian Car, Ideal, 24", NM, from $650 to **$750.00**

Captain Action, accessory, Survival Kit, complete, Ideal, MIB **$200.00**

Captain Action, figure, Action Boy, complete, Ideal, 12", EX..**$400.00**

Captain Action, figure, Captain America, complete, Ideal, 12", VG..**$225.00**

Captain Action, outfit, Steve Canyon, complete, Ideal, MIB, from $400 to...**$500.00**

Captain Planet & the Planeteers, accessory, GEO Cruiser, Kenner/Tiger, MIB **$25.00**

Captain Planet & the Planeteers, figures, any character, Tiger/Kenner, MOC, ea **$15.00**

Captain Power, figures, any character, Mattel, MOC, ea from $15 to..**$20.00**

CHiPs, accessory, Rescue Bronco w/Launcher, Fleetwood, 1979, MOC...**$25.00**

CHiPs, figure, Wheels Willy, Mego, 3¾", MOC **$20.00**

Chuck Norris, figures, Kung-Fu, Battle Gear, Undercover Agent, Tabe or Ninja Warrior, Kenner, 6", MOC, ea.............**$15.00**

Dark Knight, figures, Bruce Wayne, Iron Winch Batman, Shadow-Wing Batman or Tec-Shield Batman, Kenner, MOC, ea...**$20.00**

DC Comics Super Heroes, figures, Aquaman, Green Lantern, Hawkman or Two Face, Toy Biz, 3¾", MOC, ea.**$25.00**

DC Comics Super Heroes, figures, Batman, Flash, Joker, Penguin, Riddler or Robin, Toy Biz, 3¾", MOC, ea.**$20.00**

Dick Tracy, figure, Flattop, Playmates, MOC..............**$20.00**

Dick Tracy, figures, any character except Flattop, Playmates, MOC, ea..**$10.00**

Dukes of Hazzard, figure, Coy, Mego, 8", MOC **$40.00**

Dukes of Hazzard, figure, Uncle Jesse, Mego, 3¾" **$35.00**

Dukes of Hazzard, figures, Bo, Boss Hogg, Daisy or Luke, Mego, 8", MOC, ea **$35.00**

Fighting Yank, figure, Mego, 12", MOB **$50.00**

Flash Gordon, figure sets, any, MIB, ea......................**$40.00**

Ghostbusters, figures, Egon Spengler, Janine or Winston Zeddmore, complete, Kenner, NM, ea **$40.00**

Happy Days, figure, Ralph, Potsie, or Richie, Mego, 1976, 8", MOC, from $50.00 to $60.00 each. (Photo courtesy Greg Davis and Bill Morgan)

He-Man, figures, any character, Mattel, MIC, ea..........**$15.00**

Hercules, figure, 3 different, Toy Biz, MOC, ea **$15.00**

Incredible Hulk, figures, Leader, Rampaging Hulk, Savage Hulk or She-Hulk, Toy Biz, MOC, ea....................**$15.00**

James Bond (Goldfinger), figure, Oddjob, Gilbert, 12", M (EX box) **$385.00**

James Bond (Moonraker), figures, Drax or Holly, Mego, 12", NMIB, ea **$135.00**

Kung Fu, figure, Kane, 6", MOC...............................**$60.00**

Land of the Lost, accessory, Jeep, Tiger, MOC...........**$20.00**

Land of the Lost, figures, Annie Porter, Kevin Porter, Tom Porter, Tasha or Shung, MOC, ea **$10.00**

Land of the Lost, figures, Talking Annie, Talking Kevin or Talking Stink, MOC, ea...................................**$15.00**

Land of the Lost, playset, Villain, Tiger, MOC............**$20.00**

Legends of Batman, figure, Ultimate Batman, Kenner, 15", MIB **$50.00**

Legends of Batman, figure set, Egyptian Batman & Catwoman, Kenner, MOC.............................**$25.00**

Legends of Batman, figure set, Pirate Batman & Two-Face, Kenner, MOC..**$25.00**

Legends of the Wild West, figures, Buffalo Bill, Cochise, Wild Bill Hickok or Wyatt Earp, 9½", NMIB, ea from $45 to...**$55.00**

Lone Ranger Rides Again, accessory, Landslide Adventure, Gabriel, MIB, from $25 to **$35.00**

Lone Ranger Rides Again, figures, Butch Cavendish or Little Bear, Gabriel, 9", NRFB, ea $50.00

Lost World of the Warlords, figures, any character, Remco, 6", MOC, ea from $15 to.....................................$20.00

Major Matt Mason, accessory, Astro Trac Vehicle, Mattel, MIB $150.00

Major Matt Mason, carrying case, vinyl spaceship, Mattel, 20", EX................................$65.00

Major Matt Mason, figure, Calisto, complete, Mattel, EX ...$75.00

Major Matt Mason, figure, Captain Lazer, complete, Mattel, 12", EX..................................$150.00

Man From UNCLE, accessory, Uncle Husky Car, Gilbert, MOC.$225.00

Man From UNCLE, figure, Illya Kuryakin, Gilbert, 12", VG (VG box) $150.00

Marvel Super Heroes, figure, Aquaman, complete, Mego, EX $45.00

Marvel Super Heroes, figure, Green Goblin, complete, Mego, NMIB..................................$200.00

Marvel Super Heroes, figure, Iron Man, complete, Mego, NMIB..................................$175.00

Marvel Super Heroes, playset, Super Vator, Mego, EX .$50.00

Marvel Super Heroes Secret Wars, figure, Daredevil & His Secret Shield, Mattel, 3¾", MOC...........................$40.00

Masters of the Universe, accessory, Slit Stalker, Mattel, MOC.$10.00

Masters of the Universe, figures, Moss Man, Roboto, Spiker, Sy-Klone or Two Bad, Mattel, MOC, ea.............$20.00

Masters of the Universe, playset, Fright Zone, Mattel, MIB.$85.00

Micronauts, figure, Acroyear, Mego, 3¾", MOC $50.00

Mortal Combat, figure set, Goro Vs Johnny Cage, complete w/Battle Arena, Hasbro, 1994, 4", MIP.................$20.00

Official Scout High Adventure, accessory, Avalanche at Blizzard Ridge, complete, Kenner, EX $25.00

Official Scout High Adventure, figures, Craig Cub or Steve Scout, Kenner, NRFB, ea $30.00

Official World's Greatest Super Heroes, figure, Spider-Man, complete, Mego, 12", M $35.00

Official World's Greatest Super Heroes, figures, Aquaman or Tarzan, 8", EX, ea $45.00

Pee Wee's Playhouse, figure, Miss Yvonne, Matchbox, 6", MOC.........................$30.00

Planet of the Apes, figures, Cornelius or Astronaut, complete, Mego, 8", EX, ea from $65 to $75.00

Power Rangers, figures, any character, Bandai, MIB, ea from $15 to.................................$20.00

RoboCop, figures, any character, Kenner, MOC, ea....$25.00

Robotech, figures, Dana Sterling, Lisa Haynes or Lynn Minmei, Matchbox, 12", MIB, ea..........................$30.00

Six Million Dollar Man, accessory, Bionic Mission Vehicle, Kenner, 20", EX.....................................$25.00

Six Million Dollar Man, figure, Bionic Bigfoot, complete, Kenner, 12", EX......................................$70.00

Space: 1999, figures, Commander Koenig, Dr Russell or Professor Bergman, Mattel, 9", MOC..................$50.00

Space: 1999, playset, Moon Base Alpha, complete, Mattel, MIB $300.00

Spider-Man (Animated Series), figures, any character, Toy Biz, MOC, ea.......................................$15.00

Super Mario Brothers, figures, any character, Ertl, 1993, MOC, ea $10.00

Super Powers, accessory, Darkseid Destroyer, Kenner, MIB.$45.00

Super Powers, figure, Joker, complete w/ID card & comic book, Kenner, NM $35.00

Super Powers, figures, Batman or Robin, Kenner, MOC....$45.00

SWAT, figures, Decon, Hondo or Luca, LJN, 8", MOC, ea..$25.00

Terminator 2, figure, John Conner, Kenner, MOC.......$25.00

Terminator 2, figures, any except John Conner, Kenner, MOC, ea.............................$20.00

Toxic Crusaders, figure, Toxic Crusader, Playmates, 1991, 5", MOC..............................$15.00

Universal Monsters, figure, Mummy, glow-in-the-dark, Remco, 3¾", MOC $75.00

Venom, figures, any character from 1st or 2nd series, Toy Biz, MOC, ea.............................$15.00

World Championship Wrestling, figure sets, Hulk Hogan & Sting or Nasty Boys, San Francisco Toymakers, MOC, ea .$25.00

World Wrestling Championship, figure, Hulk Hogan, Johnny Badd, Ric Flair or Sting, Vader, SF Toymakers, MOC, ea $15.00

World Wrestling Federation, figure, any from Jakks Stomp Series, MOC, ea......................$15.00

World Wrestling Federation, figure, Bart or Billy Gunn, Hasbro, MOC (green), ea....................$35.00

World Wrestling Federation, figure, Jesse Ventura, Hasbro, MOC.................................$45.00

X-Force, figures, Deadpool, Domino or The Blob, MOC, ea .$20.00

X-Men, figures, any character from Animated Series or Flashback Series, Toy Biz, MOC, ea.....................$15.00

X-Men, figures, any character from Mutant Armor Series, Toy Biz, MOC, ea from $15 to $20.00

Battery Operated

It is estimated that approximately 95% of the battery-operated toys that were so popular from the '40s through the '60s came from Japan. The remaining 5% were made in the United States by other companies. To market these toys in America, many distributorships were organized. Some of the largest were Cragstan, Linemar, and Rosko. But even American toy makers such as Marx, Ideal, Hubley, and Daisy sold them under their own names, so the trademarks you'll find on Japanese battery-operated toys are not necessarily that of the manufacturer, and it's sometimes just about impossible to determine the specific company that actually did make them. After peaking in the '60s, the Japanese toy industry began a decline, bowing out to competition from the cheaper diecast and plastic toy makers.

Remember that it is rare to find one of these complex toys that has survived in good, collectible condition. Batteries caused corrosion, lubricants dried out, cycles were interrupted and mechanisms ruined, rubber hoses and bellows aged and cracked, so the mortality rate was extremely high. A toy rated good, that is showing signs of wear but well taken care of, is generally worth about half as much as the same toy in mint (like new) condition. Besides condition, battery-operated toys are rated on scarcity, desirability, and the number of 'actions' they preform. A 'major' toy is one that has three or more actions, while one that has only one or two is considered 'minor.' The latter, of course, are worth much less.

In addition to the books we referenced in the beginning narrative to the toy category, you'll find more information in *Collecting Battery Toys* by Don Hultzman (Books Americana).

Alps, Accordion Bear, 1950s, remote control, 11", EXIB ..**$800.00**
Alps, Antique Gooney Car, 1960s, 9", MIB...............**$150.00**
Alps, Bongo Monkey, 1960s, 9½", EX **$165.00**
Alps, Bubble Blowing Monkey, 1959, 10", EX **$200.00**
Alps, Chippy the Chipmunk, 1950s, MIB...................**$225.00**
Alps, Drumming Polar Bear, 1960s, 12", EX..............**$200.00**
Alps, French Cat, 1950s, 10", EX **$100.00**
Alps, Trumpet Playing Bunny, 1950s, 10", EX...........**$300.00**
Aoshin, Smoking Volkswagen, 1960s, NM.................**$175.00**
Bandai, Comic Road Roller, 1960s, 9", EX **$150.00**
Bandai, Flipper the Spouting Dolphin, MIB..............**$125.00**
Bandai, Pete the Indian, MIB...................................**$175.00**
Cragstan, Dilly Dalmatian, MIB **$250.00**
Cragstan, Growling Tiger Trophy Plaque, 1950s, 10", NM...**$250.00**
Cragstan, Nautilus Periscope, MIB **$225.00**
Cragstan, School Bus, 1950s, 20½", NM **$150.00**
Daiya, Josie the Walking Cow, 1950s, EX.................**$125.00**
Frankonia, Ol' MacDonald's Farm Truck, 1960s, complete
    w/plastic animals, EX **$100.00**
Gakken, Musical Show Boat, 1960s, 13", EX.............**$250.00**
Hubley, Mr Magoo Car, 1961, 9", MIB.....................**$375.00**
Ideal, Clancy the Great, 1960s, MIB........................**$375.00**
Illco, Mickey Mouse Loop the Loop, MIB **$175.00**
Illco, Pink Panther One Man Band, 1970s, 11" **$125.00**
K, Jolly Bear the Drummer Boy, 1950s, NM.............**$275.00**
K, Merry Rabbit, 1950s, 11", EX...............................**$200.00**
K, Traveler Bear, 1950s, 8", NM...............................**$375.00**
Linemar, Dick Tracy Police Car, remote control, 1949, 8",
    EXIB...**$475.00**
Linemar, Doxie the Dog, 1950s, 9", EX....................**$65.00**
Linemar, Electro Fire Engine, MIB...........................**$175.00**
Linemar, Electro Sand Loader w/Conveyor, MIB **$225.00**
Linemar, Telephone Bear, 1950s, 7½", MIB.............**$450.00**
Linemar, Walking Donkey, 1950s, 9", EX..................**$175.00**
Marx, Honeymoon Express, 1947, EX........................**$125.00**
Marx, Hopping Astro, 4", NM **$250.00**
Marx, International Agent Car, MIB..........................**$200.00**
Marx, Sheriff Sam Whoopee Car, 1960s, 5½", EX.....**$250.00**
Mego, Roll-Over Rover, 1970s, 9", EX......................**$35.00**
MT, ABC Fairy Train, 14", EXIB...............................**$175.00**
MT, B-Z Rabbit, 1950s, 7", EX.................................**$125.00**
MT, Popcorn Eating Panda, NM **$175.00**
Nasta, Raggedy Ann Vacuum Cleaner Doll, 1973, 10",
    MIB **$35.00**
Plaything Toy, Sam the Shaving Man, 1960s, MIB....**$450.00**
Remco, Johnny Speedmobile, 1960s, 15", EX...........**$285.00**
Rosko, Pretty Peggy Parrot, 10", EXIB **$425.00**
S&E, Playing Monkey, 1950s, 10", EX **$40.00**
SAN, Smoking Grandpa, eyes open, 1950s, 9", MIB.**$300.00**

TN, Big John Indian Chief, 1960s, 12½", MIB..........**$125.00**
TN, Black Smithy Bear, 1950s, 9", EX **$375.00**
TN, Coffeetime Bear, 1960s, 10", EX.......................**$250.00**
TN, Jo-Jo the Flipping Monkey, 1970s, 10", EX........**$100.00**
TN, Jolly Penguin, 1950s, remote control, 7", EX **$200.00**

TN, Loop the Clown, 10½", EX, $125.00; MIB, from $175.00 to $200.00.

TN, Maxwell Coffee-Loving Bear, 1960s, 10", NMIB.**$250.00**
TN, Sammy Wong the Tea Totaler, 1950s, 10" **$325.00**
TPS, Dune Buggy, 1960s, 11", EX **$100.00**
TPS, New Service Car (World News), 9½", EX..........**$400.00**
Y, Cheerful Dachshund, 1960s, 8½", EX....................**$85.00**
Y, Cragston Crapshooter, 1950s, 9", MIB **$175.00**
Y, Grand-Pa Car, 1950s, 9", EX...............................**$100.00**
Yanoman, Pepi the Tumbling Monkey, 1960s, MIB..**$100.00**
YM, Acrobat Clown, 1960s, 9", EXIB **$125.00**

Guns

One of the bestselling kinds of toys ever made, toy guns were first patented in the late 1850s. Until WWII most were made of cast iron, though other materials were used on a lesser scale. After the war, cast iron became cost prohibitive, and steel and diecast zinc were used. By 1950 most were made of either diecast material or plastic. Hundreds of names can be found embossed on these little guns, a custom which continues to the present time. Because of their tremendous popularity and durability, today's collectors can find a diversity of models and styles, and prices are still fairly affordable.

See also Cowboy Character Collectibles.

Newsletter: *Toy Gun Collectors of America*
Jim Buskirk, Editor and Publisher
3009 Oleander Ave., San Marcos, CA 92069; 760-559-1054. Published quarterly, covers both toy and BB guns. Dues: $17 per year

Alps Cosmic Ray Gun, tin w/attached siren, 5", NM (EX box)...**$125.00**
Daisy Annie Oakley Holster Set, complete w/2 diecast pistols
    & bullets, 1950s, M (EX box)..............................**$650.00**
Daisy BB Target Pistol, black-painted pressed steel w/brown
    grips, 10", NM (VG box) **$85.00**
Daisy Model 76 Flintlock Rifle, brown plastic stock w/gold
    trim, black metal barrel, 37", NM........................**$50.00**

Daisy Rocket Dart Pistol, pressed steel, complete w/darts & target, 8", NMIB **$200.00**

Daisy Zooka Pop Pistol, painted pressed steel, red, yellow & blue, 7½", VG **$135.00**

Esquire Hide-Away Derringer, diecast, 1960, 3½", EX ..**$30.00**

Esquire Lugar Cap Pistol, diecast w/gold finish, 1960, NM **$50.00**

Futuristic Products Strato Gun, diecast w/chrome finish, red trim, 1950s, 9", NM **$250.00**

Hubley Army .45 Cap Pistol, diecast w/NP finish, white plastic grips, 1950s, 6½", EX.......................................**$85.00**

Hubley Cowboy Dummy Cap Pistol, cast iron w/nickel finish, white plastic grips, 1940, 8", NM.................**$175.00**

Hubley Remington .36 Cap Pistol, diecast, 1950s, 8", NM..**$125.00**

Hubley Secret Rifle Cap Gun, diecast steel & plastic, 1960, EX **$100.00**

Hubley Texan Jr Cap Pistol, diecast w/nickel finish, white plastic grips w/black steer heads, 9½", EX...........**$75.00**

Hubley 110 Ranch Cap Gun, cast iron, 1930, 11½", VG ..**$225.00**

Ja-Ru, Beetle Bailey Cork Gun, plastic, 1981, 6", MOC.......**$30.00**

Ja-Ru Dick Tracy Bullet Gun, NMOC **$25.00**

Kenton Buffalo Bill Cap Pistol, cast iron w/lacquered finish, 1931, 13½", EX **$300.00**

Kilgore Big Horn Cap Pistol, diecast w/silver finish, 1950s, 7", NMIB...**$100.00**

Kilgore Dude Derringer, diecast w/silver finish, heavy scroll work, black plastic grips, 4", MOC........................**$25.00**

Kilgore G-Man Cap Pistol, cast iron, 6", EX **$125.00**

Kilgore Police Chief Cap Pistol, cast iron w/nickel finish, 1938, 5", EX...**$75.00**

Kilgore Presto Cap Gun, cast iron, automatic, 1940, 5⅛", VG..**$65.00**

Kilgore Private Eye Cap Pistol, diecast w/silver finish, lift-up cap door, 1950s, 6½", NMIB **$35.00**

Knickerbocker Davy Crockett Water Pistol, blue plastic w/brass nozzle, 1950s, 9", MOC **$75.00**

Knickerbocker 4-Barrel Space Dart Gun, gray & black plastic, w/4 rubber-tipped darts, 10", NM **$75.00**

Larami Captain America Clicker Gun, blue plastic, 1974, MIP **$20.00**

Leslie-Henry Gene Autry .44 Pistol, diecast w/nickel finish, embossed horse head grips, 1950s, 11", NM (VG box) **$300.00**

Leslie-Henry Gunsmoke Cap Pistol, diecast w/nickel finish, brown plastic horse head grips, 1950s, 9", NM..**$150.00**

Leslie-Henry Marshal Cap Pistol, diecast w/nickel finish, white plastic grips w/black shamrock, 1950s, 10", EX.....**$125.00**

Lone Star Cisco Kid Cap Pistol & Holster, diecast w/chrome finish, brown plastic horse head grips, 1960, 9", M......**$275.00**

Lone Star Space Gun, red-painted metal, 7½", VG..**$100.00**

Lone Star 9mm Lugar Cap Pistol, diecast w/black-painted finish, brown plastic grips, 8", NM **$50.00**

Marubishi Space Gun, litho tin w/plastic barrels, friction, 1960s, 8", EX **$100.00**

Marx Davy Crockett Clicker Gun, litho tin, 1952, 10", EX..**$150.00**

Marx Flash Gordon Arresting Ray Gun, litho tin, 1930s, 10", NM **$200.00**

Marx Flash Gordon Click Ray Pistol, litho tin, 10", NM (NM box) **$300.00**

Marx Siren Signal Pistol, yellow plastic w/siren sound & bulit-in whistle, 1950, 7", NMIB......................**$75.00**

Marx Sparking Burp Gun, 1950s, 24", EX..................**$85.00**

Marx US Army Automatic Rifle, plastic BAR-type w/removable bipod, battery-op, 1960s, 32½", NM **$85.00**

Mattel, Shootin' Shell Buffalo Hunter Holster Set, complete w/6 cartridges, 1960, 9", EX..............................**$250.00**

Mattel Fanner-50 Cap Pistol, diecast w/silver finish, plastic stag grips, 1965, 11", EX......................................**$125.00**

Mattel Shootin' Shell Snub-Nose .38 Cap Pistol, diecast w/chrome finish, brown plastic grips, 1959, 7", VG .**$85.00**

Mattel Thunder-Burp Machine Gun, black plastic, 1957, EX...**$60.00**

Nichols Dyna-Mite Derringer, diecast w/nickel finish, white plastic grips, 1950s, 3", MIB **$55.00**

Nichols Hide-A-Mite Derringer, complete, MOC.........**$50.00**

Nichols Spitfire Saddle Rifle, diecast w/nickel finish, 1950s, 9", MIB...**$65.00**

Norton-Horner Buck Rogers Sonic Ray Gun, plastic, battery-op, 1950, 7", NMIB **$150.00**

Ohio Art Astro Ray Signal-Dart Gun & Target, litho tin & plastic, battery-op, 10" gun w/13" dia target, 1960s, EX.......**$100.00**

Park Plastics Dee Gee Water Gun, black plastic w/2 brass nozzles, 1950s, 3", NM..**$20.00**

Pery Super Nova Space Gun, white plastic w/red trim, friction, 1980s, 17½", MOC..**$40.00**

Ranger Steel Cosmic Ray Gun, pressed steel w/yellow plastic barrel, 1955, 8½", G.......................................**$85.00**

Remco Batman Bat Ray Gun, black plastic, battery-op, 1979, MIB...**$55.00**

Remco Electronic Signal Ray Gun, red plastic w/gray trim, internal color wheel, 1950s, 9", NM (EX box)....**$150.00**

Renwal Stratoblaster, black plastic w/missiles & rockets embossed on grips, 27", NM (VG box)...............**$150.00**

Stevens Billy the Kid Repeating Cap Pistol, diecast metal w/buffalos embossed on plastic grip, 7½", NM (G box)..**$150.00**

Stevens Western Boy Cap Pistol, cast iron w/nickel finish, white plastic grips w/& red jewels, 1940, 8", NM............**$100.00**

Thomas Western Water Rifle, gray plastic, 27", 1960s, NMIB..**$50.00**

Wicke James Bond 007 PPK Cap Pistol, black plastic w/diecast works, 1983, 6", MOC **$55.00**

Ramp Walkers

Though ramp-walking figures were made as early as the 1870s, ours date from about 1935 on. They were made in Czechoslovakia from the '20s through the '40s and in this country during the '50s and '60s by Marx, who made theirs of plastic. John Wilson of Watsontown, Pennsylvania, sold his worldwide. They were known as 'Wilson Walkies' and stood about 4½" high. But the majority has been imported from Hong Kong.

Advisor: Randy Welch (See Directory, Toys)

Astro & Rosey, Hanna-Barbera/Marx	**$95.00**
Baby Walk-A-Way, plastic, lg	**$40.00**
Big Bad Wolf & Mason Pig, Disney/Marx	**$50.00**
Black Mammy, Wilson	**$35.00**
Brontosaurus w/Monkey, Marx	**$40.00**
Bunny, pushing cart, plastic	**$60.00**
Camel w/2 Humps, head bobs, plastic	**$20.00**
Choo-Choo Cherry, Funny Face Kool-Aid	**$60.00**
Dairy Cow, plastic	**$15.00**
Dog, Pluto look-alike w/metal legs, plastic, sm	**$15.00**
Donald Duck, pulling nephews in wagon, Disney/Marx	**$35.00**
Donald Duck, Wilson	**$175.00**
Duck, plastic	**$15.00**
Elephant, Wilson	**$30.00**
Eskimo, Wilson	**$100.00**
Farmer, pushing wheelbarrow, plastic	**$20.00**
Fiddler & Fifer Pigs, Disney/Marx	**$50.00**
Figaro the Cat w/Ball, Disney	**$30.00**
Fred Flintstone & Wilma on Dino, Hanna-Barbera/Marx	**$60.00**
Hap & Hop Soldiers, Marx	**$20.00**
Hippo w/Native, Marx	**$40.00**
Horse, yellow plastic w/rubber ears & string tail, lg	**$30.00**
Horse w/English Rider, plastic	**$40.00**
Indian Chief, Wilson	**$45.00**
Jiminy Cricket w/Cello, Marx	**$30.00**
Lion w/Clown, Marx	**$40.00**
Mad Hatter w/March Hare, Marx	**$50.00**
Man, w/carved wood hat, Czechoslovakian	**$30.00**
Minnie Mouse, pushing baby stroller, Marx	**$35.00**
Nurse, Wilson	**$30.00**
Olive Oyl, Wilson	**$175.00**
Penguin, Wilson	**$25.00**
Pig, Wilson	**$30.00**
Pinocchio, Wilson	**$175.00**
Policeman, Czechoslovakian	**$60.00**
Popeye, pushing spinach can wheelbarrow, Marx	**$40.00**
Popeye, Wilson	**$175.00**
Rabbit, Wilson	**$60.00**
Root'n Toot'n Raspberry, Funny Face Kool-Aid	**$60.00**
Sailor, Wilson	**$30.00**
Santa & Snowman, faces on both sides, Marx	**$50.00**
Santa Claus, w/gold sack, Marx	**$45.00**
Santa Claus, Wilson	**$75.00**
Soldier, Wilson	**$25.00**
Spark Plug, Marx	**$200.00**
Teeny Toddler, plastic, Dolls Inc, lg	**$40.00**
Top Cat & Benny, Marx	**$65.00**
Walking Baby, w/moving eyes & cloth dress, plastic, lg	**$40.00**
Wimpy, Wilson	**$175.00**
Yogi Bear & Huckleberry Hound, Hanna-Barbera/Marx	**$50.00**
Zebra w/Native, Marx	**$40.00**

Rings

Toy rings are a fairly new interest in the collecting world. Earlier radio and TV mail-order premiums have been popular for some time but have increased in value considerably over the past few years. Now there is a growing interest in other types of rings as well — those from gumball machines, World's Fairs souvenirs, movie and TV show promotions, and any depicting celebrities. They may be metal or plastic; most have adjustable shanks. New rings are already being sought out as future collectibles.

Note: All rings listed here are considered to be in fine to very fine condition. Wear, damage and missing parts will devaluate them considerably.

Advisors: Bruce and Jan Thalberg (See Directory, Toys)

Bazooka Joe, initial ring, 1950s	**$250.00**
Buck Rogers, Ring of Saturn, 1940s, from $450 to	**$475.00**
Captain Midnight, Marine Corp, 1940s, from $350 to	**$450.00**
Captain Midnight, Skelly Oil, red V, 1940s	**$200.00**
Cisco Kid, club, 1950s	**$250.00**
Cisco Kid, saddle, 1950s	**$450.00**
Dick Tracy, monogram, 1930s	**$650.00**
Dick Tracy, secret compartment, 1940s, from $200 to	**$300.00**
Don Winslow, member, 1930s, from $850 to	**$1,200.00**
Frank Buck, elephant, 1930s	**$300.00**
Gene Autry, flag, 1950s	**$150.00**
Gerber Baby Food, 1940s	**$125.00**
Hopalong Cassidy, compass, brass w/removable black-painted hat, 1950s, EX	**$200.00**

Hopalong Cassidy, face, NM, $75.00.

Howdy Doody, face in relief, silver-tone, 1950s	**$150.00**
Jack Armstrong, crocodile, 1940s	**$900.00**
Jimmy Allen, flying club, 1930s	**$150.00**
Joe E Brown, club, 1940s	**$250.00**
Kit Carson, TV, 1950s	**$300.00**
Lassie, friendship, 1950s	**$200.00**
Laugh-In, flicker, 1960s	**$25.00**
Lone Ranger, flashlight, brass, 1940s, EX+	**$75.00**
Lone Ranger, 6-shooter, 1940s, from $135 to	**$150.00**
Martin Luther King, flicker, 1960s, set of 6	**$150.00**
Melvin Pervis, G-Man Corp, 1930s	**$100.00**
Mickey Mouse, dome top, 1940s	**$350.00**
Monster Fink, 1960s, set of 4	**$25.00**
Mr Peanut, 1950s	**$50.00**
Mr Softie, flicker, 1960s	**$125.00**
Oscar Meyer Weiner, boy's, 1950s	**$15.00**
Poll Parrot/Howdy Doody, flicker, 1950s	**$140.00**
Quaker, jingle bell, 1950s	**$30.00**
Radio Orphan Annie, face, 1940s, from $125 to	**$175.00**
Roy Rogers, branding iron, 1950s, from $225 to	**$275.00**

Roy Rogers, face, 1950s $125.00
Shadow, blue coal, 1940s, from $500 to....................$550.00
Sky King, Aztec calendar, 1940s, from $550 to $750.00
Sky King, radar, 1940s...$200.00
Straight Arrow, Good Luck, bronze, 1950s.................$50.00
Superman, crusader, 1940s, from $250 to..................$300.00
Tales of Texas Rangers, 1950s $40.00
Tom Corbett, face, 1950s $125.00
Tom Mix, circus, 1930s, from $50 to..........................$60.00
Tom Mix, target, 1930s..$300.00
Walnetto's, saddle, 1940s..$150.00
Weather Bird Shoes, 1950s..$250.00
Wheaties, compass, 1940s...$50.00
Wyatt Earp, Marshall, initial, 1950s, from $100 to.....$150.00
Zorro, logo, lg Z, 1960s..$75.00

Robots and Space Toys

Japanese toy manufacturers introduced their robots and
space toys as early as 1948. Some of the best examples were
made in the '50s, during the 'golden age' of battery-operated
toys. They became more and more complex, and today some
of these in excellent condition may bring well over
$1,000.00. By the '60s, more and more plastic was used in
their production, and the toys became inferior.

Acrobat, Y, robot does acrobatics, plastic, battery-op, EX ...$225.00
Apollo Lunar Module, Japan, litho tin & plastic, battery-op,
    9", MIB...$250.00
Apollo Space Patrol, battery-op, EX (EX box) $175.00
Apollo Spacecraft, MT, 1960s, several actions, w/detachable
    astronaut, litho tin, battery-op, 10", EX..............$250.00
Atomic Robot, Japan, advances w/step-over action, litho tin,
    wind-up, 5", NM $750.00
Blue Eagle Space Rocket, battery-op, MIB................$450.00
Cragstan Satellite, 1950s, litho tin, battery-op, 5½", VG ..$175.00
Electric Robot, Marx, 1950s, several actions, litho tin, battery-
    op, 14½", EX...$200.00
Esso Energy Rocket, battery-op, MIB.......................$375.00
Excavator Robot, SH, 1960s, several actions, plastic & tin, 10",
    EX $200.00
Fighting Spaceman, SH, 1960s, several actions, battery-op,
    litho tin, 12", EX...$300.00
Flashing Rocketship Space Patrol, Irwin, 1950s, several
    actions, plastic, battery-op, 7½", EX....................$85.00
Flying Saucer Z-101, England, 1950s, litho tin, 7", scarce,
    EX $250.00
Jupiter Jyro Set, Tomy, 1970s, mostly plastic, battery-op, 13",
    EX $125.00
King Flying Saucer, KO, 1960s, 3 actions, battery-op, 7½" dia,
    EX $150.00
Laughing Robot, Y, 1970s, 3 actions, mostly plastic, battery-
    op, 9½", EX..$125.00
Lunar Captain, TN, 1960s, several actions, battery-op, 13½",
    EX $225.00
Marching Drummer Robot (Babes in Toyland Look-Alike),
    battery-op, NM...$400.00

Mars King, SH, 1960s, advances w/light-up space scene in
    chest & sound, litho tin, battery-op, 9½", VG $200.00
Mars 3 Space Rocket, TN, 1960s, several actions, battery-op,
    15", EX...$200.00
Mercury Space Saucer X-1, Y, 1960s, several actions, battery-
    op, 8" dia, EX..$150.00
Moon Crawler X-12, battery-op, M............................$100.00
Moon Man 001, Hong Kong, 1960s, mostly plastic, battery-
    op, 6", rare, EX, minimum value.........................$175.00
Moon Orbiter, Yonezawa, advances & spins as astronaut flies
    above, plastic, wind-up, NMIB............................$150.00
Moon Patrol 11, Y, 1960s, several actions, tin & plastic, bat-
    tery-op, 9" dia, EX...$200.00
Nike Missle Sam-A7, Daiya, advances w/sparks, litho tin, fric-
    tion, 18½", NM (EX box) $300.00
Pete the Spaceman, Bandai, 1960s, battery-op, MIB...$225.00
Planet Explorer X-80, MT, 1960s, several actions, litho tin,
    battery-op, 8" dia, EX..$185.00
Radar Robot, SH, advances w/step-over action, plastic, wind-
    up, 7", NM (NM box) $125.00
Radar Tank, MT, 1950s, 3 actions, litho tin w/plastic antenna,
    battery-op, 8", NM $250.00
Robert the Robot, Ideal, 1940s-50s, red & gray plastic, bat-
    tery-op, 14", scarce, NMIB, from $250 to............$350.00
Robot Commando, battery-op, MIB $650.00
Robot YM-3, Masuraya, 1980s, gray plastic, battery-op, 5", MIB ..$25.00
Rocket X-202, Spain, 1950s, litho tin, friction, 10½", VG (G
    box) $100.00
Rocket XB-115, SH, advances w/lights & sounds, litho tin &
    plastic, friction, 12", MIB....................................$175.00
Rotating Satellite, Gesha, satellite spins around Earth, litho
    tin, 8", NM (EX box)..$150.00
Saturn V Apollo II Rocket, Hong Kong, plastic & tin, 14", EX
    (EX box) $200.00
Solar-X Space Rocket, TN, several actions, litho tin & plastic,
    battery-op, 15", EX (EX box) $125.00
Sounding Robot, SH, advances w/sound, plastic, battery-op,
    10½", MIB...$200.00
Space Capsule #5, MT, 1960s, several actions, litho tin & plas-
    tic, battery-op, 10½", EX $300.00
Space Explorer S-61, Japan, litho tin, friction, 13", EX.$65.00
Space Fighter Robot, SH, 1970s, several action, tin & plastic,
    9", NM...$150.00
Space Orbitestor, Asakusa, 1960s, 3 actions, tin & plastic, bat-
    tery-op, 8", EX...$185.00
Space Patrol XII Tank, battery-op, VG......................$185.00
Space Pioneer Vehicle, MT, 1960s, 3 actions, litho tin, battery-
    op, 12", EX...$300.00
Space Ranger Flying Saucer No 3, battery-op, MIB ..$175.00
Space Tank M-41, MT, 1950s, several actions, litho tin w/plas-
    tic antenna, battery-op, 9", EX............................$200.00
Space Tank X-4, TN, advances w/sound, litho tin, friction, 7",
    MIB..$175.00
Spacecraft Jupiter, K, advances w/sparks, litho tin w/clear
    plastic dome, windup, 5" dia, NMIB...................$150.00
Spaceship X-8, Tada, 1960s, several actions, litho tin, battery-
    op, 8", EX...$200.00

Spitz Junior Planetarium, Harmonic Reed Corp, 1956, plastic globe plugs in & shows stars, planets, etc, MIB .**$175.00**

Strange Explorer, DSK, 1960s, several actions, battery-op, 7½", EX.....................**$250.00**

Super Space Capsule, SH, 1960s, advances, stops & door opens to reveal pilot, tin & plastic, 9", EX **$200.00**

Swivel-O-Matic Astronaut, SH, 1960s, several actions, litho tin, battery-op, 11½", EX.....................**$165.00**

Twikki Robot (Buck Rogers), plastic, wind-up, 7", NM ..**$75.00**

UFO X-05, MT, 1970s, battery-op, MIB.....................**$175.00**

Vanguard Satellite Launcher, Remco, 1960s, battery-op, MIB **$275.00**

Video Robot, SH, 1960s, 3 actions, litho tin, battery-op, 10", EX **$185.00**

Yoshiya, Space Dog, windup, walks from side to side, ears flap, mouth opens, EX, $235.00.

Slot Car Racers

Slot cars first became popular in the early 1960s. Electric raceways set up in storefront windows were commonplace. Huge commercial tracks with eight and ten lanes were located in hobby stores and raceways throughout the United States. Large corporations such as Aurora, Revell, Monogram, and Cox, many of which were already manufacturing toys and hobby items, jumped on the bandwagon to produce slot cars and race sets. By the end of the early 1970s, people were losing interest in slot racing, and its popularity diminished. Today the same baby boomers that raced slot cars in earlier days are revitalizing the sport. Vintage slot cars have made a comeback as one of the hottest automobile collectibles of the 1990s. Want ads for slot cars frequently appear in newspapers and publications geared toward the collector. As you would expect, slot cars were generally well used, so finding vintage cars and race sets in like-new or mint condition is difficult. Slot cars replicating the 'muscle' cars from the '60s and '70s are extremely sought after, and clubs and organizations devoted to these collectibles are becoming more and more commonplace. Large toy companies such as Tomy and Tyco still produce some slots today, but not in the quality, quantity, or variety of years past.

Advisor: Gary Pollastro (See Directory, Toys)

Accessory, Aurora AFX Billboard Retaining Walls, set of 8, EXIB..........................**$15.00**

Accessory, Aurora Model Motoring Steering Wheel Controller, EX........................**$10.00**

Accessory, Aurora Power Passers Controller, red, EX.**$10.00**

Accessory, Tyco HO Scale 1973-74 Handbook, EX **$10.00**

Accessory, Tyco Terminal Pack, EX **$5.00**

Car, Aurora AFX, '55 Chevy Bel Air, #1913, yellow, VG.....**$16.00**

Car, Aurora AFX, Blazer, #1917, black, blue & white, VG.**$12.00**

Car, Aurora AFX, Chevy Nomad, #1760, chrome, EX .**$25.00**

Car, Aurora AFX, Chevy Nomad #1760, orange, EX ...**$20.00**

Car, Aurora AFX, Dodge Fever Dragster, white & yellow, EX **$15.00**

Car, Aurora AFX, Dodge Police Van, white w/black stripe, VG **$15.00**

Car, Aurora AFX, Firebird, #1965, black & gold, EX+.**$15.00**

Car, Aurora AFX, Turbo Porsche #3, red, white & blue, no decal, VG........................**$10.00**

Car, Aurora AFX, VW Baja Bug, #1914, lime, VG **$20.00**

Car, Aurora Cigarbox, Ferrari GTO, red w/white stripe, G....**$10.00**

Car, Aurora Cigarbox, Ford GT, white w/black stripe, NM+ .**$20.00**

Car, Aurora G-Plus, Amrac Can Am, yellow & black w/white stripe, EX **$15.00**

Car, Aurora G-Plus, Datsun 240-Z, red, white & blue, EX .**$14.00**

Car, Aurora G-Plus, Indy Valvoline, black, VG...........**$12.00**

Car, Aurora G-Plus, Rallye Ford Escort, #1737, green & blue, EX........................**$15.00**

Car, Aurora Thunderjet, '63 Corvette, #1356, yellow, EX ..**$50.00**

Car, Aurora Thunderjet, Cobra GT, #1396, candy blue & silver, EX **$60.00**

Car, Aurora Thunderjet, Ford J Car, #1430, yellow & blue, EX **$25.00**

Car, Aurora Thunderjet, Porsche 904, #1376, blue w/white stripe, EX........................**$30.00**

Car, TCR, Mack Truck, white & red, EX **$15.00**

Car, TCR, Maintenance Van, white & red, EX **$15.00**

Car, TCR, Mercury Stock Car, purple & chrome, VG ..**$15.00**

Car, Tyco, '40 Ford Coupe, #8534, black w/flames, EX..**$20.00**

Car, Tyco, A-Team Van, black w/red stripe, EX..........**$40.00**

Car, Tyco, Bandit Pickup, black & yellow, EX............**$12.00**

Car, Tyco, Camero Z-28, blue & white w/red stripe, EX.**$10.00**

Car, Tyco, Corvette Cliffhanger #2, yellow & black, EX...**$10.00**

Car, Tyco, Jam Car, yellow & black, EX **$10.00**

Car, Tyco, Jeep CJ-7, red & light blue, VG.................**$12.00**

Car, Tyco, Mustang #1, orange w/yellow flames, VG.**$20.00**

Car, Tyco, Superbird, #8533, red, white & blue, VG+ ..**$15.00**

Car, Tyco, Van-Tastic, #8539, blue & white, VG **$20.00**

Set, Atlas Racing Set #1000, HO scale, G (G box)....**$100.00**

Set, Aurora AFX Devil's Ditch, EX............................**$40.00**

Set, Aurora Home Raceway by Sears, #79N9513C, VG.**$225.00**

Set, Cox Ontario 8, #3070, w/Eagle & McLaren, G (G box) .**$75.00**

Set, Eldon Raceway Set #24, 1/24th scale, VG..........**$175.00**

Set, Mini-Motorific Set, #4939-5, EX **$85.00**

Set, Remco Mighty Mike Action Track, NMIB **$100.00**

Set, Strombecker 4-Lane Mark IV Race Set, VG (VG box).**$250.00**

Set, Tyco Racing Bandit, EX **$30.00**

Vehicles

These are the types of toys that are intensely dear to the heart of many a collector. Having a beautiful car is part of the

American dream, and over the past eighty years, just about as many models, makes, and variations have been made as toys for children as the real vehicles for adults. Novices and advanced collectors alike are easily able to find something to suit their tastes as well as their budgets.

One area that is especially volatile includes those '50s and '60s tin scale-model autos by foreign manufacturers — Japan, U.S. Zone Germany, and English toy makers. Since these are relatively modern, you'll still be able to find some at yard sales and flea markets at reasonable prices.

There are several good references for these toys: *Collecting Toy Cars and Trucks* by Richard O'Brien; *Hot Wheels, A Collector's Guide,* by Bob Parker; *Collector's Guide to Tootsietoys* by David Richter; *Collector's Guide to Tonka Trucks, 1947 – 1963,* by Don and Barb deSalle; *Collectible Coca-Cola Toy Trucks* by Gael de Courtivron; *Matchbox Toys, 1948 to 1993,* and *Collector's Guide to Diecast Toys and Scale Models* by Dana Johnson; *The Golden Age of Automotive Toys, 1925 – 1941,* by Ken Hutchinson and Greg Johnson; and *Motorcycle Toys, Antique and Contemporary,* by Sally Gibson-Downs and Christine Gentry.

Newsletter: *The Replica*
Bridget Shine, Editor
Highways 136 and 20, Dyersville, IA 52040; 319-875-2000

Newsletter: *Matchbox USA*
Charles Mack
62 Saw Mill Rd., Durham, CT 06422; 203-349-1655

AC Williams, Mack Stake Truck, cast iron, blue w/nickel-plated spoke wheels, 5", NM.....................................**$400.00**

AC Williams, 1936 Delivery Van, cast iron, blue w/white rubber tires & red hubs, 4½", VG.............................**$550.00**

AC Williams, 1936 Roadster, cast iron, blue w/nickel-plated windshield & bumper, rubber tires w/red hubs, 4¼", EX...**$450.00**

Arcade, Century of Progress Greyhound Bus, cast iron, 12", EX...**$350.00**

Arcade, DeSoto Sedan, cast iron, red w/white rubber tires & blue hubs, nickel-plated trim, decal on door, 6", EX.......**$275.00**

Arcade, Ford Model T Touring Car, cast iron, black w/spoke wheels, 6¼", VG..**$185.00**

Arcade, International Dump Truck, cast iron, green & yellow w/black rubber tires, 11", NM **$550.00**

Arcade, Mullins Red Cap Trailer & Sedan, cast iron, light blue w/white rubber tires, red hubs, 8¾", NM...........**$385.00**

Arcade, Plymouth Coupe, cast iron, yellow w/nickel-plated trim, white rubber tires, open rumble seat, 5", VG **$250.00**

Arcade, Taxi Cab, cast iron, black w/white disk wheels & rear spare, 5", G...**$250.00**

Arcade, Wrecker, cast iron, orange w/black rubber tires, nickel-plated crane, 5½", EX.................................**$275.00**

Arcade, 1927 Ford Coupe, cast iron, blue w/nickel-plated wheels & driver, 7", G...**$300.00**

Arcade, 1938 Chevy Stake Truck, cast iron, green w/red fenders, white rubber tires, 4¼", NM **$825.00**

Bandai, Cadillac Sedan, friction, black w/chrome detail, plastic taillights, 1959, 11", EX.................................**$300.00**

Bandai, 1955 Ford Custom Ranch Wagon, friction, red w/black top & chrome detail, 11½", MIB..........**$375.00**

Bandai, 1956 Ford Red Cross Ambulance, friction, white w/red cross on roof, 12", EXIB **$350.00**

Champion, Police Motorcycle, cast iron, blue w/nickel-plated wheels, 5", VG...**$200.00**

Corgi, #152, Ferrari 312 B2, MIB **$35.00**

Corgi, #154, Ferrari Formula I, MIB **$50.00**

Corgi, #158, Lotus Climax, MIB................................**$50.00**

Corgi, #161, Santa Pod Commuter, MIB....................**$45.00**

Corgi, #202, Morris Cowley, MIB.............................**$150.00**

Corgi, #204, Rover 90, white & red, MIB..................**$300.00**

Corgi, #240, Rover 90, other colors, MIB..................**$175.00**

Corgi, #248, Chevy Impala, MIB................................**$80.00**

Corgi, #262, Captain Marvel's Porsche, MIB **$65.00**

Corgi, #273, Rolls Royce Silver Shadow, MIB **$100.00**

Corgi, #275, Royal Wedding Mini Metro, MIB **$25.00**

Corgi, #301, Lotus Elite, MIB...................................**$25.00**

Corgi, #303, Porsche 924, MIB.................................**$20.00**

Corgi, #320, The Saint's Jaguar XJS, MIB **$85.00**

Corgi, #386, Bertone Runabout, MIB.........................**$50.00**

Corgi, #401, VW 1200, MIB......................................**$60.00**

Corgi, #409, Mercedes Dumper, MIB.........................**$50.00**

Corgi, #429, Jaguar Police Car, MIB.........................**$40.00**

Corgi, #486, Chevrolet Kennel Service, MIB............**$100.00**

Corgi, #508, Holiday Mini Bus, MIB.........................**$110.00**

Corgi, #513, Alpine Rescue Car, MIB.......................**$350.00**

Corgi, #703, Breakdown Truck, MIB..........................**$20.00**

Corgi, #805, Hardy Boy's Rolls Royce......................**$300.00**

Corgi, #831, Mercedes Benz 300 SL, MIB..................**$25.00**

Corgi, #906, Saladin Armoured Car, MIB...................**$50.00**

Dinky, #105, Triumph TR2, MIB..............................**$200.00**

Dinky, #116, Volvo 1800S, MIB...............................**$100.00**

Dinky, #133, Cunningham C-5R, MIB.......................**$130.00**

Dinky, #144, VW 1500, MIB **$100.00**

Dinky, #153, Aston Martin, MIB..............................**$100.00**

Dinky, #160, Mercedes Benz 250 SE, MIB.................**$90.00**

Dinky, #166, Renault R16, MIB.................................**$60.00**

Dinky, #170, Lincoln Continental, MIB....................**$120.00**

Dinky, #173, Nash Rambler, MIB.............................**$110.00**

Dinky, #184, Volvo 122S, red, MIB..........................**$130.00**

Dinky, #188, Jensen FF, MIB....................................**$75.00**

Dinky, #189, Triumph Herald, MIB..........................**$120.00**

Dinky, #261, Telephone Service Van, MIB................**$150.00**

Dinky, #272, Police Accident Unit, MIB....................**$60.00**

Dinky, #354, Pink Panther, MIB................................**$60.00**

Dinky, #384, Sack Truck, MIB..................................**$25.00**

Dinky, #412, Bedford Van AA, MIB...........................**$60.00**

Dinky, #434, Bedford Crash Truck, MIB...................**$125.00**

Dinky, #452, Trojan Van, Chivers, MIB....................**$175.00**

Dinky, #514, Alfa Romeo Giulia, MIB........................**$85.00**

Dinky, #530, Citroen DS-23, MIB..............................**$60.00**

Dinky, #622, 10-Ton Army Truck, MIB.....................**$140.00**

Dinky, #687, Convoy Army Truck, MIB......................**$25.00**

Dinky, #752, Police Box, MIB...................................**$50.00**

Dinky, #894, UNIC Boilot Car Transporter, MIB **$275.00**

Dinky, #917, Mercedes Benz Truck & Trailer, MIB...**$120.00**

Dinky, #953, Continental Touring Coach, MIB.........**$400.00**

Hot Wheels, Beach Bomb, red line tires, metallic blue w/blue interior, flower decal on roof, complete, 1969, EX+ .**$53.00**

Hot Wheels, Beach Patrol, black walls, flourescent green w/red interior, magenta, white & pink tampo, 1990, M...**$10.00**

Hot Wheels, Beatnik Bandit, red line tires, metallic aqua, 1968, M...**$24.00**

Hot Wheels, Classic '32 Vicky, red line tires, metallic brown w/medium interior, 1969, NM+..............................**$35.00**

Hot Wheels, Classic '57 T-Bird, red line tires, metallic red w/cream interior, 1969, EX+ **$20.00**

Hot Wheels, Custom Baracuda, red line tires, metallic aqua, 1968, NM **$70.00**

Hot Wheels, Custom Mustang, black walls, medium brown, 1994, M (NM card)....................................**$10.00**

Hot Wheels, Demon, red line tires, light metallic green w/cream interior, 1970, NM+ **$22.00**

Hot Wheels, Ford Aerostar, back walls, white, 1991, M (NM International box) **$7.00**

Hot Wheels, Ford Mk IV, red line tires, metallic blue w/black interior, 1969, NM+ **$20.00**

Hot Wheels, Funny Money, red line tires, plum w/orange & yellow tampo, 1974, NM+ **$60.00**

Hot Wheels, Greased Gremlin, black walls, red & blue w/yellow & white #5 tampo, 1979, M............................**$10.00**

Hot Wheels, Hot Bird, black walls, blue w/orange & yellow tampo, scarce color, 1980, VG **$20.00**

Hot Wheels, Ice T, red line tires, yellow w/black interior, 1971, EX+ **$20.00**

Hot Wheels, Lola GT-70, red line tires, metallic brown, 1969, EX...**$25.00**

Hot Wheels, Mercedes SL, black walls, 1991, M (NM International card) **$10.00**

Hot Wheels, Monte Carlo Stocker, black walls, yellow w/red, white & blue #38 tampo, 1977, NM **$15.00**

Hot Wheels, Porche Carrera, red line tires, yellow w/orange & blue tampo, 1975, NM..................................**$40.00**

Hot Wheels, Prowler, black walls, Super Chrome, 1978, NM...**$16.00**

Hot Wheels, Python, red line tires, metallic red, 1968, EX...**$8.00**

Hot Wheels, Ranger Rig, red line tires, green w/yellow tampo, gray windshield, M **$50.00**

Hot Wheels, Rapid Transit School Bus, black walls, yellow, 1984, M (NM Team Bus card) **$7.00**

Hot Wheels, Rock Buster, black walls, Super Chrome, 1977, NM **$20.00**

Hot Wheels, Rocket Bye Baby, red line tires, red, Shell promotion, 1973, MIB **$150.00**

Hot Wheels, Rolls Royce Silver Shadow, red line tires, metallic blue, 1969, NM...**$35.00**

Hot Wheels, Rumbler Bone Shaker, red line tires, white, yellow driver w/goggles & helmet, training wheels, 1973, rare, M **$300.00**

Hot Wheels, Rumbler Roamin' Candle, metallic brown, brown driver w/full face shield, no training wheels, 1972, EX..**$15.00**

Hot Wheels, Rumbler Straight Away, metallic brown, tan driver w/full face shield on helmet, training wheels, 1972, NM.**$25.00**

Hot Wheels, Short Order, red line tires, gold w/black interior, 1971, M **$40.00**

Hot Wheels, Silhouette, red line tires, metallic purple, 1968, M...**$20.00**

Hot Wheels, Sizzler Corvette 4 Rotor, yellow, scarce, 1976, NM **$80.00**

Hot Wheels, Sizzler Cuda Trans-Am, metallic orange, 1971, EX..**$60.00**

Hot Wheels, Sizzler Double Boiler, metallic yellow, scarce, 1972, NM **$50.00**

Hot Wheels, Sizzler Hot Head, metallic green, 1970, M.**$40.00**

Hot Wheels, Sizzler Juice Machine, MIB....................**$25.00**

Hot Wheels, Snake, red line tires, yellow, 1970, NM+..**$30.00**

Hot Wheels, Snake (Vintage), black walls, metal-flake green, 1994, M (NM card)...**$15.00**

Hot Wheels, Spoiler Sport, black walls, green w/black, yellow & dark red tampo, 1 lg window, 1980, MIP ...**$6.00**

Hot Wheels, Steve's Rig Wrecker, black walls, white, 1983, M (EX+ Workhorses card) **$12.00**

Hot Wheels, Street Snorter, red line tires, red w/red & orange flame tampo, 1973, NM+.....................................**$150.00**

Hot Wheels, Sugar Caddy, red line tires, metallic green, complete, 1971, NM...**$35.00**

Hot Wheels, SWAT Van Scene, black walls, dark blue, 1979, VG...**$15.00**

Hot Wheels, Thing, black walls, dark blue, 1979, M..**$15.00**

Hot Wheels, Thor Van, black walls, yellow, 1979, M.**$10.00**

Hot Wheels, Tow Truck, red line tires, metallic green w/black interior, 1970, NM................................**$25.00**

Hot Wheels, Turbofire, red line tires, metallic red w/cream interior, 1970, NM **$10.00**

Hot Wheels, Whip Creamer, red line tires, metallic pink w/black interior, 1970, NM...................................**$30.00**

Hot Wheels, Whip Creamer (Vintage), black walls, metal-flake dark red, 1994, M (NM card) **$5.00**

Marusan, Atom Racer #45, w/driver, litho tin, 1950s, 8", EX (G box)..**$550.00**

Marx, Load & Dump Truck, pressed steel, 17", MIB ..**$300.00**

Marx, Marine Corps Truck, pressed steel w/canvas top, complete w/2 plastic soldiers, 13", NMIB.................**$250.00**

Marx, Powerhouse Dump Truck, pressed steel, MIB..**$300.00**

Matchbox, Bedford Compressor Truck, regular metal wheels, 1956, NM+ **$40.00**

Matchbox, K-04D, Big Tipper, King Size, metallic red w/yellow dump, 3-stripe labels, 1974, M (EX+ box).......**$8.00**

Matchbox, K-15, Londoner, Super Kings, red w/yellow interior, 1973, MIB **$20.00**

Matchbox, K-16B, Petrol Tanker, King Size, Total label, 1974, M (NM box)..**$31.00**

Matchbox, Y-O4C, 1909 Opel Coupe, orange & black w/maroon seats, white grille, 12-spoke wheels, 1967, M (NM box)..**$17.00**

Matchbox, Y-08 C, 1914 Stutz Roadster, Models of Yesteryear, red w/smooth tan top, copper gas tank, 1969, M (EX+ box) **$15.00**

Matchbox, Y-92B, 1911 B-Type London Bus, Models of Yesteryear, unpainted wheels, 8-over-4 windows, 1956, NM+ **$55.00**

Matchbox, 01-I, Revin' Rebel Dodge Challenger, red, white, and blue, 1982, M, $6.00. (Photo courtesy Dana Johnson)

Matchbox, 04-D, Dodge Stake Truck, regular black wheels, green stakes, 1967, MIB **$10.00**

Matchbox, 04-F, Gruesome Twosome, Super Fast, gold w/cream interior, purple windshield, 1971, M (NM box) **$15.00**

Matchbox, 05-E, Lotus Europa, Super Fast, pink, unpainted base, 1969, MBP **$19.00**

Matchbox, 07-B, Ford Anglia, regular black wheels, 1961, MIB **$25.00**

Matchbox, 10-D, Pipe Truck, regular black wheels, silver grille, 1966, MIB **$15.00**

Matchbox, 10-F, Mustang Piston Popper, blue w/Rolamatics on unpainted base, no tampo, 1973, M (NM box) **$11.00**

Matchbox, 12-C, Safari Land Rover, regular black wheels, blue w/tan luggage, 1965, MIB....................**$19.00**

Matchbox, 15-B, Atlantic Prime Mover, regular black wheels, 1959, NM+ **$39.00**

Matchbox, 18-E, Field Car, regular black wheels w/red hubs, unpainted base, original top, 1969, MIB..............**$17.00**

Matchbox, 18-F, Field Car, Super Fast, yellow w/red-brown top, unpainted base, 4-spoke fat wheels, 1970, M..........**$15.00**

Matchbox, 20-C, Chevy Impala Taxi, regular black wheels, yellow w/red interior, unpainted base, 1965, MIB......**$25.00**

Matchbox, 20-E, Police Patrol, Super Fast, white w/orange spinner, unpainted base, frosted windshield, labels, 1975, NM+ **$5.00**

Matchbox, 21-D, Foden Concrete Truck, regular black wheels, 1968, NM..**$6.00**

Matchbox, 26-C, GMC Tipper Truck, regular black wheels, 1968, MIB **$10.00**

Matchbox, 28-C, Jaguar MK 10, regular black wheels, unpainted motor, 1964, MIB **$20.00**

Matchbox, 28-E, Mack Dump Truck, Super Fast, pea green axle cover, unpainted base, spiro wheels, 1970, M..........**$19.00**

Matchbox, 31-C, Lincoln Continental, regular black wheels, aqua, 1964, MIB **$20.00**

Matchbox, 34-A, VW Microvan, regular gray wheels, 1957, NM+ **$53.00**

Matchbox, 36-A, Austin A50, regular metal wheels, 1957, M **$50.00**

Matchbox, 38-D, Honda Motorcycle & Trailer, Super Fast, pink & yellow, w/labels, 5-spoke wheels, 1970, M..........**$14.00**

Matchbox, 41-D, Ford GT, Super Fast, white w/light green base, 6 labels, 5-spoke thin wheels, 1970, M (EX card)..**$15.00**

Matchbox, 44-A, Rolls Royce Silver Cloud, regular gray wheels, 1958, MIB **$46.00**

Matchbox, 44-D, GMC Refrigerator Truck, Super Fast, yellow & red, w/axle covers, 1970, M (EX+ box)............**$25.00**

Matchbox, 47-A, 1-Ton Trojan Van, regular gray wheels, 1958, NM **$50.00**

Matchbox, 50-D, Kennel Truck, Super Fast, medium green w/black base, silver grille, thin wheels, 1970, M .**$28.00**

Matchbox, 52-B, BRM Racing Car, regular black wheels, 1965, M **$15.00**

Matchbox, 56-D, Hi-Trailer, Super Fast, white w/unpainted base, blue driver, MB5 labels, 5-spoke front wheels, 1974, NM **$10.00**

Matchbox, 60-B, Site Hut Truck, regular wheels, 1966, M (NM box) **$18.00**

Matchbox, 63-D, Dodge Crane Truck, Super Fast, yellow w/black axle covers, fat wheels, 1970, M.............**$25.00**

Matchbox, 66-A, Citroen DS19, regular gray wheels, 1959, NM **$39.00**

Matchbox, 69-B, Hatra Tractor Shovel, regular black wheels w/yellow hubs, orange (scarce), 1965, M............**$25.00**

Matchbox, 72-A, Fordson Tractor, regular black wheels, 1959, M (NM+ box) **$50.00**

Matchbox, 73-D, Mercury Commuter, red w/cow label, 1970, MIB **$17.00**

Matchbox, 75-C, Ferrari Berlinetta, Super Fast, red w/unpainted grille, thin wheels, 1970, M.............**$25.00**

SAN, 1956 Ford Fairlane, friction, w/chrome detail, 13", EX (G box) **$750.00**

Schuco, Mercedes 190 SL, windup, red w/red plastic interior, chrome detail, 8", NMIB................................**$465.00**

Smith Miller, Bank of America Brinks Truck, pressed steel, 1950s, 14", VG **$300.00**

Smith Miller, Mack Custom Union 76 Tanker Truck, pressed steel, NM **$600.00**

Smith Miller, Silver Streak Trailer, pressed steel, EX.**$450.00**

Steelcraft, Railway Express Truck, pressed steel, red cab w/enclosed green screen body, 24", G..............**$600.00**

Steelcraft, US Army Truck, pressed steel, open cab w/canvas-covered bed, 22", G..**$700.00**

Structo, Army Ambulance, #416, pressed steel, 17", EX...**$275.00**

Structo, Gasoline Truck, #912, pressed steel, 1950s, 13", NM **$135.00**

Structo, US Mail Truck, #428, pressed steel, 17", NM .**$300.00**

TN, Cadillac Sedan, battery-op, brown w/chrome detail & hood ornament, 1950, 8", NM **$165.00**

TN, 1958 Ford Skyliner, battery-op, red w/chrome detail, retractable roof, NMIB......................................**$300.00**

Tonka, Allied Van Lines Truck, #1089, 1962, 16", NMIB ..**$150.00**

Tonka, Cement Truck, #620, 1963, M **$200.00**

Tonka, Fire Jeep, #425, 1963-64, M............................**$300.00**

Tonka, Livestock Van, #500, 1952-53, NM................**$275.00**

Tonka, Parcel Delivery Van, #10, 1957, NM $400.00

Tonka, Rescue Squad Van, #105, 1960-61, NM $350.00

Tonka, Suburban Pumper Truck, #926, 1960, NM $250.00

Tonka, Wrecker, #250, 1953, EX.............................$250.00

Tootsietoy, Ambulance, #0809, Graham Series, white, NM $120.00

Tootsietoy, Buick Estate Wagon, 1948, closed grille, wine & cream, NM $70.00

Tootsietoy, Dunebuggy, 1970-79, M..........................$10.00

Tootsietoy, Ford Fairlane 500 Convertible, 1957, red, M..$25.00

Tootsietoy, Jumbo Sedan, #0116, 1942-46, blue w/white top, NM $50.00

Tootsietoy, Touring Car, w/top down, #232, 1940-41, green, NM $55.00

Tootsietoy, Tow Truck, #2485, 1960s, white w/red trim, NM...$45.00

Vindex, Motorcycle, cast iron, green w/nickel-plated 4-cylinder engine, black rubber tires w/spoke wheels, 8½", G...$400.00

Vindex, PDQ Delivery Cycle, cast iron, red w/black rubber tires & spoke wheels, w/driver, 8½", VG $950.00

Wyandotte, Ambulance, #340, pressed steel, w/swinging rear door, 11", EX...$175.00

Wyandotte, Deluxe Delivery Truck, pressed steel, 1936, 11", EX+ $100.00

Wyandotte, Dump Truck w/Sand Loader, pressed steel, 1941, EX $450.00

Wyandotte, Railway Express Truck, pressed steel, 1939, 12", EX $100.00

Wyandotte, School Bus, pressed steel, 1930s, 24", EX+ ...$175.00

Wyandotte, Stake Truck, #325, pressed steel, 1931, 10", EX...$200.00

Yonezawa, 1956 Ford Crown Victoria, friction, white over red w/blue roof & chrome detail, 12", MIB...........$1,500.00

Windups

Windup toys, especially comic character or personality related, are greatly in demand by collectors today. Though most were made through the years of the '30s through the '50s, they carry their own weight against much earlier toys and are considered very worthwhile investments. Mechanisms vary; some are key wound while others depended on lever action to tighten the mainspring and release the action of the toy. Tin and celluloid were used in their manufacture, and although it is sometimes possible to repair a tin windup, experts advise against putting your money into a celluloid toy whose mechanism is not working, since the material may be too fragile to tolerate the repair.

AHI, Ben Hur Trotter, cart w/gladiator, litho tin, 7", NM (NM box) $300.00

Alps, Banjo Bunny, litho tin & celluloid, 8", EX (worn box) $200.00

Alps, Bozo, w/drum, litho tin, 8½", NM (EX box) ..$1,000.00

Alps, Bulldog, cloth over tin, 8", NM.......................$125.00

Alps, Butterfly, litho tin, friction, 5", NM (EX box)...$165.00

Alps, Chirpee Chick, litho tin & plush, MIB.............$125.00

Alps, Drumming Bear, white fur-covered tin w/cardboard drum, 5½", EX+ $100.00

Alps, Pioneer Spirit, litho tin, friction, battery-op lanterns, 11", NM (EX box) $150.00

Alps, Telephone Santa Claus, tin w/cloth clothes & vinyl face, 7", MIB...$175.00

Arnold, Howdy Doody, Acrobat, composition figure w/cloth clothes on litho tin base, 12", VG $275.00

Arnold, Stunt Racer, litho tin, 10" hoop, EXIB $350.00

Ashitoy, Super Atom Train, litho tin, 11", EXIB $100.00

Brimfield, Santa Claus, 1940s, 4", EX (original box), from $350.00 to $375.00.

Chein, Barnacle Bill, litho tin, 6½", NM....................$300.00

Chein, Fancy Groceries Truck, litho tin, 6", EX $350.00

Chein, Penguin, litho tin, 4", EX................................$125.00

Chein, Popeye Waddler, litho tin, 6½", NM $1,300.00

Chein, Racer #52, litho tin w/wooden wheels, EX ...$200.00

Chein, Roller Coaster, litho tin, 1950s, 19", EX.........$300.00

Chein, Toyville Dump Truck, litho tin, 9", NM $350.00

Cragstan, Snapping Alligator, snaps at jumping fish, litho tin, 12", MIB...$100.00

Cragstan, USA Military Vehicle Group, tin, friction, set of 5, NMIB...$250.00

Haji, Indian Chief on Horse, litho tin, 8", EX...........$250.00

K, Animal Circus Magic Garage, litho tin, 4x5" garage, EX $100.00

KO, Circus Elephant, w/spinning ball & umbrella, litho tin, 7½", NM (EX box) $175.00

Lindstrom, Skeeter Duck, litho tin, 9", EX (G box).....$75.00

Lindstrom, Sweeping Mammy, litho tin, 1935, 8", NM (EX box) $450.00

Linemar, Donald Duck Delivery Wagon, litho tin & celluloid, 6", VG (worn box)................................$500.00

Linemar, Donald Duck Motorcycle, litho tin, friction, 4", NM $275.00

Linemar, Ferdinand the Bull, tin w/rubber tail, 5½", NM (EX box) $900.00

Linemar, Hopping Carry the Crow, litho tin, 4", M (EX box) $150.00

Linemar, Lady & the Tramp, litho tin, friction, 4", NM..$275.00

Linemar, Mickey Mouse Motorcycle, litho tin, friction, 4", NM $275.00

Linemar, Old Jalopy, litho tin, 7", EX (VG box)........$150.00

Linemar, Pinocchio Walker, litho tin, 6", NM.............**$950.00**

Lionel, Peter Rabbit Chick Mobile, painted composition & steel, 1930s, 10", EX.................................**$500.00**

Marx, Barney Rubble's Wreck, litho tin w/vinyl head, friction, 1962, 7", NM..................................**$450.00**

Marx, Donald Duck Twirling Tail, plastic, 1950s, 6", NMIB...**$600.00**

Marx, Dumbo, litho tin, WDP, 1941, 4", EXIB...........**$750.00**

Marx, Dumm Dumm & Touche Turtle, plastic, friction, 1963, 4", NMIB...**$300.00**

Marx, Flintstone Flivver, w/Fred driving, litho tin w/vinyl head, 1962, 4", EX...............................**$200.00**

Marx, Parade Drummer, litho tin, 9", NM.................**$200.00**

Marx, Sheriff Sam Whoopee Car, litho tin & plastic, 1960s, 5½", EX...**$250.00**

Marx, Superman Rollover Plane, litho tin, 1940, 6", NM .**$1,700.00**

Marx, Walt Disney's Television Car, litho tin, friction, 7½", NM (EX box)...**$550.00**

Marx, Whoopee Cowboy, litho tin, 1932, 8", EX......**$350.00**

Marx, Yogi Bear Car, litho tin w/vinyl head, friction, 4", NMIB...**$275.00**

Mikuni, Jumping Rabbit w/Baby, litho tin, 4½", EXIB..**$100.00**

Mikuni, Sam the Skeleton, litho tin, 5", EX.............**$175.00**

MM, Easter Parade, celluloid w/pressed steel base, 8", NM (NM box)...**$175.00**

Nifty, Drummer Boy, celluloid w/cloth clothes, 12", NM (EX box) **$225.00**

Nifty, Rudy Ostrich (from Barney Google), litho tin, 1924, 8½", EX...**$575.00**

Occupied Japan, Boy w/Dog, celluloid w/cloth clothes, 5", EX...**$75.00**

Occupied Japan, Clown on Donkey, celluloid, w/spinning tail, 4½", NM **$100.00**

Occupied Japan, Horse Race, boy in clown suit rides horse on base, celluloid & tin, 4", NM (EX box)..........**$200.00**

Occupied Japan, Playful Little Dog, litho tin, 3½", NM (EX box)...**$165.00**

SAN, Grasshopper, litho tin, realistic movement, 7½", NM (EX box)...**$200.00**

Schuco, Black Drummer, w/cymbals & base drum, litho tin w/felt clothes, 4½", EX..**$225.00**

Schuco, Charlie Chaplin, tin w/cloth clothes, 6", EX (worn box)...**$1,000.00**

Schuco, Fox Carrying Swan in Cage, litho tin w/plush-covered head & cloth clothes, 5", M **$1,100.00**

Schuco, Mouse in Open Roadster, tin, 6", EX...........**$225.00**

Schuco, Rolly Clown, composition w/cloth clothes, 8", EXIB...**$600.00**

Schuco, Traffic Man (Flic), 5", NM (NM box)............**$275.00**

SSS, Circus Trailer, litho tin, friction, 9", NM (NM box)..**$200.00**

Technofix, Friendly Cycle, litho tin, friction, 8", EX..**$300.00**

TN, Buzzy Bee, litho tin & plush, MIB.....................**$150.00**

TN, Ko-Ko Sandwich Man, w/Eat at Joe's sign, tin w/cloth clothes, 7½", NMIB...**$175.00**

TPS, Bear Golfer, litho tin, 4", NM (EX box)............**$375.00**

TPS, Calypso Joe the Drummer, litho tin, 6½", NM (EX box)...**$375.00**

TPS, Candy Loving Canine, litho tin, 6", NM (NM box)...**$225.00**

TPS, Clown on Roller Skates, litho tin w/cloth clothes, realistic motion, 6½", NM **$350.00**

TPS, Suzy Bouncing Ball, realistic action, litho tin w/vinyl head, 5½", NM (EX box)....................................**$125.00**

Unique Art, Casey the Cop, litho tin, 8½", EX..........**$550.00**

Unique Art, Finnegan, litho tin, 13", NM (VG box)..**$275.00**

Unique Art, GI Joe & His K-9 Pups, litho tin, 9", VG **$250.00**

Wolverine, Dandy Andy Rooster, litho tin, 10", NMIB ...**$850.00**

Wolverine, Drum Major, litho tin, 14", NM **$350.00**

Wolverine, Jet Roller Coaster, litho tin, 12", NM (EX box)..**$300.00**

Wyandotte, Easter Bunny Delivery, litho tin, 9", EX.**$275.00**

Yone, Carnival Ride, litho tin, 5½", EX, $95.00. (Photo courtesy June Moon)

Transistor Radios

Introduced during the Christmas shopping season of 1954, transistor radios were at the cutting edge of futuristic design and miniaturization. Among the most desirable is the 1954 four-transistor Regency TR-1 which is valued at a minimum of $750.00 in jade green. Black may go for as much as $300.00, other colors from $350.00 to $400.00. The TR-1 'Mike Todd' version in the 'Around the World in Eighty Days' leather book-look presentation case goes for $4,000.00 and up! Some of the early Toshiba models sell for $250.00 to $350.00, some of the Sonys even higher — their TR-33 books at a minimum of $1,000.00, their TR-55 at $1,500.00 and up! Certain pre-1960 models by Hoffman and Admiral represented the earliest practical use of solar technology and are also highly valued. Early collectible transistor radios all have civil defense triangle markings at 640 and 1240 on the frequency dial and nine or fewer transistors. Very few desirable sets were made after 1963.

Values in our listings are for radios in at least very good condition — not necessarily working, but complete and requiring very little effort to restore them to working order. Cases may show minor wear. All radios are battery-operated unless noted otherwise. For more information we recommend *Collector's Guide to Transistor Radios* (there are two editions), by Marty and Sue Bunis (Collector Books).

Advisors: Marty and Sue Bunis (See Directory, Radios)

Acme, #CH-610 Tops All, 1962, horizontal, 6 transistors, 2-thumbwheel dials, perforated grill, AM.................**$35.00**

Acme, Boy's Radio, vertical, plastic, 2 transistors, window dial, round metal grill, Japan, AM.........................**$55.00**

Admiral, #Y2023 Super 7, 1960, horizontal, 7 transistors, off-center dial, crown logo, AM **$25.00**

Admiral, #Y2307GPS, 1963, vertical, plastic, 6 transistors, round window dial, crown logo, AM....................**$30.00**

Admiral, #Y2423GP, 1963, vertical, plastic, 8 transistors, slide rule dial, swing handle, crown logo, AC/DC, AM..**$30.00**

Admiral, #Y798 Starlet, 1960, horizontal, clock, 5 transistors, alarm, crown logo, AM....................................**$15.00**

Air Chief, #4-C-100, 1965, horizontal, 10 transistors, window dial, AM **$15.00**

Airline, #GEN-1297A, 1861, horizontal, 8 transistors, front dial knob, M/W logo, handle, AM......................**$30.00**

Aiwa, #AR-752, 1966, vertical, plastic, 7 transistors, slide rule dial, AM..**$10.00**

Alaron, #B-666 Deluxe HiFi, 1963, vertical, 6 transistors, window dial, AM..**$20.00**

Arvin, #60R19, 1959, horizontal, slate gray, 4 transistors, step-back top, round dial, swing handle, 'A' logo, AM.**$25.00**

Arvon, #60R58, 1960, tan cowhide, 7 transistors, round dial, checkered grill, leather handle, AM **$20.00**

Astrotone, #99-3513L, 1965, vertical, 9 transistors, window dial, horizontal bars on grill, AM..........................**$10.00**

Atkins, #61N59-11, 1964, horizontal, black leather, 8 transistors, slide rule dial, leather handle, AM................**$10.00**

Automatic, #P-990, 1962, horizontal, top control knobs, front grill w/rectangular cut-outs, leather handle, USA.**$25.00**

Blaupunkt, #22503 Lido, 1963, horizontal, 9 transistors, slide rule dial, telescoping antenna, AM/FM/SW **$45.00**

Bulova, #742 Super 6, 1962, vertical, 6 transistors, thumbwheel dial, logo, AM **$45.00**

Cameo, #64N06-03, 1964, vertical, 6 transistors, window dial, AM..**$15.00**

Captain, #YT-781 Deluxe, horizontal, plastic w/metal panel, 8 transistors, window dial, Japan, AM...................**$30.00**

Channel Master, #6506A, 1960, horizontal, 6 transistors, logo, Japan, AM **$35.00**

Claricon, #46-090, 1965, horizontal, 12 transistors, round dial, telescoping antenna, AM/FM **$15.00**

Continental, #TFM-1155, 1964, horizontal, 11 transistors, slide rule dial, telescoping antenna, handle, AM/FM....**$15.00**

Continental, #TR-716, 1965, 7 transistors, side dial, center logo, side strap, AM..**$40.00**

Coronado, #RA60-9941A, 1964, horizontal, round dial, crown logo, handle, AM **$15.00**

Crown, #TRF-1000, 1965, horizontal, 13 transistors, slide rule dial, 2 telescoping antennas, handle, AM/FM/SW..**$20.00**

Dewald, #L-414, 1958, horizontal, leather, 3 transistors, side dial, vertical cut-out grill, leather pull-up handle, AM........**$50.00**

Dumont, #1210, 1957, horizontal, leather, 6 transistors, front dial knob, grill w/diamond cut-outs, leather strap, AM ...**$40.00**

Elgin, #R-1600 Commander, 1965, horizontal, 11 transistors, slide rule dial, 2 telescoping antennas, handle, AM/FM/SW **$20.00**

Emerson, #855, 1956, horizontal, 6 transistors, front round dial knob, leather handle, AM **$45.00**

Emerson, #977 Falcon, 1961, horizontal, plastic, 7 transistors, AM..**$35.00**

General Electric, #CT-455A, 1960, horizontal, clock, 6 transistors, round dial knob, alarm clock face, AM....**$20.00**

General Electric, #P750A, 1958, horizontal, 6 transistors, side dial, plastic lattice grill, leather handle, AM..........**$15.00**

General Electric, #P797A, 1958, horizontal, beige leather, side dial knob, plastic lattice grill, leather handle, AM..**$20.00**

General Electric, #P835 Super 6, 1961, horizontal, saddle brown leatherette, 6 transistors, front dial knob, handle, AM..**$20.00**

General Electric, #P930, 1964, horizontal, 8 transistors, slide rule dial, telescoping antenna, handle, AM/2 SWs..**$20.00**

Genie, Boy's Radio, vertical, plastic, 2 transistors, window dial, metal grill, Japan, AM....................................**$55.00**

Global Imperial, #HT-8054, vertical, plastic, 8 transistors, window dial, grill w/horizontal slots, AM.............**$20.00**

Graetz, #42 H Flip, 1966, plastic, vertical, 8 transistors, slide rule dial, metal grill, strap, West Germany, AM/FM..........**$35.00**

Halex, Transonette 99U, 1964, horizontal/table, 9 transistors, slide rule dial, telescoping antenna, AM/FM/LW/SW..........**$25.00**

Hatachi, #TH-680, 1965, vertical, plastic, 6 transistors, round dial, AM..**$25.00**

Hilton, #TR108, vertical, plastic, 10 transistors, front round dial knob, metal grill, logo, Japan, AM.................**$25.00**

Hoffman, #729, 1964, horizontal, 12 transistors, slide rule dial, 3 telescoping antennas, handle, AM/FM.......**$15.00**

Holiday, #HS921 Super DX, vertical, plastic, 9 transistors, window dial, metal panel w/vertical grill slots, AM.....**$20.00**

Jade, #J-162, vertical, plastic, 6 transistors, round window dial, horizontal bars on grill, AM..........................**$10.00**

Jade, #171, vertical, plastic, 7 transistors, window dial, checkered grill, AM **$10.00**

Kent, #TR-605, 1965, vertical, 6 transistors, window dial, AM..**$15.00**

Kowa, #KT-67, 1961, vertical, 6 transistors, window dial, round perforated grill, AM **$75.00**

Layfayette, #TR-1660, 1964, vertical, 6 transistors, window dial, horizontal grill bars, AM **$10.00**

Lincoln, #TR-3422, 1963, horizontal, 14 transistors, slide rule dial, 3 telescoping antennas, handle, AM/FM/SW..**$25.00**

Lloyd's, #TR-6T, 1964, vertical, 6 transistors, window dial, side strap, AM..**$10.00**

Majestic, #6G780, vertical, plastic, 6 transistors, front round dial, bird logo on perforated grill, AM.................**$45.00**

Masterwork, #M2812, 1965, horizontal, leather, 8 transistors, slide rule dial, leather handle, AM **$10.00**

Melodic, #MT-69, 1961, vertical, 6 transistors, window dial, perforated grill, AM..**$15.00**

Mitsubishi, #7X-164, 1965, vertical, 7 transistors, window dial, logo on perforated grill, AM **$15.00**

Monacor, #RE-612, 1963, vertical, 6 transistors, window dial, perforated circular grill, AM................................**$20.00**

Motorola, #L12N Power 8, 1960, horizontal, 6 transistors, round dial, logo on grill, handle, AM **$15.00**

Motorola, #X36E, 1962, vertical, 6 transistors, lattice grill, AM...**$20.00**

Motorola, #X49E, 1962, horizontal, black leather, 6 transistors, round dial, handle, AM.................................**$20.00**

NEC, #NT-6B, horizontal, plastic, slide rule dial, textured panel w/checkered grill, AM..............................**$30.00**

Nordmende, Mikrobox, 1961, horizontal, plastic, 6 transistors, round dial, metal grill, West Germany, AM/LW.....**$30.00**

North American, #L4X05T, 1961, horizontal, 7 transistors, slide rule dial, 7 push buttons, handle, AM/3 SWs.........**$35.00**

Norwood, #MN-1000, 1965, horizontal, 10 transistors, slide rule dial, telescoping antenna, handle, AM/FM....**$15.00**

Packard Bell, #12RT1, 1964, horizontal, 12 transistors, slide rule dial, 3 knobs, telescoping antenna, AM/FM..**$15.00**

Panasonic, #R-109, 1964, horizontal, leather, 9 transistors, slide rule dial, logo in grill, AM..........................**$15.00**

Parlax, #P-1000, vertical, plastic, front dial, vinyl strap, AM...**$10.00**

Peerless, #10T-2SP, Twin Speaker, 1964, horizontal, 10 transistors, slide rule dial, AM.....................................**$15.00**

Penncrest, #1871, 1964, horizontal, 10 transistors, 1 AM dial, 1 FM dial, logo on grill, telescoping antenna, AM/FM.........**$20.00**

Philco, #T-68BKG, 1963, vertical, plastic, 6 transistors, round window dial, metal grill, AM.............................**$20.00**

Philco, #T-804, 1963, horizontal, leather, 8 transistors, front round dial knob overlaps grill bars, leather strap, AM...........**$15.00**

Plata, #L2X00T/00L, horizontal, plastic, slide rule dial, metal grill, telescoping antenna, AM/SW/LW.................**$35.00**

RCA, #RFG 25E, 1964, horizontal, leatherette/plastic, 8 transistors, front knobs, textured grill, handle, AM....**$15.00**

RCA, #1-T-1E, 1960, vertical, plastic, 6 transistors, round dial, vertical grill w/Nipper & RCA logos, swing handle, AM...**$30.00**

RCA, #1-T-4J Hawaii, 1959, vertical, plastic, 8 transistors, round dial, center grill, swing handle, AM...........**$35.00**

Realtone, #TR-1030, 1963, horizontal, leather, 10 transistors, window dial, leather handle, AM.........................**$15.00**

Realtone, #TR-1057, horizontal, 1963, 10 transistors, front dial, perforated grill, AM.....................................**$20.00**

Rhapsody, Sexetta, 1959, horizontal, plastic, 6 transistors, 2 slide rule dials (1FM/1 AM), telescoping antenna, AM/FM...**$20.00**

Roland, #4TR, 1959, horizontal, 4 transistors, dial knob, logo on grill, handle, USA, AM.....................................**$35.00**

Sampson, #BT65, 1963, vertical, 6 transistors, window dial, logo on grill, AM...**$15.00**

Seminole, #1010, 1964, horizontal, 10 transistors, front dial over wrap-around panel, AM...............................**$15.00**

Sharp, #FX-495, 1963, horizontal, 10 transistors, slide rule dial, logo on grill, telescoping antenna, handle, AM/FM...**$25.00**

Silvertone, #1019 Medalist, 1961, horizontal/table, 7 transistors, 3 front knobs, feet, AM...............................**$20.00**

Silvertone, #2224, 1962, horizontal, 8 transistors, vertical slide rule dial, telescoping antenna, AM/2 SWs.............**$20.00**

Silvertone, #5222, 1964, horizontal, leather, 9 transistors, front dial, lattice grill, leather handle, AM....................**$15.00**

Sony, #TR-627, horizontal, plastic, 6 transistors, slide rule dial, 3 knobs, handle, feet, Japan, AM.................**$30.00**

Sony, #2R-31, 1970, vertical, plastic w/chrome front, 6 transistors, window dial, vertical grill bars, Japan, AM.....**$20.00**

Sony, #6R-33, horizontal, leather, 9 transistors, wood-grain panel, H/L switch, AM..**$20.00**

Soundesign, #1177, vertical, plastic, round dial, side strap, Hong Kong, AM..**$10.00**

Sportmaster, #47900, 1965, vertical, 6 transistors, window dial, lg grill w/horizontal bars, AM.........................**$15.00**

Star-Lite, #TD-660 Duke, vertical, 6 transistors, window dial, crisscross grill, AM..**$15.00**

Sylvania, #5P16, horizontal, plastic w/metal, front dial overlaps grill w/logo, side pull-out metal handle, AM..........**$45.00**

Symphonic, #S-84, 1963, vertical, 8 transistors, ½-round window dial, logo on grill, AM..............................**$15.00**

Tonecrest, #2091, 1965, horizontal, 10 transistors, slide rule dial, telescoping antenna, AM/FM......................**$15.00**

Toshiba, #8TH-428R, 1963, horizontal/table, 8 transistors, 3 slide rule dials, 3 knobs, checkered grill, feet, AM/2 SWs...**$35.00**

Transtone, #TR-101, vertical, plastic, 6 transistors, window dial, perforated metal, grill, Japan, AM.................**$40.00**

Truetone, #DC3338, 1963, vertical, 8 transistors, 2 window dials, strap, AM..**$20.00**

Valiant, #655-HiFi, vertical, plastic, 6 transistors, window dial, horizontal bars on grill, AM...................................**$10.00**

Vista, #NTR-850, 1963, horizontal, 8 transistors, slide rule dial, oval perforated grill, AM.............................**$30.00**

Trolls

The legend of the Troll originated in Scandinavia. Nordic mythology described them as short, intelligent, essentially unpleasant, supernatural creatures who were doomed to forever live underground. During the '70s, a TV cartoon special and movie based on J.R.R. Tolkien's books, *The Hobbit* and *The Lord of the Rings*, caused an increase in Trolls' popularity. As a result, books, puzzles, posters, and dolls of all types were available on the retail market. In the early '80s, Broom Hilda and Irwin Troll were featured in a series of books as well as Saturday morning cartoons. Today trolls are enjoying a strong comeback.

Troll dolls of the '60s are primarily credited to Thomas Dam of Denmark. Many, using Dam molds, were produced in America by Royalty Des. of Florida and Wishnik. In Norway A/S Nyform created a different version. Some were also made in Hong Kong, Japan, and Korea, but those were of inferior plastic and design.

The larger trolls (approximately 12") are rare and very desirable to collectors. Troll animals by Dam, such as the giraffe, horse, cow, donkey, and lion, are bringing premium prices.

For more information, refer to *Collector's Guide to Trolls* by Pat Peterson.

Advisor: Pat Peterson (See Directory, Trolls)

Ballerina, bright red hair, green eyes, Dam, MIP........$55.00

Batman, original felt outfit, Uneeda Wishnik, 1966, 6", NM..**$100.00**

Batman, 3", $25.00.

Cheerleader, painted-on clothes, several variations, Dam, 1964, 2½", NM, ea **$20.00**

Cook-Nik, bendable, original outfit, blue hair, brown eyes, Uneeda Wishnik, 5", EX......................**$20.00**

Doll-Faced Troll, red & white petal-shaped dress, red hair, painted eyes, Uneeda Wishnik, 7", NM................**$20.00**

Eskimo, red & white painted-on clothes, brown hair & eyes, Dam, 1965, 5½", EX.....................................**$75.00**

Good Luck-Nik, Uneeda Wishnik, 1970s, M (original bag) **$30.00**

Greek Soldier, silver costume w/shield & cap, yellow hair, brown eyes, Russ, 4", NM **$15.00**

Horse, red hair, amber eyes, Dam, 1960s, NM............**$40.00**

Indian, felt outfit w/yellow feather in black hair, green eyes, Dam, 7", NM......................................**$50.00**

Mama-She-Nik, yellow felt dress w/green heart design, green ribbon in white hair, amber eyes, Uneeda Wishnik, 5", EX...**$25.00**

Norfin Seal, amber eyes, Dam, 1984, 6½", NM **$50.00**

Pirate, felt outfit, 1 gold hoop earring, red hair, green eyes, Dam, 7", NM...**$55.00**

Robin Hood, red hair, brown eyes, complete w/bow & arrow, Russ Storybook series, 4½", NM **$15.00**

Tartan Girl, original outfit w/matching ribbons in black hair, amber eyes, Dam, 1964, 12", M, from $145 to ...**$165.00**

Uglie Giraffe, black hair, amber eyes, marked Made in Hong Kong, NM **$25.00**

TV Guides

This publication goes back to the early 1950s, and granted, those early issues are very rare. But what an interesting, very visual way to chronicle the history of TV programming!

Values in our listings are for examples in fine to mint condition; be sure to reduce them significantly when damage of any type is present. For insight into *TV Guide* collecting, we recommend *The TV Guide Catalog* by Jeff Kadet, the *TV Guide* Specialist.

Advisor: Jeff Kadet (See Directory, *TV Guides*)

1953, August 7, Ray Milland $36.00
1953, October 23, Arthur Godfrey...........................$54.00
1954, January 29, Robert Montgomery.....................$24.00
1954, May 7, Nelson Family...................................$75.00
1955, April 16, Garry Moore $28.00
1955, February 19, Sid Ceasar...............................$22.00
1956, April 28, Red Skelton....................................$15.00
1956, August 4, Jackie Cooper & Cleo.....................$12.00
1956, February 11, Perry Como $12.00
1957, June 8, Lassie $47.00
1957, March 23, Ernie Ford....................................$12.00
1958, April 19, Polly Bergen $34.00
1958, August 16, cast of Wagon Train.....................$45.00
1959, July 18, Janet Blair......................................$10.00
1959, March 21, Ann Sothern.................................$15.00
1960, March 5, Jay North as Dennis the Menace $48.00
1960, May 14, Ernie Kovacs & Edie Adams................$18.00
1960, May 6, Donna Reed.......................................$25.00
1960, September 10, Dick Clark of American Bandstand...$20.00
1961, February 4, Clint Eastwood............................$95.00
1961, July 29, Captain Kangaroo $22.00
1962, January 27, Myrna Fahey $15.00
1962, September 8, cast of Bonanza........................$70.00
1963, February 9, Ernest Borgnine $15.00
1963, October 19, Judy Garland $27.00
1964, February 1, Danny Kaye $11.00
1964, November 21, Gomer Pyle..............................$15.00
1965, January 23, Chuck Conners............................$23.00
1965, November 13, Joey Heatherton $16.00
1966, February 19, Ben Gazzara, Run For Your Life.....$9.00
1966, October 22, Lucy Goes Mod in London $28.00
1967, January 14, Art Carney $6.00
1967, November 25, Garrison's Gorillas.....................$16.00
1968, January 13, Bob Hope...................................$8.00
1968, June 22, Toni Helfer & Tigers.........................$21.00
1968, November 30, Ann-Margret.............................$18.00
1969, August 2, Andrew Duggan of Lancer.................$8.00

1970, April 4, Cast of The Brady Bunch, $125.00. (Photo courtesy Greg Davis and Bill Morgan)

1970, April 18, cast of The Bold Ones.......................$10.00
1970, June 27, Liza Minnelli...................................$9.00
1970, November 21, Starlett Sally Marr $5.00
1971, July 10, Cookie Monster.................................$6.00
1971, November 13, cast of The Partners $6.00

1972, February 26, Mary Tyler Moore **$12.00**
1972, June 17, Julie London of Emergency..............**$5.00**
1972, October 14, Robert Conrad & Cloris Leachman ..**$10.00**
1973, February 3, Bill Cosby **$5.00**
1973, October 20, Telly Savalas of Kojak **$10.00**
1974, January 5, World on TV in 1973 ....**$7.00**
1974, July 20, Boom in Made-for-TV Films..............**$4.00**
1974, November 9, Sophia Loren **$4.00**
1975, April 26, cast of McCloud..............**$7.00**
1975, February 1, James Garner of Rockford Files.......**$4.00**
1975, November 1, Lloyd Bridges as Joe Forester.........**$8.00**
1976, January 24, cast of M*A*S*H..............**$8.00**
1976, October 16, World Series..............**$6.00**
1977, June 11, Grizzly Adams..............**$12.00**
1977, November 19, Frank Sinatra **$12.00**
1978, February 4, The Love Boat..............**$7.00**
1978, June 10, UFOs on TV **$6.00**
1978, October 28, cast of Mork & Mindy..............**$9.00**
1979, July 14, cast of Little House on the Prairie.......**$13.00**
1979, November 24, Pernell Roberts of Trapper John ..**$7.00**
1980, January 12, Estrada & Wilcox of CHiPS **$12.00**
1980, November 1, Reagan, Carter & Anderson..........**$6.00**
1981, April 18, Ted Koppel of ABC News **$4.00**
1981, July 18, cast of BJ & the Bear..............**$5.00**
1981, October 1, cast of Hill Street Blues..............**$7.00**
1982, June 26, Michelle Lee of Knot's Landing **$5.00**
1982, November 6, Ray & Gimpel of Fame..............**$4.00**
1983, December 31, Farrah Fawcett..............**$15.00**
1983, June 18, cast of Simon & Simon..............**$7.00**
1983, March 5, Valerie Bertinelli..............**$8.00**
1983, October 15, Larry Hagman & Joan Collins **$5.00**
1984, August 18, Jane Pauley..............**$4.00**
1984, May 12, Crystal Gayle..............**$4.00**
1985, June 22, Nancy Reagan **$4.00**
1985, March 9, Angela Lansbury..............**$5.00**
1985, October 19, cast of Golden Girls..............**$7.00**
1986, April 26, cast of Kate & Allie..............**$5.00**
1986, December 20, cast of Our House..............**$4.00**
1986, January 18, cast of Night Court..............**$7.00**
1987, April 11, cast of Newhart..............**$7.00**
1987, January 17, Davis & Hensley of Amen..............**$7.00**
1987, November 14, Danson & Alley of Cheers..........**$5.00**
1988, December 10, cast of Empty Nest **$7.00**
1988, January 9, Emma Samms..............**$5.00**
1988, May 14, Beat the Press..............**$4.00**
1988, September 24, cast of Cosby Show..............**$4.00**
1989, February 11, JR on the Couch **$5.00**
1989, May 13, Tracy Scoggins of Dynasty..............**$5.00**
1989, September 16, Rosanne Barr & Bill Cosby **$9.00**
1990, February 17, Elvis..............**$9.00**
1990, June 23, Arsenio Hall..............**$5.00**
1990, November 17, Muppets **$7.00**
1991, February 9, Lucy & Desi..............**$6.00**
1991, May 11, cast of LA Law **$4.00**
1991, November 2, Michael Jackson **$5.00**
1992, February 2, Jessica Lange..............**$4.00**
1992, September 26, Billy Ray Cyrus & Reba McEntire...**$5.00**

1993, January 30, Craig T Nelson of Coach..............**$7.00**
1993, June 5, Connie Chung..............**$4.00**
1993, September 25, Raymond Burr..............**$20.00**
1994, January 1, Tim Allen..............**$8.00**
1994, September 3, John Madden..............**$5.00**
1995, February 25, George Clooney..............**$8.00**
1995, June 17, Brett Butler & Bryant Gumbel **$6.00**
1996, August 31, Dolphin's Jimmy Johnson, NFL's 1996 Viewer's Guide..............**$17.00**
1996, January 13, Morgan Fairchild **$5.00**
1996, June 22, Conan O'Brien **$7.00**
1996, November 2, Michael Jordan **$6.00**

Twin Winton

The genius behind the designs at Twin Winton was sculptor Don Winton. He and his twin, Ross, started the company while sill in high school in the mid-1930s. In 1952 older brother Bruce Winton bought the company from his two younger brothers and directed its development nationwide. They produced animal figures, cookie jars, and matching kitchenware and household items during this time. It is important to note that Bruce was an extremely shrewd business man, and if an order came in for a nonstandard color, he would generally accommodate the buyer — for an additional charge, of course. As a result, you may find a Mopsy (Raggedy Ann) cookie jar, for instance, in a wood stain finish or some other unusual color, even though Mopsy was only offered in the Collector Series in the catalogs. This California company was active until it sold in 1976 to Roger Bowermeister, who continued to use the Twin Winton name. He experimented with different finishes. One of the most common is a light tan with a high gloss glaze. He owned the company only one year until it went bankrupt and was sold at auction. Al Levin of Treasure Craft bought the molds and used some of them in his line. Eventually, the molds were destroyed.

One of Twin Winton's most successful concepts was their Hillbilly line — mugs, pitchers, bowls, lamps, ashtrays, decanters, and novelty items molded after the mountain boys in Paul Webb's cartoon series. Don Winton was the company's only designer, though he free-lanced as well. He designed for Disney, Brush-McCoy, Revell Toys, The Grammy Awards, American Country Music Awards, Ronald Reagan Foundation, and numerous other companies and foundations.

Twin Winton has been revived by Don and Norma Winton (the original Don Winton and his wife). They are currently selling new designs as well as some of his original artwork through the Twin Winton Collector Club on the Internet at www.twinwinton.com. Some of Don's more prominent pieces of art are currently registered with the Smithsonian in Washington, D.C.

If you would like more information, read *A Collector's Guide to Don Winton Designs,* written by our advisor Mike Ellis, and published by Collector Books. Other sources of information are *The Collector's Encyclopedia of Cookie Jars* (three in the series) by Joyce and Fred Roerig.

Note: Color codes in the listings below are as follows: A — avocado green; CS — Collectors Series, fully painted; G — gray; I — ivory; O — orange; P — pineapple yellow; R — red; and W — wood stain with hand-painted detail. Values are based on actual sales as well as dealer's asking prices.

See also Cookie Jars.

Advisor: Mike Ellis (See Directory, Twin Winton)

Club: Twin Winton Collector Club
Also Don Winton Designs (other than Twin Winton)
266 Rose Lane
Costa Mesa, CA 92627; 714-646-7112 or fax: 7414-645-4919
www.twinwinton.com; e-mail: ellis5@pacbell.net

Ashtray, Bambi, W, 6x8" $100.00
Ashtray, Bronco Group, #B-208, 5½" $75.00
Bank, cop, W, I, G, A, P, O, R, 8" $65.00
Bank, Dobbin, W, I, G, A, P, O, R, 8" $40.00
Bank, lamb, W, I, G, A, P, O, R, 8" $40.00
Bank, Monk/Friar Tuck, W, I, G, A, P, O, R, 8" $40.00
Bank, owl, W, I, G, A, P, O, R, 8" $65.00
Bank, Pirate Fox, W, I, G, A, P, O, R, 8" $65.00
Bank, Ranger Bear, W, I, G, A, P, O, R, 8" $50.00
Bank, Sailor Elephant, W, I, G, A, P, O, R, 8" $50.00
Bank, shoe, W, I, G, A, P, O, R, 8" $85.00
Candle holder, Aladdin, W, I, G, A, P, O, R, 9½x6½" .$45.00
Candle holder, Ravel, W, I, G, A, P, O, R, 6x4½" .$15.00
Candle holder, Strauss, W, I, G, A, P, O, R, 5x10" $15.00
Candle holder, Verdi, W, I, G, A, P, O, R, 9½x4" $15.00
Candy jar, elf on stump, W, I, G, A, P, O, R, 8½x8" ...$65.00
Candy jar, Sailor Elephant, W, I, G, A, P, O, R, 6x9" ..$65.00
Candy jar, shack, W, I, G, A, P, O, R, 6½x9½" $65.00
Candy jar, shoe, W, I, G, A, P, O, R, 10x10" $75.00
Candy jar, train, W, I, G, A, P, O, R, 8x10" $75.00
Candy jar, turtle, W, I, G, A, P, O, R, 8x10" $85.00
Canister, Canister Farm, cookie barn, W, I, G, A, P, O, R, 8x12" $80.00
Canister, Canister Farm, sugar dairy, W, I, G, A, P, O, R, 4x8" $55.00
Canister, Canisterville, house, coffee, W, 4x8" $75.00
Canister, Canisterville, house, flour, W, 7x11" $125.00
Canister, Canisterville, house, tea, W, 3x7" $50.00
Creamer, Artist Palette Line, 4" dia $40.00
Creamer & sugar bowl, cow & bull, W, G, I, 5x6" ...$200.00
Creamer & sugar bowl, hen & rooster, W, G, I, 5x6" .$200.00
Expanimals, chipmunk, W, 7½" $125.00
Expanimals, poodle, W, 7½" $125.00
Figurine, Asian boy holding frog, #T-15, 5½" $150.00
Figurine, beaver lying down, #315, 1x2½" $8.00
Figurine, blind mouse, #208, ¾" $6.00
Figurine, boy wearing Mickey Mouse ears holding airplane hot dog, #T-1, 5½" $150.00
Figurine, cocker spaniel, W, I, G, 7" $50.00
Figurine, shaggy dog, W, I, G, 8" $65.00
Lamp, monkey, W, 13" $175.00
Lamp, raccoon, W, 12" $175.00

Lamp, seal, W, 12" $175.00
Lamp, squirrel, W, 12" $175.00
Mug, bear, W, I, G, A, P, O, R, 3¼" $85.00
Mug, elephant, 3½x5" $125.00
Mug, kitten, W, I, G, A, P, O, R, 3¼" $85.00
Napkin holder, Bambi, W, I, G, A, P, O, R, 7x6" $85.00
Napkin holder, cocktail; horse, W, I, G, A, P, O, R, 4x6" .$150.00
Napkin holder, cocktail; rabbit, W, I, G, A, P, O, R, 4x6" .$150.00
Napkin holder, cow, W, I, G, A, P, O, R, 6x7" $85.00
Napkin holder, Dobbin, W, I, G, A, P, O, R, 5x7" $65.00
Napkin holder, Dutch girl, W, I, G, A, P, O, R, 8½x5½" ..$75.00
Napkin holder, elf, W, I, G, A, P, O, R, 5x8" $85.00
Napkin holder, goose, W, I, G, A, P, O, R, 5x7" $75.00
Napkin holder, lamb, W, I, G, A, P, O, R, 5x7" $75.00
Napkin holder, Persian cat, W, I, G, A, P, O, R, 5½x7" .$75.00
Napkin holder, Ranger Bear, W, I, G, A, P, O, R, 4x9" .$75.00
Napkin holder, shack, W, I, G, A, P, O, R, 7x7" $65.00
Planter, cat, W, 8" $50.00
Planter, circus dog w/drum, W, 8" $50.00
Planter, rabbit w/cart, 7x10" $85.00
Planter, Ranger Bear, W, 8" $50.00
Planter, squirrel, W, I, G, A, P, O, R, 4x8" $50.00
Plate, dinner; Wood Grain Line, 10" $40.00
Salt & pepper shakers, apple, W, I, G, A, P, O, R, pr.$75.00
Salt & pepper shakers, barn, W, I, G, A, P, O, R, pr ..$40.00
Salt & pepper shakers, bear, W, I, G, A, P, O, R, pr...$40.00
Salt & pepper shakers, Bronco Group, saddles, #B-207, 3", pr $50.00
Salt & pepper shakers, bull, W, I, G, A, P, O, R, pr....$40.00
Salt & pepper shakers, cable car, W, I, G, A, P, O, R, pr ..$50.00
Salt & pepper shakers, cart, W, I, G, A, P, O, R, pr....$50.00
Salt & pepper shakers, chipmunk, W, I, G, A, P, O, R, pr ..$40.00
Salt & pepper shakers, cookie pot, W, I, G, A, P, O, R, pr.$30.00
Salt & pepper shakers, cop, W, I, G, A, P, O, R, pr....$40.00
Salt & pepper shakers, donkey, W, I, G, A, P, O, R, pr..$40.00
Salt & pepper shakers, Dutch girl, W, I, G, A, P, O, R, pr.$35.00
Salt & pepper shakers, elf on stump, W, I, G, A, P, O, R, pr $40.00
Salt & pepper shakers, frog, W, I, G, A, P, O, R, pr.$125.00
Salt & pepper shakers, hen, W, I, G, A, P, O, R, pr....$50.00
Salt & pepper shakers, house, W, I, G, A, P, O, R, pr ..$75.00
Salt & pepper shakers, lion, W, I, G, A, P, O, R, pr....$45.00
Salt & pepper shakers, Mother Goose, W, I, G, A, P, O, R, pr $45.00
Salt & pepper shakers, owl, W, I, G, A, P, O, R, pr....$30.00
Salt & pepper shakers, pear, W, I, G, A, P, O, R, pr...$75.00
Salt & pepper shakers, poodle, W, I, G, A, P, O, R, pr..$50.00
Salt & pepper shakers, potbellied stove, W, I, G, A, P, O, R, pr...$40.00
Salt & pepper shakers, raccoon, W, I, G, A, P, O, R, pr.$45.00
Salt & pepper shakers, sailor elephant, W, I, G, A, P, O, R, pr...$35.00
Salt & pepper shakers, shack, W, I, G, A, P, O, R, pr...$40.00
Salt & pepper shakers, Sheriff, W, I, G, A, P, O, R, pr..$50.00
Salt & pepper shakers, shoe, W, I, G, A, P, O, R, pr ..$50.00
Salt & pepper shakers, snail, W, I, G, A, P, O, R, pr...$125.00
Spoon rest, Dutch girl, W, I, G, A, P, O, R, 5x10" $40.00

Spoon rest, lamb, W, I, G, A, P, O, R, 5x10" $40.00
Spoon rest, owl, W, I, G, A, P, O, R, 5x10" $40.00
Spoon rest, pig, W, I, G, A, P, O, R, 5x10" $40.00
Spoon rest, Ranger Bear, W, I, G, A, P, O, R, 5x10" ...$40.00
Stein, Bamboo Line, 8" $35.00
Talking picture frame, Hotei, W, I, G, A, P, O, R, 11x7" .$110.00
Talking picture frame, shoe, W, I, G, A, P, O, R, 11x7"....$110.00
Wall planter, bear, W, 5½" $100.00
Wall planter, rabbit, W, 5½" $100.00

Hillbilly Line

Ladies of the Mountains, ashtray, sm, 4½x4¼" $20.00
Ladies of the Mountains, pour spout, head, 6½" $35.00
Men of the Mountains, bank, Mountain Dew Loot, 7".$75.00
Men of the Mountains, bowl, Bathing Hillbilly, 6x6"..$70.00
Men of the Mountains, bowl, pretzel; #H-104, 4½" $40.00
Men of the Mountains, candy dish, 5¼", dia..............$75.00
Men of the Mountains, cigarette box, outhouse, #H-109, 7" .$75.00
Men of the Mountains, ice bucket, man w/jug on lid, #TW-33, 7½x14" $350.00
Men of the Mountains, pitcher, #H-101, 7½" $85.00
Men of the Mountains, pouring spout, #H-104, 6½" ..$30.00
Men of the Mountains, punch cup, #H-111, 3" $15.00
Men of the Mountains, tankard, 1-gal, 15" $250.00
Men/Ladies of the Mountains, bowl, man on 1 side, woman on other, 12" dia $350.00
Men/Ladies of the Mountains, salt & pepper shakers, 4", pr..$40.00

Stein, $40.00 each; mug, $30.00 each. (Photo courtesy Mike Ellis)

Universal Dinnerware

This pottery incorporated in Cambridge, Ohio, in 1934, the outgrowth of several smaller companies in the area. They produced many lines of dinnerware and kitchenware items, most of which were marked. They're best known for their Ballerina dinnerware (simple modern shapes in a variety of solid colors) and Cat-Tail (See Cat-Tail Dinnerware). The company closed in 1960.

Ballerina, egg cup..$12.00

Ballerina, mug..$12.50
Ballerina, plate, luncheon; 9¼"..............................$6.00
Calico Fruit, bowl, serving; tab handles.....................$12.00
Calico Fruit, custard cup, 5-oz................................$6.00
Calico Fruit, plate, 9"..$8.00
Calico Fruit, refrigerator jar, w/lid, 5"....................$15.00
Cattail, batter jug, metal lid, part of set..................$80.00
Cattail, cookie jar, tab handled...............................$85.00
Cattail, jug, canteen; angle handle $30.00
Cattail, pitcher, glass w/ice lip..............................$100.00
Cattail, plate, Old Holland, Wheeling, 6" $6.00
Cattail, salad set, bowl, fork & spoon, 3-pc $50.00
Cattail, saucer, Old Holland, marked Wheelock...........$6.00
Cattail, tumbler, iced tea; glass $35.00
Circus, teapot, white over blue, w/lid $32.00
Holland Rose, plate, Old Holland $4.00
Iris, jug, canteen refrigerator................................$18.00
Kitchenware, bean pot, red & white, handled...........$32.00
Kitchenware, syrup pitcher, metal lid, red & white $35.00
Largo, creamer..$6.00
Largo, plate, dessert; 6" $3.00
Largo, sugar bowl, no lid $4.00
Rambler Rose, plate, 9" $6.00
Refrigerator ware, bowl set, blue & white, 3-pc +lids .$27.00
Refrigerator ware, canteen jug, blue & white, various decals, ea $20.00
Windmill, bowl, utility; w/lid...............................$8.00
Woodvine, bowl, soup; flat.....................................$4.00
Woodvine, gravy boat...$12.00
Woodvine, plate, 9"..$6.00
Woodvine, tray, utility; tab handles.........................$15.00

Valentines

As public awareness of Valentine collecting grows, so does the demand for more categorization (ethnic, comic character, advertising, transportation, pedigree dogs and cats, artist signed, etc.). Valentine cards tend to be ephemeral in nature, but to the Valentine elitist that carefully preserves each valuable example, this is not true. Collectors study of their subject thoroughly, from the workings of the lithography process to the history of the manufacturing companies that made these tokens of love. Valentines are slowly making their way into more and more diversified collections as extensions of each collector's original interest. For more information we recommend *Valentines for the Eclectic Collector, Valentines With Values,* and *100 Years of Valentines,* all by Katherine Kreider (available from the author).

Advisor: Katherine Kreider (See Directory, Valentines)

Newsletter: *National Valentine Collectors Bulletin*
Evalene Pulati
P.O. Box 1404
Santa Ana, CA 92702; 714-547-1355

Dimensional, Cinderella coach, Hallmark, 1960s, 9¾x7½x 4½", EX **$10.00**

Dimensional, pink 4-door sedan, ca 1930s, 9x12x3", EX.**$25.00**

Dimensional, swan carriage, ca 1930s, 8½x11x3", EX.**$25.00**

Flat, cowboy stick man, USA, ca 1940s, 5½x4¾", EX...**$3.00**

Flat, cowboy w/glitter, USA, 1960s, 4¾x2", EX ....**$.50**

Flat, Dear Little Daughter, Hallmark, USA, 1950s, 7½x6½", EX...**$2.00**

Flat, dog selling heart accented w/sparkles, ca 1960s, EX ..**$1.00**

Flat, Dollie Dingle, USA, 1940s, 10x5", EX **$10.00**

Flat, duck in a stew, ca 1940s, 6x5", EX **$2.00**

Flat, Flintstone, 1960s, 4¾x3", EX.................................**$3.00**

Flat, foxy, ca 1960s, USA, 5x3", EX...............................**$1.00**

Flat, girl throwing darts, felt accented, ca 1950s, 5x3½", EX **$1.00**

Flat, Letter K, by: Carrington, 1940s, 3¾x2½", EX **$1.00**

Flat, Little Red Riding Hood, 1950s, 5½x2½", EX **$5.00**

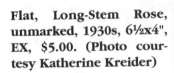

Flat, Long-Stem Rose, unmarked, 1930s, 6½x4", EX, $5.00. (Photo courtesy Katherine Kreider)

Flat, Lux Soap, USA, 1940s, 3½x3", EX........................**$2.00**

Flat, Margaret (Dennis the Menace), USA, 1950s, 5x3¼", EX.**$2.00**

Flat, merry-go-round, USA Carrington Comp, 6x6½", EX....**$3.00**

Flat, miniature flower greeting cards w/child's head inside, 2x3", EX **$1.00**

Flat, Morton salt caricature, USA, 1940s, 4½x3", EX **$2.00**

Flat, Native American, JG Scott, ca 1940s, Gibson, 4x3½", EX..**$3.00**

Flat, owl w/glitter, USA, 1960s, 4¾x2", EX ....**$.50**

Flat, picketer, made in Chicago IL, Carrington Comp, 4¼x4", EX..**$1.00**

Flat, South American child, USA, Golden Bell Greetings, 5½x4½", EX **$3.00**

Flat, streamline engine, unsigned CT, ca 1920, USA, 8½x2", EX **$5.00**

Flat, stuffed soldier, ca 1940s, 4½x4½", EX **$2.00**

Flat, trolley filled w/circus animals, ca 1960s, 3x5½", EX.**$1.00**

Flat, Winnie the Pooh, USA, 1960s, 5½x2¾", EX..........**$2.00**

Flat, Wizard of Oz, USA, 1988, 5x2¾", EX....................**$2.00**

Folded-flat, girl in car, ca 1940s, USA, 6x3", EX...........**$1.00**

Folded-flat, Henry, USA, ca 1940s, 4x4", EX.................**$3.00**

Folded-flat, sailor w/his ship, ca 1940s, 4x3½", EX **$3.00**

Gift-giving flat, w/original toilet water, Fuller Brush, 1950s **$10.00**

Gift-giving greeting card, original candy, Barker Cards, 1950s, 7½x3¾", EX...**$1.00**

Greeting card, bathing beauty, ca 1940s, 3x3½", EX....**$3.00**

Greeting card, cabbage, ca 1940s, 3x3½", EX **$2.00**

Greeting card, carrot w/child, ca 1940s, 3x2½", EX......**$2.00**

Greeting card, clockwork musical, Hallmark, 1950s, 9½x7½", EX...**$10.00**

Greeting card, dog w/felt ears, Hallmark, 1940s, 8¾x6½", EX...**$3.00**

Greeting card, fan, Norcross, ca 1950s, 4x3½", EX.......**$2.00**

Greeting card, Jack & Jill, 4½x3½", EX...........................**$1.00**

Greeting card, jar of honey, A-meri-card, ca 1940s, 5x5", EX...**$5.00**

Greeting card, Nestle Chocolate coupon, ca 1991, 8¼x5", EX...**$3.00**

Greeting card, Pixie, Norcross, 5½x4½", EX...................**$.50**

Greeting card, plaid kitten, Hallmark, ca 1950s, 8x6½", EX.**$5.00**

Greeting card, walnut, ca 1940s, 3x2½", EX..................**$2.00**

Greeting card booklet, Jack Horner, USA, 6½x3¾", EX .**$3.00**

Greeting card w/dimension, castle, Hallmark, 1950s, 9½x15x4¾", EX **$10.00**

Greeting card w/dimension, house, Hallmark, ca 1950s, 7½x9x2", EX **$15.00**

Greeting card w/dimension, Loveland Train Station, ca 1940s, 4x7x11", EX **$15.00**

Honeycomb paper-puff basket, Biestle, USA, 1920s, 10x7x6", EX..**$10.00**

Honeycomb paper-puff basket (sm), Biestle, USA, 1920s, 5x4", EX...**$5.00**

Honeycomb paper-puff clown, Biestle, USA, 1920s, 6¾x6x2", EX..**$5.00**

Honeycomb paper-puff costumed lady, Biestle, USA, 1920s, 7½x7½x8", EX **$15.00**

Mechanical-flat, Army men, USA, no maker, ca 1940s, 9¾x7½", EX..**$10.00**

Mechanical-flat, camel w/Shirley Temple caricature, ca 1930s, 6½x5½", EX..**$5.00**

Mechanical-flat, child in prison w/ball & chain, unsigned CT, 10x7", EX **$10.00**

Mechanical-flat, children swinging, A-meri-card, ca 1940s, 8x5½", EX **$2.00**

Mechanical-flat, fan, made by Biestle, USA, ca 1920s, 5x8", EX..**$10.00**

Mechanical-flat, girl w/bouquet, unsigned CT, PIG, 1940s, 6¾x4¼", EX..**$3.00**

Mechanical-flat, girl w/daisy, Germany, 1940s, 6¾x4", EX....**$5.00**

Mechanical-flat, kaleidoscope style, unsigned CT, PIG, 1920s, 7x4", EX **$3.00**

Mechanical-flat, knife, Biestle, USA, 7¼", EX **$5.00**

Mechanical-flat, sailor & girl doing hula, 1950s, 7x3¾", EX....**$1.00**

Novelty, button boy, ca 1940s, 3½x3½", EX **$3.00**

Novelty, clockwork, Heart Beat, Fishlove & Co, 1950s, 7x3¾", EX...**$1.00**

Novelty, fan, American Greetings, ca 1960s, 7x6", EX..**$5.00**

Novelty, kitten w/toilet water, ca 1950s, 5x2", EX **$5.00**

Novelty, lollipop card w/pirate motif, E Rosen Co, ca 1940s, w/out pop, 6x5", EX...**$2.00**

Novelty, Loveland, CO Cachet, dated 1956, EX $10.00
Novelty, Loveland, CO Cachet, dated 1960, EX $6.00
Novelty, paper doll sailor, ca 1940s, 9½x3½", EX $15.00
Novelty, puzzle, 1940s, 5½x5½", EX..................................$10.00
Novelty flat, Avon scratch-off, USA, 1970s, EX.............$1.00
Novelty flat, cat w/plastic eyes, 1940s, 3¾x3", EX........$2.00
Novelty flat, pig finger puppet, USA, 1950s, 6½x3¼", EX ..$2.00
Novelty greeting card, cabbage, USA, 3½x4", EX $1.00
Novelty greeting card, Paint Book, Carrington, 6¾x5",
     EX...$5.00
Novelty greeting card, prune, USA, 3½x4", EX $1.00
Novelty greeting card, red beet, USA, 4x4", EX $1.00
Novelty mechanical-flat, pocketknife, USA, 1950s, 4x5",
     EX $3.00

Vallona Starr

Triangle Studios opened in the 1930s, primarily as a gift shop that sold the work of various California potteries and artists such as Brad Keeler, Beth Barton, Cleminson, Josef Originals, and many others. As the business grew, Leona and Valeria, talented artists in their own right, began developing their own ceramic designs. In 1939 the company became known as Vallona Starr, a derivation of the three partners' names — (Val)eria Dopyera de Marsa, and Le(ona) and Everett (Starr) Frost. They made several popular ceramic lines including Winkies, Corn Design, Up Family, Flower Fairies, and the Fairy Tale Characters salt and pepper shakers. There were many others. Vallona Starr made only three cookie jars: Winkie (beware of any jars made in colors other than pink or yellow); Peter, Peter, Pumpkin Eater (used as a TV prize-show giveaway); and Squirrel on Stump (from the Woodland line). For more information we recommend *Vallona Starr Ceramics* by Bernice Stamper.

See also Cookie Jars.

Advisor: Bernice Stamper (See Directory, Vallona Starr)

Bowl and mug, Humpty Dumpty, minimum value, $125.00. (Photo courtesy Bernice Stamper)

Bowl, stump design, shadow gray & green $15.00
Butter dish, corn design, natural green & yellow, w/lid..$40.00
Candy dish, Cosmos, various color combinations, ea..$20.00
Cigarette box, man in doghouse $70.00
Cotton dispenser, rabbit, white w/gold trim..............$20.00
Creamer, blue, hand-painted floral............................$20.00

Creamer & sugar bowl, snowbirds, blue w/gold trim or yel-
     low w/gold trim, ea set..$35.00
Figurines, kneeling Indian boy & canoe, green & brown,
     set $75.00
Honey jar, Cosmos, bee on lid, blue or yellow, ea $20.00
Mug, corn design, natural yellow & green $30.00
Salt & pepper shakers, Aladdin & lamp, white w/gold
     Aladdin, gold lamp, pr $100.00
Salt & pepper shakers, clover, 3- & 4-leaf, natural color,
     pr $20.00
Salt & pepper shakers, ears of corn, natural green & yellow,
     4½", pr $40.00
Salt & pepper shakers, Gingham dog & Calico cat, pr.$50.00
Salt & pepper shakers, man in doghouse & wife w/rolling
     pin, pr...$125.00
Salt & pepper shakers, snowbirds, blue & yellow w/gold
     trim, pr $20.00
Salt & pepper shakers, toadstool (brown) & frog (green),
     pr...$15.00
Salt & pepper shakers, tortoise & hare, pr $60.00
Spoon rest, corn design $25.00
Spoondrip, Honeymoon design, yellow $30.00
Sugar bowl & creamer, corn design, natural green & yellow,
     4½"..$40.00
Vase, red-headed woodpecker on side, med $35.00

Vandor

For more than thirty-five years, Vandor has operated out of Salt Lake City, Utah. They're not actually manufacturers but distributors of novelty ceramic items made overseas. Some pieces will be marked 'Made in Korea,' while others are marked 'Sri Lanka,' 'Taiwan,' or 'Japan.' Many of their best things have been made in the last few years, and already collectors are finding them appealing — anyone would. They have a line of kitchenware designed around 'Cowmen Mooranda' (an obvious take off on Carmen), another called 'Crocagator' (a darling crocodile modeled as a teapot, a bank, salt and pepper shakers, etc.), character-related items (Betty Boop and Howdy Doody among others), and some really wonderful cookie jars reminiscent of '50s radios and jukeboxes.

For more information, we recommend *The Collector's Encyclopedia of Cookie Jars, Vol II,* by Joyce and Fred Roerig (Collector Books).

Advisor: Lois Wildman (See Directory, Vandor)

Ball & Bat, salt & pepper shakers, paper label, pr $20.00
Baseball, bank, unmarked, paper label missing..........$30.00
Bellhop, salt & pepper shakers, Vandor in mold, paper label,
     pr..$25.00
Betty Boop, ashtray, Betty sitting at piano, #0618, from $75
     to..$80.00
Betty Boop, bookends, jukebox, 1981, pr................$165.00
Betty Boop, chalkboard $30.00
Betty Boop, clock, Betty's Kitchen, 1995...................$50.00

Betty Boop, dish, Betty sitting on crescent moon face, #0676, 1989, from $30 to...$35.00
Betty Boop, figurine, hula girl, 1984, rare................$350.00
Betty Boop, mask, head, 1981.................................$65.00
Betty Boop, music box, piano, 4-pc........................$125.00
Betty Boop, salt & pepper shakers, wooden boat, 2nd series, pr..$40.00
Betty Boop, string holder..$65.00
Betty Boop, utensil holder, 1995, sm......................$15.00
Cowboy, salt & pepper shakers, paper label, pr........$20.00
Crocagator, bank, Vandor in mold, paper label.........$25.00
Crocagator, teapot, Vandor in mold, paper label.......$35.00
Crocagator Shoes, salt & pepper shakers, Vandor in mold, paper label, pr..$20.00
Crocagator w/Parasol, salt & pepper shakers, Vandor in mold, paper label, pr..$20.00

Flintstones, mug, Betty, paper label, from $15.00 to $25.00. (Photo courtesy Fred and Joyce Roerig)

I Love Lucy, mug, Forever Friends, Lucy & Ethyl in heart, 1996..$15.00
I Love Lucy, teapot, 1996, MIB................................$50.00
Mona Lisa, bank, stamped..$35.00
Mona Lisa, salt & pepper shakers, stamped, pr..........$25.00
Mona Lisa, teapot, stamped......................................$40.00
Swamp, soap dish, Vandor in mold, paper label........$20.00

Vernon Kilns

Founded in Vernon, California, in 1930, this company produced many lines of dinnerware, souvenir plates, decorative pottery, and figurines. They employed several well-known artists whose designs no doubt contributed substantially to their success. Among them were Rockwell Kent, Royal Hickman, and Don Blanding, all of whom were responsible for creating several of the lines most popular with collectors today.

In 1940 they signed a contract with Walt Disney to produce a line of figurines and several dinnerware patterns that were inspired by Disney's film *Fantasia*. The figurines were made for a short time only and are now expensive.

The company closed in 1958, but Metlox purchased the molds and continued to produce some of their bestselling dinnerware lines through a specially established 'Vernon Kiln' division.

Most of the ware is marked in some form or another with the company name and in some cases the name of the dinnerware pattern.

If you'd like to learn more, we recommend *The Collector's Encyclopedia of California Pottery, Second Edition,* by Jack Chipman; and *Collectible Vernon Kilns, An Identification and Value Guide,* by Maxine Feek Nelson. (Both are published by Collector Books.)

Newsletter: *Vernon Views*
P.O. Box 945
Scottsdale, AZ 85252
Published quarterly beginning with the spring issue

Anytime, bowl, chowder...$8.00
Anytime, relish..$20.00
Brown-Eyed Susan, bowl, chowder; tab handle, 6"....$12.00
Brown-Eyed Susan, bowl, serving; 9".......................$20.00
Brown-Eyed Susan, cup & saucer............................$10.00
Brown-Eyed Susan, plate, bread & butter; 6"..............$5.00
Brown-Eyed Susan, plate, chop; 12⅜".....................$25.00
Calico, bowl, vegetable; divided.............................$40.00
Calico, creamer..$20.00
Calico, pitcher, bulbous, 1-pt.................................$35.00
Calico, plate, bread & butter; 6½"...........................$7.50
Calico, plate, chop; 14"..$75.00
Calico, salt & pepper shakers, pr............................$25.00
Chintz, bowl, fruit; 5½"...$8.00
Chintz, cup..$8.00
Chintz, plate, luncheon; 9½"..................................$10.00
Chintz, saucer..$4.00
Coral Reef, cup & saucer.......................................$26.00
Desert Bloom, coffeepot...$65.00
Fantasia, bowl, satyr, #124...................................$250.00
Fantasia, plate, salad; Nutcracker, 7½"...................$165.00

Fantasia, vase, Pegasus, #127, $700.00.

Frontier Days, plate, chop; 14"..............................$175.00
Gingham, casserole, individual, w/lid & stick handle.$35.00
Gingham, coaster..$26.00
Gingham, spoon rest..$40.00
Hawaiian Flowers, coffeepot..................................$125.00
Hawaiian Flowers, plate, chop; 12", from $60 to........$85.00
Hawaiian Flowers, salt & pepper shakers, pr.............$35.00
Homespun, creamer & sugar bowl, w/lid...................$25.00
Homespun, pitcher, 2-qt...$47.50
Homespun, plate, dinner; 10½"...............................$12.00
Homespun, plate, 6"..$5.00

Homespun, salt & pepper shakers, pr	**$18.00**
Lei Lani, creamer	**$35.00**
Lei Lani, plate, chop; 12"	**$55.00**
Lei Lani, plate, chop; 14"	**$125.00**
Lei Lani, plate, dinner; 10"	**$45.00**
Lei Lani, plate, salad; 7"	**$27.00**
Lei Lani, salt & pepper shakers, Ultra shape, pr	**$45.00**
Lei Lani, tumbler	**$65.00**
Linda (#838), cup & saucer	**$12.00**
May Flower, bowl, salad; 12"	**$60.00**
May Flower, bowl, vegetable; 9"	**$38.00**
May Flower, butter tray, w/lid	**$45.00**
May Flower, cup & saucer	**$12.00**
May Flower, plate, dinner; 10¼"	**$15.00**
May Flower, platter, 14"	**$40.00**
Moby Dick, bowl, fruit; 5½"	**$50.00**
Moby Dick, mug, maroon	**$75.00**
Moby Dick, plate, chop; 12"	**$145.00**
Moby Dick, plate, 10½"	**$55.00**
Moby Dick, salt & pepper shakers, pr	**$145.00**
Modern California, bowl, fruit; 5½"	**$9.00**
Mojave, bowl, mixing; 5"	**$15.00**
Mojave, sugar bowl, w/lid	**$14.00**
Organdie, bowl, chowder; tab handle, 6"	**$10.00**
Organdie, bowl, fruit; 5½"	**$5.00**
Organdie, bowl, vegetable; round	**$18.00**
Organdie, cup & saucer	**$7.00**
Organdie, egg cup	**$15.00**
Organdie, plate, bread & butter	**$3.00**
Organdie, plate, salad; 7½"	**$6.00**
Organdie, salt & pepper shakers, pr	**$12.00**
Organdie, teapot	**$45.00**
Our America, cup & saucer	**$100.00**
Our America, plate, 6"	**$50.00**
Plate, Alaska Scrimshaw, 10½"	**$45.00**
Plate, Bits Mission, San Diego, 14"	**$95.00**
Plate, Bits of the Old South, Down on the Levee, 14"	**$95.00**
Plate, Edward Grieg, Composer, 8½"	**$25.00**
Plate, Historic Baltimore, John's Hopkins Hospital, 8½"	**$20.00**
Plate, Moors Mans, advertising, 10½"	**$45.00**
Plate, Mount Rushmore, 10½"	**$15.00**
Plate, Texas, spindle top	**$45.00**

**Raffia: Plate, dinner; 10", $8.00;
Platter, 9½", $15.00; Bowl, 6", $3.50.**

Salamina, bowl, fruit; 5½", from $60 to	**$70.00**
Salamina, cup & saucer	**$100.00**
Salamina, plate, bread & butter; 6½"	**$55.00**
Salamina, plate, chop; 12"	**$285.00**
Salamina, plate, luncheon; 9"	**$95.00**
Santa Maria, bowl, serving; 9"	**$42.00**
Shadow Leaf, pitcher, 1-qt	**$32.00**
Tam O'Shanter, bowl, mixing; 5"	**$20.00**
Tam O'Shanter, bowls, mixing; nesting set of 5	**$125.00**
Tam O'Shanter, casserole, handles, w/lid	**$50.00**
Tam O'Shanter, plate, bread & butter; 6¼"	**$6.00**
Tam O'Shanter, plate, salad; 7½"	**$8.00**
Tickled Pink, bowl, chowder	**$12.00**
Tickled Pink, bowl, vegetable; 8"	**$12.00**
Tickled Pink, butter dish	**$35.00**
Tickled Pink, creamer	**$12.00**
Tickled Pink, gravy boat	**$18.00**
Tickled Pink, plate, dinner; 10"	**$9.00**
Tickled Pink, platter, 11"	**$18.00**
Tickled Pink, sugar bowl, w/lid	**$18.00**
Trade Winds, pitcher, 2-qt	**$40.00**
Tweed, plate, chop; 12"	**$55.00**
Tweed, sugar bowl, w/lid	**$40.00**
Vernon 1860, coffeepot	**$75.00**
Vernon 1860, plate, chop; 14"	**$50.00**
Vernon 1860, teapot	**$65.00**
Winchester 73, cup & saucer	**$75.00**
Winchester 73, mug	**$45.00**
Winchester 73, plate, chop, 12"	**$100.00**
Winchester 73, plate, 6"	**$32.00**
Winchester 73, platter, 12½"	**$130.00**
Winchester 73, salt & pepper mill, pr	**$125.00**
Winchester 73, tumbler	**$45.00**

Viking Glass

Located in the famous glassmaking area of West Virginia, this company has been in business since the 1950s; they're most famous for their glass animals and birds. Their Epic Line (circa 1950s and '60s) was innovative in design and vibrant in color. Rich tomato-red, amberina, brilliant blues, strong greens, black, amber, and deep amethyst were among the rainbow hues in production at that time. During the 1980s the company's ownership changed hands, and the firm became known as Dalzell-Viking. Viking closed their doors in 1998.

Some of the Epic Line animals were reissued in crystal, crystal frosted, and black. If you're interested in learning more about these animals, refer to *Glass Animals of the Depression Era* by Lee Garmon and Dick Spencer (Collector Books).

Bookend, elephant, amber, w/label, pr	**$40.00**
Bookends, Wise Old Owl, figural, green, ca 1950, 5", pr	**$30.00**
Bowl, teal, 8 deep scallops at rim, footed, 7x8"	**$35.00**
Figurine, angelfish, amber, 7x7"	**$125.00**
Figurine, bird, orange, long tail, 9½"	**$35.00**
Figurine, bird, Orchid, 9½"	**$40.00**

Figurine, duck, ashtray, dark blue, 9" $45.00
Figurine, duck, dark teal, Viking's Epic Line, 9" $45.00
Figurine, duck, ruby, round, footed, 5" $40.00
Figurine, ducks, fighting; orange, pr $50.00
Figurine, horse, aqua blue, 11½" $95.00
Figurine, Jesus, crystal w/Crystal Mist, flat back, 6x5".$65.00
Figurine, penguin, crystal, 7" $35.00
Figurine, rooster, red, Viking's Epic Line, 9½" (+)......$65.00
Figurine, swan, bowl, amber, 6"................................$45.00
Lamp, fairy; Fine Cut, pink satin, footed $25.00

Candle holder, girl praying, clear and frosted, two-piece, 6", from $25.00 to $30.00.

Wade Porcelain

If you've attended many flea markets, you're already very familiar with the tiny Wade figures, most of which are 2" and under. Wade made several lines of these miniatures, but the most common were made as premiums for the Red Rose Tea Company. Most of these sell for $3.50 to $7.00 or so, with a few exceptions such as the Gingerbread man. Wade also made a great number of larger figurines as well as tableware and advertising items.

The Wade Potteries began life in 1867 as Wade and Myatt when George Wade and a partner named Myatt opened a pottery in Burslem — the center for potteries in England. In 1882 George Wade bought out his partner, and the name of the pottery was changed to Wade and Sons. In 1919 the pottery underwent yet another change in name to Geroge Wade & Son Ltd. The year 1891 saw the establishment of another Wade Pottery — J & W Wade & Co., which in turn changed its name to A.J. Wade & Co. in 1927. At this time (1927) Wade Heath & Co. Ltd. was also formed.

These three potteries plus a new Irish pottery named Wade (Ireland) Ltd. were incorporated into one company in 1958 and given the name The Wade Group of Potteries. In 1990 the group was taken over by Beauford plc. and given the name Wade Ceramics Ltd., remaining so until the present time. In early 1999, Wade Ceramics Ltd. was bought out from Beauford plc. by the Wade management.

If you'd like to learn more, we recommend *The World of Wade, The World of Wade Book 2,* and *Wade Price Trends — First Edition* by Ian Warner and Mike Posgay.

Advisor: Ian Warner (See Directory, Wade)

Newsletters: *The Wade Watch, Ltd.*
8199 Pierson Ct.
Arvada, CO 80005
303-421-9655 or 303-424-4401 or fax: 303-421-0317

Wade's World
The Official International Wade Collector's Club
Wade Ceramics Ltd.
Royal Works, Westport Rd., Burslem, Stoke-on-Trent, Staffordshire, ST6 4AP, England, UK
e-mail: club@wade.co.uk; http:www.wade.co.uk/wade

Teapot, duck figural, ca 1938, $95.00.

Aquarium set, 1976-1980, Bridge, 1¾" $125.00
Aquarium set, 1976-1980, Diver, 2¾" $30.00
Aquarium set, 1976-1980, Lighthouse, 3" $40.00
Aquarium set, 1976-1980, Mermaid, 2½" $50.00
Aquarium set, 1976-1980, Snail, 1¼" $100.00
Bride & groom (all-over white), 1992, 4¼" $45.00
Disney Miniature Figurine, 1981-1987, Am, 1⅞" $45.00
Disney Miniature Figurine, 1981-1987, Dumbo, 1⅜" ..$85.00
Disney Miniature Figurine, 1981-1987, Peg, 1½".........$25.00
Disney Miniature Figurine, 1981-1987, Si, 1¾" $75.00
Disney Miniature Figurine, 1981-1987, Thumper, 1⅞" ..$35.00
Irish Porcelain, child's tankard, 3" $20.00
Irish Porcelain, Donkey & Cart Vase, 6¼" $45.00
Irish Porcelain, Leprechaun on pig, 1¾" $55.00
Irish Porcelain, Leprechaun-Cobbler, 1½"...................$20.00
Irish Porcelain, Leprechaun-Crock of Gold, 1½".........$20.00
Irish Porcelain, Leprechaun-Tailor, 1½" $20.00
Nursery Favourites, 1972-1981, Bo-Peep, 2⅞" $80.00
Nursery Favourites, 1972-1981, Miss Muffet, 2⅝"........$50.00
Nursery Favourites, 1972-1981, Three Bears, 2⅞".......$60.00
Nursery favourites, 1990-1991, Goosey Gander, 2⅝"..$45.00
Nursery Favourites, 1990-1991, Polly Kettle, 2⅞"........$35.00
Nusery Favourites, 1972-1981, Queen of Hearts, 2⅞"...$55.00
Red Rose Tea (US), 1998, Clown w/drum, 1⅝" $3.00
Red Rose Tea (US), 1998, Clown w/pie, 1½"...............$3.00
Red Rose Tea (US), 1998, Human Cannonball, 1⅛" $3.00
Red Rose Tea (US), 1998, Ringmaster, 1¾"..................$3.00
Red Rose Tea (US), 1998, Strongman, 1½" $3.00
Westminister piggy bank, Annabel, 6⅜" $35.00
Westminister piggy bank, Lady Hillary, 7" $45.00
Westminister piggy bank, Maxwell, 6¾" $70.00

Westminister piggy bank, Sir Nathaniel, 7¼"..............$45.00
Westminister piggy bank, Woody, 5"........................$30.00
Whimtray, 1958-1965, Lion Cub.............................$30.00
Whimtray, 1958-1965, Llama................................$30.00
Whimtray, 1958-1965, Panda................................$30.00
Whimtray, 1971-1987, Duck.................................$20.00
Whimtray, 1971-1987, Fawn.................................$20.00
Whimtray, 1971-1987, Trout................................$20.00

Wall Pockets

A few years ago there were only a handful of avid wall pocket collectors, but today many are finding them intriguing. They were popular well before the turn of the century. Roseville and Weller included at least one and sometimes several in many of their successful lines of art pottery, and other American potteries made them as well. Many were imported from Germany, Czechoslovakia, China, and Japan. By the 1950s, they were passè.

Some of the most popular today are the figurals. Look for the more imaginative and buy the ones you especially like. If you're buying to resell, look for those designed as animals, large exotic birds, children, luscious fruits, or those that are particularly eye catching. Appeal is everything. Examples with a potter's mark are usually more pricey (for instance Roseville, McCoy, Hull, etc.), because of the crossover interest in collecting their products. For more information refer to *Made in Japan Ceramics* (there are three in the series) by Carole Bess White; *Collector's Guide to Wall Pockets, Affordable and Others,* by Marvin and Joy Gibson; *Wall Pockets of the Past* by Fredda Perkins; and *Collector's Encyclopedia of Wall Pockets* by Betty and Bill Newbound.

Advisor: Carole Bess White (See Directory, Japan Ceramics)

Bird and flowers, Japan, 6", from $28.00 to $40.00 each. (Photo courtesy Bill and Betty Newbound)

Basket w/glossy multicolored floral motif on white, gold trim, Japan, 9", from $30 to...............................$45.00
Basket w/handle, embossed flower vine in yellow & green gloss on blue lustre ovoid shape, Japan, 7½", from $30 to $45.00

Bird on a flowerpot, multicolored lustre & glossy glazes, Japan, 6¾"..$50.00
Bird on bamboo pole w/nest hole, glossy blue & green bird on greenish white pole, Germany, 7", from $22 to.......$34.00
Bird on branch w/blossoms, porcelain w/glossy multicolored bird & yellow flowers on blue lustre, Japan, 9", from $50 to..$75.00
Bird on tree trunk w/blossoms, porcelain w/multicolored glossy glazes on blue lustre trunk, Japan, 7", from $50 to ..$75.00
Bird on wishing well, brown on cream, semigloss, 6¼", from $40 to..$50.00
Birdhouse (white & pink), w/2 multicolored airbrushed birds on branch, 5½", from $18 to $28.00
Bottle, yellow horizontally ribbed bulbous body w/brown trumpet neck, glossy, Japan, 4¼", from $18 to $25.00
Carrots (3) in a bunch, orange w/green tops, glossy, Japan, 5½", from $28 to..$40.00
Champagne glass, brown & black airbrushed glossy glazes, marked Ceramicraft, 5½", $15 to $20.00
Colonial couple w/bass fiddle, multicolored glossy glazes, Japan, 6½", from $25 to $30.00
Colonial lady in high relief on ornate vessel w/fruit, multicolored lustre & glossy glazes, Japan, 6½", from $30 to $40.00
Conical form w/flower & butterfly, chalkware w/red & yellow matt glazes on green, Japan, 6½" $25.00
Conical form w/flower & butterfly, multicolored glossy glazes on white w/gold lustre & black trim, Japan, 7", from $40 to...$50.00
Conical form w/geisha girls embossed on ornate background, multicolor w/gold trim, semigloss, Japan, 8¾", from $30 to...$45.00
Conical form w/moriage bird & rose-bud motif on blue & tan lustre, black trim, Japan, 6¼", from $50 to...........$65.00
Conical form w/moriage bird on tan lustre, matt blue top, 7½", from $50 to......................................$65.00
Conical form w/moriage dragon on matt white w/green airbrushed top & bottom, gold trim, 7½", from $35 to.$45.00
Corner pocket, 3 horizontally ribbed cones in tan glossy glaze w/blue drip-glazed rim, 6", from $30 to $45.00
Devils' heads in flower petals, whimsical boy & girl in green & red w/black trim, Japan, 4¾", ea, from $35 to.$50.00
Elf sitting in nook of tree trunk w/pointed grassy base, semigloss, marked SylcaC, England $40.00
Fan w/bow & applied flowers, gold-lined bow & multicolored flowers on cream w/textured gold, Lefton, 8x6", from $25 to...$38.00
Flamingo & pond lilies on circular form w/open center, multicolor painting/airbrushing, Japan, 6½", from $30 to.$40.00
Flower vine & butterfly on handled vessel, multicolored glossy glazes on tan lustre, Japan, 6¼", from $40 to.........$55.00
Flower vine entwined around tree trunk, multicolored glossy glazes, Japan, 7½", from $50 to.......................$65.00
Flower w/ruffled petals, yellow w/green stem, glossy, Japan, 6½", from $20 to..$30.00
Girl & doll buggy against garden wall, multicolored glossy glazes, Japan, 5½", from $25 to...........................$35.00

Girl w/lute against lg rose w/leaves, porcelain w/multicolored glossy glazes, Japan, 6", from $25 to............**$35.00**

Hat w/flower & bow, white hat w/med brown bow & blossom, gold trim on green leaves, glossy, marked USA, 6", from $20 to.......................................**$30.00**

Indian head, multicolored lustre & glossy glazes, Japan, 7¼", from $50 to.......................................**$75.00**

Japanese peasant couple w/baskets on backs, multicolored glossy glazes, Japan, 8", ea, from $40 to **$65.00**

Lady (eyes closed) w/rose on hat & bodice, yellow roses w/airbrushed blue, green leaves, gold trim, 4½", from $25 to.......................................**$35.00**

Lady holding skirt, green hat, yellow bodice & white lustre skirt, 5¼", from $25 to.......................................**$35.00**

Lady's head in blue hat & painted features on glossy white, Japan, 3", from $30 to **$40.00**

Man's head w/mustache, yellow or brown hair, polka-dotted bow tie, Japan, 4¼", from $25 to **$35.00**

Mexican man w/basket on back & flowers at feet, glossy blue, cream, yellow & green, Japan, 5¾", from $15 to **$25.00**

Oil lamp, floral design on white w/22k gold trim, Elynor China, 6¾", from $15 to.......................................**$22.00**

Pitcher w/multicolored stylized bird on white w/green & black trim, Japan, 6¾", from $25 to **$30.00**

Polar bear w/penguin, white lustre bear against glossy blue & white background, Japan, 5½", from $30 to.....**$45.00**

Rose blossom & bud on stem w/leaves, semigloss pink & green, Czechoslovakian, 10½", from $35 to **$40.00**

Sack w/circular handles decorated w/scenic view of road, cottage & trees, blue trim, European, 5", from $15 to..**$25.00**

Sailboat, blue & gold lustre, marked Brown China Co, 5¾", from $20 to.......................................**$30.00**

Scottie dog against fence, white w/brown spots & black collar, orange fence, Japan, 5", from $30 to **$45.00**

Scottie dog head embossed, w/bottom finial, black w/yellow neck ribbon on orange, Japan, 3½", from $30 to .**$45.00**

Shell, pink glossy glaze, marked Continental Ceramics, 6¼", from $18 to.......................................**$28.00**

Straw hat w/brown bird, marked Stewart B McCulloch, 6½", from $18 to.......................................**$28.00**

Swirled conical form in dark green glossy glaze, European, 10", from $12 to **$18.00**

Urn w/multicolored floral motif on white basketweave design, caramel tan trim, Japan, 6¼", from $25 to **$30.00**

Watt Pottery

The Watt Pottery Company operated in Crooksville, Ohio, from 1922 until sometime in 1935. It appeals to collectors of country antiques, since the body is yellow ware and its decoration rather quaint.

Several patterns were made: Apple, Autumn Foliage, Cherry, Dutch Tulip, Morning-Glory, Pansy, Rooster, Tear Drop, Starflower, and Tulip among them. All were executed in bold brush strokes of primary colors. Some items you'll find will also carry a stenciled advertising message, made for retail companies as premiums for their customers.

For further study, we recommend *Watt Pottery, An Identification and Price Guide,* by Sue and Dave Morris, published by Collector Books.

Advisor: Sue Morris (See Directory, Watt Pottery)

Club/Newsletter: *Watt's News*
Watt Collectors Association
P.O. Box 1995
Iowa City, IA 52240
Subscription: $12 per year

Apple, bean server, individual, #75, 2¼x3½"............**$250.00**
Apple, bowl, #106, 3½x10¾"...............................**$350.00**
Apple, bowl, #55, 4x11¾"...................................**$250.00**
Apple, bowl, ribbed, w/lid, #05, 4x5"...................**$145.00**
Apple, bowl, ribbed bottom, shallow, straight tapered sides, plain rim, #603, 2x5¾".................................**$150.00**
Apple, bowl, spaghetti; #44, 1½x8".......................**$400.00**
Apple, casserole, stick-handled, #18, 3¾x7½"..........**$175.00**
Apple, cereal/salad; #94, 1¾x6".............................**$50.00**
Apple, cheese crock, #80, 8x8½"..........................**$1,500.00**
Apple, creamer, #62, 4¼x4½"...............................**$100.00**
Apple, mug, #61, 3x3¼"......................................**$500.00**
Apple, pitcher, #15, 5½x5¾"................................**$75.00**
Apple, plate, pie; w/advertising, #33, 1½x9"............**$150.00**
Apple, sugar bowl, w/lid, #98, 4½x5"......................**$400.00**
Apple, teapot, #505, 5¾x9" **$3,000.00**
Apple (Double), baker, w/lid, w/metal stand, #96, 5½x 8½"..**$225.00**
Apple (Open), bowl, mixing; #7, 4x7".....................**$150.00**
Autumn Foliage, baker, w/lid, #96, 5¾x8½" **$90.00**
Autumn Foliage, bowl, cereal; #94, 1¾x6"................**$30.00**
Autumn Foliage, mug, #501, 4½x2¾".....................**$175.00**
Autumn Foliage, pitcher, #15, 5½x5¾"....................**$65.00**
Banded (Blue & White), pitcher, 7" **$95.00**
Banded (Green & White), bowl, mixing; #5, 2¾x5"..**$35.00**
Banded (Light Blue & White), bowl, mixing; 4x7" **$25.00**
Basketweave, bowl, 5 sizes, ea **$30.00**
Basketweave (Brown), casserole, 6¼x8¼"................**$40.00**
Brown Glaze, carafe, #132, 11x8½" **$175.00**
Brown Glaze, warmer, electric, 2x7".......................**$125.00**
Brown-Banded, teapot, #112, 6x9".........................**$700.00**
Butterfly, ice bucket, w/lid, 7¼x7".........................**$800.00**
Cabinart (Brown/Cream), pitcher, w/lid, 6x7"............**$35.00**
Cherry, cookie jar, #21, 7½x7"..............................**$275.00**
Cherry, salt shaker, barrel shape, 4x2½"....................**$90.00**
Cut-Leaf Pansy, casserole, stick-handled, 3¾x7½"....**$125.00**
Cut-Leaf Pansy, casserole, 4½x8¾".........................**$75.00**
Cut-Leaf Pansy, pitcher, 6½x6¾".............................**$175.00**
Cut-Leaf Pansy (Bull's Eye w/red swirls), platter, 15" **$90.00**
Cut-Leaf Pansy (Bull's Eye w/red swirls), saucer, 6½"..**$20.00**
Cut-Leaf Pansy (Bull's Eye), plate, 7½".....................**$55.00**
Dogwood, plate, bread; 6½"..................................**$55.00**
Dutch Tulip, bowl, mixing; #6, 3½x6".....................**$100.00**
Dutch Tulip, canister, tea; #82, 7x5" **$400.00**

Dutch Tulip, pitcher, #15, $250.00.

Dutch Tulip, plate, divided; 10½" $800.00
Eagle, bowl, mixing; #12, 6x12" $145.00
Eagle, pitcher, ice-lip; 8x8½" $450.00
Esmond, cookie jar, w/wooden lid, 8½x7½" $100.00
Esmond, platter, 15".......................................$175.00
Kitch-N-Queen, bowl, mixing, #5, 2¾x5".............$45.00
Kla Ham'rd, casserole, 2-handled, #43-18, 6x9" $60.00
Morning Glory, cookie jar, #95, 10¾x7½" $400.00
Morning Glory (Yellow), bowl, mixing; #6, 3½x6".....$75.00
Old Pansy, bowl, spaghetti; 3x13"............................$80.00
Old Pansy, platter, 15"..$100.00
Old Pansy (Cross-Hatch), cookie jar, 7x7½"............$275.00
Panel-sided, bowl, mixing; #10, 5x10"....................$35.00
Peedeeco, casserole, stick-handled, 4x11½"..........$25.00
Raised Pansy, pitcher, 7¾x7".................................$225.00
Rooster, baking dish, rectangular, 10" handle to handle,
   5¼x2¼"...$1,000.00
Rooster, bowl, w/lid, #67, 6½x8½".....................$200.00
Rooster, ice bucket, 7¼x7½".............................$275.00
Rooster, pitcher, refrigerator; square, #69, 8x8½"...$550.00
Rooster, salt & pepper shakers, hourglass shape, 4½x2½",
   pr $400.00
Starflower, bowl, #53, 3x7½" $40.00
Starflower, bowl, #73, 4x9½" $65.00
Starflower, casserole, tab-handled, w/lid, individual, #18,
   4x8"..$125.00
Starflower, cookie jar, #21, 7½x7".......................$185.00
Starflower, pitcher, refrigerator; square, #69, 8x8½" .$700.00
Starflower, plate, pie; w/advertising, #33, 1½x9"......$200.00
Starflower (Green on Brown), casserole, w/lid, #54,
   6x8½" $90.00
Starflower (Green on Brown), pitcher, #15, 5½x5¾" .$190.00
Starflower (Pink on Black), sugar bowl, open, 2¾x6½" ..$75.00
Starflower (Pink on Green), platter, #31, 15" $110.00
Starflower (White on Blue), bowl, spaghetti; #39, 3x13"..$250.00
Starflower (White on Green), bowl, 3x13" $100.00
Swirl-sided, bowl, green, #9, 5x9".......................$25.00
Swirl-sided, bowl, 5 sizes, multicolored, ea.............$30.00
Tear Drop, bowl, #05, 2½x5"...............................$45.00
Tear Drop, cheese crock, #80, w/lid, 8x8¼"............$375.00
Tear Drop, pitcher, #15, 5½x5¾" $60.00
Tulip, creamer, #62, 4¼x4½"................................$225.00
White Daisy, casserole, stick-handled, 3¾x7½".......$145.00
Woodgrain, chip 'n dip bowl set, #611.....................$75.00

Weeping Gold

In the mid- to late 1950s, many American pottery companies produced lines of 'Weeping Gold.' Such items have a distinctive appearance; most appear to be covered with irregular droplets of lustrous gold, sometimes heavy, sometimes fine. On others the gold is in random swirls, or there may be a definite pattern developed on the surface. In fact, real gold was used; however, there is no known successful way of separating the gold from the pottery. You'll see similar pottery covered in 'Weeping Silver.' Very often, ceramic whiskey decanters made for Beam, McCormick, etc., will be trimmed in 'Weeping Gold.' Among the marks you'll find on these wares are 'McCoy,' 'Kingwood Ceramics,' and 'USA,' but most items are simply stamped '22k (or 24k) gold.'

Basket, Dixon Art Studios, 22k Gold, 8½x5"..............$35.00
Bud vase, gold draping in combination w/cream gloss on
   gold pedestal foot, Made in USA, 8" $12.00
Candy dish, flattened apple form.................................$24.00
Candy dish, footed ball form w/elongated finial, 8½"..$42.50
Candy dish, swirl design, w/lid, marked Hand Decorated 22k
   Gold USA Weeping-Bright Gold, 3½x7" $22.50

Candy dish, with sticker marked Kingwood Ceramics, 6½" across, from $25.00 to $30.00.

Candy dish, 3-compartment w/center handle, 7"........$16.00
Cup & saucer, demitasse: 2½", 5", scarce, up to........$35.00
Ewer, straight flaring sides, handle wraps from rim to base,
   8"...$22.00
Pin dish, flower blossom form, Elynor China, USA 22k Gold,
   6" dia..$12.00
Pitcher, straight sides, unmarked, 9x4" $45.00
Planter, horses figural, facing pr, rearing before opening,
   10"...$70.00
Planter, panther, pacing, opening in back, 24k Gold, 14¾"
   L $55.00
Planter, tiger figural, marked 24k Gold, Made in USA,
   5¾x9½", from $30 to.....................................$40.00
Teapot, McCoy, ca 1957 ....$80.00
Tidbit tray, 2-tier, marked 22k Gold Weeping-Bright Gold,
   bottom plate: 10" dia......................................$25.00
Vase, cornucopia; marked 22k Gold USA Weeping-Bright
   Gold, 6½x5½" $22.50
Vase, dripping gold, 10-petal flower form, 5x5" dia ...$15.00
Vase, fan shape, pleated sides, chevron design along rim,
   6½"..$22.50

Vase, scalloped square, 22k Gold, 3x4½".................**$10.00**

Vase, shoe figural, marked Diamond Fire Studio (slightly illegible), 4½x4½"............................**$60.00**

Vase, swirls in gold, Swetye Salem O (star in circle), square, 7x4¼".................................**$24.00**

Wall pocket, apple form, 24k Gold, USA, 5", from $25 to ..**$30.00**

Wall pocket, goblet form, 24k Gold, Made in USA, 7", from $20 to.................................**$30.00**

Weil Ware

Though the Weil company made dinnerware and some kitchenware, their figural pieces are attracting the most collector interest. They were in business from the 1940s until the mid-'50s, another of the small but very successful California companies whose work has become so popular today. They dressed their 'girls' in beautiful gowns of vivid rose, light dusty pink, turquoise blue, and other lovely colors enhanced with enameled 'lace work' and flowers, sgraffito, sometimes even with tiny applied blossoms. Both paper labels and ink stamps were used to mark them, but as you study their features, you'll soon learn to recognize even those that have lost their labels over the years. Four-number codes and decorators' initials are usually written on their bases.

If you want to learn more, we recommend *The Collector's Encyclopedia of California Pottery, Second Edition,* by Jack Chipman.

Advisors: Pat and Kris Secor (See Directory, California Pottery)

Baker, Mango, 9x6½" **$15.00**

Bowl, lug soup; Blossom, tab handles...................**$20.00**

Bowl, serving; Blossom...........................**$18.00**

Bowl, vegetable; Bambu, 9x5¾".....................**$16.00**

Butter dish, Blossom, ¼-lb.........................**$22.00**

Cigarette box, raised ming tree design, w/2 ashtrays.**$50.00**

Creamer & sugar bowl, Bambu **$30.00**

Cup & saucer, Blossom **$10.00**

Figurine, girl in green with flowers, 10½", $55.00.

Flower holder, boy & girl, ea w/bouquet, standing on base attached to fan-shaped vase, #4032 & #4033, pr..**$60.00**

Flower holder, Dutch boy #3040, 7¼" **$45.00**

Flower holder, Dutch girl, 3041, 7¼" **$45.00**

Flower holder, girl in short dress seated on step by vase, 11½"................................**$65.00**

Flower holder, girl wearing scarf, carrying long pointed basket ea side, #4024, 10½" **$50.00**

Flower holder, lady in pink dress holding parasol, blond hair, 10" **$60.00**

Flower holder, lady in yellow dress w/wide blue flounce at bottom, light blue shawl, #1728, 11" **$85.00**

Flower holder, lady seated by stump, applied roses/lace, hand-painted flowers, 7¾" **$70.00**

Flower holder, sailor boy, stamped mark, 10¾" **$50.00**

Flower holder, woman, hands to hair, w/flower holder behind her, 11"...............................**$55.00**

Gravy boat, Blossom **$22.00**

Plate, Blossom, 9¾"...............................**$12.00**

Plate, chop; Bambu, 13" dia, from $35 to..................**$45.00**

Plate, dinner; Blossom, yellow **$10.00**

Platter, Bambu, 11"...............................**$25.00**

Salt & pepper shakers, 5-petal flower-shaped top, conforming sides, pr...............................**$12.00**

Snack tray & cup, Birchwood, rare **$15.00**

Sugar bowl, Blossom, w/lid...........................**$16.00**

Tray, Bambu, 6x12"...............................**$25.00**

Tumbler, Blossom, 4¼" **$16.00**

Wall pocket, lady holding horn of plenty, stamped logo, 9"...**$75.00**

Weller

Though the Weller Pottery has been closed since 1948, they were so prolific that you'll be sure to see several pieces anytime you're 'antiquing.' They were one of the largest of the art pottery giants that located in the Zanesville, Ohio, area, using locally dug clays to produce their wares. In the early years, they made hand-decorated vases, jardinieres, lamps, and other useful and decorative items for the home, many of which were signed by notable artists such as Fredrick Rhead, John Lessell, Virginia Adams, Anthony Dunlavy, Dorothy England, Albert Haubrich, Hester Pillsbury, E.L. Pickens, and Jacques Sicard, to name only a few. Some of their early lines were First and Second Dickens, Eocean, Sicardo, Etna, Louwelsa, Turada, and Aurelian. Portraits of Indians, animals of all types, lady golfers, nudes, and scenes of Dickens stories were popular themes, and some items were overlaid with silver filigree. These lines are rather hard to find at this point in time, and prices are generally high; but there's plenty of their later production still around, and some pieces are relatively inexpensive.

If you'd like to learn more, we recommend *The Collector's Encyclopedia of Weller Pottery* by Sharon and Bob Huxford.

Alvin, vase, stump shape, unmarked, 8½", from $50 to ..**$75.00**

Ansonia, batter jug, embossed ring decor on body, unmarked, 14½", from $200 to........................**$250.00**

Ansonia, strawberry pot, hand marked, 10", from $95 to...**$110.00**

Ardsley, candle holders, flower form, ink stamp, 3", pr, from $75 to..**$85.00**

Baldin, Blue; red apples on blue, unmarked, 11", from $400 to..**$500.00**

Baldin, bowl, red & yellow apples on brown, unmarked, 4", from $100 to..**$150.00**

Barcelona, ewer, floral medallion on tan, rim-to-hip handle, pouring spout, ink stamp, 9½", from $200 to....**$225.00**

Barcelona, vase, floral medallion on tan, rim-to-hip handles, hand marked, 6½", from $175 to **$225.00**

Blo' Red, vase, shouldered, paper label, 9½", from $125 to..**$140.00**

Blossom, wall vase, ivory flowers on blue, impressed mark, 7½", from $110 to.....................................**$140.00**

Blue Drapery, bowl, pink roses on shirred blue drapery background, unmarked, 3", from $55 to...............**$65.00**

Blue Drapery, candlestick, pink roses on blue shirred drapery background, unmarked, 9½", from $100 to.**$125.00**

Blue Ware, comport, fruit swags on blue, impressed mark, 5½", from $175 to **$225.00**

Blue Ware, jardiniere, 2 angels on blue, unmarked, 8½", from $250 to..**$300.00**

Bonito, vase, flower branch on white, sm rim-to-shoulder handles, signed NC, paper label, 10", from $300 to.....**$400.00**

Bonito, vase, multicolor flowers on white, waisted cylinder, hand marked, 5", from $100 to...........................**$135.00**

Bouquet: vase, in-mold mark, 15", from $125.00 to $150.00; vase, in-mold mark, 12", from $100.00 to $125.00.

Brighton, flamingo, unmarked, 6", from $400 to **$500.00**

Brighton, parrot on perch, impressed mark, 7½", from $600 to...**$700.00**

Burntwood, vase, 2-tone brown floral, 6-sided, impressed mark, 5", from $100 to **$125.00**

Cactus, camel, recumbent, brown, hand marked, 4", from $75 to...**$100.00**

Cactus, Sylvia the Dancer, shiny tan, script mark, 8", from $375 to...**$575.00**

Candis, vase, embossed flowers on ivory, handles, in-mold script mark, 9", from $55 to **$65.00**

Chase, vase, fox hunt scene in white on dark blue, bulbous, hand marked, 6½", from $250 to **$350.00**

Chengtu, ginger jar, Chinese Red w/upturned handles, ink stamp, 8", from $175 to..................................**$200.00**

Chengtu, vase, Chinese Red, shouldered, paper label, 8", from $70 to...**$95.00**

Classic, bowl, cut-out scallops along rim on white, script mark, 8", from $30 to **$40.00**

Classic, planter, cut-out scallops at rim on green, paper label & script mark, 4", from $60 to **$70.00**

Claywood, candle holder, 2-tone brown floral, flared foot, unmarked, 5", from $65 to.................................**$85.00**

Claywood, plate, floral 2-tone brown decor, unmarked, 7", from $125 to..**$150.00**

Cloudburst, vase, brown & white lustre crackle, shouldered, unmarked, 5", from $95 to.................................**$110.00**

Colored Glaze, jardiniere, green runs on wine w/embossed decor, impressed mark, 8", from $250 to...........**$300.00**

Coppertone, basket, embossed floral decor on dark green w/bronze patina, twig handle, unmarked, 8½", from $175 to...**$225.00**

Coppertone, console bowl, dark green lily-pad form w/bronze patina, 3x12" w/frog figural flower arranger, from $300 to..**$350.00**

Coppertone, vase, dark green w/bronze wash, frog handles, ink stamp mark, 8", from $800 to **$900.00**

Creamware, bowl, lady cameo on ivory, unmarked, 6", from $50 to...**$60.00**

Creamware, Decorated, teapot, floral decal on cream, unmarked, 5½", from $100 to...........................**$125.00**

Creamware, Decorated; mug, floral decal on cream, unmarked, 5", from $50 to **$75.00**

Creamware, Decorated; mug, hand-painted flower on cream, unmarked, 5", from $100 to **$125.00**

Creamware, planter, reticulation along sides, 4-footed, linear decor on ivory, impressed mark, 4", from $75 to ..**$85.00**

Dupont, planter, flowers in vases in grid-like panels on ivory, impressed mark, 5", from $65 to **$75.00**

Elberta, bowl, brown to green, 3-part, hand marked, 3½", from $65 to...**$75.00**

Eocean, vase, flower on shaded brown, flared cylinder, unmarked, 9", from $275 to....................................**$325.00**

Etna, vase, embossed rose on gray to cream, shouldered, unmarked, 10½", from $375 to...........................**$425.00**

Etna, vase, lizard on side of gourd shape, sm die impressed mark, 4½", from $575 to **$675.00**

Evergreen, console bowl, scalloped rim, green tones, script mark, 5", from $65 to **$75.00**

Evergreen, triple candle holder, 3 flower-like forms on base green tones, script mark, 7½", from $95 to.......**$115.00**

Flask, Never Dry, unmarked, 5", from $185 to **$235.00**

Flemish, jardiniere, embossed ivory roses w/brown leaves on light brown, impressed mark, 8", from $250 to .**$350.00**

Flemish, jardiniere, pink roses & green leaves in panels on brown, unmarked, 7½", from $125 to................**$150.00**

Fleron, bowl, green w/plum wash, folded/ruffled rim, hand marked, #J-6, 3", from $75 to...........................**$85.00**

Florala, candle holders, multicolored flowers on ivory, 6-sided, impressed mark, 5", pr, from $125 to **$150.00**

Floretta, ewer, embossed grapes on dark brown, cylindrical, circle seal mark, 10½", from $175 to **$225.00**

Floretta, vase, embossed grapes, gourd shape, circle seal mark, 5½", from $125 to **$150.00**

Forest, bowl, woodland scene in earth tones, shape #3, unmarked, 2½", from $65 to................................**$75.00**

Forest, jardiniere, trees in earth tones, unmarked, 8½", from $400 to..**$450.00**

Forest, tub planter, woodland scene in earth tones, impressed mark, 6", from $125 to **$150.00**

Fruitone, vase, brown tones, 6-sided, impressed mark, 8", from $125 to...**$150.00**

Geode, vase, 6-point star-shaped rim, folded sides, #C-10, Weller...Since 1872 mark, 13", from $125 to **$150.00**

Glendale, vase, bird in flight, brown tones w/blue sky, unmarked, 6½", from $400 to.............................**$450.00**

Greora, strawberry pot, mottled red to brown, script mark, 8½", from $175 to...**$225.00**

Hobart, candle holder, draped nude kneels at side of holder, pastel green, unmarked, 6", from $250 to **$300.00**

Hobart, figurine, kneeling nude, unmarked, 3", from $225 to..**$275.00**

Hudson, Blue & Decorated; flower band along rim, cylindrical, impressed mark, 8½", from $175 to.............**$225.00**

Hudson, Light; vase, floral on pink to gray, bulbous, impressed mark, 4½", from $125 to.....................**$175.00**

Hudson, Light; vase, lg flowers on shaded tan, signed HP, impressed mark, 9", from $350 to **$450.00**

Hudson, vase, flowers on shaded blue, signed Timberlake, hand marked, 7", from $300 to.........................**$350.00**

Hudson, vase, mixed flowers on blue to tan, signed M Timberlake, impressed mark, 12", from $600 to ..**$800.00**

Hudson, White & Decorated; bowl, flowers along rim, unmarked, 4", from $150 to................................**$200.00**

Hudson, White & Decorated; flower decor along rim, 6-sided, impressed mark, 9½", from $200 to.........**$250.00**

Hudson-Perfecto, vase, floral on shaded pink, impressed mark, 5½", from $350 to **$400.00**

Ivoris, ginger jar, embossed floral panel on ivory, sm upturned handles, sm foot, hand marked, 8½", from $100 to...**$125.00**

Ivoris, powder box, ivory w/conical finial, hand marked, 4", from $40 to...**$50.00**

Ivory, jardiniere, embossed diamond geometrics on 2-tone ivory, ink stamp, 7½", from $125 to **$150.00**

Ivory (Clinton Ivory), window planter, embossed floral decor, die stamp mark, 6x15½", from $200 to ...**$225.00**

Klyro, bowl, embossed floral swags w/in fence-like brown panels, impressed mark, 3½", from $75 to...........**$85.00**

Klyro, wall pocket, floral swag w/in fence-like panel w/reticulation along rim, paper label, 7½" **$150.00**

Knifewood, vase, daisy-like flowers on brown, impressed mark, 7", from $200 to **$250.00**

Knifewood, vase, peacock, brown tones, inverted cylinder, impressed mark, 9", from $400 to **$450.00**

Knifewood, wall vase, daisy-like flowers on brown, impressed mark, 8", from $225 to **$275.00**

L'Art Nouveau, vase, embossed Nouveau lady, glossy, double circle seal, 12", from $475 to....................**$525.00**

Lamar, vase, landscape scene in deep plum & black, bottle neck, shouldered, unmarked, 6", from $150 to..**$200.00**

Lorbeek, vase, pink pleated shape, footed, ink stamp mark, 7", from $95 to..**$115.00**

Lustre, basket, blue w/faintly pleated body, unmarked, 6½", from $85 to...**$95.00**

Lustre, candlestick, orange w/embossed ribs, flared foot, block letters w/ink stamp mark, 8", from $50 to .**$70.00**

Luster, vase, deep pink cylinder w/slightly incurvate rim, unmarked, 8½", from $50 to.............................**$65.00**

Lustre, vase, tan w/flared rim, block letters w/ink stamp, 9½", from $40 to..**$50.00**

Malverne, vase, flower embossed on side, script mark, 5½", from $75 to...**$85.00**

Marbleized, vase, swirling brown tones, bulbous, hand marked, 4½", from $65 to......................................**$75.00**

Marbleized, vase, swirling brown tones, 6-sided, hand marked, 10½", from $150 to................................**$165.00**

Marvo, double bud vase, allover embossed flowers & leaves, unmarked, 5", from $85 to.....................................**$95.00**

Marvo, vase, allover embossed flowers & leaves, cylindrical, unmarked, 10", from $95 to................................**$115.00**

Melrose, vase, rose branch on ivory, twig handles, scalloped rim, unmarked, 5", from $75 to **$85.00**

Mirror Black, bowl, faint scallop along rim, impressed mark, 11", from $50 to...**$60.00**

Mirror black, bud vase, trumpet neck, unmarked, 5½", from $30 to..**$40.00**

Montego, vase, green runs over burnt umber, angle handles, ink stamp mark, 8", from $200 to **$300.00**

Muskota, bowl w/goose applied at side of rim, impressed mark, 4½", from $275 to....................................**$375.00**

Muskota, fence, 2 posts support 2 cross-piece boards, brown wood look, impressed mark, 5", from $100 to...**$125.00**

Noval, comport, applied multicolor fruit handles on ivory w/black trim, tall foot, unmarked, 5½", from $85 to..**$95.00**

Novelty, monkey on peanut (ashtray), hand marked, 5x8", from $70 to..**$90.00**

Novelty, teapot wall vase, impressed mark, 9½", from $350 to..**$400.00**

Novelty, 3 Pigs (ashtray), unmarked, 4", from $125 to .**$150.00**

Paragon, vase, allover embossed floral decor w/blue wash over white, bulbous, script mark, 6½", from $150 to.....**$200.00**

Patra, basket, floral decor along handle w/pebbly brown bowl, hand marked, 5½", from $150 to..............**$175.00**

Patra, vase, pink & blue floral decor on pebbly brown w/green trim, 4 green feet, hand marked, 7", from $100 to..**$125.00**

Ragenda, vase, draped decor on deep plum, ...Since 1872 mark, 12", from $110 to **$135.00**

Raydance, embossed leaf spray on white, sm upturned handles, Weller Since 1872 mark, 7½", from $25 to ..**$35.00**

Roma, bowl, floral decor on ivory, 4 sm feet, handles, impressed mark, 7", from $75 to **$85.00**

Roma, bud vase, multicolor floral swag on ivory, square sides, unmarked, 6½", from $65 to **$75.00**

Roma, comport, multicolor floral decor on ivory, low handles, unmarked, 5", from $75 to...........................**$85.00**

Roma, console bowl, grapes & leaves on ivory, unmarked, 6½x18", from $200 to......................................**$250.00**

Roma, letter pocket, floral branch on ivory, unmarked, 4½x7½", from $250 to......................................**$300.00**

Roba, vase, #R-20, 13", from $125.00 to $150.00.

Rosemont, jardiniere, apple branch on ivory w/black grid, impressed mark, 5", from $125 to **$150.00**

Sabrinian, basket, shells form bowl, sea horses form handle, half kiln stamp mark, 7", from $250 to..............**$300.00**

Sabrinian, vase, pastel pink to green, sea horse handles, half kiln stamp mark, 10½", from $200 to.................**$225.00**

Softone, vase, embossed linear decor on pink, script mark, 5½", from $15 to...**$25.00**

Stellar, vase, blue stars on white, script mark, 5½", from $400 to...**$500.00**

Suevo, vase, geometric bands, brown tones, trumpet neck, unmarked, 8", from $125 to................................**$150.00**

Sydonia, double candle holder, 2 textured blue lily forms on dark green vase, hand marked, 7", from $75 to...**$100.00**

Trellis, wall shelf, fan-shaped trellis w/round support, unmarked, 10½", from $150 to............................**$200.00**

Turkis, vase, over-glaze runs on dark plum, rim-to-hip handles, hand marked, 14", from $275 to.................**$350.00**

Tutone, basket, flowers, berries & arrowhead leaves on green to brown, ink stamp mark, 7½", from $95 to........**$120.00**

Tutone, vase, flowers, berries & arrowhead leaves on red, footed cylinder, ink stamp mark, 12½", from $200 to..**$250.00**

Velva, vase, floral panel on green, sm upturned handles, footed, paper label, 9½", from $75 to...................**$85.00**

Velvetone, pitcher, blended pastels w/embossed rings, unmarked, 10", from $175 to.............................**$200.00**

Warwick, basket, flower bud on textured brown w/twig handle, ink stamp mark, 9", from $150 to.................**$200.00**

Warwick, planter, bud decor on textured brown, twig handle, foil label/paper label, 3½", from $85 to................**$95.00**

Woodcraft, basket, acorn form w/twig handle, brown tones, impressed mark, 9½", from $300 to.....................**$400.00**

Woodcraft, bowl, reticulated twigs along sides, brown wood tones, impressed mark, 3½", from $85 to.............**$95.00**

Woodcraft, tankard, foxes in den, twig handle, brown wood tones overall, unmarked, 12½", from $650 to....**$750.00**

Woodcraft, wall vase, fruit at base of tree-trunk form, impressed mark, 9", from $125 to **$150.00**

Woodrose, vase, pink embossed floral decor on brown barrel form, tub handles, impressed mark, 7", from $75 to..**$85.00**

Wooodcraft, candle holder, stump form, wood tones, impressed mark, 8½", from $100 to....................**$125.00**

Zona, bowl, rabbit & bird on ivory, molded mark, 5½", from $75 to...**$85.00**

Zona, dinner plate, apple branches along rim on ivory, unmarked, 10", from $25 to................................**$30.00**

Zona, jardiniere & pedestal, multicolor floral band w/black trim on ivory, ink stamp, 28½", from $350 to....**$450.00**

Zona, pickle dish, ivory w/brown twig handle, impressed mark, 11" L, from $85 to **$95.00**

Zona, pitcher, red flowers w/green leaves on ivory w/blue linear decor, unmarked, 7½", from $200 to........**$250.00**

Western Collectibles

Although the Wild West era ended over one hundred years ago, today cowboy gear is a hot area of collecting. These historic collectibles are not just found out west. Some of the most exceptional pieces have come from the East Coast states and the Midwest. But that should come as no surprise when you consider that the largest manufacturer of bits and spurs was the August Buemann Co. of Newark, New Jersey (1868 – 1926).

For more information refer to *Old West Cowboy Collectibles Auction Update & Price Guide*, which lists auction-realized prices of more than 650 lots, with complete descriptions and numerous photos. You can obtain a copy from our advisor, Dan Hutchins.

Advisor: Dan Hutchins (See Directory, Western Collectibles)

Badge, Special Agent, Wells Fargo & Company, round, heavy brass w/pin-back, 1½" dia **$150.00**

Book, Smokey, by Will James, Scribner's reprint, green hardback cover, VG **$35.00**

Catalog, Porter's Cowboy #34, ca late 1940s, VG **$45.00**

Chaps, black woolies, marked EM Stern San Jose CA, long nap, VG **$1,400.00**

Cuffs, dark brown leather w/tooled border, B Leather Co, 7"...**$250.00**

Cuffs, heavy leather w/5½" plain dark cuffs, narrow border design, buckle & rivet closure **$90.00**

Gauntlets, black bear hide, elbow length, heavy leather palms, EX **$145.00**

Gold poke, buckskin, drawstrings, used in Klondike gold rush, from $110 to **$135.00**

Longhorns, red velvet cover in center, 32"...............**$125.00**

Mitts, winter; sheep hide, long wrists **$65.00**

Powder can, metal container used to measure powder at store, painted green, 11" **$65.00**

Powder flask, full fluted shell design, green shoulder cord, American Flask Company, 50% original lacquer ..**$125.00**

Powder horn, leather shot bag, original strap, from $225 to **$425.00**

Quirt, braided leather, white w/black & red strips woven in **$50.00**

Saddle, lady's astride, padded seat, sm metal horn, narrow stirrup leathers & metal stirrups **$300.00**

Saddle, Moran Bros, Miles City, Montana Territory, slick fork, high back, EX **$2,800.00**

Snowshoes, leather laces, from $150 to.....................**$225.00**

Spurs, Mexican, some silver on heel band & swing buttons, 8-point rowels, dark patina, lg **$195.00**

Spurs, North & Judd, w/star on shank, new leathers, cast iron, EX **$150.00**

Spurs, Spanish, unmarked (California), carved shank, engraved body, 4⅝" diameter, $550.00.

Strongbox, painted black w/gold pinstriping, no handles, heavy hinges, loop for lock, 14x9x8"..................**$275.00**

Tongs, blacksmith's; iron, hand-forged, down-turned jaws ..**$25.00**

Westmoreland Glass

The Westmoreland Specialty Company was founded in 1889 in Grapeville, Pennsylvania. Their mainstay was a line of opalware (later called milk glass) which included such pieces as cream and sugar sets, novel tea jars (i.e., Teddy Roosevelt Bear Jar, Oriental Tea Jars, and Dutch Tea Jar), as well as a number of covered animal dishes such as hens and roosters on nests. All of these pieces were made as condiment containers and originally held baking soda and Westmoreland's own mustard recipe. By 1900 they had introduced a large variety of pressed tablewares in clear glass and opal, although their condiment containers were still very popular. By 1910 they were making a large line of opal souvenir novelties with hand-painted decorations of palm trees, Dutch scenes, etc. They also made a variety of decorative vases painted in the fashion of Rookwood Pottery, plus sprayed finishes with decorations of flowers, fruits, animals, and Indians. Westmoreland gained great popularity with their line of painted, hand-decorated wares. They also made many fancy-cut items.

These lines continued in production until 1939, when the Brainard family became full owners of the factory. The Brainards discontinued the majority of patterns made previously under the West management and introduced dinnerware lines, made primarily of milk glass, with limited production of black glass and blue milk glass. Colored glass was not put back into full production until 1964 when Westmoreland introduced Golden Sunset, Avocado, Brandywine Blue, and Ruby.

The company made only limited quantities of carnival glass in the early 1900s and then re-introduced it in 1972 when most of their carnival glass was made in limited editions for the Levay Distributing Company. J.H. Brainard, president of Westmoreland, sold the factory to Dave Grossman in 1981, and he, in turn, closed the factory in 1984. Westmoreland first used the stamped W over G logo in 1949 and continued using it until Dave Grossman bought the factory. Mr. Grossman changed the logo to a W with the word Westmoreland forming a circle around the W.

Milk glass was always Westmoreland's main line of production. In the 1950s they became famous for their milk glass tableware in the #1881 Paneled Grape pattern. It was designed by Jess Billups, the company's mold maker. The first piece he made was the water goblet. Items were gradually added until a complete dinner service was available. It became their most successful dinnerware line, and today it is highly collectible, primarily because of the excellence of the milk glass itself. No other company has been able to match Westmoreland's milk glass in color, texture, quality, or execution of design and pattern.

Advisor: Cheryl Schafer (See Directory, Westmoreland)

Covered Animal Dishes

Camel, emerald green or turquoise carnival, ea **$175.00**

Cat on rectangular lacy base, Antique Blue **$160.00**

Cat on rectangular lacy base, caramel, green or purple marbled, ea...**$175.00**

Cat on rectangular lacy base, milk glass...................**$125.00**

Cat on vertical rib base, black carnival or ruby marbled, 5½", ea **$125.00**

Cat on vertical rib base, purple marbled, 5½" **$75.00**

Dove & hand on rectangular lacy base, milk glass ..**$150.00**

Duck on wavy base, Almond, Almond Mist, Antique Blue or Antique Blue Mist, 8x6", ea...................................**$85.00**

Duck on wavy base, caramel or purple marbled, 8x6", ea **$125.00**

Duck on wavy base, Crystal, Dark or Light Blue Mist, 8x6", ea **$50.00**

Duck on wavy base, purple marbled carnival, 8x6", ea .**$150.00**

Fox on diamond or lacy base, chocolate or Electric Blue carnival, ea...**$200.00**

Fox on diamond or lacy base, milk glass w/hand-painted realistic fur, ea..**$300.00**

Fox on diamond or lacy base, purple marbled, purple marbled carnival, ruby or green marbled, ea **$275.00**

Fox on lacy base, milk glass.....................................**$255.00**

Hen on basketweave base, Antique Blue, Golden Sunset or any mists, 3½", ea...**$30.00**

Hen on basketweave base, milk glass, 3½" **$20.00**

Hen on basketweave base, milk glass w/hand-painted accents, 3½", ea **$25.00**

Hen on basketweave base, Mint Green w/hand-painted accents, 3½" $30.00

Hen on diamond base, chocolate, 7½" $195.00

Hen on diamond base, milk glass with blue head, 5½", $65.00. (Photo courtesy Everett Grist)

Hen on diamond base, milk glass, 7½" $40.00

Hen on diamond base, purple, green or ruby marbled, 7½", ea $200.00

Hen on diamond base, ruby or purple marbled (noniridized), 5½", ea $85.00

Hen on diamond base, ruby or purple marbled carnival, 5½", ea $100.00

Hen on lacy base, milk glass, 7½" $60.00

Lamb on picket fence base, Antique Blue, 5½" $60.00

Lamb on picket fence base, caramel or purple slag carnival, 5½" $125.00

Lamb on picket fence base, milk glass, 5½" $40.00

Lion on diamond base, Electric Blue carnival (500 made), turquoise or emerald green carnival, 8", ea $225.00

Lion on diamond base, milk glass, 8" $135.00

Lion on diamond base, purple marbled, 8" $200.00

Lion on lacy base, milk glass, 8" $150.00

Lion on picket fence base, milk glass w/blue head, 5½"...$125.00

Lovebirds on base, black or pink carnival, 6½", ea .$100.00

Lovebirds on base, Butterscotch carnival or vaseline (400 made), 6½", ea $125.00

Lovebirds on base, Crystal Mist, Moss Green or Olive Green, 6½", ea $45.00

Lovebirds on base, Dark or Light Blue, Green, Pink or Yellow Mist, 6½", ea $55.00

Lovebirds on base, Golden Sunset, Bermuda Blue or Brandywine Blue, 6½", ea $55.00

Lovebirds on base, milk glass or milk glass carnival, 6½", ea $50.00

Mother eagle & babies on basketweave base, Crystal Mist on Brown Mist base, 8", ea $65.00

Mother eagle & babies on basketweave base, purple marbled carnival (160 made), 8" $250.00

Mother eagle & babies on basketweave base, purple or ruby marbled, 8", ea $200.00

Mother eagle & babies on basketweave base, turquoise carnival (limited edition) or chocolate, 8", ea $225.00

Mother eagle & babies on basketweave or lacy base, milk glass, 8", ea $130.00

Rabbit (mule-eared) on picket fence base, caramel or purple marbled, 5½", ea $100.00

Rabbit (mule-eared) on picket fence base, hand-painted milk glass or pink opaque top, on milk glass base, 5½", ea $60.00

Rabbit (mule-eared) on picket fence base, white carnival (1,500 made) or caramel marbled carnival, 5½", ea $130.00

Rabbit w/eggs on diamond or lacy base, blue opaque, 8", ea $175.00

Rabbit w/eggs on diamond or lacy base, chocolate, ruby or purple marbled, 8", ea $200.00

Rabbit w/eggs on diamond or lacy base, milk glass, 8", ea $125.00

Rabbit w/eggs on diamond or lacy base, purple slag carnival (150 made), 8", ea $250.00

Rabbit w/eggs on diamond or lacy base, white carnival (1,500 made) or Electric Blue carnival (500 made), 8", ea $200.00

Robin on twig nest base, any mist color, 6¼" $60.00

Robin on twig nest base, caramel, vaseline, purple marbled, or turquoise carnival, 6¼", ea $150.00

Robin on twig nest base, milk glass, 6¼" $50.00

Robin on twig nest base, pink (160 made), black carnival (experimental) or ruby (2,000 made), 6¼", ea ...$150.00

Rooster on diamond base, crystal (1,500 made), turquoise carnival (1980) or Electric Blue Carnival, 7½", ea....$175.00

Rooster on diamond base, milk glass, 7½" $70.00

Rooster on diamond base, milk glass w/Minorca decoration (hand-painted realistic feathers), 7½" $125.00

Rooster on diamond base, ruby, purple marbled or purple marbled carnival, 7½", ea $200.00

Rooster on ribbed base, milk glass, 5½" $35.00

Rooster on ribbed base, purple marbled, 5½" $85.00

Rooster on ribbed base, ruby, caramel or marbled carnival, made for Levay, 1978, limited edition, 5½", ea..$100.00

Rooster standing, Antique Blue, 8½" $85.00

Rooster standing, milk glass, 8½" $35.00

Rooster standing, milk glass w/Minorca decoration, hand-painted, 8½" $75.00

Rooster standing, purple marbled or Almond w/hand-painted accents, 8½", ea $125.00

Swan (closed neck) on diamond base, milk glass or blue opaque, ea $95.00

Swan (raised wing) on lacy base, black milk glass, 6x9½" $275.00

Swan (raised wing) on lacy base, emerald green, purple marbled, pink or cobalt carnival, 6x9½", ea $225.00

Swan (raised wing) on lacy base, Ice Blue or turquoise carnival, 6x9½", ea $200.00

Swan (raised wing) on lacy base, milk glass, milk glass mother-of-pearl, Light Blue or Pink Mist, 6x9½", ea..........$175.00

Toy chick on basketweave base, Brandywine Blue, Dark Blue Mist, Moss Green, 2", ea $20.00

Toy Chick on basketweave base, milk glass or milk glass w/red accents, 2", ea $15.00

Toy chick on basketweave base, milk glass w/any fired-on color, 2", ea $20.00

Figurals and Novelties

Bird, ashtray or pipe holder, green marbled **$35.00**

Bulldog, Crystal Mist, painted collar, rhinestone eyes, 2½" **$35.00**

Butterfly, Almond, Mint Green, Mint Green Mist or milk glass, 2½", ea...**$25.00**

Butterfly, Almond, Mint Green, vaseline or Antique Blue, lg, ea **$40.00**

Butterfly, any mist color, lg, ea....................**$40.00**

Butterfly, Green Mist, 2½"...........................**$25.00**

Butterfly, mist colors other than Mint Green Mist, 2½", ea..**$20.00**

Butterfly, pink opaque or purple carnival, 2½", ea **$30.00**

Butterfly, purple, caramel or green marbled, lg, ea...**$50.00**

Butterfly, purple carnival, 1977 limited edition, lg, ea..**$55.00**

Cardinal, crystal, solid **$20.00**

Cardinal, Green Mist..................................**$20.00**

Cardinal, purple marbled, solid **$35.00**

Cardinal, ruby carnival, solid......................**$30.00**

Cardinal, ruby or any mist color, solid, ea **$25.00**

Cat in boot, Green, Dark Blue or Yellow Mist, hollow, ea.**$35.00**

Duck, salt cellar, crystal carnival (1,500 made) **$35.00**

Duck, salt cellar, milk glass, Apricot, or Green Mist, ea...**$25.00**

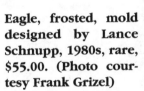

Eagle, frosted, mold designed by Lance Schnupp, 1980s, rare, $55.00. (Photo courtesy Frank Grizel)

Egg, trinket box, any color w/beaded bouquet, w/lid.**$35.00**

Egg, trinket box, any Crystal Mist w/decal, w/lid.......**$25.00**

Egg, trinket box, ruby w/Mary Gregory style or cameo, w/lid, ea **$40.00**

Egg on gold stand, Almond w/any decal or Crystal Mist w/floral spray, blown, hollow, ea **$50.00**

Egg on gold stand, Almond w/any hand-painted decor, blown, hollow, ea..................................**$60.00**

Egg on gold stand, black milk glass (plain), blown, hollow.**$40.00**

Egg on gold stand, black milk glass w/Oriental Poppy, blown, hollow..**$60.00**

Egg on pedestal, any color or decoration, blown, hollow, 1-pc, ea..**$125.00**

Grandma's slipper, Antique Blue, Antique Blue Mist, Almond, Mint Green, Dark Blue or Green Mist, ea **$30.00**

Grandma's slipper, black milk glass or milk glass Mother of Pearl, ea..**$35.00**

Grandma's slipper, brown, Crystal or Yellow Mist, ea.**$25.00**

Grandma's slipper, Honey, Ice Blue carnival or Cobalt Blue carnival, ea **$40.00**

Mantel clock, candy container, Brandywine Blue, hollow, no markings **$35.00**

Mantel clock, candy container, milk glass w/hand-painted clock face, hollow, no markings **$45.00**

Mantel clock, milk glass or Moss Green, hollow, no markings, ea **$30.00**

Napkin ring holder, brown, Light Blue or Pink Mist w/flower, 6 sided **$35.00**

Napkin ring holder, milk glass w/holly decor, 6-sided..**$50.00**

Napkin ring holder, milk glass w/pink flower, 6-sided..**$35.00**

Owl on 2 stacked books, Almond, Mint Green, Antique Blue or black milk glass, 3½", ea................................**$30.00**

Owl on 2 stacked books, any mist color, 3½", ea **$25.00**

Owl on 2 stacked books, blue, pink, yellow opaque or Brandywine Blue, 3½", ea **$25.00**

Owl on 2 stacked books, milk glass, 3½" **$20.00**

Owl on 2 stacked books, purple marbled, 3½" **$40.00**

Owl standing on tree stump, Almond Mist, Antique Blue or Antique Blue Mist, not marked, 5½", ea..............**$40.00**

Owl standing on tree stump, Crystal, Dark Blue or Yellow Mist, not marked, 5½", ea.....................................**$35.00**

Owl standing on tree stump, crystal carnival, ruby or milk glass w/22k gold-rubbed feathers, 5½", ea **$45.00**

Owl standing on tree stump, milk glass or milk glass mother-of-pearl, not marked, 5½", ea...............................**$30.00**

Owl standing on tree stump, purple marbled or ruby carnival, 5½", ea..**$55.00**

Owl toothpick holder, aqua, milk glass, Moss Green or pink, 3", ea..**$20.00**

Owl toothpick holder, crystal, 3"....................................**$15.00**

Owl toothpick holder, green, ruby or purple marbled, 3", ea.**$30.00**

Penguin on ice floe, blue or Blue Mist, ea................**$100.00**

Penguin on ice floe, Crystal Mist or milk glass, ea.....**$80.00**

Porky pig, cobalt carnival, 3"..**$40.00**

Porky pig, Crystal Mist w/hand-painted decor, yellow opaque, milk glass, crystal, Dark Blue Mist or Mint Green, 3", ea **$30.00**

Porky pig, milk glass or Mint Green w/hand-painted decor, 3", ea **$35.00**

Pouter pigeon, Apricot, Dark or Light Blue, Green or Pink Mist, ea **$35.00**

Pouter pigeon, Lilac Mist...**$40.00**

Revolver, black milk glass or crystal w/black hand-painted grips, solid, ea..**$90.00**

Revolver, crystal, solid..**$70.00**

Robin, Almond, Antique Blue, Antique Blue Mist or ruby, solid, 3¼", ea...**$30.00**

Robin, crystal, solid, 3¼"..**$20.00**

Robin, crystal, solid, 5¼"..**$20.00**

Robin, Dark Blue, Green or Pink Mist, solid, 3¼", ea.**$25.00**

Robin, ruby or any mist color, solid, 5¼", ea.............**$25.00**

Robin, Smoke, 5⅛" **$24.00**

Swallow, Almond, Antique Blue or Mint Green, solid, ea **$30.00**

Swallow, Green or Yellow Mist, solid..........................$25.00

Turtle, ashtray or pipe holder, green, Pink Mist, dark or light blue, ea...............................$25.00

Turtle, paperweight, Dark Blue, Green or Lilac Mist, no holes, ea.................................$50.00

Turtle, paperweight, milk glass, no holes....................$75.00

Wren, Almond, Almond Mist or any opaque color, solid...$35.00

Wren, milk glass or any other color mist, solid, ea....$30.00

Wren, pink, 2½"...$20.00

Wren, Smoke, 2½"......................................$20.00

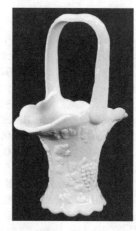

Basket, Paneled Grape, 8", $125.00. (Photo courtesy Frank Grizel)

Wren on square-base perch, any color combination, two-piece, $55.00. (Photo courtesy Lee Garmon and Dick Spencer)

Lamps

Boudoir, English Hobnail/#555, milk glass, stick type w/flat base.........................$45.00

Candle, Almond, Mint Green or ruby w/hand-painted decor, w/shade, mini, ea..........................$45.00

Candle, any mist color w/out decal, w/shade, mini...$27.50

Candle, Crystal Mist w/any decal, w/shade, mini.......$30.00

Candle, Crystal Mist w/child's decal, w/shade, mini...$65.00

Candle, Crystal Mist w/roses & bows, w/shade, mini.$75.00

Candle, milk glass w/child's decal, w/shade, mini...$125.00

Candle, milk glass w/roses & bows, w/shade, mini.$135.00

Electric, any child's decor, w/shade, mini...................$80.00

Electric, any color w/Mary Gregory-style decor, w/shade, mini.........................$80.00

Electric, any color w/roses & bows, w/shade, mini.$100.00

Electric, Brown Mist w/floral bouquet or spray, w/shade, mini, ea.........................$35.00

Electric, Colonial; any color or decor, brass base w/scroll work, glass shade, ea.........................$125.00

Electric, Crystal Mist w/decal, w/shade, mini..............$35.00

Electric, Dolphin; crystal.........................$125.00

Electric, Dolphin; green or pink, ea..........................$175.00

Fairy, Almond w/hand-painted flowers, footed, 2-pc.$65.00

Fairy, Brandywine Blue carnival, footed, 2-pc............$75.00

Modern Giftware

Ashtray, Beaded Grape/#1884, Brandywine Blue, 6½x6½".........................$30.00

Ashtray, Colonial, purple slag.........................$30.00

Basket, English Hobnail/#555, Light Blue Mist, 9"......$45.00

Basket, Paneled Grape/#1881, Brandywine Blue, split handle, oval.........................$45.00

Basket, Pansy/#757, purple slag, split handle.............$35.00

Basket, Rose Trellis/#1967, milk glass w/hand-painted decor, 8½".........................$35.00

Bell, Cameo/#754, w/Beaded Bouquet trim, Dark Blue Mist.........................$35.00

Bonbon, Daisy/#205, Brown Mist.........................$30.00

Bonbon, Waterford/#1932, ruby on crystal, handled..$38.00

Bowl, centerpiece; Colonial/#1776, Bermuda Blue, w/2 candle holders, 3-pc set.........................$125.00

Bowl, console; Paneled Grape/#1881, milk glass, round, 12"..$55.00

Bowl, Lotus/#1821, black, round, lg.........................$50.00

Bowl, Lotus/#1921, milk glass, oval.........................$30.00

Bowl, Lotus/#1921, ruby or crystal, round, lg............$75.00

Bowl, purple slag, leaf form, #300.........................$45.00

Bowl, Rose Trellis/#1967, milk glass w/hand-painted decor, 10".........................$75.00

Bowl, Striped/#1814, Apricot Mist, round, footed, lg.$35.00

Bowl, wedding; ruby on crystal, #1874, 10"................$65.00

Bowl, wedding; ruby on crystal, #1874, 8"................$50.00

Bowl (Grandfather), Sawtooth/#556, Brandywine Blue.......$80.00

Box, jewel; Crystal Mist w/blue China rose, #275, square...$20.00

Box, trinket; Purple Mist, heart form, #1902.............$25.00

Candle holders, ruby on crystal, #1874, matches wedding bowl, 4½", pr.........................$45.00

Candy dish, Beaded Bouquet/#1700, Colonial pattern, milk glass.........................$35.00

Candy dish, Beaded Grape/#1884, Bermuda Blue, 5", w/lid.........................$45.00

Candy dish, Beaded Grape/#1884, Brandywine Blue, 3½", w/lid.........................$35.00

Candy dish, Paneled Grape/#1881, Dark Blue Mist, crimped, 3-footed, 7½".........................$35.00

Candy dish, Paneled Grape/#1881, Mist Pink, open ruffled edge, 3-toed.........................$35.00

Cup plate, Stippled Hearts/#502, Brandywine Blue, 3½"..$15.00

Flowerpot, purple Beaded Bouquet trim, #1707........$45.00

Grandma's slipper, hand-painted Christmas decor, #1900..$40.00

Pin tray, Heart/#1820, Blue Mist.........................$30.00

Sweetmeat, ruby on crystal, 2-handled, #1700............$35.00

Urn, ruby on crystal, footed, #1943, w/lid.................$95.00

Plates

Beaded edge/#22, milk glass w/birds, florals or poultry, 7", ea **$20.00**

Bicentennial decoration, Paneled Grape/#1881, limited edition, 14½" **$225.00**

Forget-me-not/#2, black Mary Gregory style, 8" **$55.00**

Forget-me-not/#2, Blue or Brown Mist, Mary Gregory style, 8", ea...**$60.00**

Hearts, heart shape/#HP-1, Almond or Mint Green w/dogwood decal, 8", ea..**$30.00**

Hearts, heart shape/#HP-1, any color w/daisy decal, 8", ea **$25.00**

Lattice edge/#1890, black milk glass or milk glass w/any hand-painted decor, 11", ea **$95.00**

Lattice edge/#1890, Dark Blue Mist, Mary Gregory style, 11" **$65.00**

Luncheon, Paneled Grape/#1881, milk glass w/hand-painted decor, 8½" **$40.00**

Plain, dinner/#PL-8; black milk glass w/Christmas nativity decor, 8½" **$80.00**

Tableware

Bowl, banana; Old Quilt/#500, milk glass, footed, 11"..**$125.00**

Bowl, banana; Paneled Grape/#1881, Electric Blue carnival, footed, 12"...**$150.00**

Bowl, banana; Paneled Grape/#1881, milk glass, footed, 12" **$125.00**

Bowl, Paneled Grape/#1881, milk glass, belled or lipped, footed, oval, 11"..**$75.00**

Bowl, Paneled Grape/#1881, milk glass, cupped, 8" ..**$45.00**

Bowl, Paneled Grape/#1881, milk glass, shallow, skirted foot, 6x9" **$60.00**

Bowl, relish; Old Quilt/#500, milk glass, round, 3-part....**$35.00**

Box, chocolate; Paneled Grape/#1881, milk glass, w/lid, 6½" dia **$45.00**

Butter/cheese dish, Old Quilt/#500, milk glass, w/lid, round **$45.00**

Butter/cheese dish, Old Quilt/#500, purple marbled, w/lid, round **$75.00**

Butter/cheese dish, Old Quilt/#500, purple marbled carnival, w/lid, round **$125.00**

Butter/cheese dish, Paneled Grape/#1881, milk glass, w/lid, round, 7"..**$50.00**

Butter/cheese dish, Paneled Grape/#1881, purple marbled, w/lid, round, 7"...**$75.00**

Cake plate, Irish Waterford/#1932, ruby on crystal, low footed, 12"..**$95.00**

Cake plate, Paneled Grape/#1881, milk glass, skirted, 11"...**$65.00**

Cake salver, Beaded Grape/#1884, milk glass, square, footed, 11" **$95.00**

Cake salver, Old Quilt/#500, milk glass, skirted, bell footed, 12" **$125.00**

Candelabra, Lotus/#1921, any mist color, 3-light, pr....**$70.00**

Candelabra, Lotus/#1921, milk glass, 3-light, pr.........**$60.00**

Candelabra, Paneled Grape/#1881, milk glass, 3-light, pr....**$400.00**

Candle holder, Paneled Grape/#1881, milk glass, arc shape, 2-light, 8", ea **$45.00**

Canister, Paneled Grape/#1881, green or purple marbled, footed, w/lid, 11½x6¾".......................................**$200.00**

Canister, Paneled Grape/#1881, green or purple marbled, footed, w/lid, 10x5¾"...**$175.00**

Canister, Paneled Grape/#1881, green or purple marbled, footed, w/lid, 7½x4½"..**$150.00**

Canister, Paneled Grape/#1881, milk glass, footed, w/lid, 10x5¾"..**$500.00**

Canister, Paneled Grape/#1881, milk glass, footed, w/lid, 11½x6¾"..**$400.00**

Canister, Paneled Grape/#1881, milk glass, footed, w/lid, 7½x4½"...**$300.00**

Cup & saucer, Paneled Grape/#1881, milk glass.........**$21.00**

Decanter, Paneled Grape/#1881, Lime Green carnival, w/stopper **$175.00**

Decanter, Paneled Grape/#1881, milk glass, w/stopper..**$150.00**

Egg tray, Paneled Grape/#1881, milk glass, w/center handle, 10" **$90.00**

Egg tray, Paneled Grape/#1881, milk glass, w/center handle, 12" **$125.00**

Epergne, Paneled Grape/#1881, Almond or Mint Green, flared, 3-pc set, 14", ea.......................................**$300.00**

Epergne, Paneled Grape/#1881, milk glass, flared, 3-pc set, 14" **$275.00**

Epergne, Paneled Grape/#1881, milk glass, lipped, 2-pc set (no base), 9"...**$175.00**

Epergne, Paneled Grape/#1881, milk glass, lipped, 3-pc set, 12" **$275.00**

Goblet, water; Paneled Grape/#1881, milk glass, footed, 8-oz **$15.00**

Goblet, water; Princess Feather, Golden Sunset, $15.00, and low sherbet, $12.50. (Photo courtesy Frank Grizel)

Goblet, wine; Paneled Grape/#1881, milk glass, footed, 2-oz **$22.00**

Plate, dinner; Paneled Grape/#1881, milk glass, 10½"...**$55.00**

Plate, dinner; Paneled Grape/#1881, Mint Green, 10½".**$55.00**

Plate, luncheon; Old Quilt/#500, milk glass, 8½" **$35.00**

Plate, luncheon; Paneled Grape/#1881, milk glass, 8½"..**$22.00**

Plate, Old Quilt/#500, milk glass, 10½" **$70.00**

Plate, salad; Della Robbia, crystal...............................**$15.00**

Punch bowl set, Fruits, Honey or Ice Blue carnival, 15-pc...**$350.00**

Punch bowl set, Fruits, Lilac Opalescent, 15-pc **$350.00**

Punch bowl set, Old Quilt/#500, milk glass, bowl/base/ladle/12 cups...................................**$960.00**

Punch bowl set, Paneled Grape/#1881, milk glass, bowl/base/ladle/12 cups....................................**$575.00**

Tray, tidbit; Beaded Grape/#1884, milk glass, 2-tier...**$95.00**

Tray, tidbit; Paneled Grape/#1881, Light Blue Mist, 1-tier, 8"..**$35.00**

Tray, tidbit; Paneled Grape/#1881, milk glass, w/Christmas decor, 1-tier, 10½"....................................**$85.00**

Tray, tidbit; Paneled Grape/#1881, milk glass, 1-tier, 10½"...**$50.00**

Tray, tidbit; Paneled Grape/#1881, milk glass, 2-tier, 8½" & 10½" plates......................................**$80.00**

Tray, tidbit; Paneled Grape/#1881, milk glass, 2-tier, 8½" & 10½" plates w/Poinsettia decor **$100.00**

Tumbler, iced tea; Paneled Grape/#1881, milk glass, 12-oz...**$22.50**

Tumbler, juice; Old Quilt/#500, milk glass, flat, 5-oz .**$25.00**

Tumbler, old-fashioned; Paneled Grape/#1881, milk glass, flat, 6-oz..**$35.00**

Tumbler, water; Old Quilt/#500, milk glass, flat, 9-oz..**$12.00**

Water set, Old Quilt/#500, purple slag, 3-pt pitcher & 6 9-oz tumblers...**$280.00**

Water set, Paneled Grape/#1881, Lime Green carnival, 1-qt pitcher & 6 8-oz tumblers **$290.00**

Water set, Swirl & Ball, purple carnival, 3-pt pitcher & 6 8-oz tumblers..**$265.00**

Wheaton

The Wheaton Company of Millville, New Jersey, has produced several series of bottles and flasks which are very collectible today. One of the most popular features portraits of our country's presidents. There was also a series of twenty-one Christmas bottles produced from 1971 through 1991, and because fewer were produced during the last few years, the newer ones can be hard to find and often bring good prices. Apollo bottles, those that feature movie stars, ink bottles, and bitters bottles are among the other interesting examples. Many colors of glass have been used, including iridescents.

Apollo XIII, blue carnival, 8½", $10.00.

American Indian face, cobalt w/bank slot, 6" **$18.00**

Apollo XI, First Moon Flight, cobalt carnival, 8" **$10.00**

Apollo XII, Great American **$10.00**

Apollo XIII, smoky amber carnival, MIB **$12.00**

Apothecary canister, clear, #6 on bottom, metal screw-down lid holder..**$20.00**

Ball & Claw Bitters, amber, 9½".............................**$14.00**

Bell, Proclaim Liberty..., pink, w/cork, 8x4¾"............**$20.00**

Benjamin Franklin, turquoise carnival, 8", MIB, from $10 to..**$15.00**

Bicentennial, Independence Hall/Signers, blue carnival ...**$15.00**

Calvin Coolidge, light amber, disk form, 1st edition, w/cork, MIB...**$55.00**

Carter's Ink, ruby red w/6 cathedral panels, 2½" **$40.00**

Cathedral Brand, Celebrated Remedy, topaz, 4 cathedral panels to body, 3"..**$10.00**

Christmas, 1988, light green, disk shape w/embossed Santa Lucia figure, rare..**$45.00**

Christmas, 1991, light purple, disk shape w/embossed dove, rare..**$55.00**

Christmas tree, green, 9½" **$12.00**

Clark Gable, brown star shape, $15.00.

Coffin shape, blue, mini...**$16.00**

Daniel Webster's Recorder Ink.................................**$26.00**

Dr Fisch's Bitters, 5" **$12.00**

EC Booz Old Cabin Whiskey, amber, house shape, 9" .**$45.00**

EC Booz Whiskey, cabin, blue, 3"............................**$7.00**

Fisch's Bitters, red, fish shape, 3" **$8.00**

Frank's Safe Kidney & Liver Cure, green, 7½" **$15.00**

Horse Shoe Bitters, green w/embossed horse's head w/in horseshoe, 7½"...**$9.00**

Ink (embossed on front & back), warm red, 8-sided.**$35.00**

Ink (embossed on front), ruby red, 6-sided, 2½" **$35.00**

Ink (embossed on side), green, paneled flaring sides, 2½"...**$18.00**

James Buchanan, dark amethyst, disk form, 1st edition, w/cork, MIB...**$35.00**

Jean Harlow, topaz carnival, star shape, 7" **$15.00**

Jenny Lind, red, flask form, 5½"..............................**$15.00**

John Quincy Adams, dark amethyst, disk form, 1st edition, no cork, M (VG box)..**$25.00**

John Tyler, light amber, disk form, 1st edition, w/cork, MIB...**$50.00**

Lantern, blue, 9¾" $20.00
Lincoln Head penny, coin shape, light carnival, 7½" ...$8.00
Millard Fillmore, blue, disk form, 1st edition, w/cork,
    MIB..$60.00
Nascar, Southern 500, 25th Anniversary, med blue $30.00
Nevada City, CA, In Silver We Trust embossed on coin shape,
    5" $16.00
Old Doc's Celebrated Cure, med blue, corn shape, 3¾" ..$22.00
Pocahontas Bitters, amethyst, 5¼".............................$15.00
Poison, skull, crossbones & RIP on front, green, 3" ...$24.00
Rutherford B Hayes, pink, disk form, 1st edition, w/cork,
    MIB $60.00
Schoolhouse, Tuckahoe Country School 1891 on side,
    green...$22.00
Schoolhouse, Tuckahoe Country School 1891 on side,
    ruby $75.00
Scroll flask, med blue, 3" $6.00
Skull, green, 5¼"..$25.00
Skull, med amethyst, 5¼"...$60.00
Thomas Jefferson, flask shape, ruby, 3".......................$8.00
Tonic series, red, 8-sided, 6"...................................$10.00
Tree of Life, Straubmuller's Elixir, dark red, mini, 3¼" ...$15.00

Union, shield and clenched fists embossed on blue, 9", $14.00.

Violin flask, clear, 7½"..$25.00
Warren Harding, green, disk shape, 1st edition, w/cork,
    MIB $60.00

World's Fairs and Expositions

Souvenir items have been issued since the mid-1800s for every world's fair and exposition. Few fairgoers have left the grounds without purchasing at least one. Some of the older items were often manufactured right on the fairgrounds by glass or pottery companies who erected working kilns and furnaces just for the duration of the fair. Of course, the older items are usually more valuable, but even souvenirs from the past fifty years are worth hanging on to.

Advisor: Herbert Rolfes (See Directory, World's Fairs and Expositions)

Newsletter: *Fair News*
World's Fair Collectors' Society, Inc.
Michael R. Pender, Editor
P.O. Box 20806
Sarasota, FL 34276; 941-923-2590; Dues: $12 (12 issues) per year in USA; $13 in Canada; $20 for overseas members

Chicago, 1933

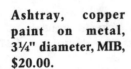

Ashtray, copper paint on metal, 3¼" diameter, MIB, $20.00.

Ashtray, Cuckoo Tower stamped design, brass, dated 1934,
    4½" dia...$5.00
Ashtray, 1933 A Century of Progress Chicago, Plymouth
    Dodge, De Soto Chrysler, copper, 2¾" square.......$8.00
Ashtray, 1934 A Century of Progress Chicago, Fire-
    stone, miniature tire, glass & rubber, 5½" dia, from
    $50 to $100.00
Badge, Annual Convention Chicago Coin Club 1833-1933,
    nickel-plated brass, on blue ribbon, 3"................$40.00
Badge, identification; A Century of Progress, blue & black
    enamel on tin, 55mm L $80.00
Book, Official Views, multicolored illustrations, RH
    Donnelley, 64 pages, 12x9"..................................$22.50
Bracelet, 1933 A Century of Progress, various views of Fair
    Buildings, brass, ⅜" W $20.00
Candle holders, silvered metal, embossed designs, 4x2"
    square, pr $30.00
Cane, varnished wood, brass plate: 1833-1933 A Century of
    Progress Chicago, bentwood grip handle, 36" $20.00
Cigar, White Owl w/band reading: Made at World's Fair,
    Our Grade A Vintage Filler, Chicago 1933, original cel-
    lophane..$35.00
Cigarette case, 1933 Fort Dearborn, Century of Progress,
    leather, snap closure.....................................$25.00
Coat hanger, Congress Hotel & Annex, At The Gateway of
    the 1933 World's Fair Chicago, wood, 16" W.......$35.00
Compact, metal, from $35 to $90.00
Mirror, purse; colorful Chinese Temple depiction, oval,
    2¾"..$50.00
Mug, ceramic, green, nude female handle, embossed
    designs, 3½x6½" $45.00

Needle card, 1933 A Century of Progress, multicolored holder, 4½x6½" **$15.00**

Pencil sharpener **$38.00**

Poker chip, A Century of Progress, white composition w/blue lettering & design, 38mm dia.................... **$25.00**

Salt & pepper shakers, 1933-34 Chicago World's Fair, various images on sides, nickle-plated white metal, 3" **$25.00**

Seashell, 1933 Chicago Fair carved on top, also 'Evaline' & '3' **$10.00**

Shoe, wooden; Belgium Village, red & brown lettering, 98mm L.. **$15.00**

Spoon, fair scene in bowl, sterling, marked handle, 5½"...**$25.00**

Ticket, admission; Good for One Admission to Fort Dearborn, 25¢ tax free, multicolored, w/stub **$5.00**

Token, Good Luck, depicts symbols of good luck, Dodson, copper, 1¼" dia.................................... **$10.00**

Uniform, Lieutenant of Guards, jacket & trouser, gray knit w/orange & red bands, brass Expo button **$275.00**

New York, 1939

Bandana, Boy Scout, dark blue w/orange border, 30" square **$150.00**

Button, for Deutsche tag, w/swastika banner, yellow, from $75 to.. **$100.00**

Cane, black & brown painted wood w/tin edging & tip, 36", EX+ **$85.00**

**Dish, Japan, 7½", from $35.00 to $50.00.
(Photo courtesy Carole Bess White)**

Envelope, multicolored design of Railroads of New York Worlds Fair, letter size, 2½x1½"........................**$5.00**

Game, Going to the World's Fair, multicolored board, box repaired **$100.00**

Mirror, 1939 NY WF, fair logo & printing in blue on glass, 64x89mm, MIB.. **$25.00**

Pie server, image of George Washington on handle, logo, silverplate, 8" L.. **$25.00**

Pin, Trylon & Unisphere on gold-tone metal, oval, 1½" dia **$25.00**

Pocketknife, Trylon & Perisphere, faux mother-of-pearl handles, 2-blade, bottle shape, red, white & blue, miniature **$45.00**

Program, Billy Rose's Arcade, background on show & aquabelles.. **$30.00**

Ticket, blue, orange & white, T&P, no stub, 4x2¼"......**$2.00**

Whistle, saxaphone; NY WF 1940, Made in USA, tin, 4½" ...**$40.00**

San Francisco, 1939

Booklet, Ziegfeld Follies, history, expo events, 20 pages, 9x12".. **$30.00**

Folder, Map of San Francisco, aerial view, Bekin's Van Storage, 20x20".. **$5.00**

Map, Arizona Roads, 1939, marked Arizona Commission San Francisco World's Fair Exhibit............................ **$5.00**

Ticket, w/stub, 1940, 5x2½" **$10.00**

New York, 1964

Badge, Ford, plastic, glows in dark............................ **$15.00**

Bank, Unisphere design, plastic, minimum value **$75.00**

Booklet, Lincoln-Mercury Treasury of World's Fair & New York Attractions, illustrated, 64 pages, 5x7"..........**$12.00**

Bowl, maroon background w/design of Unisphere in silver, plastic, 8" dia.. **$15.00**

Camera, Kodak, MIB **$50.00**

Cheese-cutting board, Switzerland Pavilion.................. **$10.00**

Coaster, Schaefer Center, cardboard............................ **$3.50**

Coaster set, wood w/multicolored views, set of 6, 4" dia..**$15.00**

Dish, Frontier Palace 1964-65 Texas Pavilions — New York World's Fair in black lettering on heavy oval china, 9x11", EX.. **$45.00**

Fan, Zefyr, battery-powered, EX w/box...................... **$15.00**

Figurine, Pieta, white plaster figure on wooden oval base, 6", NM **$50.00**

Guide, Official; Time-Life, illustrated, 312 pages **$12.50**

Hat (beret), orange, blue & white cloth w/buildings & Unisphere on colorful design, center, EX............ **$35.00**

License plates, pr **$20.00**

Map, Official; detailed, multicolored, courtesy of Esso, foldout, 16x24" open.. **$7.50**

Paper doll book, Spertus Publishing Co, w/2 cardboard dolls, Unisphere punch-out & 6 pages of outfits, 10x14", NM+ **$55.00**

Phonograph record, The Triumph of Man, Travelers Insurance Co, 33 1/3 rpm, original colorful fold-out jacket **$12.00**

Pin-back, Meet Me at the Smoke Ring........................ **$15.00**

Pop-Up book, by Mary Pillsbury, Spertus Publishing Co, 24 pages w/5 elaborate pop-ups, 8½x11", NM **$65.00**

Puzzle, frame-tray; multicolored view of fair, Milton Bradley, complete, EX+.. **$22.50**

Salt & pepper shakers, Unisphere form, silver-colored metal, 2x1¼" dia.. **$20.00**

Slide-tile puzzle, plastic, spells out New York World's Fair & pictures the Unisphere, EX **$45.00**

Tumbler, frosted glass, mc scene of Shea Stadium, 7", NM **$10.00**

Unisphere, 3-D, w/Statue of Liberty & buildings in background, silver-colored metal, 4x1x2", NM............**$10.00**

Viewer, color slide; pop-up magnifying lens..............**$25.00**

Auction Houses

Many of the auction galleries we've listed here have appraisal services. Some, though not all, are free of charge. We suggest you contact them first by phone to discuss fees and requirements.

Aston Macek Auctions
2825 Country Club Rd.
Endwell, NY 13760-3349
phone or fax: 607-785-6598
Specializing in and appraisers of Americana, folk art, other primitives, furniture, fine glassware, and china

Bill Bertoia Auctions
2413 Madison Ave.
Vineland, NJ 08630
609-692-4092
fax: 609-692-8697
Specializing in antique toys and collectibles

Cincinnati Art Gallery
225 E. Sixth St.
Cincinnati, OH 45202
513-381-2128
Specializing in American art pottery, American and European fine paintings, watercolors

Collectors Auction Services
RD 2, Box 431
Oil City, PA 16301
814-677-6070
Specializing in advertising, oil and gas, toys, rare museum and investment-quality antiques

David Rago
Auction hall: 333 N. Main St.
Lambertville, NJ 08530
609-397-7330
Gallery: 17 S Main St.
Lambertville, NJ 08530
Specializing in American art pottery and Arts & Crafts

Dunbar's Gallery
76 Haven St.
Milford, MA 01757
508-634-8697; fax: 508-634-8698
Specializing in quality advertising, Halloween, toys, coin-operated machines; holding cataloged auctions occasionally, lists available

Dynamite Auctions
Franklin Antique Mall & Auction Gallery
1280 Franklin Ave.
Franklin, PA 16323
814-432-8577 or 814-786-9211

Early Auction Co.
123 Main St.
Milford, OH 45150

Flying Deuce
1224 Yellowstone
Pocatello, ID 83201
208-237-2002
fax: 208-237-4544
e-mail: flying2@nicoh.com
Specializing in vintage denim apparel; catalogs $10.00 for upcoming auctions; contact for details on consigning items

Garth's Auctions, Inc.
2690 Stratford Rd.
Box 369, Delaware, OH 43015
740-362-4771

Jackson's Auctioneers & Appraisers of Fine Art & Antiques
2229 Lincoln Street
Cedar Falls, IA 50613
www.jacksons@jacksonsauction.com
Specializing in American and European art pottery and art glass, American and European paintings, decorative arts, toys, and jewelry

James D. Julia
P.O. Box 830 Rt. 201
Showhegan Rd.
Fairfield, ME 04937
207-453-7125

Kerry and Judy's Toys
1414 S. Twelfth St.
Murray, KY 42071
270-759-3456
e-mail: kjtoys@apex.com
Specializing in 1920s through 1960s toys; consignments always welcomed

L.R. 'Les' Docks
Box 691035
San Antonio, TX 78269-1035
Providing occasional mail-order record auctions, rarely consigned (the only consignments considered are exceptionally scarce and unusual records)

Lloyd Ralston Toys
447 Stratford Rd.
Fairfield, CT 06432

Manion's International Auction House, Inc.
P.O. Box 12214
Kansas City, KS 66112
913-299-6692
fax: 913-299-6792
e-mail: manions@qni.com
www.manions.com

Michael John Verlangieri
Calpots.com
PO Box 844, Cambria, CA 93428
805-927-4428
www.calpots.com
Specializing in fine California pottery; cataloged auctions (video tapes available)

Noel Barrett Antiques & Auctions
P.O. Box 1001
Carversville, PA 18913
215-297-5109; fax: 215-297-0457

Richard Opfer Auctioneering, Inc.
1919 Greenspring Dr.
Timonium, MD 21093
410-252-5035

Smith House
P.O. Box 336
Eliot, ME, 03903
207-439-4614
fax: 207-439-8554
Specializing in toys

Toy Scouts Inc.
137 Casterton Ave.
Akron, OH 44303
330-836-0668
fax: 330-869-8668
e-mail: toyscouts@toyscouts.com
www.toyscouts.com
Specializing in baby-boom era collectibles

Treadway Gallery Inc.
2029 Madison Rd.
Cincinnati, OH 45208
513-321-6742; fax: 513-871-7722
Member: National Antique Dealers Association, American Art Pottery Association, International Society of Appraisers, and American Ceramic Arts Society

Clubs and Newsletters

There are hundreds of clubs and newsletters mentioned throughout this book in their respective categories. There are many more available to collectors today; some are generalized and cover the entire realm of antiques and collectibles, while others are devoted to a specific interest such as toys, coin-operated machines, character collectibles, or railroadiana. We've listed several below. You can obtain a copy of most newsletters simply by requesting one. If you'd like to try placing a 'for-sale' ad or a mail bid in one of them, see the introduction for suggestions on how your ad should be composed.

America's Most Wanted To Buy
P.O. Box 171707, CB
Little Rock, AR 72222
800-994-9268
Subscription $12.95 per year for 6 issues; up to date information about what collectors big and small are buying now

American Matchcover Collecting Club
  (AMCC)
P.O. Box 18481
Asheville, NC 28814
828-254-4487
fax: 828-254-1066
www.matchcovers.com
e-mail: bill@matchcovers.com
Dues $25 yearly + $3 registration fee for first year, includes *Front Striker Bulletin*; also available: *Matchcover Collector's Price Guide*, 2nd edition, $25.20+$3.25 shipping and handling

Antique Advertising Assoc. of America
  (AAAA)
P.O. Box 1121
Morton Grove, IL 60053
708-446-0904
Also *Past Times* newsletter for collectors of popular and antique advertising. Subscription: $35 per year

Antique and Collectors Reproduction News
Mark Chervenka, Circulation Dept.
P.O. Box 12130
Des Moines, IA 50312-9403
800-227-5531
Monthly newsletter showing differences between old originals and new reproductions. Subscription: $32 per year

Antique Journal
Michael F. Shores, Publisher
Jeffery Hill Editor/General Manager
2329 Santa Clara Ave. #207
Alameda, CA 94501

The Antique Trader Weekly
P.O. Box 1050 CB
Dubuque, IA 52004-1050
800-334-7165
Subscription: $37 (52 issues) per year

Antique Week
P.O. Box 90
Knightstown, IN 46148
Weekly newspaper for auctions, antique shows, antiques, collectibles and flea markets. Write for subscription information.

The Bicycle Trader Newsletter
510 Frederick
San Francisco, CA 94117
415-876-1999 or 415-564-2304
fax: 415-876-4507
e-mail: info@bicycletrader.com
www.bicycletrader.com

Bobbing Head Doll Newsletter
Tim Hunter
4301 W. Hidden Valley Dr.
Reno, NV 89502
775-856-4357; fax: 775-856-4354
e-mail: thunter885@aol.com

The Carnival Pump
International Carnival Glass Assoc., Inc.
Lee Markley
Box 306
Mentone, IN 46539
Dues: $20 per family per year (US & Canada) payable each July 1st

Cast Iron Marketplace
P.O. Box 16466
St. Paul, MN 55116
Subscription $30 per year, includes free ads up to 200 words per issue

Coin-Op Newsletter
Ken Durham, Publisher
909 26th St., NW; Suite 502
Washington, DC 20037
Subscription (10 issues): $15; Sample: $5

Dorothy Kamm's Porcelain Collector's Companion
P.O. Box 7460
Port St. Lucie, FL 34985-7460
561-465-4008

Dragonware Club, c/o Suzi Hibbard
849 Vintage Ave.
Fairfield, CA 94585

Grandpa's Depot, John Grandpa White
1616 17th St., Suite 267
Denver, CO 80202
303-628-5590; fax: 303-628-5547
Publishes catalogs on railroad-related collectibles

International Golliwog Collector Club
Beth Savino
PO Box 798
Holland, OH 43528
800-862-TOYS; fax 419-473-3947

International Ivory Society
11109 Nicholas Dr.
Wheaton, MD 20902; 301-649-4002
Membership: $10 per year; includes 4 newsletters and roster

National Bicycle History Archive
Box 28242
Santa Ana, CA 92799; 714-647-1949
e-mail: Oldbicycle@aol.com
www.members.aol.com/oldbicycle
Resource for vintage and classic cycles from 1920 to 1970; collection of over 1,000 classic bicycles; over 30,000 original catalogs, books, photos; also over 100 original old bicycle films 1930s–70s; restoration and purchase
Newspaper Collectors Society of
  America
517-887-1255
e-mail: info@historybuff.com
Publishes booklet with current values and pertinent information

Nutcracker Collectors' Club
Susan Otto, Editor
11204 Fox Run Dr.
Chesterland, OH 44026
$15.00 annual dues, quarterly newsletters sent to members, free classifieds

Old Stuff
Donna and Ron Miller, Publishers
336 N Davis
P.O. Box 1084
McMinnville, OR 97128
Published 6 times annually; Copies by mail: $3.50 each; annual subscription: $18 ($32 in Canada)

Paper Collectors' Marketplace
470 Main St.
P.O. Box 128
Scandinavia, WI 54977-0128
715-467-2379; fax: 715-467-2243
Subscription: $19.95 (12 issues) per year in USA; Canada and Mexico add $15 per year

Paper Pile Quarterly
P.O. Box 337
San Anselmo, CA 94979-0337
415-454-5552
Subscription: $20 per year in USA and Canada

Pen Fancier's Club
1169 Overcash Dr.
Dunedin, FL 34698
Bimonthly catalog of vintage pens and mechanical pencils; Subscription $20 per year; sample $4

Southern Oregon Antiques and Collectibles Club
P.O. Box 508
Talent, OR 97540
541-535-1231
Meets 1st Wednesday of the month; promotes 2 shows a year in Medford, OR

Stanley Tool Collector News
c/o The Old Tool Shop
208 Front St.
Marietta, OH 45750
Features articles of interest, auction results, price trends, classified ads, etc.; subscription: $20 per year; Sample: $6.95

Statue of Liberty Collectors' Club
Iris November
P.O. Box 535
Chautauqua, NY 14722
216-831-2646

Table Toppers
1340 West Irving Park Rd.
P.O. Box 161
Chicago, IL 60614
312-769-3184
Membership $19 (single) per year, includes *Table Topic*, a bimonthly newsletter for those interested in table-top collectibles

Thimble Collectors International
6411 Montego Rd.
Louisville, KY 40228

Three Rivers Depression Era Glass Society
For more information call:
Edith A. Putanko
John's Antiques & Edie's Glassware
Rte. 88 & Broughton Rd.
Bethel Park, PA 15102; 412-831-2702
Meetings held 1st Monday of each month at DeMartino's Restaurant, Carnegie, PA

Tiffin Glass Collectors
P.O. Box 554
Tiffin, OH 44883
Meetings at Seneca Cty. Museum on 2nd Tuesday of each month

View-Master Reel Collector
Roger Nazeley
4921 Castor Ave
Philadelphia, PA 19124

The Wheelmen
Wheelmen Magazine
63 Stonebridge Road
Allen Park, NJ 07042-1631
609-587-6487; e-mail: hochne@aol.com
www.thewheelmen.org
A club with about 800 members dedicated to the enjoyment and preservation of our bicycle heritage

The '50s Flea
April and Larry Tvorak
P.O. Box 94
Warren Center, PA 18851
570-395-3775; e-mail: april@epix.net
Published once a year, $4 postpaid; free classified up to 30 words

Special Interests

In this section of the book we have listed hundreds of dealers/collectors who specialize in many of the fields this price guide covers. Many of them have sent information, photographs, or advised us concerning current values and trends. This is a courtesy listing, and they are under no obligation to field questions from our readers, though some may be willing to do so. If you do write to any of them, don't expect a response unless you include an SASE (stamped self-addressed envelope) with your letter. If you have items to offer them for sale or are seeking information, describe the piece in question thoroughly and mention any marks. You can sometimes do a pencil rubbing to duplicate the mark exactly. Photographs are still worth a 'thousand words,' and photocopies are especially good for paper goods, patterned dinnerware, or even smaller three-dimensional items.

It's a good idea to include your phone number if you write, since many people would rather respond with a call than a letter. And suggesting that they call back collect might very well be the courtesy that results in a successful transaction. If you're trying to reach someone by phone, always stop to consider the local time on the other end of your call. Even the most cordial person when dragged out of bed in the middle of the night will very likely *not* be receptive to you.

With the exception of the Advertising, Books, Bottles, Character Collectibles, and Toys sections which we've alphabetized by character or type, buyers are listed alphabetically under bold topics. A line in italics indicates only the specialized interests of the particular buyer whose name immediately follows it. Recommended reference guides not available from Collector Books may be purchased directly from the authors whose addresses are given in this section.

Abingdon
Louise Dumont
318 Palo Verde Dr.
Leesburg, FL 34749
e-mail: LOUISED452@aol.com

Advertising
Aunt Jemima
Fee charged for appraisal
Judy Posner
P.O. Box 2194 SC
Englewood, FL 34295
www.judyposner.com
e-mail: judyandjef@aol.com

Big Boy
Steve Soelberg
29126 Laro Dr.
Agoura Hills, CA 91301
818-889-9909

Campbell's Soup
Authors of book
Dave and Micki Young
414 Country Ln. Ct.
Wauconda, IL 60084
541-664-6764

Cereal boxes and premiums
Author of books; editor of magazine: Flake
Scott Bruce; Mr. Cereal Box
P.O. Box 481
Cambridge, MS 02140
617-492-5004
Buys, sells, trades, appraises; books available from author

Gerber Baby dolls
Author of book ($44 postpaid)
Joan S. Grubaugh
2342 Hoaglin Rd.
Van Wert, OH 45891
419-622-4411
fax: 419-622-3026

Green Giant
Edits newsletter
Lil West
2343 10000 Rd.
Oswego, KS 67356
Also other related Pillsbury memorabilia

Jewel Tea products and tins
Bill and Judy Vroman
739 Eastern Ave.
Fostoria, OH 44830
419-435-5443

Mr. Peanut
Judith and Robert Walthall
P.O. Box 4465
Huntsville, AL 35815
256-881-9198

Poppin' Fresh (Pillsbury Doughboy)
Editor of newsletter
Lil West
The Lovin' Connection
2343 10000 Road
Oswego, KS 67356
Also other related Pillsbury memorabilia

Reddy Kilowatt and Bordon's Elsie
Lee Garmon
1529 Whittier St.
Springfield, IL 62704

Smokey Bear
Glen Brady
P.O. Box 3933
Central Point, OR 97502
541-664-6764

Tins
Author of book
Linda McPherson
P.O. Box 381532
Germantown, TN 38183
e-mail: KPCY12A@prodigy.com

Watches
Editor of newsletter: The Premium Watch Watch
Sharon Iranpour
24 San Rafel Dr.
Rochester, NY 14618-3702
716-381-9467
fax: 716-383-9248
e-mail: SIranpour@aol.com

Airline Memorabilia
Richard Wallin
P.O. Box 1784
Springfield, IL 62705
217-498-9279

Aluminum

Author of book
Everett Grist
P.O. Box 91375
Chattanooga, TN 37412-3955

Author of book
Dannie Woodard
P.O. Box 1346
Weatherford, TX 76086

American Bisque

Author of book
Mary Jane Giacomini
P.O. Box 404
Ferndale, CA 95536-0404

Animal Dishes

Author of book
Everett Grist
P.O. Box 91375
Chattanooga, TN 37412-3955
423-510-8052
Has authored books on aluminum, advertising playing cards, letter openers, and marbles

Appliances

Jim Barker
Toaster Master General
P.O. Box 746
Allentown, PA 18105

Arts and Crafts

Timothy Northup Gallery
190 Cemetery Hill Rd.
Oneonta, NY 13820; 607-433-0191
e-mail: tnorthup@catskill.net
Also period pottery, lighting, furniture, and 19th and 20th century decorative arts

Ashtrays

Author of book
Nancy Wanvig
Nancy's Collectibles
P.O. Box 12
Thiensville, WI 53092

Autographs

Don and Anne Kier
2022 Marengo St.
Toledo, OH 43614
419-385-8211
e-mail: ozrktrmn@clandjop.com

Automobilia

Leonard Needham
118 Warwick Dr. #48
Benicia, CA 94510; 707-748-4286
www.tias.com/stores/macadams

Tire ashtrays
Author of book ($12.95 postpaid)
Jeff McVey
1810 W State St., #427
Boise, ID 83702

Autumn Leaf

Gwynneth Harrison
P.O. Box 1
Mira Loma, CA 91752-0001
909-685-5434
e-mail: morgan99@pe.net

Avon Collectibles

Author of book
Bud Hastin
P.O. Box 11530
Ft. Lauderdale, FL 33339

Banks

Modern mechanical banks
Dan Iannotti
212 W Hickory Grove Rd.
Bloomfield Hills, MI 48302-1127S
248-335-5042
e-mail: modernbanks@ameritech.net

Barware

Especially cocktail shakers
Arlene Lederman Antiques
150 Main St.
Nyack, NY 10960

Specializing in vintage cocktail shakers
Author of book
Stephen Visakay
P.O. Box 1517
W Caldwell, NJ 07707-1517

Beanie Babies

Jerry and Ellen L. Harnish
110 Main St.
Bellville, OH 44813
419-886-4782
Also character toys, dolls, GI Joe, general line; catalogs available

Amy Hopper
2161 Holt Rd.
Paducah, KY 42001

Beatnik and Hippie Collectibles

Richard M. Synches
208 Summit Dr.
Corte Madra, CA 94925
415-927-8844
Also Peter Max

Beatrix Potter

Nicki Budin
679 High St.
Worthington, OH 43085
614-885-1986
Also Royal Doulton

Beer Cans

Dan Andrews
27105 Shorewood Rd.
Rancho Palos Verdes, CA 90275
310-541-5149
e-mail: brewpub@earthlink.net

Bells

Unusual; no cow or school
Author of books
Dorothy J. Anthony
2401 S Horton St.
Ft. Scott, KS 66701-2790

Bicycles and Tricycles

Consultant, collector, dealer
Lorne Shields
Box 211
Chagrin Falls, OH 44022-0211
440-247-5632; fax: 905-886-7748
e-mail: vintage@globalserve.net
Alternate address: P.O. Box 87588
300 John St. Post Office
Thornhill, Ontario, Canada L3T 7R3

Black Americana

Buy, sell, and trade; lists available
fee charged for appraisal
Judy Posner
R.R. 1, Box 273
Effort, PA 18330
www.tias.com/stores/jpc
e-mail: judyandjef@aol.com
Also toys, Disney, salt and pepper shakers, general line

Black Glass

Author of book
Marlena Toohey
703 S Pratt Pky.
Longmont, CO 80501
303-678-9726

Blue Danube

Lori Simnionie
Auburn Main St. Antiques
124 E. Main St.
Auburn, WA 98002
253-927-3866 or 253-804-8041

Blue Ridge

Author of several books; columnist for
The Depression Glass Daze
Bill and Betty Newbound
2206 Nob Hill Dr.
Sanford, NC 27330
Also milk glass, wall pockets, figural
planters, collectible china and glass

Bobbin' Heads by Hartland

Author of guide; newsletter
Tim Hunter
4301 W. Hidden Valley Dr.
Reno, NV 89502
702-626-5029

Bookends

Author of book
Louis Kuritzky
4510 NW 17th Pl.
Gainesville, FL 32605
352-377-3193

Books

Big Little Books
Ron and Donna Donnelly
6302 Championship Dr.
Tuscaloosa, AL 35405

Children's illustrated, Little Golden, etc.
Ilene Kayne
1308 S Charles St.
Baltimore, MD 21230
410-685-3923
e-mail: kayne@clark.net

Little Golden Books, Wonder and Elf
Author of book on Little Golden Books
Steve Santi
19626 Ricardo Ave.
Hayward, CA 94541

Bottle Openers

Charlie Reynolds
2836 Monroe St.
Falls Church, VA 22042
703-533-1322
e-mail: reynoldstoys@erols.com

Bottles

Bitters, figurals, inks, barber, etc.
Steve Ketcham
P.O. Box 24114
Minneapolis, MN 55424
612-920-4205
Also advertising signs, trays, calendars, etc.

Dairy and milk
Author of books
John Tutton
R.R. 4, Box 929
Front Royal, VA 22630; 703-635-7058

Painted-label soda
Author of books
Thomas Marsh
914 Franklin Ave.
Youngstown, OH 44502
216-743-8600 or
800-845-7930 (book orders)

Boyd

Joyce M. Pringle
Antiques and More
3708 W Pioneer Pky.
Arlington, TX 76013
Also Summit and Mosser

Boyd's Bears

Editor of secondary market price guide
Rosie Wells Enterprises, Inc.
R.R. #1
Canton, IL 61520
Also Hallmark, Precious Moments,
Cherished Teddies

Breweriana

Dan Andrews, The Brewmaster
27105 Shorewood Rd.
Rancho Palos Verdes, CA 90275
310-541-5149
e-mail: brewpub@earthlink.net

Breyer

Carol Karbowiak Gilbert
2193 14 Mile Rd. 206
Sterling Hts., MI 48310

British Royal Commemoratives

Author of book
Audrey Zeder
1320 SW 10th St. #5
North Bend, WA 98045
Catalog available

Brush-McCoy Pottery

Authors of book
Steve and Martha Sanford
230 Harrison Ave.
Campbell, CA 95008; 408-978-8408

Bubble Bath Containers

Matt and Lisa Adams
1234 Harbor Cove
Woodstock, GA 30189-5467
770-516-6874
e-mail: mattradams@earthlink.net

Cake Toppers

Jeannie Greenfield
310 Parker Rd.
Stoneboro, PA 16153-2810
724-376-2584

Calculators

Author of book
Guy Ball
14561 Livingston St.
Tustin, CA 92780
www.mrcalc@usa.net

California Perfume Company

Not common; especially items marked
Goetting Co.
Dick Pardini
3107 N El Dorado St., Dept. G
Stockton, CA 95204-3412
Also Savoi Et Cie, Hinze Ambrosia,
Gertrude Recordon, Marvel Electric Silver
Cleaner, and Easy Day Automatic Clothes
Washer

California Pottery

Author of several books
Jack Chipman
California Spectrum
PO Box 1079
Venice, CA 90294-1079
Specializing in various California ceramics, Bauer in particular; order books from
author

Author of several books
Susan N. Cox
800 Murray Drive
El Cajon, CA 92020
619-697-5922
email: antiqfever@aol.com
Want to buy: California pottery, especially
Brayton, Catalina, Metlox, Kay Finch, etc.;
Also examples of relatively unknown companies. Must be mint. (Susan Cox has

devoted much of the past 15 years to California pottery research which caught her interest when she was the editor and publisher of the *American Clay Exchange*. She would appreciate any information collectors might have about California pottery companies and artists.)

Especially Hedi Shoop, Brad Keeler, Howard Pierce, Kay Finch, Matthew Adams, Marc Bellaire, Twin Winton, Sascha Brastoff; many others
Pat and Kris Secor
P.O. Box 158
Clarksville, AR 72830

Editor of newsletter: The California Pottery Trader
Michael John Verlangieri Gallery
Calpots.com
P.O. Box 844
W Cambria, CA 93428-0844; 805-927-4428
www.calpots.com
Specializing in fine California pottery; cataloged auctions (video tapes available)

Cleminson
Robin Stine
P.O. Box 6202
Toledo, OH 43614; 419-385-7387

Camark
Tony Freyaldenhover
P.O. Box 1295
Conway, AR 72033; 501-329-0628
e-mail: camarket@cyberback.com

Cameras
Classic, collectible and usable
C. E. Cataldo
4726 Panorama Drive, S.E.
Huntsville, AL 35801; 256-536-6893
e-mail: genecams@aol.com

Wooden, detective and stereo
John A. Hess
P.O. Box 3062
Andover, MA 01810
Also old brass lenses

Candy Containers
Glass
Jeff Bradfield
90 Main St.
Dayton, VA 22821; 540-879-9961
Also advertising, cast-iron and tin toys, postcards, and Coca-Cola

Glass
Author of book
Doug Dezso
864 Paterson Ave.
Maywood, NJ 07607
Other interests: Tonka Toys, Shafford black cats, German bisque comic character nodders, Royal Bayreuth creamers, and Pep pins

Cape Cod by Avon
Debbie and Randy Coe, Coes Mercantile
Lafayette School House Mall #2
748 3rd (Hwy. 99W)
Lafayette, OR 97127
Also Elegant and Depression glass, art pottery, Golden Foliage by Libbey Glass Company, and Liberty Blue dinnerware

Carnival Chalkware
Author of book
Thomas G. Morris
P.O. Box 8307
Medford, OR 97504-0307
e-mail: chalkman@cdsnet.net
Also Ginger Rogers memorabilia

Cast Iron
Door knockers, sprinklers, figural paperweights, and marked cookware
Craig Dinner
P.O. Box 4399
Sunnyside, NY 11104; 718-729-3850

Cat Collectibles
Editor of newsletter: Cat Talk
Marilyn Dipboye
33161 Wendy Dr.
Sterling Hts., MI 48310; 810-264-0285

Ceramic Arts Studio
BA Wellman and John Canfield
P.O. Box 673
Westminster, MA 01473
e-mail: bawellman@net1plus.com

Character and Personality Collectibles
Author of books
Dealers, publishers, and appraisers of collectible memorabilia from the '50s through today
Bill Bruegman, Toy Scouts, Inc.
137 Casterton Ave.
Akron, OH 44303
330-836-0668; fax: 330-869-8668
e-mail: toyscouts@toyscouts.com
www.toyscouts.com

Any and all
Terri Ivers
Terri's Toys
206 E Grand
Ponca City, OK 74601
580-762-8697 or 580-762-5174
fax: 580-765-2657
e-mail: toylady@poncacity.net

Any and all
Norm Vigue
3 Timberwood Dr., #306
Goffstown, MA 03045; 603-647-9951

Batman, Gumby, and Marilyn Monroe
Colleen Garmon Barnes
114 E Locust
Chatham, IL 62629

Beatles
Bojo
Bob Gottuso
P.O. Box 1403
Cranberry Twp., PA 16066-0403
phone or fax: 724-776-0621
e-mail: bojo@zbzoom.net

California Raisins
Ken Clee
Box 11412
Philadelphia, PA 1911; 215-722-1979

California Raisins
Larry De Angelo
516 King Arthur Dr.
Virginia Beach, VA 23464; 757-424-1691

Dick Tracy
Larry Doucet
2351 Sultana Dr.
Yorktown Hts., NY 10598

Disney, Western heroes, Gone With the Wind, character watches ca 1930s to mid-1950s, premiums, and games
Ron and Donna Donnelly
6302 Championship Dr.
Tuscaloosa, AL 35405

Disney
Buy, sell and trade; lists available fee charged for appraisal
Judy Posner
R.R. 1, Box 273
Effort, PA 18330
www.tias.com/stores/jpc
e-mail: judyandjef@aol.com

Elvis Presley
Author of book
Rosalind Cranor
P.O. Box 859
Blacksburg, VA 24063

Elvis Presley
Lee Garmon
1529 Whittier St.
Springfield, IL 62704

Garfield
Adrienne Warren
1032 Feather Bed Ln.
Edison, NJ 08820
Also Smurfs and other characters, dolls, monsters, premiums; Lists available

The Lone Ranger
Terry and Kay Klepey
c/o *The Silver Bullet* newsletter
P.O. Box 553
Forks, WA 98331

Lucille Ball
Author of book
Ric Wyman
408 S Highland Ave.
Elderon, WI 54429

Peanuts and Schulz Collectibles
Freddi Margolin
P.O. Box 5124P
Bay Shore, NY 11706
516-666-6861
fax: 516-665-7986
e-mail: snupius@li.net

Roy Rogers and Dale Evans
Author of books; biographer for Golden Boots Awards
Robert W. Phillips
1703 N Aster Pl.
Broken Arrow, OK 74012-1308
918-254-8205
fax: 918-252-9362
e-mail: rawhidebob@aol.com
One of the most widely-published writers in the field of cowboy memorabila and author of *Roy Rogers, Singing Cowboy Stars, Silver Screen Cowboys, Hollywood Cowboy Heroes*, and *Western Comics: A Comprehensive Reference*; research consultant for TV documentary *Roy Rogers, King of the Cowboys* (AMC-TV/Republic Pictures/Galen Films)

Shirley Temple
Gen Jones
294 Park St.
Medford, MA 02155

Smokey Bear
Glen Brady
P.O. Box 3933
Central Point, OR 97502
541-664-6764

Wizard of Oz
Bill Stillman
Scarfone & Stillman Vintage Oz
P.O. Box 167
Hummelstown, PA 17036
717-566-5538

Character and Promotional Drinking Glasses
Authors of book; editors of Collector Glass News
Mark Chase and Michael Kelly
P.O. Box 308
Slippery Rock, PA 16057
412-946-2838
fax: 412-946-9012
e-mail: cgn@glassnews.com
www.glassnews.com

Character Clocks and Watches
Author of book
Howard S. Brenner
106 Woodgate Terrace
Rochester, NY 14625

Bill Campbell
1221 Littlebrook Ln.
Birmingham, AL 35235
205-853-8227
fax: 405-658-6986
Also character collectibles, advertising premiums

Character Nodders
Matt and Lisa Adams
1234 Harbor Cove
Woodstock, GA 30189
770-516-6874
e-mail: mattradams@earthlink.net

Chintz
Mary Jane Hastings
310 West 1st South
Mt. Olive, IL 62069
phone or fax: 217-999-1222

Author of book
Joan Welsh
7015 Partridge Pl.
Hyattsville, MD 20782
301-779-6181

Christmas Collectibles
Especially from before 1920 and decorations made in Germany
J.W. 'Bill' and Treva Courter
3935 Kelley Rd.
Kevil, KY 42053
phone or fax: 270-488-2116

Clocks
All types
Bruce A. Austin
1 Hardwood Hill Rd.
Pittsford, NY 14534
716-387-9820

Clothes Sprinkler Bottles
Ellen Bercovici
5118 Hampden Ln.
Bethesda, MD 20814
301-652-1140

Clothing and Accessories
Author of book
Sue Langley
101 Ramsey Ave.
Syracuse, NY 13224-1719
315-445-0113
e-mail: langshats@aol.com

Teresa Clawson, Customer Service
Flying Deuce
1224 Yellowstone
Pocatello, ID 83201
208-237-2002
fax: 208-237-4544
e-mail: flying2@nicoh.com

Coca-Cola
Also Pepsi-Cola and other brands of soda
Craig and Donna Stifter
P.O. Box 6514
Naperville, IL 60540
630-789-5780

Coin-Operated Vending Machines
Ken and Jackie Durham
909 26th St., NW
Washington, D.C. 20037

Colorado Pottery (Broadmoor)
Carol and Jim Carlton
8115 S Syracuse St.
Englewood, CO 80112
303-773-8616
Also Coors, Lonhuda, and Denver White

Comic Books
Avalon Comics
Larry Curcio
P.O. Box 821
Medford, MA 02155
617-391-5614

Compacts
Unusual shapes, also vanities and accessories
Author of book
Roselyn Gerson
P.O. Box 40
Lynbrook, NY 11563

Cookbooks
Author of book
Bob Allen
P.O. Box 56
St. James, MO 65559
Also advertising leaflets

Cookie Cutters
Author of book and newsletter
Rosemary Henry
9610 Greenview Ln.
Manassas, VA 20109-3320

Cookie Jars
Joe Devine
1411 3rd St.
Council Bluffs, IA 51503
712-323-5233 or 712-328-7305
Also Russel Wright

Buy, sell, and trade; lists available fee charged for appraisal
Judy Posner
R.R. 1, Box 273
Effort, PA 18330
www.tias.com/stores/jpc
e-mail: judyandjef@aol.com

Cow Creamers
Shirley Green
1550 E. Kamm Ave. #116
Kingsburg, CA 93631; 209-897-7125
e-mail: granas@psnw.com

Cracker Jack Items
Phil Helley
Old Kilbourn Antiques
629 Indiana Ave.
Wisconsin Dells, WI 53965
Also banks, radio premiums, and wind-up toys

Wes Johnson, Sr.
106 Bauer Ave.
Louisville, KY 40207

Author of books
Larry White
108 Central St.
Rowley, MA 01969-1317
978-948-8187
e-mail: larrydw@erols.com

Crackle Glass
Authors of book
Stan and Arlene Weitman
101 Cypress St.
Massapequa Park, NY 11758
516-799-2619; fax: 516-797-3039

Cuff Links
National Cuff Link Society
Eugene R. Klompus
P.O. Box 346
Prospect Hts., IL 60070
phone or fax: 847-816-0035
e-mail: genek@cufflink.com
Also related items

Currier & Ives Dinnerware
Author of book
Eldon R. Bud Aupperle
29470 Saxon Road
Toulon, IL 61483
309-896-3331
fax: 309-856-6005
(See also Clubs and Newsletters)

Dakins
Jim Rash
135 Alder Ave.
Egg Harbor Township, NJ 08234

Decanters
Homestead Collectibles
Art and Judy Turner
R.D. 2, Rte. 150
P.O. Box 173
Mill Hall, PA 17751
570-726-3597; fax: 717-726-4488

Degenhart
Linda K. Marsh
1229 Gould Rd.
Lansing, MI 48917

deLee
Authors of book
Joanne and Ralph Schaefer
3182 Williams Rd.
Oroville, CA 95965-8300
916-893-2902 or 800-897-6263

Depression Glass
Also Elegant glassware
John and Shirley Baker
673 W Township Rd. #118
Tiffin, OH 44883
Also Tiffin glassware

Dinnerware
Cat-Tail
Ken and Barbara Brooks
4121 Gladstone Ln.
Charlotte, NC 28205

Fiesta, Franciscan, Russel Wright, Lu Ray, Metlox, and Homer Laughlin
Fiesta Plus
Mick and Lorna Chase
380 Hawkins Crawford Rd.
Cookeville, TN 38501
931-372-8333

Homer Laughlin China
Author of book
Darlene Nossaman
5419 Lake Charles
Waco, TX 76710

Johnson Brothers
Author of book
Mary Finegan
Marfine Antiques
P.O. Box 3618
Boone, NC 28607
828-262-3441

Liberty Blue
Gary Beegle
92 River St.
Montgomery, NY 12549
914-457-3623
Also most lines of collectible modern American dinnerware as well as character glasses

Restaurant China
Author of book
Barbara J. Conroy
P.O. Box 2369
Santa Clara, CA 95055-2369
e-mail: restaurantchina@earthlink.net
www.home.earthlike.net/~restau-
rantchina/index.html
(lists contents and details of books and
links to restaurant china sites)

Royal China
BA Wellman and John Canfield
88 State Rd. W
P.O. Box 673
Homestead Farms #2
Westminster, MA 01473-1435
e-mail: bawellman@net1plus.com
Also Ceramic Art Studios

Russel Wright, Eva Zeisel, Homer
Laughlin
Charles Alexander
221 E 34th St.
Indianapolis, IN 46205
317-924-9665

Dolls

Annalee Mobilitee Dolls
Jane's Collectibles
Jane Holt
P.O. Box 115
Derry, NH 03038

Betsy McCall and friends
Marci Van Ausdall, Editor
P.O. Box 946
Quincy, CA 95971-0946
916-283-2770

Celebrity and character dolls
Henri Yunes
971 Main St., Apt. 2
Hackensack, NJ 07601
201-488-2236

Dolls from the 1960s – 70s, including Liddle
Kiddles, Dolly Darlings, Petal People, Tiny
Teens, etc.
Author of book on Liddle Kiddles;
must send SASE for info
Paris Langford
415 Dodge Ave.
Jefferson, LA 70121
504-733-0667

Chatty Cathy and Mattel talkers
Authors of books
Don and Kathy Lewis
Whirlwind Unlimited
187 N Marcello Ave.
Thousand Oaks, CA 91360
805-499-8101
e-mail: chatty@ix.netcom.com

Dolls from the 1960s – 70s, including
Liddle Kiddles, Barbie, Tammy, Tressy, etc.
Co-author of book on Tammy
Cindy Sabulis
P.O. Box 642
Shelton, CT 06484; 203-926-0176

Holly Hobbie
Helen McCale
1006 Ruby Ave.
Butler, MO 64730-2500

Holly Hobbie
Editor of newsletter: The Holly Hobbie
  Collectors Gazette
Donna Stultz
1455 Otterdale Mill Rd.
Taneytown, MD 21787-3032
410-775-2570

Ideal
Author of book; available from author
or Collector Books
Judith Izen
P.O. Box 623
Lexington, MA 02173-5914
781-862-2994
e-mail: jizenrez@aol.com

Liddle Kiddles and other small dolls
from the late '60s and early '70s
Dawn Parrish
20460 Samual Drive
Saugus, CA 91530-3812; 661-263-TOYS

Strawberry Shortcake
Geneva D. Addy
P.O. Box 124
Winterset, IA 50273

Vogue Dolls, Inc.
Co-author of book; available from
author or Collector Books
Judith Izen
P.O. Box 623
Lexington, MA 02173-5914
781-862-2994
e-mail: jizenres@aol.com

Vogue Dolls, Inc.
Co-author of book; available from
author or Collector Books
Carol J. Stover
81 E Van Buren St.
Chicago, IL 60605

Dollhouse Furniture and
Accessories

Renwal, Ideal, Marx, etc.
Judith A. Mosholder
186 Pine Springs Camp Rd.
Boswell, PA 15531; 814-629-9277

Door Knockers

Craig Dinner
Box 4399
Sunnyside, NY 11104
718-729-3850

Egg Beaters

Author of Beat This: The Egg Beater
  Chronicles
Don Thornton
Off Beat Books
1345 Poplar Ave.
Sunnyvale, CA 94087

Egg Cups

Author of book
Brenda Blake
Box 555
York Harbor, ME 03911
207-363-6566

Egg Timers

Ellen Bercovici
5118 Hampden Ln.
Bethesda, MD 20814; 301-652-1140

Jeannie Greenfield
310 Parker Rd.
Stoneboro, PA 16153-2810
724-376-2584

Elegant Glass

Cambridge, Fostoria
Deborah Maggard Antiques
P.O. Box 211
Chagrin Falls, OH 44022
440-247-5632
e-mail: debmaggard@worldnet.att.net
Also china and Victorian art glass

Roselle Schleifman
16 Vincent Rd.
Spring Valley, NY 10977

Erich Stauffer Figurines
Joan Oates
685 S Washington
Constantine, MI 49042; 616-435-8353
e-mail: koates@remc12.k12.mi.us
Also Phoenix Bird china

Ertl Banks
Homestead Collectibles
P.O. Box 173
Mill Hall, PA 17751
Also decanters

Eyewinker
Sophia Talbert
921 Union St.
Covington, IN 47932
765-793-3256

Fast-Food Collectibles
Author of book
Ken Clee
Box 1142
Philadelphia, PA 19111
215-722-1979

Authors of several books
Joyce and Terry Losonsky
7506 Summer Leave Lane
Columbia, MD 21046-2455
Illustrated Collector's Guide to McDonald's® Happy Meal® Boxes, Premiums and Promotions ($9 plus $2 postage), McDonald's® Happy Meal® Toys in the USA and *McDonald's® Happy Meal® Toys Around the World* (both full color, $24.95 each plus $3 postage), and *Illustrated Collector's Guide to McDonald's® McCAPS®* ($4 plus $2) are available from the authors.

Bill and Pat Poe
220 Dominica Cir. E
Niceville, FL 32578-4085
850-897-4163
fax: 850-897-2606
e-mail: McPoes@aol.com
Also cartoon and character glasses, Pez, Smurfs, and California Raisins; send $3 (US delivery) for 70-page catalog

Fenton Glass
Ferill J. Rice
302 Pheasant Run
Kaukauna, WI 54130

Figural Ceramics
Especially Kitchen Prayer Lady, Enesco, and Holt Howard
April and Larry Tvorak
P.O. Box 94
Warren Center, PA 18851
570-395-3775
e-mail: aprilandlarry@softhome.net

Fire-King
Authors of price guide
April and Larry Tvorak
P.O. Box 94
Warren Center, PA 18851
570-395-3775
e-mail: aprilandlarry@softhome.net

Fisher-Price
Co-author of book
Brad Cassity
1350 Stanwix
Toledo, OH 43614; 419-389-1100

Fishing Collectibles
Publishes fixed-price catalog
Dave Hoover
1023 Skyview Dr.
New Albany, IN 47150
Also miniature boats and motors

Flashlights
Editor of newsletter
Bill Utley
P.O. Box 4094
Tustin, CA 92681
714-730-1252; fax: 714-505-4067

Florence Ceramics
Author of book
Doug Foland
1811 NW Couch #303
Portland, OR 97209

Jerry Kline
Florence Showcase
3070 Sugarwood Dr.
Kodak, TN 37764
423-933-4011; fax: 423-933-4492

John and Peggy Scott
4640 S Leroy
Springfield, MO 65810

Flower Frogs
Nada Sue Knauss
12111 Potter Rd.
Weston, OH 43569; 419-669-4735

Frankoma
Authors of book
Phyllis and Tom Bess
14535 E 13th St.
Tulsa, OK 74108

Author of books
Susan N. Cox
800 Murray Dr.
El Cajon, CA 92020
619-697-5922
Also unsharpened advertising pencils, complete matchbooks, Horlick's advertising, women's magazines from 1900 to 1950. (Susan Cox has written three books and five price guides and is currently working on an updated price guide and a Frankoma advertising book. She has devoted much of the past fifteen years to California pottery research and welcomes any information have about California companies and artists.)

Fruit Jars
Especially old, odd or colored jars
John Hathaway
3 Mills Rd.
Bryant Pond, ME 04219
Also old jar lids and closures

Games
Paul Fink's Fun and Games
P.O. Box 488
59 S Kent Rd.
Kent, CT 06757
860-927-4001

Paul David Morrow
1045 Rolling Point Ct.
Virginia Beach, VA 23456-6371

Gay Fad Glassware
Donna S. McGrady
154 Peters Ave.
Lancaster, OH 43130
740-653-0376

Geisha Girl Porcelain
Author of book
Elyce Litts
P.O. Box 394
Morris Plains, NJ 07950
e-mail: happy-memories@worldnet.att.net
Also ladies' compacts

Glass Animals
Author of book
Lee Garmon
1529 Whittier St.
Springfield, IL 62704

Glass Knives
Michele A. Rosewitz
3165 McKinley
San Bernardino, CA 92404
909-862-8534
e-mail: rosetree@sprintmail.com

Glass Shoes
Author of book
The Shoe Lady
Libby Yalom
P.O. Box 7146
Adelphi, MD 20783

Graniteware
Author of books
Helen Greguire
864-457-7340
Also carnival glass and toasters

Griswold
Grant Windsor
P.O. Box 3613
Richmond, VA 23235-7613

Hallmark
The Baggage Car
3100 Justin Dr., Ste. B
Des Moines, IA 50322
515-270-9080

Halloween
Author of books; autographed copies available from the author
Pamela Apakarian-Russell
Chris Russell & The Halloween Queen Antiques
P.O. Box 499
Winchester, NH 03470
e-mail: halloweenqueen@top.monad.net
Also other holidays, postcards, and Joe Camel

Hartland Plastics, Inc.
Author of book
Gail Fitch
1733 N Cambridge, Ave. #109
Milwaukee, WI 53202

Specializing in Western Hartlands Buy and sell; hold consignment auctions specializing in vintage toys
Kerry and Judy Irwin
Kerry and Judy's Toys
1414 S. Twelfth St.
Murray, KY 42071
270-759-3456
e-mail: kjtoys@apex.net

Specializing in sports figures
James Watson
25 Gilmore St.
Whitehall, NY 12887

Holt Howard
Pat and Ann Duncan
Box 175
Cape Fair, MO 65624
417-538-2311

April and Larry Tvorak
P.O. Box 94
Warren Center, PA 18851
570-395-3775
e-mail: aprilandlarry@softhome.net

Homer Laughlin
Author of book
Darlene Nossaman
5419 Lake Charles
Waco, TX 76710

Horton Ceramics
Darlene Nossaman
5419 Lake Charles
Waco, TX 76710

Hull
Author of several books on Hull
Brenda Roberts
R.R. 2
Marshall, MO 65340

Mirror Brown, also Pfaltzgraff Gourmet Royale; rare items only
Bill and Connie Sloan
4965 Valley Park Rd.
Doylestown, PA 18901

Imperial Glass
Joan Cimini
67183 Stein Rd.
Belmont, OH 43718-9715
Also has Candlewick matching service

Imperial Porcelain
Geneva D. Addy
P.O. Box 124
Winterset, IA 50273

Indy 500 Memorabilia
Eric Jungnickel
P.O. Box 4674
Naperville, IL 60567-4674
630-983-8339

Insulators
Mike Bruner
6980 Walnut Lake Rd.
W Bloomfield, MI 48323; 313-661-8241
Also porcelain signs, light-up advertising clocks, exit globes, lightening rod balls, and target balls

Jacqueline Linscott
3557 Nicklaus Dr.
Tutusville, FL 32780

Japan Ceramics
Author of books
Carole Bess White
PO Box 819
Portland, OR 97207

Jewel Tea
Products or boxes only; no dishes
Bill and Judy Vroman
739 Eastern Ave.
Fostoria, OH 44830; 419-435-5443

Jewelry
Marcia Brown (Sparkles)
P.O. Box 2314
White City, OR 97503
541-826-3039
fax: 541-830-5385

Men's accessories and cuff links only; edits newsletter
The National Cuff Link Society
Eugene R. Klompus
P.O. Box 346
Prospect Hts., IL 60070
phone or fax: 847-816-0035

Josef Originals
Authors of books
Jim and Kaye Whitaker
Eclectic Antiques
P.O. Box 475, Dept. GS
Lynnwood, WA 98046

Kay Finch

Co-Authors of book, available from authors
Mike Nickel and Cynthia Horvath
P.O. Box 456
Portland, MI, 48875
517-647-7646

Kentucky Derby and Horse Racing

B.L. Hornback
707 Sunrise Ln.
Elizabethtown, KY 42701

Kreiss; Psycho Ceramics

Authors of book
Michelle and Mike King
P.O. Box 3519
Alliance, OH 44601
330-829-5946
www.quest-for-toys.com
Exclusive source for Kreiss book; international mail-order vintage toy company specializing in toys and memorabilia from the 1960s – 1980s; collect novelty and character ceramics, vintage Barbie dolls, ad characters, Arts & Crafts home furnishings

Kitchen Prayer Ladies

Issues price guide
April and Larry Tvorak
P.O. Box 94
Warren Center, PA 18851
570-395-3775
e-mail: aprilandlarry@softhome.net

Lamps

Aladdin
Author of books
J.W. Courter
3935 Kelley Rd.
Kevil, KY 42053
502-488-2116

Figural Lamps
Dee Boston
2299 N Pr. Rd. 475 W
Sullivan, IN 47882
Also dresser, pincushion, and half dolls

Motion lamps
Eclectic Antiques
Jim and Kaye Whitaker
P.O. Box 475, Dept. GS
Lynwood, WA 98046

Authors of book
Sam and Anna Samuelian
P.O. Box 504
Edgmont, PA 19028-0504
610-566-7248
Also motion clocks, transistor and novelty radios

Lefton

Author of books
Loretta DeLozier
1101 Polk St.
Bedford, IA 50833
712-523-2289 (M-F, 9 am to 4 pm)
fax: 712-523-2624
e-mail: LeftonLady@aol.com

Letter Openers

Author of book
Everett Grist
P.O. Box 91375
Chattanooga, TN 37412-3955; 423-510-8052

License Plates

Richard Diehl
5965 W Colgate Pl.
Denver, CO 80227

Longaberger Baskets

*The **only** reference tool for consultants, collectors, and enthusiasts of Longaberger Baskets®*
The Bentley Collection Guide®
5870 Zarley Street, Suite C
New Albany, OH 43054
Monday through Friday, 9:00 am – 5:00 pm (est) 1-800-837-4394
www.bentleyguide.com
e-mail: Bentcol@aol.com
The most accurate and reliable reference tool available for evaluating Longaberger Products®; full color with individual photographs of most baskets and products produced since 1979; published once a year in June with a free six-month update being sent in January to keep the Guide current for the entire year

Holds exclusive auctions
Greg Michael
Craft & Michael Auction/Realty Inc.
PO Box 7
Camden, IN 46917
219-686-2615 or 219-967-4442
fax: 219-686-9100
e-mail: gpmmgtco@netusal1.net

Lunch Boxes

Norman's Ole and New Store
Philip Norman
126 W Main St.
Washington, NC 27889-4944
252-946-3448

Terri's Toys and Nostalgia
Terri Ivers
206 E. Grand
Ponca City, OK 74601
580-762-8697 or 580-762-5174
fax: 405-765-2657
e-mail: toylady@poncacity.net

Magazines

Issues price guides to illustrators, pin-ups, and old magazines of all kinds
Denis C. Jackson
Illustrator Collector's News
P.O. Box 1958
Sequim, WA 98382
360-452-3810
e-mail: ticn@olypen.com

Pre-1950 movie magazines, especially with Ginger Rogers covers
Tom Morris
P.O. Box 8307
Medford, OR 97504
e-mail: chalkman@cdsnet.net

National Geographic
Author of guide
Don Smith's National Geographic Magazines
3930 Rankin St.
Louisville, KY 40214
502-366-7504

Pulps
Issues catalogs on various genre of hardcover books, paperbacks, and magazines of all types
J. Grant Thiessen, Pandora's Books Ltd.
Box 54
Neche, ND 58265-0054
fax: 204-324-1628
e-mail: jgthiess@mts.net
www.pandora.ca/pandora

Marbles

Author of books
Everett Grist
P.O. Box 91375
Chattanooga, TN 37412-3955
423-510-8052

Match Safes

George Sparacio
P.O. Box 791
Malaga, NJ 08328
609-694-4167
fax: 609-694-4536
email: mrvesta@aol.com

Matchcovers

Author of books
Bill Retskin
P.O. Box 18481
Asheville, NC 22814
704-254-4487
fax: 704-254-1066
e-mail: bill@matchcovers.com
www.matchcovers.com

McCoy Pottery

Authors of book
Robert and Margaret Hanson
16517 121 Ave. NE
Bothell, WA 98011

Melmac Dinnerware

Co-author of book
Gregg Zimmer
4017 16th Ave. S
Minneapolis, MN 55407

Co-author of book
Alvin Daigle, Jr.
Boomerang Antiques
Gray, TN 37615
423-915-0666

Metlox

Author of book; available from author
Carl Gibbs, Jr.
P.O. Box 131584
Houston, TX 77219-1584
713-521-9661

Miller Studios

Paul and Heather August
7510 West Wells St.
Wauwatosa, WI 53213
414-475-0753
e-mail: packrats@execpc.com

Morton Pottery

Authors of books
Doris and Burdell Hall
B&B Antiques
210 W Sassafras Dr.
Morton, IL 61550-1245

Motion Clocks

Electric; buy, sell, trade, and restore
Sam and Anna Samuelian
P.O. Box 504
Edgmont, PA 19028-0504
610-566-7248
Also motion lamps, transistor and novelty radios

Motorcycles

Bob 'Sprocket' Eckardt
P.O. Box 172
Saratoga Springs, NY 12866
518-584-2405
Buying and trading

Bruce Kiper
Ancient Age Motors
2205 Sunset Ln.
Lutz, FL 33549
813-949-9660
Also related items and clothing

Movie Posters

Movie Poster Service
Cleophas and Lou Ann Wooley
Box 517
Canton, OK 73724-0517
580-886-2248; fax: 580-886-2249
e-mail: mpsposters@pldi.net
In business full time since 1972; own/operate mail-order firm with world's largest movie poster inventory

Napkin Dolls

Co-Author of book
Bobbie Zucker Bryson
1 St. Eleanoras Ln.
Tuckahoe, NY 10707
914-779-1405
e-mail: napkindoll@aol.com
www.reamers.org
To order a copy of *Collectibles for the Kitchen, Bath & Beyond* (featuring napkin dolls, egg timers, string holders, children's whistle cups and baby feeder dishes, razor blade banks, pie birds, laundry sprinkler bottles, and other unique collectibles from the same era), contact Antique Trader Books, PO Box 1050, Dubuque, IA 52004-0880, 1-800-334-7165; fax: 1-800-531-0880.

Newspaper Collector Society
Rick Brown
517-887-1255

Novelty Radios

Authors of several books
Sue and Marty Bunis
R.R. 1, Box 36
Bradford, NH 03221-9102

Orientalia and Dragonware

Suzi Hibbard
849 Vintage Ave.
Fairfield, CA 94585

Paden City Glassware

George and Mary Hurney
Glass Connection (mail-order only)
312 Babcock Dr.
Palatine, IL 50067
847-359-3839

Paper Dolls

Author of books
Mary Young
P.O. Box 9244
Wright Bros. Branch
Dayton, OH 45409

Pencil Sharpeners

Phil Helley
629 Indiana Ave.
Wisconsin Dells, WI 53965
608-254-8659

Advertising and figural
Martha Hughes
4128 Ingalls St.
San Diego, CA 92103
619-296-1866

Pennsbury

Author of price guide; video book available
BA Wellman and John Canfield
88 State Rd. W
P.O. Box 673
Homestead Farms #2
Westminster, MA 01473-1435
e-mail: bawellman@net1plus.com

Joe Devine
1411 3rd St.
Council Bluffs, IA 51503
712-323-5322 or
712-328-7305

Shirley Graff
4515 Graff Rd.
Brunswick, OH 44212

Pepsi-Cola
Craig and Donna Stifter
P.O. Box 6514
Naperville, IL 60540
630-789-5780
Other soda-pop memorablia as well

Perfume Bottles
*Especially commercial, Czechoslovakian,
Lalique, Baccarat, Victorian, crown top,
factices, miniatures*
*Buy, sell, and accept consignments for
auctions*
Monsen and Baer
Box 529
Vienna, VA 22183
703-938-2129

Pez
Richard Belyski
P.O. Box 124
Sea Cliff, NY 11579
e-mail: peznews@juno.com

Pfaltzgraff
Gourmet Royale
Bill and Connie Sloan
4965 Valley Park Rd.
Doylestown, PA 18901

Pie Birds
Linda Fields
158 Bagsby Hill Lane
Dover, TN 37058
931-232-5099
e-mail: Fpiebird@compu.net
Organizer of piebird collector's convention and author of *Four & Twenty Blackbirds;* Specializing in pie birds, pie funnels, and pie vents

Pin-Back Buttons
Michael and Polly McQuillen
McQuillen's Collectibles
P.O. Box 50022
Indianapolis, IN 46250; 317-845-1721
e-mail: buttons@oaktree.net

Pinup Art
Issues price guides to pinups, illustrations, and old magazines
Denis C. Jackson
Illustrator Collector's News
P.O. Box 1958
Sequim, WA 98382
360-452-3810 or fax 360-683-9807
e-mail: ticn@olypen.com

Pocket Calculators
Author of book
International Assn. of Calculator Collectors
Guy D. Ball
P.O. Box 345
Tustin, CA 92781-0345
Phone or fax: 714-730-6140
e-mail: mrcalc@usa.net

Political
Michael and Polly McQuillen
McQuillen's Collectibles
P.O. Box 50022
Indianapolis, IN 46250
317-845-1721
e-mail: buttons@oaktree.net

Before 1960
Michael Engel
29 Groveland St.
Easthampton, MA 01027

Pins, banners, ribbons, etc.
Paul Longo Americana
Box 5510
Magnolia, MA 01930; 978-525-2290

Poodle Collectibles
Author of book
Elaine Butler
233 S Kingston Ave.
Rockwood, TN 37854

Porcelier
Jim Barker
Toaster Master General
P.O. Box 746
Allentown, PA 18105

Author of book
Susan Grindberg
1412 Pathfinder Rd.
Henderson, NV 89014; 702-898-7535
e-mail: porcelier@anv.net
www.coyote.accessnv.com/porcelier

Postcards
C.J. Russell & Pamela Apakarian-Russell
Halloween Queen Antiques
P.O. Box 499
Winchester, NH 03470
Also Halloween and other holidays

Powder Jars
John and Peggy Scott
4640 S Leroy
Springfield, MO 65810

Sharon Thoerner
15549 Ryon Ave.
Bellflower, CA 90706
562-866-1555
Also slag glass

Purinton Pottery
Author of book
Susan Morris
P.O. Box 1519
Merlin, OR 97532-1519
541-955-8590
e-mail: sue@wattpottery.com
www.wattpottery.com
www.applebarrel.com

Purses
Veronica Trainer
P.O. Box 40443
Cleveland, OH 44140

Puzzles
Wooden jigsaw type from before 1950
Bob Armstrong
15 Monadnock Rd.
Worcester, MA 01609

Especially character related
Norm Vigue
3 Timberwood Dr.
Goffstown, MA 03045
603-647-9951

Radio Premiums
Bill Campbell
1221 Littlebrook Ln.
Birmingham, AL 35235
205-853-8227
fax: 405-658-6986

Radios
Authors of several books on antique, novelty, and transistor radios
Sue and Marty Bunis
R.R. 1, Box 36
Bradford, NH 03221-9102

Author of book
Harry Poster
P.O. Box 1883
S Hackensack, NJ 07606
201-410-7525
Also televisions, related advertising items, old tubes, cameras, 3-D viewers and projectors, View-Master, and Tru-View reels and accessories

Railroadiana

Also steamship and other transportation memorabilia
Fred and Lila Shrader
Shrader Antiques
2025 Hwy. 199
Crescent City, CA 95531
707-458-3525
Also Buffalo, Shelley, Niloak, and Hummels

Any item; especially china and silver
Catalogs available
John White, 'Grandpa'
Grandpa's Depot
1616 17th St., Ste. 267
Denver, CO 80202
303-628-5590; fax: 303-628-5547
Also related items

Razor Blade Banks

Debbie Gillham
47 Midline Ct.
Gaithersburg, MD 20878; 301-977-5727

Reamers

Co-author of book, ordering info under Napkin Dolls
Bobbie Zucker Bryson
1 St. Eleanoras Ln.
Tuckahoe, NY 10707
914-779-1405
e-mail: napkindoll@aol.com
www.reamers.org

Records

45 rpm and LP's
Mason's Bookstore, Rare Books, and Record Albums
Dave Torzillo
115 S Main St.
Chambersburg, PA 17201
717-261-0541

Picture and 78 rpm kiddie records
Peter Muldavin
173 W 78th St. Apt. 5-F
New York, NY 10024; 212-362-9606
e-mail: kiddie78s@aol.com

Especially 78 rpms
Author of book
L.R. 'Les' Docks
Box 691035
San Antonio, TX 78269-1035
Write for want list

Red Wing

B.L. and R.L. Dollen
Dollen Books & Antiques
P.O. Box 67
Minden, IA 51553; 712-483-2150
Collector Books authors specializing in Red Wing art pottery and dinnerware

Red Wing Artware

Hold cataloged auctions
Wendy and Leo Frese
Three Rivers Collectibles
P.O. Box 551542
Dallas, TX 75355; 214-341-5165
e-mail: rumrill@ix.netcom.com

Regal China

Van Telligen, Bendel, Old MacDonald's Farm
Rick Spencer
Salt Lake City, UT
801-973-0805
Also Coors, Shawnee, Watt, silverplate (especially grape patterns)

Rooster and Roses

Jacki Elliott
9790 Twin Cities Rd.
Galt, CA 95632
209-745-3860

Rosemeade

NDSU research specialist
Bryce Farnsworth
1334 14½ St. S
Fargo, ND 58103; 701-237-3597

Royal Bayreuth

Don and Anne Kier
2022 Marengo St.
Toledo, OH 43614; 419-385-8211

Royal Copley

Author of books
Joe Devine
1411 3rd St.
Council Bluffs, IA 51503
712-323-5233 or 712-328-7305
Buy, sell, or trade; also pie birds

Royal Haeger

Author of book
David D. Dilley, D&R Antiques
P.O. Box 225
Indianapolis, IN 46206; 317-630-5448
e-mail: bearpots@aol.com

Co-author of book
Doris Frizzell
Doris' Dishes
5687 Oakdale Dr.
Springfield, IL 62707
217-529-3873

RumRill

Hold cataloged auctions
Wendy and Leo Frese
Three Rivers Collectibles
P.O. Box 551542
Dallas, TX 75355; 214-341-5165
e-mail: rumrill@ix.netcom.com

Ruby Glass

Author of book
Naomi L. Over
8909 Sharon Ln.
Arvada, CO 80002; 303-424-5922

Russel Wright

Author of book
Ann Kerr
P.O. Box 437
Sidney, OH 45365

Salt and Pepper Shakers

Figural or novelty
Buy, sell, and trade; lists available
fee charged for appraisal
Judy Posner
R.R. 1, Box 273
Effort, PA 18330; 717-629-6583 or
www.tias.com/stores/jpc
e-mail: judyandjef@aol.com

Scouting Collectibles

Author of book: A Guide to Scouting Collectibles With Values; available by sending $30.95 (includes postage)
R.J. Sayers
P.O. Box 629
Brevard, NC 28712

Sebastians

Jim Waite
112 N Main St.
Farmer City, IL 61842; 800-842-2593

Sewing Machines

Toy only
Authors of book
Darryl and Roxana Matter
P.O. Box 65
Portis, KS 67474-0065

Shawnee
Rick Spencer
Salt Lake City, UT
801-973-0805

Shot Glasses
Author of book
Mark Pickvet
Shot Glass Club of America
5071 Watson Dr.
Flint, MI 48506

Silhouette Pictures (20th Century)
Author of book
Shirley Mace, Shadow Enterprises
P.O. Box 1602
Mesilla Park, NM 88047
505-524-6717; fax: 505-523-0940
e-mail: shadow-ent@zianet.com

Silverplated Flatware
Rick Spencer
Salt Lake City, UT
801-973-0805

Skookum Indian Dolls
Jo Ann Palmieri
27 Pepper Rd.
Towaco, NJ 07082-1357

Snow Domes
Author of book and newsletter editor
Nancy McMichael
P.O. Box 53310
Washington, DC 20009

Soda Fountain Collectibles
Harold and Joyce Screen
2804 Munster Rd.
Baltimore, MD 21234
410-661-6765
e-mail: hscreen@home.com

Soda-Pop Memorabilia
Craig and Donna Stifter
P.O. Box 6514
Naperville, IL 60540
630-789-5780
e-mail: cocacola@enteract.com

Painted-label soda bottles
Author of books
Thomas Marsh
914 Franklin Ave.
Youngstown, OH 44502
216-743-8600 or 800-845-7930 (order line)

Sports Collectibles
Sporting goods
Kevin R. Bowman
P.O. Box 471
Neosho, MO 64850-0471
417-781-6418 (Mon through Fri after 5 pm CST, Sat and Sun after 10 am CST); e-mail: ozrktrmnl@clandjop.com.

Equipment and player-used items
Don and Anne Kier
2022 Marengo St.
Toledo, OH 43614; 419-385-8211

Bobbin' head sports figures
Tim Hunter
4301 W Hidden Valley Dr.
Reno, NV 89502; 702-856-4357
fax: 702-856-4354
e-mail: thunter885@aol.com

Golf collectibles
Pat Romano
32 Sterling Dr.
Lake Grove, NY 11202-0017

St. Clair Glass
Ted Pruitt
3350 W 700 N
Anderson, IN 46011
Book available ($15)

Stangl
Birds, dinnerware, artware
Popkorn Antiques
Bob and Nancy Perzel
P.O. Box 1057
3 Mine St.
Flemington, NJ 08822; 908-782-9631

Statue of Liberty
Mike Brooks
7335 Skyline
Oakland, CA 94611

String Holders
Ellen Bercovici
5118 Hampden Ln.
Bethesda, MD 20814; 301-652-1140

Swanky Swigs
Joyce Jackson
900 Jenkins Rd.
Aledo, TX 76008
817-441-8864
e-mail jjpick@fastlane.net

Syroco and Similar Products
Doris J. Gibbs
3837 Cuming #1
Omaha, NE 68131
402-556-4300
ddgibbs@top.net

Teapots and Tea-Related Items
Author of book
Tina Carter
882 S Mollison
El Cajon, CA 92020

Tiara
Mandi Birkinbine
P.O. Box 121
Meridian, ID 83680-0121
www.shop4antiques.com
e-mail: tiara@shop4antiques.com

Tire Ashtrays
Author of book ($12.95 postpaid)
Jeff McVey
1810 W State St., #427
Boise, ID 83702-3955

Toothbrush Holders
Author of book
Marilyn Cooper
P.O. Box 55174
Houston, TX 77055

Toys
Any and all
June Moon
245 N Northwest Hwy.
Park Ridge, IL 60068
847-825-1441; fax: 847-825-6090

Aurora model kits, and especially toys from 1948 – 1972
Author of books
Dealers, publishers, and appraisers of collectible memorabilia from the '50s through today
Bill Bruegman
137 Casterton Dr.
Akron, OH 44303
330-836-0668; fax: 330-869-8668
e-mail: toyscout@salamander.net

Diecast vehicles
Mark Giles
P.O. Box 821
Ogallala, NE 69153-0821
308-284-4360

Fisher-Price pull toys and playsets up to 1986
Co-author of book; available from author
Brad Cassity
1350 Stanyx
Toledo, OH 43614; 419-389-1100

Hot Wheels
D.W. (Steve) Stephenson
11117 NE 164th Pl.
Bothell, WA 98011-4003

Model kits other than Aurora; edits publications
Gordy Dutt
Box 201
Sharon Center, OH 42274-0201

Puppets and marionettes
Steven Meltzer
1255 2nd St.
Santa Monica, CA 90401; 310-656-0483

Rings, character, celebrity, and souvenir
Bruce and Jan Thalberg
23 Mountain View Dr.
Weston, CT 06883-1317; 203-227-8175

Sand toys
Authors of book
Carole and Richard Smyth
Carole Smyth Antiques
P.O. Box 2068
Huntington, NY 11743

Slot race cars from 1960s – 70s
Gary T. Pollastro
5047 84th Ave. SE
Mercer Island, WA 98040

Tin litho, paper on wood, comic character, penny toys, and Schoenhut
Wes Johnson, Sr.
3606 Glenview Ave.
Glenville, KY 40025

Tops and spinning toys
Bruce Middleton
5 Lloyd Rd.
Newburgh, NY 12550; 914-564-2556

Toy soldiers, figures, and playsets
The Phoenix Toy Soldier Co., Bob Wilson
16405 North 9th Place
Phoenix, AZ 85022; 602-863-2891

Transformers and robots
David Kolodny-Nagy

3701 Connecticut Ave. NW #500
Washington, DC 20008; 202-364-8753

Walkers, ramp-walkers, and wind-ups
Randy Welch
Raven'tiques
27965 Peach Orchard Rd.
Easton, MD 21601-8203
410-822-5441

Trolls
Author of book
Pat Peterson
1105 6th Ave. SE
Hampton, IA 50441-2657
SASE for information

TV Guides
Price guide available
TV Guide Specialists
Jeff Kadet
P.O. Box 20
Macomb, IL 61455

Twin Winton
Author of book; available from the author or through Collector Books
Mike Ellis
266 Rose Ln.
Costa Mesa, CA 92627
949-646-7112; fax: 714-645-4697

Valentines
Author of books, available from author; fee charged for appraisal
Katherine Kreider, Kingsbury Antiques
P.O. Box 7957
Lancaster, PA 17604-7957; 717-892-3001

Vallona Starr
Author of book
Bernice Stamper
7516 Eloy Ave.
Bakersfield, CA 93308-7701; 805-393-2900

Van Briggle
Dated examples, author of book
Scott H. Nelson
Box 6081
Santa Fe, NM 87502; 505-986-1176
Also UND (University of North Dakota), other American potteries

Vandor
Lois Wildman
175 Chick Rd.
Camano Island, WA 98282

Wade
Author of book
Ian Warner
P.O. Box 93022
Brampton, Ontario
Canada L6Y 4V8

Watt Pottery
Author of book
Susan Morris
P.O. Box 1519
Merlin, OR 97532; 541-955-8590
e-mail: sue@wattpottery.com
www.wattpottery.com
www.applebarrel.com

Western Collectibles
Author of book
Warren R. Anderson
American West Archives
P.O. Box 100
Cedar City, UT 84721; 435-586-9497
Also documents, autographs, stocks and bonds, and other ephemera

Author of books
Dan Hutchins
Hutchins Publishing Co.
P.O. Box 529
Marion, IA 52302; 505-425-3387

William Manns
P.O. Box 6459
Santa Fe, NM 87502; 505-995-0102

Western Heroes
Author of books, ardent researcher, and guest columnist
Robert W. Phillips
Phillips Archives of Western Memorabilia
1703 N Aster Pl.
Broken Arrow, OK 74012
918-254-8205; fax: 918-252-9363

Westmoreland
Cheryl Schafer
RR 2, Box 37
Lancaster, MO 63548
660-457-3510; email: cschafer@nemr.net

World's Fairs and Expositions
Herbert Rolfes
Yesterday's World
P.O. Box 398
Mount Dora, FL 32756
352-735-3947
e-mail: NY1939@aol.com

Index

Abingdon 13,153-154
Action Figures 252-254,434-435,435-436,446,447
Action Jackson..446
Adams, Matthew..95
Advertising.........................41,43-45,63-65,87-89,131,138-141
153,247-249,313,357-358,370,
388-390,443-444
Advertising Character Collectibles................................13-30
Advertising Tins..30-31
Advertising Watches...31-34
Airline Memorabilia...34
Akro Agate...34-36
Aladdin (Disney)..190
Aladdin Lamps...308-309
Alps..449,457
Aluminum..36-37,406-407
Amazing Stories...326
Amberstone..276
American Art Potteries..342-343
American Bisque 37-38,154
American Modern..406
Americana...76
AMT..336-337
Anchor Hocking...290-291
Angels..38-40
Animal Dishes With Covers.........40,178,179,314-315,477-478
Animal Yackers..200
Annalee Dolls..196-198
Applause..98,206
Appliances...304
Arby's..219
Arcade Toys..454
Archies..116
Argosy...326
Ashtrays.....................40-42;23,27,70,85,275,287,291-292,
329,356,440-441,443-444
Aunt Jemima...14-15
Aurora..337,453
Autographs..42-43
Automobilia..43-45
Autumn Leaf Dinnerware......................................45-47
Aviation Collectibles..390
Badges 287;247,368,380,483
Bakelite..355-356
Bandai..449
Banks.................17,27,43,263,312,329-330,338,368,463
Banners...247
Barbie and Her Friends 47-51
Barware..51-52
Baseball Cards...52-53
Baseballs (Signed)..431

Baskets 221,480
Bathing Suits..136
Batman.........................118,121-122,141,376,447
Battery-Operated Toys 448-489
Bauer Pottery..53-54
Beam Decanters 175-176
Beanie Babies..54-59
Beanie Buddies...58-59
Beatles Collectibles...59-61
Beatnik Collectibles......................................61-62,307
Beatrix Potter..62-63
Beer Cans...63-65
Bellaire, Marc..95
Bells.........................65-66,67,91,177,221,432
Bendel Shakers..388
Betsy Wetsy...203
Better Homes and Gardens 149
Betty Boop..122,466-467
Bibendum..23
Bicycle Collectibles...66-68
Big Boy and Friends...15-16
Big Little Books...78-79
Birthday Angels...38-39
Black Americana..................68-70,213,409-410
Black Cats...70-72
Blair Dinnerware..72
Blotters..138,366
Blue Danube...72-74
Blue Garland...74
Blue Ridge Dinnerware......................................74-76
Blue Willow Dinnerware 76-77,276,399
Bonanza...167
Book of Knowledge Banks.....................................338
Bookcases...244
Bookends...77-78,330,441
Books 78-83;61,69,263,271,380,423,429-430
Borden's..19
Boru, Sorcha..95
Bottle Openers..83-84
Boy George...391
Boy Scouts...415
Boyd Crystal Art Glass..84
Boyds Bears and Friends.....................................84-85
Bozo the Clown..200
Bracelets...295
Brastoff, Sascha...85-86
Brayton Laguna...86-87
Breweriana..87-89
Breyer Horses...90-91
British Royal Commemoratives 91-92
Brock of California..95

Brooches 295-296
Brooks Decanters 176
Brown Drip Dinnerware 332
Brundage 370
Brush 154-155
Bubble Bath Containers 92-93
Bugs Bunny 118,122,143,200
Burger Chef 116
Burger King 16,219
Butter Pats 378
Buttons 380
Cake Toppers 93-94
Calculators 95-95
Calendars 138-139,247,357,380-381,427
California Originals 155
California Potteries 95-97
California Potteries, See Also Specific Categories
California Raisins 97-99
CALRAB 98-99
Camark 99-100
Cambridge Glassware 100-103
Cameras 103-105
Campbell Kids 16-17
Candle Holders 275
Candlewick Glassware 105-106
Candy Containers 106-107,129,263
Canisters 305,306,354,356,443,444,463,481
Cap'n Crunch 17
Cape Cod by Avon 107-108
Captain America 122
Captain Midnight 451
Cardinal China Company 108,155
Carnival Chalkware 108-109
Carnival Glass 221,285-286
Carryalls 145
Casper the Friendly Ghost 123
Cast Iron 78,83-84,209-210
Cast Iron, See Also Griswold Cast-Iron
Cat Collectibles 109-111
Cat in the Hat 111-112,200
Cat-Tail Dinnerware 112
Catalin Napkin Rings 112-113
Catalogs 345,430
Cattail 464
Cecil the Seasick Serpent 200
Celebrity Dolls 198-200
Ceramic Arts Studio 113-114
Cereal Boxes and Premiums 114-116
Chairs 244-245
Character and Promotional Drinking Glasses 116-118
Character Banks 118-119
Character Clocks and Watches 119-121
Character Collectibles 141-142

Character Collectibles, See Also Specific Categories
Charlie Tuna 17-18
Chatty Cathy and Other Mattel Talkers 200-202
Chein 457
Chessie 111
Chicago World's Fair 483-484
Children's Miscellaneous Books 79-80
Chiquita 35
Christmas Collectibles 128-131;243,257,273,307,
                                                   342,371,411,423,461,482
Chub Creek 234
Cigarette Lighters 131-132;22,44,70
Clay Art 155
Cleminson Pottery 132-133,156
Cliftwood Art Potteries 342
Clocks 21,44,88,119-120,224,343-344,345
Clothes Sprinkler Bottles 133-134,306
Clothing and Accessories 134-135
Coats and Jackets 135
Coca-Cola Collectibles 138-141
Cocktail Shakers 51-52,249
Coffeepots 46,255
Colonel Sanders 18
Coloring and Activity Books 141-142,423
Comic Books 143-144
Compact and Purse Accessories 144-147
Compacts 145-146
Concentric Rib, Concentric Ring 35
Condiment Sets 147-148
Cookbook and Recipe Leaflets 148-151
Cookie Cutters 151-152
Cookie Jars 152-164;86,165,306,317
Coors Rosebud Dinnerware 164
Corgi 454
Corn Ware 417
Cottage Ware 164-165
Covered Dishes, See Animal Dishes With Covers
Cow Creamers 165-166
Cowboy Character Collectibles 166-168
Cracker Jack Toys 169-170
Crackle Glass 170-171
Crazy Green-Eyed Monsters and Friends 307
Crown Dinnerware 442
Cruets 71,305,394
Cuff Links 171-172
Cupboards 245
Currier and Ives by Royal 400
Czechoslovakian Glass and Ceramics 172-174
Daisy 449-450
Dakin 174-175
Davy Crockett 167
Dawn Dolls by Topper 202
Day Wear 135-137

Decanters 175-177;71,170,215-216,287
deForest of California 95,156
Degenhart 177-179
deLee Art Pottery 179-180
Dell Comics 143-144
Denim (Vintage) 137-138
Department 56 156
Depression Glass 181-190
Dick Tracy 123,376,447
Dinky 454-455
Disney 190-193;117,445,469
Dispensers 22
Displays 88
Dog Collectibles 193-194
Dogwood 276
Dollhouse Furniture 194-195
Dolls 196-209;15,16,20,21,24,25,29,
47-49,69,139,423,427-428
Donald Duck 190-191
Door Knockers 209
Doorstops 209-210
Doranne of California 156
Dr. Dolittle 123,201
Dr. Seuss 123
Dresses 135,136
Duncan and Miller Glassware 211-212
Earrings 297
Easter 257,342,371,411
Econolite 309-310
Egg Cups 212-213,313,378
Egg Timers 213-214
Elegant Heirs 307
Ellery Queen 326
Elmer Fudd 123
Elsie the Cow and Family 19
Elvis Presley Memorabilia 214-216
Embossed Line 276
Enesco 156
Epergnes 481
Epicure 276-277
Erich Stauffer Figurines 217
ET 123
Evening Wear 135,137
Everlast 36-37
Eye Winker 217-218
Family Affair 123
Famous Firsts Decanters 176
Fast-Food Collectibles 218-219
Fenton Glass 220-225;66
Fiesta 225-228
Figural Lamps 309
Figurals and Novelties 479-480
Finch, Kay 228-229

Finger Puppets 26
Fire-King 229-231,290-291
Fishbowl Ornaments 231-232
Fisher-Price 232-233
Fishing Lures 233-235
Fitz & Floyd 235;156-157
Flash Gordon 123-124
Flintstones 124
Florence Ceramics 235-237
Flower Frogs 237-238,403
Flower Holders 473
Fostoria 238-241
Francie 48
Franciscan Dinnerware 241-242
Frankoma 242-244
Freeman-McFarlin 95-96
Furniture 244-245
Gadgets 304-305
Games 245-247,264,369
Garfield 111
Gas Station Collectibles 247-249
Gay Fad Glassware 249-250
Geisha Girl China 250-252
Gerber Baby 19-20
GI Joe 252-254
Gilligan's Island 124
Gilner 96
Girl Scouts 415-416
Glass Knives 254
Goebel 157,214
Golden Foliage 254-255
Good Housekeeping 150
Gourmet Royale 360-361
Graniteware 255-256
Graters 305
Green Giant 20-21
Green Hornet 124
Greeting Cards 465
Gremlins 124
Griddles 257
Griswold Cast-Iron Cooking Ware 256-257
Gumby 124
Guns (Toy) 449-450
Gunsmoke 376
Gurley Candle Company 257-258
Haddon Clocks 344
Hadley, M.A. 258
Hagen-Renaker 96
Hall China 258-262
Hallmark 157,262-263
Halloween 263-265;257,371
Happy Days 124
Hardee's 219

Harker Pottery 265-266
Harlequin 277
Hartland Plastics, Inc. 266-267
Harvey Cartoon Characters................................117
Hats..135,136,137
Hayes, Gabby 167
Head Vases 267-268
Headlamps...68
Hearth & Home (H&HD) 157
Heddon 234-235
Heisey Glass 268-270
Hillbilly Line 464
Hippie Collectibles......................................270-272
Hobnail 223
Hoffman Decanters 176
Holly Hobbie 202-203
Holt Howard...272-275
Homer Laughlin China Co. 276-278
Honey Boxes...442
Hopalong Cassidy 167
Horns 264
Horton Ceramics...278-279
Hot Wheels 455
Howdy Doody..124-125
Huckleberry Hound 125
Hull...279-282;157
Ideal..194-195,203
Imperial Glass..282-284
Incredible Hulk 125
Indiana Glass..285-287
Indianapolis 500 Racing Collectibles 289-289
Interior Panel..35
Intimate Apparel/Lounge Wear 136
Iroquois Casual..406
Italian Glass 288-289
Jade-ite Glassware 289-291
Japan Ceramics........................291-293,470-471
Jeans...138
Jem 204
Jewel Tea Company......................................293-294
Jewelry 295-297
Joe Camel 21-22
Johnson Bros. 298-299
Josef Originals 299-300
Jubilee..277
Juvenile Series Books 80-81
Keeler, Brad...300-301
Kellogg's...28-29
Kellogg's Pep Pins.......................................365-366
Ken Dolls...48-49
Kentucky Derby Glasses 301-303
Kindell, Dorothy 96
King's Crown Thumbprint 303

KISS 391
Kitchen Collectibles..........................303-306;254
Kitchen Kraft..227-228,277
Kitchen Prayer Ladies 306
Kitty Cucumber...111
Kliban...111
Knickerbocker 206
Knives 248
Knowles 406
Kodak 104
Kontinental Decanters 176
Kozy Kitten 273
Kreiss & Co. 306-308,348
L.E. Smith 311-312
L.G. Wright..314-315
LA Goodman 309-310
Ladies' Home Journal..324
Lamps 308-311;25,223-224,315,
330,340,342,403,480
Land of the Lost 447
Lanterns 264,379
Lassie 377
Lefton China...................................312-313;39,157-158
Letter Openers 313-314
Li'l Abner 125
Liberty Blue 315-316
License Plates...316-317;68
Liddle Kiddles 204-205
Life Magazine...324
Light Bulbs...129-130
Linemar 449,457-458
Linens...379
Lionstone Decanters 176
Lipsticks 146
Little Golden Books 81-82
Little Orphan Annie 125
Little Red Riding Hood 317
Little Tikes 317-318
Littlechap Family 205
Lobby Cards...346-347
Lobster Ware...417
Locks 379-380
Lone Ranger 168,447-448,451
Longaberger Baskets....................................318-320
Look Magazine...324
Looney Tunes..117
Louise Piper Decorated Pieces.........................224
LP Albums...385
Lu Ray Pastels..320
Lunch Boxes...320-322
M&M Candy Men..22-23
Maddux of California 322-323;158
Magazines 323-326;62,271,366,431

Mammy 410
Marbles 326-327
Marvel Super Heroes 125,448
Marx 195,449,450,458
Mastercrafters Clocks 344
Match Safes 327-328
Matchbox 455-456
Mattel 195,200-202
Max, Peter 328-329
McCormick Decanters 176
McCoy Pottery 329-333;158-160
McDonald's 59,117,219-220
McKee 40
Melmac Dinnerware 332-333
Men of the Mountains 464
Metlox Pottery 333-335;160-161
Mexican Decaled Lines 277
Michelin Man (Bibendum or Mr. Bib) 23
Mickey Mouse 117,120,121,191-192,445
Midwest Potteries, Inc. 342
Milk Bottles 335-336,379
Milk Glass 40,477-478
Milton Bradley 245-247
Mirror Almond and Mirror Brown 281-282
Mirrors 146-147
Miss America 35
Mission Ware 349-350
Model Kits 336-338
Modern Mechanical Banks 338
Modern Screen Magazine 324
Monkees 392
Monogram 337-338
Moon and Star 339-340
Moon Beings 307
Mortens Studios 340-341
Morton Pottery 341-342
Moss Rose 343
Motion Clocks (Electric) 343-344
Motion Lamps 309-310
Motorcycle Collectibles 344-346
Movie Collectibles 42-43,346-347,354-355
Movie Posters and Lobby Cards 346-347
Mr. Bib 23
Mr. Peanut 23-24,32
Muggsy 361
Muppets 126
Nancy Ann Storybook Dolls 205
Napco 39,40
Napkin Dolls 348
Napkin Holders 463
National Geographic Magazine 325
Necklaces 297
New Martinsville 348-349

New York World's Fairs 484
Newspapers 271-272
Nichols 450
Niloak Pottery 349-350
Nodders 18,60
Noise Makers 264
Novelty Radios 350-351
Novelty Telephones 351
Nudies 307
Occupied Japan Collectibles 351-353,356
Octagonal 35
Old Commonwealth Decanters 176-177
Old Crow 24-25
Old Fitzgerald Decanters 177
Old MacDonald's Farm 353-354
Omnibus 161
Ornaments 130-131
Pacific Pottery 96
Paper Dolls 354-355
Paperback Books 272
Paperweights 44,432
Parrish 371
Peanuts 119,126
Pencil Sharpeners 355-356
Pennants 287
Pennsbury Pottery 356-357
Pepsi-Cola 357-358
Perfume Bottles 358-359
Pez Candy Dispensers 359-360
Pfaltzgraff Pottery 360-362
Phantom 126
Photographs 371-372
Pie Birds 362-363
Pierce, Howard 363-364
Pillsbury 25-26,150
Pin-Back Buttons 27,61,272,364-366,368-369,430
Pincushions 293
Pinocchio 192
Pins, See Brooches
Pinup Art 366-367
Pixie Ware 274
Planters 38,71,279,280,313,330-331,
353,401-402,403,416
Planters Peanuts 23-34
Plastic 355-356,406
Playing Cards 367-368
Playsets 435,436
Pocket Tins 444
Pocket Watches 120
Political Memorabilia 368-369
Ponytail Girl 274
Popeye 126
Poppets 334

Poppin' Fresh (Pillsbury Doughboy) and Family 25-26
Porcelier China 369-370
Postcards........................370-372;92,415,430,431
Posters 28,272,328-329,345,346-347,369
Potato Mashers 305
Powder Jars..372-373
Premiums 115-116
Prints 367
Priscilla 277-278
Programs............................287,345,423,431
Psycho Ceramics 30
Pulp Magazines 325-326
Puppets..70
Purinton Pottery 373-375
Purses 135,136,137
Puzzles..375-377;248
Radios 18,68,350-351,458-460
Raggedy Ann and Andy..............................127,205-206
Railroadiana 377-381;372
Raised Daisy 36
Ramp Walkers 450-451
Rattles 265
Razor Blade Banks 381
Reamers..381-383
Records 383-385;62,70,272
Red Rose Tea 469
Red Wing 385-387;161
Reddy Kilowatt..26-27
Regal China 387-388;161,353-354
Relco 39
Renwal 195
Restaurant China 388-390
Restaurant Ware..290-291
Return of the Jedi, See Star Wars
Revell..338
Rhythm..278
Ring Ware 54
Rings..297
Rings (Toy) 451-452
Riviera 278
Robinson-Ransbottom 161-162
Robots and Space Toys..................................452-453
Rock 'n Roll Memorabilia 390-392
Rocketeer 192
Rocky and Bullwinkle...127
Rogers, Roy; See Roy Rogers
Rolling Stones...392
Rookwood 392-393
Rooster 274-275
Rooster and Roses..393-394
Roselane Sparklers 394-395
Rosemeade..395-396
Roseville Pottery..396-399

Roto-Vue Jr..309-310
Roy Rogers 116,168,355,451-452
Royal China 399-401
Royal Copley...401-402
Royal Haeger..402-403
Rozart 404-405
RumRill..405
Russel Wright Designs....................................405-407
Salt Shakers 407-414;14,17,18,26,71,76,89,114,164,177,
                    235,275,313,354,388,396,416,431,463-466
Sandwich Pattern...442-443
Saucy Walker 204
Schoop, Hedi 414-415
Schuco..458
Scottie Collectibles 194
Scouting Collectibles 415-416
Serenade 278
Sesame Street 119,127
Shawnee Pottery..416-417;162
Sheet Music 417-422;70,216
Shelf Sitters 114
Shell Pink Glassware...422
Sherman, Bobby..391
Shirley Temple..422-423
Shirts...137
Shoes...135,136
Shot Glasses..423-424;303
Sierra Vista...162-163
Signs................................45,89,139-140,248,345,
                                358,367,428,444-445
Silhouette Pictures.......................................424-425
Silverplate 380
Silverplated Flatware.....................................425-427
Simmons, Robert..96-97
Simpsons...127
Ski Country Decanters 177
Skillets...257
Skookum Indian Dolls 427-428
Sleeping Beauty..192
Slot Car Racers...453
Smiley Pig...416
Smokey the Bear...27-28
Smurfs...127
Snap!, Crackle!, and Pop!......................................28
Snow White & the Seven Dwarfs...............192-193
Soda Bottles With Painted Labels 429
Soda-Pop Memorabilia...................................428-429
Solid Perfumes..147
Spartus Clocks..344
Spice Sets...71,293
Spoons...92
Sporting Goods...429-432
Sports Collectibles...430-432

St. Clair Glass..432
Stacked Disk...36
Stanford Corn..432
Stangl Birds..432-433
Stangl Dinnerware..433-434
Star Trek Memorabilia..434-435
Star Wars...435-436
Steamship Collectibles...372
Steiff Animals..437-438
Stippled Band...36
Strawberry Shortcake and Friends.................................207
String Holders..438-439
Suits..135
Super Heroes...118
Superman...119,128,142,377
Swanky Swigs..439-440
Sweaters...136
Syroco..440-441
Syrups...380
Tablecloths..379
Tables...245
Tammy and Friends..207-208
Taylor, Smith and Taylor......................................441-442
Teapots.............................47,75-76,235,252,256,262,
293,370,378-379,416-417
Telephones...351
Thanksgiving...258,342
Thermometers..45,445
Thermoses..322
Tiara Exclusives..442-443
Tire Ashtrays...443-444
Tires...68
Toasters...304
Tobacco Collectibles..444-445
Tom and Jerry..128
Tom Mix..168
Tomy...195
Tonka...456-457
Tony the Tiger...28-29
Toothbrush Holders..445-446
Toothpick Holders....................................177,178,432
Tootsietoy...195,457
Toppers...23
Toy Story..193
Toys...446-458;19,21,24,116,
140,232-233,252-254
Transistor Radios...458-460
Trays..........................52,89,140-141,358,380
Treasure Craft...163

Tressy...208
Trolls..460-461
TV Guides...461-462
TV Lamps..310-311,323
Twin Winton..462-464;163
Tyco...453
Uneeda Dolls..208-209
United Clocks..344
Valencia...417
Valentines..........................464-466;342,371
Vallona Starr..466
Van Telligen Shakers...388
Vandor...466-467;163-164
Vehicles (Toy)..453-457
Vernon Kilns..467-468
Viking Glass..468-469
Village...361-362
Virginia Rose..278
Vistosa..442
Wade Porcelain..469-470
Wall Pockets..................470-471;132-133,343,394
Wallace China...97
Warner Bros..164
Watch Fobs..45,345
Watt Pottery..471-472
Weeping Gold..472-473
Weil Ware..473
Weller..473-476
Wells Art Glaze..278
Wendy's..220
West Coast Pottery..97
Western Collectibles..476-477
Westmoreland Glass..477-483
Wheaton...482-483
Wild Turkey Decanters..177
Will-George...97
Willow Dinnerware, See Blue Willow Dinnerware
Windups...457-458
Winfield..97
Winnie Pig...416
Wizard of Oz...128
Woman's Home Companion...325
World's Fairs and Expositions.................................483-484
Wristwatches....................32-34,120-121,369
Yearbooks..288,432
Yogi Bear..128
Yona..97
Zodiac Angels..39-40
Zorro..168

COLLECTOR BOOKS
Informing Today's Collector

DOLLS, FIGURES & TEDDY BEARS

2079	**Barbie** Doll Fashion, Volume I, Eames	$24.95
3957	**Barbie** Exclusives, Rana	$18.95
4557	**Barbie**, The First 30 Years, Deutsch	$24.95
3810	**Chatty Cathy** Dolls, Lewis	$15.95
4559	Collectible **Action Figures**, 2nd Ed., Manos	$17.95
1529	Collector's Encyclopedia of **Barbie** Dolls, DeWein/Ashabraner	$19.95
2211	Collector's Encyclopedia of **Madame Alexander Dolls**, 1965-1990, Smith	$24.95
4863	Collector's Encyclopedia of **Vogue Dolls**, Stover/Izen	$29.95
4861	Collector's Guide to **Tammy**, Sabulis/Weglewski	$18.95
3967	Collector's Guide to **Trolls**, Peterson	$19.95
1799	**Effanbee Dolls**, Smith	$19.95
5253	Story of **Barbie**, 2nd Ed., Westenhouser	$24.95
1513	**Teddy Bears & Steiff** Animals, Mandel	$9.95
1817	**Teddy Bears & Steiff** Animals, 2nd Series, Mandel	$19.95
2084	**Teddy Bears, Annalee's & Steiff** Animals, 3rd Series, Mandel	$19.95
1808	Wonder of **Barbie**, Manos	$9.95
1430	World of **Barbie** Dolls, Manos	$9.95
4880	World of **Raggedy Ann Collectibles**, Avery	$24.95

TOYS, MARBLES & CHRISTMAS COLLECTIBLES

3427	**Advertising Character** Collectibles, Dotz	$17.95
2333	Antique & Collectible **Marbles**, 3rd Ed., Grist	$9.95
4934	**Breyer Animal** Collector's Guide, Identification and Values, Browell	$19.95
4976	**Christmas** Ornaments, Lights & Decorations, Johnson	$24.95
4737	**Christmas** Ornaments, Lights & Decorations, Vol. II, Johnson	$24.95
4739	**Christmas** Ornaments, Lights & Decorations, Vol. III, Johnson	$24.95
2338	Collector's Encyclopedia of **Disneyana**, Longest, Stern	$24.95
4958	Collector's Guide to **Battery Toys**, Hultzman	$19.95
5038	Collector's Guide to **Diecast Toys** & Scale Models, 2nd Ed., Johnson	$19.95
4566	Collector's Guide to **Tootsietoys**, 2nd Ed, Richter	$19.95
3436	Grist's Big Book of **Marbles**	$19.95
3970	Grist's Machine-Made & Contemporary **Marbles**, 2nd Ed.	$9.95
5267	**Matchbox** Toys, 3rd Ed., 1947 to 1998, Johnson	$19.95
4871	**McDonald's Collectibles**, Henriques/DuVall	$19.95
1540	**Modern Toys** 1930–1980, Baker	$19.95
3888	**Motorcycle** Toys, Antique & Contemporary, Gentry/Downs	$18.95
5168	Schroeder's Collectible **Toys**, Antique to Modern Price Guide, 5th Ed	$17.95
1886	Stern's Guide to **Disney** Collectibles	$14.95
2139	Stern's Guide to **Disney** Collectibles, 2nd Series	$14.95
3975	Stern's Guide to **Disney** Collectibles, 3rd Series	$18.95
2028	**Toys**, Antique & Collectible, Longest	$14.95

JEWELRY, HATPINS, WATCHES & PURSES

1712	Antique & Collectible **Thimbles** & Accessories, Mathis	$19.95
1748	Antique **Purses**, Revised Second Ed., Holiner	$19.95
1278	Art Nouveau & Art Deco **Jewelry**, Baker	$9.95
4850	Collectible **Costume Jewelry**, Simonds	$24.95
3875	Collecting Antique **Stickpins**, Kerins	$16.95
3722	Collector's Ency. of **Compacts, Carryalls & Face Powder Boxes**, Mueller	$24.95
4940	**Costume Jewelry**, A Practical Handbook & Value Guide, Rezazadeh	$24.95
1716	Fifty Years of Collectible **Fashion Jewelry**, 1925-1975, Baker	$19.95
1424	**Hatpins** & Hatpin Holders, Baker	$9.95
1181	100 Years of Collectible **Jewelry**, 1850-1950, Baker	$9.95
3830	Vintage **Vanity Bags & Purses**, Gerson	$24.95

FURNITURE

1457	American **Oak** Furniture, McNerney	$9.95
3716	American **Oak** Furniture, Book II, McNerney	$12.95
1118	Antique **Oak** Furniture, Hill	$7.95
2132	Collector's Encyclopedia of **American** Furniture, Vol. I, Swedberg	$24.95
2271	Collector's Encyclopedia of **American** Furniture, Vol. II, Swedberg	$24.95
3720	Collector's Encyclopedia of **American** Furniture, Vol. III, Swedberg	$24.95
1755	Furniture of the **Depression Era**, Swedberg	$19.95
3906	**Heywood-Wakefield** Modern Furniture, Rouland	$18.95
1885	**Victorian** Furniture, Our American Heritage, McNerney	$9.95
3829	**Victorian** Furniture, Our American Heritage, Book II, McNerney	$9.95

INDIANS, GUNS, KNIVES, TOOLS, PRIMITIVES

1868	Antique **Tools**, Our American Heritage, McNerney	$9.95
1426	**Arrowheads** & Projectile Points, Hothem	$7.95
2279	**Indian** Artifacts of the Midwest, Hothem	$14.95
3885	**Indian** Artifacts of the Midwest, Book II, Hothem	$16.95
5162	Modern **Guns**, Identification & Values, 12th Ed., Quertermous	$12.95

2164	**Primitives**, Our American Heritage, McNerney	$9.95
1759	**Primitives**, Our American Heritage, Series II, McNerney	$14.95
4730	Standard **Knife** Collector's Guide, 3rd Ed., Ritchie & Stewart	$12.95

PAPER COLLECTIBLES & BOOKS

4633	**Big Little Books**, A Collector's Reference & Value Guide, Jacobs	$18.95
4710	Collector's Guide to **Children's Books**, 1850 to 1950, Jones	$18.95
1441	Collector's Guide to **Post Cards**, Wood	$9.95
2081	Guide to Collecting **Cookbooks**, Allen	$14.95
2080	Price Guide to **Cookbooks & Recipe Leaflets**, Dickinson	$9.95
3973	**Sheet Music** Reference & Price Guide, 2nd Ed., Pafik & Guiheen	$19.95
4654	**Victorian Trade Cards**, Historical Reference & Value Guide, Cheadle	$19.95
4733	**Whitman Juvenile Books**, Brown	$17.95

OTHER COLLECTIBLES

2269	Antique **Brass & Copper** Collectibles, Gaston	$16.95
1880	Antique **Iron**, McNerney	$9.95
3872	Antique **Tins**, Dodge	$24.95
1128	**Bottle** Pricing Guide, 3rd Ed., Cleveland	$7.95
3718	Collectible **Aluminum**, Grist	$16.95
4560	Collectible **Cats**, An Identification & Value Guide, Book II, Fyke	$19.95
4852	Collectible **Compact Disc** Price Guide 2, Cooper	$17.95
2018	Collector's Encyclopedia of **Granite Ware**, Greguire	$24.95
3430	Collector's Encyclopedia of **Granite Ware**, Book II, Greguire	$24.95
4705	Collector's Guide to Antique **Radios**, 4th Ed., Bunis	$18.95
4857	Collector's Guide to **Art Deco**, 2nd Ed., Gaston	$17.95
4933	Collector's Guide to **Bookends**, Identification & Values, Kuritzky	$19.95
3880	Collector's Guide to **Cigarette Lighters**, Flanagan	$17.95
4887	Collector's Guide to **Creek Chub Lures** & Collectibles, Smith	$24.95
3966	Collector's Guide to **Inkwells**, Identification & Values, Badders	$18.95
3881	Collector's Guide to **Novelty Radios**, Bunis/Breed	$18.95
4652	Collector's Guide to **Transistor Radios**, 2nd Ed., Bunis	$16.95
4864	Collector's Guide to **Wallace Nutting Pictures**, Ivankovich	$18.95
1629	**Doorstops**, Identification & Values, Bertoia	$9.95
3968	**Fishing Lure** Collectibles, Murphy/Edmisten	$24.95
5259	**Flea Market Trader**, 12th Ed., Huxford	$9.95
4945	**G-Men and FBI Toys**, Whitworth	$18.95
3819	**General Store Collectibles**, Wilson	$24.95
2216	**Kitchen Antiques**, 1790–1940, McNerney	$14.95
4950	The **Lone Ranger**, Collector's Reference & Value Guide, Felbinger	$18.95
2026	**Railroad** Collectibles, 4th Ed., Baker	$14.95
1632	**Salt & Pepper Shakers**, Guarnaccia	$9.95
5091	**Salt & Pepper Shakers** II, Guarnaccia	$18.95
2220	**Salt & Pepper Shakers** III, Guarnaccia	$14.95
3443	**Salt & Pepper Shakers** IV, Guarnaccia	$18.95
5007	**Silverplated Flatware**, Revised 4th Edition, Hagan	$18.95
1922	Standard **Old Bottle** Price Guide, Sellari	$14.95
3892	**Toy & Miniature Sewing Machines**, Thomas	$18.95
5144	Value Guide to **Advertising Memorabilia**, 2nd Ed., Summers	$19.95
3977	Value Guide to **Gas Station** Memorabilia, Summers	$24.95
4877	Vintage **Bar Ware**, Visakay	$24.95
4935	The W.F. Cody **Buffalo Bill** Collector's Guide with Values, Wojtowicz	$24.95
5281	**Wanted to Buy**, 7th Edition	$9.95

GLASSWARE & POTTERY

4929	**American Art Pottery**, 1880 – 1950, Sigafoose	$24.95
4938	Collector's Encyclopedia of **Depression Glass**, 13th Ed., Florence	$19.95
5040	Collector's Encyclopedia of **Fiesta**, 8th Ed., Huxford	$19.95
4946	Collector's Encyclopedia of **Howard Pierce Porcelain**, Dommel	$24.95
1358	Collector's Encyclopedia of **McCoy Pottery**, Huxford	$19.95
2339	Collector's Guide to **Shawnee Pottery**, Vanderbilt	$19.95
1523	Colors in **Cambridge Glass**, National Cambridge Society	$19.95
4714	**Czechoslovakian Glass** and Collectibles, Book II, Barta	$16.95
3725	**Fostoria**, Pressed, Blown & Hand Molded Shapes, Kerr	$24.95
4726	**Red Wing Art Pottery**, 1920s – 1960s, Dollen	$19.95

This is only a partial listing of the books on collectibles that are available from Collector Books. All books are well illustrated and contain current values. Most of our books are available from your local bookseller, antique dealer, or public library. If you are unable to locate certain titles in your area, you may order by mail from COLLECTOR BOOKS, P.O. Box 3009, Paducah, KY 42002-3009. Customers with Visa, MasterCard, or Discover may phone in orders from 7:00–5:00 CST, Monday–Friday, Toll Free 1-800-626-5420; www.collectorbooks.com Add $3.00 for postage for the first book ordered and $0.40 for each additional book. Include item number, title, and price when ordering. Allow 14 to 21 days for delivery.

Schroeder's
ANTIQUES
Price Guide

. . . is the #1 bestselling antiques & collectibles value guide on the market today, and here's why . . .

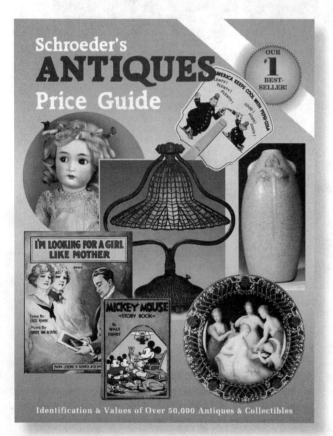

Schroeder's ANTIQUES Price Guide

OUR #1 BEST-SELLER!

Identification & Values of Over 50,000 Antiques & Collectibles

8½ x 11, 608 Pages, $12.95